THE ROUGH

C000319528

French Hotels & Restaurants

le guide du **ROUTARD**

Rough Guides and France

In addition to this guide, Rough Guides
publish eight guidebooks on France:

**France • Brittany & Normandy • Corsica
The Dordogne & Lot • Languedoc & Roussillon
Provence & the Côte d'Azur • Paris
The Pyrenees** (French and Spanish)

There is also a
Rough Guide French phrasebook

Credits

Rough Guides

Managing editor: Jonathan Buckley
Series editor: Mark Ellingham
Text editor: Andrew Dickson
Translator for this edition: Vanessa Dowell
Production: Susanne Hillen, Maxine Repath, Julia Bovis, Michelle Draycott,
    Ed Wright, Katie Lloyd-Jones, Katie Pringle
Design: Henry Iles

Routard

Directeur de collection: Philippe Gloaguen
Rédacteur: Amanda Keraval

Acknowledgements

Thanks to Monique Lantelme, Amanda Keraval and all those at Lexus who
worked on the first edition: Jane Goldie, Céline Reynaud, Peter Terrell, Sophie
Curien, Alice Grandison, Leslie Harkins, Sarah Cartwright, David Alun Jones,
Anita Leyerzapf. Thanks also to Sam Cook for invaluable help with editing and to
Katie Pringle for patient typesetting.

Cover credits

Front small bottom pictures © Joe Cornish
Back top picture © Robert Harding
Back lower picture © Joe Cornish

This translation © The Rough Guides Ltd
848pp, includes index
A catalogue record for this book is available from the British Library.
ISBN 1-85828-879-7

Distributed by the Penguin Group:
Penguin Books Ltd, 80 Strand, London WC2R ORL
Penguin Putnam, Inc., 375 Hudson Street, New York 10014, USA
Penguin Books Australia Ltd, 487 Maroondah Highway, PO Box 257, Ringwood, Victoria 3134,
    Australia
Penguin Books Canada Ltd, 10 Alcorn Avenue, Toronto, Ontario, Canada M4V 1E4
Penguin Books (NZ) Ltd, 182–190 Wairau Road, Auckland 10, New Zealand

Printed in England by Clays Ltd, St Ives PLC

THE ROUGH GUIDE TO

French Hotels & Restaurants

Le guide du ROUTARD

ENGLISH EDITION
2002

LE GUIDE DU ROUTARD
EDITOR: PHILIPPE GLOAGUEN

Translated by
Vanessa Dowell and Lexus

ROUGH GUIDES

CONTENTS

CONTENTS

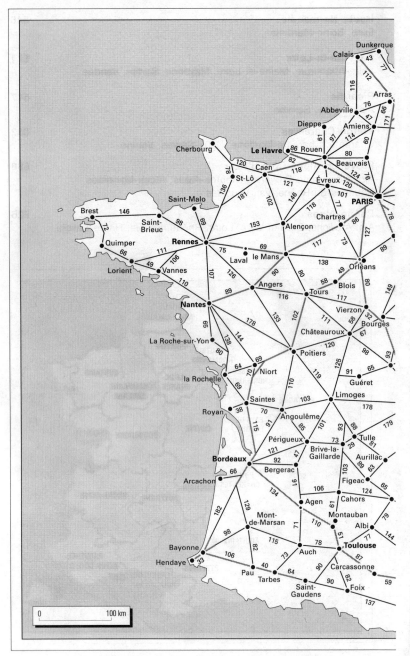

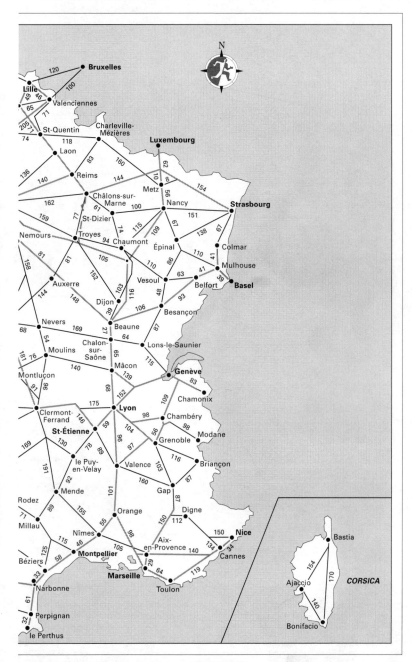

About this book

This is the fifth edition of the **Rough Guide to French Hotels & Restaurants**, a translation of the Routard guide, the best-selling French guide to good-value restaurants and accommodation in France. Revised every year, *French Hotels & Restaurants* is up-to-date, comprehensive and opens up the country in a way that no other guide does. Its listings include everything from simple hostels and family-run bistros to high-comfort rural retreats and city-centre three-stars. All selected are reviewed by Routard's team of locally based writers, who re-assess the entries for each edition.

The hotels and restaurants selected tend to be small, independent establishments – look out for the Routard stickers on their front doors. There may also be a *Logis de France* sticker, too – a fireplace symbol with one, two or three fires to indicate the level of facilities provided. This denotes membership of a scheme that promotes family-run hotels, often in rural locations well away from major towns.

The guide's layout
The Routard/Rough Guide is divided into twenty-two **chapter regions**, each with a regional map. The regions are listed alphabetically and within each chapter the **main towns** (marked by black circles on the maps) are listed in alphabetical order, their names appearing in a dark heading that also shows the postcode:

QUIBERON   **57170**

Small towns and villages within a radius of 30km of a larger town are included after the entries for that town (and marked by white circles on regional maps); these places are listed in the order of their distance from the main town, and their names are displayed in a light heading:

LEVERNOIS   **21200 (4KM SE)**

Within each town **hotels** are listed first, followed by **restaurants**, and both are listed in **ascending order of price**. Note that stars indicated are the official ratings of the French hotel industry and **not of this guide**.

After the address of the establishments, tips on **how to get there** are given wherever possible, plus phone number, fax number, email address, closing times and a summary of facilities where relevant.

In addition to regional maps, certain key cities are covered by detailed **city maps**. Hotels and restaurants in these places are given a two-part map code (eg **MAP B2-13**) comprised of a grid reference and the establishment's number in the map key. Sometimes city establishments are located outside the area covered by the map; these are marked **Off map** and correspond to an arrow pointing in the direction you'll need to travel in order to get there.

Symbols
The following symbols have been used:

⌂	hotel
|O|	restaurant
🌿	discount

The **discount symbol** indicates that an establishment offers some sort of benefit to readers of this guide. In the case of hotels, it's usually a discount (generally 10%) on the price of the room. You are usually obliged to stay for a minimum of two nights to qualify but sometimes the period or the amount of the discount can be different. The benefit can also be limited to certain periods of the year. Where possible these conditions have been indicated in the text. In some instances, the concession consists of a free breakfast or free garage space; many restaurants in this guide offer a free coffee, house apéritif or house *digestif*, but you qualify only when you order a complete meal and, more often than not, the choice of drink will not be up to you. All establishments will insist that you are entitled to the benefit only if you are carrying the **current year's edition** of this guidebook. In all cases, show your copy when you check in at the hotel or before you order your meal in a restaurant. Hotels and restaurants are familiar with the French Routard guide, and should you have any difficulties claiming the benefits with this translation, point to the front cover where the Routard logo is clearly displayed.

The Euro

The **Euro** (€), the European single currency, became the only legal tender in France in February 2002 when its coins and notes replaced the French Franc. Prices in this guide are quoted in Euros and are as accurate as possible, but while everyone is getting used to the exchange there may be small variations when you get to your hotel or restaurant.

The French way

It pays to know what's what in French hotels and restaurants and your basic rights as a consumer.

• When you're reserving a room by phone or in writing, it's not unusual for the hotel to ask for a **deposit** by way of a guarantee. There's no law to say how much this deposit should be, but don't pay any more than around 25–30% of the total. The French have two words for deposit – *arrhes* and *acompte*. The first is refundable, the second is not. So in the event of cancellation your *arrhes* can be returned in full if you give the hotel reasonable notice. If it's the hotel that cancels the booking, then under Article 1590 of the Civil Code (which dates back to 1804) you're entitled to double the amount of the *arrhes*

you paid. So if you do make a deposit, be very specific in your letter as to whether it's *arrhes* or *acompte*.

• Hotels and restaurants are required by law to **display their prices**. You won't get anywhere arguing about extortionate charges if they're clearly marked on a price list.

• Hotels are **not permitted to try to sell you something you haven't requested**; for example they can't force you to book for several nights if you only want to stay for one. Similarly, they can't insist you have breakfast or any other meal at the hotel unless it's clearly stated that **half** or **full board** is compulsory. Make sure you find this out before you book into a hotel with a restaurant, and bear in mind that half-board prices often apply to a minimum stay of three nights. This is permitted by law.

• In restaurants the cheapest **set meals** are often served at lunchtimes on weekdays only. This should be clearly marked on the board outside. The same menu may cost more at night.

• **Wine lists** aren't always very clear so be sure that you know precisely what you're ordering. For example, you might select a bottle of Burgundy at €8 and be charged €16; when you check the list again, you find (maybe in small print) that the price was for a half-bottle. A bottle of wine must be opened in front of the customer – otherwise you've no way of knowing that you're getting what you ordered. A jug of tap water is free as long as you're ordering a meal.

• Occasionally restaurants **refuse to serve** customers if they feel they haven't ordered enough. But no one can force you into ordering something you don't want and refusing to serve you is technically against the law.

Alsace

67 Bas-Rhin

68 Haut-Rhin

ALTKIRCH   68130

🏃 🏠 |●| AUBERGE SUNDGOVIENNE**

1 route de Belfort; it's 3km out of town on the D419 in the direction of Dannemarie.
☎ 03.89.40.97.18 ➡ 03.89.40.67.73
e mail@auberge-sundgovienne.fr
Closed Mon, Tues until 5pm, Sun eve and 23 Dec–1 Feb. **Restaurant closed** Sept to end June. **TV**. **Disabled access**. **Garden**. **Lock-up garage**.

A cross between an American motel (it's near the road), a Swiss chalet (Switzerland isn't far) and a traditional Alsace hotel. Rooms cost €46–53, are clean and comfortable and some have a balcony. Even though they are all double-glazed, the ones at the back are quieter. The cooking provides a pleasant surprise. It's inspired by the fresh produce in the market and shows plenty of imagination: Scotch salmon with leeks and Riesling, sole fillet with purple-tipped asparagus and a sauce of top quality Tokay Pinot, and so on. There is a three-course set menu at €11 – not available for Saturday dinner or on Sunday – and others at €18–40. Half board €43–46. The terrace is a great place to sit over a drink, admiring the Sundgau countryside. 10% discount on the room rate.

HIRTZBACH   68118 (4KM S)

🏠 |●| OTTIÉ

17 rue de-Lattre-de-Tassigny; it's just as you come into the village, heading towards Ferrette and Hirsingue.
☎ 03.89.40.93.22 ➡ 03.89.08.85.19
e ottierest@aol.com
Closed Mon evening, Tues, a fortnight in June–July, and

25 Dec–6 Jan. **Garden**. **Car park**.

This lovely little inn is set in the heart of Sundgau – sadly it's by the road, not on a hill. Simple, well-maintained rooms; the ones with garden view are quiet. Doubles with washing facilities €23, with shower €24, and with bath €31. Half board €30–36. The food is unusual – try the *terrine* of artichokes with *foie gras* or the dandelion salad. There's a weekday lunch menu at €9, then others up to €35. The chef has worked in some of Alsace's better kitchens so the cooking has personality: bream with lime and ginger, *fricassée* of kidneys and sweetbreads and *moelleux* with caramelized pears. Nice terrace.

GOMMERSDORF   68210 (12KM W)

🏃 🏠 |●| L'AUBERGE DU TISSERAND**

28 rue de Cernay; it's on the D103 as you leave the village.
☎ 03.89.07.21.80/03.89.07.26.26 ➡ 03.89.25.11.34
TV. **Disabled access**. **Car park**.

This is a typical Alsace inn with a long history. Parts date from the seventeenth century when it was a weaver's house, and other parts are even older. On the first floor, reserved for smokers, the wooden floor has buckled with age. Good cooking and enormous portions at reasonable prices. The weekday lunch menu, €7, is one of the cheapest around; other menus are €12–27. They offer Alsace specialities, bake their own bread and serve flambéed tarts every night. A really delightful place with a few rooms for €41–45 with shower/wc. Breakfast €5. 10% discount on the room rate and free coffee or apéritif.

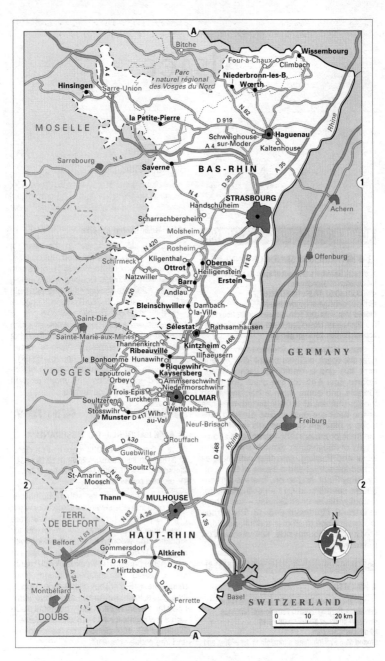

BARR
67140

♫ ♠ |●| HÔTEL MAISON ROUGE**

1 av. de la Gare (South); it's near the post office.
☎ 03.88.08.90.40 ➡ 03.88.08.90.85
e maisonrouge@wanadoo.fr
Closed Sun evening, Mon, the Feb school holidays and a fortnight in June–July. **TV**. **Car park**.

This place is far enough away from the centre not to attract too many tourists but there's a little square planted with trees and a pedestrian area across from the hotel. In the restaurant, which has been completely refurbished, set menus start at €15. Alsace specialities include fillet of salmon with *choucroute*, chicken in Riesling sauce and flambéed kidneys. Good choice of beers. Pleasant rooms €45–49 with en-suite bath. Breakfast €7. Free apéritif if you dine in.

HEILIGENSTEIN
67140 (1.5KM N)

♫ ♠ |●| RELAIS DU KLEVENER**

51 rue Principale.
☎ 03.88.08.05.98 ➡ 03.88.08.40.83
Closed Mon, Tues lunchtime. **TV**. **Garden**. **Car park**.

This inn has wonderful views over the vineyards, the Rhine and Germany beyond. The rooms are simple with no great appeal but some have views. Doubles at €40–46. There's a brasserie and a separate restaurant. Generous set menus €15–20 and *à la carte*. Specialities include home-made *foie gras* and the fish is good too. Half board €41. Sit out on the terrace and have a glass of Klevener – it's an old grape variety peculiar to Heiligenstein and pretty rare elsewhere in Alsace. Free house apéritif.

ANDLAU
67140 (4KM SW)

♠ |●| LE ZINCK HÔTEL

13 rue de la Marne; it's at the bottom of the village.
☎ 03.8808.27.30 ➡ 03.88.08.42.50
e zinck.Hotel@wanadoo.fr
Closed 10 days in Feb and 10 days in Dec. **TV**.
Disabled access.

Charming hotel in a restored water-mill. The eighteen comfortable rooms have been tastefully decorated, each with a distinctive look. They have names rather than numbers – the *Vigneron* has a bed with a canopy. Doubles €53–92. The hall has been beautifully decorated and they have preserved the mill wheel. The hotel doesn't have its own restaurant but the owner runs the *Relais de la Poste* at 1 rue des Forgerons (closed Mon

and Tues). It's a wine cellar with a good reputation.

BLIENSCHWILLER
67650

♠ HÔTEL WINZENBERG**

58 route du Vin; on the N422.
☎ 03.88.92.62.77 ➡ 03.88.92.45.22
e winzenberg@visit-alsace.com
Closed 3 Jan–20 Feb. **TV**. **Disabled access**. **Car park**.

The Dreschs believe that it's the division of labour that makes their family tick: mother and daughter run the hotel while father and son take charge of the vineyard. They seem to have got it about right. The comfortable rooms, with pretty Alsace furniture and brightly coloured bedspreads and curtains, prove good value: doubles cost €41–45. The whole family is very welcoming – they will show you the wine cellar, built in 1508, and invite you to taste the wine.

COLMAR
68000

♫ ♠ HÔTEL COLBERT**

2 rue des Trois-Épis (West); next to the station, overlooking the railway tracks.
☎ 03.89.41.31.05 ➡ 03.89.23.66.75
TV. **Pay garage**.

A hotel with no particular charm but the rooms are air-conditioned, comfortable and clean, with double glazing to keep out the noise from the railway. Doubles with bath or shower/wc €37–46. A small detail that will keep beer drinkers happy: there's a bottle-opener on the wall in the bathroom. The disco-bar, *The Toucan*, is in the hotel basement, so noise levels aren't too bad. 10% discount on the room rate.

♫ ♠ |●| HÔTEL BEAU SÉJOUR**

25 rue du Ladhof (East).
☎ 03.89.41.37.16 ➡ 03.89.41.43.07
e resa@beausejour.fr
Restaurant closed Sat lunchtime and Sun evening out of season. **TV**. **Disabled access**. **Garden**. **Car park**.

This hotel has been run by the Keller family since 1913 and they ran the eighteenth-century post house that stood here before that. They have added lots of annexes with around forty rooms, most of which now have modern facilities (€53–84). There's a sauna and a gym, a lovely sitting room with blue armchairs, and, in the garden, a terrace with wisteria clambering over the pergola. The dining room is elegant but the chef can get a shade too daring with his interpretations of local dishes. Menus €17–46. Free parking and 50% reduction on the third night when you stay over the weekend, except on public holidays.

☎ |●| HÔTEL TURENNE**

10 route de Bâle (Southeast).
☎ 03.89.21.58.58 ┣ 03.89.41.27.64
e helmlinger@turenne.com
TV. **Pay car park**.

A good establishment made up of a collection of buildings with pink, green and cream walls hung with geraniums. The contemporary-looking rooms have been renovated in a functional style, but they're pleasant enough. The ones over the road are noisier than those at the back. Doubles with bath or shower/wc €54–65, and the buffet breakfast, at €8, is generous. Professional, warm welcome. Good value.

|●| LE CAVEAU SAINT-PIERRE

24 rue de la Herse (Centre), Petite Venise.
☎ 03.89.41.99.33 ┣ 03.89.23.94.33
Closed Sun evening, Mon, Fri lunchtime and Jan.

Elegant but affordable, this is undoubtedly the best restaurant in the romantic area known as *Petite Venise* (Little Venice). It's up against the old town walls and you can only get to it by walking over a wooden footbridge which crosses a charming canal lined with half-timbered houses and beautiful gardens. It's a lovely spot, and when it's sunny, tables are set out by the water. The dining room has lots of alcoves, painted furniture and checked cloths on the tables. The prices are reasonable – set menus €12–22 or €21 as a minimum *à la carte*. Service is polite without being fussy. Mouthwatering specialities include oxtail with shallots in Pinot Noir and beef fillet with a Munster cheese sauce. They make *baeckeoffe*, a stew of beef, mutton and pork marinated in local wine, every Saturday and Sunday in winter.

|●| LE PETIT GOURMAND

9 quai de la Poissonnerie; riverside in Petite Venise.
☎ 03.89.41.09.32
Closed Mon evening and Tues, Nov and Jan.

This pretty little restaurant, in the heart of the Petite Venise district, seats just fourteen people – though in summer there's outdoor seating on the waterside terrace. The décor is low-key, with just a few photos of old Colmar on the white walls. The owner makes a

fuss of you. Large portions of tasty regional fare, like the extremely good *tartiflettes* of Munster cheese with salad and smoked pork, for a modest price (set menus €12–23). If you're struck by the quality of the *baeckeoffe* (a beef, mutton and pork stew), it's because the meat is left to marinate for three days. A real treat.

⅍ |●| RESTAURANT GARBO

15 rue Berthe-Molly; it's in the centre.
☎ 03.89.24.48.55 ┣ 03.89.24.57.68
e garbo@restaurantgarbo.com
Closed Sat lunchtime, Sun, public holidays, 1–7 Jan and 11–19 August.

This restaurant dedicated to the screen goddess is in one of the town's mansion-lined old streets. The huge dining room is part bistro, part gastronomic restaurant and offers good regional cuisine – dishes change with the seasons. Regular specialities include duck *foie gras* terrine with *Gewürztraminer*, zander fillet with lavender and cold beer *sabayon* with a beer sorbet. There's a lunchtime menu at €30 and a *menu-carte* at €15. The chef offers a *carte blanche* from €44–61. The hushed atmosphere makes it ideal for a romantic dinner. Free apéritif.

⅍ |●| WINSTUB BRENNER

1 rue de Turenne; it's just beside Petite Venise.
☎ 03.89.41.42.33 ┣ 03.89.41.37.99
Closed Tues, Wed, 14–27 Feb, 16–24 June, 18–27 Nov and Christmas–New Year.

Gilbert Brenner is a real character. He's stocky, rosy-cheeked, loves life – and it shows. He does the cooking and the serving, helped by his wife (who always manages to laugh at his jokes). They keep things simple here, with hearty dishes like salad of deep-fried Munster cheese, tripe in Riesling, ham knuckle with potatoes and *bibalakas* (curd cheese flavoured with horseradish and herbs). Gilbert trained as a pastry cook so leave room for dessert. A meal costs around €23. The beer flows into the small hours and students, regulars, wine-growers and tourists all come to have a good time. Free coffee.

WETTOLSHEIM   68920 (8KM SW)

☎ |●| HÔTEL AU SOLEIL**

20 rue Sainte-Gertrude; it's on the D17.
☎ 03.89.80.62.66 ┣ 03.89.79.84.45
Closed Thurs, 17 June–18 Jul and 19 Dec–6 Jan. **TV**.
Garden. Car park.

Run by a young couple, this is a great little place just outside Colmar in a tiny, little-known village on the *Route des Vins d'Alsace*. A good choice if you want to be near but not actually in the town, and, unlike many other hotels in the vineyards, it's reasonably priced. Reception is in a renovated half-timbered building, but you actually stay in a quiet annexe where rooms look out either onto the hotel car park or across acres of vineyards. Double rooms with shower/wc at €37. There's a short weekday lunch menu at €8 and another at €15. Half board is compulsory June–Sept, at €39 per person. Breakfast €6. Credit/debit cards not accepted.

NIEDERMORSCHWIHR   68230 (5KM W)

|●| RESTAURANT CAVEAU MORAKOPF

7 rue des Trois-Épis (South); N415 and the D11.
☎ 03.89.27.05.10 ➡ 03.89.27.08.63
Closed Sun, Mon lunch, last fortnight in Jan and last fortnight in June. **Disabled access. Garden.**

This big pink and green house can be found in a charming village tucked away among the vineyards. There is a glorious garden in the summer. The restaurant is all wood and comfortable benches and the window panes have been decorated with a "Morakopf" (the same Moorish head that adorns T-shirts in Corsica). The food is meticulously prepared and served in generous portions. Excellent home-made *presskopf* (brawn) and *baeckeoffe*, layers of different meats and potatoes marinated for twelve hours (for four people minimum and to order in advance). Specialities include trout in Riesling, and their duck *confit* on *choucroute* is not to be missed. Good local wines. Attentive, friendly service and unpretentious décor. A main course and a pudding will set you back about €20.

TROIS ÉPIS (LES)   68410 (10KM W)

🎿 🏠 |●| HÔTEL-RESTAURANT VILLA ROSA**

4 rue Thierry-Schoéré, on the Turckheim road; it's about 400m from the village.
☎ 03.89.49.81.19 ➡ 03.89.78.90.45
ℰ ar@wanadoo.fr
Closed lunchtimes, Thurs and 8 Jan–19 March. **Swimming pool. Garden.**

A gorgeous house run by a lovely couple who are committedly green and really make their guests feel at home. The rooms are delightful – ask for one with a view of the garden and swimming pool. Doubles with shower/wc or bath are €46–52. They even have some very

simple rooms in a separate guest house at €31 for two or €38 including breakfast – the shower is along the landing. Half board is compulsory in season at €48 per person. The restaurant serves evening meals only, with a menu at €18. Produce comes from the garden or local growers, and the cooking has an engaging personal touch. They run all sorts of courses too, including cookery, wild food and painting. Free apéritif.

ERSTEIN   67150

🎿 🏠 |●| HÔTEL ET L'ESTAMINET DES BORDS DE L'ILL**

94 rue du Général-de-Gaulle (Centre) near the Centre Nautique.
☎ 03.88.98.03.70 ➡ 03.88.98.09.49
ℰ bords-ill@reperes.com
TV. Disabled access. Garden. Car park.

You get a lovely welcome in this country-style hotel, beautifully situated near the banks of the Ill river and refurbished in typical Alsace style. Doubles with shower or bath at €48. The owners serve carefully cooked local dishes and huge, complicated salads using fresh local produce. The restaurant is across the road and has a terrace and a garden by the water. Set menus to suit all budgets: €7 (lunchtimes only), a *menu terroir* at €13 and another at €25. Wonderful wine from Alsace and elsewhere. 10% discount on the room rate.

HAGUENAU   67500

🎿 |●| S'BUEREHIESEL–CHEZ MONIQUE

13 rue Meyer; it's next to the theatre.
☎ 03.88.93.30.90 ➡ 03.88.06.13.22
Closed Sun, Mon, last week in May, first fortnight in Sept and Christmas–New Year.

A *winstub*, a typical Alsatian wine tavern, serving only wine from the region (as opposed to a *bierstub*, which serves beer). All the stars from the nearby theatre come here, and their photos – complete with beaming smiles and red-eye from the flash – smother the walls in the main dining room. Weekday lunch menu €7 or around €20 *à la carte*. They concentrate on regional dishes including *choucroute*, of course, braised knuckle of pork with local Munster cheese sauce, *quenelles* of liver, house *spaetzle* (a type of noodle) and snails *à l'alsacienne* cooked in local wine. Friendly welcome and warm, pleasant surroundings. Free coffee.

⅍ |●| RESTAURANT AU TIGRE

4 pl. d'Armes (Centre); it's in the pedestrian precinct.
☎ 03.88.93.93.79 ➡ 03.88.93.96.06

The handsome dining room has high ceilings, wood panelling and lots of wrought iron. This is a classic brasserie serving typical fare: *andouillette* and seafood platters in winter, kebabs and salad in summer. Set menus €14 and €18. When the sun comes out, they open a large terrace where they serve grills. Free coffee.

SCHWEIGHOUSE-SUR-MODER   67590 (3KM SW)

⅍ |●| AUX BERGES DE LA MODER

8 rue de la Gare.
☎ 03.88.72.01.09 ➡ 03.88.72.63.16
e clarisse.jost@wanadoo.fr
Closed Sun evening, Mon, a fortnight at All Saints' and 3 weeks in March. **Disabled access.**

The view over the industrial park is hardly idyllic but the two dining rooms are typical Alsace, with a lovely dresser, tiled floor, vermillion walls and decorated beams. The specialities – fish, game and rhubarb strudel – are quite delicious. Lunch menu of the day is €7, or €15–18 *à la carte* for dinner. A place to enjoy. Free aperitif.

KALTENHOUSE   67240 (5KM SE)

☎ |●| LA CRÉMAILLÈRE (CHEZ KRAEMER)

32 rue Principale (Centre).
☎ 03.88.63.23.06 ➡ 03.88.63.67.48
Closed Friday evening, Saturday lunchtime and Aug. **TV**. **Car park**.

An inn which is also the village bistro, located only 5km from the frontier. Locals, pensioners and passing travellers create a convivial atmosphere. It's a family-run place and, even at 86, Marthe Kraemer still keeps a watchful eye over proceedings while her grandson cooks up tasty dishes. Menus €19–30. Doubles at €46–54 have good facilities though they're slightly gloomy; it's best to avoid the ones overlooking the road.

KAYSERSBERG   68240

|●| AUBERGE DE LA CIGOGNE

73 route de Lapoutroie.
☎ 03.89.47.30.33 ➡ 03.89.78.16.42
Closed Fri, Sun evening, the first fortnight in July and between Christmas and New Year. **Car park**.

A restaurant popular with long-distance lorry drivers and workers from the Lotus paper factory next door. This is the type of roadside establishment where you get a good, hearty meal without forking out lots of money. Weekday menu €8 and others up to €27. The food ranges from brasserie classics to a few house specialities like fillet of zander, trout in Riesling and *choucroute*. A good place to stop. It has a terrace for outdoor dining.

|●| RESTAURANT ST-ALEXIS

lieu-dit Saint-Alexis.
☎ 03.89.73.90.38
Closed Fri.

Service noon–8pm. This appealing converted farmhouse, covered in ivy and hidden away in the forest, is very popular with locals. Inside, there's an appetizing smell of soup and *choucroute*. Set menus €10–16 and all are very filling: good home-made soup, a large, succulent ham omelette and *crudités* are the appetizers, which set you up for a deliciously cooked free-range chicken which has been simmering in the pan for hours. To round it all off, there's a lovely *tarte Alsacienne* (a kind of jam tart). In nice weather you can eat outside.

LAPOUTROIE   68650 (9KM W)

⅍ ☎ |●| L'ORÉE DU BOIS**

6 rue Faudé (South); it's on the N415.
☎ 03.89.47.50.30 ➡ 03.89.47.24.02
Closed lunchtimes and 1 Nov–5 Dec. **TV**. **Disabled access. Garden. Car park**.

To get to this place, you take a lovely little winding road up the mountain past fields of cows and pine forests. The view is nothing short of superb. This very modern-looking inn was originally a farmhouse and later transformed into a holiday camp. It is ideal for outdoor types looking for a nice quiet break with plenty of beautiful countryside to walk in. Each room has its own cooking area and a bucolic name; *Pâturages* has the best view. €38 for a double room; half board per person costs the same. The food is mostly traditional but not particularly original. Set menus €14–23.10% discount outside school holidays.

⅍ ☎ |●| HÔTEL LES ALISIERS

Lieu-dit Faudé; it's 3km out of the village, follow the signs.
☎ 03.89.47.52.82 ➡ 03.89.47.22.38
e hotel.restaurant-lessalisiers@wanadoo.fr
Closed Tues, 6 Jan–3 Feb, 22–25 Dec.

Way out in the wilds at an altitude of about

700m, this friendly and unusual little place is classified as a "Hôtel au Naturel" by the Regional Parks administration. It used to be a farm and the old stone sink and bread oven are still visible. There's a stunning view over the valley and the peaks of the Vosges. The bedrooms and the sitting room, with an open fire where they burn whole logs, are charming and cosy. Double rooms €47–92. Appetizing cooking using updated versions of old family recipes – veal kidneys steamed with leeks and old-style *choucroute*. Menus €13–37.10% discount on the room rate and half board from 15 Nov to 31 March.

⅍ ☎ |O| HÔTEL-RESTAURANT DU FAUDÉ

28 rue du Général Dupieux (Centre).
☎ 03.89.47.50.35 ➡ 03.89.47.24.82
℮ info@faude.com
Closed 24 Feb–16 March and 4 Nov–1 Dec. **Swimming pool. TV**.

A traditional hotel that has kept up-to-date. Besides the extremely comfortable rooms, facilities include a covered and heated swimming pool, Jacuzzi, steam room and gym. Double rooms with shower/wc or bath €54–74. The quality extends to the restaurant, where they serve authentic local dishes with a dash of individuality. Try the *Menu Welsh*, which lists *djalaïe* (a local version of brawn), troutlet salad with bacon and cream sauce and suckling pig Cordon Bleu with Munster cheese. Menus start at €14 and go up to €64. They also have a menu of the day served in the bar – a favourite with local workers. Courteous and friendly welcome. Free house apéritif.

ORBEY　　　　　　　　68370 (10KM W)

☎ |O| HÔTEL PAIRIS

Lieu-dit Pairis; it's 2km from Orbey on the way to Lac Blanc.
☎ 03.89.70.20.15 ➡ 03.89.71.39.90
Closed Wed and Nov. **Car park**.

An unusual hotel in a superb 1900s house run by a delightful German woman. The entrance hall is modish and miniminalist, with designer furniture and white everywhere. Lots of natural materials have been used in the rooms. Doubles with shower/wc €44–58; weekly rates available. Sumptuous buffet breakfast, with freshly squeezed fruit juices, *charcuterie* and cheese. Cakes and cappuccino are served at all times. Half board by arrangement (vegetarian menus available). There's a TV room with a wide

choice of books and games. A favourite with German visitors.

LE BONHOMME　　　　　　68650 (18KM W)

⅍ ☎ |O| HÔTEL DE LA POSTE – RESTAURANT LA BÉHIME**

48 rue du 3e-Spahi-Algérien; it's next to the post office.
☎ 03.89.47.51.10 ➡ 03.89.47.23.85
℮ hposte@club.internet.fr
Closed Tues and Wed out of season, Wed lunchtime in season and Jan–March. **TV**. **Disabled access. Swimming pool. Car park**.

A good inn with really nice rooms, some with a small sitting room. The ones near the road are noisy. Doubles with shower/wc €46. Six rooms have been specially adapted for disabled visitors. Regional cooking, as you would expect: *spätzle* (local noodles) and house *foie gras* are specialities. Menus €10–34. The friendly, professional woman who runs the place will even let you cancel your skiing holiday if there's no snow. 10% discount on the room rate.

MULHOUSE　　　　　　　　68100

☎ HÔTEL SCHOENBERG*

14 rue Schoenberg (Southwest); it's at right angles to av. d'Altkirch, behind the station.
☎ 03.89.44.19.41 ➡ 03.89.44.49.80
TV. Garden. Lock-up garage.

A good little hotel with clean, well-kept rooms where you'll sleep soundly. Prices are modest: €22 for a double room with basin and €34 with shower/wc. The toilet and the shower are behind sliding cupboard doors. There's a little garden at the back – numbers 1, 5 and 15 look over it – where you can laze in the sun and eat breakfast.

⅍ ☎ HÔTEL SAINT-BERNARD**

3 rue des Fleurs (Centre).
☎ 03.89.45.82.32 ➡ 03.89.45.26.32
℮ stber@evh.net
TV. Pay car park.

The *Saint-Bernard* is probably the nicest hotel in Mulhouse and it's run by a guy who's travelled the world – the hotel is named after his Saint Bernard dog. You can borrow a bike (free of charge), relax in the library or connect with the world in an Internet corner under the gaze of General de Gaulle's portrait. The rooms are all impeccable and have high ceilings; number 16 has a hundred-year-old fresco of the four seasons that you could spend the whole day admiring. Numbers 14 and 15 have water beds. Doubles with shower or bath €37–43, prices varying according to size and which floor they're on. 10% discount after the third night.

|●| LE PETIT ZINC

15 rue des Bons-Enfants (Centre).
☎ 03.89.46.36.38
Closed Sun, the three weeks in Aug and between Christmas and New Year's Day.

A chic but cool bar/restaurant that's a gathering place for artists, musicians, writers and their mates. There are loads of photos on the wall and a big bar with a huge old calculating machine. Local dishes with unexpected twists: *choucroute* salad with grilled Cerevelas, lentil soup and regional dishes like *haxala* (pork knuckle) or smoked ox tongue. Weekday lunch starter-main course *formule* for €8 or a meal *à la carte* from around €21.

|●| WINSTUB HENRIETTE

9 rue Henriette (Centre); it's off pl. de la Réunion.
☎ 03.89.46.27.83
Closed Sun.

This wine tavern is named after the first woman in the town officially to become a French citizen in 1798. The interior, decorated in typical Alsace style, has seen many years and many gourmets come and go. Classic regional dishes on the menu include *choucroute*. The chef's specialities include pan-fried *foie gras* with apples or fillet of beef with Munster cheese. At lunchtime, there's a starter/main course *formule* at €9. You'll pay about €20 *à la carte*. There's a terrace open in summer. The welcome, food and surroundings are all attractive, and it's a great refuge when it's cold outside – but the service isn't always up to snuff.

SOULTZ   68360 (21KM NW)

🏃|●| RESTAURANT METZGERSTUWA

69 rue du Maréchal-de-Lattre-de-Tassigny; it's on the main street.
☎ 03.89.74.89.77
Closed Sat, Sun, three weeks in June–July and 3 weeks from Christmas to 5 Jan.

Veggies be warned: this little restaurant in a green house is run by a man who owns the butcher's next door. It serves meat, meat and more meat – boned pig's trotters, skirt with shallots, calves' brains with capers, homemade black pudding, veal sweetbreads, and bulls' testicles with cream. Big local following. The servings are vast but you can ask for

a half portion. There is an unbeatable *menu du jour*, served with a smile, at €7 and others are €15–20. You can also buy home-made products to take away. Free *digestif* if you order a coffee after your meal.

MUNSTER   68140

🏠|●| HÔTEL AUX DEUX SAPINS**

49 rue du 9e-Zouave (Southwest).
☎ 03.89.77.33.96 ➡ 03.89.77.03.90
Closed Sun evening, Mon out of season and 10 Nov–20 Dec. **TV**. **Garden**. **Car park**.

You must reserve very early to get into this excellent place where the emphasis is on quality at reasonable prices. Excellent trout with almonds – you can really taste the Riesling. Set menus at €11–35. The rooms are small and simple but very pleasant and good value. Doubles €35–46. Windows are double-glazed and decently soundproofed from the traffic noise, but light sleepers should ask for a room at the back.

🏃🏠|●| HÔTEL-RESTAURANT DU CHALET*

col de la Schlucht (West); from the centre take the D417 to col de la Schlucht on the Alsace-Vosges border.
☎ 03.89.77.04.06 ➡ 03.89.77.06.11
Restaurant closed Wed evening, Thurs out of season.
Hotel closed a fortnight in June and 12 Nov–20 Dec.
TV. **Garden**. **Private garage**.

The hotel is one of the busiest passes over the peaks of the Vosges but being in such a prime location doesn't mean they take their patrons for granted. The rooms, restaurant and brasserie have all been refurbished. Doubles with shower/bath €43–46. In the vast dining room, welcoming especially on cold days, they serve simple but good regional dishes: *choucroute*, *baeckeoffe* in winter, *schiffele* with potatoes and salad in summer and wild boar stew in the autumn. Half board, €38 with evening meal, is compulsory in peak season. The lunch menu in the brasserie costs €9, and others are €17–19. Free apéritif.

|●| RESTAURANT À L'ALSACIENNE

1 rue du Dôme (Southeast); it's behind the Protestant church.
☎ 03.89.77.43.49
Closed Tues lunchtime and Wed.

Locals and tourists alike enjoy sitting at the tables on the pavement alongside the church. The décor is typical of the Alsace region but somewhat lacking in character. They serve individual dishes or set menus at €12–24. A meal *à la carte* will set you back around €23. Specialities include *choucroute garnie*, stuffed pig's trotters, *escalope* of veal with Munster cheese, game in season – or simply try a plate of local Munster served with a glass of *Gewürztraminer*. At lunch the fresh pasta and herbs is excellent. Delightful welcome.

SOULTZEREN   68140 (4KM NE)

🎋 🏠 I●I VILLA CANAAN – CHEZ LÉOPOLDINE

8 chemin du Buchteren; take the D47 in the direction of col de la Schlucht; after the village it's signposted on the right.
☎ 03.89.77.05.64. ➡ 03.89.77.35.73
Closed lunchtimes, Tues, Sun evening, Nov, Jan and March. **Garden. Car park.**

This huge yellow house, set high on a rock, dominates the Munster valley and lives up to the "promised land" implied in the name. Prices are reasonable: €43 for a double with basin, €49 with bath and €45–48 per person half board. The bathrooms are all different, with nice personal touches. You'll get a good night's sleep here, and in the morning you can fling open the shutters to an amazing view. The cooking is organic, and be warned – Léopoldine doesn't stint on the portions. This place is perfect for ramblers: the *col* of the Schlucht is barely an hour's walk away. Free apéritif.

STOSSWIHR-AMPFERBACH   68140 (8KM W)

🎋 I●I AUBERGE DES CASCADES

How to get there: leave Stosswihr by the route des Crêtes, turn left before the church at the signpost.
☎ 03.89.77.44.74
Closed Mon and Tues out of season, Tues only 14 July–20 Aug, and Jan.

Service until 10pm, last orders taken about an hour earlier. A very good inn which hasn't been spoiled by too many tourists (yet). The pretty house, which has recently been done up, is in a flower garden where you can hear the peaceful play of a waterfall nearby. There's a hearty weekday lunch menu at €8, one at €20 on Sundays or, *à la carte*, there are rather unusual specialities such as flambéed tart of frogs' legs prepared under the attentive gaze of Madame Decker and her flights of china ducks on the walls. If you fancy something more classic, there are traditional flambéed tarts baked in a wood-fired stove, trout fillet with sorrel and an awesome *entrecôte* with ceps. Treat yourself to the house Edelzwicker wine, which isn't expensive but is among the best in the region. Free coffee.

STOSSWIHR   68140 (8KM W)

I●I AUBERGE DU SCHUPFEREN

Centre; take the D417 out of Munster to the col de la Schlucht and turn right towards Le Tanet ski resort. About 4km down the road, you'll see a sign to the Auberge on a tree. Take the dirt track (it's OK for cars) for about 3km. Pass the Sarrois refuge on your left and continue along the road on your right (there is a sign).
☎ 03.89.77.31.23
Closed Mon, Tues and Fri.

Service 9am–7pm. Although this place is off the beaten track, it's definitely worth the effort to get here. It's popular with skiers in winter and walkers in summer. Christophe Kuhlman, the easy-going owner, will give you a warm welcome. He cooks great dishes like *Fleischsnecke*, pastry filled with mince, or a salad with leaves and vegetables from the garden. The menu is written on a blackboard. It's around €15 *à la carte*. Don't forget to order a small jug of house Edelzwicker, a white wine made from a blend of Alsace grapes. The view over the forest and valleys from this high pasture (1100m) is amazing.

WIHR-AU-VAL   68239 (9KM E)

I●I LA NOUVELLE AUBERGE

9 route Nationale; it's on the D417 in the direction of Colmar.
☎ 03.89.71.07.70
Closed Mon evening and Tues.

The talented chef has worked in some great kitchens but he hasn't let it go to his head. His roadside restaurant packs them in at lunchtime because of the €8 *menu-ouvrier*, which is amazing – you'll be lucky to find a parking space. The other menus, €15–43, list dishes such as cockerel in Riesling and Tricastin lamb with thyme *jus*, and the dishes are remarkable value given the quality of the produce and the chef's skill. The simple dining room is very pretty, and the welcome is unaffected and kindly. Excellent place.

NIEDERBRONN-LES-BAINS   67110

🏠 I●I HÔTEL-RESTAURANT CULLY**

33–37 rue de la République (West); it's near the station.
☎ 03.88.09.01.42 ➡ 03.88.09.05.80
📧 hotel-cully@wanadoo.fr
Closed Feb. **TV. Disabled access. Garden. Car park.**

The hotel is low-key and comfortable; most of

the big rooms have a balcony. Doubles €52 with shower/wc or bath. The restaurant is typical in the Alsace style and they serve classic local specialities. Good weekday set menu for €9, another at €15 or around €23 for *à la carte*. There's a shady arbour where you can sit and have a drink or a quiet meal. The hotel is right beside a park with recreation facilities – a golf driving range and games for the kids.

🏃 |●| RESTAURANT LES ACACIAS**

35 rue des Acacias (Northwest); it's near the station.
☎ 03.88.09.00.47 ➡ 03.88.80.83.33
e acacias@free.fr
Closed Fri and Sat lunchtimes, 31 Aug–7 Sept and 27 Dec–28 Jan. **Garden. Car park.**

This is a very classy place on the edge of the forest with a terrace for the summer. Stylish service. They do a nice set menu for weekday lunchtimes at €11; others €15–30. Traditional Alsace cooking with dishes such as zander with *choucroute* and *civet* of young wild boar. The view of the valley is sadly marred by a factory. Free coffee.

OBERNAI 67210

🏃 ☎ HÔTEL DU GOUVERNEUR

13 rue de Sélestat.
☎ 03.88.95.63.72 ➡ 03.88.49.91.04
Closed 20 Oct–31 Dec.

This building dates from 1566, and was the residence of the town's governor. It's generously proportioned and has an interior courtyard; one wall forms part of the town ramparts. There's a gallery and a Louis XV balustraded staircase. The bright, clean rooms have been refurbished in a sedate, contemporary style and some are very spacious (sleeping 3 or 4 people). Double with shower/wc €40–56. The owner makes you feel welcome. Free breakfast.

🏃 ☎ HOSTELLERIE LA DILIGENCE**

23 pl. de la Mairie (Centre).
☎ 03.88.95.55.69 ➡ 03.88.95.42.46
e hotel.la.diligence@wanadoo.fr
TV. Pay car park.

It would be difficult to find anywhere more central – the rooms at the front look out onto place de la Mairie in the town centre. With such a great location, you'd think the owners would just sit back and wait for the customers to roll in. In fact, they go out of their way to make you feel welcome. The rooms are of an excellent

standard, and there is a lovely breakfast room with bay windows which make you feel that you're almost in the square itself. Rooms with shower/wc €43–70. 10% discount on the room rate for a minimum of three nights.

|●| L'AGNEAU D'OR

99 rue du Général-Gouraud; it's on the main street.
☎ 03.88.95.28.22
Closed Sun evening and Mon, 3 weeks in Jan and a fortnight of June.

This is an authentic *winstub* serving wine from the region only. The painted ceiling, cuckoo clock, prints and decorated plates all make for a cosy atmosphere. Tasty local dishes are served up in generous portions. Good weekday lunch *menu du jour* at €11, others €21–32 and a children's menu at €7. *À la carte* are rack of suckling pig, stuffed pig's trotters and lamb from the Alps.

KLINGENTHAL 67530 (6KM SW)

🏃 ☎ |●| HÔTEL-RESTAURANT AU CYGNE

23 route du Mont-Sainte-Odile (Southwest); take the D426. ☎ 03.88.95.82.94
Hotel closed a fortnight June–July and a fortnight in winter. **Restaurant closed** Tues evening and Wed. **Car park.**

This is a nice little place in a good location on the Mont-Sainte-Odile road. It has a traditional atmosphere with clean simple rooms. Doubles €21–31. Menus, €14–18, all include good home cooking served in enormous portions. The delicious fruit tarts are made in the family bakery next door. 10% discount on the room rate Nov–March.

SCHARRACHBERGHEIM 67310 (18KM N)

🏃 ☎ |●| RESTAURANT LAUTH & FILS

82 rue Principale; take the Molsheim road then the D422 in the direction of Marlenheim.
☎ 03.89.50.66.05 ➡ 03.888.50.60.76
Closed Mon, Tues and lunchtimes, and Christmas–15 Jan. **Car park. Disabled access. TV.**

The vast dining room used to be a dance hall and is now a popular, relaxed restaurant. Daniel Lauth has set up a small brewery, and the beer flows freely. The place has the atmosphere of a tavern and the dishes on offer are in appropriate style: *choucroute*, *pot-au-feu*, horse steak with port. If you've got a sweet tooth, save some room for the flambéed apple tart – a favourite – and the iced kirsch soufflé. There's a cheap menu at €6 and others up to €38, as well as a children's menu for €5. The serving staff wear traditional costume. Across the courtyard in the other part of the building there are seven guest rooms. Number 104 is furnished in Alsace style with a canopied bed and a mirrored ceiling. Double with bath €43. Free apéritif.

OTTROTT   67530

🚶 🏠 |●| À L'AMI FRITZ***

8 rue des Châteaux.
☎ 03.88.95.80.81 ➡ 03.88.95.84.85
📧 hotel@amifritz.com
Closed Wed, a fortnight June–July and the first week in Jan. **TV. Disabled access. Garden. Car park.**

This seventeenth-century house is impressive both outside and in, and it's one of the least touristy places in town. It's beautifully decorated and very quiet. Bedrooms andbathrooms are pretty, and are fitted with all mod cons; those in the annexe, *Le Chant des Oiseaux*, 600m away, are cheaper but not so nice. The rooms overlooking the street are air-conditioned. Doubles €67–70. Pleasant dining room with rustic décor and efficient, attentive service. Patrick Fritz, the owner, prepares regional dishes in his own fresh style, depending on what is good at the market – black pudding strudel with horseradish, *choucroute royale*, gratinéed tripe braised in Sylvaner. Set menus €19–54. Free coffee.

NATZWILLER   67130 (19KM W)

|●| AUBERGE METZGER

55 rue Principale; take the D214 then the D130.
☎ 03.88.97.02.42 ➡ 03.88.97.93.59
Closed Sun evening and Mon except July–Aug, 7–28 Jan and 24 Jul–1 Aug. **TV. Disabled access.**

A pleasant place to stop in this beautiful valley. Mme Metzger takes her guests' comfort very seriously, and the rooms are huge and comfortable – particularly the ones that have been renovated. Prices have stayed fair: €47–53 for a double room. Typical local dishes – *salade Vosgienne*, pigeon with *choucroute* or zander with Riesling – on the menus, which start at €11 for lunch or €23–53 for dinner.

PETITE-PIERRE (LA)   67290

🏠 |●| HÔTEL DES VOSGES**

30 rue Principale.
☎ 03.88.70.45.05 ➡ 03.88.70.41.13
Closed Tuesday in winter and the last week in July. **TV. Disabled access. Garden. Car park.**

Even for such a large place it's a surprise to

find such a range of inventiveness and variety in the decoration. You're bound to find a room to your taste (whether that's modern blond wood or traditional Alsace). Comfortable double rooms, €46–75, with bath or shower/wc. Underneath the hotel there's a traditional *winstub* serving a range of local dishes; *foie gras*, trout, coq with Riesling. Menus start at €18 and go up to €48.

🚶 🏠 |●| HÔTEL-RESTAURANT AU LION D'OR***

15 rue Principale; it's opposite the town hall.
☎ 03.88.01.47.57 ➡ 03.88.01.47.50
📧 phil.lion@liondor.com
Closed 2 Jan–2 Feb and 1–10 July. **Swimming pool. TV. Disabled access. Garden. Car park.**

A rather chic little village in the Vosges regional park, popular with German holidaymakers. The *Lion d'Or*, which has just qualified for its third star, is top of the range and you will receive a warm welcome. In summer, try something from the grill and eat in the garden, or head for the affordable *winstub*. The restaurant has been refurbished and prices reflect the quality: set menus €18–50, and a children's menu at €10. The hotel has double rooms with shower/wc for €60–76. They are big, comfortable and smart, and some have wonderful views of the valley and the forest. Facilities include an indoor swimming pool and a sauna. 10% discount on the room rate for a stay of more than two nights and free apéritif when you dine.

RIBEAUVILLÉ   68150

🏠 HÔTEL DE LA TOUR**

1 rue de la Mairie (Centre).
☎ 03.89.73.72.73 ➡ 03.89.73.38.74
📧 hoteldelatour@aol.com
Closed Jan to mid-March. **TV. Garden. Pay car park.**

An old wine-grower's house in the middle of a little medieval town – it offers pleasant rooms for €60 with shower/wc, €75 with bath. Guests can use the sauna, Turkish baths and Jacuzzi for free. There is no restaurant but try the local wine and specialities in the typical Alsace *winstub*. Very pleasant, even stylish, place.

|●| L'AUBERGE AU ZAHNACKER

8 rue du Général-de-Gaulle (Centre).
☎ 03.89.73.60.70
Closed Thurs and mid-Jan to mid-Feb.

Service 9am–10pm. This inn, owned by the local wine co-operative, is a little oasis of calm off a main street jammed with tourists. Even though it's grey and next to a round-about, in summer, when the sweet-smelling wisteria is in full bloom, you can sit out on the terrace and savour a glass of Pinot Blanc while you wait for your *presskopf* (brawn) or onion tart. In winter the *winstub* has a warm and pleasant atmosphere and is full of locals and tourists. Classic house specialities, like calf's head vinaigrette, tripe in Riesling and *baeckeoffe*. €23 minimum *à la carte*. Good local wines.

ILLHAEUSERN   68970 (11KM E)

⌘ |●| À LA TRUITE

17 rue du 25-Janvier (Centre).
☎ 03.89.71.83.51 ➡ 03.89.71.85.19
Closed Tues evening, Wed, three weeks in Feb and a week at the end of June. **Garden**.

A nice country inn with a terrace looking onto the river and the weeping willows. The simple, relaxed dining room is full of office and factory workers, farmers, long-distance lorry drivers and many others looking for an inexpensive meal. The chef's speciality, which has to be ordered in advance, is *matelote Marie-Louise*, a fish stew served with noodles. Alternatively try the *foie gras*, fried fillet of carp or *coq au Riesling*. The bill is always easy on the pocket: weekday lunch menu €10 or others €14–34; *à la carte* you'll pay around €24. Free coffee.

THANNENKIRCH   68590 (11KM N)

⌘ ☗ |●| AUBERGE LA MEUNIÈRE**

30 rue Sainte Anne; take the D1 then the D42.
☎ 03.89.73.10.47 ➡ 03.89.73.12.31
ℯ info@aubergelameuniere.com
Closed Mon and Tues lunchtimes and 20 Dec–25 March. **TV**. **Garden**. **Car park**.

From the road it's a classic Alsace inn, festooned with geraniums. From the valley, it's one of a rash of buildings that sprang up in the Alps in the 1970s. The rooms are rustic but contemporary in style, done out in a superb combination of natural materials. Most have a balcony or a terrace and splendid views – you can watch the deer coming for a drink at daybreak. Doubles with shower/wc or bath €49–67. Sauna and billiards for guests. The fine, inventive cuisine in the restaurant is reasonably priced, with a set weekday lunch menu at €14 and others up to €30. *À la carte*, you'll find tasty dishes like *baeckeoffe* of snails in Riesling, wild boar

with juniper berries and ox tongue with a horseradish sauce – but the selection of dishes changes at least twice a year. The prices overall are fair, given the quality of the place, the perfect welcome and the attentive service. Free coffee.

RIQUEWIHR   68340

⌘ ☗ HÔTEL DE LA COURONNE**

5 rue de la Couronne.
☎ 03.89.49.03.03 ➡ 03.89.49.01.01
ℯ couronne@hoteldelacouronne.com
Car park.

This attractive sixteenth-century hotel is spot-on. It has a delightful gateway, and the owners' warm smiles make for a welcoming atmosphere. There are inviting little wooden benches and tables in the porch where you can enjoy a glass of *Gewürztraminer* before going off to explore the forests. All the rooms have been tastefully refurbished and the plain walls are stencilled; some have beams. The prices are pretty decent for the location – doubles with bath €55–62. Everything about this hotel is pleasing, making it one of the nicest in Riquewihr. Free house apéritif.

HUNAWIHR   68150 (4KM N)

|●| WINSTUB SUZEL

2 rue de l'Église.
☎ 03.89.73.30.85
Closed Tues; Jan–end March. **TV**. **Disabled access**. **Garden**.

The Mittnacht family, who run this wine tavern, make it a warm, welcoming place. There's a view of the church tower and in summer the shady terrace is covered with flowers. The big wooden doors at the back of the restaurant lead to the cellars, where you can sample good Alsatian wine. But the main reason to come here is the food – whatever you have it'll be good. An onion tart with salad is more than enough for smaller appetites, while the *Katel* menu would satisfy a hungry Obélix: you get onion tart, *roulades farcies* (rolled meat or fish with stuffing), sautéed potatoes, green salad and dessert. The *formule* for €14 is served at lunch and dinner, or there are menus at €16, €18 and €22. On Sunday evenings they do flambéed tarts.

SAVERNE 67700

🏠 HÔTEL EUROPE***

7 rue de la Gare (Centre).
☎ 03.88.71.12.07 ➡ 03.88.71.11.43
✉ info@hotel-europe-fr.com
TV. Disabled access. Lock-up garage.

This is the best hotel in town, and it's open every day of the year. Good facilities in the rooms, some of which have whirlpool baths. €57–78 for a double with shower or bath. Some are more spacious and have cable TV. The ritzy atmosphere, the first-rate service and the excellent buffet breakfast (€8) make sure that the customers – including a large number of staff from the European Parliament in Strasbourg – keep coming back. For families there's a flat in an adjoining house.

🍴 TAVERNE KATZ

80 Grand-Rue (Centre); it's near the town hall.
☎ 03.88.71.16.56
Closed Tues evening, Wed and a fortnight in Jan.

This beautiful place was built in 1605 as the residence of a man called Katz, the archbishop's tax collector – the house's history is retold on a board outside just above the menu. Beautiful dining room with wood panelling. The first-rate cooking focuses on traditional dishes and excellent desserts – the dishes rarely change and are totally reliable. Menus start at €15 and go up to €37. Specialities include *timbale* of chicken in pastry served with *spaetzles* (noodles), marinated *baeckeoffe* (which they make with fish) and goose *choucroute*. The terrace looks out onto the pedestrianized street. Suzie and Jos, the friendly owners, have also bought a hotel, *Hôtel Villa Katz*, at 42 rue du Général Leclerc. It is in an old colonial-style residence and offers 8 spacious rooms priced at €53–69.

SÉLESTAT 67000

🍴 🏠 🍴 HÔTEL VAILLANT**

pl. de la République (Centre); it's on the way to the station from the town centre.
☎ 03.88.92.09.46 ➡ 03.88.82.95.01
✉ hotel-vaillat@rmcnet.fr
Restaurant closed Sat and Sun lunchtimes out of season, the last week of the year and a week in the Feb school holidays. **TV. Disabled access. Car park.**

The rooms in this large modern hotel, built in 1967, all have personality and are individually furnished with contemporary pieces that are brightly coloured without being overpowering.

Double rooms are €41–49 with shower/wc, €60 with bath. In the restaurant specialities include fish, *choucroute* and other Alsace dishes. Set menus range from €14 to 38 or you can dine *à la carte*. There is a small gym with sauna for residents. Free house apéritif.

🍴 🏠 🍴 AUBERGE DES ALLIÉS**

39 rue des Chevaliers (Centre).
☎ 03.88.92.09.34 ➡ 03.88.92.12.88
✉ auberge-des-allies@libertysurf.fr
Closed Sun evening, Mon, 1–16 July. **TV.**

The history of this building starts in 1372; it was a bakery in the first half of the nineteenth century when Louis-Philippe ruled France, and it's been a restaurant since 1918. In the middle of the dining room is an impressive old Alsatian stove, and there's also a beautiful fresco showing the place aux Choux in the first half of the nineteenth century – note that the women are not wearing the typical Hansi-style head-dress. The *à la carte* menu is typical of this kind of restaurant, with local dishes such as ham hock, *choucroute* and zander with Riesling. Try the house *foie gras*. Set menus €15–25. Double rooms with bath €55. 10% discount May–Nov.

RATHSAMHAUSEN 67600 (3KM E)

🏠 🍴 🍴 HÔTEL-RESTAURANT À L'ÉTOILE**

Grande-Rue; it's on the D21 in the direction of Muttersholz.
☎ 03.88.92.35.79 ➡ 03.88.82.91.66
Closed Feb. **Swimming pool. TV. Garden. Car park.**

A young couple have cleverly modernized this old house by adding an extension with a bright foyer and a stairway in wood and glass. Pleasant doubles with shower/wc cost €38–53. The dining room is warm and intimate in the evenings. The *à la carte* menu is limited but lists good dishes, particularly the fried carp or fried small fry. Expect to pay €17 for a meal or opt for the cheap set menu at €6 or others €11–18. In summer the terrace is covered with flowers and there's an open-air pool. A really nice little place.

DAMBACH-LA-VILLE 67650 (10KM N)

🏠 HÔTEL LE VIGNOBLE**

1 rue de l'Église.
☎ 03.88.92.43.75
Closed Sun out of season, 20 Dec–15 March and ten days in Nov. **TV. Disabled access. Car park.**

Charming hotel, tastefully converted from an

eighteenth-century gabled barn. Stylish, comfortable rooms, with doubles €45–50, extra bed €14 and breakfast for €6 or €9.

STRASBOURG 67200

SEE MAP OVERLEAF

🛏 |◉| HÔTEL SCHUTZENBOCK

81 av. Jean-Jaurès-Neudorf (Southeast). **Off map D4-3**
☎ 03.88.34.04.19 ➡ 03.88.34.04.19
Closed Sat lunchtime, Sun, Aug and 23 Dec–2 Jan.

An inexpensive, clean and friendly hotel. Some of the rooms at the back overlook the garden. Doubles €24 with handbasin. Set lunch menu €8, other menus €15–23, with simple, regional cooking. Half board €27. Pretty fair.

🐾 🛏 HÔTEL DE BRUXELLES**

13 rue Kuhn (Centre). **MAP A2-6**
☎ 03.88.32.45.31 ➡ 03.88.32.06.22
TV.

A little place near the station. It's decent, clean and friendly. The decoration is in highly personal taste – the fabrics and carpets are a hotch-potch of colour – but it's quiet and the bedding is good. Doubles €25–42, depending on facilities. 10% discount on the room rate Jan–March and July–Aug.

🐾 🛏 HÔTEL PATRICIA*

rue du Puits (Centre). **MAP C4-4**
☎ 03.88.32.14.60 ➡ 03.88.32.19.08
e hotelpatricia@hotmail.com

A lovely sixteenth-century building in a quiet, centrally located side street. A really wonderful place with generously proportioned, clean and newly refurbished rooms. TV and smoking are outlawed, so it's quiet and pleasant too. And it's not expensive: €27 for a double with basin, €34 with shower, €37 with shower/wc. Easy-going, gentle welcome. 10% discount on the room rate 1 Jan–15 March.

🐾 🛏 HÔTEL DE L'ILL**

8 rue des Bateliers-Krutenau. **MAP D3-7**
☎ 03.88.36.20.01 ➡ 03.88.35.30.03
Closed 29 Dec–5 Jan.**TV**. **Disabled access**. **Public car park opposite**.

A good place in a quiet street with fair prices so it's advisable to book. It's well-run by the Ehrhardt family. Rooms are not very big but they're pleasant and clean and prices are reasonable – doubles €39–40 with shower, €46–60 with shower/wc or bath. Some rooms are set aside for non-smokers and two have direct access onto the lovely terrace on the first floor. It gets the sun and you can enjoy the view of Sainte-Madeleine church. Generous breakfast for €6. Free breakfast and 10% discount on the room rate in July and Aug.

🛏 HÔTEL GUTENBERG**

31 rue des Serruriers (Centre). **MAP C3-8**
☎ 03.88.32.17.15 ➡ 03.88.75.76.67
Closed 1–13 Jan. **TV**.

An eighteenth-century house that successfully combines the modern and the traditional with facilities that you would expect to find in a three-star hotel. The owner, whose grandfather was an officer in the Grande Armée, is mad about military engravings from the Napoleonic period and his collection is displayed over all the walls. This passion for the Empire carries through into the rooms which have good pieces of old family furniture. The rooms on the fifth floor (three of which have a mezzanine) give delightful views over the rooftops – you'll get more or less the same view on the fourth floor. The breakfast is pretty ordinary and at €7 seems expensive. Double rooms €53–84 with shower/wc or bath. Warm welcome.

🐾 🛏 HÔTEL COUVENT DU FRANCISCAIN**

18 rue du Faubourg-de-Pierre. **MAP B1-5**
☎ 03.88.32.93.93 ➡ 03.88.75.68.46
e info@hotel-franciscain.com
Closed Christmas to 1 Jan. **TV**. **Disabled access**. **Car park**.

A centrally located hotel near the covered market. It has been thoughtfully renovated and has lots of rooms. Doubles cost €56 with shower/wc or bath. Buffet breakfast €8. Warm welcome. 10% discount Jan–March.

🛏 HÔTEL SAINT-CHRISTOPHE**

2 pl. de la Gare. **MAP A3-9**
☎ 03.88.22.30.30 ➡ 03.88.32.17.11
e christop@tpgnet.net
TV. **Disabled access**.

This well-run hotel, named after the patron saint of travellers, is convenient for businesspeople arriving by train at the station opposite or holidaymakers travelling by car – it's hard to drive into the centre of town. Rooms are really comfortable and most have been refurbished (doubles €66–73). The top price ones look onto a pleasant inner courtyard which is bathed in sunlight nearly all day – a nice place for breakfast or a relaxing drink in the late afternoon.

⅄ 🏠 LE GRAND HÔTEL***

12 pl. de la Gare. **MAP A2-10**
☎ 03.88.52.84.84 ➡ 03.88.52.84.00
e le.grand.hotel@wanadoo.fr
TV. Disabled access. Pay parking.

You can't miss this huge, concrete, Soviet-style 1950s monstrosity on the square. It has austere lines, an oppressive vastness, wide corridors, an awe-inspiring hall, an immense, high-ceilinged sitting room and a superb glass lift, also from the '50s, that's not only a prototype but the only one now in existence. The interior, though, has been redesigned to suit modern tastes. Good facilities in rooms which are well worth the hotel's three-star status, some with air-conditioning; doubles €63–91. Service of the same standard. A "Grand" hotel that lives up to its name. Free apéritif.

⅄ 🏠 HÔTEL MAISON ROUGE***

4 rue des Francs-Bourgeois. **MAP B3-12**
☎ 03.88.32.08.60 ➡ 03.88.22.43.73
e info@maison-rouge.com
TV.

The startling red frontage gives no clue to the quality of accommodation in this hotel. Inside, the rooms are individually decorated in soft pastels with matching fabrics and they have all modern facilities (mini-bar, cable TV and so on). Doubles with shower €78 or bath €104. Very professional staff. 10% discount in July and Aug.

🏠 HÔTEL BEAUCOUR***

5 rue des Bouchers. **MAP C4-11**
☎ 03.88.76.72.00 ➡ 03.88.76.72.60
e beaucour@hotel-beaucour.com
TV. Disabled access. Public parking opposite.

This hotel is spread between five half-timbered buildings from the eighteenth century and it is in a wonderful location only a few minutes from the cathedral. Considerable refurbishment has somewhat detracted from its authenticity, but it's comfortable and has a matchless charm. All the rooms are nicely decorated. Prices €84–119 for a double with bath.

|O| RESTAURANT LA VICTOIRE

2 bd. de la Victoire. **MAP D2/3-22**
☎ 03.88.35.39.35
Closed Sat evening, Sun and first three weeks in Aug.

Closes at 1am. This place is always full, so if you can't book you'll need to go early. Though it looks anonymous from outdoors, it's pretty impressive inside with a great atmosphere – a

favourite haunt of students and teachers from the university. Classic regional dishes such as pork chop with tarragon, trout with cream, grilled Cervelas sausages (menus €7–34), but you come more for the atmosphere than the originality of the cuisine.

⅄ |O| S'THOMAS STEUBEL

5 rue du Bouclier. **MAP B3-28**
☎ 03.88.22.34.82
Closed Sun, Mon, a fortnight during the Easter school holidays and 5–18 Aug.

There's nowhere more friendly than this pocket-sized traditional *winstub*. Local wines by the glass or the jug and plate-groaning portions of the region's specialities: reasonably priced *choucroute*, duck fillet with Pinot Noir wine sauce, veal kidneys with noodles, grilled pork knuckle with mash and *bibelkäss* (cream cheese with sautéed potatoes). Lunch menu is at €8, but, on average, expect to pay €18 for a meal. Smiling staff and a relaxed atmosphere. It's a bit of a squeeze so it's best to book. Free coffee.

|O| LA COCCINELLE

22 rue Sainte-Madeleine (South). **MAP D4-27**
☎ 03.88.36.19.27
Closed Sat lunchtime, Sun and 15 July–15 Aug.

Two sisters run this place: one does the cooking and the other looks after the dining room. The restaurant is packed with regulars at lunchtime, drawn by the reasonably priced dish of the day. It's calmer in the evenings. Good regional specialities include *quenelles* of liver, *pot-au-feu* with rock salt and *vigneronne* pie. On Saturday evenings in winter, order the Alsace classic *baeckeoffe*, a stew of beef, mutton and pork. Menus €10–18. Friendly welcome and service with a smile.

|O| AU PONT CORBEAU

21 quai Saint-Nicolas. **MAP C4-21**
☎ 03.88.35.60.68
Closed Sat, Sun lunchtime, a week in the Feb school holidays and Aug.

First off, the owner here will always give you a warm, friendly welcome. Secondly, the food is great, and thirdly, it's one of the few *winstubs* in the town centre near the cathedral that's open on Sunday nights. The mineral water is from the Bas-Rhin, the draught beer from a brewery across the Rhine is excellent and they serve a big selection of Bas-Rhin wines by the glass. These little things make all the difference. The house speciality (a must),

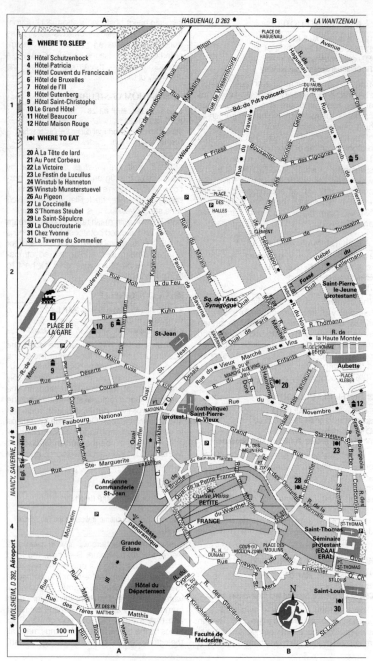

WHERE TO SLEEP

3 Hôtel Schutzenbock
4 Hôtel Patricia
5 Hôtel Couvent du Franciscain
6 Hôtel de Bruxelles
7 Hôtel de l'Ill
8 Hôtel Gutenberg
9 Hôtel Saint-Christophe
10 Le Grand Hôtel
11 Hôtel Beaucour
12 Hôtel Maison Rouge

WHERE TO EAT

20 À La Tête de lard
21 Au Pont Corbeau
22 La Victoire
23 Le Festin de Lucullus
24 Winstub le Hanneton
25 Winstub Munsterstuevel
26 Au Pigeon
27 La Coccinelle
28 S'Thomas Steubel
29 Le Saint-Sépulcre
30 La Choucrouterie
31 Chez Yvonne
32 La Taverne du Sommelier

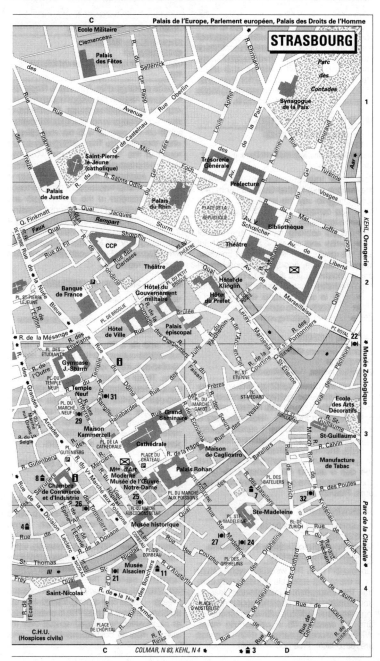

C   Palais de l'Europe, Parlement européen, Palais des Droits de l'Homme

STRASBOURG

Ecole Militaire
Clemenceau
Palais
des Fêtes
Sellénick
Parc
des
Contades
Synagogue
de la Paix

des
Rue
Avenue
du
Gal de Castelnau
Saint-Pierre-
le-Jeune
(catholique)
Trésorerie
Générale
Préfecture
Palais
de Justice
Palais
du Rhin
PLACE DE LA
RÉPUBLIQUE
Bibliothèque
Théâtre

Quai   Jacques
Rempart   Sturm
Faux
CCP
Théâtre
Banque
de France
Hôtel du
Gouvernement
militaire
Hôtel de
Klinglin
Hôtel
du Préfet
Brûlée
Hôtel
de Ville
Palais
épiscopal

R. de la Mésange
Gymnase
J.-Sturm
Temple
Neuf
31
29
Maison
Kammerzell
Cathédrale
Grand
Séminaire
Maison
de Cagliostro
St-Guillaume
Ecole
des Arts
Décoratifs
Manufacture
de Tabac

8
Chambre
de Commerce
et d'Industrie
26
Mée d'Art
Moderne
Musée de l'Œuvre
Notre-Dame
Palais Rohan
1
32
Ste-Madeleine
4
Musée historique
27   24
III
Musée
Alsacien
21   11
Saint-Nicolas

C.H.U.
(Hospices civils)

C   COLMAR, N 83, KEHL, N 4   3   D

[17]

is grilled ham with sautéed potatoes at €11; you might also try the salad with a selection of meats and *crudités* with sautéed potatoes or the calves' brains fritters in *rémoulade* sauce served with steamed potatoes and salad. Menus at €11 or around €23 for *à la carte*. This place is a showcase for everything that's great about Alsatian food and drink.

|●| LE FESTIN DE LUCULLUS

18 rue sainte-Hélène. **MAP B3-23**
☎ 03.88.22.40.78
Closed Sun evening, Mon and 8–15 Dec and 12 Aug–1 Sept.

Four years' training under the eagle eye of the famous chef Michel Guérard is character-forming to say the least, and the chef here was certainly inspired by his time at Eugénie-les-Bains – everything from the well-judged cooking times to the use of fresh herbs and seasonings is thoughtful and the results are excellent. The cheerful, friendly welcome, good service and honest prices mean that you'll want to come back, too. Weekday lunch menu €11 or another at €25; *à la carte* around €31. The only slight drawback is the somewhat overformal décor in the long dining room.

🎎 |●| AU PIGEON

23 rue des Tonneliers. **MAP C4-26**
☎ 03.88.32.31.30
Closed Sun evening, Mon and Tues evening.

In one of the oldest buildings in town, a glorious, half-timbered, gabled residence built in the sixteenth century, this historic *winstub* has been going for years. Above the door is a wooden frieze featuring a carved pigeon. The faultless dining room is sobre and classic in style, and serves dishes such as *baeckeoffe*, *choucroute* and knuckle of pork. Dish of the day is around €9, menus €13–21. A shining beacon in a galaxy of lesser wine taverns. Free coffee.

🎎 |●| WINSTUB LE HANNETON

5 rue Sainte-Madeleine **MAP D4-24**
☎ 03.88.36.93.76
Closed Mon except public holidays, Tues lunch and a fortnight at the beginning of Nov.

Open until 11pm. This *winstub* is worlds away from the tourist scramble yet still pretty central. The atmosphere is intimate and pleasant and Monsieur Denis' good humour is refreshing. Very good *tartiflette* with Munster cheese and the *baeckehoffe* is wonderfully moist. With a meal costing between €12–18, prices are reasonable. Free house apéritif.

🎎 |●| LA CHOUCROUTERIE

20 rue Saint-Louis. **MAP B4-30**
☎ 03.88.36.52.87
Closed Sun evening, a week in Jan and three weeks in Aug.

Service evenings only, 7pm–1am. Roger Siffer was an Alsatian folk singer before he went into the restaurant business. From time to time he still sings in his restaurant-theatre – either on his own or with his musical pals when they drop by. The building was a post house in the 18th century and was then home to the last *choucroute* makers in Strasbourg – apparently they made the best in town. The owner has brought his own touch to the decoration of the dining room and hung a collection of beautiful musical instruments on the walls. But you can still get *choucroute* here – seven varieties, in fact. Alternatively, try the Munster cheese rissoles with salad or the "Siffer" veal dish. Set menus €13–27. Free coffee.

|●| LA TAVERNE DU SOMMELIER

ruelle de la Bruche. **MAP D3-32**
☎ 03.88.24.14.10
Closed Sat, Sun, New Year holidays and a week now and then through the year.

The ruelle de la Bruche is extremely narrow but widens out just by the tavern to make a bit of space. It's a nice place with lots of regulars. There is typical *winstub* fare on the menu – *croustillant* of calf's head, grilled tuna and pan-fried *foie gras* escalopes – but the thoughtfully prepared dishes range more widely than the basic regional classics. *Á la carte* around €18. Good little wines by the glass. Down-to-earth, smiling staff.

🎎 |●| RESTAURANT À LA TÊTE DE LARD

3 rue Hannomg. **MAP B3-20**
☎ 03.88.32.13.56
Closed Sat lunchtime, Sun and the first fortnight in Aug.

An unpretentious bistro that's always has a lively atmosphere. Flambéed tart, goose breast with honeyed apples, *choucroute*, baked potatoes with Munster cheese, winemakers *tourte* and a menu with seasonal dishes – all the regional specialities, with a few variations, are here. Their *flammenküche*, or flambéed tart, is made with bacon, onions and cheese – share one among friends and get stuck in with your fingers! This is a very popular place which has stayed special over the years. A meal will cost around €19 *à la carte*. Free coffee.

⦿ LE SAINT-SÉPULCRE

15 rue des Orfèvres. **MAP C3-29**
☎ 03.88.32.39.97
Closed Sun, Mon and 7–15 July.

This is one of the most extraordinary places in town and one of the best-known in Strasbourg. The owner's renowned for his playful rudeness – he'll accost you brusquely at the door and demand to know your business. He's actually a lovely man who thrives on a joke, but come prepared. The food is excellent, solid Alsace cuisine – there's *confit* of pork tongue, potato salad, ham *choucroute*, goose *foie gras* and a fabulous ham *en croûte* which is sliced in front of you. The typical little bistro glasses, carafes of wine, checked napkins, polished floors and the wooden stove in the middle of the room all create the right atmosphere for an unforgettable meal. It'll cost about €23 per person.

⦿ WINSTUB MUNSTERSTUEVEL

8 pl. du Marché aux Cochons-de-Lait. **MAP C3-25**
☎ 03.88.32.17.63
Closed Sun and Mon.

Patrick Klipfel and his wife Marlène, both professional to their fingertips, have a solid fan club who gravitate here – and they keep their customers satisfied. The prices are slightly higher – €23 *à la carte* – than in a traditional *winstub* but the quality is undeniable. Oxtail *pot-au-feu* with vegetables, marrowbone and *crudités* with horseradish sauce, pork cheek, and *choucroute* are typical of the hearty fare on offer. Good selection of wines, spirits and draught Météor. The terrace gets crowded on sunny days.

⦿ CHEZ YVONNE

10 rue du Sanglier. **MAP C3-31**
☎ 03.88.32.84.15
Closed Sun, Mon lunchtime, mid-July to mid-Aug and Christmas to New Year.

Yvonne Haller's *winstub* is a Strasbourg institution. Showbiz celebs and politicians – including President Chirac, who appreciates good food and drink – often come here when they're in town and it's also very popular with locals, who flock in to enjoy this great lady's cooking. Calf's head, milk-fed veal chops, *choucroute* tart, oxtail *terrine* and stuffed fresh quails are all first-class. Expect some expense – a meal will cost about €31 (no set menus). The impressive *stammtisch*, or regulars' table, is a tradition. No credit cards.

HANDSCHUHEIM   67117 (13KM W)

⦿ L'AUBERGE À L'ESPÉRANCE

5 rue Principale; take the N4 from Strasbourg.
☎ 03.88.69.00.52 ➔ 03.88.69.10.19
Closed Mon, Tues and the second fortnight in Jan. **Car park**.

The restaurant in this attractive half-timbered house is welcoming but open only for dinner. You go up the stairs and there's a choice of five pretty dining rooms. *Flammenküche* (flambéed tart) is a particular speciality, cooked here in the old-fashioned way on wood cinders – which gives it its unique flavour and lightness. The place appeals to families and groups of friends, so the atmosphere is warm and friendly. They have some good wines, and they don't push the local vintages too hard. Expect to pay €18 *à la carte*.

THANN   68800

🍴 🏠 ⦿ HÔTEL-RESTAURANT KLÉBER**

39 rue Kléber (Centre).
☎ 03.89.37.13.66 ➔ 03.89.37.39.67
Hotel closed 1–20 Feb. **Restaurant closed** Sat and Sun. **TV**. **Disabled access**. **Car park**.

This hotel is in a residential area away from the hustle and bustle of town. It's quite new and stylish, with fair prices. Rooms 24 and 26 in the annexe are really quiet, with balconies overlooking the orchards. Doubles with shower/wc €38–60. The restaurant, which has a good reputation, offers a weekday lunch menu at €11 and others at €15–21, with dishes like beef with morels, game, wild boar or kid and iced *Kugelhopf*. Good value for a two-star. Pleasant welcome. 10% discount on the room rate except July–Aug.

MOOSCH   68690 (7KM NW)

🏠 ⦿ FERME-AUBERGE DU GSANG

How to get there: from Moosch, head for the Mine d'Argent campsite, follow the forest road for 7km, and park in the car park in the Gsang. Then it's a 20-minute walk – there's only one path.
☎ 03.89.38.96.85
Closed Fri except in July and Aug, and Sun evening.

It's worth making the effort to find this delightful farmhouse, where they have yet to discover electricity. You eat very well: they do sandwiches at any time of the day, smoked scrag of mutton, roasts, *fleischschnake*, vegetable stew and the most wonderful soup *fermière*. For €11 per person you get a really good meal. On Sundays the dining rooms are full to bursting and if you want to stay, you should book. Accommodation is in clean, basic dormitories but bring a sleeping bag and a torch. Half board €22. You have to walk everywhere and the view is fabulous. Great atmosphere – you'll have a memorable stay.

SAINT-AMARIN   68550 (8KM NW)

☎ |●| AUBERGE DU MEHRBÄCHEL*

Route de Geishouse. Leave the N66 at Saint-Amarin signposted to Geishouse; about 3km along the main road, before the village, turn off left and keep going (where all the pine trees are) until you come to the inn.
☎ 03.89.82.60.68 ➡ 03.89.82.66.05
Closed Thurs evening, Fri and All Saints' school holidays. **Car park**.

The chalet, with woods on one side and pastures on the other, is set on the side of the mountain dominating the Thur valley. The views of the valley from the bedrooms – which are in a modern annexe – are splendid. Doubles with shower/wc or bath €46–49. The restaurant is well worth the effort of getting here. Cooking is traditional, but the chef has added his own touches. Specialities include trout with almonds, lamb shank, pan-fried fresh *foie gras* and whisky soufflé. The fried Munster cheese coated with breadcrumbs and served with salad and cumin is also a treat. Menus from €17 (except on Sun) to €27. The generous breakfast buffet features smoked bacon, ham, cereal, yoghurt and more. And outside there's the soothing sound of cowbells.

WISSEMBOURG   67160

⅍ ☎ |●| HÔTEL-RESTAURANT WALK**

2 rue de la Walk (Northwest); it's next to the hospital.
☎ 03.88.94.06.44 ➡ 03.88.54.38.03
℮ hotel.moulin.la.walk@wanadoo.fr
Closed Fri lunchtime, Sun evening, Mon, 8–31 Jan and 15–30 June. **TV. Disabled access. Car park**.

This place, outside the town's fortifications and surrounded by lots of greenery, has a relaxing atmosphere. In an annexe there are ten comfortable, cheery rooms with wood-panelled walls and new bathrooms – a few with lovely views of the park. They go for €51–55; half board costs €55 per person. The restaurant is housed in another building. The cooking is pretty upmarket: goose *foie gras*, a duo of zander and salmon with scallops and iced *parfait* with kirsch. Menus at €27 and €33. Free apéritif.

CLIMBACH   67510 (9KM SW)

|●| RESTAURANT AU COL DE PFAFFENSCHLICK

Col du Pfaffenschlick. Climbach is on the D3; turn left up to the pass.
☎03.88.54.28.84 ➡ 03.88.54.39.17
Closed Mon, Tues and 15 Jan–15 Feb. **Disabled access. Car park**.

The Séraphin family will give you a genuinely warm welcome to their little inn in the heart of the forest. The dining room, with its hefty beams and wood panelling, has a friendly atmosphere, and there's a terrace for summer. They serve ham, snails, salads, cheeses, quiches, onion tarts and regional specialities including free-range chicken in Riesling, wild boar stew or *baeckeoffe* (to order in advance). Weekday menu €8, another at €18 or about €19 *à la carte*. Madame Séraphin goes out of her way to make your meal as pleasant as possible. A good place, and only a few kilometres from Four à Chaux, an important sector of the Maginot Line.

WOERTH   67630

⅍|●| RESTAURANT SANS ALCOOL ET SANS FUMÉE

11 rue de la Pépinière; it's at the entrance to the town.
☎ 03.88.09.30.79 ➡ 03.88.54.06.42
Closed Mon, evenings and the Feb school holidays. **Disabled access**.

This establishment in a huge traditional residence is one of a kind in Alsace. Just think – it's in the middle of the vineyard and they don't serve alcohol or allow smoking. Its origins date back to 1944 when Mme Bender swore that if she got out alive from a devastating bombardment she would open an alcohol-free inn. She kept her word but had to cope with the most challenging of times: the traditional patrons left in droves and it took a while to build up a new clientele – but the quality of the cuisine ensured that she did. Now people come from far and wide. The pastries and desserts prepared by her daughter are second to none – apple tart, cheese flan, smooth chocolate mousse, meringues and iced *vacherin*. In the week there are cold platters and charcuterie. Dish of the day €6, menus €10–17. There's a wonderful smell of cooking in the warmly welcoming dining room, which is set with long tables. It's absolutely packed at the weekend. Free coffee.

AQUITAINE

AGEN   47000

🍴 🛏 HÔTEL DES AMBANS*

59 rue des Ambans (Centre); it's near the station.
☎ 05.53.66.28.60 📠 05.53.87.94.01
TV.

A simple one-star hotel on a quiet street in the old part of town. It's well run and clean, even if the décor in all nine rooms is a bit tired. The prices are very attractive, though: doubles €24 with shower/wc and €29 with bath. The owner will welcome you like a friend. One free breakfast per room per night.

🛏 HÔTEL DES ILES

25 rue Baudin (Centre).
☎ 05.53.47.11.33 📠 05.53.66.19.25
TV.

Behind the white stone façade, this lovely hotel is arranged around a central light well. There's every chance the owner himself will check you in, his cheroot clamped in the corner of his mouth. The laidback feel is deceptive as it's actually a well-organized place. The ten clean rooms are clean and nicely maintained and you'll have peace and quiet in this residential area. Doubles €24 with shower/wc and €32 with bath. It doesn't have an official star rating but deserves one for its character alone.

🍴 🛏 ATLANTIC HÔTEL**

133 av. Jean-Jaurès (Southeast).
☎ 05.53.96.16.56 📠 05.53.98.34.80
Closed 24 Dec–3 Jan. **Disabled access**. **TV**.
Swimming pool. **Pay garage**.

Neither the surroundings nor the '70s architecture of this building are particularly attrac-
tive, but the rooms are spacious and quiet, and the air-conditioning helps beat the heat. Six rooms overlook the garden. Doubles with shower/wc go for €44; with bath they're €50. Very warm welcome. Free garage and 10% discount on the room rate.

🍴 LES MIGNARDISES

40 rue Camille-Desmoulins (Centre).
☎ and 📠 05.53.47.18.62
Closed Sun, Mon evening and a fortnight in August.

Though it has no pretentions to being gourmet cuisine, the food here is good value. They do remarkably cheap menus at €10 (available lunchtimes as well as Tuesday and Wednesday evenings), which include soup, starter, main course and dessert. Settle down on one of the green moleskin-covered benches and get stuck into a seafood platter (€46 for two), the veal stew, the fine trout *meunière* and the smooth *crème caramel*. The place is always packed at lunchtime.

🍴 🍴 LA BOHÊME

14 rue Émile-Sentini (Centre).
☎ 05.53.68.31.00
Closed Sat lunchtime, Sun and Wed evenings except July–Aug; also 12–17 Feb, 16–21 April and 3–15 Sept.

The décor doesn't have the warm bohemian feel you might expect from the name but the owner certainly injects spirit into the place. He contributes creativity and adventure to the food: dishes include spiced duck breast, pan-fried *foie gras* with girolles, pork *colombo*, creole stew followed with either chocolate *fondant* or banana *croustillant* with rum to follow. Weekday lunch menu €11; others are €15–28, including a West Indian menu

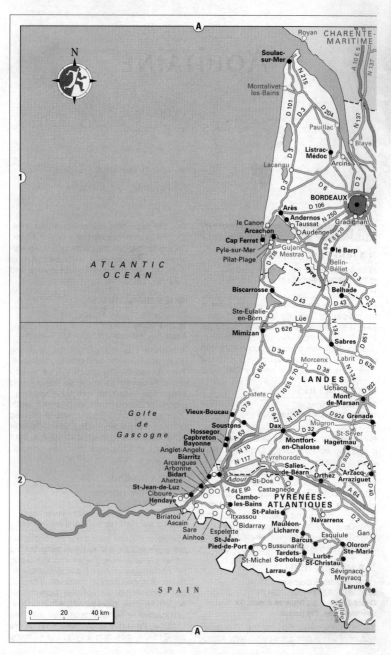

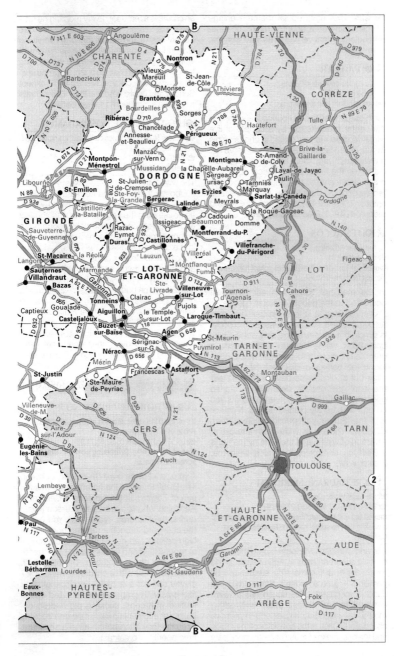

for €24. They host regular theme evenings concentrating on a country, region or wine. Particularly attentive welcome and service. Free apéritif.

🏃 |●| L'ATELIER

14 rue du Jeu-de-Paume (Centre).
☎ 05.53.87.89.22
Closed Sat, Sun; Mon lunchtimes.

Everyone comes to this sparky, lively place in the centre of town, run by a couple of live wires. Monsieur is very skilled in choosing his wines while Madame takes time to serve her guests attentively. There are quite a lot of fish dishes on the menu and the local speciality, duck, also features: amazing carpaccio and *tartare* of duck, duck breast with honey and spices. There's a lunch *formule* at €13 and menus €14–25. Free house apéritif.

🏃 |●| LES AUCOS

33 rue Voltaire (Centre).
☎ 05.53.48.13.71
Closed Sat lunchtime, Tues, the Feb school holidays and the first fortnight in Sept.

In the medieval town, this establishment dedicated to the goose (*aucos* is "goose" in Provençal) is on a little street that becomes an outdoor café in summer. Inside, the décor is simple but creates a nice atmosphere with bare brick walls, Basque table cloths, a grandfather clock and classical music playing in the background. Lunch is a speedy affair but you have time to savour the local gastronomic delicacies – stuffed goose neck with herbs, goose ham fillets and so on – in carefully crafted dishes. Menu at €15 (not Saturday or public holidays), then €22–29. There's a wide and interesting selection of wines, and the wine by the jug is *appellation contrôlée*. Very nice welcome. Free *digestif*.

🏃 |●| RESTAURANT MARIOTTAT

25 rue Louis-Vivent (Centre).
☎ 05.53.77.99.77 ➡ 05.53.77.99.79
Closed Sat and Mon lunchtimes, Sun evening, Mon, and a week in the Feb school holidays. **Disabled access**. **Car park**.

Éric and Christiane Mariottat turned their back on their suburban hotel in Agen to set up this restaurant in a fine mansion surrounded by parkland – just a stone's throw from the Jacobin monastery. The house has a warm atmosphere and a cosy décor with ceiling mouldings, splendid parquet and impressive chandeliers. Duck is the speciality of the region and the chef makes full use of it – his duck pâté

en croûte is a real treat. Every morning he reinvents his dishes depending on what he's bought fresh at the market that day. Everything is wonderful, from the potato *millefeuille* with warm *foie gras* and truffle gravy to the suckling lamb medley with basil. To finish, try prune ravioli in wine with orange. Menus €17, except Sunday and public holidays, then €26–46 with a children's menu at €11. Free coffee.

|●| RESTAURANT LE NOSTRADAMUS

40 rue des Nitiobriges, Vallon de Verone; it's on the road to Vérone.
☎ 05.53.47.01.02
Closed Sun evening and Mon.

The wife of the medieval seer Nostradamus is supposed to have come from around here – hence this restaurant's name. This all-wooden house is on the edge of town and you feel as if you've gone to eat in the country. In summer you can have a meal on the terrace in the dappled shade of the trees. Inside the décor is a successful balance between rustic and modern. If you order the €20 *formule*, you start by helping yourself from the twenty starters on the buffet and finish with a choice of ten desserts. In between, there's a small selction of tasty and original main courses: semi-cooked *foie gras* with quince jelly, quail with grapes, duck with orange, a selection of meats grilled over the open fire and parsleyed scallops with curry. Cordial welcome.

SÉRIGNAC-SUR-GARONNE 47310 (8KM W)

🏃 🏠 |●| HÔTEL LE PRINCE NOIR★★★

It's on the D119 in the direction of Nérac, after the bridge over the Garonne.
☎ 05.53.68.74.30 ➡ 05.53.68.71.93
Closed Sun evening. **Swimming pool**. **TV**. **Disabled access**. **Car park**.

A wonderful place in a 17th-century convent. The Black Prince of the hotel's name was the son of Edward III, the Lieutenant-General of Aquitaine who laid waste to the southwest during the Hundred Years' War. You get to the courtyard through a turreted porch. With high ceilings and period furniture, the rooms at ground level and upstairs are all very good, and some are sumptuous. Doubles €49. Menus €16–58 with a children's menu at €7 or you can eat *à la carte*: escalope of duck *foie gras* with grapes, roasted rolled capon stuffed with ceps, suckling pig and so on. Luxury at affordable prices; it's worth booking because they often host business seminars. Free apéritif or breakfast.

AIGUILLON 47190

🏃 🏠 |●| HÔTEL-RESTAURANT LA TER-RASSE DE L'ÉTOILE**

Centre; it's in a part-pedestrianized street.
☎ 05.53.79.64.64 ➡ 05.53.79.46.48
Swimming pool. Disabled access. TV. Car park.

A superb little hotel built in white stone. There are seventeen rooms – all different but equally charming – and they're decorated in 1930s style with iron bedsteads and country furniture. Doubles €41 with bath. The dining room is quite elegant (apart from the plastic chairs, that is) and there's a terrace overlooking the swimming pool. The menus start at €12 (except weekends and public holidays) with others at €15–24, featuring dishes like scallops *au gratin*, salmon with fennel mousse and confit of duck with prunes – but because the menu changes frequently this is just a guide. Charming welcome. Free apéritif.

CLAIRAC 47320 (8KM NE)

🏃 |●| L'ECUELLE D'OR

22 rue Porte Pinte.
☎ 05.53.88.19.78
Closed Sat lunchtime, Sun evening and Mon (except in July–Aug).

A typical village house in rough brick with oak beams. The dining room is relaxing and there's an open log fire. Fresh produce appears in imaginative dishes (how about *millefeuille* of courgette flowers or spiced *foie gras* terrine?) and the menu changes frequently. They make everything in their own kitchens, including the bread, and also do more traditional fare such as *confit* of duck. Weekday menu €12, with others €21 to €44. Excellent welcome. Free house apéritif.

ANDERNOS-LES-BAINS 33510

🏠 HÔTEL DE LA CÔTE D'ARGENT

180 bd. de la République.
☎ 05.56.03.98.58 ➡ 05.56.03.98.68
TV. Disabled access.

This roadside hotel with ten well-equipped rooms offers the best value in the area. €37–46 with shower/wc or bath. There's a small flowery patio with a small fountain – the two rooms at garden level have the view. Breakfast includes fresh fruit and real orange juice. Smiling welcome.

TAUSSAT 33148 (3KM SE)

🏃 |●| RESTAURANT LES FONTAINES

Port de plaisance de Taussat; from Bordeaux take the expressway in the direction of Cap Ferret.
☎ 05.56.82.13.86 ➡ 05.57.70.23.43
Closed Sun evening, Mon. **Car park.**

This modern building near the marina doesn't exactly ooze charm, but it has a pleasant terrace where you can sit on a warm evening and enjoy the inspired cooking of chef Jean-Pascal Paubert. Try his *tartare* of salmon with chives the roast *langoustines* in an aubergine marinade. Menus €17–35. As with many of the restaurants in the region, you can bring your own wine. The owner is chairman of the local *sommeliers* association. Free house apéritif.

AUDENGE 33980 (8KM SE)

🏠 |●| LE RELAIS GASCON

24 av. de Certes.
☎ 05.56.26.83.94 ➡ 05.56.26.95.11
Closed Sun evening out of season. **Car park.**

In these parts, it's hard to find a restaurant offering anything other than seafood. This place is an exception: though the menus do list seafood, the chef here specializes in authentic Girondin dishes: goose neck stuffed with *foie gras*, goose *rillettes* and Médoc salad. Menus €10 (not served Sunday or public holidays), with two others at €24. There are a few simple double rooms with basin and bidet – shower and wc are on the landing – which go for €29.

ARCACHON 33120

🏠 HÔTEL LA PERGOLA

40 cours Lamarque-de-Plaisance.
☎ 05.56.83.07.89 ➡ 05.56.83.14.21
TV. Car park.

A centrally located, delightfully renovated hotel which is also quiet (thanks to the double glazing) and well-run. Doubles €23–60 with shower, shower/wc or bath. The top-priced ones have a terrace.

🏃 🏠 HÔTEL LES MIMOSAS**

77 [bis] av. de la République (Centre); it's near pl. de Verdun.
☎ 05.56.83.45.86 ➡ 05.56.22.53.40
Closed Jan and Feb. **TV. Car park.**

This hotel is in a fine and large Arcachon house not far from the ocean. Warm welcome and clean, neat rooms. Doubles €39–56 with shower/wc, or with bath €43–61. 10% discount on the room rate Oct–April

⅍ ≙ |●| VILLA TÉRÉSA – HÔTEL-RESTAURANT SÉMIRAMIS***

4 allée Rebsomen (Centre).
☎ 05.56.83.25.87 ➡ 05.57.52.22.41
Closed 10 Jan–28 Feb. **Swimming pool. Garden. TV. Car park**.

A 19th-century villa in a variety of architectural styles – Hispano-Moorish, neo-Gothic, Swiss and colonial – in the part of Arcachon known as the "winter town". Saved from demolition in the 1970s, the house was listed as a historic monument and renovated from top to bottom. The rooms are attractive, but all very different; some have a balcony. There are others in a little pavilion next to the pleasant swimming pool. Doubles €76–89 with shower/wc or €99–125 with bath. The restaurant facility is exclusively for seminars or weddings. 10% discount on the room rate 1 Sept–31 May.

⅍ |●| RESTAURANT LE CHIPIRON

69 bd. Chanzy (East); it's near the marina.
☎ 05.57.52.06.33
Closed Tues evening, Wed and Jan.

A Spanish bistro off the tourist track. The décor boasts little more than a few hams hanging from the ceiling and the cuisine deals in basic dishes: tapas, grilled fish and meat and – unsurprisingly given the restaurant's name – *chipirons à la plancha* (grilled baby squid). Generous servings. There's a weekday lunch menu for €11 or reckon on paying around €21 *à la carte*. Friendly welcome, pleasant service, regular clientele — it's a simple place where you feel at ease and eat well. Free glass of sangria.

|●| LES GENÊTS

25 bd. du Gl Leclerc (Centre).
☎ 05.56.83.49.28
Closed Sun evening, Mon out of season, 2–22 Jan and 1–15 Oct.

The dining room is a classic, serving traditional local cuisine and regional dishes. There's a weekday lunch menu at €12, with others up to €23. Some include a dish of oysters and other local classics like duck *confit*. Sadly, it's in a poor location with a view of the railway and a petrol station.

PYLA-SUR-MER   33115 (5KM SW)

≙ HÔTEL MAMINOTTE**

allée des Acacias (Northeast); take the D217 or the D218 and it's 200m from the Archacon basin.
☎ 05.56.54.05.05 ➡ 05.57.52.06.06
Garden.

This small, twelve-room hotel looks just like all the other houses in this peaceful part of town, lost among the pine trees and 100m from the ocean. Friendly welcome. Fresh, comfortable and pleasant rooms; some have little balconies. €40 for a double but it's up to €79 in July and August – pricey but not untypical.

≙ |●| HÔTEL-RESTAURANT CÔTÉ DU SUD**

4 av. du Figuier.
☎ 05.56.83.25.00 ➡ 05.56.83.24.13
Ⓦ www.cote-du-sud.fr
Closed mid-Nov to early Feb. **TV**.

This unpretentious, single-storey, blue and yellow hotel faces south (as you might guess), and is right by the sea. The whole place has been done up, soundproofed and double-glazed. Wonderful welcome. Comfortable rooms with shower/wc or bath are €53–69, but they're €69–84 in July and August. The restaurant is highly rated. Sit on the south-facing terrace experience house specialities such as tuna tartare *Côté du Sud*, steamed sea bream with basil butter, cured Bayonne ham in a cream sauce, seafood platter and a genuine home-made nougat served cold with a summer fruit *coulis*. Set menus are €17–25, or it'll cost around €30 *à la carte*.

PILAT-PLAGE   33115 (10KM SW)

⅍ ≙ |●| HÔTEL-RESTAURANT LA CORNICHE**

46 bd. Louis-Gaume.
☎ 05.56.22.72.11 ➡ 05.56.22.70.21
Ⓦ www.corniche-pyla.com
Closed Wed except July–Aug; All Saints' to Easter. **TV. Garden**.

Wonderfully located between pine trees and the foot of a large dune with steps down to the beach. There's a large communal terrace with deckchairs and hammocks. Very warm welcome. Doubles with shower/wc €53, and with bath €61–76. Rooms over the kitchens are noisy; others have balconies overlooking the ocean. The panoramic restaurant offers menus €15–23 and a speedy *formule* for €11, served at lunchtime during the week. Fish and seafood predominate and only fresh ingredients are used: creole-style stuffed crab, Spanish-style sea bream and fresh cod with pickled onions and *piquillos*. It's more expensive *à la carte* – you'll pay an average of €26, which is a bit pricey for such simple cooking. Here dishes include Arcachon-style mussels, *escalope* of meagre (similar to sea bass) with sorrel and fillet of beef with *gigas*. Half board, compulsory in July and August, costs €61–57 per person. Free apéritif.

ARÈS   33740

⌖ 🏠 |●| LE SAINT-ÉLOI

11 bd. de l'Aérium.
☎ 05.56.60.20.46 📠 05.56.60.10.37
e nlatour@free.fr
Closed Sun evening and Mon out of season.

Situated among the pines in a quiet location 500m from the beach. Clean, spacious double rooms with good beds; €24 with basin and €28 with shower. The elegant restaurant has a particularly good reputation as all the dishes are perfectly prepared. Menus from €20 with one for kids at €9; *à la carte*, expect to pay €38 Good wines and competent service. Free house apéritif.

ARZACQ   64410

|●| LA VIEILLE AUBERGE

Place du Marcadieu; it's in the centre of the town.
☎ 05.59.04.51.31

A friendly old house with an old-style dining room and a village bistro with formica tables and a TV beaming the world in. The new chef has the energy of youth and an equal measure of creativity. Try his stuffed, filleted sardines or his pan-fried mussels – tasty, generously served and inexpensive. Menu for €8 (including wine) and others €12–21. A good place.

ASTAFFORT   47220

⌖ 🏠 |●| LE SQUARE – MICHEL LATRILLE***

5–7 pl. de la Craste (Centre).
☎ 05.53.47.20.40
ᗯ www.latrille.com
Closed Sun evening, Mon, Tues lunchtime, a fortnight in Jan and a week in Nov. **TV. Disabled access. Pay car park**.

Michel Latrille is passionate about using high-quality produce for his dishes and he plays around with different flavours. The results are excellent: semi-cooked duck foie

gras, boned pigeon perfumed with sweet spices and honey, warm monkfish salad with pickled tomato petals and parsley oil, *croustillant* of veal sweetbreads, and his famous *moelleux au chocolat* dessert. Menus €20 (except weekends and public holidays) and €32 or €46 *à la carte*. There are also fourteen comfortable rooms decorated in bright Provençal colours. Doubles €56. Free coffee.

BARCUS   64130

🏠 |●| CHILO***

Centre.
☎ 05.59.28.90.79 📠 05.59.28.93.10
e matiné.club@wanadoo.fr
Closed Sun evening and Mon out of season, and Jan.
Swimming pool. Garden. TV. Pay car park.

A popular place on the borders of Béarn and Basque country. It has been extended but hasn't lost its soul, and it's still family-run. Attractive, nicely appointed rooms are €58 for a double with shower/wc or €76 with bath. Unusual, original cooking: farmers' salad with breaded pigs' ears, milk-fed lamb chops with ravioli stuffed with sheep's cheese, hot *foie gras* with apples. Keep a space for the speciality desserts, *macaron à l'Izarra* and a *charlotte* made with ewe's milk. *Menu du jour* €11; other menus €20–39.

⌖ |●| RESTAURANT CHEZ SYLVAIN

pl. du Fronton (Centre).
☎ 05.59.28.92.11 📠 05.59.28.94.37
Closed Thurs and 8–15 May.

You'll get a charming welcome in this family-run restaurant. It's like a country inn, and has a mainly local clientele. The country-style cooking is prepared with a great deal of care and taste. Dishes include lamb in wine, lamb sweetbreads with parsley, delicious omelettes and an excellent home-made *garbure* (Béarnaise vegetable broth). Menus €11 and €12. Worth going out of your way for. Free coffee.

BARP (LE)   33114

⌖ 🏠 |●| LE RÉSINIER**

Route de Bayonne; it's on the N10, 36km south of Bordeaux.
☎ 05.56.88.60.07 📠 05.56.88.69.74
Closed Sun evening. **TV. Car park**.

This small hotel and restaurant is a good place to stop on the dusty and often congested N10. They offer a few rooms – doubles €43 with shower/wc or bath – and honest local cooking. Dishes include pan-fried *foie gras* with figs or grapes, roast monkfish with red peppers and a duck trio of *foie gras*, *confit* and breast. Set lunch menu €14 during the week or €23–32. Free digestif.

BAYONNE   64100

⅔ ≙ HÔTEL DES BASSES-PYRÉNÉES**

1 pl. des Victoires and 14 rue Tour-de-Sault (Centre); it's in the old town.
☎ 05.59.59.00.29
Restaurant closed Sun and Mon lunchtimes except July–Aug; Jan. **TV. Pay car park**.

Extremely well-managed family hotel, strategically situated near the ramparts. The rooms overlooking the square are quiet, and if you're not scared by the creaking floorboards the one in the executioner's tower is superb. Doubles €49 with shower/wc. In the restaurant, menus go for €14–26. Specialities include grilled steak with panfried *foie gras*, duck breast with peaches and sole stuffed with ceps in a special sauce. 10% discount on the room rate Nov–April.

⅔ ≙ ❙●❙ HÔTEL LOUSTAU***

1 pl. de la République (Centre); it's near pont Saint-Esprit on the river bank.
☎ 05.59.55.08.08 📠 05.59.55.69.36
ℯ loustau@aol.com
TV. Disabled access. Car park.

On the River Adour, with an uninterrupted view of old Bayonne and the Pyrenees, this 200-year-old hotel offers clean, well-soundproofed rooms which are excellent value. Doubles with bath or shower €60–73. The restaurant offers specialities such as *piperade* with dried duck breast and Serrano ham, roast suckling lamb and cod Spanish-style. Set menus €11–23. 10% discount on the room rate Oct–July.

❙●❙ LE BISTROT SAINTE-CLUQUE

9 rue Hughes; it's opposite the train station.
☎ 05.59.55.82.43
Closed Mon Oct–July. **Disabled access**.

The place to eat in Bayonne. David is an excellent English chef who plays around with flavours, mixing them inventively and using simple produce. Prices are reasonable. Try the house paella or duck with honey and lemon. There's a basic weekday lunch menu for €9, then ones at €13 and €15 in the evening; *à la carte* you can dine for about €17. You are strongly advised to book; the place is always full both inside and on the terrace – it's particularly popular with the gay community.

❙●❙ AUBERGE DU PETIT BAYONNE

23 rue des Cordeliers.
☎ 05.59.59.833.44
Closed Tues.

Kattalin's the owner; she comes from the Mixe area, a region where tradition is valued and her CV includes a spell cooking in a convent. She must have been sorely missed when she left – she cooks like an angel. The menus are very filling but, as an alternative, opt for the platter "canaille" (a selection of fried diced bacon and duck offal served on a crisp salad) or the panfried monkfish with garlic. The house *piperade* is the best there is, with the peppers and tomatoes almost cooked like preserves – and Kattalin swears that all the vegetables come from her kitchen garden at Lantabat. Menus are at €9, €12 and €15; platters €9; and main dishes €11.

⅔ ❙●❙ LE CHISTERA

42 rue Port-Neuf; in the pedestrian area between the town hall and the cathedral.
☎ 05.59.59.25.93
Closed Mon, Tues and Wed evenings (except in season); and 1–8 May.

Jean-Pierre manages to combine being a restaurateur and a professional *pelota* player. The food in this local canteen-style place is typical of Bayonne, with fabulous tripe and fish, and daily specials are chalked up on the blackboard: hake *koskera*, cod *Viscayenne*, chicken *basquaise*. If you see pig's trotters or *louvines* (wild bream), order them at once. Prices are reasonable – menus from €13 or around €18.30 *à la carte* – and service is friendly. Free sangria.

❙●❙ LE BAYONNAIS

38 av. quai des Corsaires.
☎ 05.59.25.61.19

Fresh, tasty food, perfectly produced; portions that make "generous" sound mean; quantity that equals quality. It's all here, along with a rare selection of dishes: Basquaise trpe with good Espelette pimentos, grilled milk-fed lamb, scallops with the perfect amount of garlic and duck with mashed potatoes. The €15 menu is a filling three courses and you should pay about €26 per person for a meal *à la carte*. The wine list has a selection from different regions with bottles for €15. Very friendly welcome and a nicely rustic dining room. You get the full flavour of Bayonne.

🖈 |●| RESTAURANT EL ASADOR

pl. Montaut (Centre); it's near the cathedral.
☎ 05.59.59.08.57
Closed Sun evening and Mon, three weeks Christmas–New Year and a fortnight in June.

Set on the Montaut square, with its many antique dealers and junk shops, this small restaurant specializes in grills over the open fire – *asador* is the Spanish word for a grill chef, and the man in question is Maris-Jésus. The line-caught fish is splendid, particularly the cod with garlic and the sea bream *à l'espagnole*. Menu €19, or about €27 *à la carte*. Free apéritif.

|●| AUBERGE DU CHEVAL BLANC

68 rue Bourg-Neuf; it's in the Petit Bayonne area near the Bannat museum and the St André church.
☎ 05.59.59.01.33
Closed Sun evening and Mon except Aug, mid-Feb to mid-March, last week in June and first week in Aug.

Rather than following the menus, you'll have a much more interesting meal if you allow the chef to guide your gastronomic journey and choose his daily or seasonal dishes; you might be tempted by the cream of chestnut and cep soup with *xingar;* or what about the *louvine* (wild bream) with salt? He also cooks "peasant" dishes such as ham bone *xamango* served with wholesome mashed potatoes and glamorized with truffle *jus*. Sublime desserts, in particular his grapefruit and grape soup with figs. There's a weekday menu for €21 and others up to €50. The setting is cosy and there's a family atmosphere. It's worth putting aside part of your holiday budget to eat here.

BAZAS   33430

🖈 ▲ HOSTELLERIE SAINT-SAUVEUR**

14 rue du Général-de-Gaulle (Centre).
☎ 05.56.25.12.18
📧 mlatry@gironde.com
Closed Sun in winter and 10–25 Oct. **TV. Disabled access. Pay car park**.

A fifth-generation business that has been handed down from mother to daughter since 1886. The exterior is pretty dull, and it's hard to imagine that it was the residence of the last bishop of Bazas, Grégoire de Saint-Sauveur. The rooms are somewhat cluttered, with a kitsch, 1970s-style décor. They are, nonetheless, pretty good value at €31 for a

double with shower/wc or €36 with bath. No restaurant, but there's a bistro, the *Saint-Sô*, on the ground floor. Free coffee.

🖈 |●| RESTAURANT DES REMPARTS

Espace Mauvezin (Centre); it's near the cathedral.
☎ and ➡ 05.56.25.95.24
Closed Sun evening and Mon. **Disabled access**.

Park near the cathedral and walk through the passage to this restaurant. It's superbly situated next to the Mairie, on the *brèche de Bazas*, overlooking the Sultan's garden. You can enjoy these quite exceptional surroundings from the terrace when the weather is fine. The very classic décor is understated, and the cuisine is inspired, using quality produce like Bazas beef or Grignol capon. Set menus (€12–43) feature semi-cooked *foie gras,* grilled rib-eye steak, cabbage stuffed with duck and prune and Armagnac mousse. *À la carte* choices include shellfish *millefeuille* in cream and port sauce, and veal sweetbreads in Sauternes with mushrooms. Free coffee.

GOUALADE   33840 (16.5KM SE)

🖈 |●| RESTAURANT L'AUBERGE GAS-CONNE

How to get there: it's in the centre, on the main road opposite the church.
☎ 05.56.65.81.77
Closed Mon, Sun evening and 15 Aug–3 Sept.

This inn is in the middle of nowhere. It's deep in the woods across the road from an old village church. Inside, though, it is unexpectedly smart and comfortable, and air-conditioned too. A group of regulars, including lorry drivers and electricity board employees, flock here for good cooking and low prices. No one would dream of "reinventing" local dishes here. The simple country food comes from good old recipes and is substantial, filling and unpretentious. Large slices of Bayonne ham, wood-pigeon stew, *confit* of turkey, duck, pork, wild boar casserole and *poule-au-pot* all come with as many *frites* as you can eat. Set menu €9 (including wine and coffee) and around €14 *à la carte* – try grilled quails with sweet herbs, roast guineafowl or pressed *foie gras* with leeks. Free coffee.

CAPTIEUX   33840 (19KM S)

▲ |●| HÔTEL-RESTAURANT CAP DES LANDES

rue Principale (Centre); it's on the D932 in the centre of

town opposite the church.
☎ 05.56.65.64.93 ➡ 05.56.65.64.75
Closed Sun evening and Mon. **Disabled access**. **TV**. **Car park**.

This hotel is in the middle of a small market town on a noisy road with lorry traffic at night – so try to get one of the simple rooms at the back. Doubles €30–35 with bath. Nice family atmosphere. The hotel may be a bit on the noisy side but there are no complaints about the food. Though you can get a meal in the little room by the bar, the dining room next door is more stylish with a weekday menu at €10 and others up to €31. Choose from local duck specialties, various gourmet salads and *escalope* of *foie gras* with apples and fresh grapes.

BELHADE   40410

|●| RESTAURANT EULOGE-LE CHÊNE PASCAL

☎ 05.58.07.72.01
Closed Sun evening and Mon out of season.

A charming little inn with kindly staff. The quality of the tasty meat and fish dishes they serve make it worth the detour, the full flavours of the ingredients brought out in the cooking process. There's a very good weekday menu for €15 then others at €20 and €24. One of the better restaurants in the Haut-Pays Landais.

BERGERAC   24100

☖ |●| FAMILY HÔTEL – RESTAURANT LE JARDIN D'EPICURE**

pl. du Marché-Couvert (Centre).
☎ 05.53.57.80.90
Closed Sun except in summer. **TV**.

One of the cheapest hotels in town, in a great location in the old centre. The atmosphere is relaxed and youthful. The rooms are bright and good value given they're air-conditioned, €29 for a double with basin or shower/wc, €37 with bath. If you like a bit of space go for numbers 1, 4, 7 or 10, which have been refurbished and fitted with air conditioning. The restaurant is decent enough but not special.

⚇ ☖ |●| HÔTEL-RESTAURANT LA FLAMBÉE***

153 av. Pasteur (North); it's 2km north of Bergerac on the N21 towards Périgueux.

☎ 05.53.57.52.33 ➡ 05.53.61.07.57
📶 www.laflambee.com
Restaurant closed Sun evening and Mon out of season. **Swimming pool**. **TV**. **Garden**. **Car park**.

This hotel is on the edge of the Pecharmant hills set in substantial gardens screened by trees with a tennis court and a swimming pool – so it's as quiet as anything. The twenty or so individualized rooms are split between a large Périgord residence and a summer house. Doubles are €34–58 with shower/wc or bath; rooms have a small terrace. The restaurant is *the* place to be seen on the Bergerac circuit, thanks to its opulent décor and the finely cooked local dishes. It's best to book. Set menus €15–30. À la carte dishes include pan-fried *foie gras* with seasonal fruit, truffles with scrambled eggs, stuffed sole with ceps and crayfish tails, *escalope* of salmon in Monbazillac wine and strawberries *au gratin* in a Monbazillac *sabayon*. Pleasant terrace for when the weather is fine. 10% discount on the room rate.

|●| RESTAURANT LA SAUVAGINE

18–20 rue Eugène-Leroy (Centre).
☎ 05.53.57.06.97
Closed Sun and Mon evenings, mid-Jan to Feb, a week in June and ten days in Sept.

Modern air-conditioned restaurant that serves traditional, well-prepared cuisine at honest prices. Go for fish such as lamprey from the Bordeaux region or game in season, and make room for the delicious desserts. Great little menu at €12 and others up to €27. Classy clientele but a friendly, natural welcome.

|●| RESTAURANT L'ENFANCE DE LARD

rue Pélissière (Centre).
☎ 05.53.57.52.88 ➡ 05.53.57.52.88
Closed Tues, Wed lunchtime and mid-Sept–early Oct.

A charming restaurant on the first floor of a 12th-century house on one of Bergerac's finest squares. It's small and soon fills up, so it's essential to book. It has a warm, intimate atmosphere and a fantastic view of the medieval church. Classical music plays in the background. The remarkable regional cuisine from the southwest includes quality meats grilled over vines in the superb fireplace, Sarlat-style potatoes which melt in the mouth, rack of lamb with mint, ceps in parsley *vinaigrette*, grilled sirloin of steak pricked with cloves of garlic and *foie gras* served with peaches in the summer or lentils in winter. Generous helpings. €23 menu or around €40 *à la carte*.

SAINT-JULIEN-DE-CREMPSE 24140 (12KM N)

🎄 🏠 🍴 LE MANOIR DU GRAND VIGNOBLE***

How to get there: take the N21 then the D107.
☎ 05.53.24.23.18 📠 05.53.24.20.89
📧 grand.vignoble@wanadoo.fr
Closed 15 Nov–30 March. **Swimming pool**. **TV**. **Car park**.

A very fine 17th-century manor house – also an equestrian centre – in beautiful countryside. It's a luxury establishment, with enormous, charming rooms; it'll cost you €58–104 for a double with bath. Facilities include tennis courts, heated swimming pool and fitness centre. The restaurant offers set menus for €23–43, featuring dishes such as Périgourdine pâté *en croûte*, poached *foie gras* with grapes, duck breast with ceps and pike-perch *demi-deuil*. 10% discount on the room rate.

ISSIGEAC 24560 (19KM SE)

🍴 CHEZ ALAIN

tour de Ville; it's on the edge of town, opposite the château.
☎ 05.53.58.77.88
📧 infor@chez-alain.com
Closed Sun evening and Mon except 1–30 Sept; 15 Jan–20 Feb.

An elegant residence which has been skilfully restored. There's a splendid terrace round a village fountain, and tastefully decorated dining rooms. The classic cuisine matches the same standard and dishes change with the seasons: duck with seasonal mushrooms, snail turnovers with crayfish *coulis*, pike *escalope with Monbazillac* butter, char with basil and ostrich fillet with pink pepper. The desserts are even more original. Weekday menu €11, then others €18–58. The quality is excellent and the aimiable owner, who manages front of house, ensures that everything runs smoothly. They do a Sunday brunch.

RAZAC-D'EYMET 24500 (20KM S)

🎄 🏠 🍴 LA PETITE AUBERGE**

It's on the edge of the village.
☎ 05.53.24.69.27 📠 05.53.61.02.63
📧 lparazmet@aol.com
Hotel closed Jan. **Restaurant closed** lunchtimes, Sun and Nov–March. **Swimming pool**. **Disabled access**. **Car park**.

Peace and quiet is guaranteed in this tiny vil-

lage where this former farm has been transformed into a charming hotel by an English couple. There are just seven pleasant rooms, some under the eaves, one of them a little suite; €46 for a double with shower/wc or bath. The welcoming restaurant has a lunchtime menu for €15 and there's a *table d'hôte* for €15. Dishes include soup, poached salmon in butter sauce and walnut tart. You can also rent self-catering houses: the *Poulailler* (henhouse) sleeps four and the *Ferme* (farm) six; rates vary. Delightful swimming pool. Free breakfast or coffee.

BIARRITZ 64200

🎄 🏠 HÔTEL LE SAINT-CHARLES**

21 av. Foch (North).
☎ 05.59.24.10.54 📠 05.59.24.56.74
Closed end Nov to the Feb school holidays.
🌐 www.hotelstcharles.com
Garden. **TV**. **Pay garage**.

A haven of peace just out of the centre of town, very prettily done out in pink. *Patronne* Annie goes out of her way to be welcoming. If you like peace and quiet, greenery and flowers, you'll find it hard to leave – especially after breakfast in the lovely garden. Freshly refurbished rooms with period furniture; doubles are €43–67 with shower/wc and €63–70 with bath/wc. Well worth going out of your way for. Free breakfast after the fourth night.

🎄 🏠 HÔTEL LA ROMANCE**

6 allée des Acacias (South); from the centre, take av. du Maréchal-Foch, then av. Kennedy. It's near the racecourse.
☎ 05.59.41.25.65 📠 05.59.44.25.65
Closed 15 Jan–1 March.

A little off the beaten track in a residential area. The wonderful proprietor, for whom nothing is too much trouble, has decorated the ten rooms with a floral theme. Half look straight out onto the garden. Doubles with shower/wc or bath cost €43–73. Free coffee and 10% discount on the room rate 1 Oct–15 June.

🏠 HÔTEL PALYM*

7 rue du Port-Vieux; it's 100m from the sea.
☎ 05.59.24.16.56 📠 05.59.24.96.12
Closed All Saints' holidays. **TV**.

An old-fashioned hotel now run by the daughters of the previous owners with charm and a décor that strikes a nice balance between past and present. A little winding staircase leads to the rooms, which are neat and tidy; some have been modernized. Doubles cost €46 with shower/wc and €49 with bath. The rooms at the rear are quieter than those overlooking the nice (but noisy) rue du Port-Vieux. There are also some rooms sleeping three or four. Friendly staff.

⚴ 🛋 HÔTEL MAÏTAGARIA**

34 av. Carnot; it's 500m from the sea opposite the public gardens.
☎ 05.59.24.26.65 ➡ 05.59.24.27.37 **TV**. **Garden**.

You'd do well to book at this place, which attracts a host of regulars. It's a charming town house with quiet, comfortable rooms. Doubles with shower/wc for €47–56 or, with bath, €50–55. There's a very pleasant flower-filled garden. Warm welcome. 10% discount except during all school holidays and July–Aug.

⚴ 🛋 MAISON GARNIER***

29 rue Gambetta.
☎ 05.59.01.60.70 ➡ 05.59.07.60.80
e maison-garnier@hotel-biarritz.com
TV. **Car park**.

The only 3-star hotel in the town centre near everything you want to visit. This is where the owner decided to settle after a 10-year odyssey around the world. There are only seven rooms and they've all been smartly decorated and well updated. Some rooms are up in the roof and you can see the solid metal column that supports the whole house. Rooms €69–99. Professional, smiling welcome. It's essential to book because there are many regulars. 10% discount on the room rate.

🛋 LE CHÂTEAU DU CLAIR DE LUNE***

48 av. Alan-Seeger (Southeast); it's near the station on the Arbonne road.
☎ 05.59.41.53.20 ➡ 05.59.41.53.29
e hotel-clair-de-lune@wanadoo.fr
TV. **Car park**.

A secluded 18th-century residence, splendidly decorated in Art Deco style. It's in wonderful flower-filled grounds with landscaped gardens. Doubles €69–114. The enormous rooms are stylishly decorated, painted in muted tones and furnished with antiques. There are other rooms in the hunting lodge and one room sleeping 4 at €119. A dream of a place where you can relax away from the hectic life on the coast. Reservations are advisable.

⚴ 🍴 LE SAINT AMOUR

22 rue Gambetta; it's near the covered market.
☎ 05.59.24.19.64

Closed Sun, Mon, a fortnight in Feb, June and Nov.

A Lyonnais bistro in exile – this place is a real find. Besides which, they serve lots of wines from small Lyonnais vineyards. The *andouille* and sausage come from the town too but there are also inventive Basque specialities on the menu: sautéed scallops with red peppers and bacon, fresh cod with creamed lentils, *andouillette à la ficelle* with creamed potatoes. The *moelleux au chocolat* dessert is very special. There's a lunch *formule* at €12 or *à la carte* it'll cost about €23. It's frequented by lots of people who know a good thing when they eat it. Free *digestif*.

⚴ 🍴 CAFÉ DES BAINS DE MINUIT

plage du Port-Vieux.
☎ 05.59.24.36.50
e philippe.gli@wanadoo.fr

A genuine 1930s establishment that had really gone downhill until it was taken over by the old owner of the *Bistrot des Halles*. He brought in a breath of good humour, a sense of hospitality and took the menu by the scruff of the neck, shook it firmly and started again – raw or cooked fish dishes with influences from far-off countries and grand classics of French cuisine such as duckling with garlic and orange, seafood platters, cooked oysters and sole with ceps. It'll cost around €23 *à la carte*. The two best times to go are for lunch out on the shady terrace in summer and for a cosy winter dinner – when you can enjoy the views of the stormy sea. Free *digestif*.

🍴 CAMPAGNE ET GOURMANDISE

52 av. Alan-Seeger
☎ 05.59.41.10.11
Closed Wed evening and Mon lunch in summer; Wed evening and Sun evening in winter.

A classic setting with dining rooms that provide a degree of intimacy. On the *menu-carte*, €34, there's a choice of eight starters (four cold and four hot), eight main courses (four fish and four meat), and eight desserts. The chef has a quiet, inventive flair without going over the top. He uses the local ingredients in his own way – a nice balance between regional, traditional French and *nouvelle* cuisine. A decent wine will add around €13 to the bill. In summer there's a terrace with a view of the Pyrenees.

ANGLET 64600 (3KM NE)

🍴 HAVANA CAFÉ

plage de la Chambre-d'Amour.

☎ 05.59.03.77.40
Closed Sun evening in winter. **Garden**. **Car park**.

Way back, this place – which is the oldest restaurant in town – was called La Rotonde. It has a circular dining room and terrace, and looks down on the beach. The new owners have shaken out the cobwebs and changed its name – the rum-based cocktails seemed a decent enough reason. All week (except Sunday out of season) they offer a dish of the day for €7, desserts for €5 and a few wines from small properties. There's a splendid view of the sea from the terrace and the grind of the engines on the road is out of earshot. The only drawback comes from its success: it's always full, even in January. Nice welcome.

⚲|●| LA FLEUR DE SEL

5 av. de la Forêt.
☎ 05.59.63.88.66
Closed Wed and Sun evening (except July–Aug); Mon lunchtime.

A little restaurant run by a dynamic young couple in the midst of the Chiberta forest. It's a quiet contrast to the popular beach resorts and it fills quickly. Modern, inventive, carefully worked cuisine with dishes that vary depending on what's fresh in the market. Weekday lunch *formule* €14 or *menu-carte* at €24. They open the terrace on sunny days and light a fire when it's cold. Free *digestif*.

ARCANGUES 64200 (4KM SE)

⚲|●| AUBERGE DU TRINQUET

It's in the village.
☎ 05.59.43.09.64
Closed Mon and Tues out of season; Feb.

A brand new, rather charmless building. But the cuisine, which uses fresh local produce, is healthy and solid – lots of pork. The dining room looks over the *trinquet*, the playing area, where the players test their skills; it's fun to watch them expending so many calories while you eat broiled mussels, stuffed crab, *croustillant* of boned pigs' trotter or calves' head. In the evening, the bar is a-buzz with local players. There's a huge terrace which has a view over the golf course and the small pink pelota court.

ARBONNE 64210 (5KM SE)

🏠|●| ESKUALDUNA**

How to get there: take the D255.
☎ 05.59.41.95.41 ➡ 05.59.41.88.16

Closed Sun evening in winter. **Garden**. **Car park**.

Jolly place with a lively bar. Customers, most of them factory workers, are welcomed into the big dining room. Jacky the owner keeps the conversation going between courses, flinging out comments on the latest rugby match or chatting away while cooking up the sauces. He's as robust as the regional cuisine on his set menus (€10–21). The place also has double rooms with shower for €32, or €42 with bath.

⚲🏠|●| LAMINAK

route de Saint-Pée.
☎ 05.59.41.95.40 ➡ 05.59.41.87.65
Ⓦ www.hotel-laminak.com
Disabled access. **TV**. **Garden**. **Car park**.

A nice quiet spot which isn't miles away from everywhere. It's comfortably located in a thoroughly renovated Basque house with a terrace and surrounded by a garden. The owner moved here from a health spa, so he's expert at looking after the inner you. Clean rooms, fresh décor and good facilities. The rooms with shower/wc cost €53–56 and are on the small side; doubles with bath cost €73–92. Some have a private terrace onto the garden. Breakfast is served on the veranda or in the garden facing the mountains – sheer heaven. If you fancy a round of golf, the hotel has an arrangement with the local links which offer 10–20% discount in the green fees. A charming place only minutes from the sea.

AHETZE 64210 (8 KM S)

|●| HIRIARTIA

pl. du Fronton; take the D255 in the direction of Arbonne, then turn left onto the D655.
☎ 05.59.41.95.22
Closed Tues and 15 Dec–15 Jan.

A beautiful inn. You go through a bar which can't have changed for sixty years: dark beams, antique wood and practically the whole village propping up the bar. The dining room lies beyond and leads through to the terrace and the garden. Typical cuisine without frills and generous (very generous) portions: peppers stuffed with cod and crab, monkfish kebabs with *beurre blanc* and omelettes with ceps. Menus 15–21. Very agreeable service and welcome.

BIDART 64210

⚲🏠|●| L'HACIENDA***

rue de Bassilour.
☎ 05.59.54.92.82 ➡ 05.59.26.52.73

Closed 15 Nov–15 Feb.
TV. **Swimming pool**. **Car park**.

Just outside the village you'll find this inn, masked by a ravishing park of tall pines and blue hydrangeas. The architecture is wonderfully 1930s, and inside the decoration is bright and modern and stuffed with ornaments from the owners' collections. Good sized rooms with lovely bathrooms €58–137 and the welcome is more than attentive. In the restaurant, the dishes are simple but the menus are thoughtfully put together: hake *koxkera*, house *foie gras*, scallops with Basque herbs and rack of lamb with thyme. Menus €22. Free house apéritif.

☎ |●| LA VILLA D'ARCHE★★★

chemin Camboenea.
☎ 05.59.51.65.95 ➡ 05.59.51.65.99
Ⓦ www.villa-l-arche.com
Closed 15 Nov–15 Feb.
TV. **Car park**.

A fine mansion in typical Basque style, now an excellent three-star hotel. Six of the eight rooms have huge bay windows looking over the ocean. The décor is original and refined, and the bathrooms are big. Doubles €80–145. The gardens are elegantly scattered with teak furniture and there is direct access to the beach – alternatively, there's a great view looking down on the surfers from the sunbeds lined up on the terrace. And when the grey days come, snuggle up in the sofas by the bright fire on the veranda.

|●| LA TANTINA DE LA PLAYA

plage du Centre
☎ 05.59.26.53.56
Closed Sun evening, Mon, 15 Nov–15 Dec.

This is Bidart's most switched-on place and it's in a fantastic location with a superb terrace right over the beach. Inside there's a huge dining room with large communal tables and benches as well as a few smaller tables to eat in more intimate groups. Wonderfully fresh cooking which is particularly strong on fish dishes with sauce – and there are great grills too. Around €31 per person. Service is a bit busy but the waiting staff are never short of a smile. The terrace tables are very popular so it's essential to book.

BISCARROSSE   40600

☎ HÔTEL LE SAINT HUBERT★★

588 av. P. G. Latecoere; it's 500m from the centre of the village, near the lake.

☎ 05.58.78.09.99 ➡ 05.58.78.79.37
ℯ le.saint-hubert@wanadoo.fr
Disabled access. **Garden**. **Car park**.

It's just outside the village, and you feel as if you're way out in the country – yet the summer hordes simply don't come here. You can stretch out with a book in the garden, which is brimming with scented flowers. They put out tables for tea or breakfast. Double rooms €38–60 with bath or shower.

☒ ☎ |●| HÔTEL LA CARAVELLE★★

5314 route des Lacs, quartier ISPE, lac Nord. On the bank of lac Cazaux on the way to the golf course.
☎ 05.58.09.82.67 ➡ 05.58.09.82.18
Ⓦ www.lacaravelle.fr
Closed Mon lunchtime and mid-Nov to mid-Feb. **TV**.
Car park.

A fine, large building in a pleasant setting on the banks of the lake. They've painted the whole place white, and nearly all the rooms have a little balcony looking out onto the water. Doubles €46–53 with shower/wc, €60–61 with bath. There's also a villa to rent in summer, which sleeps four. A lovely restful place – though the frogs may disturb some guests on spring nights. The restaurant serves good local food, with dishes such as Landes-style salad with *foie gras*, *confit* of duck breast, lamb shin in a cream garlic sauce, monkfish kebabs, veal sweetbreads in Jurançon wine, eel *fricassée* and fillet of pike-perch with leek *fondue*. Cheapest menu at €15 (not Sunday) then others €18–37. Half board is compulsory in summer, at €49 per person. Free house apéritif, and 10% discount on the room rate in winter.

|●| RESTAURANT CHEZ CAMETTE

532 av. Latécoère (South).
☎ 05.58.78.12.78
Closed Fri evening and Sat out of season.

A popular and quaint little inn with white walls and red shutters. There's a short set menu at €10. Wonderful welcome and generous helpings. The food is simple and unpretentious: set menus €15–21. Dishes include mussels in white wine or *escalope* in cream sauce. Don't miss out on the house speciality – duck breast grilled over the open fire.

BORDEAUX   33000

SEE MAP OVERLEAF

☒ ☎ HÔTEL BOULAN

28 rue Boulan. **MAP B3-4**
☎ and ➡ 05.56.52.23.62

ⓦ www.hotelboulan.com
TV.

A simple little hotel near the cathedral and town hall. The cleanliness of the place, the obliging owners and the peaceful atmosphere (which belies its busy location) will win you over. Simple, well-maintained rooms with good beds. Doubles with basin €20; with shower (wc on the landing) €23. Breakfast is served in your room. Good value. 10% discount on the room rate Nov–March inclusive.

☎ HÔTEL DE LYON

31 rue des Remparts. **MAP B3-5**
☎ 05.56.81.34.38 ➡ 05.56.52.92.82
TV.

This small hotel in a pedestrianized street doesn't have any stars but it is well-run. It's very central, near the cathedral of Saint-André, but even the rooms overlooking the street are quiet. They all have a certain charm and are very reasonably priced. Doubles €21 with shower/wc.

☎ HÔTEL DAUPHIN*

82 rue du Palais Gallien. **MAP B2-3**
☎ 05.56.52.24.62 ➡ 05.56.01.10.91
ⓔ contact@coalachr.com
TV.

The French star Viviane Romance lived in room 7 during World War II, and even today the hotel is heavily redolent of the 1930s and 1940s. It's right in the city centre, in the quietest part of a street which gets busy in the evening. The comfortable rooms are all different. Rates are a tiny bit higher than for the other one-star hotels in the area, but it's well worth the extra money. Rooms with basin (wc on the landing) go for €24, and you'll pay €27 for rooms with shower or €30 with shower/wc. The rooms around the little patio are the quietest.

🎋 ☎ HÔTEL GAMBETTA**

66 rue Porte-Dijeaux. **MAP B2-8**
☎ 05.56.51.21.83 ➡ 05.56.81.00.40
ⓔ hogambetta@aol.com
TV. Car park.

This hotel is a good base located in a lively part of the centre of town. It's decent value for money given this and the facilities – there are TVs and mini-bars in the bright and clean rooms. Doubles €38 with shower/wc or €45 with bath. The owner is amiable. Free breakfast.

🎋 ☎ HÔTEL NOTRE-DAME**

36 rue Notre-Dame. **Off map C1-9**

☎ 05.56.52.88.24 ➡ 05.56.79.12.67
TV. Pay car park.

At the heart of the Les Chartrons district, which used to be full of wine merchants, this stone-fronted 19th-century house has been beautifully cleaned. It is almost overwhelmed by the monumental Cité Mondiale du Vin – where you can find hydraulic and everything related to wine. In contrast to the modern and somewhat neutral décor of the rooms, the rue Notre-Dame overflows with antique dealers and bric-à-brac shops. Doubles with shower/wc €40; with bath €44. Pay car park nearby. 10% discount July–Aug.

☎ ACANTHE HÔTEL**

12–14 rue Saint-Rémi. **MAP C2-6**
☎ 05.56.81.66.58 ➡ 05.56.44.74.41
ⓦ www.acanthe-hotel-bordeaux.com
TV.

Just twenty metres from the superb place de la Bourse and the riverside, in the picturesque Saint-Pierre area. When the hotel was taken over the new owners refurbished it tastefully, creating personalized rooms and offering good facilities. Doubles €40 with shower/wc or €46 with bath. The owner greets you warmly and can organize visits to the great wine châteaux of Bordeaux. Parking is fiendishly difficult around here, though.

🎋 ☎ HÔTEL DE LA TOUR INTENDANCE**

16 rue de la Vieille-Tour. **MAP B2-10**
☎ 05.56.81.46.27 ➡ 05.56.81.60.90
TV. Pay car park.

Two sisters take turns on reception in this charming establishment, and guests always encounter the same friendly and obliging service. Here the welcome includes numerous thoughtful touches like freshly-squeezed orange juice served at breakfast. Everything is efficient and well-organized. In the cellar, you can see a few vestiges of the 3rd-century tower of the hotel's name. The rooms on the pedestrianized street can be noisy in summer due to the lively restaurants nearby – but it's completely quiet at the rear where the cheapest rooms (singles) have a nice view over the rooftops. On the whole the rooms aren't large but they've done their best with the décor. Doubles with shower/wc €41, with bath €44. Overnight car park €6, free on Sunday and public holidays 7.30pm–9am. 10% discount at weekends and during school holidays.

☎ HÔTEL DE L'OPÉRA**

35 rue Esprit-des-Lois. **MAP C2-1**
☎ 05.56.81.41.27 ➡ 05.56.51.78.80

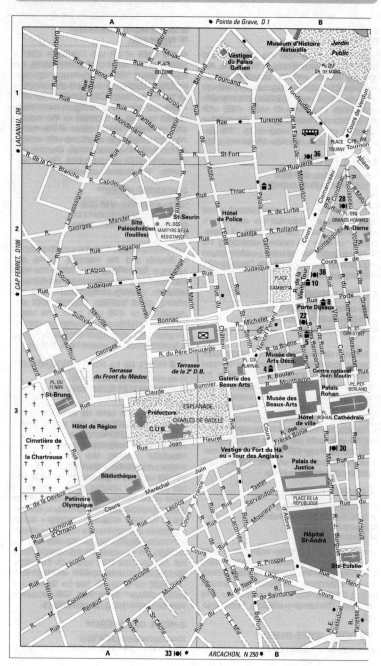

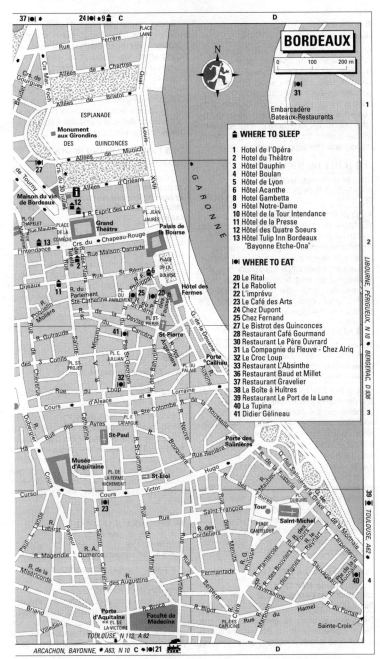

BORDEAUX

0   100   200 m

🛏 **WHERE TO SLEEP**

1 Hotel de l'Opéra
2 Hotel du Théâtre
3 Hôtel Dauphin
4 Hôtel Boulan
5 Hôtel de Lyon
6 Hôtel Acanthe
8 Hotel Gambetta
9 Hôtel Notre-Dame
10 Hôtel de la Tour Intendance
11 Hôtel de la Presse
12 Hôtel des Quatre Soeurs
13 Hôtel Tulip Inn Bordeaux
      "Bayonne Etche-Ona"

🍽 **WHERE TO EAT**

20 Le Rital
21 Le Raboliot
22 L'imprévu
23 Le Café des Arts
24 Chez Dupont
25 Chez Fernand
27 Le Bistrot des Quinconces
28 Restaurant Café Gourmand
30 Restaurant Le Père Ouvrard
31 La Compagnie du Fleuve - Chez Alriq
32 Le Croc Loup
33 Restaurant L'Absinthe
36 Restaurant Baud et Millet
37 Restaurant Gravelier
38 La Boîte à Huîtres
39 Restaurant Le Port de la Lune
40 La Tupina
41 Didier Gélineau

LIBOURNE, PERIGUEUX, N 10 ✦ BERGERAC, D 936

TOULOUSE, A 62

e hotel-opera.bx@wanadoo.fr
Closed 23Dec–9 Jan. **TV**.

An elegant 18th-century house next to the Grand Théâtre. The splendid stone staircase is original, while the rooms have been decorated in more classical style. Doubles €44 with shower/wc, €49 with bath. The drawback is the location – it's right on one of the busiest streets in the centre of town. It's advisable to ask for a room at the back which will be quieter, though not so bright. Warm, friendly and charming welcome.

🏠 HÔTEL DU THÉÂTRE**

10 rue Maison-Danrade. **MAP C2-2**
☎ 05.56.79.05.26 ➡ 05.56.81.75.06
TV.

A pair of 18th-century private mansions form this hotel, which is in a pedestrianized street right in the middle of the Triangle district. Animated and friendly welcome. The rooms are rather ordinary but they have good facilities and are kept beautifully clean. Doubles with shower/wc are €44 or €49 with bath; there are also twin and triple rooms available for €47–50 and rooms sleeping four at €54. 5% discount on the room rate.

🏠 HÔTEL DES QUATRE SŒURS***

6 cours du 30-Juillet. **MAP C2-12**
☎ 05.57.81.19.20 ➡ 05.56.01.04.28
e 4soeurs@mail.city.com
Closed a week at Christmas. **TV**.

Built in the 18th century, between allées de Tourny, the Grand Théâtre and place des Quinconces, this hotel is steeped in history. The composer Wagner stayed here in 1850 when he was having an adulterous affair with a local woman. The staff are really relaxed and there are attractive, freshly decorated, classy rooms. The ones overlooking the cours de Tourny or allées de Tourny are more expensive because they are bigger – they include some family rooms with two double beds – than the quieter rooms above the inner courtyard. All are air-conditioned. Doubles with shower/wc or bath €61. Breakfast €6. 10% discount for a two-night stay except June, Sept and Oct.

🏠 HÔTEL DE LA PRESSE***

6 rue Porte-Dijeaux. **MAP C2-11**
☎ 05.56.48.53.88 ➡ 05.56.01.05.82
Closed 24 Dec–1 Jan.**TV**.

This place is close to the junction of rue Sainte-Catherine and rue Porte-Dijeaux in a central area which is pedestrianized during the day; some cars are permitted in the evening. The comfortable rooms are sound-proofed and air-conditioned. If you really can't stand any noise at all, those on the courtyard side are the quietest, but you'll miss out on the view of the Grand Théâtre – particularly good from rooms 206 and 207, which have balconies. This place offers modest luxury at a reasonable price. Doubles with shower/wc €61–69, with bath €76. One free breakfast per room per night.

🏠 HÔTEL TULIP INN BORDEAUX "BAYONNE ETCHE-ONA"***

15 cours de l'Intendance. **MAP C2-13**
☎ 05.56.48.00.88 ➡ 05.56.48.41.60 61
e bayetche@bordeaux-hotel.com
Closed last week in Dec and first week in Jan. **TV**. **Pay car park**.

A 64-room hotel, part of which is housed in an 18th-century building. It belongs to the upmarket *Golden Tulip* group, and is very in keeping with this middle-class area. Courteous staff and attractive 1930s-style lounge. On the upper floors the rooms have been completely refurbished in an impersonal, contemporary style. Doubles €74 with shower/wc or €88 with bath. There's a public car park for €2 per night. 10% discount on the room rate.

🍴 LE RABOLIOT

38 rue Peyronnet. **Off map C4-21**
☎ 05.56.92.27.33
Closed A fortnight to three weeks in Aug. Fri evening, Sat and Sun require reservations.

A friendly, lively place away from the centre. Good quality cooking at very reasonable prices, with an €8 menu of the day or others from €9. The desserts are particularly good: try the crumble or the chocolate cake, both of which are made by the English owner who usually waits at table. Her husband is in charge of the cellar and he has a selection of good-value vintages. Free Kir.

🍴 RESTAURANT LE RITAL

3 rue des Faussets. **MAP C2-20**
☎ 05.56.48.16.69
Closed Sat and Sun, public holidays and 15–30 August.

In a part of the city where restaurants come and go every few months, this little Italian place has been around for twenty years. The food is very good and you get a warm welcome. Tables are in a series of linked rooms, each of which give a view of the kitchen. The pasta is fresh: marinated aubergines and peppers, fresh pasta with *foie gras*, aubergines or pesto. Also try the *osso-bucco* or aubergine *au gratin*. Good home-made desserts. Lunchtime menu €8, and others at €10–16. *À la carte* you'll spend less than €15.

|●| RESTAURANT LA COMPAGNIE DU FLEUVE – CHEZ ALRIQ

quai des Queyries. **MAP D1-31**
☎ 05.56.86.58.49
Closed Sun evening and Mon; 3 weeks in Feb and 3 weeks at All Saints'.

An unusual place in an unusual setting – a kind of alternative self-service restaurant located in the postwar wasteland near the ruined gare d'Orléans. There are plans to redevelop the area. The restaurant has become rather trendy, and is large enough to host occasional plays and concerts: the welcome is very, *very* chic. It has an "unstructured" garden running down to the river, dotted with chairs. Set menus start at €8 but you will most likely eat *à la carte*, which will set you back around €17. The dishes available vary according to season: mussels in summer and Béarnaise vegetable broth in winter, with shad, eels and lampreys when available.

⅍ |●| RESTAURANT L'ABSINTHE

137 rue du Tondu. **Off map A4-33**
☎ 05.56.96.72.73 ➥ 05.56.90.14.23
Closed Sat lunchtime, Sun, public holidays and a fortnight in Aug.

You can almost imagine Toulouse-Lautrec sitting with a glass of absinthe in his hand at this bistro restaurant with its period décor. The food is good, too. Lunchtime *formules* and set menus €9–18. Extensive choice of dishes, including Landes-style salad, *escalope* of veal with cheese *au gratin*, *fricassée* of scallops with oyster mushrooms and veal sweetbreads in port. The sweets are home-made. Free apéritif.

⅍ |●| L'IMPRÉVU

11 rue des Remparts. **B2-22**
☎ 05.56.48.55.43
Closed Tues evening.

A few bistro tables are set out on the terrace in this pedestrianized street, with a couple of attractive dining rooms inside – one a vaulted cellar decorated with dried flowers and willow baskets. Lots of regulars chatting with the affable owner. Good, quick service and healthy cooking using fresh, market produce: *pot-au-feu*, beef skirt, pork fillet in mustard

and home-made *clafoutis*. Lunch menu €10, and others €11–15. Splendid sweet *crêpes* for dessert. It's a good idea to book. Free house apéritif.

|●| LE CAFÉ DES ARTS

138 cours Victor-Hugo **MAP D4-23**
☎ 05.56.91.78.46

A really popular brasserie in a busy, buzzing part of town. The terrace is quite wide and the dining room is like an old-style bistro with simple chairs and moleskin benches. Honest, traditional dishes in good-sized portions: deep-fried Camembert, herrings in oil, *andouillette*, scallops with ceps, coddled eggs with *foie gras* and that rarity, real *frites*! Lunch menu €10 and brasserie dishes *à la carte*. This place has been going for years and is a real favourite with the younger crowd.

⅍ |●| CHEZ DUPONT

45 rue Notre-Dame. **Off map C1-24**
☎ 05.56.81.49.59 ➥ 05.56.51.35.19
Closed Sun.

About the best value for money you'll get in the Les Chartrons district. Attractive bistro-style surroundings and traditional dishes such as *pot-au-feu* chalked up on the blackboard. The *formule*, €13, offers a main course with a choice of starter or dessert and changes every day. There's a more substantial menu with starter, main course and dessert at €20, and the *à la carte* menu is regularly updated to reflect the changing seasonal produce – eels, ceps, asparagus and so on, all bought fresh from the market. Good humoured atmosphere and the staff provide a cheery welcome. Occasional live jazz in the evenings. Free *apéritif*.

|●| CHEZ FERNAND

3 pl. du Parlement. **MAP C2-25**
☎ 05.56.52.51.72

They serve only cold food here – a panoply of oysters and three kinds of salmon – and it's very popular with the tourists. And if you can't do without a fix of red meat, try the steak *tartare*. Lunch menu €10, or others €15–26. The relaxed service is perhaps a bit too casual. Wines are reasonably priced.

|●| LE CROC LOUP

35 rue du Loup. **MAP C3-32**
☎ 05.56.44.21.19
Closed Sun, Mon and Aug.

A lovely, refined little place though it looks like a snack bar from the outside. Warm welcome. The weekday lunch menu at €12 isn't elaborate, but typically it might include duck *pâté* with green peppercorns, grilled beef with shallots and chocolate *millefeuille* with coffee sauce – amazing value for money. Other set menus, €23–27, include interesting and quite sophisticated dishes like cuttlefish ravioli with coriander, chicken drumsticks with ceps and *foie gras*, red mullet and cod with a sea-urchin coral sauce and *millefeuille* of chocolate with coffe beans.

🎄 |●| RESTAURANT LE BISTROT DES QUINCONCES

4 pl. des Quinconces. **MAP C2-27**
☎ 05.56.52.84.56
Disabled access.

Service until 11.30pm. This classic brasserie, which faces the famous monument to the Girondins, is Bordeaux's trendiest bistro. If weather permits, sit outside. Efficient service. You can get all the bistro staples like steak and roast lamb, along with more unusual offerings such as iced terrine of pickled tomatoes, mozzarella with olive paste, marinaded red peppers, cod steak with hazelnuts, Mexican-style chicken *fajitas* and desserts such as *sabayon* with Lillet vermouth. Prices are reasonable. Weekday *formule* €12; dinner will cost around €23–31 *à la carte*. Tapas are also served in the evening. Free coffee.

🎄 |●| RESTAURANT CAFÉ GOURMAND

3 rue Buffon. **MAP B2-28**
☎ 05.56.56.79.23.85
Closed Sun and Mon lunchtime.

When the sun makes an appearance, sit down at one of the tables outside this elegant restaurant and admire the covered market. Bruno Olivier comes from a well-known family of chefs, and photos of the lot of them adorn the walls. He produces sound, well-judged dishes at bistro prices, with a lunch menu at €14 and dinner menus at €19–22. The brasserie menu includes crunchy salad with mussels and pesto, ham with sage, perfect calf's head and a special version of fried eggs. Expect to pay €15 at lunch and €26 in the evening *à la carte*. Free coffee.

|●| LE PÈRE OUVRARD

12 rue du Maréchal-Joffre. **MAP B3-30**
☎ 05.56.44.11.58
Closed Sat lunchtime and Sun; one week in winter; Aug.

This colourful restaurant is a-flurry with judges and lawyers – especially with the first spring sun, when outside tables are set up opposite the École Nationale de la Magistrature. There's a huge blackboard with an appetizing selection of bistro dishes: grilled sardines *fleur de sel*, *moules marinières*, grilled chicken with cayenne pepper. The menu lists more sophisticated dishes, such as salad of caramelized *foie gras* with sea salt and cod spiced with harissa and cumin. Lunchtime menu at €15, an evening one at €20 or around €34 *à la carte*.

|●| LA TUPINA

6–8 rue Porte-de-la-Monnaie. **MAP D4-40**
☎ 05.56.91.56.37

An unmissable place serving gastronomic Bordelais dishes. It's one of those rare restaurants serving genuine dishes from the southwest: *terrine* of semi-cooked *foie gras*, potted shoulder of lamb with haricot beans, roast chicken with chips cooked in duck fat and the like. Delicious desserts. The prices reflect the quality of the cooking, with a €15 lunchtime menu and other seasonal menus up to €38. Very good wines. The dining room has a rustic feel and is quite charming, though the atmosphere is a bit prim.

|●| RESTAURANT LE PORT DE LA LUNE

59 quai de Paludate. **Off map D4-39**
☎ 05.56.49.15.55 ➡ 05.56.49.29.12
Disabled access.

Service until 2am, seven days a week. Opposite the abattoirs in a part of Bordeaux which has recently acquired a nightlife, this is a great place for jazz fans and they have live bands. It's an animated, friendly, "lived-in" place, with photos of jazz legends lining the wall. You can eat very well here, with bistro dishes – as well-chosen as the music – at reasonable prices. *À la carte* dishes (€9–15) include harbour salad, mussels and oysters, whole duck breast and traditional-style veal kidneys. For €23 you can get a *casse croûte* and seasonal dishes including baby eels *à l'espagnole*, shad in green sauce, lamprey and so on plus dessert, wine and coffee. Wines from €11. Michel, the boss, creates an easy-going atmosphere with his ready smile and chat.

🎄 |●| RESTAURANT BAUD ET MILLET

19 rue Huguerie. **MAP B1-36**
☎ 05.56.79.05.77 ➡ 05.56.81.75.48
Closed Sun.

A specialist cheese restaurant serving 200 kinds of cheese, meticulously selected by M. Baud. He has a great passion for his work and applies strict criteria. The cheeses can be eaten in their natural state but are also used in numerous specialities, which range from *raclette* and *tartiflette* to more daring concoctions. The "cheese and dessert" *formule* is a surprising but tasty combination of sweet and savoury ingredients. There is an impressive and well-chosen selection of nearly a thousand different wines from all over the world, arranged on shelves around the very pleasant, air-conditioned restaurant. Friendly staff. Menus €17–22. 10% discount on a meal with wine.

|●| RESTAURANT GRAVELIER

114 cours de Verdun. **Off map C1-37**
☎ 05.56.48.17.15 ➡ 05.56.51.96.07
Closed Sat lunchtime, Sun, Monday evening, the Feb holidays and 3–23 Aug.

One of the new wave of restaurants in Bordeaux, run by the daughter of one of the famous Troisgros brothers. Her husband, Yves Gravelier, is also a creative chef. The surroundings are modern without being flashy, and prices are reasonable. Lunch menu €19, with two more at €23 and €30. The menus change frequently – look out for mussels and cod in white wine with celery, mullet cooked in a charcoal pan with vine shoots and saddle of rabbit in cream truffle sauce.

|●| DIDIER GÉLINEAU

26 rue du Pas-Saint-Georges. **MAP C3-41**
☎ 05.56.52.84.25 ➡ 05.56.51.93.25
Closed Sat and Mon lunchtimes; Sun; a fortnight in Aug.

Its subtle blend of traditional and modern cuisine has led this restaurant to become one of the city's musts in just a few short years. The prices are still unbelievably reasonable. They offer exemplary menus of the day at €20 and €24, with others €34–49. Dishes change frequently: the cep soup, a stuffed turnip with snails followed by the *fricassée* of veal kidneys will see you right. The desserts are particularly good.

GRADIGNAN 33170 (6KM SW)

🛏 |●| HÔTEL-RESTAURANT LE CHALET LYRIQUE BIS***

169 cours du Général-de-Gaulle (Centre); take exit 16 off the outer ring road and it's just beyond pl. de l'Église.
☎ 05.56.89.11.59 ➡ 05.56.89.53.37
ⓦ www.chalet-lyrique.fr
Restaurant closed Sun in Aug. **TV. Garden. Pay garage. Disabled access**.

Less than fifteen minutes from Bordeaux-Mérignac airport in suburban Gradignan,

this resolutely modern building is arranged around a patio planted with ancient olive trees and centring on a fountain. The whole place has had the Lawrence Llewellyn-Bowen treatment to create a luminously bright mediterranean feel. They offer 44 very comfortable rooms, some with balcony. Doubles with shower/wc or bath cost €58. In the restaurant menus start at €11 (weekday lunchtimes only). All the meat dishes are wonderful – the proprietor used to work at a butcher's – but *à la carte* prices are high.

BRANTÔME 24310

🛏|●| RESTAURANT AU FIL DE L'EAU

21 quai Bertin (Centre).
☎ 05.53.05.73.65
Closed Tues and Wed except July–Aug; Nov–April.

They don't sell fishing permits behind the bar any more but the décor of this adorable little restaurant still has fishing very much as its theme. There's a boat anchored next to the lovely terrace on the banks of the Dronne. They have a system of *formules* with a wide a selection of freshwater fish – trout, perch and so on – and local dishes including duck priced €17–21. Uncomplicated but well-presented dishes. Friendly welcome and efficient service. Free *digestif*.

MONSEC 24340 (12KM NW)

🛏 |●| HÔTEL-RESTAURANT BEAUSÉJOUR

rue Principale; take the D939.
☎ 05.53.60.92.45 ➡ 05.53.60.72.38
Closed Fri evenings and Sat in low season; Christmas–1 Jan. **TV. Car park**.

Really friendly welcome and quality food served in a pleasant restaurant with a panoramic view of the garden. Fine range of set menus, which celebrate local cuisine: duck sausage, oyster mushroom omelette, *foie gras* and duck breast kebab. The cheapest menu, €10, includes a $\frac{1}{4}$ litre of wine and there are others €12–26. Simple but impeccable rooms cost €30 with shower/wc.

VIEUX-MAREUIL 24340 (13KM NW)

🛏 🏠 |●| HOSTELLERIE DE L'AUBERGE DE L'ÉTANG BLEU***

How to get there: take the D93; it's 2km before the hamlet and well indicated.
☎ 05.53.60.92.63 ➡ 05.53.56.33.20
ⓦ www.perigord-hotel.com

Closed Sun evenings in winter. **TV**. **Car park**.

In a huge park at the edge of a private lake, with a small beach where you can bathe. The spacious, nicely furnished rooms are as quiet as can be. Those overlooking the lake have a covered balcony. Doubles €46–56, with half board at €55 per person, compulsory in July–Aug. Good breakfasts, with boiled eggs. The elegant dining room has a lakeside terrace which is inhabited by noisy ducks. Good, generously flavoured dishes include salmon with cep sauce and slivers of duck breast with morel sauce. €17 weekday menu and others €20–44; à la carte it'll cost around €32. 10% discount on the room rate.

SAINT-JEAN-DE-CÔLE   24800 (20KM NE)

🏛 🏠 |●| HÔTEL SAINT-JEAN**

route de Nontron; take the D78.
☎ 05.53.52.23.20
Closed Sun and Mon evenings out of season. **TV**. **Car park**.

Nice little place on a main road that isn't too busy at night. Traditional, comfortable and meticulously kept rooms – you'll pay €31 for a double with shower/wc. The proprietor concocts quality regional dishes such as home-made duck *foie gras pâté*, monkfish fritters with parsley and duck breast *à l'orange*. Weekday lunch menu at €11, then others €14–23. 10% discount April–June and Sept.

BUZET SUR BAÏZE   47160

🏛 |●| AUBERGE DU GOUJON QUI FRÉTILLE

rue Gambetta; it's opposite the church.
☎ 05.53.84.26.51
Closed Tues evening and Wed; Nov to 15–30 March.

The village is quiet and pretty – and so is this inn, literally "The Inn of the Wriggling Gudgeon", which stands opposite the church. You sit down to generous helpings of fine food in peaceful surroundings. There is a weekday lunch *formule* at €13, others €17–29, and a children's menu at €8. Dishes include duck breast *carpaccio*, raw*choucroute* salad with grilled *cervelas* sausage and bream with lentils. House speciality is pan-fried fresh *foie gras* with a port *jus*. Free coffee.

CAMBO-LES-BAINS   64250

🏛 |●| L'AUBERGE DE TANTE URSULE**

fronton du Bas-Cambo; it's by the *pelota* court.
☎ 05.59.29.78.23 📠 05.59.29.28.57
Closed Mon evening,Tues and mid-Feb to mid-March.
TV. **Disabled access**. **Car park**.

This old farm, painted all in white, offers decent rooms for €27 with basin and from €38 with shower. Good food, with a range of set menus €14–23. Dishes include gourmet salad, monkfish with green pepper, wood-pigeon stew and duck breast *à l'orange*. Look out for specialities such as braised lamb sweetbreads with ceps, home-made grilled black pudding with pickled garlic and grilled mullet. The welcome could be warmer but it's good value.

ESPELETTE   64250 (5KM W)

🏛 🏠 |●| HÔTEL-RESTAURANT EUZKADI**

285 Karrika-Nagusia; take the D918 towards Saint-Jean-de-Luz.
☎ 05.59.93.91.88 📠 05.59.93.90.19
📧 hotel.euzkadi@wanadoo.fr
Closed Mon, Tues out of season and 1 Nov–20 Dec.
Swimming pool. **Garden**. **Car park**.

This is one of the most popular country hotel-restaurants in the Basque area and it's a good idea to book well in advance. Michèle and André Darraïdou, both completely mad about Basque cooking, search out old recipes and revamp them. In their enormous restaurant you'll discover dishes you would have very little chance of finding elsewhere: *tripoxa* (black pudding made from veal and served with a tomato and capiscum sauce); *axoa* (cubed veal browned with onions); *merluza en salsa verde* (poached hake with pea and asparagus sauce); cockles and hard-boiled eggs in a sauce made with Jurançon wine and fish stock; *elzekaria* (vegetable soup). Set menus €15–27. The lovely little rooms are €44 for a double with bath. Now that there's a by-pass, there's no noisy through-traffic. In the back there's a pleasant garden, tennis court and swimming pool. Free house apéritif.

ITXASSOU   64250 (5KM S)

🏛 🏠 |●| HÔTEL-RESTAURANT ONDORIA**

It's 100m from the Pas de Roland.
☎ 05.59.29.75.39 📠 05.59.29.24.99

Closed Mon and 20 Nov–27 Dec. **Car park**.

A quiet place with lots of flowers out in the countryside. A easy family atmosphere with nice rooms with shower from €33. The dining room has a picture window with a view of the mountains to admire while you enjoy parsleyed eel, cep omelette or chicken basquaise. Fairly priced menus €8–23.

⚥ ✿ |●| HÔTEL-RESTAURANT DU CHÊNE**

How to get there: take the D918 towards Saint-Jean-Pied-de-Port, then the D349 as you enter the Nive valley.
☎ 05.59.29.75.01 ➡ 05.59.29.27.39
Closed Mon, Tues out of season, Jan and Feb. **TV**. **Car park**.

This establishment is superbly situated. Doubles cost €37 with bath, and they serve unpretentious but delicious local cuisine. Set menus €14–27. Specialities include a mix of traditional and Basque dishes: lamb blanquette, chillies stuffed with cod with a red pepper *coulis*, chicken with rice and red peppers, risotto of monkfish and chorizo, Biscay-style cod, *escalopes* of *foie gras* in cherry vinegar and tuna with capsicums. Free glass of sangria.

AINHOA   64250 (12KM SW)

✿ |●| ITHURRIA***

rue principale (Centre); it's at the beginning of the village when you come from Cambo-les-Bains.
☎ 05.59.29.92.11 ➡ 05.59.29.81.28
🌐 www.ithurria.com
Closed Wed out of season and 2 Nov–Easter. **Garden**. **Swimming pool**. **TV**. **Car park**.

A very fine inn in a large 17th-century house and former coaching inn on the pilgrim route to Santiago de Compostela. The gorgeously furnished rooms go for €99–114. There's an attractive dining room with hand-made floor tiles and a vast fireplace. Dishes include pepper stew, Basque *cassoulet* with red kidney beans and roast pigeon with garlic. Menus from €28 to €43. Fine garden and swimming pool to the rear. The welcome is a bit cool.

CAPBRETON   40130

|●| LE BISTRO

pl. des Basques; (Centre).
☎ 05.58.72.21.98
Closed Sun, Mon and Wed evenings. **Disabled access**. **Car park**.

An innocuous-looking restaurant from the outside, but it's delightful within. The owner, his apron wrapped round his waist, will take your order and cook your food. Chalked up on the blackboard are delicious dishes that are carefully prepared and perfect in their simplicity: pork fillet with mirabelle plums, grilled ham with honey or hake fillet with red peppers. Menu of the day €9 or €18 *à la carte*.

|●| RESTAURANT LA PÊCHERIE DUCAMP

rue du Port-d'Albret; near the beach and the casino.
☎ 05.58.72.11.33 ➡ 05.58.72.26.00
Closed Mon and Tues lunchtimes, then evenings and Sat lunchtime out of season.

Direct from the fishmonger to the consumer – the tables are arranged around the fish counter, and the waitresses wear boots and plastic aprons. Set menus €14–38. You'll find cuisine such as seafood platter and grilled fish; the house specialities is *parillada*, a dish containing seven varieties of fish and seafood.

⚥ |●| LES COPAINS D'ABORD

Port des Mille-Sabords.
☎ 05.58.72.14.14
Closed Thurs out of season.

There's a strong holiday feel to the décor: sea colours, green echoing the forests of the Landes and sunshine gold. The restaurant has a lovely terrace which is at its best on summer evenings – it can get too hot at lunchtime. Weekday menu at €19, listing dishes that use produce straight from the farm or the ocean: chillis with garlic, panfried mussels, squid with garlic and parsley. Or you could go *à la carte*, which will cost not much more. There's a surprise gift at the end of your meal.

CAP-FERRET   33970

✿ LA FRÉGATE**

34 av. de l'Océan.
☎ 05.56.60.41.62 ➡ 05.56.03.76.18
🌐 www.hotel-la-fregate.net
Closed Jan and mid-Nov–mid Dec.
Swimming pool. **Disabled access**. **TV**. **Pay car park**.

The hotel is named after the frigate bird and is in an ideal location between the pleasure port and the ocean, 300m from where the Arcachon boat docks. The grounds are big enough for a swimming pool which is kept impeccably clean, and the rooms – €42–46 with shower/wc or €47–122 with bath – are spotless too. The nicest have a wide balcony and terrace looking over the pool and three-star facilities. The place is smoothly run by attentive owners.

🕍 🛏 |●| HÔTEL DES PINS**

23 rue des Fauvettes (Centre).
☎ 05.56.60.60.11 ➡ 05.56.60.67.41
Closed 15 Nov–April.

A delightful house dating from the early part of the century with a garden full of flowers. It's quietly situated between the bassin d'Arcachon and the ocean. The meticulously planned décor, all classic advertisements and old billiards tables, creates the impression that time has stood still. Rooms are €39–68 with shower or bath. You eat on a veranda adjacent to the garden or on the lawn. There's a single set menu at €18, which lists fresh cod steak with garlic mayonnaise, Bordeaux-style grilled tuna and Pauillac lamb, or you can dine *à la carte* for about €23. Warm welcome. Free apéritif.

🕍 |●| PINASSE CAFÉ

2 [bis] av. de l'Océan (Centre); it's on the seafront.
☎ 05.56.03.77.87 ➡ 05.56.60.63.47
Closed Mon and 12 Nov–10 Feb.

An attractive turn-of-the-century house painted blue and white, near to the landing stage. The restaurant is something of a youthful hang-out, and its young staff offer wonderfully laid-back yet efficient service. From the terrace, with its background beat of house and techno music, there's a brilliant view of the ocean, the oyster beds and the dune du Pyla. They offer a series of *menus du marché* which change almost daily and list dishes such as fried squid, mussels *en papillote* cooked with pine needles in parchment paper, grilled mullet in green sauce, whelks, grilled meat and pork spare ribs. These cost €15–21, or there's *à la carte* for about €30. Free *digestif*.

CANON (LE)   33950 (6KM N)

🕍 |●| RESTAURANT DE LA PLAGE

L'Herbe, 1 rue des Marins.
☎ 05.56.60.50.15
Closed Mon out of season and Jan–10 Feb.

A typical wooden house just by the water with a small grocer's and an old-fashioned telephone. Thankfully it's resisted the pressure to modernize. The restaurant is simple and cheap: fish soup, sole with ceps, hake, sea bream and fish cooked Basque-style. Careful cooking and home-made pastries. Set menus €15 and 24.

CASTELJALOUX   47700

🕍 🛏 |●| LA VIEILLE AUBERGE

11 rue Posterne (Centre).
☎ 05.53.93.01.36 ➡ 05.53.93.18.89
Closed Sun evening and Wed out of season, 18–28 Feb, 17–30 June and 18–30 Nov.

In one of the oldest streets in town, this inn has a thoroughly local flavour. Enjoy all the tastes Gascony has to offer with produce skilfully selected according to season: asparagus, *foie gras* cooked in a cloth, duck breast with truffles, monkfish Arles-style, bass with chicory, local lamb stew, fillet of beef with morels, duck breast Périgourdine. Set menus €18–37 with one for children at €11. A few simple rooms with shower for €27. Free coffee and 10% discount on the room rate.

CASTILLONÈS   47330

🕍 🛏 |●| HÔTEL-RESTAURANT DES REMPARTS

26–28 rue de la Paix (Centre).
☎ 05.53.49.55.85 ➡ 05.53.49.55.89
🅔 ludwig47@libertysurf.fr
Restaurant closed Sun evenings and Mon out of season. **TV.**

A beautiful and sturdy stone house in the middle of the village. Its conversion into a hotel has been carefully performed, to respect its original proportions. The rooms are spacious and painted in pale, soothing colours and the bathrooms are odd shapes; €37 for a double with shower, €44 with shower/wc and €50 with bath. The traditional regional dishes in the restaurant are predictable but well-prepared: duck breast with *foie gras* sauce and prunes preserved in Monbazillac wine, red mullet fillet with thyme butter and a platter of duck. The bread is especially good. €11 *formule*, €15 *menu terroir* and others up to €26. Attentive, pleasant welcome. Free coffee and 10% discount on the room rate Nov–15 June.

DAX   40100

🕍 🛏 |●| HÔTEL-RESTAURANT BEAUSOLEIL**

38 rue du Tuc-d'Eauze (Centre).
☎ 05.58.74.18.32 ➡ 05.58.56.03.81
Closed Jan. **Restaurant closed** Mon and Thurs evenings. **Garden. Disabled access. TV. Pay car park.**

This is the most charming and friendly hotel in

town, quietly situated near the centre. It's a pretty white house with a terrace and 32 comfortable rooms with shower/wc. Doubles €42 with shower/wc or €57 with bath. The food is conventional but good, all of it prepared with quality produce. Menu €10 (except Sun) and others €17–31. Your bottle is already set on the table next to your napkin ring. Excellent value. Free house apéritif and, if you stay, one free breakfast per room per night.

🕭 🏠 🍽️ LES CHAMPS DE L'ADOUR**

5 rue Morancy (Centre).
☎ 05.58.56.92.81 ☎ 05.5856.98.61
📧 leschampsdel'adour@club-internet.fr
Restaurant closed evenings in the week (open Tues evening in summer); 24 Dec–4 Jan.

This little hotel, very close to the covered market, looks more like a private house. The outside walls and the wooden staircase are original but inside it's been totally rebuilt with seven quiet rooms; doubles €38–41. The restaurant produces tasty dishes prepared with fresh, natural ingredients. The lunch *formule,* €8, includes a glass of wine or a coffee. If you eat *à la carte,* expend to spend around €15; you'll find marinated salmon Scandinavian style, hiziki seaweed *à la martime,* beef skirt with pickled shallots and, to order, oysters *au gratin*. 10% discount on the room rate 1 Dec–1 April.

🍽️ LA GUITOUNE

pl. Roger-Ducos.
☎ 05.58.74.37.46
Closed evenings, Sun and Mon. **Disabled access**.

Ideal if you don't want to spend too much. It's best to come on a Saturday when all local life is on show; the place teems with stall-holders from the market and it's a rendezvous for lots of Dax inhabitants. On offer are plates of good food like omelette with asparagus tips or mushrooms or a dozen oysters with a glass of local white wine. Dishes of the day €5–9.

🕭 🍽️ L'AMPHYTRION

38 cours Galliéni.
☎ 05.58.74.58.05
Closed Sat lunchtime; Sun evening and Mon; 2–20 Jan and 18 Aug–3 Sept.

Eric Pujos will delight you with dishes from the Landes and the Basque country in his bright, modern little restaurant, one of the gourmet establishments in the area. Dishes include rustic-style *foie gras*, Dublin Bay prawn salad, lamb stuffed with *axoa* (cubed

lamb browned with onions), *pimientos del piquillo* (spicy peppers), hake with squid cooked in the ink and, to finish, a delicious *pastis* from the Landes region. Very reasonable set menus €18–34. The *à la carte* menu changes every month. Prompt and pleasant service under the watchful eye of Mme Pujos. Free apéritif.

🕭 🍽️ LA TABLE DE PASCAL

4 rue de la Fontaine-Chaude (Centre).
☎ 05.58.74.89.00
Closed Sun, Mon lunchtime and three weeks in Feb.

A genuine little bistro with attractive decor and good food. Dishes include frogs' legs, *piquillos* stuffed with hake, calf's liver with parsley, salted belly pork and beef and duck with potatoes. No set menu; you'll pay around 18–€21 *à la carte*. Free apéritif.

🕭 🍽️ EL MESÓN

18 place Camille-Bouvet.
☎ 05.58.74.64.26
Closed Sat lunchtime, Sun, Mon lunchtime, a fortnight in Aug, 25 Dec–1 Jan and a week in April.

You're in Spain here. The décor and the cooking tell you so: panfried squid, grilled whole turbot, *paella*, gazpacho and juicy grilled lamb chops. If all you want is a snack, lean against the bar and order from the range of tapas and wash the delicacies down with a strong Spanish wine or the house sangria. Complete meals from €23. Free digestif.

DURAS   47120

🕭 🏠 🍽️ L'HOSTELLERIE DES DUCS**

bd. Jean-Brisseau; it's near the castle.
☎ 05.53.83.74.58 📠 05.53.83.75.03
📧 hostellerie.des.ducx@wanadoo.fr
Closed Sat lunchtime, Sun evening and Mon except July–Sept. **Swimming pool**. **TV**. **Garden**. **Car park**.

Originally a convent, these two fine semi-detached buildings now house the region's most prestigious hotel and restaurant. It's quietly situated, with a pleasant terrace, lovely swimming pool and prize-winning garden. There's a friendly atmosphere in the restaurant, where the food enjoys an excellent reputation. You can choose from a €14 weekday lunch menu and others at €20–45. Specialities include beef fillet with morels, rolled duck breast with pears, leeks with smoked salmon and perfumed plums, escalope of duck *foie gras* with white asparagus and a *crème brûlée* with Mandarine Impériale. The chef puts regional produce before originality and the result is good, high-quality cooking. The wine list has a fine selection of Duras bottles. Comfortable rooms go for €47 for a double with shower/wc or €60–83 with bath. It's pretty much essential to book in season. 10% discount on the room rate Oct–July.

EUGÉNIE-LES-BAINS — 40320

|●| LA FERME AUX GRIVES

Le bourg (Centre).
☎ 05.58.51.19.08
Closed Weds and Thurs (except public holidays); mid-July to end Aug; 5 Jan–7 Feb. **Car park**.

This restaurant is in the hands of famous chef Michel Guérard, who owns several local hotels, a spa and two other restaurants. This place is cheaper than some of his others, with *menu-cartes* starting at €37 – well worth it for perfectly simple dishes based on wonderfully fresh produce. Cured hams hang from the ceiling while a suckling pig turns slowly on the spit in the fireplace. You feel good as soon as you sit down. Dishes include braised *foie gras* with pigs' feet in a parcel of cabbage and for dessert there's Paris-Brest (a large *choux* pastry ring) with praline-flavoured cream, *crème brûlée* with grilled oats and fruit tarts. It's a wonderful celebration of culinary art; you will rarely eat better.

EYZIES-DE-TAYAC (LES) — 24620

♠ |●| HÔTEL-RESTAURANT DU CENTRE**

Centre; it's opposite the museum.
☎ 05.53.06.97.13 ➡ 05.53.06.91.63
Closed lunchtimes, Tues lunchtime only July–Aug, and 5 Nov–5 Jan. **TV. Car park**.

On a small, peaceful pedestrian square by the river. The white shutters add a touch of charm to the old ivy-covered walls. Very attractively decorated rooms. Doubles €45–76 with shower/wc or with bath. Beautifully restored rustic restaurant serves well-prepared, reasonably priced traditional dishes. Set menus, €15–34, are good value and list dishes such as *délice périgourdin* with *foie gras*, chicken breast with walnuts and chicken *confit*, three styles of *foie gras*, veal sweetbreads with morels, pan-fried scallops with ceps, rabbit *confit* in truffle juices, chocolate *rissoles* with pine kernels and almonds and hot nut *soufflé*. Half board (€53) is compulsory Aug–Sept.

♠ |●| LE MOULIN DE LA BEUNE – RESTAURANT LE VIEUX MOULIN**

le bourg (Centre).
☎ 05.53.06.94.33 ➡ 05.53.06.98.06
Hotel closed Nov–March. **Restaurant closed** Tues, Wed and Sat lunchtimes.
Disabled access. Garden. Car park.

This place, which used to be a mill, is on the water's edge at the quiet end of the village. The décor of the rooms is understated, a little austere for some tastes, but they're comfortable and good value. Doubles €49 with shower/wc and €50 with bath. Tasty, well-prepared food is served in *Le Vieux Moulin*, which houses the original mill machinery. The €19 menu lists dishes such as country-style Périgord medallion, chicken *ballotine* and trout supreme with almonds. On the other menus, up to €45, you'll see things like chicken *pâté* in aspic and duck *confit* with Périgord *mojettes*. In summer you eat in the garden on a delightful terrace, lulled by the murmuring river.

♠ |●| HÔTEL DE FRANCE – AUBERGE DU MUSÉE**

rue du Moulin.
☎ 05.53.06.97.23 ➡ 05.53.06.90.97
e hotel-de-france24@wanadoo.fr
Hotel closed Nov. **Restaurant closed** Mon and Sat lunchtimes except for groups and on public holidays.
Swimming pool. Garden. Car park.

Two establishments standing opposite each other at the foot of a cliff. The inn, which serves traditional and regional food, has two dining rooms – or you can eat outside under the wisteria-covered arbour. Set menus €16–33. There are a few rooms in the main building and others in an annexe on the banks of the Vézève, where there is a garden and a swimming pool. Doubles with bath from €52. Half board is compulsory 1–20 Aug.

⅍ ♠ |●| HÔTEL-RESTAURANT LE CENTENAIRE***

rocher de la Penne; it's in the main street.
☎ 05.53.06.68.68 ➡ 05.53.06.92.41
ⓦ www.hotelducentenaire.fr
Hotel closed 1 Nov to mid-April. **Restaurant closed** Mon, Tues and Wed lunchtimes out of season.
TV. Car park.

This exceptional establishment is quite simply the best restaurant in Périgord. Chef Roland Mazère is a culinary artist and his flavours are subtle, intense and original – try hot wild cep terrine, creamy black truffle risotto or fillet of goose "Rossini" (with *foie gras*) served with macaroni with Cantal cheese au gratin. Weekday lunch menu €31, with others €53–107. Despite its cachet, the dining room is not in the least stuffy. Alain Scholly and his wife offer you a genuine welcome and the service is perfect in its discreet efficiency. Décor is luxurious without being ostentatious, and the rooms are wonderfully furnished. Doubles from €107 with bath. 10% discount on the room rate except at weekends.

TURSAC   24620 (6KM N)

⅍ |●| RESTAURANT LA SOURCE

Le bourg; on the D706 between Eyzies and Montignac.
☎ 05.53.06.98.00 ➡ 05.53.35.13.61
📧 leoierschen@aol.com
Closed Sat in low season and Dec–March. **Garden**.

Decent little village inn run by a friendly young couple. It's a rustic-style restaurant, and when the weather is fine you can eat out on the terrace and admire the spring running through the garden. Modern cuisine with a good selection of local dishes: rabbit *terrine* with hazelnuts, semi-cooked duck *foie gras*, cep mushroom omelette, cod *au gratin* and rack of lamb with mild garlic. Menus, €12–21, include a vegetarian option. Staff are unobtrusive and pleasant. Free coffee.

TAMNIÈS   24620 (14KM NE)

🏠 |●| HÔTEL-RESTAURANT LABORDERIE**

Centre; take the D47 and the D48 – it's equidistant between Sarlat and Montignac.
☎ 05.53.29.68.59 ➡ 05.53.29.65.31
Closed 1 Nov–1 April. **Swimming pool. TV. Car park.**

Set on a peaceful square in this hillside market town, surrounded by exceptional countryside, *Laborderie* started off as a farm, became a country café and restaurant, and is now a rather chic – though relatively inexpensive – hotel-restaurant. Lovely rooms at reasonable prices; you'll pay €28–75 for a double with shower or bath. Some rooms are in the turreted main house, which has a great deal of charm, while others are in a garden annexe looking onto open countryside – those on the ground floor face the swimming pool. The large, bright restaurant has become one of the most popular in Périgord. The chef skilfully prepares generous helpings of classics such as Périgord platter, semi-cooked *foie gras* and duck with peaches. Menus €18–40. There's a terrace.

GRENADE SUR ADOUR   40270

⅍ 🏠 |●| PAIN, ADOUR ET FANTAISIE***

14–16 pl. des Tilleuls; it's on the village square under the arcade.
☎ 05.58.45.18.60 ➡ 05.58.45.16.57
📧 pain.adour.fantaisie@wanadoo.fr
Closed Sun evening, Mon, Wed lunchtime and Feb school holidays. **TV. Garden. Car park.**

This gorgeous old village dwelling stands between the main square and the Adour river. It has eleven comfortable, tastefully decorated rooms with great views. Doubles €64–122. The food is unforgettable, served in the sophisticated surroundings of the restaurant or on the riverside terrace. Dishes include *foie gras* marinated in Jurançon wine, risotto with glazed prawns, potatoes stuffed with ribbons of pork, pan-fried red mullet in lavender vinegar, braised rabbit with ceps in chestnut *jus* and milk-fed lamb from the Pyrenees. The service is unobtrusive and refined without being over-formal. Menus €27–82. Unbeatable charm and value for money. Free house apéritif.

HAGETMAU   40700

⅍ 🏠 |●| LE JAMBON**

27 ave Carnot (Centre); it's opposite the covered market.
☎ 05.58.79.32.02. ➡ 05.58.79.34.78
Closed Sun evening, Mon lunchtime and 20 Oct–10 Nov. **Swimming pool. TV. Car park.**

Behind the freshly painted pink-and-white exterior is a nice little place famous for its good cooking: *foie gras* with spices, scallop stew with ceps, pigeon with fine sliced liver and spleen, hot oysters in champagne sauce, beef with baby vegetables and hot Grand Marnier *soufflé*. Menus €17–27. The rooms are also recommended; doubles go for €43 with shower/wc or €46 with bath. Free apéritif.

HENDAYE   64700

🏠 |●| HÔTEL-RESTAURANT BERGERET-SPORT**

4 rue des Clématites; it's right in the middle of the beach area 150m from the sea.
☎ 05.59.20.00.78 ➡ 05.59.20.67.30
📧 bakea@club-internet.fr
Closed Sun evening and Mon.

The family photos on the walls are pictures of long-term guests, which creates a friendly atmosphere. The family-run hotel with comfortable rooms, €41–46 with bath. They are well-maintained by a charming, talkative lady. Her chef husband is a real pro – his classic, regional dishes are to be recommended and the portions are substantial: fish soup, fish *cassoulet*, free-range chicken Basquaise and home-made pastries. Menus from €13 to 18. Half board, €53, is compulsory 1 July–31 Aug. You can eat in the garden and the shade of the plane trees.

🛏️ |●| LE PARC À HUÎTRES

4 rue des Orangers
☎ 05.59.20.32.38
Closed Tues evening out of season.

This is a grocer's shop which also serves a fine array of seafood and salads. They're all cold: ultra-fresh oysters are €8–11 for a dozen, mixed platters €3–6 and there are a variety of salads €4–5. Service is inside or on the terrace. Tempting desserts and local wines served by the glass. A really good place.

🌿|●| LA CABANE DU PÊCHEUR

quai de la Floride; it's in Hendaye Plage on the fishing port.
☎ 05.59.20.38.09
Closed Mon 15 Oct–15 April. **Disabled access**.

Given its name and its location, there are no prizes for guessing that fish is king in this restaurant. You'll find the freshest of fish landed on the quayside opposite and cooked simply: either char-grilled, Spanish-style with pickled garlic or Basque-style. The large dining room is sparse and has a view of the boats. Menus €14–24. Charming welcome by the owner – who learned his trade with some of the best chefs in the region. Free green apple brandy.

BIRIATOU   64700 (4KM S)

🌿 🏠 |●| HÔTEL-RESTAURANT BAKEA**

How to get there: take the D258 and follow the signs.
☎ 05.59.20.76.36 ➡ 05.59.20.58.21
🌐 www.bakea.fr.st
Closed Sun evening and Mon Oct–March; Mon and Tues lunchtimes April–Sept; and 28 Jan–28 Feb. **TV**.
Disabled access. Car park.

A gorgeous, isolated place where you'll get complete rest and relaxation– though they've recently acquired the hotel next door so there is some work in progress. In the meantime, double rooms cost €38–61. Excellent restaurant where specialities include warm duck liver *tarte tatin*, joint of monkfish and

fresh anchovy lasagne marinated in basil. Set menus €28–55. 10% discount on the room rate Sept to end-June.

HOSSEGOR   40150

🌿 🏠 HÔTEL LES HÉLIANTHES**

av. de la Côte-d'Argent (West); 10min on foot from the beaches and 300m from the centre.
☎ 05.58.43.52.19 ➡ 05.58.43.95.19
🌐 www.helianthes.com
Closed mid-Oct to end March. **Swimming pool. TV**.

This stunning little white building with its red shutters is a family-run establishment where you'll get a warm welcome, peace and quiet, and excellent value. Doubles with shower/wc €35–54 and €65–80 with bath/wc. Breakfast is included in high season, and there's an evening menu on request out of season. The swimming pool is hidden among the pine trees. 10% discount 15 Sept–22 June for two nights or more.

🌿 🏠 |●| HÔTEL-RESTAURANT LES HUÎTRIÈRES DU LAC**

av. du Touring-Club.
☎ 05.58.43.51.48 ➡ 05.58.41.73.11
Closed Mon and Jan. **TV. Garden. Car park**.

Doubles €46–61 – reserve well in advance to be sure of getting a room overlooking the lake. It's very well-kept (if slightly pricey for the area), the food is excellent and there's a nice family atmosphere. Whether or not you spend the night here, it's worth stopping to eat: *foie gras* with peaches, roast pigeon with honey and sea bass in a salt crust. Set menus €15–29 with a children's menu for €9. 10% discount on the room rate except July–Aug and public holidays.

LALINDE-EN-PÉRIGORD   24150

🌿 🏠 |●| HÔTEL-RESTAURANT LE CHÂTEAU***

rue de Verdun (Centre); off pl. des Martyrs-du-21-Juillet-1944.
☎ and ➡ 05.53.61.01.82
Closed Sun evening and Mon in winter; Mon in autumn and spring; Mon lunchtime July–Aug; 15 Dec–15 Feb.
Swimming pool. TV. Lock-up garage.

This is a proper little castle with its corbelled turret, pepper-pot towers and balcony overlooking the sleepy Dordogne. Guy Gensou, who has redecorated the entire place, is in charge of the kitchen and gives you a very warm welcome. He adds his own touch to local dishes and uses superb fresh produce. The dining rooms are peaceful and the staff pleasant. The €21 menu includes apéritif. Good, traditional dishes on the menus or *à la carte*: *pâté* with truffle fragments, goose neck stuffed with sorrel, smoked salmon, stuffed trout in white Bergerac, black pudding with apples, barbecued meats, smoked goose with onion preserve, knuckle of lamb with vegetables, pig's trotter stew in red wine, roast Rocamadour cheese with walnut salad, *fromage frais* with melon jam. Comfortable double rooms with shower/wc or bath at €49–145. Guy rides a motorbike himself so fellow bikers are warmly welcomed. The small swimming pool overlooks the Dordogne. Half board is compulsory from May to the end of Sept. Free apéritif and 10% discount on the room rate or 5% on the price of half board (bikers only).

LAROQUE-TIMBAUT   47340

|●| LE ROQUENTIN

Centre; it's opposite the church.
☎ 05.53.95.78.78
Closed Thurs and Sun evenings, Mon, evenings on public holidays.

Recently built in the style of a stone Provençal house, and with bright décor. The chef has acquired a good reputation for regional cooking, using the finest quality produce and the traditional methods of the southwest. Dishes include duck with honey, sautéed chicken with ceps, zander in a butter sauce, frogs' legs in parsley, and scrambled eggs with truffles. Weekday menu €9 and others €19–34 with an option for children at €6. There's a fine wine list, with a good Cahors La Coutale 1992 or a Madiran 1991 from Bouscassé.

LARRAU   64560

🏠 |●| HÔTEL-RESTAURANT ETCHEMAÏTE**

☎ 05.59.28.61.45 ➡ 05.59.28.72.71
Ⓦ www.hotel-etchemaite.fr
Closed Sun evening and Mon out of season. **TV. Car park**.

It's easy to fall in love with this contemplative spot, and the welcome and kindness of the Etchemaïte family help to make it a magical experience. Simple, comfortable doubles go for €40 with shower/wc or €49 with bath. Chef Pierre's aim is to combine tradition with originality; he conjures up dishes such as

salad *souletine*, peasant soup, cep terrine with *foie gras jus*, grilled hake fillet with herb butter, cutlets of suckling lamb, grilled veal with a mushroom crust and, for dessert, pear *clafoutis* or apple tart with cinnamon ice cream. Set menus €14–40, or you can eat *à la carte*. The rustic dining room has a view over the mountains and the wine list is full of pleasant surprises at reasonable prices.

LARUNS   64400

|●| L'ARRÉGALET

37 rue du Bourguet (Centre).
☎ 05.59.05.35.47
Closed Sun evening, Mon, 15 April to end May, and last three weeks in Dec. **Disabled access**.

A warmly welcoming restaurant in an old street with a small terrace. The Coudouy family cook typical local dishes using the best ingredients the mountain can produce. The owner's brother makes the *charcuterie* and the bread is baked in the kitchens. Their *garbure* and duck *foie gras* with leek *fondue* are both special. But the *poule-au-pot*, with the chicken served whole in a vegetable broth, is the house speciality. Menus €10–23. *Arrégalet* is the local word for a crust of garlic-spread bread fried in goose grease.

🍴 |●| AUBERGE BELLEVUE

55 rue Bourguet (Centre).
☎ 05.59.05.31.58
Closed Tues evening, Wed and 5 Jan–20 Feb.

An attractive, friendly place with appetising set menus at €12–27. The chalet is festooned with flowers and there is an uninterrupted view of the mountains. Try the salmis of pigeon *à l'ancienne*, the duck *confit* with ceps or the chicken *fricassée* with freshwater crayfish. Don't overlook their chocolate pudding with raspberry coulis. Free *digestif*.

SÉVIGNACQ-MEYRACQ   64260 (8KM S)

🍴 🏠 |●| HÔTEL-RESTAURANT LES BAINS DE SECOURS**

How to get there: take the D934 for Laruns; after Rébénacq; as you come into the vallée d'Ossau, it's signposted.
☎ 05.59.05.62.11 ➡ 05.59.05.76.56
ⓔ jp.paroix@wanadoo.fr
Closed Sun evening, Mon and Jan. **TV. Car park**.

A scenic road leads to this restored Béarn farm, now an inn adorned with flower-filled

balconies. Well-appointed rooms go from
€45 with shower/wc to €55 with bath. Delicious food is served by the open fire in winter
and on the terrace in summer. Set menus €13
(residents only) and €14, featuring crayfish
salad with sheep's cheese, three fillets of beef
in three sauces, squid stuffed with *foie gras*
and ceps and lamb sweetbread *fricassée*. A
very good place to eat, close to the old spa.
10% discount on the room rate.

LESTELLE-BETHARRAM   64800

🏃 🏠 |●| LE VIEUX LOGIS***

Route des Grottes (Southeast); it's on the outskirts of the
village on the D937, towards the caves.
☎ 05.59.71.94.87 ➡ 05.59.71.96.75
e hotel-levieuxlogis@wanadoo.fr
Closed Sun evening and Mon out of season, 25 Oct–4
Nov and 25 Jan–1 March. **Swimming pool. TV.
Disabled access. Car park**.

Sizeable modern roadside hotel at the foot of
the mountains, with a swimming pool and
extensive grounds. An ideal place to relax.
It's excellent value, with impeccable double
rooms €34–49. There are separate wooden
chalets in the grounds where the rooms have
balconies. Quality regional cooking with particularly good desserts. Menus €15–34. Free
apéritif.

LISTRAC-MÉDOC   33480

🏠 |●| L'AUBERGE MÉDOCAINE

13 pl. du Maréchal Juin; it's in the centre on the N215.
☎ 05.56.58.08.86
Closed evenings in Jan.

The patio, which is set back from the road, is
a very pleasant place to eat good local dishes. The set lunch menu, €10, gets you a
selection of starters from the buffet, a dish of
the day, dessert and wine, and there are others €14–34. Rooms are simple and clean,
some with beamed ceilings. Doubles €34
with shower and €38 with bath/wc.

ARCINS   33460 (8 KM E)

|●| CAFÉ-RESTAURANT DU LION D'OR

It's in the centre of the village.
☎ 05.56.58.96.79
Closed Sun and Mon. **Disabled access**.

The owner can be brusque but the cooking is
superb, with game in season and fish from the
estuary prepared to local Médoc recipes. The

€10 menu offers starter, main course,
cheese, dessert and a $1/2$-litre of country wine.
The dishes of the day are always good – try
roast lamb, *tournedos*, or a simple omelette. À
la carte, expect to pay €31 with wine.

LUBRE-SAINT-CHRISTAU   64660

🏃 🏠 |●| AU BON COIN***

route d'Arudy; it's about 1km outside the village.
☎ 05.59.34.40.12 ➡ 05.59.34.46.40
e valerielassala@worldonline.fr
Closed Sun evening, and Mon 1 Nov–15 April. **TV.
Swimming pool. Car park. Disabled access**.

A good, comfortable, modern hotel set in
quiet countryside in the foothills 300m from
a spa. The swimming pool is across the road.
Double rooms €46–69. In the restaurant they
serve unusual dishes at reasonable prices
with lots of wild mushrooms: *terrine* with
Jurançon wine, shoulder of milk-fed Pyrenean lamb, pigeon with ceps *en croûte*.
Menus €14–50. Free coffee.

MAULÉON-LICHARRE   64130

🏠 |●| HÔTEL BIDEGAIN

13 rue de la Navarre.
☎ 05.59.28.16.05 ➡ 05.59.19.10.26
e bidegain-hotel@wanadoo.fr
Closed Sun evening and Mon 30 Sept–30 June, and
Jan. **TV. Pay car park. Garden**.

One of the oldest and most beautiful town-
centre hotels, once inhabited by the smart
set, has undergone a renaissance. Pierre and
Martine Chilo have taken it in hand and in a
few brief months it has been acknowledged
as the best gourmet restaurant in town. You'll
find cod terrine with a spicey pimento paste
smeared on good bread, barbecued beef
and chocolate soufflé on the costliest menu
at €23 (it'll cost around the same *à la carte*);
on the cheapest at €11 there are delicious
dishes such as salmon lasagne with fresh
pasta. Rooms go for €27 for double with
handbasin to €46 with shower/wc or bath.

MIMIZAN-PLAGE   40200

🏃 🏠 |●| HÔTEL-RESTAURANT
ATLANTIQUE

38 av. de la Côte-d'Argent; it's on the north end of the
beach.
☎ 05.58.09.09.42 ➡ 05.58.82.42.63
ⓦ www.cortix.fr/atlantique

Restaurant closed 7 Jan–2 Feb. **Disabled access**.
Garden. **Car park**.

This modest and friendly family establishment stands on the seafront but only enjoys
a limited sea view. The façade of the old
wooden building is intact and they've built a
forty-room modern hotel on the back.
Rooms with shower or basin are modestly
priced at €21, while those with shower/wc
go for €37–50. The best rooms are in the
main house, and four of them have that sea
view. It's also a nice place to eat, with a
weekday lunchtime menu at €8 and others
up to €24; there's a children's menu for €6.
Simple, nourishing dishes include duck
breast with *foie gras* with Balsamic vinegar,
scallop salad with mango and chicken with
prawns. Half board is compulsory in
July–Aug. 10% discount for a two-night stay
Sept–June.

🏃 🏠 |●| HÔTEL-RESTAURANT
L'ÉMERAUDE DES BOIS**

66–68 av. du Courant; take the D626.
☎ 05.58.09.05.28 ☛ 05.58.09.35.73
e emeraudedesbois@wanadoo.fr
Hotel closed Oct to end March. **Restaurant closed**
lunchtimes 20 May–20 Sept. **TV**. **Car park**.

This hotel-restaurant is another good family
establishment in a charming house surrounded by large trees and decorated in traditional style. Very warm welcome. Double
rooms €40–58 with shower/bath. Half
board, compulsory in July and August, costs
€44–49 per person – well worth it given the
quality of the cooking. Excellent menus
€15–27. Try the fish or cream of courgette
soups, home-made *foie gras*, roast rabbit in
mustard sauce, monkfish *à la provençale*,
duck breast with honey and walnut *gâteau*.
A great deal of care goes into the preparation
and cooking. The verandah and terrace provide welcome shade in summer. Free house
apéritif or coffee and 10% discount out of
season.

🏃 🏠 LE PATIO

6 av. de la Côte d'Argent.
☎ 05.58.09.09.10.
ⓦ www.le-patio.fr
Closed Mon end Sept–April and Jan **TV**. **Swimming**
pool. **Car park**.

It's advisable to book well in advance for this
place because the oceanfront location
means it gets full. Stunning little rooms, nicely furnished in Provençal style. Doubles are
€53–104, or you could choose to stay in the
quiet bungalows at the back near the swim-

ming pool. There's a small *crêperie* next door
belonging to the same family. 10% discount
on the room rate 15 Sept–15 June.

SAINTE-EULALIE-EN-BORN   40200 (12KM NE)

🏃 🏠 |●| AUBERGE DU MOULIN DES
CYGNES

quartier Mauras.
☎ 05.58.09.72.63 ☛ 05.58.09.74.35
Restaurant closed weekdays 1 May–15 Sept. **TV**. **Car**
park.

A nice little surprise. Lovely rooms where you
sleep quietly – doubles are €38–44. The
restaurant is near the lake with a view of an
odd-looking windmill. The food is delicious:
roulade of duck *foie gras* with figs marinated
in port or pan-fried with raspberry butter,
profiteroles with *foie gras* and apple *clafoutis*
– that sort of thing. Menus €23 and €27.
Free house apéritif.

LÜE   40210 (22KM E)

|●| RESTAURANT L'AUBERGE LANDAISE

In the village; take the D626.
☎ 05.58.07.06.13 ☛ 05.58.07.05.90
Closed Sun evening, Mon, Oct and three weeks in Jan.
Car park.

A jolly little inn where they serve a string of
set menus to suit every pocket, from €9
(excluding Sun in July–Aug) up to €29.
Unless you're a veggie, it's impossible not to
find something you fancy: wood-pigeon
stew, duck gizzard salad, *foie gras*, duck
breast and duck *confit*, baby squid in ink or
monkfish *à l'armoricaine*. The quality of Monsieur Barthet's cooking and the range of
prices cut through all social barriers.

MONT-DE-MARSAN   40000

🏃 🏠 |●| HÔTEL-RESTAURANT DES
PYRÉNÉES*

4 rue du 34ème R.I.
☎ 05.58.46.49.49 ☛ 05.58.06.43.57
Closed Fri evening, Sun in July–Aug. **TV**.

You can't miss this wonderful old pink house.
At lunchtimes – when there's an €11 menu –
it's rather like a canteen for local workers.
Other menus, up to €30, list good, tasty
dishes such as duck breast, *foie gras* and
confit of chicken, pork or lamb. When it's hot,
the dining room's large bay windows are
opened onto a terrace surrounded by trees
and flowers. The rooms are attractive,

particularly those which overlook the garden – the ones on the crossroads side are noisier. Doubles €21 with handbasin and up to €38 with shower/wc or bath. Pleasant service. Free coffee.

🛏 |●| HÔTEL-RESTAURANT ZANCHETTIN**

1565 av. de Villeneuve; 2km on the road to Villeneuve de Marsan, next to the campsite in the Saint-Médard district.
☎ and ➡ 05.58.75.19.52
Closed Mon and 3 weeks from mid-Aug. **TV**. **Car park**.

Relatively quiet hotel and restaurant with a bar. Nine good rooms with shower/wc or bath €33–43. You can eat on a terrace under the plane trees or in the sweet little restaurant. The weekday menu, €11, includes wine and coffee, and there are others up to €25. It's a little off the beaten track, but it's a well-run place and well worth the trip.

🍴 🛏 |●| HÔTEL-RESTAURANT RICHELIEU**

rue Wlérick (Centre); it's behind the theatre.
☎ 05.58.06.10.20 ➡ 05.58.06.00.68
Restaurant closed Sat except for group bookings.
TV. **Pay car park**.

Central hotel with a crisp, starchy, rather provincial feel. Good-value doubles with shower/wc are €41; €44 with bath. In the restaurant you get some of the best cooking in town. Set menus, at €14–28, list tasty traditional dishes: chicken salad with leek vinaigrette, sea bream slices with squid, pigeon stuffed with ceps, strawberry *millefeuille* with strawberry sorbet. This is where the locals come for their business lunches. 10% discount on the room rate except during July and August.

|●| CHEZ DESPONS

20 rue Plumaçon; it's at the foot of the train station steps.
☎ 05.58.06.17.56
Closed evenings, Sun and the first 3 weeks in Aug.

A whole range of *formules* and menus: for €6.50 you get the dish of the day, a salad and a dessert; for €7 there's a self-service buffet of crudités and charcuterie followed by a choice of dessert; and the €9 menu has three courses and includes wine. Prices go all the way up to €14. Good family food – the kind you dream of finding on your travels through France. The best dish is grilled entrecôte steak with sauces or peppered and served with a salad.

|●| LE BISTROT DE MARCEL

1 rue du Pont-du-Commerce (Centre).
☎ 05.58.75.09.71
Closed Sun; Mon lunchtime.

Despite the name, this isn't an old-style bistro but a good restaurant with fine cooking and a rather wonderful setting – and there's an enclosed, heated terrace with a view over the Midouze, too. The cooking is defiantly representative of the Landes region and the chef uses excellent local produce. Menus €7–13.

UCHACQ — 40090 (4KM W)

🍴 |●| RESTAURANT DIDIER GARBAGE

It's on the RN134, on the way to Sales and Bordeaux.
☎ 05.58.75.33.66
Closed Sun evening, Mon and 7–14 Jan. **Car park**.
Disabled access.

The chef moved to this small village restaurant – and all his previous regulars followed. The dining room is a pleasant place in which to sit and enjoy his fine cooking. Recommended are pan-fried *foie gras* with figs, lamprey with the white of leek, duck *confit* and *tournedos* of pig's trotter with truffle oil. Menus in the restaurant start at €23 and go up to €43 while the bistro corner is regularly under seige from friends and regulars. Here there's a dish of the day for €8, or the *menu du jour* costs €11. If you don't fancy that, have a slice of country ham and a glass of wonderful wine. Free house *digestif*.

MONTFERRAND-DU-PÉRIGORD — 24440

🍴 🛏 |●| HÔTEL-RESTAURANT LOU PEYROL

La Barrière; it's on the D26.
☎ 05.53.63.24.45 ➡ 05.53.63.24.45
Closed Wed lunchtime April–June and Sept; 30 Sept–29 March. **Car park**.

A pretty little country hotel with a restaurant run by Sarah and Thierry, a friendly Anglo-French couple who also run the snack bar across the road. Simple, clean double rooms (some of which have a view of the gorgeous village of Montferrand) go for €31 with basin and up to €39 with bath/wc. Good cooking, too: roast Barbary duck; omelettes with ceps, morels or girolle; chocolate and walnut gâteau. Menus €13–27. Free apéritif.

MONTFORT EN CHALOSSE   40380

♠ |●| AUX TAUZINS**

It's on the D2 (the route to Baigts and Hagetmau), about 500m outside the village.
☎ 05.58.98.60.22 ➡ 05.58.98.45.79
Closed Sun and Mon out of season; the first fortnight in Oct; Jan. **Swimming pool. TV. Car park**.

A fine example of a traditional hotel and restaurant, but with some welcome modern facilities – such as the pool. The owners have been hotel-keepers for three generations, so the establishment has a comfortable family feel with old-style bedrooms looking over the grounds; it's wonderfully peaceful. Doubles €45 with shower/wc and €48 with bath. The bright restaurant has a view over the valley. Dishes are from the region: *tournedos* Landais, *fricassée* of monkfish and John Dory with ceps. Menus €17 (except weekends) and €22–32.

MONTIGNAC   24290

♠ |●| RESTAURANT BELLEVUE

Regourdou; it's on the Lascaux road, after the caves at the top of the hill.
☎ 05.53.51.81.29
Closed Sat, evenings and a week each in June, Oct and Jan. **Car park**.

Located close to the Lascaux caves, with superb views from its bay windows and terrace, this place is a restaurant with a few rooms. It serves decent food with a regional bent: chicken *confit* and *enchaud*, baked loin of pork, pig's trotters with garlic and truffles, gizzard salad, cep mushroom omelette. Prices are reasonable – a weekday menu for €9 and others up to €21. Rooms €32 with shower/wc or €38 with bath.

♣ ♠ |●| HÔTEL-RESTAURANT DE LA GROTTE

3 rue du 4-Septembre (Centre); it's opposite the Lascaux road.
☎ 05.53.51.80.48 ➡ 05.53.51.05.96
Closed Jan. **TV. Disabled access. Lock-up garage**.

A coaching inn which became a hotel around the time that the Lascaux caves were discovered. It's right in the centre, so ask for a room looking onto the garden. Prices are competitive for the area – €27 for a double with basin, €38 with shower/wc and €43 with bath. Dishes include cep and girolle *millefeuille* with walnut

cream sauce, warm salad of poached goose with light *choucroute*, veal picata with cream and morel sauce, zander pie with snails in a garlic cream sauce and escalope of *foie gras* with coriander. There's a weekday lunch *formule* for €10, and menus are €15–18. There are two terraces for when the weather is fine. Free apéritif and use of garage.

♠ |●| HOSTELLERIE LA ROSERAIE***

11 pl. d'Armes; (Centre)..
☎ 05.53.50.53.92 ➡ 05.53.51.02.23
🌐 www.laroseraie.fr.st
Closed lunchtime (except weekends between 15 April–15 June and 15 Sept–15 Nov); 15 Nov–20 Dec and 2 Jan–15 April. **TV. Swimming pool**.

A solid, elegant 19th century town house which stands proudly to attention on the place d'Armes. Polite welcome. The staircase is wooden and there are several small sitting rooms; it's a charming house. The fourteen rooms are exquisite; though they're all different, they have en-suite bathrooms. They cost €69–79 with shower/wc and €79–99 with bath. It feels more like an old-style guest house or a family *pension* than in a stylish 3-star establishment – they even cork your unfinished wine and leave it on the table for the next meal. The small, enclosed grounds have high walls so it's easy to imagine you're out of town, and behind the swimming pool you'll find the rose garden the hotel is named after. The restaurant – which has a delightful terrace – serves sophisticated local dishes, adroitly prepared: duck breast and tartare, duckling *pot-au-feu* with creamed horseradish. Set menus €16–31. Half board is compulsory in July and August and on public holidays (€71–82 per person).

SAINT-AMAND-DE-COLY   24290 (8KM E)

♣ ♠ |●| HÔTEL-RESTAURANT GARDETTE**

In the village.
☎ and ➡ 05.53.51.68.50
📧 hotelgardette@free.fr
Closed 15 Oct to Easter. **Car park**.

Two pale stone houses overshadowed by a fantastic church. Quiet, modernized rooms at reasonable prices – €27 with shower and wc along the landing, €33 with shower/wc or bath. Some have a balcony with a view of the abbey. The restaurant across the lane has a few small tables in one corner – the owner cooks for the local schoolchildren during term time. For taller customers, set menus are €11 (except Sunday) and €14–20, offering salads and dishes from the southwest including omelette with cep mushrooms or truffles, duck breast and *confit*. In summer, it's advisable to book during the classical music festival. 10% discount on the room rate Sept–June.

SERGEAC   24290 (8.5KM S)

⚞|●| RESTAURANT L'AUBERGE DU PEYROL

How to get there: it's on the D65, between Montignac and Les Eyzies.
☎ 05.53.50.72.91
Closed Mon except in July–Aug and the school holidays; Dec. **Garden. Car park.**

A traditional stone-built inn standing on its own just outside a quaint little village. A large bay window looks out over the lovely Vézère valley. The fine rustic restaurant has a big fireplace where they smoke fillets of duck breast. Decent welcome and tasty food. Jeanine concocts rare country dishes – fresh goose liver, baked loin of pork, pig's trotters with garlic and truffles, duck liver *confit*, duck breast with Périgueux sauce, walnut salad, Sarlat-style potatoes. Menus €11–34. It's best to book. Free apéritif.

CHAPELLE-AUBAREIL (LA)   24290 (12KM S)

⚞🏠|●| HÔTEL-RESTAURANT LA TABLE DU TERROIR**

From Montignac or Les Eyzies take the road to Lascaux II, from there on, it's signposted.
☎ 05.53.50.72.14 ➡ 05.53.51.16.23
Closed 30 Nov–28 Feb. **Swimming pool. TV. Disabled access. Car park.**

The Gibertie family have developed a tourist complex around their smallholding, which deep in the country. The restaurant is on a hill 100m from the hotel; midway between them there's a swimming pool with views over the countryside. The buildings are new, but in traditional Périgord style, and they blend well with their surroundings. Rooms are pleasant, and the rates include breakfast, €34 with shower/wc, €36 with bath (though these prices rise in high season). Half board, compulsory in July and August, costs €48 per person, per night. Set menus, €11–32, list sliced duck, duck *confit*, stuffed chicken, country salad, pan-fried *foie gras* and truffles cooked in hot coals. They can even make you a packed lunch and are happy to show you around the farm. Free apéritif and a serving of *foie gras* on toast.

MONTPON-MÉNESTÉROL   24700

|●| AUBERGE DE L'ÉCLADE

In the village. Take the D708 from Ribérac, turn right at the crossroads before going into town and it's signposted.
☎ 05.53.80.28.64
Closed Tues evening and Wed; 1–20 March; Oct.

This rustic, flower-filled restaurant is off the beaten track but it has built a large following through word-of-mouth recommendation. Warm welcome and good atmosphere. The food is creative but rooted in tradition: duo of asparagus tips and panfried *foie gras* with a sesame seed sauce, flash-fried red mullet with ratatouille perfumed with Mandarine vinegar and duck breast with truffle shavings. The menus, €13 (weekday lunchtimes only) and €21–37, are good value.

NAVARRENX   64190

⚞🏠|●| HÔTEL-RESTAURANT DU COMMERCE**

pl. des Casernes (Centre).
☎ 05.59.66.50.16 ➡ 05.59.66.52.67
🌐 hotel-du-commerce.fr
Closed Jan. **TV.**

One of the oldest houses in Navarrenx. They light a fire in the large fireplace in the foyer at the first sign of cold weather. Pleasant rooms – the nicest up in the attic – are €45 with shower/wc or bath. Wonderful Béarn flavours in the restaurant, which has plush surroundings, or there's a cool terrace for the summer. Menus are very reasonably priced: €11 for the weekday lunch one and others up to €24. Kindly owner. Free coffee.

NÉRAC   47600

⚞|●| AUX DÉLICES DU ROY

7 rue du Château; on the pl. de la Mairie.
☎ and ➡ 05.53.65.81.12
Closed Wed.

The food is a winning combination of tradition, subtle flavours and high-quality produce. Menus (€16–40) include unusual fish or meat dishes: canelloni of raw salmon, *foie gras* with baby spinach, cockles in butter with lamb's lettuce, grilled red mullet with olive *pâté*, calf's head *ravigotte*, braised ox cheek with vegetables and seasonal shellfish. Young and attentive staff. The wine list features regional wines. Free apéritif.

FRANCESCAS   46600 (13KM SE)

|O| LE RELAIS DE LA HIRE

In the village; take the D930 for 9km towards Condom, then left onto the D112.
☎ 05.53.65.41.59 ➡ 05.53.65.86.42
📧 la.hire@wanadoo.fr
Closed Sun evening and Mon.

This restaurant, set in a stunning 18th-century manor house, has a peaceful atmosphere. After working with Roger Verger and Robuchon at the *Ritz* and running the kitchens at the *Carlton*, Jean-Noël Prabonne returned to Gascony. He is fussy about buying from local suppliers when creating his masterful dishes: local ceps *en cocotte*, Albret artichokes with a *soufflé* of *foie gras*, red sea bream poached with herbs, farm-bred pigeon with mushrooms, rack of roast lamb with garlic cloves and thyme, braised leg of maize-fed chicken. Weekday menu €21, with others €29–49; it costs around €35 *à la carte*, and there's a children's menu for €12. Pleasant reception from Mme Prabonne and attentive service. An unforgettable gastronomic experience.

SAINT-MAURE-DE-PEYRIAC   47170 (17KM SW)

|O| RESTAURANTS DUFFAU-LES 2 GOURMANDS

rue Principale.
☎ and ➡ 05.53.65.61.00
Closed Sat, end Jan.

At lunchtime during the week this place is like many others, with a clientele of travelling salesmen, local workers and lost tourists – though the food is slightly better than average and dishes are substantial. The lunch menu costs €10 and lists soup, *terrine* or omelette as typical starters. But Sunday lunch is a different story: the restaurant is a magnet for gourmands so you have to book in advance. The chef has worked at the *Ritz* and *Chez Lasserre* (two of the very best kitchens in Paris) and on Sundays he and his associates give flight to their skill and imaginations at prices that would be unthinkably cheap in the capital – the menu is €25. They sell prepared meals as well. Splendid welcome.

NONTRON   24300

🏃 ⭐ |O| HÔTEL-RESTAURANT PELISSON**

pl. Alfred-Agard (Centre).

☎ 05.53.56.11.22 ➡ 05.53.56.59.94
Swimming pool. TV. Disabled access. Car park.

This grand hotel, right in the centre, has an elegant – if rather austere – exterior and a pleasant garden with a lovely swimming pool. The rooms are particularly quiet at the rear; doubles €40 with shower and up to €49 with shower/wc or bath. Huge, cosy, rustic restaurant with attractive, locally-made tableware. The terrace looks onto the garden. They serve traditional local food which has a good reputation: veal pâté *ravigotte*, foie gras, sliced beef in red wine and casseroled sole with ceps. Set menus €13–40 and a good wine list. 10% discount on the room rate for a two-night stay Oct–May.

OLORON-SAINTE-MARIE   64400

|O| ⭐ HÔTEL DE LA PAIX **

24 ave Sadi-Carnot; it's opposite the train station.
☎ 05.59.39.02.63 ➡ 05.59.39.98.20
TV. Lock-up car park.

The new owner has made visible changes to this place: some of the rooms have already had a makeover with double glazing and new beds and linen. They are huge and bright. Doubles €30 with shower on the third floor and €40 with bath.

GURMENÇON   64400 (3KM S)

🏃 |O| ⭐ RELAIS ASPOIS**

Route du col du Somport; 3km south of Oloron-Sainte-Marie; take the D55 and the N134, in the direction of Zaragoza
☎ 05.59.39.09.50 ➡ 05.59.39.02.33
Closed Mon lunchtime and the second fortnight in Nov.
TV. Children's playground. Garage.

The dining room here is full of character, with slate tiles, bare stone and beams and, in cool weather, a fire crackling in the hearth. Set menus are €8–27 – try Béarnaise vegetable broth, *foie gras* or *confit* of duck leg. They also prepare good regional dishes: ceps with parsley, Basque tripe *pâté*, *foie gras*, trout, duck breast with ceps. Rooms from €24 with basin, €30 with shower and €43 with bath. Free apéritif.

ESQUIULE   64400 (12KM S)

|O| CHEZ CHÂTEAU

It's in the village.
☎ 05.59.39.23.03
Disabled access.

What a place! What a village! And what a

chef! Jean-Bernard Houçourigaray's cheapest menu lists *garbure* (a local speciality, a substantial soup), troutlets with parsley, duck *confit* and a strawberry soup. That will set you back €14. For the same price you can order a *garburade*; as you dig down to the bottom of the dish you uncover duck drumsticks, chunks of ham, duck meat *confit* and you have to excavate for a long time before you've finished. If you're on a gastronomic indulgence trip, opt for the sweet-and-sour salad of duck with fresh duck liver and oyster mushrooms or the simple lamb sweetbreads with fresh ceps. Menus €24–33, and there's a superbly selected list of wines at more than reasonable prices. The dining room is country-inn in style and the hosts are from the area – which explains why the portions are so big. Another option, even better value, is to eat in the bar with the villagers. The innkeeper is young, energetic (like his friendly team), attentive and chatty. This is the place to brush up on your Basque – although the village is elsewhere, its population is exclusively from that area . . .

ORTHEZ   64300

⅍ ☎ |●| HÔTEL-RESTAURANT AU TEMPS DE LA REINE JEANNE**

44 rue du Bourg-Vieux (Centre); it's opposite the tourist office.
☎ 05.59.67.00.76 ➡ 05.59.69.09.63
Closed 1–15 March. **TV. Disabled access. Pay car park**.

The mother of Henri IV, Jeanne d'Albret, bravely professed her Protestantism in this house at a time when it was risky to criticize the Catholic Church. Today it's a peaceful and quiet hotel with lovely rooms overlooking the patio. Doubles with shower or bath €45. The restaurant is a pleasant surprise: the décor is modest but the cuisine is opulent – delicate cream of celery soup, *foie gras* terrine with artichokes, joint of monkfish with bacon, duck *cassoulet*, Béarn black pudding on split bread, suckling pig. A festival of flavours at honest prices. The cheapest menu is at €9 (weekday lunchtimes only); others up to €25. Perfect service. Free apéritif.

|●| AUBERGE SAINT-LOUP

20 rue du Vieux Pont.
☎ 05.59.69.15.40
✉ brosse.p@wanadoo.fr
Closed Sun evening and Mon.

A very beautiful house, characteristic of the region, in a street which is typical of the town. This used to be a coaching stop on the way to Santiago de Compostela; it has a superb half-timbered façade. Patrick Brosse's dishes blend the traditional and the modern: prawns with salt cod mousse with chorizo and chilli, sea bass with lemon and star anis, roast pigeon with rosemary. Lunch menu €15, with others from €15 to €31. In summer, they open the cool terrace in a peaceful garden. Friendly service.

PAU   64000

☎ HÔTEL D'ALBRET*

11 rue Jeanne-d'Albret (Centre); it's near the château of Henri IV.
☎ 05.59.27.81.58

You get a warm welcome in this pretty 19th-century house. Rooms are quite large and very well kept; €19 with washing facilities and €23 with shower/wc.

⅍ ☎ HÔTEL LE POSTILLON**

10 cours Camou; it's two minutes from the château and just by the place de Verdun.
☎ 05.59.72.83.00 ➡ 05.59.72.83.00
✉ hotel-le-postillon@wanadoo.fr
TV. Car park.

A hotel in the neo-Romantic style. There's a little flower garden in the courtyard and a trickling fountain. Doubles with shower/wc or with bath €39. A good place, particularly given the value for money. 10% discount.

☎ |●| HÔTEL-RESTAURANT LE COMMERCE**

9 rue du Maréchal-Joffre (Centre); it's opposite the Préfecture de Police.
☎ 05.59.27.24.40 ➡ 05.59.83.81.74
✉ hotel.commerce.pau@wanadoo.fr
Restaurant closed Sun and public holidays, except for groups. **TV. Pay car park**.

Traditional hotel in the centre of town, with a certain charm and a warm welcome. Comfortable, soundproofed rooms €39–50 with shower/wc or bath. No lift. There's a bar and a fine restaurant with rustic décor with walls built from smooth stones. Menus €14–24; specialities include fillet *mignon* with morels, sole with ceps and duck breast with prawns. Pleasant courtyard terrace with good service.

⅍ |●| DON QUICHOTTE

30–38 rue Castetnau (Northeast).
☎ 05.59.27.63.08

Closed Sat lunchtime, Sun and Mon lunchtime.

One of the cheapest restaurants of quality in Pau – you can eat well for €8. They list 15 dishes (including *tapas*, *paella* and *zarzuela*) for derisory prices and provide a generous welcome. In winter they specialize in pork and even have a menu which is exclusively pork-based – the menu "extrêmités" for €15 includes dishes featuring ears, tail and trotters and there's another at €20 using only the fine cuts. Free sangria.

⚗️❖❘ RESTAURANT LA BROCHETTERIE

16 rue Henri-IV (Centre); it's near the château d'Henri IV.
☎ 05.59.27.40.33 ➡ 05.59.27.30.58
Closed Sat lunchtime.

Service until 11pm. Attractive stone-built restaurant where they grill duck breast and meats over the fire. The lunchtime clientele consists mainly of people who work nearby. Menus €10–18. Attentive staff. *À la carte*, try grilled hake flambéed with anis, wild boar cutlets and various fresh salads. A real treat, so it's best to book. Free apéritif.

❖❘ LE MAJESTIC

9 pl. Royale (Centre).
☎ 05.59.27.56.83
Closed Sun evening and Mon. **Disabled access.**

Locally-born chef Jean-Marie Larrère, who has worked at the *Trou Gascon* and *Le Pressoir* in Paris, is a little ill-served by the dull surroundings – though the shady terrace on the Place Royale makes up for it on sunny days. In any case, Larrère produces remarkable dishes: hot *foie gras* with caramelized pears, salad of *croustillant* of pig's trotters with fresh morels, pot-roast pigeon with ceps, saddle of monkfish with a chorizo *jus* and mushrooms. Menus €14 (weekdays) to €30. Mme Larrère is very welcoming, and runs the dining room to perfection.

❖❘ AU FIN GOURMET

24 av. Gaston-Lacoste (Centre).
☎ 05.59.27.47.71 ➡ 05.59.82.96.77
Closed Sun evening, Mon, the Feb school holidays and a fortnight July–Aug.

This place, a firm favourite with the people of Pau, really lives up to its name. Quality cooking is on all the menus, which start at €17 (except at the weekend) then go from €27 up to €53. Dishes are finely prepared – stars include the *foie gras terrine* with pistachios, rabbit and potato pie, and roast pigeon with *foie gras* toast.

⚗️❖❘ RESTAURANT LA TABLE D'HÔTE

1 rue du Hedas; it's 5 minutes on foot from the château.
☎ 05.59.27.56.06
Closed Sun, Mon and the school holidays at Easter and All Saints'.

In one of the oldest parts of Pau, Pierre will welcome you like a regular to his impressive restaurant which has stained-glass windows and beams. The richly flavoured cuisine is spot-on, and uses lots of quality produce: crayfish *fricassée* with *foie gras* and fresh noodles, salad of quail in sherry, duck pie scented with truffle, duck tart with truffles, sole braised in Jurançon wine and lamb sweetbreads with peppers. Menus €18 and 24. Free coffee.

GAN   64290 (8KM S)

⚗️🏠❖❘ HOSTELLERIE L'HORIZON**

chemin de Mesplet.
☎ 05.59.21.58.93 ➡ 05.59.21.71.80
✉ eytpierre@aol.com
Closed Sun evening and Mon out of season, 22–31 Dec and 31 Jan–28 Feb. **TV. Garden. Car park. Disabled access.**

A pink house with a garden full of flowers and a peaceful terrace, in extensive grounds. Attractive, well-equipped rooms for €47. Sophisticated cuisine *à la carte*: trilogy of *foie gras*, braised sole with *foie gras*, salmon trout with ceps, lambs sweetbreads with girolles and so on. There are menus priced €15–46. Free apéritif.

PÉRIGUEUX   24000

⚗️🏠❖❘ HÔTEL-RESTAURANT DU MIDI**

18 rue Denis-Papin; northwest of town opposite the train station.
☎ 05.53.53.41.06 ➡ 05.53.08.19.32
Closed Sat 20 Oct–15 April, and Christmas–New Year. **TV. Pay car park.**

A typical station hotel which has been completely renovated by the friendly young couple who run the place. Nice family atmosphere. Very clean modern rooms, at €23 for a double with basin or €38 with bath; those at the back are bigger and quieter. The restaurant is peaceful. Set menus, €12–35, offer traditional cooking with local dishes such as truffle omelette, veal sweetbreads with morels and duck breast with *foie gras* cream. Free use of pay garage.

⚗️❖❘ LES BERGES DE L'ISLE

2 rue Pierre Magne.
☎ 05.53.09.51.50

Closed Sun evening and Mon.

This restaurant is in a picturesque spot – on the shore of the island opposite the cathedral – and they have the only waterside terrace in town. Unusual cooking such as *cassoulet* with four different meats and walnut oil, *soufflé* of *foie gras* with *vigneronne* sauce and lamprey with Bordelais sauce. Menus €14–22. Some wines are served by the glass. Friendly atmosphere. Free coffee.

⅍ |◉| RESTAURANT HERCULE POIREAU

2 rue de la Nation (Centre); it's in a small street opposite the main door of the Saint-Front cathedral.
☎ 05.53.08.90.76
Closed 24–27 Dec and 31 Dec–3 Jan.

The name of this restaurant is a play on words – Inspector Hercule Poirot was fastidious about what he ate, while *poireau* means leek. Brasserie-style food includes *andouillette*, veal *blanquette*, and, their speciality, a splendid duck Rossini with *foie gras*. The dining room is an impressive 16th-century vaulted cellar. *Formule* at €19 for two courses and menus €18–35. Free house apéritif.

⅍ |◉| RESTAURANT LE 8

8 rue de la Clarté (Centre); it's next to the Saint-Front cathedral.
☎ 05.53.35.15.15
Closed Sun, Mon.

Regional and creative dishes served in a sunny dining room – home-made *foie gras* or *croustillant* of duck are the star turns. Set menus €26–61, and it'll cost around €27 *à la carte*. They take their cooking seriously here and are happy to serve half-portions of any dish on the menu. They have a courtyard and garden, and the cellar has been turned into a sitting room. Free coffee.

CHANCELADE   24650 (3KM W)

✿ |◉| LE PONT DE LA BEAURONNE**

4 route de Ribérac; it's at the crossroads of the D710 and D939.
☎ 05.53.08.42.91 ➡ 05.53.03.97.69
Closed Sun evening, Mon lunchtime and 20 Sept–15 Oct. **TV. Garden. Disabled access.**

Service until 9.30pm – last orders half-an-hour before. The crossroads doesn't exactly enhance the charm of the place, but the rooms are reasonable and well-kept. Doubles with basin or shower €23 and €35 with bath – try to get one at the back, looking onto the garden. There's a half-board option for €46. Family atmosphere. The cooking is straight-

forward, with an emphasis on the regional. Menus from €11 to €22.

ANNESSE ET BAULIEU   24430 (12KM)

⅍ ✿ |◉| CHÂTEAU DE LALANDE – RESTAURANT LE TILLEUL CENDRÉ***

How to get there: take the D3 in the direction of Saint-Astier.
☎ 05.53.54.52.30 ➡ 05.53.07.46.67
🌐 www.hotels-restau-dordogne.org/chateau-lalande
Garden. Swimming pool. Car park.

Situated in an estate on the banks of the Isle, this is luxury without ostentation. You are welcomed with old-fashioned charm. The rooms are attractively furnished and most of them have a river view; they are all quiet and cosy. Doubles €49–63 with shower/wc and €56–78 with bath. The cuisine is resolutely regional and prepared to the most exacting standards: salmi of pigeon with truffle, guineafowl breast with green peppercorns, trilogy of duck in *pot-au-feu* and fillet of zander in parchment paper. Menus 23–47. Half board is compulsory in high season for €55–66. There's a swimming pool down by the river. Free apéritif or coffee and 10% discount for a minimum three-night stay March–April and Oct–Nov except public holidays.

MANZAC-SUR-VERN   24110 (20KM SW)

✿ |◉| HÔTEL-RESTAURANT LE LION D'OR**

pl. de l'Église (Centre): take the D43 and the D4.
☎ 05.53.54.28.09 ➡ 05.53.54.25.50
Closed Sun evening and Mon except July–Aug, and Feb. **Garden. TV.**

This place is quiet: it's in the heart of a region largely bypassed by tourists, in the centre of a small village where nothing happens after 7pm. Doubles with shower or bath €21–37 – some look onto the garden. The restaurant features modern décor with a few older elements and traditional cooking. Weekday lunch menu €12 and others €18–34. The chef's specialities include a platter of three types of *foie gras*, salmon with mead, duck breast with fresh fruit and balsamic *jus*, *millas* (maize flour porridge) with apples and cinnamon ice cream. You can eat outside in summer. Half board €43 per person.

SORGES   24420 (23KM NE)

⅍ ✿ |◉| AUBERGE DE LA TRUFFE***

N21 (Centre).

☎ 05.53.05.02.05 ➡ 05.53.05.39.27
🌐 www.auberge-de-la-truffe.com
Closed Sun evening in winter and Mon lunchtime. **TV**.
Swimming pool. **Garden**. **Car park**.

Good traditional food in a region famous for truffles: duck with *foie gras*, stuffed carp *à l'ancienne*, cep omelette and beef with *foie gras* or sliced duck. The restaurant is popular with local businesspeople as well as tourists. Friendly service. The limited €14 set menu is well-priced and there's a self-service buffet and fresh dishes daily. Other menus, €17–53, include pressed vegetables with *foie gras*, goat stew with *verjus*, duck aiguillettes with foie gras and there's a truffle menu – featuring *marbré* of veal sweetbreads with *foie gras* and truffle vinaigrette, medallions of lamb with truffle and truffle omelette. Though the inn is right on the road, the rooms look out over the open countryside; some have a garden view. Doubles with shower/wc €40, or with bath €53. Good breakfast buffet. 10% discount on the room rate Sept–June.

RIBÉRAC   24600

🎿 |●| RESTAURANT LE CHEVILLARD

Gayet (Southwest); 2km from Ribérac, on the D708, Montpon to Bordeaux road.
☎ 05.53.90.16.50
Closed Mon except July–Aug, and 15 Nov–15 Dec.
Garden. **Car park**.

Restaurant in an old farm surrounded by a huge garden. The owner, formerly a sales rep, knows how to make you feel welcome, and he offers large portions of quality food: fresh farm chicken, oysters from the display and good meats grilled over an open fire (the place's name literally means "Restaurant of the Wholesale Butcher"). They do a €11 lunch menu and others €18–69. Seafood is also served at reasonable prices, and they offer a good selection of local wines. Free apéritif.

SABRES   40630

🎿 ⬧ |●| L'AUBERGE DES PINS***

rue de la Piscine.
☎ 05.08.30.00 ➡ 05.58.07.56.74
☎ www.auberge-des-pins.com
Closed Sun evening and Mon out of season, Mon lunchtime in season, and a fortnight in Jan.
Disabled access. **TV**. **Car park**.

A large timber-framed house, typical of the Landes, with a lovely balcony. The Lesclauze family are only happy when you're happy and

will pull out all the stops to ensure that you leave with fond memories of the place. The rooms have some fine furniture, pretty ornaments and supremely comfortable beds. Doubles with shower or bath €58–64. The surroundings are rustic but classy, and the quality of the food is equally high. Tempting dishes include turbot with creamed carrots, stuffed roast pigeon with risotto, crayfish ravioli with ceps and strawberry soup with a cream cheese sorbet. The choice is made exquisitely difficult because of the tireless inventiveness of the chef. First menu €18, excluding Sunday; others €27–69 with a children's menu €12. 10% discount on the room rate out of season.

SAINT-ÉMILION   33330

⬧ L'AUBERGE DE LA COMMANDERIE**

rue des Cordeliers (Centre).
☎ 05.57.24.70.19 ➡ 05.57.74.44.53
✉ contact@aubergedelacommanderie.com
Closed 15 Jan–15 Feb. **TV**. **Disabled access**. **Car park**.

A senior officer of the Order of the Knights Templar used to live here, and during the French Revolution the disgraced Girondins used it as a hiding place. Very little of its rich past is visible today, however. It's now a conventional family hotel with romantic rooms in the main building and more futuristic ones in the annexe. Doubles €46–69 with shower or bath. There is also an apartment that sleeps four.

⬧ HÔTEL AU LOGIS DES REMPARTS***

rue Guadet.
☎ 05.57.24.70.43 ➡ 05.57.74.47.44
✉ logis-des-Remparts@wanadoo.fr
Closed mid-Dec to mid-Jan. **Swimming pool**. **TV**.
Garden. **Car park**.

A fine three-star in a very old building which has kept the original stone staircase to the entrance, the terrace and the garden bordering the ramparts. Doubles with shower/wc €61–85, with bath €84–114. Some rooms can sleep five people. The owners have recently brought the neighbouring *Maison des Templiers*, doubling the number of rooms with views over the garden. When the weather's fine, breakfast is served on the elegantly paved terrace or in the garden. It's substantial and very good – just try the cake.

🎿 |●| RESTAURANT FRANCIS GOULLÉE

27 rue Guadet (Centre).
☎ 05.57.24.70.49 ➡ 05.57.74.47.96

Closed Sun evening and Mon.

Hidden away in a narrow old street, this is the least touristy restaurant in Saint-Émilion. Francis Goulé, ably assisted by his chatty wife, prepares very good local cooking in the warm, comfortable dining room. Prices are very fair, with a €15 *formule* (not served on Sundays), and menus €21–38. Choices include pigeon with ceps, pastry case filled with chicory and gravadlax, breast of duck *en aiguillettes*, roast potatoes with onion *fondue*, marvellous *foie gras*, pigeon *en croûte* with mild spices and Szechuan pepper, casserole of *brandade de morue* (creamed salt cod) with morels, dried figs with spices and pear *dacquoise*. Attractively-priced wine list. Free apéritif.

SAINT-JEAN-DE-LUZ 64500

涂 🛌 LE PETIT TRIANON**

56 bd. Victor-Hugo.
☎ 05.59.26.11.90 ➡ 05.59.26.14.10
℮ le petittrianon@wanadoo.fr
Closed Jan. **TV. Car park**.

This hotel is charming, simple, clean and unpretentious. And reasonably priced. The new owners have retained the family character of the place, while coming up with a few new ideas to bring it more up-to-date, and they are refurbishing and redecorating the rooms systematically. The third-floor rooms have handbasins or shower only (no wc) but the sloping ceilings make them rather romantic. Doubles €34–64. Pretty private terrace. 10% discount on the room rate Oct–March.

涂 |●| HÔTEL OHARTZIA**

28 rue Garat; it's in a little street between the church and the sea, 40m from the beach.
☎05.59.26.00.06 ➡ 05.59.26.74.75
℮ benoit.audibert@libertysurf.fr

The façade is appealing with its Spanish ceramic flower pots overflowing with geraniums and petunias. Inside, the peaceful garden seems far from the hubbub of the tourists and it's perfect for breakfast. Most of the rooms are tastefully decorated. The ones on the first floor have rattan twin beds lacquered in navy blue while those on the third are more rudimentary – but the view of the Rhune is great compensation. Double rooms for €52–73 with shower/wc and €60–81 with bath. 10% discount on the room rate Oct–June.

涂 🛌 HÔTEL LA DEVINIÈRE***

5 rue Loquin (Centre); it's 100m from the beach.

☎ 05.59.26.05.51 ➡ 05.59.51.26.38

A family house right in the middle of the old town. It's a haven of peace if you want to stay a while. There's a music room and likewise the cosily decorated rooms strike a chord. All the rooms are different and furnished with antique furniture, pictures and ornaments. Doubles €99–130 with bath/wc. Free house apéritif or coffee. Perfect welcome.

|●| LA BUVETTE DES HALLES

bd. Victor-Hugo; it's opposite the covered market.
☎ 05.59.26.73.59
Closed Mon in winter.

There's a great atmosphere on market days. Jean Laborde's customers provide him with the best produce from the market; they bring it in at 5am, he opens at 5.30 and cooks it up later in the day – fish soup (€6), grilled line-caught tuna with *piperade* (€10) and *axoa* of veal (€10). The mussels and grilled sardines are delicious, too. It's the oldest and smallest place in town – just three tables and the terrace.

涂 |●| PIL-PIL ENEA

3 rue Sallagoïty; it's near the covered market and the post office.
☎ 05.59.51.20.80
Closed Sun; Tues evening except in the school holidays; Jan.

The small dining room houses a dozen tables and a minimalist décor. The chef is king of line-caught hake – and it's super fresh because his wife, the only woman who owns a fishing boat in the port, is responsible for catching it. Her whole crew is female and off they sail to bring the fish back for Monsieur to cook. The menu is short and depends on what she lands. Menu for €21 or €18 upwards *à la carte*. The clientele is local and a mixture of fishermen and fishmongers and the chat is mainly about the price of fish.

|●| LE KAIKU

17 rue de la République (Centre).
☎ 05.59.26.13.20
Closed Mon lunchtime and Wed out of season.

Service until 11pm. A superb medieval house with elegant mullioned windows and wonderful natural stonework. They specialize in fish and seafood, and the cooking is of a very high standard – though it's a bit touristy. Set menus from €22; try the exquisite oysters *gratinée*, the langoustine ravioli or the milk-fed Pyrenees lamb. Some recipes, like braised pork cheeks with Irouléguy, hark back to the past.

CIBOURE   64500 (1KM S)

⅍ |●| CHEZ MATTIN

pl. de la Croix-Rouge.
☎ 05.59.47.19.52 ➡ 05.59.47.05.57
Closed Mon; Jan–Feb.

Service until 9.30pm out of season and
10.15pm in season. One of the best-known
fish restaurants in the area. The agreeable
dining room is bright white with a few good
pictures of the region on the wall. The place
is famous for the "ttoro", a fish soup costing
€19 per portion. It may seem expensive but
on its own it will do for a whole meal. All the
fish landed at the quay make an appearance
on the menu unless you fancy deep-fried,
breadcrumbed tripe for €8 or pig's cheeks
with potato terrine for €12. It may lighten the
bill but it's weighty food. Free apéritif.

ASCAIN   64310 (7KM SE)

⅍ ⚑ |●| HÔTEL OBERENEA***

route des Carrières; it's on the edge of the village going
towards the Saint-Ignace pass.
☎ 05.59.54.03.60 ➡ 05.59.54.47.39
Ⓦ www.oberenea.com
Disabled access. **TV**. **Swimming pool**. **Car park**.

The hotel is in huge grounds with views of
the mountains. It has 25 rooms and is run by
an energetic woman who is systematically
doing them up. She'll make time to give you
a lovely welcome. Doubles with shower/wc
or bath €53–91 – the priciest have a balcony. An alternative is to book one of the
chalets in the garden for €76–109 (they
sleep four).There's a heated indoor pool,
another outside, a Jacuzzi, a sauna and an
exercise room.

SARE   64310 13.5KM E

⅍ ⚑ |●| HÔTEL-RESTAURANT PIKASSARIA**

How to get there; it's just outside Sare in the hamlet of
Lehenbiscay and is well signposted.
☎ 05.59.47.19.52 ➡ 05.59.47.05.57
Ⓦ www.hotel-rest-pikassaria.com
Closed Wed out of season and 12 Nov–19 March.
Disabled access. **TV**. **Car park**.

Located in breathtaking countryside, this
place has built quite a reputation for itself.
However, with its success it's lost that touch
of intimacy which is the charm of country
hotels. Big, bright rooms with terrace from
€40. Nonetheless, the local specialities in
the restaurant make the punters come back

time after time – try the pigeon and lamb
dishes and you'll understand why. Menus
€14–27. Free house apéritif.

⚑ |●| HÔTEL ARRAYA***

It's on the village square.
☎ and ➡ 05.59.54,20.46
Ⓦ www.arraya.com
Closed 4 Nov–31 March. **TV**. **Car park**.

This place was originally an old coaching on
the pilgrim route to Santiago de Compostel-
la, then it became a presbytery in the 19th
century before being bought by the wealthy
Fagoaga family. Now it's a hotel again and
the rooms are decorated very attractively.
Some are very spacious, others are at garden level, others have balconies. Superb
period furniture and hand-sewn bed linen
decorated with the Basque symbol of a flam-
ing torch. Doubles €60–91. The restaurant
also has a good reputation and a quota of
regulars. The €15 menu is served only on the
terrace and there are others €21–30. They
boast pan-fried troutlets with ham and garlic
vinegar, méli-mélo of lamb and prawns with
girolles.

⅍ |●| RESTAURANT LASTIRY

It's on the village square.
☎ 05.59.54.20.07
Closed Mon, Mon and Tues Feb–April and Nov–Dec and
Jan.

Guillaume Fagoaga is still very young but he
has a passion for his craft, his region and its
produce. With his brother Jean in charge
front-of-house, he opened this restaurant,
which in just a few months became the talk of
the area – perhaps because both brothers
are equally perfectionist in their approach.
Guillaume's dishes are prepared with artistry
and invention and they change as often as
the produce is available – a particular house
classic is the char-grilled squid. Menus
€15–25. On the terrace they serve an assiette du randonneur for €7 – slices of ham
and cheese and a portion of Basque gâteau.
It's barely more expensive than a hamburger
but it's good, clean, tasty food.

SAINT-JEAN-PIED-DE-PORT   64220

⅍ ⚑ |●| CENTRAL HÔTEL**

1 pl. du Général-de-Gaulle (Centre).
☎ 05.59.37.00.22 ➡ 05.59.37.27.79
Closed 10 Dec–1 March. **TV**. **Car park**.

Rooms here are luxurious and impeccably
clean; they cost €53 with shower and €61

with bath. Ask for one with a view of the Nive and the waterfall. Similarly high standards in the restaurant, which offers set menus at €17–37. The dining room has charm and the cooking is first-rate: roast milk-fed lamb, lamb sweetbreads with *piquillos*, wild salmon, *soufflé* with Izarr (a liqueur similar to Chartreuse). Good welcome and attentive service. Free apéritif.

⋔ |●| LES PYRÉNÉES***

19 pl. du Général-de-Gaulle (Centre).
☎ 05.59.37.01.01 📠 05.59.37.18.97
Closed Mon evening Nov–March, Tues excluding July–Aug, 5–28 Jan and 20 Nov–22 Dec.
Swimming pool. **TV**. **Car park**.

On paper, €92–145 might seem a lot to pay, but this is a high-class hotel, the rooms are impeccable and there's a very pleasant indoor swimming pool. The restaurant, which has a well-established reputation throughout the Basque country, offers fine cuisine artistically conjured from local produce – delicious *pipérade*, peppers stuffed with cod, *foie gras*, lasagne with truffles, roast pigeon with cep ravioli and remarkable desserts and sorbets. Menus €38–84.

|●| RESTAURANT ARBILLAGA

8 rue de l'Église; it's inside the fortified part of town.
☎ 05.59.37.06.44
Closed Tues evening and, out of season, Wed.

Grand dining room in a stunning location between the fortified walls and the old houses. Delicious food is served in generous portions, both on the set menus (€13–26) and *à la carte* – try the scrambled eggs with truffle and *foie gras*, the scallops with smoked bacon or the spit-roast milk-fed lamb. Spirited welcome and service in an intimate atmosphere.

SAINT-MICHEL   64220 (4KM S)

⋔ ⋔ |●| HÔTEL-RESTAURANT XOKO-GOXOA**

How to get there: it's on the D301.
☎ 05.59.37.06.34 📠 05.59.37.34.63
Closed Tues. **Car park**.

This is a large traditional house surrounded with greenery. Most of the rooms look straight onto the countryside. Comfortable double rooms €31–34. Atmospheric rustic-style dining room and no-nonsense, good value cooking. Set menus, at €11 (not Sunday) to €21, list specialities such as trout *etxekoa*, steak *à la navarraise* (with sweet peppers, onions and garlic), salad *gourmande* and so on. The *à la carte* prices are very reasonable. Large terrace with a wonderful panoramic view. Free apéritif when you stay three nights.

BUSSUNARITZ   64220 (7KM E)

⋔ |●| HÔTEL-RESTAURANT DU COL DE GAMIA**

col de Gamia; take the D933 then the D120.
☎ 05.59.37.13.48 📠 95.59.37.96.96
Closed Jan–end March. **Car park**.

The little road to this place is one of the loveliest in the region. When you get to the top of the col de Gamia, the view is tremendous. The clean and comfortable rooms are €30 with shower or €34 with bath. The excellent Basque cuisine includes delicious wild boar stew in season. Set menus €10–26. The charming owners are warm and friendly.

BIDARRAY   64780 (14KM NW)

⋔ |●| HÔTEL-RESTAURANT BARBERAENEA**

pl. de l'Église (Centre).
☎ 05.59.37.74.86 📠 05.59.37.77.55
Closed 15 Nov–15 Dec. **Disabled access**. **TV**. **Car park**.

A very old country inn belonging to the Elissetche family. It has been beautifully renovated after a lengthy closure. Cheery welcome and attractive, charming rooms with white walls, period furniture and shining parquet floors. They look out onto the square and its 12th-century church; some have a view of the countryside. Doubles €29 with basin, €42–52 with shower/wc. In the restaurant you can get appetising dishes including salad of warm cod with garlic sauce, pan-fried lamb chops and bread-and-butter pudding. *Menu du randonneur* €14, *menu du terroir* €21.

SAINT-JUSTIN   40240

⋔ |●| HÔTEL DE FRANCE**

pl. des Tilleuls.
☎ 05.58.44.83.61 📠 05.58.44.83.89
Closed Sun evening, Mon, Thurs evening and 14 Oct–12 Nov. **TV**. **Disabled access**.

1930s-style decor in this hotel in the middle of a 13th-century fortified town. Peace and quiet reigns here, along with a traditional family atmosphere. Lovely rooms at €37 with shower/wc and up to €46 with bath. The restaurant is at the back. The chef comes up with delicious flavours and prepares everything from fresh produce: salad of duck gizzards, prawns with diced cep and ginger with green chilli, suckling pig with *ratatouille*, duck breast with mushrooms and *foie gras*. The house speciality is goose simmered in red wine. Set menus €11, except Sun, then €19–40. Friendly welcome and relaxed atmosphere.

SAINT-MACAIRE   33490

☎ |●| L'ABRICOTIER

2 rue Borgoeing; it's on the N113 between Langon and La Réole.
☎ 05.56.76.83.63 ➡ 05.56.76.28.51
Closed Mon and Tues evenings; 12 Nov–12 Dec. **TV**. **Car park**.

This restaurant would be one of the most beautiful in the region were it not on the edge of the N113. At least the little dining room looks out onto the terrace at the back with its apricot tree – lovely when the sun is out. The kitchen turns out imaginative dishes including *gazpacho* of scallops with Jerusalem artichokes, roast sea bass with asparagus, braised shoulder of lamb, *cassolette* of snails with *confit* of pig's trotters, salad of duck's neck with artichokes, fillet of bream with mixed vegetable *confit*, vegetables with *foie gras* and, for dessert, roast pineapple with vanilla. Weekday lunch menu €18, and others €24–37. Very good wine list – exclusively Bordeaux. A handful of rooms with bath for €46.

SAINT-PALAIS   64120

🏃 ☎ |●| HÔTEL-RESTAURANT DE LA PAIX**

33 rue du Jeu-de-Paume (Centre).
☎ 05.59.65.73.15 ➡ 05.59.65.63.83
Closed Fri evening, Sat lunchtime except July–Aug, and Jan. **Disabled access**. **TV**. **Car park**.

You'd never think from the outside that this hotel has been around for 200 years – it's been entirely rebuilt and has all mod cons. Rooms €44–46 with shower/wc or bath. Good regional cooking, with a weekday menu at €11 and others €18–25. Dishes include lamb's sweetbreads with ham and ceps, monkfish, marinated salmon and ewe's-milk cheese *millefeuille*, *ttoro* (fish

stew), and game in season. Charming welcome, but it'll be some time before it gets its old character back. Free house apéritif.

SARLAT-LA-CANÉDA   24200

🏃 ☎ HÔTEL LE MAS DE CASTEL

Sudalissant (South); it's 3km from the town – take the D704 in the direction of Souillac, then La Canéda, and after that it's signposted.
☎ 05.53.59.02.59 ➡ 05.53.28.25.62
Closed 11 Nov to Easter. **Swimming pool**. **Disabled access**. **TV**. **Car park**.

A charming hotel built in beautiful white stone in the local style and surrounded by greenery. Excellent welcome. The rooms are comfortable, pleasant and restful; numbers 2, 3, 4, 5 and 14 are larger than the others. Expect to pay €42–53 for a double with shower/wc or bath. There's a beautiful swimming pool where you can cool off in summer. 10% discount April and Oct.

🏃 ☎ HÔTEL LES RÉCOLLETS**

4 rue Jean-Jacques-Rousseau (Centre); it's in the middle of the medieval city.
☎ 05.53.31.36.00 ➡ 05.53.30.32.62
🔘 www.hotel-recollets-sarlat.com
Closed Jan. **Car park**. **TV**.

This place is in a quiet, picturesque lane away from the cars and the tourist crowds. Sarlat is an old town so it's good to stay in a hotel with a bit of history – this used to be the cloisters of a 17th-century convent. Today it's managed by a father-and-son team and you get a convivial welcome. The rooms have been tastefully refurbished; doubles with shower/wc or bath cost €38–46. A few look out onto a quiet courtyard where you have breakfast. Number 15 is particularly light and has a lovely view over the tiled rooftops in the old town, while number 8 has elegant stone archways. Free bottle of regional wine.

🏃 ☎ |●| LA MAISON DES PEYRAT**

Le lac de la Plane; pass the police station and follow the signs for 2km.
☎ 05.53.59.00.32 ➡ 05.53.28.56.56
✉ maisondespeyrat@net.up.com
Open weekends only 15 Nov–1 April. **Swimming pool**. **Disabled access**. **TV**. **Car park**.

A 17th-century hermitage that has been converted and refurbished by the new owners. It's become a charming hotel and is in a delightful place. The thoughtful decor makes the most of the old stonework. Bright, spacious rooms are €38–89 with shower/wc or bath. Very charming welcome. Menu at €15, featuring tomato *tarte Tatin*, sautéed shrimps. Free coffee.

🏊 🛏 |●| HÔTEL-RESTAURANT SAINT-ALBERT ET HÔTEL MONTAIGNE**

10 pl. Pasteur et 11 rue Émile Faure (South); behind the main post office.
☎ 05.53.31.55.55 ➡ 05.53.59.19.99
Closed Sun evening, and Mon out of season. **Disabled access**. **TV**. **Car park**.

Two hotels and a restaurant on the edge of the old town. Behind the tasteful façade of *Hôtel Montaigne* you'll find pretty rooms which are well equipped and attractively decorated in modern style. The ones on the top floor have ceilings criss-crossed with beams. There's a glassed-in terrace where you have breakfast. On the other side of the street, in *Hôtel Saint-Albert*, the rooms have been refurbished and the ones over the street have double glazing. In both establishments doubles with shower or bath cost €43–53. In the huge dining room you'll rub shoulders with faithful regulars and local worthies – people who appreciate culinary classics such as calf's head and pig's trotters as well as regional food like salad *périgourdine*, omelette with cep mushrooms and *confit* of duck with walnuts. At lunchtime on weekdays, the bistro serves a dish of the day, a set menu for €10 or *à la carte*; at other times, you'll pay €18–26. Free apéritif.

🏊 🛏 HÔTEL DE COMPOSTELLE**

64 av. de Selves; near the centre of town on the road to Montignac/Brives.
☎ 05.53.59.08.53 ➡ 05.53.30.31.65
✉ hotel.compostelle@perigord.com
Closed Sun lunchtime and 15 Nov to end-March. **Disabled access**. **TV**. **Garden**.

Friendly welcome. Excellent, large and pleasant rooms; doubles €46 with shower/wc or €50 with bath. A few have a glassed-in balcony but they look out onto the street. The quieter rooms at the back overlook a tiny garden. Families can go for the small suites with two bedrooms and bath. 10% discount on the room rate in low season, except for public and school holidays.

🏊 🛏 |●| LA HOIRIE***

La Giragne; take the Souillac road out of Sarlat and it's well signposted.
☎ 05.53.59.05.62 ➡ 05.53.31.13.90
🌐 www.lahoirie.com
Closed 15 Nov–15 March. **Swimming pool**. **TV**. **Car park**.

Some parts of the original 13th-century

house remain, and a recent refurbishment has brought out the brilliance of the pale stone. There are large grounds with a pool so you can sunbathe and cool down afterwards. The rooms are spacious and more like comfortable apartments; they're €58–104. The kitchen cooks everything fresh – look out especially for the semi-cooked house *foie gras* with fennel *compote*, boned pig's trotter stuffed with goose *foie gras*, duck breast with leeks and chocolate *moelleux*. Menus €14–40. Free apéritif.

|●| RESTAURANT CHEZ MARC

4 rue Tourny (Centre).
☎ and ➡ 05.53.59.02.71
Closed Sun, and Mon evening out of season.

You'll need to book at this minuscule bistro, which has two or three tables set on the terrace on a busy old street. Ideal for lunch. There are menus €14–34 (with an €8 one on weekdays), or you might pay around €15 *à la carte*. Dishes include duck *andouillette* in Cahors wine, duck breast with red fruit, a choice of fish, and apple *fondant*. Reasonably priced wine.

|●| RESTAURANT LES 4 SAISONS

2 côte de Toulouse (Centre).
☎ 05.53.29.48.59 ➡ 05.53.59.53.74
Closed Wed out of season.

A newly opened restaurant in a steep, narrow street. The two dining rooms have been knocked into one and there's a terrace with a panoramic view. Dishes are cooked using only fresh produce. The set menu at €14 offers some of the best value for money in town; others, €18–34, list dishes like *croustillant* of pig's trotters with ceps and truffle sauce, duck confit with truffle *jus* and original desserts including *gratin* of seasonal fruit. They also do great chocolate creations and a truffle ice cream with saffron sauce.

|●| LE PRÉSIDIAL

6 rue Landry; it's next to the town hall.
☎ 05.53.28.92.473 ➡ 05.53.59.43.84
Closed Mon and Jan–Mar.

Great gastronomic feats are accomplished in this restaurant, which is run by a charming couple. This jewel is their new enterprise and already it's become *the* place to eat in Sarlat. The building is classified as a historic monument and is a gorgeous house from 1552, set in a large, quiet garden in the old town. The dining room is very elegant and the terrace is the loveliest around. The €18 short menu offers a good choice and value for money. On the others, €22–27, you'll find perfect *foie gras*, a stew of snails and pig's trotters and beautifully cooked guineafowl supreme in pastry. An extensive wine list with fair prices. Courteous and efficient service.

ROQUE-GAGEAC (LA) 24250 (9KM S)

☎ |●| HÔTEL-RESTAURANT LA BELLE ÉTOILE**

rue Principale (Centre); it's on the D46.
☎ 05.53.29.51.44 ➔ 05.53.29.45.63
e hotel.belle-etoile@wanadoo.fr
Restaurant closed Mon and Wed lunchtime; end Oct–early April. **TV.**

Charming, stylish hotel in a glorious setting in one of the most beautiful villages in France. The rooms are individually decorated and tastefully furnished. A few have a great view of the slow-moving Dordogne. Great efforts have been made to update the décor. Doubles €31–76 with shower or bath. The elegant dining room has a vine-smothered terrace overlooking the river, and the food is excellent – the kitchen concentrates on the classics but adds the odd unexpected modern touch such as *millefeuille* of *foie gras* and apple and walnut tart with caramel sauce. Set menus from €20.

DOMME 24250 (12KM S)

☎ |●| NOUVEL HÔTEL*

rue Maleville and Grande-Rue (opposite pl. de la Halle).
☎ 05.53.28.38.67 ➔ 05.53.28.27.13
Closed Mon or Tues, Jan–Feb.

A pretty stone house ideally situated in the centre of the old fortified town. Good prices for the area. The pleasant rooms cost €38 for a double with shower/wc or €53 with bath. The restaurant, which has set menus at €10–29, offers regional cuisine. Specialities include snails in flaky pastry, pan-fried *foie gras*, *confit* or breast of duck and goose gizzard stew.

MARQUAY 24620 (12KM NW)

⅍ |●| HÔTEL DES BORIES – RESTAURANT L'ESTÉREL**

North of Sarlat take the D47 for Les Eyzies then the D6 signposted for Marquay.
☎ 05.53.29.67.02 ➔ 05.53.29.64.15
Restaurant closed Tues lunchtime. **Swimming pool. Disabled access. Garden. TV. Car park.**

A delightful hotel in a very good location – a nice village off the beaten track. It has a big garden, a swimming pool and a superb view.

Bright, clean rooms €31–83. Thirty-two of these have a corner sitting room, a big fireplace and a view, and some have separate rooms for children. Breakfast is served on the two terraces. Friendly welcome. The restaurant next door, now part of this establishment, has a good reputation. They serve dishes such as *aiguillette* of duck with ceps and *foie gras*, scallops and prawns with ceps and pan-fried *foie gras* with roast pears. Menus €14–31. 10% discount on the room rate April–June and Oct (excluding long weekends and school holidays).

MEYRALS 24220 (12KM NW)

⅍ ☎ HÔTEL DE LA FERME LAMY***

How to get there: take the D47 in the direction of Les Eyzies/Périgueux, then turn left at Benive signposted to Meyrals.
☎ 05.53.29.62.46 ➔ 05.53.59.61.41
w www.ferme-lamy.com
Swimming pool. Disabled access. TV. Car park.

Charming hotel in an old farmhouse hidden in the depths of the country. Parts of the building date from the 17th century. It's the height of luxury; ravishing doubles, some with air conditoning, cost €64–119 with shower/wc or €90–157 with bath. In good weather you can eat breakfast – walnut bread, *brioche* and home-made jam – outside in the garden under the lime trees. A superb swimming pool overlooks the fields and hills. Simple, genuine welcome. 10% discount Sept–June.

PAULIN 24590 (24KM NE)

⅍ |●| LA MEYNARDIE

How to get there: from Sarlat, go in the direction of Salignac-Eyvignes, then towards Archignac.
e la-meynardie@wanadoo.fr
☎ 05.53.28.85.98 ➔ 05.53.28.82.79
Closed Wed; Dec to mid-Feb. **Car park.**

An old farmhouse set deep in the country. The dining room has been carefully restored and has a certain appeal with its paved floor and massive fireplace dating from 1603. Courteous welcome, though the atmosphere's a little on the chic side. The €12 weekday lunch menu and others €16–40 are all based on traditional dishes, but include creative variations like *carpaccio* of duck breast and goose stew with Bergerac wine. Good desserts include an iced *soufflé* with walnuts. Sit out on the terrace in summer, or stroll through the chestnut tree forest after your meal. Best to book. Free coffee.

LAVAL-DE-JAYAC   24590 (25KM NE)

ᐯᓐ �🏠 |●| HÔTEL-RESTAURANT COULIER**

It's in the village; take the D60.
☎ 05.53.28.86.46 ➡ 05.53.28.26.33
Ⓦ www.hotelcoulier.com
Closed Sat out of season; and mid-Dec to Feb.
Swimming pool. Disabled access. TV. Car park.

You'll find this hamlet in an almost deserted part of darkest Périgord. The pretty converted farm buildings make a U-shape around a courtyard, on a hillock set well away from the road. The fairly small rooms, which are scattered around the building, go for €31 with shower and €46 with shower/wc or bath. Friendly welcome. The restaurant serves regional dishes like semi-cooked *foie gras*, scrambled eggs with truffle, warm semi-cooked *foie gras*, veal sweetbreads and breast of duck with violet mustard. Menus are €15–38, and there's a children's menu at €6. If you don't want to spend all day by the pool, there are several short trails in the surrounding area – the owners know the area very well so don't hesitate to ask them for advice. 10% discount on the room rate Sept–June.

SAUTERNES   33210

|●| AUBERGE LES VIGNES

pl. de l'Église.
☎ 05.56.76.60.06 ➡ 05.56.76.69.97
Closed Mon and 15 Jan–15 Feb. **Disabled access.**

A gorgeous country inn with log fires and tables laid with checked cloths. Friendly welcome from the American owner, and a warm, homely atmosphere. The authentic local cuisine changes with the seasons – try steak, lamb or duck breast grilled over vine shoots, or the smoked ham, or pick a speciality such as rabbit in Sauternes or *foie gras* with apples. The puff pastry fruit tart comes straight from the oven to your plate and the ceps for the mushroom omelette will have been picked that morning. Menus €11–25. Superb selection of wines in the cellar – many of them very affordable.

|●| RESTAURANT LE SAPRIEN

11 rue Principale; it's opposite the tourist office.
☎ 05.56.76.60.87
Closed Sun evening; Mon; Wed evening; Feb and Christmas school holidays.

A little house with thick stone walls on the outskirts of the village. It's ever so slightly chic

and the elegant interior is a successful blend of old and new. It has a delightful reading room and also a huge terrace that opens out onto the vineyard. They grill food over vine shoots and offer Sauternes by the glass. Primarily they offer dishes that reflect the changing seasons and what the market has to offer: warm salad of *foie gras*, lamprey in Sauternes or roasted veal sweetbreads in a Sauternes and curry sauce. Various menus, at €21–40, list *foie gras terrine* with Sauternes jelly, lamprey in Sauternes, grilled duck breast and pan-fried *foie gras*.

SAUVETERRE-DE-BÉARN   64390

CASTAGNÈDE   64270 (10KM NW)

🏠 |●| LA BELLE AUBERGE

It's in the centre of the village.
☎ 05.59.38.15.28➡ 05.59.65.03.57
Closed Sun evenings and Dec to end Jan.
Swimming pool. Disabled access.TV.

A good old country inn in a pretty village. Prices for the twelve rooms are very reasonable at €30–38. There are lots of flowers and a swimming pool and you can sunbathe in the garden. It's popular with travelling businesspeople and pensioners. The restaurant is busy all week; they offer menus €10–20, listing dishes such as *pipérade basquaise*, pot-roast pigeon and chocolate *fondant*.

SOULAC-SUR-MER   33780

🏠 HÔTEL MICHELET**

1 rue Baguenard (Centre); it's on the sea port.
☎ 05.56.09.82.18 ➡ 05.56.73.65.25
Closed Sun evening, Nov and Jan. **Disabled access.**
TV. Garden.

A typical seaside villa. The staff are beyond compare – their thoughtful gestures include giving out little gifts to the kids. The rooms have been redecorated and are pleasant and comfortable (if a little noisy); eight have a balcony and three lead out into a sandy garden. Doubles with bath €37–44, or €50–71 in July and August (confirm the prices before you book). It's 50m from the sea and 250m from the town centre.

SOUSTONS   40140

ᐯᓐ |●| LA FERME DE BATHURT

route de l'Étang Blanc.

☎ 05.58.41.53.28
Closed Tues evening and Wed out of season; Nov–mid-Dec. **Swimming pool. Garden. TV.**

A gorgeous half-timbered 16th-century house surrounded by oak trees (a rarity in the Landes) and close to the magnificent Étang Blanc and the Lac d'Hardy – where you can ramble or fish in peace. Succulent, tasty local dishes such as parsleyed eels, foie gras terrine with Jurançon, grilled squid and lamprey stew. The asparagus or cep omlettes are big enough to satisfy any appetite. Menus €12–29; you can eat on the terrace. Free house apéritif.

TARDETS-SORHOLUS   64470

🏠 |●| HÔTEL-RESTAURANT DU PONT D'ABENSE*

Abense-de-Haut; it's 500m outside the town on the banks of the Saison.
☎ 05.59.28.54.60 ➡ 05.59.28.75.91
e uhaltia@wanadoo.fr
Closed Sun evening and Mon; Dec–Jan (except for New Year's Eve). **Car park.**

This riverside hotel is a lovely place to stay, with nice quiet rooms. Doubles with shower from €34–46 or €38–46 with bath. There's a friendly bar where you can drink the local light ale. The restaurant has a good reputation and the chef, who's also the owner, loves preparing simple dishes using the freshest ingredients. Dishes change often but are in the style of warm cep terrine, pig's trotter and potato pie, pan-fried hake and aiguillettes of duck with wine. Superb desserts. Menus €15 or menu-cartes around €24. You can eat on the terrace.They prefer you stay on a half-board basis in the summer; it'll cost €32–41.

TONNEINS   47400

🎋 🏠 |●| CÔTÉ GARONNE

36 cours de l'Yser.
☎ 05.53.84.34.34 ➡ 05.53.84.31.31
w www.cotegaronne.com
Closed Sun evening, Mon, 1–15 Jan, 1–15 Nov.
Disabled access. TV. Car park.

The street doesn't look particularly appealing – neither does the town, for that matter – so this beautiful building really stands out. It's like entering a different world when you step inside. In the restaurant, Jean-Luc Rabanel's combinations of local produce and spices are unexpected but his meticulous preparation and presentation are a triumph. Highlights include duck foie gras in a terrine, roast or confit, lob-

ster with baby vegetables, Tonneins ham in parsley jus and remarkable desserts like the millefeuille and a tart with soft almond filling. Weekday lunch menu €25; others €30–69. There are five luxurious rooms from €129 for a double. 10% discount on the room rate.

VIEUX-BOUCAU-LES-BAINS   40480

🎋 🏠 |●| HÔTEL-RESTAURANT DE LA CÔTE D'ARGENT**

4 Grand'Rue; it's in the old village.
☎ 05.58.48.13.17 ➡ 05.58.48.01.15
Restaurant closed Mon Oct–June; 1 Oct–15 Nov.
TV. Car park.

The owners have passed on the torch through four generations so the extensive experience of running the place is in evidence. Forty well-kept, comfortable rooms, a few of which have a balcony. Doubles €41–52 with shower/wc or bath. Very simple, traditional food in the restaurant, with no surprises. Go for the confit of duck, the salmis de palombes (wood-pigeon in red wine sauce), hake, blanquette of scallops, pan-fried prawns with garlic or sole with ceps. Set menus €15–23 and a children's menu is €8. Free house apéritif out of season.

VILLANDRAUT   33730

🎋 🏠 |●| HÔTEL-RESTAURANT DE GOTH**

pl. Principale; it's right in the centre of the village.
☎ and ➡ 05.56.25.31.25 ➡ 05.56.25.30.59
e evelyne.abadie@online.fr
Closed Sun evening; Mon out of season; Jan. **Pay car park.**

A pretty village inn with stone walls. The rooms are clean and well cared-for. Doubles €37 with shower/wc and €40 with bath. Decent traditional local dishes include chicken confit, assiette landaise, whole breast of duck with peaches, duck foie gras with apples and lamb medallions persillé. Set menus €10–24. In fine weather, sit on the terrace on the square. One free breakfast per person, per night.

VILLEFRANCHE-DU-PÉRIGORD   24550

🎋 🏠 |●| HÔTEL-RESTAURANT LA PETITE AUBERGE**

How to get there: it's 800m before you reach the village and well signposted.
☎ 05.53.29.91.01 ➡ 05.53.28.88.10
Closed Fri evening, Sat lunch and Sun evening out of

season, a fortnight in Nov and a fortnight Feb–March. **Garden**. **TV**. **Car park**.

A large house, typical of the region, deep in the countryside. It's got an enormous garden and very inviting sun-loungers. The rooms are tastefully decorated. Doubles with shower/wc €38 or €40 with bath. In the restaurant, there's a weekday menu for €11 and others up to €25, listing dishes based on regional and seasonal produce like Périgord ceps, *foie gras* and duck. A haven of peace and serenity, with a terrace for the summer. Free apéritif.

VILLENEUVE-SUR-LOT   47300

⅔ ☎ HÔTEL LA RÉSIDENCE**

17 av. Lazare-Carnot (Centre); it's near the old station.
☎ 05.53.40.17.03 ➡ 05.53.01.57.34
Closed 20 Dec–5 Jan. **TV**. **Garden**. **Car park**.

A pretty little hotel with a pink façade, green shutters and lots of character, in a very quiet neighbourhood near the old station. As soon as you set foot inside you can see the garden at the end of the corridor. Doubles €22 with washing facilities, €34 with shower/wc and €40 with bath. It's ideal if you like things simple and if you're looking for peace and quiet. 10% discount on the room rate for a two-night stay Sept–June.

|●| CHEZ CÂLINE

2 rue Notre-Dame (Centre).
☎ 05.53.70.42.08
Closed Tues.

A pleasant, cheery place overlooking the Lot river which will not fail to surprise you. They serve honest local dishes such as breast of duck stuffed with *foie gras*, fillet of salmon with sorrel, eggs *vignerons* (fried in walnut oil and served with a white wine, shallot and garlic sauce) and cherry soup with mint. Set menus €11–18 or about €20 *à la carte*. Câline is the cocker spaniel. Nice welcome. Best to book.

|●| RESTAURANT AUX BERGES DU LOT

3 rue de l'Hôtel-de-Ville; next door to the Hôtel de Ville.
☎ 05.53.70.84.81 ➡ 05.53.70.43.15
Closed Sun evening, Mon, and a fortnight in Nov.

This nice restaurant, with a shady terrace and a view of the Lot, has become something of an institution in a town that's rather short on good places to eat. The chef sticks to conventional dishes with a dollop of imagination: *foie gras* with dried fruit, roast zander with pistachio sausage, duck breast on the bone

with red fruit nectar and *foie gras* chips. Set weekday lunch menu €13; others €21–32.

PUJOLS   47300 (5KM S)

⅔ ☎ HÔTEL DES CHÊNES***

Lieu-dit Bel-Air.
☎ 05.53.49.04.55 ➡ 05.53.49.22.74
🌐 www.hoteldeschenes.com
Closed 30 Dec–5 Jan.
Swimming pool. **TV**. **Car park**. **Disabled access**.

Look out for the restaurant *La Toque Blance* – the hotel is next door. They stand on their own on the side of the valley so they're both very quiet. Lovely, well-equipped rooms looking onto the medieval village; they're all decorated differently. Doubles with shower/wc or bath, €47–64. Cool down in the pool. Free house apéritif.

LE TEMPLE-SUR-LOT   47110 (17KM W)

⅔ ☎ |●| LES RIVES DU PLANTIÉ***

It's on the D13 between Castelmoron and Le Temple-sur-Lot.
☎ 05.53.79.32.06 ➡ 05.53.79.32.05
Swimming pool. **Disabled access**. **TV**.

This place was a crumbling wreck before a brave young couple took it on and converted the house and some of the outbuildings into a hotel and restaurant. The grounds are planted with ancient trees and they slope down towards the river, leaving space for the swimming pool. The rooms – €49–60, depending on the size – are spacious and have good facilities but rather ordinary furniture. The view over the park is splendid. The cooking has a Mediterranean accent with lots of sea fish alongside the duck and local meat dishes. Weekday *formule* €13 or other menus €20–37. Free house apéritif.

MONCLAR   47380 (18KM E)

|●| LE RELAIS

rue du 11-Novembre; take the D911 to Sainte Livrade, follow the D667 for 5km, then turn onto the D113.
☎ 05.53.49.44.74
Closed Sun evening and Mon.

Locals crowd in here for lengthy lunches on Sunday and public holidays. Simple dishes and generous portions; the service is attentive. The rustic dining room has beautiful terraces overlooking the valley. The cooking has a strong regional bias, with a few fish dishes such as *piccata* of salmon and prawns. Menus €10–23.

AUVERGNE

03 Allier

15 Cantal

43 Haute-Loire

63 Puy-de-Dôme

AMBERT   63600

🏠 |●| HÔTEL-RESTAURANT LES COPAINS**

42 bd. Henri-IV; it's opposite the town hall.
☎ 04.73.82.01.02 ➡ 04.73.82.67.34
e hotel.rest.les.copains@wanadoo.fr
Closed Sat, Sun, and 15 Sept–15 Oct.

The dining room is fresh, flowery and air-conditioned and boasts an unusual pianola from 1935. The traditional cuisine, based largely on local produce, is simple, but Thierry Chelle, the fourth generation of his family to be in charge, picked up some tricks from the time he spent in the Robuchon kitchens. Thus the menu has a touch of class: *terrine* of trout with lentil salad and raspberry vinegar, fillet of sea bream roasted in its skin with a Maury sauce, duck *compote* with Chartreuse and tart sauce. Set menus €11–38. Completely refurbished bedrooms €44 with shower/wc or €46 with bath.

🎿 🏠 |●| HÔTEL-RESTAURANT LA CHAUMIÈRE**

41 av. Foch; from the town centre go towards Puy-en Velay.
☎ 04.73.82.14.94 ➡ 04.73.82.33.52
Closed Sun; Sat Oct–May; 26 Dec–21 Jan. **TV.**
Disabled access. Garden. Private car park.

A reminder that you can eat well at reasonable prices. Nothing fancy – just good plain cooking and substantial set menus (€15–33). The restaurant has been enlarged and there's a south-facing terrace overlooking the garden. The dining room is in classical style, with a fireplace where they do grills,

and the cooking similarly sticks to old faithfuls: *Potée Auvergnate* (a local soup), crayfish in saffron-scented broth, mutton tripe, *millefeuille* of sorbets. The bedrooms are clean, modern and fresh; doubles €47. Free apéritif.

ARCONSAT   63250

🎿 🏠 |●| L'AUBERGE DE MONTONCEL**

Les Cros d'Arconsat; take the N89 then the D86.
☎ 04.73.94.20.96 ➡ 04.73.94.28.33
e moncatel@aol.com
Closed Mon Oct–May; Jan. **TV. Disabled access. Car park**.

You'll find this building, housing an old-style restaurant and a simple hotel, nestling in the depths of the forest above Chabreloche. Very substantial €11 *menu du jour* – smoked ham, lamb stew, a fine platter of mature cheeses and fresh fruit. Other menus, €12–24, list dishes like crayfish grilled with butter, frogs' legs, steak skirt with local *bleu d'Auvergne* cheese and fillet of duck with brandy and ceps. The hotel is quiet and clean, occupying a modern annexe, with doubles from €31 with shower/wc or bath. Some rooms have balconies overlooking the pleasant garden. 10% discount on the room rate Sept–June.

ARDES-SUR-COUZE   63420

🏠 |●| L'AUBERGE DE LA BARAQUE D'AUBIAT**

How to get there: take the D23 from Ardes in the direction of Anzat and drive for 11km.
☎ 04.73.71.74.33 ➡ 04.73.71.74.99

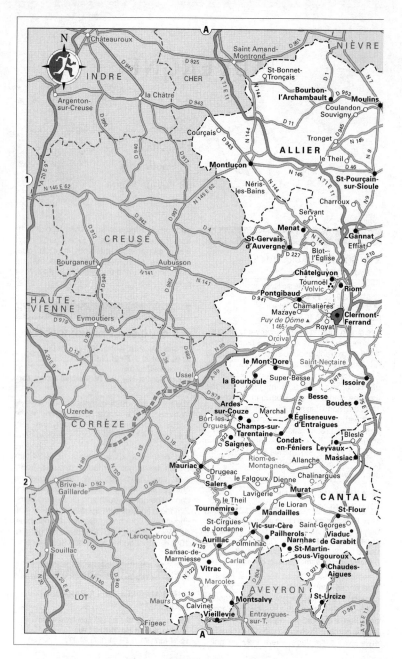

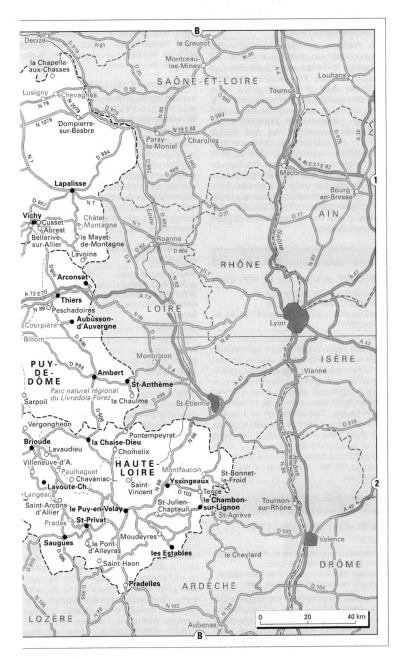

Closed Tues evening and Wed except school holidays; Jan. **Disabled access. Car park**.

This refurbished old farm – located on the Cézalier plateau south of Puy-de-Dôme – will be heaven for hikers and people who love peace and quiet. The owners, who have made the most of the restaurant's rustic style, offer generous portions of simple traditional dishes: good house *terrines*, stuffed cabbage, guineafowl with chanterelle mushrooms and home-made fruit tarts. Menus €12–17. The comfortable rooms are cosy and practical – some have a mezzanine, ideal if you're travelling with children. Doubles are €31 with shower, €32–41 with shower/wc or bath. Or you can sleep in a *gîte* for €8 a night. Good-sized breakfasts include a selection of home-made jams and cost €5. You'll receive a very friendly welcome and good advice on daytrips.

AUBUSSON-D'AUVERGNE   63120

☎ |●| HÔTEL-RESTAURANT AU BON COIN

Centre; the town is between Thiers and Ambert.
☎ 04.73.53.55.78 ➡ 04.73.53.56.29
Closed Sun evening and Mon out of season; 20 Dec–20 Jan. **Car park**.

A little inn decorated in pleasant country style – the only problem being that it can get a bit noisy when the big dining room is opened up. The proprietor-chef uses quality ingredients in his cooking and serves generous portions: good house *terrines*, poached trout with crayfish sauce, *entre-deux* of veal with cream sauce, fillets of zander on a bed of cabbage, pear in flaky pastry with egg custard. During the crayfish season they have lots of special dishes. Menus €12–37 or about €28 *à la carte*. There are a few rooms which go for €21 with basin or €37 with shower/wc.

AURILLAC   15000

⚥ ☎ |●| HÔTEL-RESTAURANT DU PALAIS**

4–6 rue Beauclair (Centre); behind the Palais de Justice.
☎ 04.71.48.24.86 ➡ 04.71.64.97.92
Restaurant closed Sun; public holidays; a fortnight in summer; 12 days in winter. **TV**. **Pay car park**.

This classic hotel has a striking façade and is quiet inside. Nice rooms, particularly the ones giving onto the Provençal-style patio; doubles €40–43 with shower/wc or bath. The restaurant offers a good taste of Auvergne: fillet of Salers beef with girolles or ceps, rack of pork *à l'Auvergnate*, stuffed pig's trotter salad, grilled fish. Menus €11–23. The owner is welcoming. 10% discount on the room rate.

⚥ ☎ GRAND HÔTEL DE BORDEAUX***

2 av. de la République; it's opposite the public gardens.
☎ 04.71.48.01.84 ➡ 04.71.48.49.93
e bestwestern@hotel-de-bordeaux.fr
TV. Car park.

A charming hotel with lots of character, built in 1812 and located in the centre of town. You'll be welcomed with great courtesy and in a very professional manner. Bedrooms are exceptionally comfortable and cost €58–70 with shower/wc or €60–89 with bath – some have air-conditioning. Stylish bar and lounges and a good breakfast. 10% discount on the room rate, except in Aug.

⚥ ☎ |●| HÔTEL-RESTAURANT LA THOMASSE***

28 rue du Docteur-Mallet.
☎ 04.71.48.26.47 ➡ 04.71.48.83.66
e accueil@hotel-la-thomasse.com
Closed Sun and 20 Dec–10 Jan. **TV. Swimming pool. Car park**.

In a residential area 1km from the centre, this charming hotel overlooks a large park. Pretty rooms in rustic style with proper bathrooms go for €61. Regional dishes and gastronomic cuisine are served in the restaurant, which attracts large parties on some evenings. Menus €22–38. More often than not, the owner will serve you a free glass of champagne as you sit down to eat. He's welcoming and talkative, and the club bar gets lively in the evenings. Free house apéritif.

⚥ |●| L'ARSÈNE

24 rue Arsène-Vermenouze (Centre).
☎ 04.71.48.48.97
Closed lunchtimes; Sun evening; Mon; the third week in March.

A warm and cosy dining room, with exposed stonework and modern paintings. It's very popular with locals attracted by the cheap, hearty food. The restaurant specializes in *fondue*, rump of beef, *tartiflette* and either pork fillet or breast of duck – which you cook yourself on a hot stone. Or opt for the wonderful onion soup, which is the genuine article. Set menus €11, except Saturday evenings and public holidays, and around €18 *à la carte*. Reasonably priced wine. Free coffee.

|●| LE BOUCHON FROMAGER

rue du Buis; pl. des Docks.
☎ 04.71.48.07.80
Closed Sun and public holidays.

A cheese and wine bar which is perfect if you're in a hurry or simply want a snack. You can grab a plate of cheese with a glass of wine bought direct from the vineyards – Auvergne wines cost from €2. Also try their toasted cheese (which comes in about 24 different varieties) or the platter of *charcuterie* and cheese. They also do a stew of the week and *potée auvergnate* to order. Menu €14. There's a nice terrace where you can enjoy an apéritif or take a meal.

|●| LE TERROIR DU CANTAL

rue du Buis; pl. des Docks; it's near the cheese market.
☎ 04.71.64.31.26
Closed Sun, Mon and public holidays.

A delightful restaurant specializing in Cantal dishes, located in the old part of town known as Saint-Géraud. The restaurant is decorated in conventional country style and has a good atmosphere and a large choice *à la carte* – *pavé du Cantal* (breaded Cantal cheese with local ham), salad of *cabecou* (goat's cheese) and honey, *pounti* (a mixture of bacon and Swiss chard), a slab of Salers beef with truffles, *bouriol* (a local pancake), stuffed cabbage and a cheese platter. Menus €15–22. Wine by the glass €1–6.

SANSAC DE MARMIESSE   15130 (8KM W)

⅍|●| LA BELLE ÉPOQUE

Lesfargues; take the Aurillac exit off the N122 and follow the signs for 4km to the golf course of La Cère.
☎ 04.71.62.87.87 ➡ 04.71.62.81.05
Closed Sun evening and Mon (except July–Aug); Jan.

This restaurant is a restored farmhouse deep in the country near the tiny villages of Haut-Cros and Labattude. The large dining room is decorated in *belle époque* style – a welcome change from the rustic look prevalent around here. Its reputation has grown by word of mouth, so it's almost always full – even on a weekday evening out of season. It has a lively atmosphere, very friendly staff and great local cooking. Prices are very reasonable: menus €15–35 or €37 *à la carte*. They use fresh produce and pick soft fruit and vegetables from the garden. *À la carte* you're faced with plenty of classic dishes: semi-cooked or pan-fried *foie gras*, mutton tripe, woodland mushrooms, zander and a red wine *jus*, duck breast with orange. The

chef is a wild mushroom enthusiast and uses many different varieties in his cooking. The terrace is very pleasant in fine weather. Free house *digestif*.

POLMINHAC   15800 (14KM E)

⅍|●| LE BERGANTY

pl. de l'Église; take the N122.
☎ 04.71.47.47.47
Closed Sat and Sun; reservations only on Sat in summer; Christmas and New Year holidays.

The square is superb, with its church and its crowd of stone-roofed houses. And the dining room is absolutely wonderful, too. Seating only twenty, it has an old polished sideboard, a massive table positioned in front of the fireplace and large bouquets of flowers from the garden. The chef prefers to prepare dishes to order and uses only fresh seasonal produce enhanced with herbs from his vegetable plot: trout with bacon, *truffade* (a potato cake with Cantal cheese) and ham are served at any time, but you have to order in advance for the stuffed cabbage, the *pounti* (a mixture of bacon and Swiss chard), and the *potée auvergnate*, the hearty local soup. Other specialities include rabbit with prunes and carrots and shoulder of local beef. Expect to pay around €13 for the menu of the day – dishes change as the seasons turn. The young owner has a flair for making people feel welcome. Free coffee.

BESSE-EN-CHANDESSE   63610

⅍ 🏠 |●| HÔTEL-RESTAURANT LE CLOS**

La Villetour.
☎ 04.73.79.52.77 ➡ 04.73.79.56.67
Restaurant closed Mon–Thurs lunchtimes except school holidays. **TV**. **Swimming pool**. **Car park**.

This modern establishment just out of the town centre offers a wide range of facilities – indoor pool, well-equipped gym, Turkish bath and games room. Bedrooms are pleasant and very clean; doubles cost €37–50 with shower/wc or bath and there are a few family rooms too. The owners can provide suggestions for excursions and walks. The food is decent and traditional. Set menus go from €14, and a meal *à la carte* will cost around €17. Free apéritif.

🏠 |●| HOSTELLERIE DU BEFFROY**

26 rue de l'Abbé-Blot.
☎ 04.73.79.50.08 ➡ 04.73.79.57.67

Closed Mon and Tues except Feb; July–Aug; a fortnight in April; a fortnight at the beginning of Dec. **TV**. **Car park**.

A fifteenth-century building owned and run by Thierry Legros, who has a fine reputation as a chef: try his *fricassée* of wild salmon, the pan-fried Salers beef with woodland mushroom *jus*, the Cantal turnover or the *pounti* (a mixture of bacon and Swiss chard). Weekday menu €20 and others €26–45. Rooms are decent but facilities are not all good. Doubles €46 with shower/wc and €53 with bath.

SUPER-BESSE   63610 (7KM W)

|●| RESTAURANT LA BERGERIE

Route de Vassivières (West); take the D149.
☎ 04.73.79.61.06
Closed weekdays out of season; 15 Sept–15 Dec.

It would be a crime to come here without trying the *truffade* (potato cake with Cantal cheese). The young owner serves a hearty portion straight from the frying pan with local ham; it's cooked to order and probably the best you'll get in the region. Extremely satisfying, well worth the thirty-minute wait and yours for €11. Lots of other local delicacies at €15–25: ham *truffade*, trout pâté with ceps and pig's trotters in red wine. You'll really feel at home in this country inn with its delightful décor and atmosphere. It's popular in winter and summer alike – when you can eat on the terrace overlooking the lake.

BOUDES   63340

⅄ ≙ |●| LE BOUDES LA VIGNE**

pl. de la Mairie.
☎ 04.73.96.55.66 ➡ 04.73.96.55.55
Closed Sun evening; Mon; 2–20 Jan; from the last week in Aug to the beginning of the school term. **TV**.

This popular little hotel-restaurant, in a pleasantly renovated building, is in the centre of a small wine-growing village south of Puy-de-Dôme. The cooking is quite delightful: salmon and goat's cheese pancake served on salad leaves, ravioli with garlic sauce, *blanquette* of chicken with honey, iced nougat with walnuts and Boudes honey. For dessert, it's hard to resist the peach soup with fresh mint. Weekday lunch menu €11 or €18–40. You're right in the midst of the best vineyards of the Auvergne so the wine list is splendid and wine is also served by the glass. The hotel was built only recently and is very quiet. Doubles €34 with shower/wc. Free apéritif and 10% discount Sept–May.

BOURBON-L'ARCHAMBAULT   03160

⅄ ≙ |●| GRAND HÔTEL MONTESPAN-TALLEYRAND***

1–3 pl. des Thermes (Centre).
☎ 04.70.67.00.24 ➡ 04.70.67.12.00
e hotelmontespan@wanadoo.fr
Closed late Oct to early April. **TV**. **Disabled access**. **Car park**.

A superb hotel in a fine building full of old-fashioned charm. It's an oasis of peace and quiet – there are reading rooms and card rooms hung with velvet and tapestries, a bright flower-filled dining room and a pool among the greenery of the garden. Bedrooms are tastefully and stylishly decorated. Doubles with shower/wc are €46–50 and €63–70 with bath, which is very reasonable given the standard of accommodation. The restaurant sticks to old favourites – fillet steak *Ducs des Bourbons*, lamb chop from the Allier region, rabbit with mustard and white wine, *coq au vin* (the wine in this case being Saint-Pourçain). The cooking is worth the trip. Menus €14–27. Friendly staff and excellent service. Free apéritif.

SAINT-BONNET-TRONÇAIS   03360 (23KM NW)

⅄ ≙ |●| LE TRONÇAIS**

rond de Tronçais; take the N144, then the D978 in the direction of the forest of Tronçais as far as the Rond de Tronçais. It's 3km south of Saint-Bonnet-Tronçais.
☎ 04.70.06.11.95 ➡ 04.70.06.16.15
Closed Sun evening; Mon out of season; mid-Nov to mid-March. **TV**. **Car park**.

A peaceful, very comfortable lakeside hotel with lots of charm. The forest of Tronçais, one of the oldest and most beautiful in France, becomes every shade of green in spring and every shade of yellow, red and brown in autumn. Spacious bedrooms €47–67 with shower/wc or bath/wc. The restaurant is strong on traditional local dishes: snails with walnuts, eel terrine with blackberries, zander *au gratin*, pike in Saint Pourçain wine. Menus €18–31. The two dining rooms are very elegantly and tastefully decorated, and the staff are delightful. Pleasant view of the grounds and surrounding countryside. Free coffee.

TRONGET   03240 (23KM S)

≙ |●| HÔTEL DU COMMERCE**

D945; take the D1 towards Montet.
☎ 04.70.47.12.95 ➡ 04.70.47.32.53

TV. **Car park**.

A hotel that contrasts the new and the traditional. The building is practically brand-new and has comfortable, modern and well-equipped bedrooms (€40), though they're a bit lacking in character. Contrast that with the cooking of the chef, Monsieur Auberger, which is packed with personality: house *foie gras*, scallops with Noilly, Charolais steak with Saint Pourçain wine sauce, local lamb, *andouillette* with Charroux mustard. Menus €11–26.

BOURBOULE (LA)   63150

🎿 🏠 |●| HÔTEL-RESTAURANT LE PAVILLON**

av. d'Angleterre.
☎ 04.73.65.50.18 ➡ 04.73.81.00.93
e francois.montrieul@wanadoo.fr
Closed Nov–March. **TV**.

Pretty Art Deco façade. The young owners greet you kindly and there's a warm family atmosphere. The rooms are modern and clean, if a little functional. Doubles €23–31 with basin, €35–40 with shower/wc and €38–48 with bath. Simple family cooking using regional ingredients; menus €9–18. Free house apéritif or coffee.

🎿 🏠 |●| HÔTEL LE CHARLET**

94 bd. Louis-Chousy.
☎ 04.73.81.33.00 ➡ 04.73.65.50.82
e hotel.lecharlet@wanadoo.fr
Closed mid-Oct to mid-Dec. **TV**. **Car park**.

An attractive family-run place in a quiet residential area – indeed, the whole town is quiet and residential. The décor in the 38 pleasant bedrooms has been brightened up with pictures of Auvergne country scenes and they come equipped with modern facilities. Doubles overlooking the street with shower/wc go for €35–49, or with bath and a mountain view they're €49–55. There's a very nice pool with a wave machine, a Turkish bath and a gym. The cooking is traditional and local, with dishes like poté Auvergnate (a local soup), *coq au vin*, stuffed trout, rabbit *foie gras* and truffles. Menus €15–27. Free house *digestif* and 10% discount on the room rate 25 Aug–1 July.

BRIOUDE   43100

🎿 🏠 |●| HÔTEL DE LA POSTE ET CHAMPANNE**

1 bd. du Docteur-Devins (West).
☎ 04.71.50.14.62 ➡ 04.71.50.10.55

Closed Sun evening Oct–June; Feb. **TV. Car park.**

An old country hotel which has been updated to suit modern tastes. The bedrooms facing the street are rather noisy, while those in the annexe at the back are very quiet. Doubles €24 with shower and shared wc, €41 with shower/wc and €46 with bath and balcony. There's a bar on the ground floor; the restaurant on the floor above has long had a reputation for good food and does a number of set menus at €13–34 and also *à la carte*. Traditional, unpretentious food: pressed cod with Roseval potatoes and caper *vinaigrette*, blue cheese mouse with walnuts, lamb's trotters with Fourme d'Ambert cheese and lentils and fillet of zander with ham. The star attraction is the owner – a jolly, chubby man with a ruddy face and twinkling eyes. With the assistance of a team of waitresses, he serves the food himself in the way that innkeepers used to – if you want bigger helpings, just ask. Free coffee.

🎿 🏠 |●| HÔTEL LE BAUDIÈRE – RESTAURANT LE VIEUX FOUR**

Saint-Bauzire; it's 8km west of Brioude before Saint-Bauzire, at the D588 and D17 junction.
☎ 04.71.76.81.70 ➡ 04.71.76.80.66
Closed Mon and 26 Dec–26 Jan. **Swimming pool**. **TV**. **Disabled access**. **Car park**.

A pleasant modern hotel with sauna, indoor and outdoor swimming pools and very comfy bedrooms. Doubles with bath and satellite TV €46. Right next door is the restaurant, which has a handsome stone oven in the main dining room. The grilled meat is as good as the *escalope* of veal muzzle with mushrooms, the zander with baby vegetables, the *crépinette* of pig's trotters and the *crème brûlée*. Set menus €14–38. It's quite well-known, and some of the wealthier customers arrive by helicopter on the landing strip nearby. Free apéritif.

🎿 🏠 |●| LA SAPINIÈRE***

av. Paul-Chambriard (South); take the N102 through Brioude.
☎ 04.71.50.87.30 ➡ 04.71.50.10.55
e hotel.la.sapiniere@wanadoo.fr
Hotel closed Feb. **Restaurant closed** Sun evening, Mon and lunchtimes. **TV**. **Disabled access**. **Car park**.

An appealing modern building built from wood, brick and glass, located between two old farm buildings. The spacious rooms look out over the grounds and are decorated in different styles. They're named rather than numbered – "Vulcania" has a bedhead carved from lava. Doubles with shower/wc

€69, with bath €99. Friendly welcome. The restaurant serves dishes with interesting flavour combinations, such as bitter dandelion with ham and honey-roast radish, Salers beef with ground ceps, salmon with simmered green Puy vegetables, cabbage stuffed with *foie gras* and poultry *mousseline*. Menus €18–34. Free coffee.

VERGONGHEON   43360 (8KM N)

🎿 |●| LA PETITE ÉCOLE

Rilhac.
☎ 04.71.76.00.44
e petite.ecole@wanadoo.fr
Closed Sun evening; Mon; Tues evening Oct–Easter; the last week in June. **Car park**.

The décor takes you straight back to school – blackboards, maps of France, school photos and desks. Françoise and Éric run the place and produce delicious dishes (no school dinners here): scallops *Alienor d'Aquitaine*, eggs *à la Jules Ferry*, orange meringue tart. You choose from an excercise book full of menus €15–22 with a children's menu at €11. Good salads, roast pork with apricot sauce and a fabulous dessert trolley. Best to book. Free house apéritif.

LAVAUDIEU   43100 (9KM SE)

|●| AUBERGE DE L'ABBAYE

Centre.
☎ 04.71.76.44.44
Closed Sun evening and Mon, Mon only in summer. **Car park**.

A charming village inn on the little street opposite the church. It has a rustic interior – complete with log fires in winter – which has been very nicely renovated and decorated. The carefully prepared traditional dishes, based on local produce, include jellied trout and lentil terrine, lamb *Bizet* with potatoes and Cantal cheese and ice-cream with green verbena. Set menus €12 in summer; at other times of year they're €16–19.

VILLENEUVE-D'ALLIER   43380 (14KM S)

🎿 🏠 |●| HOSTELLERIE SAINT-VERNY*

route D585; from Brioude go towards the gorges of Allier and Lavoute-Chilhac.
☎ 04.71.74.73.77 ➡ 04.71.74.74.20
Closed All Saints' Day to Easter. **Swimming pool. TV. Car park**.

Located a few kilometres from the wonderful village of Lavoute-Chilhac, here's a genuine, simple country inn that's very well run. It's on the south bank of the Allier, across from the romantic ruined château of Saint-Ilpize. Bedrooms look onto the street or have a superb view of the valley. They're small and nicely laid-out, and there are bunk beds for children. Doubles with shower/wc or bath €38–43. The food in the restaurant is perfectly done, with dishes based largely on local produce. Set menus €14–23 or around €15 *à la carte*. The house speciality is the *plateau du vigneron* – grilled Cantal cheese, local ham and a salad with walnut oil. There's a bar on the ground floor and a quiet terrace at the back, facing a garden where you can enjoy your meals in summer. Free coffee or *digestif*.

BLESLE   43450 (24KM W)

🎿 🏠 |●| HÔTEL-RESTAURANT LA BOUGNATE

pl. de Vallat; take the D588.
☎ 04.71.76.29.30 ➡ 04.71.76.29.39
Closed Tues and Wed except April–Sept; Jan. **Car park**.

Gérard Klein has been a successful actor, producer and cattle farmer, and now he's an innkeeper. He and his wife Françoise started this establishment a couple of years ago. They began by renovating the building and created a few quiet, pretty doubles which go for €56–61 with shower/wc or bath. The speciality in the restaurant is their own Salers beef, served with stuffed cabbage. Menu for €23. Free apéritif.

CHAVANIAC-LAFAYETTE   43230 (27KM SE)

🎿 🏠 |●| HÔTEL-RESTAURANT LAFAYETTE*

Centre; take the N102 after Saint-Georges-d'Aurac, turn left onto the D513 then continue ahead for 2km.
☎ 04.71.77.50.38 ➡ 04.71.77.54.90
Closed Tues Nov–March; 20 Dec–1 April. **Garage**.

As you might gather from the name, this nice family hotel is in the village where General Lafayette, one of the heroes of the American War of Independence, was born. In the ground-floor bar a sprightly old woman pours drinks for the regulars, and the adjoining restaurant is simple and inviting. The chef's specialities are veal kidneys in red wine sauce and veal sautéed with Puy lentils. Prices are very reasonable – menus €9–20 with a children's menu at €7. The bedrooms are unpretentious and very well-maintained; numbers 10 and 11 overlook the Lafayette château. Doubles are €35 with shower/wc or bath. Very friendly staff. Free house apéritif and 10% discount on the room rate Sept–June.

CHAISE-DIEU (LA)　43160

♣ ☎ |●| HÔTEL DE LA CASADEÏ**

pl. de l'Abbaye (Centre); it's near the steps to the abbey.
☎ 04.71.00.00.58 ➡ 04.71.00.017
Restaurant closed Sun evening and Mon. **TV**. **Car park**.

You get to the hotel through a flower-filled terrace and an art gallery. The best rooms have a view of the abbey and are nicely furnished; doubles €35–48 with shower/wc. Friendly staff. In the restaurant they serve *potée auvergnate* (a thick local soup), omelette of chanterelle mushrooms, mutton tripe and *truffade* (potato cake with Cantal cheese). Set menus €13–21. The photos you'll see everywhere are of artists who've stayed at the hotel during the town's sacred music festival. There's a little terrace at the back. Free apéritif and 10% discount on the room rate May–June and Sept–Oct.

♣ ☎ |●| HÔTEL-RESTAURANT DE L'ÉCHO ET DE L'ABBAYE**

pl. de l'Écho (Centre).
☎ 04.71.00.00.45 ➡ 04.71.00.00.22
Closed Wed lunchtime out of season, and 15 Nov–10 Feb. **TV**. **Car park**.

This delightful inn is fully booked during the festival – all the big names have stayed here. The handsome dining room with its antiques and Louis XIII décor is housed in the former monastery kitchens. You'll find tasty, regional dishes using plenty of wild mushrooms, truffles and *foie gras*: a *timbale* of wild mushrooms with cep coulis, rabbit thigh stuffed with hazelnuts on a bed of lentils and a trolley of fresh desserts. Menus €17–49. Eleven bedrooms are available; doubles go for €41–52 with shower/wc and €52–61 with bath. Number 7 has a wonderful view of the abbey. 10% discount on the room rate.

CHOMELIX　43500 (15KM SE)

♣ ☎ |●| AUBERGE DE L'ARZON**

How to get there: take the D906 then the D135.
☎ 04.71.03.62.35 ➡ 04.71.03.61.62
Closed Mon evening and Tues except July–Aug; All Saints' Day to Easter. **TV**. **Car park**.

This is a good village inn and the restaurant is extremely popular. It's best to book in

summer, especially during the music festival in nearby La Chaise. The bedrooms are impeccable and situated in a quiet modern annexe with shower/wc upstairs and bathroom downstairs; doubles €38 with shower/wc and €53 with bath. The restaurant uses local produce in carefully prepared regional dishes: *foie gras*, duck breast with blackcurrants. It also has excellent fish and a good selection of home-made desserts. Set menus €15 (not Sun) and up to €40. Decent service. 10% discount on the room rate Sept–June.

PONTEMPEYRAT　43500 (25KM E)

♣ ☎ |●| HÔTEL-RESTAURANT MISTOU***

How to get there: take the D498.
☎ 04.77.50.62.46 ➡ 04.77.50.66.70
℮ moulin.de.mistou@wanadoo.fr
Restaurant closed lunchtimes except weekends, public holidays and 1 Nov to Easter. **TV**. **Car park**. **Disabled access**.

The setting, deep in the Ance valley, is as pastoral as you could wish for: the river runs past fir trees at the bottom of the garden. There used to be an eighteenth-century water mill here; its old turbine still runs, producing enough electricity to light the hotel. The rooms are enormous, quiet and perfectly decorated; those with a view of the garden are the nicest. Doubles €82–105 with shower/wc or bath. In the stylish restaurant Bernard Royx, one of the gurus of regional cuisine in these parts, mans the stove, churning out platters of *foie gras* prepared in four different ways, roast lamb with sea salt, marinated guineafowl with spices and roast strawberries with szechuan pepper. Menus €27–50. Half board is compulsory in high season. Free coffee and 10% discount on the room rate Sept–June (excluding public holidays).

CHAMBON-SUR-LIGNON (LE)　43400

♣ ☎ HÔTEL-BEAU RIVAGE*

rue de la Grande-Fontaine (Centre).
☎ 04.71.59.70.56
Closed Oct to end April. **Car park**.

If you're after peace and quiet, this is the place. The staff greet you with big smiles and everything is done thoughtfully; doubles with shower/wc €38. Two terraces give you a view of the river. Although a bit kitschy, it's a very nice place with genuine people. 10% discount on the room rate.

♯ ♠ |●| HÔTEL LE BOIS VIALOTTE**

Le Bois Vialotte; from Chambon take the D151 going towards Le Mazet, then turn left onto the route de la Suchère and left again onto a smaller road (there is a signpost).
☎ 04.71.59.74.03 ➡ 04.71.65.86.32
Closed 1 Oct–30 May. **Car park**.

This lovely place, surrounded by woods and meadows, boasts fifteen acres of beautiful grounds – but it feels more like a family guesthouse than a country-house hotel. The attentive but unobtrusive proprietress takes great pride in her new house. The décor of the simple bedrooms is rather old-fashioned but they're comfortable and very clean. You'll pay €42–50 for a double with shower/wc and €47–53 with bath; ask for one with a view over the fields and the trees. The restaurant offers home cooking and simple traditional dishes. Menus €12–21. It's worth going on a half-board basis since the hotel is rather isolated, but it's not compulsory. Free apéritif and 10% discount on the room rate

TENCE 43190 (8.5KM N)

♯ ♠ |●| CAFÉ-RESTAURANT BROLLES

Mas-de-Tence.
☎ 04.71.65.42.91

An authentic country inn run by friendly people. The restaurant has been tastefully decorated and the stone floor makes the place feel nice and cool. Sit at the table beside the fireplace and enjoy home-made *saucisson* or omelette made from eggs laid by the owner's hens. Also recommended are the sautéed baby potatoes and the snails, and people come from miles around to taste the warm ewe's-milk cheese. Set menu €11. Simple but clean rooms with basin at €18; breakfast costs €4. Best to book. Free apéritif.

SAINT-BONNET-LE-FROID 43290 (20KM NE)

♠ |●| AUBERGE ET CLOS DES CIMES***

rue Principale.
☎ 04.71.59.93.72 ➡ 04.71.59.93.40
Closed Mon evening, Tues, Wed lunchtime (Tues only July–Aug); mid-Nov to Easter. **Disabled access**.

One of the culinary high points of the area, run by Régis Marcon, who is constantly scaling new heights with his inventive, inspirational cuisine. His preparation is meticulous, everything he buys is of the freshest quality and he's well-acquainted with the traditional dishes of the Velay and the Vivarais. Subtle,

delicate dishes full of unexpected flavours – the house speciality is plateau-raised lamb cooked *en croûte*. Menus, €51–100, reflect the quality of his work. There are rooms of the same calibre for €130–206 with bath.

CHAMPS-SUR-TARENTAINE 15270

♯ ♠ |●| L'AUBERGE DU VIEUX CHÊNE**

34 route des Lacs.
☎ 04.71.78.71.64 ➡ 04.71.78.70.88
✉ danielle.moins@wanadoo.fr
Closed Lunchtimes except Sun; Sun evening and Mon out of season; 15 Nov–15 March. **TV**. **Garden**. **Car park**.

A renovated old farm in northern Cantal. Bedrooms have been nicely done up in bright, cheerful colours and all have bathrooms; doubles €50–78. There's an enormous fireplace on the back wall of the restaurant, and though the dining room is on the large side it's laid out in such a way that it actually feels rather intimate. The menus, €21–29, feature regional specialities alongside classic dishes – try the *foie gras* with green peppercorns, snails in pastry, trout with diced bacon or *entrecôte* steak with Roquefort cheese. Attentive and courteous service and pleasant garden. 10% discount out of season.

MARCHAL 15270 (5KM NE)

♠ |●| HÔTEL-RESTAURANT L'AUBERGE DE L'EAU VERTE

Centre; take the D679 then the D22.
☎ 04.71.78.71.48
Closed a fortnight in Feb and a fortnight at the end of Sept. **Car park**.

A traditional little inn on a small hill beside the church. Super-friendly welcome in the restaurant, where you'll find special "taste of Auvergne" menus. These have to be ordered in advance and offer a delicious plate of cold meat, *truffade* (potato cake with Cantal cheese), salad, cheese and dessert. Prices €10–27. There are a few bedrooms with basin for €31. Half board €27 per person. A good place to appreciate traditional Auvergne cuisine.

CHÂTELGUYON 63140

♠ |●| HÔTEL-RESTAURANT CASTEL RÉGINA**

rue de Brocqueville.

☎ 04.73.86.00.15 ➡ 04.73.86.19.44
Closed Oct–April. **TV**. **Car park**.

A stylish spa hotel. The *belle époque* décor gives it a delightful old-fashioned atmosphere, and it has a relaxed atmosphere. You'll receive a charming welcome. The guests seem to have come out of the same mould as the hotel – after all, no one comes to Châtelguyon for the nightlife. Clean, well-kept bedrooms €27 with shower/wc or €29 with bath. The €10 *menu du jour* features more substantial fare than you might expect while the one at €16 includes wine.

🍴 🏠 |●| LES CHÊNES**

15 rue Guy-de-Maupassant; take the D985.
☎ 04.73.86.02.88 ➡ 04.73.86.46.60
e leschênes@wanadoo.fr
Closed 2 Jan–10 Feb. **TV**.

A good establishment a bit out of the way in the old village of Châtelguyon. The restaurant is particularly lovely in fine weather, when you can eat on the terrace. Expect refined classic cooking: veal sweetbreads in pastry with ceps, salmon with sorrel sauce, quail salad with *foie gras*. *Menu du jour* €10 and others at €21 and €26. The rooms are quiet and pleasant and some have balconies. Doubles €27 with basin/wc, €34 with shower/wc. The owner is charming and full of life. 10% discount on the room rate for a two-night stay.

🍴 🏠 |●| LE CANTALOU**

17 rue du Lac-Saint-Hippolyte; it's on the D985 on the outskirts of Châtelguyon in the Saint-Hippolyte district.
☎ 04.73.86.04.67 ➡ 04.73.86.24.36
Closed Mon lunchtime, except for guests, and 11 Nov–15 March. **Car park**.

A family guesthouse on the edge of town offering good value for money. Bedrooms are clean and well-maintained but the décor is a bit old-fashioned. Some have a view of the Monts d'Auvergne and Le Puy de Dôme. Doubles €31 with shower/wc, €34 with bath. The restaurant serves generous helpings of local staples: house *terrines*, country omelette and veal escalope with Auvergne blue cheese sauce. Set menus €12–20. 10% discount on the room rate for a two-night stay in March, April, Oct and Nov.

🍴 🏠 |●| HÔTEL BELLEVUE – RESTAURANT LE CÈDRE BLEU**

4 rue Punett; it's opposite the spa park
☎ 04.73.86.07.62 ➡ 04.73.86.02.56
Closed Tues, Wed and Oct–May.

This hotel has been completely renovated

and offers quiet rooms with excellent facilities. Smiling, warm welcome. Doubles with shower/wc €46 or €56 with bath. They serve local dishes in the restaurant: Cantal truffles, salmon with lentils, pigs' trotters *croustillant* with lentils, pan-fried duck breast with honey and szechuan pepper. Menu of the day €15, regional menu €20 and gastronomic menu €24. Free apéritif. 10% discount on the room rate March–April and Oct–Nov.

|●| RESTAURANT LA POTÉE

34 av. Baraduc.
☎ 04.73.86.06.60
Closed Oct to end March.

The façade of this restaurant is beautifully timbered. The *patronne* is larger than life and carefully scans the dining room from her vantage point behind the bar to ensure her guests are being looked after. You sit at nice tables with proper cloths to sample classic dishes: *andouillette* (a type of sausage), mutton tripe, *truffade* (a potato cake with Cantal cheese), pork knuckle and trout with bacon. Menu of the day €10 or around €18 *à la carte*.

CHAUDES-AIGUES   15110

🏠 |●| HÔTEL LES BOUILLONS D'OR**

10 quai du Remontalou (Centre).
☎ 04.71.23.51.42
Closed Sun evening and Mon out of season; Jan–March. **TV**. **Car park**.

This is a conventional and well-kept hotel, set back from the main street. You'll get a courteous welcome. Comfortable rooms (€29–38) and classic cooking, both in keeping with the style of the hotel. Menus, €10–21, list dishes like *briochin* with Cantal cheese, *aligot saucisse* (mashed potatoes and Aligot cheese with sausage), local mutton tripe, *paupiettes* of chicken with cabbage and *quenelles* of pike with prawn sauce.

VENTUEJOLS   15110 (5KM N)

🍴 🏠 |●| AU RENDEZ-VOUS DES PÊCHEURS

Pont-de-Lanau; take the D921.
☎ 04.71.23.51.68
Closed Sat.

An unobtrusive little inn at the side of the road which has been modernized and freshened up. The owner's son is carrying on the long tradition of friendly and unpretentious service. He's a big music fan and has lined the walls with pictures and caricatures of musicians and famous local characters. There's a single menu at €11 (€14 for Sun lunch), with good, reliable home cooking: rabbit stew, *potée*, tripe, home-made ice creams and sorbets. A few basic but clean rooms with handbasin go for €26 and there's a half-board option at €31. Free coffee.

CLERMONT-FERRAND   63000

SEE MAP OVERLEAF

☎ HÔTEL RAVEL**

8 rue de Maringues. **MAP D2-7**
☎ 04.73.91.51.33 ➡ 04.73.92.28.48
Closed Christmas to New Year. **TV**. **Car park**.

This little family-run hotel is in a quiet neighbourhood tucked away between the station and the town centre. It has a captivating mosaic façade and the proprietress will give you a warm welcome. She runs the place virtually single-handed and creates a nice relaxed atmosphere – if you want more bread at breakfast, she'll nip across to the baker's. The décor in the bedrooms is simple and charming and they're good value at €31 with shower or €38 with bath/wc.

☎ HÔTEL FOCH*

32 rue du Maréchal-Foch. **MAP A3-8**
☎ 04.73.93.48.40 ➡ 04.73.35.47.41
✉ jm.fragne@wanadoo.fr
TV. **Car park**.

The entrance is easy to miss in spite of the sugar-coloured frontage. Reception is on the first floor but the rooms here are best avoided; opt for preference for the ones on the upper floors, even though they're quite small. Rooms with basin €29, or €37 with shower/wc.

🏃 ☎ HÔTEL DE BORDEAUX**

39 av. Franklin-Roosevelt. **MAP A3-3**
☎ 04.73.37.32.32 ➡ 04.73.31.40.56
TV. **Pay garage**.

This hotel is just outside the centre in an unprepossessing area, but it's quiet and convenient for the main tourist attractions. Doubles €31 with basin/wc, €43–47 with shower/wc. Staff are pleasant and unobtrusive. Free use of garage.

🏃 ☎ HÔTEL ALBERT-ÉLISABETH**

37 av. Albert-Élisabeth. **MAP D2-4**
☎ 04.73.92.47.41 ➡ 04.73.90.78.32

✉ hotel-albertelisabeth@massifcantal.com
TV. **Garden**. **Car park**.

This place is marked by a big red neon sign – you won't miss it. Well-soundproofed rooms, some overlooking the courtyard, though on the whole they lack character. Doubles €42 with shower/wc and €45 with bath and TV. 10% discount for a two-night stay at weekends Sept–June.

🏃 ☎ ▐●▌ HÔTEL DE LYON***

16 pl. de Jaude. **MAP B3-6**
☎ 04.73.93.32.55 ➡ 04.73.93.54.33
✉ hotel.de.lyon@wanadoo.fr
TV. **Garage**.

You can't get more central than place de Jaude – it's in the very heart of town. Comfortable if conventional rooms with good facilities, double glazing and telephones; doubles with shower/wc €54 or €60 with bath. Self-service breakfast is served in the pub downstairs or brought to your room. Simple menus €10–20 and a *carte brasserie*. Parking fee included in the price of the rooms. 10% discount on the room rate and free coffee.

▐●▌ L'OLIVEN

5 rue de la Boucherie. **MAP B2-17**
☎ 04.73.90.38.94
Closed Sat lunchtime, Sun and Mon. **TV**. **Garage**.

This place has pretty décor in orange hues and is run by a bright, friendly team. Weekday lunch menu €10 and *menus-cartes* at €16 and €22. Specialities include salad with sheep's milk cheese; prawns with lime, coriander and tomato croutons; warm smoked salmon with marinated red peppers and *aïoli*; sea bass with herbs and aubergine stew; coconut cake with ricotta and almond liqueur cream. This place offers a fresh look at Provençal and Mediterranean cooking and dishes are light and tasty.

🏃 ▐●▌ RESTAURANT LE BOUGNAT

29 rue des Chaussetiers. **MAP B2-21**
☎ 04.73.36.36.98
Closed Sat lunchtime; Sun and Mon; 9 July–18 Aug.

You might think this is a tourist trap, but it's not. The restaurant has a regional-rustic feel and offers a wonderful selection of well-prepared regional dishes – mutton tripe, *pounti* (a mixture of bacon and Swiss chard), pig's trotters with white kidney beans and *potée auvergnate*, the thick local soup. There's a splendid wood-burning stove in the foyer, which the chef uses to prepare Auvergne pancakes. The €12 set menu is very decent and there are good wines from the Auvergne. If you're on your own, try to get one of the stools at the counter where the regulars sit. Free coffee.

⅔ |●| LES JARDINS D'HISPAHAN

11 ter rue des Chaussetiers. **MAP B2-27**
☎ 04.73.90.23.07
Closed Sun, Mon and public holidays.

Persian cooking with subtle, flowery, aromatic flavours rather than heavily spiced dishes. The décor's not particularly exciting but it's not intrusive either. The kebab *bargue*, made with grilled veal marinated in lemon, is delicate and delightful. Menus €12–19. If you think you don't like rice, the way they cook basmati here will change your mind forever. Free apéritif.

⅔ |●| RESTAURANT LE CAFÉ DE LA PASSERELLE

22 rue Anatole-France. **MAP D3-23**
☎ 04.73.91.62.12
Closed Sun and 15 July–15 Aug.

With left-wing politicians and ex-ministers among its regulars, this is one of Clermont's liveliest places, thanks mostly to its extrovert owner. Alain Aumaly hails from the south but his cooking is typical of the Auvergne region, with generous portions of pig's trotters, *potée* (a thick soup), stuffed cabbage and satisfyingly thick, juicy steaks. There's a weekday lunch menu €14, with a starter, main course, cheese and dessert. A good restaurant, but it's small so it's best to book. Free apéritif.

⅔ |●| LE CHARDONNAY

1 pl. Philippe-Marcombes. **MAP C2-26**
☎ 04.73.90.18.28

Service 3pm–1.30am. It's the wine that really matters here, as you can see from the shelves of bottles displayed behind the bar. The owner's a trained *sommelier* and will pick out delightful vintages for you, some sold by the glass. On the food front, there are earthy, robust dishes like *andouillette* with green lentils, calf's head *gribiche* with capers, gherkin and herb mayonnaise, stuffed pig's trotters and waffles with preserves for dessert. €14–18 *à la carte*. Friendly but unobtrusive staff and there's a piano to add a bit of atmosphere. Free apéritif.

|●| LE 5 CLAIRE

5 rue Saint-Claire. **MAP B2-18**

☎ 04.73.37.10.31
Closed Sun; Mon; a week in Feb; 3 weeks in Aug.

A typical Clermont restaurant with retro-chic décor and welcoming staff who readily offer information about the food or advice about the wines. It's not the cheapest place in town, but the dishes are tasty and imaginatively prepared: marinated fresh anchovies on a bed of pickled onions, roast sea bass with squid, shoulder of lamb with pickled lemons, saddle of rabbit with cinnamon served with rigatoni and herby ricotta. Menu of the day €18 then others at €27–41 depending on the number of dishes, which can get elaborate – creamed peas and asparagus with curried croutons, sea perch with artichokes with a sliver of warm *foie gras,* veal chop in a parmesan crust with an aubergine and thyme *compote*. Good cheeses and delicious desserts, too.

ROYAT   63130 (2KM W)

⅔ ♠ |●| LA PÉPINIÈRE CHALUT

11 av. Pasteur; (Centre).
☎ 04.73.35.58.81 ➡ 04.73.35.94.23
Closed Sun evening and Mon, Sun only June–Sept. **TV**.
Car park.

You are warmly welcomed by Madame Chalut when you arrive at her charming inn. Her husband's cuisine is appetizing and imaginative, concentrating on fresh regional produce used in old family recipes: potato sausage, boned pigs' trotters. But his palette is not limited – he also handles fish with great skill, particularly in the *choucroute* and the crayfish ravioli with herb *jus*. Menus €11–46. A few rooms for €20 with basin and €31–35 with shower/wc.

CHAMALIÈRES   63400 (3KM W)

⅔ ♠ |●| HÔTEL RADIO***

43 av. Pierre-Curie; take the D941b in the direction of Pontgibaud.
☎ 04.73.30.87.83 ➡ 04.76.36.42.44
@ hotel.radio@wanadoo.fr
Restaurant closed Sat lunchtime; Sun evening, Mon lunchtime except for public holidays, and Jan. **TV**.
Secure parking.

Built as a radio station in the 1930s, this hotel-restaurant was owned by Michel Mioche for many happy years. Now it's run by his daughter, who gave up her career as a journalist in Paris to do so. She, her young chef and a head waiter make up the trio running this successful enterprise. The dining room and sitting room are period and have been carefully

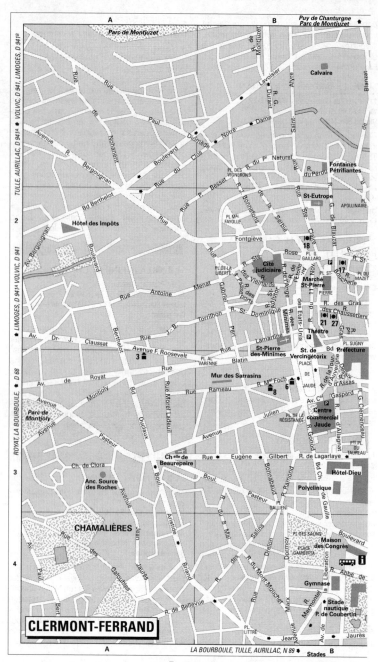

CLERMONT-FERRAND

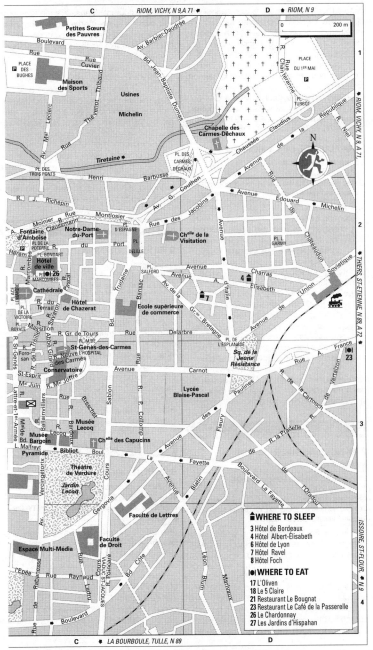

0   200 m

RIOM, VICHY, N 9, A 71 ◆
THIERS, ST-ÉTIENNE, N 89, A 72 ◆
ISSOIRE, ST-FLOUR, N 9 ◆

WHERE TO SLEEP
3 Hôtel de Bordeaux
4 Hôtel Albert-Élisabeth
6 Hôtel de Lyon
7 Hôtel Ravel
8 Hôtel Foch

WHERE TO EAT
17 L'Oliven
18 Le 5 Claire
21 Restaurant Le Bougnat
23 Restaurant Le Café de la Passerelle
26 Le Chardonnay
27 Les Jardins d'Hispahan

restored. Only top-quality produce is used and dishes are as skilfully prepared as they are imaginative – a revival of real French cooking. There is a fish menu designed around the catch brought in by the fishermen, and a themed menu inspired by the Orient. Dishes include rabbit *tartare*, casserole-roast pigeon and spiced John Dory with fruit and hot Caribbean chocolate *soufflé*. Menus €27–56. Beautiful bedrooms with lots of style; doubles €74 with shower/wc and €89–121 with bath. 10% discount for a two-night stay.

🎿 |●| AUBERGE DE LA MORÉNO

Col de la Moréno; it's on the D941A.
☎ 04.73.87.16.46
Closed evenings in the week, lunchtimes at weekends out of season, and from All Saints' Day to Jan. **TV**. **Car park**.

The inn was built in 1905 and it's run by a welcoming couple. The dining room, which has changed little over the years, has polished floors, stone walls and a wide hearth, and you can glimpse the kitchens through the door. You'll find interesting menus with appetizing dishes. In summer they serve a weekday lunch menu for €13, while others range from €17 to €29. Local specialities include *tripou* (a local gateau with herbs and prunes), frogs' legs with braised cabbage and diced smoked bacon, eggs with truffles and *andouillette*. The menu *Auvergnat* is exceptional: it lists pig's trotters stuffed with sweet herbs or char with Cantal and cream sauce with lentils. Try the local wine with *truffade* and the local ham. Of the desserts, don't miss their warm *tarte à Tine,* their version of *tarte Tatin*. Free apéritif.

CONDAT-EN-FENIERS   15190

🏠 |●| HÔTEL-RESTAURANT CHÉ MARISSOU

Le Veysset, it's 3km from Condat on the D62.
☎ 04.71.78.55.45
✉ marissou@aol.com
Open school holidays and weekends Feb–11 Nov.
Disabled access. **Garden**. **Car park**.

This hotel, the smallest in the world, was born out of the genuine passion of a Laval industrialist – a local boy made good – and helped along by an elaborate marketing campaign. He had a holiday home in Veyssat, between Condat and Montboudif, birthplace of President Pompidou, and decided to turn it into an inn. You'll be welcomed by the owner himself in a dining room that looks as much like a living museum as it

does a restaurant. Marissou's job is to send you away full, no matter how hungry you were when you arrived. You can go back as often as you like to the table of traditional cold meat and *crudités*. That will be followed by the day's special – *potée*, the thick local soup, or mutton tripe – then you serve yourself from a table bearing a selection of perfectly matured regional cheeses and dessert. With the cheese you'll get a chance to sample (on the house) a glass of rare wine made from late-harvested regional grapes. How much you pay depends on how old you are – it's free for children under 7 and centenarians, €21 if you're aged 10–65, €19 if you're 65–100. The one and only bedroom, at €76 including champagne, is traditionally decorated. Perfect for a special night away.

ÉGLISENEUVE-D'ENTRAIGUES   63850

🏠 |●| HÔTEL DU NORD*

rue principale.
☎ 04.73.71.90.28.
Closed a week in June and a week in Sept. **Car park**.

After a day's walking in the Cézallier, this pretty little country inn is a lovely place to stop for an Auvergnat snack or something a bit more substantial. *Menu ouvrier* €8 and others €10–20. Dishes are a compendium of local cooking: salmon with green lentils, warm goat's cheese with hazelnuts and bacon, home-made liver *terrine*, stuffed cabbage, pig's trotters. Make sure you try the iced soufflé with green verbena or the chocolate tart. Doubles €23 with shower/wc. Credit cards not accepted.

GANNAT   03800

🏠 |●| HÔTEL DU CHÂTEAU**

9 pl. Rantian; it's opposite the château.
☎ 04.70.90.00.88 📠 04.70.90.30.79
Closed Sat out of season; mid-Dec to 5 Jan. **TV**. **Car park**.

This hote is charming in a way that only nineteenth-century buildings in provincial towns can be. The kitchen provides the kind of traditional cooking from generations back: *andouillette bonne femme*, sautéed veal and chicken with creamed garlic. They also do a wonderful *pâté bourbonnais*, a potato and bacon pie, and a delicious walnut cake. Set menus €11–21. Clean simple bedrooms are €36 with shower/wc, or €46 with bath.

CHARROUX   03140 (10KM NW)

|●| LA FERME DE SAINT-SÉBASTIEN

Chemin de Bourion; take the N9, then turn right onto the D42.
☎ 04.70.56.88.83
Closed Mon and Tues except July–Aug; four weeks in Jan; a week in June; a week in Sept. **Disabled access. Garden. Car park.**

This delightful restaurant was opened in 1994 in one of France's most beautiful villages and it has quickly become a local favourite. The building was an old farm which has been renovated, and it provices an intimate atmosphere in which to enjoy Valérie Saignie's fresh, creative *bourbonnais* cooking. Menus (€15–49) feature courgette fritters with a cream chive sauce, chicken in Charroux mustard, Jerusalem artichokes with bacon, local cheeses (Lavor and smoked Lavor) and a good choice of desserts. They have an excellent cellar and the staff are warm and attentive. It's very popular, so you'll definitely need to book.

ISSOIRE   63500

⅔ 🏠 |●| AU BON COIN, CHEZ YVES

34–36 rue Aug-Bravard (Centre).
☎ 04.73.89.21.15 ➡ 04.73.89.21.15
Closed Sun evening and a fortnight in Nov. **Car park.**

A place with something of the warm south about it. The owner is an exile from Nice, and he'll serve you a drink at the bar before he sets about cooking your meal. The dishes have a *Provençal* accent and are liberally served: squid fritters with two sauces, fresh salmon carpaccio, local salt lamb with pesto, fish stew, a mini-*bouillabaisse*. There's a good choice of fish and, from September to the end of April, plenty of oysters and seafood. Lunch *formules* (dish and dessert) are priced at €8, or there are menus €12–20. There are a few rooms: €27 with basin, €32 with shower but wc on the landing. An unpretentious place with definite personality. Free coffee.

⅔ 🏠 HÔTEL DU TOURISME**

3 av. de la Gare.
☎ 04.73.89.23.68 ➡ 04.73.89.65.28
Closed Sun 11am–6pm and 23 Dec–21 Jan. **TV.**

A pretty house set back from the avenue, near a green park and the twelfth-century abbey. It's run by a man who's obsessed with aeroplanes – so much so that he's even built

one. Unsurprisingly, it's the place the pilots and paragliders go. Double rooms with shower/wc or bath €38. Free Kir.

SARPOIL   63500 (9KM SE)

|●| LA BERGERIE DE SARPOIL

From Issoire, take the D996 then the D999 in the direction of Saint-Germain-l'Herm.
☎ 04.73.71.02.54 ➡ 04.73.71.02.99
Closed Sun evening and Mon except July–Aug. **Car park.**

The best restaurant in the region. Laurent Jury and Éric Moutard produce marvels using the finest Auvergne produce: free-range pork, Salers beef, suckling lamb with wild ceps and morels from the forest. Menus €21–56. Dishes include mouthwatering *andouille* pancake with pickled onions, nettle soup with frogs' legs and sweet garlic and veal sweetbreads braised with Boudes wine. On the *Saint Cochon* menu you'll find black-pudding tart with chestnuts and *foie gras* cream, a morsel of pork smoked over rye stalks stuffed with ceps and cooked in a straw crust and the sublime Caraïbe chocolate tart. There's a little rhyme on the menus: "the art of the cook begins where nature's work ceases". So now you know.

LAPALISSE   03120

⅔ 🏠 |●| HÔTEL-RESTAURANT GALLAND**

20 pl. de la République.
☎ 04.70.99.07.21 ➡ 04.70.99.34.64
Closed Mon and Sun evenings out of season; Feb school holidays; last week in Nov. **TV. Car park.**

A delightful place where you can eat Dublin Bay prawns *Nantais*, sliced Charolais steak with Saint-Pourçain wine sauce and *escalope* of duck *foie gras* pan-fried with figs. The cooking is fresh and brings out subtle flavours. *La patronne* is adorable, good-humoured and very stylish, and the staff are keen and attentive. Menus €21–43. The bedrooms are spick-and-span and cost €41 for a double with shower/wc or €46 with bath. Ask for one overlooking the interior courtyard. A very good establishment. Free apéritif.

LAVOUTE-CHICHAC   43380

🏠 |●| HOSTELLERIE LE PRIEURÉ**

Centre.
☎ 04.71.77.47.93 ➡ 04.71.77.48.00

Closed Tues evening and Wed except July–Aug; 31 Oct–1 April.

The priory was built in the eighteenth century, and the comfortable rooms have been thoughtfully renovated – all have a startling view of the Allier. The kindly owner is absolutely emphatic that General Lafayette slept in room 3, which has a view of the humpback bridge. Doubles with washing facilities €32, or €39 with en-suite bathrooms. Several menus, €15–24, list dishes concocted from fresh local produce – the cabbage stuffed with salmon is a *tour-de-force*, as is the summer fruit sorbet. The cheapest menu includes apéritif, dessert, cheese and a $1/_4$-litre of red wine. Pleasant terrace on the Allier.

SAINT-ARCONS-D'ALLIER   42300 (8KM SE)

🏠 |◉| LES DEUX ABBESSES

In the village; it's on the D585 in the direction of Prades.
☎ 04.71.74.03.08 ➡ 04.71.74.05.30
Closed 15 Nov–15 March. **Swimming pool**.

The mayoress had the inspired idea of renovating seven houses to make a sort of hotel village, gathered around the twelfth-century château on an outcrop of rock between the Allier and the Sioule rivers. There are twelve charming, comfortable and spacious rooms with period furniture. The garden, where you eat breakfast in summer, has a Romanesque church to one side built of volcanic rock. The owner is also the cook and she produces simple, tasty dishes – her spiced lamb is splendid, slowly roasted for seven hours and served with potatoes topped with cheese and cinnamon. There's a single menu at €38, breakfast for €11, and rooms with en-suite are €107–229. There's even a swimming pool with a breathtaking view.

MANDAILLES-SAINT-JULIEN   15590

🏠 |◉| HÔTEL-RESTAURANT AU BOUT DU MONDE

Centre.
☎ 04.71.47.92.47 ➡ 04.71.47.95.95
Closed 15 Nov–27 Dec.

A nice place in the Jordanne valley which is a starting point for hillwalkers going up the Puy-Mary. The hotel is quiet, simple, and well run; doubles €31. The restaurant, with its traditional *cantou* (inglenook fireplace), armchairs and gleaming copperware is as cosy as you could wish. The cooking will satisfy even the hungriest hiker – portions are generous

beyond belief. Everything's delicious, from the selection of *charcuterie* to the vegetable soup and regional specialities like *truffade* (potato cake with Cantal cheese). Menus €13–16. Stuffed cabbage and *potée*, the substantial local soup, is made to order. You'll get a pleasant smiling welcome. 10% discount on the room rate except in school holidays.

🏠 |◉| HÔTEL-RESTAURANT AUX GENÊTS D'OR*

Centre.
☎ 04.71.47.96.45 ➡ 04.71.47.93.65
Closed 15 Nov–20 Dec. **TV**.

A small hotel with a homely atmosphere in the centre of the village. It's set back from the road down a cul-de-sac, so it's quiet. Good cooking, with set menus at €11–38. They concentrate on a few specialities: pie of duck *confit* with ceps, *tournedos* with gentian sauce, scallops on a bed of *fondant* leeks, venison with morels. They offer half board if you like. Doubles €31 with shower/wc. 10% discount on the room rate.

SAINT-CIRGUES-DE-JORDANNE 15590 (8KM SE)

🏠 |◉| HÔTEL-RESTAURANT LES TILLEULS**

Centre; take the D17.
☎ 04.71.47.92.19 ➡ 04.71.47.91.06
✉ hoteltilleuls15@aol.com
Closed Feb. **Swimming pool**. **TV**. **Garden**. **Car park**.

A beautiful building overlooking the road and the Jordanne valley. You can relax in the garden, swimming pool or sauna when you come back from a walk on the Puy-Mary. The quiet, pleasant bedrooms all have en-suite bathrooms and some have a terrace too; doubles €38–41 with shower/wc or bath. The dining room is equally pleasant and the open fire is welcome in winter. You'll get a warm reception from Yvette Fritsch, who creates her own recipes with wonderful results – duck breast in honey with dandelions, pork chops with Cantal cheese and noodles, *pounti* with raisins, profiteroles with coconut. Menus €11–38, half board €38–41. 10% discount on the room rate.

MASSIAC   15500

🏠 |◉| GRAND HÔTEL DE LA POSTE**

26 av. du Général-de-Gaulle (Centre).
☎ 04.71.23.02.01 ➡ 04.71.23.09.23
Closed the first fortnight in Dec.

Swimming pools. TV. Garden. Car park.

32 bedrooms renovated in trendy, elegant, Neoclassical style. Doubles with all mod cons weigh in at €40–50. There's a pleasant restaurant at the back; it offers a set menu at €11 (not served on Sunday or public holidays), and others €17–27. À la carte there are a few specialities: Auvergne ham, Cantal cheese tart, the chef's own *tournedos*, potato in flaky pastry, two types of fish in *beurre blanc* and warm apple tart. 10% discount on the room rate 1 Oct–31 May.

MAURIAC   15200

☎ ◉ HÔTEL DES VOYAGEURS – LA BONNE AUBERGE**

pl. de la Poste.
☎ 04.71.68.01.01 ➡ 04.71.68.01.56
E auberge.des.voyageurs@wanadoo.fr
Closed Sat and Sun evening Nov–April; 21 Dec–6 Jan.
TV. Garden. Car park.

A nice hotel with twenty rooms which have been prettily redecorated in modern colours. Good bathrooms. Doubles €23 with shower (wc on the landing), €30 with shower/wc and €37 with bath. Straightforward, honest menus, €11–29, list regional specialities like Salers beef with ceps and traditional dishes. Very hospitable.

DRUGEAC   15140 (12KM SE)

☀◉ L'AUBERGE DES SAVEURS

Centre.
☎ 04.71.69.15.50.
Closed Mon evening and Wed.

A village inn with a simple, inviting dining room and sophisticated cooking. It's run by a husband-and-wife team – David will welcome you warmly front of house, while Nicole is in charge of the kitchen. She worked in a number of restaurants on the Côte before settling here and developing her own style. The menu features Auvergne ravioli with baby vegetables, poussin *terrine*, Mediterranean prawns *provençale* and home-made desserts and bread. She bakes her own bread. Dishes change with the seasons. Weekday lunch menu €9, and others €15–23. Pleasant sunny terrace. Free apéritif.

MONT-DORE (LE)   63240

☀☎◉ HÔTEL DE LA PAIX**

8 rue Rigny.

☎ 04.73.65.00.17 ➡ 04.73.65.00.31
Closed a fortnight Nov–Dec.

A hotel built in 1880 with a wonderfully old-fashioned décor. It's run by a friendly woman who greets you warmly. Simple, functional rooms go for €38 with shower/wc. Superb *belle époque* dining room and a charming sitting room. Classic cooking, as is appropriate in such surroundings, using simple, fresh produce: lobster *au gratin*, St Nectaire cheese tart, truffles with scrambled eggs and salmon *escalope* with Cantal cheese. Menus €14–26. Half board at €37 per person is compulsory in the Feb school holidays and during Aug. Free house apéritif.

☀☎◉ HÔTEL LE CASTELET**

av. Michel-Bertrand (Northwest); it's near the town centre.
☎ 04.73.65.05.29 ➡ 04.73.65.27.95
E castelet@compuserve.com
Closed 25 March–15 May and 1 Oct–20 Dec.
Swimming pool. TV. Garden. Car park.

They don't emphasize spa cures here as much as they do in the other hotels in town. Nevertheless there's a swimming pool, garden and terrace, and they have lots of facilities to keep you and the kids amused – ping-pong, snooker, toboggans, video games and outdoor activities – as well as cots and high-chairs, all free of charge. There are 34 rooms, with doubles at €51 with bath. Sophisticated cuisine in the restaurant: smoked duck breast and mango with walnut oil, trout with gentian sauce and salmon *escalope* with green lentils, raspberry *gratin* and fruit *fondue* with chocolate. Menus €15–26. 10% discount on the room rate Jan–March, May–Jun and Sept, and a free house apéritif.

◉ RESTAURANT LE BOUGNAT

23 av. Georges-Clémenceau.
☎ 04.73.65.28.19
Closed Tues except during school holidays and 8 Nov–15 Dec. **Garden. Car park.**

Traditional cooking with a modern slant – nobody in Mont-Dore does it better. An old stable has been very nicely transformed to make a delightful dining space with little tables and tiny sideboards. The *pounti (*a mixture of bacon and Swiss chard) is one of the best we've ever tasted, and the *truffade* (potato cake with Cantal cheese), is excellent. The garlic soup, the sautéed rabbit *à la gentiane* and the stuffed cabbage are also good. Set menus €13–21. This is a great place to come on cold winter evenings after a good day's skiing. Best to book – it's very popular. They've opened a shop, "La Petite Boutique du Bougnat", where you can buy home-made delicacies.

MONTLUÇON 03100

⌂ HÔTEL DE LA GARE**

42 av. Marx-Dormoy (Southwest); it's close to the station.
☎ 04.70.05.44.22 ➡ 04.70.05.90.89
Closed 22 Dec–4 Jan. **TV**. **Car park**.

This little hotel, the headquarters of the *Contact-hôtel* chain, is a good example of a traditional, family-run establishment. It's pleasant, quiet and very handy for the station. Bedrooms are simple and well-maintained, and cost €37 with shower/wc and €40 with bath. Free hearty breakfasts, usually €5. Good staff on hand to help.

⋨ ⌂ |●| HÔTEL DES BOURBONS – RESTAURANT AUX DUCS DE BOURBON**

47 av. Marx-Dormoy (Southwest); it's near the station.
☎ 04.70.05.28.93 ➡ 04.70.05.16.92
Brasserie ☎ 04.70.05.22.79
Closed Sun evening and Mon except public holidays. **TV**.

This beautiful eighteenth-century townhouse has been stylishly renovated and offers comfortable, bright bedrooms. Doubles €43 with shower/wc or bath. The brasserie is cosier than the restaurant; set menus, €12–31, offer dishes such as skate wings with capers, grilled salmon and scorpion fish with two sauces and profiteroles with chocolate sauce. Very professionally run. Free apéritif.

|●| LA VIE EN ROSE

7 rue de la Fontaine; it's beside Notre-Dame church.
☎ 04.70.03.88.79
Closed Sun lunchtime.

If you find yourself in the old part of Montluçon, unwind here in the relaxed atmosphere created by the friendly owner. The dining room is decorated in warm colours and there's new lighting to make for a more cosy feel. The walls are hung with old photos of the town and adverts from the 1950s and 1960s, and the background music is not muzak but a collection of great French songs. The cooking is good – various thick and tasty steaks and fresh, big salads. Excellent potato pie in particular. €17 *à la carte*. Menus €8–14.

|●| LE SAFRAN D'OR

12 pl. des Toiles (Centre); it's in the pedestrian part of

the medieval town.
☎ 04.70.05.09.18 ➡ 04.70.05.55.60
Closed Sun evening, Mon, Feb school holidays and 15 Aug–15 Sept.

The yellow marbled façade looks like the front of a Parisian brasserie and the cooking is of the kind you'd get in a high-class bistro. You'll get a warm welcome from the owner. The service is quick and efficient but you won't feel rushed, and the excellent cooking won't cost you a fortune. Set menus €15–21.

NÉRIS-LES-BAINS 03310 (8KM SE)

⋨ |●| LE RELAIS DU VIEUX MOULIN

rue des Moulins; take the N144.
☎ 04.70.03.24.88
Closed Tues; 30 Oct–1 March. **Garden**. **Car park**.

A lovely place, especially in summer, when you can sit outside on the delightful terraces below the viaduct. You're in Charolais country and they sell the cuts by weight; this is the best place for miles around for beef grilled over the open fire. You'll find a wide variety of sweet and savoury pancakes and salads as well. Free apéritif.

COURÇAIS 03370 (21KM NW)

⌂ |●| BAR-HÔTEL-RESTAURANT JOSETTE LAUMONIER

Take the D943; it's on the pl. de l'Eglise.
☎ 04.70.07.11.13
Closed Sun evening, Mon and 1–22 Sept.

Located in a peaceful village, this is a simple, pleasant and relaxing place which is ideal for families. There's a cosy atmosphere in the rustic restaurant – the fireplace has a lot to do with that – or you might prefer the terrace on sunny days. Menus €11–20 and you won't go hungry. The free-range poultry from the neighbouring farm is excellent and, if you order in advance, they can provide snails or veal sweetbreads. Four bedrooms at €20 with basin. Half board, €23, is compulsory April–August.

MONTSALVY 15120

⋨ ⌂ |●| L'AUBERGE FLEURIE**

pl. du Barry (Centre).
☎ 04.71.49.20.02 ✉ info@auberge-fleurie.com
Restaurant closed 2 Jan–15 Feb.

Everything's well-maintained and has a rustic feel here – ivy clambering up the front wall, a fireplace, exposed beams and ancient doors. There's always a good crowd in the bar and restaurant, and you'll find the staff very friendly. The menu of the day, €9, is not available on Sunday, but others (€15–28), are good value. Dishes changes with the seasons but expect cuisine like *foie gras* escalope with mushroom *fricassée*, breast of duck with Marcillac butter and chestnut charlotte with a quince *coulis*. Wines are reasonably priced. Rooms with shower/wc €37–46; half board is €35–60 per person. Free apéritif.

🧖 🛏 |●| INTER-HÔTEL DU NORD**

Centre.
☎ 04.71.49.20.03 📠 04.71.49.29.00
📧 hotel@hotel-du-nord.com
Closed Jan–March. **TV**. **Garden**. **Car park**.

Situated in the heart of the Châtaigneraie, this chic hotel has colourful, comfortable rooms equipped with telephone, TV and mini-bar. They cost €43–47 with shower/wc or €45–49 with bath. The quiet, plush restaurant has an excellent reputation for its traditional local dishes. A husband-and-wife team runs the place – he deals with the dining room while she does the cooking. Menus (€15–40) include *crépinette* of pig's trotters, trout *soufflé* with lentil sauce, *falette* (stuffed breast of mutton), stew of suckling pig, pan-fried snails with ceps and walnuts, fresh *foie gras* in Sauternes, locally grown beef and iced *mousse* flavoured with gentian liqueur. 10% discount April–June and Sept–Dec. Free coffee.

CALVINET   15340 (17.5KM W)

🧖 🛏 |●| HÔTEL DE LA TERRASSE*

pl. Jean-de-Bonnefon (Centre); take the D19.
☎ 04.71.49.91.59
Closed Nov–May. **Garden**. **Car park**.

The chatty lady who's been running the hotel since 1936 has a gift for taking care of her guests. She has created a wonderful and homely atmosphere, with lovely rustic décor including copper pans, an old clock and a sideboard. Her specialities are pear tart and stuffed pig's trotters and she has set menus at €16–26 (the most expensive of which features two starters). The bedrooms are furnished with period furniture; doubles are €26–38 with bath/wc or shower/wc. Half board €37 per person. Free house apéritif.

🛏 |●| HÔTEL BEAUSÉJOUR**

Route de Maurs; get there by the D66, the D45 and the D51.
☎ 04.71.49.91.68 📠 04.71.49.98.63

Closed Mon; Sun evening out of season; mid-Jan to 1 March. **TV**.

Michelin has awarded the restaurant a coveted star – it's the only place in Cantal to have one – and it's won regional awards too. In spite of the chef's success, this establishment remains as down-to-earth as ever, so he hasn't lost the support of his regulars – travelling executives and local farmers who come here for family celebrations. Staff are particularly friendly and offer efficient service in a classic dining room. Amazingly high-quality cooking and reasonable prices. Dishes include stuffed cabbage, black pudding with duck livers, *marbré* of *foie gras* with oxtail, guinea fowl *gourmandises*, roast crayfish with raw ham, casserole of milk-fed veal, medallions of lamb spiked with anchovies, ham hock with pea *purée*, *fricassée* of Breton lobster and farm-raised pigeon. Menus €15–49. Good wines at reasonable prices. Comfortable and pretty bedrooms cost €53.

MOULINS   03000

🧖 🛏 |●| LE GRAND HÔTEL DU DAUPHIN**

59 pl. d'Allier (Centre).
☎ 04.70.44.33.05 📠 04.70.34.05.75
TV. **Disabled access**. **Garden**. **Car park**.

A seventeenth-century coaching inn with an air of romance. The tables are nicely laid and the refined cooking is classical in style. Regional specialities include *salmis* of duck in Saint-Pourçain, frogs' legs with garlic cream and duck leg *confit*. Menus €11–23. You can order chicken with blue Auvergne cheese, *potée* Bourbonnais, Royal couscous and *coq au vin* with Saint Pourçain wine. Delightful and comfortable bedrooms are €25 with basin or €42 with bath. 10% discount on the room rate Jan–March.

🧖 🛏 |●| LE PARC**

31 av. du Général-Leclerc (East); it's near the train station.
☎ 04.70.44.12.25 📠 04.70.46.79.35
Restaurant closed Sat; 23 Dec–4 Jan; 5–19 July; 28 Sept–5 Oct. **TV**. **Car park**.

The Barret family have been running this hotel since 1956 and they offer a kindly welcome. It's a beautiful building, classic in style and exceptionally well-appointed. The bright dining room is relaxing, and the furniture, fabrics and colours are simple and harmonious. The restaurant serves traditional and local dishes interpreted with imagination: zander fillet with Charroux mustard, roast saddle of rabbit with cream and morel sauce, chocolate and hazelnut *délice*. Set menus €15–34. Rooms are well-soundproofed; doubles with shower/wc cost €34–43 or €56 with bath. Some are in an annexe. Free apéritif.

|●| LE GRAND CAFÉ

49 pl. d'Allier (Centre).
☎ 04.70.44.00.05
Car park.

Service until 11pm. This superb 1900s brasserie is a listed building, and it's the most popular place in the area – people come for the atmosphere as much as as the food. Dishes of the day include grilled pig's trotters, calf's brawn, oxtail and steak.

⅔ |●| RESTAURANT LA PETITE AUBERGE

7 rue des Bouchers (Centre); it's near the main post office.
☎ 04.70.44.11.68 ➡ 04.70.44.82.04
Closed Sun except public holidays; Mon evening; 22 July–12 Aug.

The dining room is long and narrow and very traditionally decorated. The chef's expertise with first-rate ingredients produces results which are full of flavour – scallop *fricassée* with salad, Charolais steak with Auvergne blue cheese and Saint-Pourçain *andouillette* with Charroux mustard. There's a *formule rapide* in the brasserie for €10 or menus at €15–29. Delightful welcome. Free Kir.

COULANDON   03000 (6KM W)

⅔ ♠ |●| HÔTEL LE CHALET-RESTAURANT LE MONTÉGUT***

It's on the D945.
☎ 04.70.44.50.08 ➡ 04.70.44.07.09
Closed 15 Dec–1 Feb. **Swimming pool. TV. Disabled access. Garden. Car park.**

If you're on the lookout for a relaxing break in a hotel where service always comes with a smile, this late nineteenth-century chalet nestling in the depths of the countryside is ideal. Bedrooms have been tastefully decorated and they're all different; doubles €63–73 with shower/wc or bath. From the rooms you'll either have a view of the countryside or the park, which has an ornamental lake. The restaurant is in a separate building, and when summer arrives you can lunch or dine by the swimming pool. The €18 weekday menu is based on fresh market produce and there are others with bigger portions and more elaborate dishes priced up to €38 – fillet of lamb *en*

croûte, pan-fried crayfish with fresh noodles, iced mousse with Chivas Regal. Service is good. Free apéritif.

SOUVIGNY   03210 (11KM W)

⅔ |●| AUBERGE LES TILLEULS

pl. Saint-Éloi.
☎ 04.70.43.60.70 ➡ 04.70.44.85.73
Closed Sun evening except July–Aug; Mon; the second week in Feb; the third week in June; 1–10 Oct.

There's a magnificent basilica surrounded by buildings dating from the tenth to the fifteenth centuries in this delightful village. The inn is welcoming, fresh and clean; on the walls there are paintings of village life in the 1940s and 1950s. €11 weekday lunch menu and others up to €31. Specialities include pan-fried duck *foie gras escalope*, chicory *charlotte* with walnuts and scallops, home-smoked salmon and sea bream *andouillette* with smoked crayfish sauce. The selection of local cheeses, whether from cow's milk or goat's, is perfect. Free apéritif.

CHAPELLE-AUX-CHASSES (LA) 03230 (22KM NE)

⅔ |●| L'AUBERGE DE LA CHAPELLE-AUX-CHASSES

Centre; take the N79 towards Bourbon-Lancy, then the D30 as far as the village; the restaurant is beside the church.
☎ 04.70.43.44.71
Closed Tues evening, Wed, Mon and Thurs evening Oct–April; a fortnight in Jan; a fortnight in Sept. **Garden**.

This building looks like a child's picture of a house. You walk through the garden accompanied by the sound of birdsong, then past reception to a pretty little dining room. The cooking is classic, imaginative and bursting with freshness: *terrine* of semi-cooked duck *foie gras*, *fricassée* of farmed rabbit with rosemary and lime, ham braised in a hay box, fisherman's stew with a mandarin and almond sauce, fillet of zander with creamed lettuce, iced *soufflé* flavoured with verbena liqueur. The prices make it one of the more popular places in the area. *Formule* during the week at €11 and menus €15–23. There's a shady terrace where they serve in summer. Free coffee.

DOMPIERRE-SUR-BESBRE   03290 (30KM E)

⅔ ♠ |●| AUBERGE DE L'OLIVE**

129 av. de la Gare; take the D12.
☎ 04.70.34.51.87 ➡ 04.70.34.61.68

Closed Fri (except July–Aug); 10 days during the Feb school holidays; a fortnight in Nov. **TV**.

A handsome, well-maintained building covered in Virginia creeper. Care is taken with the cooking and the service is faultless. Set menus range from €11 (except Sunday and public holidays) to €40. Freshly refurbished doubles with shower/wc or bath go for €40. There are seventeen newly renovated rooms and now that the bypass has been built lorries don't go thundering through the village. Free coffee.

MURAT   15300

🏠 AUX GLOBE-TROTTERS**

22 av. du Docteur-Louis-Mallet (South).
☎ 04.71.20.07.22 ➡ 04.71.20.16.88
Closed Sun except summer; a week in July; the Nov school holidays. **TV**. **Garden**. **Car park**.

There are twenty very clean, modern rooms here, costing from €27 to €37. The attic ones on the second floor are absolutely delightful, though watch your head if you're tall! Very laid-back atmosphere in the downstairs bar which is popular with young people.

🏠 HÔTEL LES BREUILS**

av. du Docteur-Louis-Mallet (Centre).
☎ 04.71.20.01.25 ➡ 04.71.20.02.43
Swimming pool. Garden. Pay car park.

A substantial nineteenth-century private house which has been turned into a hotel. It has aristocratic charm and an old-fashioned feel that's a world away from the sterility of some modern establishments. They play soft music and there's a restful garden too. Charming welcome. Ten cosy, comfortable rooms, stylishly redecorated. Doubles €42–73. 10% discount Sept–June.

�‖❙ RESTAURANT LE JARROUSSET

RN122; it's 4km from Murat heading in the direction of Massiac.
☎ 04.71.20.10.69 ➡ 04.71.20.15.26
Closed Mon–Wed except July–Aug; Jan. **Garden**. **Car park**

You can't miss this restaurant at the end of the road; the setting is elegant and the service faultless. Eliane Andrieu runs this place with exceptional know-how and is always courteous and attentive to her guests. Only the best local produce is used in the cooking, and clever combinations of flavours and subtle aromas are created. The cheeses are good, and the *crème brûlée* and chocolate tart are

both excellent. They have a brilliant menu at €21, a veritable feast, but it's not available Saturday evenings or Sunday lunchtimes; others go up to €55. *À la carte* you can get dishes such as leg of duck *au sel*, braised cabbage with a *coulis* of peppers, quail stuffed with *foie gras*, *escalope* of *foie gras* with caramelized apples, *blanquette* of veal sweetbreads, cabbage stuffed with truffles and fillet of sea bass with *fondue* of fennel. Expect to spend €53 *à la carte*. Good choice of wines.

CHALINARGUES   15170 (9KM S)

🏠❙❙❙ AUBERGE DE LA PINATELLE

☎ 04.71.20.15.92 ➡ 04.71.20.17.90
e pinatel@club-internet.fr
Closed Wed evening; a fortnight Sept–Oct.

A pretty, popular inn. The young owners have five comfortable rooms, which they have decorated tastefully; doubles €34. The convivial dining room has been done up in modern style and menus are €11–24. There are Auvergne and Mediterranean specialities and good fish – trout with bacon, *coq au vin*, duck breast, salad with truffles and other Périgord delicacies such as *foie gras* served in a *brioche*. Attentive, smiling service. Free house apéritif.

DIENNE   15300 (11KM NW)

🏠❙❙ RESTAURANT DU LAC SAUVAGES

How to get there: take the D3 from Murat then the D23.
☎ 04.71.20.82.65
Closed Oct–June. **Garden**. **Car park**.

Paradise for fishermen and walkers on the banks of a private lake 1230m up. The restaurant is the place to be when summer comes to Dienne – it's a magnificent setting. It is run by the head of the Super-Lioran ski school, and you'll get a nice welcome. The kitchen uses local produce to prepare tasty regional specialities, served up in generous portions: especially good are trout with bacon, *truffade* (potato cake with Cantal cheese), *pounti* (a mixture of bacon and Swiss chard) and mutton tripe. €11 set menu or around €15 *à la carte*. You can even catch your own trout – no permit needed and there's equipment for hire. Free coffee.

LIORAN (LE)   15300 (12KM SW)

🏠❙❙ HÔTEL-RESTAURANT LE ROCHER DU CERF**

How to get there: take the N122 from Murat then the D67.

☎ 04.71.49.50.14 ➡ 04.71.49.54.07
Closed 15 April–30 June and 15 Sept–19 Dec. **TV. Car park**.

A typical family hotel in a ski resort. Located near the slopes, this is the nicest place in the area and the staff are always friendly and helpful. Bedrooms have been refurbished, and all rooms have views of the mountains. Doubles €23 with basin, €31 with shower/wc and €37 with bath. The restaurant has the same kind of homely atmosphere and the set menus for full-board guests are planned over a two week period so that you don't get the same thing every day. Set menus in the restaurant are €11–18. Specialities include stuffed cabbage, trout with bacon, *truffade* (the local potato cake with Cantal cheese), *pounti* (a mixture of bacon and Swiss chard), *coq au vin*, steak with bleu d'Auvergne (a local blue cheese), *escalope cantalienne* and bilberry fruit tart. 10% discount on the room rate July– Aug.

LAVIGERIE   15300 (15KM W)

◗◗ AUBERGE ADRIENNE NIOCEL

Route de Dienne; take the D680 – it's just after Dienne.
☎ 04.71.20.82.25
Open Nov–Jan by reservation only.

An authentic Cantal house with a superb dining room. It's got a flagstoned floor and a vast chimney piece where the old beds in the alcoves have been preserved. Adrienne Niocel is a gifted cook who prepares excellent regional dishes – good mountain ham, one of the tastiest *truffades* (potato cake with Cantal cheese) in the area, cheese, *poulacre* (lamb's liver with pork belly), home-made fruit tart. Warm and unpretentious welcome. A single menu for €12.

ALLANCHE   15160 (23KM NE)

⌂◗◗ RESTAURANT AU FOIRAIL

Maillargues; take the N122 from Murat, then the D679.
☎ 04.71.20.41.15
Closed evenings except July–Aug; Sun; the first week in Jan.. **Car park**.

You'll find this place on a little hill 1km outside Allanche in the middle of the summer pastures and near one of the Auvergne's biggest cattle markets. It's a simple place serving Salers beef which is particularly full of flavour. Hearty dish of the day €7, *menu du jour* €11 and others up to €15.There are panoramic views from the dining-room windows and friendly staff. Free coffee.

NARNHAC   15230

⌂⌂◗◗ L'AUBERGE DE PONT-LA-VIEILLE**

Pont-la-Vieille.
☎ 04.71.73.42.60 ➡ 04.71.73.42.20
Closed Nov. **TV. Garden. Car park**.

This is a welcoming and relaxing little hotel which has been nicely restored. It's set back from the main road and has a pretty garden in front. Quiet and pleasant double rooms with shower/wc are €35, or €38 with bath. Half board, from €31–35 per person, is compulsory in July–August. Set menus, €10–21, feature regional specialities – choose from dishes like stuffed cabbage, trout with bacon *à l'ancienne*, *rissole Saint-Flour* (a sort of fritter with a cabbage and bacon filling) and lamb's trotters. There are two shady terraces on the river bank. 10% discount on the room rate May–June and Sept.

PAILHEROLS   15800

⌂⌂◗◗ L'AUBERGE DES MONTAGNES**

Centre; east of Vic-sur-Cère, take the D154 then the D54.
☎ 04.71.47.57.01 ➡ 04.71.49.63.83
Closed Tues out of season and 8 Oct–20 Dec. **Swimming pool. TV. Disabled access. Garden. Car park**.

A pretty little winding road from Vic-sur-Cère will lead you up to this excellent family hotel on the outskirts of the village. It's been thoughtfully renovated and there's a new building constructed in the traditional style with a beautiful turret. The pond and the wonderful view complete the setting. There's a terrace, indoor and outdoor swimming pools, a climbing wall and a games room in the old barn across the road – it also offers horse-drawn carriage rides. The bedrooms are on the small side, but they're cosy and well decorated; the bigger ones are in the new building. Doubles €34–45. There are two very bright dining rooms, one with the traditional *cantou* (inglenook) fireplace. The €13 *menu du jour*, and others €16–21, list local dishes such as *pounti* (a mixture of bacon and Swiss chard) and *truffade* (potato cake with Cantal cheese). It's popular, so it would be a good idea to book ahead. Free house apéritif and 10% discount on the room rate 1 June–15 July.

PONTGIBAUD   63230

⌂◗◗ HÔTEL-RESTAURANT DE L'UNIVERS

How to get there: take the D941, it's opposite the station.

☎ 04.73.88.70.09.
Car park.

This family guesthouse looks like a picture postcard. Charlot grows the vegetables and milks the cows, and Marie-Antoinette is the highly competent chef – she can feed the local fire brigade on her tripe dish while at the same time beating up a few eggs for an omelette for another customer. The dining room, with its flowery wallpaper, is clean and bright. You can have a meal here at any time: calf's head, terrific grilled *andouillette*, good pig's trotters. There's no rush to leave, so sit a while and play cards – and if you're missing a player, Charlot or Marie-Antoinette will happily make up the numbers. *Menu ouvrier* €9 and others up to €11. Double rooms €25 with shower on the landing or €35 for ones sleeping three or four.

𝒳 ⌂ |●| HÔTEL DE LA POSTE**

pl. de la République.
☎ 04.73.88.70.02 ⟼ 04.73.88.79.74
Closed Sun evening and Mon except July–Aug; Jan; the first fortnight in Oct.**TV**. **Car park**.

A traditional hotel-restaurant with appealing, old-fashioned rooms. Doubles €32 with shower/wc or €34 with bath. Delicious local and seasonal dishes in the restaurant: roasted local rabbit with honey and ginger, *crepinette* of pigs' trotters, chard with *mousserons* (small white or yellow mushrooms). Menus €13–43. Free apéritif.

MAZAYES   63230 (7KM S)

⌂ |●| AUBERGE DE MAZAYES**

How to get there: take the D578, the D62, then the D52.
☎ 04.73.88.93.90 ⟼ 04.73.88.93.80
Closed Mon and Tues lunchtime in summer; 17 Dec–25 Jan. **TV**. **Car park**.

At the end of a winding road, a magnificent stable has been turned into a comfortable inn. It has an authentic rustic air – they've kept the stone drainage gully from the original stable – with sophisticated overtones. It's almost completely silent, and the terrace is a perfect spot for an apéritif while you enjoy the sunset. Proper regional dishes, with an excellent *potée auvergnate* and a tasty *coq au vin* leading the way. Weekday menu €13, and another €22. The attractive rooms cost €44–50 with bath, breakfast included. The ideal place for a weekend in the country.

PUY-EN-VELAY (LE)   43000

⌂ DYKE HÔTEL**

37 bd. Maréchal-Fayolle (Centre).
☎ 04.71.09.05.30 ⟼ 04.71.02.58.66
Closed Christmas to 1 Jan. **TV**. **Lock-up garage**.

All the advantages of a chain hotel, plus a central location and a lock-up garage. Everything's clean and brand new, the décor is low-key and the service is efficient. Bedrooms are identical and the mattresses very firm. Doubles €29 with shower/wc and €43 with bath. Breakfast, €5, is served in the bar. "Dyke" refers to the local sugarloaf rock formations which give the area its character.

⌂ |●| HÔTEL BRISTOL**

7 and 9 av. Maréchal-Foch (Centre).
☎ 04.71.09.13.38 ⟼ 04.71.09.51.70
Closed Mon out of season and 23 Nov–10 Dec. **TV**.
Disabled access. **Garden**. **Car park**.

A very English hotel – as the name suggests. It's a tall old building, the kind you generally find in a spa town in the Auvergne, with an entirely renovated and modernized interior. There is a brand-new annexe overlooking the garden with impeccable bedrooms that are very bright and very quiet; doubles €40–49 with shower/wc or bath. It may look smart but *Hôtel Bristol* is not at all stuffy, and you'll always get a warm welcome. Try the carefully prepared traditional cooking in the *Taverne Lyonnaise* – the best dish is ham hock with lentils. The €9 menu includes wine, and there are others at €14–26.

𝒳 ⌂ |●| HÔTEL-RESTAURANT LE VAL VERT**

6 av. Baptiste-Marcet; it's at the side of the road near the Puy south exit heading for Aubenas.
☎ 04.71.09.09.30 ⟼ 04.71.09.36.49
ℯ info@hotelvalvert.com
Restaurant closed Sat lunchtime; 21–29 Dec. **TV**. **Car park**.

They've just finished a complete refurbishment of the hotel and though it looks rather like a chain establishment from the outside, inside you'll find a friendly, homely atmosphere with smiling and attentive staff. The comfortable, modern rooms are well-maintained and decorated. The ones overlooking the road are soundproofed, but if it's absolute quiet you're after, ask for one at the back. Bedrooms with shower or bath €44–49. The restaurant serves carefully prepared classics; weekday lunch menus €10–11 and others up to €40 with seasonal specialities. Free house apéritif.

🎿 🏠 |O| HÔTEL LE RÉGINA***

34 bd. Maréchal-Fayolle (Centre).
☎ 04.71.09.14.71 ➡ 04.71.09.18.57
TV. Disabled access. Car park.

This hotel, in a beautiful old building right in the centre of town, is something of an institution. Prices are very reasonable for a three-star, especially considering the high standard of the facilities and service: doubles with shower/wc or bath €53–57. If you're a light sleeper, ask for a room at the back rather than one overlooking the street. The ground-floor restaurant offers some of the best cooking in Puy; menus are €13–30. Staff are courteous and friendly. Free coffee.

🎿 |O| LA PARENTHÈSE

8 av. de la Cathédrale (Centre).
☎ 04.71.02.83.00
Closed Sat and Sun.

A friendly restaurant in a quiet paved street at the foot of the imposing cathedral. It serves regional dishes that are simple and tasty: smoked trout salad with Puy lentils, duck with honey vinegar sauce and *aligot* (potatoes cooked with Tome du Cantal cheese). Desserts include *crème brûlee* with chestnut honey. Menus €15 and €20. Free coffee.

|O| RESTAURANT L'OLYMPE

8 rue du Collège (Centre); 200m from the Mairie and the Collegiate church.
☎ and ➡ 04.71.05.90.59
Closed Sun evening and Mon; Sun only in Aug; last week in March; first week in April; last week in Nov; first week in Dec.

A delightful restaurant in a cobbled alleyway in the conservation area. You'll get a warm welcome. The young chef sticks resolutely to local specialities but interprets them in his own, sometimes exotic, way; lentils, trout, game and verbena play star roles. In just a few years he's made this one of the best eating places in Puy. Menus €17–48 and a children's menu at €10.

|O| RESTAURANT TOURNAYRE

12 rue Chênebouterie (Centre); it's behind the town hall.
☎ 04.71.09.58.94 ➡ 04.71.02.68.38
Closed Sun and Wed evenings; Mon; Jan.

The exterior may be lovely, but the sixteenth-century vaulted dining room decorated with murals is simply magnificent – it's the most beautiful restaurant in Puy. The service is pleasant and unobtrusive and Eric Tournayre is a first-rate chef who creates imaginative dishes of a very high order: knuckle of veal,

croustillant of pig's trotters, *truffade* (potato cake with Cantal cheese) with a Saint-Agur sauce, *galette* of veal sweetbreads, pan-fried *foie gras* with ceps. A good range of desserts served in generous helpings. Menus at €18–38 include a vegetable option and a filling children's one for €11. Best to book in summer.

SAINT-VINCENT   43800 (18KM N)

🎿 |O| RESTAURANT LA RENOUÉE

Cheyrac; take the D103 that follows the gorges of the Loire.
☎ 04.71.08.55.94
Closed Sun evening and Mon except July–Aug; Jan–Feb; a week in Oct.

The most delightful place in the area. It's a romantic house in a tiny garden where you'll find a warm welcome and fine, imaginative cooking: zander with crispy onions, morels stuffed with duck *foie gras*, *fricassée* of pike with *velouté* of green lentils. Set menus €15–29 and children's menu €9. Nice set tea on Sunday afternoons. Free apéritif.

MOUDEYRES   43151 (20KM SE)

🎿 🏠 |O| LE PRÉ BOSSU***

It's at the beginning of the village on the D361.
☎ 04.71.05.10.21
Closed weekday lunchtimes and Nov to Palm Sunday.
Disabled access. Car park.

A cosy, characterful cottage in the middle of a field; the air is clean and it's very quiet. There are ten smart, comfortable rooms, some of which overlook the field; others have a view of the vegetable garden. Doubles with shower/wc €60, or €65 with bath. The red mullet with *ratatouille* and peach soup with coconut are particularly tasty. Menus for €28, a vegetarian one for €30 and others €39. Quick, efficient service. There's a pleasant terrace in summer. There are building projects in the pipeline so prices may rise from the ones listed here. 10% discount on the room rate April–June and Sept–Oct.

SAINT-JULIEN-CHAPTEUIL   43260 (20KM E)

🎿 |O| RESTAURANT VIDAL

pl. du Marché; take the D15.
☎ 04.71.08.70.50 ➡ 04.71.08.40.14
Closed Sun, Mon evening and Tues out of season; Mon evening in July–Aug. **Car park.**

Jean-Pierre Vidal is a brilliant and creative chef and one of the most important in the

Haute-Loire, though he modestly describes himself as "a country cook". All the menus, €18–53, display his exquisite skill, and he makes sure to use seasonal produce – game, wild mushrooms, duck and local beef. Courteous, attentive service in the quiet, pleasant dining room next to the bar. It's worth making the journey. Free coffee.

PONT-D'ALLEYRAS 43580 (29KM S)

🏠 I●I HÔTEL-RESTAURANT DU HAUT-ALLIER***

How to get there: take the D33.
☎ 04.71.57.57.63 ➡ 04.71.57.57.99
Closed Sun evening and Mon except high season and public holidays; Dec–Feb. **TV**. **Disabled access**.

This delightful hotel-restaurant, tucked away in a little village in the Haut-Allier valley, has been run by the same family for three generations – you'll get a warm welcome. The building was renovated recently and the large restaurant has a classical décor. The elaborate cuisine is prepared by Philippe Brun Cacaud, a fine chef who specializes in regional dishes full of authentic flavours. There's a wide choice on the set menus, €19–73; the civet of mussels and the young rabbit with herbs are both excellent, or try the pigeon deglazed with honey vinegar. The simpler yet substantial menu du jour is served at speed in the bar or on the terrace. Well-stocked cellar. Doubles €46–53 with shower/wc or bath.

SAINT-HAON 43340 (29KM SW)

🏕 🏠 I●I AUBERGE DE LA VALLÉE**

Centre; take the N88 in the direction of Pradelles/Langogne, travel 7km on the D33 to Cayres and then take the D31.
☎ 04.71.08.20.73 ➡ 04.71.08.29.21
Closed Mon Oct–May; Jan to mid-March.

The village is out in the wilds at 970m and just a few kilometres away the Allier cascades down the rocks of a deep gorge. This rustic, welcoming inn stands in a square dominated by a church with an unusual tower. It has ten comfortable rooms, furnished with solid old furniture, at €35 for a double with shower/wc and €40 with bath. Nights are quiet. In the restaurant they serve a series of menus, €13–31, featuring the chef's specialities: duo of smoked trout and goose fillet with Puy lentils, veal escalope with mushrooms and cream, pear turnover. 10% discount on the room rate Sept–June.

RIOM 63200

I●I RESTAURANT L'ÂNE GRIS

13 rue Gomot (Centre).
☎ 04.73.38.25.10
Closed Sun; Mon lunchtime; 15–30 Aug.

Whether you think this place is insane, ghastly or heaven on earth will depend on how you feel about the owner, Casimir. He's slightly mad but ever so nice – forever making jokes at his customers' expense. He used to just call his chef "baboon" but now he uses the nickname for his favourite customers, too. To hear him talk, you might think the food wasn't up to much, but the kitchen produces good traditional dishes: truffade (potato cake with Cantal cheese or ham), aligot (fried potato cakes with Aligot cheese and sausage), salt pork with lentils and Charolais steaks. Brilliant list of local wines which Casimir chooses with a genuine passion. No set menus; you'll pay €17–20 à la carte. A great place if you're prepared for Casimir's outsized personality.

TOURNOËL 63530 (1.5KM N)

🏕 🏠 I●I HÔTEL-RESTAURANT LA CHATELLENIE

It's on the D986.
☎ 04.73.33.63.23
Closed Wed out of season and mid-Oct to end March.

Located on the road going up to Tournoël, this hotel is peaceful and the rooms overlook the valley. Doubles €27 with shower, €31 with shower/wc and €34–38 with bath/wc. The dining room is decorated in rustic style and has a panoramic view. In it you'll find wholesome local dishes: ceps in pastry, potée, coq au vin, trout with smoked bacon, duck breast with ceps, a good blanquette of veal kidneys and sweetbreads. Menus at €14–24 offer regional specialities and portions are generous. Children's menu €8. Friendly service. Free apéritif.

EFFIAT 63260 (27KM NE)

🏕 I●I LE CINQ MARS

Lieu-dit Les Peytoux; it's a hamlet between Chardonnières-les-Vieilles and Blot-l'Eglise.
☎ 04.73.97.44.17
Closed lunchtimes; Fri and Sat evenings; 11 March–25 March; 16–31 Aug.

Behind a deceptively anodyne exterior lies a very good restaurant, formerly owned by the chef's mother-in-law. The man himself has worked with some of the greats, including a Michelin star recipient, and his cooking is excellent. The generous, expertly prepared dishes use the season's best ingredients: highlights include *coq au vin*, salmon *tartare*, frogs' legs, salmon croquettes, Auvergnat soup and fillet of cod with creamed lentils. Modestly priced dishes of *charcuterie* are served with Auvergne wine. Menus are €9, €17 and €21 in the week and €20–24 at weekends. Wonderful welcome. It's best to book. Free coffee.

SAIGNES   15240

🕊 🏠 |●| HÔTEL RELAIS ARVERNE*

Centre; it's on the main square.
☎ 04.71.40.62.64 ➡ 04.71.40.61.14
📧 info@hotel-relais-arverne.com
Hotel closed Feb school holidays and the first fortnight in Oct. **Restaurant closed** Fri and Sun evenings out of season. **TV. Car park**.

This stone building has a huge corner watchtower and the tables on the terrace are made from ancient stone wheels. The bedrooms are comfortable and accessed via the terrace, so you can come and go as you please. Doubles €37 with shower, €40 with shower/wc and €41 with bath. The hotel is full of interesting nooks and crannies. The dining room, where they serve dishes from the Dordogne and elsewhere, has a big clock and a huge fireplace. Specialities include monkfish with bilberries, *escalope* of *foie gras* with a cider sauce, mutton tripe *bonne femme*, veal sweetbreads in flaky pastry with morels, grilled steak *au bleu* and calf's liver with port caramel. Menus €11–34. Free apéritif.

SAINT-ANTHÈME   63660

🕊 🏠 |●| HÔTEL-RESTAURANT AU PONT DE RAFFINY**

It's 4km along the Saint-Romain road.
☎ 04.73.95.49.10 ➡ 04.73.95.80.21
Closed Sun evening and Mon out of season, weekdays in March and 1 Jan–15 Feb. **TV. Disabled access. Car park**.

If you're looking for a gourmet meal, head for this place, located on the banks of a little river near Saint-Anthème. The main attraction is Alain Beaudoux's light, creative cooking, typified by *andouillette* of fish with shellfish *coulis*, young rabbit *en crépine*,

croustillant of guinea fowl with morels and verbena *parfait*. €12 weekday menu and others up to €26. Excellent wine list with reasonable prices. The hotel is quiet and comfortable, and rooms with shower/wc or bath cost €34–39. They've built some single-storey bungalows with facilities for disabled visitors, which are available by the week. 10% discount on the room rate Sept–June.

CHAULME (LA)   63660 (10KM S)

🕊 🏠 |●| AUBERGE DU CREUX DE L'OULETTE

By the D67 then the 258.
☎ 04.73.95.41.16 ➡ 04.73.95.80.83
📧 auberge.oulette@wanadoo.fr
Closed Tues evening, Wed and 15 Nov–1 March. **Swimming pool. Car park**.

This village hotel has recently been renovated, and it's an ideal spot if you want to go hiking in the region – the owners are a dynamic pair who have organized discovery trails for you to follow. Double rooms with shower/wc €34. The chef is passionate about cooking and his wholesome family dishes have a good reputation locally; expect to be offered snail stew with mushrooms, fish fillet with Fourme cheese sauce or *coq au vin*. Menus €9–26. You can eat on the terrace in summer. Free apéritif and 10% discount on the room rate.

SAINT-FLOUR   15100

🏠 |●| HÔTEL-RESTAURANT DES ROCHES**

pl. d'Armes; it's opposite the museum.
☎ 04.71.60.09.70. ➡ 04.71.60.45.21
📧 fillesgauthier@wanadoo.fr
Closed Sat and Sun out of season. **TV**.

Very central place with bright, pleasant bedrooms priced at €34–40. You'll be warmly greeted. Classic and regional styles dominate in the restaurant: *bavette* steak with blue Auvergne cheese sauce, John Dory with fresh tomato sauce, *potée Auvergnate*, truffade, aligot and so on. Menus €9–27. They're not clock-watchers here: if you turn up at 9pm they'll still be happy to serve you.

🕊 🏠 |●| AUBERGE DE LA PROVIDENCE**

1 rue du Château-d'Alleuze (South).
☎ 04.71.60.12.05 ➡ 04.71.60.33.94
📧 auberge.provence@free.fr
Closed Mon lunchtime, Fri and Sun evenings out of

season; 1 Nov–1 Dec. **TV**. **Garden**. **Car park**.

This old inn has been completely refurbished. The décor is generally low key and the ten rooms are decorated in pastel shades; all have good bathrooms. Doubles €43 with shower/wc. Set menus, €17–27, offer some of the best value in town: quail fillet with mushroom sauce, St Nectaire cheese tart, morels in season. Free apéritif.

SAINT-GEORGES   15100 (4KM SE)

🏠 |●| HÔTEL-RESTAURANT LE BOUT DU MONDE**

Le Bout du Monde.
☎ 04.71.60.15.84 ➡ 04.71.73.05.10
e jean.pierre.albisson@wanadoo.fr
Closed Sun evening out of season. **Swimming pool**.
TV. **Disabled access**. **Garden**. **Car park**.

As its name says, this place is indeed at the end of the world, deep in a valley in the countryside outside Saint-Flour – ideal for anglers and walkers. The restaurant serves a range of delicious regional specialities. Menus (€10–24) feature *tourte de caillé* (curds), *pounti* (a mixture of bacon and Swiss chard), stuffed rabbit with cabbage, black pudding salad with walnuts, scallops and prawns with a hazelnut *tuile*, quail in pastry with Armagnac, duck breast with blackberries and *millefeuille* with spiced bread and ice-cream. Simple, well-maintained rooms cost €35 with shower/wc or €36 with en-suite bath.

GARABIT   15320 (12KM SE)

🦌 🏠 |●| HÔTEL-RESTAURANT BEAU SITE**

How to get there: take exits 30 or 31 on the A75.
☎ 04.71.23.41.46 ➡ 04.71.23.46.34
e garabitbeausite@wanadoo.fr
Closed Nov–March. **Swimming pool**. **TV**. **Disabled access**. **Garden**. **Car park**.

The hotel looks down on Eiffel's viaduct (he of tower fame), and you get wonderful views of the lake. It's a huge building with bright, roomy doubles for €34 with shower/wc or €35 with bath. Excellent facilities include a heated swimming pool and tennis courts in wonderful surroundings: an excellent base for fishing, windsurfing and long walks. The restaurant serves classic French dishes and gourmet cuisine. Set menus, €9–33, list specialities such as *chiffonade* with two types of Cantal cheese, liver escalope in its juices and frogs' legs *provençal*. Free apéritif or coffee. 10% discount on the room rate April–June and Sept–Oct and free use of the lock-up car park.

SAINT-GERVAIS-D'AUVERGNE   63390

🦌 🏠 |●| LE RELAIS D'AUVERGNE**

Route de Châteauneuf-les-Bains (Centre).
☎ 04.73.85.70.10 ➡ 04.73.85.85.66
e relais.auvergne.hotel@wanadoo.fr
Closed 25 Dec–1 March. **TV**. **Car park**.

A good place in the middle of the village, with an orange-tinted façade. It's run by an energetic and friendly young couple. Bedrooms are regularly decorated and new facilities added – all have feather eiderdowns and hairdryers. Doubles €37 with en-suite bath. The dining room is cosy and there's a huge chimney piece where they light an open fire in winter. Honest, traditional food: *tripoux*, *truffade* (potato cake with Cantal cheese), chicken *aiguillette* with Fourme cheese, stuffed cabbage and pork knuckle with lentils. Menus, €12–28, are good value. Half board costs €37 per person. One free breakfast per room per night.

🏠 |●| HÔTEL-RESTAURANT CASTEL HÔTEL 1904**

rue du Castel (Centre).
☎ 04.73.85.70.42 ➡ 04.73.85.84.39
Closed 1 Jan–15 March. **TV**. **Car park**.

This house first belonged to Monsieur de Maintenon, the husband of Louis XIV's most influential mistress, then to the monks of Cluny. More recently, it's been in the same family since 1904 and if you have a taste for the simple pleasures of days gone by, you'll enjoy the genuine feel of this place. There are two restaurants: the tiny *Comptoir à Moustaches* is open every day and serves traditional cuisine based on local produce. The second, closed on Monday and Tuesday, serves gourmet cuisine delicately prepared by Jean-Luc Mouty, who trained with Robuchon. It's cooking from a lost age: *pavé* of zander with cider, *fondant* of cabbage with stewed young rabbit, *cromesquis* of veal sweetbreads (fried and battered), tomato salad with fresh chanterelles. Menus start at €13 and go up to €46. The hotel is spacious and very quiet, and the refurbished rooms are affordable at €57 for a double with shower/wc or bath.

🦌 |●| CAFÉ TALLEYRAND, CHEZ MARIE

Lieu-dit Talleyrand-Saint-Gervais; it's 3km on the D531 to Queuille, going towards the dam.
☎ 04.73.85.78.47
Closed Tues and Thurs evenings. **Car park**.

This remote farm on the road leading to the

dam is a special place. For lunch or dinner there's an appetizing €10 *menu du jour*, or you could have a plate of delicious *charcuterie*, or perhaps an omelette made with eggs from the farm's own chickens. But if you want to sample some of Marie's fabulous specialities – potato cake, stuffed rabbit and game in season – you'll have to give her a call the night before to place your order. A glass of Auvergne costs only €1. Free coffee.

SERVANT   63560 (6KM E)

🎋 🏠 |●| HÔTEL-RESTAURANT LE BEAU SITE*

Gorges de la Sioule; take the N144 from Menat then the D915 for Gorges de Chauvigny.
☎ 04.73.85.50.65
Closed Wed and Thurs out of season; Feb; Jan reservations only.

Located in a really wonderful place which you reach on the road that follows the Sioule, this is a perfect place to stay while you explore the area and do a bit of fishing. Six double rooms cost from €26 with shower up to €38 with bath/wc. You can have a meal or just a drink on the terrace overlooking the river. Menus €14–37, one of which lists only house specialities: Rocquefort *terrine* with chestnuts, *pochouse* (a freshwater fish stew), veal with grain mustard sauce and iced *nougat* with sour cherries. The gastronomic menu includes a meat and a fish course. Free house apéritif.

SAINT-MARTIN-SOUS-VIGOUROUX   15230

🎋 🏠 |●| LE RELAIS DE LA FORGE*

Centre; take the D990; it's west of Pierrefort.
☎ 04.71.23.36.90 ➡ 04.71.23.92.48
Closed Wed out of season. **Lock-up car park**.

A simple, welcoming country hotel with a restaurant that has a very substantial *menu du jour* for €12. It includes a selection of *charcuterie* and dishes such as farm-bred quail and *truffade* (potato cake with Cantal cheese). Other menus €9–27. Ten clean and simple rooms, yours for €31 with shower/wc or bath. Half board costs €29. There's a lock-up for bikes and motorcycles. Free apéritif.

SAINT-POURÇAIN-SUR-SIOULE   03500

🎋 🏠 |●| HÔTEL-RESTAURANT LE CHÊNE VERT**

35 bd. Ledru-Rollin (Centre).

☎ 04.70.45.40.65 ➡ 04.70.45.68.50
Closed 7 Jan–21 Feb. **Restaurant closed** Sun evening and Mon out of season; 7 Jan–4 Feb. **TV**. **Pay car park**.

An unmissable landmark, across from the river Sioule, on the main road through the town. It's a classic, conventional establishment with excellent facilities at decent prices. Pleasant rooms with fresh décor cost €43 for a double with shower/wc or €46 with bath. Good traditional cooking with lots of game in season, served in an attractive dining room; menus €15–34. Free coffee.

SAINT-URCIZE   15110

🎋 🏠 |●| HÔTEL-RESTAURANT REMISE

In the village; take the D12 then the D112.
☎ and ➡ 04.71.23.20.02
Closed Mon evening. **Disabled access**. **Car park**.

A good country inn that's very popular with anglers, hunters and cyclists. The home cooking is wonderful and dishes of the day (€8) might be *aligot*, nettle soup or trout – it all depends on what's good in the market. Menus €11–13. Since so many anglers stay here, they make up picnic baskets to see you through a day's fishing. The owner can probably tell you anything you want to know about the region, from local history to the best walks and places to visit. Friendly, easygoing atmosphere. Doubles €34. Free house apéritif and 10% discount on the room rate.

SALERS   15140

🎋 🏠 |●| HÔTEL DU BEFFROI**

rue du Beffroi (Centre); it's in the old town.
☎ 04.71.40.70.11 ➡ 04.71.40.70.16
Closed 31 Nov–31 March. **TV**. **Car park**.

This old building, which was renovated not so long ago, looks onto a busy pedestrianized street. It has ten bedrooms at €38 for a double with shower/wc or bath, with some small, well laid-out attic rooms that have a rooftop view. Substantial regional menus – €10 at lunch and others €14–18 – feature *truffade* (potato cake with Cantal cheese), *potée*, *pounti* (a mixture of bacon and Swiss chard), Salers beef and duck stew with chestnuts. Being too small for groups, the place specializes in looking after independent travellers and there's a good friendly atmosphere. Free house apéritif and 10% discount on the room rate 1 April–1 June and 15 Sept–12 Nov.

🕏 |●| LE DRAC

pl. Tyssandiers-d'Escous (Centre).
☎ 04.71.40.72.12

In the early 1900s this early sixteenth-century house was used as a cellar for maturing Salers cheese, and now it's a restaurant. It's tucked away in the nicest part of this well-preserved medieval town, which swarms with tourists at the height of the season. The house has been in the family for nine generations, so you'll feel a sense of that history. Good regional dishes on the €11 set menu and a dish of the day plus pizzas, salads and ice-cream. They specialize in foreign beers and there's also a tearoom and a *crêperie*. It really buzzes in summer, but the staff are friendly and the service is fast. Free house *digestif*.

THEIL (LE)   15140 (3KM W)

🕏 ⬛ |●| HOSTELLERIE DE LA MARONNE***

Centre; take the D680 or the D37.
☎ 04.71.69.20.33
e hotelmaronne@cfi15.fr
Swimming pool. **Garden**. **TV**. **Car park**.

A substantial nineteenth-century Auvergnat residence that has been tastefully renovated by a talented designer. Part of the *Relais du Silence* group, it's set among the greenery of a wide park and has a garden, swimming pool, tennis court and a peerless view over the valley. Monsieur Decock keeps thinking up new ideas while Madame, the chef, toils to produce the highest quality cuisine: zander in salted butter, braised and stuffed vegetables and warm cake with bitter chocolate. Menus €26–46. A classy place, reflected in the price of the rooms: doubles €79–113 with bath/wc. Free apéritif.

FALGOUX (LE)   15380 (16KM NE)

🕏 ⬛ |●| HÔTEL-RESTAURANT L'ÉTERLOU**

Centre; take the D680 or the D37.
☎ 04.71.69.51.14 ➡ 04.71.69.53.26
Closed 12 Nov–1 April. **TV**. **Disabled access**. **Garden**.

Halfway between Salers and Puy-Mary, this hotel is beautiful, traditional and very welcoming, and the restaurant serves up hearty portions of tasty dishes. The set menus, €11–25, give pride of place to Auvergne and the chef's own specialities – monkfish *à l'américaine*, zander with *beurre blanc*, pounti and stuffed cabbage. Bedrooms are

clean and pleasant; doubles with bath €38–56. Half board costs from €36 per person. Nice staff. Free apéritif.

SAUGUES   43170

🕏 ⬛ |●| LA TERRASSE**

cours Gervais (Centre).
☎ 04.71.77.83.10 ➡ 04.71.77.63.79
e laterrasse.denis@wanadoo.fr
Closed Sun evening and Mon out of season; Dec–Jan.
TV.

The owner is friendly and particularly attentive to his guests. Rooms have been refurbished, and doubles go for €42–55 with shower/wc or bath. The ones at the back are particularly quiet and have an uninterrupted view of the tour des Anglais. The brasserie serves classic dishes but the restaurant is a bit fancier, with specialities such as *croustillant* of calves' sweetbreads with ceps, upside-down tart with *foie gras* and apple, lamb noisettes with garlic and *délice glacé*. Set menus €19–26. Ultra-friendly service. Free apéritif.

THIERS   63300

🕏 ⬛ HÔTEL DE LA GARE

30 av. de la Gare; it's opposite the train station.
☎ 04.73.80.01.41 ➡ 04.73.80.01.41
Hotel closed 23 Aug–3 Sept. **Restaurant closed** Sun out of season

The cheapest and friendliest hotel in town, completely hidden under a covering of wisteria. Simple, clean rooms €14 with basin and €20 with shower or bath (wc on the landing). Friendly welcome and a small bar which closes at 7pm. Free apéritif or coffee and 10% discount for a stay of three nights or longer.

🕏 |●| RESTAURANT LE COUTELIER

4 pl. du Palais; it's in the middle of the old town.
☎ 04.73.80.79.59
Closed Mon evening except July–Sept; 3 weeks in June; a fortnight in Oct.

Thiers is the centre of France's cutlery industry and this restaurant is in a converted cutler's workshop. It's a museum and a restaurant in one, and they're both first-rate – there's an intriguing collection of old implements and knives displayed on the walls. Good classic dishes like Puy lentils with smoked bacon, sausage with cabbage, mutton tripe and *coq au vin*. Incredible value given the quality. Menus €11–23. Free apéritif.

PESCHADOIRES 63920 (4KM SW)

🎋 |O| RESTAURANT LA FERME DES TROIS CANARDS

Lieu-dit Biton; take the N89, then the D212 and head for Maringues – turn left at the sign and you'll find the restaurant 300m further along.
☎ 04.73.51.06.70
Closed Sun evening and a fortnight in early Jan.
Garden. **Car park**.

The most delightful place in the area. It's a beautifully renovated, single-storey farmhouse in the heart of the countryside but it's not far from the motorway exit. Dishes on the set menus at €20–49 are perfectly cooked and presented: pan-fried *foie gras*, snails with bacon, stewed oxtail and hot chocolate *fondant* with pistachios. Cheeses are matured to perfection and there are light, delicate desserts. Friendly, attentive staff. Terrace in summer. Free coffee.

TOURNEMIRE 15310

🎋 🏠 |O| AUBERGE DE TOURNEMIRE

rue principale; take the D60, the D160 and the D260 – you'll find it about 20km north of Aurillac.
☎ 04.71.47.61.28 ➡ 04.71.47.68.76
e louisfert@wanadoo.fr
Closed 10 Jan–3 Feb. **TV**. **Garden**.

In one of Cantal's prettiest villages, you'll find this delightful inn set on the side of a hill; the views of the valley are gorgeous, especially at sunset. The six simple bedrooms are all well-maintained and one or two have lovely sloping ceilings. Doubles with shower/wc €34–38 and up to €56 with bath/wc. Good cooking in the restaurant, with Auvergnat dishes such as black pudding and a *fondue* of onions, *foie gras*, fillet steak with morels and lobster with vanilla sauce. Half board from €34 per person. By reservation only out of season. 10% discount on the room rate.

VICHY 03200

🎋 🏠 À L'HÔTEL DE NAPLES**

22 rue de Paris (Centre); it's opposite the station.
☎ 04.70.97.91.33 ➡ 04.70.97.91.28
TV. **Garden**. **Car park**.

The hotel, located in the most famous (and busiest) street in town, isn't luxurious but it does have modern facilities. Doubles €23 with basin/wc, €25–29 with shower/wc. Ask for a room overlooking the pretty garden, which is full of flowers in summer. Cordial welcome. They've done a deal with three nearby restaurants so they can offer half board for €27–40 per person. 10% discount on the room rate.

🎋 🏠 |O| HÔTEL DU RHÔNE**

8 rue de Paris (Centre).
☎ 04.70.97.73.00 ➡ 04.70.97.48.25
e hotel@hoteldurhone.fr
Closed 1 Nov to Easter. **TV**. **Disabled access**. **Car park**.

The owner is dynamic and quite a character; he'll cheerfully announce that he deliberately hasn't installed a lift so his guests get a bit of exercise. It's an elegant building with a cosy décor. The rooms are clean and simple – go for one overlooking the patio, which is particularly lovely when the hydrangeas are in flower. Doubles €27 with shower or €40 with shower/wc or bath. Menus range from €11 (weekday lunch) to €38 (gastronomic menu). The cooking features a variety of Auvergne and Normandy dishes: veal *escalope* flambéed with Calvados in a cream and mushroom sauce, sea bass with sorrel and ham on the bone in Saint-Pourçain wine – this isn't the place to begin your diet. Free house apéritif, coffee or *digestif* and 10% discount on the room rate Sept–May; state that you're using this guide when you book.

🎋 🏠 |O| LE PAVILLON D'ENGHIEN***

32 rue Callou; it's in the spa area of the town.
☎ 04.70.98.33.30 ➡ 04.70.31.67.82
Hotel closed Jan. **Restaurant closed** Sun evening and Mon. **Swimming pool**.

This hotel-restaurant has recently been renovated and offers some of the best value for money in town. The spacious double rooms, €38 with shower/wc and €46–73 with bath/wc, are individualized and sound-proofed. Weekday lunch menu €11, a *menu terroir* at €15 and others at €23. They do a good slab of Charolais beef with blue Auvergne cheese sauce, *marbré* of young rabbit with herbs, escalope of salmon in Saint-Pourçain and rather fine desserts. Nice swimming pool. 10% discount on the room rate.

🏠 |O| MIDLAND HÔTEL – RESTAURANT LE DERBY'S**

2–4 rue de l'Intendance (North).
☎ 04.70.97.48.48 ➡ 04.70.31.31.89
e hotelmidlandvichy@wanadoo.fr
Closed 15 Oct–15 April. **TV**. **Car park**.

This hotel has retained its warmth and turn-of-the-twentieth-century style. Some rooms are traditionally decorated, others are more modern, but in each case they're quiet and the facilities good. Doubles €46–49 with shower or €50–53 with bath/wc, colour TV and phone. The cuisine is varied and dishes are generously served. Every lunchtime there's a huge spread of *hors-d'œuvres* to choose from. Lunch *formule* for €12 and menus €8–17.

❙●❙ L'AUTRE SOURCE

10 rue du Casino (Centre).
☎ 04.70.59.85.68
Closed Sun, Mon and the first week in Sept.

They close around 11.30pm. Just behind the casino, this is probably the nicest and brightest restaurant in the centre of town – and a change from the "spa" feel you find in some places around here. The atmosphere is relaxed and cheerful and you can choose from inexpensive salads and sandwiches made mostly from local produce, as well as a cheese platter containing unusual varieties. A meal will cost around €9. It's also a wine bar, and Patrice chooses the wines himself; he'll gladly introduce you to the local vintages, some of which he serves by the glass at very reasonable prices.

⅍ ❙●❙ L'ENVOLÉE

44 av. E-Gilbert.
☎ 04.70.32.85.15
Closed Tues evening, Wed and the Feb and All Saints' school holiays. **Car park**.

Way off the traditional visitor track in Vichy, this restaurant is a nice surprise. The service and welcome are very agreeable but the fresh-flavoured cuisine is what you'll remember. The chef plays around with classic dishes: duck *foie gras* terrine with onion marmalade, crayfish sausage with cream of fennel sauce, veal kidneys with grain mustard, zander fillet with creamed nettles. The pear charlotte with raspberry *coulis* or the *millefeuille* of spiced bread served with jam would appeal to anyone. *Formule* at €12 and menus €16–21. Free glass of sparkling wine with dessert.

❙●❙ LA BRASSERIE DU CASINO

4 rue du Casino (Centre).
☎ 04.70.98.23.06 ➡ 04.70.98.53.17
Closed Sun evening, Wed and Nov. **Car park**.

This restaurant has got more character than any other in Vichy. Big prewar brasseries have a certain something, and this one, built in 1920, is no exception. The walls are covered

in photos of stars who used to dine here after performing at the opera house. The *à la carte* menu has a long list of classic dishes and balanced set menus are also available. The weekday lunch menu will cost you €14 and others €23 – they feature oven-roasted goat, calf's liver with onions and a killer chocolate dessert. They serve a special after-show dinner. Fairly priced wines. Free apéritif.

CUSSET   03300 (1KM E)

⅍❙●❙ LE BRAYAUD

64 av. de Vichy; it's on the outskirts coming from Vichy.
☎ 04.70.98.52.43
Closed Tues, Wed, a fortnight late Aug and one week end April.

This is where you come if you want to stay out late in Vichy, but more importantly it's the best place to eat meat around here. Exceptional steak – the *entrecôte* of Charolais beef weighs close on 400g and the *onglet* 300g. Lunch menu €9 or at €15, with a good variety of salads, a meat dish, cheese and dessert. There's nough to satisfy even the biggest appetites. Friendly staff. Free apéritif or coffee.

BELLERIVE-SUR-ALLIER   03700 (2KM SW)

⅍ 🏚 LA RIGON**

route de Serbannes.
☎ 04.70.59.86.46 ➡ 04.70.59.94.77
Closed Sun evening out of season, Dec and Jan.
Disabled access. Swimming pool. TV. Garden. Car park.

A little haven of peace and quiet up in the Bellerives hills above Vichy, just five minutes from the town centre. You'll get the best of both worlds here – the excellent service and hours you'd expect from a hotel and the intimacy of a good-quality guesthouse. It's a beautiful building, with its own extensive grounds and the bedrooms, decorated in a subtle tones, are all lovely. Doubles €46–55 with shower/wc or bath. Hearty breakfast for €6. Brilliant swimming pool in a large 1900s glasshouse. Very friendly welcome. 10% discount.

ABREST   03700 (3KM S)

⅍ 🏚 ❙●❙ LA COLOMBIÈRE

Route de Thiers; take the D906, it's 2km after Abrest.
☎ 04.70.98.69.15 ➡ 04.70.31.50.89
Closed Sun evening; Mon; mid-Jan to mid-Feb. **TV. Garden. Car park**.

An old dovecote converted into a restaurant and set high above the Allier. Menus €15 to

€46. The cuisine is imaginative and dishes change with the seasons, mixing tradition and new ideas: cock's comb salad, house *foie gras* terrine and fresh ox liver, duck breast, local chicken. The home-baked bread is excellent and served with an impressive selection of cheeses. Four huge, bright, charming bedrooms at €42 with shower/wc and €51 with bath. The ones decorated yellow and green have a lovely view of the river. Free apéritif or *digestif*.

MAYET-DE-MONTAGNE (LE)   03250 (23KM SE)

|●| LA VIEILLE AUBERGE

9 pl. de l'Église; take the D62.
☎ 04.70.59.34.01
Closed Mon evening in season, Wed out of season, three weeks in Jan, and the last fortnight in Sept.

Time seems to have stopped in this old inn, which stands near the church in this wonderful little village deep in the Bourbonnais mountains. Décor of stone and wood brightened up by posters. Traditional dishes: hot goat's cheese salad with almonds, duck *confit*, *coq au vin* and wonderful home-made desserts. *Menu campagnard* at €8 with a selection of *charcuterie*, sausage and ham; others €10–21. *À la carte* also available.

LAVOINE   03250 (30KM SE)

|●| AUBERGE CHEZ LILOU

Le Fau; take the D49.
☎ 04.70.59.37.49 ► 04.70.59.79.95
Closed evenings exept Sat and Sun July–Aug, four weeks over the All Saints' holidays and the last week in June. **Garden. Car park.**

Bookings by reservation only. The dark woods and mountain views are breathtaking at 1000m, where *Chez Lilou* is to be found. It's always crowded on Sunday, and has an extremely good reputation locally. It's a simple, unpretentious restaurant where they use exclusively local produce in the kitchen. Menus €13–15, plus a *menu ouvrier* at €9 – offering two starters, two main courses and a choice of cheeses or desserts. Try their *fino* (potatoes with bacon), *coq au vin*, charcuterie and bilberry tart. They're really kind people, and make you feel like one of the family.

VIC-SUR-CÈRE   15800

⁂ 🏠 |●| HÔTEL-RESTAURANT BEL HORIZON**

rue Paul Doumer.

☎ 04.71.47.50.06 ► 04.71.49.63.81
e info@hotel-bel-horizon.com
Closed 20 Nov–20 Dec and 4–25 Jan

A pleasant place on the edge of town where you'll get a warm greeting. It gets full at the weekends because the cooking is totally reliable. Menus €12–31 – the *menu du terroir* lists stuffed cabbage, *pounti* (a mixture of bacon and Swiss chard), trout with bacon and *coq au vin*. The chef rings the changes frequently, but his specialities are dishes such as salmon fillet with light-flavoured Cantal cheese, *coq au vin* and *foie gras*. The home-made ice creams are as delicious as the pear charlotte. The dining room is unprepossessing except for the big bay window. Rooms are comfortable, and cost €35 with shower/wc or bath. Free house apéritif.

VIEILLEVIE   15120

🏠 |●| HÔTEL LA TERRASSE**

rue principale; take the D141.
☎ 04.71.49.94.00 ► 04.71.49.92.23
e hoteldelaterrasse@wanadoo.fr
Closed 1 Jan–1 April. **Swimming pool. TV. Disabled access. Garden. Car park.**

At 200m, this hotel is apparently at a lower altitude than any other in Cantal. It's to be found between an eleventh-century château and the river Lot. Comfortable rooms priced at €39–44 for a double with shower/wc, €40–46 with bath/wc. Good outdoor facilities: shaded terrace, beautiful swimming pool, garden and tennis courts. You'll enjoy the cooking: specialities include char in wine sauce, pig's trotters *en crépine* and *feuillantine* of caramelized pears. Menus €9–24. Free house apéritif.

VITRAC   15220

⁂ 🏠 |●| L'AUBERGE DE LA TOMETTE**

Centre.
☎ 04.71.64.70.94 ► 04.71.64.77.11
e latomette@wanadoo.fr
Closed 15 Dec–Easter. **Swimming pool. TV. Disabled access. Car park.**

This is a delightful village inn set in a large flower-filled garden overlooking the countryside. The hotel is pleasant and has comfortable, ultra-modern double rooms at €47–57 depending on the season. A few duplexes are available for families and there's a new fitness centre. The cosy rustic dining room offers good hearty food and a choice of set menus at €15–32. Try the chef's specialities: fish *pot-au-feu*, vegetable stew *crépinette* of pig's trotters with chanterelles, Puy lentil terrine and traditional dishes such as stuffed cabbage, *truffade* (potato cake with Cantal cheese) and *potée*. Mme Chausi is friendly and helpful. Free apéritif.

YSSINGEAUX 43200

🏃 🏠 I●I AUBERGE AU CREUX DES PIERRES

It's in Fougères; 5km south of the town on the D152 in the direction of Queyrière.
☎ 04.71.59.06.81
Open Fri evening, Sat and Sun except at Christmas and during the winter holidays. **Restaurant closed** Mon and Tues except July–Aug. **Disabled access**. **Car park**.

A charming inn in a superbly renovated property that's surrounded by a lovely garden. They offer well-arranged rooms with views of the countryside and the volcanic peaks. Doubles with shower/wc for €32. The cui-sine is uncomplicated – tasty family dishes with seasonal veg, fresh starters, moist home-made tarts. Menus €11–14 and a kid's *formule* for €7. Excellent food matched by the winning smiles of the charming hosts. It's a favourite with walkers and cyclists.

🏃 🏠 I●I LE BOURBON**

5 pl. de la Victoire (Centre).
☎ 04.71.59.06.54 ➡ 04.71.59.00.70
✉ le.bourbon.hotel@wanadoo.fr
Closed Sun evening; Mon all year; and Friday evening except July and Aug. **TV**. **Car park**.

The hotel has been refurbished, but it may have lost some of its character in the process. Doubles €46 and a handsome dining room decorated in English-garden style. The kitchen serves regional dishes that have been re-thought and made considerably lighter. Set menus from €14 (not available Sun) to €37 to suit all tastes and pockets; like the *à la carte* menu, they change every three months. You'll find a list of local suppliers beside the dishes. A reliable and first-rate establishment. Free coffee.

BOURGOGNE

21 Côte-d'Or

58 Nièvre

71 Saône-et-Loire

89 Yonne

ANCY-LE-FRANC   89160

☎ |●| HOSTELLERIE DU CENTRE**

pl. du Château (Centre)
☎ 03.86.75.15.11 ✆ 03.86.75.14.13
✉ hostellerieducentre@diaphora.com
Closed 15 Nov–15 Mar. **Swimming pool. TV. Car park**.

In an old, much-refurbished building in the main street. The hotel looks quite classy but the atmosphere is easy-going.The cosy, restful bedrooms, decorated in pastel tones, are €45–52 with shower/wc or bath (half board is often compulsory, so check). The restaurant – the larger of the two dining rooms is the prettier – offers traditional local dishes including snails, veal kidneys in a wine sauce, and *andouillette en croûte* in a Chablis sauce. Set menus are as varied as the portions are generous. A weekday lunch menu is €13; others start from €18 and range up to €32. The terrace is opened when the weather gets fine and there's a heated indoor swimming pool.

CHASSIGNELLES   89160 (4KM SE)

☎ |●| HÔTEL DE L'ÉCLUSE No. 79

chemin de Ronde; take the D905 then take the small left turn.
☎ 03.86.75.18.51 ✆ 03.86.75.02.04
Closed mid-Dec to New Year. **TV**.

A delightful family-run country hotel alongside the banks of the Burgundy canal. Grandmother still runs the bar, which has a delightful terrace by the waterside, and her daughter runs the hotel. The rooms are charming and tastefully decorated at prices that are very reasonable for the region; dou-

bles with shower/wc or bath at €40. The cooking is done by the granddaughter, who specializes in local dishes: *œufs en meurette*, duck *bourguignon*, *terrine* of *andouillette*, and blackcurrant tart. Menus €15–24. You can hire bikes to ride along the towpath.

ARNAY-LE-DUC   21230

🎋 ☎ HÔTEL LE CLAIR DE LUNE**

4 rue du Four (Centre).
☎ 03.80.90.15.50 ✆ 03.80.90.04.64
✉ chez-camille@wanadoo.fr **TV. Car park**.

The Poinsot family, who also run *Chez Camille* (see below), originally had a few rooms over the restaurant but they were smart enough to open a proper hotel in the neighbouring street. This pretty, simple place is the result. It offers bright, modern and attractive accommodation at €27 for a double with shower/wc. They do an overnight option including dinner with a special menu and breakfast for €67 for two – you eat in the flower-filled conservatory. Or there's a gastronomic option at the hardly astronomic price of €104 for two. Otherwise menus are at €17, €32 and €76. Children under eleven eat and sleep for free.

🎋 |●| CHEZ CAMILLE***

1 pl. Édouard-Herriot (Centre).
☎ 03.80.90.01.38 ✆ 03.80.90.04.64
🌐 www.chezcamille.fr
TV. Car park.

This authentically old-fashioned inn with blue shutters, located at the foot of the old town, looks as if it's straight out of an operetta. Waitresses in flowery dresses enter the lounge,

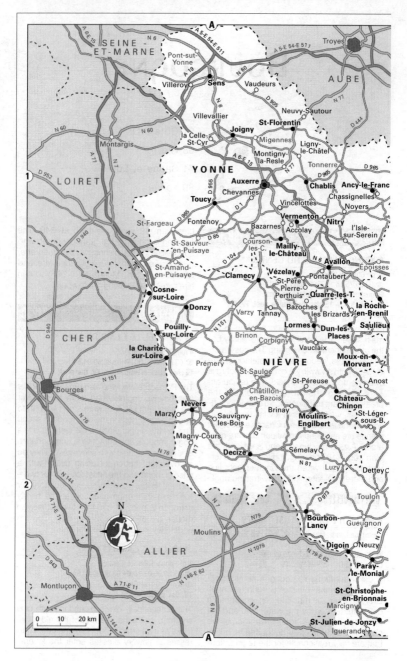

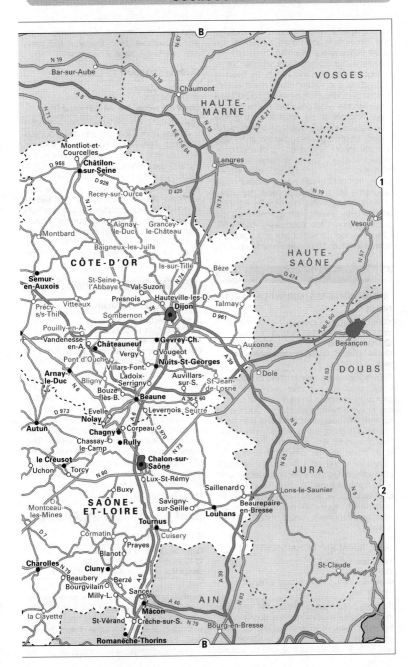

serving apéritifs with cheesy *choux* pastries and home-made ham before conducting you to the conservatory, which has been converted into a dining room. Here you can sit as though in a theatre and watch the ballet of sous-chefs and kitchen staff, which is performed on a kind of stage raised up behind a large window – on one side you've got the pastry kitchen, on the other an awning. The whole scene is enacted beneath a glass roof in a room full of pot plants and wicker armchairs. The cheapest menu at €17 is of traditional, refined cuisine – satisfying dishes like pan-fried duck *foie gras*, Burgundy snails in their shells, fillet of Charolais beef and *bœuf bourguignon* – which will tempt you to try others next time (at €32–75). The wine list is terrific, and the cellar is worth visiting. There are a few plush bedrooms, too; doubles with bath €69. Children under 11 eat for free and there's no charge for them if they share your room.

AUTUN   71400

𝔄 🏠 |◉| HÔTEL-RESTAURANT DE LA TÊTE NOIRE**

1–3 rue de l'Arquebuse (Centre).
☎ 03.85.86.59.99 ➡ 03.85.86.33.90
Ⓦ www.hoteltetenoire.fr
Closed 15 Dec–20 Jan. **TV**. **Disabled access**. **Car park**.

There's imposing frontage to this comfortable hotel, which gets prettier every year. The rooms are charming and a good deal of work has repaired the ravages of time. Doubles go for €49 with shower/wc and €52 with bath. The food is good, with a starter, main course and dessert for €11 and other menus up to €39. These change three times a year but always list sound, attractive dishes: hot duck pâté with orange sauce, fillet of Charolais beef with bone marrow, monkfish with green peppercorns, scallops, bread and butter pudding with apples. Wine is available by the glass and the carafe. Friendly reception. Free coffee.

𝔄 |◉| RESTAURANT CHATEAUBRIANT

14 rue Jeannin (Centre).
☎ 03.85.52.21.58
Closed Sun evening, Mon, a fortnight in Feb and three weeks in July.

Centrally positioned just behind the town hall, this reliable establishment offers quality cooking year in, year out. Classic dining room and decent reception. Set menus €12 (weekdays) and €19–34. Good meat specialities include

beef fillet, rack of lamb, *andouillette*, frogs' legs *Provençale*, fresh *foie gras* and salad with pan-fried prawns. Free coffee.

𝔄 |◉| RESTAURANT LE CHALET BLEU

3 rue Jeannin (Centre).
☎ 03.85.86.27.30
Closed Mon evening, Tues and a fortnight in Feb.

The exterior is nothing to write home about – in no way does it look like a chalet – but you can eat here with confidence. Philippe Bouché, who trained in the kitchens of the Elysée Palace, offers five set menus from €14 (weekdays only), then €21–€41. The cooking is gloriously imaginative: perch and frogs' legs with baby onions; pigeon breast; veal sweetbread rissoles with almond milk; tureen of Burgundy snails with wild mushrooms; Bresse chicken caramelized with sour cherry brandy and broad beans – and the helpings are generous. Wonderful dessert menu. Not to be missed. Free apéritif.

SAINT-LÉGER-SOUS-BEUVRAY 71990 (20KM W)

𝔄 🏠 |◉| HÔTEL DU MORVAN

pl. de la Mairie (Centre); take the D3.
☎ 03.85.82.51.06 ➡ 03.85.82.45.07
ⓔ hotel.du.morvan@wanadoo.fr
Closed Mon evening and Tues out of season, Tues lunchtime in summer, and mid-Nov to mid-Feb.

This little village hotel, in the increasingly depopulated Morvan region, survives by keeping its prices reasonable and by prioritizing the comfort and well-being of its guests. A good base for climbing Mont-Beuvray. Seven bedrooms with a wonderful country feel; €30 with handbasin or €37 with shower/wc. The owner, Mme Els O'Sullivan, has a great sense of hospitality and she serves good regional cooking; menus €9–24 and children's menu €7. 10% discount on the room rate for two nights or more July–Aug.

ANOST   71550 (22KM NW)

🏠 HÔTEL FORTIN**

Centre; take the D978, then the D2
☎ 03.85.82.71.11 ➡ 03.85.82.79.62
Closed Mon except July–Aug; Feb. **TV**. **Car park**.

This hotel in the Morvan national park has an interesting history. The owner's an extremely friendly guy who travelled the world before returning to his native land. He then played a vital role in giving a new lease of life to the village – which, like so many others in the region, is threatened by decay and depopulation – by setting up this little hotel with its ancillary bar, restaurant and travellers' lodge. It's basic, clean and inexpensive, and no two rooms are alike. Tourists and walkers enjoy meeting for a drink in the friendly ground-floor bar – a little oasis of conviviality in the middle of the Morvan tundra. The owner also runs *La Galvache* (see below). Doubles with shower €34; with bath €40.

|●| LA GALVACHE

Grand-rue.
☎ 03.85.82.70.88
Open Easter to 11 Nov.

A wonderful little village restaurant, run by the owner of the *Hotel Fortin*, offering generous helpings of terrific regional cooking. Their €11 *menu du jour* (not served Sunday lunch) is amazing value for money. Dishes include *terrine*, zander fillet *à la Bourguignonne*, escalope of salmon with a leek *fondue*, delicious crayfish *à l'Américaine*, Charolais steak and *croustade* of veal sweetbreads with morels. And there's soft cream cheese to finish, of course. Other menus €14–27.

DETTEY   71190 (28KM S)

⅍ 🏠 |●| RELAIS DE DETTEY

Centre; take the D994, then the D224.
☎ 03.85.54.57.19 ➡ 03.85.54.57.09
Closed Mon evening and 15 Dec–15 Jan.
Disabled access. TV. Car park.

Situated in one of the smallest villages of the Saône-et-Loire and at the top of one of its highest "mountains", this inn is a must. Good reasons to come include the charm of the village and the inn, and the delicious regional cooking. You'll get a friendly reception from Daniel and Monique. He's in charge of the dining room – a cosy, low-ceilinged room with two enormous exposed beams and a big fireplace – while she takes care of the cooking. It's popular with families for Sunday lunch. Everything is tasty and served in generous helpings, and the limited choice makes it easier to make up your mind. The cheapest menu at €11 is served every day (including weekends) and there are others from €15 to €26. Dishes include panfried frogs' legs with Aligoté wine, duck confit with honey and four spices, snails *au gratin*. On fine days you can eat on the terrace in the shade of the church while the horses frolic opposite. If you want to stay, there's only one room – a big studio with its own entrance, almost like a two-roomed flat with a bedroom, a lounge that sleeps two

extra people, a large bathroom and really nice décor. It costs €38 for two. 10% discount on the room rate for a two-night stay.

AUXERRE   89000

⅍ 🏠 HÔTEL NORMANDIE**

41 bd. Vauban (West).
☎ 03.86.52.57.80 ➡ 03.86.51.54.33
🌐 www.acom.fr/normandie
Disabled access. TV. Pay car park. Garden.

Surrounded by a small garden, this large bourgeois house dates from the late 19th century. It's named after a famous French liner, and the atmosphere in the elegant, slightly dated hotel (complete with uniformed night porter) is indeed reminiscent of a luxury transatlantic cruise ship. The stylishly furnished rooms are very comfortable and extremely well looked after. Prices range from €51 to €73 for a double room with shower/wc or bath. A gym, sauna and billiard room are also at your disposal. There's a lock-up garage for cars and bikes. 10% discount for a stay of two nights or more.

|●| LE JARDIN GOURMAND

56 bd. Vauban; it's in the pedestrian precinct, 50m from the Carrefour de Paris.
☎ 03.86.51.53.52
📧 le.jardin.gourmand.auxerre@wanadoo.fr
Closed Tues, Wed, 25 Feb–13 Mar and 12 Nov–4 Dec.
Disabled access. Car park.

The chef here is an artist and frequently makes sketches of his dishes. His cooking is very inventive, too, and the service is perfection itself – the staff will guide you expertly through an *à la carte* menu that changes according to the whims of the chef and the season. The cheapest menu costs €29 and others are at €38 and €44, all offering an ideal introduction to what is truly imaginative cooking. The menus change eight times a year but here's a taster: rabbit in sage jelly, Charolais beef steak, veal shin with vegetables and morels. They have a small selection of Burgundies. The dining room is cosy, and there's a nice terrace for good weather. Best to book.

CHEVANNES   89240 (8KM SW)

⅍ 🏠 |●| LA CHAMAILLE***

La Barbotière – 4 route de Boiloup. From Auxerre, take the Nevers-Bourgnes road then the D1.
☎ 03.86.41.24.80 ➡ 03.86.41.34.80
🌐 www.la-chamaille.com

Closed Mon evening and Tues 1 March–31 Sept, Mon and Tues 1 Oct–28 Feb, Sun evening, Mon and Tues 14 Nov–15 Dec and 2–18 Jan. **Car park**.

An excellent place located in the middle of wonderful scenery within minutes of Auxerre. It's in an old turreted farm smelling reassuringly of polish, with a little stream running through the garden where ducks splash about. There's an open fire when the weather gets cold. The cooking is traditional but shows considerable skill and the ingredients are first-rate. A weekday menu is available for €23 and a range of others from €35 to €56. Familiar ingredients are combined with unusual new ones: skate with potato croustille and sesame jus; pork and vegetable stew with coconut milk. Wine is by the glass at prices that won't make you wince. Two doubles with shower €38 or €46 with shower/wc. Free coffee and 10% discount on the room rate 1 Oct–30 April.

MONTIGNY-LA-RESLE 89230 (12KM NE)

🏃 🏠 |O| HÔTEL-RESTAURANT LE SOLEIL D'OR**

How to get there: on the N77.
☎ 03.86.41.81.21 ➡ 03.86.41.86.88
Disabled access. **TV**. **Car park**.

The hotel and restaurant are housed in old farmhouses that have been comprehensively renovated. The rather pretty bedrooms with shower/wc or bath cost €50. The kitchen turns out classical dishes that are consistent in quality and sometimes show a touch of imagination. The weekday lunch menu, €12, includes a ¼ litre of wine; others range between €15 and €50. Try the pan-fried *foie gras* with bananas and runny caramel, pigeon with sweet cider or crayfish tails with Imperial Mandarin liqueur. Wine by the glass is rather expensive. Essential to book in the hotel. Free apéritif.

VINCELOTTES 89290 (14KM SE)

🏠 |O| AUBERGE LES TILLEULS

12 quai de l'Yonne.
☎ 03.86.42.22.13 ➡ 03.86.42.23.51
Closed Wed evening and Thurs Oct–Easter (just Weds the rest of the year); 20 Dec–20 Feb. **TV**.

A lovely place to stop near Irancy and Saint-Bris-le-Vineux overlooking the Yonne and shaded by lime trees. Doubles with shower/wc at €49 or €65 with bath. When the weather is dismal the restaurant, which is full of flowers and paintings, will cheer you up. And if the weather's fine, sit on the shady

waterside terrace. The cooking, like the chef, has considerable character and the dishes change constantly. Dishes feature unusual produce like Chinese artichokes, Jerusalem artichokes and swedes that the chef ferrets out on the market in Auxerre. He chooses the freshest and best, and uses wild rather than farmed fish. The €22 menu is served on weekdays before 1.30pm and 8.30pm or other menus are €36–44. The select location is matched by a charming welcome.

AVALLON 89200

🏃 🏠 |O| HÔTEL-RESTAURANT DES CAPUCINS

6 av. Paul-Doumer; the road leads to the station.
☎ 03.86.34.06.52 ➡ 03.86.34.58.47
Closed Tues and Wed out of season, Wed in season.
TV. **Private car park**.

The bright dining room is decorated with a collection of biscuit barrels in glass and opaline, and the remarkable cooking is prepared by a chef who's a real pro. He makes everything himself – from the *foie gras* to the *nougat* – and gets his ingredients and produce from local suppliers. There's a weekday menu at €14 and others are €20–40. Wines served by the glass. Although the rooms are all different, they're quiet – even the ones overlooking the road. Doubles with handbasin €29; with bath €46. Free coffee and 10% discount 1 Nov–28 Feb.

🏃 🏠 DAK'HÔTEL**

119 rue de Lyon, étang des Minimes (Southeast); it's on the edge of town, on the Dijon road.
☎ 03.86.31.63.20 ➡ 03.86.34.25.28
Disabled access. **TV**. **Car park**.

New hotel with all mod cons. The warmth of the reception makes up for the starkness of the building. Lots of little extras such as tea or coffee, a magazine, a chocolate on your pillow – at no extra cost. No restaurant, but you can order a snack meal and there's a buffet breakfast for €6. Doubles with bath from €49. Free coffee.

🏃 |O| RELAIS DES GOURMETS

47 rue de Paris; it's 200m from the main square.
☎ 03.86.34.18.90
📧 relaisdesgourmets@wanadoo.fr
Closed Sun evening and Mon, 1 Nov–1 May. **Car park**.

This used to be the *Hôtel de Paris* in the days when Avallon was still a staging post and – unlike its contemporaries, which have long since disappeared – it's found a new lease of life. It's no longer a hotel but you can have a good meal in a pleasant atmosphere. Set menus €14 (served daily except Easter Sun) and €20–58. The chef prepares fish with as much skill as he does the meat from neighbouring Charolais herds. There's a terrace in summer. Free coffee.

ISLE-SUR-SEREIN (L')   89440 (15KM NE)

🕊 ✿ |●| AUBERGE DU POT D'ÉTAIN

24 rue Bouchardat (Centre).
☎ 03.86.33.88.10 ➡ 03.86.33.90.93
Closed Sun evening except July–Aug; Mon; Feb and 3 weeks in Oct. **TV**. **Pay car park**.

This charming and tiny country inn is one of the best places to eat in the entire region. There's a new team in the kitchen – a pair of chefs and a pastry chef, all of whom trained in Michelin-cockaded kitchens. The cooking is a mixture of the traditional and the modern. There's a *menu du jour* at €17 (not available Sun), and other menus are €22–49. They have the most fantastic cellar – the spectacular wine list features about 900 vintages. Nine pleasant rooms, ranging from €43 for a double with shower/wc to €64 for a small suite. The charming ones at the back of the flower-filled courtyard are quieter. Free coffee.

BEAUNE   21200

🕊 ✿ HÔTEL GRILLON***

21 route de Seurre (East).
☎ 03.80.22.44.25 ➡ 03.80.24.94.89
Closed Feb.

It's difficult to see why people make do with chain hotels when, in a charming place like this, you can fall into bed after a visit to the wine cellar and wake up to the sound of chirping birds. The rooms in this old family house have style and all are decorated with a modern touch: doubles €45–46 with shower and €48–55 with bath. In the summer you can eat breakfast in the garden or on the terrace. 10% discount Dec–March.

🕊 ✿ LE HOME**

138 route de Dijon (North); it's at the Beaune-Sud exit of the A31, on the outskirts of Beaune, going towards Dijon.
☎ 03.80.22.16.43 ➡ 03.80.24.90.74
Disabled access. TV. Garden. Car park.

It's rather hard to spot this old Burgundian house, swathed in Virginia creeper – it's tucked away at the bottom of a garden. It

makes a very pleasant place to stop, and this an ideal spot in which to relax. The décor may raise a few eyebrows but the welcome is as charming as the location. Two annexes have bedrooms that lead straight out into the garden. €52–64 for a double with shower/wc or bath. 10% discount Dec–March.

🕊 ✿ |●| HÔTEL CENTRAL***

2 rue Victor-Millot (Centre).
☎ 03.80.24.77.24 ➡ 03.80.22.30.40
e hotel.central.beaune@wanadoo.fr
Closed 20 Nov–20 Dec. **TV**.

An aptly named hotel that everyone – from trendy motorcyclists to fun-loving couples – enjoys. Spacious bedrooms with good facilities at €63–75 with shower/wc or bath. The cooking (which might look a bit austere, but isn't) also enjoys a good reputation. The owner has delved into his history books, unearthing 17th- and 18th-century dishes which he interprets in his own way. Try the *coq au vin à l'ancienne* or the *oeufs en meurette à l'andouille*. Menus €22–38. 10% discount on the room rate.

|●| AU BON ACCUEIL

La Montagne. Take the D970, turn right, and at the Beaune exit head towards La Montagne.
☎ 03.80.22.08.80
Closed Mon and Tues evening, Wed, 4–13 March, 21 Aug–5 Sept and 23–31 Dec. **Car park**.

The town centre often features more tourists than locals. But this restaurant, barely a kilometre from the Hospices, is a thoroughly local preserve. It's filled with families at Sunday lunchtime, when the menu includes *terrine*, *crudités* and *pâté* (as much as you can manage) and their star dish, roast beef, followed by a cheese platter and home-made tart. Other specialities include snails, beef with morels, *coq au vin* and iced Vacherin. Menus €11 (weekdays) and €20–40. Bask in the warm reception and, in summer, on the wonderful tree-shaded terrace.

|●| RESTAURANT LE P'TIT PARADIS

25 rue Paradis (Centre).
☎ 03.80.24.91.00
Closed Mon evening, Tues, 19 Nov–3 Dec, last week in Feb, the first week in March and 12–20 Aug.

Beaune's road to paradise was a gastronomic purgatory until this restaurant opened opposite the Musée du Vin. It's painted in colours as fresh as the cooking, which is very reasonably priced. Jean-Marie Daloz is a fine chef: cream of snails with Aligoté and creamed garlic, crayfish salad with orange butter, chicken breast stuffed with spiced bread and Charolais steak with époisses butter are particular highlights. Weekday menu at €11 and others at €15–26. Choice of wines at equally good prices. Terrace in summer.

I●I RESTAURANT LA CIBOULETTE

69 rue de Lorraine (Centre); it's in the old part of town, opposite the theatre.
☎ 03.80.24.70.72
Closed Mon, Tues, Feb and a fortnight in Aug.

The renovated premises are small and the décor is restrained. Two well-priced set menus (€16 and €21) bring in tourists and locals alike, which is reassuring. Choose between sautéed rabbit with fresh thyme and grain mustard mash, cod with tomato and fresh mint coulis, veal chops with asparagus tips and rack of lamb with rosemary. An ideal spot to gather your strength for a tour of the Hospices or the city's numerous wine cellars. Friendly atmosphere.

I●I RESTAURANT LE VERGER

21 route de Seurre (East).
☎ 03.80.24.28.05
Closed Tues, Wed lunchtime and Feb.

Shared entrance with the *Hôtel Grillon* (see above). The smiling, rosy-cheeked owner is slowly building up a local reputation – with the help of her husband – in a region famous for dishes such as *œufs meurette* and *bœuf bourguignon* by adding a few of her own. Try the tureen of Burgundy snails with bottled tomatoes and cream of baby vegetables, or the veal sweetbreads with pistachios and mussels.The cooking is light and well-seasoned. Menus €19–18. Madame is from a wine family in Gevrey-Chambertin, so she or her husband will help you choose something to suit your taste. Enjoy the terrace in summer.

I●I LE BENATON

25 faubourg Bretonnière; it's five minutes from the town centre, heading towards Autun.
☎ 03.80.22.00.26
Closed Wed, Thurs lunchtime and the first week in Dec.

Though it's not ideally located, this restaurant is worth seeking out. The cooking is of the traditional local variety but it is by no means dull: pan-fried snails, courgette caviar served on a reduced tomato sauce and custard cream. The €20 weekday menu is a model of its type, and there are others at €29 and €40 featuring panfried snails, pancake with pigs' trotters in mustard with sweet garlic broth, fried crayfish with mustard and gribiche broth, roast fillet of beef with mashed potato and beef *jus*.

LEVERNOIS   21200 (4KM SE)

☗ LE PARC**

rue de Golf: take the D970 in the direction of Verdun-sur-le-Doubs then turn left.
e hotel-le-parc@wanadoo.fr
☎ 03.80.22.22.51 ➡ 03.80.24.21.19
Closed 25 Nov–25 Jan. **Disabled access**. **TV**. **Car park**.

An old house, now a charming hotel. The trees in the grounds are a hundred years old and full of birds – the ideal spot to be lazy. And the nearby tennis court, golf course and pool mean you can exhaust yourself should you feel so inclined. In the evening, you can recover in the bar with a glass in your hand, chatting to the other guests about your day. The bedrooms are full of character; doubles €32 with handbasin, €44 with shower/wc and €50 with bath. A lovely place – it's best to book.

BOUZE-LÈS-BEAUNE   21200 (7KM NW)

I●I LA BOUZEROTTE

It's on the side of the D970.
☎ 03.80.26.01.37
Closed Mon evening, Tues, Feb, a week in Sept and the Christmas–New Year holidays. **Car park**.

A real country inn, ten minutes from the centre of Beaune, with real Burgundians and real Burgundy cooking. Real flowers (so unusual nowadays you have to mention the fact) decorate the old wooden tables, and there's an old-fashioned sideboard and a fireplace where a fire burns in cold weather. More to the point, they also have good wines from small local vineyards which Christine, who used to be a *sommelière*, can recommend. The freshest produce of the highest quality is used in the dishes and the presentation is lovely. Cheap menu at €14 and others up to €41. It'll cost about €31 *à la carte*.

LADOIX-SERRIGNY   21550 (7KM NE)

🏃 I●I LES COQUINES

N74; it's in the direction of Dijon.
☎ 03.80.26.43.58
Closed Wed, Thurs and Feb. **Car park**.

On one side of this house there's an old storeroom and on the other large windows offer views of the surrounding countryside. They know all about cooking and looking after guests here. Opt for one of the set menus and you will eat well without spending a fortune.

The €25 one, which offers *coq au vin* and calf's head salad with a *sauce gribiche*, is quintessentially good Burgundian fare and designed for people who are serious about food. Others up to €37. Free *digestif*.

BOURBON-LANCY 71140

🏃 🏠 I●I LE GRAND HÔTEL***

Parc Thermal.
☎ 03.85.89.08.87 ➡ 03.85.89.25.45
Ⓦ www.thermes-bourbon-lancy.com
Closed end Oct to end March. **TV**. **Car park**.

This is technically a place for people with rheumatism or heart problems – but it's also great if you want to spend a few days exploring the region. The hotel is a good example of spa-town chic and has an extensive park where people play *pétanque*. The rooms are clean, the bathrooms enormous, and the prices reasonable: doubles € 28 with handbasin and €57–74 with shower/wc or bath. The restaurant offers set menus at a range of prices, €11–20. Traditional cuisine and a good choice of wines. 10% reduction on the room rate April, May and Oct. Free coffee.

CHABLIS 89800

🏠 I●I HOSTELLERIE DES CLOS***

rue Jules-Rathier.
☎ 03.86.42.10.63 ➡ 03.86.42.17.11
Ⓦ www.hostellerie-des.clos.fr
Closed 20 Dec–18 Jan.
Disabled access. **TV**. **Car park**.

In this hostelry, housed in a former hospital and chapel, the waiters wear tails, the tinkling chandeliers gleam luxuriously, the illuminated gardens are delightful and Madame sports elaborate jewellery. Despite all this, the waiters don't take themselves too seriously and Madame's laugh makes you feel welcome. Her husband uses only the finest ingredients and his best-known dishes are subtly flavoured with Chablis, so take your credit card – menus start at €34 and go all the way up to €69. If you're eating *à la carte*, choose just a main course and a dessert and they won't object. Double rooms with bath €69–92.

I●I LE VIEUX MOULIN DE CHABLIS

18 rue des Moulins (Centre).
☎ 03.86.42.47.30
Car park.

A lot of water from the Serein river has flowed under the bridge since this restaurant started up in a house which used to belong to a wine-growing family. The large dining room has walls of local stone, the regional cuisine is well up to standard and the prices are fair. The best dishes are the local ham in Chablis and the beef fillet in Pinot noir. And the rest aren't bad either. Menus €15–40.

LIGNY-LE-CHÂTEL 89144 (15KM NW)

🏃 🏠 I●I RELAIS SAINT-VINCENT**

14 Grande-Rue (Centre).
☎ 03.86.47.43.42 ➡ 03.86.47.48.14
Ⓔ saint.vincent@libertysurf.com
Closed New Year holidays. **Disabled access**. **TV**. **Car park**.

The village and the street are from another age, and the ancient half-timbered house dates all the way back to the 12th century. It has been tastefully converted by the welcoming owner and the rooms have all mod cons. Doubles €39–63 with shower/wc or bath. Set menus €13–26. Excellent, authentic local dishes are produced by the chef. There's a remarkable cheese selection including a local Époisses. You can sit out in the quiet flowery courtyard. Free apéritif.

I●I AUBERGE DU BIEF

2 av. de Chablis; it's next to the church.
☎ 03.86.47.43.42
Closed Sun evening, Mon, Tues evenings, evenings out of season and the Christmas school holidays..

Very popular locally for lunch on Sunday. There aren't many tables so it's advisable to arrive early or book – otherwise you might find a small space on the terrace. Well-presented dishes and refined cooking: *gâteau* of artichokes with lemon and herb butter, ham on the bone with Chablis sauce, Burgundy snails with butter and Bavrois with Chablis and a *coulis* trio. Good value for money with a first menu at €14 and others at €18–37. Charming, smiling welcome. There's a big public car park nearby.

CHAGNY 71150

🏃 🏠 HÔTEL DE LA FERTÉ**

11 bd. de la Liberté (Centre).
☎ 03.85.87.07.47 ➡ 03.85.87.37.64
Closed 23–27 Dec. **TV**.

This substantial house has been attractively refurbished and turned into a welcoming hotel. There are thirteen rooms with open fires, flowery wallpaper and antique furniture. And, without detracting from the period style, all the bathrooms are modern. The rooms are also efficiently soundproofed. Doubles €38–46 with en-suite bath. A country breakfast is served in a room overlooking the garden, or outside in good weather. One of the best hotels in the price range in the area. 10% discount Oct–April except weekends and public holidays.

🏠 |●| LAMELOISE★★★★

36 pl. d'Armes (Centre).
☎ 03.85.87.08.85
e reception@lameloise.fr
⊕ www.lameloise.fr
Restaurant closed Tues lunchtime, Wed, Thurs lunchtime; 23 Dec–8 Jan. **Disabled access**. **TV**. **Car park**.

The third generation of the Lameloise family runs this establishment, which attracts a varied clientele from local businessmen and committed foodies to well-heeled couples. The decoration in the five small dining rooms is stylish – stone walls, hefty beams, comfortable chairs, fresh flowers and so on. The service is unobtrusive, precise and perfect. The cooking has its foundations in local produce: snail ravioli, *gâteau* of liver with crayfish, roast pigeon with truffle fragments, *aiguillettes* of duck with spiced bread, and caramelized pears in a flaky pastry case. In between each course, delicious morsels, both savoury and sweet, appear out of nowhere. The desserts are served in gargantuan portions. Menus €69 to €99. In the hotel, doubles with bath/wc are €114–244.

CORPEAU   21190 (2KM NE)

🎋|●| L'AUBERGE DU VIEUX VIGNERON

Route de Beaune (Centre); it's opposite the town hall.
☎ 03.80.21.39.00
Closed Mon, Tues, a fortnight in Jan, a fortnight in Feb and three weeks in Aug. **Car park**.

This village wouldn't merit a special trip were it not for the inn. In the dining room, the atmosphere feels a bit like it's time for harvest supper: old tables, old furniture and a wide fireplace where lamb cutlets and *andouillettes* are cooked. The must-have dishes include salmon in Chassagne-Montrachet, crayfish tales flambéed in Marc de Bourgogne au gratin, rib of Charolais beef and *crème brûlée* with spiced bread. Menus €14–18. House wines include a Chassagne-Montrachet and a Puligny, both affordable; try a few other vintages grown by the owner

in their newly refurbished cellar. It's a simple place and a good one. Free apéritif.

CHASSEY-LE-CAMP   71150 (5KM SW)

🎋 🏠 |●| AUBERGE DU CAMP ROMAIN★★★

How to get there: take the D974 in the direction of Santenay then turn left; it's down the hill from the ruins of a Roman camp.
☎ 03.85.87.09.91 ➡ 03.85.87.11.51
e auberge.du.camp.romain@wanadoo.fr
Closed 2 Jan–10 Feb. **Swimming pool**. **Disabled access**. **TV**. **Car park**.

The inn overlooks a lush green valley and you'd think you were in the mountains. It's a sort of mini *Club-Med* with tennis courts, crazy-golf, a heated pool and even a helipad! The inn has 44 spacious rooms with en-suite bathrooms for €54–69 and there are some for families who spend their whole holidays here. Set menus €22 and €39. Specialities include duck *foie gras* with a *confit* of rabbit fillet, grilled red mullet with a red pepper coulis, *fricassé* of Bresse chicken with vinegar and raspberry dessert with its *coulis*. Good itineraries for hiking and biking, while the less actively inclined can play billiards. Nice place for a weekend of sport with the family or for lounging around – though perhaps it's not ideal for a romantic weekend à deux. Free apéritif and 10% discount on the room rate.

CHALON-SUR-SAÔNE   71100

🎋 🏠 HÔTEL SAINT-JEAN★★

24 quai Gambetta (South).
☎ 03.85.48.45.65 ➡ 03.85.93.62.69
Disabled access. **TV**.

If you have to spend a night in Chalon, the *Saint-Jean* is the only hotel on the Saône riverbank and it's away from the traffic – so booking is advisable. The mansion has been tastefully decorated by a former restaurateur who gave up cooking in favour of hotel-keeping, and there are friendly and professional staff. A quiet, clean and welcoming establishment with magnificent views, where everything is pleasing and the prices are reasonable. Large double rooms decorated in fresh colours go for €46. You feel there should be some sort of preservation order on the handsome imitation marble staircase, which dates from the late 19th century. 10% discount for two nights or more.

🎋 🏠 HÔTEL CLARINE★★

35 pl. de Beaune (Centre).

☎ 03.85.90.08.00 ➡ 03.85.90.08.01
TV.

Small hotel in a renovated old house. Accommodation is in the main building or in two annexes, the more recent of which overlooks an inner courtyard and is quieter. Some rooms have parquet floors, open fireplaces and old furniture. Doubles €49–56. There's a sauna, a solarium and a gym. 10% discount.

♠ |●| LE SAINT-GEORGES***

32 av. Jean-Jaurès (Centre); it's opposite the station.
☎ 03.85.90.80.50 ➡ 03.85.90.80.55
ℯ reservation@lesaintgeorges71.fr
Restaurant closed Sat lunchtime **Hotel closed** 1–15 Aug. **TV**. **Pay car park**.

A classic station hotel. All the rooms have been refurbished with good facilities – although they're rather lacking in personality, the armchairs will appeal to fans of modern design. All in all, it's value for money with double rooms €61–70. The gastronomic restaurant may beckon but try your luck at the friendly bistro *Le Comptoir d'à Côté* instead, where you can have a meal of Burgundian specialities – parsleyed ham with Aligoté, *foie gras* escalope with spiced bread – for around €16. Menus in the restaurants are €18–38, and there's good quality food in both.

⚶ |●| RESTAURANT RIPERT

31 rue Saint-Georges (Centre).
☎ 03.85.48.89.20
Closed Sun, Mon, 2–7 Jan, a week at Easter and 5–25 Aug.

Alain Ripert has created something of an institution. The dining room is small with a few touches reminiscent of a 1950s bistro (adverts, enamel signs and so on) and fills up rapidly with locals. Dishes change daily with the fresh produce in the market but might include escalope of veal sweetbreads with spices and honey, monkfish stew with saffron, *croustillant* of oxtail, lobster tail *timbale*, and, for dessert, warm *gratin* of raspberries, *nougat* with blackcurrant sauce, and hot apple tart. Set daily menus are €12–27. Unusually for this part of the world, they serve some good wines in carafes as well as bottles. Free coffee.

|●| RESTAURANT CHEZ JULES

11 rue de Strasbourg (Southeast); it's on île Saint-Laurent.
☎ 03.85.48.08.34
Closed Sat lunchtime, Sun, a fortnight in Feb and 3 weeks in Aug.

This small restaurant, located in a quiet neighbourhood, is popular with the locals, and the salmon-pink walls, sturdy beams, copper pots, paintings and old sideboard add to the cosy atmosphere. The cooking is inventive. *Menu du jour* at €15; others at €22 and €18. They list mackerel charlotte with new potatoes, sauteéd rabbit with pickled tomatoes and at least another eight imaginative main courses, followed by dessert or fresh, creamy cheese. Good wine list available by the glass, bottle and carafe. After all that, a post-prandial stroll along the embankment might well be called for.

⚶ |●| LE GOURMAND

13 rue de Strasbourg (Southeast); it's on île Saint-Laurent.
☎ 03.85.93.64.61
Closed Mon evening, Tues, a fortnight at the end of Jan and three weeks in Aug.

Everything in this establishment is yellow, beige or golden, and the owner has a similarly sunny smile. The restaurant itself is richly decorated, with tastefully stylish décor and atmosphere, but it's not posh or over-the-top. There are lots of regulars, and everyone seems to know each other. Faultless presentation, refined cooking and combinations of tasty herbs make for very successful sauces, and the fish dishes are cooked to perfection. There are several house classics but try the crayfish tails with lentils, the roast pigeon or the pig's trotter *tournedos* with *foie gras*. Menus €15–30. Free apéritif.

LUX-SAINT-RÉMY   71390 (4KM W)

⚶ ♠ |●| MA CAMPAGNE

quai Bellevue (Centre).
☎ 03.85.48.33.80 ➡ 03.85.93.33.72
Closed. Sun eve, Mon, Jan. **TV**. **Car park**.

A lovely, huge country house, standing alone on the banks of the Saône. The rooms have been given the names of precious stones and decorated in the appropriate colour. It's an elegant idea and it works. Rooms are from €38 and the difference in price depends on the size – the biggest are suites. Sadly, none have views of the river. On sunny days, you eat on a wide terrace protected by an awning and accompanied by birdsong. The classic cooking is very decent and the chef has a preference for fish dishes. Good quality service and the welcome is excellent. Menus €15–27. There are games for the kids and you can walk along the river too.

BUXY   71390 (15KM SE)

⌂ HÔTEL FONTAINE DE BARANGES

rue de la Fontaine de Baranges (Centre).
☎ 03.85.94.10.70 ➡ 03.85.94.10.79
Ⓦ www.hotelfb.com
TV. Disabled access. Car park.

A substantial early-19th-century residence in grounds planted with shady trees, right next to a pretty old stone wash-house. The whole place has been completely restored, and the attractive rooms are spacious and peaceful; all come with bath or shower. Three of them and three suites have private terraces overlooking the park. Doubles with shower/wc €53–84 or €84–114 with bath. No restaurant but there is a charming bar. Breakfast in the cellar or the terrace.

CHARITÉ-SUR-LOIRE (LA)   58400

⌂ HÔTEL LE BON LABOUREUR**

quai Romain-Mollot; it's on the île de Loire.
☎ 03.86.70.22.85 ➡ 03.86.70.23.64
TV. Garden.

An ancient building where each room is a different size (some sleep three or four) and each has different facilities. They've all been refurbished; doubles cost €40–47 with shower/wc or bath. There is an interior garden with a terrace and a bar. Reasonable prices and a warm welcome.

⚒ I◉I L'AUBERGE DE SEYR

4 Grande-Rue (Centre).
☎ 03.86.70.03.51
Closed Sun evening, Mon, a week in Feb and a fortnight end Aug–beginning Sept.

A simple, unpretentious restaurant serving cooking with character. Dishes change daily but the *menu du jour* at €10 includes a starter – various salads or home-made *terrine* – and a main dish of meat or fish followed by cheese or dessert. Other menus €15–26. Free coffee.

⚒ I◉I AUBERGE DE LA POULE NOIRE

9 pl. des Pêcheurs; it's next to the Saint-Laurent church.
☎ 03.86.70.10.71 ➡ 03.86.57.66.99

Housed in a 12th-century priory, this restaurant features a long dining room with a grandiose wooden staircase leading up to a mezzanine level. In summer, it's wonderfully cool inside – certainly more so than on the sunny south-facing terrace. Carefully prepared dishes draw on traditional Burgundian

food but add a few new ideas as well: medallion of pork with Chavignol goat's cheese; fricassée of eel; strawberry and rhubarb dessert with honey. The weekday menu costs €14 and there are others at €22–30. Dishes *à la carte* cost around €15. One of the best tables in town. Welcoming greeting and free coffee.

CHAROLLES   71120

⌂ I◉I HÔTEL-RESTAURANT LE LION D'OR**

6 rue de Champagny (Centre).
☎ 03.85.24.08.28 ➡ 03.85.88.30.96
Closed Sun evening and Mon except mid-June to mid-Aug; Dec and Jan. **TV. Car park**.

This 17th-century coaching inn is on the banks of a small river. Large double rooms with shower go for €52–55. Numbers 23 and 25 have a view of the river. The top-notch restaurant serves good regional cooking, with exceptional meat dishes, as you would expect in Charolais country. Set menu €14 except Sunday, with others €24–42.

⚒ ⌂ I◉I HÔTEL-RESTAURANT DE LA POSTE***

2 av. de la Libération (Centre).
☎ 03.85.24.11.32 ➡ 03.85.24.05.74
Closed Sun evening, Mon and Nov. **TV. Car park**.

This is a very important establishment in the Charolais – it's run by Daniel Doucet, the ambassador of Burgundy gastronomy, and his cooking is as fresh and tasty as ever. The dining room is richly decorated and the service is faultless and attentive, but this place is definitely not affected. You'll get great advice on wine to suit your taste and an excellent choice of dishes – don't miss the Charolais rib steak with Guérande salt, the *truffe* of potatoes with snails in garlic sauce, the *cassolette* of scallops with a leek *fondue* or the *croustillant* of veal sweetbreads with morels and chanterelle mushrooms. Magnificent cheese platter and desserts. Set menus at €20 during the week, others at €26–49. Eat out under the maple trees in the interior garden on fine days. Comfy bedrooms from €55 to €76. Free coffee.

BEAUBERY   71220 (12KM SE)

⚒ I◉I AUBERGE DE BEAUBERY

La Gare; take the N79 from Charolles, then the D79.
☎ 03.85.24.84.74

Closed Wed evening; Sat; Christmas holidays.

Little inns like this offering a complete meal with wine and coffee for €10 are few and far between. Basic home cooking, lovingly prepared and served in generous portions, is dished up in a dining room decorated with prints and a kitschy old clock. It's full of regulars and local travelling salesmen. You can get a sandwich filled with local ham, omelette and soft white cheese. There's a pricier menu at €13, which features dishes such as *coq au vin*, frogs' legs and Charolais steak. *À la carte* will cost you around €15. Free apéritif.

CHÂTEAU-CHINON 58120

⅙ ⚑ |●| HÔTEL DU PARC – LE RELAIS GOURMAND**

route de Nevers; it's on the left as you leave the village on the Nevers road.
☎ 03.86.79.44.94 ➥ 03.86.79.41.10
Closed Sun evening 15 Nov–15 March; Feb. **TV. Car park**.

This place is named after the Morvan national park nearby, but there the pastoral theme ends. It's a modern, modestly functional place looking rather like a chain hotel; all the corridors and rooms are identical. Double rooms with bath go for €40. Though the hotel offers little more than a place to sleep, you can enjoy a decent, cheap meal in the restaurant. The €10 menu (not available on Sunday) is particularly good value, and there are others up to €32. Dishes such as calves' head, salmon tartare and home-made terrines. Free coffee.

CHÂTEAUNEUF 21320

⚑ |●| HOSTELLERIE DU CHÂTEAU**

rue de Centre. How to get there: take the Pouilly-en-Auxois exit off the A6.
☎ 03.80.49.22.00 ➥ 03.80.49.21.27
Closed Mon and Tues except July–Aug; Dec and Jan. **Disabled access**.

Despite the fact that it looks as if it hasn't changed for years, nearly all the 12th- and 14th-century houses in this picturesque hilltop village have been bought by outsiders. Similarly misleading is the medieval exterior of this hotel, which stands in the shadow of a 12th-century castle – inside it's modern and comfortable. It would be nice, though, if the welcome were a bit warmer and the *à la carte* menu a little more imaginative. Set menus €23–40 with traditional local dishes. Doubles

with shower or bath, €45–69; some look out over the countryside.

|●| LE GRILL DU CASTEL

☎ 03.80.49.26.82
Closed Wed out of season, Tues in winter, and 15 Dec to 15 Jan.

Facing the *hostellerie* and the château, this is a lovely old stone building in one of France's prettiest villages. In summer, don't bother with the two parasols on the lawn – the real terrace is in the courtyard. Set menus at €15–29 include various meats simply grilled over a wood fire, *jambon persillé*, *bœuf bourguignon*, salads, cream cheese, home-made tart and local wine. Congenial welcome.

VANDENESSE-EN-AUXOIS 21320 (5KM W)

⅙ |●| RESTAURANT DE L'AUXOIS

How to get there: it's very close to Châteauneuf-en-Auxois on the banks of the canal.
☎ 03.80.49.22.36
Closed Sun evening and Mon Oct–June, and 20 Dec–28 Jan. **Car park**.

The whole village has benefitted from the reopening of the grocer's and this restaurant, both run by the Walloons. Food served here spices up the local style of cooking: snail and oyster mushroom *millefeuille*, fillet of beef with Époisse cheese sauce and duck *foie gras*. There's a weekday menu at €12 and others at €16–29. The garden is superb in summer, and there's an old-fashioned dining room for greyer days. Free apéritif.

CHÂTILLON-SUR-SEINE 21400

⅙ ⚑ SYLVIA HÔTEL**

9 av. de la Gare.
☎ 03.80.91.02.44 ➥ 03.80.91.47.77
ⓦ www.sylvia-hotel.fr
Disabled access. TV. Car park.

The previous owners transformed this enormous old family home, set in parkland, into a delightful hotel and named it after their daughter. Then Sylvia grew up and the family moved on. The present owners decided to keep the name, though, and do their utmost to make you enjoy your stay, offering cosy rooms and wonderful breakfasts. Simple doubles €21 and up to €43 with bath. 10% discount on the room rate Oct–April.

⅙ |●| LE BOURG-À-MONT "CHEZ JULIE"

27 rue du Bourg-à-Mont; it's in the old town, opposite the old courthouse.

☎ 03.80.91.04.33
Closed Sun evening and Mon out of season; a fortnight in Oct. **Disabled access**.

This is a pleasant surprise in a quiet little town chiefly known for the remarkable 5th-century BC Vix burial vessel displayed in the museum. The house, decorated with old adverts, original paintings and bright colours, belonged to a grandmother who apparently had a bit of money, but there's a youthful spirit about the place nowadays. There are log fires in winter, while in summer the windows, overlooking a little flower garden, are thrown wide open and you can have lunch or dinner there. Lunch menu €10 with others €15–29; there's a vegetarian menu for €17. The best dishes are *terrine* of local trout, roast rabbit with prune stuffing, *bœuf Bourg à Mont* (a souped-up version of *bœf bourguignon* flavoured with Crème de Cassis) and pancake millefeuille with chocolate. Free coffee.

MONTLIOT-ET-COURCELLES 21400 (3.5KM N)

|O| CHEZ FLORENTIN

It's on the N71, on the outskirts of the village.
☎ 03.80.91.09.70
Closed Sun evening and Mon except public holidays (when it's closed Tues instead). **Disabled access**.

You enter through the bar, where the lorry drivers eat, and go through to a large dining room used for banquets and christenings. The crowds you'd expect only on high days and holidays are an everyday occurrence here, the local accents and laughter of the evening contrasting with the business atmosphere at lunchtime. The reception is friendly and the prices are unbeatable – the €11 menu consists of three courses, with dishes such as fresh mushrooms with cream, *blanquette de veau* and tart. Other menus cost €13–26.

CLAMECY 58500

♨ ≜ |O| HOSTELLERIE DE LA POSTE**

9 pl. Émile-Zola (Centre).
☎ 03.86.27.01.55 ➡ 03.86.27.05.99
TV.

A substantial building in the centre that looks the part – like a post house that's been there forever. The rooms are clean and comfortable and it's obvious that the hotel is seriously well-run. Doubles €40–45. The menu *du jour* is pricey at €16, though the cooking is of good quality; other menus are €26–30. The

beef is local Charolais and there are fresh river fish too. Free coffee.

♨|O| LA CRÊPERIE DU VIEUX CANAL

18 av. de la République (Centre); it's opposite the museum.
☎ 03.86.24.47.93
Closed Mon.

One of Clamecy's friendliest spots to eat, a place where you can have a good, quick lunch. The decor is Breton and they serve savoury and sweet pancakes (also to take away), as well as pasta dishes and *bruschetta*. Menus €10–20. Welcoming owner. Free coffee.

|O| RESTAURANT AU BON ACCUEIL

3 route d'Auxerre.
☎ 03.86.27.91.67
Closed evenings Oct–May, Sat, Sun and Wed evenings in summer, the Feb school holidays and the first ten days in July and Dec. **Disabled access**.

A restaurant with a welcome that lives up to its name. It also has a peaceful dining room that has views of the Yonne and the collegiate church. François Langlois cooks with flair and passion – dishes change as the mood takes him and there are many regional options on the menu. Attentive service and a delightful welcome from Madame Langlois. Weekday menu €18, with others €23 and €31. It's not a very big place, so it's best to book.

TANNAY 58190 (13KM S)

♨ ≜ |O| HÔTEL DU RELAIS FLEURI**

2 rue de Bèze (Centre); take the D34 from Clamecy.
☎ 03.86.29.33.88
Closed Sun evening, Mon, Feb and end Sept–Oct.
Swimming pool. Disabled access. Car park.

A comfortable hotel in a period house. The interior has been attractively refurbished and you'll be greeted with a smile. Doubles with shower/wc €37–43. The cooking has a good reputation with an emphasis on the regional: *œufs en meurette* and beef and potato pie. Weekday lunch menu at €9 and others €14–23. Free coffee.

CLUNY 71250

♨ ≜ HÔTEL DU COMMERCE*

8 pl. du Commerce (Centre).
☎ 03.85.59.03.09 ➡ 03.85.59.00.87
TV.

In this expensive town, this is a small, well-maintained and central hotel that offers basic, clean accommodation at reasonable prices. Wonderfully friendly reception to boot. Doubles with handbasin €23, with shower €32 and bath €37. Discount on breakfast.

♠ HÔTEL SAINT-ODILON**

rue Belle-Croix; it's beside the racecourse.
☎ 03.85.59.25.00 ➡ 03.85.59.06.18
Closed 12 Dec–20 Jan.
e saint-odilon@acmtel.com
Disabled access. **TV**. **Car park**.

Surrounded by fields full of grazing Charolais cattle, this is a modern establishment but one in sympathy with its surroundings. The building is low and squat, and the two wings create a square courtyard reminiscent of the local farms. A nice place to stay – it has modern facilities and everything has been newly refurbished. You'll get a friendly welcome from Monsieur and Madame Berry, too. Rooms with phone, TV and satellite channels are €46; breakfast costs extra.

BOURGVILAIN   71520 (9KM S)

🎋 |●| AUBERGE LAROCHETTE

le bourg; take the D980 then the D22 and it's on the village square.
☎ 03.85.50.81.73
Closed Sun evening, Mon and 15 Feb–15 March.

A welcoming provincial dining room in this large, traditional village inn. There are reproductions of Millet paintings on the wall and a country clock in the corner. The excellent cooking likewise carries on the best French traditions: dishes are finely judged by Monsieur Bonin and generously served. Weekday menu at €12, with others €17–33. À la carte you can get warm *foie gras* with apple and cinnamon sauce, frogs' legs and *trompette* mushrooms in flaky pastry, zander *mille-feuille*, salmon and bacon *paupiette*, duck breast with seasonal fruits and a tasty Charolais steak. Free apéritif.

🎋 |●| LA PIERRE SAUVAGE

Col des Enceints.
☎ 03.85.35.70.03
Closed Tues evening and Wed except July–Aug; weekdays 1 Oct to Easter; Jan. **Disabled access**. **Car park**.

Service until 9.30pm (10pm in summer). This place is on a hilltop 529m high. Some fifteen years ago, it was a ruin which has since been wonderfully restored and is now an appealing place to stop. Start off with a hunk of bread and strong cheese or house *terrine* before getting onto the main courses: game or some Charollais lamb chops. Specialities include *cassolette* of snails *forestière*, guinea fowl with vanilla and fresh figs, chicken with seasonal fruits and pigeon with *pêche de vigne*. Menus €17–26. They also do good platters of country ham or *terrines*. The terrace is superb in summer. Best to book. Free *digestif*.

BERZÉ-LA-VILLE   71960 (10KM SE)

♠ |●| RELAIS DU MÂCONNAIS**

La Croix-Blanche (Northwest); take the D17.
☎ 03.85.36.60.72 ➡ 03.85.36.65.47
e lannuel@aol.com
Closed Sun evening, Mon in low season and 6 Jan–4 Feb. **TV**.

The quiet atmosphere here will be to many people's liking and the well-spaced tables mean that you won't overhear your neighbours. Fittingly, Christian Lannuel's cooking has a very personal touch. The small *tartare* of beetroot is so original that it deserves to be upgraded from an appetiser to a starter. Other dishes, based on local produce, are finely flavoured: try milk-fed veal cutlets with vegetables *au gratin* or roast pigeon with garlic purée and sautéed mushrooms. Good dessert trolley. Menus €23–46. Comfy double rooms with shower or bath at €50; half board at €53 is compulsory in season.

BLANOT   71250 (10KM NE)

🎋 ♠ |●| AUBERGE DU MONT SAINT-ROMAIN

Mont St-Romain; take the D15.
☎ 03.85.33.28.93
Closed Tues out of season and 11 Nov–1 April.
Disabled access.

An inn with a beautiful panoramic terrace, right up on one of the peaks of the Saône-et-Loire. Excellent reception from the very nice young couple (who have to cope with scorching winds in summer and snowdrifts in winter); their dishes are prepared with professional care for a clientele of walkers, horseriders and nature lovers who drop in for a meal. Hearty portions of regional specialities, cooked using fresh produce. The set menus, €11–19, are good value: the supreme of chicken with liver is very fine and so is the chicken *aiguillette* with wild mushrooms. Lodge for those who want to stay. Free apéritif or coffee.

COSNE-SUR-LOIRE 58200

🏠 🏨 |●| HÔTEL-RESTAURANT LE SAINT-CHRISTOPHE**

pl. de la Gare; it's opposite the train station.
☎ 03.86.28.02.01 ➡ 03.86.26.94.28
Closed Sun evening, Fri, 25 July–22 Aug and 25 Dec–2 Jan.

Delightfully refurbished and comfortable rooms with good facilities. Doubles with shower/wc or bath €36–40. The owner will welcome you with a smile and she seems to be doing things right in the restaurant too, which is popular with the locals. The *formule* of main course with a choice of starter or dessert costs €12, and there are menus €18–33 and options *à la carte*. Straightforward, robust cooking; *foie gras* with oxtail and veal kidneys with *confit*. Free *digestif* and 10% discount on the room rate at the weekend.

🏨 |●| LE VIEUX RELAIS***

11 rue Saint-Agnan; it's near the Eden Cinema.
☎ 03.86.28.27.50
€ contacts@le-vieux-relais.fr
Closed Fri evening, Sat lunch and Sun evening Sept–April. **TV. Pay car park**.

A coaching inn straight out of the 19th century. The double rooms are cosy and spacious, as you would expect for the price range (€76–80), and the cooking is one of the establishment's great strengths. Father and son team up in the kitchen, while mother and daughter-in-law run the dining room. It's a popular place. The cheapest menu is €18, with others up to €44. There's a dream of a courtyard with a balcony overgrown with Virginia creeper and a puzzle of higgledy-piggledy roofs.

CREUSOT (LE) 71200

🏠 |●| LE BISTROT DE LA GRIMPETTE

16 rue de la Chaise (Centre).
☎ 03.85.80.42.00
Closed Sun and the week of 15 Aug.

Exactly halfway up the stairway connecting the lower and upper town, this is an inexpensive restaurant serving genuine Lyons specialities. The décor is wine-red, and the place is full of the aromas of hot sausage, guinea fowl with mushrooms and salt pork with lentils. Attentive service and friendly welcome. There's a basic set menu at €12 and others up to €20; they include perch fillet

with cream and shallot sauce, salad with warm calves' feet and flank of beef *Lyonnais* and guinea fowl with mushrooms. Free apéritif.

|●| LE RESTAURANT

rue des Abattoirs (South); it's in a cul-de-sac.
☎ 03.85.56.32.33
Closed Sun evening and 1–20 Aug.

Somewhat bizarrely located, this place is hidden among the abattoirs in an area which is dark and deserted in the evenings – but it's a real gastronomic beacon. You get a warm reception and the bright dining room is painted in fresh colours. It feels lofty on account of its mezzanine, and looks elegantly bare with a beautiful zinc counter. The well-designed cooking aims to preserve the taste of good produce by clever seasoning. Set menus €12 (weekdays) and €17–29. Dishes include parsleyed eels with pickled onions, roast lamb with fresh mint and calves' kidneys with liquorice *jus*. Excellent selection of wines at reasonable prices and some high-quality (but affordable) Burgundies. It's advisable to book for dinner; this little establishment is going places.

TORCY 71210 (3KM S)

🏠 |●| LE VIEUX SAULE

route du Creusot (South).
☎ 03.85.55.09.53
Closed Sun evening and Mon.

One of the best restaurants in the region, located in an old country inn at Torcy, on the outskirts of Le Creusot. Excellent welcome and brilliant décor. Good €15 weekday menu, others €23–61. The cooking is particularly tasty, and nicely presented to boot – *foie gras* escalope with rhubarb, pheasant and *foie gras* tart, fish stew and a delicious lamb shank. Desserts along the same lines. Excellent choice of local wines. Free *digestif*.

UCHON 71190 (16KM W)

🏠 🏨 |●| AUBERGE LA CROIX MESSIRE JEAN

La Croix Messire Jean; head for Montcenis, then take the D228.
☎ 03.85.54.42.06 ➡ 03.85.54.32.23
Closed Wed in winter and Christmas–New Year. **Car park**.

Ideal base for walkers and mountain bikers planning to tackle one of the splendid routes up one of the highest mountains (684m) in the département. This is a friendly inn and one of only three that have been classified as a "Bistrot Accueil du Parc du Morvan", all of which offer authentic dishes using local ingredients. It offers basic but perfectly adequate doubles with handbasin for €27. Tasteful rustic décor and prices to suit all pockets. There's a half board option for €36. It's best to book in high season; if you yearn for peace and quiet, this won't be your scene. There's a large shaded terrace where you can enjoy the €8 four o'clock Morvan snack or the exceptionally reasonabe set menus, which range from €13 to €19. Mountain bikes for hire. Free coffee, and 10% discount on full board if you stay a minimum of three days.

DECIZE   58300

|●| SNACK DU STADE NAUTIQUE

promenade des Halles. Take the street that goes past the tourist office to the end; it's next to the camp site.
☎ 03.86.25.00.99

This is a waterside café and, when it's sunny, it's the prettiest place in Decize. Happiness is sitting at a table in the shade of the plane trees with a plate of country ham, an omelette with salad or some fresh cream cheese. They do *frites* to take away. A couple of menus at €8, with dessert extra. You can play volleyball or have a pony ride, and some evenings in summer they have live music. Really friendly welcome.

🧍 |●| RESTAURANT LA GRIGNOTTE

57 av. du 14-Juillet (North).
☎ 03.86.25.26.20
Closed Sun, and Mon evening.

An unpretentious restaurant unfortunately situated on a busy road. The dining room is lovely with floral decoration. You can eat decently and cheaply: the lunch menu (not Sun) costs €10 or there are others €18–25. Seafood, *fondue* and *tartiflette* are specialities. Free apéritif if you opt for a set menu over €15.

|●| AUBERGE DES FEUILLATS

Hameau Les Feuillats. At the tourist office go along the bd. Voltaire; after the bridge over the Rl152, take the road to Moulind. 1km further on, turn left onto the route des Fuillats and it's 1km on the left.
☎ 03.86.25.05.19
Closed Wed evening.

This is the place for a slab of "Red Label" Charolais beef – a Red Label means its ori-

gins can be tracked. The terrace at the back is right on the bank of a canal that runs lateral to the Loire and it's busy with pleasure boats wherever you look. There's a pleasant welcome. Menus 15–27, with a weekday lunch *formule* at €10.

|●| LE CHAROLAIS

33 [bis], route de Moulins.
☎ 03.86.25.22.27
Closed Sun evening and Mon.

An attractive dining room with quiet service and classic, well-judged cuisine. The cheapest menu, at €14, will allow you to judge, or there's a dish of the day for €13. Other menus are €24–50. The terrace at the back is well sheltered.

DIGOIN   71160

🧍 🏠 |●| LES DILIGENCES**

14 rue Nationale (Centre); it's in a pedestrian street in the town centre.
☎ 03.85.53.06.31 ➡ 03.85.88.92.43
Ⓦ www.les-diligences.com
Closed Mon evening and Tues except July–Aug; 18 Nov–10 Dec. **TV. Car park.**

In the 17th century, travellers arriving in the town by mail coach or boat stayed at this inn. It has recently been restored and the exposed stonework, beams, polished furniture and gleaming coppers make it look very smart. But that doesn't mean the prices in the restaurant are insane: set menus start at €15 and go up to €51. Dining *à carte*, however, is a different story: lobster and crayfish tail salad with raspberry vinegar, Charolais fillet steak with five peppers, *fricassée* of ceps Bordeaux-style and John Dory fillet with watercress sauce – all are a bit pricey. Six tastefully furnished and decorated rooms, €38 with shower or €46–53 with bath, overlook the quiet banks of the Loire. There's a duplex with a private spa in the vast bathroom. Reservations advisable. Free apéritif.

NEUZY   71160 (3KM NE)

🧍 🏠 |●| LE MERLE BLANC***

36 route de Gueugnon-Autun; take the D994 going towards Autun.
☎ 03.85.53.17.13 ➡ 03.85.88.91.71
Closed Sun evening and Mon lunchtime Oct to end April. **Disabled access. TV. Car park.**

The hotel is set back from the road. Doubles with shower/wc €31, or up to €43 with bath. The substantial set menu at €13 (weekdays only) and others at €18–35 offer dishes such as pan-fried duck foie gras with spices, savoury île flottante with smoked salmon, Charolais sirloin and apple and walnut crumble. Friendly, efficient staff. Be warned, though: there's renovation work scheduled for May 2002. Free house apéritif.

DIJON 21000

SEE MAP OVERLEAF

♨ ♠ HÔTEL LE CHAMBELLAN**

92 rue Vannerie. **MAP C2-1**
☎ 03.80.67.12.67 ➡ 03.80.38.00.39
TV. Car park.

This is the place if you're after the splendours of yesteryear combined with the convenience of mod cons. It's an old building and a delightfully old-fashioned establishment with extremely reasonable prices. Doubles with basin at €21; with shower or bath they go up to €43. They've all got character, but go for one overlooking the seventeenth-century courtyard. 10% discount.

♨ ♠ HÔTEL LE JACQUEMART**

32 rue Verrerie. **MAP B1-3**
☎ 03.80.60.09.604 ➡ 03.80.60.09.69
Ⓦ www.hotel-lejacquemart.fr
TV.

Book to avoid disappointment. A lovely hotel whose many regulars include opera singers during the season. The rooms are quiet and comfortable and all have cable TV. An ideal spot for a well-earned rest after a day spent absorbing the old part of Dijon. Doubles €27–46 depending on facilities. 10% discount Dec–March inclusive.

♨ ♠ HÔTEL DU PALAIS**

23 rue du Palais. **MAP B2-2**
☎ 03.80.67.16.26 ➡ 03.80.65.12.16
Disabled access. TV.

Ideally situated right in the centre of the old town, opposite the public library – which is worth a visit in itself – but totally quiet. The clean, welcoming double bedrooms are soundproofed, and they go for €32–35 with shower or €43 with bath. Beautiful breakfast room. Credit cards not accepted. 10% discount Dec–March inclusive.

♠ HÔTEL VICTOR HUGO**

23 rue des Fleurs. **MAP A1-5**
☎ 03.80.43.63.45 ➡ 03.80.42.13.01
TV. Lock-up car park.

Located in Dijon's sedate, middle-class neighbourhood, this isn't the place to let your hair down: it's quiet, spotless and has an atmosphere that is ever so slightly staid. There are twenty or so comfortable, welcoming rooms; doubles with shower/wc or bath €41–43. Free locked car park.

♠ HÔTEL DES ALLÉES**

27 cours Général-de-Gaulle. **OFF MAP C3-6**
☎ 03.80.66.57.50 ➡ 03.80.36.24.81
Ⓦ www.hotelallees.com
Reception closed Sun afternoon. **Disabled access. TV. Car park.**

Small modern hotel on a smart tree-lined avenue leading to the parc de la Colombière. It used to be a maternity hospital – and, appropriately, they allow children (and pets) to stay at no extra charge. The garden is alive with birds and you can be sure of peace and quiet. Doubles with shower/wc are €43 or €53 with bath. They lock the doors at 11pm, so remember to ask for the entry code just in case.

⦿ LE PASSÉ SIMPLE

18 rue Pasteur. **MAP B2-13**
☎ 03.80.67.22.00
ⓔ marc.balducci@infonie.fr
Closed Sat lunchtime, Sun and 24 Dec–1 Jan.

Old-school bistro decorated in antique style with cosy décor and informal service – the owner is on first-name terms with his customers. It's where friends come to have a glass of wine at the bar or relax in the sun on the terrace. The €9 lunch menu gives you the opportunity to try the most traditional of dishes – œufs en meurette, salad with grilled Époisse cheese and perch fillet with pink peppercorns. Other menus at €12–21.

♨ ⦿ LE CHABROT

36 rue Monge. **MAP A2-16**
☎ 03.80.30.69.61
Closed Sun and the first fortnight in Aug.

Service until 10.30pm. Plates of Burgundian specialities available all day long – although there's a new owner, the tried-and-tested approach of this place hasn't changed. You can eat in the bistro or the restaurant upstairs, and there's a tiny terrace. The cooking is emphatically local with a few twists: try the pressed goat and smoked salmon or the signature dish, salmon unilatérale (cooked on one side). There's a €11 weekday lunch menu and others at €18–26. You go through the wine cellar to get to the dining areas so you can choose your bottle on the way to your table. Wines are also served by the glass:

Coteaux de l'Auxois and Epineuil red for €2. Free apéritif.

|●| LE BOUCHON DU PALAIS

4 rue Bouhier. **MAP B2-12**
☎ 03.80.30.19.98
Closed Sat and Sun lunchtimes.

An old favourite under new ownership – and the décor hasn't changed a bit. Guests are still asked to decorate the paper tablecloths which are then put up on the walls. The cooking remains straightforward and of the same quality and the helpings are ample: gratinéed marrow bone, *andouillette* terrine, veal escalope with St Marcellin cheese sauce, and tasty lamb chops, followed by *clafoutis* or *crème brûlée*. There's a *formule* based around the dish of the day comprising main and dessert for €12; with a starter as well it costs €16. Knock back a glass of wine at the bar with the chef. Service is efficient, attentive and kindly.

衤|●| SIMPLE SIMON

4 rue de la Chouette. **MAP B2-14**
☎ 03.80.50.03.52
Closed Mon.

This is an ideal spot for a snack in the oldest part of town; it's just round the corner from the carving of the good-luck owl. Cheese and onion pies, cheese scones, cold meat and desserts – all on offer in this little corner of Burgundy that is forever Britain. Ideal for a break or breakfast any time between 10am and 7pm. Also one of the few places in Dijon where you can get breakfast on Sunday. Menu for €12 which is around the same price as a meal *à la carte*. Very pleasant staff. Free coffee.

衤|●| LE BISTROT DES HALLES

10 rue Bannelier. **MAP B1-19**
☎ 03.80.49.94.15
e billoux@club-internet.fr
Closed Sun evening.

This is the place everyone in Dijon goes to eat. It's an old-style bistro, complete with large mirrors and checked napkins. The man responsible for the cooking is Jean-Pierre Billoux, a wonderful chef and one of Burgundy's six great masters. Every dish – home-made *pâté en croûte à l'ancienne*, terrine of *jambon persillé*, pig's trotters, or *terrine* of lamb and leeks – bears his mark. Add to that some good country dishes, superb grills and reasonably priced wines (even though the stuff by the jug isn't great), and you'll understand

why it's such a success. Set lunch menu €15 or around €17 *à la carte*. There's a very nice terrace looking onto the covered market. Free house apéritif.

衤|●| RESTAURANT LE BISTINGO

13 passage Darcy. **MAP A1-11**
☎ 03.80.30.61.38
Closed Sun, Mon and Aug.

This place, half-pub, half-restaurant, serves substantial portions of inexpensive food for €9 to €14 – salmon with lemon butter, skate with capers and *andouillette*. You'll pay €18–24 *à la carte*. It's a friendly spot where it's easy to get into conversation with the regulars. The owner is a colourful character reminiscent of Figaro (of opera fame), while the waiter uses the familiar *tu* with everybody. In the evening, you'll be served the delicious steak *tartare* almost automatically. Free Kir.

衤|●| LE CÉZANNE

40 rue Amiral-Roussin. **MAP B2-20**
☎ 03.80.58.91.92
Closed Sun, Mon lunchtime.

Located in an old pedestrianized street, the restaurant has vintage stonework and beams and an intimate atmosphere brightened up by the Provençal decor. The chef's cooking has become a gastronomic yardstick in the town. You won't be disappointed by the quality even on the cheapest menu, at €15: red mullet and scallops with saffron and basil; steak flambéed with *Pastis* and fennel; pigeon with hazelnuts and dried figs; and chocolate soufflé with pistachio ice cream. Other menus go up to €27 and you'll pay about 40 *à la carte*. Pleasant little terrace. Free coffee.

HAUTEVILLE-LES-DIJON   21121 (8KM NW)

衤 ⋒ |●| LA MUSARDE**

7 rue des Riottes; it's on the N71 road to Troyes.
☎ 03.80.56.22.82 ➡ 03.80.56.64.40
e hotel.rest.lamusarde@wanadoo.fr
Closed Mon and 15 Dec–15 Jan. **TV. Car park**.

A place with a risqué past – it used to be a discreet rendezvous for intimate dalliances. Nowadays it's also a restaurant and it's best to book, especially at the weekends, to be sure of a table. The informal, relaxed atmosphere is at the same time sophisticated and professional. It's run by Marc Ogé, a true Breton with his feet planted firmly on the ground. His dishes brighten Breton and Burgundy traditions with a little North African sun: turbot

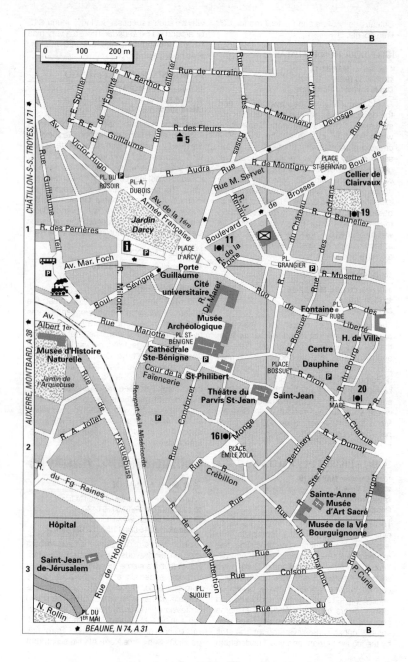

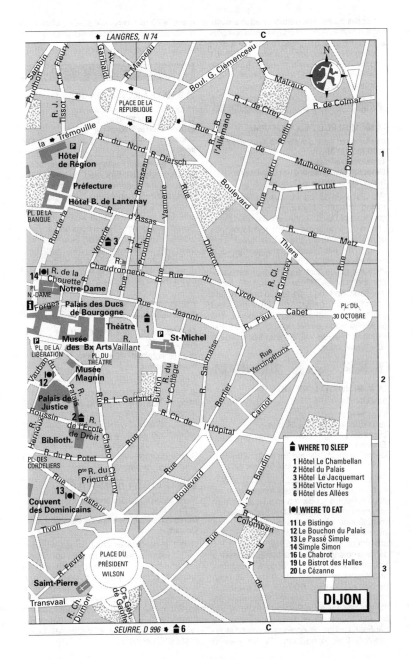

with basil purée; *foie gras* cooked in a cloth; pigeon tajine; *terrine* of shellfish with *foie gras* and *confit* of aubergines; roasted sea trout with *coulis* of mussels. Set menus €25–61 and there's a weekday menu at €18 including wine and coffee. Nice terrace. Attractive bedrooms €42–52. 10 % discount.

PRENOIS   21370 (12KM NE)

🎋 |●| AUBERGE DE LA CHARME

It's a turning off the road that goes to Darois aerodrome.
☎ 03.80.35.32.84
e davidlacharme@aol.com
Closed Sun evening, Mon and Tues lunchtimes,the February school holidays and 1–15 Aug.

Prenois used to be famous for its motor-racing circuit. Nowadays the culinary creations of David Zuddas are the main draw, and even though the chef's reputation has grown considerably the prices remain very attractive. He uses good-quality local produce from which he concocts interesting dishes: pressed duck and *foie gras* with sage; chickpea *galette* with sweet onion. All dishes are seasoned and presented with a rare attention to detail. This is the best establishment in these parts. Set menus €15 at weekday lunchtimes; others €21–64 and eating *à la carte* will set you back around €53. Free coffee.

VAL SUZON   21121 (15KM NE)

🎋 🏠 |●| HOSTELLERIE DU VAL SUZON***

It's on the N71.
☎ 03.80.35.60.15 ➡ 03.80.35.61.36
Closed Sun evening, Mon and Tues lunchtimes
e hotelvalsuzon@magdos.com
Closed Sun evening, Mon and Tues lunchtime Oct–May, Mon, Tues lunchtime and Wed June–Sept and 15 Nov–20 Dec. **TV. Car park**.

A peaceful, comfy establishment serving good food. It's a bewitching site, just fifteen minutes from Dijon, in a valley surrounded by magnificent parkland and gardens. The owner gives a country-style welcome and still offers some rural dishes while at the same time catering for the tastes of passing Parisians and other "strangers". Peaceful and comfy bedrooms which have all been renovated. Doubles €69 with shower/wc or bath, half board €77 minimum (compulsory in high season). Yves Perreau is the chef and he likes to use spices and flavours from the Far East, though his cooking remains fundamentally true to tradition. Weekday lunch

menu €20 and others €33–74. Ideal for a romantic weekend. Wonderful terrace. Free coffee.

DONZY   58220

🎋 🏠 |●| LE GRAND MONARQUE**

10 rue de l'Étape; it's near the church.
☎ 03.86.39.35.44 ➡ 03.86.39.37.09
e grandmonarque@hotmail.com
Closed Mon evening, Tues and 10 Jan–10 Feb. **TV. Car park**.

This is a delightful village with a number of 15th-century half-timbered buildings. The hotel is the old stone house practically next door to the Romanesque church, but don't worry – the bells don't ring between 11pm and 8am so you won't be woken too early. Rustic charm with all mod cons and a warm, tastefully decorated interior. Spacious doubles with shower/wc are €41, with bath €47. Set menus at €14 and €18. Good-quality regional cooking with a number of fish dishes. Free house apéritif.

DUN-LES-PLACES   58230

🎋 🏠 |●| L'AUBERGE ENSOLEILLÉE

Centre; it's on the D6 Lormes to Saulieu road.
☎ 03.86.84.62.76 ➡ 03.86.84.64.57
Closed Christmas.

A typical Morvan inn run by three women – one at the bar, one in the restaurant and one in the kitchen. They offer a smiling welcome. Traditional local recipes include ham with cream sauce, calf's head with two sauces, perch with saffron and steak with morels. Substantial weekday menu at €14 with others €21–34. Simple country-style rooms at €27–43 for a double with shower or bath. Free coffee.

🏠 |●| LE CHALET DU MONTAL

How to get there: it's 1.5km northeast of the village.
☎ 03.86.84.62.77
Closed Mon evening and Tues out of season, and Jan. **Car park**.

Here's a genuine chalet perched above a river in wild surroundings straight out of *Twin Peaks*. It has a bar and an enormous central fireplace, and is popular with campers from round about. The cooking is simple but a lot of care goes into the preparation of the dishes. Set menus €14–24. If you want to spend the night, they offer four basic but newly refurbished rooms for €36–38; half board costs €39 per person.

GEVREY-CHAMBERTIN   21220

🏃 🛏 |●| AUX VENDANGES DE BOURGOGNE

47 route de Beaune.
☎ 03.80.34.30.24 📠 03.80.58.55.44
📧 aux.vendanges.de.bourgogne@wanadoo.fr
Closed Sun and a fortnight Christmas–New Year. **TV.**
Car park.

Among the gourmet restaurants, world-renowned cellars and inflated prices of the area is this old-fashioned hotel restaurant. It has a warm Art Deco décor with a stencilled ceiling and stained glass lampshades and there's an interior terrace. Good local dishes in hearty portions at reasonable prices, all charmingly served. Specialities include snails in a pastry case with garlic, pig's trotters, *coq au vin*, ox cheek, home-made parsleyed ham and pears poached in blackcurrant liqueur. Weekday menu at €14; others €20 and €24. Despite being in the epicentre of great Burgundies, here they even serve wine by the glass. Simple rooms with period furniture €44–50. 10% discount on the room rate for a two-night stay.

🏃 |●| CHEZ GUY

3 pl. de l'Hôtel-de-Ville.
☎ 03.80.58.51.51
Closed Wed and the Feb school holidays.

This is the restaurant Gevrey-Chambertin has been waiting for. Up to now life in this most famous of famous wine-growing villages has been focused solely on the famous cellars but this restaurant has brought a good deal of new life to the place. There's a terrace and in summer there are jazz concerts on Tuesday and Friday. When the weather gets cold, there's a rotisserie churning away in the dining room. The cooking is bright and inventive, with a few new twists on traditional Burgundian dishes: *coq au vin* with parsley; poached eggs with mustard and oyster mushrooms; ox cheek with red wine sauce; and Burgundy bread and butter pudding. The *menu-carte*, where you make up your own menu to go with a dish of the day, is superb and among the set menus (€17–24) there's one of Burgundy specialities. An attractive choice of Gevrey wines at appealing prices. Free coffee.

JOIGNY   89300

🏃 🛏 |●| LE PARIS-NICE**

Rond-point de la Résistance (Centre).

☎ 03.86.62.06.72 📠 03.86.62.56.99
Closed Sun evening and Mon. **TV. Car park.**

The N6 from Paris to Nice used to be known as the "Route des Anglais" before the motorway to the Côte d'Azur was built. Those were the glory days of this establishment, though it's never really been done up by its new owners. There are ten simple rooms, all with double glazing; they're yours for €38 with shower or bath. You eat in the *Bistrot de Joingy*, a decent place with good-value menus of typical bistro fare and regional dishes – €9 and €12 on weekdays only, then €15 and €20. There's a fine, shady terrace. Free coffee.

🏃 🛏 |●| LE RIVE GAUCHE***

Chemin du Port-au-Bois; it's on the banks of the Yonne, very close to the old town.
☎ 03.86.91.46.66 📠 03.86.91.46.93
📧 lorain@relaischateaux.com
Closed Sun evening Nov–Feb inclusive. **Garden. TV.**
Car park. Swimming pool.

The Lorains realized that things were changing – so they built a modern building looking just like a chain hotel opposite their world-famous Côte Saint-Jacques (not reviewed here). The new establishment is welcoming and has good-looking, comfortable and functional rooms – doubles with bath €58. There's a pool, a tennis court and a garden. You can eat outside on the terraces or in the dining room, where the décor and the food both reflect modern tastes. The cooking is bistro-style, with set menus €16 in the week and others at €26–34. 10% discount on the room rate for a two-night stay.

CELLE-SAINT-CYR (LA)   89116 (8KM W)

🏃 🛏 |●| AUBERGE DE LA FONTAINE AUX MUSES**

How to get there: take exit 18 off the motorway and head for Joigny on the D943; after 3km, turn left when you come to the village of La Motte – the inn is 3km further.
☎ 03.86.73.40.22 📠 03.86.73.48.66
Closed Mon and Tues until 5pm (except July–Aug).
Hotel open for bookings only on Mon in July–Aug.
Swimming pool. Disabled access. TV. Car park.

Hidden away in the Burgundy hills, this country house inn is covered in Virginia creeper, and the rooms are wonderfully rustic: doubles with shower or bath for €55–96. The cooking is passionately Burgundian: foie gras, snails, pigeon and Burgundy beef. Set weekday menu €28, or à la carte. The Langevin family are musicians (father Claude composed the European anthem, no less), so their friends often turn up at weekends and a jam session frequently results. They also have their own vineyard, the Fontaine aux Muses, which produces white (Chardonnay) and red (Pinot Noir) wines. Tennis court and heated swimming pool. 10% discount on the room rate Oct–March inclusive.

VILLEVALLIER 89330 (9KM NW)

⅍ ☎ |●| LE PAVILLON BLEU**

31 rue de la République
☎ 03.86.91.12.17 ☏ 03.86.91.17.74
Closed Sun evening, Mon lunchtime and 1–15 Jan. **TV**. **Car park**.

It's worth coming to this place simply for the welcome. Besides that, the prices are attractively low for the region. Though the rooms are small, they're charming and comfortable. Doubles with shower/wc €35 or €41 with bath. Equally welcoming is the family-style cooking, which is served in substantial portions: snail salad, eggs *en meurette*, fillet of beef with grilled Époisse cheese, pike-perch and trout. Free house apéritif.

LORMES 58140

⅍ ☎ |●| HÔTEL PERREAU**

8 route d'Avallon (Centre).
☎ 03.86.22.53.21 ☏ 03.86.22.82.15
Closed Sun evening and Mon from Oct–end of May; also 1 Jan–15 Feb. **TV**.

This imposing building, which has had a successful face-lift, is large enough to accommodate an army of backpackers. The restaurant is very pretty and rustic-looking with a large fireplace and superb ceiling. The cooking is equally refined and there's the superb Burgundian menu, with prices running from €11 to €25. Rooms are spacious – the ones overlooking the garden have been renovated – and cost €41 with shower or bath. 10% discount on the room rate Sept–June.

VAUCLAIX 58140 (8KM S)

☎ |●| HÔTEL DE LA POSTE**

Vauclaix (Centre); it's 8km south of Lormes on the D944.
☎ 03.86.22.71.38 ☏ 03.86.22.76.00
e hoteldelaposte@ifrance.com
Swimming pool. Garden. Disabled access. TV. Car park.

Located in deepest, darkest Morvan, this is a popular and friendly hotel. Five generations of Desbruères have run the place and they're constantly doing it up and introduc-

ing new ideas – there's a swimming pool in the garden, a giant chess game and ping-pong. The rooms are big but cosy; doubles €31 with basin and €51 with shower/wc or bath. It's worth the trip here for the cooking alone. The two-page menu changes regularly and offers traditional dishes like beef fillet with morels and innovative ones like scallops and crayfish tails on leek purée. €9 weekday menu and others €15–40.

BAZOCHES-DU-MORVAN 58190 (17KM N)

⅍ |●| LE TIRE-BOUCHON

How to get there; take the D2 from Lormes in the direction of Clamecy, turn right on the D958 and it's at the beginning of the village.
☎ 03.86.22.11.66
Open Out of season, Mon–Sat lunchtimes; Fri and Sat evenings. **Closed** In season, Tues evening and Weds. **Car park.**

The café-restaurant has an atractive décor with bacchanalian paintings on the wall. Good, reliable French cuisine which is both substantial and tasty. Menus at €14 and €20, with two lunch menus (not Sat). There's a choice of local wines. A good place to stop if you're visiting the château de Bazoches. Free house apéritif.

LOUHANS 71500

☎ |●| LE MOULIN DE BOURGCHÂTEAU**

route de Châlon; from the centre of town take the D978 and turn right before the Citroën sign.
☎ 03.85.75.37.12 ☏ 03.85.75.45.11
e bourgchateau@francemel
Closed Lunchtimes, Sun from Oct–Easter and 20 Dec–20 Jan. **TV. Car park.**

If you feel the urge to do something romantic, try a trip to this old mill built in 1778 on the banks of the Seille, a tributary of the Saône. The location is superb and the rooms are very cosy – especially the ones under the eaves on the top floor. Those on the second floor have a rather vertiginous view of the river. Doubles €38–53 with shower/wc and €53–84. Very filling breakfast for €7. The restaurant overlooks the river and offers refined cooking. Set menus €20–29 and the *à la carte* dishes change regularly: *terrine* of duck with onion marmalade; roast pigeon with chopped liver sauce; walnut and currants in a pastry case. The ideal spot for a weekend away – whether you're with that special person or not.

🍴 |●| RESTAURANT LA COTRIADE

4 rue d'Alsace.
☎ 03.85.75.19.91
Closed last week in Feb. **Disabled access. Car park**.

Eating here can be agonizing if you find it hard to make decisions – there's a shoal of menus to choose from, all at reasonable prices (€11–32). Fresh ingredients are all-important and the fish and seafood are brought straight from Brittany – monkfish with seaweed, *cotriade* (a white fish stew with mussels, potatoes and cream), fish soup and sole with sorrel. If you fancy trying the local speciality, which is Bresse chicken, here they prepare it with a cream and morel sauce. The service can be a bit vague, so just remind them you're there. Free apéritif.

SAVIGNY-SUR-SEILLE   71440 (11KM W)

🍴 |●| AUBERGE LA RIVIÈRE

Tiellay.
☎ 03.85.74.99.03
Closed Tues evening, Wed in winter and 10 Jan–13 Feb.

This adorable country inn on the banks of the Seille was once the ferryman's home, and the attractive wood-framed building certainly has charm. You'll get a good reception and the cooking enjoys an excellent reputation. The owner, a keen angler, catches the fish for the restaurant. Set menus €15–28 or *à la carte*; dishes include Bresse chicken with morels or baked in a salt crust and served with a cream sauce, *gâteau de foies de volaille* (pounded chicken livers with *foie gras*), *suprême* of freshwater crayfish, whitebait, snails and salads. If *silurid* "house-style" is on the menu, order it – it's a monster fish from the local rivers and lakes. *Pocheuse*, a freshwater fish stew with garlic and white wine, is made to order. Attractive desserts. There's a dreamy terrace for fine days, and the lawn rolls down to the water. Free coffee.

BEAUREPAIRE-EN-BRESSE   71580 (14KM E)

🍴 🏠 |●| AUBERGE LA CROIX BLANCHE**

Centre; take the N78 in the direction of Lons-le-Saunier.
☎ 03.85.74.13.22 ➡ 03.85.74.13.25
Closed Sun evening and Mon 30 Sept–15 June;mid-Nov to mid-Dec.
Disabled access. TV. Car park.

There's a real country atmosphere in this genuine 17th-century coaching stop, which has been sensitively renovated. The first-rate free-range *poulet de Bresse* is irresistible, prepared in different ways at different times of the year by chef Gilles Poulet. Weekday menu €14, then others at €19–34. *À la carte* you can get rabbit with a spinach *mille-feuille*, breast of *poulet de Bresse* with *foie gras*, monkfish with garlic and game in season. All main courses change six times a year to reflect what the market has to offer. The hotel is at the back hidden among the trees. It dates from the 1970s but is not unattractive, and you'll get a good night's sleep as long as you don't have noisy neighbours (the partitions are a bit thin). Doubles with shower or bath €38. Free house apéritif or coffee.

SAILLENARD   71580 (20KM NE)

🍴 🏠 |●| AUBERGE LE MOULIN DE SAUVAGETTE

How to get there: take the D87 signposted to Saillenard and Bletterans – it's 3km from Saillenard.
☎ and ➡ 03.85.74.17.58
Closed Sun evening, Mon and Feb and Dec–Jan.

For lovers of country retreats (or for lovers pure and simple), this is the ultimate hideaway on the Burgundy borders, with all the delights of deepest, darkest Bresse. It's an old mill way out in the country, attractively converted and decorated. Wonderful bedrooms are furnished in old style at €38–44 with shower and bath. The miller's room is particularly fine, but each has its own charm. Rooms on reservation only. You'll get a very friendly reception and sample excellent regional cooking served in a beautiful, rustic dining room. Dishes are cooked using seasonal produce: local *terrine*, free-range chicken, fillet of zander with hazelnuts and frogs' legs *sauce poulette*. Set menus €18–20 or country platter €11; breakfast is €7. Worth visiting more than once. 10% discount on the room rate for a minimum three-night stay.

MÂCON   71000

🍴 🏠 HÔTEL D'EUROPE ET D'ANGLETERRE**

92 quai Jean-Jaurès (Northeast); it's near the train station.
☎ 03.85.38.27.94 ➡ 03.85.39.22.54
TV. Pay garage.

This 18th-century building has character and, with its original staircase and large public rooms, it offers the charm of a long-past era.

The hotel has been tastefully renovated and is well-located on the riverside; although it's right on the N6, the rooms are soundproofed. You'll get a nice welcome from the owner. Doubles are €41–49, and there are rooms to sleep four at €49 or five at €60. 10% discount and free garage space, except in July and August.

🚶 🏠 |O| INTER HÔTEL DE BOURGOGNE**

6 rue Victor-Hugo (Centre).
☎ 03.85.38.36.57 ➡ 03.85.21.10.23
Restaurant closed Sat lunchtime, Sun. **TV. Car park**.

Lovely hotel on a shady, flower-filled square just a step away from the pedestrian area. Delightful interior with a foyer that's straight out of a Chabrol film. Rooms are painted in pastel shades. Lots of twists and turns, half-landings, nooks and crannies. Doubles with shower/wc are €58, with bath €69. In the restaurant there's a 2-course lunch menu for €9 or others €12–23. Specialities include Bresse chicken in cream sauce and Burgundy snails. 10% discount on the room rate and free apéritif.

🚶 |O| MAISON MÂCONNAISE DES VINS

484 av. de-Lattre-de-Tassigny (North); it's on the bank of the Saône as you come into town from Chalon-sur-Saône.
☎ 03.85.22.91.11
📧 maisondesvins@wanadoo.fr
Open 1 Sept–30 June, 8am–6pm Mon to Thurs, Fri–Sat 8am–11pm and Sun 8am–10pm. **Disabled access**.
Car park.

This establishment represents a considerable number of vineyard owners from the Côtes Chalonnaises, Beaujolais and Mâcon. You can buy wine by the bottle or fill up a plastic container. They also serve a selection of regional specialities from €14 *à la carte* – *bœuf bourguignon*, *andouillette Mâconnaise*, salt pork with lentils, omelettes, salads, *fromage blanc* and particularly good house Mâconnais tarts and waffles. These are the perfect accompaniment to a Saint-Véran, a Pouilly-Fuissé, a Rully or a Givry, many of which are served by the glass. You'll be spoilt for choice – decide who's driving in advance! There's a terrace overlooking the Saône. Free house Kir.

|O| LA VIGNE ET LES VINS (SCOUBIDOU)

42 rue Joseph-Dufour (Centre).
☎ 03.85.38.53.72
Closed Sun, Mon and 29 July–20 Aug.

Service noon–2pm and 7.30–11pm. It's often hard to get a table in this rather ordi-nary-looking little restaurant, because they serve the best meat and the most generous portions in Mâcon. The owner – known as Scoubidou to his regulars – has a real passion for chunky and tasty slabs of the stuff. The sirloin literally melts in your mouth; eat it plain grilled or with mouthwatering sauces and crisp French fries. There's a pretty good choice – fillet, Châteaubriand, lamb chops, oriental kebabs. On Fridays and Saturdays in winter, they do couscous too. Large first-floor dining room for big groups on a night out – and it won't ruin you. €18 *à la carte*.

|O| LE POISSON D'OR

Allée du Parc (North); it's on the marina, 1km from the centre of town.
☎ 03.85.38.00.88 ➡ 03.85.35.82.55
Closed Tues evening in winter, Wed all year and Feb.
Disabled access. Car park.

Contemplate the glinting lights in the water and the shady river banks from the large picture windows of this plush but informal establishment, which also has a large, shaded terrace. Regional specialities include rabbit compote with prunes and onion marmalade, pike soufflé with frogs' legs, duck breast roasted with blackcurrants and fresh-fried river fish. Menus €17–40. It's a refined place with tables covered in thick white cloths and enormous vases of flowers everywhere. Attentive service.

|O| RESTAURANT LE ROCHER DE CANCALE

393 quai Jean-Jaurès (Centre).
☎ 03.85.38.07.50 ➡ 03.85.38.70.47
Closed Sun evening and Mon except on public holidays.

The 18th-century house on the river is a refined, elegant setting for this restaurant. The excellent €16 menu is not the kind of loss-leader you often find in slightly upmarket restaurants; the dishes are delicious and satisfying. If you want to eat more lavishly, there are other set menus at €21–38. The house specialities include warm flan of *foie gras*, Burgundy snails with garlic butter, *poulet de Bresse* with a cream and morel sauce and soufflé pancakes with lemon and apricot *coulis*. À la carte, a meal will cost around €38. They care about the little things here – the bread rolls are served fresh and hot from the oven.

|O| L'AMANDIER

74 rue Dufour (Centre); it's near the tourist office.
☎ 03.85.39.82.00

Closed Sun evening and Mon.

Salad of pig's trotters *gribiche* is the house speciality, but Florent Segain often rejigs his €16 and €20 set menus (not available on public holidays) to use what's best in the market. It's easy enough to find the restaurant since it's painted blue – the flowers and the plates are the same colour, complemented by the yellow fabrics in the cosy, comfortable dining room. They offer a string of other set menus from €25 up to €46. *À la carte* there are many delights, including Burgundy snails with parsley butter, perch with smoked bacon and a red Mâcon wine infusion, roast noisette of lamb with a rosemary and jus, boned pigs' trotters *gribiche* with vinaigrette sauce, roast fillet of red mullet with a four-spice infusion and tomato *timbale* with scallops. Flowers adorn the terrace.

SANCÉ   71000 (3KM N)

🏠 |●| LA VIEILLE FERME**

N6 motorway, exit Mâcon North.
☎ 03.85.40.95.15 ➡ 03.85.40.95.16
e vieil.ferme@wanadoo.fr
Closed 20 Nov–10 Dec.
Disabled access. Swimming pool. Garden. TV. Car park.

An old farm which has been restored in good taste and turned into a small hotel complex. It is particularly well-positioned on the banks of the Saône, surrounded by real cornfields and real cows, patient anglers and peaceful cyclists riding along the tow-path. The modern part is built like a motel and most of the bedrooms, €43, overlook the Saône or the countryside. They are spacious and pleasant and you hardly notice the high-speed train hurtling past. The lovely dining room has rustic décor and old-fashioned furniture, but on fine days the terrace is everyone's favourite place to be. Dishes, executed with care, are perfectly affordable – parsleyed frogs' legs, house *foie gras*, perch fillet with sherry sauce and breast of guinea fowl stuffed with ceps. Set menus €13–25, or a fairly standard *à la carte* menu. Beautiful swimming pool in summer and a generous lunchtime buffet.

CRÈCHES-SUR-SAÔNE   71680 (8KM S)

⅍ 🏠 |●| CHÂTEAU DE LA BARGE**

Centre; take the Mâcon sud exit on the A6 and follow the signs to the train station.
☎ 03.85.23.93.93 ➡ 03.85.23.93.39

ⓦ www.hoteldelanbarge.fr.st
Closed Sat and Sun 1 Nov–Easter; Tues April–Oct; 21 Dec–6 Jan. **TV. Car park**.

Château life at affordable prices. This enormous house, covered in Virginia creeper, dates from 1679, and it's surrounded by ancient trees. Quite a friendly welcome. The sturdy furniture, the large rooms echoing with birdsong, the wallpaper that's seen better days – everything seems to have come from another age. Doubles €43 with shower, €52 with bath. The restaurant offers tasty, simple cooking that showcases the quality of the ingredients – Burgundy snails with almond butter, house *foie gras* terrine, pike *terrine* with tarragon, rump steak with pepper. Menus start at €15 with others from €23 to €33. Really lovely terrace. Free house apéritif.

MILLY-LAMARTINE   71960 (10KM W)

⅍ |●| CHEZ JACK

pl. de l'Église (Centre); take the N79 from Mâcon and turn off at Milly-La Roche Vineuse.
☎ 03.85.36.63.72
Closed Sun evening, Mon and Tues evening, a fortnight Aug–Sept and a week in Dec. **Disabled access.**

A lovely little village restaurant in the shadow of a beautiful church and Lamartine's house, boasting good Beaujolais cooking. Tables are set outside on fine days. Weekday lunch menu €8; dinner menu €13. *À la carte* a meal will cost €13 on average and dishes include calf's foot *remoulade*, veal kidneys in cream, oven-baked *andouillette*, *entrecôte* steak, hot sausage and *tablier de sapeur* (a slab of ox tripe egged, crumbed and fried). Good wine selection by the jug or the bottle: Mâcon rouge, Régnié, Pouilly-Fuissé and so on. Free coffee.

SAINT-VÉRAND   71570 (13KM S)

⅍ 🏠 |●| L'AUBERGE DE SAINT-VÉRAN**

How to get there: leave the A6 at exit 29 to Vinzelles, Juliénas and Saint-Vérand.
☎ 03.85.23.90.90 ➡ 03.85.23.90.91
Closed Tues out of season. **Garden. TV. Car park.**

In an unspoilt village in the hills among the vineyards lies this lovely stone house with a terrace and garden and a stream flowing nearby. Inside is a clean, simple hotel with good facilities. The restaurant specialises in regional cooking, with menus €20 (weekdays) and €24–40 and attractively priced regional wine. *À la carte* it offers casserole of *andouillette* sausage and veal spleen with Saint Véran, monkfish medallions and tail in Pouilly, *ballotine* (aspic) of free-range chicken stuffed with morels and *coq au vin*. Double rooms at €53–60 with shower/wc, and they do half board arrangements on request. Free apéritif, and free bed for children under two.

MAILLY-LE-CHÂTEAU   89660

🎿 🏠 I●I LE CASTEL**

pl. de l'Église.
☎ 03.86.81.43.06 ➡ 03.86.81.49.26
✉ michelbreerette@waika9.com
Closed Wed and 15 Nov–15 March. **Disabled access. Garden. Car park**.

It's straight out of a picture book – a 13th-century church, a town hall and a solid, turn-of-the-19th-century house in a courtyard shaded by lime trees. The hotel and restaurant are both good value for money. Rooms are being renovated one by one and the bathrooms are being refitted so, if you wish, you can see them and choose the one that suits you. Doubles €23 with washbasin and up to €50 with bath. Local dishes predominate – snails with hazelnuts, Charolais steak with mustard, *coq au vin* and raspberry *au gratin*. The €11 menu is served every day and there are others €16–27. Free kir as a welcome.

MOULINS-ENGILBERT   58290

🎿 🏠 I●I AU BON LABOUREUR**

pl. Boucaumont (Centre).
☎ 03.86.84.20.55 ➡ 03.86.84.35.52
Closed first fortnight in Jan. **TV. Car park**.

One of the most reliable places in the south of the Morvan where you can have a scrumptious meal at an attractive price. The dishes are generously served and carefully prepared: Burgundy snails with smoked bacon, ceps, poached egg and *meurette* sauce; veal with cumin and truffle; *mille-feuille* of apples; *foie gras* with rhubarb jelly. Weekday menu €11 and others €17–36. The rooms range from simple to quite comfortable – €24–45. Free coffee and 10% discount on the rooms with en-suite bathrooms 11 Nov–30 April.

BRINAY   58110 (11KM NW)

🎿 I●I L'ANCIEN CAFÉ

In the village (Centre); take the D10 signposted Cergy-

La-Tour and turn left at Biches.
☎ 03.86.84.90.79
Closed Sun evening.

A modest bar-cum-grocery-cum-bread store-cum-garage with a real restaurant attached. Tasty dishes, generously served: Morvan ham, calf's head, Charolais steaks and house *terrine*. There's a 2-course *formule* for €8 and menus cost €10–17. Run by the owners and their daughter. There's a shaded terrace.

SAINTE-PÉREUSE   58110 (14KM N)

I●I AUBERGE DE LA MADONETTE

Centre; from Châtillon-en-Bazois, take the D978 and follow the signs for Château-Chinon, turning left 8km beyond Châtillon-en-Bazois.
☎ 03.86.84.45.37
Closed Tues and Wed evenings except July–Aug, and 15 Dec–5 Feb. **Car park**.

Marie-Madeleine Grobost used to look after disabled children before changing career and going into the restaurant business. She set about transforming this enormous house, decorating it in gingham throughout and making the most of its magnificent terraced garden with a stunning view of the Morvan hills. She offers tasty country cooking and dishes like calf's head *à l'ancienne*, pan-fried lamb with parsley and garlic and pan-fried sweetbreads on *rosés* mushrooms. Set weekday menus €11 and others up to €41.

SÉMELAY   58369 (19KM S)

I●I RESTAURANT GILLES PERRIN

In the village; it's on the D158 in the direction of Saint Honoré-les-Bains.
☎ 03.86.30.91.66
Closed Mon, every evening except Sat except in July and Aug, and mid-Jan to mid-Feb.

A traditional restaurant with a good local reputation. This is the place to go for a meal with friends, or if someone's just dropped in. Weekday lunch menu €11 and others €15–25, with an amazing salmon and bream in Chablis sauce, veal sweetbreads in Noilly or *noisette* of Charolais steak cooked exactly as you order. The dining room has a countrified, provincial feel.

CHIDDES   58360 (27KM SE)

🎿 I●I LA BOUILLE À MALYS

In the village; take the D985 in the direction of Saint Honoré-les-Bains and Luzy; it's signposted off to the left.

☎ 03.86.30.48.90
✉ labouilleamalys@aol.com
Closed Wed, Jan–Feb. **Disabled access. TV.**

This place is run by a couple from the Morvand who wanted to stay in their native area and do something fun. They've created a really matey café-restaurant, decorating it in soft, warm colours. Absolutely reliable local cuisine – *andouillette*, grilled salmon fillet, the *patronne's* home-made stew or Charolais steak with Roquefort cheese sauce. Lunch menu for €8 and others €10–18. On Saturday they have karaoke or theme evenings with dishes from further afield – couscous, paella, *choucroute* and so on. Free coffee or, if there are four of you ordering the €14 menu, a T-shirt.

MOUX-EN-MORVAN 58230

🏃 🛏 |●| HÔTEL-RESTAURANT BEAU SITE*

Bellvue-Moux-en-Morvan: it's on the D121.
☎ 03.86.76.11.75 ➡ 03.86.76.15.84
Closed Sun evening and Mon in March, Nov and Dec; Jan–Feb. **Locked car park.**

An ordinary-looking place but the name's appropriate – it's in a fantastic setting. Sound home cooking at good prices, specializing in traditional dishes with lots of sauce. First menu at €11 is very respectable; others €14–29. In the hotel, a five-minute walk away, there are cheap, simple and spacious rooms; doubles with basin €23 and up to €39 with bath. Free apéritif.

NEVERS 58000

🏃 🛏 HÔTEL BEAUSÉJOUR**

5 [bis] rue Saint-Gildard; it's opposite the shrine of St Bernadette.
☎ 03.86.61.20.84 ➡ 03.86.59.15.37
Closed end Dec. **TV. Garden. Car park.**

Cheap, simple, functional rooms which are spotlessly clean. Just out of the town centre in a busy street but everything is well soundproofed and the garden rooms are very quiet. Doubles with washing facilities €22, up to €35 with bath. The welcome is really charming and breakfast is available on the veranda from a self-service buffet. 10% discount on the room rate in Aug and €1.5 deduction other times. Free car park.

🏃 🛏 HÔTEL DE CLÈVES**

8 rue Saint-Didier (Centre).

☎ 03.86.61.15.87 ➡ 03.86.57.13.80
Closed 26 Jan–2 Jan. **TV. Garden.**

Well placed, not far from the station in a quiet street in the town centre. A small establishment, very well run by an affable woman who's happy to chat while you have breakfast. The rooms have been updated with quality bedding. There's a small, pleasant corner of a garden. Double with shower €23, €44 with bath. 10% discount at weekends.

🏃 🛏 HÔTEL MOLIÈRE

25 rue Molière. Take the boulevard du Maréchal-Juin; when you get to the BP garage turn right into the rue de Vauzelles and follow the signs.
☎ 03.86.57.29.96
Closed the first fortnight in Aug. **TV. Car park. Garden.**

A small hotel in a quiet spot near the town centre run by a kindly, welcoming lady. The rooms are bright and cheerful and half of them have views over the garden. Excellent beds. Double rooms €41 with shower/wc and €43 with bath. There are some non-smoking rooms. There's a big, enclosed (and free) car park across the road. One free breakfast per room 1 Oct–31 March.

🏃 🛏 |●| HÔTEL-RESTAURANT LA FOLIE

Route des Saulaies.
☎ 03.86.57.05.31 ➡ 03.86.57.66.69
🌐 www.hotel-lafolie.com
Restaurant closed Fri and Sun evening Sept–May, and Fri lunchtime June–Aug. **Swimming pools. Garden. TV. Car park.**

It's well worth choosing this place – its park, tennis court and swimming pools give it an atmosphere of a holiday club. Bedrooms are contemporary in design and €45 with shower or bath – no charge for children under two and cots are available. You eat either in the dining room or on the terrace, which has a distant view of the Loire. Cheapest menu at €15 and others €20–25. No charge for parking. It's advisable to book. Free kir and 10% discount on the room rate.

🏃|●| LE GOÉMON – CRÊPERIE BRETONNE

9 rue du 14-Juillet; it's near the town hall and the cathedral.
☎ 03.86.59.54.99
Closed Sun, Mon, and end-Aug into early Sept.

Somewhat dreary setting, but the savoury *crêpes* are anything but dull. There's an excellent variety, the tastiest filled with *Guéméné andouillette* sausage, and the sweet ones are good too. At lunchtime there's a €9 menu of starter, savoury *galette* and dessert. Expect to pay about €14 *à la carte*. Friendly service. Free apéritif.

|●| RESTAURANT AUX CHŒURS DE BACCHUS

25 av. du Général-de-Gaulle (Centre); near the station.
☎ 03.86.36.72.70
Closed Sat lunchtime, Sun, mid-Dec to beginning of Jan, and the first three weeks in Aug.

Very good – very, very good – little restaurant. Service is slick, fast and friendly. The cuisine has been honed and improved over the years; it's self-confident and delicious, and the dishes strictly follow the seasons. Enjoy wine carefully chosen to complement each dish, turning your meal into a feast fit for a king – at affordable prices. The €13 menu is also served in the evenings and there are others €19–28.

|●| LA COUR SAINT-ÉTIENNE

33 rue Saint-Étienne (Centre); it's behind the church of Saint-Étienne.
☎ 03.86.36.74.57
Closed Sun, Mon, 1–18 Jan and 1–25 Aug.

Two dining rooms decorated in gentle colours, a discreet classical interior and competent service. So far, so good. Better still are the dishes which change regularly with the seasons; delicate salmon stuffed with artichoke and aubergine or supreme of chicken stuffed with ceps. On the dessert front, the *croquant* of pear with chicory is a triumph. Menus €14 (not served Sat) to €24. In summer they set a few tables on the terrace opposite the beautiful church of Saint-Étienne.

|●| RESTAURANT JEAN-MICHEL COURON

21 rue Saint-Étienne (Centre); it's near the church of Saint-Étienne.
☎ 03.86.61.19.28
Closed Sun evening, Mon and Tues lunchtime, 2–18 Jan and 15 Jul–5 Aug.

A Michelin star for the star restaurant of Nevers. Three small, elegant rooms, one in a particularly charming gothic style. Fine, well-balanced cuisine. More surprising are the realistic prices: menus start at €18 (weekdays only), including cheese or dessert, and go up to €40. Particularly good are the tomato and apple tart and the

stewed plaice fillet with a red pepper and sage compote. For dessert, the warm spiced chocolate soup is a delight. Probably worth booking.

MARZY · 58000 (5KM W)

⅍ ♠ |●| LE VAL DE LOIRE

Corcelles village; take the D131, it's on the edge of the village on the way to Corcelles.
☎ 03.86.38.86.21
Disabled access. Car park.

A quiet, cheap place with a nice family feeling. Doubles €20 with basin to €31 with bath. The rooms are in a new annexe and are very well-maintained. The only drawback is that it's a bit far from Nevers and there are only two buses a day. Uncomplicated dishes – snails, frogs' legs, steaks – in ambitious portions and honestly-priced menus €9–18. Free apéritif.

SAVIGNY-LES-BOIS · 58160 (10KM E)

⅍ |●| RESTAURANT LE MOULIN DE L'ÉTANG

64 route de l'Étang. Take the D978 from Nevers–Château–Chinon then turn right on the D18. It's just outside the village on the D209.
☎ 03.86.37.10.17
Closed Mon, Wed evening and 2–15 Jan. **Car park.**

One of the good tables in the area; excellent brawn on the €18 menu served with all the fat, a "slimline" *sauce gribiche* and a tasty *mignon* of pork in game marinade. The desserts are a little disappointing – the *crème brûlée* is heavy and over-sweet – but it's still a good place. Attentive, friendly service in the large, provincial-feeling dining room. Other menus €23–38. Free coffee.

MAGNY-COURS · 58470 (12KM S)

⅍ ♠ |●| HÔTEL-RESTAURANT LA RENAISSANCE***

2 rue de Paris. It's in the village; take the N7.
☎ 03.86.58.10.4 📠 03.86.21.22.60
e hotel-la-renaissance@wanadoo.fr
Closed Sun evening, Mon, three weeks in Feb–Mar and a fortnight in Aug. **TV. Car park.**

A smart hotel-restaurant where the cooking has a good local reputation. It's about 3km from Magny-Cours car racing circuit, and it's full of guys from the pits who like the chef's tasty cooking. He uses the freshest produce: frogs' legs *à la bourguignonne*;

grilled monkfish with an escalope of duck *foie gras* and Saint-Émilion wine sauce; sole with foaming butter; duck breast with *jus nerveux*. Good Loire wines at affordable prices, served in a pleasant dining room with attentive service. The €38 menu includes wine and there are others at €46–67. Bedrooms have good facilities and cost from €76 for a double. A seriously good place in this category. Free house apéritif.

NITRY   89310

I●I AUBERGE LA BEURSAUDIÈRE

Chemin de Ronde (northwest); it's on the Sacy road.
☎ 03.86.33.69.69
Closed 2–3 weeks in Jan. **Car park**.

A superb Morvan building with a medieval dovecote. There's an emphasis on "local" character here: waitresses in regional costume, quaint menu titles and the like, but the terrace is great – it really sizzles in summer. Sturdy local dishes built for robust appetites. In the week, there's a €11 *formule* of starter and a main course, but the first real menu costs €15, with others €28–35. A hotel is currently being built.

NOYERS-SUR-SEREIN   89310 (10KM NE)

♠ I●I HÔTEL DE LA VIEILLE TOUR

pl. du Grenier-à-Sel (Centre).
☎ 03.86.82.87.69 ➥ 03.86.82.66.04
Closed 10ct–1 April.

This elegant 17th-century edifice, swathed in creepers, was the home of the writer Charles-Louis Pothier, famed throughout France for the song *Les Roses Blanches*. It's since become a picture gallery with a few rooms and a simple place to eat. The *patronne* is Dutch and, fittingly, she's also an art-historian. The setting is warm and informal; the place is more a guest house than a hotel-restaurant. Double rooms are €31 with basin and €38–53 with shower/wc or bath. Menus €13–15. They use lots of fresh vegetables and herbs from the garden. Overall, an amazing place – something from another era, just like the village.

NOLAY   21340

♣I●I RESTAURANT LE BURGONDE

35 rue de la République; Nolay lies between Beaune and

Autun.
☎ 03.80.21.71.25
Closed Tues, Wed and the Feb school holidays.

Service noon–2pm and 7–9pm. They've kept the shop front of this small department store, but today a restaurant occupies the sales floor. The dining room has a strong bourgeois style with green plants everywhere and a beamed wooden ceiling; it's absolutely charming. In the second dining room there's another surprise: a winter garden on a veranda, enclosed by a conservatory. All very pleasant, very plush. There's a regional menu and the chef uses produce bought from the neighbouring farms and local producers – pancakes made from spelt flour, eggs *en meurette*, snails with creamed garlic, *millefeuille* of perch with spiced bread, Bresse chicken with morel sauce. Menus from €16 and up to €43; wine at reasonable prices. Good service. Free apéritif.

NUITS-SAINT-GEORGES   21700

♣ ♠ I●I HÔTEL IRIS

1 av. Chamboland (South); it's on the edge on the Beaune side of town.
☎ 03.80.61.17.17
Ⓦ www.hotel-iris.fr
Disabled access. TV. Car park.

This used to be a dreary chain hotel which closed and fell into serious disrepair. But it's been taken over and turned into a small, welcoming establishment – ideal for an overnight stay. It's a place worth supporting, even if it falls short of perfection. Double rooms €45. The restaurant serves local dishes: *foie gras* cooked in a cloth, Burgundy snails in a pastry case, eggs in *meurette* sauce, *bœuf bourguignon*, *coq au vin*, perch *pocheuse* style. Weekday lunch menu €10; others €12–29. There's a corner bar where you can try the local vintage, as well as a terrace. Free apéritif and breakfast Nov–April.

I●I LE RESTAURANT DE LA TOUR

14 rue Général-de-Gaulle (Southwest); it's on the Beaune road.
☎ 03.80.61.17.20
Closed Sun evening and Mon.

A very well-run family establishment offering attractive prices, a good choice of wines and cuisine cooked using fresh ingredients of the highest quality. Regional dishes include the famous chicken Gaston-Gérard, a recipe inadvertently created by the first wife of the former mayor of Dijon. The mayor was entertaining a gastronome and critic when Madame, in her nervousness, dropped a small tin of paprika into a pan of chicken cooking in white wine and Gruyère cheese. The result was a triumph. There's a €10 lunch menu in the week and others at €12–26.

VOUGEOT   21640 (5KM N)

🎨 🏠 HÔTEL DE VOUGEOT

18 rue du Vieux-Château.
☎ 03.80.62.01.15 ➡ 03.80.62.49.09
📧 info@castel-tres.girard.com
TV. Car park.

Vougeot is world-famous for the wine festivals organized by the Confrérie du Clos Vougeot, founded to maintain the quality of Burgundy's wines and to promote them across the globe. This odd hotel, with its dreary façade, is not what you'd expect to find here, but the lovely courtyard and the peace and tranquillity make up for that. Rooms, some with a view of the château, are €53–75. It has a bar where they serve local wine. Everyone is treated well – even tourists clutching guide books. 10% discount Nov–May.

CURTIL-VERGY   21220 (5KM NW)

🏠 HÔTEL LE MANASSES

rue Guillaume de Tavanes; as you leave the village, take the side road going up to the Hautes Côtes de Nuits.
☎ 03.80.61.43.81 ➡ 03.80.61.42.79
Closed Dec–Feb. **TV. Car park.**

There's a splendid view over the vineyards and a remarkable silence to this place. The Chaleys and other winegrowers in the area have built up the reputation of the wines from the Hautes Côtes. In his younger days, the grandfather used to deliver his wines himself; his son does the same today, but at least he has a car. They have constructed this charming little hotel and turned a barn into a wine museum where you can sample the goods. Breakfast is Burgundy style. Very comfortable doubles €69–92.

VILLARS-FONTAINE   21220 (5KM W)

🍴 AUBERGE DU COTEAU

It's in the centre.
☎ 03.80.61.10.50 ➡ 03.80.61.30.32
Closed Tues evening and Wed, a fortnight in Feb and 15

Aug–10 Sept. **Car park.**

This is a real country inn, serving home-made terrine, coq au vin, snails and lots of other lovely local dishes. They'll satisfy your hunger after a walk through the vineyards and your thirst will be more than slaked by the local wines from the Hautes Côtes. There's an open fire, checked tablecloths and old-fashioned prices – the weekday lunch menu costs €9, and there are others at €12–19. It's a perfect place to come after an afternoon exploring the countryside behind the Côte de Nuits – a region famous for its goats, artisan craftsmen, hilltop chapels and ruined castle museums.

AUVILLARS-SUR-SAÔNE   21250 (12KM SE)

🍴 AUBERGE DE L'ABBAYE

route de Seurre.
☎ 03.80.26.97.37
📧 auberge-abbaye@wanadoo.fr
Closed Sun and Tues evenings, Wed and 6–13 Jan and 30 June–7 Jul. **Car park.**

You simply have to stop here – it's only 1km from Citeaux Abbey, the mother house of the Cistercian order. And the restaurant offers enough reasons of its own: the chef creates succulent dishes and you can try his specialities at almost prix fixe prices. Eat in the bistro corner (which is as delightful as can be) and opt for the menu of the day – chicken liver terrine, pork with apples and bread and butter pudding are typical. The bistro formule at lunchtime in the week costs €13, and there are other menus €19–37. Their specialities include crayfish salad with hazelnuts, spiced bread terrine, veal and chicken pie and, in winter, cream of morel soup. There's a picturesque terrace. Free coffee.

PARAY-LE-MONIAL   71600

🎨 🏠 🍴 GRAND HÔTEL DE LA BASILIQUE**

18 rue de la Visitation (Centre); it's 100m from the basilica, opposite the chapel of the Visitation.
☎ 03.85.81.11.13 ➡ 03.85.88.83.70
🌐 www.hotelbasilique.com
Closed 1 Nov–15 March. **TV. Pay car park.**

Double rooms go for €40–49, all with new bathrooms, and regional dishes are served in the restaurant – menus €11–27. Of the specialities, try the turbot, the Charolais beef steak label rouge (which means its origins can be traced) and œufs en meurette.

Delightful hotel but best behaviour is required – it's a favourite of visiting pilgrims. 10% discount on the room rate Sept–July.

🏃 🏠 |●| HÔTEL TERMINUS***

27 av. de la Gare (North); it's opposite the train station.
☎ 03.85.81.59.31 ➡ 03.85.81.38.31
Restaurant closed Sat, Sun and 1–15 Nov. **TV**. **Car park**.

Big, well-restored hotel. Don't let the austere façade put you off; once inside you'll be warmly greeted and you'll see that the owners pay great attention to detail. The spacious rooms have been revamped and decorated in matching floral fabric. The bathrooms in particular are fantastic: the marriage of materials – wood, perspex and high-pressure jets in the shower – is rather futuristic. Rooms from €50 with shower/wc to €61 with bath. A limited number of good dishes in the brasserie, with a lunch menu at €13. Free coffee.

POUILLY-SUR-LOIRE   58150

🏃 🏠 |●| LE RELAIS FLEURI – COQ HARDI***

42 av. de la Tuillerie; it's 1km southeast of the centre, opposite the wine cellars.
☎ 03.86.39.12.99 ➡ 03.86.39.14.15
e le-relais-fleuri-sarl@wanadoo.fr
Closed Tues evening and Wed Oct–April; mid-Dec to mid-Jan. **TV**. **Garden**. **Car park**.

Typical *Logis de France* hotel, with rustic furniture and flowers everywhere. The rooms are good, particularly those with a view over the Loire. Doubles with shower or bath €46–70. The restaurant serves regional cooking worth its salt: smoked salmon pancake with vine stems, roast turbot with meat *jus* and honey-roast Nivernais pigeon. Menus start at €17 then €26 and €41. A pleasant, reliable establishment. Free digestif.

QUARRÉ-LES-TOMBES   89630

🏠 |●| HÔTEL-RESTAURANT LE MORVAN

6 rue des Écoles (Centre).
☎ 03.86.32.29.29 ➡ 03.86.32.29.28
Closed Mon and Tues (except July–Aug); 2 weeks in Oct; Jan–Feb. **Disabled access**. **Garden**. **TV**. **Car park**.

One of those places where you feel at ease as soon as you walk through the door – largely because of the smiling welcome. The rooms

are decorated in individual style; doubles €46–66. The cooking is pure Burgundy and dishes show off the freshness of the seasonal market produce. Menus €17–40. Things are done simply but well.

🏃 🏠 |●| AUBERGE DE L'ÂTRE***

Les Lavaults; take the N6 then the D10 in the direction of Lac des Settons.
☎ 03.86.32.20.79 ➡ 03.86.32.28.25
Closed Tues evening and Wed out of season, 25 Nov–10 Dec and 1 Feb–10 March. **Disabled access**. **Garden**. **TV**. **Car park**.

This inn is in an isolated spot in the tough country of the Morvan. The bar is like an old-fashioned bistro with warm, rustic décor. The chef plays around with the plants and mushrooms he picks locally to create his delicious dishes – this is probably the most inventive cooking in the area and it's at realistic prices too. Menus from €23 (weekdays) then €37–45 at other times. It's a charming place where you may well be tempted to stay. If so, they have seven pleasant rooms, €61–92, with good facilities. 10% discount on the room rate 1 Oct–Easter.

BRIZARDS (LES)   89630 (8KM SE)

🏃 🏠 |●| AUBERGE DES BRIZARDS**

How to get there: take the D55 and follow the signs.
☎ 03.86.32.20.12 ➡ 03.86.32.27.40
Closed 5 Jan–8 Feb. **Disabled access**. **TV**. **Car park**.

An isolated fairytale of a place in the depths of the bewitching Morvan forest. Doubles with shower/wc or bath €38–84. In the winter they light a wood fire so you can snuggle up, while in the summer the old stones prove nice and cool. Service is conducted with a smile in a bright dining room, which looks nothing like it used to when Grandma Odette ran the place. Try the zander stewed in red wine, the pork pie or the genuine black pudding with home-grown apples and spiced bread. The cheapest of their range of menus costs €22 and includes wine; others go up to €46. Free apéritif.

ROCHE-EN-BRENIL (LA)   21530

🏃 |●| AUX PORTES DU MORVAN

It's on the RN6.
☎ 03.80.64.75.28
Closed Tues evening, Wed, Christmas to early Jan and a fortnight June/July. **Disabled access**. **Car park**.

Tasty, healthy food that won't turn your

stomach when you see the bill. The chef's specialities include *terrine façon Ginette*, ham with cream, eggs in wine sauce and Morvan tarts at the weekend. Get into the swing before your meal by having a drink at the bar, which is full of local regulars. Menus €10–23 and they also provide snacks like omelettes at any time of the day. Free coffee.

ROMANECHE-THORINS   71720

⅓ ☎ |●| HÔTEL-RESTAURANT LA MAISON BLANCHE**

N6 (Centre); it's south of Mâcon, on the border of Rhône.
☎ 03.85.35.50.53 ➡ 03.85.35.21.22
Closed Sun evening, Mon and 6 Jan–6 Feb. **Swimming pool**. **TV**. **Car park**.

The roadside location of this establishment doesn't make you feel like stopping, but here you get fantastic regional cooking created with great professional skill. The décor is pretty conventional but the service is attentive and they score points where it counts – for the quality of the food. Highlights from the menus include salmon smoked over beechwood, pan-fried frogs' legs, lobster with spring vegetables and coral sauce, *andouillette au gratin*, and tournedos with morels – and their *coq au vin* is the best you're likely to eat. Menus start cheaply at €14 and go up to €38. They've a few comfy bedrooms, doubles €27–31; the ones at the front are soundproofed. Half board, which is compulsory, costs €44. Free apéritif.

RULLY   71150

☎ |●| LE VENDANGEROT**

6 pl. Sainte-Marie (Centre).
☎ 03.85.87.20.09 ➡ 03.85.91.27.18
Closed Tues, Wed, 1–15 Jan and 15 Feb–10 March.
Garden. **TV**. **Car park**.

On the square of this picturesque wine village stands a substantial house surrounded by flowers and greenery. As a reminder of its previous incarnation, the old *Hôtel du Commerce* sign stills hangs outside. Inside it's new and run by excellent staff. The chef, Armand, creates wonderful things. Weekday menu is at €15 with others up to €38; these include things like oxtail with vegetables and morels, perch with Chardonnay Marc, crayfish tails in a white Rully wine broth, grain-fed pigeon with a

truffle sauce and *coq au vin* in white wine. Try the wine of the village – they serve Rully by the glass. The rooms have heavy wooden shutters and the village is quiet – altogether an ideal escape from the stress of town. Rooms for €43–46 with shower or bath.

SAINT-CHRISTOPHE-EN-BRIONNAIS 71800

|●| BAR-RESTAURANT DU MIDI

Grand-Rue (Centre); either on the D34 from Paray-le-Monial or from Clayette on the D989.
☎ 03.85.25.87.06 ➡ 03.85.25.90.63
Closed Mon and Jan.

Thursday is market day and for a good number of years Marielle and Dominique Lauvernier have opened at 6am to feed and water the horse-dealers and traders. They all pile into the big dining room-cum-canteen beyond the bar and the kitchen; dishes include tasty brawn, ham hock, delicious *pot-au-feu* (meat poached with vegetables), good sirloin and skirt – they use only top quality meat. If you don't fancy the bustle, it's quieter the rest of the week. Menus €9–19. Decent Côtes-du-Rhône, Mâcon Village and Saint-Véran.

SAINT-FLORENTIN   89600

☎ |●| LES TILLEULS**

3 rue Decourtive (Centre).
☎ 03.86.35.09.09 ➡ 03.86.35.36.90
ℯ alliances.tilleuls@wanadoo.fr
Restaurant closed Sun evening, Mon, a week at the end of Dec, and Feb. **Garden**. **TV**. **Lock-up car park**.

Service noon–2pm and 7.30–9pm. In a quiet side street just outside the centre. You can have a peaceful lunch under the lime trees here, on a pretty terrace surrounded by an equally pretty garden and far from the stress of daily life. Set menus start at €15 and go up to €38. Staff are rather reserved. Comfortable rooms with good facilities cost €47–50 with shower/wc or bath.

SAINT-JULIEN-DE-JONZY   71110

☎ |●| HÔTEL-RESTAURANT-BOUCHERIE PONT BERNARD**

Le bourg; it's 8km south of Saint-Christophe-en-Brionnais – from Paray-le-Monial, take the D34 and the D20.
☎ 03.85.84.01.95 ➡ 03.85.84.14.61

Closed Mon eening and the Feb school holidays. **TV**. **Swimming pool. Car park**.

This is Charolais country, 30km north of Roanne, and they don't do things by halves. Monsieur Pont is both butcher and cook so the meat is of superb quality, cooked up in generous portions; this is simple, tasty home cooking. Dishes on the middle-priced menus include *coq au vin* and fillet of sea bream with champagne sauce; others include home-made *foie gras*, *tournedos* and farm-raised veal escalope in cream sauce. Excellent desserts. There's a weekday lunch menu at €9 and others are €14–24. Simple and comfortable rooms with bath at €34–43. Kind, congenial hosts.

SAULIEU   21210

⅔ 🏠 |O| LA VIEILLE AUBERGE

15 rue Grillot (South).
☎ 03.80.64.13.74
Closed Tues evening and Wed except July–Aug, and 10 Jan–10 Feb. **Garden. Car park**.

Everyone who drove south on the N6 to the coast knew Saulieu well, but when the *autoroute* opened the old town fell on leaner times. A new generation of restaurateurs have put Saulieu back on the gastronomic and touristic map, however, and two of them took over this inn. Having said that, you could drive past without even noticing; it's tucked away behind a bend in the road. The cooking is well worth finding: try the brilliant mousse of zander *soufflé* with Aligoté, the *terrine* of Charolais, *marbré* of rabbit or roast zander with red wine. Menus €11–27. Absolutely delightful dining room and an attractive hidden terrace. Rooms with shower/wc or bath €32. 10% discount on the room rate for two nights minimum.

⅔ 🏠 |O| LA BORNE IMPÉRIALE**

14–16 rue d'Argentine (Centre).
☎ 03.80.64.19.76
Closed Tuesday evening, Wed and 15 Nov–15 Dec. **Garden. TV. Car park**.

Near Pompom's famous sculpture of a bull – a Saulieu landmark – you'll find *La Borne Impériale*, a gastronomic landmark and one of the last old-fashioned inns in Burgundy. It has seven rooms at €34–46, the best of which have a view of the attractive garden. The beautiful dining room has a terrace for fine days. Weekday menu at €14 and others up to €26, listing good, regional cooking:

coddled eggs with snails, braised ham with morels and warm strawberries with vanilla ice. The welcome is variable. Free coffee.

SEMUR-EN-AUXOIS   21140

⅔ 🏠 |O| HÔTEL DU LAC**

10 rue du Lac.
☎ 03.80.97.11.11 ➡ 03.80.97.29.25
ⓦ www.hoteldulacdepont.com
Closed Sun evening, Mon out of season, and 5 Nov–9 Jan. **Garden. TV. Car park**.

Just below the lake, this huge building reeks of the 1950s. Some pleasant rooms but some are fairly dreary; €43–48. There's a family atmosphere in the restaurant and the kind of regional cooking you'd eat during a traditional Sunday lunch: dishes like *jambon persillé* made with local ham, chicken *fricassée* with mushrooms, *coq au vin* and calf's head in a spicy *vinaigrette*. A set menu at €14 is served in the week; others are €16–24. Try the local *blanc de l'Auxois*, which is very drinkable and deserves to be more widely known. There's a terrace with a canopy for fine summer days. Free house apéritif.

⅔ 🏠 HÔTEL DES CYMAISES**

7 rue du Renaudot (Centre).
☎ 03.80.97.21.44 ➡ 03.80.97.18.23
ⓔ hotel.cymaises@libertysurf.fr
Closed 10 Feb–1 March and a fortnight in Nov. **Disabled access. TV. Car park**.

In the heart of the medieval city, just behind Porte Sauvigny, there's a beautiful 18th-century building which has adapted extremely well to life as a 21st-century hotel. It's cool, clean and comfortable, and you can come and go as you please. Breakfast is served under the pergola. Nicely furnished rooms at €49–55. 10% discount on the room rate Nov–March.

|O| LE CALIBRESSAN

16 rue Feveret.
☎ 03.80.97.32.40
ⓔ le.calibressan@wanadoo.fr
Closed Sat lunchtime, Sun evening, Mon and Jan.

A twist of California in this Bresse kitchen, which is why it's called *Calibressan*. An attractive little restaurant combining authentic rustic decor – beams, unadorned brick walls, flowers and pretty curtains – with the vitality and exoticism of America, well-represented by Madame at reception. You'll also detect flavours of the New World in certain sauces and side dishes.

Try the roast kangaroo fillet with Grand Veneur sauce or the house chilli con carne. Weekday lunch menu €13 and others €16–28.

|●| RESTAURANT DES MINIMES

39 rue Vaux; it's 500m from the town centre.
☎ 03.80.97.26.86
Closed Sun evening, Mon and the end of Dec except for New Year's Eve. **Disabled access**.

Service noon–2pm and 7.30–9.30/10pm. This "local" bistro below the ramparts has become an absolute must for tourists in search of the soul and the cooking of Semur. There's a pastoral feel to the décor and an informal atmosphere; on offer are a €15 menu and a *menu-carte* at €23. The *patronne* loves good wine and good banter and she's completely unfazed by anyone – from local politicians to people who quibble about the bill. You can have *œufs en meurette* in a red wine sauce, salmon *à l'unilatéral* (grilled on just one side), steak with Époisses cheese, boned and caramelized pig's trogger, calf's head *ravigote*, *clafoutis* with sour cherries and iced nougat.

ALÉSIA   21150 (20KM NE)

|●| L'AUBERGE DU CHEVAL BLANC

Rue du Miroir (Centre).
☎ 03.80.97.11.11 ➡ 03.80.97.29.25
Closed Sun evening, Mon and 7 Jan–4 Feb. **Disabled access**.

Repair here after a morning reviewing the excavations at Alesia, where Vercingetorix and the Gauls fought their last battle against the armies of Julius Caesar. The brasserie menu lists parsleyed ham with salad and other simple dishes, and good regional cooking is served in the bigger dining room. The chef uses vegetables from the garden and the market: *fricassée* of chicken with cream and mushrooms or grilled steak with shallot butter. Weekday lunch menu €12; others €15–12. The place has lots of energy with a team of young serving staff. Have a glass of local Chardonnay or Pinot Noir.

SENS   89100

⚇ 🛎 HÔTEL L'ESPLANADE*

2 bd. du Mail.
☎ 03.86.83.14.70 ➡ 03.86.83.14.71
Closed Sun out of season, Aug, Christmas and New Year. **TV**.

Lovely hotel in a fancy house in the centre of town – the place is so old that even the owner can't tell you when it was built! Rooms are on the small side but have been well renovated and refurbished; there's double glazing in those looking over the road, and new beds and linen. Doubles with basin €29, or €37 with shower/wc. No restaurant, but they do have a really nice bar where you also have breakfast. One free breakfast per room.

|●| RESTAURANT LE SOLEIL LEVANT

51 rue Émile-Zola (Southwest); it's close to the station.
☎ 03.86.65.71.82
Closed Sun and Wed evenings; Aug.

A restaurant, very classic in both décor and cuisine, which is well known for its fish – particularly the signature dish of salmon with sorrel. They also do good meat dishes such as house duck *foie gras*, along with some heavenly desserts. The cheapest menu costs €11 (not served on Sun); others are €17 and €26 and there's *à la carte* too.

VILLEROY   89100 (7KM SW)

⚇ 🛎 |●| RELAIS DE VILLEROY**

Route de Nemours (centre).
☎ 03.86.88.81.77 ➡ 03.86.88.84.04
Closed Sun, Mon, Christmas and Feb school holidays; first week in July. **Garden**. **TV**. **Car park**. **Disabled access**.

This smart-looking establishment is one of the nicest in the area. The owners are trying to create a homely atmosphere and to offer a warm welcome with good food, and they're doing it with considerable success. The restaurant smells wonderfully of furniture polish and good cooking. There's a lot of fish on the menu and they do home-made pastries that melt in the mouth; set menus €18–53. The prices in the bistro next door, *Chez Clément*, are more affordable with a menu at €12. The bedrooms, with their flowery wallpaper and antique furniture, are in keeping with the rest of the establishment and double glazing means you don't have to worry about traffic noise. Doubles €37 with shower/wc and €43 with bath. 10% discount on the room rate and a free glass of champagne with dessert Oct–May.

VAUDEURS   89320 (24KM S)

⚇ 🛎 |●| HÔTEL-RESTAURANT LA VAUDEURINOISE*

10 route de Grange-Sèche; take the N60 for Troyes then the D905 towards Saint-Florentin.

☎ 03.86.96.28.00 ➡ 03.86.96.28.03
Closed Tues and Wed evenings except in July–Aug, and Jan. **Garden**.

Classic country hostelry in the green and pleasant land of the Othe river. It's a relatively new building, just outside the village and nice and quiet. They offer six basic but bright rooms, some of which overlook the garden and all of which have en-suite bath; doubles €27–38. In the restaurant, set menus range from €14 (weekdays only) to €35. They are dominated by regional cuisine: snail fritters *à la bourguignonne*, a pastry of Chaource cheese with salad and a mousse of *crémant de Bourgogne* with poached fruit. *À la carte* are *brioche* filled with ox marrow *à la bourguignonne*, *salmis* of quail with Ratafia liquor and Burgundy cherries. Particularly friendly atmosphere. Free breakfast Sept to the end of June.

TOUCY 89130

♔ 🛏 |●| LE LION D'OR

37 rue Lucile-Cormier (Centre).
☎ 03.86.44.00.76
Closed Sun evening, Mon and 1–20 Dec. **Car park**.

An old hotel in the Yonne with a magnificent wooden staircase – it's difficult not to fall in love with this place. Everything smells of beeswax, and the rooms are simple but cosy and meticulously clean. Doubles €29 with basin and €46 with shower/wc or bath. The dining room is delightful. Regional specialities include snails in a pastry case, ham cooked in Chablis, fish *en croûte* with sorrel and (in season) roast wild boar in a pepper sauce. Menus €12–25. 10% discount on the room rate.

FONTENOY 89420 (10KM S)

♔ 🛏 |●| LE FONTENOY

34 rue Principale (Centre); from Tournus take the D14 towards Chapaize.
☎ 03.86.44.00.84 ➡ 03.86.44.16.36
Garden.

The Marseillais boss and his wife embrace the regulars and create a very friendly, easy-going atmosphere in this café-restaurant-hotel – in fact, the whole of the village seems to pass through the place. Cheap, standardized rooms: €26 for a double with all facilities. Good, honest, friendly cooking, too: duck breast with a sweet and sour sauce, *bœuf bourguignon* and *andouillette*. They even ask you if you've had enough to eat.

The €9 weekday menu includes a $1/4$ litre of wine; others €13–18. There's a terrace and a space for the kids to play in the garden. It's best to book at the weekend. Free apéritif.

TOURNUS 71700

♔ 🛏 |●| HÔTEL-RESTAURANT DE SAÔNE**

Rive Gauche (Centre).
☎ 03.85.51.20.65 ➡ 03.85.51.05.45
Closed Mon from 1 April to 1 Oct. **Disabled access**. **Car park**.

A lovely, peaceful location away from traffic noise on the riverbank. Most of the rooms, €40–43, are situated in the annexe and though they're small, they have a river view. The restaurant offers good regional cooking and set menus €14–25. They lists frogs' legs and main courses like sirloin or free-range chicken with a morel sauce. If you feel like fish, they have *petite friture* like whitebait, fillets of sole in an Aligoté wine sauce and zander in a cream and white wine sauce. The terrace is very pleasant in summer, overlooking the houses down by the water and the abbey. Have a post-prandial stroll along the velvety green banks of the Saône. Free coffee or 10% discount on the room rate April–June.

♔ 🛏 |●| HÔTEL-RESTAURANT AUX TERRASSES**

18 av. du 23-Janvier (South).
☎ 03.85.51.01.74 ➡ 03.85.51.09.99
Closed Sun evening except July–Aug, Mon, Tues lunchtime, and Jan. **TV**. **Car park**.

This place is known primarily for the quality of the cooking in the restaurant. It's set in an enormous roadside establishment, probably a former coaching inn. The lounge separates two large, richly decorated dining rooms. Reception's a bit on the smart side but not overly so, and service is attentive. Set menus start at €15 (weekday lunch only), which is good value, and go up to €35. *À la carte* lists a variety of dishes: zander with oyster mushrooms, Bresse chicken with morel and cream sauce, and *millefeuille* with pears and gingerbread ice cream. And there's an excellent fish soup. Comfortable rooms with shower/wc €46 or €52 with bath. Free coffee.

♔ 🛏 |●| HÔTEL LE SAUVAGE***

pl. du Champ-de-Mars (Centre).
☎ 03.85.51.14.45 ➡ 03.85.51.14.45

e lesauvage.tournus@wanadoo.fr
TV. **Pay car park**.

They say you can't miss this Virginia-creeper-smothered house – but then they all say that. It's just a little set back from the main road. This old establishment has been ticking over quietly for ages. Pleasant rooms €62 with shower/wc, or €65 with bath. The restaurant does a good range of set menus from €14 to €39 – one is dedicated to regional dishes like parsleyed frogs' legs, snails, Bresse chicken in cream and morel sauce and flambéed fillet of Charolais beef. *À la carte* is also excellent and there are wines at good prices. 10% discount on the room rate Oct–March

PRAYES   71460 (20KM W)

🎋 🏠 |●| AUBERGE DU GRISON

hameau de Prayes; from Tournus take the D14 towards Chapaize, and it's near Chissey-les-Mâcon.
☎ 03.85.50.18.31 ➡ 03.85.50.18.31
Closed Mon evening and Tues out of season and three weeks from 15 Nov.

Set in a tiny village in one of the most delightful parts of Saône-et-Loire, this charming inn has nine bedrooms at €34 with shower/wc; no two are the same but all are colourful, smart and cosy. Excellent regional cooking is served in the lovely dining room which features wooden panels and beams. Snacks are available at all hours, and they do salads of cold meats or cheese, thick local *crêpes*, *andouille* in white wine and Charolais steak with mushrooms. Set lunch menu at €11 then others €14–18. Small shaded terrace. It would be nice to come across an inn like this in every French hamlet. Free apéritif.

VERMENTON   89270

🎋 |●| AUBERGE L'ESPÉRANCE

3 rue du Général-de-Gaulle (Centre).
☎ 03.86.81.50.42
Closed Sun evening, Mon and Jan. **Disabled access**.

However glum you're feeling, the mere mention of this inn's name (*espérance* means "hope") should perk you up. You'll get a delightful welcome, and the kitchen turns out wonderful dishes which change with the seasons – but try the house *foie gras*, which is a regular. Set menus €14–34. The place has been redecorated throughout and they've provided a play area for the kids.

Everyone will find the air conditioning a blessed relief in summer. Free coffee.

ACCOLAY   89460 (3KM W)

🎋 🏠 |●| HOSTELLERIE DE LA FONTAINE**

16 rue de Reigny.
☎ 03.86.81.54.02 ➡ 03.86.81.52.78
e hostellerie.fontaine@wanadoo.fr
Closed Sun evening and Mon mid-Nov to 31 March, Jan and Feb. **Car park**.

A traditional Burgundy house in a lovely little village in the Cure valley. On fine evenings you can relax in the garden while feasting on salad of snails with mustard dressing, *quenelles* of pike, fried *entrecôte* steak with soft creamy Chaource cheese sauce, a medallion of monkfish with a leek upside-down tart and *clafoutis* with fresh fruit and raspberry *coulis*. Set menus €18–38. Doubles €41–44, and there's a good breakfast for €5. In winter the small cellar is pressed into service and they serve traditional local dishes down there for €14, including cheese and dessert with jugs of Aligoté or Pinot Noir. Free apéritif.

BAZARNES   89460 (6KM W)

🎋 |●| RESTAURANT LA GRIOTTE

3 av. de la Gare; it's opposite the Cravant-Bazarnes station.
☎ 03.86.42.39.38
Closed Mon–Wed.

A nice little restaurant with a great chef who's an expert in seeking out fantastic local suppliers. With this fresh produce, his imagination takes him to culinary heights. The dishes really taste of the country – you just have to try the pork *andouille* to know what we mean. Two menus at €10 and the *menu du marché* is €14. Delightful service. Free apéritif.

VÉZELAY   89450

🎋 🏠 LE COMPOSTELLE**

pl. du Champ-de-Foire (Centre).
☎ 03.86.33.28.63 ➡ 03.86.33.34.34
Closed a month from end of first week in Jan–Feb. **Disabled access**. **TV**. **Garden**.

Vézelay was one of the assembly points for pilgrimages to Santiago de Compostela in north-western Spain. That fact is commemorated by the name of this pretty house, which has reverted to being an inn – as it was at the beginning of the 20th century. The service is first-rate and the modern, well-equipped bedrooms have views of the countryside or the garden; doubles €43 or €52 for a family room. 10% discount.

⊼ 🛏 ΙΟΙ HÔTEL DE LA POSTE ET DU LION D'OR***

pl. du Champ-de-Foire.
☎ 03.86.33.21.23 ➡ 03.86.32.30.92
Closed Mon, Tues lunchtime and 2 Nov–23 March.
Disabled access. **TV**. **Car park**.

This former coaching inn, a superb ivy-clad building, is an extremely pleasant place to stay. Rooms are well-kept and tastefully decorated; they overlook the basilica on one side and the valley on the other. Doubles with shower/wc start at €50 and go up to €99 with a bath. The restaurant has a beautiful terrace. Menus at €18–35, while the rather expensive à la carte menu features a mixture of classic and regional dishes such as œufs en meurette in red wine sauce, snails, rack of lamb with sage, roast pigeon and fricassée of chanterelles and ceps in season. Free apéritif.

ΙΟΙ RESTAURANT LE BOUGAINVILLE

26 rue Saint-Étienne.
☎ 03.86.33.27.57 ➡ 03.86.33.35.12
Closed Tues, Wed, and Dec to mid-Feb.

This restaurant, in a beautiful old building overflowing with flowers, is very good value for money (menus €12–32) – a pleasant surprise in a town where low prices are a rarity. Traditional local dishes: œufs en meurette, ham knuckle à la morvandelle. The dining room, with its magnificent old fireplace, is a pleasant place to sit.

SAINT-PÈRE-SOUS-VÉZELAY   89450 (2KM S)

⊼ 🛏 ΙΟΙ À LA RENOMMÉE**

19–20 Grande Rue; it's on the D957, at the foot of Vézelay hill.
☎ 03.86.33.21.34 ➡ 03.86.33.34.17
Closed Tues except from Easter to 11 Nov, and 15 Jan–15 Feb. **Disabled access**. **TV**. **Garage**.

This hotel is also a newsagent's and a tobac-

conist's so there's a relaxed atmosphere. The more expensive rooms are spacious and have a small terrace with a view over the countryside and the Saint-Pierre church. Doubles €30 with basin; up to €44 with bath. The small brasserie, open in season, will do if you're stuck for somewhere to eat. 10% discount on the room rate for a two-night stay except over public holiday weekends and July-Aug.

PONTAUBERT   89200 (10KM NE)

⊼ 🛏 LE MOULIN DES TEMPLIERS**

Vallée du Cousin; coming from Vézelay, turn right as soon as you cross the bridge and follow the arrows.
☎ 03.86.34.10.80 ➡ 03.86.34.03.05
Ⓦ www.hotel-moulin-des-templiers.com
Closed Nov–Mar. **Car park**.

This large ochre-coloured house, deep in the Cousin valley and covered with Virginia creeper, is now a waterside hotel with oodles of charm. It's an old 12th-century mill that's been wonderfully restored; there are intimate sitting rooms for intimate conversations and a a flowery terrace for when the sun shines. Lovely walks and mountain-bike rides in the surrounding woods. Double rooms €41– 60, depending on the size, with shower or bath. Free coffee and a 1/2-bottle of Burgundy for a two-night stay.

⊼ 🛏 ΙΟΙ LES FLEURS**

route de Vézelay; take the D957.
☎ 03.86.34.13.81 ➡ 03.86.34.23.32
Closed Wed, Thurs lunchtime and 15 Dec–1 Mar.
TV. **Car park**.

This beautiful hotel is surrounded by a delightful garden overflowing with flowers. It's been tastefully decorated by the owners, with lovely wood panelling in the dining room. The bedrooms are pretty, and bathrooms have shower or bath; they cost €46–56. The restaurant gets things just right and the prices are reasonable – the cheapest set menu is €14 (not served on Sun), with others €21–36 – and there's a wealth of specialities like trout terrine with basil sauce, fillet of beef Morvandiau, cockerel à la façon des Ducs and pavé de Pontaubert. 10% discount on the room rate Oct–April.

BRETAGNE

22 Côtes-d'Armor

29 Finistère

35 Ille-et-Vilaine

56 Morbihan

ARZON 56640

🕯🍴 CRÊPERIE LA SORCIÈRE

59 rue des Fontaines; it's near the naval port.
☎ 02.97.53.87.25
Closed Wed in mid-season and Mon–Thurs in winter; Nov to mid-Dec; Jan.

You'll be bewitched by this pretty stone house, where they conjure up devilishly delicious recipes. All the *crêpes* have names: *la Pensardine*, *la Vendéenne*, *la Périgourdine*, *l'Irlandaise* – and you'll only have to cross their palm with a (small) amount of silver. Quality produce and ingredients are used – such as the black wheat. Around €10 for a meal of good *crêpes* with interesting fillings. Smiling service. There's a terrace. Free coffee.

AUDIERNE 29770

🕯🍴 HÔTEL DE LA PLAGE

21 bd. Emmanuel-Brusq; it's 2km from the ferry terminal to the Île de Sein.
☎ 02.98.70.01.07 ➡ 02.98.75.04.69
Hotel closed Oct–April. **TV. Car park.**

Located on the seafront, this hotel smells of summer holidays. Fresh, maritime-influenced décor in the very pleasant rooms, most of which have a sea view. Lots of charm and good value for money. Doubles with bath €39–65; half-board €50–63.

AURAY 56400

🍴 RESTAURANT L'ÉGLANTINE

pl. Saint-Sauveur, Saint-Goustan, port d'Auray.
☎ 02.97.56.46.55

Closed Wed.

Traditional cuisine prepared with great care in this restaurant – it's probably the only one on the port worth recommending. Dishes include fish *choucroute*, sole, smoked fish, sea bass roasted in its skin, five-fish *cotriade*, house-smoked fish, monkfish blanquette with leeks. True Breton cuisine and menus €13–30. On the walls there are portraits of the most important leaders of the Chouanne army. Pleasant welcome.

SAINTE-ANNE-D'AURAY 56400 (6KM N)

🕯🕯🍴 L'AUBERGE

56 route de Vannes.
☎ 02.97.57.61.55 ➡ 02.97.57.69.10
Closed Tues except July–Aug; Wed; 5–21 Feb; 12 Nov–5 Dec. **TV. Car park.**

One of the best restaurants in the locality; John-Paul II dined here when he visited the region in 1996. You can savour the delicacy of Jean-Luc Larvoir's culinary approach on all the menus, from the cheapest at €16 (not served Sat evening, Sun lunchtime or public holidays) to those up to €24: try crab *tartare*, home-smoked salmon, chopped oysters, sea bass with Guéméné *andouille*, stewed veal with truffle *coulis* and the like. The extensive wine list proves excellent value for money. You may find the service and atmosphere a little cool, but it won't detract from your enjoyment. Rooms €33–37. Free coffee.

ERDEVEN 56410 (10KM W)

🕯🍴 LA CRÊPERIE DU MANOIR DE KERCADIO

Lieu-dit Kercadio: from Auray, take the road to Ploërmel

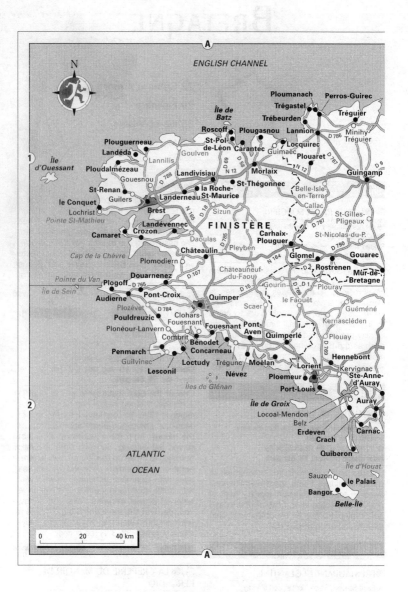

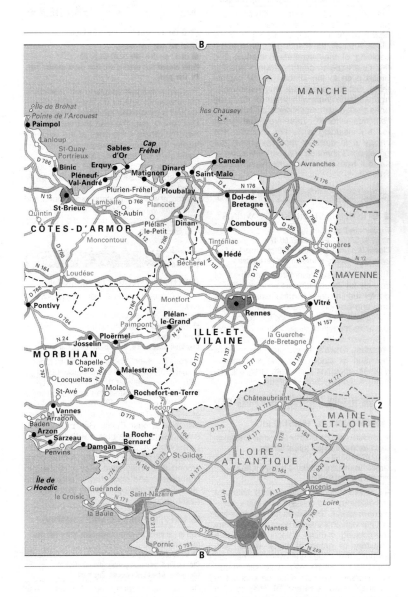

then Erdeven.
☎ 02.97.24.67.57
Closed Sept to Easter, except school holidays. **Garden**.

The elegance of the setting with its wood-panelled walls, original fireplace and wide hearth might lead you to expect a pricey place. After all, the manor goes back to the begining of the seventeenth century and there's a fifteenth century tower – and the bread oven in the kitchen is the original thing. But the prices are very reasonable, from a simple crêpe with butter for €2 to the ones stuffed with mushrooms or scallops *à l'amoricaine* for €6. There are crêpe menus for €9 including a ¼-litre of cider; the choice *à la carte* is more extensive but prices don't shoot up. You can hire a bike or set out from here along the hiking paths. Free Kir.

BADEN   56870 (10KM SE)

☎ |●| HÔTEL-RESTAURANT LE GAVRINIS

Toulbrock-en-Baden; take the D101
☎ 02.97.57.00.82 ➡ 02.97.57.09.47
Closed Mon lunch; Mon from mid-Sept to mid-Jun; Sun evening Oct–March; mid-Nov to end Jan **Garden**.

This venerable establishment is renowned not only for for its comfortable accommodation but for the fine cuisine in the restaurant. The chef and his son are equally skilful and use high quality, fresh fish and local produce: fish in sauces, saddle of rabbit stuffed with ceps. They even bake the fresh *viennoiseries* for breakfast. There's a lunch *formule* for €15 (not Sun or public holidays) and menus €18–31. Doubles with bath and balcony €66–74. An excellent establishment.

LOCOAL-MENDON   56550 (10KM NW)

🎿 |●| MANOIR DE PORH KERIO

route d'Auray; take the D120 for 5km, in the direction of Locoal Mendon, then turn right at the sign.
☎ 02.97.24.67.57
Closed Tues evening and Wed; a fortnight in Nov; a fortnight end Jan. **Garden**.

A splendid fifteenth-century manor, miles out in the country – it's only a shame that it does-n't have rooms. The tables are elegantly laid in a hall with an immense open fireplace. Very fine cooking: a menu of local dishes has a speciality of *gratin* of black wheat with *andouille* from Guéméné, while the seafood menu lists roast monkfish with saffron-suf-fused cream. Lobster must be ordered in advance. Menus €14 and 19. They serve in the garden in summer. Service is efficient and

easy-going so it's a pleasure to while away the time over the free coffee.

BELZ   56550 (12KM W)

🎿 ☎ |●| LE RELAIS DE KERGOU

It's on the road from Auray.
☎ 02.97.55.35.61 ➡ 02.97.55.27.69
Hotel closed Sun evening and Mon out of season; Feb. **TV. Car park**.

This place was built as a farm with a smithy in the nineteenth century. It's thoroughly charm-ing and is remarkably furnished. Three rooms look directly over the road so they're noisier than the others – the ones at the back are quieter. The bathrooms vary in size, also, and some are a real squeeze. Doubles with basin €31–36 or with bath €44–48. The garden is lovely and the beaches are only 4km away. Good cooking is served in the imposing din-ing room with its majestic proportions and large bay window. Menus €10–21 feature lots of fish dishes. 10% discount on the room rate Sept–June.

BANGOR   56360

☎ |●| HÔTEL-VILLAGE LA DÉSIRADE

Le Petit Cosquet; it's outside Bangor on the Port-Colon road.
☎ 02.97.31.70.70 ➡ 02.97.31.89.64
✉ hotel-la-desirade@liberty.surf.fr
Hotel closed 15 Nov–25 Dec and 5 Jan–1 March. **Disabled access. TV. Swimming pool. Car park**.

A cross between a hotel and a B&B, in local architectural style – a series of low buildings with painted walls and shutters. Twenty-six thoughtfully decorated and spacious rooms €59–107; half board is compulsory July–Aug at €73–94. The owner-chef offers delicate dishes like roast Dublin Bay prawns with sweet peppers, sea bream with fennel and preserved lemons and small *crêpes* gar-nished with pears and apples. A meal costs around €33. They have a lot of regulars in high season and since they've enlarged the restaurant it's also open to non-residents. It's best to book.

|●| CRÊPERIE DES QUATRE CHEMINS

How to get there: it's at the crossroads of the two main roads on Belle-Île.
☎ 02.97.31.42.13
Closed Wed except July–Aug, and mid-Nov to Christmas. **Disabled access. Car park**.

Service noon–2pm and 7–11pm. This isolated establishment serves some of the best *crêpes* on the island – hearty, delectable, cooked to perfection and stuffed with unusual fillings. Humorous menus – lots of word-play – and a jovial atmosphere. Brightly decorated, complete with a small children's play area, and there's soft jazz and blues in the background. A meal costs about €13.

🎿 |❍| FERME-AUBERGE DE BORDROUHANT

Lieu-dit Bordrouhant; it's about 1km outside Bangor.
☎ 02.97.31.57.06 ➡ 02.97.31.57.06
Closed weekday lunchtimes in July and Aug; weekdays out of season.

A simply, friendly place, just outside touristy Belle-Île, making a nice change from the more traditional type of restaurant. It's an old farmhouse and the man in charge welcomes you before going off to the kitchens to prepare your order. Tasty and filling dishes and house *charcuterie*, the *terrine* is splendid and they stick to old local recipes that are rarely cooked these days – try the stewed chicken *aux Krassens* with dumplings or the house lamb dishes. Single menu at €16. It's worth calling to reserve. Reservations only so phone in advance. Free house apéritif.

BÉNODET   29950

♠ HÔTEL L'HERMITAGE

11 rue Laënnec (Centre); it's 300m from the beach, part way up the hill overlooking the town centre.
☎ 02.98.57.00.37
Closed Oct–June. **Garden. Car park.**

In a small, quiet street, just minutes from the beach there's a large white house with blue shutters set in a garden full of hydrangeas. It's really lovely, has a 1950s feel and the prices are very reasonable: plain but pleasant rooms cost €38–45 with shower or bath. Some have a view of the sea. There are studio apartments in a neighbouring building which can be rented by the week. Breakfast is €4.

🎿 ♠ |❍| HÔTEL LES BAINS DE MER**

11 rue de Kerguelen (Centre); it's up a steep street 100m from the sea.
☎ 02.98.57.03.41 ➡ 02.98.57.11.07
📧 bainsdemer@portdebenodet.com
Closed 15 Nov– 1 March. **Swimming pool. Garden. TV. Pay car park.**

This hotel is very comfortable, even plush, but it's retained a family atmosphere. Very friendly welcome and lovely double rooms

with shower/wc €44–56. If the weather is cloudy, dive into the swimming pool or try a relaxing sauna. Excellent cuisine in the restaurant. There are two places to eat: the *Domino*, open until 11pm (midnight in summer) offers a speedy *formule* every lunchtime at €13, listing grilled meat or pizza, dessert and coffee, as well as salads, pasta, pizzas and grilled dishes. The restaurant has set menus at €17–24. Half board at €43–53 is a good option in July–Aug. Free house apéritif.

|❍| FERME DU LETTY

quartier du Letty; it's 1km from the town centre, well signposted.
☎ 02.98.57.01.27
Closed Wed; Thurs lunchtime; 15 Nov to end Feb.

The superbly restored building is full of Breton delights: exposed beams, wide fireplace, stone walls, sumptuous furniture and an army of waiters in bow-ties rushing about in all directions (though admittedly with little effect on the speed of the service). There's no requirement to wear a tie, especially in summer, but the customers are only a tad less smartly dressed than the staff. This is the best table in Finistère, offering wonderful cuisine and some genuinely inspired dishes: Sizun lamb, asparagus flan with prawns and some more exotic dishes such as curried monkfish and chicken *confit* with peanuts. Incredible desserts. Menus €30–63.

CLOHARS-FOUESNANT   29950 (3KM NW)

|❍| RESTAURANT LA FORGE D'ANTAN

It's on the road to Quimper.
☎ 02.98.54.84.00 ➡ 02.98.54.89.11
Closed Mon; Tues lunchtime; Sun evening out of season; Tues lunchtime July–Aug. **Garden. Car park.**

Way out in the country. Friendly welcome and superb rustic décor, with a stylish atmosphere and clientele to match. The imaginative seasonal cuisine doesn't come cheap: set weekday lunch menu €20 and others €27–53. À la carte you get turbot *à la Fouesnantoise*, oyster and prawn *tartare*, pan-fried prawns with champagne sauce, gratinéed rabbit with morels, veal kidneys in spices and sole fillets with vanilla.

COMBRIT   29121 (5.5KM W)

🎿 ♠ |❍| HÔTEL-RESTAURANT SAINTE-MARINE*

19 rue Bac; it's in the port of Sainte-Marine.
☎ 02.98.56.34.79 ➡ 02.98.51.94.09

e guydiquelou@wanadoo.fr
Closed Wed Oct–Easter. **TV**.

A favourite with ocean-racing seafarers, novelists and film-makers. The wonderful dining room is decorated in a nautical style and has a magnificent view of the River Odet and pont de Cornouaille; there's also a terrace. Double rooms with shower/wc €50–58 or €58–62 with bath. Menus €15–30. *À la carte* you get marinated scallops with seaweed, pan-fried sole with aubergine caviar, fresh braised cod, pork fillet with leeks and seafood *tartare* with smoked salmon. Half board, obligatory July–Aug, costs €54 per person. Excellent place. 10% discount on the room rate Sept–June.

PLONÉOUR-LANVERN   29720 (18KM NW)

𝕁 🛏 |⦿| HÔTEL-RESTAURANT DES VOYAGEURS**

1 rue Jean-Jaurès; it's behind the church; take the D2 from Pont-l'Abbé.
☎ 02.98.87.61.35 ➡ 02.98.82.62.82
Closed Fri evening; Sat and Sun evening out of season; Sun evening in season and 1–15 Nov. **TV**.

A nice, classic village hotel. Pleasant rooms €28–42. Numbers 4,5 and 9 are the biggest – avoid the ones over the street if possible. Excellent cuisine at decent prices: lunch menu €11 and others €37–45. Dishes include house fish soup, Breton lobster and duck breast with raspberry vinegar. Free house apéritif.

PENMARCH   29760 (25KM W)

|⦿| LE DORIS

port de Kerity, pointe de Penmarch; take the D785 in the direction of Plomeur.
☎ 02.98.58.60.92
Closed All Saints' to Easter.

Right on the harbour of this little port, this place is something of an institution, with a reputation for serving good seafood and fresh fish. It's run by a fishing family so the fish appear direct from the sea and served in traditional ways: scallops on a skewer, poached turbot with *beurre blanc* and medallions of monkfish cooked to a Cancale recipe. Good meat too – sliced leg of lamb with herbs, duck breast with a spiced wine sauce. Menus €10–55.

BINIC   22520

🛏 |⦿| HÔTEL BENHUYC***

1 quai Jean-Bart.

☎ 02.96.73.39.00 ➡ 02.96.73.77.04
e mprovoos@fr.packardbell.org
Restaurant closed Sun evening; Mon lunchtime; Sept––June except over the Easter holidays.
Hotel closed 15 Dec–1 Feb **TV**. **Pay car park**.

Overlooking the boats moored in the pleasure port, this modern hotel is easy to recommend. The bright, comfortable rooms are well-maintained, and most have a view of the harbour or the Banche beach. Doubles with shower €45–65; the smaller ones are the cheapest but they're still pleasant. Competent welcome. The restaurant serves seafood – *waterzooï*, seafood stew, pan-fried scallops – and a few Belgian specialities from the owners' homeland. Weekday lunch menu €10 and others €14–33. Free apéritif if you book half-board.

BREST   29200

𝕁 🛏 HÔTEL ASTORIA**

9 rue Traverse (Centre); it's between the station and the château, close to the rue de Siam.
☎ 02.98.80.19.10 ➡ 02.98.80.52.41
e infor@hotel-astoria-brest.com
Closed 15 Dec–7 Jan. **TV**. **Pay car park**.

A hotel that looks like so many other buildings in Brest, but it offers good value for the town considering its excellent position. Bright, cheerful rooms; the six with balconies overlooking the quiet street are double-glazed, but if you need absolute quiet, ask for one at the back. Doubles with basin €23 and €38–41 with shower/wc or bath. Warm welcome. In July and Aug the Brest *jeudis* are just seven minutes' walk away. The car park costs €5 per day or €27 for a week. 10% discount Sept–June.

🛏 HOTEL ABALIS**

7 av. Georges-Clémenceau: it's 100m from the tourist office and the train station.
☎ 02.98.44.21.86 ➡ 02.98.43.68.32
Disabled access. **TV**. **Car park**.

Very central, with double rooms from €27 with handbasin and €43 with shower/wc. They all have double glazing, though they're a bit small; some have a sea view. Breakfast, €6, is served until noon and reception is open round the clock.

🛏 HÔTEL LE PASTEUR*

29 rue Louis-Pasteur; it's between the rue de Siam and the covered market.
☎ 02.98.46.08.73 ➡ 02.98.43.46.80
TV.

An establishment that holds its own in its category. It's clean and the welcome is pleasant, and though the soundproofing between rooms is not great, the beds are OK and at least the windows are double-glazed. Doubles €29 with shower.

☎ HÔTEL DE LA GARE**

4 av. Gambetta (Centre); it's opposite the station.
☎ 02.98.44.47.01 ➡ 02.98.43.37.07
✉ info@hotelgare.com
Disabled access. TV.

Practical and friendly place with lovely views of the harbour – you can get at those views from the 3rd floor upwards. Doubles with shower/wc €44 or €47 with bath.

☎ RELAIS MERCURE – LES VOYAGEURS***

2 rue Yves-Collet (Centre); it's on the corner of av. Clémenceau and rue Yves-Collet.
☎ and ➡ 02.98.80.31.80
✉ mercure.voyageurs@mail.dotcom.fr
TV.

It's rare for a chain hotel to fight its way into this guidebook but this brilliant three-star is one of the best of its category in town. The hotel has retained its superb 1940s entrance hall. The well-equipped bedrooms have bathrooms with character; doubles €65–85 with shower/wc or bath. Pleasant, competent staff.

|●| CRÊPERIE MODERNE

34 rue d'Algésiras (Centre).
☎ 02.98.44.44.36 ➡ 02.98.80.58.32
Closed Sun lunchtime. **Disabled access.**

Service 11.30am–10pm. The façade is an arresting lemon yellow while the 90-seat dining room is uninspiringly classical. The crêpes (from €8) are delicious, however, and served simply with butter or more elaborately with scallops in vermouth. This establishment has been going since 1922, so they know what they're about.

♿ |●| RESTAURANT LA PENSÉE SAUVAGE

13 rue d'Aboville and rue de Gasté; behind Saint-Michel church.
☎ 02.98.46.36.65
Closed Sat lunchtime and Sun; Mon; end July to mid-Aug.

Service noon–1.30pm and 7.30–10pm. You have to hunt a little for this restaurant – it's way off the beaten track. But it has two simple little dining rooms that generate a great atmosphere so it's worth the effort. The cooking is tasty: try the home-made cas-

soulet and duck confit or the crayfish Ouessant-style. It's excellent value with a lunch menu at €8, or you can eat for about €18 à la carte. Portions are huge and they'll give you a doggy bag to take away what you can't manage. Free apéritif.

|●| LE VOYAGE DE BRENDAN

23 rue Danton: 300m from Saint-Martin church.
☎ 02.98.80.52.84
✉ Dominique-Perrin@wanadoo.fr
Closed Sat lunchtime; Sun; Sept.

You have to search out this tiny place – they can only seat 22. The super-friendly owner offers traditional, quality French cooking using only fresh produce: huge salads like the one with warm Plougastel goat's cheese, duck breast in cider and fish choucroute, the house speciality. Weekday lunch menu €9, another for €18 or around €15 à la carte. Every couple of months they have an exhibition of local artists' work.

|●| AMOUR DE POMME DE TERRE

23 rue des Halles (Centre); it's behind the Saint-Louis covered market.
☎ 02.98.43.48.51 ✉ amourPDT@wanadoo.fr
Disabled access. Car park.

Open at lunchtime and in the evening until 11pm. This restaurant is unique in Brest and indeed in the whole of Finistère; they serve only potatoes, and just the "samba" variety, which was developed for its baking qualities, at that. A multitude of preparations: with parsley, stuffed with different cheeses or grilled meats, with fish and shellfish. Menus €9–19. The lunchtime the dishes of the day change daily with one of the excellent (potato-free!) desserts. The walls and the menus give you glimpses of the owner's sense of humour. The setting is pretty nice, sort of revisited rustic. And since the tables are rather tightly packed, you may well make new friends.

|●| RESTAURANT LE MARRAKECH

14 rue de la Traverse.
☎ 02.98.46.45.14
Closed Sun; Wed lunchtime; mid-July to mid-Aug.

Service noon–2.30pm and 7–11pm. This restaurant offers an attractive, restrained décor and good-quality cooking. Excellent lamb tajines with onions and raisins, chicken, lamb or mixed meat couscous, all generously served for the price. Lunch menu €9, dish of the day €10 and around €15–18 à la carte. The delicate and aromatic dishes are expertly spiced according to secret recipes that have been passed down from mother to daughter for generations. The mint tea is divine.

|●| TONNERRE DE BIO

1 rue Kerfautras.
☎ 02.98.443.35.80
Closed Sun and 1–22 Aug.

All dishes here are prepared using only fresh and organic ingredients. It's straightforward, natural cuisine where quality is all-important. Menus from €10.

|●| RESTAURANT L'ABRI DES FLOTS

port de Commerce: on the quayside.
☎ 02.98.44.07.31
Closed Sun, Mon evening.

The really nice owner is a live wire and he has created a welcoming restaurant with a personal touch. It's on the merchant port, but the dining room's cosy and in summer there's a pretty verandah and pleasant terrace. Various menus from €17 with lots of fish. Their speciality is a seafood couscous and they do *crêpes* as well.

|●| MA PETITE FOLIE

plage du Moulin-Blanc (Southwest); it's close to the marina and Océanopolis.
☎ 02.98.42.44.42 ➡ 02.98.41.43.68
Closed Sun.

One of the best fish restaurants in Brest, set in a superb, sturdy old Mauritanian fishing boat which landed hundreds of tons of crayfish on the coast of Mauritania between 1952 and 1992. The skipper dropped anchor in well-earned joint retirement and set about cooking with real passion, giving his vessel a second lease of life in the process. He and his wife welcome you warmly and serve up an unmissable culinary experience. Looking around to check the bill is being overheard, the hostess will whisper conspiratorially in your ear, offering a fish which isn't on the menu – accept without hesitation. There's one menu only at €18, or it's about €38 *à la carte*. Booking is very strongly advised, and pretty much essential at the weekend.

GUILERS 29820 (5KM NW)

|●| CRÊPERIE BLÉ NOIR

bois de Keroual; from Brest head towards Penfeld – the restaurant is near the Parc des Expositions.
☎ 02.98.07.57.40 ➡ 02.98.07.47.83

Almost hidden by trees and bushes next to a

small lake and located in an ancient mill, this *crêperie* is a dream of a place. Friendly service, delicious *crêpes* and plenty of opportunity for wonderful country walks after the meal. A meal will cost €9–12. Specialities include buckwheat pancakes with medallions of monkfish *armoricaine*, with scallops or smoked salmon and *crêpe suzette* with lime.

GOUESNOU 29850 (10KM N)

|●| CRÊPERIE LA FINETTE

rue du Bois-Kerallenoc; from Gouesnou it's signposted and 1km along the road to Kerallenoc.
☎ 02.98.07.86.68
Closed Mon and Tues lunchtime out of season; Mon and Tues lunchtimes July–Aug; a week at the end of June; a fortnight in Nov. **Garden.**

Lydie and Jean-Yves Pirou used to run one of the best *crêperies* in Brest before setting up in this lovely old house with a beautiful garden. The interior is old stone with a huge fireplace; you get a real sense of Brittany and the sea. Very tasty, traditional *crêpes*. A meal costs about €11. Best to book.

CAMARET 29570

🎿 🏠 |●| HÔTEL-RESTAURANT DU STYVEL**

quai du Styvel: one of the last restaurants at the end of the quay, opposite the Rocamadour chapel.
☎ 02.98.27.92.74 ➡ 02.98.27.88.37
Closed Jan.

The thirteen well-kept rooms are generally comfortable and have been redecorated. Some have a view of the harbour. Reasonable prices – €28–40 with shower/wc. They've engaged a new chef and serving staff and while the cooking is inevitably inspired by the fish landed in the harbour, there's an unusual feel to the menus: scallop kebabs with Choron sauce, a duo of yellow ling and John Dory *à la Ouessanne* and platters of seafood. Menus €12–30 with a children's menu at €7. Free house apéritif and 10% discount on the room rate Sept–June.

|●| LA VOILERIE

7 quai Toudouze; it's on the harbour facing the tower and the chapel.
☎ 02.98.27.99.55
Closed Wed. **Disabled access. Car park.**

One of Camaret's most serious restaurants, offering consistent quality, a friendly welcome and service late into the evening. It's in a building that used to be the main sailmaker's – which makes for a very pleasant dining room. Lots of fish dishes and regional specialities but what's available in the market or the fish-market dictates what you'll find. Set menus, €15–55. Best to book – only twenty covers.

CANCALE   35260

♠ |●| LE GRAND LARGE

4 quai Jacques-Cartier.
☎ 02.99.89.82.90 ➡ 02.99.89.79.03
e rietz.alain@wanadoo.fr
Closed a few days in Jan.

A very old and very lovely house festooned with ivy. It's got an unimpeded view of the sea (which is just the other side of the road). Numerous bright and comfortable rooms; doubles €38–58, some accommodating 3, 4 or 5 people. The breakfast is beautiful and has a sea view. They also run a restaurant service but it's not up to the quality of the rest of the establishment.

♠ |●| LE QUERRIEN**

7 quay Duguay-Trouin; it's on the port.
☎ 02.99.89.64.56 ➡ 02.99.89.79.35
Disabled access. TV.

You find some of the loveliest rooms in Cancale at this place. They're all brand-new, huge, bright and equipped with good bath-rooms. Doubles with shower/wc €53–79. The restaurant is decorated like a smart brasserie with wood panelling, copper pans on the walls and a large fish tank. Good cooking and highly competent service. Menus €13–29 list grilled lobster, hot oysters, seafood platters and *crêpes* in orange butter. They take their work seriously here.

♠ |●| HÔTEL DE LA POINTE DU GROUIN**

How to get there; take the signs to Pointe du Grouin, about 3km from the centre of town.
☎ 02.99.89.60.55 ➡ 02.99.89.92.22
Restaurant closed Tue and Thurs lunchtimes **Hotel closed** Oct–Easter.

A solidly-constructed building out on the Pointe du Grouin, facing the sea. The site is exceptional and the smart hotel is built of local stone and has a cosy interior. The small, simple rooms have been smartened up. You pay for the location and the supert views: doubles €69–84. Three of them have a pri-vate terrace. Quiet is guaranteed. It's a good starting-point for walks in the wild country around. The dining room has a panoramic

view of the bay of Mont-Saint-Michel. Tradi-tional cuisine and menus €18–50.

|●| AU PIED D'CHEVAL

10 quai Gambetta.
☎ 02.99.89.76.95
Closed weekdays from mid-Nov to Palm Sunday except for the Christmas school holidays; weekend lunchtimes 15 Nov–1 April.

Unbeatable oysters are what they claim to serve here, and the osyter-farming family who run the place certainly deliver. Their claim also holds good for all the other seafood and cooked dishes – the ingredients are ultra-fresh. Try the *écuelle du Père Dédé*, a mixture of shellfish in a creamy lemony sauce, or the *patouillou* (whelks) *à l'armori-caine*. The tables and stools on the ground floor are rustic but the upstairs dining room is more done up. You'll pay between €13 and €20 for a meal depending on how hungry you are. Energetic service and good wines.

|●| LA CANCALAISE

3 rue de la Vallée-Porcon; it's 2 mins from the Musée des Arts et Traditions Populaires.
☎ 02.99.89.66.08 ➡ 02.99.89.89.20
Closed Mon–Thurs except in school holidays; July–Aug.

A place frequented by locals and tourists alike. The walls are made from dressed stone and adorned with old photographs, and the tables are nicely set. At the back of the dining room there's a long range with a double line of hot plates to cook the *crêpes* – all the dishes are made to order. The *crêpes* and *galettes* are crispy and delicate. Savoury stuffings include *andouille* while the sweet specialities are curdled milk with superb home-made jam and apple compote flavoured with cinnamon. There's nothing revolutionary here but everything is very tasty. About €15 for a meal; they also do a take-away service.

|●| LE SURCOUF

7 quai Gambetta; (Centre).
☎ 02.99.89.61.75
Closed Wed and Thurs ecept July–Aug; mid-Dec to end Jan.

This gourmet restaurant stands out from the rest of the establishments along the port. The produce used is not only wonderful but the ingredients are deftly and creatively prepared and cooked. For €16 – their cheapest menu – you get a splendid meal: appetizer, nine oysters, *effiloché* of cod and a warm kouing aman with a few surprises such as the home-baked buckwheat bread. The setting is carefully designed in quiet good taste. Professional welcome. Other menus up to €50.

⦿ RESTAURANT LE SAINT-CAST

route de la Corniche; it's a 5-min walk from the centre.
☎ 02.99.89.66.08 ➡ 02.99.89.89.20
Closed Sun evening and Tues out of season; Wed; the Feb school holidays; 25–29 June; 15 Nov–18 Dec.

A delicious restaurant in all senses of the word. It's just outside the town in an elegant building overlooking the sea – with Mont-Saint-Michel away in the distance – and an ideal place to spend a delightful evening dining on fresh seafood expertly but simply cooked; try fresh cod with shellfish or *tajine* of lobster. The €17 menu served at lunch and dinner during the week is remarkable for quality and balance. Other menus up to €33 feature specialities prepared in the same vein.

SAINT-MÉLOIR-DES-ONDES　　35350 (5KM S)

⦿ RESTAURANT LE COQUILLAG, BISTROT MARIN

Maison Richeux; it's next to the *Hotel Bricourt*.
☎ 02.99.89.24.24
Closed Mon and Thurs lunchtimes Jul–Aug. **Disabled access. TV. Car park**.

A ravishing 1920s manor house looking down over the Mont-Saint-Michel bay. The prices are fair when all is said and done and even the wines are affordable: Menus €17–35; seafood platter for two at €87 including a choice of desserts from the trolley. It's the pinnacle of refinement and good taste. The décor has created a country interior with checked and plaid fabrics, leather chairs, a bar and a wide fire place. The views over the sea are breathtaking. Olivier Roellinger, the *enfant-chéri* of Breton cuisine, produces the best dishes from what the sea has to offer: Cancale oysters, sea bream *tartare*, lemon sole with butter and wonderful seafood and shellfish.

CARANTEC　　　　　　　　29660

⦿ LA CAMBUSE – LE CABESTAN

It's on the harbour.
☎ 02.98.67.08.92 ➡ 02.98.67.90.49
Closed Mon except July–Aug; Tues; 1 Nov to first week in Dec.

Two restaurants in one here: *La Cambuse* and *Le Cabestan*. Choose the one that suits your mood; the chef is the same for both but

the serving staff and atmospheres are very different. *La Cambuse* is a mixture of a brasserie, a bar and an inn, with a lively, even raucous atmosphere in summer; it can get overwhelming at the weekends. It's a popular meeting place for young people, with rock and Irish music at full-blast. A mixture of locals and extrovert holiday-makers of all nationalities are drawn by the atmosphere and the reputation of the cuisine. Generous portions of filling food at reasonable prices – pancake of pollack and crab sausage *des monts d'Arrée* with young garlic, lamb curry with coconut milk, *fario de Camaret* with sorrel. Next door at *Le Cabestan* the mood is quieter, even hushed. With its smart décor and softly spoken diners, this is the place for a romantic dinner. The cuisine is more refined, too, featuring scallops and prawns with thyme and a lightly smoked sea bream with red butter. In either establishment, expect to pay around €15 *à la carte*.

CARHAIX-PLOUGUER　　　　29270

⦿ CRÊPERIE LES SALINES

23 rue Brizeux; it's near the tourist office.
☎ 02.98.99.11.32
Closed Sun out of season and at Christmas; Mon and Tues; Wed evening; Jan.

They've tried to create a maritime feel in the dining room. The tasty *crêpes* are made from Breton organic flour and stuffed with unusual fillings. Various *formules* for €5 except Sun and public holidays and others up to €14. The most expensive will give you salmon in seaweed preserve and a Breton *crêpe* with apple flambéed in Calvados, or you can choose *à la carte* from dishes such as the *Fleur Grand Cru* with Guéméné *andouille* and cider preserve. A quality place for all budgets.

CARNAC　　　　　　　　　56340

⚐ ⬧ ⦿ HÔTEL LE RÂTELIER**

4 chemin Douët.
☎ 02.97.52.05.04 ➡ 02.97.52.76.11
Closed Sun evening and Mon end Sept to end March; 10 Jan–10 Feb. **TV. Car park**.

A charming little hotel in an attractive house weighed down by ivy, tucked away down an alley in the town centre. Well-kept rooms for €38–46; most have shower/wc but a few have washing facilities only. Half board, from €61 per person, is compulsory in summer.

The setting in the restaurant is very *vielle France*, both comfortable and charming. Lunch menu for €14 and others €23–39. Specialities are seafood and fish often served with complicated but delicious sauces. One menu offers nothing but lobster in all shapes, sizes and styles. Attentive, polite service. Free coffee. 10% discount on the room rate, except in school holidays.

I●I LES KERGUELEN

It's on the D781, the road to La Trinité-sur-Mer.
☎ 02.97.52.28.21
Closed Mon and Tues out of season. **Disabled access**.

They've invented a specially modified dish here – the "quzza". It's a cross between a pizza and a quiche and the chef has created a special base which is neither bread or short-crust pastry. It is, however, firm and soft and it's filled will all kinds of good things. The *crèpes* themselves sell for €2–6 and the pasta dishes for €7–9. The dining room is uninteresting but restful, the boss is amusing and very welcoming. The food is well-served and the prices are very modest. This is a place where everything is made in-house and every mouthful proves the point. You'll be reluctant to eat in those beach-side tourist traps after this.

I●I RESTAURANT LA CÔTE

Kermario. It's 1km from the centre of town; take the Auray road and turn left at the first lights. It's near the standing stones of Kermario.
☎ 02.97.52.02.80
Closed Sun and Mon out of season; a week early Dec; 3 weeks Jan; a week early March. **Car park**.

The owners' son, Pierre, a virtuoso chef fresh out of hotel school, has decided to transform the family restaurant into a temple of gastronomic delights. This has not been a hollow ambition; you will taste dishes of rare subtlety here. Starting with the menu at €20 you are in for an uplifting experience: try sea bream *galette à la tomate confite* or the egg casserole with scallops (on the winter menu). Other menus €27–41 and around €30 *à la carte*.

CHÂTEAULIN 29150

⅍ 🏠 I●I HÔTEL-RESTAURANT AU BON ACCUEIL**

av. Louison-Bobet; 2km from Châteaulin on the D770.
☎ 02.98.86.15.77 ➡ 03.98.86.36.25
Closed Sun evening and Mon out of season; Jan.
Swimming pool. Garden. TV. Car park.

A group of buildings on the side of the

Nantes-Brest canal make up this establishment. It's in a lovely spot in spite of being on the main road. The hotel's name means "Good welcome" and the owners keep their staff on their toes to live up to it. The rooms are elegantly decorated and vary in size but they all have good facilities; they're €40–61 with shower/wc or bath. The restaurant serves classic dishes that are well-executed and good value, with a weekday menu for €12 and others €17–28. Specialities include flambéed scallops with garlic butter and *aiguillette* of duck with raspberry. 10% discount on the room rate Oct–April.

⅍ I●I CRÊPERIE MARC PHILIPPE

29 quai Cosmao; it's very close to the tourist office.
☎ 02.98.86.38.00

A very small, very central *crêperie*. The *crêpes* are honestly priced and taste great. A meal will cost around €9 – the buckwheat *crêpe* stuffed with onions or goat's cheese and the *crêpe* with a prune cream are both good. It's a cheerful place where they use quality local produce, including Fouesnant cider and local beer; the flour is produced from grain grown 100% in Brittany. The place has recently been enlarged, but they've kept the terrace. Free coffee.

PLOMODIERN 29550 (28KM NW)

I●I AUBERGE DES GLAZICS

rue de la Plage.
☎ 02.98.81.52.32
Closed Tues lunchtime; one week in Feb; Nov. **Garden**.

At the beginning of the twentieth century this place was a smithy where grandmother made soup for clients waiting their turn. Now the third generation has taken over, following on in the culinary tradition. Olivier Bellin left school at fifteen and became an apprentice in a great kitchen; in ten years he accumulated a sheaf of diplomas and an array of awards. He was voted best young chef in Brittany and went off to work all over France before returning home and turning part of the dining room into a gastronomic restaurant. They changed the decoration and brought in stylish linen and plates. Menus €23–50 or you can choose *à la carte*. Specialities vary all the time, but here's a taster: pan-fried lobster with a lemon *noisette* or soup of *foie gras* with lentil cream, while for dessert choose a *cristalline* of strawberries with soft sugar or a *chaud-froid* of sweet chestnuts. This is a splendid place, one of the best in the region. Booking is essential.

COMBOURG 35270

🛏 |●| HÔTEL DU LAC**

2 pl. Chateaubriand; it's on the Rennes road.
☎ 02.99.73.05.65 ➡ 02.99.73.23.34
Closed Fri and Sun evening out of season; Nov. **TV. Car park. Garden.**

This place has a tranquil charm, and it's just a little old-fashioned. On one side there is the château and on the other the lake which was so dear to the writer Chateaubriand. Rooms for €44–61 depending on the facilities. The restaurant has two dining rooms – one is air-conditioned and there's a terrace looking over the lake and a garden. Set menus, €13–30, offer good, classic dishes with specialities of hot oysters Chateaubriand, roast sea bream with salt butter and raspberry dessert swathed in dark chocolate.

|●| RESTAURANT L'ÉCRIVAIN

pl. Saint-Gilduin (Centre); it's opposite the church.
☎ 02.99.73.01.61
Closed Wed evening, Thursday and Sun evening except mid-Feb to mid-March; the second fortnight in Oct. **Disabled access. Garden. Car park.**

This restaurant has a good reputation, built up over a number of years. The prices are astonishingly low considering the inventive flavours presented to you, and though there's a limited choice à la carte, that's because the chef uses only fresh produce: try the home-smoked fish or *millefeuille* of foie gras and artichokes. Set menus €14 in the week then €20–25. The restaurant name means "The Writer" and they sell illustrated books here too.

HÉDÉ 35630 (15KM SW)

🌿 |●| RESTAURANT LE GENTY HOME

Vallée de Hédé; it's on the N137 in the direction of Tinténiac, 500m outside Hédé.
☎ 02.99.45.46.07
Closed Tues evening; Wed; a fortnight in March; 3 weeks in Nov.

It's hard not to fall for this charming, flower-bedecked hostelry with natural stone walls and a huge fireplace. It's run by a highly talented young chef who has already attracted a following of food lovers. He constantly strives to embellish and improve his art. His cooking is excellent and even the most demanding of foodies will be intrigued by the selection of dishes he puts on his menus. Delicious weekday lunch menu at €10 and a long list of others €15–35. Specialities include asparagus tips with Cancale oysters,

escalope of foie gras with a scallop kebab, pigeon breast with foie gras and sea bass with leeks and balsamic sauce. Free coffee.

CONCARNEAU 29110

🛏 |●| HÔTEL-RESTAURANT LES OCÉANIDES

3 and 10 rue du Lin (Centre); it's near the harbour.
☎ 02.98.97.08.61 ➡ 02.98.97.09.13
Closed Sun Oct–April; Sun evening only May–June. **TV.**

For generations this place has been known as *La crêpe d'or*. Yvonne and family have maintained a homely atmosphere and they'll make you welcome at the bar, telling you about the region and its traditions. They may even serenade you – especially during the Filets Bleus festival. Set menus start at €12. À la carte the choice includes monkfish in pepper *coulis*, scallop *brochettes à la crème*, duck *aiguillettes aux baies roses* and *crépinette* of crab. Equally attractive room prices, with doubles from €40; half board is a good deal at €39 per person.

🌿 🛏 HÔTEL DE FRANCE ET D'EUROPE**

9 av. de la Gare (Centre).
☎ 02.98.97.00.64 ➡ 02.98.50.76.66
Closed Sat evening and 15 Nov–15 March. **TV. Car park.**

Well-positioned in the centre of town, this hotel offers the kind of pleasant, comfortable rooms – with telephones, alarm clocks, good-quality linen on the beds and double-glazing – that you would expect from a modern hotel. They're putting in a lift and a new sitting room, and reception is on the ground floor. Enjoy a drink on the terrace. All this plus a cheerful welcome, a professional attitude and excellent information services. Double rooms €46 with shower/wc or €53 with bath; buffet breakfast €6. 10% discount 1 Oct–1 May.

🛏 HÔTEL KERMOR**

Les Sables Blancs.
☎ 02.98.97.02.96 ➡ 02.98.97.84.04
🌐 www.kermorlespiedsdansleau.com

The *Kermor* is a characterful turn-of-the-(twentieth)-century hotel right on the beach. Inside it's been beautifully decorated with lithographs, etchings and photographs from the 1920s. Rooms are bright and fresh, with wood panelling and, to complete the illusion, portholes for windows. Each one has a sea view. Double with shower/wc €58–80 and those on the first floor have pretty wooden balconies. The splendid breakfast room has a fantastic view of the sea too. Breakfast, €8, is served until 11.30am.

|●| CRÊPERIE LE GRAND CHEMIN

17 av. de la Gare; it's 300m from the tourist office.
☎ 02.98.97.36.57
Closed Mon except July–Aug.

The touristy atmosphere in town can get a bit much, but this appealing *crêperie*, which has clocked up fifty years of quality service, doesn't rely on the tourist trade to make a living: some regulars have been coming here for nearly as long and so it has a friendly feel. It's not at all chi-chi; the *patronne* simply sees her job as serving generous portions of *crêpes* at reasonable prices. The menu at €7 gets you two buckwheat *galettes* and a chocolate *crêpe*. Other menus up to €11 with choices including *crêpe* with scallops and leek *fondue*.

|●| RESTAURANT CHEZ ARMANDE

15 [bis] av. du Docteur-Nicolas; it's opposite the marina.
☎ 02.98.97.00.76
Closed Tues out of season; Wed in summer; Christmas to New Year; the Feb school holidays.

One of the best seafood restaurants in Concarneau and the prices won't make you feel queasy. Lovely panelling and pleasant furniture in the dining room, which also has a fish-tank brimming with crustaceans. Excellent fresh fish and seafood straight from the quay, which is just a stone's throw away. The cheapest set menu costs €17 and is only served during the week. There are others at €23–30. The *cotriade*, a Breton five-fish soup, is the signature dish. You would return to this place for that alone – otherwise try the lobster stew or the seafood platters and a dessert from the selection on the trolley.

CONQUET (LE)   29217

⚥ ☎ |●| LE RELAIS DU VIEUX PORT

1 quai dy Drellac'h.
☎ 02.98.89.15.91
Closed Jan.

In times gone by this old harbour inn provided simple rooms and a restaurant. But after substantial alterations it has been upgraded to the standards of a modern hotel. It's a friendly place, run by a family who know how to make you feel welcome and at home. Stripped wooden floors and white walls gently brightened up with blue stencilling. Very good beds. Five rooms with a view of the

estuary go for €33–52 with shower/wc – really excellent prices for the quality. Each room bears the name of a Breton island. Avoid *Bannalec*, the cheapest but the smallest, which has a cramped shower. Breakfast of white or brown bread with a selection of home-made preserves is set out on a large refectory table. The dining room is a relatively new addition to the building and they've put in an open fireplace – it's about €11–18 for a meal in the restaurant. In the *crêperie*, you'll pay more but there's a good selection of *crêpes*, a savoury *complète*, fried mussels and chips and a good wine cellar. There's live music on Wednesday evening in summer. Free house apéritif and 10% discount on the room rate except during school holidays and weekends.

LOCHRIST   29217 (2KM S)

⚥ |●| LA FERME DE KERINGAR

It's in the village.
☎ 02.98.89.09.59
Restaurant closed lunchtimes in summer; during the week the rest of the year.

The farm is sheltered from the wild sea storms between Le Conquet and the Pointe de Saint-Mathieu and has been in the same family for over two hundred years. Alain Larsonneur used to teach primary school kids and is a passionate advocate of organic farming: he's turned the farm into a teaching centre and it also provides a welcome stopping place for walkers. There are eight attractively arranged rooms with shower/wc for €32–26. In the reataurant there's a massive granite fire place and wooden tables and benches. Old tools and photographs of the owners' ancestors decorate the walls. The cuisine is a mixture of fish and meat and offers good value for money: *cotriade*, *Kig ha farz*, Molène sausage smoked over seaweed as well as oat broth and Guéméné *andouille*. Bread is baked on-site. Menus €15–34. There's a shop selling their produce.

CRACH   56400

⚥ |●| RESTAURANT CRÊPERIE L'HERMINE

12 rue d'Aboville.
☎ 02.97.30.01.17
Closed Mon–Wed Oct–March; Mon lunchtime and Wed April–June and Sept; the Feb school holidays.

You can't miss this lovely house, festooned with flowers. The dining room is bright and pleasant, and there is also a lovely verandah opening onto the rock garden. Their famous *crêpes* come in about twenty varieties; all are equally delicious. There are also numerous fish and seafood dishes, not least the mussels *façon Hermine*. Anyone with a sweet tooth will be spoilt for choice between the tempting desserts. Crêpes cost different from €2–5 with specialities for €1–7. There's a children's play area, too. Free Breton Kir or coffee.

CROZON   29160

犬 🏠 |●| HÔTEL DE LA PRESQU'ÎLE – RESTAURANT LE MUTIN GOURMAND

1 rue Graveran; it's on the church square.
☎ 02.98.27.29.29 ➡ 02.98.26.11.97
e mutin-gourmand@wanadoo.fr
Closed Sun evening and Mon out of season; Mon lunchtime in season. **Disabled access**. **TV**.

A charming hotel that radiates the true style of Brittany. The décor is inspired by the yellow and ochre of local costumes, Breton pottery and the sea. Double rooms €42–65 and half board €48–59. There are several dining rooms decorated in the same style. Very good cuisine using fresh market produce: egg *chaud-froid* and sea-urchin coral, fillet of yellow pollack with black wheat pancake and very good desserts. Everything from the bread to the *foie gras* is prepared in their kitchens. 10% discount on the room rate Oct–March except during school holidays.

DINAN   22100

犬 🏠 HÔTEL LES GRANDES TOURS**

6 rue du Château (Centre); it's opposite the château.
☎ 02.96.85.16.20 ➡ 02.96.85.16.04
e carregi@wanadoo.fr
Closed 15 Dec–15 Feb. **TV**. **Car park**.

Victor Hugo and Juliette Drouet stayed here on 25 June 1836 while they were on a five-week tour of the west of France. "They dined, spent a pleasant night and dined there again the following evening. They found the hotel to their taste." The recommendation still holds good, especially considering the recent updating that's been done. It's a quiet place even though five of the thirty-six rooms overlook the road; €30 with handbasin and €45 with shower/wc or bath. You can park in the courtyard, though there's a charge in summer. Free breakfast for one person if there are two of you staying.

🏠 |●| HÔTEL LES ALLEUX**

Route de Ploubalay (North); take the D2 in the direction of Ploubalay and it's in a ZAC.
☎ 02.96.85.16.10 ➡ 02.96.85.11.40
e hotel.alleux@wanadoo.fr
Closed Jan. **Garden**. **TV**. **Car park**. **Disabled access**.

A modern hotel surrounded by greenery and with little charm – but it's a good place to stop on the road between Saint-Malo and Dinard. The rooms have been refurbished and there is one adapted for disabled visitors. Doubles cost €43–50. Menus in the restaurant for €10–27. It's popular with groups.

犬 🏠 |●| HÔTEL LE CHALLONGE**

29 pl. Du-Guesclin.
☎ 02.96.87.16.30 x02.96.87.16.31
Closed access. **TV**.

Eleven of the eighteen rooms look over the square but don't worry about noise – the double glazing is efficient. All the rooms have good bedding and doubles cost €52–65 with shower/wc or bath. Some doubles communicate with a twin room for the children. There's also a room especially adapted for disabled visitors. All the bathrooms have heated towel rails. Honest value. Weekday lunch menu €10 and others €11–22. One free breakfast per room per night.

|●| CRÊPERIE DES ARTISANS

6 rue du Petit-Fort (Centre); it's by the Jerzual gate.
☎ 02.96.39.44.10
Closed Mon except July–Aug, and mid-Oct to March.

A beautiful building in a charming street in the old town. It's an ancient residence with a rustic setting, bare stone walls and wooden tables. The relaxed atmosphere is enlivened by the really friendly owners. Excellent traditional *crêpes* and cider from the barrel. There's a €8 lunch menu, one at €11 in the evenings and a *menu terroir* for €10. They play nice music and, in summer, set up a large wooden table in the street.

|●| RESTAURANT LA COURTINE

6 rue de la Croix; it's opposite the town hall
☎ 02.96.39.74.41
Closed Wed lunchtime in summer; Wed and Sun evening out of season; 15–30 Nov; 1–15 Jan.

A warm and cosy dining room in a quiet side street. The fresh, friendly decoration provides a nice setting for the cuisine. Everything comes straight from the market and the fish and seafood are skilfully prepared. Weekday *formule* €11 with main course and a choice of starter or dessert (wine and coffee included) then menus €15–30.

|●| LE BISTROT DU VIADUC

22 rue du Lion-d'Or, Lanvallay; take the road to Rennes, just after the viaduct on the left at the bend.
☎ 02.96.85.95.00
Closed Mon; the second fornight in June; mid-Dec to mid-Jan.

Incredible views of the Rance valley from this restaurant, which is in a splendid setting and has a pleasant interior with pastel colours and a stove in the dining room. They serve delicious local cuisine, including *croustillant* of pig's trotters, the celebrated oxtail, cod *à la Bretonne* and marrowbone. There's a short weekday lunch menu for €14 and others €26 and 38, or *à la carte* you'll pay somewhere in the region of €46 plus wine. Booking is essential.

PLÉLAN-LE-PETIT   22980 (13KM W)

|●| LE RELAIS DE LA BLANCHE-HERMINE

Lieu-dit Lourmel; take the N176 towards Jugon-les-Lacs. At the roundabout take the road to Plélan-le-Petit along the old road signposted for the *zone artisanal*.
☎ 02.96.27.62.19 📠 02.96.27.05.93
Closed Tues except July–Aug.

This restaurant has a good reputation in the region and is housed in a long stone building by the road. Spacious, lively dining room. Classy, cooking with an €11 menu (not served Sun lunch), and others €15–24. Seafood or shellfish must be ordered in advance. On the first and third Thursday of every month they roast suckling pig on the spit.

DINARD   35800

🎿 🛏 HÔTEL LES MOUETTES

64 av. George-V; it's 50m from the Yacht Club.
☎ 02.99.46.10.64 📠 02.99.16.02.49
Closed Jan.

A pleasant family hotel with ten charming, cosy rooms which are freshly decorated with a touch of the sea – they're €25–38, depending on facilities and season. It's friendly, simple and inexpensive, with a very warm welcome. Ask at reception for information about parking. 10% discount except for school holidays and long weekends.

|●| DIDIER MÉRIL

6 rue Yves-Verney (East).
☎ 02.99.46.95.44
Closed 4–25 Jan.

Didier Méril has created restaurants in Dinard yet he old. He's full of passion and c recruited a dynamic young te come comes with a smile and ....humour. The setting is a tad minimalistic but not unappealing. The presentation on the plates is original and meticulous and matches the inventive and delicious cuisine. Seafood dishes predominate *à la carte* and they change frequently: *craquant* of salmon and *andouille de Guéméné*, John Dory with spiced caramel. Weekday lunch menu €14 and others €20–42. One of the great temptations is the home-made bread – there are eight different types of rolls so go easy because the desserts are too good to miss.

|●| RESTAURANT L'ESCALE À CORTO

12 av. George-V (East).
☎ 02.99.46.78.57
Closed lunchtimes and Mon evening except for school holidays.

A lively little restaurant, popular with young locals. It is also known as *restaurant des Marins*. Dod is the barman, while Marie runs the kitchen, producing seafood salad, oysters, salmon *tartare* and various other fish dishes. There are no set menus, but for about €23 you will enjoy a good, healthy meal. Seafood platter available to order. This restaurant is only open in the evening, as Corto likes to take a nap on the beach in the afternoon.

DOL-DE-BRETAGNE   35120

🛏 GRAND HÔTEL DE LA GARE*

21 av. Aristide-Briand (Southwest).
☎ 02.99.48.00.44 📠 02.99.48.13.10
Closed Mon Oct–April. **Private garage**.

A small, plain and unpretentious hotel with double rooms at €26–38. The new owners have implemented a programme of refurbishment. Good, spacious restaurant cheerfully decorated in a conventional style in shades of old rose. There's also a lively café on the ground floor.

🎿 🛏 |●| RESTAURANT DE LA BRESCHE-ARTHUR**

36 bd. Deminiac (Centre).
☎ 02.99.48.01.44 📠 02.99.48.16.32
Closed Sun evening unless you book. **TV**. **Car park**.

One of the best restaurants in the region,

⌐rving excellent food in a lovely dining room. Menus at €12–30 are astonishing value for money. The chef is a star who makes wonderful sauces and solemnly respects the seasons. Naturally, he uses only fresh produce to produce mussel soup with citrus fruit juice, chicken with cockles and cider and grilled, pickled cuttlefish. Rooms also available for €27–58. 10% discount on the room rate out of season except public holiday weekends. Free breakfast and free apéritif.

🏃🍴 AUBERGE DE LA COUR VERTE

route de Rennes (Centre).
☎ 02.98.48.41.41
Closed Mon, Tues and Wed lunchtimes out of season; Mon and Tues; Christmas–New Year. **Disabled access**. **TV**.

This long, low-built farm has been expertly renovated and it's surrounded by greenery. There is a children's playground in the courtyard. The monumental fireplace that dominates the dining room is used for grilling splendid hunks of meat. Other dishes, *crêpes* and salads (*medium* or *senior* according to your appetite) and desserts are prepared in the kitchen, which you can peer into from the dining room. Lunchtime *formule* for €8 or around €20 *à la carte*. The chef is Belgian and includes various specialities from home on the menu – notably mussels and a remarkable *sirop de Liège*. There's a warm atmosphere and young staff. A small shop across the courtyard sells foodie goodies. Free glass of "Magic Potion" offered at the end of your meal.

DOUARNENEZ   29100

🏃🏨🍴 HÔTEL DE FRANCE – LE DOYEN**

4 rue Jean-Jaurès (Centre).
☎ 02.98.92.00.02 ➡ 02.98.92.27.05
Restaurant closed Sun evening and Mon except July–Aug; the second week in Jan. **TV**.

A local institution right in the town centre which feels both chic and homely. The rooms in the annexe are quieter, while those in the main building are being done up in authentic Breton style like the dining room. Rooms €38–54. The cooking in the restaurant is resolutely from the region (meaning that there's lots of seafood and fish) but it has the imprint of the chef's individuality. Menus €15–33; dishes change constantly as fresh produce comes to market. House apéritif and 10% discount on the room rate Oct–April, but

make sure you mention this guide when you book.

🏃🏨🍴 HOSTELLERIE LE CLOS DE VALLOMBREUSE***

7 rue Estienne-d'Orves (Centre); it's near the Sacré-Cœur church.
☎ 02.98.92.63.64 ➡ 02.98.92.84.98
TV. **Car park**.

An elegant, early twentieth-century building very close to the church and overlooking the sea. Inside, wide fire places, wood panelling, tapestries and leather armchairs create a cosy interior. The rooms are charming and bright, some with a sea view; they go for €50–120. Charming welcome. The food in the restaurant is in harmony with the surroundings: *cotriade* (a local soup made with five types of fish), grilled lobster glazed with coral and apple tart with a caramel *coulis*. Menus €15–51. 10% discount on the room rate.

🏃🍴 CRÊPERIE AU GOÛTER BRETON

36 rue Jean-Jaurès (Centre).
☎ 02.98.92.02.74
Closed Sun and Mon in winter except during school holidays; a fortnight in mid-June; a fortnight in Nov. **Disabled access**.

Service from noon to 10pm in the summer. Lots of character here: the proprietor gets around on a Harley-Davidson or in a Cadillac and inside the décor is very Breton with a soundtrack of Breton bagpipe music mixed with plenty of jazz and rock. It's no surprise to find American hamburgers among the list of *crêpes*. House specialities have names such as *Moscovite*, which comes with smoked salmon, sour cream and lemon, and *La Nordique*, with herrings, onions and potatoes. *Crêpe* menus from €7 upwards and a children's menu for €7. Flower-filled terrace to the rear. Free apéritif or coffee.

ERQUY   22430

🏨🍴 HÔTEL BEAUSÉJOUR**

21 rue de la Corniche.
☎ 02.96.72.30.39 ➡ 02.96.72.16.30
✉ hotel.beausejour@wanadoo.fr
Restaurant closed Sun evening and Mon Oct–June; the first fortnight in Feb.
Disabled access. **TV**. **Car park**.

Only 100m from the port lies this small, traditional holiday hotel. Very warm welcome. Well-maintained doubles with shower/wc or bath for €40–49. Moderately priced restau-

rant with generously served set menus at
€12–21: cockles with garlic and parsley butter, seafood *choucroute*, scallop kebabs with
crab *coulis*, *tarte Tatin*. Half board, obligatory July–Aug, is good value at €43–52 per
person.

⦿ RESTAURANT LE RELAIS SAINT-AUBIN

Saint-Aubin; 3km from Erquy-bourg, it's signposted off
the D34.
☎ 02.96.72.13.22 ➡ 02.96.63.52.31
Closed Mon; Tues out of season; the Feb school
holidays; the last week in Sept; 19–26 Dec. **Car park**.
Garden.

Situated in a small hamlet, this beautiful seventeenth-century priory in exceptional surroundings is full of character. There's a ravishing dining room with ancient beams,
antique furniture and a monumental granite
fireplace. In summer you can eat on the
terrace. A variety of set menus: one at weekday lunchtime for €12 and others €18–31.
There's also a dish of the day written up on
the slate. Warm welcome and excellent service. A good selection of wines, including
white or red Menetou Salon. Best to book in
season and at the weekend.

⦿ RESTAURANT L'ESCURIAL

21 bd. de la Mer; it's next to the tourist office.
☎ 02.96.72.31.56 ✉ escurial@wanadoo.fr
Closed Sun evening and Mon except in Aug; 20 Nov–5
Jan.

The other "best-known" restaurant in the
region. View the ocean in the dining room
from comfortable green-and-white leather
armchairs. Menus €18–43. Specialities are
seafood, of course, like pan-fried John Dory
with *foie gras* and tagliatelle. Reliable value.

⥯⦿ LA CASSOLETTE

6 rue de la Saline (Centre).
☎ 02.96.72.13.08
Closed Thurs and Fri lunchtime out of season; Dec; Jan.

The locals are lucky enough to have two
excellent restaurants in town (the other is
L'Escurial). This one is run by a nice woman
who was smart enough to hire a young chef
who trained in some excellent kitchens. He
uses the best seafood straight from the sea:
scallop raviolis, *cassolette* of crayfish with
orange, *andouille* with cider butter, veal kidneys with Pommeau sauce and, for dessert,
a *Byzantin* with two chocolates. Prices are
reasonable – there's a weekday lunch for
formule at €10, menus for €19–37 or €38 *à
la carte* plus wine. Free glass of champagne.

FOUESNANT   29170

⥯ ⌂ HÔTEL À L'ORÉE DU BOIS**

4 rue de Kergoadig.
☎ 02.98.56.00.06 ➡ 02.98.56.14.17
TV. Pay garage.

Small, classic family hotel that's been completely renovated. Genuine welcome. Good
rooms at good prices: €30 with basin/wc,
€40–45 with shower/wc and bath. Some
have a sea view of the Cap-Coz or of the forest of Fouesnant. There are also have rooms
sleeping three or four. Walking trails start just
nearby and the beach is three minutes away
by car. 10% discount Sept–June.

GLOMEL   22110

⌂ ⦿ LA CASCADE

5 Grande-Rue; it's on the main street.
☎ 02.96.29.60.44.

A pleasant little country hotel with four pretty rooms – each has a different décor and is
clean and neat. Two have handbasins only
and share the bathroom (€24) while for
(€27) there's one with a shower and another with shower/wc and bath. They serve a *menu
ouvrier* at €9 in the restaurant; in the
evenings and at weekends it's open to hotel
guests only.

GROUX (ÎLE DE)   56590

⥯ ⌂ HÔTEL DE LA JETÉE**

It's on the port.
☎ 02.97.86.80.82 ✉ laurencetonnerre@freesbee.fr
Hotel 5 Jan–15 Feb.

The very last house on the right before you
drive into the sea, this is a picture-postcard
of a place, fronted by a jetty with a lighthouse
at the end, with anchored boats bobbing,
gulls wheeling and squealing and the sea
practically licking the hotel walls. The décor
inside is tasteful and the rooms are pretty.
Doubles with shower/wc €40 or €64 with
bath. Breakfast €6. Free coffee.

GUINGAMP   22200

⦿ RESTAURANT LA ROSERAIE

parc Styvel; 1km from the town centre on the Tréguier
road, and signposted on the right.
☎ 02.96.21.06.35
Closed Mon evening out of season; the first fortnight in

Sept. **Car park**.

This restaurant is in a lovely bourgeois house, delightfully set in the middle of large grounds. Attractive dining rooms serving tasty grills and seafood. You'll pay €15–23. Booking highly recommended.

HENNEBONT 56700

⊜ |●| HÔTEL-RESTAURANT DU CENTRE

44 rue du Maréchal-Joffre (Centre).
☎ 02.97.36.21.44 ➡ 02.97.36.44.77
Closed Mon except July and Aug.

A likeable young couple have taken over this grand old hotel and brought it up-to-date without sacrificing its simple provincial appeal. You will appreciate the *patronne*'s charm and the hotel's excellent value. Doubles €26 with shower (wc on the landing) and others up to €32. Set menus – €12 in the week and others €18–36 – list good, honest dishes, particularly fish and seafood: grilled crayfish with cream, salmon with two sauces. One of the best restaurants in town.

HOËDIC (ÎLE DE) 56170

⊜ |●| LES CARDINAUX

☎ 02.97.52.37.27 ➡ 02.97.52.41.26
℮ lescardinaux@aol.com
Closed Sun evening and Mon out of season; a fortnight in Feb; a fortnight in Oct.

Ten rooms with a sea view. Doubles €43–53. Half board, from €46 per person, is compulsory in summer. There's also a restaurant with menus at €21–30; the house speciality is fish *choucroute*. Good idea to book – it's the only hotel on the island. Rather serious welcome.

JOSSELIN 56120

⅔ ⊜ |●| HÔTEL DE FRANCE**

pl. Notre-Dame (Centre).
☎ 02.97.22.23.06 ➡ 02.97.22.35.78
Closed Sun evening and Mon; Jan. **TV**.

Superb location opposite the basilica. The lovely rooms are well maintained, with some spacious ones in the roof; €43 with shower/wc or bath. Stalwart, traditional cooking: hot oysters with leeks *julienne*, sole braised in red Saumur wine. Menus €13–23 or *à la carte*. Decent value for money. Professional and courteous staff. Free coffee.

LANDÉDA 29870

⊜ HÔTEL LA BAIE DES ANGES***

350 route des Anges; it's on Aber-Wrac'h port.
☎ 02.98.04.90.04 ➡ 02.98.04.92.27
Closed Jan and Feb. **Disabled access**. **TV**. **Car park**.

The chatty owner is justifiably proud of his establishment. It's a lovely house, dating from the early 1900s, with a yellow façade set just above the beach and overlooking the ocean. The views and sunsets are breathtaking. Attractively decorated rooms with sitting rooms from €67 with shower/wc or bath. Breakfast €10 with a choice of coffees, home-made jams, and bread from the baker next door – delicious. There's a splendid terrace.

LANDERNEAU 29220

⊜ |●| L'AMANDIER**

55 rue de Brest; coming down from the station, turn right at the first set of traffic lights, 500m from the town centre.
☎ 02.98.85.10.89 ➡ 02.98.85.34.14
Restaurant closed Sun evening and Mon. **TV**.

This hotel offers remarkable value. Very elegant interior, with attractive paintings and refined furniture. The rooms are particularly pleasant and have superior facilities. Doubles from €40. The traditional cuisine comes with a good reputation and there are some delightful new dishes. Menus from €16; choose from *roulade* of roasted pig's trotters and pork knuckle, guineafowl, stuffed mussels and clams, seafood *mouclade* and *croustade* of queen scallops in a butter sauce. Excellent desserts such as *gourmandise* with almond milk and red fruit, pear *tulipe* with chocolate and iced Grand Marnier soufflé.

|●| RESTO DE LA MAIRIE

9 rue de la Tour-d'Auvergne; it's on the quay opposite the town hall.
☎ 08.98.85.01.83 ➡ 08.98.85.37.07
Closed Tues evening.

A long, thin, friendly bar-restaurant. Plush décor with stained glass, red carpet and lush plants. The *patronne* has been running the place for thirty years with infectious *bonhomie*. For the kids, there's a tortoise called Nono which hides in the patio. Among the specialities try the *marmite Neptune*, a seriously good fish stew, made with scallops, monkfish, shrimps and prawns expertly cooked with cream and cognac (you'll have to wait half-an-hour for this, because it's prepared to order). Otherwise, depending on the season, try the mussels *maison*, scallops, monkfish and spring vegetable stew or, for carnivores, the *fricassée* of veal kidneys. Good-value dishes *à la carte*. The *menu express* costs €9, and there are others up to €28. You can get wine by the glass. They make you feel very welcome.

ROCHE-MAURICE (LA)   29800 (4KM NE)

IOI AUBERGE DU VIEUX CHÂTEAU

4 Grand-Place.
☎ 02.98.20.40.52
Closed evenings in the week. **Car park**.

A fine inn set in a peaceful village square near a lovely Breton church and in the shadow of a ruined eleventh-century château. It undoubtedly offers the best value for money in the Landerneau region. The first menu, €9 at lunchtime, is really astonishing, attracting crowds of local farmers and people who travel for their job. The restaurant appeals to people from all walks of life who know a good place to eat when they find one.

LANDVÉNNEC   29560

🏃 🏠 IOI SAINT-PATRICK

rue Saint-Guénole; it's next to the church.
☎ 02.98.27.70.83
Closed Wed and Sun evening out of season; 17 Oct–17 March.

A charming little hotel in a peaceful village on the Crozon peninsula, with an unspoilt bistro where old wooden chairs scrape noisily on the tiled floor. There's a parade of aged Irish whiskeys on the shelf behind the cramped bar. Good home cooking in the restaurant with a lot of fish dishes. Menus start at €15 and go up in tiny increments to €17, or there's *à la carte*. The lovely rooms are just like you'd find in a private home: marble chimney pieces and scattered ornaments. Rooms 1, 4 and 7 have windows overlooking the Rade de Brest. Doubles with basin €30–34. Friendly, easy-going welcome. 10% discount on the room rate after three nights Sept–June.

LANDIVISIAU   29400

🏠 IOI RESTAURANT LE TERMINUS

94 av. Foch (Northeast).
☎ 02.98.68.02.00

Closed Fri and Sun evenings; Sat lunchtime. **TV**. **Car park**.

One of the best *Routier* restaurants in Finistère. The impressive €9 *menu-ouvrier* comprises two starters (including seafood), a main course with as many vegetables as you can eat, salad, cheese, dessert, coffee and a litre carafe of red wine – it's unbeatable. The line-up of lorries parked outside are evidence of its winning formula. They have a few double rooms with shower/wc starting at €20.

LANNION   22300

IOI LA VILLE BLANCHE

Lieu-dit la Ville-Blanche; it's 5km along on the Tréguier road, by Rospez.
☎ 02.96.37.04.28 ➡ 02.96.46.57.82
Closed Sun evening except July–Aug; Mon; Wed evening; 10 Dec–4 Feb.

Great cooking prepared by a pair of brothers who have gone back to their roots. If they offer to show you their aromatic herb garden, don't refuse. Their specialities are seasonal – scallops from November to March, Breton lobster from April to October. Try the pork knuckle pâté with *foie gras*, the roast brie with rhubarb or the *millefeuille* with caramalized apples. Weekday menu at €24 and others €38–64. You can also buy good wines by the glass, which is rare in a place of this quality.

LESCONIL   29730

🏠 IOI GRAND HÔTEL DES DUNES**

17 rue Laennec.
☎ 02.98.87.83.03 ➡ 02.98.82.23.44
Closed mid-Oct to end March. **TV**.

This huge establishment is in a fabulous location: one side looks out over a sand dune which falls away to the sea 100m beyond. There's a lovely walk from the hotel along the shore. The rooms have been refurbished; doubles from €52. They're spacious and well-appointed – obviously the ones with sea view are the best. The food is pretty good value, and even on the half-board menu there's lots of choice. Menus start at €18 (not served Sun lunch). The friendly, professional *patron* makes you feel welcome.

LOCQUIREC   29241

🏠 IOI HÔTEL LES SABLES BLANCS

15 rue des Sables-Blancs; it's on the road to Morlaix.

☎ 02.98.67.42.07 ➡ 02.98.79.33.25
Closed Tues and Wed March–Sept; Wed in July–Aug; Jan–Feb. **Car park**.

Small hotel and *crêperie*, tucked away in the dunes facing Lannion Bay. Wild, magnificent setting and warm welcome. Decent rooms, some with superb sea views. Doubles for €43. *Crêperie* and salad buffet on a veranda looking out over the sea. Set menus from €9 listing mussels *au chouchen* and *crêpes à l'andouille* or filled with feta cheese. Oysters served at any time.

GUIMAËC   29620 (3KM W)

ı⊙ı LE CAPLAN AND CO

Lieu-dit Poul-Rodon; take the Plouganou road out of Guimaëc and turn right at the third crossroads.
☎ 02.98.67.58.98
Closed Sat lunchtime; noon–9pm Sun; public holidays out of season.

Right at the end of a track, at the mercy of the howling winds, *Le Caplan* stands defiantly against the elements. Push open the door and you'll find a warm, friendly café-book-shop that is almost unique in France – a brilliantly successful combination of reading room and bar. Piles of books are strewn here and there on the tables, selected by Lan and Caprini, who used to work in publishing. The menu is even more of a surprise in Brittany – it features a platter of Greek specialities at €9, served with Greek wine. There's a games corner for the kids.

LOCTUDY   29750

🧖 🏠 HÔTEL DE BRETAGNE**

19 rue du Port.
☎ 02.98.87.40.21
e hoteldebretagne@hotmail.com
Swimming pool.

The renovation work they've done on this old building is exquisite – they two owners have added excellent facilities yet retained the building's character and charm. Lavishly decorated rooms, all with shower/wc and telephone, €41–51. Breakfast costs €6 per person. Walkers and cyclists especially welcome. There's a new swimming pool, sauna and a Jacuzzi. Free house apéritif.

🧖ı⊙ı RELAIS DE LODONNEC

3 rue des Tulipes, plage de Lodonnec; it's 2km south of Loctudy.
☎ 02.98.87.55.34
Closed Mon July–Aug; Tues evening and Wed out of

season; 15 Jan–15 Feb.

This old granite fisherman's house, just 20m from the beach, is home to one of the region's up-and-coming restaurants. Pleasant ambience, with blond wood and exposed beams. Depending on the menu (they're €11–40), you get platters of oysters or seafood and gratinéed sea trout or red mullet fillets in a sea urchin sauce. *À la carte* dishes include scallops *rosace* with two sauces, hot *foie gras* in a pastry case and grilled bass with basil. The wine list has affordable bottles to satisfy most tastes. Booking advised at weekends. Free house apéritif.

LORIENT   56100

🏠ı⊙ı HÔTEL-RESTAURANT GABRIEL**

45 av. de la Perrière (South); it's on the main road from Keroman fishing port.
☎ 02.97.37.60.76 ➡ 02.97.37.50.45
Restaurant closed Sat lunchtime and Sun Oct to end June. **TV**.

Small, unfussy hotel with a cheap and friendly restaurant. Modern, very clean doubles for €20–30; they add a supplement of €12 during the Interceltic Festival. The set menu costs €9 including wine (lunchtime and evening) and there are others €10–15. There's a nice atmosphere.

🏠 HÔTEL LES PÊCHEURS

7 rue Jean-Lagarde.
☎ 02.97.21.19.24 ➡ 02.97.21.13.19
Closed Sun and public holidays **TV**.

The rooms here are simple but impeccably clean. The cheapest ones don't have private facilities and there are communal ones along the corridor. Doubles €21 with shower up to €32 with shower or bath/wc – excellent value for money for this town-centre establishment. On the ground floor, there's a bar with a very welcoming owner.

🧖 🏠 ı⊙ı HÔTEL-RESTAURANT VICTOR HUGO**

36 rue Lazare-Carnot (Southeast); it's near the ferry terminal for Île de Groix.
☎ 02.97.21.16.24 ➡ 02.97.84.95.13
TV. **Private garage**.

Warm welcome from the cheery *patronne*. Clean doubles with handbasin go for €26, €46 with good bathrooms providing shower/wc or bath. Those overlooking the street are well-soundproofed. Children under ten get a free breakfast. The restaurant has a range of menus €13–49 and a very extensive *à la carte* selection: *foie gras* and lots of fish are specialities. 10% discount on the room rate Nov–March and free breakfast for kids under the age of 10.

|●| TAVARN AR ROUE MORVAN

17 rue Poissonnière; (Centre).
☎ 02.97.21.67.47
Closed Sun

A genuine Celtic establishment with a typical décor and serving a couple of dishes of the day for lunch and dinner – one meat, one fish – priced €6–8. Tasty dishes, particularly the *triskèle* (a Breton soup with cabbage and sausage) and the Irish mutton stew, and they have a good range of red, white and rosé wines with dry cider as an alternative. There's lots of noisy music, creating a young, energetic atmosphere. They hold regular folk concerts and on Monday evenings there are classes in the Breton language.

|●| RESTAURANT LE PIC

2 bd. du Maréchal-Franchet-d'Esperey (North); it's near the post office.
☎ 02.97.21.18.29 ➡ 02.97.21.92.64
Closed Sat lunchtime and Sun. **Disabled access**.

A pleasant spot with Parisian bistro décor and a terrace for sunny days. Simple, tasty cooking including crab *croustillant* with a prawn *coulis*, cod with *aïoli*, pig's trotters stuffed with oxtail, chocolate *fondant* and pears with cream tea sauce. Cheapest set menu at €13 and others €17–36. The restaurant has just been included in the *Qualité de France* list, and the owner, Pierre Le Bourhis, is a wine connoisseur who was voted Brittany's best wine waiter in 1986. Have a good look in the cellar.

|●| RESTAURANT LE JARDIN GOURMAND

46 rue Jules-Simon (Northwest); it's near the train station.
☎ 02.97.64.17.24 ➡ 02.97.64.15.75
Closed Sun and Mon; the Feb school holidays; 1–10 Aug.

Delicious dishes concocted from the freshest local produce are served outside under a pergola and in the airy, elegant dining room. Courteous service from the host and skilful, creative cooking by his wife, who uses fresh market produce. Weekday lunch menu €17; otherwise it's €27, or €38 *à la carte* for an excellent meal including wine. There's a selection of coffees or teas on a special menu. One of the best restaurants in Lorient so it's best to book.

KERVIGNAC   56700 (10KM E)

|●| CRÊPERIE HENT ER MOR

Hot to get there; from the N165, take the turning marked Kervignac and it's in the village
☎ 02.97.65.77.17
Closed Tue.

There's such a range of crêpe fillings to choose from that it's hard to decide: sardines, chilli, pork belly and prunes, mussles with garlic butter – the choice is huge. You'll pay between €1–5 for a savoury one while the sweet ones cost around €4. This place has been run by the same man since 1967 and he has a genuine passion for good crêpes; he's also a bit of a painter so the restaurant serves as an art gallery as well. You're invited to do your own painting on a pancake – the possibilities are limitless.

PORT-LOUIS   56290 (20KM S)

🏄 🏠 |●| HÔTEL-RESTAURANT DU COMMERCE**

1 pl. du Marché (Centre); take the N165 to Port Louis.
☎ 02.97.82.46.05 ➡ 02.97.82.11.02
Closed Sun evening and Mon out of season; 15 Jan–15 Feb. **Disabled access**. **TV**. **Garden**.

A quiet, comfortable hotel in the centre of town on a tranquil, tree-lined square with a small orchard behind. There are thirty-odd rooms, not all in the first flush of youth. Double rooms €25 with handbasin, €38 with shower and TV and €59 with bath/wc. The cheapest menu in the week is €11, and there are others €14–33 and you'll pay around €22 *à la carte*. They prefer you to stay half-board in July–Aug, priced from €55 per person. 10% discount on the room rate Nov–March, and free apéritif.

|●| LA GRÈVE DE LOCMALO

18 bis, rue Locmalo; (South).
☎ 02.97.82.48.41
Closed Wed evening and Thurs except in summer; All Saints' to March.

The recipe they use for the *crêpe* batter must have something unusual in it to produce such light yet firm ones. And there are some unusual fillings, too: *La Grève* is stuffed with bacon, garlic butter and onions cooked in cider. The flambéed one with crayfish is very tasty. They also do fish dishes, depending on the catches landed, and their speciality is mussels. The place is a charming stone building with a dining room in bright yellow and blue, on a charming little harbour with bobbing boats.

MALESTROIT   56140

▐●▌ RESTAURANT LE CANOTIER

pl. du Docteur-Queinnec.
☎ 02.97.75.08.69 ➡ 02.97.75.13.03
Closed Sun evening and Mon.

Good value and the best cooking in town at this split-level restaurant. *Formule* for €9 served for weekday lunch, then menus €12–26. They feature the obligatory seafood platter and dishes as different as fillet of zander – unusual to find a freshwater fish in these parts – and duck. There's also a daily menu served weekday lunchtimes. There's a choice between the romantic dining room or the terrace which has a bright green carpet. Easy to park on the market square.

CHAPELLE-CARO (LA)   56460 (8KM N)

𝄪 🛏 ▐●▌ LE PETIT KERIQUEL**

1 pl. de l'Église (Centre).
☎ and ➡ 02.97.74.82.44
Closed Sun evening and Mon out of season; the Feb school holidays; 1–15 Oct. **Garden**. **TV**. **Car park**.

This pretty hotel has been rebuilt and now has eight decent, inexpensive rooms mostly facing the church; doubles €27–37 with shower/wc or bath. Though part of the often stuffy *Logis de France* chain, there's a relaxed, young feel about the place, created by the friendly husband-and-wife team who run it. In the restaurant, classic dishes are made from really fresh ingredients and are generously served. There's a weekday lunch *formule* at €8, an evening menu for €10 and others €14–28. Half board is compulsory in July/Aug and costs €27–32 per person. Dishes include queen scallops in pastry cases with baby vegetables, zander with shellfish butter, country salad and pork *confit* with apple and cabbage. Half board at €32 per person is compulsory in summer. Free coffee.

MOLAC   56230 (13KM S)

𝄪 🛏 ▐●▌ HÔTEL-RESTAURANT À LA BONNE TABLE

pl. de l'Église.
☎ 02.97.45.71.88 ➡ 02.97.45.75.26
Closed Sun evening; Fri evening out of season; 21 Dec–3 Jan.

The old coaching house standing on the church square dates back to 1683. It offers clean and simple rooms with good beds above the restaurant for €18 with washing facilities

only. The annexe, 100m from the restaurant, provides rooms with shower, common entrance hall but private doors and a small sitting room; these are €24 with shower/wc. There's a weekly rota of dishes of the day: fish couscous is Thursday's special, for example, though you can order it in advance on other days. Weekday menu €8 or €16. Cheerful, welcoming, busy atmosphere; well-served traditional dishes; attractively laid tables. You can really do yourself proud here. Free coffee.

MATIGNON   22550

𝄪 ▐●▌ CRÊPERIE DE SAINT-GERMAIN

Saint-Germain-de-la-Mer, on the village square; from Matignon, drive 1km on the D786 in the direction of Fréhel, turn right for Saint-Germain and continue 2km.
☎ 02.96.41.08.33
Closed 1 Oct to Easter except for school holidays.
Garden.

It's worth making the trip to this seaside village for the best pancakes and girdle cakes in the area. They're made using local black wheat flour and while the fillings are not unusual, Mme Eudes uses top-quality ingredients. And it's not pricey – expect to pay €8–9 for a meal. The old house is lovely and so is the garden terrace in summer. Free coffee.

MOËLAN-SUR-MER   29350

𝄪 🛏 MANOIR DE KERTALG****

Route de Riec: on the D24, 2km outside Moëlan, take right fork to Riec.
☎ 02.98.39.77.77 ➡ 02.98.39.72.07
TV. **Car park**.

An impressive building of hewn stone, smothered in ivy and set in grounds in the forest. The rooms are vast and individually decorated – they have huge beams and are carpeted in blue or red. Doubles and duplex rooms €80–160. You can eat breakfast (€10) on the magnificent terrace, which has a panoramic view over the countryside. They hold exhibitions in the tearoom. 10% discount Sept–June. Free house apéritif.

MORLAIX   29600

🛏 ▐●▌ HÔTEL-RESTAURANT SAINT-MÉLAINE

75 rue Ange-de-Guernisac (Centre); it's close to the viaduct on the harbourside.
Closed Sat evening and Sun in winter; the school

holidays.

Small, well-maintained family hotel in a quiet street. Plain rooms in which the furnishings are sometimes mismatched but the wallpaper is fresh. Doubles €23; it's difficult to find cheaper in this area. The very friendly boss serves traditional dishes. Menus from €9; the cuisine is reassuringly traditional and the cheapest menu features starters from the self-service buffet.

⬥ HÔTEL DU PORT**

3 quai de Léon (North); it's 400m from the viaduct on the quayside.
☎ 02.98.88.07.54 ➡ 02.98.88.43.80
TV.

With its harbour view and reasonable prices, this little hotel offers value for money. Fresh, pleasant rooms with shower/wc for €32 and €35 with bath. Very warm welcome. Breakfast €5.

▮❶▮ LE BAINS-DOUCHES

45 allée du Paon-Ben; it's opposite the Palais de Justice on the river bank.
☎ 02.98.63.83.83
Closed Sat lunchtime, Sun and Mon evening.

One of the most original restaurants in town. They've kept the turn-of-the-century feel, with the railings, tiles and etched glass from the old public baths. Decent bistro food at very reasonable prices. Start with a dozen *carantecoises* oysters or fresh anchovies marinated *à l'orientale*, followed by *noisette* of stuffed lamb, peppered duck steak or *fricassée* of rabbit in cider with gingerbread. Good desserts include coconut and pear *gratin* and caramelized apples in flaky pastry. Weekday lunch menu €10 (except Sun), €21 in the evening.

▮❶▮ LA MARÉE BLEUE

3 rampe Saint-Mélaine (Centre).
☎ 02.98.63.24.21
Closed Sun evening and Mon out of season; 3 weeks in Oct.

A good fish and seafood restaurant. Elegant and intimate surroundings on two levels, with lots of wood and stone. Dishes are seasonal – the menus change every three months – and they're carefully prepared using very fresh ingredients. Set menus from €14 or around €20 *à la carte*.

MUR-DE-BRETAGNE 22530

⅔ ⬥ ▮❶▮ AUBERGE GRAND-MAISON***

1 rue Léon-le-Cerf (Centre); it's near the church.

☎ 02.96.28.51.10 x02.96.28.52.30
e grandmaison@armornet.tm.fr
Closed lunchtimes out of season; Sun evening and Mon July–Aug; a fortnight in Feb; 3 weeks in Oct.

A smart place that will set you back a bit. Jacques Guillo is one of the best respected chefs in the *département*. You need to be good to make a success of a restaurant out in the country, but just read his menus: *foie gras* profiteroles with a truffle *coulis*, lobster *fricassée* with crisp vegetables, *tournedos* of pigs' trotters, potato pancakes with *andouille* and and honey ice-cream. This is a serious gastronomic experience, as demonstrated by the prices: weekday lunch menu €27, with others €33–58. The magnificent rooms have been confidently redecorated and they're worth the price: doubles €58–104 with shower/wc or with bath. Breakfast, €14, is a really solid meal. This is an exceptional place. Free coffee. 10% discount on the room rate Sept–June except for weekends.

GOUAREC 22570 (17KM W)

⅔ ⬥ ▮❶▮ HÔTEL DU BLAVET**

It's on the RN 164.
☎ 02.96.24.90.03 ➡ 02.96.24.84.85
Hotel closed Christmas and Feb. **Restaurant closed** Sun evening and Mon out of season. **TV. Car park**.

A sturdy, stone-built house on the banks of the river Blavet with the relaxed atmosphere you find in remote Brittany. Nice, comfortable rooms for €34 with basin/wc and €40 with shower/wc or bath. The restaurant offers an interesting range of six menus; weekday lunch menu for €13 and others €24–38. Traditional dishes are well worked by the owner-chef. A pleasant dining room with big mahogany cupboards and a lovely view of the river Blavet. You can have a sauna for €7. 10% discount on the room rate except in Aug.

NÉVEZ 29920

⬥ ▮❶▮ HÔTEL AR MEN DU

It's at Raguenez-Plage
☎ 02.98.06.84.22 ➡ 02.98.06.76.09
Open only during school holidays

This is a seasonal holiday hotel. It has a peaceful atmosphere and all the rooms have been decorated in lovely colours. It's luxurious and quiet with a lovely Breton atmosphere. Rooms have teak shelves, maritime furniture and rooms with lovely views of the countryside and the island. Doubles €60–75. The two most expensive have huge bay windows overlooking the sea. The restaurant is decorated in similar colours. Dishes are prepared using lots of local produce; menus €20–30. Very friendly welcome.

OUESSANT (ÎLE D') 29242

◉ CRÊPERIE TI À DREUX

Le bourg.
☎ 02.98.89.00.19 ⌦ 02.98.89.15.69
Closed afternoons, Oct–April except for school holidays.

Ti à Dreux means "crooked house", and the leaning stone façade looks as if was built in a force ten gale. Inside it's painted blue and white. There's a huge choice of *crêpes*, stuffed with a variety of fillings – try scallops and *sauce aurore* or *fario* (sea trout) from Camaret. The best pudding is the *Joséphine*; nothing to do with Napoleon, but a concoction of home-made lemon preserve, pineapple and vanilla ice-cream. *Crêpes* are individually priced and you'll have €12–80 for a meal. Nice family-run feel, and they have a real eye for quality.

PAIMPOL 22500

🏠 ◉ HÔTEL K'LOYS***

21 quai Morano (Centre); it's on the harbour.
☎ 02.96.20.93.80 ⌦ 02.96.20.72.68
Disabled access. TV.

The *Hotel K'Loys* is in the nineteenth-century shipfitter's house, now an elegant hotel with an intimate atmosphere and a new lift put in to assist disabled access. The eleven rooms, €60–106, have been tastefully furnished in keeping with the period; some look over the harbour and one has a sitting room with a bow window.

🏠 ◉ LE REPAIRE DE KERROC'H***

29 quai Morand; it's on the marina.
☎ 02.96.20.50.13 ⌦ 02.96.22.07.46
Restaurant closed Tues and Wed lunchtime out of season; 15 Nov–23 Dec. **Disabled access. TV**.

Dating back to 1793, this house, in a style originating in St Malo, was built by a privateer who pillaged the seas for Napoleon. Its thirteen stylish, scrupulously clean and spacious rooms cost €44–113. In the elegant dining room, done out in shades of green, the new chef is getting into his stride and offers menus €21–75.

◉ RESTAURANT DE L'HÔTEL DE LA MARNE**

30 pl. de la Marne; it's near the train station.
☎ 02.96. 20.82.16 ⌦ 02.96.20.92.07
Closed Sun evening and Mon except July–Aug and public holiday weekends; the Feb school holidays. **Car park**.

This restaurant is in the hotel istelf, which looks rather like an ordinary provincial establishment. But there's a good reason why it is a favourite with the locals. The chef is inventive: Breton lobster poached in chicken stock, roast sea bream with a stock flavoured with crayfish, fresh *foie gras* marinated in *verjus* and fresh herbs. Whatever your choice, you will relate to Curnonsky's motto, printed on the menu: "True happiness is things that taste the way they should." Menus €20 (not Sunday) and €24–70; drinks are included in the more expensive ones. An impressive wine list, with at least 300 different wines.

◉ CRÊPERIE-RESTAURANT MOREL

11 pl. du Martray.
☎ 02.96.20.86.34
Closed Sun out of season; a fortnight in Feb; 3 weeks in Nov.

A genuine Breton *crêperie* in a welcoming room that heaves with a lively regular clientele. Delicious *crêpes*, such as *à l'andouille de Guémené* (a type of sausage). Dish of the day €8 and around €11 *à la carte*. Excellent cider. For an apéritif, try the *pommeau des Menhirs*.

PALAIS (LE) 56360

🏠 HÔTEL LA FRÉGATE

quai de l'Acadie; it's opposite the ferry terminal.
☎ 02.97.31.54.16
Closed mid-Nov to 31 March, but open during Christmas and Feb holidays.

Nice, cosy little hotel that's pleasantly furnished and excellent value for money. Cheery welcome. Most of the rooms look out onto the harbour. They cost €21–29 with basin or €38 with shower/wc. There'sa good atmosphere in the ground-floor bar – fortunately the noise doesn't disturb you in the rooms.

◉ CRÉPERIE LA CHALOUPE

10 av. Carnot; it's near the market place.
☎ 02.97.31.88.27

Non-stop service. Excellent crêpes served in an appealing setting and you get a lovely welcome as well. The batter is made using organic milk, eggs and flour – the pancakes come out light and crispy and stuffed with prawns, seafood, smoked fish and so on. If you don't want salad with your food, you have to say so. They also do fish soup, big salads and good ice-creams. A meal costs €15–18.

SAUZON   56360 (8KM NW)

⚘ |●| LE PETIT BAIGNEUR

Rampe des Glycines.
☎ 02.97.31.67.74

There are nice photographs on the wall of the pleasant dining room and the dishes of the day are inscribed on the blackboard. The cuisine is tasty, well executed and combines lovely flavours using only fresh produce. The tuna mousse with lemon and oregano is light, the marinated anchovies and sardines are tasty then there's a clam *fricassée* and grilled lamb chops. Mussels come in a variety of preparations and there are also more substantial dishes such as veal *escalope* and sea bream with crayfish *bisque*. Keep some room for a dessert. Menus from €14. In summer they put a few tables outside. Free Kir.

|●| LE ROZ-AVEL

rue du Lieutenant-Riou.
☎ 02.97.31.61.48
Closed Wed out of season; Jan–Feb.

An elegant venue that is without doubt the best restaurant on the island. Sophisticated cuisine. There's a single menu for €21 but *à la carte* can get pricey. Belle-Île *cotriade* or fish soup, skate with lemon verbena, pan-fried Dublin Bay prawns and monkfish *osso buco* with spices. Lobster to order. The setting and service match the excellence of the food.

⚘ |●| LA MAISON

As you come into Sauzon, it's on the left.
☎ 02.97.31.69.07

Service until 11pm. This place has been going since 2000 and it's already vying with the best restaurant on the island, *Le Roz-Avel*. The house is a solid construction; they converted the old bistro but had the good sense to retain its character. There are three areas: the bistro is the haunt of local fishermen, the dining room inside is the restaurant and there's also a heated terrace. The decoration changes – they've recently put up a Barton Fink mural on disposable wallpaper, just for fun. The cooking is done by a chef

aged only 24. He's full of inspirational ideas and the flavours he puts together blend brilliantly: tender lamb in pastry, succulent grilled pepper tortellini with crab meat, rib of beef, subtly flavoured *hors d'oeuvres*. The desserts include an unusual tart with preserved fennel. You will pay a minimum of €40 for a meal. You choose your own wine; they're fairly priced. The terrace is the place if you want musical accompaniment with your meal – they often have a singer or a band. And if you want intimacy, opt for the dining room.

PERROS-GUIREC   22700

⚘ 🏠 |●| HÔTEL-RESTAURANT LA BONNE AUBERGE

pl. de la Chapelle; it's in the hamlet of La Clarté, 3km from Perros-Guirec on the road to Plonmanach.
☎ 02.96.91.46.05 ➡ 02.96.91.62.88
Restaurant closed Sat lunchtime 1 Oct–31 May except for public holidays; the last 3 weeks in Nov. **TV**.

Warm welcome, charming place. There's a huge wood fire, a piano and sofas that you won't want to get up from and they serve very more-ish little *canapés*. Rooms, €24–33, are small and simple but all have shower/wc. Numbers 1, 2 and 3 have a sea view. Half board, €32–36 per person, is compulsory in July–Aug and on public holiday weekends. The restaurant has a terrace. Lunchtime menu €11 during the week then €17–30. The new chef has introduced his own specialities: crayfish and goat's cheese tart with baby vegetables in *vinaigrette*, earshell salad, roast ling with walnut and sweet wine sauce, hot apple tart with honey butter, roast pineapple with ginger. You can hire bikes. A really reasonable, pleasant place of a type that is getting harder to find. 10% discount on the room rate 15 Sept–15 June for a stay of several nights or on a half-board basis.

🏠 |●| LE GULF STREAM

26 rue des Sept-Îles; it's at the start of the road to the plage de Trestraou.
☎ 02.96.23.28.82 ➡ 02.96.49.06.61
Closed Wed and Thurs except July–Aug, and 2 Jan–2 Feb. **TV. Garage for motorbikes**.

There is a pleasant turn-of-the-last-century feel to this charming establishment. Some of the simple, pretty and well-maintained rooms have splendid views of the ocean and cost €27–38 with handbasin or €46–61 for a double with shower/wc or bath. The owners enjoy their work, and it's obvious from the way they welcome you. Bikers and hikers welcome. In the restaurant there's the same atmosphere. The well-spaced tables are attractively laid and the dining room is brightened up with green plants. The views from here are also spectacular. Menus €15 (not Sun or public holidays) and €23–37. Fish and seafood are the dishes of choice, though the menus changed through the season: scallop stew with leeks, pollack *en papillote* with a pancake stuffed with seasonal vegetables, *cotriade*. The local wines are well-chosen, too.

|●| CRÊPERIE HAMON

36 rue de la Salle; it's in a steep little street opposite the marina.
☎ 02.96.23.28.82
Closed Mon and Fri except school holidays.

This place is a local institution. It would be a secret little hideaway if its reputation didn't go before it – *Hamon* is known for miles around as much for its rustic setting and good atmosphere as for the spectalular way the host tosses the *crêpes* to the waitress to catch. A meal costs about €11. Booking essential.

PLÉLAN-LE-GRAND   35380

|●| AUBERGE DES FORGES

How to get there: take the D724 to the lake of the Hameau des Forges; it's right next to the lake in the middle of the Brocèlioande forest.
☎ 02.99.06.81.07

The traditional cuisine makes the best of the quality of local produce. They place a substantial terrine on the table or you could opt for a 'lighter" pan-fried *andouille* with potatoes. The fish, game, meat and fish cater for all tastes and budgets – and they even serve frogs' legs. There's pretty amazing value for money on the menus €10–23, with a weekend menu for €12. A really good country inn – it's been run by the same family since 1850.

PLÉNEUF-VAL-ANDRÉ   22370

|●| AUBERGE DU POIRIER

Rond-point du Poirier at Saint-Alban; it's next to the petrol station.
☎ 02.96.32.96.21 **e** ternet.olivier@wanadoo.fr
Closed Sun evening and Mon out of season; Feb; June; Oct.

Olivier Termet has made such a success of

his restaurant that he's had to build a new dining room. The chef trained in some of the most famous kitchens before bringing his talent home. The first menu at €11 (Tues–Sat lunchtime) includes a main course, dessert, wine and coffee.There are more original dishes on the menus at €15–30, which change four times a year. Each dish is prepared with meticulous care.

|●| AU BINIOU

121 rue Clémenceau; it's near Val-André beach.
☎ 02.96.72.24.35
Closed Tues evening and Wed out of season; Feb.

This has long been a favourite locally. It's a traditional, elegant restaurant with excellent cuisine prepared by the owner-chef. Specialities include fish and meat dishes: *fricassée* of crayfish and scallops in *Noilly*, cauliflower with coriander, fillet of sea bass braised in fennel-scented milk, pigeon in bread crust and *foie gras escalope* with garden vegetables. Menus €14–36 or around €31 *à la carte*. Whet your appetite with a bracing walk on the wind-blown Val André beach or along the customs officers' tracks.

PLOEMEUR   56270

⚐ 🛏 |●| LE VIVIER**

au fort de Lomener.
☎ 02.97.82.99.60 **e** levivier.lomener@wanadoo.fr
Closed Sun evening except in July–Aug. **Garden**. **TV**. **Car park**.

One of the really good tables in the region, with a view of the Île de Groix and the sea beyond. Specialities from the sea, naturally enough, and other dishes besides – saltwater crayfish, oysters, boned quail with *foie gras vinaigrette* and truffle *jus*, *fricassée* of squid in cider, grilled sea bass with fennel. There's a €18 menu (not served at weekends or on public holidays) and others €27–41. Good value. The welcome comes with a smile and the service is attentive without making you feel crowded. The rooms, €67–82 with shower/wc or bath, have terraces with sea view. 10% discount on the room rate weekends Oct–March.

⚐ |●| CRÊPERIE LE GRAZU

It's on the harbour near the car park.
☎ 02.97.82.83.47
Closed Tues and Wed in winter except in school holidays; Nov.

The young owners are making a real success of this place. They have sorted out a network of local suppliers for their *crêpes*, so they use buckwheat as well as ordinary wheat and the fillings are fresh and very interesting. They do huge salads as well. Weekday menu €7 and there's another at €9. Free coffee.

PLOËRMEL   56800

🏃 🏠 |●| HÔTEL LE COBH**

10 rue des Forges (Centre).
☎ 02.97.74.00.49 ➡ 02.97.74.07.36
📧 le.cobh@wanadoo.fr
TV. Car park.

The reputation of this hotel, with its brilliant yellow façade, is totally justified – you'll appreciate the convivial and comfortable Irish atmosphere, and there are lovely furnishings in the spacious rooms (€30–40). The meal they bring to your room on a tray is excellent, so you won't have to dress for dinner. Otherwise they do a bar menu for €13 and others at €18–30 including a menu *terroir*: veal *mignon*, *fricassée* of chicken with mussels, brill fillet with leek *fondue* and caramelized apples with honey ice-cream. 10% discount on the room rate, free house apéritif with a meal and 10% discount on meals.

🏃 🏠 |●| HÔTEL-RESTAURANT SAINT-MARC**

1 pl. Saint-Marc (West).
☎ 02.97.74.00.01 ➡ 02.97.73.36.81
Closed Sun evening. **Garden. TV**.

Trains rarely call at the neighbouring station so it's quiet here. The well-maintained rooms have been redecorated; they cost €32–53 depending on facilities. The bar is a popular local watering-hole, while the restaurant, which attracts the smarter set, is generally regarded as the best in Ploërmel. They list dishes such as *cassoulette* of four scallops with a light curry sauce, fillet of salmon with a *hollandaise* sauce and goat's cheese salad. Menus €11 in the week then €14–26. 10% discount on the room rate 15 Sept–15 June.

🏠 LE THY**

19 rue de la Gare (Centre).
☎ 02.97.74.05.21 ➡ 02.97.74.02.97
TV. Car park.

Each room is dedicated to a painter and decorated in the style of the artist: *Klimt* is spacious and sensual while *Pratt* has a travel theme complete with globe and packed

trunk. The "studio" is bright and the light streams through the windows and decorated with sketches on the wall – it's as if the painter has just left; other rooms are named after Tapies and van Gogh. Each room is large and the bathrooms are superb; doubles €43–53. On the ground floor, there's a bar and a concert room that looks like a chapel; the apse is flanked by books and hung with purple curtains. Concerts every Friday.

PLOGOFF   29770

🏃 🏠 |●| HÔTEL DE LA BAIE DES TRÉPASSÉS**

On the seafront; it's 3km from pointe du Raz and pointe du Van.
☎ 02.98.70.61.34 ➡ 02.98.70.35.20
📧 hoteldelabaie@aol.com
Closed 12 Dec–10 Feb. **Garden. TV. Car park**.

This large, prosperous hotel stands on a broad beach in an exceptionally wild situation. Doubles €48–59. Menus in the restaurant cost €14–27; house specialities are scallop *brochettes*, grilled lobster in cream sauce and baked Alaska. Free coffee.

PLOUARET   22420

🏃 |●| CRÊPERIE TY YANN

24 impasse des Vergers (Centre); it's in a cul-de-sac next to the curch.
☎ 02.98.38.93.22 📧 ty-yann@club-internet.fr
Closed Mon–Thurs from Oct to June except evenings during the school holidays; Jan and Feb.

One of the best *crêperies* of the legion in the Côtes d'Armor – but there are only a few tables. Pretty décor and an open, friendly welcome. They use the best black flour for the savoury pancakes, and the fillings are varied and interesting, including *la Bigoudène*, an unusual sweet and sour one. It won't cost a fortune – €9 for a meal in a very friendly place. Free house apéritif.

PLOUBALAY   22650

|●| RESTAURANT DE LA GARE

4 rue des Ormelets.
☎ 02.96.27.25.16 📧 zavier.termet@wanadoo.fr
Closed Tues evening and Wed; the first fortnight in March; Oct.

They closed the station long since as well as the ragged bar that used to be here. The three dining rooms are attractively decorated with floral designs. The menu is like some public declaration of intent with the chef explaining his involvement in no uncertain terms: "the scallops are fished locally and placed in the marinade instantly". This is excellent cuisine using fresh Breton produce; black pudding, whole pigeon and wonderful seafood dishes. Menus €17 (not Sun) and €26–35. Around €23 *à la carte*. Smiling service.

PLOUDALMÉZEAU   29830

🎋 I●I LA SALAMANDRE

pl. du Général-de-Gaulle (Centre).
☎ 02.98.48.14.00
Closed Wed out of season; weekdays from Oct to Easter; mid-Nov to mid-Dec.

Grandma opened this place and her grandson is the present owner; he and his wife are now carrying on the tradition in this pleasant and bright *crêperie*. The *crêpes* are tasty – try the one with scallops and baby vegetables, the *bigoudène* (stuffed with *andouille*, fried potatoes and cream) or the *paysanne* (bacon, potatoes, cheese and cream). Children are very welcome. Around €12 for a full meal. Free apéritif.

POULDREUZIC   29710

🎋 🏠 I●I HÔTEL-RESTAURANT BRIEZ-ARMOR

It's on the beach of Penhors.
☎ 02.98.51.52.53 ➡ 02.98.51.52.30
Closed Mon except July–Ang; 2 Jan–15 March

A beautifully located hotel right on the sea shore which, over the years, has spread – it's built of concrete but in the Breton style. Lovely rooms with fabulous views of the sea. Double rooms €49–60; half-board is compulsory in July and Aug for €60–67 per person. It's easy to put up with the building because the location and the cuisine make all the difference. You'll find traditional dishes with an oriental streak – recipes have been brought back from holidays in Thailand, Madagascar and Tahiti – including slow-baked salmon with Berber spices and cod in salt. Menus €12 (lunch in the week) and €17–37. Free Breton Kir.

PLOUGASNOU   29630

🎋 🏠 I●I HÔTEL ROC'H VELEN

Saint-Samson.

☎ 02.98.72.30.58 ➡ 02.98.72.44.57
e roch.velen@wanadoo.fr
Closed Sun evening out of season; a fortnight in Jan. **TV**.

This hotel is a small place located on the sea road with 10 pretty rooms decorated in a maritime style. Each has the name of an island from the area; *Molène*, *Houat*, *Hoëdic* and *Sain* have views of the sea. Doubles with shower.wc or bath for €36–50. The restaurant offers lots of seafood and fish dishes cooked by the owner's wife. Lunch menu for €11 and others up to €18. In summer they have a week-long festival featuring local singers. 10% discount on the room rate out of season.

PLOUGUERNEAU   29880

🎋 I●I RESTAURANT TROUZ AR MOR

plage du Corréjou-Saint-Michel; it's north of Plouguerneau, near Correjou beach, 2km from the town centre, towards Saint-Michel.
☎ 02.98.04.71.61
Closed Mon and Wed evening out of season except public holidays; Feb. **Car park**.

From the outside this looks like a totally typical Finistère building with a terrace for fine weather. Inside the décor is rustic but cosy and well-tended, and the service is efficient. Typical dishes from Finistère are of a high quality and very good value. Seafood and fish feature on all the set menus at €9–39: *fricassée* of ear-shell with tarragon, fish *pot-au-feu*, brill with a Loire wine stock. The speciality dessert is apple *au gratin* with almond cream. Free Kir.

PONT-AVEN   29930

🎋 I●I CRÊPERIE LE TALISMAN

4 rue Paul-Sérusier; it's on the way into the town on the Riec road.
☎ 02.98.06.02.58
Closed Sun lunchtime out of season; Mon; a fortnight mid-Oct. **Garden**.

This place doesn't exactly offer gourmet dining: Marie-Françoise is in charge, cooking recipes her grandmother taught her – both the *crêpes* and the other dishes are satisfying and the prices reasonable. A meal of *crêpes* will set you back €9. The house specials include the *Talisman* – with ham, chipolata, spicy *merguez* sausage, smoked sausage, garlic and anchovies – along with seafood specialities. Also there's flambéed potato *galette*, omelettes, salads and ice-cream. It's a charmingly renovated old house with a quiet terrace facing the garden. Free house apéritif.

|●| CAFÉ DES ARTS

11 rue du Général-de-Gaulle (Centre).
☎ 02.98.06.07.12
Closed Thurs out of season.

A traditional café-brasserie with a convivial atmosphere and excellent music. A lively, though not overpowering, place – artists and young people (and the not-so-young, too) use this as their local. Wine is served by the glass and the beer is good; swig it down with a Lyon sausage served with sautéed potatoes simmered in white wine. They also serve Mexican dishes like *fajitas* with chicken and Thai chicken, which is the house speciality. Expect to pay €13 *à la carte*. They have live concerts from time to time – sea songs, jazz evenings, rock and local folk music.

⚑|●| RESTAURANT LE TAHITI

21 rue Belle-Angèle; it's on the Bannalec road.
☎ 02.98.06.15.93 ☛ 02.98.71.85.60
Closed Mon and Tues lunchtime; 15–28 Feb; 15–30 Nov.

This is run by a local man and his Tahitian wife. The restaurant has been prettily decorated, and the cooking is exotic because Madame is in the kitchen – Tahitian *chow mein* with chicken, yellow noodles, black mushrooms and vegetables, Tahitian fish marinated in lemon and blanched with onion. Divine desserts start with a *compote* of banana with vanilla pod cream. There's a weekday lunch menu at €11 and you'll pay about €18 *à la carte*. They also do a takeaway service. The table staff don't rush to serve you, however. Free coffee or *digestif*.

TRÉGUNC · 29910 (6KM SW)

⚑ 🏠 |●| HÔTEL-RESTAURANT LE MENHIR

17 rue de Concarneau.
☎ 02.98.97.62.35 ☛ 02.98.50.26.68
Closed Wed evening Oct–May; the Feb and All Saints' school holidays. **Car park**.

A place that has built a good reputation. There's a cheerful, sincere welcome. The cuisine is refined, which is hardly surprising considering that Patrice has worked with some top chefs. His creations have a touch of the inspirational – at once tasty, aromatic, traditional and imaginative. Set lunch menu €8 and another at €27, listing suckling pig

braised in wine, roast sea bream with fennel, medallions of monkfish with Guémenée *andouille* and pears with liquorice *sabayon*. They've opened a shop called "Au Menhir Gourmand", selling prepared dishes to take away. For an overnight stay, decent rooms, cost €37–43. 10% discount on the room rate Sept–June.

PONT-CROIX · 29790

⚑ 🏠 |●| HÔTEL-RESTAURANT TY-EVAN**

18 rue du Docteur-Neis (Centre); it's next to the town hall.
☎ 02.98.70.58.58 ☛ 02.98.70.53.38
Closed Feb.

Pont-Croix is a delightful, characterful town, definitely worth visiting for its magnificent cathedral portal. If the crashing waves have got too much for you, this is an ideal place to come for some gentle charm. This hotel on the quiet main square has good double rooms for €34–45. Warm welcome and honest food with set menus at €13–40. Half board, €39–43 per person, is obligatory 1–15 Aug. 10% discount on the room rate Sept–June and free coffee.

PONTIVY · 56300

⚑ |●| CRÊPERIE LA CAMPAGNARDE

14 rue de Lattre-de-Tassigny; it's on the Vannes road on the edge of town.
☎ 02.97.25.23.07
Closed Tues; the first 3 weeks in Sept. **Disabled access**.

This country restaurant is decorated like a farm with old farm implements, cartwheels, forks and threshers that the owners have gleaned from here and there. Good crêpes made from Breton black wheat, stuffed with everything from cheese and seafood to apples and pears. All the cooking methods are respectful of the quality of the produce used. A good meal will cost about €12. They serve "chistr per" – a rare Breton pear cider made locally.

QUIBERON · 56170

🏠 |●| PARC TEHUEN*

1 rue des Tamaris; it's 500m from the town centre.
☎ 02.97.50.10.26 ✉ pujol@wanadoo.fr
Closed 30 Sept–3 April. **Car park**. **Garden**.

A really nice family pension. It's got a huge garden and is only 300m from the beach.

They have doubles with shower/wc but the hotel works only on a half-board basis which costs €37–40 per person. Full board costs around €45 per person in July–Aug for a room with shower/wc. Good value for money.

⚹ ☗ |●| HÔTEL-RESTAURANT BELLEVUE***

rue de Tiviec, BP 30341, 56173 Quiberon Cedex.; it's set back from the beach, by the casino.
☎ 02.97.50.16.28 ➡ 02.97.30.44.34
Closed Oct–March. **Swimming pool. TV. Car park. Garden.**

This is a big, angular 1970s block which, while not having the appeal of a more traditional building, is quiet, comfortable and boasts lots of facilities – heated swimming pool, solarium and gardens. Warm welcome, too. Doubles with shower and swimming pool view €54 in low season; large double with bath with a sea view from €84. In high summer, half-board is compulsory and, roughly speaking, the room prices quoted are about the same as the half board price per person. Menus in the restaurant are €15, €20 and €23, with a selection of local and other dishes: semi-cooked duck *foie gras* with Beaumes-de-Venise sauce served with home-made bread, pan-fried scallops with exotic spices and asparagus tips. 10% discount on the room rate April–June.

⚹ |●| CRÊPERIE-RESTAURANT DU VIEUX PORT

42–44 rue Surcouf; the street is above the old port of Port-Haliguen.
☎ 02.97.50.01.56
Closed part of the Feb school holidays; the end of the All Saints' holidays. **Car park.**

Non-stop *crêpes* from noon to 10pm and from 7pm in the restaurant. In a street overlooking the harbour you'll find this *crêperie*, which, though a tad more expensive than others around, is in a lovely spot. An all-inclusive menu of *crêpes* and cider at €10 will limit your cash outlay, and you shouldn't spend much more than €15 for a meal *à la carte*. Their speciality *crêpe* is served with salt butter and caramel but they do also do sound seafood one involving lobster *à l'Armoricaine*. Free coffee.

|●| LA CHAUMINE

36 pl. du Manémeur; it's in the village of Manémeur.
☎ 02.97.50.17.67
Closed Sun evening and Mon; Mon only July–Aug; 12 Nov–18 Dec; a fortnight in March. **Disabled access. Swimming pool. Car park.**

The restaurant is in an adorable spot, surrounded by fishermen's cottages. Arrive in time for an apéritif at the bar and join the fishermen and locals sipping a Muscadet – it's a million miles from the stress and traffic jams of city life. The set menus have no frills, just good, honest ingredients – mussels, prawns, fish – while specialities include sole with morel *jus* and soft fruit *au gratin*. The menu at €13 is served at lunchtime though not on Sun, and there are others €22–45.

⚹ |●| RESTAURANT LA CRIÉE

11 quai de l'Océan; it's on the fishing port opposite the fish market.
☎ 02.97.30.53.09
Closed Sun evening except July–Aug; Mon lunchtime in July–Aug; Jan.

One of the best seafood and fish specialists of the peninsula – *La Criée* means "fish market" and it's the restaurant belonging to the Lucas smoke-house. Not surprisingly, the shellfish and seafood are of the freshest. Good value for money and fast service with a smile. There are dishes of the day on the €14 menu and *à la carte* they do *sole meunière*, fish *choucroute*, grilled fish, house smoked fish and seafood platters; expect to pay €38. Free coffee.

QUIMPER   29000

|●| CRÊPERIE AU VIEUX QUIMPER

20 rue Verdelet (Centre).
☎ 02.98.95.31.34
Closed Sun lunchtime; Tues; the first fortnight in June.

A *crêperie* that deserves its reputation. The little dining room has bare stone walls and Breton furniture and it quickly gets full. There's a friendly family atmosphere and everyone tucks into the tasty *crêpes*, swigging down tumblers of cider and milk *ribot*. The pancakes are delicate and crispy. The mushroom and cream filling is gorgeous, and the speciality of the house is the scallop filling. You'll pay between €10 and €13 for a meal. It's an excellent place so it's good to book.

|●| CRÊPERIE DU SALLÉ

6 rue du Sallé (Centre).
☎ 02.98.95.95.80
Closed Sun and Mon.

This *crêperie* is in an ancient half-timbered building in the heart of the old town. This is the most touristy area but the welcome is as good as anywhere in the depths of Brittany. In theory it closes around 10pm, but the owner will always greet you with a smile and declare: "We're open as long as the lights are on…!". Pleasant, rustic surroundings for delicious *crêpes*. Home-made batter is carefully and skilfully made, and they use only the freshest of ingredients. Attentive service. House special *crêpes* include *paysanne*, warm goat's cheese, scallop *provençale*, *forestière* and candied orange zest. You'll pay around €11 for a meal.

⅍ ⅼ◉ⅼ LA CAMBUSE

11 rue Le Déan (Centre); going towards the train station, it's on the right after the theatre.
☎ 02.98.53.06.06
Closed Sun.

A friendly establishment with a small garden. The colourful décor evokes the style of a ship's cabin, with varnished wood, portholes and maritime bric-a-brac. Try the delicious home-made *tartes* – which are out of the ordinary and filled with aubergines and Saint-Marcellin cheese or walnuts, asparagus and Brie – or go for *crêpes* with vegetables, cheese and meat. A great selection of wheat and buckwheat *crêpes* and appetising mixed salads. Prices are reasonable: you'll pay around €12 for a meal. Free house apéritif.

ⅼ◉ⅼ KERFATY

15 rue Le Dean (Centre).
☎ 02.98.90.36.78
Closed Sat lunchtime, Sun and Mon.

Fatima hails from Grenoble, where, a few years ago, she thought she'd open a restaurant. The banks frowned on the project and gave her no support, so she decided to head to Brittany and started up her bar-restaurant. *Kerfaty* means "Faty's place" and everything in the décor pays tribute to the spirit that created it – hundreds of photographs of friends cover the walls and ceiling. The couscous is excellent but you should also try the Algerian *briks*, including grilled peppers and meat (the Tunisian *briks* of tuna, onion and spices) or her *tajine* of lamb. On the second Friday of each month, she prepares *Kig Ha Farz*, a local dish from north Finistère, but you have to book. Expect to pay about €18 *à la carte*, while individual dishes start at €11. The desserts, however, are not up to the standard of the rest of the cuisine.

⅍ ⅼ◉ⅼ LE CLOS DE LA TOURBIE

43 rue Elie-Fréron (Centre); take the road going uphill from the cathedral.
☎ 02.98.95.45.03
Closed Wed and Sat lunchtime.

Chef Didier le Madec started his training in the kitchens of the *Tour d'Argent* in Paris and then with Jacques Cagna; he worked in London, Jersey and Ireland before coming home to open this lovely restaurant next to the cathedral. It's elegant yet warm in restful shades of orange and mahogany, and full of fresh flowers and leafy plants. A charming welcome. The quiet atmosphere allows you to concentrate on the conscientious yet inspired cuisine. Superb set menus €14–24. The freshest ingredients are used and the menu changes with the seasons. The chef has revived some classics, such as stewed pig's trotters with oysters, braised veal sweetbreads with truffles or oyster mushrooms, spiced duck *fricassée* and fisherman's hot pot. Very good desserts. The wine list is short but has a good choice in each category. Free house apéritif or coffee.

ⅼ◉ⅼ LE STEINWAY

20 rue des Gentilshommes; it's in the centre of the old town.
☎ and ➜ 02.98.95.53.70
Closed Sun lunchtime and Mon except July–Aug.

The décor hails from the 1950s, with local ornaments and memorabilia; there's also an old petrol pump, a trombone, lots of old radios and plenty of telephones. The whole place feels warm and welcoming, with solid wooden floorboards and red checked tablecloths. They do an excellent slab of steak and servings are ample. Normally they produce good peasant food but occasionally they'll spice it up with Mexican or American dishes. Menus €17–24 or around €20 *à la carte*. Wine by the glass. A live band plays in the corner in summer.

ⅼ◉ⅼ AU P'TIT RAFIOT

7 rue de Pont-l'Abbé; near the quay.
☎ 02.98.53.77.27 ➜ 02.98.52.96.19
Closed Sat and Mon lunchtimes, and Sun.

Don't be put off by the rather dull exterior: inside is thoughtfully decorated in marine style with portholes. In the middle of the room there's a splendid aquarium full of sea creatures with huge claws – the cook will only work with the freshest ingredients, and all fish and shellfish come from the *patron's* own tanks. The dishes are excellently served, very tasty and good value; try Breton *bouillabaisse*, seafood couscous or lobster of the *P'tit Rafiot*. The waiter gives very clear descriptions of the dishes, and you'll pay about €30 for a complete meal.

QUIMPERLÉ   29300

|●| LA CIGALE ÉGARÉE

5 rue Jacques-Cartier (Centre).
☎ 02.98.39.15.53
Closed Sun and Mon and Tues evenings out of season;
Sun only in season.

This place feels as though it comes from much further south, with its two delightful dining rooms with colour-washed walls and the terrace. The chef prepares dishes combining original flavours: *carpaccio* of salmon with Breton honey, *croustillant* of fresh sardines with ginger and lime, *fricassée* of scallops with royal jelly and grilled bacon with pesto. Desserts include strawberries with *pastis* and a *coulis* of aromatic herbs. Dishes change every four months. Menus €15–29, children's menu €10.

|●| LE RELAIS DU ROCH

Forêt Domaniale de Toul Foën; 2km out of town following the river on the Pouldu road, it's on the right.
☎ 02.98.96.12.97 ➡ 02.98.39.22.40
Closed Sun evening and Mon; a fortnight in Jan.
Garden. Car park.

Well-run restaurant in the heart of the forest. There's a gastronomic dining room with an open fireplace, pink tablecloths and abundant floral arrangements. The chef puts his favourite dishes on the menu: grilled lobster with coral butter, *confit* of duck, smoked salmon and a home-made *foie gras* which is so good that it challenges the stuff they produce in the southwest for quality. Lunch menu at €13 and a range of others €17–40. Children's menu for €6 and quick lunchtime *formule* for €10.

|●| LE BISTRO DE LA TOUR

2 rue Dom-Morice; it's in the *ville basse*, by the covered market, opposite Sainte-Croix church.
☎ 02.98.39.29.58 ➡ 02.98.39.21.77
Closed Sat lunchtime; Sun evening out of season.

This place is beautifully furnished – the owners are also in the antique trade. Traditional cuisine is prepared by the very friendly host, who is a great wine connoisseur. There's a new cellar if you feel like a visit. Specialities include fresh fish of the day such as Breton salmon, bass and sole, hot and cold scallops, pan-fried prawns *à la façon de ma grand-mère*, peppers stuffed with cod, tuna *tournedos*, oxtail *compotée*, lamb *roulade* with aubergine and cold *escabèche* of Breton sardines. Weekday lunchtime menu at €16 and others up to €49. Children's menu for €12.

RENNES   35000

SEE MAP OVERLEAF

☎ HÔTEL LE RIAVAL*

9 rue Riaval. **Off map B3-1**
☎ 02.99.50.65.58 ➡ 02.99.41.85.30
Closed 14–22 July. **Garden**.

A simple, unpretentious hotel conveniently located behind the station in a pleasant part of town. The building has been refurbished and is well-maintained. Brightly painted, modern rooms. Doubles €22–32 depending on facilities. The ones with a garden view look onto a huge lime tree.

☎ HÔTEL DE LA TOUR D'AUVERGNE

20 bd. de la Tour-d'Auvergne. **MAP A2-8**
☎ 02.99.30.84.16
TV.

Plain but spotless rooms €23 with basin, then €28–35 with shower/wc or bath – a bargain. Ideal family hotel for limited budgets, run by a very kindly woman. Breakfast is served in your room – there's no breakfast room. Parking in the street.

☖ ☎ LE GARDEN**

3 rue Duhamel. **MAP B2-4**
☎ 02.99.65.45.06 ➡ 02.99.65.02.62
Garden. TV. Car park.

Charming, tasteful hotel, set between the station and the old town. There's a café decorated in apple-green and a small internal garden. Friendly welcome. Very nice, individualized rooms in fresh colours; doubles for €35–53 with shower. Some rooms sleep four. 10% discount July–Aug.

☖ ☎ HÔTEL LANJUINAIS**

11 rue Lanjuinais. **MAP A2-6**
☎ 02.99.79.02.03 ➡ 02.99.79.03.97
TV.

A quiet, well-maintained hotel in a small street leading towards the quai Lamennais. Most rooms look over the street but some look into the (rather dark) courtyard. They have reasonable facilities and cost €43 with shower/wc or €46 with bath. 20% discount on the room rate Fri–Sun including public holidays out of season.

☎ HÔTEL DES LICES**

7 pl. des Lices. **MAP A1-7**
☎ 02.99.79.14.81 ➡ 02.99.79.35.44
Disabled access. TV. Car park.

On one of the most beautiful squares in the

old town. They've completely modernized this hotel, it's full of light and well-appointed. The very pleasant rooms have balconies and the ones on the upper floors have good views over the rooftops and the old town. Doubles €45 with shower/wc and €53 with bath. Bright, efficient welcome.

🍴 🛏 HÔTEL DE NEMOURS**

5 rue de Nemours; it's near the pl. de la République. **MAP B2-9**
☎ 02.99.78.26.26 ➡ 02.99.78.25.40
TV. Car park.

This hotel has what feels like the smallest lift in the world. In reception the walls are covered with autumn leaves, engravings and butterflies. The rooms have undergone a programme of refurbishment and they're pretty and clean; doubles with shower/wc or bath €48–57. The quieter rooms face onto the courtyard. Good welcome. 10% discount June–Aug.

🛏 HÔTEL ASTRID

32 av. Louis Barthou. **Off map B3-11**
☎ 02.99.30.82.38 ➡ 02.99.31.85.55
Closed New Year's Eve and New Year's Day. **Disabled access. TV. Garden**.

Well-located near the station and only a ten-minute walk from the town centre. A pretty, chic hotel where you'll get a friendly welcome. It's spotless and the rooms are modern, large, quiet and well-equipped – cost €51–54 with shower/wc or bath. The whole place is quiet and pleasant. The breakfast room looks out onto a small garden. A reliable establishment, run very professionally. 10% discount in school holidays and public holidays (not applicable on the lower weekend rates).

🍴 CRÊPERIE SAINT-ANNE

5 pl. Sainte-Anne. **MAP B1-22**
☎ 02.99.79.22.72
Closed Sun.

This crêperie is one of the best in Rennes. The pancakes are crispy on the outside and soft inside and they're made in front of you. They don't stint on the butter or on any of the fillings – they're all generously served and delicious. Crêpes from €6.

🍴 LE BOCAL-P'TY RESTO

6 rue d'Argentré. **MAP A2-16**
☎ 02.99.78.34.10
Closed Sun, Mon and 1–20 Aug.

This friendly restaurant is overflowing with creative ideas. The décor is lovely: glass jars are filled with all sorts of strange things col-

lected here and there and the lids have been used to decorate the walls and even the doors in the toilet. The dishes of the day – like chicken with spices topped with grilled cheddar and grilled squid with butter and lemon – are scrawled up on a blackboard. There's a particularly delicious sticky moelleux au chocolat. Formules from €9. There's a well-chosen, cheaply priced wine list and they're all served by the glass. Trendy, young and appealing.

🍴 LE TIRE BOUCHON

2 rue du Chapitre. **MAP A2-13**
☎ 02.99.79.43.43

A new approach to the wine bar. You sit side by side at the big counter or at one of the small wooden tables. There's a choice of only three or four dishes of the day – the kind that are slowly and carefully cooked. Alternatively, opt for a plate of charcuterie or farmhouse cheese. Otherwise go for the toasted sandwiches – with cheese, fruit and charcuterie. Prices are modest – you'll pay €9 for a dish, €6 for the toasties and €4 for a dessert. The wine is thoughtfully chosen and include some unusual vintages from overseas vineyards. They're sold by the glass. Super décor, lovely welcome – it's very popular. Best to book.

🍴 LA BISCORNE

8 rue Saint-Mélaine. **MAP B1-17**
☎ 02.99.30.18.37
Closed Sun, Mon and Wed evenings; public holiday weekends; 3 weeks in Aug.

Warm, rustic charm, harmonizing well with the traditional cuisine. The young chef offers a range of set menus at €12–30, à la carte dishes and a lunch menu at €9. The dishes change every four months, but the following are typical: mackerel terrine with a chive cream and pickled shallots, pork kebab with apple served with cauliflower and tomato. The wine is reasonably priced. Free Kir.

🍴 LÉON LE COCHON

1 rue du Maréchal-Joffre. **MAP B2-15**
☎ 02.99.79.37.54
Closed Sunday July–Aug. **TV**.

A lot of thinking has gone into creating this restaurant, which is at once modern, refined and authentic – not an easy achievement. Dried flowers, walls hung with chilli peppers and windows full of leaves are the backdrop for unpretentiously prepared local cooking. There's a lunchtime formule for €10 and menus from €19. Try the chef's oxtail of his

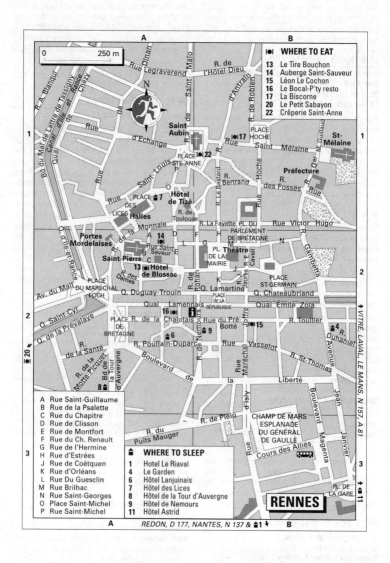

WHERE TO EAT

13	Le Tire Bouchon
14	Auberge Saint-Sauveur
15	Léon Le Cochon
16	Le Bocal-P'ty resto
17	La Biscorne
20	Le Petit Sabayon
22	Crêperie Saint-Anne

A Rue Saint-Guillaume
B Rue de la Psalette
C Rue du Chapitre
D Rue de Clisson
E Rue de Montfort
F Rue du Ch. Renault
G Rue de l'Hermine
H Rue d'Estrées
J Rue de Coëtquen
K Rue d'Orléans
L Rue Du Guesclin
M Rue Brilhac
N Rue Saint-Georges
O Place Saint-Michel
P Rue Saint-Michel

WHERE TO SLEEP

1	Hotel Le Riaval
4	Le Garden
6	Hôtel Lanjuinais
7	Hôtel des Lices
8	Hôtel de la Tour d'Auvergne
9	Hôtel de Nemours
11	Hôtel Astrid

RENNES

REDON, D 177, NANTES, N 137 & ⌂1

pig's trotter *du Petit Jésus en culotte de velours* or the *andouillette à la ficelle*. Best to book. Free house apéritif.

⚐ |●| AUBERGE SAINT-SAUVEUR

6 rue Saint-Sauveur. **MAP A2-14**
☎ 02.99.79.32.56
Closed Sat lunchtime; Sun; Mon lunchtime; 3 weeks end Aug to Sept.

In a lovely sixteenth-century canon's house behind St-Pierre cathedral, this restaurant has a warm, intimate, sophisticated atmosphere. Weekday lunch *formule* €12 and two menus for €17 and €46. They offer quality traditional cuisine in dishes such as roast monkfish with cabbage, grilled lobster and good duck *foie gras*. Free coffee.

|●| LE PETIT SABAYON

16 rue des Trente. **MAP A2-20**
☎ 02.99.35.02.04
Closed Sat lunchtime; Sun evening; Mon; 4–21 Aug.

One of the best tables in town, with simple décor and diligent, smiling service. Try the salad with two kinds of *foie gras*, the *tournedos* of sardines with rhubarb sauce or the *marquise* with chocolate and an arabica coffee sauce. Realistic prices: lunch menu for €12 and others €18–25. Good wine list at reasonable prices. The restaurant is a smoke-free zone.

ROCHE-BERNARD (LA)   56130

☎ |●| LES DEUX MAGOTS**

3 pl. du Bouffay (West).
☎ 02.99.90.60.75 ➡ 02.99.90.87.87
Closed Sun evening and Tues lunchtime out of season; Mon; a week in June; a week in Oct; 20 Dec–15 Jan. **TV**.

This comfortable hotel has a lovely façade with arched windows and fifteen pleasantly furnished rooms. Doubles €43–53 with shower/wc or bath. Seafood dishes predominate – warm crayfish salad, braised sea bream with baby vegetables, roast turbot in cider and onions. Menus start at €13 at lunch then there are others €23–49. Lengthy wine list. The bar has an impressive collection of miniature bottles of apéritifs, cognac, whisky and so on. Friendly welcome.

ROCHEFORT-EN-TERRE   56220

|●| HOSTELLERIE DU LION D'OR

rue du Pélican.

☎ 02.97.43.32.80 ➡ 02.87.43.30.12
Closed Sun and Tues evenings and Wed; 20 Sept–1 May; 20 Jan–10 Feb; 25 Nov–5 Dec.

The best restaurant in town, located in a sixteenth-century posthouse. Even the cheapest menu at €13 is just fine while there are others €27–43. The cooking uses wealth of local produce to great benefit and specialities include grilled pigeon in a caul and red mullet with pickled lemon. It's a bit uptight and traditional but this suits the surroundings – this is one of the most beautiful houses in Rochefort.

ROSCOFF   29680

☎ HÔTEL LES ALIZÉS**

Quai d'Auxerre; go along the rue Courbet, in the direction of the Saint-Barbe chapel and the fish ponds.
☎ 02.98.69.72.22 ➡ 02.98.61.11.40
Car park.

Located just away from the lively centre of town. It has comfortable rooms with shower/wc for €28–40. The view over the port is excellent; other rooms look over the rue Courbet. Nice welcome.

☎ HÔTEL AUX TAMARIS**

49 rue Édouard-Corbière; it's next to the Kerléna clinic.
☎ 02.98.61.22.99 ➡ 02.98.69.74.36
@ auxtamaris@dial-olcome.com
Closed mid-Oct to 1 March. **TV**.

A nearly great location – although this welcoming hotel looks out towards the Île de Batz it's separated from the sea by the coast road. Bright, comfortable rooms, some with the view for €40–53 with shower/wc or bath. Breakfast for €6. No restaurant, but some of the best hospitality in Finistère.

☎ |●| LES CHARDONS BLEUS**

4 rue Amiral-Réveillère; from the bridge, it's towards the church.
☎ 02.98.69.72.03 ➡ 02.98.61.27.86
Closed Thurs except July–Aug; Sun evening in Oct–Easter. **TV**.

Good value for money for this town and a good atmosphere. There's a weekday lunch menu at €10 and others up to €26. Lots of classic dishes, cooked well: marinated salmon with warm potatoes, crayfish *au gratin*, fillets of John Dory with cream. Comfortable rooms at reasonable prices; doubles €44–53 with shower/wc or bath. The owner is warm and welcoming so it's a pity the staff are sniffy.

|●| L'ÉCUME DES JOURS

quai d'Auxerre.
☎ and ► 02.98.61.22.83
e Michel.Quévé@wanadoo.fr
Closed Tues evening and Wed out of season.

This fine granite building was a shipwright's house. Comfortable, warm, intimate interior with a wide fireplace. The chef combines produce from land and sea in extraordinary ways: pan-fried scallops with smoked duck breast, *foie gras* and scallops with oyster mushrooms and balsamic vinegar, braised emperor fillet with vegetables from the garden. Menus €14–35 and childrens' menu for €8.

ROSTRENEN   22110

|●| COEUR DE BRIEZH

14 rue Abbé Gibert (Centre).
☎ 02.96.29.18.33
Closed Tues evening and Wed.

Situated in the middle of the hamlet, in a substantial house. The owners raised the money to get started through friends and clients who had been trying to persuade them to open a bar and restaurant; it worked. The setting is totally seductive – stone walls and a Breton décor. Roger is a natural front-of-house and Anne-Laure is a self-taught chef with talent. She cooks local dishes using fresh, good-quality produce – organic for the most part – which she sources through local farmers and producers. Delicious main courses and an array of seductive sweets. Weekday lunch menu for €10 and menus €15–23. À la carte, prices are fair.

SABLES-D'OR-LES-PINS   22240

⅔ ♚ |●| HÔTEL DES PINS**

allée des Acacias (Centre); it's 400m from the beach.
☎ 02.96.41.42.20 ► 02.96.41.59.02
Closed Oct–March.

A holiday hotel with the kind of charm that suits the slightly old-fashioned feel of the resort. Doubles €34 with shower/wc and €43 with bath. Half board €43–49 per person, obligatory July–Aug. Set lunch menu €13 and others up to €30 feature lots of seafood and fresh fish. Mini-golf and a garden. 10% discount on the room rate April–September.

PLURIEN-FRÉHEL   22240 (2KM S)

⅔ ♚ MANOIR DE LA SALLE**

rue du Lac; it's 1km from Sables-d'Or-les-Pins, just

before you get to Fréhel.
☎ 02.96.72.38.29 ► 02.96.72.00.57
e Aude.Labruyere@manoir-de-la-salle.com
Closed 30 Sept–24 March. **Disabled access**. **TV**. **Car park**.

A stone, sixteenth-century manor house which you enter through a beautiful gothic portal built a century earlier. Bright, comfortable rooms furnished with modern pieces; doubles with shower/wc or bath for €38–61. They've converted another old building to make a couple of apartments with kitchens sleeping four to six. Lots of things to keep you amused – such as the solarium and ping-pong – and there's a golf course nearby. There are even stalls for horses and ponies if you're on a riding holiday. It's an excellent place, run by a delightful young couple, and is very fashionable in these parts. Free house apéritif.

FRÉHEL   22240 (5KM E)

♚ HÔTEL LE FANAL**

Lieu-dit Besnard; take the road to Cap-Fréhel and when you get there turn right for Plévenon – the hotel is on the left after 1.5km.
☎ 02.96.41.43.19
Closed 30 Sept–1 May. **Garden**. **Car park**.

A tall chalet, the sort of architecture you'd expect to find in Scandinavia – perfect for this barren Breton wasteland stretching to the ocean. Comfortable rooms with shower/wc or bath for €38–52. TV is outlawed. Rooms 6–9 are more spacious than the others. Children under ten get a free breakfast.

SAINT-BRIEUC   22000

⅔ ♚ HÔTEL DU CHAMP DE MARS**

13 rue du Général-Leclerc.
☎ 02.96.33.60.99 ► 02.96.33.60.05
e hoteldemars@wanadoo.fr
Closed 22 Dec–8 Jan. **Disabled access**. **TV**.

This well-run, pleasant establishment with all the facilities you expect of a two-star hotel has the merit of being reasonably priced: €74 for a double including breakfast. Friendly owners. 10% discount on the room rate Sept–June.

♚ |●| HÔTEL-RESTAURANT DU GUESCLIN**

2 pl. Duguesclin; it's in the pedestrian area.
☎ 02.96.33.11.58 ► 02.96.52.01.18
Disabled access. **TV**.

Centrally located and completely refurbished

with bright, comfortable rooms. Doubles with shower/wc or bath for €41–43. There's a bar-brasserie on the ground floor and an elegant dining room serving menus at €14–26; specialities include *mousseline* of scallops, bream with fennel, home-smoked fish and chocolate *fondant*.

❑❙ RESTAURANT LE SYMPATIC

9 bd. Carnot; it's behind the train station.
☎ 02.96.94.04.76
Closed Sat lunchtime; Sun; public holidays; the first fortnight in Aug.

Open until 11pm. A happy combination of a good atmosphere and good food grilled over a vine fire. The ambience is warm with lots of wood and bare stone. The service is friendly and efficient; dishes using quality ingredients are served on huge plates with a side vegetable, and they're inexpensive. Set menus €11–30 or *à la carte*.

❑❙ AUX PESKED

59 rue du Légué; it's 1km north of the town centre.
☎ 02.96.33.34.65
Closed Sun evening; Mon; 24 Dec–15 Jan; 28 Aug–12 Sept.

The gastronomic reputation of this restaurant is highly regarded in Saint-Brieuc. It's got lots going for it – a sober, elegant, modern setting and a terrace which gives superb views of the Légué valley. Delightful light, mouth-watering dishes, with a €17 weekday menu and others at €29–44. Some days they offer a seven-course *menu dégustation*. The extensive cellar contains a modest collection of 13,000 bottles! Some are rare and expensive, lots are Loire wines but many are less prestigious and more affordable.

SAINT-MALO   35400

🛏 HÔTEL NAUTILUS**

9 rue de la Corne de Cerf (Centre).
☎ 02.99.40.42.27 ➡ 02.99.56.75.43
TV.

A little hotel inside the old town, just five minutes from the beach. It's newly decorated in bright, young colours. Smallish rooms with good facilities for €38–53 for a double with shower/wc. On the ground floor, there's a lively pub with psychedelic walls – more Yellow Submarine than Nautilus.

🎋 🛏 HÔTEL DU LOUVRE**

2 rue des Marins (Centre).
☎ 02.99.40.86.62 ➡ 02.99.40.86.93

TV. **Car park**.

Although it has an impressive number of rooms – fifty – this is still a family hotel has appeal. Very comfortable doubles for €44–58 with shower/wc or with bath. The ones overlooking the pretty courtyard are more spacious. They have rooms sleeping three and one sleeping seven. From Nov to March they offer a 50% (yes, 50%!) discount; at other times it's 10%.

🎋 🛏 ❑❙ HÔTEL DE L'UNIVERS**

Place Châteaubriand; (Centre)
☎ 02.99.40.89.52 ➡ 02.99.40.07.27
Restaurant closed Wed

This establishment is right next to the legendary Bar de l'Univers and the hotel stands as testimony to a splendid past. It's one of those local places with style and an almost British charm. The reception is spacious, the corridors and sitting rooms well-proportioned. The atmosphere in the huge rooms is lovely – some of the rooms can sleep 3 or 4. The new management have undertaken work to restore the rooms and the stucco in the dining room to their former glory; the renovations should be completed for the summer of in 2002. Double rooms €52–72 depending on the view and the season. 10% discount on the room rate except for weekends and July–Aug.

❑❙ LE PETIT CRÊPIER

6 rue Sainte Barbe (Centre).
☎ 02.99.40.93.19 ✉ LePcrepeir@aol.com
Closed Wed out of season; a fortnight in Nov; a fortnight in Jan.

The pancakes and girdle cakes here are as good as they are surprising. Excellent produce and subtle, often unexpected, combinations of flavours. The man behind them is talented: try his mussel flan, girdle cake with fish *mousse* or pancakes with Breton *andouille* and onion marmalade. He also does monkfish liver and king prawn salad. Equally unusual sweet pancakes: poached pear with orange caramel, one with seaweed marmalade. There's an interesting list of beers and Breton ciders. You'll pay around €13 for a meal.

❑❙ RESTAURANT CHEZ GILLES

2 rue de la Pie-qui-Boit (Centre).
☎ 02.99.40.97.25
Closed Wed and Thurs out of season; Wed only in Aug; mid-Nov to mid-Dec.

The gloriously fresh seafood here is cooked

with enthusiasm and served in a cosy, comfy, bourgeois dining room with intimate corners. There's a €12 lunch *formule* and other menus €14–28. The owner/chef cooks fish to perfection in delicate, aromatic sauces: slivers of John Dory with oysters and bacon pieces, brill in a chicken stock and *foie gras*. You get the same quality of cooking on all the set menus.

|●| LE BÉNÉTIN

Les Rochers Sculptés de Rothéreuf, Paramé.
☎ 02.99.56.97.64

The owners of this restaurant also have a Michelin-starred restaurant in town. Here the approach is simpler and the atmosphere more relaxed but the quality of the cooking is identical. A retinue of little dishes arrive on the table: sautéed baby vegetables cooked crisp accompany a delicious pollack fillet. It's generously served, full of flavour and tasty. The desserts are equally delicious. *Formule* of the day (main course and dessert) for €14 or, if you dine *à la carte*, expect to pay around €20. The décor is inspired by some of the most beautiful photographs of the coast – rope floors, teak furniture and marine ornaments– and the view of the sea is quite simply wonderful. There's a big terrace for good weather. Youthful, smiling serving staff. Best to book.

|●| LA CORDERIE

Saint-Servan, chemin de la Corderie; it's next to the Alet camping site.
☎ 02.99.81.62.38
Closed mid-Nov to mid-March.

La Corderie is off the tourist track and wonderfully lacking in traffic noise. It's an old family house filled with old furniture, books and paintings. From the terrace and dining room, there is a beautiful view of the sea, the Solidor tower, La Rance and Dinard beyond. They serve light, well-presented dishes at reasonable prices, and they change practically every day – Greek salad, grilled fish. Menus from €15 or *à la carte* a meal will cost around €23.

|●| RESTAURANT BORGNEFESSE

10 rue du Puits-aux-Braies; it's inside the town walls.
☎ 02.99.40.05.05
Closed Sat lunchtime; Sun evening; a fortnight end June to July; a fortnight end Nov.

A restaurant with a pirate theme run by a larger-than-life *patron*, a poet and seafarer – a legendary character in Saint-Malo. At the

drop of a hat he'll weave tales of pirates and derring-do and tell you how the restaurant got its name. On the food front, the *crêpes* are made with local organic eggs and full-cream milk. The house specialities are the savoury *galette Borgnefesse* (stuffed with black pudding and served with buttered apples) and the sweet *Saint-Patrick* (apple compote flavoured with cinnamon, raisins, whisky and cream). They serve dishes of the day – lamb chops with creamed garlic and mussels in season. One set menu for €19.

SAINT-SULIAC   35430 (10KM S)

★ |●| LE GALICHON

5 La Grande Cohue; it's on the N17
☎ 02.99.58.49.49
Open June and Sept 19–21; July and Aug daily 11am–11pm; out of season open Fri–Sun. **TV**.

A really nice place, this. A handful of the rustic, a shake of refinement and a pinch of nostalgia combine to make a delicious place where they serve dishes using old recipes cooked over the fire and good pancakes. There's also a modern feel engendered by the bright young lady who owns the place and her team of friends. They serve meat stews, quails with grapes, roast pork with great mashed potato and melting beans. Pudding could be rice pudding made with unpasteurised organic milk. It works a treat. No set menu; dishes around €8 and desserts for around €2.

SAINT-POL-DE-LÉON   29250

★ |●| LE PASSIFLORE-LES ROUTIERS

28 rue Penn-Ar-Pont; it's near the station.
☎ and ➔ 02.99.69.00.52
Closed Sun evening; Christmas; New Year's Day. **TV**.

This really unpretentious little hotel offers a genuine welcome and pleasantly classic rooms at low prices – from €32 with shower/wc. *Les Routiers*, the restaurant on the ground floor, is excellent, so don't be surprised if it's packed at lunchtime, when €9 menu is very popular. There are others up to €26. Seafood platters, Breton lobster and other fish dishes.

SAINT-RENAN   29290

|●| LA MAISON D'AUTREFOIS

7 rue de l'Église.
☎ 02.98.84.22.67

Closed Sun; Mon evening; mid-Jan to mid-Feb.

Superbly attractive, half-timbered house. Inside, the natural stone walls are decorated with old farm implements and beautiful furniture. Good, traditional *crêpes* – the *Bretonne* is stuffed with scallops, chopped leeks and cream and flambéed with Calvados, while the *Sauvage* drips with wine caramel and honey ice-cream. Weekday lunch menu for €8 and a children's menu for €5.

SAINT-THÉGONNEC · 29410

✿ IOI AUBERGE DE SAINT-THÉGONNEC***

6 pl. de la Mairie.
☎ 02.98.79.61.18 ☛ 02.98.62.71.10
e auberge@wanadoo.fr
Closed Sun lunchtime and Mon from mid-Sept to mid-June; 20 Dec–10 Jan. **Disabled access**. **TV**. **Car park**.

This is recommended as one of the best restaurants in Finistère and it's located just opposite one of the most lovely walled towns in the area. Come here for seriously good cooking in elegant, sophisticated surroundings. The service is faultless. Seasonal dishes are excellently prepared from fresh produce: fillet of ling with an aubergine *tian* and fresh tomato *coulis*, braised veal *mignon* with morels, a pocket of veal sweetbreads with oyster mushrooms and grain mustard, orange *terrine* with nutmeg and mint. Menus from €18 but the bill is much higher *à la carte*. Three lovely rooms with good facilities from €58, with breakfast served in the comfortable lounge.

IOI RESTAURANT DU COMMERCE

1 rue de Paris; it's in the centre of the village.
☎ 02.98.79.61.07
Closed evenings; Sat and Sun; 3 weeks in Aug.

A roadside restaurant of the *routier* variety, open for breakfast and lunch only. Friendly welcome, good cooking, huge portions and cheap prices. For €9 you get soup, starter, dish of the day, cheese and dessert – the menu states that a drink is included for "workers" but not for people "passing through"! They also have a few specialities like *pot-au-feu*, a broth with large chunks of meat and vegetables, *choucroute*, *Kig-ha-Farz* and couscous. Pleasant dining room with stone walls. It's a lively place.

IOI CRÊPERIE STEREDENN

6 rue de la Gare (Centre).

☎ 02.98.79.43.34 ☛ 02.98.79.40.89
Closed Mon and Tues from Oct to mid-June. **Disabled access**.

Christine and Alain offer a friendly greeting and an open fire. A choice of 150 delicious, cheap *crêpes*: the *Picardie*, with leek sauce; the *Indien*, with white sauce, onions, mushrooms and curry; the sweet *Druidique*, with marmalade, almonds and Grand Marnier. About €11 *à la carte*. Wash it down with cider brewed on the premises.

SARZEAU · 56370

IOI RESTAURANT L'HORTENSIA

La Grée Penvins.
☎ 02.97.67.42.15 ☛ 02.97.67.42.16
Closed Mon evening; Tues out of season; a week end March; a fortnight end Nov.

The restaurant is in an old house where you go through one dining room to get to the next. They're all painted hydrangea-blue, contrasting attractively with the starkness of the granite walls. The full range of seafood, shellfish and meat provide the fare here: goujons of sole with sesame, asaparagus tips with parmesan, pigs' trotters stuffed with *foie gras* with Pont-Neuf potatoes and cream cheese. The couple trained at the Auberge Grand-Maison in Mur-de-Bretagne which is a good school. There's a lunch menu for €14, others at €24–36 and a lobster one for €49.

✿ IOI AUBERGE DE KERSTÉPHANIE

Route du Roaliguen; it's on the right at the end of a cul-de-sac.
☎ 02.97.41.72.41 ☛ 02.97.41.99.15
Closed Tues evening and Wed out of season and Jan to mid-Feb. **Car park**.

In all respects one of the best restaurants in the Morbihan. Elegant setting and service without excess formality. Virtuoso cuisine by the chef-owner Jean-Paul Jego, ably supported by his wife. The €15 lunch menu and others at €22–36 all change with the seasons and the *à la carte* choice is fairly priced: pan-fried squid with potatoes and onions sprinkled with wine vinegar, salmon *unilatéral* (cooked only on one side), *granité*, sorbet and an exquisite dessert of honey *sabayon* with apples and *nougat* ice-cream. Mr Jego found a spit made in 1952, renovated it and set it up in the dining room. It's used to cook the day's special, like leg of ham on the bone served with a *sauce Malaga*. The lobster is grilled fresh from the fish tank. Absolutely fabulous food at excellent prices. Free apéritif.

PENVINS   56370 (7KM E)

♠ |●| LE MUR DU ROY**

Lieu-dit Le Mur-du-Roy à Penvins.
☎02.97.67.34.08 ➡ 02.97.67.36.23
Closed Wed lunchtime out of season; Jan.

Well-situated with direct access to the beach. This comfortable hotel offers impeccably clean rooms, four of which have views of the sea. Doubles €51–68 with shower/wc or bath. The excellent restaurant has a good range of fish and seafood. Menus €15–30; half board is compulsory July–Aug and costs €50–54. There's a wonderful terrace and the service is faultless.

TRÉBEURDEN   22560

♠ |●| HÔTEL-RESTAURANT KER AN NOD**

rue de Pors-Termen (Centre); it's opposite île Millau.
☎ 02.96.23.50.21 ➡ 02.96.23.63.30
ℯ keranod@infonie.fr
Closed Thurs lunchtime except in school holidays; 5 Jan–31 March. **TV**.

Peaceful beachside hotel run by a nice couple in sight of the Île Millau. Of the twenty rooms, fourteen look out to sea. Doubles with shower/wc or bath €44–58. They're comfortable and bright with great picture windows. The dining room is equally pleasant; you dine here on fresh fish, seafood and local dishes – gratinéed oysters with nutmeg butter, fisherman's soup, Trégor chicken with crayfish, duckling with caramelized apples. Menus €15–28.

TRÉGASTEL   22730

♠ |●| HÔTEL-RESTAURANT DE LA CORNICHE**

38 rue Charles-Le-Goffic (Centre); it's in the town centre, 300m from the beaches.
☎ 02.96.23.88.15 ➡ 02.96.23.47.89
Closed Wed and Oct. **TV**. **Garden**. **Car park**.

A bright place where rooms have a range of facilities. They're €30–43 with handbasin and €38–53 with en-suite shower/wc or bath. The cheery décor puts you in a good mood. The weekday menu for €14 and others at €20–40 list lots of local dishes.

|●| AUBERGE DE LA VIEILLE ÉGLISE

Place de l'Église; it's the old town, 2.5km from the beach.

☎ 02.96.23.88.31
Closed Sun evening; Mon out of season; the Feb school holidays.

This place used to do it all: canteen for local workers, butcher's, fruit and veg shop, minimarket – the lot. But it's been completely transformed since the owner and his family bought the place in 1962. They've turned it into an unmissable restaurant and you *won't* miss it – the outside is smothered in flowers. Weekday lunch menu at €13 (not served Sun or public holidays) and others €18–33; *à la carte* a meal costs about €30. Tagliatelle with scallops, fish *choucroute*, fish *pot-au-feu* and John Dory roast with bacon are house specialities. Exceptionally high-quality cuisine, served by attentive staff in delightful surroundings. It's best to book in the evening during the season and at weekends.

TRÉGUIER   22220

♨ ♠ |●| HÔTEL AIGUE MARINE ET RESTAURANT DES 3 RIVIÈRES***

It's on the marina.
☎ 02.96.92.97.00 ➡ 02.96.92.44.48
Closed Sat lunchtime, Sun evening and Mon out of season; 7 Jan–17 Feb. **Disabled access**. **Swimming pool**. **Garden**. **TV**. **Car park**.

A recently built establishment on the harbour, with 48 very comfortable rooms for €64–88 with shower/wc or bath. There's a heated swimming pool and a garden, and they've built a sauna and Jacuzzi. The owners have passed on responsibility in the restaurant to a talented young chef who shows his skill with local dishes. Menus at €17 (in the week) and €25–33. The prices are good for such high-quality cuisine. 10% discount on the room rate March–April and Oct–Nov.

|●| LA POISSONNERIE DU TRÉGOR

2 rue Renan (Centre).
☎ 02.96.92.30.27
Tasting rooms open daily July–Sept.

A warm yet unusual establishment which has been run by Mme Moulinet for the last thirty or so years. Jean-Pierre Moulinet runs a fishmonger's where you can buy fish to cook – or you try fish, seafood and shellfish dishes in the tasting rooms upstairs. Crab mayonnaise €8, *moules marinières* €5, and platters of shellfish €17–30. The *formule Petit Mousse*, specially designed for kids, is brilliant. Marine frescoes line the walls – you'd think you were at sea. No desserts.

VANNES 56000

🏕 🏠 |●| HÔTEL-RESTAURANT LE RELAIS DE LUSCANEN**

Zone commerciale de Luscanen (West); N165, route d'Auray and the zone commerciale is sign-posted.
☎ 02.97.63.15.77 ➡ 02.97.63.30.45
Closed Fri and Sat evenings; Sun; a fortnight in August. **TV. Car park.**

A real roadside hotel-restaurant. The €58 set menu gives a choice of a hot or cold starter, a choice of main course, cheese, dessert and as much wine, bread and butter as you can manage. Twenty-four clean simple rooms; all doubles €29. Welcome with a smile. Free house apéritif.

🏠 HÔTEL LE MARINA**

pl. Gambetta (Centre).
☎ 02.97.47.22.81 ➡ 02.97.47.27.34
TV.

This hotel is above L'Océan bar, one of the drinking holes around the square; it's ideal if you like to be where the action is. Pretty rooms with double glazing have views of the harbour and town walls, and good facilities including TV. Doubles at €30–53 offer good value for money in the heart of the old town. The only drawback is that you have breakfast in the bar – a noisy way to drag yourself into the day.

🏠 HÔTEL LE BRETAGNE**

36 rue du Mené (Centre); it's 50m from the Prison gateway.
☎ 02.97.47.20.21 ➡ 02.97.47.90.78
Closed Sat evening; Sun; Ascension day weekend; a fortnight in Aug. **TV.**

Old-fashioned charm. Quiet, smallish rooms, some overlooking the town walls, are all well-maintained. Doubles €31–38 with shower/wc or bath. Good value, courteous welcome and it's often full.

|●| LA MORGATE

21 rue de 6 Fontaine.
☎ 02.97.42.42.39
Closed Sun evening, Mon and Tues lunchtime except in July–Aug; a fortnight in June; a week in Sept; 26 Dec–3 Jan.

A gourmet restaurant in a street that just climbs and climbs. Fine, flavoursome cuisine firmly based in local traditions. It mainly attracts people on business lunches and expense accounts but the menus offer good value for money: weekday lunch menu for

€13, then others from €20 (which includes a cheese course) to €24. Courteous and dynamic service.

|●| RESTAURANT DE ROSCANVEC

17 rue des Halles (Centre); it's in the pedestrian area.
☎ 02.97.47.15.96 ➡ 02.97.47.86.39
📧 le-pavé-des-halles@wanadoo.fr
Closed Mon except July–Sept; Sun evening; 1–23 Jan.

This cosy, traditional restaurant occupies two floors of a characterful fourteenth-century house. The owner-chef is full of talent and ambition and he has succeeded in attracting a clientele of informed gourmets. Things get serious right from the first menu at €17 (served at lunch and before 8.30pm), and there are others up to €53; try the hochepot de bœuf (boned oxtail) or the lobster dishes. The menus change regularly to reflect what's good in the market. First-rate wine list.

SAINT-AVÉ 56890 (5KM N)

|●| RESTAURANT LE TOURNESOL

2 pl. Notre-Dame-du-Loc; Saint-Avé is on the Vannes-Pontivy road.
☎ 02.97.44.50.50
📧 restaurant.le.Tournesol@wanadoo.fr
Closed Mon; Wed evening; 3 weeks in Oct.

A doll's house decorated in sunflower yellow with copies of Van Gogh's pictures on the wall. Seven tables in the dining room with fine cuisine and prices that are a throwback to another era: €13, €17 and €24. Dishes such as queen scallops and Dublin Bay prawn kebabs, medallions of filet mignon with oyster mushrooms, excellent cheeses and a bewildering choice of desserts. Seafood platters to order. The wine list is well-priced. Service is friendly and efficient. Best to book.

|●| LE PRESSOIR

7 rue de l'Hôpital; it's 1km out of Saint-Avé.
☎ 02.97.60.87.63 ➡ 02.97.44.59.15
Closed Sun evening; Mon and Tues; 4–20 March; the first week in July; 1–24 Oct. **Car park.**

Exceptional surroundings and facilities, a warm welcome and gastronomic delights in an attractive house just outside town. It's quite simply the best restaurant in these parts, serving galette of red mullet with potato and rosemary, foie gras ravioli with wild mushroom broth and baked apples. The cheapest set menu at €30 is served only on weekday lunchtime, but it's worth going out of your way to try it. Others €38–75.

LOCQUELTAS   56390 (6KM N)

🕏 🏠 |●| HÔTEL LA VOLTIGE**

8 route de Vannes (North); from Vannes, take the D767
for Pontivy, the turning to Meucon aerodrome, then it's
signposted.
☎ 02.97.60.72.06 ➡ 02.97.44.63.01
Restaurant closed Sun evening and Mon out of
season; Mon lunchtime in season; a fortnight in March;
a fortnight in Oct. **Garden. TV. Car park**.

A dozen impeccably clean rooms – €35–49
with shower/wc or bath – all of which have
been refitted, redecorated and are meticulously maintained. Check out the great split-
level rooms for three or four people. 5–20
Aug they prefer you to stay on a half board
basis at €35–44, and it's an attractive option
because of the rather good traditional food.
to be found on even the cheapest menu
(€13). Efficient, unobtrusive service. There's a
garden with an area set aside for games.
Free coffee and 10% discount on the room
rate 15 Sept–25 March.

ARRADON   56610 (8KM SW)

🏠 |●| HÔTEL-RESTAURANT LE STIVELL***

rue Plessis-d'Arradon; take the D101.
☎ 02.97.44.03.15 ➡ 02.97.44.78.90
Restaurant closed Sun evening and Mon out of
season; a week in Jan; 15 Nov–15 Dec. **TV. Car park**.

A *Logis de France*, located on one of the
prettiest stretches of the coast of the Gulf of
Morbihan. It's very well-run, with comfortable
double rooms at €43–71 and an appealing
half board option for €40–48 per person
based on the €18 menu. The dishes are
inspired by the sea: seafood *choucroute*,
warm oysters in champagne. Fabulous
seafood platters to order 48 hours in
advance and there's an astonishing gourmet
menu for children's for only €6 offering half-
portions of the dishes on the main menu. The
patronne makes you feel welcome. Ideal for
those who like the serenity of the sea without
having to stray too far from Vannes and,
since the owner is a fisherman himself, he'll
tell you where to fish hereabouts.

🏠 |●| HÔTEL-RESTAURANT LES VENÈTES***

Pointe d'Arradon.
☎ 02.97.44.85.85 ➡ 02.97.44.78.60
Restaurant closed Sun evening and Mon Sept–June.
TV.

Some ten rooms – a few under the eaves,

others with teak terraces. They've all been
thoroughly renovated in ultra-modern, maritime style and have marvellous views of the
bay. The bathrooms are luxurious with corner
baths. The huge bay windows and the way
the beds are placed make you feel you're
sleeping in a yacht. Doubles €104–134. The
dining room enjoys the same exceptional
view of the sea. The cuisine is fine but prices
are high-end – €24 (weekday lunchtimes)
and €35. Fish and seafood have the place of
honour on the menus and the excellent wines
are selected with these dishes in mind. The
welcome is variable, however.

VITRÉ   35500

🏠 HÔTEL LE MINOTEL**

47 rue Poterie (Centre).
☎ 02.99.75.11.11 ➡ 02.99.75.81.26

Really pretty hotel in the old town; they've
virtually rebuilt the house but have respected the local style while providing modern
facilities. Perhaps, if you're being very picky,
the result is rather unimaginative. The green
and tartan décor makes the place look a bit
like a golf clubhouse – and aptly enough
they've done a deal with the local golf club
and offer packages if you want to play a
round or two. Doubles €46 with bath and
there are family rooms for 4 people. Good
welcome.

|●| LA GAVOTTE

7 rue des Augustins (Centre).
☎ 02.99.74.47.74
Closed Mon; Tues except in the shool holidays; the first
fortnight in March; a fortnight in Sept.

This restaurant fits in well with the surroundings in this charming village. It's a *crêperie*
with a large, pink and gree dining room. They
serve excellent girdle cakes and pancakes
with fillings from the traditional to the unusual: Darley cheese, *andouille*, various
sausages and an apple preparation which is
somewhere between *purée* and chutney. The
delicious dishes are accompanied by cider
and local beverages There are two menus at
€8 and €11; *à la carte* you'll pay around €16
for a complete meal.

|●| AUBERGE SAINT-LOUIS

31 rue Notre-Dame (Centre).
☎ 02.99.75.28.28
Closed Sun evening; Mon; a week in Feb; a week in
March; a week in Sept. **Disabled access**.

An elegant fifteenth-century house which has

built up a solid reputation. The wood panelling in the dining room creates a warm, sophisticated yet family-style atmosphere. The young *patronne* will bring you a small plate of appetizers to nibble while you select your meal. You're in for a feast in a cosy setting. Menus €11–22. There's a good selection of grilled meats and superb fish, accompanied by well-crafted sauces.

CENTRE

AMBOISE   37400

⬦ HÔTEL LE CHANTELOUP**

12 av. Émile Gounin; it's 1.5km from the château.
☎ 02.47.57.10.90 ➡ 02.47.57.17.52
Closed end Sept to early April. **TV**. **Car park**. **Garden**.

Staying in Amboise tends to be expensive so it's good to find a hotel, open in season only, offering good value for money. This big block of a house, with a private car park front and back, is just outside the centre of town. There's no consistent style to speak of – armchairs are in fake leather, surfaces in Formica. There are three floors (with lift), and very simple rooms; a double with shower/wc costs €38 or with bath €43–49. The rooms up in the roof have skylights. It's very well maintained but the welcome is a bit impersonal. There's a small garden, a terrace behind the hotel.

⦿ RESTAURANT L'ÉPICERIE

46 pl. Michel-Debré (Centre); it's opposite the château car park.
☎ 02.47.57.08.94
Closed Mon evening and Tues except 15 June–30 Sept; 2 Nov–22 Dec. **Car park**.

A magnificent half-timbered building painted a lovely olive green. There are pretty curtains at the windows, screening the dining room from the waves of tourists surging past outside. Good cooking with tasty little dishes: *filet mignon* of spiced pork with vinegar and aged cider, duck with peppercorns preserved in Chinon wine, crayfish ravioli with anisé butter and roast pigeon with crumbled truffles. The €10 set menu is not served on Sunday or evenings in season; others

€18–34. The service is efficient and relaxed which is slightly at odds with the rather classical style of the dining room.

⦿ LE MANOIR SAINT-THOMAS

1 Mail Saint-Thomas
☎ 02.47.57.22.52
Closed Mon and Tues lunchtime. **Garden**.

The manor and garden make a harmonious setting for the luxurious dining rooms and well-proportioned salons. The tables are beautifully laid and the waitresses all wear uniforms. There's cooking to match: even on the cheapest menu, €27, you're served *amuse-bouches* (a melon cocktail with Muscat de Beaumes de Venise) and *petits-fours* with your coffee. The menu at €31 includes a cheese course and the one at €45 has three mains. The sweetbread and morel *terrine* is fine and delicate, while the pigeon *confit* is flavoured with junipers and served with green cabbage and a highly concentrated *sauce glace*. The *Gâteau Dame Anne* is a white chocolate dessert served with a kiwi *coulis*. Gastronomic cooking at affordable prices in a restaurant devoted to the art of good living.

LIMERAY   37150 (8KM NE)

⦿ LES GRILLONS

30 rue Nationale; it's on the road to Montrichard.
☎ 02.47.30.11.76
Closed Wed lunchtime to Friday inclusive.

A genuine farm with décor that can only be described as operatic. It's run by a family team – grandma's at the stove, the son grows the wine, a second raises chickens and the daughter-in-law runs the dining

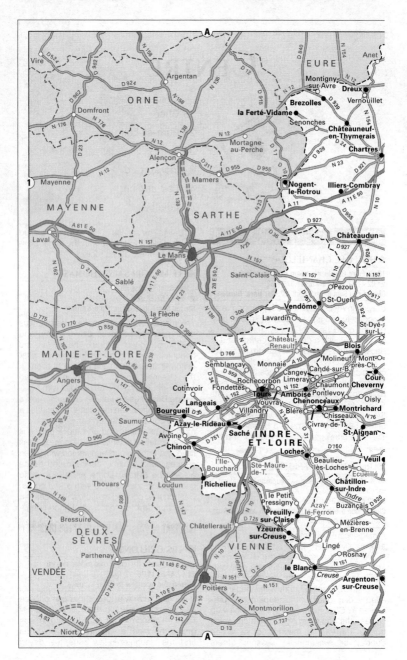

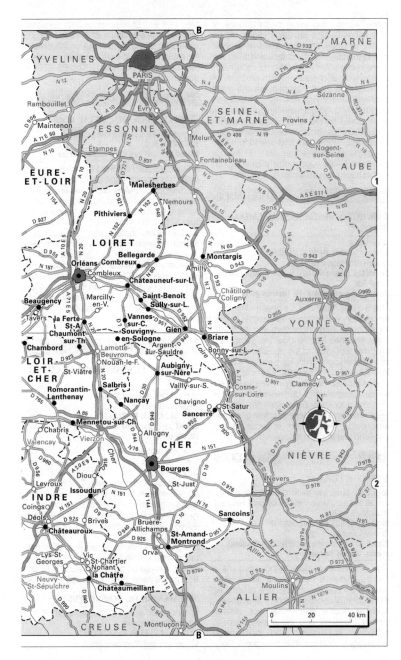

room. Grandpa has a walk-on part whenever he's needed. All three generations of the Guichard family are very attentive to their guests' needs. The charcuterie and pâtés are home-made – try the astonishingly good rabbit and juniper one served with crudités, or the excellent poultry or perhaps the roast beef with tasty juices. The fine cheeses and tasty desserts are also excellent, and the rum baba would be the envy of many a pastry cook. Everything is served in substantial portions. Red, white, rosé and sparkling wines are available. Menus from €18. There are three simple but huge rooms with skylights, and all have en-suite facilities: €26–46.

BLÉRÉ   37150 (10KM S)

🏠 I●I HÔTEL-RESTAURANT LE CHEVAL BLANC**

pl. de l'Église.
☎ 02.47.30.30.14 ➡ 02.47.23.52.80
Ⓦ www.lechevalblancblere.com
Closed Sun evening and Mon except July–Aug, and Jan to mid-Feb.
Swimming pool. Garden. TV. Lock-up garage.

This is a delightful hotel in a seventeenth-century residence. Prettily arranged rooms at €50 for a double with shower/wc and €53 with bath. The reputation of the place is mainly due to Michel Blériot's fresh, light, inventive cooking. The €16 set menu (not Sun) offers some of the best value for money in the area; there's serious gastronomic cuisine on the other menus (up to €53). Good wine list with fine Loire wines and a superb selection of vintage armagnacs. Reservation essential at the weekend and public holidays.

CANGEY   37530 (12KM NE)

🏠 I●I LE FLEURAY**

Route Dame-Marie; take the N152 Amboise–Blois road, turn left onto the D74 signposted to Cangey, Fleuray and Dame-Marie-les-Bois. ➡
☎ 02.47.56.09.25 ➡ 02.47.56.93.97
Ⓦ www.lefleurayhotel.com
Closed during the winter school holidays. **Disabled access. Garden. Car park.**

This nineteenth-century manor house is a cross between a hotel and a guesthouse. Hazel and Peter Newington have called their eleven prettily decorated rooms after flowers such as *bouton d'or* (buttercup), *cerisier* (cherry blossom) and *clochette* (bluebell); *capucine* (nasturtium) and *perce-neige* (snowdrop) are larger than the others. Dou-

bles €76 with shower/wc or bath. Gourmet cooking, with set menus at €25–35, is served in a pleasant dining room or out on the terrace. Nice welcome, and a very international clientele, but you must book. Half board €72 per person.

CHISSEAUX   37150 (17KM SE)

🏕️I●I AUBERGE DU CHEVAL ROUGE

30 rue Nationale; it's on the road to Montrichard.
☎ 02.47.23.86.67
Closed Mon, and Tues out of season. **Garden.**

A few steps lead out from this lovely country bistro into a charming and tastefully decorated dining room. Mme Feron serves her husband's cooking with great kindness – though when the restaurant is packed she has her hands full. On offer are a *feuillantine* of Sainte-Maure cheese with tart apples, a salmon *bavarois* with cream and chives, saddle of rabbit "Grand-mère Julienne", a good *entrecôte* steak and a fish *choucroute*. The chef devotes a lot of care to his food, particularly to his wine and cream sauces: this is a place where cooking is taken very seriously. Menus €15–31. There's a lovely garden and a terrace. Free coffee.

ARGENTON-SUR-CREUSE   36200

🏕️🏠 I●I HÔTEL-RESTAURANT LE CHEVAL NOIR**

27 rue Auclert-Descottes (Centre); it's on the road to Gargilesse-Dampierre.
☎ 02.54.24.00.06 ➡ 02.54.24.11.22
Closed Sun evening and Mon lunchtime out of season.
TV. Car park.

The restoration work done on this nineteenth-century posthouse has been particularly well-executed. The rooms are quiet, comfortable and have been freshly decorated. Doubles €37–43 with shower/wc and €43 with bath. The large dining room has a highly polished parquet floor. The elegant, subtle cuisine is prepared by chef Christophe Jeannot, whose skill shows in his specialities: *foie gras* with Guérande sea salt, pigs' trotters *parmentier*, fillet of zander. Set menus at €9 (not served on public holidays), €14 and €21 or *à la carte*. Free house apéritif.

🏕️🏠 MANOIR DE BOISVILLERS**

11 rue du Moulin-de-Bord (Centre); beside the N20 in the direction of Limoges.
☎ 02.54.24.13.88 ➡ 02.54.24.27.83
🅔 maison.de.boisvilliers@wanadoo.fr

Closed 20 Dec–6 Jan. **Swimming pool. Garden. TV. Car park.**

The foundation stone of the riverside residence of the Chevalier de Boisvillers was laid in 1759. This unusual manor house is elegantly set on the banks of the Creuse and it deserves more than two stars. The décor is tasteful, the carpet is luxuriously deep and there's a friendly little lounge next to the bar. You can have a drink by the pool in the grounds. The rooms are decorated in various styles; those under the eaves are the prettiest. Doubles with shower €37 or with bath €44–60 – which is reasonable considering the facilities. 10% discount on the room rate.

AUBIGNY-SUR-NÈRE 18700

☎ |●| HÔTEL-RESTAURANT LA CHAUMIÈRE**

1 av. du Parc-des-Sports; it's next to the château, on the Sancerre road.
☎ 02.48.58.04.01 ☛ 02.48.58.10.31
Closed Sun evening except July–Aug; Mon lunchtime; the Feb school holidays. **TV. Pay car park.**

A comfortable little thatched cottage. The decoration of the rooms is well up to standard, as is the reception. Doubles – €37 with shower/wc or bath – are on the small side. Traditional dishes are served on all menus, which start at €14 and go up to €35. Specialities include duck *foie gras*, fillet of beef with truffle sauce and assorted sorbets with fresh fruit.

ARGENT-SUR-SAULDRE 18410 (10KM N)

☎ |●| LE RELAIS DU COR D'ARGENT

39 rue Nationale; it's set back from the D940, coming from Aubigny-sur-Nère.
☎ 02.48.73.63.49 ☛ 02.48.73.37.55
Closed Tues and Wed except July–Aug, 15 Feb–15 March and a week in Oct. **TV.**

This is a country place with country style: hunting trophies on the walls, stuffed partridges and pheasants, a few copper pots dotted around and flowers on the tables. Delicious smells drift out of Laurent Lafon's kitchen, hinting at the gastronomic delights to come. In game season, duck *confit*, and *fricassée* of lobster in Noilly with leeks are all excellently prepared. Menus €13–49. This is a good place to spend the night; the seven tastefully decorated rooms combine the charm of old-fashioned furniture and the comfort of modern bedding. Doubles €32–38.

VAILLY-SUR-SAULDRE 18260 (17KM E)

|●| LE LIÈVRE GOURMAND

14 Grand-Rue; by the D923 in the direction of Sancerre.
☎ 02.48.73.80.23 ☛ 02.48.73.86.13
℮ le.lievre.gourmand@wanadoo.fr
Closed Sun evening, Mon and end Jan.

Service noon–2pm and 7.30–9.30pm. This old Berry house belongs to one William Page from Australia. His cooking is exceptional and makes inspired use of spices – *roulade* of semi-cooked *foie gras* and fig *compote*, boned quail stuffed with roast dates in Maghreb spices, caramelized pineapple kebab with poached dried fruits and *anise* ice-cream. The menu changes with the seasons but the inventiveness is constant. Set menus at €17, €24, €35 and €44. Mr Page has some Australian vintages in the cellar which is a bit daring in France. Give it a whirl – it's one of a kind.

AZAY-LE-RIDEAU 37190

♣ ☎ HÔTEL DE BIENCOURT**

7 rue Balzac (Centre); it's on the pedestrianized street leading to the château.
☎ 02.47.45.20.75 ☛ 02.47.45.91.73
Closed 15 Nov–1 March. **Disabled access. TV. Car park.**

This is a very beautiful eighteenth-century house in a typically Tours style. The eighteen comfortable rooms are variously furnished along Directoire or rustic themes, and some overlook the flower-filled patio at the back. Charm and tranquility guaranteed. Good value, with doubles for €42 with shower/wc, and €51 with bath and TV. 10% discount in March, Oct and Nov.

♣ |●| RESTAURANT L'AIGLE D'OR

10 av. Adélaïde-Richer; head for Langeais.
☎ 02.47.45.24.58 ☛ 02.47.45.90.18
Closed Sun evening and Wed; Tues evening out of season; the Feb school holidays; the last fortnight in Nov. **Disabled access. Garden.**

Service noon–2pm and 7.30–9pm. One of the best gastronomic restaurants in Touraine, with a welcoming and refined setting – even the beams in the dining room are a relaxing soft green. Attentive service. Meals served in the garden in summer. Weekday lunch menu €16; others €24–40 with one for €56 including wines. The *à la carte* menu changes frequently but retains a few classics: *langoustine* salad with *foie gras*; *blanquette* of zander in Azay wine sauce; and *la griottine* with chocolate. The wine list is most instructive, with maps showing the provenance of numerous wines. Free glass of Azay-le-Rideau sweet wine Nov–April.

VILLANDRY   37510 (10KM N)

🏃 |●| L'ÉTAPE GOURMANDE

Domaine de la Giraudière; take the D121 from Villandry in the direction of Druye; cross the Loire on the D57, then at Libinières take the D7 for Tourain.
☎ 02.47.50.08.60 ➡ 02.47.50.06.60
Closed 12 Nov–15 March reservations only. **Disabled access. Garden.**

This is a splendid seventeenth-century farm which, despite the complicated-looking directions, is easy to find. The superb dining room has a huge fireplace and you can also eat outside on the terrace. The chef gave up a career as a diplomat to start the place – expect a courteous welcome and punctillious service. They serve their own goat's cheese and there are plenty of local dishes, complicated salads, omelettes, quiches and lovely Loire wines. Set menus €15–21 or *à la carte*. On the first Saturday of the summer they give concerts with singers and storytellers. You can buy goat's cheeses and fruits preserved in wine and they will even show you the goats and take you round the dairy. A refreshing place. Free coffee.

BEAUGENCY   45190

🛏 |●| HOSTELLERIE DE L'ÉCU DE BRETAGNE**

pl. du Martroi (Centre).
☎ 02.38.44.67.60 ➡ 02.38.44.68.07
🌐 www.ecu-de-bretagne.fr
Closed Sun evening. **TV. Garden. Car park.**

There are heraldic shields on the wall and an atmosphere reminiscent of a Chabrol film, but no visible connection with Brittany – although this place gets its name from the Breton family who have owned the place since the fifteenth century. Ask for a room in the coaching inn rather than in the annexe across the way; they cost €31–43 with shower/wc or €45–78 with bath. The restaurant is pricey but the quality is good, and the house speciality is zander. Menus €15–34 and a children's menu at €8.

🛏 HÔTEL DE LA SOLOGNE**

6 pl. Saint-Firmin (Centre).
☎ 02.38.44.50.27 ➡ 02.38.44.90.19
Closed weekends in Jan; a fortnight from Christmas.

Garden. TV. Car park.

The medieval rue de l'Evêché leads to a delightful little square dominated by an tenth-century keep. This is the historic heart of the town, and the hotel's handsome stone façade, festooned with geraniums, fits in perfectly. There's a pretty lounge with ceiling beams and fireplace, a balcony overlooking a flower-filled courtyard and a conservatory where an enormous philodendron has pride of place. All quite charming. Quiet, well-equipped rooms. Doubles €37–43 with shower/wc or €46–58 with bath. And you won't be able to fault the reception.

TAVERS   45190 (3KM SW)

🏃 🛏 |●| LA TONNELLERIE****

12 rue des Eaux Bleues.
☎ 02.38.44.68.15 ➡ 02.38.44.10.01
📧 latonnellerie@chateaux-france.com
Closed Sat and Mon lunchtimes, and Jan–Feb.
Swiming pool. TV. Car park.

An austere building in the centre of the village – but inside it's a different story. By general consent, this is the best place in Beaugency: very chic, with relaxing, comfortable décor. It's so quiet that you can hear the birdsong and the chimes of the church bell, and you can stroll through the park, which is full of chestnut trees. The cooking is luxurious and fragrant: *mesclun* of chicken, skate wings with pickled onions, *foie gras* soufflé and chocolate *moelleux*. The rooms are super-comfortable. The ones in the eaves are the nicest and the best value. Doubles with shower or bath/wc cost €75–93. Free house apéritif.

BLANC (LE)   36300

🛏 HÔTEL DU THÉÂTRE**

2 [bis] av. Gambetta (Centre); it's near the tourist office.
☎ 02.54.37.68.69 ➡ 02.54.28.03.95
TV.

This hotel is bang in the middle of town. The clean, small rooms, all with en-suite bathrooms, are soundproofed. Even so, the street is extremely busy in summer – it's an alternative route to Paris – so ask for a room that isn't over the street. Doubles €38.

🛏 |●| DOMAINE DE L'ÉTAPE***

Route de Bélâbre; drive 5km along the D10 in the direction of Bélâbre
☎ 02.54.37.18.02 ➡ 02.54.37.75.59
Disabled access. TV. Car park.

This magnificent nineteenth-century estate is

a magical place. It's set in huge grounds, with a lake, woods and fields, and the 35 rooms are spread between the château itself, the modern lodge and the rustic farm by the stables. The most splendid are on the first floor in the château: they're immense and beautifully furnished – ideal for a honeymoon or an intimate weekend *à deux*. Doubles €38–92 with shower/wc or bath. There are set menus from €21 to €55 or you can dine *à la carte*. Recommended are the duck *foie gras carpaccio* with balsamic vinegar and hazelnut oil, the zander escalope with cider vinegar sauce and the chocolate *marquise* with marmalade.

|●| LE CYGNE

8 av. Gambetta (Centre).
☎ 02.54.28.71.63 ☛ 02.54.28.32.13
Closed Mon and Tues (Mon only in July).

A fairly new restaurant with a reputation which has spread well beyond the town. The décor is fresh – pinkish walls, blond floor and pale green chairs. The first-floor dining room is more rustic, with big beams and walls painted straw-yellow, and there's an intimate salon which is perfect for groups of four to nine. Cordial welcome from the owners, and the chef comes out of the kitchen to chat to his clients. Menus €15–30; specialities include *cassolette* of snails Berry-style and ox kidneys cooked whole and flambéed in Marc.

ROSNAY · 36300 (15KM NE)

⅍ |●| LE CENDRILLE

1 pl. de la Mairie (Centre).
☎ 02.54.28.64.94 ☛ 02.54.28.64.93
Closed Tues evening, Wed and 2 Jan–28 Feb.

This delightful restaurant, in the middle of a village in the Brenne, has been stylishly done up by Florence and Luke Jeanneau with the aid of a grant from the town hall. They have chosen strong yellows and blues and created a warm atmosphere; they'll welcome you warmly, too. The cooking is simple, tasty and traditional: pike *mousseline*, roast honeyed goat's cheese, simmered oxtail and warm apple tart. All their cheeses are local. Menus start at €9, then go up to €27. Free house apéritif.

LINGÉ · 36220 (16KM N)

⅍ ▲ |●| AUBERGE DE LA GABRIÈRE**

La Gabrière; take the D6 at Lingé, follow the signs for La Gabrière and the inn is across from the lake.

☎ 02.54.37.80.97 ☛ 02.54.37.70.66
Restaurant closed Mon evening and Tues except July–Aug. **Disabled access. Garden. TV.**

The inn is beautifully situated on Lake Gabrière. The restaurant is crowded all year because the cuisine is good and you can enjoy the view while you eat; try the €15 menu with clam and oyster mushroom salad, roast shoulder of lamb spiked with green garlic and fillet of zander with cream and chives – just the thing to set you up for a walk in the surrounding countryside. Other menus range from €10, served on weekdays, to €24. *À la carte* there's fillet of carp *paysanne*, pike with cream and chive sauce and *fricassée* of frogs' legs *provençale*. The inn has a number of rooms, some with a lake view; doubles with shower/wc or bath €31. Free coffee.

BLOIS · 41000

▲ HÔTEL SAINT-JACQUES*

7 rue Ducoux (West); it's opposite the train station.
☎ 02.54.78.04.15 ☛ 02.54.78.33.05

Large, bright rooms, neither particularly pretty nor especially ugly, but they're particularly well-maintained. Doubles range from €34 for a big room with shower/wc down to €21 for a simpler, smaller room with handbasin.

⅍ ▲ HÔTEL LE SAVOIE**

6 rue Ducoux (Northwest); it's in the street opposite the train station.
☎ 02.54.74.32.21 ☛ 02.54.74.29.58
Closed 24 Dec–3 Jan. **TV.**

This is a nice little hotel, reminiscent of a guesthouse, away from the hustle and bustle of the tourist area. Rooms are clean and bright; doubles start at €37 with shower/wc or €46 with bath. You'll get a very nice welcome. Best to book. 10% discount Sept–May.

⅍ ▲ HÔTEL DE FRANCE ET DE GUISE**

3 rue Gallois (Centre); it's opposite the château.
☎ 02.54.78.00.53 ☛ 02.54.78.29.45
Closed Nov–March. **TV.**

Very, very *Vieille France*, from the welcome to the atmosphere – and particularly in the floral wall coverings and sofas in the hall and the dining room. The rooms are in the same style, but brighter and freshly decorated. Some are particularly attractive, with plaster mouldings and big fireplaces, and a few have a view of the castle. All are wonderfully maintained. Double room with shower/wc €44 or €69 with bath. 10% discount April–May and Sept–Oct. They don't accept American Express or Diner's Club cards.

☆ ☎ HÔTEL ANNE DE BRETAGNE**

31 av. Jean-Laigret; it's 300m from the château and the city centre, near the tourist office.
☎ 02.54.78.05.38 ➡ 02.54.74.37.79
Closed 6 Jan–3 Feb. **TV. Car park**.

A family hotel, stylishly provincial and situated in the middle of town. The rooms overlook the rear of the building and have double glazing; those at the front have a nice view of the square and the bar terrace, which is set back from the road. Pleasant rooms for €48–55 with shower or bath and phone. Free coffee.

◉ RESTAURANT LA GARBURE

36 rue Saint-Lubin (Southwest); it's between the market and the steps leading up to the château.
☎ 02.54.74.32.89
Closed Wed (lunchtime only in season), and Sat and Thurs lunchtimes.

This restaurant, located in a Louis XV-era building, has two dining rooms. The main has exposed beams while the tiny second one in the cellar is used only for groups. There is also a non-smoking area. They specialize in dishes from southwestern France: duck *foie gras* and gizzards *confits* with Sarlat potatoes and truffles and, of course, the hearty traditional *garbure* soup, made with cabbage, swedes, turnips, Toulouse sausage, duck wing and drumsticks. Set menus €12 (weekdays) and €14.

◉ L'EMBARCADÈRE

16 quai Ulysse Besnard (Southwest); it's on the N6, in the direction of Tours.
☎ 02.54.78.31.41
Closed Mon evening 15 Nov–15 April.

A splendid country-style place decorated as if it were a boat tied up on the banks of the Loire, with views over the mudflats and sand dunes. Come rain or shine, this is the place for mussels, chips, river fish and seafood and a few tasty meat dishes such as rabbit *terrine* with *trompette* wild mushrooms. Prices are reasonably cheap, with a €12 *formule* served weekdays at lunchtime. There's also a fish dish of the day; a meal *à la carte* will cost about €18. They also serve good local wine by the jug. Dance evenings on Fridays and an open-air cinema in the summer.

◉ LE BISTROT DU CUISINIER

20 quai Villebois-Mareuil; it's on the left bank of the Loire, 50m from the pont Gabriel.
☎ 02.54.78.06.70 ➡ 02.54.74.81.75
e bistrot.du.cuisinier@wanadoo.fr
Disabled access.

Service noon–3pm and 7–11pm. It's only 50m from the pont Gabriel (also known as the Vieux Pont), and there's a wonderful view of the city from here. Simple, unpretentious dining room with decent, good-value food. There's a *formule* at €16 and a set menu at €24. The cuisine is really delicious and portions are big. Specialities include *marbré* of rabbit and *foie gras* with sweet Vouvray; roast salmon with Chinon wine; and *nougatine* with honey, hazelnuts and chocolate sauce. Very interesting list of wines from the Loire. About once a month the chef takes you on a gastronomic tour, producing dishes from other French regions as well as further afield.

◉ AU BOUCHON LYONNAIS

25 rue des Violettes (Centre); head for pl. Louis-XII.
☎ 02.54.74.12.87
Closed Sun and Mon except in summer and public holidays; Jan.

Blois has everything, including, surprisingly, a genuine traditional Lyon-style bistro serving genuine traditional Lyon-style specialities: calf's head, warm *saucisson*, salad *lyonnaise* with warm lentils, grilled salmon escalope and sirloin with Beaujolais wine sauce The prices are really very reasonable given quality and quantity. Set menus €18–26. The setting is a superb Louis XII house and there's a terrace for sunny days. Best to book or turn up early.

MOLINEUF   41190 (9KM W)

☆ ◉ RESTAURANT DE LA POSTE

11 av. de Blois; take the D766 in the direction of Angers.
☎ 02.54.70.03.25 ➡ 02.54.70.12.46
e thierry@poidras.com
Closed Sun and Tues evening out of season, Wed, and the first fortnight in Nov.

This little restaurant on the outskirts of Molineuf is a good place to stop and treat yourself to some of the delicious creations of chef Thierry Poidras. Try his duo of hot and cold *foie gras*, crayfish tail stew with morels, fillet steak with morel and cream sauce or *fondant* of bitter chocolate and iced mousse with nuts. Menus start at €16 and you should expect to pay about €39 if you eat *à la carte*. Attentive service. An extremely good restaurant, decorated in bright citrus colours. Free coffee.

CANDÉ-SUR-BEUVRON   41120 (15KM SW)

🛉 ☎ |●| LA CAILLÈRE**

36 route des Montils (South); take the D173 along the south bank of the Loire.
☎ 02.54.44.03.08 ▶ 02.54.44.00.95
📧 lacaillere@mageos.com
Closed Wed; Thurs lunchtime; Jan; Feb. **Disabled access. TV. Car park**.

A delightful hotel with a restaurant in a sympathetically converted eighteenth-century farmhouse. There are fourteen rooms; doubles with shower/wc are €55–60, some of which have been designed for the disabled. The restaurant has a good reputation locally, so it's advisable to book. Weekday menu at €15 and others €16–45. Specialities vary with the season: you might find skate and *foie gras* salad, pigeon *pot-au-feu* with pine nuts, pickled turnips with sautéed *foie gras*, roast peaches or *brioche* and butter pudding. In summer, meals are served in the very pleasant garden. They prefer you to stay half board, €62 per person, June–Aug. Free house apéritif.

CHITENAY   41120 (15KM S)

🛉 ☎ |●| L'AUBERGE DU CENTRE**

pl. de l'Église (Centre); take the D956 as far as Cellettes and then the D38.
☎ 02.54.70.42.11 ▶ 02.54.70.35.03
Closed Sun evening, Mon out of season and Feb.
Disabled access. Garden. TV. Car park.

The classical frontage doesn't really give any clue to the handsome interior of this hotel and its delightfully peaceful garden. The rooms are well-equipped and decorated in sophisticated style. Doubles with shower/wc or bath go for €38–61. The restaurant is of a similar standard. Set menus start at €18 (not Sat evening, Sun or public holidays), and go up to €36. Specialities from the Sologne include *ballotine* of rabbit with morels and *foie gras*, pike *brandade* with a shrimp *coulis*, game in season and *feuilleté* of roast pears with an *anise* ice-cream. Friendly welcome. Free house apéritif and 10% discount on the room rate.

CHAUMONT-SUR-LOIRE   41150 (18KM SW)

|●| RESTAURANT LA CHANCELIÈRE

1 rue de Bellevue; it faces the Loire very near the château, on the way out of the village.
☎ 02.54.20.96.95 ▶ 02.54.33.91.71
Closed Wed; Thurs; 16 Jan–5 Feb; 10–30 Nov. **Disabled access**.

This is a restaurant to savour and its reputa-

tion continues to grow. There are two dining rooms: one in a restrained rustic style, the other prettier and more quaint. The cooking is fresh and the flavours are delicate. The chef comes with a good track record, having trained in the kitchens of Barriers and the Troisgros brothers: he offers quail *pâté* in *brioche*, zander with *beurre blanc* and a house *terrine* of *foie gras*. The meat is tender and the desserts first-rate. Excellent value, too: the cheapest set menu is €13 and there are others €20–32. Nothing is too much trouble, and service comes with a smile.

BOURGES   18000

SEE MAP OVERLEAF

🛉 ☎ HÔTEL LE CHRISTINA**

5 rue de la Halle. **MAP A2-14**
☎ 02.48.70.56.50 ▶ 02.48.70.58.13
📧 christina-hotel-bourges@wanadoo.fr
TV. Pay car park.

Well-located on the edge of the historic town, near the pedestrianized area. Good facilities. All rooms have effective soundproofing; some have attractive rustic furniture and a toilet separate from the bathroom. Doubles €39–71. Nice welcome. 10% discount at the weekend Nov–March.

🛉 ☎ HÔTEL DE L'AGRICULTURE**

18 bd. de Juranville and 15 rue du Prinal. **MAP A2-3**
☎ 02.48.70.40.84 ▶ 02.48.65.50.58
Closed Christmas and New Year. **TV. Car park**.

You'll get a very warm welcome from Madame Maigret, who likes to talk delightedly about how she realized her dream of having a farm in the Sologne. If you arrive by car, use the door opposite the car park on boulevard de Juranville. Rooms are pretty as well as quiet, having been completely refurbished. Doubles €46 with shower/wc or bath. Some are air-conditioned and have exposed beams, but they're on the top floor. Studios are available for rent. 10% discount Nov–March.

🛉 ☎ |●| INTER HÔTEL LES TILLEULS**

7 pl. de la Pyrotechnie. **Off map C3-2**
☎ 02.48.20.49.04 ▶ 02.48.50.61.73
📧 lestilleurls.bourges@wanadoo.fr
Closed 24 Dec–2 Jan. **Disabled access. Swimming pool. Garden. TV. Car park**.

The hotel is on a little square just out of the centre but will suit very well if you're tired or desperate for peace and quiet. It has a beautiful garden and pretty rooms with bath. The

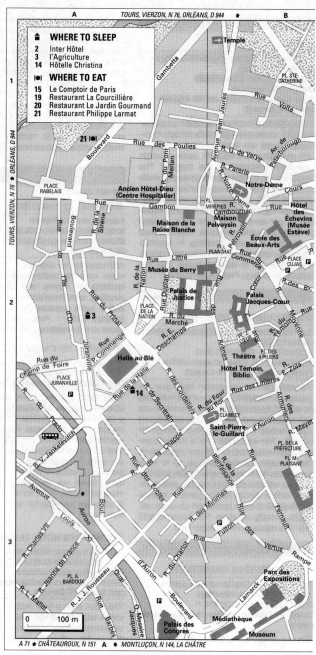

TOURS, VIERZON, N 76, ORLÉANS, D 944

WHERE TO SLEEP
2   Inter Hôtel
3   l'Agriculture
14 Hôtelle Christina

WHERE TO EAT
15 Le Comptoir de Paris
19 Restaurant La Courcillière
20 Restaurant Le Jardin Gourmand
21 Restaurant Philippe Larmat

Temple
PL. STE-CATHERINE

Gambetta

Rue   Volta

Boulevard   Rue des Poulies

21

PLACE RABELAIS

Avenue Jean Jaurès
R. G. de Varye
Av. de Peterborough
R. Pareria
Notre-Dame
Cours

Ancien Hôtel-Dieu
(Centre Hospitalier)

Rue   Gambon

Rue de la Sirène

Boulevard   Rue de Pila

Maison de la
Reine Blanche

PL. MIREPIED
R. Cambournac
Maison
Pelvoysin
Hôtel
des
Échevins
(Musée
Estève)

École des
Beaux-Arts

PL. PLANCHAT
Rue du Commerce
Rue des Cujas
PLACE CUJAS

Littré

Musée du Berry

Palais de
Justice

Rue Dupian
PLACE DE LA NATION
R. de la Nation
R. du Marché

Palais
Jacques-Cœur

PLACE
DE LA
NATION

R. E. Deschamps

Arènes
PL. J. CŒUR

R. du Primal
Rue Commengé
Juranville

Théâtre
PL. DES 4 PILIERS
R. E. Zola

Halle au Blé

Hôtel Témoin,
Biblio.

Rue du
Champ de Foire
PLACE JURANVILLE

Rue de la Halle
R. de Secretain
14

Rue des Cordeliers
Rue des Linières

R. du Four
au Roi
PL. CLAMECY

R. V. Jankelevitch

Rue de la Chappe
Rue des Écoles

Saint-Pierre-
le-Guillard

PL. DE LA
PRÉFECTURE

PL. M.
PLAISANT

Avenue   Louis
Auron
Bour.

R. Charles VII
R. Jeanne de France

R. L. Mallet

R. de la
Bienfaisance

R. des Minimes

Fernault

Rue des Vertus
Rampe

Rue   d'Auron
R. du Chariot

Parc des
Expositions

PL. A.
BARDOUX
Quai   R. J. J. Rousseau
R. Barbès
Q. Messire Jacques

Boulevard
Lamarck

Médiathèque

Muséum

0   100 m

Palais des
Congrès

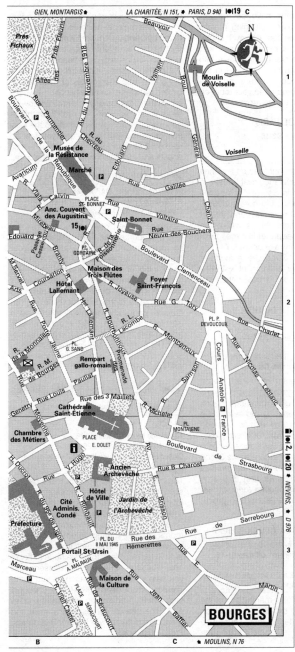

rooms and bathrooms have been refurbished, and there's air-conditioning in eighteen of them; doubles cost €55 with shower/wc or bath. The mini-bars are well stocked, but if you prefer to wind down with physical exercise you can work out in the gym, swim in the pool or hire a mountain bike. Meals can be brought to your room on a tray. 10% discount on the room rate.

|●| LE COMPTOIR DE PARIS

1 rue Édouard-Vaillant. **MAP B2-15**
☎ 02.48.24.17.16
Car park.

This place is painted bright red so it stands out from the wonderful medieval houses in the prettiest square in Bourges. Inside the décor is wood, so it's a bit more subdued. There's a friendly atmosphere and lots of animated conversation; this is where the lively and creative people of Bourges congregate. The speciality is andouillette à l'ancienne. There's a €12 formule, a menu at €15 and a meal for children at €4. The downstairs dining room is cosier than the one upstairs.

🎋 |●| RESTAURANT LE JARDIN GOURMAND

15 [bis] av. Ernest-Renan. **Off map C3-20**
☎ 02.48.21.35.91
Closed Sun evening, Mon, Tues lunchtime and 8–26 July. **Disabled access**. **Garden**. **Car park**.

This is a very pleasant restaurant, much appreciated by local gourmands who enjoy a good meal in delightful surroundings. Handsome building with panelling and beams; the dining room is decorated with flowers and watercolours on the walls. Staff are pleasant, the service is unobtrusive and the cooking shows the same refinement as the décor. Specialities include fish pot-au-feu, braised veal, house duck foie gras, fillet of beef in Chinon sauce and chocolate fondant. Set menus €14–37. You can eat in the garden, weather permitting. Free coffee.

🎋 |●| RESTAURANT LA COURCILLIÈRE

rue de Babylone; head for av. Marx-Dormoy and look for a narrow street off to the right. **Off map C1-19**
☎ 02.48.24.41.91
Closed Tues evening, Wed, and a fortnight in winter. **Disabled access**. **Car park**.

This magical, mysterious, marshy part of the region is watered by the river Yèvre, which runs directly alongside this restaurant – you can opt to dine on the terrace, admiring the waterlilies flowering at the water's edge. Inside, the regional dishes are lovingly prepared by Denis Julien; set menus at €15 and €21 feature excellent house terrines, frogs' legs, coq au vin with calf's head and couilles d'âne (don't worry – it's nothing more frightening than eggs in wine sauce). They've renovated the place, and the handsome wooden furniture, small aviary and copious flowers make it very easy on the eye. Everything's genuine here, from Annie's smile to the local accent of the gardeners, and you feel so relaxed that time just slips by. Free house apéritif and 10% discount on the room rate.

|●| RESTAURANT PHILIPPE LARMAT

62 [bis] bd. Gambetta. **MAP A1-21**
☎ 02.48.70.79.00
Closed Sun evening, Mon and 16 Aug–2 Sept.

Gourmet heaven courtesy of the culinary god Philippe Larmat. The pampering starts as you're guided gently to your place, your feet sinking into the deep pile of the carpet. There's lots of space around the tables and the colours are soft and subtle. Larmat's refined cooking produces well-balanced dishes: crispy zander with apples, pigeon en crépine, goat's cheese ravioli, lobster salad with fresh mint, red mullet in a sharp curry sauce. This is a well-known, stylish restaurant but it's not too fashionable for its own good. Menus €20–38 and children's menu €9 – good value for money.

SAINT-JUST   18340 (6KM SW)

🎋 🏠 |●| HÔTEL-RESTAURANT LE CHEVAL BLANC*

18 route de Bourges; take the N76.
☎ 02.48.25.62.18 ➡ 02.48.25.63.41
Closed Mon evening; Tues; the first 3 weeks in Jan. **Garden**. **Car park**.

The neon lights that edge the roof can be seen from some distance, making this place look like a motorway stopover. In fact, you find excellent cooking and a proper welcome. The hotel is comfortable and the rooms are well-soundproofed; doubles with shower/wc €28. The restaurant has a sort of "holiday club" feel: there's a huge buffet of hors-d'œuvres, cheeses and desserts and you help yourself to as much as you want. The self-service deal applies for the cheapest menu, at €10, and others are available up to €15. The service comes with a smile and great care is taken over the smallest details. Free house apéritif.

ALLOGNY 18110 (18KM NW)

|●| RESTAURANT LE CHABUR

route de Mehun-sur-Yèvre; take the D944 in the direction of Neuvy-sur-Barangeon.
☎ 02.48.64.00.41
Closed Wed, 23 Dec–15 Jan and 1–15 Sept. **Disabled access. Car park.**

The infamous witches of Berry were supposed to gather in the forest near here. They must have left something good behind – this is a rather nice place. Marie-Jo and Gérard serve tasty snacks, warm goat's cheese salads and cheese dishes including *fromage blanc* with herbs and cream. Lunch dishes are generously proportioned and of the order of *coq au vin* at lunchtime. Set menus €11–18 or around €16 *à la carte*.

BOURGUEIL 37140

♠ LE THOUARSAIS

10 pl. Hublin.
☎ 02.47.97.72.05
Closed Sun evening Oct–Easter; 5–20 Oct. **Garden.**

A simple yet well-maintained hotel in a quiet, centrally-located square. The rooms in the annexe are more comfortable and they look out over a garden. Doubles €24 with basin and €35–38 with shower or bath and wc. When the weather is warm, breakfast is served outside in the flower garden, which is full of tweeting birds. Other than these, animals are not welcome. Prices go down if you stay for more than three nights.

⚶|●| RESTAURANT L'AUBERGE LA LANDE

On the D35, follow the signs for the *cave touristique*.
☎ 02.47.97.92.41 ➡ 02.47.97.99.91
Closed Sun evening; Mon; Jan. **Car park.**

The restaurant, situated in a pleasant old house, stands a little way outside the village. Good honest traditional cooking with no pretentions; using fresh, seasonal, regional produce. Menus €13–24; dishes include a seafood *mousseline* with a crayfish *coulis*, trout fillet with a *julienne* of vegetables and lamb shank with Guérande sea salt. Meals are served out on the terrace. Free coffee.

BREZOLLES 28270

⚶ ♠ |●| LE RELAIS DE BREZOLLES**

4 rue Berg-op Zoom; it's on the outskirts of town, in the direction of Chartres.
☎ 02.37.48.20.84 ➡ 02.37.48.28.46
Closed Fri and Sun evenings, Mon lunchtime, the first fortnight in Aug and three weeks in Jan. **TV. Garden. Car park.**

When you first clap eyes on this large pink and brown inn with its window boxes overflowing with flowers, you might wonder if you've taken a wrong turning and ended up somewhere in the Black Forest. Whatever your confusion, though, the proprietors make you feel welcome and the rooms are comfortable (especially those that have been refurbished); €38 with bath/wc or €28 with shower. The décor in the restaurant is appealing and the range of set menus from €11 to €31 offer the added enticement of a few innovations among the local dishes. *À la carte*, you'll find enough interesting meat, fish and vegetables to satisfy any gourmet and the specialities change with the seasons. 10% discount on the room rate 1 Feb–30 May and Oct–Jan; free house apéritif with a meal.

MONTIGNY-SUR-AVRE 28270 (8KM NW)

⚶ ♠ |●| HÔTEL-RESTAURANT MOULIN DES PLANCHES**

How to get there; it's 10km from Brezolles on the D102.
☎ 02.37.48.25.97 ➡ 02.37.48.35.63
€ moulin.des.planches@wanadoo.fr
Closed Sun evening; Mon; Jan. **Disabled access. TV. Car park.**

This old flour mill looks like it's out of a picture book, but it can be found on the banks of the River Avre. It's been turned into a very handsome inn by an ex-farming couple. There's a friendly simplicity in the welcome – even the light has a special quality. Delightful, comfortable rooms €46–60. Set menus start at €18 with *terrine* and *fricassée* of chicken in cider, and with others €24–43. The chef specializes in *foie gras* and veal sweetbreads. Free apéritif.

BRIARE 45250

⚶|●| RESTAURANT LE BORD'EAU

19 rue de la Liberté; it's on the main street.
☎ 02.38.31.22.29
Closed Wed and Sun Dec–March.

This is a region of rivers and canals and, aptly, the chef puts lots of fish on the menu – braised salmon, sea bass with shallots, zander fillets *persillade* and bream in a

Sancerre sauce. The food is good and simple and portions are generous, as is the welcome – the *patronne* treats her guests like family. Set menus €15–30. Best to book. Free coffee.

BONNY-SUR-LOIRE   45420 (10KM SE)

≜ |●| LES VOYAGEURS

10 Grande-Rue (Centre).
☎ 02.38.27.01.45 ➡ 02.38.27.01.46
Hotel closed Sun evening, three weeks in the Feb school holidays and a fortnight Aug/Sept. **Restaurant closed** Sun evening, Mon and Tues lunchtime.
TV. Car park.

Given the prices – menus are listed at €13 (weekdays) and €21–34 – you might not realize that this is one of the best gourmet restaurants in the area. Philippe Lechauve is a local, but he was the chief *saucier* for the renowned Troisgros brothers for years; the prices are even more unbelievable given his pedigree. The cheapest menu lists *émincé* of calf's tongue, fillet of pollack with a *fondue* of chicory and sour cherry *charlotte*. He manages to provide such interesting dishes by simplifying the ingredients and relying on his talent to produce something wonderful. Take the second menu: *terrine* of monkfish cheeks, *croustillant* of cod joint with spices and celery *purée*, cheeses, and *chocolat fondant* – the chocolate oozes over the pistachio sauce as you cut the cake. There are also some decent wines on the list. Double rooms with shower/wc €31–44.

CHAMBORD   41250

⅍ ≜ |●| HÔTEL DU GRAND SAINT-MICHEL

Château de Chambord.
☎ 02.54.20.31.31 ➡ 02.54.20.36.40
Closed 15 Nov–20 Dec. **TV. Car park**.

This hotel is in an exceptional location opposite the château, and it boasts spacious, comfortable and pleasant rooms – even without the view. Doubles €45–50. The dining room is traditionally decorated, providing an appropriate setting for the cuisine, which includes salmon, zander with fennel seeds and wild boar stew in game season. Menus €17–22. Considerate, attentive service and a friendly welcome – not at all the mechanical toil you might expect in such a touristy place. In summer you can eat on the terrace with the château right in front of you. Book well in

advance. 10% discount on the room rate Oct–March.

SAINT-DYÉ-SUR-LOIRE   41500 (5KM N)

⅍ ≜ |●| LE MANOIR DE BEL-AIR

1 route d'Orléans.
☎ 02.54.81.60.10 ➡ 02.54.81.65.34
TV. Car park.

This old ivy-smothered building is on the banks of the Loire. It has a delightfully provincial feel and there's a lovely smell of beeswax polish. Rooms are honestly priced given the facilities and cleanliness: doubles go for €53–89. (The ones with a view of the river are the best.) The dining room, which also has the view, is bright and spacious. Specialities include salmon steak in Chinon sauce, *andouillette* braised in Sauvignon, scorpion fish *mousseline*, game and quail *à la Solognote*. Set menus €20–38. There's a track along the riverbank if you fancy a post-prandial walk. 10% discount on the room rate Oct–April.

MONT-PRÈS-CHAMBORD   41250 (10KM SW)

⅍ ≜ |●| HÔTEL-RESTAURANT LE SAINT FLORENT**

Le bourg; take the D33 to Huisseau then the D72.
☎ 02.54.70.81.00 ➡ 02.54.70.78.53
Closed Mon lunchtime and 1 Jan–8 –8 Feb. **Disabled access. Garden. TV**.

A neat hotel in the heart of the châteaux of the Loire just 8km from Cheverny. Bright, cheerful rooms at good prices: €34–58 with shower/wc or bath. They have a sauna. Weekday lunch menu at €13 and others up to €33. Their specialities are worth trying; pig's trotters *Solognote* (stuffed with *foie gras*), eel casserole with vegetables, pan-fried *foie gras* with honey vinegar. They make you feel pleased that you came. 10% discount on the room rate Nov–March.

CHARTRES   28000

⅍ ≜ |●| HÔTEL-RESTAURANT DE LA POSTE**

3 rue du Général-Kœnig (Centre); it's between the post office and the *Hôtel Grand Monarque*.
☎ 02.37.21.04.27 ➡ 02.37.36.42.17
✉ hotelposte.chartres@wanadoo.fr
Restaurant closed Fri and Sun evenings. **Disabled access. TV. Pay garage**.

A practical place to stay, given its excellent location. It's not exactly a bundle of laughs, but you can sleep well. Clean, comfortable rooms €52 with shower/wc, €56 with bath; some have a lovely view of the cathedral. Menus €14–26 in the restaurant; dishes include duck with honey and lemon, beef steak *à la Chartres* and zander fillet with pepper *sabayon*. The breakfast is particularly good. There's a charge for the garage. Free apéritif.

I●I BRASSERIE BRUNEAU

4 rue du Maréchal-de-Lattre-de-Tassigny; it's 30m from the town hall.
☎ 02.37.21.80.99
Closed Sat lunchtime, Sun and 5–21 Aug.

There's a 1940s atmosphere in this brasserie with its classic zinc-topped bar, bistro tables, benches covered in red velvet and posters advertising operettas covering the walls. Traditional food cooked using exclusively fresh produce, speedy yet relaxed service and a forthcoming, youthful welcome. Prices start with the €11 *formule*.

⅔ I●I AU P'TIT MORARD

25 rue de la Porte-Morard.
☎ 02.37.34.15.89
Closed Sun evening, Wed, a fortnight in Feb and three weeks end Jul.

No middle-class girl from a good family would have ventured into the lower end of town 25 years ago, but it's now the liveliest, friendliest, greenest, loveliest part of Chartres. It's full of attractive cafés, and everyone loves the old doorways and mill buildings. You'll be as happy inside the *P'tit Morard* as out on the terrace – where you pick up a buzz from the cheerful crowds in the street. Set lunch menu €14 during the week, others up to €22. Advisable to book. Free apéritif.

⅔ I●I LE DIX DE PYTHAGORE

2 rue de la Porte-Cendreuse; it's about 200m from the back of the cathedral.
☎ 02.37.36.02.38
Closed Sun evening, Mon and July.

Good old-fashioned classics – steak with truffles, ox kidneys, salmon *à la Dugléré*, snails flambéed with Sauvignon – are served up in the basement dining room under the watchful eye of the *patronne*. Good service and affordable prices make this place popular. Menus €14–22 or around €30 *à la carte*. Free apéritif.

I●I RESTAURANT LE SAINT-HILAIRE

11 rue du Pont-Saint-Hilaire; it's between pl. Saint-Pierre and pont Saint-Hilaire.
☎ and ➡ 02.37.30.97.57
Closed Sat and Mon lunchtimes; Sun; 28 Jul–18 Aug; 22 Dec–5 Jan.

You can't possibly go to Chartres without eating in this delightful little restaurant – it has just ten tables. Everything is of a piece: the welcome, the service, the cooking and the décor. Benoît Pasquier's family have been in the Beauce for five generations and he makes a point of showing off local produce to its best advantage. The dishes change with the seasons, though favourites such as *petit-gris* snails with a *fondue* of tomato and veal sweetbreads cooked in a haybox are available all year. Set menus €15–38. Good selection of wines at reasonable prices.

⅔ I●I LE MOULIN DE PONCEAU

21–23 rue de la Tannerie; it's below the collegiate church of Saint-André.
☎ 02.37.35.30.05
Closed Sat lunchtime and Sun evening.

Arguably the most attractive table in Chartres. It's in a romantic, charming situation on an arm of the river, just behind the cathedral. There's a terrace at the waterside and another made from an old wash-house – once numerous in these parts. It serves attentively and laboriously produced dishes that are a bit pricey but the setting adds considerably to the pleasure. Menus €20–38. Free coffee.

MAINTENON   28130 (18KM NE)

⅔ I●I LE BISTROT D'ADELINE

3 rue Collin-d'Harleville; it's in the main street, 100m from the chateau.
☎ 02.37.23.06.67
Closed Sun and Mon.

A little restaurant in a rustic style – evidenced by the old iron cooking pot in the entrance. It's one of the best in Maintenon both for its welcome and the family dishes the boss prepares. He's particularly famous for his calf's head and makes sauces that will never go out of fashion. It's essential to book because of the cheap €11 menu; others €19–23. Free apéritif.

CHÂTEAUDUN   28200

🏠 I●I LE SAINT-LOUIS**

41 rue de la République (East).
☎ 02.37.45.00.01 ➡ 02.37.45.16.09
TV. Garden. Car park.

Ben Maamar pulled off quite a stunt in a very

few years, first by turning a ruin into a decent, comfortable hotel and then by adding a restaurant and a brasserie next door. Menus in the traditional restaurant are €15, grills €9–15 and pizzas €5–10. For an encore, he opened up a brasserie next door which is *the* place to eat in Châteaudun, especially in summer when the piano bar gets going outdoors. It's the loveliest terrace in town. Mussels, salads, grills – dishes to satisfy all tastes at €14–23. A real success. And the hotel rooms are fairly priced, at €40 for doubles with shower/wc or bath.

|●| LA LICORNE

6 pl. du 18-Octobre (Centre); it's in the main square.
☎ 02.37.45.32.32
Closed Tues evening; Wed; 20 Dec–15 Jan; a week in June.

The dining room is long and narrow and decorated in salmon pink. You'll find solid cooking in big portions; dishes include pan-fried skirt of beef with shallots, chicken in mushroom sauce, oysters and leeks *au gratin*, breast of duck with orange and honey and – if you're famished – a *millefeuille* of *crêpes*. They've only got two people to wait tables, so when things get busy they are a bit pushed. Nice terrace on sunny days. Set weekday menu €11, then others €13–27.

|●| AUX TROIS PASTOUREAUX

31 rue André-Gillet (South); it's between pl. du 18-Octobre and espace Malraux.
☎ 02.37.45.74.40
Closed Sun evening; Mon; Thurs evening; 29 April–8 May; 29 July–13 Aug.

This is the oldest inn in Châteaudun and there's a calm atmosphere – choose between the simply set tables in the green dining room and a seat in the sun on the terrace. There's a wide variety of *à la carte* dishes, including some unusual ones – *petit-gris* snails with oyster mushrooms and Szechuan peppercorns, roast pigeon stuffed with wheat and lemon juice, veal kidneys in Chenonceau sauce, and so on – this is sophisticated cooking. €19 weekday lunch menu, then others €25–58.

CHÂTEAUMEILLANT   18370

⌂ |●| HÔTEL-RESTAURANT LE PIET À TERRE**

21 rue du Château; it's next to the Gendarmerie.
☎ 02.48.61.41.74 ➡ 02.48.61.41.88
Closed Sun evening; Mon; Tues lunchtime; Jan–Feb.

TV. Car park.

A two-star hotel with a three-star restaurant. The dining room has blue shutters and a fine chimney place for open fires in winter and there's a new veranda too. Thierry Finet is passionate about cooking and he makes the bread and breakfast rolls on the premises. The cuisine is designed around fresh produce from the market and reflects the mood of the chef and the *menu tradition*, specializing in local dishes. Menus €19–69. The vegetables and herbs come from grandfather Piet's kitchen garden. The bedrooms are named after flowers. Doubles €43 with shower/wc or €53 with bath. No dogs admitted.

CHÂTEAUNEUF-EN-THYMERAIS   28170

⌂ |●| L'ÉCRITOIRE

43 rue Emile Vivier.
☎ 02.37.51.85.80 ➡ 02.37.51.86.87
Closed Sun evening; Mon; school holidays in Feb; Oct.

This is an old posthouse and the restaurant is one of the best places to eat in the Eure et Loire. Chef Luc Pasquier travelled widely in Asia, Africa and elsewhere before returning home. His cuisine is excellent in the classical style, which means he uses a lot of local produce: *petit-gris* snails, rabbit from Thimerais, honey from the Beauce. Impressive menus and the prices start very reasonably at €23. Expect to pay €38 for a meal *à la carte*, where you'll find some appetizing specialities like salmon *tartare* with yoghurt and fillet of roast lamb with a *croustille* of small snails. If you feel like staying, there are a few clean, simple rooms with balconies (€44) looking into the interior courtyard. Attentive welcome and perfect service.

SENONCHES   28250 (13KM W)

⋇ ⌂ |●| AUBERGE LA POMME DE PIN**

15 rue Michel Cauty; take the D928 to Digny then the D24.
☎ 02.37.37.76.62 ➡ 02.37.37.86.61
Closed Sun evening; Mon lunchtime; 25 Dec–25 Jan.
Garden. TV. Car park.

A half-timbered inn which used to be a posthouse on the edge of the Zandere area. Ten comfortable rooms from €46 with shower/wc. They serve good quality, wholesome food with an emphasis on local specialities like carp with crayfish, Chartres pâté, Zandereronne salad or game and wild mushrooms in season. Menus start at €14, then €16–38. Free coffee and 10% discount on the room rate from end Oct to end Feb.

CHÂTEAUROUX   36000

🏠 HÔTEL BONNET**

14 rue du Marché; it's not far from the town hall.
☎ 02.54.22.13.54 ➡ 02.54.07.56.78
📧 hotel-bonnet@wanadoo.fr
Closed Sun afternoon. **Disabled access. TV. Pay garage.**

The rooms are clean, comfortable and well looked-after and the place has a quiet family atmosphere. The extremely nice managers do a wonderful breakfast. Doubles €31 with basin/wc and €35 with shower/wc. There's access to a lock-up garage for a small fee.

🏠 HÔTEL LE BOISCHAUT**

135 av. de la Châtre (Southeast).
☎ 02.54.22.22.34 ➡ 02.54.22.64.89
Closed 27 Dec–7 Jan. **Disabled access. TV. Garage.**

Boischaut is the area around Châteauroux and it's where Gérard Depardieu comes from. The hotel has large, comfortable double rooms at €33–38 with shower/wc and €35–38 with bath. There are also some family rooms sleeping three or four. There are two drawbacks, though: it's a 20-minute walk from the centre and there's no restaurant – but there is a bar, and they provide a meal on a tray for €9 with a hot main dish, cheese and dessert. Free lock-up parking for two-wheelers.

🕏 🏠 ÉLYSÉE HÔTEL***

2 rue de la République (Centre); it's practically opposite the Équinoxe cultural centre.
☎ 02.54.22.33.66 ➡ 02.54.07.34.34
📧 elysee36@aol.com
Closed 24 Dec–2 Jan. **TV. Disabled access.**

An excellent little hotel run by a Norman couple who used to run a newsagent's. It's in the centre of town, with spotlessly clean, pleasant rooms; doubles €45–52. They've opened a salon-bar where they serve a good breakfast and offer wine tastings with wines at under €15 a bottle. Though there's no restaurant they offer a meal on a tray service. 10% discount at weekends and 1 July–15 Aug.

🕏 🍴 RESTAURANT LA CIBOULETTE

42 rue Grande (Centre).
☎ 02.54.27.66.28
Closed Sun, Mon, public holidays, 23 Dec–8 Jan, 30

April–5 May and 28 July–22 Aug.

This is Châteauroux's gourmet restaurant – everybody dines here. It has pleasant décor and friendly service, and the menus have been thoughtfully put together. There's a weekday menu at €15 and others at €19–32; they include such local specialities as *couilles d'âne* (eggs poached in red wine and shallot sauce), *foie gras* and lentil terrine, roast pigeon with balsamic vinegar and vanilla Bavarois. The "Premier cru" and "Grand cru" menus include a glass of wine. Around fifteen wines are sold by the glass; some local ones are produced by vineyards owned by Gérard Depardieu (who lives nearby). 20% discount on the price of a meal when you show your guide in advance.

🕏 🍴 LE BISTROT GOURMAND

10 rue du Marché (Centre).
☎ 02.54.07.86.98
Closed Sun, Mon lunchtime, a fortnight in Feb and three weeks in Aug/Sept.

The dining room is bright yellow and soft green – it's really cheerful. A huge blackboard displays the dishes of the day and they only use fresh produce here: *foie gras* of duck with sea salt, rib of beef for two, duck thigh *confit* on a bed of oyster mushrooms, *tarte tatin*, pear soup with preserved orange. You'll pay around €20 *à la carte*. Free house apéritif.

DÉOLS   36130 (2KM N)

🍴 L'ESCALE VILLAGE

How to get there: it's on the N20.
☎ 02.54.22.03.77 ➡ 02.54.22.56.70

This restaurant attracts people of all ages from across the region – whole families crowd in. Good traditional dishes include seafood platter, sole *meunière*, beef with shallots and *moules marinière*. Menus start at €10, then go up to €24. They serve excellent draught beer as well as white Reuilly and Valençay. Long-distance lorry drivers prefer the brasserie where they can watch TV while they eat. It's open round the clock – you never know who you'll bump into. A lively, vibrant place.

COINGS   36130 (8KM N)

🏠 🍴 LE RELAIS SAINT-JACQUES***

How to get there: take exit 12 off the A20 going in the direction of the airport, then Coings. Turn left before Céré.

☎ 02.54.60.44.44 ➡ 02.54.60.44.00
Restaurant closed Sun evening. **TV. Garden. Car park**.

Don't let the dreary setting near the airport put you off: this modern hotel is pleasant, comfortable and quiet. Each of the 46 rooms is decorated differently and looks onto the garden or over the countryside at the rear. Doubles start at €49. But the establishment is best known for the excellent cuisine of the chef/proprietor, Pierre Jeanrot. The dishes change frequently and the lunchtime menu at €15 is the cheapest. In good weather, there's a more affordable brasserie service with carpaccio, tuna *tartare* and various salads served on the terrace.

LEVROUX   36110 (21KM NW)

𝒜 ≜ |O| HÔTEL-RESTAURANT DE LA CLOCHE**

3 rue Nationale; use the D956.
☎02.54.35.70.43 ➡ 02.54.35.67.43
Cosed Sun evening, Mon evening, Tues and 1–27 Feb.
TV. Car park.

The same family has run this friendly village inn since 1895 – and it's kept its friendly atmosphere. You'll get a really warm welcome and they've maintained their traditional approach to cooking: they make their own duck terrine with prunes and there's a good mixture of fish cooked with tarragon. Set menus €12–37. Rooms with handbasin €27; with shower/wc or bath €40. Free apéritif or coffee.

𝒜 |O| RESTAURANT RELAIS SAINT-JEAN

34 rue Nationale; it's near pl. de la Collégiale-de-Saint-Sylvain.
☎ 02.54.35.81.56
e acceuil.relais.saint.jean@wanadoo.fr
Closed Wed, Sun evening except public holidays, the last week in Feb and a fortnight in Oct.

The chef who owns this old coaching inn studied with Vergé, and he's made this one of the best restaurants in the Indre départements. His skilful use of first-rate ingredients, and the charming welcome you get from his wife, make for a winning combination. The dining room is pleasant and from some tables you have a view of the chef in his spotless kitchen. In summer you can admire the dramatic sunsets over the Saint-Sylvain collegiate church from the terrace. There's a menu at €14 (not served on Sun or public holidays), and others are €20–34 with an impressive children's menu at €10 including a drink. Specialities include scallop ravioli with a cep sauce, fillet of beef with *foie gras*

and *marbré* with two chocolates. The cooking is judged to perfection and practically sings with flavour. Free coffee.

BUZANÇAIS   36500 (25KM NW)

𝒜 ≜ |O| HÔTEL-RESTAURANT L'HERMITAGE**

Route d'Argy–Écueille; take the N143 then follow the signs for Argy.
☎02.54.84.03.90 ➡ 02.54.02.13.19
Hotel closed first fortnight of Jan and 9–18 Sept.
Restaurant closed Sun evening and Mon. **TV. Garden. Car park. Pay garage**.

It really is as peaceful as a hermitage. The hotel is covered in Virginia creeper and overlooks a broad expanse of greenery on the banks of the Indre. There's a big kitchen garden and a really nice terrace. Bedrooms in the main building have been carefully decorated and have a view of the grounds. The ones in the annexe are slightly less attractive, but they too have been redecorated and overlook the courtyard. Comfortable double rooms with bath or shower/wc €40–57. Set menus at €15 (not Sun) and others €20–47. The cooking is fairly sophisticated, featuring specialities from Berry and the Landes with lots of fish. 10% discount if you stay half board 1 Nov–30 March.

CHÂTILLON-SUR-INDRE   36700

𝒜 ≜ |O| L'AUBERGE DE LA TOUR**

2 route du Blanc.
☎ 02.54.38.72.17 ➡ 02.54.38.74.85
TV. Garden. Car park.

A lovely seventeenth-century house which has been nicely renovated; there are flowers everywhere. In summer, people eat on the terrace rather than in the rustic dining room, which has a fireplace and exposed beams. The chef's specialities include fillet of beef in Chinon wine sauce, zander with sorrel, gratinéed fish flavoured with curry and veal escalope *forestière*. Set menus €13–34 and a children's menu at €8. Rooms are decorated in up-to-date style and have bathrooms; they're €26 with shower or €40 with bath. 10% discount on the room rate.

MÉZIÈRES-EN-BRENNE   36290 (20KM S)

≜ |O| HÔTEL-RESTAURANT AU BŒUF COURONNÉ**

9 pl. Charles-de-Gaulle; it's on the D43.
☎ 02.54.38.04.39 ➡ 02.54.38.02.84

Closed Sun evening and Mon except public holidays, and 20 Nov–31 Jan. **TV**.

The gateway that leads you into this former coaching inn dates from the middle of the sixteenth century. In the restaurant, try the carp with shellfish butter, carp *rillettes* with onion marmalade, frogs' legs, fried smelt, pigeon breasts, game in season and iced nougat with Brenne honey. The dining room is a little old-fashioned and lacking in warmth. Set menus from €14 (not available Sun) to €38. Children's menu – for under eights – is €7. Doubles with shower/wc €37. It's best to book at the weekend.

CHÂTRE (LA)   36400

⊀ ☎ HÔTEL NOTRE-DAME**

4 pl. Notre-Dame (South).
☎ 02.54.48.01.14 ➠ 02.54.48.31.14
Disabled access. Garden. TV. Car park.

La Châtre is a very pleasant town to live in, and this hotel is a similarly nice place to stay. It's in a fifteenth-century building with a flower-filled balcony. They've painted the spacious bedrooms cream – some are particularly big and well laid-out. It overlooks a quiet little square that echoes with birdsong. Doubles €38 with shower/wc, €41 with bath. There's a private garden with a terrace. Hotels like this are rare. 10% discount Jan–May.

NOHANT-VIC   36400 (6KM N)

☎ |●| L'AUBERGE DE LA PETITE FADETTE***

pl. du Château; it's on the D943.
☎ 02.54.31.01.48 ➠ 02.54.31.10.19
TV. Garden. Car park.

This beautiful building, covered in Virginia creeper, is totally in keeping with the world of novelist George Sand, who spent the greater part of her life in Nohant. The bedrooms are very prettily decorated in assorted shades of blue. Doubles with shower/wc from €53 and with bath €76–92.The nineteenth-century wood panelling in the dining room has a gleaming patina, a pendulous chandelier and is hung with Aubusson tapestry. Menus €14–38 with tasty, classic dishes.

SAINT-CHARTIER   36400 (8.5KM N)

⊀ ☎ |●| HÔTEL-RESTAURANT LA VALLÉE BLEUE***

Route de Verneuil.

☎ 02.54.31.01.91 ➠ 02.54.34.04.48
Restaurant closed Mon and Tues lunchtimes.
Hotel closed Tues lunchtime March to end April, and Oct. **Swimming pool**. **Garden**. **TV**. **Car park**.

This house, once owned by George Sand's doctor, has been wonderfully converted, retaining many original features. Everything is in keeping – the dining rooms, the lounge and the bedrooms. You'll have a pleasurable stay here and the restaurant is pretty good too. Set menus at €27, €38 and €45, so there's a lot of choice. À la carte lists a dish for vegetarians and the specialities change regularly; try the medallions of crayfish tail "George Sand", poached eggs with creamed lentils, smoked duck breast, *civet* with fresh noodles, chocolate *fondant* with sour cherries in Kirsch or honey ice-cream. Children's menu €12. There are two terraces and a swimming pool in nine acres of grounds. Very comfortable rooms €60–98 with shower/wc or €65–111 with bath. Free house apéritif.

LYS-SAINT-GEORGES   36230 (23KM NW)

⊀ |●| LA FORGE

How to get there: take the D927 in the direction of Neuvy-Saint-Sépulcre and then the D74. It's opposite the château.
☎ 02.54.30.81.68
Closed Mon, Tues from Sept to June, three weeks in Jan and a fortnight in Oct.

Service noon–2pm and 7.30–9.30pm. This rather good inn is the only commercial enterprise in a village of 180 souls. It has handsome beams, pictures by local artists, an open fire in winter and a terrace with a pergola in summer where you can enjoy the peace, the quiet and the birdsong. The *patronne* is friendly and very witty, and her husband, the chef, prepares tasty classic dishes with clearly marked flavours. These change regularly with the seasons – though there are a few constants like grilled goat's cheese salad, duck *foie gras* and braised duckling in honey. The cheapest menu at €15, served on weekdays, is substantial, and there are others €23–37. Children's menu €8. Free house apéritif.

CHAUMONT-SUR-THARONNE   41600

|●| RESTAURANT LA GRENOUILLÈRE

Route de La Ferté-Saint-Aubin; take the Chaumont exit and follow the signs for La Ferté-Saint-Aubin.
☎ 02.54.88.50.71
Closed Mon evening and Tues except in July–Aug.

Garden. Car park.

An old house, deep in the forest, which has been converted into a luxurious country inn. It's surrounded by a wildlife park where peacocks and Japanese golden pheasants shimmer in the sunlight. Meals are served in a glassed-in terrace from where you can see the lake, which is full of golden carp, moorhens, swans and forty different species of wild duck. There is a set weekday menu at €15 and others are €24–35. You get a choice: *terrine* of duck *foie gras*, boned quail stuffed with *foie gras* and truffle *jus*, veal fillet with Roquefort cheese, *pot-au-feu* terrine with creamed chives. Your post-prandial stroll in the garden will take you past the aviaries and their exotic occupants.

CHENONCEAUX   37150

🏠🍽️ RESTAURANT AU GÂTEAU BRETON

16 rue du Docteur-Bretonneau (Centre); it's in the main street.
☎ 02.47.23.90.14
Closed Tues and Wed evenings in season, Tues evening and Wed out of season, and Christmas–New Year's Day.

A large terrace for the summer and a small dining room for the winter. Menus €10–18, for which you get a cold or a hot starter and a main course from their specialities: chicken *à la tourangelle* with green beans and haricot beans, *andouillette* with Vouvray wine, rabbit *chasseur* or *coq au vin* – all of which are delicious and served generously. Nice welcome. Free house apéritif or coffee.

CIVRAY-DE-TOURAINE   37150 (1KM W)

🏠🍽️ L'HOSTELLERIE DU CHÂTEAU DE L'ISLE**

☎ 02.47.23.63.60 ➔ 02.47.23.64.62
📧 chateaudelisle@wanadoo.fr
Restaurant closed lunchtime (unless you book). **Car park**.

The staff go to a lot of trouble to make you feel welcome in this beautiful eighteenth-century house. It has ten comfortable rooms with shower/wc or bath ranging in price from €53 to €92. All the rooms are different so ask to see them and choose the one that suits. The chef prepares first-rate dishes with the freshest produce from the market and prices reflect this quality, starting with a *menu-carte* at €26. There are two dining rooms, both with an open fireplace. You can eat on the terrace and then go for a stroll in the tree-filled grounds, or go on a boat trip on the Cher.

CHINON   37500

🏠🏢 LE POINT DU JOUR

102 quai Jeanne d'Arc; you get there via the Quai de la Vienne.
☎ 02.47.93.07.20
Closed 10 Dec–4 Jan. **TV**.

This simple, quiet hotel has eight rooms and is positioned above a bar. It's easy to find a parking space across the road, on the banks of the Vienne. This is a really good place which has appeared in this guide for ten consecutive years, and it won't let you down. The owners have kept standards high: the rooms are very clean, some have a view of the river, while others, higher up the house, have Velux windows. Doubles €20 with wash basin, €27 with shower/wc or €29 with bath. 10% discount out of season.

🏢 HÔTEL DIDEROT**

4 rue Buffon; it's away from the centre, 100m from pl. Jeanne-d'Arc.
☎ 02.47.93.18.87 ➔ 02.47.93.37.10
Closed mid-Jan to mid-Feb.
Disabled access. TV. Car park.

Through the big gateway at the end of the courtyard you'll see a very handsome eighteenth-century house covered in Virginia creeper. Inside there's a fifteenth-century fireplace, an eighteenth-century staircase and beams everywhere. It's all very lovely. The 28 cosy rooms are all decorated differently, and range in price from €47 to €62. Breakfast comes with wonderful preserves. Very professional and welcoming greeting. Note that the car park closes at 10pm. 20% discount Nov–March.

🏢🍽️ HÔTEL DE FRANCE – RESTAURANT AU CHAPEAU ROUGE***

47–49 pl. du Général-de-Gaulle; (Centre).
☎ 02.47.93.33.91 ➔ 02.47.98.37.03
📧 elmachinon@aol.com
Closed Sun evening, Mon, 15 Feb–9 March and 15–30 Nov. **TV. Pay car park**.

This beautiful sixteenth-century building has been pleasantly renovated and is now a *Best Western* hotel. The rooms are comfortable – some have views of the château and the rue Voltaire, a pedestrianized medieval street. Doubles with shower or bath €61–89. The public spaces are pleasant, with little seating areas here and there. Banana, orange, lemon and bay trees grow in the Mediterranean garden in the inner courtyard. Traditional dishes predominate in the restaurant, with specialities such as zander with beurre blanc, duck terrine with *foie gras*, braised lamb's sweetbreads with white truffle and pears with Chinon wine preserve. Menus start at €21. Free house apéritif and 10% discount Oct–March.

AVOINE   37420 (5KM N)

🛐 🛏 |●| HÔTEL LA GIRAUDIÈRE – RESTAURANT LE PETIT PIGEONNIER**

Beaumont-en-Véron; take the D749 towards Beaumont for about 4km, turn left at Domaine de la Giraudière and the restaurant is 800m further on.
☎ 02.47.58.40.36 ➡ 02.47.58.46.06
e giraudiere@hotels-france.com
Disabled access. TV. Car park.

This delightful country seat of some seventeenth-century gentleman has been made into an incredibly peaceful hotel; the sixteenth-century dovecote has been turned into a sitting room and library with a piano. 25 rooms with shower/wc or bath go for €31–53. Good gourmet cooking at affordable prices is served in the restaurant; menus €18–35. Half board ranges in price from €32 to €63 per person. They've also got Internet access. Free house apéritif or coffee.

COMBREUX   45530

🛐 🛏 |●| L'AUBERGE DE COMBREUX**

35 route du Gâtinais. Take the D10 then the D9; it's on the outskirts of the village.
☎ 02.38.46.89.89 ➡ 02.38.59.36.19
Closed Mon lunchtime and 15 Dec–25 Jan. **Swimming pool. TV. Car park**.

This magnificent nineteenth-century coaching inn, swathed in ivy and Virginia creeper, has been thoughtfully refurbished. There's a cosy little sitting room with an open fire and a rustic dining room with a veranda overlooking the flower garden. In fine weather you can sit under the trees. Weekday menu €17 and others up to €32. Well-prepared dishes include house *terrines*, escalope of *foie gras*, veal kidneys with raspberry vinegar, game in season, warm fruit tarts and a Grand Marnier soufflé. The bedrooms are in the main building or in one of the little annexes hidden among the trees. They're delightful, with flower-sprigged wallpaper, beams and large wardrobes. Prices from €50 with shower/wc to €60 with bath. Half board, compulsory at weekends and May–Oct, costs €60 per person. You can hire a bike to explore the Orléans forest nearby and there's a tennis court and a heated swimming pool. It's one of the best hotels around. 10% discount on the room rate.

COUR-CHEVERNY   41700

🛐 🛏 |●| HÔTEL-RESTAURANT DES TROIS MARCHANDS**

rue Nationale (Centre); it's on the main street next to the church.
☎ 02.54.79.96.44 ➡ 02.54.79.25.60
Closed Mon and early Feb to mid-March. **Garden. TV. Car park**.

This half-timbered village inn has a lot of charm. 36 rooms, some overlooking the garden, from €27 with basin, €41 with shower/wc and €55 with bath. Avoid the rooms in the annexe across the way if you can. The cooking has earned the place a good reputation. In the dining room specialities include frogs' legs with garlic and herbs, sea bream in a sea-salt crust, roast pigeon with truffle *jus* and game. The other one serves traditional dishes and grills. Menus €20 (not Sun lunch), €31 and €43, with a children's menu at €8. 10% discount on the room rate.

🛐 |●| RESTAURANT LE POUSSE-RAPIÈRE

5 rue du Chêne-des-Dames (Centre); it's opposite the path that leads to the château.
☎ 02.54.79.94.23
Closed Tues, Wed and 1 Dec–30 Jan **Disabled access**.

You'll get a friendly welcome in this comfortable restaurant. The choice of good, original dishes includes goat's cheese quiche, *foie gras* with grapes, *paupiette* of zander in a chard and bacon parcel, pike with smoked bacon and goat's cheese sauce, shin of beef in Cheverny wine and game in season. Set lunch menu €12 and then €18–26, with a children's menu at €8. Free coffee.

DREUX   28100

🛏 HÔTEL LE BEFFROI**

12 pl. Métézeau (Centre).
☎ 02.37.50.02.03 ➡ 02.37.42.07.69
Closed Sun noon–5.30pm and 29 July–10 Aug. **TV**.

This is a good place to spend the night when you're just passing through, with its bright, quiet, comfortable rooms overlooking the river or the square (where there's an underground garage). Doubles with shower/wc €54; some rooms sleep three.

🛐 |●| AUX QUATRE VENTS

18 pl. Métézeau (Centre).

☎ 02.37.50.03.24
Closed evenings except Sat and during the summer.

They've given this bistro a good retro look. The best options are the menus where you help yourself to as many *hors-d'œuvres* from the buffet as you like: choose from salmon, shellfish, excellent *charcuterie* and *crudités*. Follow that with a main course like rack of veal *à l'ancienne* or roast chicken, then finish with dessert. Prices range from €18 to 22. Make the most of the terrace when the weather's good. Free apéritif.

VERNOUILLET   28500 (3KM S)

☎ |●| AUBERGE DE LA VALLÉE VERTE

6 rue Lucien-Dupuis; it's in the centre near the church.
☎ 02.37.46.04.04 ➡ 02.37.42.91.17
Closed Sun, Mon, 1–24 Aug and 24 Dec–8 Jan. **TV. Car park**.

This recently refurbished hotel offers cosy rooms with all amenities for €60. But the big draw is the cooking: there's a brigade of professionals in the kitchen and they produce classic cuisine using locally farmed produce and fresh seasonal fish. Menus start at €22. You can dine either in the pretty rustic dining room or under the eaves on the mezzanine. There's an intimate atmosphere and a convivial, smiling welcome. It's best to book at weekends.

FERTÉ-SAINT-AUBIN (LA)   45240

|●| L'AUBERGE DES CHASSEURS

34 rue des Poulies; it's in a street behind the tourist office.
☎ 02.38.76.66.95
Closed Mon evening and Tues.

This place used to be a hunting lodge and the name stuck – along with some of the culinary traditions. In other words, you'll get a warm welcome and in season you'll be served game in front of the impressive fireplace. The food is good, simply cooked and served in generous portions. There's a dish of the day at €9, a weekday menu at €11 and others at €16 and €24. One departure from local tradition is the mussel menu which offers mussels, chips and beer for €8.

MÉNESTREAU-EN-VILLETTE   45240 (7KM E)

🏕️|●| LE RELAIS DE SOLOGNE

63 place du 8-Mai; take the D17 from La Ferté-Saint-Aubin.
☎ 02.38.76.97.40 ➡ 02.3849.60.43
Closed Sun evening, Wed and the first week in Sept.

Thierry Roger runs this place. He's the chef

and one of the virtuosos of French gastronomic cooking. The dining room is traditional for the Sologne region: red brick walls, substantial beams, soft, warm lighting and an abundance of fresh flowers and plants – a harmonious setting for the refined local dishes. The menus change frequently and make the most of seasonal produce: pressed quail with vintage port, *foie gras* with Muscat, poached white fillet of zander with preserved tomatoes and basil. The desserts are so good they'll make you weep for joy – try the aptly-entitled mandarine chocolate tears or the strawberry soup with Kummel honey. Exquisite wines. Menus start at €15 and go up to €44. Free coffee.

MARCILLY-EN-VILLETTE   45240 (8KM NE)

☎ |●| AUBERGE DE LA CROIX BLANCHE*

118 pl. de l'Église; take the N20 and then the D921.
☎ 02.38.76.10.14 ➡ 02.38.76.10.67
Closed Fri, 13 Feb–5 March and 15–31 Aug.
TV. Garden. Car park.

When this inn opened in the seventeenth century a sign went up: "Tapholot, wigmaker, serves drink and food; soup with vegetables at any time. We also cut hair". It's good to know that the sign's still there – and though they've stopped cutting hair, they still sell food. A *menu-ouvrier* is served in the bar, and you can also buy a newspaper. It's best to book. In the pleasant dining room, you'll get good-natured service and traditional dishes prepared by a skilled chef. The menus, €16–20, change almost daily because the chef is uncompromising when it comes to the quality of his raw ingredients; you'd come back just for the desserts. The pleasant, simple rooms overlook the Place de l'Église, which looks like it comes from another era. Rooms €31 with basin and €41 with bath or shower/wc. Half board costs €46 per person.

FERTÉ-VIDAME (LA)   28340

|●| LA TRIGALLE*

How to get there: coming from Verneuil, as you come into the village it's on the right at a crossroads.
☎ 06.12.97.82.00
Closed Mon and Tues except public holidays, and from the second week in Jan to the third week in Feb.
Garden. Car park.

This restaurant is a real pleasure: classical music plays in the restaurant but Emmanuel's cooking is far from classical. He invents delicious concoctions, changing the specialities on a regular basis: fillets of red mullet with preserved lemon and basil oil, quails with truffles, steamed turbot steak with *andouille de Vire*, olive paste with duck breast, honey ice-cream with almond crackling, Bavarois with sweet wine and raspberry and basil coulis. Set weekday lunch menu at €10 and others €15–21, all of them good and generously served. The wine list is exceptional and, if you're feeling flush, there are a number of bottles with four-figure prices! Saint-Simon, the famous eighteenth-century diarist who chronicled events at the court of Louis XIV, had a château here. It's in ruins now but it's worth a visit – the grounds are enormous.

GIEN 45500

☎ SANOTEL**

21 quai de Sully; it's on the left Loire riverbank, opposite the château.
☎ 02.38.67.61.46 ➡ 02.38.67.13.01
Disabled access. Garden. TV. Car park.

This is a fairly ordinary two-star hotel on the banks of the Loire, but the prices make it stand out: a double with air-conditioning and bath costs €35 and there's a clear view of the town, huddled at the foot of the château. The rooms overlooking the garden are quieter. Nice welcome. The Italian brasserie in the hotel is run by separate management.

|●| RESTAURANT LE RÉGENCY

6 quai Lenoir; it faces the Loire, near the bridge.
☎ 02.38.67.04.96
Closed Sun evening, Wed, the Feb school holidays, a fortnight 1–15 July and Christmas.

The restaurant specializes in freshwater fish from the Loire as well as local dishes cooked simply and with care: chicken liver *terrine* with sour cherries, duckling fillet with thyme, haddock with red pepper sauce, snail *fricassée* with oyster mushrooms, zander fillet with sorrel sauce and *foie gras terrine*. Prices are reasonable with menus €14–34. The terrace is on the banks of the river – but there's a road running in front of it.

ILLIERS-COMBRAY 28120

|●| LE FLORENT

13 pl. du Marché; it's near the church.
☎ 02.37.24.10.43 ➡ 02.37.24.11.78
Closed Sun, Mon and Wed evenings except on public holidays. **Disabled access**.

An elegant, unpretentious restaurant – they don't flog the Proust connection to death. The little dining rooms are delightful, and Hervé Priolet is an excellent and imaginative chef whose speciality is fish. There are tempting set menus at €18 (Mon–Fri except public holidays) and €27–48 – but, yes, one is named after Proust. They offer a wide range of dishes priced from €12 to 18.

ISSOUDUN 36100

🏃 ☎ |●| HÔTEL DE FRANCE – RESTAURANT LES TROIS ROIS**

3 rue Pierre-Brossolette (Centre).
☎ 02.54.21.00.65 ➡ 02.54.21.50.61
Closed Sun evening, Mon evening except July–Aug, the first fortnight in Feb and the last three weeks in Sept.
TV. Car park.

Most rooms here are large and spotlessly clean but there are some smaller ones which could do with a makeover. All the doubles have en-suite bath and cost €44. The dining room is comfortable and stylish, with superb mirrors, *fleur-de-lys* wallpaper and woodwork showing the patina of age – but it gets unpleasantly smoky when it's full. You'll get an exuberant welcome from the owner, a very efficient woman who keeps an eye on everything. The cooking is conventional but doesn't disappoint. Weekday menu at €14 and others €15–21. Specialities include calf's head *à l'ancienne*, duck breast with Berry honey, house *foie gras* cooked in a cloth and a tureen of crayfish. In fine weather they serve on a flower-filled terrace overlooking the courtyard. Free house apéritif.

🏃 ☎ |●| HÔTEL-RESTAURANT LA COGNETTE***

2 bd. Stalingrad; take the N151, go into the town centre and it's near the big marketplace.
☎ 02.54.21.21.83 ➡ 02.54.03.13.03
📧 alain.nonnet@wanadoo.com
Closed Sun evening and Mon except public holidays and during summer; Jan. **TV. Disabled access**.

Balzac gives a very vivid description of this hotel in *La Rabouilleuse*. Then, it was run by a pair called Cognet and a widow from Houssaye who had a reputation as a fine cook. Nowadays the kitchens are in the hands of Alain Nonnet and his son-in-law, Jean-Jacques Daumy, and they're reputed to be some of the best in the area. The dining room décor is a mixture of Empire, Restoration and

Louis-Philippe, which would have delighted Balzac. He'd also have liked the way the ornaments, wall-hangings and pictures look as if they've just been put there – though the formality may feel a bit awkward if you're dining alone. Set menus €25–54. The hotel rooms are comfortable and perfect in every particular; they even supply a dressing gown and hairdryer. Doubles €75 with bath. Each room has its own terrace where you can have breakfast in fine weather and enjoy the scent of roses. It thoroughly deserves its three stars. Free apéritif.

⅍ I●I LE PILE OU FACE

rue Danielle-Casanova (Centre).
☎ 02.54.03.14.91
Closed Sun evening, Mon, the Feb school holidays and 15 Aug–early Sept.

Whether you choose to eat in the conventional dining room or out on the more pleasant covered terrace, the menus are the same. Weekday lunch menu €13, then €20–49. Children have their own menu for €7. Specialities include *cassolette berrichonne*, lobster *croquant*, veal kidneys with Pinot Gris and zander with herbs. Free coffee with all menus.

DIOU   36260 (12KM N)

I●I L'AUBERGEADE

Route d'Issoudun; by the D918, heading for Vierzon.
☎ 02.54.49.22.28
Closed Wed and Sun evenings. **Disabled access**.

A warm welcome, a pretty terrace, a pleasant, comfortable dining room and beautifully simple cooking – though inside the tables are rather packed. Menus run from €15 to €33 and there's one for children at €11. Dishes have the aroma of oriental cuisine. On the cheapest menu, starters might be quail *terrine*, then Thai fish curry with coconut milk or pan-fried farmhouse chicken with rosemary *jus*, followed by well-ripened cheeses and the house dessert of the day. Their specialities include stewed monkfish cheek Thai curry and laqueured half-duck with sweet spices and ginger.

BRIVES   36100 (13KM S)

⅍ I●I RESTAURANT LE CÉSAR, CHEZ NICOLE

Centre; take the D918; it's beside the church.
☎ 02.54.49.04.43
Closed Mon.

There are remains of the old dyke built by

Caesar's legions close to this restaurant, and it's also near to the village church. The ceiling of the large dining room is supported by enormous beams. Weekday menu at €9 and others €10–14 or around €20 *à la carte*. Try the house *terrine César*, calf's head with lentils or *coq au vin* with potatoes. Free apéritif.

LANGEAIS   37130

⅍ ⛊ I●I HÔTEL-RESTAURANT ERRARD-HOSTEN

2 rue Gambetta.
☎ 02.47.96.82.12 ➡ 02.47.96.56.72
Closed Sun evening, Mon and Tues lunchtime except in May–Sept, and mid-Feb to March. **TV**. **Car park**.

An old inn right in the centre of the town with eleven cosy rooms boasting lots of facilities. Doubles with shower/wc are €46, or €58–69 with bath. The ones overlooking the courtyard are the quietest. There's a warm dining room on the ground floor with a small bar just off it. High-quality gastronomic cooking with dishes precisely cooked and seasonings finely judged: eel *rillettes*, pigeon with honey and ginger and a classic zander with *beurre blanc*. All delicious. Menus at €24–39. Exemplary service and welcome. Free coffee.

LOCHES   37600

⛊ I●I HÔTEL-RESTAURANT DE FRANCE**

6 rue Picois (Centre).
☎ 02.47.59.00.32 ➡ 02.47.59.28.66
Closed Sun evening, Mon and Tues lunchtime except July–Aug; 8 Jan–15 Feb. **TV**. **Garden**. **Car park**.

This is an old posthouse with a wide courtyard and flower garden where you can have lunch in the summer. Lovely rooms priced €47–58 with shower/wc or bath. Some are split-level, and they're all very cosily furnished. They serve inventive and refined cooking prepared with great care and attention: the dishes are produced from under domed covers, the plates are hot and there's not a paper napkin in sight. After some *amuse-bouches* to get your appetite going, the €13 weekday menu includes dishes such as coddled eggs *basquaise*, haddock with a *julienne* of baby vegetables and lemon butter, roast pork with prunes, carrot purée and wild mushrooms and Norwegian salad with smoked salmon. On the €18–40 menus, specialities include pastry-cases filled with langoustine in wine sauce, *tourne-dos Rossini* (fillet steak with *foie gras*), prune ice-cream with Touraine Marc and a Grand-Marnier soufflé. The desserts are prepared on the premises. Apparently Lodovico Sforza, the duke of Milan, was imprisoned by Louis XI in the dungeons in Loche and had his meals brought in from the hotel – if the quality was anything like this, it can't have been much of a hardship.

BEAULIEU-LÈS-LOCHES   37600 (1KM E)

🖈 🏠 HÔTEL DE BEAULIEU**

3 rue Foulques-Nerra; take the D760 in the direction of Valençay; it's opposite the church.
☎ 02.47.91.60.80
Closed Oct to end-March.

This handsome sixteenth-century building, which originally belonged to the abbey opposite, is typical of the Touraine. It offers nine bedrooms framing a beautiful inner courtyard, all decorated in an appropriately rustic style. Doubles with shower/wc from €33. 10% discount April and May.

🖈 |●| RESTAURANT L'ESTAMINET

14 rue de l'Abbaye (Centre).
☎ 02.47.59.35.47
Closed Sun evening, Mon and the last week in Aug

The kind of café-restaurant that every French village should have. It's in a sixteenth-century building in the middle of the town, next to the abbey and its 61 metre-high bell tower. There's a 1900s coffee percolator behind the brass bar. Fresh cooking and local specialities are the watchwords here. The dishes of the day are prepared with care by Madame, while Monsieur serves in the dining room. He also catches the fish and picks wild mushrooms for his wife to cook. Dishes include goat's cheese salad, rabbit in mustard sauce, *coq au vin* and squid *à l'Espagnole*. Menus at €11–17 and inexpensive *à la carte*. Free apéritif or coffee.

MALESHERBES   45330

🏠 |●| L'ÉCU DE FRANCE**

10 pl. du Martroy (Centre).
☎ 02.38.34.87.25 📠 02.38.34.68.99
Restaurant closed Thurs and Sun evenings and the second fortnight in Aug. **TV**.

The courtyard, where the stagecoaches used to turn in, has been transformed into the reception hall. Comfortable, well-maintained

double rooms with shower/wc for €44 or €55 with bath. The restaurant won't blow you away, but the *formule brasserie* served in the bistro is tasty and good value with menus at €16–26. They offer decent dishes of the day and a particularly good dessert with cream and cream cheese beaten together – it's even better with strawberries. A good place to stop if you're driving on the A13, which is just 13km away, and Fontainebleau is also nearby.

MENNETOU-SUR-CHER   41320

🏠 |●| LE LION D'OR

2 rue Marcel-Bailly (Centre); it's on the edge of the N76.
☎ 02.54.98.06.10 📠 02.59.98.06.13
@ ronan.lecieux@free.fr
Closed Sun evening and Mon.

Delicious cooking like *cassolette* of snails with girolle mushrooms and Mennetou *andouillette*. The dining room is attractively rustic and there is a brasserie area with a menus at €9, €15 and €23. They have fifteen rooms at €23 with basin or €33 with shower/wc – they're adequate for an overnight stay. The ones overlooking the courtyard give you a view of the medieval walls rather than the main road.

MONTARGIS   45200

🖈 🏠 HÔTEL LE BON GÎTE*

21 bd. du Chinchon (Centre).
☎ 02.38.85.31.01 📠 02.38.93.28.06
Disabled access. TV. Car park.

Good place for a decent night's sleep at a reasonable price. It's not much from the outside, but inside it's clean and quiet. A few simple rooms on the upper floors look over the inner courtyard and you could imagine you were near the Mediterranean in summer. Doubles cost €23 with basin and bidet, and up to €36 with shower/wc or bath. The very nice owners have been here for more than thirty years; let them know if you'll be arriving after 8pm. Free coffee.

|●| RESTAURANT LES PETITS OIGNONS

81 [bis] av. du Général-de-Gaulle; it's near the train station.
☎ 02.38.93.97.49
Closed Sun evening, Mon, a fortnight in the Feb school holidays and the first 3 weeks in Aug. **Disabled access. Garden.**

The bright décor is uncluttered and a bit

modern, but it's the garden and terrace that really make the place. You can be sure of peace and quiet away from the gaze of the passers-by and the noise of the street. Take a look at what's going on in the kitchen – something they encourage you to do. Try the home-smoked salmon, the *confit* of duck, lamb's brains *meunière* or the fillet of zander in cream and saffron. You'll get a cheerful welcome and impeccable service and the menus are realistically priced at €11, €15, €22 and €29.

AMILLY   45200 (2KM SE)

|●| L'AUBERGE DE L'ECLUSE

74 rue des Ponts.
☎ 02.38.85.44.24
Closed Sun evening; Mon; Thurs evening.

From the dining room you can watch while the keeper opens the lock on the nearby canal; there's also a terrace on the waterside. Inside, the classic décor contrasts with the modern and inventive cooking. Try zander with shredded leek and wild *mousseron* mushrooms, turbot with samphire or the delicious home-made desserts and ice-creams. Prices are a little high – €20 menu in the week, €28 on Sunday – but the dishes are in no way disappointing.

MONTRICHARD   41400

♠ HÔTEL DE LA CROIX-BLANCHE**

64 rue Nationale.
☎ 02.54.32.30.87 ➡ 02.54.32.91.00
Closed Nov to end March.

This hotel has been completely renovated and is wonderfully clean. It started life as a coaching inn in the sixteenth century and it's right next to the dungeons. The rooms are well-appointed, some with a view over the River Cher, and have en-suite bathrooms and phones; doubles around €45–54. There's an attractive patio where they serve breakfast and a bar.

﹩|●| BISTROT DE LA TOUR

34 rue du Sully, (Centre); it's near the tourist office.
☎ 02.54.32.07.34
Closed Sun.

A lovely house with a pretty terrace on the town square. The stone and wood décor inside is warm and attractive. Weekday lunch menu €10, others €14 and €19, or you'll pay around €20 *à la carte*. Classic, carefully

prepared dishes like poached eggs in Gamay sauce, ox kidneys with basil, zander fillet and a particularly good dish of snails, bacon and oyster mushrooms. There's also a selection of substantial salads.

CHISSAY   41400 (4KM W)

﹩ ♠ |●| CHÂTEAU DE CHISSEY

Centre; it's on the right bank of the Cher, on the D176, in the direction of Tours.
☎ 02.54.32.32.01 ➡ 02.54.32.32.01
e chateau-chissay@wanadoo.fr
Swimming pool. Garden. TV. Car park.

When in château country, stay in a château. This one was immortalized in the charming illuminations of the *Très Riches Heures du Duc de Berry* and was built by Charles VIII. It's a wonderful, meticulously restored building, and located in the heart of the Cher valley. The terrace is under the arcades, while the splendid dining room is luxuriously decorated with period furniture. Menus €31–48 and double rooms €106–244; there's an off-season weekend deal that includes dinner and breakfast for two nights. Free house apéritif.

PONTLEVOY   41400 (7KM N)

♠ |●| HÔTEL-RESTAURANT DE L'ÉCOLE**

12 route de Montrichard (Centre); it's on the main road coming from Montrichard.
☎ 02.54.32.50.30 ➡ 02.54.32.33.58
Closed Sun evening and Mon except public holidays; 19 Nov–12 Dec; 16 Feb–14 March. **Garden. TV. Car park.**

This is a pleasant place to stop after you've visited the tenth-century abbey. It's a charming little hotel with eleven comfortable rooms with shower/wc at €40 or bath at €43. The cooking is very traditional but sophisticated and nicely presented. They do several set menus starting at €16 and going up to €40. Try their calves' head sauce *gribiche*, the pike balls with crayfish tails and their crackling vanilla dessert with chocolate sauce. In fine weather, you can eat under the pergola in the garden. Excellent service.

OISLY   41700 (16KM NE)

﹩ |●| RESTAURANT LE SAINT-VINCENT

Centre; take the D764 as far as Pontlevoy then turn right onto the D30.
☎ 02.54.79.50.04
Closed Tues; Wed; 20 Dec–3 Feb.

This is quite an exceptional restaurant. It doesn't look like much – the sign is very ordinary and you might mistake it for just another restaurant in just another village square. But step inside and notice the attention to detail: the décor is fresh, there's a decent amount of space between the tables, and the linen and cutlery have been chosen to match the rustic ambience. The menu is varied and full of tempting and original dishes: crab cake with onion chutney, fruit served with *tabbouleh* and green curry, venison *civet* with cocoa beans and desserts such as pears poached in Oisly wine and blackcurrant sorbet. The creative chef will probably have invented even more culinary delights by the time you read this. Set menus €21 (weekdays) and €27–40. Best to book. Free coffee.

NANÇAY · 18330

|●| LE RELAIS DE SOLOGNE

2 rue Salbris.
☎ 02.48.51.82.26 ➡ 02.48.51.10.70
Closed Tues evening, Wed, a fortnight in Feb and a fortnight in Sept. **Disabled access**.

Alain-Fournier, who wrote the bewitching tale *Le Grand Meaulnes*, spent his childhood in this little village. The house is almost hidden under all the flowers and it's hard to resist going up and pushing open the door. Alain Bonnot is the owner and chef, and his forte is sauces. He is unbeatable when it comes to preparing game and other regional dishes. His specialities are *poulet en Barbouille* – *coq au vin*, in other words – salmon with sorrel sauce and *meringue Relais* – You can eat in the elegant dining room, decorated mainly in royal blue, or on the terrace. Set menus at €16 and €24 or there's a weekday lunch menu at €12.

NOGENT-LE-ROTROU · 28400

🏠 LE LION D'OR**

28 pl. Saint Pol (Centre).
☎ 02.37.52.01.60 ➡ 02.37.52.23.82
TV. Car park.

Once you've dealt with the shock of the 1970s wallpaper in the corridor, you'll find the rooms are mostly spacious and comfortable. The hotel is in a brilliant location right on the town's main square but try to avoid the rooms overlooking it on a Friday night because there's a market there on Saturday and setting up starts really early. Doubles with shower/wc €40–55 according to size.

Lovely welcome. There's a separate restaurant next to the hotel.

🏠 INTER HÔTEL SULLY***

12 rue des Viennes (North).
☎ 02.37.52.15.14 ➡ 02.37.52.15.20
Closed 21 Dec–2 Jan. **Disabled access. TV.**

Sure, it's a chain hotel but you get a genuine, smiling welcome that inspires confidence. The prices are affordable given that it's a three-star establishment; doubles with en-suite bathrooms start at €53. It's quietly located just away from the centre of town in an area that's recently been built. A problem-free place.

|●| LA PAPOTIÈRE

3 rue Bourg-le-Comte.
☎ 02.37.52.18.41
Closed Sun evening and Mon.

A really odd name for this superb sixteenth-century stone house. Inside it's warm, and the pleasant service helps you relax very quickly. There's a bistro *formule* menu at €11 (a big hit) and more complete ones for €23–32 with excellent traditional cuisine. They do guinea fowl with figs and a good *noisette* of lamb – and don't miss the house dessert, *kanougat* with chocolate.

ORLÉANS · 45000

🏠 |●| HÔTEL DE PARIS

29 faubourg Bannier (North).
☎ 02.38.53.39.58
Closed Sat lunchtime and Sun except by reservation. **Garage**.

You'll get a nice, very laid-back welcome – something the boss learned from his years in the US. The rooms are simple but pleasant and a lick of paint and new wallpaper have smartened them up. The beds are good, too. Doubles with basin go for €23, or there are some with bath. Guests here range from American students to travelling workmen. The bistro on the ground floor, where they serve a dish of the day every lunchtime at €7, is popular with locals, as are the other menus €9 and €11. There's a garage where you can park a bike. Credit cards not accepted.

🏠 HÔTEL MARGUERITE**

14 pl. du Vieux-Marché (Centre); it's 50m from rue Royale, near the main post office.
☎ 02.38.53.74.32 ➡ 02.38.53.31.56
Closed Sat and Sun noon–4.30pm.

Disabled access. TV. Car park.

A handsome and delightfully old-fashioned building – the rooms are comfortable, the prices are reasonable and it's run like a three-star. The jovial owner will greet you at reception on the first floor; he's helpful and friendly. They offer 25 large, comfortable, well-maintained rooms; you'll pay €27 for a room with a basin up to €40 with bath and TV. The rooms over the street have double glazing to cut down the noise. Breakfast includes as much hot coffee as you can drink, fruit juice and honey for only €5 – they'll bring it to your room for no extra charge. 20% discount for weekends and throughout July–Aug.

🏠 HÔTEL DE L'ABEILLE**

64 rue d'Alsace-Lorraine (North); it's in a street that flanks the Palais de Justice.
☎ 02.38.53.54.87 ➔ 02.38.62.65.84
📧 hotel-de-labeille@wanadoo.fr
TV.

There's something very special about this hotel. It was opened by the family that still runs it way back in 1919, which makes it one of the oldest hotels in town. There's a creaky old sign and they've put green shrubs and flowers out all over the pavement. The old wooden staircase gleams from years of polishing and the rooms – all decorated differently – have a quiet, antiquated charm. Prices are fair: €26 for a room with basin, €44 with shower/wc and €47 with bath. Pleasant staff.

🍴 🏠 HÔTEL SAINT-MARTIN**

52 bd. Alexandre-Martin (Centre); turn left as you come out of the train station and make for the theatre.
☎ 02.3862.47.47 ➔ 02.38.81.13.28
Closed Sunday 11am–4pm and Christmas–New Year.
Garden. TV. Pay car park.

A little, old-fashioned hotel in a detached building with some rooms that look onto a tiny flower-filled courtyard. Prices start at €27 for a double with washing facilities; it's €39–41 with shower/wc and TV. 10% discount July–Sept or free use of shower if you're in a room with basin only.

🏠 JACKOTEL**

18 cloître Saint-Aignan (Southeast); follow quai du Châtelet in the direction of Montargis and turn before you get to the bridge.
☎ 02.38.54.48.48 ➔ 02.38.77.17.59
Closed Sun afternoon and public holidays 1–6pm.
Disabled access. Garden. TV. Car park.

A nice hotel, recently built, with a flower-filled

courtyard. There are 61 comfortable, neat rooms that are worthy of a three-star establishment. Doubles €46 with bath, TV and phone. There's a display of carved parrots in the reception; the real birds are outside, twittering in the lovely little square in the shadow of the church of Saint-Aignan. Pets are welcome.

🍴 🍽 RESTAURANT LES FAGOTS

32 rue du Poirier (Centre); it's near the Châtelet covered market.
☎ 02.38.62.22.79 ➔ 02.38.77.99.87
Closed Sun; Mon; the first week in Jan; the second fortnight in Aug. **Disabled access. Pay car park.**

The décor includes old posters on the wall, enamel and china coffee pots here and there and a few photographs of actors. But you'll come here for the grills, which they do over the open fire – their speciality is donkey meat steak, though you have to order this a day in advance. The lunchtime set menu costs €10, there's another at €15, and à la carte you'll pay around €17. Friendly welcome and service. It's better in the evening but on a sunny days, the terrace makes it a thoroughly nice place for lunch. Free Kir.

🍴 🍽 L'ARCHANGE

66 faubourg Madeleine (West); starting from la pl. Croix Morin, take the rue Porte Madeleine; it's on the right after bd. Jean-Jaurès.
☎ 02.38.88.64.20 ➔ 02.38.45.08.81
Closed Sun, Tues–Thurs evenings; a week in the Easter school holidays, 3 weeks in Aug; Christmas to New Year's Day.

The chef, Monsieur Schnitt, won the *grand prix d'honneur* at France's national academy of cuisine, so prepare yourself: duck *foie gras*, veal beef with morels, sole *paupiettes* with crayfish *jus* and a white chocolate dessert with apricot *coulis*. This is serious cooking prepared with great art. Menus €13–27. There's an eclectic wine list with some excellent vintages – such as red and white Cheverny – at affordable prices. The dining room is elegantly decorated and there are engravings of the local countryside on the walls. Free coffee.

🍽 LA DARIOLE

26 rue Étienne Dolet (Centre).
☎ 02.38.77.26.67
Closed Wed and Sat lunchtimes, Sun and 3–26 Aug.

Wood panelling, old-rose tones and refined cuisine in this lovely restaurant. The specialities change frequently – pressed sardines with pickled tomatoes and creamed olives, steamed turbot and vegetables, rhubarb and strawberry tart. Menus €17–31. In summer you eat outside on a pedestrianized square. Charming welcome but the service is tentative and edgy; maybe it will relax with time.

🕏 |●| LA PETITE MARMITE

178 rue de Bourgogne (Centre); it's near the préfecture.
☎ 02.38.54.23.83 ➡ 02.38.54.41.81
Closed Sat lunchtime; Sun; public holidays.

The best place in a street full of restaurants. It's open seven nights a week 7–11pm. They stick to traditional local dishes served in a pretty, rustic dining room, with a choice of three menus at €18–29 or *à la carte*. Dishes include *foie gras à l'ancienne* or with truffles, *coq au vin*, rabbit *à l'Orléanaise*, game in season and *crème brûlée* with pears. Nice proprietress who spoils her customers. Free *digestif*.

CONBLEUX   45800 (7KM E)

🕏 |●| LA MARINE

How to get there: take the N460
☎ 02.38.55.12.69

The house is smothered in wisteria and there's a terrace on the canal bank. The Loire flows through the village, revealing sandy beaches on the banks. The specialities are freshwater fish from the Loire – eel, lampray and zander – in dishes which complement each other expertly. Menus from €19. The superb dining room is built from stone and pale wood. Warm welcome. Free house apéritif.

PITHIVIERS   45300

🕏 🏠 |●| LE RELAIS DE LA POSTE**

10 Mail-Ouest (Centre).
☎ 02.38.30.40.30. ➡ 02.38.30.47.79
Restaurant closed Sun evening. **TV. Pay car park**.

A good provincial hotel dominating a square, with a reliable restaurant serving classic dishes. Menus €14–24; the cheapest one lists dishes such as brawn, steak with shallots, cheese and a choice of desserts including the famous local delicacy, Pithiviers with puff pastry and almond paste. The rooms have wooden wainscotting and the ones up in the eaves boast beamed ceilings; doubles €44 with shower/wc or bath. A good place to stop. Free house apéritif.

PREUILLY-SUR-CLAISE   37290

🏠 |●| AUBERGE SAINT-NICOLAS

6 Grande-Rue (Centre).
☎ 02.47.94.50.80. ➡ 02.47.94.41.77
Closed Sun evening and Mon except July–Aug; mid-Sept to 3 Oct. **TV. Lock-up car park**.

This hotel near the abbey has nine rooms with bathrooms which have been completely refurbished and cheerfully decorated in shades of yellow. Doubles with shower/wc €37 and €43 with bath. Pleasant welcome and good value for money. The dining room is also brightly coloured and they serve good regional cooking, with menus at €10, €17, €27 and €36.

PETIT-PRESSIGNY (LE)   37350 (9KM N)

|●| RESTAURANT LA PROMENADE

11 rue du Savoureulx; take the D41 in the direction of Loches, then the D50.
☎ 02.47.94.93.52 ➡ 02.47.91.06.03
Closed Sun evening; Mon and Tues lunchtimes; 3 weeks in Jan; a fortnight Sept–Oct.

Some of the most ordinary-looking villages hide real treasures – this is one. Jacky Dallais was a pupil of Robuchon, and he's converted his father's old smithy into a splendid restaurant with two pretty, contemporary-looking dining rooms. He's a chef with integrity and imagination and creates dishes of great distinction. The menu changes constantly and the prices are pitched to accommodate different budgets. The *menu du marché*, served on weekdays, is excellent value at €21, while the one at €64 would suit appetites verging on the Rabelaisian – five dishes plus cheese and dessert. The specialities are an absolute must, and include free-range pork chop with beans and black pudding *parmentier* with mashed potatoes. The wine list is sumptuous and there's efficient service. Best to book at weekends.

RICHELIEU   37120

🕏 🏠 |●| LES MOUSQUETAIRES

4 av. du Colonel-Goulier (Centre).
☎ 02.47.58.15.17
Closed Tues until 6pm. **Disabled access. TV. Garden**.

An unpretentious and comfortable little hotel outside the old ramparts. It has five double rooms leading straight out into the garden. Prices start at €24 with shower/wc and they have one room that sleeps four; for a small charge, you can have a TV. There's a small bar from which you can order meals – one menu at €9. Stay ten nights and you get the eleventh free. Free coffee.

ROMORANTIN-LANTHENAY   41200

🎿 🛏 |O| HÔTEL-RESTAURANT LE COLOMBIER**

18 pl. du Vieux-Marché; it's 150m from the town hall.
☎ 02.54.76.12.76 ➡ 02.54.76.39.40
Closed Sun evening and Feb. **Garden**. **TV**. **Car park**.

Rooms are comfortable, though nothing more; those overlooking the courtyard are quieter. Doubles €37 with shower/wc or €41 with bath. Pleasant garden. The cosy restaurant specializes in cooking from the Sologne and the carefully prepared dishes change with the seasons – *papillotte* of zander with lime, ox kidneys with shallot marmalade, duck *foie gras* with horn of plenty mushrooms, raspberry shortcake. Menus €17–27. 10% discount on the room rate

SACHÉ   37190

|O| AUBERGE DU XIIᴱ SIÈCLE

It's in the main street.
☎ 02.47.26.88.77
Closed Sun evening; Mon; Tues lunchtime; 7–29 Jan; 3–11 June; 2–10 Sept.

This village is enough to make many a restaurateur green with envy. It's a place of pilgrimage for devotees of Balzac and the splendid restaurant is one of the best in the region – the old beams and wide fireplace can't have changed in centuries. Xavier Aubrun and Thierry Jimenez are the two excellent chefs. They have put together a Balzac menu on which the dessert is loaded with caffeine. Other delights include dishes with contemporary combinations of flavour such as pigeon salad, zander with rhubarb and capers. Set menus are priced at €26–49.

SAINT-AIGNAN   41110

🎿 🛏 |O| GRAND HÔTEL SAINT-AIGNAN**

79 quai J. J. Delorme (Centre).
☎ 02.54.75.18.04 ➡ 02.54.75.12.59
Closed Sun evening; Mon and Tues lunchtime Nov to end March; the second fortnight in Feb and a week in March.

An old coaching inn covered in ivy, standing on the banks of the Cher. Warm greeting, friendly setting and chic atmosphere – the walls are hung with medieval tapestries. Pretty rooms at a range of prices from €23 with shower on the landing to €51 with en-suite bathroom; some have a view of the river. Specialities in the restaurant include smoked salmon with onion rings, braised ox kidneys with ceps and *assiette de trois provinces*. All delicious, but portions are a little small. Menus €15, €22, €27 and €33. 10% discount on the room rate Nov–March.

CHABRIS   36210 (25KM E)

🎿 🛏 |O| HÔTEL DE LA PLAGE**

42 rue du Pont; it's on the Valençay to Romorantin road, in the direction of the Sologne.
☎ 02.54.40.02.24 ➡ 02.54.40.08.59
Closed Sun evening; Mon except Sept to Jun; Jan. **Garden**. **TV**. **Car park**.

A nice little stop to eat and sleep. Mme d'Agostino cooks traditional dishes while her husband extends a genuine Berry welcome. The dishes on the menu change every three months and the fresh fish available depends on the catches at the ports. There's a €14 *formule* and other menus €14–29. In summer, they serve meals in the garden near the fountain. The rooms are comfortable; the ones on the first floor are older and more spacious, while those on the second floor have been modernized. Doubles €38 with shower/wc or bath. Free house apéritif or coffee.

SAINT-AMAND-MONTROND   18200

🎿 🛏 |O| HÔTEL-RESTAURANT LE NOIRLAC**

215 route de Bourges; it's 5km from the A71 motorway exit on the N144 in the direction of Bourges and 2.5 km from the twelfth-century Cistersian abbey of Noirlac.
☎ 02.48.82.22.00 ➡ 02.48.82.22.01
Hotel closed 22 Dec–1 Jan. **Restaurant closed** Fri evening; Sat lunchtime; Sun evening Nov–Easter. **Swimming pool. Disabled access. TV. Car park**.

A perfect overnight stop if you're driving through – even if it looks like an unattractive chain hotel at first. It's ultra-modern, with a pool, tennis courts and putting green, and the whole place has a clear view of the Lac de Vinlay. The super-comfortable, practical rooms cost €54 with bath; two have been specially adapted for disabled visitors. Staff in both the hotel and the restaurant are efficient. The cheapest set menu at €11 is substantial and is served daily; others go up to €23. Specialities are *fricassée* of snails, *cassolette* of ox kidneys, calf's head in balsamic vinegar and *crème brûlée* with Bourbon vanilla. In summer there's a salad menu, and grills and ice-creams all served by the swimming pool. 10% discount on the room rate.

🎋 |●| RESTAURANT LE SAINT-JEAN

1 rue de l'Hôtel-Dieu; it's near the Saint-Vic museum.
☎ 02.48.96.39.82 **e** lesaintjean@wanadoo.fr
Closed Sun, Tues and Wed evenings; Mon; a week in the Feb school holidays; a fortnight Aug–Sept.

A restaurant which is well worth a visit. It has a rustic dining room complete with flowers, beams and a wonderful old parquet floor. Chef Philippe Perrichon prepares a quite incredible set menu for €15 that includes cheese and dessert. That's the best value for money in town, so you might not feel the need to venture into the realms of the others (€17–23), though the specialities might tempt you: home-smoked zander with *blinis* and seaweed, salmon stuffed with green Berry lentils. Booking essential at weekends. Free coffee.

BRUÈRE-ALLICHAMPS   18200 (9KM NW)

|●| AUBERGE DE L'ABBAYE DE NOIRLAC

How to get there: at Saint-Amand, take the N144 in the direction of Bourges; 4km further on, turn onto the Noirlac road. It's opposite the abbey.
☎ 02.48.96.22.58
Closed Tues evening and Wed Oct–March. **Disabled access**.

One of the old abbey chapels has been transformed into a restaurant with a bistro where, in summer, you can get cheap snacks – sandwiches, an omelette or a plate of *charcuterie* at reasonable prices. The restaurant proper, which serves more serious food, has red quarry-tiles on the floor, beams and exposed stonework. Chef Pascal Verdier cooks meat and fish with equal skill; try his fresh salmon with fish purée, the Charolais steak, the goat's cheese terrine or the flambéed pineapple with chocolate. Prices are good – the cheapest set menu at €15 includes cheese and dessert, with others at €21 and €26.

SAINT-BENOÎT-SUR-LOIRE   45730

🏠 HÔTEL DU LABRADOR**

7 pl. de l'Abbaye; it's opposite the basilica.

☎ 02.38.35.74.38 **F➤** 02.38.35.72.99
e oteldulabrador@wanadoo.fr
Closed 25 Dec–25 Jan. **Disabled access**. **Garden**. **TV**. **Car park**.

The hotel is in a little square which is wonderfully peaceful; it's a charming place. The rooms in the main building are a little old-fashioned, while those in the newer annexe are more comfortable and tastefully decorated. Some have beams; others a view of the abbey or the countryside. Doubles with hand basin €27 and €49–55 with shower or bath. There's no restaurant but there is a tearoom with a very pleasant terrace, and half board can be arranged in conjunction with the *Grand Saint-Benoît*.

🎋 |●| LE GRAND SAINT-BENOÎT

7 pl. Saint-André.
☎ 02.38.35.11.92 **F➤** 02.38.35.13.79
e oteldulabrador@wanadoo.fr
Closed Sat lunchtime; Sun evening; Mon; 26 Aug–4 Sept; 22 Dec–22 Jan.

This establishment quickly earned a reputation as one of the best tables in the region – but it's not one of the most expensive. The heavenly cuisine is simple, unusual and stamped with the personality of the chef. The weekday menu, €15, is less interesting though perfectly adequate, but the €22 menu is splendid: snail pancake, roast zander with Chinon wine, veal chop in coriander *jus* and a caramel and hazelnut soufflé. Other menus up to €42. Free coffee.

SAINT-VIÂTRE   41210

🎋 🏠 |●| AUBERGE DE LA CHICHONE**

pl. de l'Église; by the N20 and then the D93.
☎ 02.54.88.91.33 **F➤** 02.54.96.18.66
Closed Wed and 2-3 weeks in March. **TV**.

In summer, you'll have to book a table in the garden – it's popular with the regulars. The interior is typical of a Sologne farmhouse, decorated in rustic style with hunting trophies on the walls and beams that show the patina of age. The subtle cooking is inspired by the immediate region and showcases dishes like *petit-salé* made with duck and stuffed carp. Set menus from €13 (not available Sun) to €28; they're all pretty substantial. Doubles €38 with shower/wc and €50 with bath. There's a fourteenth-century church just across from the inn and the *route des étangs* starts here, so make sure you have a fresh film in your camera. Free coffee.

NOUAN-LE-FUZELIER   41600 (10KM E)

|●| LE RABOLIOT

1 av. de la Mairie (Centre).
☎ 02.54.94.40.00
Closed Wed and mid-Jan to mid-Feb. **Car park**.

The chef is a local personality with a reputation that goes before him; he's very welcoming and really passionate about what he does. Try the specialities: fresh *fois gras*, snail ravioli, beef with marrowbone or *foie gras*, veal kidneys, zander with sliced Belles de Rontenay potatoes, rabbit leg stuffed with girolle mushrooms, pan-fried eel. There's plenty of game in season and the desserts are tempting – particularly the apricot tart with thyme granita and the rhubarb *mousseline*. *Menu touristique* €15 (weekdays only), and others up to €34. At lunchtime they serve simpler dishes – like free-range chicken with sage and potatoes *gratinée* with Sauvignon – for €6–8.

🏕 |●| LE DAHU

14 rue Henri-Chapron; take the N20 in the direction of La Ferté-Saint-Aubin.
☎ 02.54.88.72.88 ➡ 02.54.88.21.28
Closed Tues except July–Aug and 2 Jan–8 Feb.
Car park.

Marie-Thérèse and Jean-Luc Germain have created an incredible garden around their restaurant dedicated to the mythical "dahu". In an otherwise drab suburb their wonderful half-timbered farmhouse is surrounded by greenery, and the cosy interior manages to be both rustic and elegant. The menus start at €20 (not available Sat evening or Sun), with others at €23–40, and list all sorts of delights: salmon *chaud-froid* flavoured with pink peppercorns and red onion and ginger marmalade, red mullet with pimentos, farm-raised guineafowl marinated in sweet spices. Free apéritif.

SANCERRE   18300

|●| RESTAURANT LA POMME D'OR

pl. de la Mairie (Centre). If you're coming from Sancerre, follow the signs for the town hall.
☎ 02.48.54.13.30
Closed Tues and Wed in low season; Wed in high season; end Dec to mid-Jan.

An elegant restaurant in a narrow street in the old part of town. The cooking uses fresh, seasonal produce and it's traditional without being too heavy. Dishes have some original rustic touches: breaded Chavignol goat's cheese, veal kidneys, *andouillette* with mustard, roast zander in Sancerre, home-made *profiteroles*. The €14 menu is excellent value and there are others at €21–37. The proprietor, Didier Turpin, is the master of his cellar and offers a wonderful selection of wines – including some venerable Pouilly-Fumés – at very attractive prices.

SAINT-SATUR   18300 (3KM NE)

🏕 🏠 |●| HÔTEL-RESTAURANT LE LAURIER**

29 rue du Commerce; by the D955.
☎ 02.48.54.17.20 ➡ 02.48.54.04.54
Closed Sun evening and Mon except in July–Aug; Thurs out of season; the first fortnight in March; the last three weeks in Nov. **TV**.

After buying some good bottles in Sancerre, carry on to Saint-Satur. In it you'll find this place swathed in Virginia creeper and a stone's throw from a handsome abbey. The dining room, with its copperware, exposed beams and old wooden furniture, has clearly been decorated by someone with a taste for authenticity. You'll pay €18 for a double with basin and €38 for a larger room with bath – prices are truly reasonable for this very touristy area. The restaurant offers good regional cooking with set menus at €12 (weekdays only) and €17–29. Its specialities are poached eggs in wine *à l'ancienne*, calf's head and tongue with two different sauces, zander with chive butter and game in season. Free coffee. 10% discount on the room rate Dec–March.

CHAVIGNOL   18300 (5KM W)

🏕 |●| RESTAURANT LA CÔTE DES MONTS DAMNÉS

It's in the village; from Sancerre, take the D955 in the direction of Cosne/Gien and then the D183.
☎ 02.48.54.01.72 ➡ 02.48.54.14.24
Closed Sun evening; Mon; Tues in low season; Feb.

The "damned mountains" give their name both to a highly reputed vineyard in Sancerre and to this inn, a rustic place with beams, patterned curtains and a cosy atmosphere. Local produce plays the central role in robust dishes with a very distinct character: try *tagliatelle* with *crottin* (a reasonably strong goat's cheese made in the village), saddle of lamb stuffed with veal kidneys or the very good salmon with a sauce made from wine lees. Menus start at €16. The wine list is full of bargains from all parts of France. Nice staff. Free coffee.

SANCOINS · 18600

🏃 🔒 HÔTEL DU PARC**

8 rue Marguerite-Audoux.
☎ 02.48.74.56.60 📠 02.48.74.61.30
Closed 1–15 Jan. **Garden. Car park**.

This classy place looks like a château and is set in extensive grounds. The rooms are lovely, with Baroque mirrors and velvet bedspreads, and they're quiet. Pleasant welcome. Doubles with shower or bath €35, or €44 for rooms sleeping up to 4. 10% discount in July and Aug.

SOUVIGNY-EN-SOLOGNE · 41600

🏃 |◉| LA PERDRIX ROUGE

22 rue du Gattuces.
☎ 02.38.54.88.41.05.
Closed Mon; Tues; 15 Feb–4 March; 29 June–6 July; 25 Aug–3 Sept.

The dining room manages to be at once sophisticated and rustic, with tasteful furniture and good linen. They offer *amuse-bouches* while you peruse the menu. The food is light and tasty: *foie gras* with Muscat de Beaume-de-Venise, *aiguillette* of roast pigeon with honey and baby cabbage, rack of lamb with garden herbs and zander with *beurre blanc*. Many dishes are based on local recipes and use only fresh produce. Weekday menu €13 and others €22–46. Free house *digestif*.

SULLY-SUR-LOIRE · 45600

🏃 🔒 |◉| HÔTEL-RESTAURANT DE LA POSTE**

11 rue du Faubourg-Saint-Germain (Centre).
☎ 02.38.36.26.22 📠 02.38.36.39.35
TV. Car park.

Some of the rooms in this old coaching inn have a view of the Loire; in others, you'll have to make do with the TV. Doubles from €31 with washing facilities to €46 with shower/wc or bath – some are for non-smokers. Menus at €15–32 feature lots of fish dishes, with crab cakes with sorrel or fillet of zander as a main course. This place is a bit of an institution in Sully and the large cage full of parrots is equally renowned. 10% discount on the room rate.

TOURS · 37000

SEE MAP OVERLEAF

🏃 🔒 HÔTEL SAINT-ÉLOI*

79 bd. Béranger. **MAP A2-2**
☎ 02.47.37.67.34 📠 02.47.39.34.67
TV. Garden.

There's a superb magnolia tree in the garden, and the hotel is set back from the boulevard in a courtyard. This is a small place, run by a young couple, and it's clean, quiet, simple and friendly. Rooms come with washing facilities or shower/wc. Doubles €21–29. Street parking available in the boulevard or behind the hotel in rue Jules-Charpentier. 10% discount on the room rate.

🏃 🔒 HÔTEL RÉGINA*

2 rue Pimbert. **MAP C1-4**
☎ 02.47.05.25.36 📠 02.47.66.08.72
Closed last fortnight Dec.

A cheap, cheerful, simple and clean hotel with window-boxes full of flowers. It's really pretty and you feel so welcome that you wouldn't think it out of place to go down to breakfast in your slippers. Annie and Gérard Lachaize ran a hotel in Lyons for ten years so they know their job. The soundproofing is good and the cleanliness is evidenced by the nice smell of polish A double room with hand basin is €22 or €30 with shower/wc. 5% discount.

🏃 🔒 |◉| HÔTEL-RESTAURANT MODERNE**

1–3 rue Victor-Laloux. **MAP C2-3**
☎ 02.47.05.32.81 📠 02.47.05.71.50
📧 hotel.moderne37@wanadoo.fr
Restaurant closed Sat and Mon lunchtimes; Sun. **TV**.

This hotel, a fine building in traditional Touraine style, is on a corner in a quiet neighbourhood. There are 23 rooms in all (€30 with basin, €35 with shower), twelve with bathrooms (€44–52); the ones in the attic are cosy and have sloping ceilings. Nothing will stop you enjoying the excellent cooking. Set menus, €12 and €15, feature things like zander with softened leaks, roasted goat's cheese, flambéed prawns, steak *tartare* and pears in Chinon. There's a pay car park nearby. 10% discount on the room rate.

🔒 |◉| HÔTEL DU MUSÉE

3 pl. François Sicard. **MAP C1-19**
☎ 02.47.66.63.81 📠 02.47.20.10.42

Though this establishment needs to be refurbished it would lose its charm in the process. The façade is worn but all the rooms are decorated differently, with lovely wood panelling, and either a terrace or a fireplace. The furni-

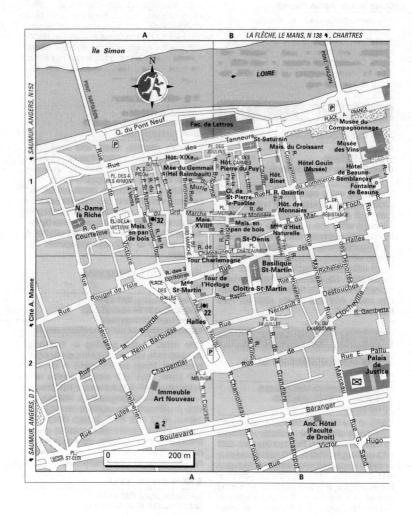

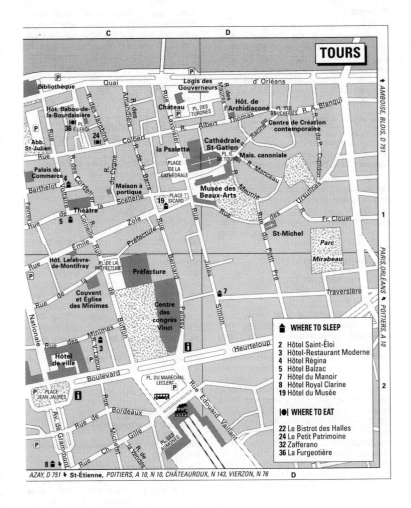

TOURS

AMBOISE, BLOIS, D 751 →

WHERE TO SLEEP

2 Hôtel Saint-Éloi
3 Hôtel-Restaurant Moderne
4 Hôtel Régina
5 Hôtel Balzac
7 Hôtel du Manoir
8 Hôtel Royal Clarine
19 Hôtel du Musée

WHERE TO EAT

22 Le Bistrot des Halles
24 Le Petit Patrimoine
32 Zafferano
36 La Furgeotière

PARIS, ORLÉANS ✈ POITIERS, A 10

AZAY, D 751 ↓ St-Étienne, POITIERS, A 10, N 10, CHÂTEAUROUX, N 143, VIERZON, N 76

ture is old but not rickety. Double rooms start at €32. They have a lovely dining room, too; menus start at €10.

⅍ 🏠 HÔTEL BALZAC**

47 rue de la Scellerie. **MAP C1-5**
☎ 02.47.05.40.87 ➡ 02.47.05.67.93
TV. Garden.

Right in the middle of town, this friendly and rather plush establishment has eighteen rooms, fifteen with shower or bath (€45–48) and five with basin only (€34). Some are particularly quiet and spacious. In fine weather, eat your breakfast on the terrace or sit quietly over a drink. 10% discount after two nights.

⅍ 🏠 HÔTEL KYRIAD***

65 av. de Grammont. **MAP C2-8**
☎ 02.47.64.71.78 ➡ 02.47.05.84.62
e kyriad.tourscentre@wanadoo.fr
Disabled access. TV. Pay lock-up garage.

This is a modern hotel with no great charm but a pleasant atmosphere. The bedrooms and the dining room are tastefully furnished in Louis XV and Louis XVI or contemporary style and they're very comfortable. All fifty have bath, satellite TV and phone; doubles from €64. 10% discount.

◉ LE PETIT PATRIMOINE

58 rue Colbert. **MAP C1-24**
☎ 02.47.66.05.81
Closed Sun evening.

A regional restaurant of quality with a dining room decorated in bright colours. The owner has a real interest in preserving the cuisine of the Touraine, though he's always looking for ways to take it gently forward. The specialities are quite delicious: Touraine tart with *rillons* and goat's cheese, pike Bourgueil-style, entrecôte steak with Saint-Maure sauce, salmon envelope stuffed with Saint-Maure cheese, *andouillette à la Vouvrillonne* (sausage in Vouvray, a white Loire wine), *matelote* of veal with red wine, onions and mushrooms and a superb selection of cheeses. If you've got room for dessert, try the pears in wine or the goat's cheese with blackberry jelly. Menus €11–25, dish of the day €6 and good Touraine wines from €9. Best to book.

◉ LE BISTROT DES HALLES

31 pl. Gaston-Paillhou. **MAP A2-22**
☎ 02.47.61.54.93

Service until 11pm. Outside this old-fash-

ioned brasserie there's an eye-catching red and green frontage, while inside the walls are covered with pictures from the turn of the (last) century. It attracts everyone from the great and the good to ordinary folk. The service is faultless but that doesn't stop the place being relaxed and informal. Regional specialities – *pot-au-feu* with three meats, *rillons* (a local dish of diced pork), pork *rillettes*, *bouillabaisse* fish soup from the south and so on – have pride of place in here. Try their *tarte Tatin*, an upside-down apple tart with caramelized fruit. *Formule* at €11 and a menu at €21, while from Sept–May there are two seafood *formules* at €25 and €30. Reckon on €17 *à la carte*. Good selection of Loire wines.

⅍ ◉ LA FURGEOTIÈRE

19 pl. Foire-le-Roi. **MAP C1-36**
☎ 02.47.66.94.75
Closed second week in Jan, second week in Feb school holidays and a week in July.

Furgeot is the family name of Marie-Hélène, who runs this place with her husband Michel. The walls are in local stone, and there are wooden beams and French-style ceilings. They change their dishes each season so you might find traditional dishes – semi-cooked duck *foie gras*, oxtail *parmentier* (with mashed potato), saddle of rabbit with tarragon – or less conventional ones such as grilled St Nectaire cheese on country bread with caramelized garlic and *croustillant* of pig's trotters in cider with sautéed potatoes and celeriac *purée*. Four menus €16–39 and a lunch *formule* at €24 (not Sunday), which includes a Kir, a ¼-litre of Chinon wine and coffee. The service is efficient, and the wines reasonably priced. In summer they put tables out on the square. Essential to book in the evening. Free *digestif*.

⅍ ◉ ZAFFERANO

7-9 rue de la Grosse Tour **MAP A1-32**
☎ 02.47.38.90.77
Closed Sun; Mon; the Feb school holidays; the second fortnight in Aug.

Let's get this straight from the start: this is not any ordinary pizzeria. They serve an array of Italian dishes from different regions and the pasta is fresh and home-made. Forget about turgid tomato sauce and let them surprise you with dishes like *pasta zafferano* (fresh home-made ribbons of pasta with smoked bacon and saffron cream sauce). And their meat dishes are amazing – the *saltimbocca alla romana*, the veal escalope with fontina cheese and the *osso bucco* are prepared with precision. Killer desserts, too, especially their ultra-light *tiramisù*. Menus €15 and €25 or around €27 *à la carte*. You'll find the same quality on the mainly-Italian wine list, and there's a small grocery counter selling Italian specialities. Great atmosphere. Free plate of *charcuterie* and house aperitif.

ROCHECORBON 37210 (3KM NE)

⌂ HÔTEL LES FONTAINES**

6 quai de la Loire.
☎ 02.47.42.42.86 ➡ 02.47.52.85.05

A charming manor-house hotel on the banks of the Loire. Unfortunately it fronts onto the main road but the trees and grounds protect it from noise. Rooms are on the ground and first floors. They're all differently decorated and attractively furnished, and are both size-able and comfortable. Doubles €37–56 with shower/wc or bath/wc; the ones in the annexe are a little cheaper at €36. Faultless welcome and service, with a pleasant salon for breakfast. Shady grounds and private car park.

|●| L'OUBLIETTE

34 rue des Clouets.
☎ 02.47.52.50.59 ➡ 02.47.52.85.65
Closed Sunday evening; Mon; the Feb school holidays; end Oct to Nov.

Local people say they serve "modern cook-ing" here – code for imaginative and inventive cuisine. The chef uses lots of spices and herbs but with great subtlety and finesse. And no *nouvelle cuisine* portions, either: they're perfectly judged, as is the refined presentation. The décor is equally appealing with tapestries on the stone walls. The sig-nature dish is lobster *civet* and they serve good *foie gras* too. Menus start at €21 and go up to €50.

FONDETTES 37230 (5KM E)

⅍ |●| AUBERGE DE PORC-VALLIÈRES

Vallières; it's on the N152 in the direction of Langeais.
☎ 02.47.42.24.04 ➡ 02.47.49.98.83
Closed Mon and Tues evenings; Wed; a fortnight in winter; a fortnight in Aug.

Because the inn is right on the edge of the N152, you might hesitate to stop. But it's worth it. There are lovely tiles on the floor, armfuls of wild flowers from the fields in

huge vases and a relaxed, pleasant atmos-phere; you hardly hear the traffic at all. The welcome is friendly and straightforward and the cuisine brilliantly judged. There's a €14 menu in the week and another for €18 at the weekend. They list original dishes and various specialities: a mixture of fried fish from the Loire, eel stew, pike. Free coffee.

VOUVRAY 37210 (8KM NE)

⌂ |●| LE GRAND VATEL

8 av. Léon Brulé.
☎ 02.47.52.70.32 ➡ 02.47.52.74.52
Closed Sun evening and Mon.

Everything here is made on the premises and the results are brilliant: *terrine* of *foie gras*, warm oyster ravioli with a light cream and herb sauce, joint of rabbit stuffed with onion preserve. Informed advice on the dish-es from the chef's delightful wife, who clear-ly has a fine palate. Menus 18–53. There's an impressive list of Vouvray wines, some served by the glass. Upstairs there are a few well-maintained rooms; a double with show-er/wc or bath costs €34–41.

SEMBLANÇAY 37360 (12KM NW)

⅍ ⌂ |●| HOSTELLERIE DE LA MÈRE HAMARD**

pl. de l'église (Centre); take the N138 in the direction of Le Mans.
☎ 02.47.56.62.04 ➡ 02.47.56.53.61
Closed Sun evening, Mon, Tues lunchtime and Feb.
TV. Car park.

You'll dine on delicious regional dishes and gourmet cuisine. The dining room is com-fortable and welcoming. Menus from €16 (not Sun) up to €43. Specialities include duck *foie gras* with morels, pigeon with truf-fles and potato cakes with *foie gras*. There are nine lovely double rooms in a delightful annexe from €40–44 with shower/wc. Free coffee.

MONNAIE 37380 (14KM NE)

⅍ |●| RESTAURANT AU SOLEIL LEVANT

53 rue Nationale (Centre); it's on the N10 north of Tours.
☎ 02.47.56.10.34 ➡ 02.47.56.45.22
Closed Sun and Wed evenings; Mon; the first fortnight in Jan; the first fortnight in Aug.

This is among the best gourmet restaurants in the area, with a stylish interior decorated in bright, luminous colours. They produce exceptional dishes that bear no resemblance to the usual things that pass for regional specialities. The best ingredients of the season are imaginatively combined to create wonderful results. However hungry you are and whatever you plan to spend, there's a set menu to suit you: they start at €15 (except Sun) and continue at €24–32. They list fillet steak in Chinon, roast zander with *beurre blanc* and veal sweetbreads with morel mushrooms – all delicious. Free coffee.

VANNES-SUR-COSSON   45510

I●I RESTAURANT LE VIEUX RELAIS

route d'Isdes.
☎ 02.38.58.04.14
Garden. Car park.

It's obvious that this superb Solognote manor house is pretty old – but you probably wouldn't guess that the original buildings go back to 1462 and that the beams come from a building in the 800s. It's been an inn since 1515 and is one of the six oldest in France. It's an absolutely sumptuous place and the cooking doesn't let the surroundings down. You should certainly go for the chef's *foie gras* if it's on the menu. He uses seasonal produce for all his dishes so it's hard to list his specialities but the game is superb, as are the calf's sweetbreads with whisky – and don't miss out on the *crème brûlée* either. Menus start at €15. Essential to book.

VENDÔME   41100

♠ I●I HÔTEL-RESTAURANT L'AUBERGE DE LA MADELEINE

pl. de la Madeleine (Centre); head in the direction of Blois.
☎ 02.54.77.20.79 ➡ 02.54.80.00.02
Hotel closed Feb. **Restaurant closed** Wed. **TV. Car park.**

An unpretentious place with attractive rooms; numbers 7 and 8 are the largest. Doubles €33 with shower/wc and €37–45 with bath. Good plain cooking with set menus €13–34. The one at €22 is really worth a try given a choice of dishes like calf's head, zander with vanilla and rabbit with mushrooms. You can eat out in the garden. Friendly welcome.

☆ I●I RESTAURANT LE PARIS

1 rue Darreau (North); go up faubourg Chartrain and it's

after the train station.
☎ 02.54.77.02.71 ➡ 02.54.73.17.71
Closed Sun and Tues evenings; Mon; 20 July–13 Aug.

An excellent gourmet restaurant. It's run by a charming woman, the service is faultless and the chef – who has a particular talent for sauces – is inspired. Try the calf's head *ravigote* in a spicy *vinaigrette*, the ox kidneys with Rougier, the rolled sole fillets with crayfish or the duck thigh *confit* and cep pancakes. Delicious dishes, all of which go well with a good local wine like the Bourgueil Domaine Lalande. Set menus €14–29. Free coffee.

SAINT-OUEN   41100 (2KM N)

I●I LA VALLÉE

34 rue Barré-de-Saint-Venant; from Vendôme, take the D92 and head for Paris and the centre of Saint-Ouen.
☎ 02.54.77.29.93 ➡ 02.54.73.16.96
Closed Mon and Tues; 7–30 Jan; the last fortnight in Sept.

Don't let the uninspiring exterior put you off – go straight in and take a look at the menus. You won't regret it: even the cheapest at €15 (not served Sun) boasts a selection of delights. Other menus €21–36.The specialities change with the seasons, the cooking is sophisticated and the dishes are beautifully presented. Courteous welcome.

PEZOU   41100 (15KM N)

I●I AUBERGE DE LA SELLERIE

Fontaine; it's on the RN10.
☎ 02.54.23.41.43
Closed Mon, Tues and three weeks in Jan.

Rustic but chic décor. It's a good inn set back from the main road from Chartres to Vendôme. There's an appetizing menu at €15, which changes nearly every day and includes half a bottle of wine and coffee. Dishes are of the order of warm *andouille* salad, *brandade* of salt cod, farmhouse cheeses and strawberry *au gratin*. The cuisine is rich, inventive and of good quality. Other menus €23–43. They serve until a decent time, and even if you show up late they still give you a smile.

LAVARDIN   41800 (18KM W)

☆ I●I LE RELAIS D'ANTAN

6 pl. du Capitaine du Vignau (Centre); take the D917, when you get to Saint-Rimay, turn left on the road to Montoire.
☎ 02.54.86.61.33

Closed Mon evening; Tues; fortnights in the Feb and autumn school holidays.

You're in for a real feast – and at a reasonable price. The choice is deliberately limited so the chef can ensure only the freshest ingredients are used to create his refined, inventive dishes: crayfish lasagne with parmesan cheese, grilled zander with *beurre blanc*. Two menus at €24 and €29. The service is friendly and the dining room is pretty; they only have a few tables so you need to book. Free coffee.

VEUIL 36600

⚷ I●I AUBERGE SAINT-FIACRE**

Le bourg (Centre).
☎ 02.54.40.32.78
Closed Tues evening and Wed except public holidays; the Feb school holidays. **Disabled access.**

A seventeenth-century inn in a flower-filled village with a stream running through it. In summer you dine under the ancient chestnut trees to the accompaniment of the trickling fountain and in winter around the giant fireplace. The chef changes his menus frequently, inspired by fresh seasonal produce. Light, tasty dishes include snails and veal sweetbread salad or Dublin Bay prawns *croustillant*, pan-fried *escalope* of *foie gras* with figs and moist fig and almond cake with vanilla ice-cream. Menus €20 (not Sun), €28 and €34. Free *digestif*.

YZEURES-SUR-CREUSE 37290

⌂ I●I HÔTEL-RESTAURANT LA PROMENADE***

1 pl. du 11-Novembre (Centre); it's on the D104 opposite the church.
☎ 02.47.91.49.00 ➡ 02.47.94.46.12
Closed Tues; 10 Jan–10 Feb. **TV. Car park.**

This hotel is in a handsome eighteenth-century building which used to be a coaching inn. The fifteen rooms are decorated in restrained rustic style in delicate pale green, grey and dark red; doubles with bath €49. There's a small sitting room with a piano on the mezzanine. Mme Bussereau creates delicious dishes that bear her own inventive imprint from the best produce she can find on the market – game in season, free-range poultry and excellent fish. She also makes the house *terrines* and bakes the bread. Set menus €21–55. The cheapest is not served after 8.30pm or on Sunday.

Champagne-Ardennes

08 Ardennes

10 Aube

51 Marne

52 Haute-Marne

AIX-EN-OTHE   10160

衣 ♠ |●| AUBERGE DE LA SCIERIE***

3 route de Druisy, lieu-dit La Vove; it's 1.5km from Aix-en-Othe on the D374.
☎ 03.25.46.71.26 ➡ 03.25.46.65.69
Closed Mon and Tues 1 Sept–30 April. **Swimming pool. Garden. TV. Car park**.

The stream winding through the peaceful grounds of this hotel used to power the saw-mill, and much of the original charm of the seventeenth-century building has been retained. There are fifteen stylish rooms, all €62 with shower/wc or bath. In summer they set tables out in the garden for lunch or dinner. There's a €13 lunch menu (not Sun or public holidays), and others €23–40. Specialities include trout stuffed with mushrooms, Troyes *andouilette* in pastry, house *foie gras terrine* and *crème brûlée* with cider Ratafia. 10% discount on the room rate 1 Sept–15 May.

BAR-SUR-AUBE   10200

衣 ♠ HÔTEL SAINT-PIERRE

5 rue Saint-Pierre (Centre).
☎ 03.25.27.13.58
Closed Sun and public holidays. **Car park**.

A simple, well-run family-style hotel just opposite Saint-Pierre church (worth a visit for its wooden gallery and tombstones). Rooms 8, 9 and 10 have a view of the church but be warned: the bells start ringing at 7am. Doubles with basin €20, shower with wc along the landing €21, or shower/wc €27. There's no restaurant, but there is a lively bar. A nice

place at very reasonable prices. Free glass of local champagne.

|●| UN P'TIT CREUX

pl. du Corps-de-Garde (Centre); entrance 24 rue Nationale.
☎ 03.25.27.37.75
Closed Sun and Mon except in Aug.

This bright, friendly *crêperie* is in a modern shopping centre in the old centre of Bar: it's ideal if you fancy a quick bite. The specials menu brings together pancakes and pizzas in a curious alliance between Brittany and Italy. There are several other menus, based mostly on *galettes*; they cost €9–21. It's great in summer, when you can sit outside on the terrace.

|●| LA TOQUE BARALBINE

18 rue Nationale.
☎ 03.25.27.20.34
Closed Sun evening and Mon except public holidays, and a fortnight in Jan.

After years working in different establishments on the Côte d'Azur, the owner returned to his roots and opened his own gourmet restaurant – and won a loyal local following within months of opening. Sophisticated cooking in very pleasant surroundings: *foie gras* with Guérande salt, seafood pancake with Champagne sauce and hot prune and Ratafia soufflé. Menus €16–46. Friendly, unaffected staff. Free coffee.

衣 |●| LE CELLIER AUX MOINES

rue du Général-Vouillemont; it's behind St-Pierre church.
☎ 03.25.27.08.01
Closed Sun–Thurs evenings; two weeks in Feb.

This twelfth-century cellar is remarkable in

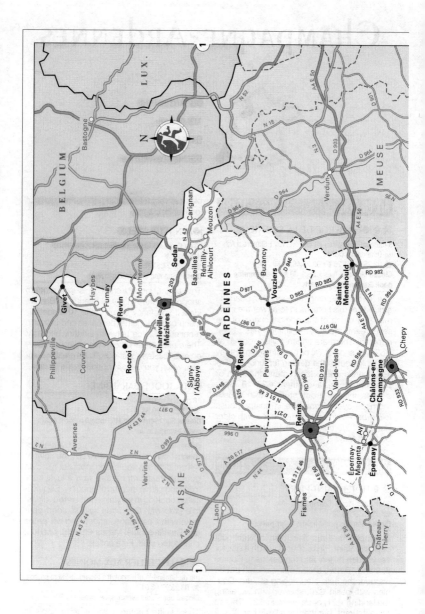

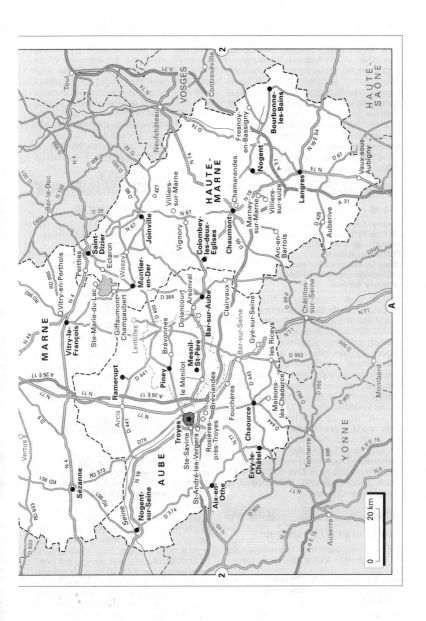

more than one way. It's the site local wine-growers chose to meet when the local sparkling wine lost the right to be called "champagne" in 1912, and scrawled inscriptions on the walls recount the suffering of the local villages. After a struggle, the wine was reclassified – you'll find it on the pricey end of the wine list. Make the most of the confident cooking: *lentillons* salad with champagne, smoked salmon and haddock, stuffed chicken with a sweet and sour onion marmalade, grilled Chaource cheese. Menus €12–27. The décor is a bit spartan, though the candles on the tables soften the general appearance. Service is on the brisk side of efficient, but perhaps it will relax in time. Free coffee.

ARSONVAL   10200 (6KM NW)

🎿 🏠 |●| HOSTELLERIE LA CHAUMIÈRE**

How to get there: take the N19 in the direction of Troyes and it's on the left on the way out of Arsonval.
☎ 03.25.27.91.02 ➤ 03.25.27.90.26
📧 lachaumiere@pem.net
Closed Sun evening and Mon except in summer and public holidays; mid-Feb to mid-March. **Disabled access. TV. Car park.**

This old village inn, run by an Anglo-French couple, has an old red English telephone box to add a bit of "couleur locale". Carefully prepared meals are generously served in a lovely dining room with wooden beams. In fine weather you can have lunch or dinner on the shady terrace, and they have opened a new dining room as well. Dishes include house *foie gras*, chicken supreme with melting Chaource cheese and fish in champagne sauce. Weekday menu €15 with others at €23–46. There are some rooms in the main building and others in a stark modern structure which is somewhat out of keeping with the old half-timbered house – but they all have views of the grounds and the river. Doubles with shower/wc €49 or €52 with bath. Good, friendly welcome. 10% discount on the room rate Oct–April

DOLANCOURT   10200 (9KM NW)

🎿|●| LE MOULIN DU LANDION***

How to get there; going towards Troyes on the N19, take the left fork 2km after Arsonval and follow the signs in the village.
☎ 03.25.27.92.17 ➤ 03.25.27.94.44
Closed 1 20 Nov–20 Feb. **Swimming pool. Garden. TV. Car park.**

This place is ultra-classy. The shady garden

has a swimming pool and inside the décor is smart – the bright, spacious rooms have small balconies. They are modern in contrast to the rustic dining room in the old mill. The restaurant overlooks the river, while the bay windows open onto the working millwheel; tables are also set at the waterside. Prices reflect the quality of the surroundings: double rooms range from €62 to €72; breakfast costs €7 extra. The cheapest set menu at €17 is not served at the weekend; others are €25–52. Dishes inlude trout fillet with Champagne cream sauce and pear *sabayon* with champagne and glazed sugar. This is a tranquil spot not far from the mad world of the Nigoland amusement park. 10% discount on the room rate.

CLAIRVAUX-SUR-AUBE   10310 (14KM SE)

🎿 🏠 |●| HÔTEL-RESTAURANT DE L'ABBAYE*

18–19 route de Dijon; where the D12 and D396 cross.
☎ 03.25.27.80.12 ➤ 03.25.27.75.79
Closed 20 Dec–10 Jan. **Garden. TV. Car park.**

Once you've arrived here, you'll have left Champagne behind and crossed into the vast forests of Burgundy. Saint Bernard of Clairvaux founded the first Cistercian abbey in these very woods in the twelfth century; the same building is now a prison, with high walls and watchtowers. The hotel is just opposite, which some may find a little strange – if you do, avoid room 17, which looks directly onto it. Doubles from €23 with basin to €35 with bath. Perhaps unsurprisingly, it's very quiet at night. Weekday menu €10, then others €12–19. 10% discount on the room rate.

BOURBONNE-LES-BAINS   52400

🎿 🏠 |●| HÔTEL D'ORFEUIL**

29 rue d'Orfeuil (Southwest); 80m from the spa.
☎ 03.25.90.05.71 ➤ 03.25.84.46.25
Closed Wed evening and 1 Nov–1 April. **Swimming pool. Disabled access. TV. Car park.**

This lovely eighteenth-century house has aged beautifully. It's on a hillside surrounded by a leafy garden in which they've built a very pleasant pool. Very tasteful inside, with antique family furniture, rugs and fireplaces. It's a welcoming place where you get good value for money: €41–46 for a double with shower/wc in the new annexe — the old part is reserved for people taking the waters. Ask for a room with a balcony and a view over the park. Informal restaurant with set menus

€9–24. Healthy buffet breakfasts for the diet-conscious. Free coffee.

⅍ ≙ |●| HÔTEL DES SOURCES**

12 rue de l'Amiral Pierre (Centre); it's next to the baths.
☎ 03.25.87.86.00 ➡ 03.25.87.86.33
e hotel-des-sources@wanadoo.fr
Closed Nov–March. **TV. Garden. Car park.**

A dynamic young couple run this establishment and offer modern, functional and pleasant rooms. Ask to see a selection, because their size varies considerably – number 34 is big and has a corner sitting room and a garden view. All rooms have en-suite facilities and some have a separate wc; doubles with shower/wc and corner kitchen are €41–46. Half board €47–54 per person. Unlike others in town, the restaurant doesn't limit itself to slimmed-down cuisine: specialities include salmon tartare, sole fillet *à la Provençale* and an excellent chocolate *trufflon*. Menus €11–24. Professional yet personal welcome. 10% discount on the room rate.

⅍ ≙ |●| LES ARMOISES – HÔTEL LE JEANNE D'ARC***

12 rue de l'Amiral Pierre (Centre).
☎ 03.25.90.46.00 ➡ 03.25.88.78.71
e hoteljda@free.fr
Closed Sun evening and Nov to mid-March. **TV. Swimming pool. Garden. Car park.**

Not surprisingly, this is the only gourmet restaurant in this health-obsessed spa town. The standard is good: supreme of chicken with *vin jaune* and morels, pork *filet mignon* with mirabelle plums and chocolate *marquise*. Set menus €15–27. There's service in the garden in fine weather. The rooms are simple rather than charming and a double with shower or bath will cost you €41–54. Most people come to the town to take the waters so it's quiet in the evenings; last orders here are at 9pm. Free apéritif with dinner.

▨ FRESNOY-EN-BASSIGNY 52400 (12.5KM NW)

⅍ |●| RESTAURANT DU LAC DE MORIMOND

Le Lac de Morimond; take the D139 and 2.5km after Fresnoy-en-Bassigny, take the right turn and follow the signs.
☎ 03.25.90.80.86
Closed evenings except June–Sept; 15 Oct–15 March. **Disabled access. Garden. Car park.**

In the depths of the country, close to the ruined Cistercian abbey, there's a little lake

encircled by forest where anglers come to tickle carp in the dark of the night. It's the ideal spot to enjoy some freshly caught fish or a nice fillet steak with wild girolle mushrooms, which you eat on the terrace overlooking the water. The dining room is also lovely, with an attractive, welcoming fireplace. You get a good selection of dishes on the lengthy menu: zander fillet *meunière*, crayfish tail salad, whitebait of lake fish, grilled *tournedos*, sirloin steak. One menu at €20 or it'll be about €23 *à la carte*. Free apéritif.

▨ CHÂLONS-EN-CHAMPAGNE 51000

⅍ ≙ HÔTEL PASTEUR**

46 rue Pasteur (East); it's about 600m from the church of Notre-Dame-en-Vaux.
☎ 03.26.68.10.00 ➡ 03.26.21.51.09
Disabled access. Garden. TV. Car park.

Part of this hotel used to be a convent which explains the superb, grand staircase. The quiet rooms over the courtyard at the back get the sun. Doubles €26 with shower but no TV, €35 with shower/wc and telephone or €41 with bath. 10% discount on the room rate.

⅍ ≙ HÔTEL DE LA CITÉ**

12 rue de la Charrière (Northeast); take rue J-J Rousseau, turn right after pl. des Ursulines and follow the signs to the Cité Administrative.
☎ 03.26.64.31.20 ➡ 03.26.70.96.21
Disabled access. Garden. TV.

This is a peaceful, provincial place, very much like a family guesthouse, with a regular clientele of businessmen, sales reps and students. Everyone is warmly greeted by the owners, who spare no effort in keeping their hotel nice – it's clean though not luxurious. A few rooms look onto the garden where you can enjoy breakfast (€5) in fine weather or just relax with a book. €27 for a room with a shower, and €34 with a bath. Room 1 is bright and spacious with an enormous bathroom. There's a pool table and TV room. 10% discount.

⅍ ≙ |●| RESTAURANT JEAN-PAUL SOUPLY

8 faubourg Saint-Antoine; it's 500m from the town centre opposite the young workers' hostel.
☎ 03.26.68.18.91 ➡ 03.26.21.76.47
e Restaurant.souply@wanadoo.fr
Closed Sun except Easter Day and Whitsun; Aug. **Car park.**

A family affair which involves members of three generations. Grandmother runs the bar

– she's been in the business more than 65 years – the daughter-in-law manages the restaurant and the son is the owner and chef, who carefully prepares traditional dishes using fresh market produce. He specializes in traditional dishes served in portions which would satisfy a famished giant. Menus €11–22 and a weekday *formule* at €9. They have a few modest rooms where you can stay half-board at €33 per person. Free coffee.

☂ ☗ HÔTEL DU POT D'ÉTAIN**

18 pl. de la République (Centre).
☎ 03.26.68.09.09 ➡ 03.26.68.58.18
e hotel.le.pot.detain@wanadoo.fr
TV. Pay car park.

This impressive fifteenth-century house has been beautifully renovated by the family that owns it. Double rooms with shower/wc and telephone €49, with bath €52. There's also a pleasant single room and six family-size ones which sleep four; number 102 has a view of the square, which is lively day and night. Monsieur Georges, who used to be a baker, prepares the croissants for breakfast and all the tarts and puddings – he'll bake different things as the mood takes him. You can leave your car parked outside the hotel and explore Châlons on foot. There's a weekend deal: stay Fri, Sat and Sun and you get the third night free – Jan–March only.

☗ |●| HÔTEL LE RENARD***

24 pl. de la République (Centre).
☎ 03.26.68.03.78 ➡ 03.26.64.50.07
Closed Sat lunchtime, Sun evening and Christmas–New Year. **TV. Car park**.

The décor in the 35 rooms of this establishment has stood the test of time and still looks good – though some may not like the beds being positioned in the middle of the room. The walls are also rather thin and the hotel's noisy. Doubles €58 with bath. The brasserie terrace is very popular because it opens out onto the square and serves pretty decent food. There is also a gourmet restaurant which offers a balance between modern tastes and traditional dishes. Menus €15, €18 and €29. Credit cards not accepted.

☂ |●| LE PRÉ SAINT-ALPIN

2 [bis] rue de l'Abbé Lambert (Centre).
☎ 03.26.70.20.26 ➡ 03.26.68.52.20
Closed Sun evening.

This magnificent establishment dates back to 1850 and still has its resplendent stained-glass windows and moulded ceilings. It's a fine example of nineteenth-century architecture, displaying both nobility and elegance. But when you're sitting on the terrace on a beautiful summer evening in a wonderfully serene atmosphere, you could be sitting down to dinner in your own home. Inventive cuisine: snails in pastry cases with melted Reblochon cheese and a wonderful tart with chocolate and pistachio. The chef, who trained in some of the best kitchens, achieves the perfect balance between tradition and innovation. Menus €15–36. The separate bistro serves a *formule* with cold starters, main course and dessert. Free coffee.

CHEPY   51240 (7KM SE)

☂ |●| COMME CHEZ SOI

49 route Nationale; from Châlons, take the N44 in the direction of Vitry-le-François.
☎ 03.26.67.50.21
Closed Sun and Mon evenings; Tues; a fortnight in Jan; a week in Aug.

Both the setting and the cooking are unreconstructedly provincial. Weekday menu €11 and others €18–31. The regional menu gives you a good idea of the local specialities: snails with red cabbage, panfried *foie gras* with Ratafia, braised trout with juniper berries, regional cheeses and sorbet with *marc de Champagne*. You can also get a straightforward menu with a choice ranging from steak and chips to more elaborate dishes like potatoes Maxime and scallops. Friendly welcome. Free house apéritif.

CHAOURCE   10210

☂ ☗ |●| HÔTEL-RESTAURANT LES FONTAINES

1 rue des Fontaines (Centre); D443.
☎ 03.25.40.00.85 ➡ 03.25.40.01.80
ℯ Alain.Musnier@wanadoo.fr
Closed Mon evening; Tues; 2–23 Jan; the last week in July. **TV. Car park**.

Chaource is located where Champagne borders Burgundy and the restaurant serves authentic regional dishes from both departments. The €12 set menu (not Sat evening, Sun or public holidays), offers a choice of four dishes at each course, the a *menu surprise* at €15 and a *menu du terroir* at €23. Specialities include fresh mushroom upside-down tart with farmhouse Chaource cheese, salmon escalope with foaming Champagne sauce and *croustillant* of Troyes *andouillette*. Half a dozen rooms with shower/wc, telephone and TV for €27; half board at €35, is compulsory at weekends. 10% discount on the room rate weekdays.

MAISONS-LÈS-CHAOURCE 10210 (6KM S)

⬛|●| HÔTEL-RESTAURANT AUX MAISONS***

How to get there: take the D34.
☎ 03.25.70.07.19 ➡ 03.25.70.07.75
Swimming pool. Disabled access. TV. Car park.

A large, well-kept family hotel in a little village in the south of the Aube, the region famous for Chaource cheese. The hotel has undergone substantial refurbishment and has recently gained a third star. Doubles €53 with shower or bath – some overlook the garden and the swimming pool. The restaurant has been renovated, too, and the main dining room boasts a splendid monumental fireplace. In the kitchens, the owner and her son concoct exquisite regional dishes served in substantial portions. Set menus €18, €23 and €29. Service can take time.

RICEYS (LES) 10340 (22KM SE)

⬛ ⬛ |●| HÔTEL-RESTAURANT LE MAGNY**

Route de Tonnerre; it's on the D453.
☎ 03.25.29.38.39 ➡ 03.25.29.11.72
Closed Tues evening; Wed; Jan–Feb. **Disabled access. Swimming pool. Garden. TV. Car park.**

Les Riceys is not content with having three churches. It's also the only village in France to produce three AOC wines – one of them a famous rosé that was once Louis XIV's favourite tipples. The chef uses the wine in the sauces of a number of dishes and he also uses Chaource cheese and Troyes *andouillette*. Set menus €11–35. Peaceful rooms; €43–46 for a double with shower/wc and telephone. There's a small garden with a heated swimming pool in summer, or you can visit the park nearby, designed by Le Nôtre. Free coffee.

GYÉ-SUR-SEINE 10250 (28KM E)

⬛ |●| HÔTEL LES VOYAGEURS – LE RELAIS

It's on the D70, on the edge of the village.
☎ 03.25.38.20.09 ➡ 03.25.38.25.37
Closed Wed; Sun evening; the Feb school holidays. **Car park.**

An old posthouse run by a young, smiling pair. It's in the midst of the Champagne vineyard. Bottles of champagne for €18 each

and robust cuisine. The chef's specialities vary according to his fancy and the weather: asparagus in pastry cases, calves' head *gribiche*, zander with garden herb butter. You might well catch him gathering fresh herbs from the garden below the veranda. Simple, traditional, tasty dishes. When the sun shines, you can have breakfast or savour an apéritif in the garden.

CHARLEVILLE-MÉZIÈRES 08000

⬛ ⬛ HÔTEL DE PARIS**

24 av. G-Corneau (Southeast); it's opposite the station.
☎ 03.24.33.34.38 ➡ 03.24.59.11.21
✉ hotel-de-paris-08@wanadoo.fr
Closed 24 Dec–4 Jan. **TV.**

Rimbaud was born here, and although he cursed the arrival of the railway, his statue stands proudly in the station square. The hotel owner and her cat provide a friendly welcome, and the rooms are classically decorated. The ones on the street side are soundproofed, while those overlooking the inner courtyard couldn't be quieter. Doubles with shower €43–67 and €45–67 with bath, and there are three family rooms. 10% discount Sept–June.

⬛ |●| RESTAURANT LE DAMIER

7 rue Bayard (South); coming from Charleville, take the avenue d'Arches and take the second on the right after the bridge over the Meuse.
☎ 03.24.37.76.89
Closed Mon–Thurs evenings; Sat; Aug.

This is a unique restaurant run by an association set up to give young and disadvantaged people training and experience, so be patient if the service is sometimes a bit below par. The €6 dish of the day and the €8 menu make this place good value for money, and the food is simple but tasty. The restaurant is bright with a chequered floor. Prices go up a notch on Fri and Sat evening, when menus go for €9–17 and the cooking is slightly more sophisticated: *feuilleté du Carolo*, beef *à l'Ardennaise*, trout soufflé with a scallop sauce, game in season. The menus change every week. An initiative that deserves support. Free house apéritif.

CHAUMONT 52000

⬛ ⬛ |●| HÔTEL-RESTAURANT LE RELAIS

20 faubourg de la Maladière (Northeast); it's 1km from the centre of Chaumont, on the N74 to Nancy.

☎ 03.25.03.02.84
Closed Sun evening, Mon, a fortnight in Jan and a
fortnight July–Aug. **TV**.

A former coaching inn on the outskirts of
Chaumont, this is an unpretentious place set
between the roadside and the banks of the
canal linking the Marne and the Saône.
Seven fairly peaceful rooms which have been
renovated – numbers 6 and 7 are particularly quiet – and prices are reasonable: €31–37
for a double with shower or bath. Carefully
prepared, sophisticated cuisine with seafood
as a speciality – prawn kebab, scallops with
whisky, salmon *escalope* with mustard.
There's a *formule* for €10 and menus
€13–18. Friendly welcome. Free coffee.

⅔ ≜ I●I HÔTEL-RESTAURANT DES
REMPARTS***

72 rue de Verdun (Centre); very close to the town walls.
☎ 03.25.32.64.40 ➡ 03.25.32.51.70
Closed 25 Dec and 31 Dec.
Disabled access. **TV**. **Public car park** opposite hotel.

This place offers the best value for money in
Chaumont. The rooms, decorated with
posters from the Chaumont Arts Festival, are
clean and efficiently soundproofed, and there
are newer, more spacious ones in the
annexe. Doubles with shower/wc or bath
€44–56. Classic setting in the classy restaurant and first-rate, imaginative cooking: pan-
fried *foie gras* with tart apples, *tournedos
Rossini* with truffles, salmon in Pinot Noir
sauce and veal sweetbreads in flaky pastry
with morels. Set menus €11–37. The *Lucifer*
grill provides a more relaxed atmosphere and
brasserie dishes at modest prices. 50% discount on the room rate for a two-night stay
between 15 Nov and 15 April, if you stay over
a weekend and have two meals in the restaurant each day. 10% discount on the room
rate.

≜ I●I GRAND HOTEL TERMINUS
REINE***

pl. Charles-de-Gaulle (Centre); it's opposite the train
station.
☎ 03.25.03.01.11 ➡ 03.25.32.35.80
TV. **Car park**.

The former residence of the Counts of
Champagne. It was rebuilt in the middle of
the twentieth century and its turreted, yellow
façade and blue shutters give it a modern air.
All the facilities you'd expect in a three-star
hotel are provided in this establishment.
Nearly all the 63 rooms have been refurbished; they're spruce and spacious with

modern bathrooms. Doubles with shower
€49, €64 with bath. The restaurant serves
classic dishes at rather high prices, but
there's a more modestly priced pizzeria and
grill. Appropriately professional service.

CHAMARANDES   52000 (2KM SE)

⅔ ≜ I●I AU RENDEZ-VOUS DES AMIS**

4 pl. du Tilleul (Southeast).
☎ 03.25.32.20.20 ➡ 03.25.02.60.90
Hotel closed 1–20 Aug. **Restaurant closed** Fri and
Sun evenings, Sat. **Disabled access**. **TV**. **Car park**.

The River Marne runs through this unspoilt
little village where the old church and school
stand near the shady banks. You can
glimpse the manor house through the trees
of the estate. This is a genuine, quiet country
inn with charm, and you get a friendly welcome – all in all, a great place to stop. Rooms
have been tastefully renovated and doubles
cost €40 with shower or €52–58 with show-
er/wc or bath; one room has been adapted
for disabled visitors. The restaurant is full of
hunters, fishermen, businessmen and people
travelling through. In summer they serve outside on a lovely terrace shaded by an ancient
lime tree. Creative gourmet cooking – duck
foie gras with monkfish liver, salmon cooked
in leaves, roast duck with a *foie gras fondant*.
The wine list has 320 different vintages.
Weekday menu €15 and €22–37. Free
house apéritif.

MARNAY-SUR-MARNE   52000 (18KM SE)

⅔ ≜ I●I HÔTEL-RESTAURANT LA VALLÉE

It's on the N19, in the direction of Langres.
☎ 03.25.31.10.11 ➡ 03.25.03.83.86
Closed Sun evening except July–Aug; Mon; a fortnight
Sept–Oct; a fortnight at the beginning of March. **TV**. **Car
park**.

Monsieur Farina produces such good food
that it's easy to forget the noise of the main
road outside. His place has a good reputation, and rightly so, because his local dishes
are skilfully prepared. Try his *cassolette* of
snails with Marc de Bourgogne or his chick-
en supreme with oyster mushrooms, and finish with a *gratin* of soft fruit. The small, rustic
dining rooms are crammed with diners – the
overflow goes onto the terrace when the
weather is good. Menu of the day €10 or
€15–34 listing dishes such as snail stew with
Burgundy Marc, scallops with cream, chives
and toungue in a pastry case and red fruit
with burned sugar. The half-dozen rooms,
decorated in provincial style, are fresh and

pleasant but quite noisy because of the main road. Doubles with shower/wc €38. Really warm welcome and a family atmosphere. Free house apéritif.

VIGNORY 52320 (20KM N)

☎ |●| LE RELAIS VERDOYANT**

rue de la Gare; take the N67 inn the direction of Saint-Dizier then signs to Vignory gare.
☎ 03.25.02.44.49 ➡ 03.25.01.96.89
Closed Sun evening; Mon lunchtime; Mon evening Oct–April; Nov; 22 Dec–15 March. **TV. Garden. Disabled access. Car park**.

This house was built in the early 1900s to provide accommodation for travellers getting off the train at Vignory station. There aren't so many trains nowadays, but the hotel and garden are as elegant as ever The small, stylish rooms are named after flowers and cost €36 for a double with shower/wc or bath. They're as charming now as they look in the sepia photos of the hotel in the reception area. Traditional cuisine at reasonable prices, offering duck breast with shallots, chicken liver *terrine* with port and iced nougat with a fruit *coulis*. Set menus €13–22.

VILLIERS-SUR-SUZE 52210 (20KM S)

⅍ ☎ |●| AUBERGE DE LA FONTAINE**

2 place de la Fontaine; take the N19 in the direction of Langres, then the D143 to Villiers-sur-Suze.
☎ 03.25.31.22.22 ➡ 03.25.03.15.76
Closed evenings except by reservation, a fortnight in Sept and a fortnight in March. **Disabled access. TV**.

A nice little inn with red shutters smothered in creepers, set in a village surrounded by woods and fields. It's a lovely place to stop for a drink, buy your papers or have a bite to eat. Settle down like the locals in the bar with its shiny ceiling, in the corner sitting room in front of the open fire, in the restaurant with its ancient stone walls, or, in sunny weather, on the terrace. Dish of the day €9 and set menus €15–26 with good, simple, flavoursome dishes that change frequently: try steak with shallots, *bœuf bourguignon*, rabbit with mustard or *civet* of wild boar in season. Seven or so newly decorated, comfortable rooms in a separate building just a step away. They're €37 for a double with shower/wc or €43 with bath. And if you've forgotten your toothpaste, no worries – the village grocery is in the hotel. Genuine, warm welcome extended by the young owner: this place has brought life back to the village. Free pot of honey.

COLOMBEY-LES-DEUX-ÉGLISES 52330

☎ |●| L'AUBERGE DE LA MONTAGNE**

17 rue de la Montagne.
☎ 03.25.01.51.69 ➡ 03.25.01.53.20
Closed Mon evening and Tues out of season; mid-Jan to mid-Feb. **TV. Car park**.

Small inn, little village, great man – this was General de Gaulle's home. The owner, Gérard Natali, was one of the twelve pall-bearers at the general's funeral in 1970. Today people from all over the world come to stay here, from the ex-King of Yemen to the Japanese ambassador, and Breton quarry-owners to French ex-pats. It offers gourmet dining in a chic, rustic setting, and the seasonal dishes feature fresh, local produce. Extensive menus at €20 on weekdays or €29–73 at weekends. Specialities include boned pigeon with regional truffles, zander cooked in its skin with a crayfish turnover and game in season. The charming rooms are really peaceful; they're €43–72 with shower/wc or bath. Breakfast is pricey.

ÉPERNAY 51200

☎ HÔTEL DE CHAMPAGNE***

30 rue Eugène-Mercier (Centre).
☎ 03.26.53.10.60 ➡ 03.26.51.94.63
e infos@loc-hotel-champagne.com
Closed first fortnight in Jan. **TV. Car park**.

The best hotel in the town centre. It's modern and comfortable, and has double glazing. Room prices depend on facilities: €69 with shower to €85 with bath. About ten rooms are due to be fitted with air conditioning. Unlimited self-service buffet breakfast for €9.

⅍ |●| LA GRILLADE

16 rue de Reims; it's near the station.
☎ 03.26.55.44.22
Closed Sat lunchtime and Sun except public holidays; a fortnight in Sept. **Garden**.

This place is more commonly known as *Chez Blanche*, after the owner. The speciality is grilling things over an open fire: sardines, bass with fennel, T-bone steak, *andouillettes* cooked to perfection. More surprising is the dessert: banana grilled over the open fire then flambéed. There's usually a full house. The pretty flower-filled garden and shady terrace are at their best in summer. Set menus €13–27. Free apéritif.

EPERNAY-MAGENTA   51530 (1KM N)

☆ |●| CHEZ MAX

13 av. A. Thevenet; it's 1km from the town centre on the Dizy road.
☎ 03.26.55.23.59
Closed Sun and Wed evenings; Mon; a fortnight in Jan; 3 weeks in Aug.

This popular restaurant has been going since 1946 and has kept up its good reputation. Weekday set menu €11 with a choice of five starters, three main courses – braised ham, scorpion fish *bouillabaisse* or veal stew – then salads or cheese and dessert. Other menus are priced at €15–33 and dishes change frequently because they are all cooked using fresh seasonal produce. There's also a celebration menu available at the weekend. Free *digestif*.

ERVY-LE-CHATEL   10130

☆ |●| AUBERGE DE LA VALLÉE DE L'ARMANCE

It's opposite the station.
☎ 03.25.70.66.36
Closed Sun evening; Mon; 16–31 Aug. **Car park**.

You don't go through the bar to get to the restaurant – it has its own entrance round the back. The dining room has been converted from an old cowshed: part of an old wooden manger has been left in its place and it's decorated with old implements – hay forks and wooden bread paddles hang on the wall. Good regional food includes *gratin d'andouillette*, house *foie gras* and veal sweetbreads with oyster mushrooms. The menu at €10 includes wine and coffee, there's a bistro *formule* and another for €19. Free coffee.

GIVET   08600

☆ 🛏 |●| HÔTEL-RESTAURANT DU NORD*

27 rue Thiers (North).
☎ 03.24.42.01.78 ➡ 03.24.40.46.79
Closed Fri, Sun evening and 23 Dec–13 Jan. **Disabled access**. **TV**. **Car park**.

This is a little place with low prices. The street's quiet despite being in the middle of town. Rooms are basic and situated above the restaurant or opposite in an annexe – and you've got to like psychedelic wallpaper. Doubles with washing facilities €22, or €33

with shower/wc. Unpretentious bar-restaurant with classic cooking and a slighty old-fashioned atmosphere. Set menus at €10–24. Free house apéritif.

☆ 🛏 LES REFLETS JAUNES***

2 rue du Général-de-Gaulle.
☎ 03.24.42.85.85 ➡ 03.24.42.85.86
e reflets-jaunes@wanadoo.fr
Disabled access. **TV**. **Lock-up car park**.

A brand-new hotel with colourfully painted rooms and particularly good facilities: hair dryer, mini-bar, air conditioning, video-player and Internet access. The rooms are sound-proofed too, which is just as well because the hotel is in the centre of town. Doubles €43–73. Buffet breakfast. 10% discount on the room rate and free apéritif with a meal.

☆ 🛏 HÔTEL LE VAL SAINT-HILAIRE**

7 quai des Fours; coming from Charleville, it's on the left as you enter the town.
☎ 03.24.42.85.85 ➡ 03.24.42.85.86
e hotel-val-saint-hilaire@wanadoo.fr
Closed 20 Dec–5 Jan. **Disabled access**. **TV**. **Car park**.

The area is famous for its blue stone – back in the eighteenth century, it was used in the construction of this old printer's. The bedrooms are pleasant and subtly decorated in contemporary style. The ones overlooking the road and the river Meuse have double glazing (triple glazing on the ground floor) but if you're very sensitive to noise, ask for a room overlooking the courtyard. Doubles with bath €53. The restaurant specializes in local dishes – veal sweetbreads in champagne, turkey, trout *à l'ardennaise*. Menus €17–28. The bar has a terrace on the waterside where the pleasureboats tie up. You get the best welcome in town and the owners are very informative about the walks you can do in the area. Free house apéritif.

FUMAY   08170 (20KM S)

☆ |●| HOSTELLERIE DE LA VALLÉE

146 pl. Aristide-Briand; it's on the N51.
☎ 03.24.41.15.61
Closed Sun evening, Mon and the end of Feb.

The country inn you were looking for. The owner is in charge of the dining room and serves the varied local dishes in substantial portions: Ardennes *charcuterie*, frogs' legs and white pudding in pastry with port sauce. Weekday menu €10 or €15–34. Free coffee.

JOINVILLE 52300

🏠 |O| HÔTEL-RESTAURANT DE LA POSTE★★

pl. de la Grève; it's on the St-Dizier road.
☎ 03.25.94.12.63 ➡ 03.25.94.36.23
Closed Sun evening in winter; 10 Jan–10 Feb. **TV**. **Car park**.

They do have rooms here but the main draw is the chef's delicious cooking: *emincé* of monkfish with baby vegetables, duck breast with raspberry vinegar, veal kidneys, trout *sire de Joinville.* The weekday set menu for €12 is remarkable value, providing starter, meat or fish main course, cheese and dessert. Other menus are €21–34. Impeccable service and comfortable, quiet rooms for €31–43 with double glazing and shower/wc or bath.

🎋 🏠 |O| LE SOLEIL D'OR★★★

9 rue des Capucins (Centre); it's beside Notre Dame church.
☎ 03.25.94.15.66 ➡ 03.25.94.39.02
Closed Sun evening; Mon; second fortnight in Feb; first week in Aug; a week in Nov. **TV**. **Pay garage**.

If you're a fan of cosy rooms with stone walls this is the hotel for you. It's spacious and light, and offers good value for money. Doubles €37–61 with shower/wc or €40–69 with bath. The vaulted dining room looks rather gothic with its wooden beams, stained glass, stone and wood. It's warm and refined and provides the perfect setting for the chef's specialities: zander turnover with shrips, quail from Dombes with cinnamon, pan-fried scallops with saffron sauce. The food doesn't come at giveaway prices, though: €32 and €49 for the two gourmet menus, but there's a more basic weekday menu for €18. Free use of garage.

VILLIERS-SUR-MARNE 52320 (17KM S)

🎋 |O| LA SOURCE BLEUE

Lieu-dit La Source; take the N67 in the direction of Chauon, at Villiers, take the Doulaincourt road and follow the signs.
☎ 03.25.94.70.35 ➡ 03.25.05.02.09
Closed Sun evening; Mon; 15 Dec–15 Jan. **TV**. **Garden**. **Car park**.

An ideal country retreat in an old mill by a river way out in the country. It's run by a young couple who have decorated it thoughtfully and created a warm atmosphere. Dynamic service and modest prices. Trout *tartare* with red peppercorns, duck fillet with blackberries, zander fillet with cream and goat's cheese sauce, and an array of delicate desserts. A short menu at €11, another at €15, a *menu dégustation* at €30, or around €27 *à la carte.* In summer they serve out on the front lawn. It's a genuinely charming place and you get good value for money. Take a quick look at the spring that feeds the trout lake, right next to the house – it's a truly remarkable colour. Free house apéritif.

LANGRES 52200

🎋 🏠 |O| GRAND HÔTEL DE L'EUROPE★★

23–25 rue Diderot (Centre).
☎ 03.25.87.10.88 ➡ 03.25.87.60.65
Closed Sun evening in winter. **TV**. **Pay car park**.

This hotel displays all the charm of pre-revolutionary France: seventeenth-century wood panelling, squeaking floorboards and huge rooms with blue shutters. It has rare provincial style, friendly staff and reasonable prices considering the quality. Doubles €49 with shower/wc and €61 with bath. The rooms on the second floor have been refurbished and painted yellow and blue – they're undoubtedly more functional but a good deal more impersonal. The older-style rooms are located in the annexe in the courtyard and they're quieter too. The restaurant is splendid: weekday set menu at €13 and others up to €40. There's a charge for use of the private car park. Free house apéritif.

🎋 🏠 |O| L'AUBERGE DES VOILIERS★★

Lac de la Liez (East); it's 4km from Langres, on Vesoul road.
☎ 03.25.87.05.74 ➡ 03.25.87.24.22
Closed Sun evening; Mon except May–Sept; 1 Feb–15 March. **TV**. **Garden**.

This is about the best place in Langres, close to a peaceful lake. Fair prices, wonderful welcome and great food. Doubles €46 with shower/wc and telephone or €53 with bath. Room 4 has a balcony with a view of the lake and numbers 8 and 11 look over the countryside towards the walled city of Langres. Set menu €12 (€15 on Sun), then others €15–31. Children's menu €8. Their fillet of pike with nettles is a speciality, and you should try the *nougat glacé* with fresh fruit. In summer the shady terrace adds to your enjoyment. €8 discount on the room rate if you dine in the restaurant.

🏠 |●| LE CHEVAL BLANC**

4 rue de l'Estres (Centre).
☎ 03.25.87.07.00 ➡ 03.25.87.23.13
✉ cblangres@aol.com
Restaurant closed Tues evening except July–Aug; Wed lunchtime; 15–30 Nov. **Disabled access. TV. Car park**.

The *Cheval Blanc* is a converted medieval abbey and has gothic arches in some rooms, a terrace overlooking the medieval church, rough-hewn stone walls and exposed beams on every floor. The décor is simple yet refined: all the rooms have been refurbished and they are as quiet as monks' cells. The new rooms in the *Pavillon Diderot*, opposite, are equally well-equipped but don't have the same charm. Doubles with shower or bath €50–70. The cuisine in the restaurant offers a panoply of gastronomic delights which change with the seasons: scallops *vinaigrette* with green apples, morel stew with egg, pan-fried *foie gras* with spiced honey and, for dessert, a warm soup of soft fruit perfumed with violet. Set menus €23–60. One of the best tables in the area.

|●| BANANAS

52 rue Diderot (Centre); it's on the main street.
☎ 03.25.87.42.96
Closed Sun; Sun lunchtime July–Aug; 15–30 Nov.

The décor here is sparkling, and the tables are covered with red and white checked cloths. They play country music and there's a buffalo head hanging on the wall – you're in John Wayne country. The atmosphere is great, as is the service and everything on the Tex-Mex menu: tacos, enchiladas, chilli con carne, burgers and steaks. Evenings are usually very busy. A meal will cost about €20.

VAUX-SOUS-AUBIGNY   52190 (25KM S)

|●| AUBERGE DES TROIS PROVINCES

rue de Verdun; it's on the N74.
☎ 03.25.88.31.98
Closed Sun evening; Mon; 15 Jan–4 Feb. **Car park**.

The wonderful paved stone floor and impressive fireplace are from another era. This décor goes well with the food, which makes good use of local produce with a glimmer of originality. It's not long since the chef was running the kitchen of a top restaurant in Saint-Maxime and it shows. Good set menu at €15 featuring home-made country *terrine*, salmon-trout *pouchouse* in red wine and a selection of cheese. Desserts include pears

poached in wine and *moelleux* of bitter chocolate with roasted sesame seeds. Other menus go up to €21. The wine list contains one or two curiosities from the little-known neighbouring vineyard in Montseaugeon.

AUBERIVE   52160 (27KM SW)

🏠 |●| HÔTEL-RESTAURANT DU LION D'OR

How to get there: from Langres take the Dijon Road then the D428 to Auberive.
☎ 03.25.84.82.49 ➡ 03.42.79.80.92
Closed Tues and Oct to April. **Disabled access. Car park**.

This adorable seasonal country hotel is set right beside a twelfth-century Cistercian abbey in a peaceful village near the forest. The Aube is nothing more than an overgrown stream here and it runs directly past the house. The eight rooms are all different and so tastefully decorated they wouldn't look out of place in a magazine: doubles €52. There's also a restaurant with a handful of tables around the fireplace. The cooking is based primarily on fresh, seasonal, local produce: snails, rabbit *à la Dijonnais*e and *profiteroles de Langres*. Set menu €15 or *à la carte*.

MESNIL-SAINT-PÈRE   10140

🌲 🏠 |●| HÔTEL-RESTAURANT AUBERGE DU LAC***

How to get there: take the N19 from Troyes, it's at the beginning of the village.
☎ 03.25.41.27.16 ➡ 03.25.41.57.59
✉ auberge.lac.p.gublin@wanadoo.fr
Closed Sun evening out of season and 12–30 Nov.
Disabled access. TV. Car park.

This is a stylish timber-framed house near to the lake in the Orient forest – the ideal place for a romantic weekend. There's a suite at €151 and quiet, air-conditioned doubles with shower or bath are €63–105. The restaurant *Au Vieux Pressoir* is really charming. The chef's cooking is excellent and prices reflect that: weekday lunch menu €19–58 or €47 *à la carte*. Free coffee.

MENILOT (LE)   10270 (3KM W)

🌲 🏠 |●| LA MANGEOIRE***

It's to the left of the N19.
☎ 03.25.41.20.72 ➡ 03.25.41.54.67
✉ lamangeoire@wanadoo.fr
Closed Sun evening out of season. **Swimming pool**.

TV. **Lock-up garage**.

This village teems with visitors to the lakes of the Orient forest, and although this attractive wooden building is right on the main road, the restaurant is on the other side, away from any noise. The appealing, comfortable rooms (€43) all have en-suite bathrooms: prices are reasonable given the amenities. A €11 *menu routier* is served in the bar for both lunch and dinner on weekdays only, or you can get others, €18–38, in the restaurant. Boat trips on the lake can be arranged from the hotel. 10% discount on the room rate.

MONTIER-EN-DER   52220

🏃 🏠 |●| AUBERGE DE PUISIE

54 av. Victor-Hugo (East).
☎ 03.25.94.22.94
TV. **Car park**.

There's a twelfth-century abbey in this town, just five minutes from the Lake de Der. This simple hotel, which is a nice place to stop, offers prices that are far from ruinous: doubles €30 with shower/wc and TV. The six rooms are not very big but they're pretty enough and have good facilities; numbers 1 and 2 look over the quiet courtyard. Traditional cooking and family dishes are served in the yellow and blue dining room or out on the shaded terrace. Menus €11–20, or around €15 *à la carte*. It's probably worth booking, because the area is a magnet for bird-watchers who come to watch the autumn migrators on the lake. Kindly welcome. Free coffee.

|●| AU JOLI BOIS

route de Saint-Dizier; it's 1km out of the village on the left, in the direction of Saint-Dizier.
☎ and ➡ 03.26.60.80.15
Closed evenings except Sat Oct–April; the Feb school holidays; a week at the beginning of Sept; Christmas and New Year's Day.

This big building is easy to miss even though it's by the road – it's slightly set back and hidden by a tall hedge. Keep your eyes peeled because you eat well here. The dining room is rustic-modern and the terrace on the edge of the wood is very pretty. Try the zander fillet with lemony butter, the *mignon* of pork with grain mustard or the pan-fried *tournedos* with girolles. The €9 weekday menu is good value and offers a choice of five starters and six main courses followed by cheese and dessert. Other menus are €16–21 or you'll pay around €20 *à la carte*. Unusually, they have a list of 30 beers.

NOGENT   52800

🏃 🏠 |●| HÔTEL DU COMMERCE**

pl. Charles-de-Gaulle (Centre).
☎ 03.25.31.81.14 ➡ 03.25.31.74.00
Restaurant closed Sun from Oct to June and Christmas to New Year. **TV**. **Lock-up garage**.

This town is famous for its cutlery and this establishment has keen prices. Well-kept and pleasant doubles €27 with basin/wc, €40–43 with shower/wc or bath. The entrance hall is huge and welcoming, as is the restaurant with its exposed beams and eigteenth-century-style décor. Set menus are generous and well thought out; weekday lunch menu €9, and others €15–24. Try the snail soup with Burgundy butter or the spiced fillet of duck with honey. The ideal place to stay if you're visiting the cutlery museum. Free coffee.

NOGENT-SUR-SEINE   10400

🏃 🏠 |●| HÔTEL-RESTAURANT BEAU RIVAGE**

20 rue Villiers-aux-Choux (North); it's about 1km from pl.de l'Église.
☎ 03.25.39.84.22 ➡ 03.25.39.18.32
Closed Sun evening; Mon; 31 Jan–21 Feb; 16–30 Feb.
TV. **Garden**.

A friendly, peaceful place with a beautiful garden. There are a few pleasant rooms, all of which have been renovated; €46 for a double with shower/wc or bath. Rooms 1, 2, 4 and 5 have a view of the Seine, the trees, the countryside and, in the distance, the incongruous outline of a nuclear power station. Breakfast €6. Cheapest set menu €15 and others €21–33. The chef uses fresh herbs generously and expertly — and he smokes his own salmon. 10% discount on the room rate Sept–June.

PINEY   10220

🏃 🏠 |●| LE TADORNE**

1 pl. de la Halle.
☎ 03.25.46.30.35 ➡ 03.25.46.36.49
📧 le.dadorne@wanadoo.fr
Closed Sun evening Oct–March; the Feb school holidays. **Disabled access**. **Swimming pool**. **TV**. **Car park**.

Near to the Orient forest nature park, this huge half-timbered building houses a bar, a restaurant and a hotel in a peaceful, relaxing setting. Cosy, stylish, impeccably clean rooms in a recently converted annexe cost €40 for doubles with shower/wc or €44 with bath. Half board, compulsory July–Aug and public holidays, is €46 per person. Prices include use of the pleasant hotel pool. If you want to spend less, there are basic rooms in the main building. These start at €24 a night with basin and shower along the landing. In the restaurant they serve a lunch menu at €9 and others €14–30. 10% discount on the room rate 15 Oct–31 March.

BREVONNES   10220 (5KM E)

🕺 🏠 |●| AU VIEUX LOGIS

1 rue de Piney; it's on the D11
☎ 03.25.46.30.17 📠 03.25.46.37.20
📧 annick.baudesson@worldonline.fr
Closed Sun evening and Mon mid-Sept to end-May; Mon lunchtime in season; March. **Swimming pool**. **TV**. **Car park**.

This old Champenois house has kept its style – exposed beams, antique furniture, a large ceramic cauldron hanging in the fireplace. Appropriately, they serve traditional dishes prepared with great care: tasty Bernon snails, home-made *terrines*, chicken *mignardise*. The service is wonderfully efficient. The €12 menu (not served Sun) is good value, and there are a couple of others for €21 and €31. *À la carte* you can choose between dishes like baby cabbage with crayfish *à la vigneronne*, stuffed supreme of chicken in Ratafia sauce and oxtail salad with vegetable *terrine*. The rooms are warm and cosy – doubles €36 with shower/wc and €39 with bath. Free coffee.

RAMERUPT   10240

🕺 |●| RESTAURANT LE VAL D'AUBE

rue Cour-Première.
☎ 03.25.37.39.45
Closed Tues and Aug.

After enjoying great success cooking for the diplomats in the French foreign office at the Quai-d'Orsay, the young chef, Hervé, came back to join his family in their country bar-restaurant. He creates decent traditional food: set weekday menu at €10. They don't take credit cards. Free coffee.

REIMS   51100

SEE MAP OVERLEAF

🕺 🏠 AU SAINT MAURICE HÔTEL*

90 rue Gambetta. **MAP C3-3**
☎ 03.26.85.09.10 📠 03.26.85.83.20
TV.

The hotel frontage looks rather like a shop window. The rooms mostly look out onto the peaceful little courtyard, where the guests sit out in the open air as they might in Andalucia – and in fact there's a Spanish feel to the place. The atmosphere is warm and friendly, and regulars have their "own" room, as people used to in old guesthouses. There are a number of singles which aren't quite as nice as the others, but they're good for anyone on a budget. Doubles with shower (wc along the hall) at €24, or €34 with bath or shower/wc. 10% discount.

🏠 ARDENN HÔTEL**

6 rue Caqué. **MAP A2-4**
☎ 03.26.47.42.38 📠 03.26.09.48.56
📧 ardennhotel@wanadoo.fr
Closed 20 Dec–7 Jan. **TV. Pay car park**.

A place in the town centre that doesn't cost an arm and a leg. The hotel has been renovated but has a flagrantly kitsch décor which seems to appeal to artists appearing at the nearby theatres. Doubles with shower €26 and €43 with bath.

🕺 🏠 |●| AUX BONS AMIS

13 rue Gosset. **Off map B1-17**
☎ 03.26.07.39.76 📠 03.26.07.73.06
Restaurant closed Fri evening, Sat and Sun. **TV**.

The popular restaurant is always crammed at lunchtime with businessmen, workers and other locals who've heard about the excellent lunch menu – a steal at €10. There's a choice of two starters and three main courses, then cheeses, dessert and a drink. The dishes are real classics – ox tongue with rice, *blanquette de veau* (a type of veal stew), veal *sauté* – and you get good-sized portions. Good, quick service guaranteed by the friendly waitresses, who work really hard. *Aux Bons Amis* is also a very basic, clean hotel. No shower in the rooms (€27), but they all have a TV. Breakfast €4. Half board, from €26 per person, is compulsory. Free coffee.

🕺 🏠 AZUR HÔTEL**

7 rue des Écrevées. **MAP B1-6**
☎ 03.26.47.43.39 📠 03.26.88.57.19
TV. Lock up garage.

In a quiet street in the town centre this unobtrusive, tranquil hotel has an English sort of charm. You are greeted warmly and the rooms are neat and tidy. Doubles cost €31 with washing facilities, €40 with shower/wc and €46 with bath; numbers 12, 17, 22, 27 and 37 are brighter than the others. Nearby are the *Henry IV* bar and the rather chic *Au Comptoir* bistro. They don't take credit cards. 10% discount from the third night of your stay.

🕏 🏠 |●| HÔTEL-RESTAURANT LE BON MOINE**

14 rue des Capucins. **MAP B2-8**
☎ 03.26.47.33.64 ➡ 03.26.40.43.87
e le-bon-moine@nc.consult.com
Hotel closed Sun. **TV**.

The rooms have been freshly painted in bright colours – choose the one that matches the colour of your favourite ice-cream. Doubles €36. They're all located above the café-restaurant and the establishment is in the centre of town. Weekday menu €9, and others €13 and €15. Nice welcome. 10% discount on the room rate June–Sept.

🏠 HÔTEL CRYSTAL**

86 pl. Drouet-d'Erlon. **MAP A1-5**
☎ 03.26.88.44.44 ➡ 03.26.47.49.28
e hotelcrystal@mintel.net
TV.

Two good reasons to stay here: its location, near the liveliest square in Reims, and its wonderful antique interior, with a beautiful old lift. The comfortable and quiet rooms have modern bathrooms; they're €37–49 for a double with shower/wc or €53–59 with bath. There's also a pretty little courtyard where they serve breakfast in good weather.

🕏 🏠 |●| COTTAGE HÔTEL**

8 av. Georges-Pompidou (South). **Off map C4-7**
☎ 03.26.36.34.34 ➡ 03.26.49.99.77
Restaurant closed Sun evening.
Garden. TV. Car park.

This place is perfect if you're looking for somewhere quiet out of the town centre. Rooms €41 for a double with shower/wc and telephone. In the restaurant there's a decent menu at €11 (not served weekends) and others at €17 and €26. Warm, professional welcome. Free coffee.

🕏 🏠 |●| HÔTEL LE BARON**

85 rue de Vesle. **MAP B2-9**
☎ 03.26.47.46.24
Closed Sun. **TV**.

Don't let the name mislead you – "baron" is slang for a 50cl glass of beer and there's

nothing aristocratic about this place. *Le Baron* deserves some respect, nonetheless: the hotel has been totally renovated and the rooms have all mod cons; those looking onto the street have been soundproofed. Doubles €44 with shower/wc; a few sleep three. The restaurant serves lunch only, with a €8 menu. 10% discount on the room rate 1 Sept–30 April.

|●| RESTAURANT LE CHAMOIS

45 rue des Capucins. **MAP B3-16**
☎ 03.26.88.69.75
Closed Wed; Sun lunchtime; the first 3 weeks in Aug.

This intimate, relaxing restaurant draws its inspiration from the mountains, with a menu of *fondues savoyardes* and *raclette valaisanne* or *vaudoise*. Short traditional menu at €8 (weekday lunchtime only) and others €9–11. The service and food here are tremendous.

🕏 |●| BISTROT HENRI IV

29 rue Henri-IV. **MAP B1-15**
☎ 03.26.47.56.22
Closed Sun, Mon and Tues evenings; 20 July–15 Aug; 25 Dec–5 Jan.

As good a local bar-restaurant as you could hope to find. By 7am they're already serving the first customers, who swallow a shot of coffee and exchange news on their way to work. On the stroke of midday the lunchtime rush starts and the place is packed with people grabbing a quick snack. Dishes of the day change regularly; tripe *à la mode de Caen*, *bœuf bourguignon*, lamb *navarin* or, *à la carte*, dishes such as *andouillette* with mustard, *entrecôte* steak with red wine sauce and calf's head. The place is packed on Saturday, which is market day. *Formule* at €8 and a weekday menu at €10. Free coffee.

🕏 |●| CHEZ ANITA

37 rue Ernest-Renan. **Off map A1-18**
☎ 03.26.40.16.20
Closed Sat lunchtime, Sun and first three weeks in Aug.

If you like Italian food, *Chez Anita* is for you. Come here for brilliant oven-baked pizza with a choice of toppings and pasta galore. The portions are generous and very filling – so go easy ordering lunch if you want to stay awake to explore the town in the afternoon. A really popular place with a good local reputation. Set menus €10 and €14 at lunchtime, then another at €21. Free coffee.

|●| BRASSERIE DU BOULINGRIN

48 rue de Mars. **MAP B1-21**

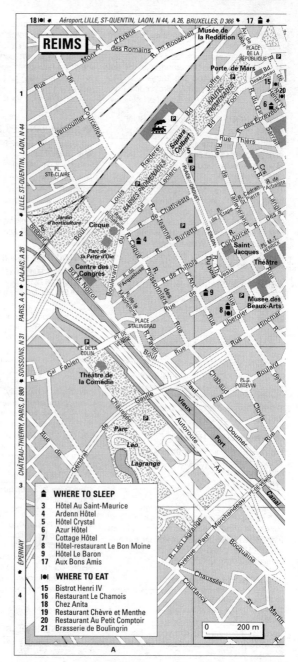

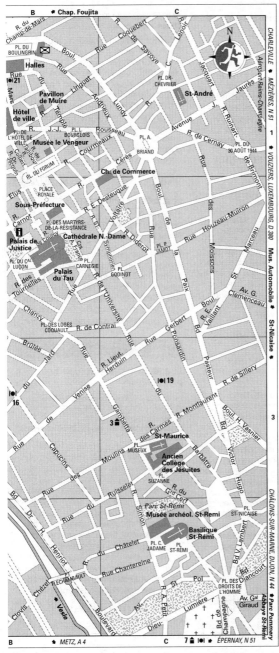

☎ 03.26.40.96.22 **e** au.petit.comptoir@wanadoo.fr
Closed Sun.

A genuine brasserie which has been running since 1925 – it does credit to its kind. The lunchtime din echoes in the vast Art Deco dining room but in the evening it's warm and convivial. The walls are painted with murals and there's an army of uniformed waiters. The excellent €15 *formule* offers a choice of three starters, three main courses, cheese or desert with a 1/2-litre of wine and coffee included. Other menus at higher prices.

❚●❚ RESTAURANT CHÈVRE ET MENTHE

63 rue du Barbâtre. **MAP C3-19**
☎ 03.26.05.17.03
Closed Sun; Mon; a week at Easte; 3 weeks in Aug; a week between Christmas and New Year.

This place has had an excellent reputation for years, so you won't be disappointed. The plate-glass windows are decorated with pictures and inside there are two small dining rooms, the nicer one reserved for smokers. The food sounds modest enough but is actually very impressive: try the house tart of goat's cheese with mint or the *papillotte* of salmon *à la parisienne*. A meal *à la carte* will cost around €15 and there are no set menus.

❚●❚ RESTAURANT AU PETIT COMPTOIR

17 rue de Mars. **MAP B1-20**
☎ 03.26.40.58.58
Closed Sat lunchtime; Sun; the first fortnight in Aug; a fortnight at Christmas.

Fabrice Maillot has worked with famous chefs in the past and is enjoying great success with this bistro. He's a clever, creative chef who produces first-rate cooking which looks simple but is finely and precisely judged. The place appeals to people who appreciate good food and the quality of his cuisine is often amazing: cream with chicken livers, crayfish and offal stew, *tartiflette* with Val d'Ajol *andouillette*, *millefeuille* of Morteau sausage with cabbage. The desserts are delicious, too: soft caramel with salted butter, a fan of *noutagine* and ice-cream with vinegar and iced *sabayon* with champagne finished with blackcurrant. The menus, €20–26, change with the seasons, and the impressive wine list features a good selection from the Rhône valley. Expect to pay €31 for a meal *à la carte*.

VAL DE VESLE · 51360 (18KM SE)

❚●❚ L'ÉTRIER

How to get there: take the N44 to Courmelais, then the D8.

☎ 03.26.03.92.12 **➡** 03.26.03.29.72
Closed Sun–Fri evenings.

Run by a family who make a delightful team. During the week there are two menus: the one at €9 includes *crudités* and *charcuterie*, dish of the day, cheese, dessert and wine. The €21 menu is a real feast: house apéritif and savouries followed by *foie gras* of duck with toast or different *terrines* of chicken liver, then a choice of fish (fillet of zander in butter, salmon *escalope* in champagne), a choice of meat (*gigot* of lamb, steak, veal kidneys in champagne, duck breast), then salad, cheese and dessert. Enough to fill anyone.

FISMES · 51170 (23KM E)

❚●❚ À LA BOULE D'OR**

11 rue Lefèvre.
☎ 03.26.48.11.24 **➡** 03.26.48.17.08
Closed Sun evening, Mon and the first fortnight in Feb.

Worth a visit for the restaurant – it's a well-known gourmet stop in the region but it's exceptional value for money. Huge care is taken over the cooking. Weekday menu €14, others up to €30 and *à la carte* expect to pay €38. Very nice welcome. Double rooms at €44. Free glass of *Marc de Champagne*.

RETHEL · 08300

❚●❚ HÔTEL-RESTAURANT LA CHAMPAGNE**

bd. de la 2e-D-I (West); it's opposite the Aisne.
☎ 03.24.38.03.28 **➡** 03.24.38.37.70
e yves.grustiniam@wanadoo.fr
Restaurant closed Sun evening. **Disabled access. TV. Car park.**

Originally built as a block of flats surmounting a parade of shops, this place got turned into a hotel. Not exactly what you'd call charming, but the rooms are nice and clean and it's good value at €35–36 for a double with shower/wc. Half board is €33. There are two restaurants: a cafeteria where you come for the prices rather than the surroundings and a more attractive dining room with good traditional cuisine – local white pudding, calf sweetbreads, zander with ginger. Set menus €12 at weekday lunchtime, and €16 and €24 elsewhere. Free house apéritif.

❚●❚ HÔTEL-RESTAURANT LE MODERNE**

pl. de la Gare (South).

☎ 03.24.38.44.54 ➡ 03.24.38.37.84
TV. Pay car park.

For over forty years, this place – situated across from the station – has been a favourite with travellers, but there aren't many trains now so the rooms are quiet. Despite being renovated they've kept some of their old style, which fits in with the overall look of the solid brick-and-stone building. Well-equipped doubles €35 with shower/wc and €40 with bath. Decent menus €15–24; *à la carte* you'll get modern classics such as *cassolette* of white pudding and *émincée* of pigeon with *foie gras*. Free house apéritif.

PAUVRES   08310 (15KM SE)

⅔ |●| RESTAURANT AU CHEVAL BLANC

How to get there: take the D946 and it's in the centre of the village.
☎ 03.24.30.38.95
Closed Mon evening and Aug. **Car park**.

Pauvres means "poor", but this town is the richer for this gem of a place. There's a sign outside saying they welcome people on foot or on horseback – two famous French poets, Rimbaud and Verlaine, used to hang about this area, so maybe they stopped here. Today you're more likely to see vans and commercial vehicles at lunchtime, when it's full of people who work locally. They generally opt for the €10 *menu du jour*, which includes a litre of red wine. The good, hearty portions of family cooking are served with a smile, though the desserts are a little uninspired. At the weekend families flock in for the regional set menus (€15), which might include *tourte* of white pudding, veal sweetbreads with cream and saddle of rabbit. Free coffee.

SIGNY-L'ABBAYE   08460 (23KM N)

🏠 |●| AUBERGE DE L'ABBAYE**

pl. Aristide-Briand; it's on the D985.
☎ 03.24.52.81.27 ➡ 03.24.53.71.72
Closed Tues evening and Wed; 10 Jan–28 Feb. **TV**. **Car park**.

This lovely inn has been in the same family since the Revolution. It's in the middle of a small picturesque market town on the edge of a huge forest. You'll get a warm welcome and there's a nice family atmosphere. The stylish rooms, all of them different, are regularly smartened up; room 9 has its own little sitting room. Doubles with shower/wc or bath €46–53. In winter they light a fire in the

dining room and you'll find plenty of local produce in the home cooking. The Lefebvres are still farmers: the excellent beef comes from their own herd, while the rhubarb for the rhubarb tart is grown in their garden. There's a weekday menu at €11, one at €17–34, which lists local specialities, and a gastronomic menu at €31 served on Sunday lunchtime. It's rare to find this sort of place anywhere, let alone in such a wonderful spot.

REVIN   08500

⅔ 🏠 |●| AUBERGE DU MALGRÉ-TOUT

chemin des Balivaux; from Revin, go along the Hautes-Buttes road for several kms, it's signposted on the left.
☎ 03.24.40.11.20 ➡ 03.24.40.18.90
Closed Sun evening. **Car park**.

The *ferme-auberge* (a farm offering food and lodging) of your dreams, way out in the forest. There are sturdy, wooden tables and a stone fireplace. They serve *terrine*, house *foie gras*, *charcuterie* and game – and in quantity! Menus €17–23. The rooms are extremely quiet, as you'd expect, and cost €35. Lovely warm welcome but it's essential to book. Free coffee.

ROCROI   08230

🏠 |●| LE COMMERCE

4 pl. d'Armes.
☎ 03.24.54.11.15 ➡ 03.24.54.95.31
Restaurant closed Sun evening and Mon. **TV**.

The old star-shaped fortifications, in perfect condition, are well worth a visit – perhaps via this old-fashioned but well-run village hotel. Small, unoriginal rooms, but they're spotless; doubles €35–38. Regional dishes in the restaurant and there's lots of choice including local *charcuterie* and white pudding with onion. Weekday lunch menu €9, or €12–27.

SAINT-DIZIER   53100

🏠 HÔTEL PICARDY**

15 av. de Verdun; it's 200m from the train station.
☎ 03.25.05.09.12 ➡ 03.25.05.36.81
TV. Garden. Car park.

A small hotel in a former craftsman's house with old-style rooms. They're clean and comfortable; some have a view of the little garden at the back, while the others look over the street but have efficient double glazing. It's got the atmosphere of a family guesthouse –

like visiting relatives you haven't seen for ages. Doubles with shower/wc at €36. An unpretentious, friendly, relaxed place.

ÉCLARON   52290 (9KM SW)

🏠 |●| L'HÔTELLERIE DU MOULIN**

3 rue du Moulin; from Saint-Dizier, take the D384 in the direction of the Lac de Der-Chantecoq
☎ 03.25.04.17.76 ➨ 03.25.55.67.01
e hotellerie.moulin@wanadoo.fr
Closed Sun evening and Mon lunchtime (Mon evening also in winter); a fortnight in Oct and 3 weeks in Jan.
TV. Car park.

One of the few romantic spots near the Lac de Der, in an old wooden mill which is typical of the region. There are five quiet, clean rooms; number 3 has a view of the mill and the woods. Doubles €46 with shower/wc and telephone. Half board is "strongly advised", and costs from €46 per person. Simple but tasty cuisine: home-smoked salmon, *noisette* of veal with morels, red mullet fillet with vanilla, poached pear with honey and cinnamon ice-cream. *Formule du jour* €11 at lunchtime and €13 in the evening (up to 8.30pm) – it's available from Tuesday to Friday lunch. Other menus €18–27. This is a really nice place to stay.

PERTHES   52100 (10KM W)

🎍|●| LE PARIS-STRASBOURG

It's on the old Route Nationale.
☎ 03.25.56.40.64 ➨ 03.25.56.40.64
Closed Sun evening, Mon, the last fortnight in Aug and the first week in Jan.

A must for gourmands but the prices will suit all pockets. Very cosily decorated with fault-less welcome and service. The dining room is full of businessmen in the week, tourists and local residents at the weekend. Delicate dishes such as snail salad, salmon in Riesling sauce, duck *foie gras* with Ratafia, zander on *choucroute* with Pinot Noir d'Alsace sauce and scallop profiteroles. Menus €14–37. Free house apéritif.

SAINTE-MÉNEHOULD   51800

🎍 🏠 |●| HÔTEL-RESTAURANT DE LA POSTE**

54 av. Victor-Hugo (East).
☎ 03.26.60.80.16 ➨ 03.26.60.97.37
Closed Sun evening and Jan. **TV. Car park.**

An unassuming place, not far from the station, run by friendly owners. The rooms are nicely old-fashioned and have decent facilities: doubles with shower/wc and telephone go for €32. The ones at the back are quieter and number 9 is the largest. The €10 menu lists the local speciality, pig's trotters *à la Sainte-Ménehould*. Others €15–20. Free coffee.

🏠 |●| HÔTEL-RESTAURANT LE CHEVAL ROUGE**

1 rue Chanzy (Centre).
☎ 03.26.60.81.04 ➨ 03.26.60.93.11
e rouge.cheval@wanadoo.fr
Closed Mon Oct–April; 15 Nov–7 Dec. **TV**.

The €10 weekday brasserie menu is reason enough to stay here. But judge for yourself: sardine *rillettes* with onion marmalade or cucumber gazpacho, followed by sautéed gizzards *basquaise* or fillet of salmon with dill, and for dessert, rhubarb *clafoutis*. The restaurant menus, €14–43, are equally imaginative: lamb with pineapple chutney in a curry sauce, pan-fried chicken *à la chinoise*, rack of lamb *dijonnais*. *À la carte* you'll find the local speciality, pig's trotters – according to those in the know, these are really quite something. Comfortable double rooms at €40–41 with shower or bath. They have one room that sleeps four.

SEDAN   08200

🎍 🏠 |●| LE RELAIS**

rue Gaston-Sauvage (Southwest).
☎ 03.24.27.04.41 ➨ 03.24.29.71.16
Restaurant closed Sun evening. **Garden**. **TV. Car park**.

A huge brick building of some character – it was once a soap factory. Today it's a successful hotel where you will get a friendly welcome. The rooms are quiet, and although you're still in town, there's a real country feel to the place. Doubles with shower/wc €38 and €41 with bath. Rooms 31 and 32 have nicer décor and look onto the garden; rooms in the adjoining annexe are also good. In the huge restaurant there's a €11 set menu at lunch and dinner, then another at €17 or *à la carte*. Traditional cuisine with a choice of regional dishes, including Ardennes *pâté* and the *cacasse à cul nu* – a stew of potatoes, onions, bacon and beef. 10% discount on the room rate.

🏠 |●| LE SAINT-MICHEL*

3 rue Saint-Michel (Centre).
☎ 03.24.29.04.61 ➨ 03.24.29.32.67

Restaurant closed Sun evening. **TV**.

This is in an ideal spot in a quiet little street beside the high castle walls – the castle is said to be the largest in Europe, and the town is no less than a thousand years old. Decent rooms are €42 with shower and up to €46 with shower/wc or bath. The restaurant is fairly traditional in its approach, with one menu at €11 (lunchtime and evening except Sun), and others €15–30. They do a few local specialities, like sautéed wild boar, seafood platters and fish dishes. But the service could be a bit more attentive.

|●| LE MÉDIÉVAL

51 rue de l'Horloge; (Centre).
☎ 03.24.29.11.52

Just by the château in the centre of the old town you'll find this charming little restaurant. The rustic, bistro-style dining room has an open fire, beams and stone walls. The establishment offers a range of Franco-Belgian dishes often featuring beer in the recipes: pork fillet mignon with Orval cheese, beef cheek stewed in brown Chimay ale and tart of meat marinated in stout. Menus are €11–27, listing affordable wines. Excellent, smiling service.

⅄ |●| RESTAURANT LA DÉESSE

35 av. du Général-Margueritte (Northwest); it's about 200m from the Dijonval Museum of Industry.
☎ 03.24.29.11.52
Closed Sat; a week in Feb; Aug.

This little bar-restaurant is always full of regulars so you have to grab a table when you get the chance. The atmosphere is warm, friendly and definitely informal. Good set weekday lunch menu at €10.83. They use only fresh ingredients, even in the desserts – and there's not a microwave in sight. It's authentic, simple and classy – they do game in season. The service is relaxed but efficient, and the owner goes round to make sure everyone's all right. The weekend set menu, €14.90, caters more for families. This is the best value in town. Free coffee.

BAZEILLES   08140 (4KM SE)

⅄ ⬧ |●| AUBERGE DU PORT**

Route de Rémilly (Southeast); from Bazeilles take the D129 towards Rémilly for about 1km.
☎ 03.24.27.13.89 ➡ 03.24.29.35.58
e auberge-du-port@wanadoo.fr
Closed Sat lunchtime; Sun evening; 16 Aug–5 Sept; 20 Dec–5 Jan. **Garden. TV. Car park**.

This pretty white house stands at the end of a little mooring berth on the River Meuse. There's a rather polite atmosphere to the place, and the garden and surrounding meadows make it really charming. The characterful bedrooms are in a separate building; those looking out over the river are brighter. They cost €51 for a double with shower or bath. There's an excellent menu at €15 (not Sun), and others €22–34. The food is beautifully presented and quite imaginative: try herb-covered veal sweetbreads *en crépinette* or steamed medallions of pork in a ginger sauce. On the fish front, there are *rillettes* of salmon with spices and roast monkfish with artichokes and ginger. Game in season. Shaded terrace for the summer months. 10% discount on the room rate.

⬧ |●| CHÂTEAU DE BAZEILLES ET RESTAURANT L'ORANGERIE

It's on the D129, on the edge of the village.
☎ 03.24.26.75.22 ➡ 03.24.26.75.19
e bazilles@chateaubazilles
Restaurant closed Sat and Mon lunchtimes, Sun evening and 18–28 Feb. **Disabled access. TV. Car park**.

Within the precincts of the château, this lovely establishment offers quiet, spacious rooms with modern décor and great views. There's a special one, number 201, in a huge separate pavillion with its own open fireplace. They're excellent value at €76 with shower/wc or bath. The restaurant is of superb quality and is situated in the old orangery in the middle of the grounds. It offers inventive cooking with constantly changing menus, (€15–31): caramelized scallops with chicory *crème brûlée*, roast venison haunch with hazelnuts and brill flambéed with *anise*.

RÉMILLY-AILLICOURT   08450 (6KM SE)

⅄ ⬧ |●| HÔTEL-RESTAURANT LA SAPINIÈRE**

How to get there: take the D6 towards Raucourt Vouziers.
☎ 03.24.26.75.22 ➡ 03.24.26.75.19
Hotel closed Jan and the third week in Aug.
Restaurant closed Sun evening and Mon lunchtime.
Disabled access. Garden. TV. Car park.

This is a traditional country hotel-restaurant which used to be a coaching inn. The rooms are clean and smart with good facilities, and because they look out onto the garden, they're quiet too; doubles €44 with shower/wc, €47 with bath. The restaurant has a large dining room which is often used for wedding parties and the like. Weekday menu €15, then others €21–34. Cuisine is traditional and uses a lot of local produce, sometimes with a nice original touch: house *foie gras* terrine, *fricassée* of scallops with girolles and sirloin *gourmand*. Game is served in season, as are summer salads. Pleasant terrace. Free breakfast per room per night and house apéritif with a meal.

MOUZON   08210 (18KM E)

|●| LES ECHEVINS

33 rue Charles-de-Gaulle.
☎ 03.24.26.10.90
Closed Mon and Sat lunchtimes; Sun evening; the first 3 weeks in Aug and the 3 last weeks in Jan.

The dining room is on the first floor of a glorious seventeeth-century Spanish house. The excellent cuisine combines traditional style with a modern approach and the dishes are meticulously prepared. While you order, a profusion of *amuse-bouches* and other delicacies are served by the smiling, professional waiting staff. The menus, €15–29, list dishes such as asparagus and leeks with *ravigote* sauce and fish *paupiettes*. One of the best restaurants in the area.

CARIGNAN   08110 (20KM SE)

|●| RESTAURANT LA GOURMANDIÈRE

19 av. de Blagny; take the N43 and it's 300m from the centre.
☎ 03.24.22.20.99
Closed Mon; 3 weeks in Jan; Feb. **Disabled access.**
Car park.

The rather fancy dining room is in keeping with the style of this elegant bourgeois residence, and there's still a very homely atmosphere about the place. The talented and daring chef mixes local produce with foreign spices: try the *chiffonnade* of Ardennes ham powdered with garam masala; the pan-fried duck *foie gras* with seasonal fruit; the braised fillet of smoked haddock with pickled lemons, saffron and cumin; or the pastry case of crab on a salmon cushion. The weekday lunch menu at €12 gives you a choice from two starters, two main courses and a dessert; others are €19–43. Lovely terrace in the garden for sunny days. Free coffee.

SÉZANNE   51120

🌿 🏠 |●| HÔTEL-RESTAURANT DE LA CROIX D'OR**

53 rue Notre-Dame (Centre).
☎ 03.26.80.61.10 ➡ 03.26.80.65.20

Closed Tues and 2–17 Jan.**Disabled access. TV. Car park**.

Gun dogs and birds of prey patrol the car park of this modestly priced establishment. Attractive rooms with renovated bathrooms are €37 with shower/wc or €53 with bath. The set menu at €13 is ideal for travellers on a budget, and others, €22–36, might tempt you if you feel like indulgence. The chef regularly goes to the fruit and vegetable market at Rungis on the outskirts of Paris to get fresh, seasonal produce. Free coffee.

🏠 |●| HÔTEL-RESTAURANT LE RELAIS CHAMPENOIS**

157 rue Notre-Dame; it's on the Troyes road.
☎ 03.26.80.58.03 ➡ 03.26.81.35.32
e relaischamp@infonie.fr
Closed Sun evenings out of season; 15 Nov–6 Jan.
Disabled access. TV. Car park.

As you come into the village you enter real Champagne country. This is a friendly old inn with ancient walls. The lovely rooms have been delightfully renovated – from €38 with shower/wc to €47 with bath. Monsieur Fourmi is the chef here, and he prepares superb food inspired by local produce: scallop salad in Reims vinegar, medallion of monkfish with wild nettles and cockerel in champagne sauce. Set menus €15 (in the week) to €38. Over more than twenty years, Monsieur and Mme Fourmi have built up a well-deserved reputation for offering quality service and a great welcome. Ask to try a glass of Ratafia de Champagne – it's a real discovery.

TROYES   10000

🌿 🏠 HÔTEL DES COMTES DE CHAMPAGNE**

54–56 rue de la Monnaie (Centre); it's in a street in the old town between the town hall and the station.
☎ 03.25.73.11.70 ➡ 03.25.73.06.02
Disabled access. TV. Pay garage.

A twelfth-century building, which was originally the bank of the counts of Champagne. The walls are thick and the wood panelling from the time of Louis XIV creates an authentic feeling of the past. There's also a small, quiet conservatory. Good prices for a two-star hotel: doubles from €21 with basin to €32 with shower/wc and €44–53 with bath. Some rooms are particularly spacious. There's a charge for the garage. Excellent welcome: a very good place. 10% discount on the room rate.

🧍🛏 HÔTEL ARLEQUIN**

50 rue de Turenne (Centre); it's near the church of Saint-Pantaléon.
☎ 03.25.83.12.70 📠 03.25.83.12.99
TV. Motorbike garage.

The *Arlequin* is a brightly coloured hotel where friendliness seems to be the byword. The staff take real pride in looking after guests. They have about twenty bright, spacious rooms at reasonable prices: doubles with shower €38, €41 with shower/wc and €46 with bath. They also have a number of family rooms that can sleep three, four or five. If you decide to stay in Troyes, this is the place to be. Another bonus: a loyalty card gets your seventh night free – a good deal for regular visitors or if you are staying slightly longer. Charge of €5 for use of the motorbike garage. 10% discount.

🧍🛏 HÔTEL DE TROYES**

168 av. du Général-Leclerc (Northwest).
☎ 03.25.71.23.45 📠 03.25.79.12.14
📧 hotel.de.troyes@wanadoo.fr
Disabled access. Garden. TV. Car park.

For those who prefer somewhere quiet outside the town centre. Immaculate rooms €44 with shower/wc, decorated in a contemporary style. You'll get a charming welcome. Buffet breakfast €6. There's no restaurant but the owners will gladly guide you to good places to eat nearby. 15% discount on the room rate 1 Nov–31 March.

🛏 HÔTEL LE CHAMP DES OISEAUX****

20 rue Linard Gonthier (Centre); it's near the Saint-Pierre cathedral and the modern art museum.
☎ 03.25.80.58.50 📠 03.25.80.98.34
📧 menage@champdesoiseaux.com
Disabled access. TV. Pay car park.

In a cobbled street with half-timbered houses, this four-star hotel occupies two fifteenth-century houses. There are twelve rooms and a private courtyard, which is a lovely spot to eat breakfast in the summer. Most of the rooms range between €81 and €150 for a double, but if you want the very best, the two enormous suites called *La suite médiévale* and *Les Bengalis* will set you back an extra €23. They're both gorgeous, with exposed beams, armchairs, period furniture and so on. A bewitchingly delightful place, ideal for a special occasion or a romantic break – if you're willing to pay the price.

🍴 LE COIN DE LA PIERRE

34 rue Viardin (Centre).

☎ 03.25.73.58.44
Closed Sun and a fortnight in Aug.

This is in an old sixteenth-century, half-timbered house on a street corner. You go in through a little courtyard with a spiral staircase curling upstairs. The huge room is very welcoming with its fireplace; it's the perfect setting in which to try their cheese specialities from the mountains: *raclettes*, *pierrades* and so on. Great variety of salads €6–7. Summer lunctime menu at €8 with a mega-salad and dessert or €9 in winter for a cheese dish and dessert. A good place if you can't face another *andouillette*. Nice atmosphere and regular customers.

🍴 LA GALTOUZE

18 rue Urbain-IV (Centre); it's next to the tourist office.
☎ 03.25.73.22.75

There are three chic dining rooms in this classy seventeenth-century building, one on the ground floor and two upstairs – the one at the back has a brick fireplace with a wooden chimneypiece. Cuisine is traditional yet simple, and comes in generous portions. The cheapest menu, served daily, includes *terrine de campagne*, a main course such as grilled *andouillette* or *bœuf bourguignon*, cheese and dessert. There's a *formule* at €8 and two other menus at €12 and €15.

🧍🍴 AU JARDIN GOURMAND

31 rue Paillot de Montabert (Centre); it's near the town hall.
☎ 03.25.73.36.13
Closed Sun and Mon lunchtime, a fortnight in March and the third and fourth weeks in Aug.

This stylish and intimate little restaurant is right in the old part of Troyes. It has a pretty courtyard, which is heated and sheltered in winter and which looks out onto a sixteenth-century timbered wall that the owner restored himself. Excellent welcome.There's a menu for €15 or a meal *à la carte* costs around €23. But what really makes this place stand out is its speciality: home-made *andouillettes* cooked in ten different ways. They're a must if you're a fan. All their other dishes use only fresh ingredients. Wine by the glass. Free coffee.

🧍🍴 LA PANINOTECA

27 rue Paillot-de-Montabert (Centre); near Saint-Jean church in a road at right angles off the rue Champeaux.
☎ 03.25.73.91.34

Closed Sat lunchtime, Sun and 15–30 Aug.

This street is lined with the liveliest restaurants and bars in town but there are also some splendid sixteenth-century woodfronted houses. Bernardo opened this place, which quickly became a regular haunt of the Trojan youth. It's packed. There's a warm atmosphere and tasty Italian cooking, including plenty of *panini* – rolls with all manner of fillings. The choice of pasta sauces is extensive and there are some tasty meat dishes. Prices are fair: pasta around €7, filled rolls €3–5, and around €14 for a meal. Free coffee.

🍴 |◉| RESTAURANT LE CAFÉ DE PARIS

63 rue du Général-de-Gaulle (Centre); it's next to the church of la Madeleine.
☎ 03.25.73.08.30
Closed Sun and Mon evenings; 20 July–10 Aug.

A good place with average prices and something for everyone. Set menus €19, €26 and €37 or *à la carte*. The chef takes a straightforward approach to his cooking – house brawn with tomato *fondue*, quail salad, saddle of rabbit with broad beans, *croustillant* of scorpion fish with sorrel, Troyes *andouillette gras* with Chaource cheese – and although it's essentially a lunch spot, it's a warm and friendly choice for a dinner by candlelight. Free coffee.

SAINTE-SAVINE   10300 (2.5KM WEST)

🍴 🏨 |◉| MOTEL SAVINIEN**

87 rue La Fontaine; take the N60, the "Paris par Sens" road, 2km further on turn right
☎ 03.25.79.24.90 ➡ 03.25.78.04.61
📧 motelsavinien@aol.com
Restaurant closed Sun evening and Mon lunchtime. **Disabled access**. **TV**. **Swimming pool**. **Car park**.

Numerous signposts ensure that this hotel is not hard to find. Though it looks as if it could be part of a chain, it isn't; it is, however, popular with people on the road for business. There's a swimming pool, a sauna and a gym. The rooms are pretty standard and lack character, but prices are attractive considering the quality of service: €40–46 for doubles with shower or twins with shower/wc or bath. Breakfast costs €6. Lunch menu €11, and others €13–30. Dishes include fillet of monkfish with orange, salmon and *foie gras* turover, roast fillet of duck with honey and spices and guineafowl breast with roast apple and bacon. Very warm welcome. Free coffee.

BRÉVIANDES   10450 (5KM SE)

🏨 |◉| HÔTEL-RESTAURANT LE PAN DE BOIS**

35 av. du Général-Leclerc; it's on the N71 to Dijon before the intersection on the southbound bypass.
☎ 03.25.75.02.31 ➡ 03.25.49.67.84
Hotel closed Sun evening. **Restaurant closed** Sun and Mon lunchtime. **Disabled access**. **Garden**. **TV**. **Car park**.

A fairly new, well-designed establishment with all the facilities you'd expect from a chain. The modern building is designed to suit the local style. The rooms at the back, looking out onto a row of trees, are the most peaceful. Doubles with bath €47. The restaurant is just next door in a similar building; the cheapest set menu is at €15 (not served on public holidays) and a meal *à la carte* costs about €15–26. They specialize in meats and steaks chargrilled over the open fire, and they serve good local wines. The terrace is especially pleasant in summer.

SAINT-ANDRÉ-LES-VERGERS   10120 (5KM SW)

🏨 CITOTEL LES ÉPINGLIERS**

180 route d'Auxerre; take the N77 in the direction of Auxerre, and it's 500m after the Saint-André roundabout.
☎ 03.25.75.05.99 ➡ 03.25.75.32.22
TV. **Disabled access**. **Garden**. **Car park**.

A nice hotel surrounded by greenery with about fifteen rooms offering good facilities – bath, TV, telephone and alarm. Each is decorated differently and they look out onto a bit of the flower garden. Doubles €41, and buffet breakfast costs €8.

🍴 |◉| LA GENTILHOMMIÈRE

180 route d'Auxerre.
☎ 03.25.49.35.64 📧 gentilhommière@wanadoo.fr
Closed Sun and Tues evenings, Wed and Aug. **Car park**.

A modern building which belies a stylish interior. The atmosphere, service and food are quite refined: try the slivers of sweetbreads with a concentrated sauce of *Vin de Paille*, the pressed *foie gras* with leeks in Ratafia jelly, the roast quail with spiced bread sauce, the roast shark with sea urchin cream sauce, the moist cake with runny chocolate or the banana and ginger sorbet – all served with Mozart playing gently in the background. Delicious food that's a real hit with businessmen and locals: hot *foie gras* with champagne Ratafia on a bed of salad, roast lobster with vanilla butter and try the runny chocolate cake with ginger sauce. The chef serves *andouillette* chopped into small pieces and melts Chaource cheese over the top – an absolute must. Set menus €18–50 or around €23 *à la carte*. Free coffee.

FOUCHÈRES 10260 (23KM SE)

|●| L'AUBERGE DE LA SEINE

1 faubourg de Bourgogne.; it's on the N71 between Troyes and Bar-sur-Seine.
☎ 03.25.40.71.11
Closed Wed and 15 Jan–5 Feb. **Car park**.

A charming restaurant on the banks of the Seine that looks as if it could be straight out of a de Maupassant story. The dining room has been carefully arranged: the bay windows open onto the river so you can enjoy the cool view, and quacking ducks will serenade you as you dine. The cuisine is delicate and inventiv with dishes changing regularly: Chaource cheese custard, crab and cucumber charlotte, *foie gras* with white kidney beans and river fish. There's a weekday lunch menu for €16, another for €24 or around €31 *à la carte*. A stylish place where you will be warmly welcomed.

VITRY-LE-FRANÇOIS 51300

🎭 🏠 |●| HÔTEL-RESTAURANT LE BON SÉJOUR*

faubourg Léon-Bourgeois (East); it's about 500m from the centre on the Nancy road.
☎ 03.26.74.02.36 ➡ 03.26.73.44.21
Closed Fri evening; Sat; the second fortnight in Aug; 24 Dec–3 Jan. **TV**. **Car park**.

This is a small, basic hotel which is clean and well-run. The rooms, in an annexe with a rather drab corridor, look out onto a quiet tree-lined street. Doubles with basin €25, €30 with shower/wc and €35 with bath. In thre restaurant you'll find set menus at €10, €15 and €24. There's a dish of the day and options *à la carte*. It's has the kind of atmosphere you get in a provincial bistro. Free house apéritif.

🏠 |●| HÔTEL-RESTAURANT DE LA POSTE***

pl. Royer-Collard (Centre); it's behind the Notre-Dame cathedral.
☎ 03.26.74.02.65 ➡ 03.26.74.54.71
Closed Sun and 23 Dec–4 Jan. **Disabled access**. **TV**. **Car park**.

The hotel seems better value for money than the restaurant, where the cheapest set menu is €21. There are others €30–43 and you can choose *à la carte*. They do a lot of fish,

and smoke their salmon on the premises – the fish and scallop lasagna with champagne sauce is highly recommended. You'll pay €52 for a double room with shower/wc and telephone, €56 for a double with bath. There are also family rooms sleeping three, and nine rooms with a Jacuzzi (€73) – or you can relax in the sauna or solarium. The bar has a great choice of beers and whiskies. Warm welcome.

🎭 🏠 |●| HÔTEL-RESTAURANT DE LA CLOCHE**

34 rue Aristide Briand (Centre).
☎ 03.26.74.03.84 ➡ 03.26.74.15.52
Hotel closed last fortnight in Aug and 20 Dec–2 Jan.
Restaurant closed Sun evening out of season.

A peaceful provincial town which was much damaged during World War II – as a consequence, it's not exactly an architectural jewel today. Mme Sautet will make you feel welcome in her establishment and everything is impeccable, whether it be the napkins in the restaurant, the sheets, the bedspreads or the bathroom towels. The windows have been double glazed so nothing will disturb your sleep. A double room with shower/wc or bath costs €55–58 a night. Jaques Sautet, the chef in charge, was classically trained and certainly knows his stuff – so much so that he's won three stars for the restaurant. He specializes in good traditional French food and has a talent for *pâtisseries*: eel *matelote* "Père Sautet", beef cheek braised in beer with lentils, pike balls with lobster sauce. There's a daily set menu at €20, a fish menu at €31, and a more lavish one with truffle specialities from Périgord at €43. Children's menu €11. Free house apéritif.

🎭 |●| LA PIZZA

17 Grande Rue de Vaux; it's opposite the cinema.
☎ 03.26.74.17.63
closed Sat, Sun and Mon lunchtimes.

The pizzas come in a range of sizes to suit all appetites, and with original, tasty toppings. Great welcome. There's a set menu for €9 and you'll pay roughly the same for a meal *à la carte*. The menus and the décor change often. 10% discount on the bill for your meal.

|●| RESTAURANT L'ASIE

54 rue de la Tour (Centre); it's near the cinema.
☎ 03.26.72.13.87
Closed Mon, Tues lunchtime and the last three weeks in Aug.

This terrifically popular restaurant, opened by

Cambodians in the late 1980s, is full every night. The place is exceptionally clean, you always get a really warm welcome and the food is consistently good. They specialize in both Chinese and Thai cuisine. Set lunch menu €9. In the evenings you can eat *à la carte* only, which will cost around €15. Air-conditioned dining room.

VITRY-EN-PERTHOIS   51300 (4KM NE)

|●| AUBERGE DE LA PAVOISE

Centre; on the D382, in the direction of Givry-en-Argonne.
☎ 03.26.74.59.00
Open Sat evening, in the week by reservation only.
Closed during the Christmas holidays.

A converted cowshed, formerly part of the working farm, done up in rustic style. Menus cost €16, €18 and €20. For starters try chicken gizzard salad with snail butter, chicken soufflé or creamed mushroom soup, followed by leg of duck with mirabelle plums or guineafowl with grapes. And for dessert, *charlotte*, tarts or *bavarois* – a hit with everyone. Wines include Aligoté, Morgon, Regnié, all at reasonable prices. They don't accept credit cards.

SAINTE-MARIE-DU-LAC   51290 (20KM SE)

|●| LE CYCLODER

2 rue de l'Église.
☎ 03.26.72.37.05
Closed weekdays only March–Nov, Dec, Jan and Feb.

A lovely *crêperie* where you can get great quality *galettes* costing €2–5 and *crêpes* at €1–4 – not to mention a friendly welcome. You can hire bikes by the hour for €4, for a half-day for €8 or a full day for €11. Visit the nearby model village, which features old Champagne buildings of wattle and daub. Credit cards not accepted.

GIFFAUMONT-CHAMPAUBERT   51290 (26KM SE)

⅔ ⋔ |●| HÔTEL-RESTAURANT LE CHEVAL BLANC***

21 rue du Lac; take the D384, then the D153.
☎ 03.26.72.62.65 ➡ 03.26.73.96.97
Restaurant closed Sun evening, Mon, Tues, three weeks in Jan and three weeks in Sept. **TV. Car park.**

Set in an adorable village full of half-timbered houses near the Lac du Der, the largest artificial lake in Europe and also a bird reserve.

Thierry Gérardin, the young owner, was spurred into rapid action when he took over: all the bathrooms have been renovated and there's a new reception and sitting room. The modern rooms cost €49 for a double with shower/wc and €55 with bath. Wonderful welcome. They serve meals in the open air in spring and summer or on the flower-ornamented terrace. The cheapest set menu is €20 – duck *foie gras* or duck *confit*, pan-fried scallops in raspberry wine are typical. Other menus €25–30. 10% discount on the room rate except July–Aug.

VOUZIERS   08400

⅔ ⋔ |●| ARGONNE HÔTEL**

route de Reims; it's on the way out of town on the Châlons-Retel road, by the first roundabout.
☎ 03.24.71.42.14 ➡ 03.24.71.83.69
@ argonnehotel@wanadoo.fr
Restaurant closed Sun evening and Christmas– New Year. **TV. Car park.**

This modern building in the commercial park is neither characterful nor charming, though the welcoming owners certainly are. It's an ideal place to overnight stop. The rooms are attractively decorated and good value: €46 for a double with shower/wc or bath. Menus €10–23 list classic cuisine with occasional exotic touches — try *foie gras* with Armagnac, crayfish stew with morels and duck breast with pear. Free coffee.

BUZANCY   08240 (22KM E)

⅔ ⋔ |●| LE SAUMON

pl. Chanzy; it's on the D6.
☎ 03.24.30.00.42 ➡ 03.25.30.27.47
@ h-saumon@wanadoo.fr
Closed Fri evening, Sat lunchtime, a fortnight in Feb and a fortnight in Nov. **TV.**

A charming hotel that it would be easy to fall in love with, right in the middle of the small town. The house has been totally refurbished – each of the nine rooms is decorated differently but with the same taste throughout. The rooms vary in size but all have the same facilities; some have a garden view. Doubles €37–54 with shower/wc or bath. Two dining rooms, one of them a very pleasant bistro offering a *menu-carte* assembled from the fresh produce bought at market. Menus from €11. Particularly friendly welcome. One free breakfast per room per night.

CORSICA

20 Corse

🕅 🛎 HÔTEL MARENGO**

2 rue Marengo, BP 244 (West); it's near the casino and the beaches.
☎ 04.95.21.43.66 ➡ 04.95.21.51.26
Closed 15 Nov–20 March. **TV. Car park**.

This is a lovely and very reliable little place at the end of a cul-de-sac – so it's quiet, too. Some rooms look out onto a peaceful courtyard with flowers everywhere. Warm welcome. Double rooms €39–56 with shower or bath. It's basic but well-run and has good facilities including air conditioning and double glazing. There is parking for six cars. 10% discount for a minimum two-night stay except July–Aug.

🕅 🛎 |●| HÔTEL IMPERIAL***

6 bd. Albert 1er; (Southwest).
☎ 04.95.21.50.62 ➡ 04.95.21.15.20

A three-star hotel with a lovely Napoleonic-style entrance. Take a look at the poster for Abel Gance's film epic, *Napoléon*, in reception. The rooms are cosy and feel old but they're comfortable and well-maintained. Depending on facilities and the season, doubles are €52–73. It's not cheap, but prices include a parasol and sunbed on the private beach just across the way. There are other rooms in the more modern annexe behind which are smaller and don't have air-conditioning. *Le Baroko* is the restaurant and the cooking is pretty good – which is just as well, because they like you to stay half board (€51–57 per person) in July–Aug. Free house apéritif.

🕅 🛎 HÔTEL FESCH***

7 rue Fesch (Centre).
☎ 04.95.51.62.62 ➡ 04.95.21.83.36
Ⓦ www.hotel-fesch.com
Closed 15 Dec–15 Jan.

The *Fesch* is very well located in the centre of town. The rooms are mostly comfortable and the furniture is made of chestnut wood. The price of a room depends on the facilities and the season: doubles €51–72 with shower/wc or bath. If you want a top-floor room with a balcony, it'll cost €8 extra. Professional service. Free breakfast.

|●| A CASA

21 av. Noël-Franchini (North); it's 2km north – go along the coast road towards the airport and turn left at the end of bd. Charles-Bonaparte.
☎ 04.95.22.34.78
Closed Sun except July–Aug, and 20 Dec–10 Jan.

This restaurant is outside the centre, but the originality of the place draws a lot of local people. They've squeezed about ten tables onto the patio/balcony, which is surrounded by plants, flowers and parasols. The cooking is uncomplicated but good: the *menu Corse* is particularly tasty. Weekday menu at €12 and others at €19 and 27. Excellent Sartène or Muscat wine. The real attraction is on a Friday or Saturday night when Frank the boss (also a professional magician) puts on a show. He does all the tricks – cutting people in half, levitation – and even burns his partner alive! Be sure to book. There's a single *menu spectacle*, €27. You'll have a great time.

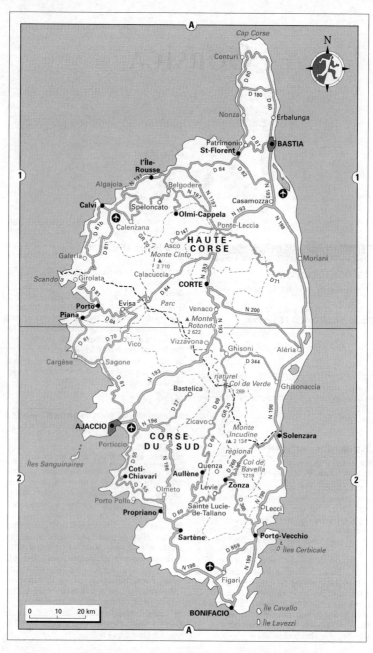

🎿|●| LE 20123

2 rue du Roi-de-Rome; it's in the old town.
☎ 04.95.21.50.05
Closed Mon and Sat lunchtimes, mid-Jan to mid-Feb.

This restaurant used to be in Pila Canale, up in the mountains behind Ajaccio, where the post code was 20123. They moved and set up with the same decor as before. Inside it's almost like a Corsican village with a fountain and small houses; they've even got an old Vespa parked there. There's a small terrace as well. They only serve dinner and there's a single menu for €25; serious Corsican *charcuterie*, *brocciu* tart made with sheep's-milk cheese, followed by a variety of meats – pork, veal or boar – which are grilled or served as stews. Finish with some genuine local cheese and a simple dessert like flan made with ground chestnuts. Good cooking in a place with character, but they don't accept credit cards. Free digestif.

BASTELICACCIA   20129 (13KM E)

🏠 HÔTEL L'ORANGERAIE**

It's on the way out of the village coming from Ajaccio.
☎ 04.95.20.00.09 ➡ 04.95.20.09.24
TV. Garden. Swimming pool. Car park.

The garden, which is filled with palms, arbutus and orange trees, is one of the most amazing in Corsica and it's maintained with passionate care by Monsieur Grisoni. The bungalows are hidden away in glorious Mediterranean vegetation. The setting is wonderful and even though the service gets overwhelmed sometimes, the welcome is warm. You can rent studios for 1–3 people or two rooms for 2–5 people; €30–61 out of season, €49–76 July–Aug. They're not brand-new but they're well-equipped, with good bedding, thermal insulation, hair-drier, kitchen, terrace and barbecue. There's a small swimming pool. Remember to book early; it's often full.

AULLÈNE   20116

🎿 🏠 |●| HÔTEL-RESTAURANT DE LA POSTE*

Centre.
☎ 04.95.78.61.21
Closed Oct–April.

This attractive stone inn with a lovely view of the mountains was built when people were travelling around in carriages; it's one of the oldest hotels in Corsica and dates back to 1880. Double rooms with basin for €31 or €36 with shower. Half board at €44 per per-

son when you stay for three nights or more (compulsory in Aug). The cooking in the restaurant is simple – in season, try the wild boar or the house *charcuterie* at any time. Menus €15 and €21. The owner, Jeannot Benedetti, knows all the interesting places to visit and even writes guide books you can borrow. Friendly welcome and efficient service. Free digestif.

QUENZA   20122 (6KM E)

🎿 🏠 |●| AUBERGE SOLE E MONTI**

Centre; take the D420, in the direction of Aullène.
☎ 04.95.78.62.53 ➡ 04.95.78.63.88
e soleemonti@wanadoo.fr
Closed Oct–April. **TV. Garden. Car park.**

Félicien Balesi, a *bon vivant* who knows how to make his guests feel at home, has run this friendly inn for more than a quarter of a century. The place is quite a new building and has a loggia that would be lovelier still with a sea view; at any rate, it's the perfect spot to admire the beauty of the Corsican mountains. There's a huge garden on the other side of the road available for the guests to enjoy. When the weather is inclement there's a cosy salon intimately arranged around the open fire where the regulars gather. The menu changes daily because only fresh produce is used and the delicious dishes are inspired by old Corsican recipes. Set menus €23 (not Sun) and €30–38. Pleasant, well-equipped rooms. They prefer people to stay half board. From 15 April–14 July half board per person sharing a double room with shower/wc costs €60–68 and, from 15 July–15 September, €61–76 per person. Free apéritif.

LEVIE   20170 (15KM E)

🎿 🏠 |●| FERME-AUBERGE A PIGNATA

Route du Pianu (Northwest); from Levie, drive 3km along the Sainte-Lucie-de-Tallano road, then turn right towards Cucuruzzu; 2km further on, turn left through the second gate, up the rising track.
☎ 04.95.78.41.90 ➡ 04.95.78.46.03
Closed 15 Nov–15 Dec. **Car park.**

A very secretive inn: you have to be in the know to find it. No signposts, no arrows, no board – nothing. And you can't just turn up, you have to book. When you get there, though, the hospitality is tremendous. There only a few rooms but they're clean and spacious and have nice linen. Half board only, at €52–58 per person. According to the locals the authentic Corsican specialities you get here are the best in the region. These include cannelloni with *brocciu* (a mild sheep's milk cheese), stuffed aubergines and braised wild boar. There's one menu only for €27; it's excellent and the portions are large. Wines are extra but there's a good house wine. A great place. Free apéritif.

BASTIA   20200

🎎 🛏 HÔTEL CYMÉA

Route du Cap.
☎ 04.95.31.41.71 ➡ 04.95.31.72.65
Closed 15 Dec–15 Jan. **Disabled access**. **TV**. **Pay garage**.

A long 1970s building, very well maintained, with air-conditioned rooms and fans. Behind, the big garden slopes down to a small pebbly beach 30m from the hotel. Depending on the season and whether you have a view of the road or the sea, doubles with shower/wc cost €46–79, including breakfast. The sea-view rooms all have a balcony – ideal for watching the sun rise over breakfast. Free use of the lock-up garage.

🛏 L'ALIVI***

Route du Cap; it's 1km from the marina on the right.
☎ 04.95.55.00.00 ➡ 04.95.31.03.95
Swimming pool. **Disabled access**. **Car park**.

Seen from the sea, this long oblong structure, three storeys high, doesn't do the coastline any favours. But inside, you really appreciate the comfort of the rooms and direct access to the pebble beach. All rooms have a sea view, a balcony and all the facilities you'd expect from a three-star hotel. A double room with shower or bath costs €91–122, depending on the season. Very professional welcome.

🎎 🍴 RESTAURANT A CASARELLA

6 rue Sainte-Croix (South); it's in the citadel near the old Genoese governors' palace.
☎ 04.95.32.02.32
Closed Sat lunchtime, Sun and three weeks in Nov.

You have to climb up to the citadel, near the Palais of the Genoese governors, to find this place. Take a seat on the terrace, with views of the old port down below, and enjoy a feast. The inventive chef prepares good authentic Corsican dishes scented with herbs from the *maquis*. Try the *casgiate*, a *fromage frais* fritter baked in the oven, the prawns in flaky pastry and the rolled veal with herbs, all of which are excellent. Desserts include the curious *storzapretti*, a stodgy cake that the people here used to

bake for the parish priest on Sundays, and the wonderful *fiadone*, a cheese and orange flan. Set dinner menu €22 or €27 *à la carte*. A good place. Free coffee.

ERBALUNGA   20222 (10KM N)

🎎 🛏 HÔTEL CASTEL BRANDO

It's in the village.
☎ 04.95.30.10.30 ➡ 04.95.33.98.18
e info@castelbrando.com
Closed mid-Oct to end March. **TV**. **Disabled access**. **Swimming pool**. **Car park**.

This hotel is in a 19th-century Corsican mansion and has great character and charm. It has been tastefully restored and furnished with antiques. The walls are colour-washed in strong pigments and there's an impressive monumental staircase; it all feels somewhat Latin American. The garden is planted with palm trees. The rooms in the annexe have air conditioning and a corner kitchen; they are quieter than those in the main building. Doubles €69–134 depending on facilities and season. The welcome is second to none.

CASAMOZZA   20200 (20KM S)

🎎 🛏 🍴 CHEZ WALTER

It's on the N193, about 4km south from the airport crossroads.
☎ 04.95.36.00.09 ➡ 04.95.36.18.92
e chez-walter@wanadoo.fr
Restaurant closed Sun out of season and New Year. **TV**. **Disabled access**. **Swimming pool**. **Garden**. **Car park**.

A fine, comfortable and reliable establishment which is run professionally. Very good facilities in the air-conditioned rooms. Doubles with shower or bath €61–76 depending on the season. There's a swimming pool, a tennis court and a lovely garden. It's a place used by ship crews stopping over or football teams come to play against Bastia. The restaurant has a good reputation and there are good fish dishes (sea bream, crayfish and seafood). Menu at €17. Free coffee.

BONIFACIO   20169

🛏 🍴 DOMAINE DE LICETTO

Route du phare de Pertusato.
Hotel ☎ 04.95.73.03.59 ➡ 04.95.73.03.59
Restaurant ☎ 04.95.73.19.48
Closed lunchtimes and out of season. **Disabled access**. **Car park**.

There's an unusual view of both the upper and

lower towns from the grounds here. The *Domaine* is right in the *maquis* and the modern hotel is in a separate building from the restaurant. The rooms are smart; €32–64 wiith shower/wc or €43–76 with bath. Dining in the restaurant is by reservation only. The single set menu, €27, is gargantuan and includes everything: apéritif, starter, two courses, cheeses, desserts, wine, coffee and *digestif*. Typically Corsican cuisine: stuffed squid, milk-fed lamb in sauce, cabbage stuffed with chestnuts and iced charlotte with chestnut cream. Credit cards not accepted.

⩗ ⌂ HÔTEL DES ÉTRANGERS*

av. Sylvère-Bohn; it's 300m from the port, hidden beneath a cliff, at the right of the road from Ajaccio.
☎ 04.95.73.01.09 ➡ 04.95.73.16.97
Closed 31 Oct–1 April. **TV**. **Car park**.

Pretty close to the road but the soundproofing is efficient. Good facilities, including shower/wc, telephone and TV. Most rooms have air conditioning and they're clean. Room prices €40–72 for a double depending on the season include breakfast. Good value for Bonifacio. Lock-up for motorbikes. 10% discount in March and April.

⌂ |●| A TRAMA

Cartarana, route de Santa-Marza; it's 1.5km from the town centre.
☎ 04.95.73.17.17 ➡ 04.95.73.17.79
Restaurant closed telephone out of season. **TV**.
Disabled access. **Garden**. **Swimming pool**. **Car park**.

In a peaceful setting surrounded by greenery, this new complex has been handsomely built and it's well maintained. There are 25 rooms at garden level, each with a private terrace facing the swimming pool – perfect for breakfast. Rooms all have modern facilities like TV, mini-bar and air conditioning, and the beds are "dorsopedic", apparently. Doubles €60–153 depending on season. It's a nice place and the welcome is calm, courteous and professional. The restaurant is called *Le Clos Vatel* and has a good reputation. Menus €21–26 or *à la carte*.

⌂ |●| HÔTEL-RESTAURANT DU CENTRE NAUTIQUE***

It's on the north side of the marina across from the quai Jérôme-Comparetti.
☎ 04.95.73.02.11 ➡ 04.95.73.17.47
TV.

This grand and beautiful building stands on its own quay – quiet compared to the one opposite. It has ten classy duplex rooms, spacious and airy, with contemporary interiors and plenty of facilities like mini-bars and air conditioning. There are sofa beds in the ground-floor sitting rooms; bedroom and shower are upstairs. A duplex with sea view costs €83 Oct–March, €33 April–June and Sept or €160 in July and August. The garden-view rooms are cheaper. There's also a restaurant serving excellent fresh pasta. The half-board rate is an extra €23 per person per day.

CALVI   20260

⩗ ⌂ |●| HÔTEL-RESTAURANT CASA-VECCHIA

Route de Santore; it's 500m from the town centre and 200m from the beach and pine wood.
☎ 04.95.65.09.33 ➡ 04.95.65.37.93
Closed Winter. **Car park**.

The accommodation is in ten simple and attractively priced bungalows in a garden full of flowers. Rooms are €30 with shower and shared outside wc, €55 with shower/wc. Half board is obligatory July–Aug at €73–98 for two people. Meals are served on a shaded terrace; good, generously served family cooking with menus at €13–17. The restaurant is closed for lunch. Nice welcome from Madame and her daughters. 10% discount for a two-night stay in bungalows over €31, except in July and Aug. Free apéritif for menus over €15.

⌂ HÔTEL LES ARBOUSIERS**

Route de Pietra-Maggiore (South); go about 800m in the direction of Bastia, then turn right at the start of the pine forest, 5 minutes from the beach, and follow the signs.
☎ 04.95.65.04.47 ➡ 04.95.65.26.14
Closed Oct–April inclusive. **Garden**. **Lock-up car park**.

It can be best to stay just outside Calvi, simply because you get more space. This hotel is in an attractive big house with pink walls, an old wooden staircase leading up to the bedrooms. The décor isn't spectacular but it's very clean and there are lots of pleasant little terraces overlooking the courtyard. Ask for a south-facing room to maximize the sun. The prices are reasonable: doubles with bath €36–48. Good welcome.

⩗ ⌂ RÉSIDENCE LES ALOÈS**

Quartier Donatéo (East).
☎ 04.95.65.01.46 ➡ 04.95.65.01.67
✉ info@hotel-les-aloes.com
Closed 15 Oct to mid-March. **TV**. **Garden**. **Car park**.

This hotel was built in the 1960s on a fabulous site above Calvi – you get a panoramic view of the bay, the citadel and the wild countryside towards Monte Cinto. The surroundings are peaceful and there are flowers everywhere. The decor in the foyer is a bit kitsch but it's reasonably elegant, while the refurbished rooms have TV, telephone and balcony. Prices range from €38–53 for a double depending on the season and the view (mountain or sea). Attentive staff. 10% discount for a minimum two-night stay 1 April–30 June.

洨 ☎ LE GRAND HÔTEL**

3 bd. Wilson (Centre).
☎ 04.95.65.09.74 ➡ 04.95.65.25.18
ⓦ www.grand-calvi.com
Closed Nov–March. **TV.**

They don't build places like this turn-of-the-(20th)-century grand hotel any more: corridors as wide as rooms, a smoking room as large as a ballroom and bedrooms as big as – well, big bedrooms, though they're spacious enough. The tea room looks a bit dated, and the armchairs need to be re-covered, but they're comfortable; the rooms themselves have been given a lick of paint and the beds are good. Doubles at €58–90 depending on the season and facilities. Nice welcome, a good atmosphere and a spectacular view from the breakfast room: it's high up, so you look down on the rooftops of Calvi to the sea beyond. 10% discount on the room rate in April and October.

洨 |●| L'ABRI CÔTIER

quai Landry; it's by the harbour.
☎ 04.95.65.12.76

The restaurant is on the first floor, over a bar and tearoom. There's a big dining room that looks over the marina. The cooking zings with fresh flavours – try their fish grilled with a drizzle of olive oil, the starters that combine fresh fruit and vegetables or their dishes using *brocciu* (mild sheep's milk cheese). Pleasant, efficient service; this is one of the most reliable places in Calvi. Menus €12–27. Free coffee.

CORTE 20250

☎ HÔTEL DE LA POSTE*

2 pl. du Duc-de-Padoue (Centre).
☎ 04.95.46.01.37
Closed Dec. **Disabled access.**

An old hotel on a shady square, with a dozen simple, reasonably-priced rooms looking

onto the square or out over the back. Doubles €30 with basin, €41 with shower/wc. Good if you're on a budget and want somewhere central. They don't take credit cards, though, and breakfast finishes at 9.30am.

洨 |●| L'OLIVERAIE

Lieu-dit Perru; head for the university, when you come to the junction with the main road, it's 150m further on the left.
☎ 04.95.46.06.32
Closed Mon evening in winter, Nov.

This very good restaurant, surrounded by greenery, is on the outskirts of town. Mme Mattei uses Corsican produce to prepare tasty dishes like *buglidicce*, *fromage frais* fritters, herb tart, squid stuffed with *brocciu* (mild sheep's-milk cheese), and for dessert, hazelnut and ground chestnut tart – the house speciality. Generous helpings. They also take lots of groups and it's popular with students and staff from the neighbouring campus. Set menus €10, €15 and €23. Free *digestif.*

|●| U MUSEU

rampe Ribanelle; head for pl. du Poilu near the citadel.
☎ 04.95.61.08.36
Closed Sun in winter, and 20 Dec–15 March.

An attractive restaurant where you'll get good food without paying a fortune. Very pleasant terrace. Set *formule* at €13 for main course and dessert or €15 for the menu (herb tart, wild boar stew, and *délice* of chestnuts), which is truly delicious. The jugs of AOC wine go down a treat. A good place to go, but the serving staff get a little stressed out in summer when it's full.

COTI-CHIAVARI 20138

洨 ☎ |●| HÔTEL-RESTAURANT LE BELVÉDÈRE

How to get there: it's on the left of the Acqua Doria road before you get to the village.
☎ 04.95.27.10.32 ➡ 04.95.27.12.99
Hotel closed 11 Nov to mid-Feb. **Restaurant closed** evenings in winter and lunchtimes in July, Aug and Sept. **Disabled access. Garden. Car park.**

A long, low and fairly modern building on its own overlooking the bay of Ajaccio. From the arc of the circular terrace, you get one of the best views of the island. Caroline, the *patronne*, really takes care of her guests. Good, generous Corsican dishes. Set menus €21 and €24. The rooms are lovely and have a view of the sea: €46–61 for a double with shower/wc. Half board, €83–99 for two, is obligatory in summer. Very reasonable prices which, unusually for Corsica, are the same throughout the year. This place is reliable and offers good service – nothing like the rip-off joints you'll find on the coast. They don't accept credit cards. Free apéritif.

ÎLE-ROUSSE (L')   20220

☎ L'AMIRAL

bd. Charles-Marie Savelli; it's about 150m from the town centre, across from the beach.
☎ 04.95.60.28.05 ➡ 04.95.60.31.21
🌐 www.hotel-amiral.com 📧 info@hotel-amiral.com
Closed 2 Oct–1 April.

A seriously appealing place in a brilliant situation across from the beach. Rooms are clean and comfortable, with air conditioning in high summer. Peaceful family atmosphere. Doubles €53–84 depending on the season or the view (sea or garden). Breakfast €6. There's also an annexe with rooms sleeping three.

SPELONCATO   20226 (26KM S)

🎿 ☎ A SPELUNCA**

pl. de l'Église; it's south of L'Île-Rousse on a very winding road.
☎ 04.95.61.50.38 ➡ 04.95.61.53.14
📧 spelunca-hotel@freesbee.fr

A hotel with charm in a characterful village sat on a rock in the Balagne – this is the real soul of Corsica. This pink house with a little turret and a lovely terrace was built in 1856 as the summer residence of Cardinal Savelli, the Secretary of State to Pope Pius IX. You can see his portrait in the grand drawing room, itself an echo of the island's Napoleonic past. The rooms lead from a superb staircase, some rooms in the attic. Doubles €53–61 with shower or bath. Great value for money and a courteous welcome. Free breakfast except in July–Aug.

OLMI-CAPELLA   20259

🎿 |●| LA TORNADIA

How to get there: it's about 2km outside Olmi-Capella on the Balagne–Pioggiola road.
☎ 04.95.61.90.93 ➡ 04.95.61.92.15
Closed mid-Nov to mid-March.

Whether you choose to eat under the chestnut trees or in the beamed dining room, the won-

derful dishes just keep on coming. There's roast, beef with ceps, pasta made from chestnut flour, killer cheeses, and brandy like fire water! Menus €18–24 or *à la carte*. They've got a shop where you can buy local products. A very good place, and it's been going more than thirty years. Warm, friendly welcome. Free apéritif.

PIANA   20115

☎ HÔTEL CONTINENTAL*

route d'Ajaccio; it's on the outskirts of town.
☎ 04.95.27.89.00 ➡ 04.95.27.84.71
Closed Oct–March. **Garden. Lock-up garage**.

An old coaching inn which has aged beautifully – it feels like a place in which some great 19th-century novelist could have spent the night. It's a bit old-fashioned, but very clean and delightfully antique. The garden is full of pines and apricot trees; the rooms have natural wooden floors, big old shutters and thick walls, though the ones over the street are pretty noisy. Doubles €30 with no private facilities, €43 with shower/wc in the annexe. No credit cards.

PORTO   20150

☎ |●| HÔTEL-RESTAURANT LE PORTO*

route de Calvi.
☎ 04.95.26.11.20 ➡ 04.95.26.13.92
Closed mid-Oct to mid-April. **Garage**.

A good restaurant in Porto, the tourist centre of Corsica. Menus, priced at €15–18, list a fine selection of tasty dishes like duck fillet with orange, veal fillet with mustard and delicious fish – all served with a smile. Good local wine at fair prices. Similar standard in the hotel, with simple spacious rooms, €36–53 depending on the season, and they all have real bathrooms. Half board, €85–106 for two, is obligatory in Aug. There's a garage for motor bikes.

EVISA   20126 (22KM E)

🎿 ☎ |●| HÔTEL RESTAURANT DU CENTRE

It's in the centre of the village.
☎ 04.95.26.20.92
Closed end Oct–1 March. **Car park**.

This typical village house contains a genuine country restaurant. The dining room is very simple and the service rudimentary, but the cooking is sublime. Only fresh produce is used in the dishes, which are skilfully prepared (try the swordfish with basil), slowly cooked (try the soup or tripe) and creatively concocted (try the wild boar with orange and bitter chocolate). Portions are colossal – you get a whole shoal of grilled prawns, for example. And the desserts are equally tasty, particularly the chestnut *parfait*. Lunch menu €14 and another at €20. It's wise to book, especially if you want a table on the terrace. The same is true for the four simple, clean rooms, which have varying toilet facilities; doubles from €37. Half board is compulsory May–Sept at €122 for two people. Free apéritif and 10% discount on the room rate March–May.

PORTO-VECCHIO   20137

☗ HÔTEL LE MISTRAL**

5 rue Toussaint-Culioli.
☎ 04.95.70.08.53 ☛ 04.95.70.51.60
Closed Nov–1 March. **TV**. **Car park**.

Located in the old town, this attractive and comfortable two-star has doubles with shower/wc or bath for €39–104 depending on the season – but check when you book because there is some variation from the listed prices. The rooms are meticulously kept and you'll get a good welcome. The high-season prices seem steep, but they tend to be in this town. You can also rent studios by the week. The shaded car park is across the road.

⅍ ☗ |●| HÔTEL LE GOÉLAND

La Marine.
☎ 04.95.70.14.15 ☛ 04.95.72.05.18
e hotel-goeland@wanadoo.fr
Closed end Oct to Easter. **TV**. **Car park**.

This, the best-located hotel in Porto-Vecchio, overlooks the gulf and has its own private beach and harbour. It's very simple but it's the only place in town to enjoy such a splendid situation. The rooms are variously sized, though most have been refurbished. Doubles with shower or basin €59–83, with shower/wc €75–124 or with bath €90–143. Nice welcome. There's a bar and a terrace with a sea view. There's not a proper restaurant but they serve simple snacks and dishes: tapas, pasta, soups. Free house apéritif.

⅍ |●| LE TOURISME

12 cours Napoléon; it's in the old town near the church.
☎ 04.95.70.39.33
Closed Sun lunchtime.

You eat well at *Le Tourisme*, where the cuisine is light and very unusual. They do an excellent

dish of spicy mussels *à la porto-vecchiaise*, and great dishes of the day like tagliatelle with asparagus and, for dessert, a soup of strawberries and bilberries. Menus €15–21 and a *formule express* with salad, a choice of pasta or *moules marinières* and carpaccio of melon; if you're really in a hurry, try the short menu with main and dessert. A little pricey for what it is but the quality is good and the service is speedy. Free apéritif.

LECCI-DE-PORTO-VECCHIO   20137 (7KM N)

☗ HÔTEL ET RÉSIDENCE CARANELLA VILLAGE

route de Cala-Rossa; 3km along the road to Bastia, at La Trinité, turn right at the Cala-Rossa signpost, turn left at the next roundabout and head straight on for 4km.
☎ 04.95.71.60.94 ☛ 04.95.71.60.80
Swimming pool. **Garden**. **Car park**.

Set in flower-filled grounds just 300m from the Cala Rossa beach are about forty self-catering studios and apartments (some with oven, microwave, TV, telephone and dishwasher). Most have a terrace and are set around the heated swimming pool. Facilities include a fitness centre, bike hire, a bar, linen hire, a cleaning service and a washing room. Given the prices in Porto-Vecchio this is a very good option. Studios with shower and corner kitchen cost €51 (Oct–May), €53 (June–Sept), €70 (July) and €82 (Aug); you pay more for a bathroom. Two-roomed apartments with shower cost €71–106. The villas or apartments sleep four to six people and cost €86–212, depending on the type and the season. Friendly welcome and easy-going atmosphere.

PROPRIANO   20110

⅍ ☗ LOFT HÔTEL

3 rue Jean-Paul-Pandolfi.
☎ 04.95.76.17.48 ☛ 04.95.76.22.04
Closed 15 Nov–15 March. **Disabled access**. **TV**. **Car park**.

An old wine warehouse huddled among a group of houses which has been converted into a hotel. As you might expect from the name, it has clean rooms boasting a modern minimalist look – pale tiles and blond wood. Doubles in low season at €39–43 and €46–58 in high season; the cheaper rooms are on the ground floor. Nice welcome. Free breakfast depending on the number of nights you stay.

☗ MOTEL ARIA MARINA**

Lieu-dit la Cuparchiata. It's in the hills above Propriano;

from Viggiarello follow the signs to the motel.
☎ 04.95.76.04.32 ➡ 04.95.76.25.01
Closed 15 Oct–1 April. **Swimming pool. Garden. Car park**.

This is a good motel, some distance from the brouhaha in Propriano and, better still, with a great view of the Gulf of Valinco. The studios or two-roomed apartments are spacious and have good facilities, and cost €53–69 in low and mid season. In July and August they rent the studios by the week only at €534–610; the two- and three-roomed apartments are more so you'll need to check. All the accommodation is sparklingly clean. They're really nice people and the pool is lovely too.

🍴 |●| RESTAURANT L'HIPPOCAMPE

rue Jean-Paul-Pandolfi (South).
☎ 04.95.76.11.01
Closed Sun out of season, and end Sept to Easter.

Antoine, aka "The American", runs this place. He loves the sea and really fresh fish – so what you eat in the evening is what he's pulled out of the Gulf of Valinco that morning. Good cuisine and good value for money too, served either in warm, simple surroundings or out on the terrace. Set menu €18 or around €31 *à la carte* including decent wine. Efficient and friendly service. Free coffee.

SAINT-FLORENT   20217

🍴 🏠 HÔTEL MAXIME**

Centre; it's in a quiet little street off place des Portes.
☎ 04.95.37.05.30 ➡ 04.95.37.13.07
TV. Garage.

A fairly new and very clean hotel, good value for the resort. Each room has a mini-bar and balcony; some of them overlook the Poggio river, where you can arrange to moor your boat. Doubles €43–61 with shower or bath; prices also vary with the season. There's a lock-up for motorbikes as well as a private car park. 10% discount in low season.

🏠 MOTEL TREPERI**

route de Bastia (East). It's 1km out of town; take the Bastia road, which goes along the beach, then turn right where you see the sign to the motel.
☎ 04.95.37.40.20 ➡ 04.95.37.04.61
Closed 15 Nov–15 March. **Swimming pool. Garden. TV. Car park**.

All the rooms are airy, spacious and well-kept, with shower and wc; each has a small terrace leading onto the flower-filled garden. A double room costs €43 out of season,

€49 in July and €73 in Aug. There's also a 7-night deal up to 10 June for €338 including breakfast. The surroundings are peaceful and there are splendid views over the gulf as well as a swimming pool and tennis courts. Lovely place.

PATRIMONIO   20253 (5KM NE)

🏠 HÔTEL U CASONE

In the village (Centre); take the D81 out of Saint-Florent, travel 250m into the village, take the right hairpin and you'll see the sign.
☎ 04.95.37.14.46 ➡ 04.95.37.17.15
Closed 15 Oct–1 April. **Garage**.

This is a large house in the upper village faced with grey rough-cast. It has a pretty garden where you can have breakfast or enjoy the sun and huge, well-maintained bedrooms with views over the countryside or the sea. Doubles €30–61, depending on facilities and season. There's a family atmosphere to this unpretentious place, and a friendly welcome from Mme Montemagni. Although there's no restaurant, make sure to try a bottle or two of the Clos Montemagni if you eat elsewhere – the vineyard isn't far. It's a good place for bikers because there's a lock-up, and the beaches are about 3km away. Credit cards not accepted.

SARTÈNE   20100

🏠 HÔTEL VILLA PIANA**

route de Propriano; it's 1km before Sartène.
☎ 04.95.77.07.04 ➡ 04.95.73.45.65
e hotel-la-villa-piana@wanadoo.fr
Closed Oct–April. **Swimming pool. Garage**.

A pretty ochre house amid trees and flowers with a delightful entrance and offering a charming welcome. The rooms have been carefully decorated, and most have a view over Sartène. Avoid the ones with a view over the back because they're not great, particularly on the ground floor. Doubles €49–84, breakfast €7. Facilities include TV (on request), tennis court, bar and a swimming pool with a superb panoramic view. Lock-up for motorbikes.

SAINT-LUCIE-DE-TALLANO   20112 (14KM NE)

🍴 |●| LA SANTA LUCIA

Centre; take the Sartène/Ajaccio road and turn right for the village.
☎ 04.95.78.81.28
Closed Sun out of season. **TV. Disabled access**.

Swimming pool. Car park.

Excellent Corsican food. The cheaper menu at €14 is decent enough – if rather ordinary – but the €20 one really showcases the talents of the two chefs, who are both from the village. The dishes are very attractively presented, the food is tasty and accurately seasoned and the cooking is judged to perfection: the roast pork with honey and rabbit with myrtle are both superb. You'll receive a smiling welcome from the boss. There's a pleasant terrace with a view of the fountain. Free house apéritif.

SOLENZARA   20145

🏛 HÔTEL LA SOLENZARA**

Centre; it's on the Bastia road on the edge of town.
☎ 04.95.57.42.18 ➡ 04.95.57.46.84
Ⓦ www.lasolenzara.com Ⓔ info@lasolenzara.com
Closed Nov and Dec. **Swimming pool. TV. Disabled access. Car park.**

This house was built 200 years ago by the Squire of Solenzara. It has been simply and tastefully redecorated and is now a charming hotel. The old rooms are vast and have newly equipped bathrooms; the high ceilings mean that they're cool in summer too. If you don't fancy these, conventional rooms are available in a new annexe. Tall palm trees sway in the garden, and there's a magnificent swimming pool. Direct access to the beach or the port. Reasonable prices for a place of such character. Doubles €53–81 including breakfast. If you stay for a week in low or mid-season, you get the seventh night free.

ZONZA   20124

🏛 I●I HÔTEL-RESTAURANT LA TERRASSE

Centre; it's set back from the main road.
☎ 04.95.78.67.69 ➡ 04.95.78.66.03
Closed 1 Nov–31 March. **Car park.**

The best thing about this place is the terrace – and, even better, you can eat on it. It's the best-positioned place in the village and boasts a view over the roofs of the town and the impressive mountains, so it's fantastic at sunset. Good Corsican food, too: the house *charcuterie* is particularly tasty and their regional dishes are the genuine article and generously served; highlights include wild boar with noodles, cannelloni and chestnut desserts. Menus €13–27. The owners, the Mondolini-Pietris, welcome you with warmth and good humour. The rooms are decent and well-maintained, and some have a terrace over the valley. There isn't a half-board requirement but they do like you to have lunch or dinner. Since the cooking is good and prices are fair, that's not much of a hassle. Double rooms €43–58, half board €44–50 per person. 10% discount on the room rate April–June and Oct.

FRANCHE-COMTÉ

25 Doubs

39 Jura

70 Haute-Saône

90 Territoire de Belfort

ARBOIS   39600

♠ HÔTEL LE MÉPHISTO

33 pl. Faramand (Centre).
☎ 03.84.66.06.49
Closed Mon except July–Aug.

Friendly and good value. All the rooms are different and the décor about as far as you can get from run-of-the-mill. Room number 7 is very bright, with a splendid view over Arbois. Doubles with basin €21; €29 with shower/wc.

🍴 ♠ HÔTEL DES MESSAGERIES**

2 rue de Courcelles (Centre).
☎ 03.84.66.13.43 ➡ 03.84.37.41.09
📧 hotel.lesmessageries@wanadoo.fr
Closed Wed 11am–5pm out of season, Dec and Jan.
TV. Pay car park.

You get a warm reception in this comfy hotel which has a pleasant, family atmosphere. It's a popular stopping point for foreign travellers passing through, so there's an international feel. Room prices vary according to facilities from €30 with basin with wc down the landing to €51 with bath/wc. Free house apéritif.

🍴 RESTAURANT LA CUISANCE

62 pl. Faramand (South).
☎ 03.84.37.40.74
Closed Tues and Wed evenings.

La Cuisance is the little river that runs through Arbois; you can enjoy a view of it from the cool terrace that looks over the water. This lively village restaurant is run by particularly welcoming proprietors. The cheapest menu at €7 includes a starter such as mountain ham, a main course which could be an omelette and dessert. Other menus €9–20. House specialities include chicken or trout with *vin jaune* sauce, mushrooms in a pastry case, sirloin with morels and game in season.

🍴 🍴 LA BALANC – METS ET VINS

47 rue de Courcelles.
☎ 03.84.37.45.00
Closed Sun evening to Wed Feb–Mar; Sun evening and Mon March to mid-Jul; 20 Aug to end-Nov; Dec and Jan.
Garden. Car park. Disabled access.

For ages this was a popular restaurant with gourmets, then it closed down. Since it re-opened, though, it's re-established its reputation. Thierry is an enormously talented chef and he launched himself on this mad adventure not long ago but he's onto a winner – the atmosphere is lively and genuinely friendly and there's a lovely terrace. The menus are varied, the dishes local with a modern touch and the prices modest. The lunch menu, €13, includes a glass of wine; the €16 menu lists a casserole of the day. There's also a *menu-carte* for €24 and a top-price one for €34. The *sommelier* helps you through the extensive and fairly-priced wine list – the owners have a lot of wine-growing friends – and most are served by the glass. Free *digestif*.

POLIGNY   39800 (9KM SW)

🍴 ♠ 🍴 DOMAINE DU MOULIN DE LA VALLÉE HEUREUSE***

route de Genève; it's on the N5.
☎ 03.84.12.13 ➡ 03.84.37.08.75

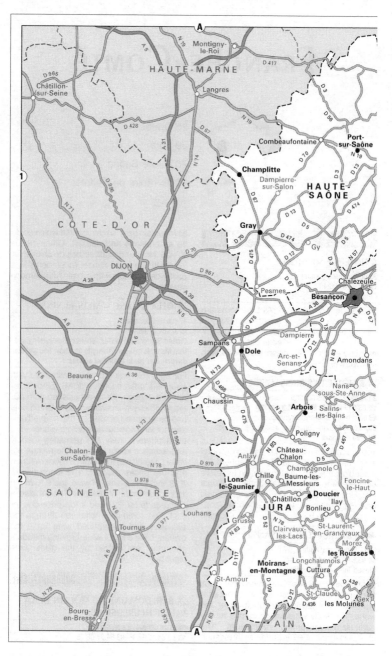

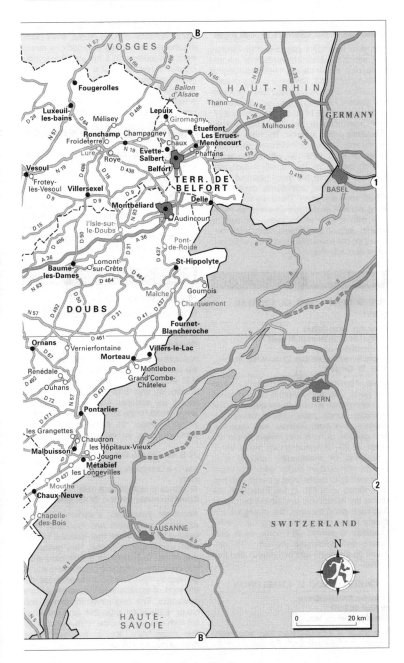

ⓦ www.hotelvalleeheureuse.com
Closed 3 Nov–30 April. **Garden**. **TV**. **Disabled access**.

The river meanders past this 18th-century mill, which has been converted into a hotel-restaurant. It's absolutely charming. Original cooking with light, flavourful dishes created by Danièle using flowers and herbs grown in the garden. Fair prices, too, with a weekday lunch menu at €14 and others from €21. Half board is compulsory over public holiday weekends and in summer. The hotel is sheer luxury and you pay for it: doubles with shower/wc or bath €69–137 with a few suites costing even more. The recently redecorated rooms are among the most beautiful to be found in the Jura, confidently mixing pale wood, rope and linen. There are two swimming pools – an outdoor one and an inside one with a view of the river – as well as sauna, Jacuzzi and fitness room. 10% discount on the room rate except on public holidays and July–Aug.

BAUME-LES-DAMES   25110

⅍ 🏠 |●| HOSTELLERIE DU CHÂTEAU D'AS***

24 rue du Château-Gaillard.
☎ 03.81.84.00.66 **➽** 03.81.84.59.67
ⓦ www.chateau-das.fr
Closed Sun evening and Mon; 22 Jan–4 Feb; 19 Nov–9 Dec. **TV**. **Car park**.

A pair of brothers – both gifted cooks – set up this place. The dining room is big and round and somewhat sombre in atmosphere. The weekday lunch menu (€21) offers two starters, two main courses, two desserts, two glasses of wine and coffee. There are others (€ 23–53) featuring local dishes with a smattering of individuality: chunky snail kebabs with peasant bacon, pike force-meat balls with crab *coulis*, pastry cases with soft fruit. Good wine list. In the hotel, half the rooms are attractively (and newly) decorated and have good facilities; the others are still dreary. Prices start at €41 and go up to €64. Breakfast is served with home-made preserves and farmhouse yoghurt. 10% discount on the room rate Nov–March and free coffee.

⅍ |●| RESTAURANT LE CHARLESTON

10 rue des Armuriers (Centre).
☎ 03.81.84.24.07
Closed Sun evening, Mon.

The décor is less cluttered than you might expect from genuine Belle Époque – but it's attractive nonetheless. The cooking sticks to strictly orthodox regional dishes: small Conté cheese tart with snails and garlic, a duo of trout and salmon on a thin cauliflower pancake and ham bone in a pastry case with green cabbage *compote*. Menus start at €10 but for a few Euros more there are more creative dishes. Friendly reception and impeccable service. Free apéritif.

LOMONT-SUR-CRÊTE   25110 (9KM E)

⅍ |●| CHEZ LA MARTHE

23 Grande-Rue.
☎ 03.81.84.01.50

A friendly, simple village café-restaurant. Nice family dishes prepared using good produce. If you want fish, whitebait or trout, you have to order them beforehand because the cook uses fresh (not frozen) fish. Menus €11–22. A surprise of a place. Free coffee.

BELFORT   90000

⅍ 🏠 NOUVEL HÔTEL*

56 faubourg de France (Centre); it's 300m from the train station.
☎ 03.84.28.28.78
Closed a week in Aug. **TV**.

A practical hotel in a pedestrianized street in the town centre. It's good value: doubles are €21 with basin, €24 with shower, €34 with shower/wc and €38 with bath/wc. All the rooms are spotless and the proprietor is always ready to be of service. Breakfast €5, or free for under 12s. At the weekend, if you take two rooms, you can have a third for free.

⅍ 🏠 AU RELAIS D'ALSACE**

5 av. de la Laurencie (Northeast); it's 500m from the centre.
☎ 03.84.22.15.55 **➽** 03.84.28.70.48
Closed Sun evening from 9pm. **TV**. **Car park**.

About ten years ago, a dynamic Franco-Algerian couple, Kim and Georges, were looking for work when they decided to take a risk and reopen this hotel. They renovated it from top to bottom, and their hard work has created a welcoming place where you're greeted by Kim's infectious cheerfulness. It's the kind of establishment increasingly rare nowadays. The bedrooms are simple and clean; €33–36 for a double, and breakfast €5 with real orange juice. 10% discount on the room rate for a two-night stay Sept–June, as well as free orange juice for guests and free breakfast for children under 10.

HÔTEL VAUBAN**

4 rue du Magasin (Centre).
☎ 03.84.21.59.37 ➡ 03.84.21.41.67
Ⓦ www.hotel-vauban.com
Closed Sun Nov–March; the Feb school holidays.
Garden. **TV**.

The hotel is in a peaceful district just a few minutes' walk from the old town. The owner has covered the walls with his paintings, adding freshness and a party atmosphere to the place. Pleasant bedrooms, some opening onto the lovely garden; doubles with shower or bath €47. On fine days, you can breakfast (yours for €6) beside the lily pond and enjoy the birdsong. Nice welcome but no animals. 10% discount.

HÔTEL-RESTAURANT LE SAINT-CHRISTOPHE**

pl. d'Armes (Centre); you can walk from the château.
☎ 03.84.55.88.88 ➡ 03.84.54.08.77
Restaurant closed Sun and 25 Dec–2 Jan. **TV**.

The dynamic owners of this establishment are always looking to improve it. The main building has comfortable and spacious double rooms from €50 with shower/wc and a view of the town's famous lion. The nearby annexe is very quiet, with has impeccable doubles with shower/wc or bath €55. A reasonable set menu for €11 is served Mon–Thurs in the restaurant; others are €18–29. In summer they open the terrace in the square, where they serve salads. 10% discount on the room rate.

GRAND HÔTEL DU TONNEAU D'OR***

1 rue Reiset (Centre); it's 100m from the police station.
☎ 03.84.58.57.56 ➡ 03.84.58.57.50
Ⓦ www.tonneaudor.fr
Disabled access. **TV**. **Car park**.

The foyer is like the hall of a palace, with an elaborately decorated ceiling, grand staircase and elegant, turn-of-the-century charm. The magnificent stained glass was created by Gruber, a local master-craftsman, and over the drawing room there's a magnificent listed dome – as you'll gather, this small luxury establishment is full of character. Spacious and exceptionally comfortable rooms are €95 with bath. The décor is modern and tasteful, and the piano bar lends a final touch of sophistication. There's a restaurant serving a single set menu for €14. Free breakfast.

L'AUBERGE DES TROIS CHÊNES

29 rue de Soissons; from the town centre take the Vesoul road (bd. Kennedy), then take the signs to the Alstour factory and Cravanche. The restaurant is opposite the factory.
☎ 03.84.22.19.45
Closed Mon–Weds evenings; the last fortnight in Aug.
Car park.

The comfortable, cosy inn, just outside town, specializes in modern cuisine which is anchored in tradition. There's a decent lunch menu for €11 on weekdays or evening set menus at €18–29, listing fillet of beef with morels, pan-fried sole with saffron sauce, monkfish with fresh noodles and mountain ham in Madeira and cream.

LA GRANDE FONTAINE

pl. de la Grande-Fontaine (Centre); it's in the old town.
☎ 03.84.22.45.38
Closed Sun evening and Mon. **Disabled access**.

In this pleasant restaurant they create inspirational dishes using only the freshest produce, combining herbs in original and intriguing ways. The lamb shank braised in a hay box is of remarkable quality, as is the baked fish with fennel, the *foie gras* risotto, the *châteaubriand en croûte* with spiced salt and all the desserts. Lunch menu €14 in the week; others up to €34, or you can eat *à la carte*. The half-bottles of wine seem pricey, though. Best to book in the evening. In fine weather they put a few tables outside on the pavement.

LE MOLIÈRE

6 rue de l'Étuve (Centre).
☎ 03.84.21.86.38 ➡ 03.84.58.01.22
Closed Tues evening, Wed, a fortnight in Feb and three weeks Aug–Sept.

This establishment is in an attractive tree-lined square, surrounded by smart buildings fronted with local sandstone. Ignore the plastic chairs – if you can – and enjoy the charm of the place and the excellence of the cuisine. Only fresh produce is used here and the owner makes a trip to Mulhouse every morning to get his fish. The dishes are delightfully flavoured and change as different meats, vegetables or salads and herbs come into season. The *à la carte* choice is almost too extensive, and there's a dazzling selection of menus for all budgets starting at €15 (not served Sun or public holidays) and going up to €38 by way of a lobster menu and a Franc-Comtois speciality one. Here's a taster: *pannequet* of snails flambéed with aniseed, lamb cutlet and *foie gras* with port and shallots, veal sweetbreads with sorrel cream and sautéed morels, fillet of zander with snails and diced bacon, large prawns in a stew and veal sweetbreads with garlic cream. Delicious desserts. The wine list is also impressive, and you should be able to pick out a good little vintage for around €12. The custom of drinking a *digestif* at the end of the meal may be going out of fashion, but here there's a large selection of liqueurs. Free coffee.

PHAFFANS   90150 (7KM NE)

|●| L'AUBERGE DE PHAFFANS

10 rue de la Mairie.
☎ 03.84.29.80.97
Closed Mon, Wed and Sat lunchtime. **Car park**.

The influence of nearby Alsace is evident in this quaint little village inn. They serve dishes you haven't eaten for years and their specialitiy is frogs' legs, guaranteed fresh year-round thanks to regular arrivals from the Vendée. The same goes for the farmed eels, served April–Dec. They also offer unmissable morel mushrooms *en croûte*, pigeon *paysanne* with prunes, quails with red and white grapes and Arbois wine, marinated leg of venison in season and raw boar ham. Dish of the day €10; weekday menus €16–19.

CHAUX   90330 (10KM N)

|●| RESTAURANT L'AUBERGE DE LA VAIVRE

36 Grande-Rue; take the D465, the Ballon d'Alsace road.
☎ 03.84.27.10.61
Closed evenings, Sat lunchtime and 15 July–16 Aug.
Car park

This inn on the Vosges road is run by a mother and daughter who have decorated it most attractively; they really make you feel welcome. It's an old barn with a mezzanine. A lot of care goes into preparing traditional dishes such as home-made terrines, monkfish *au gratin*, *confit* of duck in cider, *émincé* of liver and delicious home-made puddings like fresh fruit tarts or *biscuit* with chocolate and hazelnut dessert. The trout is caught fresh when you order it. Menus €14–31. A nicely presented wine list, served by the glass or jug.

BESANÇON   25000

SEE MAP OPPOSITE

🏠 |●| AUBERGE DE LA MALATE*

chemin de la Malate. It's 4km out of the centre in the

direction of Lausanne; after the Porte Taillée, take the Calèze-Arcier road. **Off map B2-1**
☎ 03.81.82.15.16 / 06.08.60.36.20
Closed Jan–Feb. **TV**. **Car park**.

A picturesque country inn just out of town in the forest facing the Doubs – peace and quiet are assured. Fairly comfortable, modernised rooms; doubles €34 with shower/wc. The restaurant is lovely in summer, when you can sit in the shade near the water's edge. Regional dishes with fish as the speciality – small fry or fillets of perch or zander. Menus €11–24.

🛏🏠 HÔTEL DU NORD**

8–10 rue Moncey. **MAP B1-2**
☎ 03.81.81.34.56 ➡ 03.81.81.85.96
Ⓦ www.hotel-du-nord-besancon.com
Disabled access. **TV**. **Car park**.

A pleasant city-centre hotel run by real professionals who are always ready to be of service. Lots of functional but comfortable and impeccably-maintained rooms with good facilities – several have two double beds. Good bathrooms, double glazing and room service. Reasonable prices; doubles from €37–52. 10% discount July and Aug.

🛏🏠 HÔTEL REGINA**

91 Grande-Rue. **MAP B2-4**
☎ 03.81.81.50.22 ➡ 03.81.81.60.20
Closed 24 Dec–2 Jan. **TV**. **Car park and lock-up garage**.

Charming, quiet and comfortable hotel with a pleasant inner courtyard – a haven of peace and tranquility in the city centre. The rooms are regularly redecorated, and some have balconies or terraces hung with wisteria; doubles with shower/wc €38; €40 with bath. There's also a small studio for two. Nice welcome. 10% discount on the room rate for a two-night stay.

🛏🏠 LE GRANVELLE**

13 rue du Général-Lecourbe. **MAP B2-3**
☎ 03.81.81.33.92 ➡ 03.81.81.31.77
Ⓦ www.hotel-granvelle.fr
TV. **Car park**.

An elegant stone-built hotel located in a wealthy street with many private mansions in a quiet part of the city, not far from the citadel. It's comfortable and characterful, and the owners have created a relaxing atmosphere. All the rooms look out onto an attractive paved courtyard. Doubles with wc/shower €39–43, and some are set up for families. 10% discount on the room rate.

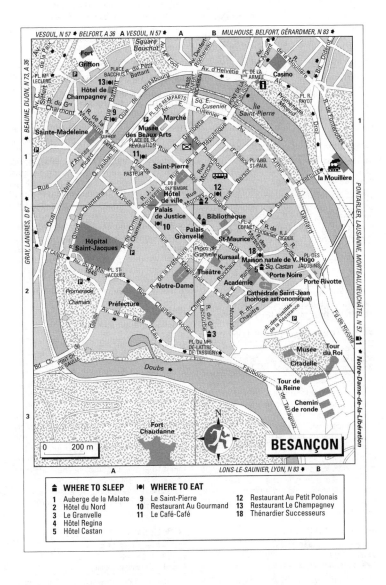

𝄞 🏠 HÔTEL CASTAN***

6 square Castan. **MAP B2-5**
☎ 03.81.65.02.00 ➡ 03.81.83.01.02
Ⓦ www.hotelcastan.fr
Closed 24 Dec–3 Jan and 1–20 Aug. **TV. Car park**.
Disabled access.

Chic and charming hotel in a private mansion
dating back to the 17th century. Wide fireplaces, wood panelling, period furniture and
a luxurious atmosphere. You can choose
your room – *Versailles*, *Pompadour*, *Pompeii*
(which has a Roman-style bathroom) and so
on. Doubles are €104–150 – not surprising
given the facilities. Breakfast €10. Free coffee.

𝄞 |●| RESTAURANT AU GOURMAND

5 rue Mégevand. **MAP A2-10**
☎ 03.81.81.40.56
Closed Sat, Sun, Mon, and Aug.

This place is small – so get here early or
book. They always take the trouble to decorate the window, and inside there's a collection of pretty jugs. The huge menu could
almost fill a book: curried *émincé* of chicken
breast, savoury *clafoutis*, egg custard with
sausage and potatoes, salads with fantasy
names like *la Javanaise* or *Metro Goldwyn*,
and desserts. Uncomplicated home cooking
using fresh produce. For a quick lunch, try
the €10 lunch menu or eat *à la carte* (which
will set you back about €18). Free coffee.

|●| RESTAURANT AU PETIT POLONAIS

81 rue des Granges. **MAP B1-12**
☎ 03.81.81.23.67
Closed Sat evening, Sun, and 14 July–15 Aug.

The dining room is very formal and the waitresses wear black-and-white uniforms: it's a
deeply traditional restaurant, a real institution. The *patronne* is charming and keeps an
experienced eye on everything. There's a
range of menus from €10 to €24 with a
choice of dishes on each one. Very classic
cuisine with a strong regional bias including
the renowned *boîte chaude* – melted Edel de
Cléron cheese with Morteau sausage and
boiled potatoes served in a birch bark box.
Excellent value for money for a popular
restaurant of its type.

|●| THÉNARDIER SUCCESSEURS

11 rue Victor-Hugo. **MAP B2-18**
☎ 03.81.82.06.18
Closed Sat lunchtime, Sun and Mon.

Victor Hugo was born in a house in the
square next door and the owners named this

establishment after one of his works. Fresh,
well-judged cooking in nicely presented dishes which veer away from the local classics.
There's a *formule* for €10 and *à la carte*
starters are €5–7 with mains €11–14. The
tables are elegantly laid, the décor is brightly
coloured and the atmosphere is relaxed. Put
it all together and that's how it's built a regular clientele.

|●| RESTAURANT LE CHAMPAGNEY

37 rue Battant. **MAP A1-13**
☎ 03.81.81.05.71 ➡ 03.81.82.19.76
Closed Sun.

This restaurant is in a splendid 16th-century
town house which has been sensitively
renovated – in summer they make use of the
old courtyard and set tables outside. Inside,
the old fireplace and the beams of the original
ceiling have been retained and the décor is a
mixture of modern and baroque with lots of
style but no stuffiness. The welcome and the
service are efficient and cool, and the cuisine
is a combination of classic favourites and
contemporary inspiration. Dishes change frequently, but the regular specialities include
rabbit with foie gras and a truffle *jus*, salmon
with scallops and baby vegetables and duck
breast with Fougerolles sour cherries. Menus
€10–26. Wines are pricey.

|●| RESTAURANT LE CAFÉ-CAFÉ

5 [bis] rue Luc Breton. **MAP A1-11**
☎ 03.81.81.15.24
Closed Sun; Mon–Wed evenings; 15–30 Aug.

A discreet, almost anonymous place, hidden
at the back of a little courtyard. You have to
keep your eyes open for the slate at the
entrance where they chalk up the dishes and
menus of the day. Dishes are around the €9
mark (you'll pay around €15 for a meal) and
are never short on imagination or exotic
touches. You'll get platters or *assiettes* with
names like *jurassienne*, *de la ferme*, *com-
toise* and so on, with selections of different
things that are a complete meal in themselves. An ideal place for lunch. Charming
welcome. Reservations are essential in this
pocket-sized dining room, which is crammed
with bric-à-brac.

𝄞 |●| LE SAINT-PIERRE

104 rue Battant. **MAP A1-9**
☎ 03.81.81.20.20.99
Closed Sat lunchtime and Sun.

There's a contrast of styles in this elegant
setting – ancient beams, bare stone walls

and contemporary pictures. Very good and sensitively prepared dishes, featuring lots of fish. The €29 menu is satisfying in all respects and the home-made bread is excellent. The atmosphere is welcoming and very relaxed even though this is one of the smart places in town. Nice terrace in warm weather. Free coffee.

CHALEZEULE   25220 (2.5KM E)

≙ HÔTEL DES TROIS ÎLES**

1 rue des Vergers; it's on the Belfort road.
☎ 03.81.61.00.66 ☛ 03.81.61.73.09
ⓦ www.hoteldes3iles.com
Closed 26 Dec–3 Jan. **TV. Garden. Car park**.

Amazing to find such a quiet village only a few minutes' drive from the town centre. It's a recently built hotel in a lovely garden enclosed by high walls; the garden and sitting room are for guests' use. It's part of the *Relais du Silence* group so the peace and quiet come as standard. Double rooms with shower/wc or bath €45–50.

CHAMPLITTE   70600

⋊ ≙ |●| HÔTEL-RESTAURANT DU DONJON**

46 rue de la République (Centre).
☎ 03.84.67.66.95 ☛ 03.84.67.81.06
ⓔ hotel.du.donjon@wanadoo.fr
Restaurant closed Fri evening and Sat lunchtime mid-Oct to mid-Jun; Mon other times. **TV. Car park**.

The only remaining medieval element here is the vaulted cellar which is used as the dining room. The cuisine is honest and traditional: trout fillet with prawn cream sauce, red mullet fillets with basil, snail casserole and asparagus pastry with hazelnut cream sauce. Weekday menu €10 and others €17–32. Clean and comfortable but not dazzling rooms; doubles with basin €27, €35 with shower/wc or bath. Free coffee.

CHAUX-NEUVE   25240

⋊ ≙ |●| AUBERGE DU GRAND-GÎT**

rue des Chaumelles; take the Mouthe road out of the village and then turn right 400m on.
☎ 03.81.69.25.75 ☛ 03.81.69.15.44
Closed Sun evening and Mon except public holidays, April and 13 Oct–21 Dec. **Disabled access. Car park**.

Quiet place on the outskirts of the village. It's fairly new, but in keeping with local architecture with a sloping roof and wooden façade.

Excellent welcome. Only eight bedrooms, but they're wood-panelled and cosy – €38–43 for a double with shower/wc and phone. Some have a lovely view of the surrounding countryside; number 5 has a mezzanine and can sleep five. There's also stopover gîte for hikers: two rooms with six beds. Classic regional dishes predominate in the restaurant; there's a weekday menu *du jour* for €11, while the €14 regional one offers ham Arbois-style or pink trout sautéed in butter and served with parsley and lemon juice. The owner is a skiing instructor and uplands guide so he knows all the local long-distance footpaths and cross-country skiing routes intimately – it's the ideal place for sporty types and nature lovers. Free house apéritif.

DELLE   90100

⋊ |●| RESTAURANT LE GALOPIN

29 Grand-Rue (Centre); it's opposite the old town hall.
☎ 03.84.36.17.52 ☛ 03.84.36.17.52
Closed Sun and Mon.

This is where local lovers of good food meet – including many Swiss customers who pop over the border. They immediately make for the restaurant cellar, which is more than a hundred years old, to celebrate the potato – the main component of many dishes. Fashionable options include potatoes with smoked salmon and shallot sauce, though there are other more local dishes such as *roësti* with Morteau sausage or *à la cancoillotte* – they also do *raclette*, mountain ham, spaghetti and a range of salads. No set menus so expect to pay €12–21 for a meal. Good, inexpensive and friendly. Free apéritif.

DOLE   39100

≙ HÔTEL DE LA CLOCHE***

1 pl. Grévy.
☎ 03.84.82.06.06 ☛ 03.84.72.73.82
TV.

A somnolent provincial hotel that started life as a coaching inn. It's conventional, with classical and rather bland décor, and the welcome just about goes through the motions. Nonetheless the rooms are clean and well maintained, the façade is pretty, there's a sauna upstairs, and it's in the middle of town – a big plus in a place where central hotels are a rare commodity. Inevitably, it's often full. Doubles with en-suite facilities from €46 up to €69 with whirlpool bath.

☎ |O| LA CHAUMIÈRE

346 av. du Maréchal Juin.
☎ 03.84.70.72.40 ➡ 03.84.79.25.60
Garden. Swimming pool.

A huge *faux* cottage by the roadside, hidden
behind Virginia creeper. It's cosy, bourgeois
and has very ordinary décor, but it gains
points for its charming grounds, flowerbeds,
terraces and swimming pool. The rooms are
particularly comfortable – though they're old-
fashioned and, at €73 for a double, overpriced. It owes its reputation to the quality of
the cooking in the restaurant. The youthful
chef is the latest in a long family line and produces delicious dishes; menus are €27–76.
He has a personal, sensitive approach and
doesn't overload the plates.

🎄 |O| CHEZ COCO

34 rue des Vieilles Boucheries (Centre).
☎ 03.84.79.10.78
Closed Sun; evenings except May–Aug; Jan.
Disabled access.

"Home cooking by the *patronne*" it says at the
top of the menu in this popular local restaurant. In a corner, there are rows of sporting
cups and photos of the town's junior teams.
Coco the manager holds the fort behind the
zinc counter, emerging to take orders and
serve the food. Weekday menu at €9 and
others €11–20. They include *crudités*, chick-
en with Comté cheese and fillet of fish cooked
in white wine; dishes are served with three different vegetables and followed by cheese and
dessert. Coco is a good-humoured, chatty
guy who provides unrushed service. Free
digestif. They don't accept credit cards.

|O| LE BEC FIN

67 rue Pasteur (Centre); it's near the marina.
☎ 03.84.82.43.43
Closed Mon; Tues (except July–Aug); the Feb school
holidays.

When you walk through the door you're
greeted by the delightful *patronne*'s kind
smile and effusive welcome. The first bright
dining room has a romantic view over the
canal des Tanneurs while the other is in the
medieval cellars. In good weather you can sit
outside on the terrace. The €15 menu
changes often and is very popular – salad of
Comté cheese *croquettes*, chicken sausage
with bacon, peach dessert flavoured with tarragon. Others €21–36. Service is a bit awkward, but it's attentive. Grown-ups have
comfortable seats and there are high chairs
for little ones too.

SAMPANS   39100 (3KM NW)

☎ |O| LE CHALET DU MONT-ROLAND**

Take the N5; before Monnières turn right towards mont
Roland.
☎ 03.84.72.04.55 ➡ 03.84.82.14.97
ⓦ www.chalet-montroland.com
Disabled access. TV. Car park.

The series of crosses leading up to this chalet
puts you in mind of Golgotha – a slightly dis-
trubing experience but the road also leads to
Notre-Dame-du-Mont-Roland, an important
pilgrimage site. From the top of the mountain
there's a superb view over Chaux Forest and
on a clear day you can even see Mont Blanc.
It's particularly delightful in the spring and definitely the place to spend a relaxing Sunday in
the country. Double rooms with shower/wc or
bath cost €41. The restaurant has its own
gastronomic pilgrims from Dole who come to
spend a weekend, giving it a chic but bustling
atmosphere. There's a glassed-in terrace so
you can make the most of the view. Robust
regional fare with a weekday lunch menu at
€12 and others €19–34, all highly calorific.

CHAUSSIN   39120 (20KM S)

🎄 ☎ |O| HÔTEL-RESTAURANT CHEZ BACH**

4 pl. de l'Ancienne-Gare; take the N73, then turn onto
the D468 at La Borde.
☎ 03.84.81.80.38 ➡ 03.84.81.83.80
ⓦ www.hotel-bach.com
Closed Sun evening, Mon lunchtime, Fri except July– Aug
and 20 Dec–10 Jan. **Disabled access. TV. Car park.**

Make a little gastronomic detour to enjoy the
fine cuisine here. The large modern building
doesn't look at promising from the outside
but its reputation has been established for a
generation or two. There are several menus of
regional specialities with sauces using the
local *vin jaune* as well as lobster stew, escalope of fresh *foie gras* and *tournedos* with
morels or soft fruit. Weekday menu at €13
and others €21–52. Half-board is compulsory July–Aug. The rooms are comfortable and
you can keep in touch with friends via the
Internet socket in the rooms; it'll cost €31–46
for a double with bath. Free coffee Oct–May.

DOUCIER   39130

🎄 ☎ |O| HÔTEL LOGIS DE FRANCE – RESTAURANT LE COMTOIS

It's in the village opposite the post office.

☎ 03.84.25.71.21
✉ restaurant.comtois@wanadoo.fr
Closed Tues, Wed and Sun evenings except 15 June–15 Sept. **TV**. **Car park**.

Wine from the best producers in the region features on the splendid and detailed wine list, which is carefully selected by the young *sommelier* – also the owner. The dining room is bright and fresh, a lovely combination of stone and beams illuminated by well-positioned lighting. There's also a solid brick chimney breast and the old Franche-Comté dresser adds a rustic touch; for those who take their wine seriously, there's even a tasting room. The cooking is in the brasserie-bistro tradition and is served in huge portions: Morteau sausage with Poulsard wine sauce, duck breast with spices, ice-cream with Macvin and *crème brûlée* with sour Fougerolles cherries. Menus €13–26. The rooms on the first floor have been refurbished and have ensuite bathrooms, €50, while the simpler ones, €40, have only a handbasin and shared facilities on the landing. 10% discount on the room rate out of season.

CHATILLON   39130 (5KM W)

🏠 |●| CHEZ YVONNE

It's on the road to Lons-le-Saulnier.
☎ 03.84.25.70-82
🌐 www.chezyvonne.com
Closed Tues and Wed (except July–Aug). **Swimming pool**. **Car park**.

There's a river running through the shady grounds of this big old house, which has been taken over by a friendly young couple and turned into a charming hotel. There's a terrace by the water's edge, grassy banks and a swimming pool. It's an ideal place to stop – you can almost feel the silence. Good food with menus from €14–40; try the duck *foie gras* with Macvin sauce, the duck breast with morels, the salmon with Vin Jaune sauce and the home-made desserts. Lovely salads (€9) are served by the water's edge. There are four modest doubles at €37–41. The drawback is that one shower serves four rooms. That given, the beds are good, the decoration adorable and four rooms have a river view.

ILAY   39150 (12KM SE)

🏕 🏠 |●| L'AUBERGE DU HÉRISSON*

5 route des Lacs.
☎ 03.84.25.58.18 ➡ 03.84.25.51.11
🌐 www.herisson.com

Closed Nov–beginning of Feb. **TV**.

A good base for local excursions and visits to the nearby waterfalls. Fourteen of the rooms have been perfectly refurbished and they're pretty and comfortable; the others are due to go through the same process. Doubles €37–46 with shower/wc or bath. Straightforward, honest dishes in the restaurant: nothing too complicated but the ingredients are fresh and the results are good. Menus start at €11 and go up to €35. The cheese selection is exceptional. There are also a few Jura specialities and *fondues*. There's an interesting children's menu offering snails or smoked salmon, chicken breast with crème-fraîche and *tagliatelle* followed by chocolate *profiteroles*. Free house apéritif.

BONLIEU   39130 (15KM S)

🏕 🏠 |●| LE POUTRE*

25 Grande-Rue; take the D67.
☎ 03.84.25.57.77 ➡ 03.84.25.51.61
Closed Tues, Wed from 11 Nov–1 May. **TV**. **Cark park**.

An excellent establishment – not in the first flush of youth but the food is high quality. The décor in the rooms (€43–58) and dining room has faded a bit and they have a provincial feel. Servings in the restaurant are as huge as they used to be in times past: there's almost more than you can manage on the €18 menu and others go to €46. House specialities include chicken and mushroom *vol-au-vent*, trout fillet with hazelnuts and pan-fried *foie gras* in Macvin. Excellent welcome and punctilious service. Free house apéritif.

ERRUES-MENONCOURT (LES)   90150

🏕 🏠 |●| LA POMME D'ARGENT

13 rue de la Noye.
☎ and ➡ 03.84.27.63.69
Closed Wed, Sun evening and a fortnight in Nov. **Car park**. **Disabled access**.

This lovely place, well off the beaten track, is a real find. It's the welcoming restaurant that's the draw, where the commitment to service has been honed over twenty years. Fine, delicate cooking on menus priced €15–40 – highlights include home-smoked salmon, frogs' legs and snail *cassolette*, and the *crème brûlée* with pistachios is to die for. The pretty terrace is opened in spring and summer. There are a couple of rooms (€20) if you need a bed for the night. Free apéritif.

ÉTUEFFONT 90170

⚐ |●| AUBERGE AUX TROIS BONHEURS

34 Grand-Rue (Centre); north of Belfort take the D23
from Valdoie.
☎ 03.84.54.71.31
Closed Sun and Tues evenings; Mon. **Car park**.
Disabled access.

___

If this elegant town-house is the *Inn of the Three Happinesses* then the fourth is the journey through flower-filled villages to get to there. It's built in brick and natural stone and occupies a delightful rustic setting. The restaurant is very popular because of the hearty, tasty cooking served in generous portions – it's a place for family gatherings and groups out on a spree. They come for fantastic home-made brawn, fried carp or zander, chanterelle mushrooms with parsley, the special *planchette des Trois Bonheurs*, *tartiflette* and good home-made desserts and fruit tarts. Lunch menu €8, or €15 at other times. Seafood stew available *à la carte*. Friendly reception and efficient service. Free coffee.

EVETTE-SALBERT 90350

⚐ |●| AUBERGE DU LAC

lac de Malsaucy; take the D24.
☎ and ➡ 03.84.29.14.10
Closed Mon and Tues evening in season, 2–16 Jan and 16–30 Oct.

___

This is a big pink house where you'll get a typical Franche-Comté welcome and good regional food. There's a large, pleasant dining room with well-spaced tables and a terrace with a view of the lake. The choice of dishes is considerable with a few specialities: fried carp, *parmentier au Morteau* (a kind of shepherd's pie made with *Jésus de Morteau*, a local sausage), fish dish of the day and *feuillantine* with two chocolates. Weekday menu €13 with others €12–24; you'll pay around €22 *à la carte*. Good wines at affordable prices or served by the pitcher. Free coffee.

FOUGEROLLES 70220

|●| RESTAURANT LE PÈRE ROTA

8 Grande-Rue.
☎ 03.84.49.12.11
e jean-pierre.kuentz@wanadoo.fr
Closed Sun evening, Mon and 2–25 Jan. **Car park**.
Disabled access.

___

Jean-Pierre Kuentz is a fantastic advocate of

the cuisine of the Haute-Saône. He uses local produce of the highest quality but introduces inspiration from way beyond regional boundaries: duck *terrine* with sour cherries, poached John Dory, lobster with *vin jaune*, zander with powdered mustard, fillet of beef with red Jura wine sauce. The service is thoughtful and the table settings and modern, bright décor have been put together with care. Weekday menu €16 and others €27–55. The atmosphere is just a tad uptight.

FOURNET-BLANCHEROCHE 25140

⚐ |●| HÔTEL-RESTAURANT LA MARAUDE**

How to get there: follow the signposts off the D464 between Fournet-Blancheroche and Charquemont.
☎ 03.81.44.09.60 ➡ 03.81.44.09.13
✉ la-maraude@wanadoo.fr
Closed Wed and Sun evening 1 Oct–30 April. **Disabled access**. **TV**. **Car park**.

___

An 18th-century farm in a remote, peaceful part of the Haut-Doubs. A nice young couple fell in love with the place and moved in. Outside there's a terrace with a view of the extensive grounds where you can have breakfast, meals or just lounge in a deckchair. The inside was completely redone a few years ago but it has retained much original charm. There are seven pretty rooms with wooden panels and beams; they're €47–62 for a double with shower/wc or bath (some are non-smoking). In the little sitting room there's an old fireplace where they used to smoke the salted meat. Relax in the sauna after a game of tennis or billiards. In the cosy dining room they serve principally regional cuisine but also dishes from further afield: *foie gras* and smoked salmon with morels, *cassolette* of snails, duo of Morteau and Montbéliard sausage. Menus €11–24.

GRAY 70100

⚐ |●| HÔTEL-RESTAURANT LE BELLEVUE**

1 av. Carnot (Centre)
☎ 03.84.64.53.50 ➡ 03.84.64.53.69
🌐 www.hotel-bellevue-gray.com
Closed Fri and Sun evenings out of season. **TV**.
Garden. **Car park**.

___

This hotel near the Saône is ageing gracefully. The rooms are still good and the ones looking onto the public gardens are quiet.

Doubles €27 with handbasin to €32 with shower/wc or bath. Two approaches in the restaurant: the brasserie does simple but substantial dishes of the day, like *coq au vin* with mashed potato, while the other dining room has menus from €11 and €16–25 with a good, standard choice. Or there's *à la carte*.

◉ RESTAURANT DU CRATÔ

65 Grande-Rue (Centre).
☎ 03.84.65.11.75
Closed Mon.

A small restaurant in a sloping lane in the old part of Gray. There aren't many restaurants in the area providing such value for money: menus €12–24. The dining room is simple and pleasant, and the chef offers a dazzling choice of starters and mains with cheese and dessert on all menus. Relaxing atmosphere, friendly service and the owner likes to play the odd joke on her guests.

LEPUIX   90200

⌂ ◉ LE SAUT DE LA TRUITE**

Malvaux; take the D465.
☎ 03.84.29.32.64 ➥ 03.84.29.57.42
Closed Fri, and Dec–Jan. **TV**. **Garden**. **Car park**.

This place is a mountain refuge that's been open since 1902 and run by the same family for forty years. It's in a superb setting in a forest clearing; you can even hear the gushing waterfall. There are some rooms but they're not ideal. It's a much better place to eat, with trout freshly caught from the pond and a fine selection of regional specialities such as cockerel in Riesling, pigeon with chanterelles and bilberry tart. Weekday menu €14 and others €17–27.

LONS-LE-SAUNIER   39000

🛇 ⌂ ◉ HÔTEL-RESTAURANT TERMINUS**

37 av. Aristide Briand (Centre).
☎ 03.84.24.41.83 ➥ 03.84.26.68.07
🌐 www.hotel-terminus-lons.com
Hotel closed 6–8pm Sun. **TV**. **Pay car park**.

A solid establishment that was gradually fading as the years passed. Luckily a massive renovation programme has been undertaken and a stop put to the process of decay: the relatively large rooms have all been modernized and painted white so they look a lot

brighter, if a little sparse. Doubles with shower or bath €44–58. The ones at the back are quieter. Simple fare is served in the restaurant, where you can get a set menu for €17 or choose *à la carte*. 10% discount on the room rate 1 Oct–30 March.

◉ LE BAMBOCHE

23 rue Perrin (Centre).
☎ 03.84.24.49.30
Closed Sun and Mon (except in season, when it's open Mon evening); 15 Aug–10 Sep.

Young, friendly atmosphere and good, original cooking. About five types of carpaccio available: fillet steak, veal, goose and rabbit. If raw meat turns your stomach, there are plenty of salads or grills cooked on the old-fashioned spit – try lamb shank, kebabs or veal kidneys. The meat is decent and the cooking perfectly judged. Enough choice to satisfy all appetites and suit all pockets with a menu for €10 or around €15 *à la carte*. The best place in town.

◉ LA COMÉDIE

pl. de la Comédie (Centre).
☎ 03.84.24.20.66
Closed Sun, Mon evening, a fortnight at Easter and three weeks in Aug.

A stylish restaurant – though it would be dreary were it not for the flowery terrace. Modern and traditional cuisine on menus at €15 and €24; it's around €35 *à la carte*. Choose from *cassolette* of snails with morels, garlic and croutons, duck breast lacquered with sesame honey and sour cherry and the like.

CHILLE   39570 (3KM E)

🛇 ⌂ ◉ HÔTEL-RESTAURANT PARENTHÈSE***

How to get there: head for Besançon on the bypass, then go 1km on the D157 and look for the signs.
☎ 03.84.47.55.44 ➥ 03.84.24.92.13
🌐 www.hotelparenthese.com
Restaurant closed Mon lunchtime, Sun evening, and a fortnight in Feb during the school holidays. **Disabled access**. **Garden**. **TV**. **Car park**.

In a small village just off the major roads, this beautiful 18th-century residence in the middle of an extensive park has been converted into a comfortable hotel and restaurant by its very friendly, welcoming proprietor. The hotel has thirty rooms, all of which are tastefully decorated and named after painters; €46–85 for a double with shower/wc or €70–119 with bath. The restaurant offers a weekday menu at €15 with others €18–41. Classic cuisine with a local bias: marbled *foie gras* with rhubarb, supreme of chicken with morels, roast bream with fennel and sherry and *chartruese* with caramelized *vin jaune*. One free breakfast per room per night 1 Oct–30 April.

CHÂTEAU-CHALON   39210 (12KM N)

|O| LA TAVERNE DU ROC

rue de la Roche.
☎ 03.84.85.24.17
Closed 15 Dec–10 Feb.

A tiny restaurant with white walls in a timeless house, right in the middle of Château-Chalon. The chef has been concocting delicious dishes for years – try her Bresse chicken with *vin jaune*, which is the best for miles around. Any of her Jura dishes are also worth a try, and on a Sunday there's a menu with trout and chicken. Menus €22 and €27.

BAUME-LES-MESSIEURS   39210 (20KM NE)

🎿 |O| RESTAURANT DES GROTTES

How to get there: take the D471 to Roches-de-Beaume, then the D70.
☎ and ➡ 03.84.44.61.59
Closed evenings and Wed 15 Oct–15 April. **Garden**. **Car park**.

The restaurant is opposite a marvellous foaming waterfall cascading down from the high rocks of the Baumes-les-Messieurs amphitheatre. Its tranquility is in sharp contrast to the racket of tourists in the nearby caves. It's open for lunch only with menus €13–24 listing mainly Franche-Comté specialities. The terrace is open in summer where you can enjoy platters of *charcuterie* or cheese washed down with a glass of Jura wine. Free coffee.

LUXEUIL-LES-BAINS   70300

🎿 🏠 |O| HÔTEL-RESTAURANT DE FRANCE**

6 rue Georges-Clémenceau; it's opposite the hospital.
☎ 03.84.40.13.90 ➡ 03.84.40.33.12
Restaurant closed Sun evening, Fri evening in winter.
Closed 3 Sept–1 April. **TV**. **Garden**. **Car park**.

This white building surrounded by greenery is behind the parc des thermes. There are twenty or so rooms – doubles with basin €32 and €37–47 with shower/wc or bath. The chef prepares good, traditional, filling dishes:

braised poultry ham with ceps and girolles in port sauce, mixed fish with *sauce américaine*, and beef *noisette*. Menus €13–34, so you can eat well without putting a hole into your bank account. Free coffee 1 Oct–30 April and at the weekend.

🎿 🏠 |O| HÔTEL-RESTAURANT BEAU SITE***

18 rue Georges-Moulimard; it's close to the casino.
☎ 03.84.40.14.67 ➡ 03.84.40.50.25
Closed Fri evening, Sat, Sun evening from mid-Nov to mid-March. **Swimming pool**. **Garden**. **TV**. **Car park**.

This is a large, very pleasing place, surrounded by a green park with a swimming pool. The rooms are comfortable and charming and the prices are attractive: doubles with bath or shower/wc €58 in both the main building and the annexe. Luxeuil ham is a must in the restaurant and, in season, the game dishes are classics – boar *civet à l'ancienne*, venison *Grand Veneur*. Weekday menu €13 or others up to €24. They do special weekend rates in conjunction with the spa. 10% discount on the room rate.

MALBUISSON   25160

🏠 |O| LE BON ACCUEIL***

Grand-Rue; it's in the centre of the village.
☎ 03.81.69.30.58 ➡ 03.81.69.37.60
e lebonaccueilfaivre@wanadoo.fr
Closed Sun, Mon and Tues lunchtime; mid-Dec to mid-Jan; a week in April; a week in Nov. **Car park**. **TV**.

The reputation of this establishment is being made by the restaurant – which gets better and better. It offers traditional cooking with a modern touch; the chef-owner, Marc Faivre, is committed to using only fresh, quality, local produce. A few specialities: fine tart with Morteau sausage, braised leeks with poached egg, tomatoes stuffed with snails and herbs with a parsley sauce and, for dessert, a gentian sorbet or *macaronade* with grapefruit. It's excellent, inventive cuisine. Menus from €24–42. A few rooms at €53–65.

CHAUDRON   25160 (3KM N)

🎿 🏠 |O| LE BROCHET D'OR

8 rue Edgar-Faure; it's 3 km north of Malbuisson, on the banks of the lake.
☎ 03.81.69.31.94
Closed Tues evening out of season and 2 weeks in Nov.
TV. **Car park**.

The owners' careful renovation of an establishment which had snoozed quietly for a while has given it a shot in the arm. There are shower cubicles in the six rooms and a shared wc along the landing; doubles are from €32. Monsieur does a sterling job in the kitchen and produces good regional dishes and a few innovations besides. There's a €9 weekday lunch menu and others for €12 and €15 with perch fillet *meunière* and roast Morteau sausage. It's a friendly place run by kindly people who've even thought to set aside a children's corner.

MÉTABIEF 25370

🎿 🏠 |●| HÔTEL-RESTAURANT L'ÉTOILE DES NEIGES**

4 rue du Village (North).
☎ 03.81.49.11.21 ➡ 03.81.49.26.91
📧 hotelrestaurant-etoiledesneiges@libertysurf.fr
TV.

A modern building a little way away from the ski resort and above a small river. The renovated rooms are cosy and comfortable; all have balconies with exceptional views of the Mont d'Or or the countryside. Eight have been renovated, including four split-level ones. Doubles with shower/wc or bath from €28. In the restaurant there's a welcoming family atmosphere. They serve exclusively local specialities and use organic produce: Morteau sausage with flaky pastry, mushrooms in a pastry case, savoury profiteroles with herbs and bacon. Menus from €10 to €20. Free coffee with a meal and 10% discount except during school holidays.

HÔPITAUX-VIEUX (LES) (4KM NE)

🎿 🏠 |●| HOTEL LAKE-PLACID

48 rue de la Seigne.
☎ 03.81.49.00.72 ➡ 03.81.49.00.42
Closed Mon evening, Tues and end March–early April
Car park. Disabled access.

It's outside the village, near the departure points for the cross-country skiing and hiking trails. There are only five rooms in this small hotel, run by Denis Sandona (who competed in the cross-country skiing at the Lake Placid Winter Olympics in 1980) and his delightful wife. Flawless, pretty rooms from €34 for a double; half board at €39 is compulsory in high season. Mountain dishes and good, honest country cooking: *pot-au-feu* and home-made tarts. Dishes from €7, menus €10–17. There's a jovial atmosphere and a warm setting – all the furniture has been

made by the contender himself. Excellent welcome. Free coffee.

LONGEVILLES MONT D'OR (LES) (4KM SE)

🎿 🏠 |●| HÔTEL-RESTAURANT LES SAPINS**

58 rue des Bief-Blanc; take the D45.
☎ 03.81.49.90.90 ➡ 03.81.49.94.43
Closed April; Oct to mid-Dec. **Car park**.

This place is situated in the centre of a little village which hasn't lost any of its character – despite being part of the Métabief resort. The pleasant rooms are the best value for money in the area; the ones on the second floor are big and have sloping ceilings. Doubles €26 with shower/wc and €29 with bath. Worthwhile menu of the day at €10 (served at lunch and dinner during the week) and others €14 and 18. Home-made regional cooking: *franc-comtoise* salad, cheese flan, *entrecôte* of beef and *gratin dauphinois*. A genuinely friendly welcome. Free house apéritif.

JOUGNE 25370 (5KM E)

🏠 |●| HÔTEL-RESTAURANT DE LA COURONNE*

pl. de l'Église (Centre); take the D9 and the N57 then head for the Swiss border.
☎ 03.81.49.10.50 ➡ 03.81.49.19.77
Closed Sun and Mon evenings out of season and Nov.
Disabled access. Garden. Car park. TV.

Set on a proper village square with a church and fountain, this small country hotel is far enough away from the main road to be nice and quiet. Pleasant rooms which have been renovated are €29 with shower, €38 with shower/wc or €43 with bath. Numbers 11, 12, 14 and 16 have a nice view over the Jougnenaz valley and you also get a lovely view from the garden. Classic cuisine with lots of local dishes from the Franche-Comté: duck fillet with wild mushrooms, morels and *petit-gris* snails in flaky pastry, trout fillet in Savagnin. Cheapest menu is at €15 (served daily), and others go up to €38.

MOIRANS-EN-MONTAGNE 39260

🎿 |●| LE REGARDOIR

It's at the Belvédère; take the north exit to Moirans.
☎ 03.84.42.01.15
Closed Mon, Tue and Wed evenings except 15 June–30 Aug; 1 Oct–15 April.

Stop for a snack here just so you can take a

seat on the terrace and enjoy the panoramic view over the Lac de Vouglans way below. There's something special about the light at sunset – it's a moment to linger over with an apéritif in hand. Nice, smiling welcome and a straightforward menu, though the cook is serious about his work. The fried small fry and the pizzas cooked in a wood-fuelled oven are tasty. À la carte, there's hot goat's cheese, zander with balsamic vinegar, chicken with prawn sauce and iced soufflé with Marc from the Jura. Weekday menu €11 and others €12–15. It's always full. Free apéritif.

MOLUNES (LES)   39310 (13KM SE)

🏠 LE COLLÈGE

How to get there: take the D436 in the direction of Septmoncel then the D25 in the direction of Moussières; it's in the middle of the village.
☎ 03.84.45.52.34
Closed Tues; 18–30 June; 26 Nov–24 Dec.

The hamlet is 1250m up and is so small it doesn't even have a church. This place used to be a bakery and grocer's shop. Its reputation has spread through the Haut-Jura – it can seat 64 but there's often a fight to get in at the weekend. There's a section set aside for non-smokers near the fireplace. The food is not only good, it's beautifully presented to boot. First-class weekday menu at €9 with *charcuterie*, followed by the dish of the day (such as sautéed veal with rice, braised chicory and spinach), then cheese and dessert. Several other menus up to €24 which are just as good: trout with morels and girolles, veal escalope Jura-style and iced nougat. Attractively priced wine list. The décor has a genuine country feel.

CUTTURA   39170 (20KM E)

🍴 L'AUBERGE DU VIEUX MOULIN

Take the D470 and it's between Moirans and St-Claude.
☎ 03.84.42.84.28
✉ aubergemoulin@aol.com
Closed Fri evening, Sat lunchtime and the Christmas school holidays.

This is a lovely old water mill and you eat down by the lakeside accompanied by ducks and moorhens. The short €11 menu – starter followed by steak or trout – draws in everyone who knows it, but that's only the half of it. Then you discover the menus and the *à la carte* options: scallop stew with Savagnin wine, escalope of *foie gras* with sour cherries, supreme of guineafowl with morels and grilled Morteau sausage with Gex blue cheese. The home-made fruit tarts are as delicious as the ice-creams. Handsome portions and fairly priced menus (€15–24). Free coffee.

MONTBÉLIARD   25200

🍴 🏠 HÔTEL DE LA BALANCE***

40 rue de Belfort (Centre); it's in the old town.
☎ 03.81.96.77.41 ➜ 03.81.91.47.16
✉ hotelbalance@wanadoo.fr
Restaurant closed Sat and Sun lunchtime. **Disabled access**. **TV**. **Car park**.

Like a lot of the other buildings in the old town, the façade of this 16th-century house has been painted and is now a dusky pink. Inside, the elegant yellow dining room, the antique furniture and a solid wooden staircase add to the charm of the place – which definitely belies the rather sad image people tend to have of the town. The rooms are stylish, all with shower/wc or bath, and cost from €64 depending on the season. If you're interested in history, ask for the room where Field Marshal Lattre de Tassigny stayed in 1944. Buffet breakfast €7. Very classic menus, at €14–32. Free breakfast or house apéritif.

🍴 RESTAURANT DU CHÂTEAU

4 rue du Château (Centre); it's on the edge of the old town, on the way to the château.
☎ 03.81.94.93.06
Closed Sun except public holidays and 8–20 August.

A small establishment which is often full. Very classical cuisine using fresh produce. You may come across the owner buying his ingredients in the local markets – he's justifiably proud of his filleted fried carp. Frogs and crayfish are served in season and if you want to try that carp for lunch it's advisable to order it before 11am. Weekday menu €13 and others €23 and €27 – fair prices given the quality of the produce. Good wine list. Free coffee.

AUDINCOURT   25400 (6KM S)

🏠 HÔTEL DES TILLEULS**

51 av. Foch (Northeast).
☎ 03.81.30.77.00 ➜ 03.81.30.57.20
✉ hotel.tilleuls@wanadoo.fr
Disabled access. **Garden**. **Swimming pool**. **TV**. **Lock-up garage**.

In a quiet street – be sure to go to the *avenue*, not the *rue* Foch. Excellent welcome. The rooms are very well equipped with fridge, power shower and hair dryer, and the décor is modern but warm. They're dotted about the main building or in annexes around the garden where there's also a lovely heated swimming pool. Singles go for €38; doubles and suites cost €45–59. There's no restaurant but they'll get meals brought in for you in the evening. One free breakfast per room.

MORTEAU   25500

♠ HÔTEL DES MONTAGNARDS**

7 [bis] pl. Carnot (Centre).
☎ 03.81.67.08.86 📠 03.81.67.14.57
Disabled access. **TV**. **Pay car park**.

This is a small, friendly hotel in the centre of the village looking out onto the surrounding countryside. You're greeted warmly. It offers attractive panelled rooms, some of which have been redecorated in pastel shades. Doubles €27 with washing facilities, €38 with shower/wc and €44 with bath.

🌲 |●| RESTAURANT L'ÉPOQUE

18 rue de la Louhière (North); it's on the Besançon road.
☎ 03.81.67.33.44
✉ jp.razurel@wanadoo.fr
Closed Wed evening and Sun (except public holidays).
Car park.

They know what they're about in this restaurant – the welcome is natural and the service friendly. There are a couple of bistro-like dining rooms where you feel instantly at home. The tasty food is inventive without ignoring its regional origins: sausage *de Morteau*, which the owner really loves, in red Arbois wine, wild mushroom pastry cases and zander fillet with Comté cheese sauce. Set menus €11–24 – flaky pastry with *filet mignon forestière*, stuffed lemon sole fillet *à la dieppoise* (poached in white wine with mussels, shrimps, mushrooms and cream). There's an impressive selection of whiskies and the owner, who is a bit of a local character, has even set up a club for whisky-lovers. Free house apéritif.

MONTLEBON   25500 (2KM SE)

♠ |●| HÔTEL-RESTAURANT BELLEVUE*

2 rue de Bellevue; it's on the D48.
☎ 03.81.67.00.05 📠 03.81.67.04.74
Closed Sun and Fri evening in winter; 15 Dec–15 Jan.
TV. **Car park**.

This Comtois farmhouse looks over the whole of the Morteau valley – truly a *belle vue*. The €9 lunchtime menu is a magnet for local people who travel in the course of their

work – plumbers, wood-cutters, gas employees and so on – and the regional dishes are generously served and well prepared. Try trout *meunière*, zander fillets, wild mushrooms in a pastry case, *filet mignon* with morels or hot mountain ham. There's a range of menus €13–24. Rooms are plain but reasonably priced at €29 for a double with washing facilities or €40 with shower/wc.

GRAND'COMBE CHÂTELEU   25500 (4KM S)

|●| RESTAURANT FAIVRE

It's on the main road.
☎ 03.81.68.84.63
Closed Sun evening, Mon and the first three weeks in Aug. **TV**. **Pay car park**.

A huge chalet with a cosy and very pleasant dining room. The classic, regional dishes betray little in the way of inventiveness but are decent and carefully prepared. A good place to stop. Lunch menu €17 and others up to €46.

ORNANS   25290

♠ |●| HÔTEL DE FRANCE***

51 rue Pierre-Vernier (Centre).
☎ 03.81.62.24.44 📠 03.81.62.12.03
✉ hoteldefrance@europost.org
Closed Sun evening and Mon depending on reservations; 1 Dec–10 Feb. **TV**. **Garden**. **Pay car park**.

A good example of traditional hotel-keeping in a place that really lives up to its old-style name. A couple of brasserie menus, €12 and €17, offer dishes like flan with Comté cheese and raw ham. The restaurant has set menus for €23 and €37, listing morels in a pastry case, house *foie gras*, pan-fried scallops with ceps and traditional trout *au bleu* with lemon. The rooms have an upmarket, rustic feel, and some look out onto the famous Grand Pont (which actually isn't that big). The road outside is noisy, but you'll get peace and quiet in the rooms at the back. Doubles €66–69 with shower/wc or €69–73 with bath, TV and mini-bar. Half board is compulsory at the weekend in season. There's a big terrace and a garden behind the hotel. Private fishing.

AMONDANS 25330   (14KM W)

♠ |●| LE CHÂTEAU D'AMONDANS

9 rue Louise-Pommery.
☎ 03.81.86.53.14
✉ chef@chateau-amondans.com

Closed Tues, Wed, Sun evening.

One of the culinary hits of the region and with good reason – the cooking is quite simply remarkable. There may be more inventive cuisine around, but chef-owner Frédéric Médique brings a personal interpretation to traditional dishes: *foie gras* with spiced bread, John Dory in *vin jaune* sauce and especially his speciality dessert, *l'Amondanais*. Menus from €30. The setting is sumptuous, the welcome friendly and the service faultless. The only drawback is that the wine list concentrates on the great classics of Burgundy, Bordeaux and Jura – meaning it's expensive and misses out on less prestigious offerings. Double rooms with bath/wc €53.

VERNIERFONTAINE 25580 (17KM E)

⅍ ☎ |●| L'AUBERGE PAYSANNE

18 rue du Stade; take the D492 in the direction of Saules, then the D392 to Guyans-Durnes then Vernierfontaine.
☎ and ➡ 03.81.60.05.21
Restaurant closed Wed,Thurs and weekday evenings. **Hotel closed** Nov–1 Feb, excluding the Christmas holidays. **Garden. Car park**.

An old farmhouse in a remote village way out in the country. The décor is cluttered but the cuisine is traditional and full of flavour, utilizing a panoply of wonderful local produce: smoked meats from the Haut-Doubs, *roësti* (grated potatoes fried in a heavy pan), flaky pastry cases with morels in rich sauce, *fondue* using Comté cheese, *poêlée paysanne* (big pans of potatoes, smoked bacon, onions, sausage and eggs), and a wonderful apple strudel prepared by the German boss. Menus start at €11 and go up to €21. There are four rooms with wood-panelling; doubles are €34 with shower/wc. Gigantic breakfast with sausage, cheese and yoghurt. 10% discount on the room rate Oct–June for a two-night stay.

PONTARLIER 25300

⅍ ☎ |●| HÔTEL-RESTAURANT LE SAINT-PIERRE*

3 pl. Saint-Pierre (Centre).
☎ 03.81.46.50.80 ➡ 03.81.46.87.80
Closed Mon out of season. **TV**.

This place sits on a square in an area that feels rather quiet and villagey. Nearly all the rooms look out on to the porte Saint-Pierre, the rather elaborate triumphal arch that has become the symbol of the town. The double rooms with shower/wc aren't exactly huge, but they are stylish as well as good value with prices at €27–37. The restaurant serves decent traditional food; menus €10–15. They have the sunniest terrace in town – the perfect spot to sip your free aperitif.

⅍ ☎ |●| HÔTEL-RESTAURANT DE MORTEAU**

26 rue Jeanne-d'Arc (Centre).
☎ 03.81.39.14.83 ➡ 03.81.39.75.07
Closed daily 3–6pm, Sun, and a week in March, June, Sept and Oct. **TV**. **Pay car park**.

This place looks vaguely like an old farmhouse, and although it's in the middle of the village, it's a quiet spot. The rooms have been completely renovated and are good value for money – doubles are €34 with shower/wc or €35 with bath. Good traditional cooking using only fresh produce; menus €10–18. 10% discount in Jan, Oct and Nov.

GRANGETTES (LES) 25160 (12KM S)

☎ |●| HÔTEL-RESTAURANT BON REPOS**

How to get there: it's on the lac de Saint-Point on the D129.
☎ 03.81.69.62.95 ➡ 03.81.69.66.62
Ⓦ www.hotelbonrepos.com
Closed Sun evening and Mon out of season; 20 Oct–20 Dec. **Garden. TV**. **Car park**.

On the edge of a little village by the lake. An old-fashioned inn – the tablecloths are white and the welcome is inviting. Substantial platters of home-made *charcuterie* and fine fish specialities like fillet of perch with mushrooms and noodles, trout *au bleu* or with almonds and *vin jaune* sauce and supreme of chicken with cabbage. Menus from €11 up to €29. The comfortable, well-maintained rooms are being renovated one by one. Doubles €33 with shower and €39 with bath.

OUHANS 25520 (17KM NW)

⅍ ☎ |●| HÔTEL-RESTAURANT DES SOURCES DE LA LOUE**

13 Grande-Rue (Centre); take the N57, at Saint-Gorgon-Main, turn left onto the D41.
☎ 03.81.69.90.06 ➡ 03.81.69.93.17
Closed Sat lunchtime and Sun evenings out of season; 25 Oct–7 Nov; 20 Dec–1 Feb. **TV**. **Car park**.

A lovely inn in an unspoilt village amidst wonderful countryside. The cooking concentrates on local dishes, as you would expect – steak with morels, trout *meunière* or in *vin jaune,* smoked ham, Morteau sausage with potatoes *au gratin,* house smoked salmon. Weekday lunch menu €11 and others €13–29. Pleasant, simple rooms (some in the roof), which are reasonably priced for the area: €34 with shower/wc and €40 with bath. They don't take debit or credit cards. Free apéritif.

RENÉDALE   25520 (24KM NW)

🕇 |⦿| AUBERGE DU MOINE

Grange-Carrée. Take the N57 to Saint-Gorgon-Main then the D41 in the direction of Ouhans and it's 400m from the Belvédère du Moine.
☎ 03.81.69.91.22
Closed Tues evening; Dec–Feb.

A lovely old farm standing on its own in the countryside. The stable has been converted into a dining room with pine panelling. On Sunday it's full of local people who have known of this fine establishment for ages so it's worth booking. Danielle runs the place and does the cooking; she uses a lot of family recipes mixed in with regional dishes: trout in *vin jaune* or pastry cases with morels. Set menu at €10 (not served Sun), then others €18–21. There are lovely walks over the *belvédère du Moine* and to the source of the Loue river. Free coffee.

PORT-SUR-SAÔNE   70170

🕇 🛏 |⦿| HÔTEL-RESTAURANT DE LA PAIX

3 rue Jean-Bogé (Centre); it's opposite the church.
☎ 03.84.91.52.80 ➡ 03.84.91.61.21
Closed Sun evening and Jan.

The hotel is in a 16th-century priory. They've recently refurbished it and the decoration is in keeping with the building. Doubles €24 with basin, €30 with shower/wc. Unpretentious cooking and traditional dishes: morels in pastry cases, duck breast *Montmorency,* salmon *pâté* in pastry and *coq au vin jaune.* Weekday menu €9 and others €13–22. Free house apéritif and 10% discount on the room rate except in summer.

|⦿| RESTAURANT LA POMME D'OR

1 rue Saint-Valère.
☎ 03.84.91.52.66
Closed Sun evening; Mon; 16 Aug–4 Sept. **Car park.**
Disabled access.

You eat in a smart little dining room right on the banks of the Saône. The cuisine is good

and dishes change with the seasons: pan-fried Jura snails with mushrooms, red mullet – and for dessert don't miss out on the house speciality, golden apples in leaves. Menus €9–24. In summer, you might find a table on the tiny terrace overlooking the water, where they serve only cold meals.

|⦿| RESTAURANT LA MARINE

15 rue de la Fontaine; it's right next to the Saône.
☎ 03.84.91.51.00
Closed Wed.

This is a genuine *guinguette,* the old type of café where they used to have dancing outside. The people who arrive in boats only have to tie up in order to eat in this pleasant establishment, where the owner treats his clients to excellent cuisine. There's a weekday menu for €12 and others at €18 and 26. Dishes change regularly, but they always list fish specialities like home-smoked salmon and fillet of plaice *grenobloise* or game in season such as boar stew. It's best to book – whether you come by boat or not.

COMBEAUFONTAINE   70120 (12KM W)

🛏 |⦿| HÔTEL-RESTAURANT LE BALCON**

Centre; take the N19.
☎ 03.84.92.11.13 ➡ 03.84.92.15.89
Closed Sun evening; Mon; 26 June–5 July; 26 Dec–12 Jan. **Garden. TV. Car park.**

A former coaching inn smothered with ivy and boasting a flower garden. It's a magnificent house with a really warm atmosphere. Pleasant, simple rooms are €38 with shower/wc or €46 with bath – because the hotel is on the main road, the ones at the back are quieter. There are delicious dishes like chicken in *vin jaune* and morels, Montbéliard sausage with lentils, pigeon in flaky pastry *à la bourguignonne* as well as more innovative ones – scallops in herb vinaigrette and slivers of duck with a cherry infusion. €11 weekday lunch menu and others €22–53.

RONCHAMP   70250

🕇 🛏 |⦿| HÔTEL-RESTAURANT CARRER**

Le Rhien; it's 2km outside Ronchamp on the N19.
☎ 03.84.20.62.32 ➡ 03.84.63.57.08
Ⓦ www.ronchamp.com
Disabled access. TV. Car park.

People come from far and wide to eat in this forest hamlet restaurant. The family cooking is very orthodox and they use the best quality fresh produce. The results are delicious: duck *terrine*, trout with Charcenne wine, zander in *vin jaune*, fried carp and game in season. Weekday lunch menu at €9 and others €18–35; the €20 menu includes apéritif and wine. There are twenty rooms, (€31–37 for a double depending on facilities). Mountain bike hire. 10% discount on the room rate Nov–1 April and free house apéritif.

CHAMPAGNEY   70290 (5KM E)

🛏 |◉| HÔTEL DU COMMERCE**

4 av. du Général-Brosset.
☎ 03.84.23.13.24 ➡ 03.84.23.24.33
🌐 www.hotel-du-commerce-70.fr
Closed Sun evening 1 Nov–1 May; 23 Dec–15 Jan.
Garden. **TV**. **Car park**.

This old house has been entirely transformed, but the family that own it have taken care to retain its original character. There are four dining rooms, each one different: one has a wide fireplace where they serve country dishes, another is more like a sitting room-cum-library. The rooms are either starkly modern or have period furniture; doubles with shower/wc or bath €35. Some things haven't changed, though – the waitresses still wear white aprons and the chef is still committed to preparing soundly-made regional and traditional dishes including casserole of lacquered pork with Champlitte wine, zander fillet with oyster mushrooms and brawn. Weekday menu €11 and a range of others up to €38. There's a fitness room, a sauna and a Turkish bath.

FROIDETERRE   70200 (10KM W)

🍴|◉| HOSTELLERIE DES SOURCES

4 rue du Grand-Bois; take the N19 in the direction of Lure and when you get to La Verrerie, take the road that goes north.
☎ 03.84.30.13.91
Closed Sun evening and Mon except public holidays; 7–25 Jan. **Car park**.

The house looks like a classic farm inn but is completely different inside: the décor is very plush, almost luxurious, and perhaps seems like too much of a contrast with the exterior. The main event is the cuisine, however, which is creative and intelligently conceived. The menus change with the seasons but everthing gets the juices flowing: Jura snails with *Maître d'Hôtel* butter, braised rack of lamb with parsley and crayfish flambéed in Cognac. It's impossible to resist the *crème brûlée* with vanilla. Menus €17–51. It's only a

pity they don't have rooms. Free apéritif or coffee.

MELISEY   70220 (10KM N)

🍴|◉| RESTAURANT LA BERGERAINE

27 route des Vosges; take the N19 towards Lure then the D73.
☎ 03.84.20.82.52
Closed Tues evening and Wed (except public holidays and July–Aug); Feb school holidays. **Disabled access**.

The chef has created a place which brings people into the country to eat – but it's not ruinously expensive. And it's so small here that, unless you want to go away hungry, it's advisable to book. He serves appetizing, classic dishes prepared with care and really well cooked. House smoked salmon, crayfish or *foie gras* with seasonal greens, veal sweetbreads with morels, morels in a pastry case with *vin jaune* sauce. Weekday lunch menu €10 with others €13–49. Free coffee.

ROYE   70200 (15KM SW)

|◉| LE SAISONNIER

56 rue de la Verrerie; it's on the edge of the village, on the N19.
☎ 03.84.30.46.80
Closed Sun evening and Wed.

You can stumble on some quite surprising places in the Haute-Saône – and this is one. It used to be a farm, as evidenced by its low ceilings and thick stone walls (which keep it warm in winter and cool in summer). Rather sober décor but pleasant nonetheless, and there's friendly service. Excellent seasonal cooking with a lot of up-to-date dishes, offering good value for money: weekday menu at €17 and others from €23 to €43. There's a quiet terrace at the back.

ROUSSES (LES)   39220

🛏 HÔTEL DU VILLAGE**

344 rue Pasteur (Centre).
☎ 03.84.34.12.75 ➡ 03.84.34.12.76
Closed Sun evening out of season. **TV**. **Pay car park**.

This ten-room hotel in the middle of the resort has been completely renovated. Large double rooms, all with shower/wc or bath, are €43–46. There's a small suite sleeping four to five on the second floor.

🛏 |◉| HÔTEL ARBEZ FRANCE-SUISSE**

La Cure (Southeast); it's 2km out of town on the D5.

☎ 03.84.60.02.20 ➡ 03.84.60.08.59
Closed Mon and Tues. **TV**.

With one foot in France and another over the Swiss border, this is an odd place – your room could be in either country. All the rooms are lovely and comfortable with blond wood panels on the walls. Doubles €49 with shower, €52 with bath. They offer two *formules* in the restaurant: a brasserie option (with filling portions) and a gourmet one. Both are solidly local – the speciality is chicken with *vin jaune* and mushrooms. Menus €13 to €32. Charming welcome.

SAINT-HIPPOLYTE   25190

⚑ ☎ I●I AUBERGE DE MORICEMAISON

route du Dessoubre, Valoreille (Southwest). Head for the Dessoubre valley on the D39 for about 11km.
☎ 03.81.64.01.72/04.30
Closed Tues evening and Wed mid-Sept to mid-May; Jan. In winter, phone ahead. **Car park**.

Very picturesque old farm with a nice view over the river and a warm, natural welcome. Anglers, walkers, cyclists and bikers all gather here – if you catch a fish the proprietors are happy to cook your catch. If your angling skills aren't up to it, though, there's trout on the menu, either cooked in *vin jaune* or fried. Good menus of the day at €8 during the week and others €15–31. Six modest, recently redecorated rooms with basins only (showers and wc are down the corridor) go for €24 each; there's one that sleeps five. 10% discount on the room rate except July–Aug. Free coffee.

GOUMOIS   25470 (20KM SE)

⚑ ☎ I●I AUBERGE LE MOULIN DU PLAIN**

Lieu-dit Le Moulin du Plain; at Goumois on the D437b follow the road along the Doubs and look for the signs.
☎ 03.81.44.41.99 ➡ 03.81.44.45.70
🌐 www.moulinduplain.com
Closed 1 Jan–25 Feb and 1 Nov–31 Dec. **TV. Car park**.

This fairly modern house, built in the local style, is on the banks of the Doubs, which cuts through a fabulous wild valley. The inn was started a few years ago by a family of farmers and it's become a thriving business. Pleasant and comfortable double rooms – all with shower/wc or bath – are €46–52; some have balconies. There's a half-board option from €42. In the restaurant there are lots of fish dishes (the trout with shallots is excellent) alongside chicken with *vin jaune* and Comté

cheese, country salad, *tournedos* with morels and gammon. Set menus €15 (not Sun) and from €18 to €20. Free house apéritif and 10% discount on the room rate March–April and Oct.

VESOUL   70000

⚑ ☎ HÔTEL DU LION**

4 pl. de la République (Centre).
☎ 03.84.76.54.44 ➡ 03.84.75.23.31
Closed Sat evening in Jan; 4–15 Aug; 26 Dec–5 Jan. **TV. Car park**.

Family-run, very traditional hotel in the centre of town. Lovely welcome – the staff know what good service is. The comfortable rooms have modern furnishings and are spacious; doubles with shower/wc cost €40, or €43 with bath. 10% discount for a two-night stay 1 Dec–31 March and July–Aug.

FROTEY-LÈS-VESOUL   70000 (3KM E)

☎ I●I EUROTEL – RESTAURANT LE SAINT JACQUES***

Route de Luxeuil.
☎ 03.84.75.49.49 ➡ 03.84.75.55.78
Closed Sun evening; a fortnight in summer. **TV. Car park and lock up garage**.

The outside is very off-putting – it looks exactly like lots of chains throughout France – and the motorway exit is hardly the most joyous view, but you leave all that behind once inside. The rooms are pleasant and contemporary; doubles with bath €55. The dining room is equally modern but the bar and dining room are truly elegant. Very professional yet warm welcome. The cuisine is splendid and has lots of personal touches – and as you'd hope, it changes with the season. Menus €15–50.

VILLERSEXEL   70110

⚑ ☎ I●I HÔTEL DE LA TERRASSE**

route de Lure; it's on the banks of the Ogno.
☎ 03.84.20.52.11 ➡ 03.84.20.56.90
Closed Sun evening and Mon lunchtime out of season; 15 Dec–4 Jan. **Garden. TV. Car park**.

Gérard Ème established the hotel, and it's now run by his daughter. It's quiet, cosy and very relaxing, and the rooms are prettily decorated and tastefully furnished. Doubles €37 with shower/wc and €46 with bath. The rustic-style restaurant is warmed by an open fire in winter; in summer you can eat on the terrace surrounded by greenery. Dishes include fillet of zander in *vin jaune* and morels and monkfish *à l'Américaine*. Weekday lunch menu at €11 and a range of others €14–27. Free house apéritif.

🏠 |●| HÔTEL-RESTAURANT DU COMMERCE**

1 pl. du 13-Septembre (Centre); it's near the château museum.
☎ 03.84.20.50.50 ➡ 03.84.20.59.57
📧 commviller@aol.com
Closed Sun evening and 1–15 Jan. **TV**. **Car park**.

Huge and absolutely classic provincial inn. It's a shame that the rooms feel like those in a chain hotel – though they're simple, clean and reasonably priced. Doubles €38 with shower/wc or bath. The owner prepares good regional dishes: smoked ham on the bone cooked in a hay box, *terrines*, poached trout with morels, grilled meats and flambéed tarts. A range of set menus at €16–33 should satisfy any appetite. There's a huge fireplace where they light a fire on cold nights.

VILLERS-LE-LAC   25130

🎋 🏠 |●| HÔTEL-RESTAURANT LE FRANCE

8 pl. Cupilhard.
☎ 03.81.68.00.06 ➡ 03.81.68.09.22
Closed Sun evening, Mon and Tues out of season; Jan; 5–15 Nov. **TV**. **Pay car park**.

Traditional *Vieille France* hotel-keeping, but souped up by a dynamic chef. Hughes Droz has improved the quality of the cooking and made a reputation for subtle, inventive cuisine contrasting textures and flavours without losing sight of simplicity. He has his own herb garden and a pungent collection of spices brought back from his travels – and uses them in delicate proportions in his cooking. His menus, €18–64 or around €47 *à la carte*, change at least four times a year but make sure you try the snails in an absinthe infusion. There are good Burgundies and clarets on the wine list and some very old vintages of *vin jaune*. The dining room is very attractive, but the rooms are getting a bit fusty – even though they're well maintained and comfortable. Doubles with bathroom are €46.

Île-de-France

75 Paris

77 Seine-et-Marne

78 Yvelines

91 Essonne

92 Hauts-de-Seine

93 Seine-Saint-Denis

94 Val-de-Marne

95 Val-d'Oise

ANGERVILLE 91670

🎿 🏠 |●| HÔTEL DE FRANCE***

2 pl. du Marché (Centre).
☎ 01.69.95.11.30 📠 01.64.95.39.59
📧 hotel-de-france3@wanadoo.fr
Closed Sun evening and Mon. **TV. Car park**.

This beautiful old inn, built in 1715, has been restored a number of times without losing its elegance or character – the old beams, fireplace, conservatory and drawing room exude an air of gracious living. There's a sitting room where you can relax over an apéritif before proceeding to the dining room. The cuisine is reassuringly traditional and reliable: cream of watercress soup (this is the region for watercress), *terrine* with watercress, *salade mérévilloise* and fresh fruit *au gratin*. Set menu €27 or expect to pay around €34 *à la carte*. There's a pair of ravishing rooms with canopied beds with shower or bath for €73. Free coffee.

ASNIÈRES 92600

🎿 |●| LE PETIT VATEL

30 bd. Voltaire; it's near the dog cemetery; M° Asnières-Gabriel-Péri.
☎ 01.47.91.13.30
Closed evenings, weekends and Aug.

Though you'd be likely to walk past this very ordinary, Formica-table lunch place with without a second look, you shouldn't. First, the welcome they extend is genuinely warm; second, the quality of the cuisine is remarkable – and, third, you almost get more than you can eat. They take tremendous care in preparing traditional family dishes like ham hock or *provençal* beef stew, and the salads are huge. Menu at €10 or *à la carte*, and reasonably priced wine. Free coffee.

🎿 |●| LA PETITE AUBERGE

118 rue de Colombes; take the overground train from Saint-Lazare to Asnières or Bois-Colombes.
☎ 01.47.93.33.94
Closed Sun and Wed evenings, Mon and a week in Aug.

Service until 9pm. The décor is completely over the top, like the set of a Grande Époque operetta – wood panelling and pictures everywhere. You're scooped up by the *patronne* or her daughter and conducted to your table; Dad, in the kitchen, produces wonderful food. There's a *menu-carte* for €23 which provides a superb meal, with dishes that change with the seasons. Of the starters, the *andouillette* in Chablis in a pastry case is meltingly delicious, the *émincé* of veal kidneys is tender and served in plenty of sauce, while the supreme of chicken *à l'indienne* is subtly flavoured with paprika and other delicate spices. The fish is as fresh as can be. Try the *gratin* of fresh fruit or the succulent soft fruit in pastry. You should definitely book. Free coffee.

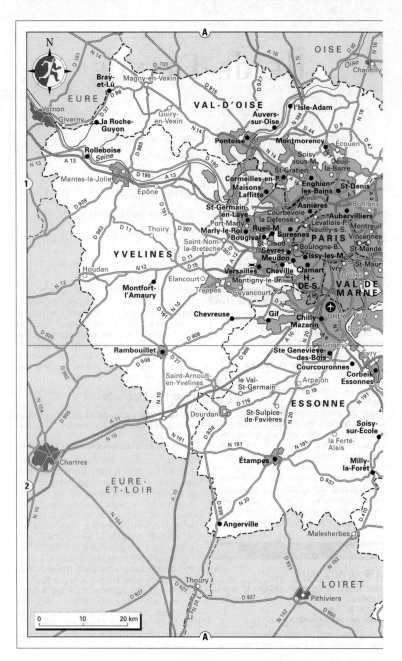

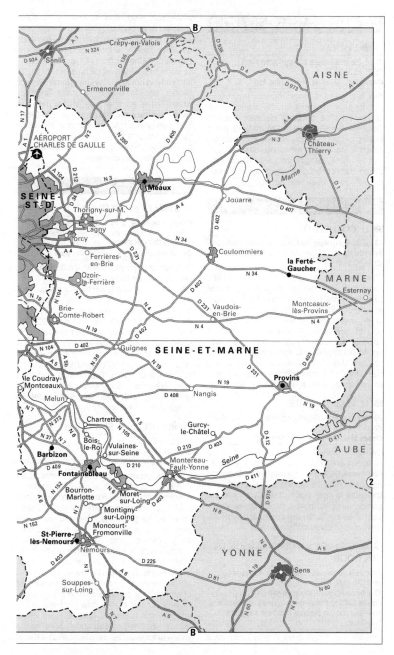

AUBERVILLIERS   93300

🕭|●| L'ISOLA

33 bd. Édouard-Vaillant; M°Fort-d'Aubervilliers
☎ 01.48.34.88.76
Closed Sun, Mon–Wed evenings and Aug.

This is a genuine Italian restaurant run by a
pair of charming sisters who are kindness
embodied. The décor is pleasant but not
ostentatious and dishes are cooked using
fresh produce from the market with a strong
Italian accent: veal escalope, osso bucco,
ricotta ravioli, lasagne and a delicious Sar-
dinian dish called coulourgionisi. You'll pay
€23–27 for a meal. Free apéritif.

AUVERS-SUR-OISE   95430

|●| LE CORDEVILLE

18 rue du Rajon; leave the A15 at exit 7 onto the N184,
then take the N322 in the direction of Méry-sur-Oise.
☎ 01.30.36.81.66

This restaurant is right in the centre of the
town that attracted so many Impressionist
painters. They serve traditional family cuisine
and don't stint on the portions. The patronne
is very sweet and sets the pot on the table for
you to help yourself, just like at home. It
appeals to a range of people, from local workers to holidaymakers, and has a brigade of
regulars. Lunch dish of the day €8 and a
menu for €13. Limited choice of wines. Booking requested in the evenings. No credit cards.

|●| LE VERRE PLACIDE

20 rue du Général-de-Gaulle; opposite the train station.
☎ 01.34.48.02.11
Closed Mon, Wed and Sun evenings; Aug.

One of the oldest restaurants in Auvers, with a
spacious and bright dining room. The weekday menu (€21) gives you starter, main course
and dessert, or it's around €31 à la carte. Try
the salad of quail confit, turbot with a fennel
compote, or lamb in a pastry case. Wines
start at €9 per bottle and service is very polite.
Advisable to book at the weekend.

🕭|●| AUBERGE RAVOUX – MAISON DE VAN GOGH

8 rue de la Sansonne; it's on the town hall square.
☎ 01.30.36.60.60
📧 auberge-Ravoux@maison-de-van-gogh.com
Closed Sun and Mon evenings in spring and summer;
Mon–Wed and Sun evenings in autumn and winter; 24
Dec–24 Jan.

Vincent van Gogh lived in this hotel for a

while, and died here in 1890 – it's been
restored to its original glory and the décor is
just as it would have been in the painter's
day. The cooking is good, and helpings are
substantial. Choose from old-fashioned dishes such as pressed rabbit on a bed of lentils
and pickled onions, slow-roast lamb de sept
heures, and, for dessert, mousse Tagliana,
which is named after one of the previous
owners of the establishment. The formule at
€24 gets you a main course plus starter or
dessert and there's a menu for €30 – not
particularly cheap, but reasonable for what
you get. Free house apéritif.

BARBIZON   77630

🕭🏠|●| LES ALOUETTES**

4 rue Antoine-Barye; at the tobacconist's on the corner
of Rue Grande, turn up the street and it's 500m along.
☎ 01.60.66.41.98 📠 01.60.66.20.69
Closed Sun evening. **TV**. **Garden**. **Car park**.

This rather chic nineteenth-century house,
set in its own substantial grounds with a garden and trees, has been turned into an inn.
It's the only hotel in the town that's away from
the main street. The décor is rustic. Doubles
€43–55 with shower/wc and €52–60 with
bath – there are also two apartments which
sleep four people. In the restaurant there's a
set menu at €26, while eating à la carte will
cost around €53. Dishes change with the
seasons and specialities include pan-fried
fresh foie gras of Landes duck served with
golden fruit and roast rabbit aux saveurs
provençales. Free apéritif.

🕭|●| L'ERMITAGE ST ANTOINE

51 Grande-Rue (Centre).
☎ 01.64.81.96.96
Closed Mon, Tues, and four weeks mid-Dec to mid-Jan.

It's an unexpected pleasure to come upon
this wine bar. More unusual still is that this is
a nineteenth-century farm house that's been
brilliantly re-arranged and decorated with
trompe-l'œil paintings. The €15 menu will
provide you with a decent meal. They scribble the dishes of the day on the blackboard
– these include gazpacho, parsleyed ham,
andouillette from Troyes, rabbit salad with
green lentils, black pudding with apples and
curried spare ribs – or you can get a plate of
charcuterie or cheeses served with a glass
of wine. If the owner offers advice about
which wine to order, take it – he really
knows what he's talking about. Most of the
wines are served by the glass; even if this is

all you order, you'll still get a smile. Free coffee.

BOUGIVAL 78380

🅰 |●| RESTAURANT CHEZ CLÉMENT

It's on the N13 about 1km outside the town.
☎ 01.30.78.20.00

Service from early morning to 1am. A huge English-style park surrounds this superb house with green shutters. You go through the smoking room – when it's cold, they light a fire – to the main room, which used to be the orangery. The simple cooking uses fresh, seasonal produce, and the oysters and shellfish are kept cool under a running waterfall. A meal will cost you around €24. This is a very pleasant place. Free house apéritif.

|●| LE CAMÉLIA

7 quai Georges-Clémenceau
☎ 01.39.18.36.06
Closed Sun evening, Mon and a fortnight in Aug. **TV**.

A welcoming, refined setting. The cuisine is prettily prepared and manages to be both solid and delicate. All the produce used is fresh and the cooking shows off the flavours extremely well. The fixed-price menu lists somewhat elaborate dishes, which change regularly – it costs €32. In addition there are two *formules*: starter and main course for €27 or main course and dessert at €24. Swift, efficient service.

BRAY-ET-LÛ 95710

🅰 🏠 |●| LE FAISAN DORÉ

12 route de Vernon.
☎ 01.34.67.71.68
Closed Sun evening, Mon, mid-Aug to early Sept and three weeks in winter. **TV**.

The balconies here are festooned with an abundance of geraniums and petunias and there's a family atmosphere. In the summer, it's pleasant to sit on the terrace under the flowery parasols. The set weekday menu is €11, while the next step up provides Burgundy snails as a starter, pepper steak and fruit Charlotte. À la carte you'll pay about €21: try *fricassée* of veal sweetbreads with morels or veal chops Normandy-style. Good value for money, with attentive service. The rooms are plain; doubles with basin €27. There is an overnight deal with evening meal and room for €41. Free coffee.

CHAVILLE 92370

🅰 |●| RESTAURANT LE MAGLOIRE

2049 av. Roger-Salengro (Northeast); it's on the N10, near pl. du Général Leclerc.
☎ 01.47.50.40.32
Closed Sun evening, Mon, and mid-July to mid-Aug. **Garden**.

A charming provincial house with a rustic dining room looking onto a pleasant garden. For quality and quantity the €14 set menu is good value, and there are others at €27 and €35. There's an interesting variety of dishes *à la carte*, like *salade gourmande*, *croustillant* of John Dory, scallops with apples and Calvados, *aiguillette* of duck with ceps and medallions of monkfish with cider. A complete meal should cost about €31. Free apéritif.

CHEVREUSE 78460

🅰 |●| AUBERGE LA BRUNOISE

2 rue de la Division Leclerc.
☎ 01.30.52.33.87
Closed Mon and Tues evenings; Wed; 3 weeks from 14 July; a week in Feb.

The village is charming and the walk over the bridges of the Yvette river and the canal is incredibly picturesque. Unpretentious cuisine is on offer here – it's honest and good on all the menus, even the €14 weekday lunch one. There are others €21–32. The speciality of the house is seafood. Natural, friendly service, and the young owners' eagerness to keep the clients satisfied has earned them a good number of regulars. The dining room has a rustic aspect, though the glorious terrace looks onto the main road. Free coffee.

CHILLY-MAZARIN 91380

🅰 |●| THYM ET BASILIC

97 rue de Gravigny; take the Longjumeau exit off the A6 and continue along the right of the motorway.
☎ 01.69.10.92.75
Closed Sat lunchtime; Sun evening; Mon; Aug.

There's a hint of Provence in the yellow and blue dining room, and a taste of the same in the dishes: pasta with lobster, king prawns, crayfish, *bouillabaisse* (to order), stuffed queen scallops and cod fillet. The €13 lunch *formule* offers a traditional main dish like *blanquette de veau*. The higher-priced menus, €16–32, are rather pricey for what you get. Free *digestif*.

CLAMART · 92140

🏠 |●| RESTAURANT LA COSSE DES PETITS POIS

158 av. Victor-Hugo (Northeast); it's a little bit outside the centre of town, 300m from the train station.
☎ 01.46.38.97.60
Closed Sat lunchtime; Sun evening; a fortnight in Aug.

They've cleverly arranged the tables so that the fireplace remains the centrepiece of this small, pleasant dining room. Service is attentive and somebody in the kitchen has considerable flair. Two *menu-cartes* at €24 and €32, and the chef produces a single *formule* with dishes that change with the season. Prices are a little high, but not unreasonable given the quality of the food and the work that goes into preparing it. Free house apéritif.

CORBEIL-ESSONNES · 91100

🏨 |●| AUX ARMES DE FRANCE

1 bd. Jean-Jaurès; it's on the N7.
☎ 01.64.96.24.04 ➡ 01.60.88.04.00
Closed Aug.

One of the oldest hotels in the *département* – it's starting to show its age but provides unbeatable value for money. The rooms over the courtyard will give you a quiet night's sleep. Doubles €26–32. Winning cuisine and dishes that change with the seasons: wild boar haunch, fresh fish of the day brought straight from the market, truffle risotto and a fish soup with garlic croutons worth running the gauntlet of the N7 for. Menus €18–36. Friendly, unobtrusive service.

🏠 |●| L'ÉPICURE

pl. de l'Hôtel de Ville/5-7 rue du Grand Pignon; it's opposite the town hall.
☎ 01.60.88.28.38
Closed Sat lunchtime and Sun except Mothers' Day; 5 weeks mid-July to mid-Aug.

Epicurean pleasures *par excellence* in this charming, aptly named restaurant. Soft music plays in the background and the setting is refined-rustic. The chef produces fine, traditional cooking: fish *pot-au-feu*, *croustillant* of duck (a must!), game *terrine*, calf's head with calf's liver and kidney. Good value on the set menus, at €21 and €25, while dishes *à la carte* are almost the same price. Stylish, friendly service. Free Kir royal with cherry brandy.

COUDRAY-MONTCEAUX (LE) · 91830 (3KM S)

🏠 |●| RESTAURANT LA RENOMMÉE

110 berges de la Seine; it's opposite the train station.
☎ 01.64.93.81.09
Closed Tues evening; Wed; Oct; the Feb school holidays.

A pleasurable place whatever the weather. In summer, you'll feel tranquil on the terrace, watching the fishermen glide along the Seine. In winter, hunker down in a dining room which is warm and cosy with a roaring fire. The €15 weekday menu lists hot sausage in flaky pastry with port sauce and roast salmon with olive butter. Other menus €24 and €30 feature scallops and crayfish *au gratin* and saddle of lamb stuffed with *foie gras*. The wine is pricey. Free vodka granita served with dessert.

CORMEILLES-EN-PARISIS · 95240

|●| LA MONTAGNE

route Stratégique; it's in the woods above Cormeilles.
☎ 01.34.50.74.04
Closed Tues; 10–25 Aug.

This is the place for robust, straightforward cooking, or so they seem to think locally – the restaurant is full every lunchtime. A typical *menu du jour* at €9 will list egg mayonnaise, seafood salad, steak and *andouillette*, sausages with lentils and *crème caramel*. There are *formules* for €15 and €23 listing goose *rillettes*, lamb tripe and *crème brûlée*. You'll pay around €27 *à la carte* and can choose from dishes such as steak with pepper and *roquefort* and escalope of *foie gras* with acacia honey. There's a small terrace in summer.

COURCOURONNES · 91080

🏠 |●| LE CANAL

31 rue du Pont-Amar; 5km south of Ris-Orangis and it's in the Quartier du Canal, near the hospital.
☎ 01.60.78.34.72
Closed Sun.

Courcouronnes is concrete city and this restaurant is a spark of life in an otherwise desolate wasteland. It's a nice place with an attractive bar and friendly service, and there's a piano bar open at the weekend. The owner cooks robust, colourful dishes – try the duo of bream and salmon with chives –and his pig's trotters are up to the standard set by many of the great-name chefs. Menus €14–27. Free coffee.

ENGHIEN-LES-BAINS 95880

⅔ 🏠 ❙●❙ VILLA MARIE-LOUISE**

49 rue de Malleville; it's behind the spa, near the lake.
☎ 01.39.64.82.21 ➡ 01.39.34.87.76
Garden. TV.

This is a fine turn-of-the-(nineteenth)-century house with a big garden in the centre of town near the spa. The 22 simply furnished, comfortable rooms have been nicely decorated. Doubles with shower/wc €40, or €45 with bath – it's probably the cheapest hotel in town. If you're looking for a meal, you have a choice of simple, tasty dishes. There's a €10 menu or it costs around €12 for a meal à la carte. They take a lot of care of you here. Free house apéritif.

DEUIL-LA-BARRE 94170 (1KM NE)

⅔ ❙●❙ VERRE CHEZ MOI

75 av. de la Division-Leclerc.
☎ 01.39.64.04.34
Closed Mon and Sat lunchtimes; Sun; 30 June–25 Aug; 24 Dec–1 Jan.

This restaurant feels like a Lyonnais tavern and occupies the ground floor of a villa which has been converted into flats. They serve good, well-prepared traditional dishes. There are no set menus, only a daily list on which you'll find *coq au vin*, *miroton* of beef – a typical Lyonnais dish with slices of boiled beef in a rich sauce with onions – or top-quality *andouillette*. Simple starters include herrings and warm steamed potatoes or *charcuterie*, and they offer a limited range of cheeses (the farmhouse Camembert is excellent) as well as basic but brilliant desserts like *crème brûlée*. The place is lovely and cosy, with a friendly feel and very fair prices: you should pay €18–23 for a meal with a jug of wine. Free coffee.

SAINT-GRATIEN 95210 (2KM E)

⅔ ❙●❙ LE PHARE DU FORUM

14 pl. du Forum; it's in the Forum district in the middle of town.
☎ 01.34.28.23.07

Deliveries of fresh fish from the market at Rungis arrive three times a week. All the produce is brilliantly fresh and cooked to order: lots of shellfish and crustaceans, oysters, stuffed mussels, *bouillabaisse*, lemon sole, Dover sole, skate – or you can fill up on pasta or home-cooked pizzas. The restaurant has a maritime décor: model ships, starfish and

fishing nets. Weekday menu €8, then others €12–20 or €23 *à la carte*. Musical entertainment on Saturday and Sunday evenings. Smiling, brisk service. Free apéritif or *digestif*.

⅔ ❙●❙ CHEZ BABER

71 bd. Pasteur; it's on the N14, on the edge of Sannois.
☎ 01.39.89.64.72
Disabled access.

You're welcomed by the gentle music of the sitar and the tabla, and the perfumed air and Indian décor transport you far from the noise of the road outside. Lunchtime menu at €9 and two dinner ones at €15 and €20. Their tandoori specialities feature delicious sauces while other dishes like lamb tikka, chicken tikka marsala and fish magala are also good. The chutneys are spicey but well tempered by the cheese nan. You'll pay around €15 *à la carte* including wine. Free coffee or *digestif*, and, if you can prove it's your birthday, a free glass of champagne.

SOISY-SOUS-MONTMORENCY 95230 (2KM NW)

⅔ ❙●❙ LE TABAC DES COURSES

34 av. Kellerman; it's 100m from the racecourse, opposite the railway line.
☎ 01.34.17.25.09
Closed Sun except on race days; evenings; 15 Aug–15 Sept. **Car park**.

This place looks like nothing special, but they serve decent, honest food which is well-cooked and generously served. Menus from €11 list *œufs en meurette* in red wine sauce, herring fillets, duck with pears, fillet of sole with sorrel and steak with the house sauce. They also do a huge steak *tartare* with a serious serving of chips. A meal *à la carte* costs about €23. There's a shady terrace which is on a rather busy avenue. Free coffee.

ÉTAMPES 91150

🏠 HÔTEL DE L'EUROPE À L'ESCARGOT**

71 rue Saint-Jacques (North). Heading in the direction of the station, go along the road parallel to the rail track for 200m turn left then left again; the entrance is down a narrow road.
☎ 01.64.94.02.96
Closed 15 June–4 Aug. **TV. Car park**.

A small, very well-run hotel offering a smiling welcome, comfortable rooms and good value for money. It's in the middle of town yet quiet. Doubles €23 with shower, €27 with shower/wc or €31 with bath.

⅄ |●| LE SAINT-CHRISTOPHE

28 rue de la République (Centre); it's next to the church Notre-Dame-du-Fort.
☎ 01.64.94.69.99
Closed Wed evening; every other Sun (phone to check); Aug.

You come here for good traditional Portuguese cooking. Ask the owner if he's changed his speciality dish – cod – and he'll ask: "Why? Change a winning formula?" It's the national dish, after all. The décor's pretty trashy, with plastic flowers and tiles on the walls, but you can eat well for less than €15. There's a set menu for €9. Free coffee.

|●| RESTAURANT LES PILIERS**

2 pl. Saint-Gilles (Centre).
☎ 01.64.94.04.52
Closed Mon evening; Tues;a week in Feb.

The restaurant is in the oldest house in town, and it dates from the twelfth century – go through the paved arcade to find the entrance. Good home cooking with a fair dash of creativity: *crépinette* of pig's trotters, house *confit* and the like. The €15 *formule* gives you a couple of courses, the one at €21 gives three but be sure to order the dishes you want. A few *appellation* wines under €15. A place with some class.

⅄ |●| AUBERGE DE LA TOUR SAINT-MARTIN

97 rue Saint-Martin.
☎ 01.69.78.26.19
Closed Mon; Tues, Wed and Sun evenings; Sat lunchtime.

Right next to the leaning tower of Saint-Martin's you'll find light, inventive cooking delicately flavoured with herbs and spices in dishes which change with seasonal produce. Just choose from the chef's suggestions: there's a *menu-carte* for €31 which includes canapés, main course and either starter or dessert. Booking is essential. Free apéritif.

SAINT-SULPICE-DE-FAVIÈRES   91910 (8km N)

|●| AUBERGE DE CAMPAGNE LA FER-RONNIÈRE

10 pl. de l'Église; take the N20 towards Orléans, after Arpajon take the Mauchamps exit onto the D99.
☎ 01.64.58.42.07
Closed Wed.

A jewel of a village with a country inn that looks like a Wild West saloon. It must have been an old coaching inn originally, with the smithy next door. You won't find a better welcome or service; there's even a shower available for use by walkers. Huge plates of wonderful traditional food with a few authentic regional dishes besides: house *pâté* under a layer of parsley, snails, duck breast, rack of lamb, steak with shallots. Weekday menu at €10. Terrace in summer. Don't miss it if you're in the area.

VAL-SAINT-GERMAIN (LE)   91530 (18KM NE)

⅄ |●| AUBERGE DU MARAIS

Lieu-dit Marais; from Dourdan, take the D116 in the direction of St Cheron; at Sermaise, turn left onto a windy road through the forest.
☎ 01.64.58.82.97
Closed Sun and Mon evenings.

A large rustic house on the edge of the forest, with a terrace that's open in summer. Traditional dishes made with fresh, quality produce; the *terrines* and the *foie gras* are particularly fine and it's definitely worth following the chef's suggestions. Weekday menus start at €11, then there are others €21–36. Free house apéritif.

FERTÉ-GAUCHER (LA)   77320

⅄ ⌂ |●| HÔTEL DU SAUVAGE**

27 rue de Paris (Centre); it's by the main square
☎ 01.64.04.00.19 ➟ 01.64.20.32.95
@ info@hotel-du-sauvage.com
Closed the second week in Jan. **Restaurant closed** Wed. **TV**.

This sixteenth-century inn was once a brothel, and its name is said to come from the wild game once abundant in the marshland that used to surround it. The Teinturier family have been innkeepers here for six generations. They've had the courage to refurbish the place, providing attractively modern and comfortable rooms while keeping the squeaky floors and its all-important character. Doubles with shower/wc €50–46, or €50–56 with bath/wc. Delicious regional dishes made with local produce are on set menus at €16, €26 and €36. Try poached eggs with Brie, fillet of beef with *Brie de Meaux*, ham on the bone with mustard *de Meaux* or iced caramel *millefeuille* with spiced bread. Good fish, too. Perfect service and smiling welcome. 10% discount on the room rate.

FONTAINEBLEAU   77300

⌂ HÔTEL VICTORIA**

112 rue de France (Centre).

☎ 01.60.74.90.00 **e** resa@hotelvictoria.com
TV. Garden. Pay car park.

Georges Sand and Alfred de Musset frequented this place in the 1830s, which gives you an idea of its quality. Here and there you'll discern the vestiges of this lovely master-craftsman's house, even though all nineteen rooms have been renovated. They're clean and pleasant, particularly the ones overlooking the large garden, and it's a real pleasure to be woken by the cooing of the birds. Paul and Isabelle will welcome you like friends. Double rooms with bath cost €56.

〽️|●| RESTAURANT-BAR LE WOODEN HORSE

10–12 rue Montebello (Centre); it's between the pl. du Jet d'Eau et the pl. d'Armes.
☎ and **➡** 01.60.72.04.05
Closed Mon and Tues lunchtime. **Disabled access**.

This place is slap-bang in the middle of the most touristy part of Fontainebleau, close to the château and the wooden statue of a horse. As you walk in, there's a large bar and a bright conservatory. There's a €9 lunch menu and others at €12–20. The cooking is exactly what you would expect in this traditional, ex-royal town: *sauté* of veal kidney with two-mustard sauce, perch fillet with red pepper butter, lobster *fricassée* with mussels, rack of lamb with garlic cream. Not very original, perhaps, but the dishes are good value for money, attentively prepared and unobtrusively served. Free *digestif*.

〽️|●| RESTAURANT CHEZ ARRIGHI

53 rue d'Alsace (Centre).
☎ 01.64.22.29.43
Closed Mon.

This is just the sort of place for a family Sunday lunch. It's got an old-fashioned feel about it, with its sturdy, stone façade and luxurious curtains. Menus at €15, €22 and €30 in a variety of combinations which include dishes like frogs' legs in parsley, boned quail in flaky pastry stuffed with *foie gras*, *goujons* of salmon with creamed spinach and lamb's tongues in sorrel sauce. They're all well-prepared and will surprise and delight any fan of good traditional cooking – though some portions are a bit skimpy. Delicious bread. The décor and the ambience are more charming than you might expect in a suburban restaurant. Free coffee.

〽️|●| LE CAVEAU DES DUCS

24 rue de Ferrare (Centre); it's near the château.
☎ and **➡** 01.64.22.05.05
Closed a week in Jan and the first fortnight in Aug.
Disabled access.

You'll know you're in Fontainebleau in this seventeenth-century vaulted cellar with its period décor and chandeliers. Classical cooking, faultlessly served. Set menus at €20 (except Sat evening), €28 (this includes apéritif, starter, main course, dessert, wine, water and coffee to finish) and €38. The chef uses excellent ingredients to produce dishes with southern influences and sometimes a touch of the exotic (a surprise in this most conventional of towns): snails with garlic in pastry, duck breast with cider vinegar, stewed monkfish *provençale*, veal sweetbreads, kidneys in madeira sauce and fine apple tart. Free *digestif*.

BOIS-LE-ROI   77590 (4KM NE)

🏠 LE PAVILLON ROYAL***

40 av. du Général-Galliéni; it's near the train station.
☎ 01.64.10.41.00 **➡** 01.64.10.41.10
e hotel-le-pavillon-royal@wanadoo.fr
TV. Disabled access. Swimming pool. Car park.

A new building in neoclassical style, plain and aesthetically pleasing. Quiet, spacious and impeccably clean rooms are €45 with shower/wc or €53 with bath. Lovely swimming pool and relaxation centre – they charge two-star prices for three-star service. A good place even though it's a little lacking in character. 10% discount Oct–May.

VULAINES-SUR-SEINE   77870 (7KM E)

〽️|●| ÎLE AUX TRUITES

6 chemin de Basse-Varenne; cross the Valvins bridge, on the D210, turn left and it's 1km along the river bank.
☎ 06.85.07.01.35
Closed Wed, Thurs lunchtime and 19 Dec–24 Jan.
Disabled access. Car park.

You're right on the Seine here, in a thatched cottage surrounded by huge willow trees and trout ponds where the children can fish for their lunch – and, as the tables are right by the water's edge, you can keep an eye on them at the same time. Very decent cuisine and perfect service make this restaurant one of the most attractive in the region. It's quite charming without being too expensive. Try the grilled trout served with baked potatoes or the *assiette de l'Île aux Truites* which includes smoked trout, marinated fillet of trout and fish *terrine*. Menus at €18 and €26, with a children's menu at €12. They also have an interesting selection of wines – including a red Mennetou-Salon. You must reserve in summer to have any hope of getting a table. Free apéritif.

BOURRON-MARLOTTE   77780 (8KM S)

⚿ |●| RESTAURANT LES PRÉMICES

12 [bis] rue Blaise-de-Montesquiou; take the N7 in the direction of Nemours-Montargis and at the Bourron-Marlott ZI exit, follow the signs to the village.
☎ 01.64.78.33.00
Closed Sun evening; Mon; a fortnight in the Feb school holidays; 1–15 Aug; a week at Christmas. **TV. Car park**.

The restaurant is in the outbuildings of the superb château Bourron-Marlotte, and they've built a conservatory so you can appreciate the glory of the countryside. Véronique will greet you charmingly; her husband, in charge in the kitchens, is a first-rate chef. *Formule* at €30, and a gourmet menu at €58: pan-fried *foie gras* with spiced bread and foyal jelly, Kobe beef, lamb with herbs, lamb shank *confit* with potatoes, grilled crayfish with beetroot *coulis*, ice-cream scented with lily of the valley The wine list is unusually good. Free *digestif*.

MONTIGNY-SUR-LOING   77690 (10KM S)

⬢ |●| HÔTEL-RESTAURANT DE LA VANNE ROUGE**

rue de l'Abreuvoir; take the D148 along the banks of the Loing river.
☎ 01.64.78.52.49 ➡ 01.64.78.52.49
Closed Sun evening and Mon except on public holidays, Tues lunchtime from end-Sept to Easter, and ten days in winter. **TV. Car park**.

Charming, super-quiet hotel with six lovely rooms that have views over the River Loing. Doubles €53 with bath/wc. There's a large sunny terrace where you're lulled by the sound of the waterfalls and you can practically trail your feet in the water while you eat. Chef Serge Granger's speciality is fish – lobster salad with fresh herbs and balsamic vinegar, cod with green peppercorns, John Dory with *beurre blanc* – but that doesn't mean you shouldn't try his *foie gras* topped with mashed potato. There's a weekday *menu-carte* at €27, rising to €34 at the weekend. There's an exceptional wine list. Altogether one of the best places in the locality so it's essential to book.

MORET-SUR-LOING   77250 (10KM SE)

|●| LA POTERNE

1 rue du Pont
☎ 01.64.31.19.89
Closed Wed afternoon and Thurs.

This restaurant is in the shortest street in France – it has one building, the gate in the town walls where the restaurant is housed. It's a fine historic dwelling with an alleyway that looks over the Loing. Inventive, local dishes that the manager, Michelle, ferrets out of old recipe books: try that sixteenth-century delight, the *ouin*, sautéed veal like grandma used to make and *casse-museau* (the favourite dessert of King Henry IV). There's no set menu but a large number of dishes priced from €7 to €23. They'll even make you up a gourmet picnic if you ask. An exceptional place.

CHARTRETTES   77590 (11KM)

|●| RESTAURANT LE CHALET

37 rue Foch; take the D39 and it's on the right by the marina.
☎ 01.60.69.65.34
Closed Mon and Tues evenings; Wed; a fortnight in March; 3 weeks Aug–Sept. **Garden. Car park**.

This place buzzes with energy and laughter. It's a friendly, popular restaurant in a private mansion that fits in well with the rest in the street. The large rustic dining room decorated in Louis XIII style extends onto an elevated terrace with a pergola, and the cuisine consists of traditional dishes with good sauces: home-made goat's cheese tart, brawn with *vinaigrette*, *coq au vin*, rabbit *chasseur*. A substantial set menu at €12 (not served Sat evening or Sun), then others €20 and €26.

MONCOUR-FROMONVILLE   77140 (11KM N)

⚿ |●| LE CHALAND QUI PASSE

10 rue du Loing.
☎ 01.64.29.12.95
Closed Tues evening and Wed Oct–March.

A nice inn on the banks of the canal near the Loing river; the shady terrace gives you a good view of the pleasure boats sliding quietly by. The dining room has a country décor with a wide chimney. The first menu, €12, is fair enough and there are others at €21 and €24. These feature dishes such as house *terrine*, lambs kidneys *à l'ancienne*, game in season and duck *confit*. Easy-going family atmosphere. Free house *digestif*.

GIF-SUR-YVETTE 91190

IØI LE BŒUF À SIX PATTES

D-128 Chemin du Moulon; take the Centre universitaire
exit off the N118.
☎ 01.60.19.29.60
Disabled access.

Service: daily 11.30am–2.30pm and
9–10pm, 10.30 on Friday. You could well get
a crick in the neck as you crane round to look
at the cow Slavik has hung up in this restaurant. Unsurprisingly, he specializes in meat
dishes, which are first-rate and served with
chips – and they're good enough that you'd
ask for a second helping if you weren't so full.
They also do fillet of lamb with rosemary,
confit of duck thigh and grilled salmon steak,
and for dessert they offer a great caramelized
rice pudding. Good menus at €9, €12 and
€20. There's a terrace.

ISLE-ADAM (L') 95290

🍴 🏠 IØI LE CABOUILLET**

5 quai de l'Oise; it's after Cabouillet bridge, on the right
as you come from the station.
☎ 01.34.69.00.90 ➡ 01.34.69.33.88
Closed Sun evening and Mon. **Disabled access. TV.**

This big, beautiful bourgeois country house
is covered with ivy. Inside, Old Masters hang
on the walls and there's a beautiful, polished
wooden staircase – five prettily decorated
rooms go for €69 each. The restaurant is the
best in L'Isle-Adam. Set menus €27 (not
Sunday) and €40, or around €27 à la carte.
The cooking is refined and tasty and the
dishes change with the seasons: trilogy of
foie gras, fried eel with a herb salad, gratin of
sole with morels, pigeon with ceps. From
some tables and from the terrace you get a
view of the Oise river. Free coffee.

IØI AU RELAIS FLEURI

61 rue Saint-Lazare; it's 300m from St Martin's church.
☎ 01.34.69.01.85
Closed Sun, Mon and Wed evenings; 3 weeks in Aug.
Garden.

The décor is absolutely classic, with blue fabric stretched across the walls and matching
curtains. The Roland brothers will give you a
courteous welcome and their delicate,
sophisticated cooking offers good value for
this town. Dishes change with the seasons.
Set menu €42 served in the bar or about €38
à la carte: mussels rémoulade, snail casse-

role, roast fillet of Dover sole with a lobster
coulis, queen scallops with beurre blanc and
fresh pasta, roast duck with spiced wine,
bouillabaisse with fish and lobster and superb
desserts. There's an enormous shady terrace
where you can enjoy a digestif after your meal.

ISSY-LES-MOULINEAUX 92130

IØI LES QUARTAUTS

19 rue Georges-Marie (North); Mº Porte-de-Versailles or
Corentin-Celton.
☎ 01.46.42.29.38
Closed weekends and Aug.

It's hard to believe that you could find such a
good establishment in a place like this: the
street's so quiet that this bistro can only have
made its reputation by word-of-mouth. Simplicity and quality are the watchwords here,
with a welcoming warmth generated by the
owners, Régine and Christophe. Succulent
home cooking is served in substantial helpings, and they do superb meat dishes.
There's a huge choice of wines from small
vineyards at very reasonable prices. The
cheese selection is impressive and the
desserts are all made on the premises.
There's a menu for €23; you'll pay about the
same à la carte.

🍴 IØI ISSY-GUINGUETTE

113 bis av. de Verdun; Mº Mairie-d'Issy, then by bus 123
to the Chemin des Vignes stop.
☎ 01.46.62.04.27
Closed Sat lunchtime; Sun; Mon evening; a week at
Christmas.

Yves Legrand, the boss of this place, is the
driving force behind the resuscitation of the
vineyard in Issy. On sunny days, sit out on the
terrace among the vines with a view of lovely
old houses – it's hard to believe you're in the
suburbs of the capital, and if it gets too hot
Yves puts up the parasols. Bistro dishes are
carefully cooked and served in generous portions. There's not an extensive choice but the
options change all the time: salmon unilatérale (cooked on one side), rolled lamb
with fresh herbs, pork with cabbage, roast
rabbit fillet with sage, stuffed breast of veal,
cod with cream sauce, duck fricassée and
pineapple preserved in red wine and ginger.
There's an excellent wine list, as you might
expect given the owner's enthusiasm. The
service is perfect and the atmosphere
relaxed and often quite festive; lunchtime
sees lots of businessmen from the area. In
winter, they serve in the bright dining room

where they light a fire in the hearth. There's a menu for €23 or you'll pay around €31 *à la carte*. Free apéritif.

|○| LA MANUFACTURE

20 esplanade de la Manufacture; Mᵒ Corentin-Celton.
☎ 01.40.93.08.98
Closed Sat lunchtime; Sun; a fortnight in Aug. **Disabled access**.

The restaurant takes up the ground floor of an old tobacco factory. It's a huge room with a high ceiling painted cream and beige, and it's brightened up with a few modern pictures and green plants. At lunchtime it's full of media execs and exhibitors from the exhibition centre – the huge space makes this a perfect place for private conversations or tricky negotations because you can hear each other without being overheard. The cooking is particularly fine, revelling in subtle flavours. Try the pigs' ears or the lamb shank braised in cider, which literally melts in the mouth. It's the best kind of home cooking rethought and served to suit modern styles and tastes. The menu changes frequently, but there are some staples: roast cod with a pepper stew, calf's brains and tongue *ravigotte*, braised beef cheek, lacquered belly of veal, crab with mashed potato and so on. Excellent desserts, and the bill won't be a shock – *menus-cartes* at €24 and €28, or about €28 *à la carte*. The only tiny quibbles are that the welcome is a bit snooty (they're not too keen on men wearing earrings, rather incredibly), and that it can be a problem booking a table for one person. The wines are attractively priced, though not by the glass.

MAISONS-LAFITTE   78600

⅔ ☗ |○| HÔTEL-RESTAURANT AU PUR-SANG*

2 av. de la Pelouse; go over the Maisons-Lafitte bridge, turn right, and skirt the racecourse until the roundabout, then turn right into av. de la Pelouse.
☎ 01.39.62.03.21 ➡ 01.34.93.48.69
Closed Sun; 3 weeks in Aug; a fortnight at the end of the year. **TV. Car park**.

Just by the entrance to the racecourse you'll find this thoroughly provincial-looking hotel-restaurant. Simple rooms with shower at €39. Take a seat in the rustic dining room or on the terrace, and opt for the €11 set menu – it will offer something along the lines of herring fillets, steak and chips and *crème caramel*; *à la carte*, served only on race days,

will set you back around €23. Free house apéritif.

|○| LA VIEILLE FONTAINE

8 av. Grétry (Centre).
☎ 01.39.62.01.78
Closed Sun evening; Mon; 12–19 Aug. **Garden**.

The building is a fine example of Second Empire architecture and it's situated in the grounds of the chateau. There's been a restaurant here since 1926, and over the years it's built up a solid reputation. The dining room and interior decoration are very attractive and there's a lovely terrace in the garden. Tasty dishes are produced with great skill: *salade folle*, roast saddle of lamb and chocolate tart. The service is beyond reproach. The *menu-carte* at €30 means you can get a good meal for a fair price, and there are affordable wines too. The place has a certain atmosphere: it was used as a movie set for a couple of (forgettable) movies and was a haunt of some of the Nazi high command during the Occupation.

MARLY-LE-ROI   78160

⅔ ☗ |○| LES CHEVAUX DE MARLY – RESTAURANT LA TEMPÊTE***

pl. de l'Abreuvoir (Centre).
☎ 01.39.58.47.61 ➡ 01.39.16.65.56
Disabled access. TV. Swimming pool. Car park.

Ten faultlessly presented rooms at €79 for a double with bath – good value for a three-star hotel in this area. Some of them have a view over the imposing Abreuvoir (the drinking fountain for horses). There's a very high standard in the restaurant, which is presided over by the *sommelier*, the master pastry chef, and the chef, who has won a string of medals. You'll understand why with dishes such as lobster stew, turbot *hollandaise* and *foie gras*. There's a menu at €30, but watch out if you order *à la carte* (it'll cost around €38), because many dishes attract supplements. Excellent fish specialities. Free coffee.

⅔ |○| LE FOU DU ROI

6 [bis] Grande-Rue.
☎ 01.39.58.80.20
Closed Sat lunchtime; Sun; 1–15 Jan; 3 weeks from 8 Aug.

A bright, simple little restaurant which you'll remember above all for the quality of the cuisine. There are three set lunch menus for €11, €14 and €18 and they include a ¼-litre of wine and coffee. The three evening ones – €18, €23 and €27 – don't include drink but offer gourmet dining instead: pan-fried duck *foie gras*, snails in pastry, turbot in butter and white rum *soufflé*. Dishes are chalked up on the slate and change according to the whim of the chef or what's best at market. Courteous service, decent prices and a satisfying meal make it a good establishment, and the dining room is tiny so it's best to book. Free coffee.

PORT-MARLY   78560 (2KM E)

⅍ 🏠 L'AUBERGE DU RELAIS DE MARLY

13 rue de Paris.
☎ 01.39.58.44.54
Closed Sun and Tues evenings; Wed; Aug. **Garden**.

The fact that the owners have been successfully running this charming country inn for over a quarter of a century suggests they're doing something right. Madame produces delicious Normandy dishes but adds a few from other regions as well. Monsieur is debonair and smiling and greets passers-by with a hearty "Bonjour", creating a lovely, relaxed atmosphere. Most people opt for a single dish at around €11 each, or there's a menu at €23. The garden is gorgeous in summer and, if you fancy fishing, you can wander across the road and drop your line in the Seine. Free coffee.

⅍ 🏠 L'AUBERGE DU RELAIS BRETON

27 rue de Paris.
☎ 01.39.58.64.33
Closed Sun evening; Mon; Aug.

The cuisine is deliciously prepared and served in substantial portions: try the stuffed sole or the chocolate tart to get the picture. Menus €24 or €36 or choose *à la carte*. Sometimes they'll encourage you to sit outside a little too early in the year, but there's good service nonetheless. Free house apéritif.

MEAUX   77100

⅍ 🏠 ACOSTEL**

336 av. de la Victoire/ Take the N3 in the direction of Châlons-en-Champagne, and it's on the right just after the Total garage; if you get to Trilport, you've gone too far.
☎ 01.64.33.28.58 ➡ 01.64.33.28.25
TV. Garden. Car park.

This unadorned concrete building is forbidding, but don't let that put you off – it's the back of the hotel. The front is much more appealing, with a lawn leading from the front door to the banks of the Marne, which is quite beautiful here. Clean rooms at garden level are €45 with shower/wc or €47 with bath. 10% discount except Aug and 31 Dec.

⅍ I●I LA MARÉE-BLEUE

8 rue Jean-Jaurès.
☎ 01.64.34.08.46
Garden.

This inn, surrounded by a lovely garden, is the good restaurant that this town was lacking until relatively recently. The dining rooms are huge and have a rustic décor. The specialities are seafood and Alsatian cooking like *baeckoffe*, fish *aioli* and fish *choucroute* – their star dish. On weekdays, the €15 *formule* is more than ample, giving you starter, main course and dessert. There's another at €22 and a gourmet one for €27. Free *digestif*.

MEUDON-LA-FORÊT   92360

⅍ I●I RESTAURANT LA MARE AUX CANARDS

carrefour de la Mare-Adam (Northwest); at the Meudon-Chaville exit on the N118, take the first left at the radio mast then head in the direction of Mare Adam.
☎ 01.46.32.07.16
Closed Sun evening and Mon.

This restaurant, miles from anywhere, is definitely isolated – the perfect place for lunch after a long walk in the Meudon woods. The big family dining room is convivial: they roast ducks on a spit in the handsome fireplace, and you're made to feel welcome. The service is fast, and the terrace pleasant in fine weather. There's a €12 *formule* of starter plus a quarter of chicken; otherwise *à la carte* is about €24 a head. Free apéritif.

I●I LE CENTRAL CHEZ PIERROT

26 rue Marcel-Allégot.
☎ 01.46.26.15.83
Closed Sun and 10–23 Aug. **Disabled access**.

Whether you've got a raging hunger or a small appetite, you'll find just what you want here. Try a few Cancale oysters at the bar with a glass or two of Pouilly or sit down in the dining room for plates of *coq au vin*. The aim of the owners is to send their customers away with a smile on their faces. To this commendable end they serve delicious calf's feet, herrings in oil with potatoes, *andouillette* (as good as you'll find in the Aveyron) and peppered steak. The boss will give you advice about the wines so you can be sure you'll get something good. Reasonably priced menus from €23.

🍴 🍽 LES TERRASSES DE L'ÉTANG

Route des Étangs, Étang de Villebon.
☎ 01.46.26.09.57
Closed Sun evening, Mon and Aug.

This is a really romantic spot for a quiet lunch *à deux*. Trees grow down to the edge of the lake, a few lonely seagulls wheel overhead, a clutch of ducks swim around and a thatched cottage completes the scene – as soon as spring arrives they open the terrace to let it all in. It's only ten minutes from Paris but it feels like a lifetime away. The chef is very skilful so you'll enjoy your meal too: pan-fried *escalopine* of *foie gras* with caramelized apples, crayfish roasted with sweet spices, *goujons* of zander, *andouillette*, hot chocolate soufflé, crêpe *millefeuille* with Grand marnier. In season they serve good game: wild boar, venison or partridge. Menus €26 and €29, and about €43 *à la carte*. Free coffee.

MILLY-LA-FORÊT   91490

🍴 🏠 🍽 HÔTEL-RESTAURANT AU COLOMBIER

26 av. de Gamay; it's in the main street.
☎ 01.64.98.80.74
Closed Fri evening, Friday April–Sept and Sat Oct–April and a week at Christmas. **Car park opposite**.

Central, simple and cheap. The rooms cost €28 with basin and €35 with shower or bath. The small, rustic dining room with sturdy beams adjoins the bar – it's where local workers come for lunch in the week and it's full of families on a Sunday. There's a huge array of appetizing crudités set out on the buffet and menus at €10 and €15. Their regional dishes are impressive, especially the *coq au vin* and the veal kidneys with cognac sauce. Lovely welcome. Free coffee and one breakfast per double room per night.

MONTFORT-L'AMAURY   78490

🍽 CHEZ NOUS

22 rue de Paris, (Centre).
☎ 01.34.86.01.62
Closed Sun evening and Mon except public holidays and during the All Saints' holidays.

The best place to eat in town. The dining

room is long and decorated in bourgeois style and warm colours. The cooking is good value but sophisticated – marinated raw salmon, duck *foie gras*, a selection of fried rish and *aiguillettes* of duck with soft fruit sauce. Monsieur cooks, while Madame organizes the service: it's a successul family affair which attracts gourmands in the know. There's a weekday *formule* at €14 and menus for €21 and €27.

🍽 L'HOSTELLERIE DES TOURS

pl. de l'Église.
☎ and ➡ 01.34.86.00.43
Closed Tues evening, Wed and mid-July to 10 Aug.

They hold the market on the pretty church square near to where this restaurant serves sound, traditional cuisine as it has for decades – in 2003 they'll celebrate their 35th anniversary. The regulars come here because they know the dishes are well prepared. Four menus from €19 to €28; they do *aioli* and *bourride* on a Friday, the herrings in cream are splendid and the lamb shank is cooked to perfection. Terrace in the summer.

MONTMORENCY   95160

🍽 LA PAIMPOLAISE

30 rue Galliéni; it's on the hill on the way to Champeaux, and signposted off to the left.
☎ 01.34.28.12.05
Closed Sun, Mon and Aug.

It's like being in Brittany but without the sea – Breton pictures, Breton furniture and Breton cuisine produced by a woman from Paimpol. Her *galettes* are the genuine article and there's a weekday menu for €7–9. Try the good *trégoroise* (*andouillette* and mustard), a fantastic *galette* with Maroilles cheese and the creamy flan with pears and whipped cream. Good dry cider, too. There's a quiet terrace.

PARIS   75000

SEE MAP OVERLEAF

1st arrondissement
🏠 HÔTEL DE LA VALLÉE*

84 rue Saint-Denis; M° Les Halles, Rambuteau or Châtelet.
☎ 01.42.36.46.99 ➡ 01.42.36.16.66
📧 hvallée@cybercable.fr

In the middle of Les Halles – you couldn't find a more central location if you tried. It's pretty decent and the price is reasonable, though the sex shops along the street may not be to everyone's taste. Rooms overlooking the street are double-glazed but if you want to be sure of a quiet night, ask for one with a view of the courtyard or on one of the higher floors. Doubles €38 with basin (shower along the corridor, though you have to pay) and €50 with shower/wc. It would be difficult to find cheaper accommodation in the area. They take credit cards but not cheques and rooms must be paid for in advance.

🎎 🏠 HÔTEL DU PALAIS*

2 quai de la Mégisserie; M° Châtelet.
☎ 01.42.36.98.25 📠 01.42.21.41.67

The rooms have a superb view of the Seine, the Conciergerie and Notre-Dame. The higher up you go the quieter it gets, but all windows are double-glazed. On the fifth floor all you can see is sky, but if you stand on a chair you can get a glimpse of the Châtelet; people come here because of the view and the location. Doubles with basin €42, €54 with shower/wc and €59 with bath/wc. Professional welcome. There's new carpet and the public areas and the rooms have been redecorated. American Express and Diners Club not accepted. 10% discount 10 Jan–28 Feb.

🏠 HÔTEL DE LILLE**

8 rue du Pélican; M° Palais-Royal, Louvre or Pyramides.
☎ 01.42.33.33.42

This hotel is in a quiet street with a notorious past. In the fourteenth century it was called "rue du Poil-au-Con" because of the brothels situated nearby, but the more respectable residents elected to rename it "rue du Pélican", which caused much less of a sensation on their address cards. It's small, with just fourteen rooms (romantic and slightly old-fashioned), but it's well looked after by a nice family. Numbers 1, 4, 7 and 10 are gloomy but quiet. Doubles €43 with basin, €49 with shower. They don't serve breakfast, but they do have a drinks machine. Ideal if you're on a budget.

🎎 🏠 HÔTEL AGORA**

7 rue de la Cossonnerie; M° Les Halles or Châtelet.
☎ 01.42.33.46.02 📠 01.42.33.80.99
📧 hotel.agora.f@wanado.fr
TV.

The street dates back to the twelfth century and owes its name to the "cossons" (second-hand dealers) who traded here. The hotel has been nicely renovated in modern colours, and has a small and tastefully laid-out reception. Rooms are pleasant and unfussy, and some are furnished with antiques. Doubles with shower or bath €87–101. It's a really great little hotel, and fairly quiet for such a lively neighbourhood. 10% discount except Sept–Oct.

🎎 🏠 HÔTEL LONDRES SAINT-HONORÉ**

13 rue Saint-Roch; M° Tuileries.
☎ 01.42.60.15.62 📠 01.42.60.16.00
📧 hotel.londres.st.honore@gofornet.com
TV.

Here's a delightful hotel with a warm family atmosphere in an area that is not exactly alluring. The rooms are spacious and comfortable with double glazing, satellite TV and mini-bar; some are air conditioned. Doubles €92 with shower or €100 with bath. There are a number of pay car parks round about the hotel. 10% discount for a minimum three-night stay.

🍴 LE RUBIS

10 fur du Marché-Saint-Honoré; M° Pyramides or Tuileries.
☎ 01.42.61.03.34
Closed Sun; public holidays; 3 weeks in Aug; a fortnight over Christmas and New Year.

Open until 10pm (4pm on Sat). The kind of typical Parisian bistro/wine bar that's on the verge of extinction – great little dishes and wines direct from producers in Beaujolais. You can have a sandwich at the bar with a glass of red. Wines are served by the glass at really decent prices. They do excellent horse *charcuterie* and dishes of the day from €8. In summer, they set up a couple of barrels on the pavement where you can prop yourself up and enjoy a cool glass of wine.

🎎 🍴 LA MOUSSON

9 rue Thérèse; M° Pyramides or Palais-Royal.
☎ 01.42.60.59.46
Closed Sun and Aug.

Service noon–2.30pm and 7.30–10.30pm. Lucile is the Chinese-Khmer chef here. Her specialities are *luk lak* (air-dried beef), sautéed beef with garlic, steamed fish *amok* (in a Cambodian sauce), minced pork with lemongrass and spare ribs. All the food is delicately perfumed and very tasty. Dishes of the day around €8, menus at €16 and €17. She also does an €11 weekday lunch *formule* with main course and dessert – chicken or beef curry, squid with basil or beef satay. Free coffee.

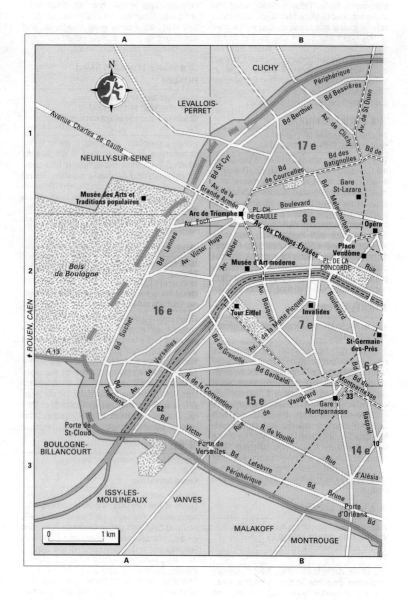

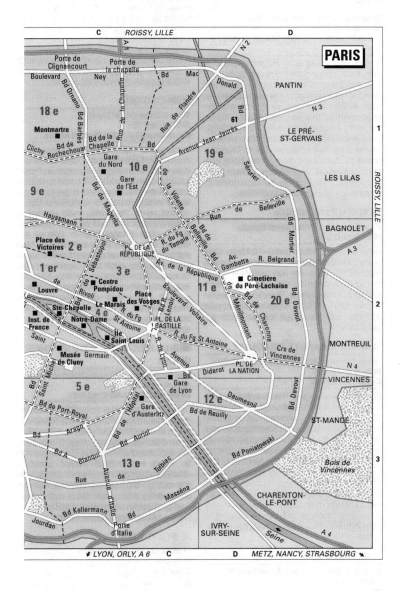

PARIS

⦿ RESTAURANT À LA CLOCHE DES HALLES

28 rue Coquillière; M° Louvre or Les Halles.
☎ 01.42.36.93.89
Closed Sat evening; Sun; public holidays; a fortnight in Aug.

Service until about 9pm. No fake beams or farm tools hanging on the walls, just a bell over the entrance which used to sound the opening and closing of the old market. As soon as this *cloche* rang, people could gather up anything that was left unsold – hence the word *clochard*, meaning tramp. Serge Lesage bottles the wine from his own vineyard and serves it in the restaurant. There are plates of *charcuterie*, ham on the bone and farm cheese. A very pleasant place with good prices. Reckon on €9 for a plate of something tasty and a glass of wine.

⦿ RESTAURANT FOUJITA

41 rue Saint-Roch; M° Pyramides or Tuileries.
☎ 01.42.61.42.93

Service noon–2.15pm and 9–10.15pm. One of the best sushi bars in Paris and prices are reasonable. They do very substantial set menus at lunchtime for €10 and €11, or €17 and €18 in the evening. There's *sushi*, *sashimi* (raw fish) and *natto*, a bowl of rice topped with raw fish. It's always full, so try to get there early.

⚹⦿ RESTAURANT LA FRESQUE

100 rue Rambuteau; M° Étienne-Marcel or Les Halles.
☎ 01.42.33.17.56
Closed Sun lunchtime.

Service until midnight. This is a friendly little restaurant in a shop that used to sell snails. The interior is lovely, with very old white tiles on the walls, brilliantly coloured frescoes and long wooden tables. It's very friendly, relaxed and cosmopolitan – you're jammed right up against your neighbour. The lunchtime *formule* offers starter, carefully prepared main course, a $^1/_4$-litre of wine and coffee for €11. Every day there are good starters, three or four traditional main course dishes, each with an original touch and a vegetarian dish (a rarity in this town). About €18 *à la carte*. Free coffee.

⚹⦿ PHARAMOND

24 rue de la Grande-Truanderie; M° Les Halles or étienne-Marcel.
☎ 01.42.36.33.93

This magnificent establishment one of the

loveliest restaurants in Paris and it was opened by an expat from Normandy in the nineteenth century. It offers very good value for money even if you eat *à la carte* – where the house speciality, their tripe dish, is always listed and black pudding with mash, fresh cod, apple tart and chocolate *fondant* are the house classics. The lunchtime *formule*, €12, is particularly apealing and you'll pay about €23 *à la carte*. Service with a smile.

⚹⦿ CA D'ORO

54 rue de l'Arbre-Sec; M° Louvre.
☎ 01.40.20.97.79
Closed Sun and 14–24 Aug. **Disabled access**.

Service until 11pm. This welcoming, unobtrusive little Italian restaurant sticks to what it does best. Go through a tiny room and down a narrow corridor and you'll come to another room where the decoration is gently evocative of Venice, the chef's home town. Before moving on to the pasta, treat yourself to grilled peppers with basil or some *bruschetta* – a slice of toast fried in olive oil and rubbed with garlic, basil and tomato. Main dishes include penne *disperata* with a sauce including garlic, anchovies, capers and olive oil; home-made ravioli; or, for two, an excellent risotto with ceps or seafood. Reckon on €24–31 with a little wine. The lunchtime *menu complet*, €14, doesn't include wine but it's very good nonetheless. Free house apéritif.

⦿ À LA TOUR DE MONTLHÉRY, CHEZ DENISE

5 rue des Prouvaires; M° Louvre, Châtelet or Les Halles.
☎ 01.42.36.21.82
Closed Sat; Sun; mid-July to mid-Aug.

Open 24 hours.This is one of the oldest all-night restaurants in Paris. It's kept the atmosphere of an old Halles bistro, but the prices have definitely gone up since those days. The welcome is off-hand but the place is lively. There are artificial leather benches, checked tablecloths and hams hanging from the ceiling. Big-hearted cooking includes *andouillette*, tripe, roast lamb with beans, beef *gros sel* and other such traditional fare. No set menu; dishes cost €14–20.

⚹⦿ JUVÉNILES

47 rue de Richelieu; M° Palais-Royal.
☎ 01.42.97.46.49
Closed Sun.

Service until 11pm. This is a very Parisian wine bar run by a Scot with a sense of humour. The place is frequented by groups who come to share a bottle of wine and tapas: squid rings, spicy chicken wings or slices of sausage. Inventive main dishes include pan-fried pollack fillet with spiced skin, sausage and mash and sautéed hare with fresh noodles. Menus €15 and €21, and à la carte you'll pay up to €34. They sell a good selection of wine and sherries by the glass, and offer an impressive array of malt whiskies. Best to book. Free house apéritif.

|●| RESTAURANT LESCURE

7 rue de Mondovi; M° Concorde.
☎ 01.42.60.18.91
Closed Sat; Sun; 3 weeks in Aug; a week at Christmas.

A very good restaurant which is often full with Members of the National Assembly who've popped across the river for lunch. They've been feeding people here since 1919 and it's passed down from grand-father to grandson. The cooking is bourgeois, and the prices are popular; you eat squashed up against your neighbour. On the €18 menu you get a starter, a generously portioned main dish, a choice of cheese or dessert, and a ½-bottle of wine. One of the best combinations to go for is hot pâté en croûte with stuffed poule-au-pot – yours for around €8. You'll pay around €23 à la carte. The dining room has a fake provincial décor but it's not too bad. In the evening, they sit people at the big communal table at the back of the room, creating a relaxed atmosphere. In summer people jostle for tables on the terrace.

|●| WILLI'S WINE BAR

13 rue des Petits-Champs; M° Pyramides, Bourse or Palais-Royal.
☎ 01.42.61.05.09
Closed Sun.

Service noon–2.30pm and 7–11pm, with various platters served at the bar 2.30–7pm. This is a chic wine bar which has been tastefully decorated. The wood gives it a cosy feel, there are pretty posters on the walls, the lighting's perfect and there are big round tables for large groups of friends. Willi's is a magnet for wine-lovers among British executives working in Paris, stock market traders and the ladies of the place des Victoires. They do a few elaborate dishes – roast cod with caramelized aubergine, roast salmon with bacon, pickled onions and sherry – as well as some some original salads including potato salad with melted Fourme cheese, bacon and grilled walnuts. The food's primary purpose, though, is to be a foil for the tremendous Côtes du Rhône, of which the

owner is a great connoisseur – though you'll also find Spanish, Californian and Italian wines listed too, many available by the glass. Excellent cheeses. Menus at €24 (lunch) and €30 (dinner).

⅔|●| L'ARDOISE

28 rue du Mont-Thabor; M° Tuileries.
☎ 01.42.96.28.18
Closed Mon, Sat lunchtime, a week in Jan, a week in May, and Aug.

Service noon–2.30pm and 7.15–11.30pm. Pierre Jay may be young, but he's been well-trained. His most interesting ideas have made their way onto the €27 menu: marinated fresh anchovies served as a *terrine*, duck *foie gras* carpaccio, scallops with caramelized Cassis liqueurand caramelized strawberries – and the list is chalked up afresh each day on the blackboard. The wines are really well-priced, too. Free *crème de cassis*.

⅔|●| RESTAURANT LA POULE AU POT

9 rue Vauvilliers; M° Louvre or Les Halles.
☎ 01.42.36.32.96
Closed Mon.

Service 7pm–5am. If you're around Les Halles at lunchtime and you suddenly feel peckish, head for this place – it's been around for more than a quarter of a century. The long room, decorated with posters and copper pots, has retro lighting, giving the place a certain intimacy, and a pleasant brasserie atmosphere. It's always busy. Service is courteous, which is not always the case in this part of town, and the menu lists solid traditional dishes such as *pot-au-feu*, *entrecôte* with marrowbone and, of course, the *poule-au-pot* from which the restaurant takes its name. Set menu €27 or about €34 à la carte. Best to book. Free *digestif*.

|●| MACÉO

15 rue des petits-Champs; M° Pyramides, Bourse or Palais Royal.
☎ 01.42.97.53.85
Closed Sat lunchtime and Sun.

Service noon–11pm. This restaurant opened in 1880 and has had a devoted following ever since. Now it's owned by Mark Williamson who also owns Willi's wine bar next door, and he changed its name from Le Mercure Gallant to Macéo, after Macéo Parker, one of James Brown's Famous Flames. The décor has a modern British flavour, and the menu is a delight just to read: smoked haddock with spinach and hazelnuts, joint of yellow pollack with a small dish of clams and asparagus, shepherd's pie with morel mushrooms, risotto with vanilla and a small orange salad, and pineapple with sweet spices. Menu €34, or €38 for the vegetarian one. The wine list is very impressive and the *fino* they serve at the bar while you're waiting for your table is excellent.

2nd arrondissement

⚥ ☗ HÔTEL SAINTE-MARIE*

6 rue de la Ville-Neuve; M° Bonne-Nouvelle.
☎ 01.42.33.21.61 ➡ 01.42.33.29.24
e sainte.marie.hotel@wanadoo.fr
TV. Car park.

This is a pretty little hotel in a quiet street, very close to the shopping area of the Grands Boulevards. It has about twenty rooms, all well-equipped. Some have beamed ceilings, but if you're tall and have a room in the attic mind your head because the ceilings slope. They're quite pleasant and even quite bright. Doubles with basin €38, with shower/wc €52–54. Breakfast €4, but it's free for children. 10% discount and free coffee.

☗ TIQUETONNE HÔTEL*

6 rue Tiquetonne; M° Étienne-Marcel or Réaumur-Sébastopol.
☎ 01.42.36.94.58 ➡ 01.42.36.02.94
Closed Aug and one week Christmas–New Year.

The pedestrianized streets leading to this one-star hotel are calm and beautiful. The rooms, which vary in size, are very well maintained, though the décor is faintly old-fashioned and the bathrooms pretty ordinary. The ones on the first two floors have double glazing and are quieter. Doubles with shower/wc €41. Breakfast €4.

☗ HÔTEL BONNE NOUVELLE**

17 rue Beauregard; M° Bonne Nouvelle or Strasbourg-Saint-Denis.
☎ 01.45.08.42.42 ➡ 01.40.26.05.81
e info@hotel-bonne-nouvelle.com
TV.

Check out the lovely screen with a *trompe-l'oeil* picture of a moonlit apartment block. Doubles with basin €46, €56 with shower or shower/wc and €61–69 with bath; they're equipped with TV, direct phone and hairdrier. Some are small and number 25 is rather dark – and the skylight in the bathroom is operated with a rather perplexing system of counterweights. There's a suite which is ideal for four; it has a splendid view of the Pompidou Centre, the Montparnasse tower and the rooftops of Paris. Really warm welcome.

☗ HÔTEL VIVIENNE**

40 rue Vivienne; M° Rue-Montmartre, Richelieu-Drouot or Bourse.
☎ 01.42.33.13.26 ➡ 01.40.41.98.19.
e paris@hotel-vivienne.com
TV.

This hotel is in a neighbourhood with lots of tiny streets and lanes filled with shops specializing in coins and medals. It's very close to the *Hard Rock Café*, the Musée Grévin, the wax museum and the Théâtre des Variétés. Warm and informal welcome. The rooms have been refurbished and are bright, clean, comfortable and quiet. Number 14 is particularly attractive, and there's a communicating door through to number 15, which makes it good for families. On the fifth and sixth floors you get a lovely view of Paris, and a few rooms have balconies. Doubles €61 with shower, €73 with shower/wc or €76 with bath.

⚥ ☗ HÔTEL FRANCE D'ANTIN***

22 rue d'Antin; M° 4-Septembre or Opéra; RER Auber.
☎ 01.47.42.19.12 ➡ 01.47.42.11.55
e carlotta.hotels@wanadoo.fr
TV. Car park.

This pleasant three-star hotel is just 100m from the Opéra Garnier and the Louvre. It is classy yet congenial, and has been completely overhauled and redecorated. Many of the public rooms have exposed stonework and vaulted ceilings. The thirty pretty rooms all have mini-bar and satellite TV, and they're air-conditioned to give you respite from the Paris summer heat. Double with shower/wc €134 and €150 with bath. Free breakfast per person – usually €6.

▐●▌ RESTAURANT CHEZ DANIE

5 rue de Louvois; M° Bourse or Quatre-Septembre.
☎ 01.42.96.64.05
Closed evenings, Sat and Sun.

This tiny restaurant, right next to the Bibliothèque Nationale, is an absolute delight. It serves good traditional dishes that change daily – *bœuf ficelle*, rabbit *en gibelotte*, beef with carrots or tarragon – and all the desserts are home-made. Great value in an area full of expensive, mediocre sandwich shops: the €8 *formule* offers a main course with a choice of starter or dessert.

|●| LE TAMBOUR

41 rue Montmartre; M° Châtelet, Les Halles or Sentier,
☎ 01.42.33.06.90

Open 24 hours. The owner, André Cam-
boulas, will immediately make you feel welcome; having built up a group of authentic
Parisian bistros similar to this one, he's had
plenty of practice. The dining room is
decorated with urban detritus –
cobblestones, drain covers and road signs.
The cooking is very French. There is a lunch
formule at €8; expect to pay €15 for lunch or
€23 for dinner *à la carte*.

|●| L'ESCALIER

80 rue Montmartre; M° Bourse.
☎ 01.42.36.95.49
Closed Sat lunch and Sun.

A tiny restaurant with a modern but warm
décor. It attracts a 30-something, intellec-
tual, hyperactive crowd including journalists
from the *Figaro* newspaper – they're always
stressed out, but this is where they come to
relax over lunch with a few mates or co-
workers. There's a chattering, laughing
atmosphere. The cuisine is cutting-edge
and incredibly fine – unusual for the price.
The dishes on the lunch *formule* (€14)
change every day: *croustillant* of goat's
cheese with pears on a salad with balsamic vinegar, rolled lamb stuffed with basil.
You can choose between a pasta course or
a dessert. Otherwise it's *à la carte* only; a
meal costs around €23. Excellent welcome.

⅍|●| LE PETIT VENDÔME

8 rue des Capucines; M° Opéra or Madeleine.
☎ 01.42.61.05.88
Closed Sat evening and Sun.

Service 7am to 8pm. This is an Auvergne
establishment with a display of local cheeses
set out on the bar counter, and Auvergne
sausage is used for their filling sandwiches.
There's a scramble for places at lunchtime,
when a dish of the day costs €11 or a complete meal around €17 *à la carte*. Reliable,
substantial offerings: pork stewed in Saint-
Pourçain wine, grilled pig's trotters, tripe and
the like. Efficient, attractive service. Free
house apéritif.

⅍|●| LA GRILLE MONTORGUEIL

50 rue Montorgueil; M° Les Halles or Étienne-Marcel.
☎ 01.42.33.21.21
Closed Sat and Sun from 4pm; Aug.

Closes at midnight in the week, 5pm on Sat

and Sun. This establishment, which has
been around a good hundred years, has
been attractively renovated – as has the
pedestrianized street it stands on. The menu
is full of traditional Parisian bistro fare: hot
goat's cheese amandine, duck thigh confit,
andouillette, grills and fish dishes and
chocolate *fondant*. Straightforward, honest
cooking with no frills. There are no set
menus but a meal will probably set you back
about €21; dishes range from €9 to €15.
There's a terrace in summer. Free house
apéritif.

|●| LE GRAND COLBERT

4 rue Vivienne; M°Bourse or Palais-Royal.
☎ 01.42.86.87.88
Closed 24 Dec.

Service daily noon–1am. This unusual
brasserie acts practically like the canteen of
the Bibliothèque Nationale. The whole place
has been freshly redecorated – the friezes,
copper bar and lamps have been restored to
their 1830s glory. Typical brasserie fare: fresh
cod with olive oil, calf's liver with small
onions, grilled slice of lamb with garlic, steak
tartare and an unexpected curried lamb.
Menus start at €24.

3rd arrondissement
⅍ 🏠 HÔTEL DU VIEUX SAULE***

6 rue de Picardie; M° République or Temple.
☎ 01.42.72.01.14 ➡ 01.40.27.88.21
✉ reserv@hotelvieuxsaule.com
TV. Garden. Pay car park.

The window boxes and tiny flower garden
brighten up the exterior of this lovely hotel;
inside, the "high-tech" décor is beginning to
date. Modern, comfortable rooms go for
€90–105 with shower/wc or €105–121 with
bath; prices increase during trade fairs. All
rooms are air-conditioned and equipped with
hairdrier, trouser press, iron, telephone, safe
and cable TV (thirty channels), and there's
free use of the sauna. Pleasant staff. Buffet
breakfast, €8, is served in a sixteenth-century vaulted cellar. One free breakfast per room
per day.

⅍|●| HÔTEL DU MONT-BLANC

17 rue Debelleyme; M° Filles-du-Calvaire.
☎ 01.42.72.23.68
Closed evenings, Sun and Aug.

Entering here is like walking back in time –
and perplexing too, seeing as this hotel is
actually a restaurant. The tables have waxed
cotton table cloths and there's a Formica

bar. The place has been going for over a hundred hears and Madame Morvan has run it since 1959. A few years ago she handed over the bar to her son and took up her saucepans; she now does the cooking, producing reassuringly old-style lunches for a regular cliental of local artists, artisans and office workers: plates of *crudités*, egg mayonnaise, steak and chips, *pot-au-feu*, cod *à la Provençale*. The prices are pretty prehistoric, too – dishes of the day €8–11 with starters and puddings between €3 and €4.

|●| LA MULE DU PAPE

8 rue du Pas-de-la-Mule. M°Bastille or Chemin-Vert.
☎ 01.42.74.55.80
Closed Sun July–Aug; 3 weeks in Aug.

This place looks more like a middle-class sitting room than a restaurant – prissy and probably bad news for your wallet. But it's not like that at all; the setting is bright and comfortable, and they welcome you with a simple kindness that immediately puts you at your ease. The menu offers dishes to satisfy anyone, whether they're on a zero-calorie diet or looking to feed a robust appetite: *œufs de la Mule* will do for the slimmers and *assiettes de la Mule* for the hungry; the *plats de la Mule* fit somewhere in between. Add to that one of their good desserts. Everything's *à la carte* and a meal will cost €9–23.

|●| AU VIEUX MOLIÈRE

12 passage Molière; M°Rambuteaul.
☎ 01.42.78.37.87
Closed Mon

This is an attractive gourmet restaurant. It's located in an untouched part of Paris in the Beaubourg area, and is surrounded by galleries and bookshops. The atmosphere is equally charming inside: the setting is attractive and there are portraits and photographs on the wall. The menu offers appetizing, bourgeois dishes: veal kidneys, cod, rabbit in Chardonnay sauce, fillet of veal in pastry and good sauces. Fine ingredients and well-judged cooking. Weekday *formule* for €15 or around €35 *à la carte*. Wines by the jug from around €8.

|●| CHEZ OMAR

47 rue de Bretagne; M° Temole.
☎ 01.42.72.36.26.
Closed Sun lunchtime.

Service until around 11pm. Omar has been here for a good twenty years, and he serves an eclectic mix of locals and visitors from all over the world in a restaurant where Paris meets North Africa. The ceilings are high, the mirrors have bevelled edges, there's a superb bar counter and the tables are snugly spaced. Waiting staff are smiling and attentive. The *couscous* is excellent (€9–15), as are the pastries, but their meat dishes are particularly tender and worthy of note. Expect to pay €23 *à la carte*.

|●| CHEZ NÉNESSE

17 rue de Saintonge; M°Filles-du-Calvairel.
☎ 01.42.78.46.49
Closed Sat; Sun; public holidays; Christmas–New Year; Aug.

Service noon–2pm and 8–10.30pm. The allure of old Paris is everywhere in this typical, traditional place with tiles on the floor and a lovely bar in Formica. Good general atmosphere and a disarmingly smiling welcome. Good, classic well-prepared French cooking with substantial portions to make up for the lack of creative flair. This is a fine example of a successful family business – at lunchtime there's hardly any elbow-room, it's so packed. There are always two or three appetising dishes of the day for around €12 with starters and desserts for €3. In the evening, the cooking is more elaborate but still in the same spirit. A meal *à la carte* will cost around €15.

4th arrondissement
≜ GRAND HÔTEL DU LOIRET*

8 rue des Mauvais-Garçons; M° Hôtel-de-Ville.
☎ 01.48.87.77.00 ➡ 01.48.04.96.56
✉ hotelloiret@aol.com

The whole building has been refurbished and the rooms are redecorated every two years – wooden staircase, marbled walls. Some are available with handbasin only for €35; those from the first to the fourth floors are in warm colours and have en-suite shower/wc (€47) or bath (€63). There is one room sleeping four on the seventh floor which has a panoramic view over the Panthéon and the Sacré Coeur – but there's no lift.

≜ GRAND HÔTEL JEANNE D'ARC**

3 rue de Jarente; M° Saint-Paul, Chemin-Vert or Bastille; RER Châtelet.
☎ 01.48.87.62.11 ➡ 01.48.87.37.31
TV.

You couldn't find a better location than this quiet neighbourhood near place Sainte-Catherine. The hotel is classy and well-run, and it's been stylishly decorated – there's an enormous mirror in the foyer made by a local artist. All of the rooms have been refurbished and have shower/wc or bath, phone and cable TV. Doubles are €67 and rooms that sleep four €78. An extra bed will cost you €11; cots are provided on request. Breakfast €6. It's essential to book.

🌾 🏠 HÔTEL DU 7E ART**

20 rue Saint-Paul; M° Saint-Paul or Sully-Morland.
☎ 01.44.54.85.00 ➡ 01.42.77.69.10
📧 hotel7art@wanadoo.fr
TV.

A fairly friendly hotel which is well-managed and original. The staircase is black, the walls white, and the rooms are decorated with photomontages and posters of films from the '40s, '50s and '60s. Rooms cost €70–120 with shower or bath and 25-channel TV. The top prices are for suites in the attic, which have sloping ceilings. Breakfast €7. There's a bar on the ground floor, and an unusual display case with plaster figures of Ray Charles, Mickey Mouse, Donald Duck and Laurel and Hardy. Free house apéritif.

🏠 HÔTEL DE LA PLACE DES VOSGES**

12 rue de Birague; M° Saint-Paul or Bastille.
☎ 01.42.72.60.46 ➡ 01.42.72.02.64
📧 hotel.place.des.vosges@gofornet.com
TV.

This place is in a grand street leading from place des Vosges to the Pavillon du Roi. The entrance is delightful. There are sixteen rooms which, though they're not spacious and have pretty ordinary furniture, are quiet, comfortable and impeccably clean. Doubles with shower/wc €76 with shower/wc or €101 with bath.

🏠 HÔTEL DE NICE**

42 bis rue de Rivoli; M° Hôtel-de-Ville.
☎ 01.42.78.55.29 ➡ 01.42.78.36.07
TV.

A very elegant and refined hotel with a small entrance and a multilingual welcome at reception. The owners used to run an antique business – they've kept a large number of attractive pieces to furnish the hotel. Breakfast is served in the television lounge, which has soft-coloured furnishings, eighteenth-century engravings and a portrait of an elegant woman surrounded by her pets. The soundproofed rooms are decorated with sumptuous wallpaper and have good bathrooms. Doubles with bath or shower cost

€92, which isn't bad value for money; in summer the rooms overlooking place du Bourg-Tibourg are particularly good.

🍴 AU JAMBON DE BAYONNE

6 rue de la Tacherie; M° Hôtel-de-Ville. It's just round the corner from the shops on the rue de Rivoli.
☎ 01.42.78.45.45
Closed Sat; Sun; a fortnight in Aug.

Not to beat about the bush, this establishment offers the best value for money in the *arrondissement*. You sit down on benches polished by years of use and tuck in to generous portions of regional cuisine. Each day they present a different classic dish – steak with *Marchand de vin* sauce, steak *tartare* and so on. These cost between €8 and €10; the cheapest menu is a modest €9 one served at lunch and up to 8.30pm, and there's another for €11. Attentive service, convivial atmosphere: you can't fail to like it.

🍴 LE PETIT PICARD

42 rue Saint-Croix-de-la-Bretonnerie; M° Rambuteau or Hôtel-de-ville.
☎ 01.42.78.54.03
Closed Sat and Sun lunchtimes; Mon; 14 July–15 Aug.

It's full to bursting at lunchtime with a mixed clientele, though in the evenings it's predominantly male. The €10 *formule* offers a starter, main course, dessert and a ¼-litre of red – without doubt one of the best deals in the area. To be fair, the food isn't going to get a Michelin star but it's good and generously served. The evening *formule*s are not much more complicated, though the prices step up to €14 and 20 – salad with snails, salmon fillet with sorrel and *flamiche* with leeks.

🍴 RESTAURANT LE TEMPS DES CERISES

31 rue de la Cerisaie; M° Bastille or Sully-Morland.
☎ 01.42.72.08.63
Closed evenings (but you can get a drink until 8pm), Sat, Sun, public holidays and Aug.

This picturesque low-ceilinged eighteenth-century building used to house the office of the Celestine convent's bursar but it's been a bistro since 1900. The décor looks immediately familiar – zinc-topped bar where you can have a drink, marble-topped tables, leather benches – and the day's menu is written up on a blackboard. These, in addition to the photos of old Paris, the cheerful atmosphere and the good-natured customers, are reminders of what a Paris bistro used to be like. You'll find cooking to match: egg mayonnaise, grilled *andouillette* with mashed potato, *pot-au-feu*, lasagne. There's a three-course menu at €10, a set menu for €11 and *à la carte* dishes from €7. It's essential to arrive before noon to get a table. There's an eclectic selection of wines. Credit cards not accepted.

⦿I RESTAURANT L'ENOTECA

25 rue Charles-V; M° Saint-Paul.
☎ 01.42.78.91.44 ➡ 01.44.59.31/72

Open daily till 2am. This wine bar, which specializes in Italian wines, is a must. The décor is typical of the Marais, with exposed beams and old stonework. It gets really full and appeals to a very Parisian clientele – it's not unusual to spot the odd TV star. The famous, the not-so-famous and the downright obscure jostle to sample some of the 450 different Italian wines – the ones available by the glass change every week. You can travel north to taste the whites of Trentino and Sicily or giving the reds of Piedmont and Basilicata a go. Accompany them with a few *antipasti misti*, *crostini* with Parma ham and mozzarella, fresh pasta with beef stew or chicken livers and tomatoes. Reckon on paying €8 for a dish at lunchtime, or there's a €11 lunch *formule* of starter plus pasta and a glass of wine.

⦿I RESTAURANT LES FOUS DE L'ÎLE

33 rue des Deux-Ponts; M° Pont-Marie.
☎ 01.43.25.76.67
Closed Sat lunchtime, Sun evening, Mon and 12–31 Aug.

Service noon–11pm. This is primarily a restaurant, but it's also a tearoom. There's a nice €12 set menu at lunchtime, while in the evening you'll pay around €23 *à la carte*; on Sundays there are three €19 *formules* for brunch. The chef's specialities are salmon *sauce ravigote* and calf's liver with Balsamic vinegar. They hold live music evenings – jazz, blues or accordion – every second Tuesday and Wednesday from 10pm.

⦿I VINS DES PYRÉNÉES

25 rue Beautreillis; M° Bastille or Saint-Paul.
☎ 01.42.72.64.94
Closed Sun lunchtime and 10–20 Aug.

A friendly cellar-bar-restaurant with a crowd of regulars – though new faces are warmly welcomed. The place is a nice mix of formal city and easy-going provincial town and it's reassuring that a place like this has managed to survive. The recipe is simple: select excellent quality meat and fish, grill it and serve with good side dishes and a decent glass of

wine in a wood-panelled dining room with engraved mirrors and moleskin chairs. Finish by issuing a reasonable bill – lunch menu for €12 or around €24 for a full meal with wine on top.

⦿I LE CAFÉ DE LA POSTE

13 rue Castex; M° Bastille.
☎ 01.42.72.95.35
Closed Sat and Sun.

This café is opposite the post office, a brick building from the 1930s. It's a stylish place, with mosaic walls, wide benches, a huge mirror and a splendid wooden bar. There's always a pasta dish on the blackboard and a few meat dishes as well – beef Strogonoff or *massalé* of lamb. Expect to pay around €18 for a meal; dishes cost €8–11.

⦿I BRASSERIE DE l'ÎLE-SAINT-LOUIS

55 quai de Bourbon; M° Pont-Marie.
☎ 01.43.54.02.59
Closed Wed; Thurs lunchtime; Aug.

Service noon–midnight. Nothing's changed at this place for ages – the waiters have worked here for 25 years on average, and they're still enthusiastic and good-humoured. A stuffed stork lords it over the bar, and there's an old clock from the Vosges nearby. Rugby fans gather here in the evening if there's a match on. Star turns include *choucroute*, *cassoulet*, ham hock with lentils, fresh skate wings and Welsh rarebit. If you choose a decent Alsace wine to accompany your meal you'll pay about €23.

⦿I RESTAURANT BARACANE

38 rue des Tournelles; M° Bastille.
☎ 01.42.71.43.33
Closed Sat lunchtime and Sun.

Service noon–2.15pm and 7pm–midnight. Cooking from Gascony predominates at this pocket-sized bistro, with dishes like homemade *cassoulet* with duck or goose *confit*, good roast lamb from Lozère, grilled duck breast and a *croustillant* of apples in aged plum brandy. Menus from €23; the *menu-carte* at €36 includes apéritif, three courses, a ½-bottle from the wine list and coffee. Faultless cooking.

⦿I RESTAURANT À L'ESCALE

1 rue des Deux-Ponts; M° Pont-Marie.
2 quai d'Orléans.
☎ 01.43.54.94.23
Closed evenings; Mon.

Lunch noon–3pm. This pleasant restaurant

gets the sun and overlooks the Seine. It's a perfect place to restore your spirits after you've trailed round Notre-Dame or the Île Saint-Louis. There's no set menu, so opt for the dish of the day at €11–12, lovingly prepared by Mme Tardieu: the *pot-au-feu*, roast veal, *coq au vin* and grills are all good. The wines are selected by Monsieur Tardieu who is quite a connoisseur. Expect to pay about €24 for a full meal.

|●| BEL CANTO

72 quai de l'Hôtel-de-Ville; M° Hôtel-de-Ville.
☎ 01.42.78.30.18
Closed Sun, Mon and Aug.

Service evenings only from 8.30pm. Between the Parma ham and the *tiramisù*, the glasses vibrate as Rodolfo and Mimì, the resident vocalists, serenade you while you dine – you come here almost as much for the show as for the offerings on the plate. The dishes are straight out of Italy – *carpaccio, osso bucco, panna cotta* – and the wine is Italian, too. The menu costs about €37.

5th arrondissement
🎄 ☎ HÔTEL MARIGNAN

13 rue du Sommerard; M° Maubert-Mutualité.
☎ 01.43.54.63.81

This has been a landing point for travellers for more than three decades. There are lots of common facilities: a dining room for picnics, a microwave, fridges, washing and drying machines, an iron and ironing board. Doubles with basin/wc €50, with shower/wc €75. 10% discount on the room rate 1 Oct–31 Jan.

☎ HÔTEL ESMERALDA

4 rue Saint-Julien-le-Pauvre; M° Saint-Michel or Muabert-Mutualité.
☎ 01.43.54.19.20 ➡ 01.40.51.00.68

This small seventeenth-century hotel is a listed monument with a listed staircase. The nineteen rooms are fussily decorated with lots of attention to detail but you should probably ignore the furniture, which is a bit dated. The whole place is really due a thorough redecoration, but because of its location, it's always full – some rooms have a glancing view of Notre-Dame or Square Viviani. Doubles €53 with shower or €73–79 with bath, though the basins are old and not always clean. Breakfast €6.

🎄 ☎ FAMILIA HÔTEL

11 rue des Écoles; M° Jussieu, Maubert-Mutualité or

Cardinal-Lemoine.
☎ 01.43.54.55.27 ➡ 01.43.29.61.77
TV.

A comfortable hotel run by the welcoming Gaucheron family, who'll go out of their way to help you. Doubles €73 with shower/wc and €81–99 with bath. The rooms on the fifth or sixth floors have views of Notre-Dame and the Paris rooftops; the bathrooms are being modernized one by one. The artist Gérald Pritchard has personalized some of the rooms by painting depictions of Notre-Dame, Île de la Cité and Pont-Neuf on the walls. 10% discount 15 Jan–27 Feb and Aug.

☎ HÔTEL DE LA SORBONNE**

6 rue Victor-Cousin; M° Saint-Michel, Cluny-Sorbonne or RER Luxembourg.
☎ 01.43.54.58.08 ➡ 01.40.51.05.18
TV.

You go through a gateway to find this small pleasant hotel, which is in the student quarter and right in the centre of things. All rooms have a phone, TV and hairdrier; doubles with shower/wc or bath are €79–84, which is very reasonable considering that the place is well-run and the reception pleasant. Some rooms could do with improved soundproofing, though. The highest prices are for the largest rooms with marble bathrooms.

☎ HÔTEL DES GRANDES ÉCOLES***

75 rue du Cardinal-Lemoine; M° Cardinal-Lemoine or Monge.
☎ 01.43.26.79.23 ➡ 01.43.25.28.15
✉ hotel.grandes.ecoles@wanadoo.fr
Disabled access. Garden. Pay car park.

The hotel is in a private lane just round the corner from place de la Contrescarpe. It's a house of some charm and character, with a small paved courtyard and a leafy garden. The owner and her daughter have long welcomed tourists from around the world and, since this is a favourite with Americans in Paris, it's worth booking well in advance. There are 51 rooms on either side of the lane, and they're carefully maintained and tastefully arranged. They have shower/wc or bath and cost €90–115. In fine weather you can have tea in the garden – even if you're not staying here.

|●| RESTAURANT TIBETAIN TASHI-DELEK

4 rue des Fossés-Saint-Jacques; RER Luxembourg.
☎ 01.43.26.55.55
Closed Sun and 10–26 Aug.

Service lunchtimes and evenings until 11pm.

This was the first Tibetan restaurant in Paris, run by people who fled their country after the Chinese invasion. The décor is restrained and the menu consists of regional dishes from U-Tsang, Kham and Amdo – it's a great place to familiarize yourself with cuisine from this part of the world. Try *momok* (beef ravioli), *chabale* (stuffed pancakes) or *baktsa markou* (pasta dumplings with melted butter and goat's cheese) and there's a selection of vegetarian dishes too. If you're feeling brave, drink your tea in the traditional way – with salted butter. Menus €8–10 or about €12 *à la carte*.

⦿ LA RÔTISSERIE GALANDE

57 rue Galande; M° Saint-Michel or Maubert.
☎ 01.46.34.70.96
Closed Mon and Aug.

Last orders 11pm. The rue Galande follows a route laid down in the thirteenth century and even in those days there was a roasting house barbecuing geese and suckling pig to calm the raging hunger of pilgrims and journeymen. The tradition has been stoutly maintained in this place where the menu lists mouthwatering dishes; you can even watch the gently-turning hunks of golden meat basting in their juices before they make their way onto your plate. There's a lunch *formule express* for €8 and menus €11–16. Platters of barbecued meats cost from €11 depending on how many types of meat you choose. Desserts from €5.

⦿ FOYER DU VIETNAM

80 rue Monge; M° Monge.
☎ 01.45.35.32.54
Closed Sun, public holidays and Aug.

Service until 10pm. This restaurant is very plain indeed. It is brightened up only by a poster of Ho Chi Minh and a TV – supposedly for the regulars' amusement but actually of more interest to the waiter. The genuine Vietnamese cooking makes no concessions to Western taste and remains resolutely authentic. They do an excellent pork soup (which, despite its small serving, is very substantial) and delicious steamed ravioli. The other dishes – fish simmered in a spicy sauce, pork kebabs and Hanoi soup – are of the same calibre. There are a few interesting specialities at the weekend, such as rice soup with tripe, duck soup and grilled prawns with vermicelli. The cheapest set menu costs €9.

⦿ RESTAURANT LE VOLCAN

10 rue Thouin; M° Monge or Cardinal-Lemoine.

☎ 01.46.33.38.33
Closed Mon.

Service noon–2.30pm and 6.30–11pm. This reliable restaurant has been around for years and has kept its natural character. Menus at €9, €14 and €22, or €23 *à la carte* – wine is included only at lunchtime. The cooking is French with a few nods in the direction of Greece, as you'll notice in their tasty *moussaka*.

⦿ RESTAURANT HAN LIM

6 rue Blainville; M° Monge.
☎ 01.43.54.62.74
Closed Mon and Aug.

This part of town is full of pleasant surprises. Right in the heart of Paris and surrounded by kebab joints, this excellent Korean restaurant is one of them: it does a lunchtime menu for €11, a barbecue menu for €14 – both of which are ridiculously cheap given the exotic cooking. Very good grills and delectable garlic chicken. €18–20 for a complete meal *à la carte*.

🍴⦿ RESTAURANT PERRAUDIN

157 rue Saint-Jacques; RER Luxembourg, it's next to the Luxembourg Gardens.
☎ 01.46.33.15.75
Closed Sat and Mon lunchtimes; Sun; the last fortnight in Aug.

Service until 10.15pm. Just around the corner from the Panthéon and the Luxembourg Gardens, here's a little bistro which is a favourite with local publishers and students from the Sorbonne. It's unpretentious and not remotely showy, with a lot of traditional dishes on the menu. Try onion tart, *quiche lorraine*, leg of lamb with potatoes *dauphinoise*, *flamiche* with Maroilles cheese, duck *confit*, beef *bourguignon* or rack of lamb with herbs. The €12 lunch menu gives a choice of three starters, two main courses and three desserts; there's a gourmet menu at €30; or it's about €23 *à la carte*. In summer you can eat in a small interior courtyard. Free apéritif.

⦿ RESTAURANT LE PORT DU SALUT

163 [bis] rue Saint-Jacques; M° or RER Luxembourg.
☎ 01.46.33.63.21
Closed Sun evening, Mon and 1–21 Aug.

Service noon–2.30pm and 7–10.30pm. If *Perraudin* is full, this is the next best thing. Lovely setting with heavy beams, a tiny staircase, a piano and paintings of pastoral scenes. The famous French singers who have passed through are too numerous to list. There's a daily €12 menu, and an extremely good *formule* of main course plus starter or dessert: you get a small casserole of mussels or warm goat's cheese salad, followed by either veal stew or roast salmon with *beurre blanc*. All in all, a very pleasant restaurant with an intimate atmosphere, cloth napkins and attentive service. There's a large cellar for groups.

🎎 |●| LE REMINET

3 rue des Grands-Degrés; M° Monge.
☎ 01.44.07.04.24
Closed Mon; Tues; 1–15 Jan; 10–25 Aug.

Service until 11pm in the week, later at the weekend. A restaurant which is situated in this quiet and charming *arrondissement* yet close to the hustling superficiality of Saint-Séverin. The cuisine is refined and the Norman chef prepares many of his region's dishes with certainty and simplicity: mussles, cockles, plaice – it'll be heaven for lovers of fresh fish and seafood. There's also rabbit and salt-flat lamb on offer, and the desserts are sublime. Weekday menu €12 and up to €17 on Wed and Thurs evening; *à la carte* expect to pay around €31. The dining room has been thoughtfully decorated in understated fashion. Diligent and natural service. Best to book.

🎎 |●| RESTAURANT PEMA THANG

13 rue de la Montagne-Sainte-Geneviève; M° Maubert-Mutualité.
☎ 01.43.54.34.34 📧 pemathang@aol.com
Closed Sun; Mon lunchtime; Aug.

Service noon–2.30pm and 7–10.30pm. The Latin Quarter is still a magnet for the various ethnic groups in the French capital. Take this restaurant, for example, which feels rather like an inn on the high plateaux of Tibet. The cooking, which involves a lot of steaming, is full of delicate, subtle flavours and deserves to be more widely known. While the dishes are pure Tibetan, the flavours might remind you of India, China or Japan – and the cuisine is just as good as any of those. The lunchtime crowd consists of students from the Sorbonne and white-collar workers; they come here to savour *sha momok* (rather like *dim sum*), *thouk* (home-made noodles in clear soup) and *pemathan* (meat balls in a sweet-and-sour sauce with sautéed vegetables). Weekday lunch menus for €13–17 with a vegetarian option. In the evening a meal can cost less than €17. Free coffee.

🎎 |●| RESTAURANT LE BUISSON ARDENT

25 rue de Jussieu; M° Jussieu.

☎ 01.43.54.93.02
Closed Sat; Sun; Aug; a week at Christmas.

This is a very French place, the kind of restaurant you'd miss if ever it closed. The décor is as comforting as the cooking, but while they use a lot of good regional produce, the approach is modern and the results tasty and full of colour. They do a lunch menu at €14 and an excellent dinner version at €26; dishes change frequently in response to the fresh market produce available. Free apéritif.

|●| RESTAURANT L'ATLAS

10–12 bd. Saint-Germain; M° Maubert-Mutualité.
☎ 01.46.33.86.98
Closed Mon.

If you've been nosing round the Institut du Monde Arabe nearby, you can prolong the experience by eating here. The food is prepared by a man whom many believe to be one of Arabic cuisine's best ambassadors in Paris. Benjamin El Jaziri, who has worked with some of the really big names, has remained faithful to the cooking of his native Morocco but goes easier on the fat and sugar. Try his incredibly light *couscous* served with meat and vegetables (it's beyond reproach), or one of sixteen superb *tajines*. As well as these classics, you can feast on grilled *gambas*, large prawns with paprika, lamb with mallow plant leaves, baked bream Moroccan style or, in season, partridge with mint and lemon. Warm welcome and attentive service. One menu at €15, or €23 *à la carte*.

|●| RESTAURANT LE LANGUEDOC

64 bd. de Port-Royal; M° Gobelins; RER Port-Royal.
☎ 01.47.07.24.47
Closed Tues, Wed, 20 July–20 Aug and 23 Dec–7 Jan.

Service noon–2pm and 7–10pm (last orders). They specialize in dishes of the southwest here, and the cooking is excellent. The service is reminiscent of the kind you'd get in a country restaurant. If you order herring, for example, they'll bring the entire dish to your table so you can help yourself. The duck *confit* with Sarlade potatoes and truffles is the star turn, but the meat dishes are well worth a try and the Rouergue wine washes it all down superbly. The white and red Gaillac from the proprietor's own vineyard aren't bad either. Set menu €18.

|●| RESTAURANT SAVANNAH CAFÉ

27 rue Descartes; M° Cardinal-Lemoine.
☎ 01.43.29.45.77

Closed Sun; Mon lunchtime; 17 Dec–3 Jan.

If you absolutely must have dinner in the Contrescarpe-Mouffetard area, try this place. Richard, the owner, is Lebanese, and he'll welcome you with a politeness that it would be nice to come across more often in French restaurants. He offers *tabbouleh* and *hummus*, naturally, but also dishes such as *ceviche*, pumpkin with nutmeg, chicken with toasted almonds, aubergines with basil, milk-fed lamb with pistachio and pine nuts, fruit and vegetable curry with cardamom – the list goes on. Try the *crème de lait* for dessert. Set menu €22. If you'd rather go *à la carte*, reckon on paying €23–27.

◉ RESTAURANT LE BALZAR

49 rue des Écoles; M° Cluny-la-Sorbonne or Odéon.
☎ 01.43.54.13.67 ➡ 01.44.07.14.91
Closed Aug.

Service noon–midnight. This fairly plush brasserie has been taken over by the *Flo* group. It's a pleasant place for supper after the theatre or the cinema, with artificial leather benches, large mirrors and waiters in white aprons. There's a long glassed-in terrace where in winter you can people-watch in the warmth. The house specialities are rabbit *terrine* at €7, skate in melted butter at €18 and *choucroute* at €13: good food of the classic variety. A meal *à la carte* will set you back about €26.

6th arrondissement
🌿 🏠 DELHY'S HÔTEL*

22 rue de l'Hirondelle; M° Saint-Michel.
☎ 01.43.26.58.25 ➡ 01.43.26.51.06
TV.

This small typical Parisian hotel is in one of the capital's least-known streets – which means that you'll find peace and quiet. It's part of a sixteenth-century town house, with exposed stonework and ancient beams; François I gave to his favourite, Anne de Pisseleu, the Duchess of Étampes. The rooms are newly and attractively furnished; €49 with basin, €63 with shower. That's pretty standard for hotels in the neighbourhood but this is definitely the most central. 10% discount after the third night.

🌿 🏠 HÔTEL DES ACADÉMIES*

15 rue de la Grande-Chaumière; M° Vavin.
☎ 01.43.26.66.44 ➡ 01.43.26.03.72

Small family hotel in a quiet street. It has been going since the 1920s, but the atmosphere is more reminiscent of the '50s. Doubles €50 with shower or €57–61 with shower/wc. One free breakfast per room per night.

🏠 HÔTEL DE NESLE

7 rue de Nesle; M° Odéon.
☎ 01.43.54.62.41 ➡ 01.43.54.31.88
Garden.

This hotel, located in a quiet street, is a throwback to the great hippy era. Anglo-Saxon and American accents mingle with Madame's North African one. She and her son shower affection on her guests and reign over their little kingdom with infinite good humour. "Relaxed" rather than "organized" best describes things here – but that means that people really do enjoy themselves. There's a small interior garden where you can have a quiet read, and when it's not open there's a pretty terrace overlooking the garden. The twenty rooms are simple, clean, well-maintained and individually decorated. Doubles overlooking the street range from €69 with basin or shower to €99 with shower/wc and a garden view; there are wcs on each floor. Each room has its own personality: number 2 has old paintings, slightly faded wallpaper and antique furniture, while number 9 has been decorated in Egyptian style. The shower is rather awe-inspiring and there's even a little *hammam*, or steam bath, in number 4. They don't take reservations, so to be sure of a room turn up before 10am.

🌿 🏠 HÔTEL DES CANETTES**

17 rue des Canettes; M° Saint-Germain-des-Prés or Mabillon.
☎ 01.46.33.12.67 ➡ 01.44.07.07.37
TV.

This establishment, situated in a very busy street full of pubs and chain stores, looks old, but inside the décor is colourful and hi-tech. The rooms overlooking the street have more light but no double glazing; those facing the courtyard are quieter but darker. Doubles with shower/wc €75, €90 with bath/wc. If you book – and it's advisable – you need to guarantee the room with a credit card at least three days before arrival. 10% discount.

🏠 GRAND HÔTEL DES BALCONS**

3 rue Casimir-Delavigne; M° Odéon; RER Luxembourg.
☎ 01.46.34.78.50 ➡ 01.46.34.06.27
ℯ resa@www.balcons.com
TV.

You'd be hard-pressed to find another place in the Latin Quarter, just 100m from the Odéon theatre, offering such value for money: doubles €83–130 with shower/wc or bath. There's an all-you-can-eat buffet breakfast for €9 – and if it's your birthday, it's free! The reception and public areas of the hotel are Art Deco style, though sadly the rooms are merely functional. Everyone gets a warm welcome.

♠ HÔTEL DU LYS**

23 rue Serpente; M° Saint-Michel or Odéon.
☎ 01.43.26.97.57 ➡ 01.44.07.34.90
TV.

A pleasant hotel on a quiet street with a nice family atmosphere – you'll get a great welcome. Rooms all have cable TV, individual safes and a hairdrier; those at the front are the best, others look onto the courtyard and are brightly decorated. Doubles with shower/wc or bath €88 including breakfast.

|●| RESTAURANT NOUVELLE COURONNE THAÏ

17 rue Jules-Chaplain; M° Vavin.
☎ 01.43.54.29.88
Closed Sun and Mon lunchtimes.

Service until 11pm. An excellent Thai restaurant in a secluded street. Someone has taken a lot of trouble over the setting, with its soft colours, subdued tones and well-spaced tables. And similar care is lavished on the cuisine: fish soup delicately flavoured with coconut milk, casserole of seafood, lacquered chicken with lemongrass, spicy duck sautéed with bamboo shoots and pork spare ribs are among the wonderful things listed on the menu, which also includes lots of Chinese dishes and some steamed specialities. The wines are priced very reasonably and they serve Thai and Chinese beer. The service is efficient, the welcome charming and the food delicious. Set menus €7 and €8 at lunchtime; €11 and €15 in the evening. All in all, it's remarkable value.

|●| RESTAURANT AUX TROIS CANETTES

18 rue des Canettes; M° Saint-Germain-des-Prés or Mabillon.
☎ 01.43.26.29.62
Closed Sat lunchtime; Sun; Aug.

Service noon–2.30pm and 7.30–11pm. Antonio is a Neapolitan who's run this place since the 1960s, and the restaurant has probably changed very little in all that time. It's a historic house which, in the nineteenth century, had a famous reading room frequented by Balzac. The ocean-and-volcano décor on the ground floor evokes Antonio's homeland, and the food does much the same: try the sardines *Antonio*, the onions *à la sicilienne* or the aubergines in olive oil. There's a good selection of pasta: *linguini* with clams, penne *à la sicilienne*, lamb Toscana. Lunch *formule* €9 and menus from €19 or around €27 *à la carte*. In June there's a poetry festival in place Saint-Sulpice, and the restaurant awards an international literary prize.

🍴 |●| RESTAURANT L'ASSIGNAT

7 rue Guénégaud; M° Odéon.
☎ 01.43.54.87.68
Closed Sun; July.

Service at the bar 7.30am–9.30pm; in the restaurant noon–3.30pm. Who would have thought you'd find a little neighbourhood restaurant in this crowded narrow street? It's popular with local art dealers, people who work at the Mint and art students – many regulars grab what they want, write down what they've had and settle up at the end of the month. You'll enjoy good, simple food in a lively atmosphere – the owner's mother, who's been doing the cooking for a very long time, clearly revels in her job. Set lunch menu €11 or around €12 *à la carte*. Free coffee.

🍴 |●| LE PETIT VATEL

5 rue Lobineau; M° Mabillon.
☎ 01.43.54.28.49
Closed Sun, Mon and 15 Jan–15 Feb.

Service noon–3pm and 7–11pm. After a period in the doldrums, this place has been revamped, re-opened and is firmly back on track. The €11 *formule* gets you main course plus starter or dessert and coffee; if you opt for individual dishes, a meal will cost about €15. Try the home-made *terrine* or, if you feel like something more elaborate, kidneys in white wine, sautéed lamb or beef *miroton*. The wines complement the cooking perfectly; they do quite a few by the glass. Free apéritif.

🍴 |●| BOUILLON RACINE

3 rue Racine; M° Cluny-Sorbonne or Odéon.
☎ 01.44.32.15.60

Service 11.45am–2.45pm and 7pm–midnight. Just when the Latin Quarter seemed set to be overrun by fast-food joints and clothes shops, this restaurant came on the scene – or, to be more accurate, made a comeback, since it first appeared at the beginning of the twentieth century as the *Bouillon Camille Chartier*. After lots of ups and downs it ended up as a civil service canteen, but luckily the building was listed so the original interior remained – albeit in a rather dilapidated state. Today this magnificent Art Nouveau establishment has been restored to its former elegance and taken on a new lease of life. It's all there: bevelled mirrors, stained glass, marble mosaics and gold-leaf lettering. Beer plays a large part in the cooking, and there are lots of varieties to drink, including famous Trappist names like Rochefort, Chimay and Orval. Set "bouillon" menus €11–15 at lunchtime (drink included), and others up to €29. Dishes include prawn *croquettes* and *waterzooi* of chicken or fish; brown sugar tarts and spiced buns are served at teatime (3–6pm); and you can get a *café liégeois* at any time of the day. Free house apéritif.

⅍ |●| MARMIET ET CASOLETTE

157 bd du Montparnasse; M° Vavin or Raspail; RER Port Royal.
☎ 01.43.26.26.53
Closed Sat; Sun; 9–17 Feb; Aug.

This is the bistro-baby brother of the grown-up gourmet restaurant *O à la Bouche*. There's a family resemblance, too, in the efficiency of both establishments and the individuality of their outlook. Come here for decent food: fish *tartare* with avocado, rabbit in mustard, warm chocolate dessert with vanilla ice-cream. Dishes of the day are chalked up on the slate and they serve some wines by the glass. *Formule* €13 with main course and a choice of starter or dessert and a menu for €17. Honest cuisine with fair prices for the area – but if you have a big appetite you may not be totally satisfied.

⅍ |●| RESTAURANT INDONESIA

12 rue de Vaugirard; M° Odéon; RER Luxembourg.
☎ 01.43.39.43.72
Closed Sat lunchtime.

Last orders 10.30pm, 11pm on Fri and Sat. Best to book for dinner. This is the only Indonesian restaurant in Paris to be set up as a workers' co-operative. The food is good and service comes with a smile. The rice tables, or *rijsttafel*, consist of a series of dishes from Java, Sumatra, Bali and Celebes; *rendang* is meat in coconut milk and *balado ikan* is fish in spicy tomato sauce. Great curries and mutton satay. Weekday lunch menu €15, then others at €17–23 or around €19 *à la carte*. Free apéritif.

⅍ |●| LA RÔTISSERIE D'EN FACE

2 rue Christine; M° Odéon.

☎ 01.43.26.40.98 **e** rotisface@aol.fr
Closed Sat lunchtime; Sun.

Service noon–2.30pm and 7–11pm, 11.30pm Fri and Sat. Top chef Jacques Cagna, whose flagship restaurant is just across the way, has every reason to be pleased. In just a few years he's made this enterprise one of the Left Bank's institutions. Try his barbecued Barbary duck, the guineafowl with aubergines and onions, the lamb moussaka, the roast free-range chicken or the duck breast with honey and spices to understand why. There are lots of things cooked on the *rotisserie*, all served with old-fashioned mashed potatoes. The food is definitely the high-point, though there have been a few hiccups – probably because of the large staff turnover. The wine list isn't very tempting and the noise from other tables is irritating. Lunch menu €15, others up to €35. Free house apéritif.

|●| L'ÉPI DUPIN

11 rue Dupin; M° Sèvres-Babylone.
☎ 01.42.22.64.56 **➡** 01.42.22.30.42
Closed Sat and Sun.

Service until 10.30pm. François Pasteau, who trained under Kérever and Faugeron, is a happy man, as you can tell from his beaming smile – his restaurant is full at lunchtime and his customers leave nothing on their plates but the pattern. You'll also get pretty good value for money: there's a lunchtime *formule* for €18 and a *menu-carte* for €28 without wine. The latter reflects what's been available at the Rungis market that day. You get a daily choice of six starters, eight main courses and six desserts; these might include rabbit turnovers with aubergines, scallops with lemons and pears and warm apples in flaky pastry with a mascarpone sorbet. Sheer delight from start to finish. Pleasant and efficient service.

|●| RESTAURANT AUX CHARPENTIERS

10 rue Mabillon; M° Mabillon or Saint-Germain-des-Prés.
☎ 01.43.26.30.05 **➡** 01.46.33.07.98
Closed Christmas Eve, Christmas Day and 1 May.

Service noon–3pm and 7–11.30pm. This restaurant used to be the headquarters of the guild of master carpenters – scale models, souvenirs and old photos fill the place, and you can find out more from the guild museum next door. They serve good traditional cuisine, with great specials: beef *papillote* with marrowbone, rack of lamb and cod aïoli, beef *à la mode* (simmered in wine, vegetables and herbs) on Tuesday, salt pork and lentils on Wednesday, *pot-au-feu* and vegetables on Thursday and so on. By comparison, the starters are expensive. They do a *formule* at lunchtime for €18, which includes a $\frac{1}{4}$-litre of wine. The equivalent costs €24 in the evening, or expect to pay €27–33 for a meal *à la carte*.

🕌 |●| RESTAURANT LE PROCOPE

13 rue de l'Ancienne-Comédie; M° Odéon.
☎ 01.40.46.79.00 ➡ 01.40.46.79.09
🄴 de.procope@blanc.net

Service 11am–1am. This is the oldest café in Paris. In 1686, an Italian called Francesco Procopio dei Cotelli came to the city and opened a café serving a then-unknown beverage called coffee. His establishment, close to the Comédie Française, soon gathered a clientele of writers and artists. In the eighteenth century it was a meeting place for Enlightenment philosophers – the idea for Diderot's famous *Encyclopaedia* was spawned here during a conversation between him and d'Alembert. During the French Revolution, Danton, Marat and Camille Desmoulins met here, and it was also a haunt of Musset, Sand, Balzac, Huysmans, Verlaine and many others. It's still a haunt for intellectuals and, incredibly, its prices are still reasonable. The cooking is unabashedly French with meat and fish dishes swathed in sauce, platters of seafood, *coq au vin*, home-made sorbets and ice-creams – you haven't been to Paris if you haven't eaten at *Procope*. Set menus €21 or about €27 *à la carte*. Reasonably priced wine list. Free house apéritif.

🕌 |●| RESTAURANT LE MACHON D'HENRI

8 rue Guisarde; M° Saint-Germain-des-Prés.
☎ 01.43.29.08.70

Service until 11.30pm. This is a good wine bar with stone walls and hefty beams. They serve a rich selection of carefully prepared classic dishes: slow-roast lamb cooked for seven hours with *gratin dauphinois*, courgette *terrine*, calf's liver with onion *compote*. €20 or thereabouts for a full meal. Free house apéritif.

🕌 |●| L'O À LA BOUCHE

124 bd. du Montparnasse; M° Vavin; RER Port-Royal.
☎ 01.56.54.01.55 ➡ 01.43.21.07.87
Closed. Sun; Mon; 1–7 Jan; 10–18 April; 3–25 Aug.

Service noon–2.30pm and 7.30–midnight.

Franck Paquier is a dynamic young master chef with genuine talent, and he's put together a brilliantly constructed three-course *menu-carte* at €30. You can mix and match with some of the dishes of the day chalked up on the board, around €40 *à la carte*. There's also a two-course menu (main course and starter or dessert) at €21. All the ingredients are fresh and the dishes freshly cooked. His creations include duck *foie gras* pan-fried with soft fruit, lobster ravioli with *Beaumes de Venise* sauce, broad beans and celery, roast rack of lamb with thyme and crispy vegetable fritters, fillet of John Dory with pickled aubergines, Grand Marnier soufflé and vanilla ice-cream, orange and grapefruit *sabayon* with a pepper sorbet – irresistible. The wines are affordable but service is somewhat slack.

|●| LA MÉDITERRANÉE

2 place de l'Odéon; M° Odéon or RER Luxembourg.
☎ 01.43.26.02.30

Time was when the stars of the silver screen and other notables would congregate here. Everyone had their own table – from Orson Welles to Aragon, Picasso to Chagal, Man Ray to Jean-Louis Barrault. It has been delicately renovated to reveal its former glory. *À la carte* there's a good number of fish dishes and a handful of starters, main courses and desserts: red tuna *tartare*, sautéed calamari with red peppers, house *bouillabaisse*, fine *crêpes* with orange. There's a *formule* of main course with a choice of starter or dessert for €24, a menu for €29 and *à la carte* expect to pay around €40.

🕌 |●| LA BAUTA

129 bd. du Montparnasse; M° Vavin.
☎ 01.43.22.52.35
Closed Sat lunchtime, Sun, and Aug.

Service noon to 2pm and 7.30–10.45pm. The décor is inspired by Venice and there's a superb collection of masks on the walls. The beautiful people who eat here are on to a good thing: everything is remarkably fresh and cooked with finesse. The pasta will satisfy everyone, and the chef cooks it perfectly *al dente* with all manner of sauces and accompaniments like *langoustine*, rosemary, cinnamon, squid ink and clams. You'll pay around €53 for a meal *à la carte*. Free *digestif*.

7th arrondissement
🕌 🏨 HÔTEL-EIFFEL RIVE GAUCHE**

6 rue du Gros-Caillou; M° École-Militaire.

☎ 01.45.51.24.56 ➡ 01.45.51.11.77
TV.

This hotel, in a peaceful street, quietly exudes a discreet charm. You reach the four floors via an elegant staircase encircling a pretty patio that leads onto a small interior courtyard with a sliding glass roof. Subtle shades of old rose and ochre predominate, almost as if you were in Andalucia. From the top floor you will catch a glimpse of the Eiffel Tower, while others look onto the patio. A double with shower costs €63, or €76 with shower/wc or bath. Buffet breakfast €7. Friendly welcome; it's best to book. 10% discount except over New Year, Easter and Whitsun.

♠ HÔTEL DU PALAIS BOURBON**

49 rue de Bourgogne; M° Varenne, Assemblée-Nationale or Invalides.
☎ 01.44.11.30.70 ➡ 01.45.55.20.21
e htlbourbon@aol.com
TV.

Pleasant reception with lofty beamed ceilings. Some of the rooms are vast, one of the benefits of being in an old building; all have double glazing, mini-bar, TV, renovated bathrooms and sockets for connnecting a fax or modem. Doubles with shower/wc or bath from €64. Good prices for the district.

🍴 ♠ GRAND HÔTEL LÉVÊQUE*

29 rue Cler; M° École-Militaire or Latour-Maubourg.
☎ 01.47.05.49.15 ➡ 01.45.50.49.36
e info@hotelleveque.com
TV.

The Eiffel Tower is very close by but you may find the picturesque street market in rue Cler even more appealing – rooms over the street get snapped up first. This is an authentic part of the district and the hotel with its fifty renovated rooms is reasonably priced. Doubles with shower/wc €69. The décor doesn't leave a lasting impression but the rooms are clean and they have safes and hairdriers. It's a well-known place, so you may have to book. And on a good day, you'll get a jovial reception. Free breakfast (usually €7).

🍴 ♠ HÔTEL LE PAVILLON**

54 rue Saint-Dominique; M° Invalides.
☎ 01.45.51.42.87 ➡ 01.45.51.32.79
TV.

This place started out as a convent, and despite becoming a hotel it has retained a provincial charm. The pretty façade really stands out and there's an internal patio.

There are just eighteen rooms, all of them soberly decorated and comfortable; the Mother Superior's old chamber is in great demand. Double rooms with shower/wc €70, €88 with bath. Try numbers 10 and 14, which have two double beds and a sizeable bathroom. But avoid the ones in the basement – they're deeply depressing. Breakfast €6. 10% discount Feb.

♠ HÔTEL MUGUET**

11 rue Chevert; M° École Militaire or Latour-Maubourg.
☎ 01.47.05.05.93 ➡ 01.45.50.25.37
e muguet@wanadoo.fr
TV. Disabled access.

This hotel has been refurbished from top to bottom, and it stands out in this quiet little road, away from the traffic noise. The rooms are air-conditioned; doubles with shower €89. Three rooms on the sixth floor have a view of the Eiffel Tower; others overlook Les Invalides.

♠ HÔTEL D'ORSAY**

93 rue de Lille; M° Solférino or Assemblée Nationale, RER Musée d'Orsay.
☎ 01.47.05.85.54 ➡ 01.45.55.51.16
e hotel.orsay@wanadoo.fr

A quiet, comfortable hotel in the buildings of the old *Hotel Solférino* and the *Résidence d'Orsay*. Attractive reception. Double rooms €95 with shower/wc or €127 with en-suite bath; that's about what you'd expect to pay in this district. Probably wise to book.

🍴 ♠ HÔTEL BERSOLY'S SAINT-GERMAIN***

28 rue de Lille; M° Rue-du-Bac.
☎ 01.42.60.73.79 ➡ 01.49.27.05.55
e bersolys@wanadoo.fr
Closed Aug. **Disabled access. TV. Pay car park**.

Gorgeous hotel in a proud mansion built in the eighteenth century, in the middle of this historic part of Paris near the antique shops. The rooms may be small, but they're absolutely lovely and perfectly clean. Each bears the name of a painter, and there's a reproduction of one of the artist's pictures on the wall; "Gauguin" and "Turner" are particularly attractive. The hushed atmosphere, period furniture and exposed beams create a nostalgic ambience. Rooms overlooking the courtyard with shower/wc cost €98–107 or €113–122 with bath. The telephones have Internet points. There's a small bar near the reception area. Breakfast, normally €7 per person, is free 1 Nov–28 Feb.

☎ |●| THOUMIEUX***

79 rue Saint-Dominique; M° Latour-Maubourg.
☎ 01.47.05.49.75 ➡ 01.47.05.36.96
TV. Disabled access.

Service noon–3.30pm and 6.30–midnight;
on Sunday it's open noon–midnight. This
large, attractive brasserie, founded in 1923,
was taken over in 1976 by Françoise
Thoumieux and Jean Bassalert. If you're
looking for a lively place with good food at
reasonable prices, this is the place. The
home-made *cassoulet* with duck *confit*, the
cep omelette and the duck breast with blackcurrants are all delicious. Menus start at €15
and there's one with specialities from the
Corrèze at €27: grilled duck breast salad,
maize flour dumplings, *cabécou* (goat's
cheese) and a $1/4$-litre of Corrèze wine. This
is also a hotel; all double rooms have bathrooms and cost €114.

|●| CHEZ GERMAINE

30 rue Pierre-Leroux; M° Duroc and Vanneau.
☎ 01.42.73.28.34
Closed Sat evening; Sun; Aug.

A simple, clean little dining room with a
slightly provincial feel and a truly warm welcome. Try the excellent creamed salt cod
and the ox tripe. They also have a lot of classic dishes, such as sautéed rabbit *chasseur*,
coq au vin, haddock fillet salad and pork
colombo; particularly excellent is their
clafoutis, an egg custard with cherries or
pear. A carafe of unassuming Bordeaux
costs €3. There's a menu for €11 or around
€15 for a full meal.

🎄 |●| RESTAURANT LE ROUPEYRAC

62 rue de Bellechasse; M° Solférino.
☎ 01.45.51.33.42
Closed Sat evening; Sun; Aug.

Service noon–2.45pm and 7–9.30pm. This is
the kind of neighbourhood restaurant you
used to find everywhere in Paris; there's none
of the flim-flam or the fancy décor that you'll
find in lesser (but commoner) places. Monsieur and Mme Fau have been running this
place for over a quarter of a century, and it's
named after the hamlet near Durenque in the
Aveyron where they hail from. Wonderful
country home cooking, with three or four
fresh dishes every day – duck with orange,
haricot de mouton (leg of lamb with haricot
beans), oxtail in a *pot-au-feu*. A weekday
lunch menu at €12, others at €18–24. Efficient, attentive service. Free apéritif.

|●| RESTAURANT LE BABYLONE

13 rue de Babylone; M° Sèvres-Babylone.
☎ 01.45.48.72.13
Closed evenings; Sun; some public holidays; Aug.

The large dining room is delightfully old-fashioned; the pictures on the walls have
yellowed with age and the imitation leather
benches are comfortable. The cooking is
good. The €17 lunch menu includes three
courses and wine. Dishes of the day cost
around €9; you'll pay about €18 for a full
meal. They don't accept credit cards.

|●| LE POCH'TRON

25 rue de Bellechasse; M° Solférino; RER Musée-
d'Orsay.
☎ 01.45.51.27.11
Closed Sat and Sun.

The restaurant has an outlandish name but
the welcoming *patronne* has a popular touch
and her husband prepares the dishes with
great care. You'll find calf's head with *sauce
gribiche*, *andouillette de Troyes*, *baeckoffe*
and all the traditional fare you'd expect in a
good bistro. You'll spend about €27 *à la
carte*. They won the Bouteille d'Or "best
bistro" award in 1996, so you can rely on the
wine list – it has particularly good bottles
from Alsace.

🎄 |●| LES OLIVADES

41 ave de Ségur. M° École-Militaire.
☎ 01.47.83.70.09
Closed Sun; first 3 weeks in Aug.

Walk through the door and you could almost
believe you were in Provence. Flora, the chef,
is from Avignon and her cooking is full of
southern flavour. The €21 menu leads with a
croustillant of red mullet and also lists sardines with balsamic vinegar, fresh crab mayonnaise, quails preserved in olive oil withrus-
set apples and scallops pan-fried in their
shells. Desserts are of the order of *millefeuille*
scented with orange blossom. There are
other menus up to €38. The wine list is com-
piled by Raphaël, Flora's husband. He knows
what he's about – if he offers advice, take it.
Free house apéritif.

|●| AU BON ACCUEIL

14 rue de Monttessuy; M° Alma-Marceau.
☎ 01.47.05.16.11
Closed Sat; Sun; 24 Dec–2 Jan.

The name evokes a quiet restaurant somewhere out in the country – which might raise
a smile when you're in the classiest part of
the 7th *arrondissement*, but it's actually

rather appropriate. The staff are delightful and the cuisine is equally good. Jacques Lacipière is as professional a restaurateur as he is an epicurean and he treks to the food market at Rungis practically every day to choose seafood, poultry and vegetables. The menus reflects what he has selected and the dishes change constantly. In the evening, seated at your table on the terrace, you have a superb view of the Eiffel Tower. Lunch menu €22 or €24 for a meal *à la carte*.

⚘ |●| LA MAISON DE COSIMA

20 rue de l'Exposition; M° École-Militaire.
☎ 01.45.51.37.71
Closed lunchtimes; Sun; 3 weeks in Aug.

Open evenings only until 10.30pm. This street is full of restaurants but here Jean-Michel Reverdy and his wife Hélène create a really lovely atmosphere with cooking to match: *pâté en croute* with duck and *foie gras*, *terrine* of veal with onion jelly, ox cheek *bourguignon*, a splendid pumpkin and cinnamon pie. All dishes are subtly flavoured and seasoned. Three-course menu at €26. They have a small private dining room you can book if the occasion demands. Free coffee.

|●| RESTAURANT LE BASILIC

2 rue Casimir-Périer; M° Solferino or Invalides.
☎ 01.44.18.94.64

Service noon–2.30pm and 7.30–10.30pm. Everyone in the 7th *arrondissement* comes to this comfortable brasserie with its welcoming terrace facing the Sainte-Clothilde church. Try the roast lamb in salt, the sole *meunière* or the other conservative classics. A complete meal comes to €27 including wine. It's a bit chintzy, but a relaxing place to come after a walk around the area admiring the splendid architecture.

8th arrondissement
⌂ HÔTEL WILSON*

10 rue de Stockholm; M° Saint-Lazare.
☎ 01.45.22.10.85

A reasonably priced one-star hotel which is conveniently near St Lazare station. It's simple, functional, clean and well-run. There's no lift, so you have to climb all the way up to the fifth floor to get to the rooms with a fantastic view over the city. Doubles with basin cost €34, €43 with shower/wc and €43 with bath. Some rooms sleep three. Breakfast is included, which makes it even better value.

⌂ HÔTEL DES CHAMPS-ÉLYSÉES**

2 rue d'Artois; M° Saint-Philippe-du-Roule or Franklin-Roosevelt.
☎ 01.43.59.11.42 ➠ 01.45.61.00.61
TV.

A clean, comfortable two-star hotel away from the racket of the Champs Élysées. The 36 spacious rooms are soundproofed and air-conditioned, and they're each decorated differently. Doubles with shower/wc €79, twins with bath €93; they include TV, minibar, room safe, hairdrier and direct dial telephone. Breakfast, €7, is served in a pretty vaulted room. Consider booking, as it's often full. They offer a dry cleaning service.

|●| RESTAURANT CHEZ LÉON

5 rue de l'Isly; M° Saint-Lazare.
☎ 01.43.87.42.77
Closed Sun and Aug.

Service noon–3pm and 7–10pm. There's a "Relais Routier" sign outside – a real poser because this place, right in the centre of town, is near a station, not a main road. But it is the real thing: waitresses in white aprons, transparent plastic table covers to protect the tablecloths, hole-in-the-ground loos and huge 1950s fridges in black and canary yellow. On the food front there are main courses like beef with tomato sauce and noodles and roast beef with mashed potato and cauliflower. The wine comes in $1/4$-litre jugs. Expect to pay €12–15. In case you're still puzzled, the only "Routier" in Paris earned its sign because the Federation of Road Hauliers is across the street.

⚘ |●| LE BOUCLÉON

10 rue de Constantinople; M° Europe.
☎ 01.42.93.73.33
Closed Sat and Sun.

Dinner served until 11pm. An easy-going local restaurant named after one of the gates of Constantinople. The décor is simple but colourful – green checked tablecloths – and they only have room for thirty, though they put a few extra tables on the pavement in summer. All the dishes chalked up on the blackboard are good: salmon *tartare*, duck *foie gras*, calf's liver pan-fried with juniper berries, *entrecôte béarnaise*, duck *pot-au-feu* with celery. All are thoughtfully prepared and well-judged. Among the desserts, go for the *financier au chocolat* served hot with pistachio cream. Around €18 for a meal. The owner serves wines by the glass and you can buy a bottle to take away. When it's hot they don't expect men to wear ties or jackets. Free coffee.

♣ |●| TANJIA

23 rue de Ponthieu; M° Franklin-D-Roosevelt.
☎ 01.42.93.73.33
Closed 1–25 Aug.

One of Paris's fashionable restaurants, put together by the "Les Bains" team. The heavy carved wooden doors swing back to reveal an astonishing décor that could be somewhere in Marrakesh. Wooden chests, dimmed lanterns, melting cushions and magical candlelit in the evening create a symphony of purple perfumed by rose petal incense. The central room has a mezzanine for dining and there are veiled alcoves for more intimate dinners; the basement bar is beautiful. It's generally full of people who come to be seen. The remarkable cuisine is truly interesting with a collection of Moroccan specialities: pigeon with almonds, generously-flavoured *couscous*, bream with coriander and filo pastry stuffed with *foie gras*. All dishes are beautifully presented and swiftly served. French or Moroccan lunch for €19 but *à la carte*, the price of a meal starts at €46 – so it's not cheap. Late on in the night, there are oriental dancers. The staff are exceedingly friendly and efficient.

|●| LA FERME DES MATHURINS

17 rue Vignon; M° Madeleine.
☎ 01.42.66.46.39
Closed Sun; public holidays; Aug.

Georges Simenon, the creator of the fictional French detective Maigret used to be a regular here in the 1930s – as the plaque tells you. The cooking is straight out of the Lyonnais area; *anduiollette* with mustard, wine sausage, ham with cream sauce, salmon fillet with sorrel, succulent chunks of Charolais steak and pears in wine. Set menus €26 or €35 or around €38 *à la carte*. They have a good selection of Burgundies – try the Irancy. The boss runs the kitchen and his wife is on duty in the dining room. Easy going welcome; most clients are, like Simenon, long-term regulars.

|●| SPOON, FOOD AND WINE

14 rue de Marignan; M° Franklin-Roosevelt.
☎ 01.40.76.34.44
Closed Sat and Sun.

Service at lunchtime and until 11pm in the evening. The minimalist, sober interior creates a peaceful atmosphere; nothing is allowed to interrupt your studious enjoyment of the flavours produced by Alain Ducasse, one of the high priests of modern cooking. It's new-concept world food: a fusion of flavours, spices and fragrances without a hint of fat. The "vegetable garden" is divine, as is the roast lamb. As well as a wine list, there's a list of waters by the bottle. A meal will set you back about €46. It's very fashionable: you have to book at least a fortnight in advance and the well-heeled regulars smile thinly to each other across the dining room.

9th arrondissement
♠ HÔTEL DES ARTS**

7 cité Bergère; M° Rue-Montmartre or Cadet.
☎ 01.42.46.73.30 ➡ 01.48.00.94.42
TV. **Disabled access**. **Car park**.

A two-star hotel with a pretty, pastel-pink façade in a lovely passageway. There's a confusing array of hotels to choose from around here – this one is the cheapest. It's far enough from the noise to be peaceful, and the rooms are clean and freshly refurbished. The ones on the fifth floor are tiny but cheaper at €58; other doubles with shower/wc cost €61 or €64 with bath. The stairway is decorated with old showbills – it is the *Hôtel des Arts*, after all. Why not engage the handsome grey parrot in the lobby in conversation? Breakfast €5.

♣ ♠ HÔTEL CHOPIN**

46 passage Jouffroy; M° Grands Boulevards or Bourse.
☎ 01.47.70.58.10 ➡ 01.42.47.00.70
TV.

This jewel of a nineteenth-century town house is in a picturesque setting at the end of a narrow street – a quiet backwater round the corner from the Grands Boulevards. The handsome façade dates from 1850 and features elegant old woodwork. The rooms are quite pretty, their walls covered in Japanese cloth, and the vista over the rooftops is reminiscent of an Impressionist painting – particularly if you're lucky enough to have a view of the setting sun. See if you can get a room on the fourth floor, as these are the brightest. It's best to avoid the ones looking onto the courtyard – all you'll see from these is a massive wall. Doubles with shower/wc or bath €69–79. Free breakfast.

♠ HÔTEL DES CROISÉS**

63 rue Saint-Lazare; M° Trinité.
☎ 01.48.74.78.24 ➡ 01.49.95.04.43
@ hotel-des-croises@wanadoo.fr
TV.

This place attracts a host of regulars, so you

really ought to book. It's in a marvellous location and looks wonderful: the superb reception area has old wood panelling and you just sink into the carpet. The wood-panelled lift with wrought iron gates takes you up to rooms which are sheer magic. They're absolutely huge and each has an individual style with period furniture and marble fireplaces; some have Art Deco wood panelling. Number 25 has an alcove which doubles as a little sitting room and some of the bathrooms are enormous. Doubles with shower/wc or bath €75–90. Breakfast costs €6, and they'll bring it to you in your room. A superb two-star hotel at reasonable prices.

🎄 🏨 HÔTEL DE LA TOUR D'AUVERGNE***

10 rue de la Tour d'Auvergne; M° Cadet.
☎ 01.48.78.61.60 ➡ 01.49.95.99.00
TV.

A pretty three-star in a quiet street near the Sacré-Cœur. The spacious, elegantly decorated rooms have beds with canopies, bath or shower, and hairdriers. There's a bar and 24-hour room service; doubles with bath €145. The fifth floor is exclusively for non-smokers. Breakfast, €10, is appetizing, with lots to choose from – yoghurt, cornflakes, *pain au chocolat* and *pain aux raisins*. 10% discount on the room rate.

❚●❚ LE BISTROT DU CURÉ

21 bd. Clichy; M° Pigalle.
☎ 01.48.74.65.84
Closed Sun; public holidays; Aug.

This eating place, located in an old church, is something of a haven in a street full of sex shops. There's a stone statue of the Virgin Mary in front of the counter and even the waiters minister to your needs with great kindness. They offer several menus (€7–16) listing simple dishes such as *crudités*, soup, egg or prawn mayonnaise, roast beef with *purée* of peppers, turkey *blanquette* with white sauce and saffron rice, steak with green peppercorns, pan-fried saddle of lamb and veal escalope. You can opt for a dish of the day if you're not very hungry. And if you wish to be confessed have a word with the priest upstairs.

❚●❚ RESTAURANT CHARTIER

7 rue du Faubourg-Montmartre; M° Grands-Boulevards.
☎ 01.47.70.86.29

Last orders 10pm and no reservations. You come in through a huge revolving door and

find yourself in an immense, turn-of-the-nineteenth-century restaurant with its original décor completely intact – in fact they've made it a listed building. Get there quickly before someone has the bright idea to refurbish it; there are only two or three places like this left and they're not half as wonderful as this one. It's always packed with regulars, local pensioners, students, poverty-stricken artists and tourists: there are 350 covers, 16 waiters and they serve 1200 meals a day. €12–15 *à la carte* including a drink. The food is passable, though not always as hot as it could be.

❚●❚ LA PETITE SIRÈNE DE COPENHAGUE

47 rue Notre-Dame-de-Lorette; M° Saint-Georges.
☎ 01.45.26.66.66
Closed Sun; Mon; the first three weeks in Aug.

This Danish restaurant offers specialities somewhat modified to appeal to gallic gourmands, all served in a bright and present bistro. It's really worth making the effort to come because their cuisine is delicious and prices are equally appealing. Fish and smoked salmon are frequent entries on the menus, flavoured with anything from juniper to curry – known to the Danish since the seventeenth century – and there's even salmon marinated in orange. The mackerel *croustillant* is very fine for such an oily fish and the guineafowl *fricassée* with ceps with beetroot sauce and juniper berries is inventive and tasty. The rhubarb soup with cream cheese sorbet is light and delicious. Menu of the day, chalked on the slate, is €21 or there's a dinner version for €26. Peter is liable to offer you a shot of aquavit – don't refuse.

🎄 ❚●❚ RESTAURANT AU PETIT RICHE

25 rue Le Pelletier; M° Richelieu-Drouot.
☎ 01.47.70.68.68
Closed Sun; weekends in July; Aug.

Closes at 1.15am. The restaurant was founded in 1880 – and with its labyrinth of intimate salons and *belle époque* décor, you might as well be dining in an Impressionist painting. They serve dishes like *rillons* from Vouvray, zander in Vouvray wine sauce, beef with sea-salt, tuna with green peppercorns, fine apple tart and other specialities from the Val de Loire. Menus at €22, €25 and €27, or *à la carte* around €31. The restaurant buzzes with atmosphere and it works with the local theatres, to offer special price "theatre-dinner" promotions. Free apéritif.

IOI CHEZ CATHERINE

65 rue de Provence; M° Chaussée-d'Antin.
☎ 01.45.26.72.88
Closed Sat; Sun; Mon; public holidays; the first week in Jan; Aug.

Service noon–2pm and 7.30–10pm. Under new management this last few years, this respected, pretty bistro, previously the *Poitou*, has undergone a revolution. Out with the dull cooking and indifferent wines, in with inventive dishes cooked to perfection and a stunning wine list. Catherine, the chef, must have inherited her cooking skills from her father (who has a great reputation): her fillet of bream with spices is splendid and her Gers duck breast is pays tribute to the traditions of southwest France. Her husband, Frédéric, loves his wine and manages his cellar with passion and intelligence. A selection is served by the glass or carafe – Côte de Brouilly, Coteaux-de-l'Ardèche du Domaine du Colombier – and the wine list proper offers real delights. Try the Comas de Robert Michel, the Côteaux d'Aix-les-Baux-de-Provence Clos Milan or a superb Saumur Champigny Clos Rougeard; prices are very reasonable. À la carte a meal costs €38–46 with drink. Excellent cuisine, excellent cellar and friendly, efficient service.

10th arrondissement
☎ HÔTEL VICQ D'AZIR

21 rue Vicq d'Azir; M° Colonel-Fabien.
☎ 01.42.08.06.70 ➡ 01.42.08.06.80
e vicqazir@club.internet.fr

Service 8am–10pm. A simple hotel with seventy low-priced rooms which look out onto a charming interior courtyard planted with bushes. You have to pay when you check in: doubles €19 with basin, €28 with shower, €31 with shower/wc. At these prices you can't expect luxury but it's good value.

☎ HÔTEL MODERNE DU TEMPLE

3 rue d'Aix; M° République or Goncourt.
☎ 01.42.08.09.04 ➡ 01.42.41.72.17
e vlado.fundarek@libertysurf.fr

This place is a pleasant surprise and you'll find it between the lock on the Saint-Martin canal and the steep section of the faubourg du Temple. It's in a narrow, busy street, where the crumbling façades are tinted with bright colours that have faded in the sun. The place is owned by a friendly Slovak who, after rather modest beginnings in 1989, now has 43 rooms with facilities that compare favourably with the nearby youth hostel;

some have been improved. Doubles €29 with washing facilities up to €40 with shower/wc. Direct dial telephone in each room. There's a bar.

🎢 ☎ NORD-EST HÔTEL**

12 rue des Petits-Hôtels; M° Gare-du-Nord or Gare-de-l'Est.
☎ 01.47.70.07.18 ➡ 01.42.46.73.50
e hotel.nord.est@wanadoo.fr
TV. Garden. Pay car park.

This hotel has a delightful provincial charm – fitting in a street with such a name. It's actually in a little garden where you can relax in good weather. Pleasant welcome. The place has recently been completely renovated and there's a good deal of oak for the sitting room, dining room and reception. Clean, functional rooms with pink-tiled bathrooms. Doubles €61–70 with shower/wc or bath. Book well in advance. There's a car park at €6 per day. 10% discount Nov–Feb, except for public holidays and during trade fairs.

🎢 ☎ HÔTEL GILDEN MAGENTA**

35 rue Yves-Toudic; M° République or Jacques-Bonsergent.
☎ 01.42.40.17.72 ➡ 01.42.02.59.66
e hotel.gilden.magenta@multi-micro.com
TV. Pay garage.

This place is a real bargain, so it's advisable to book a week in advance. It's in a quiet street between the place de la République and the Saint-Martin canal. Rooms 61 and 62 on the sixth floor are the most appealing, with their panelled ceilings and exposed beams; number 3 looks out onto a pretty patio where they serve breakfast. All rooms have TV and direct dial telephone. The owners are friendly, smiling and accommodating. Doubles with shower/wc €70, €71 for three people or €84 for four. Best to book a week in advance. Breakfast €6. They have a lock-up garage at €10 a day. 10% discount after the third night.

🎢 ☎ NEW HÔTEL**

40 rue Saint-Quentin; M° Gare-de-l'Est.
☎ 01.48.78.04.83 ➡ 01.40.82.91.22
e info@newhotelparis.com
TV. Pay car park.

Areas around train stations are notoriously grim, and it would be wrong to pretend that this place is anything other than a cheap hotel – but it does have the advantage of being quiet. The rooms are functional, and most of them have the facilities you'd expect from a two-star: multi-channel TV, hairdryer, and most have air-conditioning. The vaulted basement has been transformed into a cellar with three dining rooms, each decorated in medieval style with rough stone walls; here you can have a breakfast, €5, of *croissants*, *brioches*, cornflakes, orange juice and so on. If you turn right when you leave the hotel, you'll come to a terrace at the end of a short street affording a rare view over Paris. Double rooms €72 with shower, €83 with bath. Free use of the computer with Internet access and free breakfast.

◉ RESTAURANT DE BOURGOGNE – CHEZ MAURICE

26 rue des Vinaigriers; M° Jacques-Bonsergent or République.
☎ 01.46.07.07.91
Closed Sat evening; Sun; public holidays; the last week in July; the first fortnight in Aug.

Service at lunchtime and in the evening until 11pm. This little neighbourhood restaurant, not far from the *Hôtel du Nord* and the romantic Saint-Martin canal with its Venetian bridge, hasn't changed for years; it's got a provincial feel and still serves local people. Very inexpensive set menus at €8 and €10 for lunch or €9 and €11 for dinner. The house wine is reasonably priced at €6 or there's a Côtes de Provence for €8.

⌂ ◉ RESTAURANT BAALBECK

16 rue de Mazagran; M° Bonne-Nouvelle.
☎ 01.47.70.70.02
Closed Sun.

Service noon–3pm and 7pm–1am. A couple of pointers on how to have a successful time here: one, you absolutely *must* book; and two, come in the evening. This Lebanese restaurant has some of the best Middle Eastern cooking in Paris. If there are four of you, have the special *mezze* and you'll get eighteen different dishes. Or there's a €9 lunch menu; expect to pay around €23 *à la carte*. Things really begin to hot up after 10pm, when the belly dancers make their appearance – they're the genuine article and could rival those in Istanbul or Cairo. Don't forget to tip them. Free coffee and Lebanese pastry.

◉ LA VIGNE SAINT-LAURENT

2 rue Saint-Laurent; M° Gare-de-l'Est.
☎ 01.42.05.98.20
Closed Sat; Sun; 3 weeks in Aug; 1 week at the end of the year.

Service noon–2.30pm and 7–10pm. If you've got a train to catch or you're seeing someone off, don't just dive into the nearest brasserie – take a couple of minutes to find this pleasant wine bar instead. Inside there's a long, narrow room with a beautiful spiral staircase. At the far end, the pair of polite chaps with fine moustaches who run the place prepare delicious dishes with great care: rabbit with house *tapenade*, calf's head *sauce ravigote*, beef stewed in red wine. Menus from €11 or a meal will cost €20–23. If you want just a snack, try a plate of *charcuterie* or some perfectly ripened cheeses like the Saint-Marcellin matured in the Lyonnais style or the Arôme de Lyon matured in Marc with a salad and a glass of wine. They have a good selection wines by the glass, jug or bottle – Côteaux du Lyonnais, Bourgeuil. The *menu-assiette* is comprised of a platter of two types of sausage, green salad, two cheeses and a glass of wine.

⌂ ◉ RESTAURANT FLO

7 cour des Petites-Écuries; M° Château-d'Eau.
☎ 01.47.70.13.59
Closed Christmas.

Open daily till 1.30am. This is *the* place to go for *choucroute*. Herr Floederer's old brasserie dates from 1886 and is sparkling. Sarah Bernhardt used to have her meals delivered from here when she was at the Renaissance – others followed suit. Superb décor with stained-glass windows separating the rooms, richly decorated ceilings, leather benches, brass hat-stands and period lighting. Platters of shellfish and seafood, sensational *choucroute*, escalope of *foie gras* with apples and grapes, *sole meunière*. Given the wonderful surroundings, prices are reasonable: menus €21 and €29 or around €34 *à la carte*. The place is always buzzing with locals and lots of tourists. Free apéritif.

◉ RESTAURANT JULIEN

16 rue du Faubourg-Saint-Denis; M° Strasbourg-Saint-Denis.
☎ 01.47.70.12.06
Closed Christmas.

Service noon–3pm and 7pm–1.30am. Another restaurant – one of the oldest in Paris – which has been given a makeover by the talented Monsieur Bücher. The same old ingredients continue to work their magic: the dazzling Art Nouveau interior, efficient service and a reasonable bill. Skilfully prepared specialities include salad of duck *foie gras* and morels, warm *foie gras* with lentils, goose *cassoulet*, grilled sole and sole *meunière*. You'll spend about €30 *à la carte*; there's a lunch menu at €21 and a *menu brasserie* at €29.

⦿ CHEZ MICHEL

10 rue de Belzunce; M° Gare-du-Nord.
☎ 01.44.53.06.20
Closed Sun; Mon; the first 2 Saturdays of each month; 3 weeks in Aug; a week in winter.

Service noon–2pm and 7pm–midnight. The countless people who choose to stay in one of the many hotels near the station will be delighted to know that they can now eat in the area as well. Thierry Breton trained at two luxury hotels, the *Ritz* and the *Crillon*; his skill draws attention to this place, which is in a part of the city where greasy spoons abound. He offers a set menu for €27, and what you get for your money is sheer magic – first-rate cooking and first-rate ingredients. The *terrine* of *andouille* with peppercorns and shortbread biscuits is out of this world, while the guineafowl ravioli with a sauce of ceps and crushed walnuts is so incredibly good that you'll have to loosen your belt to make room for the *kig ha farz* of pig cheeks and pork fat, not to mention the desserts which include warm *kouign aman* (traditional Breton yeast cake) – it's worth every calorie. There's also a *table d'hôte* menu at €20.

11th arrondissement
🛏 HÔTEL NOTRE-DAME**

51 rue de Malte; M° République or Oberkampf.
☎ 01.47.00.78.76 ➡ 01.43.55.32.31
e hotelnotredame@wanadoo.fr
TV.

A well-run two-star hotel in a good location. Everything is grey, down to the business cards and the cat. The tastefully redecorated rooms have direct-dial phones, clock-radios and colour TV. The ones on the street are brighter. Singles with basin €34, €52 with shower, €61 with shower/wc or bath. Breakfast (€6) is served until 9.30am. They don't take cheques and it's best to book. 10% discount when there are no trade fairs.

🛏 HÔTEL MONDIA**

22 rue du Grand-Prieuré; M° République or Oberkampf.
☎ 01.47.00.93.44 ➡ 01.43.38.66.14
e info@hotel-mondia.com
TV.

This well-run hotel in a quiet little street is a good base if you're doing the sights on foot – Belleville, Ménilmontant and the Bastille are not too far away and the Marais-Les Halles area is very close. The comfortable rooms have shower or bath, hairdrier, safe and direct telephone – some even have marble fireplaces and the three on the top floor have

sloping ceilings. Doubles €53–58. Prices are negotiable if you're planning a long stay. Breakfast €5. 10% discount out of season.

🛏 HÔTEL BEAUSÉJOUR**

71 av. Parmentier; M° Parmentier or Oberkampf.
☎ 01.47.00.38.16 ➡ 01.43.55.47.89
TV. **Pay car park**.

A hotel with 31 rooms on six floors – with a lift. They all have bath or shower, double glazing, TV and direct telephone, and cost €58, some sleeping three or four. The little bar in the reception area is open 24 hours a day, and they offer room service. 10% discount on the room rate.

🛏 HÔTEL DAVAL**

21 rue Daval; M° Bastille.
☎ 01.47.00.51.23 ➡ 01.40.21.80.26
e hoteldaval@wanadoo.fr
TV.

A nice two-star hotel in the heart of the lively Bastille neighbourhood, near the bars of rue de Lappe and rue de la Roquette. It has modern décor and facilities – TV, double glazing and mini-safe. Doubles with shower €67. Free breakfast, usually €8 and better than the average.

🛏 HÔTEL BEAUMARCHAIS***

3 rue Oberkampf; M°Filles du Calvaire.
☎ 01.53.36.86.86 **e** hotel.beaumarchais@libertysurf.fr
TV.

An ideal situation in a lively street full of bars, close to the Bastille, the République and the Marais. It's a modern hotel, decorated in bright sunshine colours and slicked-up bathrooms. Double rooms €90 with en-suite shower/wc or €99 with bath.

⦿ LES CINQ POINTS CARDINAUX

14 rue Jean-Macé; M° Faidherbe-Chaligny or Charonne.
☎ 01.43.71.47.22
Closed Sat; Sun; Aug.

Service until 10pm. You can eat here, as Madame says, "with no worries and without being ripped off, whoever you are". Old tools belonging to local artisans of yesteryear hang from the ceiling and the benches are crammed at lunchtime. The atmosphere is relaxed and the cooking unpretentious: herring fillets, sausage and lentils, avocado with melted Roquefort cheese, duck *confit*. Lunch menu €10 then others up to €16 at dinner. Free coffee.

⦿ AU P'TIT CAHOUA

24 rue des Taillandiers; M° Bastille.

☎ 01.43.00.20.42

Philippe Jounoud has created a corner of France which is forever Morroco: ceramic tables, wrought iron, pottery, Berber hangings from the ceiling and on the walls, Arab rythms in the background. Food-wise you'll ind tangy *tagines*, soft and spicy *couscous* but make sure you try the "kemias", a selection of starters, or the *pastilla*. In the week, there's lunch *formule* for €10; à la carte a meal will cost around €23.

☆ |●| SUDS

55 rue de Charonne; M° Ledru-Rollin.
☎ 01.43.14.06.36
Closed Sat lunchtime.

"Suds" refers to "the South" of all sorts of different countries, so your choice of food will take you on a culinary tour of France, Spain, Portugal and South America. If you have a wandering spirit and a fascination with unusual cooking you'll enjoy this place. The owner has a farm in the Gers where they raise ducks: try his *foie gras* with sweet potato. The signature dish is banana mousse with white and dark chocolate – a dream. Weekday lunch menu €10 or €23 *à la carte*. On Sunday they do a family brunch with entertainment for the kids – painting workshops and dancing. *Formules* for the grown-ups are €18 and the 3–8 year-olds eat for €11. Free glass of Tariquet, a white from the Côtes de Gascogne.

☆ |●| RESTAURANT L'AMI PIERRE

5 rue de la Main-d'Or; M° Ledru-Rollin.
☎ 01.47.00.17.35
Closed Sun; Mon; 22 July–22 Aug.

Service until 2am. Marie-Jo's been in the Bastille area for more than thirty years, the last ten of them in this restaurant. She's very easy-going and treats her clients like friends. The atmosphere can get a bit heated some evenings if the rugby fans tangle with the regulars – arty types like film-makers and designers. You can have a glass or two of Pouilly, Cahors or Quincy, and fill up on a plate of *charcuterie*. Dish of the day might be beef *bourguignon*, *pot-au-feu*, oxtail or creamed salt cod. Portions are substantial, which will help prepare you for the long night ahead – things can keep going around here until dawn. €15 *à la carte* with dishes for around €9. Free *digestif*.

|●| CEFALÙ

43 av. Philippe-Auge; M° Nation.

☎ 01.43.71.29.34
Closed Sat lunchtime, Sun, and a month starting around mid-Aug.

Service noon–1.30pm and 7.30–10pm. Mr Cala comes from Mussomeli, famous for its impregnable fortress. His skill does his homeland proud, and his Sicilian restaurant is one of the best ambassadors for Italian cooking in Paris: Sicilian *antipasti*, spaghetti *à la Sicilienne* (with garlic, tomato, aubergine, capers, anchovies, olives and basil), *tagliatelle* with a choice of four sauces (cream, gorgonzola, smoked bacon, mint and basil). Try the *cannolo*, a Sicilian dessert traditionally served on Sunday, something like a brandy snap filled with fresh ricotta, candied fruit and chocolate; it's usually accompanied by a glass of Marsala. Pretty décor in the naïf style and very, very clean. Menus start at €15 and there's a *menu dégustation* offering three courses and dessert for €30. Free house apéritif.

|●| LE VILLARET

13 rue Ternaux; M° Parmentier.
☎ 01.43.57.75.56
Closed Sat lunchtime; Sun; a week in May; a week in Aug; a week at Christmas and New Year.

Joël (who used to run the dining room under the previous owner) and the young chef Olivier Gaslain are in charge. Olivier goes to Rungis market for the produce and devises his menus according to what he selects. The prices haven't changed much over the years and the wide-ranging wine list has great vintages at reasonable rates. Starters include dishes such as scallops and thyme *en papillote* (baked in a paper sack), *fricassée* of ceps with garlic and flat-leaf parsley and great fat stalks of green asparagus; for a main course try medallions of monkfish with a sauce made from small crabs, calf's liver in Banyuls vinegar, a terrific sirloin steak with shallots or a *gratin* of Jerusalem artichokes. One of the best restaurants in Paris for dinner. *Formules* at €18 (2 courses) or €23 (3 courses), or expect to pay €38 for a meal *à la carte*.

|●| LES AMOGNES

243 rue du Faubourg-Saint-Antoine; M° Faidherbe-Chaligny.
☎ 01.43.72.73.05
Closed Sat lunchtime; Sun; Mon lunchtime; 3 weeks in Aug.

Foodies flock here; the atmosphere has a welcoming and provincial feel with white beams. The chef, Theiry Coué, trained with the great Senderens. His menus are a steal at €27: it's the same price *à la carte*, more or less. Among his delicious dishes are oysters *marinière* with leeks, skate wing, red cabbage, roast veal kidneys, compote of tomatoes and celery with sage – delicate flavours and interesting combinations. For dessert try the fine pancakes stuffed with aubergine compote with cardamom. There's a very good selection of wines but sadly they're rather pricey. Efficient service and very warm welcome.

12th arrondissement
♠ HÔTEL DES TROIS GARES**

1 rue Jules-César; M° Gare-de-Lyon.
☎ 01.43.43.01.70 ➡ 01.43.41.36.58
e h3g@club-internet.fr
TV.

This is a well-located two-star in a quiet street between the Gare de Lyon, the Gare d'Austerlitz and Bastille-Plaisance. The façade is smart and the reception is decidedly modern, as are the functional rooms. Doubles with basin €37, €46 with shower, €56 with shower/wc or €61 withbath, TV and direct dial telephone. Very nice owner.

♠ HÔTEL MARCEAU**

13 rue Jules-César; M° Gare-de-Lyon or Bastille.
☎ 01.43.43.11.65 ➡ 01.43.41.67.70
Closed 20 July–20 Aug. **TV**. **Pay car park in hotel**.

It's anyone's guess as to whether General Marceau really slept here. He led the troops in who in 1793 put down the insurrections in the Vendée against the revolutionary government. But the fact that the hotel and the general share a name gives the proprietor a good excuse to display in reception a page in the general's handwriting that he bought at auction. The rooms aren't bad, and some are quite well-decorated with co-ordinating fabric, wall lights and wood panelling. Those overlooking the courtyard don't have a great view. Doubles €66 with shower or bath.

♠ NOUVEL HÔTEL**

24 av. Bel Air; M° Nation.
☎ 01.43.43.01.81 ➡ 01.43.44.64.13
e nouvelhotel@wanadoo.fr
TV. **Garden**.

This establishment is a stone's throw from place de la Nation where you can hook up with any number of buses, the Métro or the RER. The street couldn't be quieter and all the rooms have double glazing. It's as clean as a whistle, and most rooms overlook a

delightful garden where you can sit and relax in the shade of a tree. Floral décor, new flooring in all the common areas and excellent facilities. Doubles with shower €67, €77 with bath. There are connecting rooms for families sleeping three or four. Breakfast €7.

|●| AU PAYS DE VANNES

34 [bis] rue de Wattignies; M° Michel-Bizot.
☎ 01.43.07.87.42
Closed evenings; Sun; Aug.

A good local eatery with a large Breton flag on the wall – the proprietors are proud of their roots. The €9 menu includes wine and offers a choice of main courses: sautéed pork with cabbage, roast guineafowl with shredded leeks, chicken with rice, breast of veal stuffed with braised celery hearts. Starters include egg mayonnaise and dessert is included. You'll get a good simple traditional French meal and the best value for money in the *arrondissement*. There are other set menus at €13 and €18. Whole families turn up on Saturday lunchtime for a feast of oysters brought direct from Brittany. Friendly reception and service.

🎿 |●| CAPPADOCE

12 rue de Capri; M° Michel-Bizot or Daumesnil.
☎ 01.43.46.17.20
Closed Sat lunchtime; Sun; Aug.

Service noon–2.30pm and 7–11.30pm. Turkish hospitality and kindness are the hallmarks of this establishment and, together with the elaborate cooking, they have helped spread its reputation far beyond the neighbourhood. The cheese roll and the aubergine caviar are exquisite, while the *pides* (Turkish pizzas), the grilled chicken with aubergines and yoghurt, the stuffed leg of lamb with spices and the kebabs will give your tastebuds a real treat. It's obvious why the restaurant is a success and it's best to book for dinner. Two well-planned set menus at €11 and €20. Don't turn down the home-made desserts – the pumpkin in syrup is extraordinary, a bit like quince paste. Free *digestif*.

🎿 |●| SI SEÑOR!

9 rue Antoine-Vollon; M° Ledru-Rollin.
☎ 01.43.47.18.01
Closed Sun; Mon; Aug.

This Spanish restaurant, run by a group of French and Spanish friends, has nothing to do with those Parisian tapas bars – not least because it isn't a bar. This is honest, robust cooking that is very delicious: great Spanish omelettes and potatoes *ali oli* (garlic and oil), alarmingly light deep-fried *calamari*, perfectly season Argentine sirloin steak served with a spicy sauce. Different specialities from remote regions appear on the menus on a regular basis and there are good desserts. Menus €12 at lunchtime, €15 in the evening and then up to €20 or *à la carte* around €20. Nice pictures on the walls, too.

🏃 |●| LES ZYGOMATES

7 rue de Capri; M° Michel-Bizot or Daumesnil.
☎ 01.40.19.93.04
Closed Sat lunchtime; Sun; Aug.

Service noon–2pm and 7.30–10.30pm. Virtually nothing has changed here since the turn of the twentieth century – the *trompe l'œil* décor, the varnished wood and the marble were all here when this was a butcher's shop. Best of all, the prices are reasonable – there's a set lunch menu for €13, and an incredibly good one at €21 with quite complex dishes: *cannelloni* with goat's cheese and lamb's lettuce, pig's tail stuffed with morels, cheese and dessert. Considering the quality of the cooking and what they charge, this is more like a philanthropic undertaking than a restaurant, so it's best to book. Free coffee.

|●| RESTAURANT À LA BICHE AU BOIS

45 av. Ledru-Rollin; M° Gare-de-Lyon or Ledru-Rollin.
☎ 01.43.43.34.38
Closed Sat; Sun; mid-July to mid-Aug; Christmas week.

Service until lunchtime and in the evening until 10pm. If you like the old style of restaurant that does traditional dishes, this is the place for you. Even the décor, which is delightfully old-fashioned, is appealing, with prints and paintings on the walls, a Louis XIV style clock, artificial flowers and leather benches. This little restaurant gives good value on its €18 and €20 set menus with dishes such as *foie gras* with salad, fillet of beef with a cep sauce, fillet of salmon with wild mushrooms, *coq au vin* and game in season — haunch of venison, say, or venison *terrine*, pheasant casserole or wild duck with fruits of the forest. Home-made pastries and reasonably priced wines. An excellent restaurant where you can eat well for under €23.

|●| RESTAURANT SQUARE TROUSSEAU

1 rue Antoine-Vollon; M° Ledru-Rollin.
☎ 01.43.43.06.00
Closed Sun and Mon.

Service until 11.30pm. Two layers of curtains – lace and red velvet – shield you from prying eyes as you dine. In style and atmosphere the restaurant resembles an elegant 1900s bistro: there's a superb antique bar, a mosaic tiled floor, red leather benches and mouldings on the ceiling. The day's specials are chalked up on big blackboards along with a €19 set lunch menu which comprises starter, main course, dessert and coffee. Dinner menu €23. Good home cooking. The *à la carte* dishes change weekly. The presentation is pretty and the wine list has been well-researched. Reckon on €30–38 *à la carte*. A very good restaurant with lots of regulars. Terrace in summer.

13th arrondissement

🏃 🛏 HÔTEL STHRAU*

1 rue Sthrau; M° Nationale, Tolbiac, Porte-d'Ivry or Bibliotèque François-Mitterrand.
☎ 01.45.83.20.35 📠 01.44.24.91.21
TV.

A modest but clean and convenient little hotel on six floors, five minutes from the Bibliothèque François Mitterrand – it's ideal if you're on a tight budget. Doubles with €26–41 with shower or shower/wc; there are some quiet ones overlooking the courtyard. Free breakfast Jan–Feb.

🛏 HÔTEL TOLBIAC

122 rue Tolbiac; M° Tolbiac or Place-d'Italie.
☎ 01.44.24.25.54 📠 01.45.85.43.47
e info@hotel-tolbiac.com
TV.

An enormous hotel with 47 rooms just five minutes from place d'Italie. There's a pleasant reception and the rooms are clean. Doubles with basin €29 and €34 with shower/wc; all have TV. €4 for breakfast with *croissants*, *brioches*, cereals and coffee or tea, served in a bright breakfast room. Rue de Tolbiac is quite noisy but a number of the rooms are fitted with double glazing.

🏃 🛏 RÉSIDENCE LES GOBELINS**

9 rue des Gobelins; M° Gobelins; buses 27, 47, 83, 91.
☎ 01.47.07.26.90 📠 01.43.31.44.05
e hotelgobelins@noos.fr
TV. Garden.

The rue des Gobelins follows the same route it did in the Middle Ages. The château that belonged to Blanche of Castile, wife of Louis VIII and mother of Louis IX, is just round the corner. The hotel is peaceful and great value for money. Lovely double rooms €68–70 with bath and they all have satellite TV.

Breakfast €6. You can sit outside in the little garden on warm evenings. 10% discount after two nights.

🏃 🏠 RÉSIDENCE HÔTELIÈRE LE VERT GALANT***

41–43 rue Croulebarbe; M° Gobelins or Corvisart.
☎ 01.44.08.83.50 ➡ 01.44.08.83.69
Closed Sun. Disabled access. Garden. TV. Car park.

A corner of the Basque country in the middle of the 13th *arrondissement*, just across from the Gobelins gardens. It's next to the *Auberge Etchegorry* restaurant, and belongs to the same owners. It's set back from the road with a garden and lawn so it's quiet and has a certain charm. There are ten superb rooms – doubles €69–84 with shower or bath – and there are some studios with a corner kitchen, fridge and direct-dial telephone. Free breakfast after your first night, served in a room overlooking the garden.

🏃 🏠 HÔTEL LA MANUFACTURE**

8 rue Philippe-de-Champaigne; M° Place d'Italie.
☎ 01.43.35.45.25 ➡ 01.43.35.45.40
📧 lamanufact@aol.com
TV.

A very new and elegant hotel, just next to the local town hall and the old Gobelins tapestry workshop. It's managed by a trio of women who run things like clockwork. The décor is in browns and beiges with splashes of red. The entrance hall has a wooden floor and a corner bar where you can have a drink next to the open fire in winter. Rooms are not huge but go for €120 for a double with shower/wc or bath. 10% discount and free buffet breakfast.

🏃 🍴 RESTAURANT BIDA SAIGON

44 av. d'Ivry; M° Porte-d'Ivry.
☎ 01.45.84.04.85

Service 10am–10pm. A huge Vietnamese canteen at the top of an escalator at the entrance to the Terrasse des Olympiades and Paris-Store. Friendly welcome. The menu consists of the standard twenty or so savoury dishes. The soups, *phô* and Saigon soup come in large and small bowls, and helpings are generous. The spring rolls are crisp and the steamed rice cake is, well, steamed rice cake. Pork spare ribs, grilled chicken with lemongrass, and rice with pork and stuffed crab. For dessert, try the white beans with sticky rice or the lotus seeds with seaweed and *longans* – weird, but not unpleasant. A meal costs €7. It's not licensed except for beer, but naturally they

also have fizzy drinks, fresh fruit juice and tea. Free coffee.

🏃 🍴 TRICOTIN

15 av. de Choisy; M° Porte-de-Choisy.
☎ 01.45.85.51.52

One of the longest-serving establishments in the district and a veritable institution – at the weekend they even queue to get in. The big dining is pretty noisy with efficient waiters, a menu as long as your arm and your neighbour's elbow in your ribs. It's worth it for the *dim sum* – probably the finest and most varied in town – and you could even make a whole meal of it. If you're new to it all, ask the waiter how to make the accompanying sauce. If you go in a group you can try everything. À la carte only – you'll pay €8–23.

🏃 🍴 À LA BOUILLABAISSE, CHEZ KERYADO

32 rue Regnault; M° Bibliothèque or Porte-d'Ivry.
☎ 01.45.83.87.58
Closed Sun; Mon evening; the last fortnight in Aug.

Service noon–2.30pm and 7.30–10.30pm. Located on the fringes of the 13th *arrondissement* and Bercy, this is a wonderful fish restaurant run by a young couple. Bistro-type décor. The *bouillabaisse*, the house speciality, is excellent – and even better if you consider how hard it is to find a decent *bouillabaisse* in Paris. Dishes are cooked to order and prices are not too bad: weekday lunch menu €9, others at €17 and €23 or around €21 *à la carte*. If you don't want fish, there's a choice of grilled dishes and the meat is very tender. Free house apéritif.

🍴 VIRGULE

9 rue Véronèse; M° Place d'Italie.
☎ 01.43.37.01.14
Closed Sun and Mon lunchtimes and Christmas.

Service until 10.30pm. Mr Dao is a young chef originally from Cambodia and his restaurant has a lot to recommend it. The €9 lunch menu shows how he has fused the flavours of the Orient and the cuisine of the West. It changes regularly but might list cream of cauliflower soup followed by lacquered roast pork or *choucroute* with ham hock and a fruit tart or cream caramel for dessert. The other menus, €10–22, feature some astonishing dishes – sautéed scallops with oyster sauce and celeriac in a mustard mayonnaise, pan-fried scallops with chicken broth and perfumed mushrooms, and *cassoulet* like you find in the southwest of France. It's engaging food served very generously and, on top of all that, the owners are charming.

|●| L'AVANT GOÛT

26 rue Bobillot; M° Place-d'Italie.
☎ 01.53.80.24.00 ✉ rufine@club.internet.fr
Closed Sun lunchtime, Mon and the first three weeks of Aug.

Christophe Baugront was the chef at *La Courtille* up in Belleville for ages, then he decided to open a place of his own and set up in Touraine before returning to the Butte-aux-Cailles to open a restaurant here. You can tell that he's spent a lot of thought and energy on this place, from the dishes on the menus to the vintages on the wine list. He offers a triumphant combination of peasant food and elegant preparation. Try the fantastic pork *pot-au-feu*, for instance. There's a lunch *formule* at €10 which includes dish of the day, salad, a glass of wine and coffee; dishes change regularly but they include roast free-range chicken with macaroni cheese and leg of lamb with flageolet beans. Another option is the *menu-carte* at €24, which lists a choice of four starters, five main dishes and four desserts. Or push the boat out with the €31 *menu dégustation*. The wine list includes a sparkling Vouvray from Champalou, a Touraine Sauvignon du Père Aug and a red Beaume-de-Venise domaine de la Fermette-Saint-Martin. *À la carte*, a complete meal will cost about €24.

|●| NOUVEAU VILLAGE TAOTAO

159 bd. Vincent-Auriol; M° Nationale.
☎ 01.45.86.40.08.

Service until 11.30pm. This vast establishment – practically a village on its own – has dining rooms on two floors. Menus (€11 and €25 for two) are novel-length, with evocatively named Chinese and Thai dishes and pictures of the dishes next to the text. Starters include spicy duck soup with bamboo shoots and coconut milk and stuffed Thai crab, while among the main dishes are spicy chicken with honey, sautéed prawns, Peking duck, frogs' legs with dumplings or scallop fritters. There's a long dessert menu as well.

|●| RESTAURANT LA TOURAINE

39 rue Croulebarbel; M° Corvisart or Gobelins.
☎ 01.47.07.69.35
Closed Sun.

If you want a table on the terrace, you have to

book, but in the evenings there's not such a crush. There are two dining rooms, both decorated in subtle rustic style. The cuisine is filling and tasty and the dishes are what you'd expect to find in provincial France: prawns *au gratin*, *tournedos Rossini* and a *panaché* of lamb with pickled garlic. There is a selection of filling menus: lunchtime €11, others €20–29, or *à la carte* around €27.

⅍ |●| LE BISTRO DU VIADUC

12 rue Tolbiac; M° Meteor and Biblioteque François Mitterand.
☎ 01.45.83.74.66
Closed evenings, Sun and three weeks in Aug.

This bistro used to be a workman's café known as *Chez Mammy*, but the blue collars have been replaced by white ones and the cooking has become more elaborate. The €16 menu, including drink, is good value, while the one at €26 lists some great dishes – *langoustines* with poached egg and tarragon vinegar, sole *meunière*. Good classical cooking. *À la carte*, a meal costs around €33. Free apéritif.

⅍ |●| ETCHEGORRY

41 rue Croulebarbel; M° Place-d'Italie or Corvisart.
☎ 01.44.08.83.51
Closed Sun, Mon and 7–22 Aug.

On the façade of this building you can still make out the old inscription "Cabaret de Madame Grégoire". Some two hundred years ago, Victor Hugo, Châteaubriand and various poets wined and dined here. The old charm still remains; the décor is rustic and warm and the windows look onto the square. The local clientele enjoy Basque and Béarnaise cuisine: *piperade*, stuffed squid and cod with red peppers, duck and pork *confit* with garlic potatoes, sheep's cheeses and delicious desserts. Everything is cooked fresh on the premises, even the bread. There's a lunch *formule* at €18 which includes wine, and others €24–35. Free *digestif*.

|●| ANACRÉON

53 bd. Saint-Marcel; M° Les Gobelins.
☎ 01.43.31.71.18
Closed Sun, Mon, Wed lunchtime and Aug.

Service noon–2.30pm and 7.30–11pm. Situated in a rather dreary street, this restaurant offers gourmet food. The chef trained at *Prunier* and *La Tour d'Argent*. Try the splendid €23 *menu-carte*, which lists well-devised, well-prepared dishes using country produce: rabbit *terrine* with *foie gras* and vegetables, *fricassée* of snails with tomatoes, veal kidneys in a mustard sauce, cod with chicory, *parfait* with egg custard. Extremely good service and a wine list that matches the cooking. Set lunch menu €18.

𝄢 |●| CHEZ PAUL

22 rue de la Butte-aux-Cailles; M° Place-d'Italie or Corvisart.
☎ 01.45.89.22.11
Closed Sun evening; 23 Dec–3 Jan.

Service at lunchtime and in the evening until midnight. A new-style bistro that has been successfully grafted onto the Butte. Pleasant, low-key setting decorated with plenty of plants and excellent bistro cooking with friendly welcome. The menu is quite extensive, offering dishes such as marrowbone, *foie gras*, *pot-au-feu* and Celtic pork. Wine is reasonably priced with some served by the jug. Desserts are delicious. There are always one or two dishes of the day on the slate. Expect to pay €31. Free house apéritif.

14th arrondissement
𝄢 🏠 HÔTEL DU PARC MONTSOURIS**

4 rue du Parc-Montsouris; M° Porte-d'Orléans; RER Cité-Universitaire.
☎ 01.45.89.09.72 ➡ 01.45.80.92.72
e hotel-parc-montsouris@wanadoo.fr
TV.

Great location if you like an early jog – Parc Montsouris is nearby. Everyone can appreciate the peace and quiet of this delightful street. The hotel has been renovated and is resolutely modern and functional. Doubles cost from €55 with shower/wc or €65 with bath, some sleeping three and others four. Breakfast €6. 5% discount on the room rate.

𝄢 🏠 HÔTEL DES BAINS*

33 rue Delambre; M° Vavin or Edgar-Quinet.
☎ 01.43.20.85.27 ➡ 01.42.79.82.78
e des.bains.hotel@wanadoo.fr
TV. Pay car park nearby.

This one-star hotel has real character and an elegantly restrained façade. The rooms have been tastefully decorated and even the bedspreads and lampshades have been carefully chosen to complement the colour scheme. Doubles with shower/wc and TV with eleven channels are €64–67. Two-bedroom suites in a separate building in the courtyard are available for a couple with a child or two, at €86–107. They're also very quiet and comfortable. It's really not expensive considering what you get. 10% discount Sat and Sun 15 Jul–31 Aug.

𝄢 🏠 HÔTEL DELAMBRE***

35 rue Delambre; M° Edgar-Quinet or Vavin.
☎ 01.43.20.66.31 ➡ 01.45.38.91.76
Disabled access. TV.

This hotel has changed a good deal since André Breton, one of the leading lights of Surrealism, stayed here. Very reasonable prices for a hotel in this category: doubles €78–90 with shower/wc or bath. Buffet breakfast €7. In summer you can sleep with the window open without being disturbed by noise. One free breakfast per room per night.

𝄢 🏠 HÔTEL DAGUERRE***

94 rue Daguerre; M° Gaîté.
☎ 01.43.22.43.54 ➡ 01.43.20.66.84
e hotel.daguerre.paris.14@gofornet.com
Disabled access. TV.

If you have a taste for luxury but not the means, this place is for you. It's treated itself to a facelift of the kind usually reserved for great hotels: the marble, the statues, the *trompe l'oeil* painting, the co-ordinated fabrics and the exposed beams in the dining room all combine to create the illusion of a much more glamorous era. And all the rooms have been done up, too: everything is clean and shiny, and they've got safes, mini-bars and cable TV. There are even one or two rooms equipped for disabled visitors. The warm, friendly welcome comes at no extra charge. And talking of money, the rates really are incredibly reasonable considering the level of service. Doubles with shower or bath €76–99; some suites sleep four. Breakfast at the buffet or served in your room €7. 10% discount Dec–Jan and July–Aug.

|●| L'AUBERGE DE VENISE

10 rue Delambre; M° Vavin.
☎ 01.43.35.54.09
Closed Mon.

Montparnasse may no longer have the mystique it used to when *Dingo's Bar*, Hemingway's favourite watering hole, occupied these premises, but the remaining cinemas and a handful of good restaurants still give an illusion of old Montparnasse. This is one of them – an Italian inn run by Enzo, a jovial host who has the gift of putting you instantly at your ease. His clientele is a mixture of writers and show performers, and his speciality is fillet of beef in balsamic vinegar. Menus start at €18 or you'll pay €31 *à la carte*.

|●| AUX PRODUITS DU SUD-OUEST

21–23 rue d'Odessa; M° Edgar-Quinet.

☎ 01.43.20.34.07
Closed Sun, Mon, public holidays and a month end-July/Aug.

Service noon–2.30pm and 7–10pm (11pm Fri and Sat). This restaurant-cum-shop sells home-made preserves and conserves from the southwest and the prices are unbeatable. It's not gourmet cooking but decent country fare like *charcuterie*, *terrine* of rabbit or wild boar, *cassoulet* with goose *confit*, pigeon in a red wine sauce, duck *confit* served with baked sliced Salard potatoes and truffles and a terrific apple and Armagnac tart. The lunch *formule* at €5 includes dish of the day, a glass of wine and a coffee. A *terrine* costs about €3, dishes start at €8 and you'll pay around €16 *à la carte*.

☆ ● RESTAURANT LE CHÂTEAU POIVRE

145 rue du Château; M° Pernety.
☎ 01.43.22.03.68
Closed Sun; 10–27 Aug; 22 Dec–3 Jan.

Service until 11pm. A quiet neighbourhood restaurant that's popular with the locals – but the planned refurbishment might push up the prices and alter that. Dishes like *andouillette*, *cassoulet*, tripe, Hungarian goulash and steak *tartare* are prepared by the proprietor, and the service is extremely pleasant. Excellent menu at €15; *à la carte* expect to pay about €25. Free house apéritif.

☆ ● LE RESTAURANT BLEU

46 rue Didot; M° Plaisance or Pernety.
☎ 01.45.43.70.56
Closed Sun, Mon public holidays and Aug.

A quiet old bistro in a working-class district of Paris. It's worth a visit for its wonderfully old-fashioned décor alone. It's been taken over by Christian Simon, an excellent chef who used to work at *Bertie's*. The €25 *menu-carte* changes with the seasons and is full of good ingredients from the Aveyron. Depending on the month, you'll be served game, mushrooms or soft fruit. The basket of Rouergue *cochonailles*, a selection of delicacies made from pork, is a very good place to start, as is the *terrine* of mushrooms, leeks and *foie gras*. Then move on to the *truffade*, a sort of Auvergnat pancake made with cheese and potatoes, stuffed tripe or grilled fresh scallops with a parsley sauce. For dessert, try the *mascarpone* with raspberries and lime, the vanilla rice pudding with apricots or the *feuillantine* with bitter chocolate. Christian Simon doesn't ignore the other

regions of France – or indeed other parts of the world – if there's something particularly good available. On Friday, fish is the big star on the menu, as both a starter and main course. There's also a well-priced set lunch menu for €15 and a regional version at €18. Free house apéritif.

● RESTAURANT LE VIN DES RUES

21 rue Boulard; M° Denfert-Rochereau or Mouton-Duvernet.
☎ 01.43.22.19.78
Closed Sun and Mon; a week in Feb; 3 weeks in Aug.

Service from 1pm; Wed, Fri and Sat evenings from 9pm with reservations only; bar 10am–8pm. The premises used to house an old Auvergne café and the new proprietor hasn't touched the décor. Now the excellent cooking is principally in the Lyons style, with two or three very substantial dishes that change every day. For starters there's marinated sprats with red peppers or lamb's foot *ravigotte*; main dishes include things like calf's liver *à l'étouffée* or braised sweetbreads. Regional cheeses and home-made desserts. Wines and the day's menu are chalked up on a blackboard which also tells you what saint's day it is. *À la carte* only; dishes cost between €9 and €15.

● RESTAURANT LA COUPOLE

102 bd. du Montparnasse; M° Vavin.
☎ 01.43.20.14.20

Breakfast served 8.30–10.30am, brasserie noon–1am. This aircraft hangar of a restaurant is the largest in France in terms of square feet, and can house no fewer than 450 diners. Big names have been coming here since it opened in 1927 – people like Chagall, Man Ray and Josephine Baker (complete with lion cub). The bar has been restored to its original location in the middle of the room and the pillars repainted the green they used to be. The dance hall has been preserved, too, and you can trip the light fantastic at one of the early afternoon tea dances or in the evening at weekends. Lunch *formule* €29, set menu for €30, or from €31 *à la carte*. It looks better than it used to be, but it's also more expensive.

● BISTROT MONTSOURIS

27 av. Reille; M° Porte d'Orléans; RER Cité-Universitaire.
☎ 01.45.89.17.05
Closed Sun; Mon; 3 weeks in Aug.

This was once a coaching inn called the *Relais de l'Argouêt*. The name changed and so did the style, but the high quality remains the same. The décor is more country inn than city bistro, and the cuisine less trendy than traditional; it's prepared attentively. The dishes vary with the seasons and what's available at the market: *pauchouse* (a river-fish stew with white wine), free-range chicken with shrimps, *andouillette* braised in Mâcon with *dauphinoise* potatoes, pan-fried cod with parsley potatoes, authentic veal *blanquette*. The €18 *formule* includes a main course with a choice of starter or dessert; *à la carte* a meal will cost €27–31.

�‖ L'AMUSE-BOUCHE

186 rue du Château; M° Mouton-Duvernet.
☎ 01.43.35.31.61
Closed Sun, Mon, a week in March and Aug. **Disabled access**.

Service noon–2pm and 7.30–10.30pm. Gilles Lambert, formerly of *Cagna* and the *Miraville*, is a consummate artist in the kitchen. If you want proof, try his *menu-carte* at €28. Starters might be *langoustine* ravioli with tarragon, *mousseline* of pike with saffron mussels, while for a main course you can choose between dishes such as peppered tuna steak with a honey and soya sauce, cod risotto or *croustillant* of rabbit. Sweet desserts: *millefeuille* of spiced bread, white chocolate mousse and orange sauce. Lunch menu €23 and about the same *à la carte*.

❛❙ LA RÉGALADE

49 av. Jean-Moulin; M° Alésia or Porte-d'Orléans.
☎ 01.45.45.68.58
Closed Sat lunchtime, Sun, Mon, Aug and Aug.

Service noon to 2pm and evenings until midnight. This is a gem of a place, with a décor that's both low-key and refined and a chef who is inspired. Monsieur Camdeborde, the man in question, puts as much enthusiasm into his recipes and his choice of vegetables as he does into chatting to his customers. Service is efficient and unobtrusive. The *menu-carte* at €30 (not including wine), offers as a starter a basket of *charcutailles* supplied by Camdeborde senior, who owns a *charcuterie* in Pau. Try the silky smooth pumpkin soup, the delicate kidneys with pickled shallots, the roast pigeon with bacon, the scallops with shredded celery, the braised cheek of suckling pig with caramelized cabbage, the fillet of sea bass with fennel – the list of wonderful things just goes on. The wine list is astonishing, too, and all at giveaway prices. And so far, success hasn't changed this very special restaurant. You have to book at least five days ahead.

15th arrondissement
☗ LE NAINVILLE HÔTEL

53 rue de l'Église; M° Félix-Faure or Charles-Michels.
☎ 01.45.57.35.80 ┏→ 01.45.54.83.00
Closed Sat 1–7pm, Sun, and 17 July–27 Aug. **TV**.

An unobtrusive little hotel with a retro café on the ground floor, a genial proprietor and bedrooms that are old-fashioned in the nicest possible sense. It's incredible to find a place like this in a neighbourhood where they're throwing up blocks of flats everywhere. Clean and cheerful inside. Go for a room which has a view over square Violet (10, 20, 30 and 40 all do). Doubles with basin €34, €49 with shower, €59 with shower/wc.

⚤ ☗ HÔTEL AMIRAL

90 rue de l'Amiral-Roussin; M° Vaugirard.
☎ 01.48.28.53.89 ┏→ 01.45.33.26.94
TV.

This small, discreet hotel is at the back of the this area's town hall but has much to recommend it: punctillious welcome, decent rooms and honest prices. Numbers 7, 25, 26 and 31 have a balcony and a very Parisian view of the Eiffel Tower in the distance. Doubles with basin €41, with shower/wc €63 or with bath €66. 10% discount 15 July–31 Aug.

☗ DUPLEIX HÔTEL**

4 rue de Lourmel; M° Dupleix.
☎ 01.45.79.30.12 ┏→ 01.40.59.84.90
TV.

When you leave the calm of the 7th *arrondissement* and the Eiffel Tower for the hustle and bustle of this busy shopping street, you'll be aware of a huge contrast. This place is clean, family-owned and handy. Doubles all have shower/wc and double glazing and cost €49; ask for a room on the top floor. Breakfast at €5 can be served in your room if you wish. Mini-bar and satellite TV.

⚤ ☗ PACIFIC HÔTEL**

11 rue Fondary; M° Émile-Zola or Dupleix.
☎ 01.45.75.20.49 ┏→ 01.45.77.70.73
e pacifichotel@wanadoo.fr
TV.

A quiet, charming hotel and the receptionist has a ready smile. The entrance hall is brightly decorated and the rooms are simple, functional and double-glazed. They are split between different wings of the building, both of which has been completely restored. It's clean and well managed. Doubles with shower/wc or bath €59. Free buffet breakfast if you stay over the weekend.

🍴 ⊜ HÔTEL LE FONDARY**

30 rue Fondary; M° Émile-Zola.
☎ 01.45.75.14.75 ➡ 01.45.75.84.42
TV. Garden.

Good location in a quiet street in one of the liveliest parts of the 15th *arrondissement*. Modern décor and pretty patio with a well. Prices are quite high, but not excessively so for a two-star – doubles with direct phone, cable TV and mini-bar cost €63 with shower or €69 with bath. And it's quiet at night. 10% discount July–Aug.

🍴 ⊜ HÔTEL CARLADEZ CAMBRONNE**

3 pl. du Général-Beuret; M° Vaugirard.
☎ 01.47.34.07.12 ➡ 01.40.65.95.68
TV.

Carladez is a region in Auvergne where the original owners came from. This place is a charming hotel in a little square with a pretty fountain. All the rooms are soundproofed and come with mini-bar, satellite TV, hairdrier and direct-dial telephone. Doubles with shower €64, and €70 with bath. Breakfast costs €7. 10% discount during the school holidays and at weekends when there aren't trade fairs at the exhibition centre.

🍴 ⊜ HÔTEL DE L'AVRE**

21 rue de l'Avre; M° La Motte-Picquet-Grenelle.
☎ 01.45.75.31.03 ➡ 01.45.75.63.26
Disabled access. Garden. TV.

The hotel is located in a quiet and narrow street. In summer the amiable owner sets out deckchairs in the pleasant garden where breakfast is served. The prices are fairly reasonable for Paris, with doubles at €66 with shower/wc or €73 with bath. The renovated rooms are decorated in blue or yellow; numbers 22 and 28 overlook the garden. It's difficult to park in the street but there are two car parks just minutes away. 10% discount at weekends.

⦿ RESTAURANT AUX ARTISTES

63 rue Falguière; M° Falguière or Pasteur.
☎ 01.43.22.05.39
Closed Sat evening, Sun and Aug.

Service until 12.30am. This restaurant is really something. The price of the set menu has hardly increased in twelve years and the atmosphere and the décor haven't changed much either. The customers are a mixed bunch – students, teenagers from nearby housing estates, professionals, a few artists (Modigliani came here in his time) – who all enjoy their meals in a noisy, lively atmosphere. You'll have to wait for a table on weekend evenings, eat a Kir. Two-course lunch *formule* €9, and a three-course menu €12. *Hors d'œuvres* are substantial and they can prepare you a steak in many different ways. The surprise of the house is a dessert poetically entitled "young girl's dream".

🍴 ⦿ BANANI

148 rue de la Croix-Nivert; M° Félix-Faure.
☎ 01.48.28.73.92
Closed Sun lunchtime.

Open until 11pm. The dining room here is so large that it's divided into two by a low wall and has tables hidden away in bays. There's a wall painting of a Hindu temple, warm wood panelling and low lighting. The Indian dishes come from different corners of the continent and the spicing is skilfully judged: fresh tender *tandoori* dishes, mutton korma, butter chicken, prawn biryani and so on. The naan breads come both fresh and hot, and you can have your lassi salty or sweet. Portions are generous; the only drawback is that the service is somewhat slow. Lunchtime *formule* at €9, menu €15 and a substantial evening set dinner at €24. Free house apéritif.

🍴 ⦿ LE BISTROT D'ANDRÉ

232 rue Saint-Charles; M° Balard.
☎ 01.45.57.89.14
Closed Sun, 1 May, Christmas and 1 Jan.

This is one of the few survivors from the (André) Citroën era. It's been updated to cater for today's tastes by the people from the *Perraudin* (in the 5th *arrondissement*) and given a shot in the arm. "Pre-war" prices for appealing family dishes such as leg of lamb with *gratin dauphinois*, beef *bourguignon*, *andouillette* in a mustard sauce and *canard confit*. Set menu €10 at lunchtime (except Sunday). It's *à la carte* in the evening, when you should reckon on a bit more: €20 for a starter, main course, dessert and drinks. There's a children's menu at €7 with a surprise. Wine-lovers take note: there's a tasting of wines from very small vineyards every month. It's great to discover such a decent restaurant in an area where there's little else to see. Free apéritif.

🍴 ⦿ LE GARIBALDI

58 bd. Garibaldi; M° Sèvres-Lecourbe.

☎ 01.45.67.15.61
Closed evenings, Sat, Sun, and Aug.

This used to be a working-man's caff, though nowadays white collars are much more in evidence. It's almost compulsory to have the *museau vinaigrette* or *crudités* as a starter. The €11 set menu features sautéed lamb with flageolet beans, beef *bourguignon* or *blanquette de veau*, and includes wine and service. Service is friendly and there are still traces of the old décor – such as the beautiful counter at the door and a 1900 ceiling in an otherwise plain dining room. Every weekend the proprietress goes back to her native Pas-de-Calais for vegetables, salt pork, smoked sausage and other delicacies to cook for her customers. Free coffee.

⅍ |●| RESTAURANT TY BREIZ

52 bd. de Vaugirard; M° Montparnasse-Bienvenue or Pasteur.
☎ and ➡ 01.43.20.83.72
Closed Sun and Aug.

Service noon–3pm and 7–10.45pm. This pancake place is a little off the beaten track in comparison to other restaurants in the area, which fill with theatre audiences – probably why it's retained its pleasant family atmosphere. In 2000, it was voted "Best Crêperie in Paris" by a national paper. And the *crêpes* are indeed very good, especially the *savoyarde* with cheese and potato. Even the simple double butter one is great, so long as you're not worried about your cholesterol. The dessert *galettes* cost about €7: try chocolate and orange, *martiquinaise* or *Normande*. Excellent value for money – you'll pay €12–17 for a meal – and the place is as clean as a whistle. Free Kir.

|●| LE BÉLISAIRE

2 rue Marmontel; M° Convention.
☎ 01.48.28.62.24
Closed Sat, Sun and Aug.

This restaurant is named after a fifth-century Byzantine general who vanquished the Vandals and the Ostrogoths; he was an inspiration to Marmontel, after whom the street is named. There's a splendid old zinc bar, a pretty country dresser in the corner and a few Art Deco touches. Very French cuisine, but with a modern twist – the sauces, in particular, are rather special. You'll find all the standards: snails in garlic, chicken casserole, green salads with tasty dressing. There's a menu at €15 or a *menu-carte* for €24 (it's about the same *à la carte*).

|●| RESTAURANT L'AGAPE

281 rue Lecourbe; M° Convention or Boucicaut.
☎ 01.45.58.19.29
Closed Sat lunchtime, Sun and 5–26 Aug.

Service until 10.30pm. More interesting outside than in – the dining room is very plain and lacks any originality. Don't come here expecting it to be the place for a a romantic dinner for two. But you can still eat well and hordes of diners squeeze onto the old leather benches. They scrawl the menu up on the blackboard outside: *osso bucco* with ginger, lamb with baby vegetables, pigs' trotters in jelly stuffed with snails and mushrooms, *cassoulet* made with broad beans, *confit* of duck. Menus €18 and €24.

|●| LE POSTAL

279 rue de Vaugirard; M° Vaugirard.
☎ 01.48.28.11.13
Closed weekends and Aug (open Sat evening Sept–March).

This used to be a café-brasserie which was turned into a local restaurant. The decoration is warm and elegant with the distinctive character of an inn from the Champagne area – the home region of the owner. It's stuffed with lamps, curiosities from antique shops, fabrics and mirrors. Fine welcome which is as natural as it is jovial: there's no false formality, despite the fact that waiters wear bow ties. The boss takes your order and he and his wife share the service. The chef used to be with Ducasse, which tells you all you need to know. Good traditional French cuisine with fresh produce, meticulously prepared – and it's good value for money. At lunch, there's a main course-dessert option for €18 and dinner menus for €24 or €33. Good wine list.

|●| RESTAURANT LA PETITE AUBERGE

13 rue du Hameau; M° Porte-de-Versailles.
☎ 01.45.32.75.71
Closed Sun, Sat in summer, public holidays, 1–26 Aug and Christmas–New Year.

Service until 10pm. This is the informal headquarters of supporters of the local rugby team – consequently it sees lots of emotional highs and lows. If you don't fancy *après-match*, avoid this place like the plague on match days. Good plain cooking, nonetheless, with daily specials at €9–13: salt pork *à la potée*, sautéed lamb with haricot beans, *blanquette de veau*, pork spare ribs with lentils, roast chicken with herbs, steak with proper chips. The bill will come to around €20.

|●| RESTAURANT LE CLOS MORILLONS

50 rue des Morillons; M° Porte-de-Vanves.
☎ 01.48.28.04.37
Closed Sat lunchtime; Mon.

Service till 11pm. Chef Philippe Delacourcelle spent a long time in Asia, where he developed a taste for spices and sweet-and-sour combinations. East meets West here in a perfectly orchestrated and sometimes brilliant performance. The €23 set menu might feature warm calf's brains with cabbage and roast peanut *vinaigrette, parmentier* of smoked duck in China tea and baked pears with dried fruit and Marsala. There's a second menu for €27 and the *menu-dégustation* at €38 is equally inspiring. The wines are chosen by a knowledgeable *sommelier*: Vouvray by Champalou and Anjou by Richou, both of them excellent winemakers. Refined décor.

16th arrondissement
⚑ HÔTEL VILLA D'AUTEUIL**

28 rue Poussin; M° Porte-d'Auteuil.
☎ 01.42.88.97.69 ➡ 01.45.20.74.70
e villaaut@aol.com
TV.

Its location in the classy part of the 16th *arrondissement* says everything you need to know. This two-star has spotless rooms, each with private bathroom, and all at very reasonable prices (€56–59). There's efficient double glazing in the rooms overlooking the road, but the ones at the back have a prettier view over the greenery of the courtyard. The staff are particularly attentive and can't do enough for you. When you book, confirm you're using this guide and they'll only charge you €56. This offer is good all year round, and in addition they'll give you one free breakfast per double room from 15 Jul to 31 Aug.

⚑ HÔTEL LE HAMEAU DE PASSY**

48 rue de Passy; M° Passy, La Muette or RER Muette-Boulainvilliers.
☎ 01.42.88.47.55 ➡ 01.42.30.83.72
e hameau.passy@wanadoo.fr
Disabled access. **TV**.

The entrance is between a handbag shop and a baldness treatment centre. You come out into a small courtyard full of flowers and ringing with birdsong – a far cry from the luxury designer shops nearby. The hotel is run by an energetic team. Doubles with shower/wc or bath are €88–101. Free breakfast.

⚑ AU PALAIS DE CHAILLOT**

35 av. Raymond-Poincaré; M° Trocadéro.
☎ 01.53.70.09.09 ➡ 01.53.70.09.08
e hapc@wanadoo.fr
TV.

This is a delightful 28-room hotel which is fresh and clean-looking. The rooms are decorated in yellow with curtains in red or blue; all have satellite TV, phone and hairdrier. Doubles with shower/wc €95, €115 with bath. Buffet breakfast is served in a bright little room on the ground floor or they'll bring it to your room. A two-star hotel that easily deserves three – book well ahead. No restaurant but they provide room service: salads, sandwiches, pizzas, pasta and drinks. 10% discount July–Aug.

|●| LE MOZART

12 av. Mozart; M° La Muette.
☎ 01.45.27.62.45
Closed Sun.

The best *andouillette A5* from Duval, meat and mushrooms shipped in from Lozère, ice-cream from Berthillon, bread from the ovens of Michel Moizant and home-made pastries. This kind of quality is co-ordinated by a man who loves to root out quality produce and good wines. It's hardly surprising that you have to wait for a table – but the Kir they provide you with at the bar while you wait soothes your impatience. Lunch or dinner *formules* for €11 (including a platter of *foie gras* and salad) or there's a menu for €14. À *la carte* you'll pay around €23.

|●| RESTAURANT DU MUSÉE DU VIN, CAVEAU DES ÉCHANSONS

5–7 square Charles-Dickens-rue des Eaux; M° Passy.
☎ 01.45.25.63.26 **e** info@museeduvinparis.com
Closed Mon and 25 Dec–1 Jan.

Service noon–3pm. The restaurant is in the wine museum and the dining room is in a fourteenth-century vaulted cellar dug out of the Chaillot clay by the monks who used to cultivate the vines. Many of the dishes use wine in their preparation: they include *coq au vin* and perch fillets in Muscadet sauce. Menus – €15, €21 and €26 – change regularly. You sit down at a hefty wooden table and a waiter proffers you a glass of wine which you are invited to identify. The wine list is twelve pages long and lists nearly 250 vintages all the way up to a Châteay d'Yquem 1908 at €1980 a bottle. Along the way you'll come across *grand crus* from Bordeaux, Burgundy, Alsace and Jura as well as wines from lesser regions in France. Every day there's a selection of fifteen sold by the glass. Free coffee.

17th arrondissement
⅄ ♠ HÔTEL CHAMPERRET-HELIOPOLIS**

13 rue d'Heliopolis; M° Porte de Champerret.
☎ 01.47.64.92.56 ➡ 01.47.64.50.44
Disabled access. TV.

A very quiet hotel with pretty wooden balconies. Most rooms overlook a delightful patio where you can have breakfast when the weather's nice. The place is spotless, and you'll get a very friendly welcome. Rooms have everything you might need – TV, telephone, hairdrier. Doubles with bath or shower €76–52 and breakfast €7. 10% discount at weekends.

♠ HÔTEL PALMA**

46 rue Brunel; M° Porte-Maillot or Argentine.
☎ 01.45.74.74.51 ➡ 01.45.74.40.90
TV.

This hotel is a stone's throw from the convention centre and the Air France terminal. It has an attractive frontage and foyer, and offers a degree of comfort at reasonable prices. Service is polite and efficient. The rooms (single €79, double €85, triple €96) have been redecorated in Provençal style, and have a warm, bright feel. Breakfast can be served in your room. The sixth-floor rooms are extremely popular, so it's best to book.

♠ HÔTEL PRONY***

103 [bis] av. de Villiers; M° Pereire.
☎ 01.42.27.55.55 ➡ 01.43.80.06.97
TV.

Although this hotel is part of a chain, it's still got character; facilities include room service, satellite TV and double glazing. Room number 32 is huge, and ideal for families with one or two kids. Doubles cost €85–120 with bath or shower (no charge for children under twelve sharing with parents). An excellent hotel close to place Pereire and five minutes from Porte Maillot. Breakfast served until midday.

I●I RESTAURANT SHAH JAHAN

4 rue Gauthey; M° Brochant.
☎ 01.42.63.44.06

A Pakistani restaurant decked out with draperies, glittering mirrors and soft background music. À la carte, you can choose from *shish* kebab, lamb *rogan josh*, kara lamb (a very spicy curry) and chicken or lamb tikka. Accompany your main course with cheese naan and basmati rice with saffron. And there is a delicate *lassi* flavoured with cumin and cardamom. Service couldn't be nicer. Lunchtime set menus €7 and €12; others €18 and €20 including drink.

⅄ I●I LA LOGGIA

41 rue Legendre; M° Villiers.
☎ 01.44.40.47.30
Closed Sun lunchtime and Mon.

This restaurant is as much about fast cars as good food – there's a Ferrari here, another there, and a mural of magnificent machines along the wall. Even the waitresses' T-shirts are emblazoned with that famous rearing horse. The owner-chef produces tasty food: marinated fresh sardine fillets, *rigatoni* with prawn cream sauce. And let's hear it for the *tiramisù*. An enjoyable meal won't cost you a bomb, either – one menu for €11 or €20–27 à la carte.The only drawback is that the service isn't as speedy as everything else. Free Kir.

⅄ I●I L'ÉTOILE VERTE

13 rue Brey; M° Charles-de-Gaulle-Étoile or Ternes.
☎ 01.43.80.69.34

Service until 11pm. The restaurant took its name not from the square, which is just five minutes away, but from the green star that Esperanto speakers use as their emblem; the society used to hold its meetings on the first floor. It was redecorated to celebrate its half century – it was founded in 1947 – and looks fresh and pleasant. Lunchtime menu €11 and a dinner version for €17, both of which include a $1/_4$-litre of wine; another at €24 includes apéritif and bottle of wine. À la carte, a meal costs around €30. Among the star dishes, you shouldn't miss the scallops à l'Antillaise, the duck confit or their house steak tartare. Free house apéritif.

I●I RESTAURANT LE VERRE BOUTEILLE

85 av. des Ternes; M° Porte-Maillot.
☎ 01.45.74.01.02
Closed Christmas Eve and Christmas Day.

Service noon–3pm and 7pm–5am. Excellent wine bar, open until dawn. Night owls can fill up on robust main dishes like steak tartare made with chopped – not minced – steak, or very, very large salads. There's one called nain jaune, "the yellow dwarf" (also the name of an old card game), which includes Comté cheese, chicken, raisins and curry sauce. Wines come from around the world and about thirty are available by the glass. Things can get lively on weekends by the time 4am comes. Menus €17 and €26 and a lunchtime one at €14. There's a second *Verre Bouteille* at 5 bd. Gouvion-Saint Cy in the 17th *arrondissement* – but that one closes at midnight (☎ 01.47.39.99).

𝒜 |●| L'IMPATIENT

14 passage Geoffroy-Didelot; M° Villiers.
☎ 01.43.87.28.10
Closed Sat lunchtime; Sun; Mon evening; a fortnight in Aug.

The entrance is between 92 bd. de Batignolles and 117 rue des Dames. This restaurant is appropriately named – some evenings the wait for a table is extensive. The lower-priced menus (€17 at lunchtime, €20 in the evening) are excellent value for money and there's a costlier one for €46 – a meal *à la carte* will cost around €43. Dishes include pan-fried escalope of *foie gras*, squid *escabèche* salad, stew of ox cheek with baby vegetables and endive *sabayon* with cocoa sorbet. Chef Paul Blouet also prepares delicate vegetarian options like *papillotte* of lightly spiced fresh sweetcorn – he really pushes himself to produce unusual dishes that his customers appreciate. Free house apéritif.

𝒜 |●| GRAINDORGE

15 rue de l'Arc-de-Triomphe; M° Charles-de-Gaulle-Étoile.
☎ 01.47.54.00.28
Closed Sat lunchtime and Sun.

Service until 11pm. Bernard Broux is an inspired chef who uses his expertise to the greater glory of his native Flanders, re-interpreting his culinary heritage: *covet* of *jare à la Flamande* marinated in brown ale, eel in *sauce verte*, fish or poultry *waterzoï*, and for dessert go for jam *baba* in Gueuze chantilly or dark cocolate *fondant* with coffee and chicory sauce. All the produce is fresh, and dishes are cooked to order. Forget the wine list and stick to beer – any one of the many varieties goes perfectly with the food. Lunchtime menus at €22 and €27, €31 in the evening, and you'll pay around €31 *à la carte*. Best to book at the weekend. Free *digestif*.

18th arrondissement
𝒜 ☎ HÔTEL BOUQUET DE MONTMARTRE**

1 rue Durantin; M° Abbesses.

☎ 01.46.06.87.54 ➡ 01.46.06.09.09

A conventional hotel which has been taken over by a young couple and refurbished throughout. The rooms are decent if small, and they are all different. Doubles, €61, all have double glazing, their own wc and a choice of shower or bath. Excellent location, good reception and a wonderful view over Paris from room 43. 10% discount.

𝒜 ☎ HÔTEL PRIMA LEPIC**

29 rue Lepic; M° Blanche.
☎ 01.46.06.44.64 ➡ 01.46.06.66.11
e reservation@hotelprimalepic.com
TV.

This is the ideal place to set off for a stroll through the neighbourhood. The impasse Marie-Blanche is close by, and definitely worth a look. The reception is bright and fresh and there's a *trompe l'oeil* of an English garden, a theme which they've developed by choosing garden furniture. Rooms, which look like something out of a magazine, are well-maintained. Doubles €91–121 with shower/wc or bath. Avoid room numbers 11 and 17 – they're very dark. With this book, your breakfast is half-price at €3.

𝒜 ☎ TIM HÔTEL**

11 rue Ravignan (pl. Émile-Goudeau); M° Abbesses or Blanche.
☎ 01.42.55.74.79 ➡ 01.42.55.71.01
e Montmartre@timhotel.fr
TV.

This beautiful hotel, which has been recently renovated, is located in a wonderfully pretty square. Doubles with shower or bath €104. Each floor is dedicated to a painter: going from the ground floor to the fifth you have a choice of Toulouse-Lautrec, Utrillo, Dali, Picasso, Renoir and Matisse. All have direct-dial phone and TV, and those on the fourth floor and above have a view of the square or the city; number 417 is especially nice. Great place for a romantic weekend. 10% discount Dec–March and July–Sept.

|●| RESTAURANT SONIA

8 rue Letort; M° Jules-Joffrin.
☎ 01.42.57.23.17
Closed Sun lunchtime.

Service noon–2.30pm and 7.30–11.30pm. A small Indian restaurant with a pink and purple dining room seating only 25 people, so it's often full. Friendly reception. *Formules* €7 and €12, and there's a €15 menu. Everything is delicately spiced, beautifully presented and cooked to perfection – from the naan to the chicken Madras and vindaloo, not to mention the lamb korma and the aubergine bhartha.

🎿 |●| LE RENDEZ-VOUS DES CHAUFFEURS

11 rue des Portes-Blanches; M° Marcadet-Poissoniers.
☎ 01.42.64.04.17
Closed Wed, and Thurs in Aug.

Service noon–2.30pm (3pm on Sat) and evenings to 11pm. This place has a long history, and when Jeannot took it over he was wise enough to change things as little as possible: the old wood counter and mirrors are still there, the tightly packed tables are covered by glazed cotton checked tablecloths and the benches are leather – he's even kept the brownish paint so typical of old restaurants. You might start with leek *vinaigrette* or egg mayonnaise then follow it with the dish of the day – veal kidneys, calf's liver, veal escalope *à la Normande* or *pot-au-feu* – then puddings like pear tart, chocolate or fruit mousse and *crème caramel*.The €11 menu is served until 8.30pm, dishes of the day cost around €10 while a meal *à la carte* will set you back €15. Efficient, friendly service. Free Kir.

🎿 |●| LA CASSEROLE

17 rue Boinod; M° Marcadet-Poissoniers.
☎ 01.42.54.50.97
Closed Sun; Mon; public holidays; 22 July–22 Aug.

Service at lunch and until 10pm. The atmosphere, the service and the cuisine are all so good that it's worth making an effort to go to this restaurant. There's a jovial welcome and smiling service and the chef greets you at the end of your meal. The décor is an exhibition of regulars' holidays over the last 40 years: they've sent postcards and posters and brought back souvenirs which are attached to every surface. Traditional cuisine respecting the changing seasons and the fresh produce from the markets: fish *cassoulet*, duck with honey and ginger, calf's head *ravigote* and fresh fruit desserts. Menus (Tues–Fri lunch) €12 including drink with an evening one for €20. *À la carte* a meal costs €23–31 with wine on top. They won't let you use the loos unless you're over 18. House *digestif*.

🎿 |●| LA MAZURKA

3 rue André-del-Sarte; M° Château-Rouge or Anvers.
☎ 01.42.23.36.45
Closed Wed.

Reservations only at lunchtime, dinner until 11.45pm. Marek comes from Poland originally, though this corner of Montmartre has been his home for more than ten years. He produces great dishes like flambéed sausages, homemade ravioli, pork spare ribs gipsy-style, *bigos* (Poland's answer to *choucroute*), beef Strogonoff, *borscht* and *blinis* (small pancakes) topped with tarama or smoked salmon. Set menu €18 (not served Sat evening) or about €23 *à la carte*, though it all depends on your liquid intake – half a pint or so of vodka will cost you €20. If Marek is in good form, he'll get out his guitar and sing. Free coffee or *digestif*.

|●| TAKA

1 rue Véron; M° Pigalle or Abbesses.
☎ 01.42.23.74.16
Closed Sun; public holidays; the last fortnight in July.

Service 7.30–10pm. Tiny little Japanese restaurant dumped in a narrow, dingy street at the foot of the Butte. It's often absolutely crammed so it's best to book. Mr Taka is a lovely chap and attentive to your needs. Authentic Japanese cooking, perfectly executed: the quality never wavers. You'll find all the Japanese classics – *sushi*, *sashimi*, miso soup and so on. Reckon on about €24 a head *à la carte* with a large Japanese beer. Set menus €18 and €23 – when it's time to tot up the bill, Mr Taka prefers to use an abacus rather than a calculator.

|●| RESTAURANT MARIE-LOUISE

52 rue Championnet; M° Simplon.
☎ 01.46.06.86.55
Closed Sun; Mon; public holidays; 3 weeks in Aug.

Service noon–2pm and last orders for dinner 10.30pm. You'd do well to book – this is a terrific restaurant. When you walk through the door it's as if you've stepped into a *Vieille France* family dining room filled with brass and copper so highly polished you can see your face in it. The cooking is traditional and the portions enormous: *foie gras*, hare Royale, *coq au vin*, veal chops *grand-mère* and *bœuf ficelle*. The quality of the cooking hasn't changed in years. Prices are reasonable: there's a three-course set menu for €20 or you'll pay about €23 *à la carte*.

19th arrondissement
🎿 🏠 HÔTEL DE CRIMÉE**

188 rue de Crimée; M° Crimée.
☎ 01.40.36.75.29 ➡ 01.40.36.29.57
📧 hotel.crimee@free.fr
TV.

A simple, comfortable hotel not far from the

Parc de la Villet. Renovations have provided air conditioning and soundproofing in the rooms, as well as new bathrooms and new carpets everywhere. Doubles €52 with shower/wc or €56 with bath. There are also rooms for three or four. Warm welcome. 10% discount at weekends and July–Aug.

◉l AUX ARTS ET SCIENCES RÉUNIS

161 av. Jean-Jaurès; M° Ourcq.
☎ 01.42.40.53.18 ➡ 01.48.03.10.68
Closed Sat night; Christmas Day; New Year's Day.

Lunch 11.30am–2pm and dinner 7–9pm. You'll see compasses and a set square on the façade of this "canteen" for people who work at the headquarters of the carpenters' guild. Go past the bar to an extremely attractive dining room with a parquet floor, ceiling mouldings and lots of photos of guild members on the walls. The food, like the atmosphere, is provincial in style – things like escalopes, trout and grilled meats. The €9 menu is good, the helpings are generous and wine is included. Dishes of the day €6 and €9.

🎄 ◉l COK MING

39 rue de Belleville; M° Belleville or Pyrénées.
☎ 01.42.08.75.92

Service 11am–2am. This place is run by Cambodian staff, who fly and swerve round the tables providing super-efficient service. It's been going for a good 20 years. You can make up your own menu from a selection of seafood for two, arrange a fondue or a hot pot for a group of mates, throw back a bowl of soup or take your time over some of their excellent roasts and barbecued meats – Peking duck, chinese fondue and *dim sum* – and all for very fair prices. The menu is massive and includes a number of Thai dishes. Menus between €7 and €13 including a vegetarian one. There's a good choice of teas, wines and beers. Free apéritif or coffee.

◉l LE RENDEZ-VOUS DES QUAIS

10 quai de la Seine; M° Stalingrad.
☎ 01.40.37.02.81 ➡ 01.40.37.03.18

Service until midnight. Monsieur Legendre, from the legendary *Taillevent* restaurant, supervises what goes on here. Regulars include journalists from *Le Monde*, *Le Nouvel Observateur*, *Libération* and *Nova Mag*. The wide terrace, facing south, is right on the water, overlooking the pool of la Villette. When the sun shines the place heaves. Lots of wines are served by the glass and they're selected with great care – by none other than

the film director Claude Chabrol. The bistro belongs to Marin Karmitz, who also owns the cinema next door, so if you want to go to the movies, opt for the *formule menu ciné*, €23, which gets you a main course, a glass of wine, coffee and seat at the cinema. Eat *à la carte* for about the same.

◉l AU RENDEZ-VOUS DE LA MARINE

14 quai de la Loire; M° Jaurès.
☎ 01.42.49.33.40
Closed Sun; Mon; 23 Dec–2 Jan.

Service lunchtime and in the evening until 10pm. Reservations highly advisable – it's often full. A delightful bistro with flowers on the tables, a few nautical souvenirs scattered around and photos of film stars. It's *the* place to be and it's noisy, especially at lunchtime and on every other Saturday evening in the winter when a talented female singer out-Piafs Piaf. In summer, tables are set on the terrace and you have a view of the canal. Food is reasonably priced and helpingss are generous, though the cooking is pretty ordinary. Regular dishes include the house chicken liver *terrine*, mushrooms *à la provençale*, the chef's special prawns, scallops *à la provençale* and duck breast with green peppercorns. If you want paella, you have to order it the night before. There's a very good apple tart flambéed with Calvados. *À la carte* only – reckon on €23.

🎄 ◉l LE PAVILLON PUEBLA

Parc des Buttes-Chaumont; M° Buttes-Chaumont.
☎ 01.42.08.92.62
Closed Sun and Mon.

Service until 10pm. It's your wedding anniversary, you've just won the lottery and you've decided to celebrate in style? This is the place to do it. Standing in the middle of the city's most beautiful park, it has a refined setting with fresh flowers everywhere. The terrace is out of this world – the kind of place you dream about when the weather starts to improve. You'll be received with style, but there's no bowing or scraping. The cooking is first-rate and chef Christian Verges changes his dishes regularly so they reflect the seasons: delights like squid *à la catalane*, lobster stew with Banyuls wine, *pinata* (braised fish), and oyster ravioli with a curry sauce. The desserts are to die for. It's expensive – in fact it's very expensive if you go *à la carte* and have wine too – but the €31 set menu lists, for example, anchovies in a flaky pastry case, *bouillinade* (an upmarket sort of *bouillabaisse*) and chocolate *tuiles*. It's absolutely terrific and comes complete with *canapés*, home-made rolls and so on. There's also a €41 set menu. Free apéritif.

20th arrondissement
☖ TAMARIS HÔTEL*

14 rue des Maraîchers; M° Porte-de-Vincennes or Maraîchers.
☎ 01.43.72.85.48 ➠ 01.43.56.81.75
e tamaris-hotel@wanadoo.fr
TV.

Reservations advisable. An extremely well-run little hotel with prices at a level you might expect in the depths of the country. The rooms are small and pretty and have flowery wallpaper. Doubles with basin €27, with shower €36, with shower/wc €42; there are also rooms that sleep three. One of those is number 16, which has a double and a single bed. Breakfast is €4. It's a bit old-fashioned and altogether delightful – you'll get a warm welcome. Best to book.

🍴 ☖ HÔTEL PYRÉNÉES GAMBETTA**

12 av. du Père-Lachaise; M° Gambetta.
☎ 01.47.97.76.57 ➠ 01.47.97.17.61
TV.

A pleasant two-star in a quiet street near the Père-Lachaise cemetery. The rooms are perfectly adequate, with large beds pushed into alcoves, and all have TV and mini-bar. Doubles with shower/wc or bath €53–75. Breakfast is €5 – they'll serve it in your room. A good place which is quiet and cosy and in a non-touristy neighbourhood that's worth discovering. Delightful welcome. One breakfast free if there are two of you 10 Jan–20 Feb and 12 July–20 Aug.

🍴 ▮●▮ RESTAURANT ARISTOTE

4 rue de la Réunion; M° Maraîchers or Buzenval.
☎ 01.43.70.42.91
Closed Sun and a fortnight in Aug.

Service at lunchtime and until 11.30pm in the evening. This little restaurant may not be much to look at, but you won't have to go to the cashpoint before eating here. It offers generous helpings of Greek and Turkish specialities served with a smile. Starters include *firinda pastirma* or *firinda sucuk* (Turkish meat or sausage turnovers), and there are lots of kebabs and grills. Try the *hunkar beyendi* (rack of lamb with aubergines and potatoes in a sauce), the *guvec* (veal with vegetables in sauce) or the yoghurt dishes with minced steak or lamb. There are also good fish dishes for non-carnivores. The weekday lunch menu, €8,

has a main dish that changes every day. In the evening, *à la carte* costs €15–17. Local clientele, background music, pleasant setting and a good atmosphere. Free coffee or *digestif*.

▮●▮ AU RENDEZ-VOUS DES AMIS

10 av. du Père-Lachaise; M° Gambetta.
☎ 01.47.97.72.16
Closed Evenings and 20 July–15 Aug.

There's a good atmosphere in this friendly restaurant where the wine goes so fast it seems to evaporate. Robust dishes: black pudding crowned with apples, shoulder of veal and *ratatouille*, escalope of *foie gras* with apples and sirloin with blue cheese sauces – it's satisfyingly old-fashioned cooking of yesteryear. The €10 menu gives you a starter and main course, there's a *formule* for €9 and *à la carte* dishes cost around €13 each.

🍴 ▮●▮ RESTAURANT PASCALINE

49 rue Pixérécourt; M° Place-des-Fêtes.
☎ 01.44.62.22.80
Closed Sun; Mon evening; a week in Feb; a fortnight in Aug.

This restaurant has a pretty name and you'll enjoy a delightful meal of good regional dishes, generously served: sausage from Cantal, ham hock with lentils, duck *confit*, complicated salads and home-made pastries. Pleasant dining room with a large fresco and a sunny terrace where you can relax in the afternoon. Set menu €11 at lunchtime; reckon on €20 in the evening. Interesting wines. Free house apéritif.

▮●▮ RESTAURANT CHEZ JEAN

38 rue Boyer; M° Gambetta or Ménilmontant.
☎ 01.47.97.44.58
Closed lunchtimes; Sun; Aug; Christmas to New Year.

Service until about midnight. Jean says his is the best restaurant in the street and it's impossible to argue – it's the *only* restaurant in the street. He used to be a journalist but a few years ago he decided he'd rather own a restaurant. He provides home cooking in the best French tradition with a few added touches of his own. The atmosphere is a mixture of working-class and trendy so typical of the neighbourhood. It's always good fun, with an accordion player and singer at weekends. *Menu du jour* €15; it's €24 *à la carte* depending on what wine you drink.

▮●▮ LE CAFÉ NOIR

15 rue Saint-Blaise; M° Porte-de-Bagnolet or Alexandre-Dumas.
☎ 01.40.09.75.80

Closed lunchtimes Mon–Sat.

Service 7pm–midnight; noon to midnight on Sunday. This was a dispensary at the beginning of the last century, but there's little sign of its medical past – the owners collect coffee pots, hats, enamel signs and posters rather than medicine bottles. They serve generous portions of good food: dishes such as *mille-feuille* of artichokes and *foie gras, terrine* of monkfish liver, veal with violet mustard and fillet of beef with *foie gras* and spiced bread. And you can indulge in a cigar afterwards – the bar sells single Havanas. You'll pay about €23 for a meal.

NEUILLY-SUR-SEINE   92200 (0.5KM NW)

🍴 🏠 HÔTEL CHARLEMAGNE**

1 rue Charcot (West); M° Pont-de-Neuilly; it's 50m from the metro station.
☎ 01.46.24.27.63 ➠ 01.46.37.11.56
📧 info@hotelcharlemagne.com
TV. Disabled access.

Pleasant reception at this hotel, as well as comfortable, modern double rooms with mini-bar, direct phone and shower/wc or bath/wc. They cost from €69 – reasonable for Neuilly. The street is quiet in the evening and throughout the night. An ideal location for anyone who needs to get to La Défense the next day but who doesn't want to spend the night there. And the Bois de Boulogne is not far away for a morning jog. 10% discount Fri–Sun nights inclusive.

🍴 |●| LE CHALET

14 rue du Commandant-Pilot (Southeast); M° les Sablons; it's near the market square.
☎ 01.46.24.03.11
Closed Sun.

A Swiss chalet for those who didn't get away on a skiing holiday last year. There are snowscape photos on the wall to help the illusion and and bits of equipment scattered around. At lunchtime there's a super-fast *formule* at €10 and set menus at €12–24. Specialities include Canadian lobster, *raclette savoyarde* and fresh pastas. Really pleasant. It's a popular place. Free house apéritif.

🍴 |●| RESTAURANT FOC LY

79 av. Charles-de-Gaulle (Southeast); M° Sablons.
☎ 01.46.24.43.36
Closed the first fortnight in Aug. **Disabled access. Pay car park.**

You can't miss this place – it's got a pagoda roof and a pair of lions guarding the entrance.

This is undoubtedly one of the greatest Asian restaurants in the area, as the signatures of the great and the good in the foyer testify. A very refined and varied style of cooking: Peking duck, rolled monkfish with prawns, chicken with honey and ginger. Exemplary service. Weekday lunchtime *formule* €15, children's menu €11 including a drink and about €27 *à la carte*. Free apéritif.

🍴 |●| LES PIEDS DANS L'EAU

39 bd. du Parc; it's on the Île de Jatte.
☎ 01.47.47.64.07
Closed Sat lunchtime and Sun from Oct–April.

There's a feeling of time past in this riverside restaurant – an atmosphere of fishing parties and languid summer picnics. The furniture is English-style and there are old engravings on the wall, creating a sort of club-house ambience. The terraces run right down to the edge of the River Seine, under the poplars, fig trees and weeping willows. The chef landed in town from elsewhere and provides flavours from those far-off parts – grilled fish and meats, monkfish *pot-au-feu aïoli*, trout *carpaccio*, raw marinated salmon salad with whipped cream, tuna *aumônière*, chicken breasts with figs. Set menus €20–23 and €31 *à la carte*. Free apéritif.

BOULOGNE-BILLANCOURT   92100 (1KM SW)

🍴 🏠 LE QUERCY

251 bd. Jean-Jaurès (Southeast); M° Marcel-Sembat.
☎ 01.46.21.33.46 ➠ 01.46.21.72.21
📧 hotellequercy@wanadoo.fr
TV.

A freshly renovated and practical place, rather like a chain hotel – and one of the least expensive places in the area. Doubles with shower/wc €34 and €44 with bath/wc. Reassuring welcome. One free breakfast per room per night.

|●| CAFÉ LE CENTRE

120 route de la Reine; M° Marcel-Sembat.
☎ 01.46.05.47.86
Closed Sun and Aug.

A popular and genuine old bistro which feels totally out of place in the suburban setting – it's completely refused to move with the times. The walls are hung with old adverts and they're yellowed by years of nicotine. Food is simple and inexpensive: go for the tasty monkfish *à la provençale*, the *andouillette* with mustard sauce or the peppered skirt. They offer a complete set menu at €9.

I●I RESTAURANT LA TONNELLE DE BACCHUS

120 av. Jean-Baptiste-Clément (Northwest); M°
Boulogne-Pont-de-Saint-Cloud; it's 20m from the métro.
☎ 01.46.04.43.98
Closed Sat, Sun and Christmas to 1 Jan.

The white piano in the reception sets the tone – sometimes the *patronne* sits down and bangs out a tune. The chef prepares good specialities from Lyons like hot sausage with potatoes *vinaigrette*, but there's also *confit* of duck, *profiteroles* from Landes or steak with shallots, all of which are very tasty; Alsace is also represented by a decent *choucroute*. All in all, traditional cuisine of good quality; menus €18 and €22. There are some reasonably priced wines on the list if you look carefully. You can eat on the terrace when it's warm enough. Free coffee.

⚱ I●I RESTAURANT LA MARMITE

54 av. Édouard-Vaillant (East); M° Porte-de-Saint-Cloud
or Marcel-Sembat; it's 300m from porte de Saint-Cloud.
☎ 01.46.08.06.12
Closed Sat evening, Sun, public holidays and Aug.

The décor is rather run-of-the-mill, with square pillars and large mirror tiles. Simple brasserie-style cooking: kebabs, poached or grilled salmon, *entrecôte béarnaise*, and lots of fresh fish. Set menus from €18. Free house apéritif.

⚱ I●I CHEZ MICHEL

4 rue Henri-Martin; M° Porte-de-Saint-Cloud.
☎ 01.46.09.08.10
Closed Sat lunchtime; Sun; Aug; Christmas to New
Year's Day.

At lunchtime this place has the atmosphere of a noisy canteen. But in the evening, when friends come and talk more intimately, the noise levels drop. The dishes are chalked up on a blackboard so you can choose your own menu. Try *foie gras* with spiced bread, ravioli from Royans with cream and chives, monkfish tails with green peppers, veal fillet with shallots or crispy lamb with wild rosemary. The prices are reasonable, with starters and desserts at €4 and main dishes at €9, so it's not ruinous – even if you decide to have a glass of wine. Weekday menu €20. Free house apéritif.

IVRY-SUR-SEINE   94200 (1KM SE)

I●I L'EUROPE

92 bd. Paul-Vaillant-Couturier.
☎ 01.46.72.04.64.

The welcome is warm and the service effi-
cient. At lunchtime, the two dining rooms are full of noise and overflow with customers. They dish up excellent *couscous*, €8–11, and also do good grills. On Friday they also offer *choucroute* or paella.

LEVALLOIS-PERRET   92300 (1KM NW)

⌂ HÔTEL DU GLOBE

36 rue Louis Rouquier; M° Louise Michel.
☎ 01.47.57.29.39

This is a clean and unpretentious family hotel in a busy street – fortunately the rooms have double-glazing. On the other hand, they're small and don't have wc. Doubles with basin €31 or €38–46 with shower. Amiable welcome.

I●I LE PETIT POUCET

4 rond-point Claude-Monet (West); it's at the eastern
end of the île de la Jatte.
☎ 01.47.38.61.85

Lunch service noon–2.15pm, dinner 7.45–11.15pm. There's been a restaurant here for almost a century. Back in the 1900s, it was a tavern out in the country to which working-class men used to bring their sweethearts. In the 1980s it became terribly fashionable, before being transformed ten years ago into a cosy place with lots of wood panelling and a warm atmosphere. It has three lovely terraces, one on the bank of the Seine, where elegant ladies and fashionable young men come to relax as soon as the sun comes out. Good, classic French cooking with menus from €17. Fast, efficient service. Best to book.

MONTREUIL 93100   (1KM E)

I●I LE GAILLARD

71 rue Hoche; M° Mairie-de-Montreuil.
☎ 01.48.58.17.37
Closed Sun and Mon evenings.**Garden**.

It's worth braving the boulevard Périphérique to get here. Atop the Guillands hill, right in the middle of nowhere in particular, this old residence is a haven of culinary taste and *savoir-vivre*. The starters are delicate and the mains have panache: duck *parmentier* with salad, ox kidneys with puréed potato and simple but delicious desserts. Menus €23 and €34, but *à la carte* the bill can shoot up – not least because the wines are expensive. Faultless service and gracious welcome. There's an appealing open fire in winter and an amazing garden/terrace that comes into its own in the summer.

NANTERRE   92000 (1KM NW)

⚰ 🏠 HÔTEL SAINT-JEAN

24/26/33 av. de Rueil (West); RER Nanterre-Ville on the
Saint-Germain-en-Laye line or bus 258.
☎ 01.47.24.19.20 ➟ 01.47.24.17.65

The hotel is a away from the main street in a
very quiet neighbourhood. No two rooms are
alike, but all are clean and more than adequate. Doubles from €23 with basin, €31
with shower or €38 with shower/wc. Friendly
welcome. The place has been run by three
generations of the same family for over sixty
years. Free coffee.

⚰ 🏠 I●I RESTAURANT LE COIN TRANQUILLE

8–10 rue du Docteur-Foucault (Centre); RER Nanterre-
Ville.
☎ 01.47.21.11.80
Restaurant closed Sun, Christmas and 1 Jan.

Service noon–3pm and 7–9pm. Large dining
room where they serve traditional cooking at
very good prices – scallops with oyster
mushrooms and fisherman's stew, for example. Or you can have mussels and chips with
a glass of white wine. Menus from €10. Best
to book. Basic rooms with shower/wc or
bath €27–38. Free coffee, *digestif* or 10%
discount on the room rate.

SAINT-CLOUD   92210 (1KM W)

I●I LA BOÎTE À SEL

2 rue de l'Église (West).
☎ 01.47.71.11.37
Closed Sun and Mon evening.

A nice little place with a chic provincial
atmosphere and a touch of suburban refinement – just right for Saint-Cloud. It's bright,
cosy and comfortable. The cuisine is good,
and though it's not elaborate, it's carefully
prepared: grilled salmon, pork *filet mignon* in
cider, duck breast in honey, *andouillette* from
Troyes, fish *tartare*. Menus from €11.

SAINT-MANDÉ   94160 (1KM E)

I●I LE BISTROT LUCAS

8 rue Janne d'Arc; M° Saint-Mandé Tourelle
☎ 01.48.08.74.81
Closed Sun, Mon evening and Aug.

This bistro is on the outskirts of Paris and
within striking distance of the Vincennes
woods. They treat you very well here amid
the wooden tables, simple décor and post-

cards on the walls. Attractive dishes: lentils
rémoulade with hot Lyons sausage, calf's
brains with black butter, pike forcemeat balls.
For dessert, try home-made pastries or the
fruit *coulis*. One menu at €20, main courses
à la carte at €11–14 and wines around €15
a bottle. Attentive welcome.

VINCENNES   94300 (2KM SE)

⚰ I●I RISTORANTE ALESSANDRO

51 rue de Fontenay; M° Château-de-Vincennes; RER
Vincennes; it's beside the town hall.
☎ and ➟ 01.49.57.05.30
Closed Sun and three weeks in Aug. **Disabled access**.

The chef and his wife prepare a vast number
of dishes with skill and intelligence. These are
mainly Italian specialities – spaghetti with
king prawns, tagliatelle with scallops and
saltimbocca alla romana (a wonderful combination of veal, Parma ham and sage). The
antipasti – artichokes, olives, sun-dried
tomatoes, pickled onions and *charcuterie* –
are fantastic. And the pizzas are the real
thing. Set weekday lunch menu €10, then
others at €21 and €30. Reservation essential. Free house apéritif.

COURBEVOIE-LA-DÉFENSE   92400 (3KM W)

I●I PASTA, AMORE E FANTASIA

80 av. Marceau; train Saint-Lazare to Courbevoie station
or RER line A, La Défense.
☎ 01.43.33.68.30
Closed Sun; Mon evening.

Inside this place you'll be blown away by the
exuberant colours of Naples – they've even
hung washing across the room. The dining
room is vast but manages to feel intimate.
The cuisine is equally exuberant and colourful: delicious antipasti, a huge choice of pizzas, *osso bucco à la piémontaise*, Sicilian
ravioli, *piccata parmigiana* and so on. One
menu at €13 or around €31 *à la carte*. Live
music after 10.30pm on Friday and Saturday.

SAINT-DENIS   93200 (3.5KM N)

⚰ I●I LES VERDIOTS

26 bd. Marcel-Sembat (North); M° Porte-de-Paris; it's
400m from the Stade de France.
☎ 01.42.43.24.33 ➟ 01.42.43.43.44
Closed Sun, Mon and Aug.

Service noon–3pm and 7–9.30pm. Patrick
Perney specializes in cuisine from les Landes
on the Atlantic coast – ham from the
Aldudes, duck *confit*, guineafowl with figs,

crispy pigs' trotters, *foie gras* with yellow peaches. The service is friendly and charming, the dining room classic and clean, and the prices honest. There's a substantial lunch menu at €10 and a dinner one for €16; otherwise it's about €35 *à la carte*. A good place with good wines. Free apéritif.

🕸 |●| LE WAGON

14 [bis] rue Jean-Moulin (Centre); M° Porte de Paris; it's near the Baleine swimming pool.
☎ 01.48.23.23.41
Closed evenings and 14 July to end Aug.

This is an amazing restaurant, and it's housed in a railway carriage. It's run by a restaurant school, so the waiters and kitchen staff apply themselves to their tasks with great concentration. You eat cheaply but well; house specialities are fish and seafood. The *formules* and menus go for €8 or €11 and list pan-fried scallops with leeks, *terrine* with red onion marmalade, salmon fillet with grain mustard and excellent house desserts – try the duo of chocolate with bitter cocoa. It's worth booking. Free apéritif.

🕸 |●| LE MÉLODY

15 rue Gabriel-Péri (Centre); M° Porte de Paris.
☎ 01.48.20.87.73

There's a garish blue neon sign outside this pocket-sized restaurant, which offers a warm welcome and good food. The *menu-carte*, €21, lists dishes drenched in southern sun; duo of *cabécou* (a goat's cheese), roast rabbit *provençale* and *dacquoise*. And there are a modest number of well-chosen wines. Free coffee.

SAINT-MAUR-DES-FOSSÉS   94100 (10KM E)

🕸 |●| LE BISTROT DE LA MER

15 rue Saint-Hilaire; it's a turning off the A4 autoroute.
☎ 01.48.83.01.11
Closed Sun evening; Mon; Aug.

Service until 11pm. The dining room is decorated in blue and white, creating just the right atmosphere for a seafood restaurant, and dishes are prepared with style. There's lots of originality and skill in the cooking and the quality is reliable so the place has earned itself a regular following. Tues–Fri lunchtimes there's an excellent €15 menu with a salad to start, fish of the day (generously served and quite delicious), dessert, wine and coffee. The one at €24 is a veritable feast, with an even greater range of dishes – skate, scallops, monkfish and bacon kebab,

smoked salmon. They even do fried fish to take away. Free house apéritif.

|●| LE GOURMET

150 bd. du Général-Giraud (Centre).
☎ 01.48.86.86.96
Closed Sun evening, Mon, and Aug to mid-Sept.
Garden.

There are decent places to eat and there are good restaurants – and then there's *Le Gourmet*, which offers high-class cuisine at its best. The setting is wonderfully done: the dining room is elegant Art Deco with armfuls of flowers in big vases, and there's a wide bay window looking out onto a lovely terraced garden where you dine in the summer. And that's not all: the proprietor learned his profession in some of the greatest kitchens in the capital and is on absolutely top form. The food is succulent, delicious and prepared with meticulous care – flavours are delicately balanced and each dish is cooked to perfection. Menus €21–30. *À la carte* you'll pay for the quality and should expect a bill of around €34. Here dishes include lobster ravioli, duckling Marco Polo, gourmet salad with *foie gras* and smoked duck; their speciality dessert is *vacherin*.

🕸 |●| CHEZ NOUS COMME CHEZ VOUS

110 av. du Mesnil; RER Varenne-Chennevière.
☎ 01.48.85.41.61
Closed Sun evening; Mon; 1 May; a week in Feb or March; Aug.

There's an old provincial feel about this place. They've got a battery of copper pots on the walls and it would take an earthquake to disrupt the solid traditions in the kitchen, which are rooted deeply in regional cuisine. You're in the hands of real professionals who focus on providing quality rather than originality. Madame has been running front-of-house for a good quarter of a century and the service is first rate; her husband, the chef, keeps his standards similarly high. Dishes of the day include ham hock with lentils, beef and carrots and *choucroute*. There's a very full menu at €30, which includes cheese and a $1/_4$-litre of wine, and another at €34 with a children's menu at €18 (including a drink). Free coffee.

PONTOISE   95300

🕸 |●| LE PAVÉ DE LA ROCHE

30 rue de la Roche; it's a turning off the pl. de l'Hôtel-de-Ville.
☎ 01.34.43.14.05

Closed Sat lunchtime; Sun evening; Mon; 3 weeks in Aug.

You'll find this establishment on a bend of a road climbing above the Oise. Try the €12 menu, with wine included: you start by choosing from the *crudités* buffet, which has at least twenty dishes, and follow with a good main dish and home-made dessert. There's also a *menu-carte* for €23; specialities include rabbit *à la Provençale*, roast Saint-Marcellin cheese with smoked duck breast, Guémené *andouille* with apples, veal blanquette, game in season and a fine apple tart with Calvados. The *patron* and *patronne* welcome you with a broad smile. Free coffee.

PROVINS 77160

⚘ |●| LA BOUDINIÈRE DES MARAIS

17 rue Hugues-le-Grand (Centre); it's at the lower end of town.
☎ 01.60.67.64.89
Closed Tues evening; Wed; the Feb school holidays; last fortnight in Aug.

Incredible but true: they make everything on the premises, even to the point of smoking their own salmon. The locals and well-informed sales reps who come here know that on weekdays for €11 you can get a well-cooked, substantial lunch with a $1/_4$-litre of wine included, and there are other quality menus at €16–28. Traditional French cooking: rabbit *fondant* with onion marmalade, shrimps with spinach *gratiné*, grilled lamb chops with a garlic crust. The décor is neo-medieval and rather heavy, but it suits the place well. Chef Prigent wants to kick fast food out of France and he's going the right way about it. Free coffee.

GURCY-LE-CHÂTEL 77250 (21KM SW)

⚘ |●| RESTAURANT LOISEAU

21 rue Ampère; take the A5 from Paris and turn off at the Forges exit, take the D401 in the direction of Provins, go through Montigny-Lencoup and turn first left onto the D95 for Gurcy-le-Châtel.
☎ 01.60.67.34.00
Closed Sun evening; Mon; the first week in Jan; 3 weeks in Aug.

The name makes you think of the great Loiseau, Saulieu's giant of a chef, but he's no relation – it's evident that more than one Loiseau knows his way around a kitchen. Specialities are fish dishes – the roast zander with duck *brunoise* is mouthwateringly succulent, and the blends of delicate flavours in the scallop *fricassée* with *foie gras* are a sheer

delight. Set menus €15–21 and a *menu ouvrier* at €10 – at this price and quality you would come for lunch every day. At the weekend, it's essential to book. Free house apéritif.

RAMBOUILLET 78120

🏠 HÔTEL SAINT-CHARLES**

15 rue de Groussay (Northwest); from the town hall, follow the road that runs along the park for about 1km.
☎ 01.34.83.06.34 ➡ 01.30.46.26.84
Disabled access. TV. Car park.

A functional hotel near the centre. Most of the rooms are fairly spacious and they're all scrupulously clean. Rooms €47 with shower/wc or bath; breakfast is yours for €5.

⚘ |●| RESTAURANT LA POSTE

101 rue du Général-de-Gaulle (Centre).
☎ 01.34.83.03.01
Closed Mon, Thurs and Sun evenings; 1–7 Jan; a fortnight in summer.

If you want to eat here, one of the best restaurants in town, it's best to book. The two dining rooms are extremely pretty, and service is efficient and friendly. The cooking is light and refined, with dishes like house *foie gras*, lamb *noisette* cooked like game, lamb *fricassée* with crayfish and house raspberry soufflé. Set menus €20–31. Free Kir.

|●| LE LOUVETIER

19 rue de l'Étang de la Tour; take the Chevreuse/Cernay exit from the N10 then it's on the D906.
☎ 01.34.85.61.00
Closed Sun evening and Mon.

This is a fish restaurant in a brilliant white house with azure-blue shutters – you feel as if you're by the Med. That impression will be strengthened by *bouillabaisse*, *bourride* (fish stew), salad of skate and pesto and scallops with dill or basil, all of which are a tasty reminder of the owner's origins – he used to run a garage in Marseilles before he became a chef here. There's a two-course *formule* at €25, menus at €31 and 35 and a *menu-carte* for €31.

ROCHE-GUYON (LA) 95780

⚘ 🏠 |●| HÔTEL-RESTAURANT LES BORDS DE SEINE**

21 rue du Docteur-Duval; it's near the tourist office on the banks of the Seine.
☎ 01.39.98.32.52 ➡ 01.30.98.32.42
TV.

As its name suggests, you can watch the Seine flowing by from this restaurant. The cheapest menu at €13 is served at weekday lunchtime, and offers a choice of starter or dessert with your main course. There's another for €19 or it'll cost about the same *à la carte*. The food is well-cooked, served attractively and you won't go hungry. The fillet of fresh cod is perfectly judged, there's a lovely *nage* of fish, and the calf's liver is excellent. They serve a wine of the month by the glass. There's a lovely terrace with parasols for the summer which they close in and heat in winter. The hotel is well-run, and although the rooms are small they all have en-suite bathrooms and phones. Doubles €43–64 with shower or bath/wc; some have that river view. Relaxed, smiling service. Free coffee.

ROLLEBOISE   78270

🏃 🏠 |❶| CHÂTEAU DE LA CORNICHE

5 route de la Corniche; 10km northwest of Mantes-la-Jolie, when you get to the hilltops of Rolleboise it's at the end of a lane.
☎ 01.30.93.20.00 ☛ 01.30.42.27.44
Closed Sun evening; Mon; a fortnight end Dec. **TV.**

The rooms in this nineteenth-century folly have every modern comfort; doubles are €75 with bath/wc. The restaurant is elegant and there's a panoramic view from the terrace. Refined, yet somewhat daring gourmet cuisine. Lunch menu €25 Tues to Sat; others €36–55 or €46 *à la carte* – it's not cheap but definitely worth it in the category. There are lots of country walks around and it's good base from which to visit Monet's house at Giverny. 10% discount on the room rate except Sat.

RUEIL-MALMAISON   92500

🏃 |❶| LE JARDIN CLOS

17 rue Eugène-Labiche; RER Rueil-Malmaison (ligne A).
☎ 01.47.08.03.11
Closed Sun, Mon and 5–26 Aug. **Garden.**

The bland exterior doesn't really give you a clue about what you'll find inside: there's a peaceful garden with a well, and you can eat on the terrace. The cooking is seriously tasty and generously served, and you'll get a good-natured welcome. The €15 lunch menu includes a self-service buffet of *hors d'œuvres*; others are €23 and €27. Specialities include *salade gourmande* with pine nuts, *foie gras*, scallops *à la bourride*, rack of lamb, braised duck fillet, beef steak and poached turbot. Main dishes are often accompanied by rissoled potatoes. Free house apéritif.

SAINT-GERMAIN-EN-LAYE   78100

🏃 🏠 LE HAVRE*

92 rue Léon-Désoyer (Northwest); it's on the old Chambourcy road.
☎ and ☛ 01.34.51.41.05
TV.

Clean, well-run little hotel in the middle of town where a double with shower/wc will cost €43. Some overlook the cemetery, so there are no extraneous noises to wake you, and all are double-glazed. Pleasant, friendly welcome. A good place. 10% discount June–July.

🏃 🏠 |❶| L'ERMITAGE DES LOGES – LE SAINT-EXUPÉRY***

11 av. des Loges (Centre).
☎ 01.39.21.50.90 ☛ 01.39.21.50.91
TV.

This place is really smart, and there's a wide view of the avenues of trees leading through the forest to the château. Rooms are extremely comfortable and service is faultless; doubles from €98. Fine, classic cuisine is served in the Art Deco dining room. The lunchtime *menu du jour* costs €15 and includes a small bottle of water and wine; there's another at €27. Free breakfast when you stay the night or a house apéritif before your meal.

|❶| RESTAURANT LA FEUILLANTINE

10 rue des Louviers (Centre); it's in the pedestrian area.
☎ 01.34.51.04.24
Closed Sun and public holidays.

Very warm welcome, speedy service and a tasteful dining room so small you're stuffed in like sardines – but that doesn't stop you enjoying your meal. You eat very well here: excellent *foie gras* and omelette with smoked salmon. *Formules* for under €17 at lunchtime and a menu at €26.

🏃 |❶| LE TABL'O GOURMAND

18 pl. Saint-Pierre.
☎ 01.34.51.66.33
Closed Mon lunchtime.

Set on a quiet little square, this is a relaxing restaurant with a Provençal look: beams and dressed stone. The owner is an art lover and fills the dining room with pictures by local artists. He's also a fan of recipes from centuries past and he adapts them for modern tastes – try his *pantoufle de cardinal* stuffed with duck and *foie gras*, but leave room *crêpes Suzette*. Menus start at €21. Only a limited number of half-bottles but they also do wine by the glass.

SAINT-PIERRE-LES-NEMOURS 77140

겿 ≜ |●| HÔTEL-RESTAURANT LES ROCHES**

1–3 av. Léopold-Pelletier; it's opposite the church and not far from the Rochers Gréau.
☎ 01.64.28.01.43 ➡ 01.64.28.04.27
Restaurant closed Sun evening, Mon lunchtime and 15 Nov–15 March. **TV. Disabled access. Car park**.

It's a real pity that this establishment is located at a noisy crossroads, but the rooms are quiet nonetheless and they're comfortable. Doubles with bath €41; ask for the more modern and spacious ones in the annexe – they're also more expensive, of course. In the restaurant you get remarkable value for money considering the delicious food, the lovely setting and the punctilious service: weekday *menu du jour* at €15 and four others €20–41. There's a great house *terrine* and a wonderful sole fillet with morels, and some exquisite pastries to tackle after that. One of the best places to eat in the whole region. 10% discount on the room rate.

SAINTE-GENEVIÈVE-DES-BOIS 91700

|●| LA TABLE D'ANTAN

38 av. de la Grande Charmille du Parc; facing the town hall, it's the third road on the left.
☎ 01.60.15.71.53
Closed Sun; Tues and Wed evenings; Mon.

This place is in a quiet part of the town in a neat house. The décor has a completely new look, and they've also introduced a new ventilation system to make sure that non-smokers aren't disturbed by smokers' cigarettes. The chef is a duck specialist – at duck *foie gras* in particular – but menus also include tasty fish and meat dishes: zander with Puy lentils and, for dessert, *craquant* with banana and chocolate and noutagine with almonds. Menus from €25 to €45 The mistress of the house extends a charming welcome. Essential to book.

SÈVRES 92360

겿 |●| LA SALLE À MANGER

12 av. de la Division-Leclerc.

☎ 01.46.26.66.64 **e** lasalleamanger@wanadoo.fr
Closed Sat lunchtime; Sun evening; Mon; Aug.

The décor is bright and fresh and you immediately feel you're in the country. On the menu you'll find *œufs en meurette* in red wine sauce, tomato tart with Cantal cheese and mustard, *fricassée* of rabbit with herbs, calf's cheek with orange and cumin and duck breast in honey – a cornucopia of flavours. The place is a hive of activity and the service is quiet, quick and efficient; take your time to enjoy it. It's often full because prices are reasonable for the quality: menus €12–24. Free house apéritif.

SURESNES 92150

겿 |●| LES JARDINS DE CAMILLE

70 av. Franklin Roosevelt; from Porte Maillot, take bus number 244 to the Pont de Suresnes stop or take the train to the Suresnes-Mont-Valérien station.
☎ 01.45.06.22.66
Closed Sun evening.

This big house stands on the hillside of the Suresnes vineyards, way up high with a fabulous view of Paris below. They serve Burgundy rather than Suresnes wine here, and the cuisine is good – country dishes like *rillettes* of rabbit with Armagnac, snails, *bœuf bourguignon*, game in season and fresh goat from the Morvan. You'll find food like this on their *menu-carte* at €30. The Poinsots know what they're about, greet you well and really take care of you. Free *digestif*.

VERSAILLES 78000

≜ HOME SAINT-LOUIS**

28 rue Saint-Louis (Centre).
☎ 01.39.50.23.55 ➡ 01.30.21.62.45
TV.

This is a quiet, comfortable, well-looked-after hotel not far from the pretty Saint-Louis neighbourhood. Doubles with shower €38, €53 with shower/wc or €58 with bath – very good value for money.

겿 ≜ HÔTEL RICHAUD***

16 rue Richaud (Centre).
☎ 01.39.50.10.42 ➡ 01.39.53.43.36
TV. Car park.

This must be the most central and yet the most peaceful hotel in town. It has forty very clean rooms with TV and direct-dial telephone – ask for one looking over the buildings of the Hôpital Richaud opposite. The furnishings and decoration are very 1970s – they certainly didn't stint on the carpeting – and make sure you see the bar, which is a monument to kitsch. It doesn't really deserve three stars but it has two-star prices, so that's OK: doubles €37–47 with shower/wc or €52–58 with bath. 10% discount.

⅍ 🏠 HÔTEL DU CHEVAL ROUGE**

18 rue André-Chénier (Centre); it's on the market square.
☎ 01.39.50.03.03 ➡ 01.39.50.61.27
TV. Car park.

A well-located, comfortable hotel which is also a tearoom. Doubles €47 with shower, €61 with shower/wc and €70 with bath/wc – not bad for a town where prices are sky-high, especially near the château. The private car park is a definite plus. One free breakfast per room per night.

⅍ 🏠 PARIS HÔTEL**

14 av. de Paris; RER Versailles. it's 400m from the pl. d'Armes.
☎ 01.39.50.56.00 ➡ 01.39.50.21.83
ℯ contact@paris-hotel.fr
Disabled access. TV.

You will get a very warm welcome in this hotel and the proprietor will give you a friendly handshake when you come down for breakfast. Spacious, clean rooms, the nicest overlooking the courtyard; doubles €40 with shower, €53 with shower/wc, €64–73 with bath. 10% discount on the room rate and one free breakfast per room per night.

❙●❙ LE BALADIN SAINT-LOUIS

2 rue de l'Occident (Centre).
☎ 01.39.50.06.54
Closed Sun.

Not the greatest setting of all time but you can easily ignore it if you sit on the terrace, where you can appreciate the view of the Saint-Louis district. You'll find expressive and daring cuisine which is often imaginative and always of high quality: jellied rabbit with onion marmalade, fresh cod fillet with tapenade, veal kidneys. There's a *formule* (starter/main course) for €14, and menus for €20 and €29 (this one includes drink). A meal *à la carte* will cost around €20.

⅍ ❙●❙ LA CUISINE BOURGEOISE

10 bd. du roi (Centre).
☎ 01.39.53.11.38
Closed Sat lunchtime, Sun, Mon and 2–26 Aug.

This place is perfectly named. It has a very cosy dining room decorated in shades of green and they serve tasty cuisine with some gourmet dishes. The €22 lunch menu is chalked up on the blackboard and others cost €30 and €44 in the evening. *À la carte* you'll pay about €43. There's an excellent list of vintages by the glass and they have theme evenings based around wines. Free house apéritif.

MONTIGNY-LE-BRETONNEUX 78180 (10KM SW)

⅍ 🏠 ❙●❙ L'AUBERGE DU MANET***

61 av. du Manet; coming from Paris on the A12, take the St-Quentin-en-Yvelines exit.
☎ 01.30.64.89.00 ➡ 01.30.64.55.10
ⓦ www.aubergedumanet.com

The huge farm used to be part of the domaine of the Abbaye de Port-Royal-des-Champs which is about 2km away. They've converted it into a hotel-restaurant in a perfect pastoral setting and they've done it very well. The terrace looks over a pretty pond. The rooms are faultless and definitely worth the price (€87–100); all have mini-bar, satellite TV and en-suite bathroom with bath or shower/wc. In the restaurant the cooking is deftly prepared and reasonably priced starting with the menu for residents at €22 (starter, main course and cheese or dessert), €25 and €36. Menus change three times a year. Classic dishes cooked with confidence. 10% discount on the room rate.

LANGUEDOC-ROUSSILLON

11 Aude

30 Gard

34 Hérault

48 Lozère

66 Pyrénées-Orientales

AGDE   34300

🏃 🏠 HÔTEL BON REPOS*

15 rue Rabelais; it's 200m from the centre in the
direction of Béziers.
☎ 04.67.94.16.26
Closed second and third week in Jan. **TV. Pay garage.**

In previous incarnations this place, in a quiet
street, was the town brothel and later the
police station. Nowadays it's a delightful,
simple hotel run by a cheerful couple. Large,
flower–filled terraces where you can laze
around. Rooms €29–36 with shower or with
bath. 10% discount Sept–June.

🏠 HÔTEL LE DONJON**

pl. Jean-Jaurès (Centre).
☎ 04.67.94.12.32 ➡ 04.67.94.34.54
TV. Car park.

An old stone building practically next door to
the ancient cathedral of Saint-Étienne on a
pleasant square that buzzes with life in summer. The fresh-looking bedrooms are comfy,
exceptionally well-maintained and good
value for money. Doubles €43–64 with
shower/wc or bath. Easy–going atmosphere.
Nice welcome, nice prices.

🏃 🏠 |●| HÔTEL–RESTAURANT LA
TAMARISSIÈRE***

Lieu-dit La Tamarissière (Southwest); go along quai
Commandant-Réveille, then follow the D32 for 5km.
☎ 04.67.94.20.87 ➡ 04.67.21.38.40
ℯ hotel-la-Tama@wanadoo.fr
Hotel closed 5 Nov–1 March. **Restaurant closed**
Sun evening and Mon (except public holiday weekends
and in high season); Mon and Tues lunchtimes in
season.

TV.

This hotel, set on the banks of the Hérault, is
the most famous in the region and has a
lovely rose garden within a pine wood. Stylish, modernized bedrooms cost €64–116
with shower/wc or bath. The wonderful
cooking at the old–fashioned bistro is full of
the flavours of the south and successfully
combines tradition with style. Choose from
dishes such as cuttlefish with parsley, tomato and basil, *bourride*, fish stew, *bouillabaisse* and fillet of beef with Banyuls wine
sauce. Set menus €27–60. Easy-going
atmosphere. 10% discount on the room rate
15 Sept–15 June when you book in advance.

|●| LA FINE FOURCHETTE

2 rue du Mont-Saint-Loup, (Northwest); take rue
de'Richelieu then follow the "Promenade".
☎ 04.67.94.49.56
Closed evenings except Sat, Sun and Christmas–1 Jan.

A modest-looking restaurant set back from
the Grand Boulevards with a shady, flowery
terrace. This is the place to enjoy honest
regional cooking at fair prices – sardine or
mackerel tart, croustillant of pigs' trotters.
Menus €10–15. The friendly lady owner takes
care of the service.

MARSEILLAN   34340 (8KM NE)

🏃 |●| LE JARDIN DU NARIS

24 bd. Pasteur; take the D51.
☎ 04.67.77.30.07
Closed Mon evening and Tues out of season; Tuesday
lunchtime in summer; Feb.

The walled garden allows you to dine among
the flowers and the trees. Simple, traditional

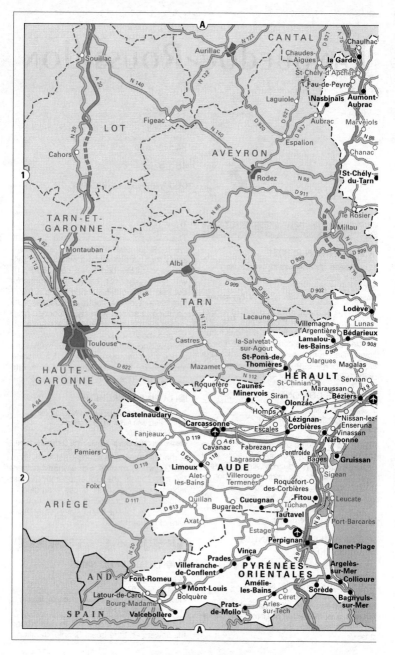

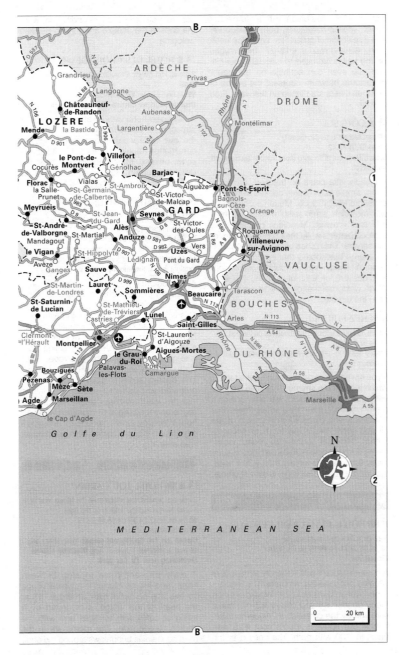

dishes include sea bream with a red pepper *coulis*, scallop *millefeuille*, pork-cheek curry and a selection of grilled fish. Weekday lunch menu €9 and menus €12–27. The crayons on the tables are used to calculate your bill, and you even can scribble on the paper tablecloths between courses; the efforts of previous diners are pinned on the walls. Free apéritif.

⅍ ⌂ CÔTÉ SUD

18 quai Antonin-Gros (Northeast).
☎ 04.67.01.72.42
Closed Thurs out of season, Thurs lunch in summer and Nov–March.

A friendly little place on the port, providing good, simple fresh dishes cooked using seasonal market produce. Madame cooks a*ï*oli with monkfish, warm salad of scallops, shellfish and prawns. Monsieur prepares the seafood platters while their son takes care of the service. The dishes of the day are written on a large blackboard that he brings to the table. Weekday lunch *formule* of *plat du jour* and dessert for €12 or a menu for €21. Warm welcome, friendly service. Good view from the terrace.

❙●❙ CHEZ PHILIPPE

20 rue du Suffren; it's behind the docks on the port.
☎ 04.67.01.70.62
Closed Mon and Tues July–Aug; Sunday evening out of season.

If you haven't booked you won't get a table – which would be a shame. This is an elegant, easy-going, fun restaurant with a terrace on a pretty square. It's run by a smart threesome from Paris who came south in search of sea air and good living. They focus on Mediterranean dishes at surprisingly cheap prices; eating such deliciously flavoured food in such lovely surroundings for less than €30 a head, including a good local wine, is almost unreal.

AIGUES-MORTES   30220

⌂ ❙●❙ HÔTEL–RESTAURANT L'ESCALE*

3 av. de la Tour-de-Constance.
☎ 04.66.53.71.14 ▸ 04.66.53.76.74
Closed Dec.

A hotel-restaurant with a friendly atmosphere situated opposite the ramparts. The regulars linger over a *pastis* or lunch. Weekday lunch *menu du jour* €8 and others €8–15; make sure you try the cuttlefish *à l'Aiguemortaise*. Simple but spotless rooms cost €25 with basin to €30 with bath. The ones over the

bar are a bit noisy but air-conditioned, while the ones in the annexe are quieter. Relaxed welcome.

⅍ ⌂ HÔTEL DES CROISADES**

2 rue du Port (West); it's outside the ramparts, near the canal.
☎ 04.66.53.67.85 ▸ 04.66.53.72.95
Disabled access. Garden. TV. Pay car park.

A fairly new hotel with an attractive, tranquil atmosphere. Some rooms have a view over the town walls and the Constance Tower. Air-conditioned doubles are €43–45 with shower/wc or bath. Most appealing of all is the delightful garden. Best value in town. 10% discount 15 Jan–15 Feb and 15 Nov–1 Dec.

⅍ ⌂ ❙●❙ HÔTEL-RESTAURANT LES ARCADES***

23 bd. Gambetta (Centre).
☎ 04.66.5381.13 ▸ 04.66.53.75.46
Closed Mon out of season; Mon lunchtime in season; Tues lunchtime; the first fortnight in March; the second fortnight in Nov. **Swimming pool. TV**.

A characterful hotel with a gastronomic restaurant of great charm in the old town, well away from the hurly-burly of the centre. This is an ancient, noble building with thick walls and spacious, stylish, beautiful rooms. Doubles with shower/wc or bath cost €76–89 including breakfast. The dining room is elegant and the tables have starched white cloths. There's also a small secluded terrace. The classic, regional cuisine is beautifully prepared and perfectly served. Specialities include warm oysters, steak with juniper sauce and medallions of monkfish with saffron. Weekday lunch menu €21 and you'll pay around €38 *à la carte* – both good value. Free apéritif.

SAINT-LAURENT-D'AIGOUZE   30220 (7KM N)

⅍ ⌂ ❙●❙ HÔTEL LOU GARBIN**

30 av. des Jardins; the village is on the Nîmes road from Aigues-Mortes and the hotel is on the right.
☎ 04.66.88.12.74 ▸ 04.66.88.91.12
e contact@bu-garbin.com
Closed Jan, Feb **Restaurant closed** reservations only all year, lunchtimes 1 July–31 Aug. **Disabled access**. **Swimming pool. TV. Car park**.

A really pleasant place to stop between Nîmes and Aigues-Mortes in a typical village for this little corner of the Camargue. It's at the heart of the village, surrounded by a string of cafés with terraces and with the church to one side. The rooms are in the main house or in bungalows around the pool;

all have TV and en-suite bathrooms. Doubles €38 with basin, €38–46 with shower/wc or bath. They offer a half-board option from Easter to the end of October at €37–39 per person, and dishes are reassuringly local with lots of beef on the menu. Unfortunately you can see and hear the main road about 200m away, but pretty soon the bushes will have grown big enough to form a screen. You can play *boules* and they do barbecues. Free coffee.

ALÈS   30100

♨ ☗ HÔTEL DURAND**

3 bd. Anatole-France; it's in a quiet street that starts opposite pl. de la Gare.
☎ 04.66.86.28.94
Disabled access. TV. Car park.

A peaceful little establishment offering good value for money. The rooms are not huge but when they were refurbished they did a thorough job. Doubles €31 with shower/wc. There's a small interior courtyard. Friendly, attentive reception and many of the customers are regulars. 10% discount on the room rate.

♨ ☗ |●| HÔTEL-RESTAURANT LE RICHE**

42 pl. Pierre-Sémard (Centre); it's opposite the train station.
☎ 04.66.86.00.33 ➡ 04.66.30.02.63
℮ riche.reception@leriche.fr
Closed Aug. **TV. Pay car park.**

This place is one of the best restaurants in town and something of an institution. The dining room is enormous and has *belle époque* mouldings on the high ceiling. Polite, efficient service. Carefully and creatively prepared dishes in classic style, showing off the fresh produce to best advantage: shellfish salad with fresh basil, fillet of sea bass with a delicate shrimp *bisque*, good Saint-Nectaire cheese, apricot tart. Menus €15, €23 and €30. The hotel is run with great professionalism and has all the comforts you need. By comparison, the rooms are modern and uninteresting but they have good facilities. Doubles with shower/wc or bath €40. 10% discount on the room rate all year.

♨ |●| LE MANDAJORS

17 rue Mandajors.
☎ 04.66.52.62.98 **℮** frederic-beguin@wanadoo.fr
Closed Sun; the first fortnight in Aug; Christmas–New Year.

The décor doesn't seem to have changed

since World War II – when the owner helped members of the Résistance disappear out of the back door. The place is now in the hands of a young man and his wife helps at lunchtime. In the evening, he's on his own to run the kitchen and the dining room. To make it work, he keeps strict opening hours. It's worth it: you'll find delectable, appetizing cuisine at more than reasonable prices – cep omelette, flavourful Cévenole *fricassée* (sautéed pork with chestnuts), good house tarts. €9 lunch menu or €10–21. Free aperitif.

|●| LE JARDIN D'ALÈS

92 av. d'Alsace (North); it's on the Aubenas road.
☎ 04.66.86.38.82 **℮** lejardinales.resto@libertysurf.fr
Closed Sun evening, Mon, 25 Jan–12 Feb and 25 June–18 July. **Garden. Car park.**

This place is located well outside the centre on the edge of an area with a number of looming high-rises – the terrace is almost too close to the roundabout for comfort. But the dining room has been decorated with great taste by the owners and they serve refined cuisine with dishes from different regions of France: *pâté en croûte cévenol*, veal stew *à la lyonnaise*, stuffed mussels *à la sétoise* (with brandy, tomato and garlic), mullet *à la Marseillaise* (baked with cheese, tomato and saffron) and chicken breast *à la Périgourdine* (cooked with truffles). Weekday lunch menu €11 and others €15–25. Warm welcome.

SEYNES   30580 (18KM E)

♨ ☗ |●| LA FARIGOULETTE**

It's in the village; take the D6 from Alès.
☎ 04.66.83.70.56 ➡ 04.66.83.72.80
Closed Sun evening; Jan–Feb.**Swimming pool. Garden. TV. Car park.**

A lovely, unfussy country establishment with a garden and swimming pool. Eleven decent double rooms at €35. Customers from far afield come to enjoy the powerfully flavoured local dishes that the owner and his family prepare – *pâtés*, *terrines*, sausage, casseroles and *confits*. They run the local *charcuterie*, and many of the dishes are home-made. Prices are reasonable – set menus €11–27. Service is in the beautifully simple, rustic dining room. You might fancy following the footpaths up Mont Bouquet (631m) after your meal. Free house apéritif.

SAINT-VICTOR-DE-MACALP   30500 (23KM NE)

☗ |●| LA BASTIDE DES SENTEURS***

It's in the centre of the village; from Alès, take the D904

then the D51 to Saint-Victor.
☎ 04.66.24.45. ▶ 04.66.60.26.10
📧 senteurs@chateauxhotels.com
Hotel closed 3 weeks in Jan. **Restaurant closed** Mon and Wed lunchtimes in season; Sun evening out of season; Jan; 10 days in Nov. **Disabled access**. **Swimming pool. TV.**

A charming hotel in a hill village which isn't overrun by tourists, set in beautiful country-side right on the edge of the Cévennes. Charming rooms with bare stone walls €53–66 with bath. The building is a collection of houses that have been soberly and tastefully renovated. Outside there's a glorious swimming pool overlooking the Cèze valley – and you get the same view from the terrace. The superb restaurant is named after the chef, Franck Subileau, who produces dishes of wonderful invention: cocks' combs and kidneys in olive oil, *crépinette* of pigs' troggers, boned pigeon with truffles, chocolate mousse and banana with rum. Weekday menu €18, or €26–64.

AMÉLIE-LES-BAINS 66110

🏠 |●| LE CASTEL-ÉMERAUDE**

Petite Provence, route de la Corniche; follow the signs to the centre sportif Espace Méditerranée.
☎ 04.68.39.02.83 ▶ 04.68.39.03.09
📧 castel.emeraude@wanadoo.fr
Closed Dec–Feb. **Disabled access. TV. Car park.**

A quiet, tranquil inn on the banks of the river and surrounded by greenery. It's a big castle-like building with two turrets, but inside the décor is modern. Double rooms are €47–64 with shower/wc; those with bath also have a terrace. The restaurant has set menus at €15, €21 and €30. The Catalan one includes scrumptious dishes: escalope and anchovies on a bed of olive paste, fillet of salt cod and *crème catalane*. Other specialities include lamb noisette with goat's cheese or tagliatelle with queen scallops in cream sauce.

ANDUZE 30140

🏕 🏠 |●| LA RÉGALIÈRE**

1435 route de Saint-Jean-du-Gard (North).
☎ 04.66.61.81.93 ▶ 04.66.61.85.94
Closed Wed lunchtime except July–Aug; 25 Nov–15 Mar. **Swimming pool. Garden. TV. Car park.**

La Régalière is a very old master-craftman's house in a vast estate – a little haven of peace and quiet. The twelve bedrooms have very modern facilities; doubles are €47–53 and half board, at €43–46 per person, is compulsory June–Sept. You can eat on the shaded terrace in summer. House specialities include *aiguillettes* of duck with honey and gentian liqueur, creamed salt cod *gratiné* with *croûtons* with olive paste and pan-fried duck *foie gras* with white chestnuts and grapes. Menus €15–37. On Fridays in high season there are jazz evenings in the restaurant. 10% discount on the room rate.

🏕 🏠 |●| LA PORTE DES CÉVENNES**

Route de Saint-Jean-du-Gard; it's on the D907, 3km out of Anduze.
☎ 04.66.61.99. 44 ▶ 04.66.61.73.65
📧 reception@porte.cevennes
Closed lunchtimes and Nov–March. **Swimming pool. TV. Car park.**

Located just outside the village of Anduze, past the bamboo fields, this modern hotel has spacious, clean and comfortable rooms. Doubles with shower/wc are €50, or €58–64 with bath, TV and a small balcony. The rather grand swimming pool is covered and heated. The restaurant, open for dinner only, serves traditional dishes: trout in a pastry case with chive sauce, soft chocolate gateau. Menus €17–29. Half board, available for a minimum of three days, costs €52–53 per person. This is a reliable place. Free apéritif.

🏕 🏠 |●| LE MOULIN DE CORBÈS

Corbès; take the route de Saint-Jean du Gard.
☎ 04.66.61.61.83
Closed Sun evening and Mon out of season; Jan–Feb. **Disabled access. Car park.**

This isn't just any old restaurant. The crunch of gravel underfoot as you approach and the grand staircase inside help to create a special atmosphere. The dining room is painted yellow and flooded with sunlight, and the flower arrangements on the tables add a touch of class. Dishes changes with the season but they're always simple and full of cleverly combined, delicate flavours – *fromage frais* ravioli in herb stock, *aiguillettes* of duckling with lavender honey and preserved ginger, beef *pot-au-feu*, fillet of pan-fried beef with spiced wine. Set menus €24–52. Double rooms with shower/wc or bath €58–61. 10% discount on the room rate.

ARGELÈS-SUR-MER 66700

🏕 🏠 |●| LA CHAUMIÈRE MATIGNON**

30 av. du Tech; it's next to the tourist office.

☎ 04.68.81.09.84 ➡ 04.68.81.33.62
e contact@chaumierematignon.com
Closed lunchtimes om seasom, Tues lunchtime and Thurs out of season and Oct to 1 April. **TV**. **Pay car park**.

Friendly welcome in a seaside hotel just 200m from the beach. Pretty, well-maintained bedrooms with air conditioning and shower or bath/wc are €37–50; four of the rooms can sleep four. Honest local dishes in the restaurant: marinated Collioure anchovies, prawns with pine nuts, duck *foie gras* with prunes, meat and fish grilled over coals. Menu at €12 and around €17 *à la carte*. Half board compulsory July–Aug. 5% discount for a minimum three-night stay on a half-board basis 10 Sept–20 June.

AUMONT-AUBRAC 48130

🕺 🛌 |●| GRAND HÔTEL PROUHÈZE***

2 rue du Languedoc; it's opposite the train station.
☎ 04.66.42.80.07 ➡ 04.66.42.87.78
e prouheze@prouheze.com
Closed Sun evening and Mon except July–Aug; Nov–March. **Garden**. **TV**. **Car park**.

Guy Prouhèze's cooking is wonderfully imaginative: his subtle dishes bring out the full flavour of salmon, asparagus, mushrooms and other fresh ingredients. There's an enormous, warm dining room decorated in charming taste. The menu at €28 is not served on Saturday evening or on public holidays; others are €38–89 with good *à la carte* choices too. Excellent cellar full of vintage wines and fantastic *vins de table*. Comfy, attractive rooms of varying size – the bigger ones have the better facilities. Doubles €61–92. 10% discount on the room rate.

FAU-DE-PEYRE 48130 (10KM NW)

🕺 🛌 |●| HÔTEL-RESTAURANT BOUCHARINC-TICHIT DEL FAÔU**

How to get there: take the D50 from Aumont-Aubral.
☎ 04.66.31.11.00 ➡ 04.66.31.30.00
Closed Sun evening out of season and 10 days at Christmas. **TV**. **Car park**.

"*Faôu*" is the local word for "tree" and the inn in this old Aubrac village is surrounded by them. The owners will give you a warm welcome and serve terrific home cooking at modest prices. Ample menus at €13 and €18: frogs' legs, trout with bacon and *manouls* (lamb breast with tripe). Just next door there's a modern building where you'll find spotless bedrooms with TV and all mod

cons. Doubles with shower/wc or bath €38. Free apéritif.

BANYULS-SUR-MER 66650

🕺 🛌 VILLA MIRAMAR**

rue Lacaze-Outhiens; it's 200m from the beach.
☎ 04.68.88.33.85 ➡ 04.68.66.90.08
e villa-miramar@wanadoo.fr
Closed 15 Oct–30 March. **Garden**. **Swimming pool**. **TV**. **Car park**.

Set on the hillside just outside the village, the hotel is surrounded by a garden which is full of trees and flowers. The place is packed with Far Eastern souvenirs, many from Thailand. The rooms are comfortable with modern facilities – mini-bar, telephone, TV – and cost €37–43 for a double with shower/wc or bath. There are also some basic bungalows in the grounds for slightly less. A well-priced place just 200m from the beach. 10% discount in April.

BARJAC 30430

🕺 🛌 |●| HÔTEL-RESTAURANT LE MAS DU TERME***

Route de Bagnols-sur-Cèze; it's 3km from the village, out in the vineyards.
☎ 04.66.24.56.31 ➡ 04.66.24.58.54
e welcome@mas-du-terme-com
Restaurant closed phone to check out of season.
Closed Nov–Feb. **Swimming pool**. **TV**. **Disabled access**. **Car park**.

This eighteenth-century silkworm-breeding house has been tastefully converted in the local style by the owners. There's a vaulted sitting room and dining room and a pretty courtyard. The hotel has 23 quiet, attractive bedrooms with modern facilities; they're €55–64 with shower/wc, €60–69 with bath. The restaurant is pretty good too: The price of a menu (half board) is €26. The local specialities, *escabèche* of red mullet fillets with garlic, cod steaks with black olive paste, stuffed rack of lamb with sea salt and so on, are carefully prepared and not bad. 10% discount on the room rate Sept–June.

BEAUCAIRE 30300

🕺 🛌 |●| HÔTEL-RESTAURANT LE ROBINSON**

route de Remoulins; it's signposted on the road to Remoulins.

☎ 04.66.59.21.32 ➡ 04.66.59.00.03
e contact@hotel-robinson.fr
Closed Feb. **Disabled access.Swimming pool**. **TV**.
Car park.

A good place just on the edge of Beaucaire.
On the *menu du terroir* you'll find beef *gardiane*, the local speciality – here they make it
like nobody else and serve it up with locally
grown rice. It goes well with a wine like a
Costières de Nîmes. Try donkey and pork
sausage as a starter, and a *crème catalane* to
finish. Menus €12–32. The bright dining room
has huge bay windows overlooking the trees in
the garden, and it's run by diligent waiting staff.
Rooms are pretty, comfortable and very clean;
doubles €52–69 with shower/wc or bath.
Smiling welcome and a family atmosphere.
They have tennis courts as well as a pool. Free
Kir made using local Sauvignon wine.

BÉZIERS 34500

🍴🏠 LE CHAMP-DE-MARS**

17 rue de Metz (Centre); it's near the pl. du 14-Juillet.
☎ 04.67.28.35.53 ➡ 04.67.28.61.42
Garden. **TV**. **Car park**.

This little hotel in a quiet side street has had
its façade thoroughly renovated and it's
smothered in geraniums. The meticulously
designed bedrooms overlook the garden and
they've all got new bedding. Double rooms
€27–43 with shower/wc or bath – it's the
best value for money in Béziers. The cheerful
owner will tell you all about the town. Free
glass of Muscat.

🏠 HÔTEL DU THÉÂTRE

13 rue de la Coquille; it's behind place de la Victoire.
☎ 04.67.49.13.43 ➡ 04.67.28.61.53
e hotel-du-theatre@wanadoo.fr
TV.

A very aged hotel which has been taken over
by a former officer on a cruise liner. He was in
charge of ensuring passengers were properly
looked after and entertained; needless to
say, he's transferred his expertise to the running of his hotel. The 30 rooms are middling
in size but they have all been overhauled and
the bathrooms are new. Doubles €35.The
walls are hung with posters advertising the
maritime and cruising companies and their
liners. Super-professional welcome. Good
buffet breakfast.

🍴 LE CEP D'OR

7 rue Viennet, (Centre); it's between the place des Trois-
six and the St-Nazaire cathedral.

☎ 04.67.49.28.09
Closed Sun and Mon; Sun and Mon lunchtimes in
summer.

This is a wonderful place which has been
going for ages but has found new energy
recently. Don't let the name mislead you –
you won't get old-style cooking here. The
chef specializes in good fish dishes without
complications. The *bourride* of monkfish is
delicious and the steamed fish served with a
garlic sauce is equally tasty. Menus from
€12–24. Charming service from the young
owner. There's a small terrace.

🍴 LE GRILLADIN, LE CARNIVORE ET LE PÊCHEUR

21 rue Française, (North-west); you get there via the rue
de la Répubiiqhe.
☎ 04.67.49.09.45
Closed Sun and Mon.

The name tells you what to expect: they do
grills, meat and fish. The restaurant is in a
cool and charming courtyard with an olive
tree in the middle. There are a couple of
menus (€15 and €21) with names suggesting great hunger – just turn up, tell them how
ravenous you are and they'll swiftly take your
order and serve your food. Nice furniture
made from wrought iron outside, while in the
dining room the setting is warm and welcoming. Very decent cooking.

🍴 L'AMBASSADE

22 bd. de Verdun (Centre); it's opposite the railway
station.
☎ 04.67.76.06.24 ➡ 04.67.76.74.05
Closed Sun and Mon.

A vast dining room with panelled walls but a
modern look. Patrick Olry is a fine chef with a
sure touch; he uses fresh produce and his
menus list dishes that change with the seasons – the food is colourful, full of aromas
and robustly flavoured. The cheese is out of
this world and so are the desserts; the weekday menu costs €23 and others are €29–57.
The waiters dress smartly but are informal in
their approach and are eager to advise –
even the bill is a pleasant surprise.

MARAUSSAN 34370 (7.5KM NW)

🍴 LE PARFUM DES GARRIGUES

37 avenue de la Poste.
☎ 04.67.90.33.76
Closed Tues and Wed; All Saints'; Shrove Tuesday.

Jean-Luc Santuré came here from Béziers and
turned this place into the best table in the area.

You'll notice the easy-going atmosphere as soon as you arrive, and the cooking is smart and subtle and full of flavour – a real *tour de force*. Menus 17–54. There isn't a garden as such, but you can stroll around the heath.

SERVIAN 34290 (10KM NE)

🏠 |●| CHÂTEAU LAROQUE

How to get there; it's 4km from Servian on the N9, half way between Pézenas and Béziers.
☎ 04.67.39.18.28 📠 04.67.32.44.28
e tbraillon@hotmail.com
Car park. Swimming pool. Garden.

The Belgian Braillon family moved here and bought this property as a ruin which, with its acres of land, no one wanted. They set about rebuilding the whole place and decorated it in rococo style, planting a small forest of trees and sinking a dreamy swimming pool. The result is neither a proper hotel nor a guesthouse, but more like a private home with some rooms; doubles cost €70 including a huge breakfast. There's a flamingo-themed bar in the entrance and a restaurant where the food is good quality and the prices won't alarm: menus €16–32. And with luck, once the motorway link to Béziers is open, the nearby N9 will get less busy.

NISSAN-LEZ-ENSERUNE 34440 (11KM SW)

🏃 🏠 |●| HÔTEL RÉSIDENCE**

35 av. de la Cave; on the A9, take the Béziers Ouest exit; it's in the centre of the village.
☎ 04.67.37.00.63 📠 04.67.37.68.63
Restaurant closed lunchtimes. **Garden. TV. Car park.**

A beautiful provincial building with bags of charm in a large village behind Béziers. There's a relaxed, informal, peaceful atmosphere with flowers everywhere, and several bedrooms have recently been added – you'll find them in the garden annexe. Doubles €46 with shower/wc or bath. They'll give you a brilliant welcome. The restaurant, open only to hotel guests, serves dinner only, with a set menu. Half board costs €42 per person. 10% discount on the room rate for a minimum two-night stay.

MAGALAS 34480 (22KM N)

|●| LA BOUCHERIE

pl. de l'Église.
☎ 04.67.36.20.82 **e** theboucherie@aol.com
Closed Sun; Mon; the Nov and Feb school holidays.

This butcher's shop doubles as a restaurant,

and a good one at that. It has two dining rooms, both decorated with odds and ends that look like they were bought in a charity shop, and there's an attractive terrace that leads out onto the village square. Menus for €15 and €20 feature fresh tapas, a selection of cold sausage, stews, steak *tartare* made in front of you and delicious *carpaccio*. If you like tripe, you'll love the way they do it here. Jazz plays gently in the background and, to cap it all, there are some good wines. It's advisable to book.

CARCASSONNE 11000

🏃 🏠 HÔTEL TERMINUS**

2 av. du Maréchal-Joffre (North); it's near the station.
☎ 04.68.25.25.00 📠 04.68.72.53.09
Closed Dec–Feb. **TV. Pay car park.**

A *belle-époque* luxury hotel with a winter garden which has even seen action as a movie set. The listed Beaux Arts foyer is fabulous and boasts a 1930s revolving door, period mouldings, a grand double staircase and a gleaming bar. It has a hundred rooms at amazing prices (considering the luxury), but some have undergone rather over-zealous renovation. Doubles with shower/wc or bath go for €60–73. The bridal suite is absolutely magnificent – stylishly furnished and vast, with a glamorous bathroom. Smiling staff welcome you and you'll have a choice of breakfast menus at €7, €8 and €9. 10% discount on the room rate.

🏃 🏠 HÔTEL DU DONJON – LES REM-PARTS***

2 rue du Comte-Roger (South); it's in the heart of the medieval city.
☎ 04.68.71.08.80 📠 04.68.25.06.60
e info@bestwestern-donjon.com
Disabled access. Garden. TV. Pay garage.

This place has everything: it's a medieval building with magnificent beams and an unusual staircase, but it also offers modern facilities such as double glazing, air conditioning, a bar, lounges, a garden and so on. There's good reason for the owner to be proud of the establishment and it's very popular with American visitors. Doubles €69 with shower and €84–92 with bath and air conditioning. The garage allows you to bring your car right into the middle of the town; it is free to readers of this guide.

🏃 |●| LE SAINT-JEAN

1 pl. Saint-Jean; it's in the old town.

☎ 04.68.47.42.43 **e** minou.cros@wanadoo.fr
Closed Tues–Sat lunchtimes; Sun evening Oct–June;
Mon in summer; 28 Dec–15 Feb.

A real find, right next to the castle in a lovely house on a pretty square near to the city walls. Expect exquisite cuisine with a light touch, showing off the delights of local ingredients: sirloin with cep sauce, *sabayon* of puréed salt cod, red mullet fillets with baby vegetables on olive-paste toast and *cassoulet*. Lunch menu for €9 then others €13–20. Good value for money. Free house apéritif.

RESTAURANT CHEZ FRED

86 rue Albert-Tomey and 31 bd. Omer-Sarrant (Centre);
it's opposite the botanic gardens.
☎ 04.68.72.02.23 **e** chez.fred@wanadoo.fr
Closed Sat lunchtime and the Feb school holidays.

This is an adorable air-conditioned restaurant with a tasteful, plush décor – plum-coloured walls and rattan armchairs. Frédéric Coste's cooking is modern and full of integrity. He changes his menus three times a year but produces dishes such as fish dressed with parsley, Languedoc *cassoulet*, *zarzuela* (a kind of fish stew), *foie gras*, *fricassée* of lamb with thyme and, for dessert, two kinds of chocolate *charlotte* or *croustillant* of apples with Armagnac and sorbet. Lunch *formule* €11 (not served weekends and public holidays), and others €17–26. There's a patio and a pleasant terrace. Free coffee.

L'AUBERGE DE DAME CARCAS

3 pl. du Château (Southeast); it's in the medieval city.
☎ 04.68.71.23.23.
Closed Mon,Tuesday lunchtime and Jan.

There's plenty of room on the terrace, in the upstairs dining room or down in the vaulted cellar. Carefully designed rustic décor. The kitchen opens onto the dining room. Given that the quality is so high and that this is a very touristy district, the set menus and dishes are cheap. The menu of regional dishes lists an absolutely terrific suckling pig with honey and house *cassoulet* – they even bake their own bread. Menus €13 and €22. Good regional wines at very reasonable prices. Free apéritif.

RESTAURANT GIL, LE STEAK HOUSE

32 route Minervoise; it's in the Ville Basse.
☎ 04.68.47.85.23
Closed Sun, Mon and three weeks in Aug.

You go down a few steps to the smallish dining room of this surprising restaurant – oddly enough given its name, it serves fish. The sea bass, red mullet, sole and salmon are all brilliantly fresh, as are the oysters, mussels and other shellfish. Some good deserts, too, including *crème catalane*. Menus €15–24. Hospitable service by Madame. Free apéritif.

LE COMTE ROGER

14 rue Saint-Louis; it's in the old town.
☎ 04.68.11.93.40
Closed Sun, the second fortnight in Nov and a fortnight Jan-Feb.

Pierre Mesa, who had a fine reputation at the *Château*, took over this restaurant formerly run by his father. Although he changed premises he brought his team and style of cooking with him. The warmth and sincerity of the welcome hasn't changed either. The menus focus on local recipes and in addition to Corbières wines, you'll find a fair selection of Bordeaux and Beaujolais too. Uncomplicated, flavourful, well-seasoned dishes with menus €18–32. The setting is very modern and really pleasant, though the dining room is rather noisy. In summer, head for the terrace. Free *digestif*.

CAVANAC   11570 (4KM S)

CHÂTEAU DE CAVANAC***

How to get there: take the D104, in the direction of St Hilaire then head for the chateau.
☎04.68.79.61.04 ➡ 04.68.79.79.76
Restaurant closed Sun evening, Mon and lunchtimes.
Establishment closed Jan and Feb. **Garden.**
Swimming pool. Car park.

An overgrown farmhouse with a very pretty garden in a quiet village. Fifteen lovely rooms (all different) with period furniture, lustrous fabrics, canopied beds and elegantly contemporary décor. Some rooms can sleep five. Doubles €60 with shower/wc and €66–134. The restaurant, in a converted stable, is the bigger draw. There's a genuine country feel – they've kept the mangers and hung some old implements on the walls. There's a single menu, €34, of delicious local dishes which change regularly: snails, *foie gras* with figs, suckling pig with honey and house *cassoulet*. The bread and wine (their own) are included and there's a tennis court, a swimming pool, a fitness centre and a sauna – it's a great place. Free apéritif, coffee or *digestif*.

ROQUEFÈRE   11380 (25KM N)

LE SIRE DE CABART

How to get there: take the Mazamet road, turn onto the

Conques road then right onto the D101 to Roquefère.
☎ 04.68.26.31.89
Closed Wed and Sun evening out of season; Nov; weeknights Dec–March.

A magnificent house in an attractive village in the middle of the Montagne Noire and the Cabardès. There's an imposing fireplace in the dining room, but it's not just a picturesque feature – it's used to char-grill meat. When you order *charcuterie*, a huge platter appears laden with sausage, *terrines* and hams, and you can help yourself to more. They also plonk down a bottle of wine. The cheese platter is equally gargantuan – don't miss the goat's cheeses, eaten smothered with honey around here. It's all handsomely served and the *charcuterie* and cheese dishes are fairly priced at €12, wine and coffee included. Lunch menu including wine for €11 (not Sun, Jan or Feb). Wine is also included in the €15 menu, but not those for €23 and 26.

CASTELNAUDARY   11400

⅍ ☖ |●| HÔTEL DU CENTRE ET DU LAURAGAIS**

31 cours de la République.
☎ 04.68.23.25.95 ➡ 04.68.94.01.66
Closed 7 Jan–7 Feb. **TV**.

A huge house on the main square in the town. The rooms are well-maintained, comfortable and cost €37 with shower/wc and €40 with bath/wc. The plush restaurant serves what is probably the best cuisine in town. It's famous for *foie gras* and *cassoulet* – the menus (€14–19) list all the local specialities but also duck breast with morels and pigeon with ceps. Slightly impersonal welcome but the service is faultless. Free coffee.

⅍ ☖ HÔTEL DU CANAL**

2 av. Arnant-Vidal.
☎ 04.68.94.05.05 ➡ 04.68.94.05.06
TV. Car park.

A recently built hotel on the edge of the Canal du Midi. There's a towpath you can walk along nearby. The rooms are modern, spacious and well-looked-after. €40–49 for a double with shower. Smiling staff. Free breakfast.

CAUNES-MINERVOIS   11160

⅍ ☖ |●| HÔTEL-RESTAURANT D'ALIBERT**

pl. de la Mairie; take the D11 for 6km then turn right for

Cannes onto the D620 and it's 2.5km further on.
☎ 04.68.78.00.54 **e** frederic.dalibert@wanadoo.fr
Closed Sun evening, Mon and 30 Nov–10 March.
Car park.

This house, thoroughly lost in the narrow lanes of this Minervois village, looks as if it's suddenly appeared from the sixteenth century. The owners, Monsieur and Mme Guiraud, have run it for years. There are only seven rooms but they're well maintained and pleasant. Doubles with basin €31, €46–53 with shower or bath. The elegant country-manor style restaurant is totally in keeping with the rest of the place, and the open fire adds to the warmth of the atmosphere in cold weather. Good, authentic local dishes like *cassoulet*, produced with great skill. Weekday menu €11, or others €18–27. The owner will give you good advice about the wines – he's a great connoisseur of the local *crus* and his pleasure is infectious. Free apéritif.

CHÂTEAUNEUF-DE-RANDON   48170

⅍ ☖ |●| HÔTEL DE LA POSTE**

L'Habitarelle: take the N88 and it's beside the Mausolée du Guesclin.
☎ 04.66.47.90.05 ➡ 04.66.47.91.41
e contact@hoteldelaposte48.com
Closed Fri evening, Sat lunchtime, All Saints' holidays and 20–31 Dec. **Disabled access**. **TV. Car park**.

Though this establishment is on the main road the traffic noise won't bother you – most bedrooms overlook the countryside. They've been modernized and are absolutely spotless; doubles cost €43 with shower/wc or €46 with bath. The restaurant is in a converted barn which has lost none of its rustic charm. José Laurens does the cooking and prepares tasty traditional dishes like farm-raised chicken *galantine*, duck breast with wild mushrooms and home-made tarts. Set menus €13–27. There's an attractively priced wine list. 10% discount on the room rate out of season.

COLLIOURE   66190

☖ LES CARANQUES**

route de Port-Vendres; it's 300m from the town centre and the beach.
☎ 04.68.82.06.68 ➡ 04.68.82.00.92
e les-caranques@little-france.com
Closed 15 Oct–1 April.

This welcoming family-run hotel is right on the sea and has a wonderful view of Collioure and the port of Avall. The 22 peaceful rooms all come with a sea view and a small balcony. Doubles with basin €37, €55–60 with shower/wc or €63–67 with bath. There's a terrace where you can sunbathe and private access to the rocky beach.

🍴 ☎ LE MAS DES CITRONNIERS**

22 av. de la République (Centre).
☎ 04.68.04.82 📠 04.68.82.52.10
Closed 12 Nov to end March. **Garden. TV**.

A generously proportioned 1930s villa with an Art Deco staircase. Well-maintained rooms with good facilities, bathrooms and air conditioning; doubles €38–75 with bath. Those in the annexe have either balconies or terraces onto the garden, surrounded by cypress hedges. There are some triple and family rooms, too. Set menus €20 and €22, and half board is available in summer at €40–58 per person. 10% discount March–April and Oct–Nov, except public holidays.

☎ |●| HOSTELLERIE DES TEMPLIERS**

quai de l'Amirauté (Centre); it's opposite the château.
☎ 04.68.98.31.10 📠 04.68.98.01.24
e info@hotel-templiers.com
Hotel closed Jan. **Restaurant closed** Thurs. **TV**.

"Chez Jojo Pous", as it's known, is *the* place to stay in Collioure. The owner's father, René Pous, used to give artists free board and lodging and they paid him with pictures they'd painted. Sounds fair enough, especially when you consider that Matisse, Maillol, Dali, Picasso and Dufy were among them. He accumulated 2000 original works of art which are on display all over the hotel, including in the bedrooms – even if some of the most precious ones, including a number of Picassos, were stolen a few years ago. The welcome is still friendly, nonetheless, and they've kept the prices reasonable: doubles with shower/wc or bath cost €44–63 depending on the season and are €34–40 in the *Villa Miranda*. Every room has a unique charm and most are simply superb: they feature painted wooden beds, quirky rustic chairs and, of course, the paintings. There are projects afoot for 2002: a lift and air conditioning. The hotel is often full, so you need to book well in advance and be sure to ask for a room in the main building – you should avoid the annexe. The restaurant specializes in fish dishes and there are tapas in the brasserie at various prices, a menu at €18 or you can dine *à la carte*.

🍴 ☎ HÔTEL CASA PAÏRAL***

Impasse des Palmiers (Centre); it's beside pl. du 8 Mai.

☎ 04.68.82.05.81 📠 04.68.82.52.10
e hotelsmascasa@wanadoo.fr
Closed Nov–April. **TV**. **Swimming pool**.

A dream of a place, with a fountain on a patio surrounded by masses of greenery, a Hollywood-style swimming pool, a cosy lounge and absolute peace and quiet: high-class luxury indeed. Comfy spacious bedrooms with period furniture; doubles €61–67 with shower/wc or €78–152 with bath. Reservations taken well in advance, especially for summer holidays. A reliable establishment run by professional staff. 10% discount April and Oct, except public holidays.

🍴 ☎ |●| L'ARPÈDE – RESTAURANT LA FARIGOLE***

Route de Port-Vendres; it's 2km from the centre of town.
☎ 04.68.98.09.59 📠 04.68.98.30.90
Hotel closed Dec–Feb. **Restaurant closed** Tues and Wed lunchtime. **Swimming pool**. **TV**. **Car park**.

This place is sturdily built on the rocks above the Mediterranean – the view is wonderful. Attractive rooms decorated in warm colours; most of them have terraces overlooking the sea. Doubles €70–92, with breakfast at €8. You walk down the hill to a lovely swimming pool. The restaurant has a spacious, bright dining room and some tables are set around the pool. Good, tasty local cooking on menus at €15–43 – grilled sea bass, sea bream or monkfish with garlic and cream sauce – and very professional welcome and service. Free coffee.

|●| CAN PLA

7 rue Voltaire; it's 50m from the port d'Avall.
☎ 04.68.82.10.00
Closed Mon and Sun evening out of season; 12 Nov–20 Dec.

A large, very simple dining room with a shaded terrace on the street. The speciality is fish and seafood, served as tapas or grilled. The boss is a solid young man who pays a lot of attention to service. He gets his fish locally or pops over the border to get it in Spain – he's a stickler for it being the freshest possible. Menu for €12; *à la carte* you'll pay around €23. Cod *aïolli*, fish paella, grilled prawns and shellfish – all of which are wonderful accompanied by a jug of white local wine.

🍴 |●| LE TRÉMAIL

1 rue Arago; it's in the old town.
☎ 04.68.82.16.10
Closed Mon and Tues out of season, and Jan.

Located in a lively part of town, with a few

tables on a streetside terrace and more in the warmly decorated dining room. They serve Catalan specialities: char-grilled squid, *boquerones* (marinated anchovies with garlic), grilled fish, shellfish stew, *paella* and, for dessert, *crème catalane* or home-made pastries. Wine is by the bottle only – a pity when there are so many good local vintages to try. It's best to book. Menu €20, and *à la carte* expect to pay €24. Free glass of Banyuls wine.

CUCUGNAN   11350

♠ |●| L'AUBERGE DU VIGNERON

2 rue Achille-Air; it's opposite the theatre.
☎ 04.68.45.03.00 ➡ 04.68.45.03.08
e auberge.vigneron@atarascie.fr
Closed Sun evening and Mon out of season; 15 Dec–15 Feb. **Car park.**

The inn offers a lovely overnight stop and rustic rooms with rough-hewn stone walls; doubles with shower/wc €39. Make your way down to the old wine store – it's been turned into a lovely restaurant. They've decorated it using some of the hogsheads and there's an open fire. You'll find regional dishes such as *cassoulet*, struffed duck, goat's cheese *croustillant* and wild boar stew. Menus start at €15. Fantastic welcome.

BUGARACH   11190 (29KM W)

🎄 |●| L'OUSTAL D'AL PECH

It's on the D14.
☎ 04.68.69.87.59
Closed Wed and Sun evening (except public holidays).

An isolated country inn in a totally unspoilt village. The rustic décor creates a lovely setting for a gourmet meal. Classic, flavourful dishes using good local produce – goose gizzard *confits*, wild boar stew and shrimps *à la Bugarach* to order (as much as a week's notice is needed) and the speciality is free-range chicken cooked in prawn sauce. Everything is made on the premises and the young team running the place are to be congratulated. Four menus €15–24. Essential to book in winter. Free coffee.

FITOU   11510

🎄 |●| LA CAVE D'AGNÈS

How to get there: it's at the top end of the village.
☎ 04.68.45.75.91
Closed Wed; Thurs lunchtime; Oct–March.

Tasteful, simple, rustic décor in this very pop-

ular place housed in an old wine cellar. You'll receive a delightful welcome from the owner, who is originally from Scotland. The cooking's good and the portions are generous; set menus are €19–24. Considerable choice on the starters buffet, local *charcuterie*, cod wrapped in red pepper, beef in Fitou wine sauce, duck breast grilled over coals of vine cuttings and some very good local wines. For dessert, there's a scrumptious mousse flavoured with rosemary honey. Free glass of *Muscat de Fitou*.

FLORAC   48400

♠ |●| GRAND HÔTEL DU PARC***

47 av. Jean-Monestier (Centre).
☎ 04.66.45.03.05 ➡ 04.66.45.11.81
Restaurant closed Mon out of season. **Disabled access**. **Swimming pool**. **TV**. **Car park**.

Set in very pleasant parkland, this is the oldest and biggest hotel in the region – in atmosphere, though, it's more like a delightful family guesthouse. They offer sixty bedrooms with good facilities, which go for €31–52 with shower/wc or bath. The cuisine has become rather ordinary, though, and the welcome could be more inviting. Set menus €14–28.

🎄 |●| LA SOURCE DU PÊCHER

1 rue de Rémuêt; it's behind the town hall on the water's edge.
☎ 04.66.45.03.01
Closed Wed; Nov–Easter.

Ideally situated in the old town on the banks of the Vibron. From the terrace there's a picture-postcard view of sloping gables, intricate roof patterns and old architecture set against the tall green mountains, while in front there are some beautiful trees, an ivy-covered façade and the gentle sound of flowing water. Good local dishes: duck breast salad, nettle soup, warm Pélardon goat's cheese with Cévennes honey and tripe made to an old recipe. Selection of mature house cheeses. Lunch *menu du jour* at €11, others €13–29. Free house apéritif.

SALLE-PRUNET (LA)   48400 (2KM S)

🎄 ♠ |●| L'AUBERGE CÉVENOLE-CHEZ ANNIE

How to get there: take the Alès road.
☎ 04.66.45.11.80
Closed Sun evening; Mon out of season except public holidays; mid-Nov to early Feb. **TV**. **Car park**.

An old building faced in local stone deep in

the Mimente valley. Take your meals on the terrace in summer or, in winter, huddle round the fire – you feel as if you're eating in the family dining room. Set menus €11–20 showcase good local *charcuterie*, *Pélardon* (hot goat's cheese salad) and the house speciality, *noisette* of veal with a cep sauce. Simple, pleasant, very well-maintained rooms; doubles €38 with shower/wc. It's advisable to book. 10% discount on the room rate Sept–March.

COCURÈS 48400 (5KM N)

🏠 |●| LA LOZERETTE**

How to get there: take the D998.
☎ 04.66.45.06.04 ➡ 04.66.45.12.93
e lalozerette@wanadoo.fr
Closed Tues and Wed lunchtime; Tues lunchtime July–Aug. **TV**. **Disabled access**. **Car park**.

This family establishment, set in a quiet little village on the picturesque road up to Mont Lozère, has kept things in the female line. Granny Eugénie once owned an inn herself, but nowadays Pierrette Agulhon's in charge. There's a weekday menu at €14 and others €20–38. The house specialities are cod with red peppers and garlic and chestnut *gateau*: overall the cuisine exhibits a successful combination of imagination, good taste and magnificent flavours. Take Pierrette's advice on the best of the local wines to complement your choice. The bedrooms are as stylish as the dining room – floral, pastel-painted and decorated with a keen eye for detail. Expect to pay €46–47 for doubles with shower/wc and €56–58 with bath. Breakfast is good.

FONT-ROMEU 66120

🏠 |●| HÔTEL CARLIT – RESTAURANT LA CERDAGNE***

rue du Docteur-Capelle (Centre).
☎ 04.68.30.80.30 ➡ 04.68.30.80.68
e carlit-hotel@wanadoo.fr
Closed early Oct to early Dec.

Though the modern building looks boring, this three-star place is more than adequate and prices are fair. Reception is professional and the rooms have good facilities – though the decoration is perhaps over-bright. Double rooms with shower/wc or bath cost €47–72. Classic dishes are served in the restaurant, where the service is friendly and warm. The chef uses good-quality fresh produce. Menus €11–27 offer dishes of scallops with orchard fruit sauce, kangaroo casserole

in *Côtes du Roussillon* and pan-fried veal with green olives. If you're planning to stay a day or two, half board is reasonably priced at €52–63 per person. Free house apéritif.

🏠 |●| RESTAURANT LA CHAUMIÈRE

av. Emmanuel-Brousse.
☎ 04.68.30.04.40 e resto.chaumiere@free.fr
Closed Sun evening; Mon out of season; a fortnight end June.

A friendly gourmet restaurant. The setting is welcoming, with wood-panelled walls and a lovely terrace. It's a popular place locally and it's even busy out of season. The cuisine is mainly local and regional: hake Catalan-style, aubergines and peppers with a *gratin* of goat's cheese, aubergine stuffed with pigs' trotters and, for dessert, *crème catalane*. There are simpler dishes, too – you could order a salad and a grilled steak with *frites*. Menus €13–25. Free coffee.

BOLQUÈRE 66210 (3KM E)

🏠 HÔTEL LASSUS*

pl. de la Mairie.
☎ 04.68.30.09.75 ➡ 04.68.30.38.11
Closed All Saints' and Whitsun holidays. **TV**.

If they gave an award for "best welcome" Jacqueline and Gérard would win hands down. They chat to their guests in the bar and are incredibly keen to help – whether it's to point out the small steps on the first floor or ask if you want an extra pillow. The rooms (€35) are clean and quiet and equipped with shower/wc or bath. €3 reduction on the room rate from the third night.

LATOUR-DE-CAROL 66760 (17KM W)

🏠 |●| L'AUBERGE CATALANE

10 av. de Puymorens.
☎ 04.68.94.80.66 ➡ 04.68.04.95.25
e carolee@club.internet.fr
Closed Mon except in school holidays; 21–31 May; 17 Nov–19 Dec. **TV**. **Car park**.

A good place to stop on the road up to the Puymorens pass. When the inn was taken over by the present owners they did up all the rooms, decorating them in attractive warm colours and fitting good soundproofing. They cost €47 with shower/wc; some have balconies and TV. There's a shady terrace and a dining room where they serve honest regional dishes: grilled black pudding with apple, chicken *à la catalane* and *crème catalane*. Menus €14–26. Free house apéritif.

GARDE (LA) 48200

🛁 🏠 ｜●｜ LE ROCHER BLANC**

Centre; it's 1km from exit 32 on the A75, which is the first in Lozère coming from the north.
☎ 04.66.31.90.90 ➡ 04.66.31.93.67.
Restaurant closed Mon and Nov to end March.
Swimming pool. Garden. TV. Car park.

The rooms here are fairly spacious and they're clean and quiet. Expect to pay €41–44 with shower/wc. Set menus are €13–34, one featuring regional specialities: zander with Banyuls wine and offal dishes with morels. Margeride is a wild and beautiful part of the country and the hotel is just 3km from France's smallest museum at Albaret-Sainte-Marie. Free apéritif.

CHAULHAC 48140 (10KM N)

🛁 ｜●｜ LA MAISON D'ELISA

How to get there: it's on the D8.
☎ 04.66.31.93.32

This isolated village, with flowers blooming everywhere, is absolutely idyllic. Originally from Lille, the owners now run a cosy and unassuming inn. They offer decent, nicely presented menus which change daily. The one at €12 includes wine and coffee, and there are others up to €22. Madame exhibits her skill in the kitchen and Monsieur serves with a smile. *Truffade* and *aligot* are made to order. Free coffee.

GRAU-DU-ROI (LE) 30240

🛁 🏠 HÔTEL BELLEVUE ET D'ANGLETERRE**

quai Colbert (Centre).
☎ 04.66.51.40.75 ➡ 04.66.51.43.78
Closed 1 Jan–6 Feb. TV.

There are quite a few rooms with a grandstand view over Grau-du-Roi. They're pretty and well maintained, and prices are competitive: doubles €31 with basin and €38–51 with shower/wc. One free night for every six 1 Nov–31 Mar.

｜●｜ LE GAFÉTOU

6 [bis] rue Frédéric Mistral.
☎ 04.66.51.60.99

Fronted by an awning, the large dining room is decorated in aquatic shades – setting the scene for the fish, seafood and shellfish you'll enjoy here. The menus, €15–26, offer good value, and the fish is as fresh as can be. Friendly welcome, perfect service and an ideal seaside location.

GRUISSAN 11430

｜●｜ LE LAMPARO

14 rue Amiral-Courbet; it's in the village beside the pond.
☎ 04.66.49.93.65
Closed Sun evening; Mon; mid-Dec to end Jan.

This is a good restaurant specializing in fish and seafood at reasonable prices. The dining room is clean and the tables are laid with salmon-pink cloths; there are more tables on the terrace, which has a view of the pond. Excellent menus €17–27 listing dishes such as roast oysters with duck breast and fillet of sea bream with olive paste.

LAMALOU-LES-BAINS 34240

🛁 🏠 ｜●｜ HÔTEL-RESTAURANT BELLEVILLE**

1 av. Charcot (Centre).
☎ 04.67.95.57.00 ➡ 04.67.95.64.18
Disabled access. Garden. TV. Car park.

This is a substantial provincial hotel, typical of a spa town; the house has character and has been entirely refurbished. It's spacious and boasts good facilities – doubles with shower/wc or bath €25–46, many overlooking the garden. The restaurant is decorated in *belle-époque* style and they serve a series of set menus at €13–32, specializing in local dishes. An excellent place. 10% discount on the room rate and free house apéritif.

｜●｜ L'ARBOUSIER**

18 rue Alphonse Daudet; (Centre).
☎ 04.67.95.63.11 ➡ 04.67.95.67.78
Disabled access. TV. Car park.

A quiet hotel in the shade of a group of old plane trees just away from the centre of town. It's a haven for regulars or a refuge if you need to stay the night – but it's often full. Doubles €32–49. The restaurant serves gourmet food served under the stars or on the terrace in summer and the dining room is in a turn-of-the-century house. Their signature dish is fillet of zander gratinéed with Laguiole cheese. Menus €14–38.

｜●｜ LES MARRONNIERS

8 ave. de Capus; it's on the way out of town after the town hall.
☎ 04.67.95.76.00
Closed Sun evening, Mon and Jan

A small and rather insignificant house above the town – but the restaurant is one of the best in Haut Languedoc at present. The chef approaches local dishes from a fresh perspective and produces seriosly good cooking: his roulade of beef with *foie gras* is a real treat. The menus for €13 and €16 offer one or two dishes (not served Saturday night, Sunday or public holidays) and there are good *menu-cartes* for €25 and €38. Efficient service and good wine by the glass. At the rear of the building, there's a terrace under an awning.

VILLEMAGNE-L'ARGENTIÈRE   34600 (8KM W)

🏕️ |●| L'AUBERGE DE L'ABBAYE

How to get there' take the D908 and follow the signs.
☎ 04.67.95.34.84
Closed Sunday evening, Mon and end Dec to end Feb.

Set in the middle of a charming village, this picturesque place has old stone walls and a terrace at the foot of an old tower. It's a very pleasing setting for authentic local cooking, carefully prepared. Menus €19–40. Free coffee.

LAURET   34270

🏕️ 🏠 |●| L'AUBERGE DU CÈDRE

Domaine de Cazeneuve; take the D17 towards Quissac.
☎ 04.67.59.02.02 ➡ 04.67.59.03.44
ℯ welcome@auberge-du-cedre.com
Hotel closed Jan–March. **Restaurant closed** lunchtimes except public holidays and for residents.
Swimming pool. **Car park**.

This old house in an ancient wine area has-been converted into a very attractive hotel and restaurant with self-catering cottages, a campsite and swimming pool. Simple but adequate bedrooms are yours for €26–37; some sleep three or four. There's a weekday menu at €13 for residents only, or for €21 you can choose between the hiker's platter – sausage, *terrine* with juniper berries, *coppa* and *chorizo* – or a succulent *croustillant* of salmon with figs and honey. There's a wide range of good Mediterranean wines, many of which are available by the glass. Courteous owners and quality food. 10% discount on the room rate out of season, and free tapas in the restaurant when you order a meal.

LÉZIGNAN-CORBIÈRES   11200

🏕️ 🏠 |●| HÔTEL LE TASSIGNY – RESTAURANT LE TOURNEDOS**

Rond-point de-Lattre-de-Tassigny; from the centre, take

av. des Corbières towards the A9 for about 2km.
☎ 04.68.27.11.51 ➡ 04.68.27.67.31
Hotel closed Sun evening; last week in Jan; first week in Feb; 1–15 Oct. **Restaurant closed** Sun evening and Mon. **Disabled access**. **TV**. **Car park**.

A great place for an overnight stay if you don't want to spend a fortune. The place is freshly refurbished and modernized, with doubles at €38–43 with shower/wc or bath; the cheaper ones are also the noisiest. The restaurant is popular locally. Weekday lunch *formule* €11 and menus €11–23. Hearty specialities include *cassoulet*, *tournedos* with morels, meats and fish grilled over a wood fire. Free coffee.

ESCALES   11200 (7KM NW)

🏕️ |●| LES DINEDOURELLES

Impasse des Pins; take the Olonzac road, the D611 for 2 km, then turn left onto the D127 and it's at the top of the village.
☎ 04.68.27.68.33
Closed Sat and Mon lunchtime May–Sept; Mon and Tues Oct–April; Nov–Feb.

A good atmosphere and a pleasant, unusual setting – unusual because you get to eat inside a variety of barrels, including a 10,000-litre one seating six. If that doesn't appeal there's always the lovely terrace under the pine trees with a panoramic view of the Montagne Noire. The cuisine is generously flavoured and original: sweet-and-sour dishes, saddle of lamb in pastry with red sugar and lemon zest, *carbonade flamande* and local cheeses. Weekday lunch menu €11 and others €15–30. Out of season on two or three Friday nights a month, they feature entertainment such as French song, jazz, storytelling and even short plays. Free *digestif*.

FABREZAN   11200 (9KM SW)

🏕️ 🏠 |●| LE CLOS DES SOUQUETS

av. de Lagrasse; take the D611 towards Lagrasse.
☎ 04.68.43.52.61 ➡ 04.68.43.56.76
ℯ clossouquets@infonie.fr
Closed Sun evening and 1 Nov–23 March. **Swimming pools**. **Garden**. **TV**. **Car park**.

This is a jewel of a place on the route to the Cathar châteaux and the Corbières caves. It only has five bedrooms; doubles €44–60. The Julien family spend the winter in the Caribbean, as you'll notice from the exotic touches in the bedrooms and the cuisine. Simple tasty food – salad *méridionale*, good home-made pizza, more unusual ones like *colombo* of lamb and best of all, the grilled fish of the day. Menus €15–28. Half board, €70–83 per person, is compulsory in summer. Free apéritif.

HOMPS   11200 (10KM N)

🏃 🏠 |●| AUBERGE DE L'ARBOUSIER

route de Carcassonne.
☎ 04.68.91.11.24 ➡ 04.68.91.12.61
Closed Mon July–Aug; Wed and Sun evening Sept–June; 3 weeks in Feb; 3 weeks in Nov. **TV. Car park**.

It's a lovely spot here, with a shaded terrace in summer and quiet comfy bedrooms; the Canal du Midi flows alongside. Doubles €35–38 with bath. The old stonework and exposed beams contrast well with the modern art you'll see on the walls. The kitchen prepares classic dishes: breast of duck with honey and pine nuts, fillets of mullet with olive oil, rabbit salad with artichokes. Set weekday menu €13 and others up to €31. Free apéritif.

|●| RESTAURANT LES TONNELIERS

Port du Canal du Midi.
☎ 04.68.91.14.04
Closed mid-Dec to mid-Feb. **Disabled access. Garden. Car park**.

The Canal du Midi runs through the village and only a few metres away from it you'll find this place. It offers good food in rustic surroundings. There's a formule for €12 and menus €15–29, listing specialities like cassoulet with confit of duck, marinated salmon with two kinds of lemon and tarte Tatin. Tourists come to see the canal in the evening. In summer, sit in the attractive garden or on the shaded terrace.

LIMOUX   11300

🏃 🏠 |●| GRAND HÔTEL MODERNE ET PIGEON***

pl. du Général-Leclerc (Centre); it's by the post office.
☎ 04.68.31.00.25 ➡ 04.68.31.12.43
🅴 modpig@chez.com
Restaurant closed Mon; Sun evening except July–Aug; Sat lunchtime; mid-Nov to mid-Jan. **TV. Car park**.

This magnificent building had many lives before being converted into a hotel in the early 1900s. Originally a convent, it became a grand town house and later a bank; make sure you take a good look at the seventeenth-century frescoes on the wall above the splendid staircase. As a hotel it's comfy

and well-run without being too formal. Lovely doubles go for €55 with shower/wc, or there are luxury rooms at €67 with bath. The dining room has sophisticated décor and a quiet atmosphere. The cheapest set menu is €25 with others at €27–36, and they list some delicious dishes: *terrine* of langoustine with *coulis* of lobster, braised duck in sparkling white wine (the house speciality – a must), followed by cheese and dessert. You can enjoy a glass of sparkling wine in the cellar where the pool players hang out. 10% discount on the room rate Sept–June.

LODÈVE   34700

🏃 🏠 |●| LA CROIX BLANCHE**

6 av. de Funel.
☎ 04.67.44.10.87 ➡ 04.67.44.38.33
🅴 hotelcroixblanche.com
Closed Fri lunchtime and 1 Dec–1 March. **TV. Pay car park**.

An impressive collection of copper pots, pans and basins decorate this place and create a welcoming atmosphere. Generations of sales reps and businessmen have stopped by to enjoy the local hospitality and simple accommodation – doubles €31–37 with shower/wc or with bath. Unfussy cooking and generous portions in the dining room, with specialities such as local snails and duck *ballotine*. Set menus €11–26. 10% discount on the room rate.

🏠 |●| HÔTEL-RESTAURANT DE LA PAIX**

11 bd. Montalangue; it's near the old watch tower.
☎ 04.67.44.07.46 ➡ 04.67.44.30.47
🅴 hotel-de-laville@wanadoo.fr
Closed Sun evening and Mon May–Aug; 1 Jan–3 March. **Swimming pool. TV. Car park.**

The same family have been running this place since 1887. It's clean and comfortable and has views of the mountains and the Lergue river. Doubles with bath at €49. The hearty cooking specializes in regional dishes and uses fresh produce. The house dishes include an unusual Roquefort flan with figs, *fricassée* of free-range chicken with a cep-flavoured sauce and Labeil trout. In summer they offer char-grilled meat served outside around the swimming pool. Set menus €13–25.

|●| LE PETIT SOMMELIER

3 pl. de la République; it's beside the tourist office.
☎ and ➡ 04.67.44.05.39
Closed Mon and Wed evening except July–Sept; the last

week in June; the All Saints' holidays.

An informal, unpretentious little place with simple bistro décor. Tasty cooking with dishes like breast of duck with apples and honey and warm mussels in a cream sauce with Banyuls wine. Set menus €10–28. You'll get a warm, friendly welcome. There's a pleasant terrace.

LUNEL   34400

⅍ |●| AUBERGE DES HALLES

26 cours Gabriel-Péri (Centre); it's next to the covered market.
☎ 04.67.83.85.80
Closed Sun evening, Mon, Feb and a week in Oct.

A well-known restaurant serving honest, traditional cuisine which respects the changing seasons. The contents of the €18 Sunday menu depend on what's good at market: it's deal for a family lunch and it might include *millefeuille* with mussels, fish *chaudrée* (a soup with a selection of fish and white wine), and good home-made desserts. Weekday menu for €10 and others €16–23. There are tables on the terrace outside and the service is charming. Free coffee.

MENDE   48000

⅍ ☗ |●| HÔTEL GTM – RESTAURANT LA CAILLE**

2 rue d'Aigues-Passes; it's in the old town.
☎ 04.66.65.01.39

Monsieur Saleil has made a large sign for *La Caille* so with that and the terrace, you can't mistake this place – but it's definitely not a tourist trap. Decent, well-maintained bedrooms at €35 with shower or bath. It's popular with sales reps who have learned to live with the owner's slightly curt manner. Brasserie-style cooking, with a €11 *menu du jour* and others €18–26. Free coffee.

⅍ ☗ |●| HÔTEL-RESTAURANT DU PONT-ROUPT***

2 av. du 11-Novembre (East).
☎ 04.66.65.01.43 📠 04.66.65.22.96
📧 hotel-pont-roupt@wanadoo.fr
Closed Sun evening out of season and March.
Swimming pool. TV. Car park.

A delightful hotel in a large house on the banks of the Lot on the edge of town. The décor is contemporary and plain but the bedrooms are comfortable. Doubles with shower/wc at €52 or €82 with bath. There's a pretty indoor swimming pool. The chef draws on a long tradition of cuisine while also creating some modern dishes: pan-fried foie gras with caramelized apples, trout with smoked bacon, frogs' legs, rabbit thigh in its own juices. Menus €20–45. 10% discount on the room rate.

|●| LE MAZEL

25 rue du Collège (Centre).
☎ and 📠 04.66.65.05.33
Closed Mon evening; Tues; 3 weeks Feb–March; a fortnight end Nov.

This is one of the few modern buildings in the town centre and although the setting isn't ideal, the dining room has been tastefully arranged. Jean-Paul Brun uses first-rate ingredients to create fine, flavoursome dishes such as *tripoux* with white wine, *terrine de campagne*, truffle omelette, fresh fish and duck with wild mushrooms. Menus €13–23. It's a popular place for business lunches and the best value for money in town – no discounts.

CHABRITS   48000 (5KM W)

⅍ |●| LA SAFRANIÈRE

How to get there: take the N88, cross the Roupt bridge, then straight ahead on the D42.
☎ 04.66.49.31.54
Closed Sun evening; Mon; March; a week in Sept.

This is the gourmet restaurant that the Mende area has been begging for. The dining room is bright and elegant, and it's in a very old building which has been attractively refurbished. The light, delicate cooking makes clever use of herbs, spices and seasonings like basil, tarragon, cumin, saffron and coconut. The choices on the various menus, €16–43, include fish *pot-au-feu* with Thai herbs, roast pigeon breast with caramelized spices, a decent selection of cheeses and a perfect *crème brûlée* perfumed with jasmine tea. Free coffee.

MEYRUEIS   48150

⅍ ☗ |●| HÔTEL DE LA JONTE**

How to get there: follow the D996 and the gorges of La Jonte.
☎ 05.65.62.60.52 📠 05.65.62.61.62
Closed 20 Nov–early March. **Disabled access.**
Swimming pool. TV.

A large establishment which is well-known for its good cooking and the warmth of its welcome – and it's cheap too. There are two dining rooms: opt for the one used by workers and travelling salesmen because the cooking is better and the prices are more reasonable, with set menus at €10–23. The rooms are very well-maintained and are above the restaurant or in an annexe overlooking the river Jonte. Doubles cost €29 with shower/wc and €31 with bath. The ones with TV and a view of the river are the most expensive. Free *digestif*.

⚲ 🏠 |●| HÔTEL FAMILY**

rue de la Barrière (Centre).
☎ 04.66.45.60.02 ➡ 04.66.45.66.54
Closed 5 Nov to Palm Sunday. **Disabled access.**
Garden. Swimming pool. TV. Car park.

A large building standing by the fast-flowing stream that runs through the village. They'll give you a friendly reception and show you to simple, well-maintained rooms; doubles cost €33 with shower/wc and €41 with bath. Those on the top floor are the best. The cuisine focuses on local dishes: calves' head *ravigote*, *civet* of suckling pig, shoulder of lamb with thyme and chestnuts. Menus are fairly priced at €11–24. There's a pleasant garden with a swimming pool opposite the hotel which you reach by crossing a little wooden bridge. 10% discount April and Oct and free house apéritif.

⚲ 🏠 |●| HÔTEL DU MONT AIGOUAL**

rue de la Barrière.
☎ 04.66.45.65.61 ➡ 04.66.45.64.25
Closed Nov to end March. **Swimming pool. TV. Car park.**

From the outside this place looks ordinary enough, but appearances are deceptive. Stella Robert is energetic and lively and she'll give you a charming welcome. There's a beautiful swimming pool at the back of the hotel in an enormous garden. The rooms have been tastefully refurbished; they're priced at €46–70 with shower or bath. The restaurant is one of the best in the area, offering consistent quality at reasonable prices. Daniel Lagrange uses authentic, tasty local produce to create appetizing local dishes: pan-fried liver with creamed lentils, saddle of lamb *confidou*, apple *galette* with Roquefort. Menus at €15, €24 and €34. They prefer you to stay half board in July/Aug; expect to pay €46–58 per person. 10% discount on the room rate April and Oct.

MÈZE   34140

⚲ |●| LE PESCADOU

33 bd. du Port; go towards the harbour.
☎ 04.67.43.81.72
Closed Tues evening; Wed; Jan.

Le Pescadou has a pretty terrace on the harbour and a spacious dining room attractively decorated with engravings of ships and lots of green plants. It's a fresh, relaxing place which is very popular with the locals. Weekday menu at €12 with others up to €29 – they list fish soup with toasted croutons, squid with *rouille*, mussels with garlic butter and snails from the Thau pond. Free coffee.

MONT-LOUIS   66210

⚲ 🏠 |●| HÔTEL-RESTAURANT LOU ROUBALLOU

rue des Écoles-Laïques (Centre); it's on the ramparts, opposite the local primary school.
☎ 04.68.04.23.26 ➡ 04.68.04.14.09
Restaurant closed lunchtimes; Wed out of season; May; Oct–Nov. **TV. Car park.**

A family guesthouse with lots of rustic character; it's comfy, delightful and full of charm. You'll be greeted warmly by Christiane Duval, who is Catalan – you can practically feel the sun in her voice when she talks about the Pyrenees. You'll feel perfectly at home in one of the seven attractive rooms, which go for €38 with shower/wc and €53 with bath. The restaurant is tastefully decorated. Pierre is likewise crazy about the mountains and his fresh, authentic cooking is up there with the best in the region. Set menus, €19–29, foreground house specialities: duck breast with fruit, *foie gras* or mushrooms; joint of locally grown lamb stuffed *à l'ancienne*; a collection of Catalan dishes. All year round there are delicious mushrooms – including the *rouballou*, which grows locally. Cheap, good and friendly. Free apéritif with every evening meal of your stay.

MONTPELLIER   34000

SEE MAP OVERLEAF

🏠 HÔTEL LES FAUVETTES*

8 rue Bonnard. **MAP A1-2**
It's on the no. 3 bus route.
☎ 04.67.63.17.60 ➡ 04.67.64.09.09nard.

Probably the cheapest hotel in its class in Montpellier. It's a small establishment in a

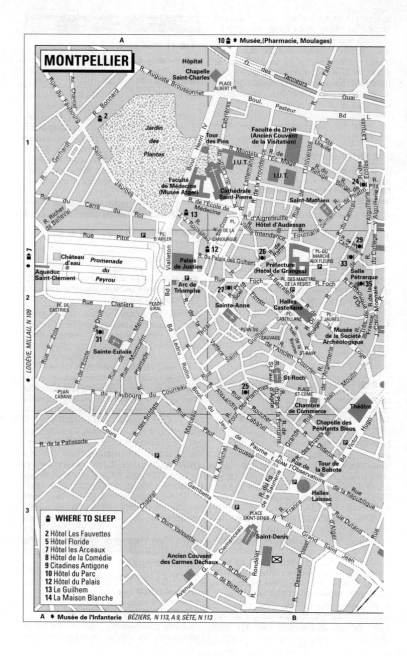

MONTPELLIER

10 🏠 ➤ Musée,(Pharmacie, Moulages)

Hôpital
Chapelle
Saint-Charles

PLACE
ALBERT I.er

Q. des Tanneuriers

Boul. Pasteur

Bd L.

Jardin
des
Plantes

Tour
des Pins

Faculté de Droit
(Ancien Couvent
de la Visitation)

I.U.T.

I.U.T.

Faculté
de Médecine
(Musée Atger)

Cathédrale
Saint-Pierre

Saint-Mathieu

24

R. de l'École de
Médecine

🚶 13

Hôtel d'Audessan

Palais
de Justice

12

Préfecture
(Hôtel de Graveso)

26

29

33

Château
d'eau

Promenade
du
Peyrou

Aqueduc
Saint-Clément

Salle
Pétrarque

35

Arc de
Triomphe

27

Halles
Castellane

Sainte-Anne

Sainte-Eulalie

31

Musée
de la Société
Archéologique

St-Roch

25

Théâtre

Chambre
de Commerce

Chapelle des
Pénitents Bleus

Tour de
la Babote

Halles
Laissac

PLACE
SAINT-DENIS

Saint-Denis

Ancien Couvent
des Carmes Déchaux

✉

A ➤ Musée de l'Infanterie   BÉZIERS, N 113, A 9, SÈTE, N 113

A   B

LODÈVE, MILLAU, N 109

[370]

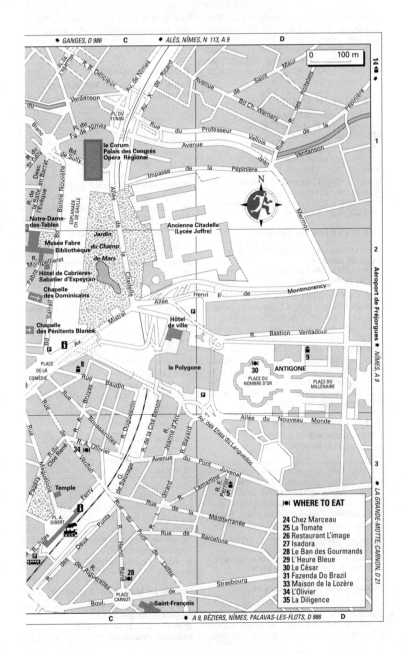

le Corum
Palais des Congrès
Opéra Régional

Notre-Dame-des-Tables

Musée Fabre
Bibliothèque

Hôtel de Cabrières-Sabatier d'Espeyran

Chapelle
des Dominicains

Chapelle
des Pénitents Blancs

Ancienne Citadelle
(Lycée Joffre)

Jardin
du Champ
de Mars

Hôtel
de ville

PLACE
DE LA
COMÉDIE

le Polygone

ANTIGONE

PLACE DU
NOMBRE D'OR

PLACE DU
MILLÉNAIRE

Temple

Saint-François

❙●❙ WHERE TO EAT

24 Chez Marceau
25 La Tomate
26 Restaurant L'image
27 Isadora
28 Le Ban des Gourmands
29 L'Heure Bleue
30 Le César
31 Fazenda Do Brazil
33 Maison de la Lozère
34 L'Olivier
35 La Diligence

quiet street, run by a friendly couple. The bedrooms may be basic but they're quiet and clean; most look onto the interior courtyard. They serve breakfast on the veranda, which is popular in summer. Doubles with shower €26, €29 with shower/wc and €35 with bath.

🏊 🏠 HÔTEL FLORIDE**

1 rue François-Perrier. **MAP D3-5**
☎ 04.67.65.73.30 ➡ 04.67.22.10.83
e hotel.floride@gofornet.com
TV.

Situated in a quiet street near the district of Antigone. You'll receive a warm welcome. Doubles €31–41 with bath and air conditioning; the best ones overlook the terrace, which is a riot of flowers. Good breakfast. 10% discount Sept–June.

🏊 🏠 HÔTEL LES ARCEAUX**

33–35 bd. des Arceaux; it's behind promenade du Peyrou. **Off map A2-7**
☎ 04.67.92.03.03 ➡ 04.67.92.05.09
Garden. TV. Pay car park.

This is an attractive house with an outside staircase leading from the garden to reception. On the other side you have a view of the seventeenth-century aqueduct near the Peyrou gardens. Homely atmosphere and comfortable bedrooms, all of which have been refurbished in fresh, pretty colours. Doubles €47 with shower/wc and €52 with bath; some have a private balcony and others can sleep three. Breakfast €6. Excellent value for money. 10% discount.

🏠 HÔTEL DE LA COMÉDIE**

1 [bis] rue Baudin. **MAP C2-8**
☎ 04.67.58.43.64 ➡ 04.67.58.58.43
TV.

You'd be hard pushed to find a more central hotel. It's good, quiet and friendly. The rooms have been refurbished and they're clean and welcoming. Doubles €47–60 with bath, satellite TV and air conditioning. Prices are negotiable for long stays. A good place.

🏠 HÔTEL DU PARC**

8 rue Achille-Bège; it's on the other side of Verdanson, 300m from the cathedral. **Off map B1-10**
☎ 04.67.41.16.49 ➡ 04.67.54.10.05
Disabled access. Garden. TV. Car park.

This is a typical eighteenth-century Languedoc building. They give you a friendly welcome and there's a quiet, attractive garden with pots of flowers on the terrace. The bed-

rooms are clean, comfy and air-conditioned, and all have mini-bar and telephone. Doubles with €49–57 with shower/wc or bath. Breakfast €7.

🏠 HÔTEL DU PALAIS**

3 rue du Palais-des-Guilhem. **MAP A2/B2-12**
☎ 04.67.60.47.38 ➡ 04.67.60.40.23
TV.

This handsome nineteenth-century building with its splendid marble entrance is near a quiet little square just five minutes from the centre. The bright, attractive bedrooms are furnished with copies of famous paintings, creating a cosy country atmosphere. They're all air-conditioned and have double glazing and mini-bar. Doubles €55–67 with shower/wc or bath. Excellent breakfast at €8. A very good hotel with a homely atmosphere.

🏊 🏠 CITADINES ANTIGONE***

588 bd. d'Antigone (and pl. du Millénaire). **MAP D2-9**
☎ 08.25.01.03.52 ➡ 04.67.64.54.65
e antigone@citadines.com
TV. Car park.

Reception open 7.30am–8pm in the week, 8am–noon and 5–8pm at the weekend and public holidays. Spacious and clean studios and apartments offering a range of hotel services (fresh linen, cleaning, breakfast, etc); from €58 for two with bath. Each has a fully-equipped kitchen which will ease the strain on your restaurant bill. There's an entry-phone system and direct-dial telephones. 10% discount.

🏠 LE GUILHEM***

18 rue Jean-Jacques-Rousseau. **MAP A1-13**
☎ 04.67.52.90.90 ➡ 04.67.60.67.67
e hotel-le-guilhem@mnet.fr
TV. Garden.

This establishment is tucked away in a delightful little street. The place has been tastefully refurbished and the bedrooms are superb (they redecorate a number of them every year), facing onto a mysterious-looking garden with a view of the cathedral beyond. Doubles €61–115 with shower/wc or bath. Good breakfast €9. Delightful reception.

🏊 🏠 ⦿ LA MAISON BLANCHE***

1796 av. de la Pompignane; it's on the corner of 46 rue des Salaisons. **Off map D1-14**
☎ 04.67.79.60.25 ➡ 04.67.79.53.39
Restaurant closed Sat lunchtime;Sun; 23 Dec–2 Jan.

Disabled access. Swimming pool. Garden. TV. Car park.

This establishment is located in a small park filled with ancient (and now officially protected) trees. The building itself looks somewhat like a mansion from the American Deep South, with spacious bedrooms elegantly decorated in shades of grey and a carpet so thick your feet sink into it. Lots of famous actors and musicians stay here – it's quiet to escape from your adoring fans. You'll pay €75–82 a night. In the restaurant, there's one set menu at €20 or you can eat *à la carte*. Breakfast for €8. 10% discount on the room rate Sept–May.

|●| LA TOMATE

6 rue du Four-des-Flammes. **MAP B2-25**
☎ 04.67.60.49.38
Closed Sun and Mon.

There are three wood-panelled dining rooms in this attractive restaurant, well-regarded locally for ages. There's an €8 *menu du jour* and others up to €18. They list generously flavoured dishes prepared with obvious skill: *charcuterie*, chicken *à la diable* (in a spicy sauce), *cassoulet* with duck confit, their speciality braised duck thigh *confit*, chocolate *gâteau*. Fairly priced regional wines.

⅔ |●| CHEZ MARCEAU

7 pl. de la Chapelle-Neuve. **MAP B1-24**
☎ 04.67.66.08.09
Closed Sun in winter and Sun lunchtime in summer.

This place is part-bistro, part-restaurant, and you'll find it on a beautiful little square shaded by plane trees – the perfect place for a spot of lunch outdoors. Good simple cooking and generous portions. It's cheap, but the standards can vary. The €10 set lunch menu is good value, and in the evening they offer menus at €14 and €18. You'll pay around €15 *à la carte*. They do a lovely breast of duck *à l'orange*, mussels *gratinée*, red mullet with peppers and bream with vermouth sauce. Free apéritif.

⅔ |●| RESTAURANT L'IMAGE

6 rue du Puits-des-Esquilles. **MAP B2-26**
☎ 04.67.60.47.79
Closed Sun and 15 July–23 Aug.

This typical old stone-built Montpellier house is something of a local hangout and is decorated with beautiful posters. If you're claustrophobic, head for the dining room upstairs. The simple dishes are suffused with Mediterranean flavours and the portions are generous. Set menus €12–20. A few specialities: fish *parillada* (a selection of fish, tastily grilled), char-grilled meat, *croustillant* of duck and pressed fresh salmon. They do musical evenings. Free *digestif*.

|●| ISADORA

6 rue du Petit-Scel. **MAP B2-27**
☎ 04.67.66.25.23
Closed Sat lunchtime and Sun; Sun and Mon lunchtime July–Aug; the All Saints' holidays.

A wonderful thirteenth-century vaulted cellar decorated in Art Deco style. Fine cooking and delicious seafood: hot oysters with braised chicory, pan-fried scallops *à la provençale* and *tournedos Rossini* (fillet of beef with *foie gras*). You'll be served by the owner, who knows how to look after his customers. Lunch menu €13 and others €23–28. In summer, the terrace on the place Sainte-Anne, overlooking the fountain, is very popular.

|●| LA DILIGENCE

2 pl. Pétrarque. **MAP B2-35**
☎ 04.67.66.12.21
Closed Sat lunchtime; Sun; lunchtimes in Aug.

The restaurant has a splendid dining room with stone walls and a vaulted ceiling – it feels gloriously old. Straightforward cuisine with a lunch menu at €15 and another for €27. The food is substantial and robust: not for tiny appetites. Efficient service. Probably best to book at the weekend.

|●| L'HEURE BLEUE

1 rue de la Carbonnerie. **MAP B2-29**
☎ 04.67.66.41.05
Closed Sun and Mon.

If you really must eat outside, ignore this place – but you'll miss out. It's charming and antique, one of those quiet tea rooms filled with smartly-dressed guests. The food is a treat, too: delicious savoury tarts, savoury and sweet platters which change daily at the whim of the chef and depending on the fresh produce in the market. Platters of the day cost €9 or you'll pay around €15–19 for a full meal.

⅔ |●| FAZENDA DO BRASIL

5 rue de l'École-de-Droit. **MAP A2-31**
☎ 04.67.92.90.91
Closed lunchtimes and Sun.

They've managed to conjure up a real Brazilian atmosphere in this bright, colourful restaurant. Their speciality is *churrascos* –

char-grilled meat served with as much cassava, *feijaos* (Brazilian black beans), onions and fried plantains as you can manage. Whatever the size of your appetite – or your wallet – there's a *formule* to suit you. They have five in all, priced at €15–25, featuring dishes such as pork marinated in lime juice and barbecued rump steak served with yams, onions or fried bananas. The service is rather slow, however, and since the meat is cooked to order, side dishes tend to go cold. They have some good Argentinian and Chilean wines and the best *piña colada* ever. Free *digestif*.

|●| LE CÉSAR

pl. du Nombre d'Or, Antigone. **MAP D2-30**
☎ 04.67.64.87.87 ➡ 04.67.22.20.39
e le.cesar@wanadoo.fr
Closed Sat, Sun evening and Christmas–New Year.

Service until 10.30pm. A good brasserie with an enormous terrace overlooking the square. There's a satisfying €20 regional menu with, for example, *fondants* of chicken or capon as a starter, followed by fresh cod with *aïoli* or *gardiane de toro* (stewed marinated beef) and rounded off by home-made dessert. The €15 menu is simpler and the €30 one more extensive. There is entertainment on the first Monday of each month at 6.30pm. 10% discount on the bill – but you must show them this book before you place your order.

|●| LE BAN DES GOURMANDS

5 place Carnot. **MAP C3-28**
☎ 04.67.65.00.85
Closed Sat lunchtime, Sun evening and Mon.

You get a warm, natural welcome in this fine restaurant, not to mention creative, delicious dishes cooked using fresh produce and served in an intimate setting. Meals cost upwards of €19. It's not a touristy place – more a haven for gourmands.

⅔ |●| MAISON DE LA LOZÈRE – RESTAURANT CELLIER MOREL

27 rue de l'Aiguillerie. **MAP B2-33**
☎ 04.67.66.46.36
Closed Sun; Mon and Wed lunchtimes; a week at the beginning of Jan; a week around 15 Aug.

Service 12.15–1.30pm and 8–10pm. This restaurant and its little sister in Paris are both showcases for Lozère specialities. Top-of-the-range cooking is served in the superb vaulted dining room down in the basement. Dishes on the €21 lunchtime menu change

constantly but there's always *aligot* and a platter of appetizing, mature cheeses. Other menus range from €38 to €46. Good choice of thoughtfully selected The place is also a high-class grocer's and there's plenty for you to take home. Languedoc wines. Free apéritif or coffee.

⅔ |●| L'OLIVIER

12 rue Aristide-Ollivier. **MAP C3-34**
☎ 04.67.92.86.28
Closed Sun; Mon; public holidays; 25 Jul–31 Aug.

Modern décor and fine cooking, both popular with local gourmands. The fish is prepared as skilfully as the meat: flaked cod on a crusty leek pancake; pigeon prepared like woodcock with roast *foie gras* and a *confit* of wings and thighs. Delicate sauces, good presentation and the boss manages the efficiently directed service. One set menu only for €37 or around €47 *à la carte*. Free apéritif.

MAUGUIO   34130 (10KM E)

|●| LE PATIO

Impasse Molière (Centre). Take the D24; it's in a cul-de-sac off Grand-Rue.
☎ 04.67.29.63.90 ➡ 04.67.29.57.75
Closed Sat and Sun lunchtimes 1 Oct–31 March; Mon.

This little restaurant with a Mediterranean atmosphere is housed in what used to be a wine cellar. The décor is a bit kitsch – the furniture in the dining room looks as if it came from a secondhand shop. But you're left in no doubt as to what's important here: the grill, where they cook duck breast, Mediterranean prawns and so on, takes centre-stage. They also do an excellent *gardiane* (marinated beef stewed in onions, tomatoes, garlic, olives and red wine). Sit out on the courtyard terrace in summer. Set lunch weekday lunch menu €11 and €15–27 in the evening.

PALAVAS-LES-FLOT   34250 (11KM S)

|●| LA ROTISSERIE PALAVASIENNE

rue de l'Église; (Centre).
☎ 04.67.68.52.12
Closed when the owner feels like it; it's best to phone and book.

A place that made its reputation by word of mouth. The eatery was the brainchild of a local man who wanted to provide cuisine that was typical of his area. The dishes are different each day because he uses only fresh produce; the fish cooked in salt water is particularly good. Around €23 for a meal.

NARBONNE   11100

🎿 ☎ WILL'S HÔTEL**

23 av. Pierre-Sémard (Centre); it's in the street opposite the station.
☎ 04.68.90.44.50 ➡ 04.68.32.26.28
Closed 25 Dec–2 Jan. **TV. Pay car park**.

There's something solidly reassuring about the beautiful façade of this bourgeois house, an impression reinforced by the hotel owner's friendly reception. The bedrooms are clean and they've been redone – though not very originally – and decorated in pastel shades. Doubles at reasonable prices: €22 with wc, €33–33 with shower/wc and €38 with bath. 10% discount Sept–June.

☎ HÔTEL DE FRANCE**

6 rue Rossini (Centre); it's near the covered market.
☎ 04.68.32.09.75 ➡ 04.68.65.50.30
e hotelfrance@worldonline.fr
TV. Pay car park.

A lovely early twentieth-century house near the covered market. It offers a number of clean, comfortable rooms; doubles with washing facilities €24 and €38–44 with shower/wc and TV. Straightforward, warm-hearted welcome.

🎿 ☎ LE GRAND HÔTEL DU LANGUDOC

22 bd. Gambetta
☎ 04.68.65.14.74 ➡ 04.68.65.81.45
TV. Private garage.

A turn-of-the-century mansion with a certain something. It's extremely well-maintained, though the corridors are a little dark and gloomy. The recently refurbished bedrooms are bright and have excellent beds and double glazing; some have a view of the cathedral. Doubles with shower/wc €46 and €53–73 with bath. There's a lift. Free house apéritif.

🎿 ⦿ L'ESTAGNOL

5 [bis] cours Mirabeau.
☎ 04.68.65.09.27 **e** lestagnol@net-up.com
Closed Sun; Mon evening; a week end Nov; a week early Feb.

A friendly brasserie with a Parisian atmosphere but local cuisine. Reasonable prices: lunch *formule* €10 and menus €15–20. A place to eat quickly and simply. The terrace is open to the sunshine in summer, closed and

heated in winter. A popular after-show hangout for actors from the theatre. Free coffee.

⦿ LA TABLE SAINT-CRESCENT

av. du Général Leclerc, it's on the Perpignan road.
☎ 04.68.41.37.37
e saint-crescent@wanadoo.fr
Closed Mon; Sat lunchtime; Sun evening.

The Palais du Vin was set up to help market local wines and is ideally located just off the motorway. But it also serves a second purpose as the site for this gourmet restaurant. The décor is extraordinary – a mixture of ancient, rough-hewn stone and modern metal sheeting – and the dining room is in an ancient chapel, adding to the feeling of displacement. The chef, Claude Giraud, brings you back to this world with his thoughtful cuisine. The lunch *formule*, €15, comprises savouries, dish of the day, cheese, dessert, a glass of wine and coffee. Everything shows off the quality of the produce he uses and the dishes change at least four times a year; other menus are €24–39 (some include wine).

VINASSAN   11110 (6KM E)

⦿ AUBERGE LA POTINIÈRE

1 rue des Arts (Centre); on the Narbonne-Plage road, turn left onto the D68, then turn onto the D31.
☎ 04.68.45.32.33
Closed lunchtimes and Sun evening out of season; 3 weeks Jan–Feb.

A pretty inn in a lovely setting where the chef concocts tasty regional dishes. Four menus at €15–39; the cheapest will include fish soup or Narbonnaise salad, then free-range chicken or salmon, followed by cheese or chocolate mousse; others feature dishes like sea bream in *beurre blanc* and rolled duckling with *Montagne Noire* sauce. The service is courteous and the food well-priced. They have just thirty seats so you may want to book.

BAGES   11100 (8KM S)

🎿 ⦿ LE PORTANEL

It's in the village: take the N9 towards Perpignan and turn left for l'étang de Bages.
☎ 04.68.42.81.66
Closed Sun evening; Mon; 1–15 Feb; 15 Oct–1 Nov.

Set in the heart of a fishing village, this unassuming restaurant has two bright, elegant dining rooms with windows overlooking the lake at Bages. Owner Didier Marty is a fisherman – he takes his nets out early to bring back the freshest catch in time for it to be creatively prepared by his wife, Rosemarie. Specialities include eel, sea bass and home-smoked fish, crab mousse, fish broth, slivers of fish in a coriander *jus* and perfect home-made desserts. Menus €18–33. Attentive, amiable service and an exceptional selection of regional wines. Free apéritif and a pot of home-made fig preserve.

ABBAYE DE FONTFROIDE   11100 (15KM SW)

🍴 |●| LA BERGERIE – LES CUISINIERS VIGNERONS

How to get there: turn off the A9 at the Narbonne-Sud exit onto the N13 in the direction of Carcassonne and then follow the D613.
☎ 04.68.41.86.06
Closed Dec–Feb.

This place is in the old sheep-fold of an abbey and dates from the Middle Ages. There are three lunch menus – €13 (except weekends), €15 and €21 – and you'll pay €31–58 at dinner. Although the prices can get high, there's wonderful food throughout. The dishes are drenched in the bold flavours of the Languedoc and the Mediterranean and the menus change with the seasons: roast shoulder of lamb, fresh cod or quail with red peppers, Roquefort in pastry, coconut and pineapple cake. In the evening the dishes are personally prepared by the chef and he's a serious contender: this is one of the best tables in the *département*. Free coffee.

NASBINALS   48260

🏠 |●| HÔTEL-RESTAURANT LA ROUTE D'ARGENT**

route d'Argent; it's the big building beside the church and the village car park.
☎ 04.66.32.50.03 ➡ 04.66.32.56.77
Disabled access. TV. Car park.

This place is something of an institution – everybody in Nasbinals drops in. It's owned by Pierre Bastide, who's a mine of information about the area, but you'll more than likely be greeted at reception (which is in a corner of the bar), by one of his sons. Guests always get a warm and friendly welcome in the restaurant too, and the chef's portions are some of the most generous you'll see. He does trout with almonds, stuffed cabbage, *truffade* (potato cake with cheese), and, of course, *aligot* made to Bastide Senior's special recipe. Set menus €10–25. Doubles with shower €31; €40 with shower/wc or bath.

Breakfast is served at the bar. The family has also opened a three-star hotel just outside the town and called it *Le Bastide* – prices are roughly the same.

NÎMES   30000

SEE MAP OVERLEAF

🍴 🏠 |●| CAT HÔTEL*

22 bd. Amiral-Courbet. **MAP C1-3**
☎ 04.66.67.22.85 ➡ 04.66.21.57.51
e cat.hotel@free.fr
TV. Pay garage.

The owners arrived from the cold, wet north determined to open a hotel in warmer climes, and they've made quite a success of it: the *Cat* is both pleasant and cheap. They've done everything up, installing double glazing, good ventilation and satellite TV. Everything is just right. Double rooms with shower/wc €26, or €32 with bath.

🏠 |●| HÔTEL ROYAL***

3 bd. Alphonse-Daudet. **MAP B1-4**
☎ 04.66.67.28.36 ➡ 04.66.21.68.97
Restaurant closed Sun and Mon. **TV. Car park.**

Most rooms look towards the fountain on the quiet pedestrian place d'Assas. The hotel is popular with actors and artists passing through, and the welcome is hospitable. The rooms are individually decorated and are attractive and charming; they don't all have the same facilities but prices are fair for this town: doubles €44 with shower/wc or up to €73 with bath. *La Bodeguita*, the newish restaurant, serves tapas and Mediterranean specialities. Lunch menu €9 or around €23 *à la carte*.

🏠 HÔTEL DE L'AMPHITHÉATRE**

4 rue des Arènes. **MAP B2-7**
☎ 04.66.67.28.51 ➡ 04.66.67.07.79
e hotel.amphitheatre@wanadoo.fr
Closed 2–20 Jan.

This is a quiet hotel in a generously proportioned eighteenth-century house just thirty metres from the Roman arena. The décor has been spruced up, the place is clean and the beds are comfortable; doubles with shower/wc or bath are €44–47. Good breakfast.

🍴 🏠 HÔTEL KYRIAD-PLAZZA**

10 rue Roussy. **MAP C2-5**
☎ 04.66.76.16.20 ➡ 04.66.67.65.99
e kyriad.nimescentre@le-plazza.fr
TV. Car park.

This place is part of a hotel chain, but you

wouldn't think so from its appearance – its a charming old Nîmes house in a quiet street. Its 28 air-conditioned rooms have shower or bath and telephone and cost €58–63. Each floor has a different colour scheme and the corridors are decorated with posters advertising bullfights and opera performances. Rooms on the fourth floor have very attractive little terraces and a view of the old tiled rooftops. 10% discount except during Easter, Whitsun, the *ferias* or the grape harvest.

為 倉 |●| L'ORANGERIE***

755 Tour l'Évêque. **Off map A3-9**
Take the A9 signposted to the airport, then left at the Kurokawa roundabout onto the N86.
☎ 04.66.84.50.57 ☛ 04.66.29.44.55
e hrorang@aol.com
Garden. Swimming pool. TV. Car park.

An unusually attractive modern hotel in a big garden with a swimming pool – though the surrounds of the commercial district and the noise from the traffic don't immediately draw you to the area. Professional staff at reception and well-maintained rooms. The prices are reasonable at €60–75 for a double with bath. This is a reliable place. The restaurant has already established a decent reputation: you'll find lack of lamb with wild herbs, scallop *tartare* and salmon and scallop tartare with asparagus. Weekday lunch menu €17 and others up to €24. 10% discount 31 Oct–1 Jan.

為 倉 |●| HÔTEL IMPERATOR CONCORDE****

15 rue Gaston-Boissier. **MAP A1-8**
☎ 04.66.21.90.30 ☛ 04.66.67.70.25
e hotel-imperator@wanadoo.fr
TV. Garden. Car park.

This is a quality four-star hotel hiding behind a somewhat ordinary façade. To the rear of the building there's an idyllic garden with an ornamental fountain and an outside bar on the terrace – a wonderful place for a drink. The superb rooms are beautifully furnished. The lift is remarkable: it's a classic Otis fitted in 1929 and guaranteed never to break down. You can stay for €90–105 in winter but the price shoots up to during the *ferias*. The restaurant serves a modest three-course *formule* with a glass of wine for €24; it has a reputation for excellent local specialities. Other menus up to €56. 10% discount Oct–Aug.

|●| RESTAURANT LA TRUYE QUI FILHE

9 rue Fresque. **MAP B2-11**

☎ 04.66.21.76.33
Closed evenings, Sun, and Aug. **Disabled access**.

A self-service restaurant under a fourteenth-century vaulted ceiling – this place has been an inn ever since then. Warm service and a lovely patio. Jean-Pierre Hermenegilde puts together a €7 *formule* consisting of hot main course and dessert; it'll cost you €8 with a starter as well. Local dishes such as *rouille du pêcheur* (fish soup with a spicy mayonnaise), *brandade* (creamed salt cod in flaky pastry) and *paella*.

為 |●| LA CASA DON MIGUEL

18 rue de l'Horloge. **MAP B2-15**
☎ 04.66.76.07.09
Closed Sun.

Service until around midnight, or 3am Friday and Saturday. There's a good atmosphere in this *bodega* and a huge range of tapas. A few cheap *formules* – which get you three or five dishes of tapas plus coffee or a drink – are on offer, or there are menus from €8. You'll pay €11 to €21 for a full meal; expect dishes like *estoufade* of beef, *chilli con carne* and *feijoada*. They do a good *piña colada*, and the sangria and the *fino* are excellent too – though they don't serve drinks without food. Lots of theme evenings, with jazz, flamenco or salsa. Free apéritif.

為 |●| RESTAURANT NICOLAS

1 rue Poise. **MAP C2-13**
☎ 04.66.67.50.47
e martin-pascal@wanadoo.fr
Closed Sat lunchtime; Mon except public holidays; 28 June–16 July; 24-26 Dec; 31 Dec–2 Jan.

The large stone-walled dining room here has been tastefully decorated; inside it you'll be served uncomplicated and reliable home cooking. The menus rarely change because that's how the regulars like it: *anchoïade provençale*, monkfish *bourride* (a fish stew with saffron and garlic), creamed salt cod in flaky pastry beef *gardiane*, house desserts such as *clafoutis*. Set menus €11–23. Free coffee.

為 |●| L'ANCIEN THÉÂTRE

4 rue Racine. **MAP B2-14**
☎ 04.66.21.30.75
Closed Sat lunchtime; Sun; the first fortnight in July.

They say that there used to be a theatre on the place du Carré nearby, but it was burned to the ground by a singer who went crazy when they didn't engage her son to sing. You'll be pleased to hear that you won't find that kind of

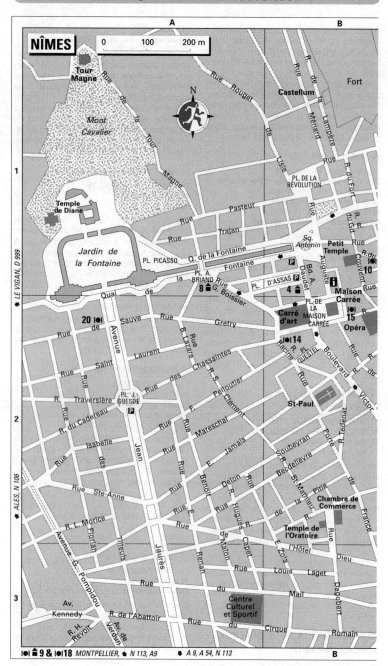

NÎMES

0   100   200 m

Tour Magne

Mont Cavalier

N

Castellum

Fort

Rue de la Tour Magne

Rue Rouget

de Liste

PL. DE LA RÉVOLUTION

Temple de Diane

Rue   Pasteur

Rue   Trajan

Sq. Antonin

Petit Temple

Rue

R. du Couvent

Jardin de la Fontaine

PL. PICASSO

Q. de la Fontaine

Rue   Fontaine

PL. A. BRIAND

8 G. Boissier

PL. D'ASSAS

Bd. A. Daudet

4

10

Maison Carrée

la   Rue   Boissier

Quai   de

Sauve   Rue

20

Carré d'art

PL. DE LA MAISON CARRÉE

15

Opéra

Rue   Grétry

Rue   B. Lazare

Avenue   de

Rue   Chassaintes

R. S.

14

R.   PL. QUESTEL   Boulevard

Racine

Rue   Saint   Laurent

PL. J. GUESDE

Rue   des   Pelloutier

Rue   F.

Clement

St-Paul

Rue   Victor

Rue   de

2

Rue   Traversière

R. du Cadereau

Rue   Mareschal

Rue   Jamais

Soubeyran

Porte

R. Tedenat

Rue   Isabelle

Rue   des

Rue   Jean

Rue   Benoit

Déton   R.

Rue

Berdelièvre

R. St-Mathieu

Pitié

Chambre de Commerce

Rue   de   France

Rue   Ste-Anne

Rue   Florian

Rue   Hugues   Capel

Temple de l'Oratoire

Rue   Dieu

R. L. Morice

Tilleuts

Rue   de   Maison

l'Hôtel

E. Zola

Laget

Dagobart

Av. Kennedy

R. H. Revoir

Av. de Jardun

R. de l'Abattoir

Jaurès

Renan

Rue

Rue   Louis

Mail

Centre Culturel et Sportif

du   Cirque

Rue

Romain

3

Av. G. Pompidou

◀ LE VIGAN, D 999

◀ ALES, N 106

|●| 9 & |●|18 MONTPELLIER, ◆ N 113, A9   ◆ A 9, A 54, N 113

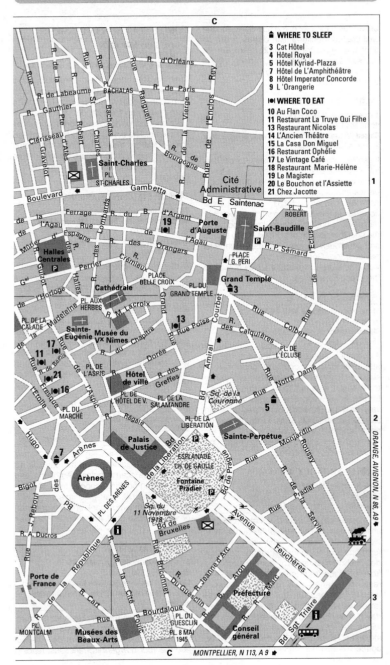

behaviour in this place: the hospitality and the well-crafted Mediterranean dishes create an altogether more tranquil atmosphere. Try the mussels *au gratin* or the cod fritters, though the menus change every two months. Menus at €12–20. Free coffee.

🍴|●| CHEZ JACOTTE

15 rue Fresque. **MAP B2-21**
☎ 04.66.21.64.59
Closed Sat lunchtime; Sun; Mon; a week in Feb; a week in June; a fortnight in Aug.

Inventive, well-prepared Nîmeois specialities, full of flavour and totally satisfying. The lunch *menu du jour* at €12 lists three starters, main dishes and desserts, or you can choose *à la carte* and pay around €31 – excellent value considering the quality. The smooth duck liver *parfait* with peppers is particularly good, while the duck breast with peaches is subtly spiced and generously served. They bake wonderful pastries, too. Good wines and attentive service. There are three or four tables outside in the street. Free coffee.

🍴|●| AU FLAN COCO

31 rue Mûrier-d'Espagne. **MAP B1-10**
☎ 04.66.21.84.81
Closed evenings except Sat and by reservation; Sun; 15–28 Feb; 15–30 Aug.

A delightful, unusual little restaurant. The two attractive dining rooms are decorated in shades of green and the tables have granite tops, or you can opt to sit on the beautiful terrace in summer. The imaginative dishes vary daily but feature potato pie, creamed salt cod, chicken leg stuffed with prawn and apple crumble with *crème fraîche*. Menus €13 and €18 (Saturday evening), or around €19 *à la carte*. Free coffee.

🍴|●| LE VINTAGE CAFÉ

7 rue de Bernis. **MAP B2-17**
☎ 04.66.21.04.45
Closed Sat lunchtime, Sun and Mon.

Tiny place based around a vintage bistro-style dining room with a fountain in the middle. It hosts frequent exhibitions of photographs and paintings. Attractive cooking, delicately seasoned to complement the fresh produce from the market. The dishes really do change daily, but expect something like Serrano ham, followed by sautéed ravioli with pesto and mixed salad, washed down with one of the interesting southern wines served by the glass. Lunchtime *formule* at €13 with a €23 *formule-carte*. Free coffee.

🍴|●| LE BOUCHON ET L'ASSIETTE

5 rue de Sauve. **MAP A2-20**
☎ 04.66.62.02.93
Closed Tues; Wed; a fortnight in Jan; 3 weeks in Aug.

The cooking here has personality and finesse: semi-cooked *foie gras* with Jamaican pepper, nutmeg caramel and white grape jelly, pan-fried zander with herb biscuits and saffron-flavoured carrot *jus*, honey ice-cream. The dining room is full of light and the renovations make a feature of the beams in the ceiling. Lunch menu €14, and others €19–37. Efficient waiting staff. Free apéritif or coffee.

🍴|●| RESTAURANT MARIE-HÉLÈNE

733 av. Maréchal-Juin; it's beside the Chambre des Métiers on the Montpellier road. **Off map A3-18**
☎ 04.66.84.13.02.
Closed Sat lunchtime; Sun; Mon–Wed evenings; a fortnight in Aug.

A paean to Provence, decorated in warm bright colours with huge vases of flowers and attractive table settings. It's a happy kind of place, enhanced by the smile of the owner and the robust cooking. They specialize in char-grilled meat and cook their fish in front of you: salmon marinated in olive oil and anise, *gardiane* of beef. There are several menus at €15–21 with choices such as chicken tikka with coriander and mint, creamed salt cod and home-made *crème catalane*. Free apéritif or coffee.

🍴|●| RESTAURANT OPHÉLIE

35 rue Fresque. **MAP B2-16**
☎ 04.66.21.00.19
Closed lunchtimes; Mon; Sun; the last fortnight in Aug.

The tiny courtyard is delightful at dusk, and when Patricia Talbot lights the candles it's nothing less than magical. Authentic and fresh-tasting cooking: choose from *gratin* of curried mussels, pan-fried *foie gras* with Muscat, roast lamb shank and red peppers, or scallops with basil. *Menu-carte* €21. Free apéritif.

🍴|●| LE MAGISTER

5 rue Nationale (or de l'Agau). **MAP C1-19**
☎ 04.66.76.11.00
Closed Sat lunchtime; Sun; Mon lunchtime; a week in the Feb school holidays; 15 July–15 Aug. **Disabled access.**

An excellent gastronomic restaurant run by chef Martial Hocquart, who has worked in the most famous kitchens in France – the *Ritz* and the *Tour d'Argent* in Paris. Just reading the menu makes you hungry: roast veal kidneys with house raspberry vinegar, sweet apples roasted with cinnamon and served with an almond sorbet. Weekday lunch menu €21 and others €31–40; even the cheaper ones are a feast. Free coffee.

SAINT-GILLES   30800 (19KM SE)

⚑ 🛏 |●| LE COURS**

10 av. François-Griffeuille (Centre); take the D42.
☎ 04.66.87.31.93 ➡ 04.66.87.31.83
Closed 15 Dec to end Feb. **Disabled access. TV. Car park.**

This beautiful white house, shaded by an avenue of tall plane trees, has 34 rooms, thirteen of them air-conditioned but all of them clean and fresh. They cost €40–51 with shower/wc or €52–61with bath; half board is at €42. Set menus – €10 and €12–25 – list dishes like scallop *terrine* and warm seafood salad, beef *gardiane* (beef stew), cuttlefish with *rouille* (spicy garlic mayonnaise) and lots of grilled fish. 5% discount on the half-board rate.

⚑ 🛏 HÔTEL HÉRACLÉE***

quai du Canal, port de plaisance (South); take the D42.
☎ 04.66.87.44.10 ➡ 04.66.87.13.65
Closed Jan–March. **Disabled access. Garden. TV. Car park.**

This Greek name graces a friendly, pretty hotel housed in a bright building. It looks onto the canal so you can watch the launches, the horse-drawn barges and the houseboats gliding by – though the view is somewhat marred by a metal monstrosity on the other bank. There are 21 tastefully decorated bedrooms; some have a terrace overlooking the canal or the peaceful garden. At €44–53, they're worth it. 10% discount April and Sept–Dec.

OLONZAC   34210

⚑ |●| RESTAURANT DU MINERVOIS "BEL"

av. d'Homps.
☎ 04.64.91.20.73
Closed Sat and Sun evening except July–Aug; evenings mid-Oct to mid-April.

The chef-proprietor's know-how and his skilful use of seasonings is evident even in the cheapest €10 set menu, which includes house *terrine* and a perfect *omelette aux fines herbes*. Other menus are €18–38, the

last of which is spectacular. The wine list has a particularly rich choice of regional vintages at good prices. A consistently good restaurant that deserves its popularity. Free coffee.

SIRAN   34210 (10KM NW)

⚑ 🛏 |●| LA VILLA D'ÉLÉIS***

av. du Château; it's in the village.
☎ 04.68.91.55.98 ➡ 04.68.91.48.34
e villadeleis@wanadoo.fr
Closed Tues evening; Wed and Sat lunchtime Oct–May; Feb–March. **Disabled access. TV. Car park.**

An old country house which has been carefully restored. The twelve stylish rooms are quiet and spacious; doubles are €73 with shower/wc or bath. Marie-Hélène will greet you warmly and the cooking is full of southern sunshine. Bernard Lafuente is a talented young chef who has won critical acclaim. Set menus €24–63. Opt for the starter of vegetables from the *poule-au-pot* topped with grilled goat's cheese, or Bernard's prize-winning cod with saffron Languedoc-style. The owners organize musical evening in summer, including piano and flute recitals, and lead walks to help you learn about the wildlife and history of the area. 10% discount on the room rate.

PERPIGNAN   66000

🛏 AVENIR HÔTEL*

11 rue de l'Avenir.
☎ 04.68.34.20.30 ➡ 04.68.34.15.63
e avenirhotel@aol.com.
Reception closed Sunday afternoon and public holidays. **Pay garage.**

A pleasing hotel in a quiet street not far from the station. The rooms are simple but well-maintained and pleasantly decorated. Prices are reasonable: double with basin €20–28 or €27–31 with shower/wc. Vacationing American students sometimes stay here, as do trainees on work placements. It has a homely atmosphere and there's a sunny terrace on the first floor where you eat breakfast. It's a place to enjoy the sun and the peace and quiet. Use of a garage in the next street costs €4 per night.

⚑ 🛏 |●| HÔTEL DE LA POSTE ET DE LA PERDRIX**

6 rue Fabriques-Nabot (Centre); it's between pl. du Castillet and the quai Sadi-Carnot.
☎ 04.68.34.42.53 ➡ 04.68.34.58.20
Restaurant closed Sun evening, Mon. **Establishment**

closed 28 Feb–5 March. **TV**.

A beautiful, characterful hotel dating from 1832. The sign bears the patina of age, the marble foyer and the gleaming old staircase are delightful and the period stained-glass windows are lovely. The pleasantly old-fashioned bedrooms are well-maintained and reasonably priced: doubles with basin €29, with shower/wc €40, and with bath €43. Simple food is served in the stunning dining room. Menus €10–18 with a few good regional specialities: snails *à la catalane*, sirloin with old Banyuls wine and *crème catalane*. 10% discount on the room rate Sept–June.

🏂 ☎ HÔTEL DE LA LOGE**

pl. de la Loge, 1 rue des Fabriques-Nabot (Centre).
☎ 04.68.34.41.02 ➡ 04.68.34.25.13
e hoteldelaloge@wanadoo.fr
TV.

A sixteenth-century mansion built around a patio with a cool fountain – especially welcome on scorching days. The décor is a mixture of Catalan and Andalusian. Comfortable, pretty rooms, though they could do with a bit of updating. Most have air conditioning and all have TV. Doubles €43 with shower/wc and €50 with bath. 10% discount.

🏂 ☎ I●I PARK HÔTEL-RESTAURANT LE CHAPON FIN***

18 bd. Jean-Bourrat (Northeast); it's opposite the tourist office in square Bir-Hakeim.
☎ 04.68.35.14.14. ➡ 04.68.35.48.18
e acceuil@parkhotel.fr.com
Restaurant closed Sun; the first fortnight in Jan; the last fortnight in Aug. **TV**. **Disabled access**.

The amazing luxury and reasonable prices on offer belie this hotel's dull modern frontage. The bedrooms are decorated in Spanish Renaissance style and have numerous mod cons, including air conditioning. Double rooms with shower/wc cost from €53 or €69 with bath. The restaurant is one of the best in town: recommended are the rock fish soup, the fillet of scorpion fish with shellfish sauce and their speciality dish, lobster *civet* with Banyuls wine. There's a wonderful selection of wines. Lunch menu €23 and others €38–61. À *la carte*, dishes are pricey but perfect.

☎ I●I HÔTEL-RESTAURANT VILLA DUFLOT****

rond-point Albert-Donnezan (South); make for the Perpignan South motorway exit then go towards Argelès. It's two minutes from the toll booth.

☎ 04.68.56.67.67 ➡ 04.68.56.54.05
e villa.duflot@little-france.com
Swimming pool. **Disabled access**. **TV**. **Car park**.

If you're planning to stay in Perpignan for a few days there are better places around, but if all you want is a night of luxury on the way to Spain, it's worth stopping. The rooms (€105 with bath/wc) have been furnished with enchanting taste – ask for one overlooking the swimming pool rather than the dreary industrial park. The restaurant tends towards modern cooking but also has traditional local dishes: try the fresh duck-liver *lasagne* with mushrooms, cod in different sauces and fish *pariade* with aïoli. There's a nice selection of Roussillon wines and they've added a wine bar with a panoply of bottles from the Pyrenees. À *la carte* only during the week, which will set you back about €31, but at weekends there's a single menu at €30 including wine.

🏂 I●I CASA SANSA

3 rue Fabrique-Couverte (Centre).
☎ 04.68.34.21.84
Closed Sun.

This is a young place full of students and travellers. It's decorated with knick-knacks, garish paintings and posters of the *corrida*. The cooking is Catalan with a few original touches – fillet of venison with liquorice, guineafowl with figs, pigs' cheeks with mushrooms, *foie gras* smoked over thyme – and generously served. There's a lunch *formule* at €11, a meal-sized selection of tapas at €21, and you'll pay about €18 à *la carte*. Free house *digestif* or coffee.

🏂 I●I AL TRÈS

3 rue de la Poissonnerie (Centre).
☎ 04.68.34.88.39
Closed Sun; Mon lunchtime 15 June–15 Sept; a fortnight end Nov to early Dec; a fortnight in Feb.

The décor in the dining room has a fresh new look but there's still plenty of old Provence and Catalonia in the sun-drenched cuisine. Start by sharing a few tapas: grilled red peppers, *calamari* with garlic, vegetable fritters or anchovies. Then follow with a dish of shellfish, the turbot with morels or a *zarzuela* (fish stew). There are also Catalan specialities: veal kidneys in Banyuls and excellent desserts. Good value generally, with a €10 lunch *formule* and a menu for €23; you'll pay around €29 à *la carte*. The wine list features 150 wines from the region. Free house apéritif.

|O| LES TROIS SŒURS

2 rue Fontfroide (Centre); it's opposite the Saint-Jean cathedral.
☎ 04.68.51.22.33
Closed Sun; Mon and Tues evenings (except July–Aug); the Feb school holidays.

The terrace, which overlooks place Gambetta, is strangely quiet and untouristy. The dining rooms are bright and air-conditioned and decorated in a cool, modern style. The dishes are made with fresh produce, and they're simple, tasty and well balanced. On offer are a panoply of tapas, fish grilled over an open fire, fresh salads and seafood. There's no set menu but *à la carte* expect to pay €23. Quick service in a relaxed atmosphere.

涨 |O| LE SUD

12 rue Louis-Bausil (Centre); take rue Élie-Delcros from the Palais des Congrès then turn left into the rue Rabelais. Rue Louis-Bausil is a continuation of that street.
☎ and ➡ 04.68.34.55.71
Closed Mon and Oct–April.

This place is in Perpignan's Romany quarter and the patio is planted with scented bushes and jasmine flowers. The delicacies on offer are a delight, combining the best from Provence, the Orient, Mexico, Greece and Catalonia. Everything they cook on the grill is recommended: the little squid with salad, the scallops with parsley, a kebab of chicken marinated in ginger, lemon and chilli, the lamb *tajine* with broad beans and coriander. *À la carte* only – you'll pay around €26. The atmosphere is calming, discreet and comfortable. Free apéritif.

CANET-PLAGE 66140 (12KM E)

涨 🏠 |O| LE CLOS DES PINS – LE MAS FLEURI***

34 av. du Roussillon.
☎ 04.68.80.32.63 ➡ 04.68.80.49.19
e masfleuri@wanadoo.fr
Open weekday lunchtimes 1 March–1 Jan; Jan–Feb.
Garden. TV.

In the restaurant the savoury cuisine is light, creative and skilful and the desserts are similarly inventive; one menu at €25. They serve regional wines only but they're a little overpriced and though the staff are very friendly, the service could be slicker. In fine weather you eat in the gorgeous garden. Quality air-conditioned rooms also available; doubles are €92–140. Free house apéritif.

|O| LA RASCASSE

38 bd. Tixador; it's parallel to the seafront.
☎ 04.68.80.20.79
Closed Mon April–June; Oct–March.

This is a very well-known fish restaurant as well as a wonderful and untouched example of *Vieille France*. All the fish, shellfish and seafood are gloriously fresh and the dishes are delicately prepared: on the menus you'll find *bouillabaisse*, skate with caper sauce, fish *pareillade* and sea bass with *sauce Rascasse*. Try the *crème catalane* for dessert. Reasonably priced menus €17–27, and affordable wines. Service is friendly and efficient.

PÉZENAS 34120

|O| LA POMME D'AMOUR

2 [bis] rue Albert-Paul-Allies (Centre); it's near the tourist office.
☎ 04.67.98.08.40
Closed Mon and Tues evening except in summer; Jan–Feb.

This is a very pleasant little restaurant in an old stone building in the picturesque old part of town. Good, simple cooking and traditional local dishes. They have a few specialities such as mussels in cream sauce and salmon with saffron. Set menus €15 and €18. You'll get a friendly welcome.

PONT-DE-MONTVERT (LE) 48220

涨 🏠 |O| LA TRUITE ENCHANTÉE

Centre.
☎ 04.66.45.80.03
Closed mid-Dec to March. **Garden. Car park.**

The hotel, run by Corinne and Edgard, has eight basic rooms which are bright, clean and spacious – they cost €24 with shower (wc on the landing). Good, hearty, regional cooking is served in the dining room next to the kitchen. Set menus €13–18 and a gourmet option for €22; salmon with sorrel, trout *meunière* and rabbit *Royale* are among the specialities. Booking advised for both hotel and restaurant. Free *digestif*.

MASMÉJEAN 48220 (7KM E)

涨 |O| CHEZ DÉDET

How to get there: take the D998 Pont de Montvert-Saint-Maurice-de-Ventalon road then turn left for Masméjean.
☎ 04.66.45.81.51

Closed Wed; weekday evenings out of season; the last fortnight in June.

The food here is out of this world. It's a real country restaurant in an old farm building with enormous beams, walls made out of great slabs of stone and a hearth you could roast an ox in. They use pigs, sheep and poultry from the family farm and get their snails, trout and mushrooms from local suppliers; in season, the wild boar and hare are also sourced from the area. Portions are enormous and you probably won't be able to finish any of the courses: *charcuterie*, stuffed duck's neck with salad, snails with herbs. The dish of the day might be a delicious fillet of pork with vegetables, along with as much as you can manage from the platter of local cheese and a perfect dessert like *crème caramel*. Set menus €10–20. The service is perfect. Credit cards aren't accepted and booking is advisable, especially in winter. Free coffee.

VIALAS   48220 (18KM E)

⅍ 🏠 |●| HOSTELLERIE CHANTOISEAU***

Centre.
☎ 04.66.41.00.02 ➡ 04.66.41.04.34
Closed Tues evening, Wed and 30 Sept–30 April.
TV. **Swimming pool**. **Car park**.

A pleasant combination of smart and rustic décor in this former coaching inn which offers authentic local cuisine of high quality. Patrick Pagès knows and loves this part of the world, its wild valleys, mushrooms, chestnut trees, its fish and its game. Try the *moche* (pork sausage with cabbage, potatoes and prunes), the *saucisse d'herbes*, the *pompétou* of trout or the *coupétade*. Menus start at €21, and continue at €31–76. Double rooms with shower/wc are €61, or €69 with bath. This gourmet restaurant is a must, and has one of the region's best wine cellars. Free coffee.

PONT-SAINT-ESPRIT   30130

🏠 |●| AUBERGE PROVENÇALE**

Route de Bagnols-sur-Cèze (South); take the N86 as you leave the village.
☎ 04.66.39.08.79 ➡ 04.66.39.14.28
Closed Sun evening Oct–March; the Christmas and New Year holidays. **Car park**.

This inn looks far better inside than out. The same family has run it for more than forty years, cheerfully welcoming travellers, long-distance lorry drivers, families and local wor-

thies alike. They serve large portions of honest traditional food in the two large and air-conditioned dining rooms. The cheapest set menu, €10, sets the tone: *charcuterie*, *crudités*, a dish of the day, seasonal vegetables, cheese platter and fresh fruit or ice-cream. There's a range of six menus from €11 to €19. Gigondas and Tavel are served by the glass and reasonably priced. The bedrooms, which cost €27, have bathrooms; the ones that overlook the courtyard are more peaceful.

⅍ |●| LOU RÉCATI

rue Jean-Jacques (Centre).
☎ 04.66.90.73.01
Closed Mon and Tues lunchtime.

"Lou Récati" is a local term to describe those little mounds of furniture or clothing thrown together to save them from the floodwaters of the Rhône. It's a rather wonderful name for a restaurant run by a talented young chef who produces delicate, skilfully cooked dishes. The prices are fair considering his professionalism: weekday lunch menu €11 and others €21 and 31. They list snail ravioli, pan-fried liver with Muscat sauce and, for dessert, an unrivalled *crème brûlée* scented with lavender. It's a real treat to dine here. Free apéritif.

AIGUÈZE   30760 (10KM NW)

⅍ 🏠 LE CASTELAS**

It's in the village: from Pont-Saint-Esprit, take the 86 for Montélimar then left onto the D901 in the direction of Barjac.
☎ 04.66.82.18.76 ➡ 04.66.82.14.98
@ dventajol@aol.com
Swimming pool. **Car park**.

Le Castelas enjoys a remarkable location in a picturesque hillside village overlooking the Ardèche. It also has some remarkable qualities of its own: the rooms and apartments are all within the ancient castle walls, and are charmingly decorated and fitted with small corner kitchens. You can stay in the main residence near the first swimming pool where the rooms have terraces and views over the gorges of the Ardèche; the annexe, just two streets away, has another pool. The owner is polite and attentive and looks after his clients very well. Double rooms with shower/wc or bath go for €53–69; rates for long stays available on request. Good, self-service buffet breakfast. They'll lend you a bicycle and tell you where to go, or advise on hiring a canoe. Free apéritif.

BAGNOLS-SUR-CÈZE   30200 (15KM S)

🌂 🛏 HÔTEL BAR DES SPORTS**

3 pl. Jean-Jaurès (Centre); take the R86 from Pont-
Saint-Esprit in the direction of Nîmes.
☎ 04.68.89.61.68 ➡ 04.66.89.92.97
TV. Pay garage.

This is a serious place which deserves its two
stars: it offers delightful, clean, comfortable
double rooms with bath and double glazing
for €41. The owner is very kind, and it's really quiet at night because the bar doesn't stay
open late. Free use of the garage at weekends (except July–Aug).

PRADES   66500

🌂 ⦿ LE JARDIN D'AYMERIC

3 av. du Général-de-Gaulle; it's opposite the lorry park.
☎ 04.68.96.53.38
Closed Sun evening; Mon; the Feb school holidays; a
fortnight June–July. **TV. Car park.**

A small restaurant with a warm dining room
where excellent cuisine is served. It's often
full, so consider booking. The generously
flavoured regional cooking uses fresh produce, so the menus change regularly and
include dishes such as roast saddle of lamb
with thyme and cappuccino of white kidney
beans. Dish of the day €9 and menus
€15–27. They serve regional wines – and the
house wine is as good as some on the wine
list. Speedy, energetic service from smiling,
chatty waiting staff. Free apéritif.

VINÇA   66320 (9KM E)

🌂 🛏 ⦿ LA PETITE AUBERGE

74 av. du Général-de-Gaulle; it's on the N116 in the
direction of Prades.
☎ 04.68.05.81.47 ➡ 04.68.05.85.80
Closed Wed and Sun evening (except July–Aug).

A little inn – as the name suggests. The
chef is chatty, and the cuisine he prepares is
as straightforward and generous as he is.
Excellent €13 menu: to start, help yourself
to the *hors d'oeuvre* buffet or go for a plate
of cooked ham; for a main course you
might get fried Catalan sausage with tomatoes, cod *à la catalane*, duck breast with
sour cherries or pan-fried monkfish with
prawns. Finally there's a home-made custard the likes of which you won't have tasted in years. Other menus €22–28, all of
which are bursting with tasty, characterful
dishes. There are a few simple rooms –

€18 with basin, €27 with shower/wc. Free
apéritif.

PRATS-DE-MOLLO   11500

🌂 🛏 ⦿ HÔTEL DES TOURISTES**

av. du Haut Vallespir; it's on the right as you arrive in the
village on the road from Amélie-les-Bains.
☎ 04.68.39.72.12 ➡ 04.68.39.79.22
✉ hotel.lestouristes@free.fr
Closed Nov–March. **TV. Car park.**

This solidly built stone hotel is an ideal spot
from which to explore the wild, mountainous
Vallespir region. The rooms are well maintained; doubles cost €21 with basin/wc or
€43–46 with shower/wc or bath. Some have
balconies, others little terraces, and the ones
at the back have a view of the river. In the
huge dining room they serve family-style
dishes – pigs' trotters *à la catalane*, *escaliva-
da*, duck stewed in Banyuls wine or scorpion
fish. Menus €14–32 or you can eat *à la carte*.
Free apéritif or free breakfast in April and
October.

ROQUEFORT-DES-CORBIÈRES   11540

🌂 ⦿ LE LÉZARD BLEU

rue de l'Église (Centre).
☎ 04.68.48.51.11
Closed Oct–July.

The lizard signs outside direct you to this
restaurant with the blue door. Inside, the
walls are white and hung with modern paintings. The food is lovingly prepared by the
owner, a friendly woman who's full of life.
There's lots of duck on the menu: *foie gras*,
tajines and *à l'orange*. Set menus €15 and
€20, though the desserts are a bit small for
what they cost. Best to book. Free glass of
Grenache.

SAINT-ANDRÉ-DE-VALBORGNE   30940

🛏 ⦿ HÔTEL-RESTAURANT BOURGADE**

pl. de l'Église.
☎ 04.66.60.30.72 ➡ 04.66.60.35.56
✉ picoboo@compuserve.com
Closed Mon–Wed evening except mid-June to mid-
Sept; 11 Nov to mid-April. **TV.**

A village that feels like the end of the
world, in the hollow of one of the prettiest valleys of the Cévennes. This place started as a
posthouse in the seventeenth century and

has been in the family for generations. The latest lot have shaken out all the cobwebs and offer an enthusiastic welcome. Simple, charming rooms overlook the church square or the stream; doubles with shower/wc or bath €44 for two or €50 for rooms sleeping three. Flavourful and inspirational cuisine by a chef who did part of his apprenticeship with the great Ducasse. He makes lots of regional dishes using fresh produce, and has kept his grandmother's famous crayfish dish on the menus, which range from €15 to €35. A lovely place.

SAINT-CHÉLY-DU-TARN   48210

🏃 ☎ |●| L'AUBERGE DE LA CASCADE*

How to get there: it's in the Gorges du Tarn, in the direction of Millau.
☎ 04.66.77.06.72
Closed Sun evening and Mon. **Disabled access.**
Swimming pool. TV.

This inn offers good value for money. Reception is in the restaurant and the rooms in a separate building – they're all brand-new and very comfortable. Doubles €33 with shower/wc and €46 with bath. The swimming pool is on a terrace overlooking the river Tarn.The restaurant offers regional dishes, crêpes and snacks but it's not the best in the area and service is slapdash. Half board is €34–40 and compulsory July–Aug. Free coffee.

SAINT-PONS DE THOMIÈRES   34220

🏃 ☎ |●| AUBERGE DU CABARETOU

route de la Salvetat; it's on the top of the Cabaretou pass on the left coming from Saint-Pons.
☎ 04.67.97.02.31
Closed mid-Jan to mid-Feb.

Here it feels like it's just you and the wild mountainside. The owner is a lovely lady and her establishment offers exceptional value for money. Single rooms with shower/wc are €38 or €43 for a double. Lovely, tasty dishes on the menu for €15 in the week with others up to €34.

SAINT-SATURNIN-DE-LUCIAN   34725

☎ |●| OSTALARIA CARDABELA

10 pl. de la Fontaine; take the D130 and it's in the centre of the village.
☎ 04.67.88.62.62 ➡ 04.67.88.62.82

Closed early Nov to mid-March.

A lovely place if you like your creature comforts – enjoy the gorgeous, cosy rooms and big beds with Egyptian cotton sheets. Great care is taken over everything, starting with the welcome. Rooms €58–80. The restaurant is *Le Mimosa*, and it's to be found in Saint-Giraud 2kms away. It's an equally stylish place in a charming old house; lunch menu €29 or €45 for dinner.

|●| LE PRESSOIR DE SAINT-SATURNIN

17 place de la Fontaine.
☎ 04.67.88.67.89
Closed Sunday evening and Mon (except July–Aug); mid-Jan to mid-Feb.

It would be easy to fall in love with this authentic Languedoc inn. You'll find some dishes prepared to very old recipes like the *escoubille* stew simmered in local red wine, and make sure you try the cheese *croquettes* or the free-range lamb. Dish of the day €8 and a menu for €14. The atmosphere on the terrace and in the dining room is always bright.

SAUVE   30610

🏃 |●| CHEZ LA MARTHE

20 rue Mazan (Centre); it's near the town hall.
☎ 04.66.77.06.72
Closed Sun evening, Mon, June and Nov.

Marthe was a woman who ran the local grocery more than two decades ago and the restaurant named after her has been delightfully decorated in local style. Weekday lunch menu €11, with others at €17 and €20. Dishes include *pieds et paquets* (lamb tripe and trotters), duck sausage with *foie gras* and Cévenole salad. They have a habit of closing unexpectedly in winter, so check in advance. Free house apéritif.

🏃 |●| RESTAURANT LE MICOCOULIER

3 pl. Jean-Astruc (Centre).
☎ 04.66.77.57.61 ✉ gail.wagman@wanadoo.fr
Closed lunchtimes July–Aug (except Sun and public holidays); Nov–March.

An unusual, pleasant little restaurant perched on a clifftop above the medieval village. There's a soothing atmosphere in the pretty dining room and the terrace is the kind of place where you can happily sit over a bottle and put the world to rights. The owner has gathered a collection of recipes during his travels, and has adapted them for here: goulash, *tajine* (Moroccan stew), curries and a number of Turkish and Mexican dishes. His American wife cooks the pastries and her chocolate cake, lemon tart and *crème caramel* are irresistible. Set menus €15 and €21. Free house apéritif.

SÈTE   34200

⬧ |●| LE P'TIT MOUSSE*

rue de Provence (West); it's in the Corniche area 100m from the beach.
☎ 04.67.53.10.66 ➡ 04.67.53.10.66
Closed Oct–March. **Garden**.

A bright ochre building in a quiet little street off the Corniche, very close to the sea. The rooms are clean but rather small. Doubles raound €28 with shower/wc, and there are also rooms sleeping four in two double beds. Simple cooking and homely atmosphere, with set menus at €12 and €20.

⬧ LE GRAND HÔTEL***

17 quai de Lattre-de-Tassigny (Centre).
☎ 04.67.74.71.77 ➡ 04.67.74.29.27
e ghsetect@sete-hotel.com
Closed 23 Dec–5 Jan. **TV**. **Pay car park**.

This magnificent grand hotel was built in the 1880s, and it hasn't lost a trace of character. It's spacious and filled with period furniture, and there's a magnificent patio with a glass roof to keep out the bad weather – lovely for breakfast. Rooms €55–72 with shower/wc or €72–101 with bath. Expect to pay more for an apartment or a suite. Faultless service, as befits a grand hotel.

🔆 ⬧ |●| LES TERRASSES DU LIDO***

rond-point de l'Europe-La Corniche (West).
☎ 04.67.51.39.60 ➡ 04.67.51.28.90
Closed Sun evening and Mon out of season; New Year holidays; 18–28 Feb. **Disabled access**. **Swimming pool**. **Garden**. **TV**. **Garage**.

Owners Michel and Colette Guironnet run this place with considerable skill and taste. Everything's just right, from the décor in the rooms to the friendly welcome and the creative cooking. There are only nine bedrooms so it's advisable to book; doubles with bath €58–76. Colette runs the kitchen and prepares dishes with artistry and style. She particularly likes to cook fish, shellfish and *bouillabaisse*, and her lobster lasagne with ceps in particular is excellent. Menus €23–53. Free coffee and 10% discount on the room rate in low season.

🔆 |●| LA GOGUETTE

30 rue Révolution (Centre); it's near the flea market.

☎ 04.99.04.07.84
Closed Sun evening and Mon.

A good-humoured local restaurant which is full of personality, located in a street where the tourists don't bother to explore. It has a colourful, Art Nouveau décor, a tiny terrace, a tiny dining room and a tiny mezzanine. On the other hand, expect large portions of simple, home cooking with a range of cheap dishes. Menus €9 or €14. Efficient service. It's popular, so book ahead. Free coffee.

🔆 |●| LA MARINE

29 quai Général-Durand (Centre); it's near the fishing harbour.
☎ 04.67.74.30.03 ➡ 04.67.74.38.18
Closed Tues out of season; Tues lunchtime July–Aug.
Disabled access.

You have a choice: to eat out on the terrace with a view of the harbour and the trawler fleet or in the pretty dining room. In both places you'll feast on authentic, traditional, local cooking. They do an €14 *menu du jour* served until 1pm and until 8pm in the evening, and other menus €18–21. They list dishes such as *bouillabaisse*, monkfish in white sauce with shellfish and turbot cooked in salt water. The desserts are excellent. You'll pay a bit more *à la carte*, but you'll have the option to try their speciality, *bourride* – a sort of fish stew with saffron and bitter orange peel. Free coffee.

|●| LE MARIE-JEAN

26 quai Général Durand
☎ 04.67.46.02.01
Closed Mon lunchtime; Mon out of season; Tues lunchtime; Jan.

A really good table which suggests that this quayside, once the pride of the town, might have an interesting future – if only it were possible to get rid of the tourist traps lining the front. Gourmet specialities here: tuna *carpaccio*, sardine tartare, stuffed squid *Sétoise*, fish grilled over the coals. Weekday menu for €14 and others €20–34. The décor is quite smart, the service stylish. The only drawback, in fact, is the racket from the traffic along the port.

|●| LA CORNICHE

pl. Édouard-Herriot; it's opposite the casino.
☎ 04.67.53.03.30
Closed Sun evening and Mon out of season; Mon lunchtime July–Aug; mid-Nov to mid-Feb.

The huge blue neon sign here might yell '"tourist trap", but actually it's not – this is a good establishment where they serve well-balanced Sète specialities prepared just as they ought to be. You can get fish soup to die for on the €15 menu, then authentic monk-fish *sétoise* with brandy, tomato and garlic to be followed by a decent *crème brûlée* – delicious and not too expensive. For €24 there's a shellfish platter, chef's fish stew, cheese and dessert.

|O| LA ROTONDE

17 quai de Lattre-de-Tassigny.
☎ 04.67.74.86.14
Closed Sat lunchtime and Sun.

This is the finest restaurant in Sète – originally it was part of the Grand Hotel which stands next door. The décor is a bit glitzy but not at all heavy; settle in and read yourself into the programme of Mediterranean delights on the menu. Philippe Mouls cooks only with fresh fish or freshly plucked vegetables and fruit: oyster lasagne with tomatoes, courgettes and ham, chicken with red peppers and saffron stock. Lunch *menu du marché* €21 and others €24–30. Dress up for a feast of delicious dishes. Charming service.

BOUZIGUES   34140 (15KM N)

🎋 |O| LES JARDINS DE LA MER

av. Louis-Tudesq.
☎ 04.67.78.33.23
Closed Thurs; the last few days in Sept; a fortnight in early Oct; Jan.

This pretty restaurant is located in an oyster farm and the shady terrace is decorated with vast white sails and hung with a torrent of shells. Try the *gratin* of mussels with leeks, the seafood platters or the meat and fish grilled over the open fire – where they use old vines as fuel. Menus €17 and €24.

🎋 |O| L'ARSEILLÈRE

av. Louis-Tudesq.
☎ 04.67.78.384.12

Jean-Pierre Molina could have been a professional footballer if things had gone badly for him. Instead he learned to prepare oysters with great skill and technique, and employs the same ingredients as lots of others round here – mussels, oysters, clams and snails, served with garlic or aïoli. Enjoy your delicious shellfish in complete confidence. The seafood platter costs €18 for two or, for twice as much, you could have the truly memorable *dégustation* option.

|O| CHEZ LA TCHÈPE

av. Louis-Tudesq; it's on the bank of the étang de Tau.
☎ 04.67.78.33.19

This little terrace catches the eye; apart from anything else, it's often chock-a-block. There are lots of places in this area where everything comes straight from the sea to the table, but this one offers the best value for money. You can get two dozen oysters, a dozen mussels, one *violet* (a small sea creature from the Mediterranean which is eaten raw and looks rather like scrambled eggs), two warm *tielles* (a small squid soufflé with tomato sauce) and a bottle of white wine for €19 – and that's for two people. There are no set menus – you just choose what you want from the display. Eat in or take away, and service at all hours of the day. No credit cards.

SOMMIÈRES   30250

🎋 🏠 |O| AUBERGE DU PONT ROMAIN***

2 rue Émile-Jamais; it's 300m from the Roman bridge.
☎ 04.66.80.00.58 ➡ 04.66.80.31.52
📧 aubergedupontromain@wanadoo.fr
Closed Mon lunchtime; 15 Jan–15 March; Nov.
Disabled access. Swimming pool. TV. Car park.

The size of this place is impressive enough, with a huge industrial chimney towering over the roof. In its time it's been a wool mill, a carpet mill, a silk farm, a distillery and a dye factory – today, it's a chic three-star hotel with affordable prices. Doubles with shower/wc are €56 or €58 with bath, some designed for disabled visitors. Half board is compulsory in summer at €66–76 per person. The restaurant is pricey with menus at €19–28 but the food is some of the best in the area: especially recommended are the snails *à la Sommieroise* with a touch of Roquefort and the gorgeous chocolate desserts. The shaded, flowery terrace and swimming pool are relaxing enough to make you feel like lazing about all afternoon. Free house apéritif.

🎋 |O| L'OLIVETTE

11 rue Abbé-Fabre.
☎ 04.66.80.97.71
Closed Tues in season; Tues evening and Wed out of season; 7–27 Jan.

They certainly know how to make you feel welcome here. The dining room is wonderful, with stone walls and wooden beams and it's air-conditioned. There's a two-course lunch menu at €11, and others €15–28. The cuisine is staunchly local – snails, salt cod with olive paste – but introduces a few flavours from further afield: scallop *mousseline* with ginger, pork with pineapple and green peppercorns. They use a great deal of butter in preference to olive oil. Free *tapenade* (homemade olive paste).

SORÈDE   66690

|O| LA SALAMANDRE

3 route de Larroque.
☎ 04.68.89.26.67
Closed Sun evening; Mon and Tues lunchtime out of season; Mon and Tues lunchtimes in summer; 15 Jan–15 March and 15 Nov–1 Dec.

The dining room is on the small side and, curiously, lacks intimacy, but the cuisine simply has to be tried. It's full of originality and combines regional gastronomic recipes with lesser-known ones. The results are delicate and flavourful: scallop flan with a crayfish *coulis*, flambéed fillet of beef with wild mushroom sauce. Menus, €15 and €21, change regularly to make the most of seasonal produce. This is a really good place. In case you're curious, a "salamandre" is the upper arch of the oven where you place dishes to caramelize them. So now you know.

TAUTAVEL   66720

🎎 🏠 |O| CHEZ DANIEL

3 rue de la République.
☎ 04.68.29.03.23
Closed Mon out of season and 3 weeks in Jan. **TV**.

This is a village bar-restaurant which is really friendly and popular – the kind of place where locals drop in for an apéritif or a tasty and cheap meal. Menus at €10 and €15 include a self-service *charcuterie* buffet, a choice of grilled lamb chops, Catalan sausages, steak, duck breast, pork belly and fish kebabs. There's ice-cream to finish – and wine is included. The rooms are clean and functional (pine furniture, white walls) and, at €27 for a double with bath/wc, offer good value for money for such a touristy location. There are also apartments to rent by the week. Free house *digestif*.

UZÈS   30700

🎎 🏠 HÔTEL SAINT-GÉNIÈS**

Quartier Saint-Géniès (southwest); it's 1.5 km from the

town centre in the direction of Saint-Ambroix.
☎ 04.66.22.29.99 ➡ 04.66.03.14.89
e saintgeniesz@wanadoo.fr
Closed 15 Dec–15 Feb.
Swimming pool. Garden. TV. Car park.

This district is very quiet, in the evenings especially. The hotel is new and there are twenty tastefully decorated bedrooms. The ones up in the roof have sloping ceilings, which makes them feel more intimate. Doubles with shower/wc €53–60 or, with bath/wc, €43–53. They offer a set meal, €12, if you don't want to venture back into town. Free coffee.

🏠 |O| HÔTEL-RESTAURANT LA TAVERNE**

4–9 rue Xavier-Sigalon (Centre); it's near the cinema.
☎ 04.66.22.47.08 ➡ 04.66.22.45.90
e lataverne.uzes@wanadoo.fr
Garden. TV.

The pleasant garden in the small courtyard provides a quiet setting for your meal, though sometimes it's overrun by groups. The owner knows the town like the back of his hand, so he's a good source of information. Good tasty cooking. Menus €19–24. They do *confit*, breast of duck and *cassoulet*, and excellent scrambled eggs with truffles. The hotel is a few metres further on and provides quiet rooms – particularly the ones at the back. They all have good facilities, and cost €52--58 for doubles with shower/wc or bath. They're all different and some have beamed ceilings and stone walls from the original house.

🎎 🏠 |O| HÔTEL D'ENTRAIGUES – RESTAURANT LES JARDINS DE CASTILLE***

8 rue de la Calade (East); it's opposite the historic bishop's palace and the cathedral of Saint-Théodorit.
☎ 04.66.22.32.68 ➡ 04.66.22.57.01
e hotels.entraigues.agoult@wanadoo.fr
Disabled access. Swimming pool. TV. Car park.

This stylish, charming establishment is a based on a group of town houses from the fifteenth, seventeenth and eighteenth centuries. The 29 air-conditioned bedrooms and apartments are furnished in classic style, and some have a private terrace. Doubles with shower/wc or bath €60–107. The restaurant has a panoramic terrace and an elegant dining room. Menus, which change with each season, are €15–49 – though you can always rely on the inspired Provençal cuisine. 10% discount if you stay half board; normal price is €18 per person.

☆ |○| LE BISTROT DU GRÉZAC

pl. Belle-Croix.
☎ 04.66.03.42.09
Closed Tues evening and Wed; a fortnight in Feb; a fortnight in Oct.

Just next to the Saint-Étienne church is this brand-new, old-style bistro which has been brilliantly done up – when it's aged a little it will be perfect. The simple, delicious cuisine is Provençal in style. Lunch menu €12; dinner costs €16. Easy-going, efficient service. Sadly, the terrace is just too close to the road for comfort. Free apéritif.

☆ |○| LE SAN DIEGO

10 bd. Charles-Gide; it's next to the town hall.
☎ 04.66.22.20.78
Closed Sun evening, Mon and a fortnight in Feb.

The frontage is unusually dull for Uzès but the restaurant is very good. There are two fresh dining rooms with vaulted ceilings, painted in grey and pink, and vases of roses on the table. A great deal of care goes into preparing dishes: duck *foie gras*, salmon *carpaccio*, fish fillet with citronella, marinated pork fillet mignon with Côte du Rhone sauce – and they're famous for their chocolate *fondant* with summer fruit *coulis*. Menus €13–16. Friendly, unobtrusive service. Free house apéritif.

SAINT-VICTOR-DES-OULES   30700 (6KM NW)

|○| RESTAURANT DU MAS DES OULES

Route de Saint-Hyppolyte.
☎ 04.66.63.17.15
Closed Sun evening, Mon and Tues.

The restaurant is in one wing of a farm in the grounds of a seventeenth-century castle. It's a small but typical Provençal house, and the atmosphere is so relaxed it's like being at home with friends. The owner comes over and goes through the menu with you, communicating her enthusiasm while doing so. The cuisine is inspirational – fresh, seasonal produce, wonderfully well cooked. It would hold its own against many a starred establishment. Menus from €23.

VERS-PONT-DU-GARD   30210 (10KM SE)

☆ ☎ |○| LA BÉGUDE SAINT-PIERRE

Les Coudoulières; it's on the D981 between Remoulins and Uzès.
☎ 04.66.63.63.63 ➡ 04.66.22.73.73
e begudessaintpierrre@wanadoo.fr
Closed Sun evening and Mon 4 Nov–30 April **Disabled**

access. Swimming pool. TV. Car park.

"Bégude" is the Provençal word for a farm that doubled as a posthouse way back when letters were carried on horseback. Times may have changed but fortunately the road that goes past isn't busy. The beautiful seventeenth-century building has been carefully restored and decorated with Provençal prints. The rooms look onto the coachyard or the swimming pool; they're air-conditioned and individually decorated. Doubles with bath €53–61. The chic restaurant serves cuisine of Provençal pedigree and has menus €29–49. The staff make you feel welcome. They have a guard dog watching over the car park at night. 10% discount on the room rate Sept–June.

VALCEBOLLIÈRE   66340

☆ ☎ |○| AUBERGE LES ÉCUREUILS***

How to get there: take the N116 and the D30 from bourg Madame.
☎ 04.68.04.52.03 ➡ 04.68.04.52.34
Closed 15 Oct–10 Dec and a fortnight in May.
Swimming pool. TV. Car park.

This cosy inn, built of solid wood and stone, lies deep in the heart of Cerdagne near the Spanish border. Étienne Laffitte's creativity blossoms in the kitchen, where he creates dishes based on local produce and serves them up in hearty portions. Set menus €19 at lunchtime and €23–38 in the evenings – or you can eat in the *crêperie* for €15. Dishes include hot duck *foie gras* with apples and honey, duck breast with ceps or morels, braised lamb fillet and hot *millefeuille* with fresh fruit. Comfortable bedrooms with marble bathrooms go for €53–84. Half-board costs €53–67. There's a gym, a sauna and pool tables. You can go on beautiful walks up the mountain, which is 2500m high and towers over the hotel. In the winter there's downhill skiing or snow-shoe hikes. 5% discount if you stay half board for ten days or more.

VIGAN (LE)   30120

☎ HÔTEL DU COMMERCE*

26 rue des Barris (Centre); it's next to the police station.
☎ 04.67.81.03.28 ➡ 04.67.81.43.20
Closed Sunday lunchtime out of season. **Garden. Car park.**

This quiet, cheap hotel is just away from the middle of the village and it's a great base from which to explore the area. Bright, simple, spacious and super-clean doubles cost €21 with basin, €27 with shower/wc, €29 with bath. Lovely place – the welcome is wonderful.

|●| LE JARDIN

8 rue du Four (Centre); it's 50m from the tourist office.
☎ 04.67.81.28.96
Closed Mon lunchtime and Feb.

This place is a wine shop as well as a restaurant and it's located in a quiet street. The dining room is as pleasant as the small terrace. Naturally enough, you'll find lots of local varieties and regional AOC wines which you can try by the glass, the jug or the bottle. Start off with a *rinquinquin*, a local peach apéritif while you meander through the menu. Dishes are seasonally inspired and the produce is fresh and local – the beef and veal come from the Aubrac, and there's also a fish menu. Weekday lunch menu €15 and others €22 and €25. The service is amiable and kind.

AVÈZE   30120 (2KM S)

🎐 🏠 |●| L'AUBERGE COCAGNE**

pl. du Château; it's on the road to Cirque de Navacelles.
☎ 04.67.81.02.70 ➡ 04.67.81.07.67
Closed Dec and Jan. **Disabled access. Car park.**

In the south of France "cocagne" means "luck", and this typical country inn, shielded by a clump of trees, couldn't be more aptly named. It's a 400-year-old building with massive stone walls, red shutters and simple yet comfortable bedrooms. Doubles €27 with basin, €43 with bath. You get a warm welcome as well as cool jazz in the dining room. The place has personality and so does the home cooking which, typical for the Mediterranean, is drenched in olive oil and strewn with spices: *terrine* with sweet onion chutney, lamb from the Causse and vegetarian dishes. The vegetables are organic and the cheeses bought direct from the farmer. The wines and apéritifs come from local winegrowers. Set menus €12–28. Half board costs €34–41 and is compulsory mid-July to mid-Aug and over long public holiday weekends. Free coffee or herbal tea.

MANDAGOUT   30120 (10KM N)

🎐 🏠 |●| AUBERGE DE LA BORIE*

How to get there: take the D170; 9km along, turn right towards Mandagout, pass the village, continue towards Saint-André-de-Majencoules, then follow a sloping street on the left for 250m.

☎ 04.67.81.06.03 ➡ 04.67.81.86.79
Disabled access. Swimming pool. Garden. Car park.

An old Cévennes *mas* on a sunny mountainside, with a swimming pool and reasonable prices. The views over the mountains, the chestnut forests and fig groves are breathtaking and the owners make you feel most welcome. There are ten nicely appointed rooms with old stone walls; doubles with basin are €26, €43 with shower/wc or €47 with bath. Numbers 8, 9 and 10, down in the ancient vaulted cellars, are wonderfully cool in summer. In the restaurant they serve home cooking based exclusively on local produce – specialities include duck breast with figs, *foie gras* with figs, frogs' legs with parsley and iced nougat with soft fruit. Set menus €12, €18 and €23. Free apéritif.

SAINT-MARTIAL   30440 (24KM NE)

🎐 🏠 |●| HÔTEL-RESTAURANT LA TERRASSE

pl. du Portail (Centre); take the D999 across Le Vigan, then the D11 and the D20.
☎ 04.67.81.33.11 ➡ 04.67.81.33.87
Closed Wed; end Feb to early March

Good living and good food go hand in hand at this mountainside inn. Dominique, the owner, boasts about the beauty spots in "her" beautiful Cévennes, including the twelfth-century Romanesque church in the village. They offer perfectly adequate bedrooms at €29 for a double with shower, but people come here primarily for the local cooking: tart *forestière* with mushrooms, bacon and potatoes, rib of beef with Roquefort cheese, *millefeuille* of onions with an olive oil *sabayon,* home-made peach tart. Menus €13–26 – you get an extra course on the most expensive menu. A brilliant find. Free apéritif.

VILLEFORT   48800

🎐 🏠 |●| HÔTEL-RESTAURANT DU LAC**

Lac de Villefort (Nord); take the D906 for 1.5km and it's a white building all by itself on the left by the lake.
☎ 04.66.46.81.20 ➡ 04.66.46.90.95
Closed Wed out of season, 15 Nov-8 March. **Car park.**

The bedrooms all have a view of the lake, where you can swim in summer, and are reasonably priced considering this excellent location: doubles with shower/wc go for €40 or €55 with bath. The restaurant also shares the view and in it you'll find traditional, old-school cooking. The €13 set menu features regional specialities like cep omelette, *troute meunière*, veal *blanquette* and chestnut gateau. It's very popular in high season, so it can get noisy. Free coffee.

🎎 🏠 |●| HÔTEL-RESTAURANT BALME**

pl. du Portalet (Centre).
☎ 04.66.46.80.14 ➡ 04.66.46.85.26
Closed Sun evening and Mon out of season; a few days in Sept; mid-Nov to mid-Feb. **TV**. **Car park**.

A well-known place which has aged elegantly. It's somewhat reminiscent of a spa hotel – same type of comfort, same English atmosphere. The cuisine is excellent, combining local dishes and specialities from the East, especially Thailand, where chef Michel Gomy spends part of every year. There's a weekday menu at €15 and others €21–31; the meals are the best value for money in the region. *À la carte* dishes change regularly so it's hard to know what you'll find – it could be ravioli stuffed with morels, pan-fried *foie gras* coated with poppy seeds, terrine of calves' head with cep oil or Thai curry with scented rice. The kitchen opens onto the dining room so you can follow what's going on, and since Micheline is a qualified *sommelier*, they've got a magnificent cellar. In the hotel, doubles go for €46 with shower/wc and €49 with bath. 10% discount on the room rate Sept–June.

VILLEFRANCHE-DE-CONFLENT 66500

|●| AUBERGE SAINT-PAUL

7 pl. de l'Église; it's in the centre of town.
☎ and ➡ 04.68.96.30.95
Closed Mon Easter–Oct; Mon and Tues Oct–Easter; three weeks in Jan; 5 days in June; 10 days end Nov.

Patricia Gomez has a remarkable culinary imagination: she combines unexpected flavours with top-quality ingredients and produces unforgettable dishes. Some of her best are ravioli with goat's cheese stuffing, roast local lamb, pig's trotters and a perfect vanilla cream. Set menus for €21, €38, €40 and €73; you'll pay around €43 *à la carte*. Brilliant wines selected by Charly Gomez. One of the best restaurants in the district, and it has a beautiful terrace to boot.

OLETTE 66360 (10KM W)

🏠 |●| HÔTEL-RESTAURANT LA FONTAINE

5 rue de la Fusterie.
☎ 04.68.97.03.67 ➡ 04.68.97.09.18

Closed Tues evening and Wed (except during school holidays); Jan. **TV**.

A substantial building painted a brilliant salmon-pink. The rooms are attractive and have good facilities – some include en-suite bathrooms. Good-value doubles with shower/wc are €29. There's a terrace with eight tables and a pretty dining room on the first floor. Try the black pudding with apricot sauce, the duck breast with honey sauce, the joint of lamb with sweet rosemary or the *tournedos* with creamed black pudding. Menus €11–31. Warm, family welcome.

VILLENEUVE-LÈS-AVIGNON 30400

🎎 🏠 HÔTEL DE L'ATELIER**

5 rue de la Foire (Centre).
☎ 04.90.25.01.84 ➡ 04.90.25.80.06
📧 hotel.atelier@wanadoo.fr
Closed 4 Nov–15 Dec. **Garden**. **TV**. **Car park**.

This is a quite delightful sixteenth-century building with nineteen bedrooms furnished with antiques. All the public spaces have been completely refurbished and rooms are scheduled for a makeover in 2002. Doubles with shower are €44–60 or €58–84 with bath. Breakfast is served in the dining room or on the patio, where plants and flowers proliferate, and there's also a rooftop terrace. It's good value for money – you'd be wise to book in season. 10% discount 1 Oct–31 March.

|●| RESTAURANT LA CALÈCHE**

35 rue de la République; it's between the Chartreuse and the village square.
☎ 04.90.25.02.54
Closed Sun.

The terrace and the patio are both very pleasant during the summer months. The restaurant also has two pretty dining rooms decorated in warm colours and the walls are covered in posters and reproductions of Toulouse-Lautrec paintings. Simple cooking, decent food and specialities from Lyon and Provence – *pieds et paquets* (lamb tripe and trotters), beef *daube* and lamb *confit*. Set menus €11–18. Friendly service.

|●| RESTAURANT LA MAISON

1 rue Montée-du-Fort-Saint-André (Centre); it's behind the town hall, overlooking pl. Jean-Jaurès.
☎ 04.90.25.20.81
Closed Tues evening; Wed; Sat lunchtime. **Car park**.

This good restaurant is attractive to look at, with lace curtains, ceiling fans and a good-looking pottery collection. Simple cooking is served in generous portions: scallops on a bed of leeks, duck breast with *beurre rouge*. You get a good meal on the €20 menu. Absolutely delightful service.

ANGLES (LES) 30133 (4KM S)

☆ |●| LE PETIT MANOIR**

15 av. Jules-Ferry; it's on the Nîmes road.
☎ 04.90.25.03.36 ➡ 04.90.25.49.13
Disabled access. Swimming pool. Garden. TV. Car park.

This group of modern buildings set around a swimming pool is hardly what you'd call a manor. But the place is not without character or comfort – and most of the quiet, clean rooms have a private terrace. Doubles €41–55 with shower/wc or bath. The restaurant serves traditional, regional cuisine with menus at €15–40. Half board costs €62 and is compulsory in July. 10% discount Sept–Aug and free house apéritif with your meal if you stay half board.

ROQUEMAURE 30150 (11KM N)

🏃 ☆ |●| LE CLÉMENT V**

route de Nîmes (Southwest); take the D980.
☎ 04.66.82.67.58 ➡ 04.66.82.84.66
📧 hotel.clementv@wanadoo.fr
Closed Sat and Sun out of season (except for reservations); 25 Oct–15 March. **Swimming pool. TV. Garden. Lock-up garage.**

A very nice place in a medieval village in the Côtes du Rhône which has so far eluded the tourists. It's in a 1970s apartment building that looks like many built along the coast at that time; the rooms are conventional but they've been renovated with a touch of Provence. The ones overlooking the swimming pool have balconies but those at the back are larger and quieter. Doubles €50 with shower/wc. Half board, €42, is obligatory in summer. The menus, €15 and €20, are available only to hotel residents. They list typical, local dishes with bags of personality. Free apéritif if you stay half board and 10% discount on the room rate Sept–June.

Limousin

19 Corrèze

23 Creuse

87 Haute-Vienne

ARGENTAT 19400

🎋 🏠 |●| HÔTEL-RESTAURANT FOUILLADE

11 pl. Gambetta.
☎ 05.55.28.10.17 ➡ 05.55.28.90.52
Closed Mon out of season; Nov. **TV**. **Car park**.

A beautiful house that's been running as a hotel-restaurant for two centuries. Scrumptious dishes include duck *confit* with chestnuts, ceps with sorrel butter and *croustade* with girolle mushrooms. Menus €11–30. The 1970s rooms are less attractive than the building itself. Doubles with shower/wc €32, €36 with bath. Free coffee.

SAINT-JULIEN-AUX-BOIS (14KM NE)

|●| AUBERGE DE ST JULIEN-AUX-BOIS

How to get there: take the D980 or the scenic Route des Écoliers.
☎ 05.55.24.41.94

This lost village on the edge of La Xaintrie and the Dordogne valley offers an unexpectedly pleasant surprise. Neither the village nor the restaurant look that appealing and even the décor in the dining room is ordinary – but it's the food that makes the place different. It's run by a German couple who fell in love with the area and decided to open a restaurant. Madame is the chef, and many of her delicious Limousin specialities have a touch of German cuisine about them: cream of lentils with scallops and pumpkin seeds, duck stew with elderflower and *verjus*, *daube* of wild boar with cornflour pancakes. There are lots of rarely used cereals, herbs and vegetables and most of the ingredients are organically grown; the choice of cheeses is amazing. There are also some vegetarian dishes. The menus offer excellent value for money: weekday lunch menu at €13 then others €19–30. A jug of good wine costs €4. Excellent welcome. An ideal spot for lunch before or after a visit to the Tours de Merle.

ARNAC-POMPADOUR 19230

🎋 🏠 |●| AUBERGE DE LA MANDRIE**

Route de Périgueux; 5km from Pompadour on the D7 going towards Payzac and Périgueux.
☎ 05.55.73.37.14 ➡ 05.55.73.67.13
e auberge.mandrie@laposte.fr
Swimming pool. **TV**. **Garden**. **Car park**.

This place, near the Cité du Cheval and the medieval village of Ségur-le-Château, looks like a holiday club with its little chalets dotted around in a park. There is a fabulous heated pool and a play area for children. The bedrooms are all at ground level and have a tiny terrace and either a shower or bath; doubles €38. The owners take pride in their work, and you'll get a warm welcome. The regional dishes are particularly tasty and are often prepared with an individual touch – salad of ceps with flambéed chestnuts, poached eggs with violet mustard, snail *profiteroles* with cream of parsley and warm *cabécou* cheese with apples Limousin-style. Set menus €11 (except Sun lunchtime) and €15–29. You can eat in the dining room or on the enormous terrace. A shame that the breakfast is poor. Free apéritif.

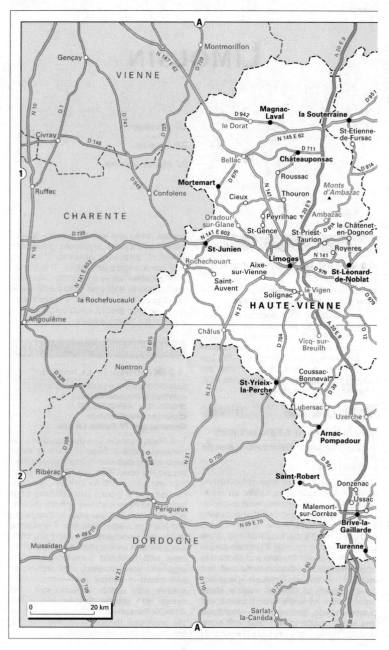

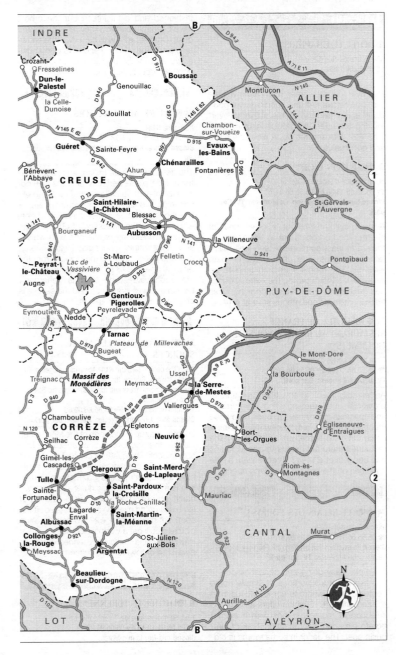

AUBUSSON   23200

⌂ HÔTEL LE CHAPITRE**

53–55 Grande-Rue (Centre).
☎ 05.55.66.18.54
TV.

Run by a friendly woman who also owns the bar downstairs. All the rooms have good facilities with tiled bathrooms and those overlooking the street are double-glazed. Doubles €29 with shower/wc. A nice little place and good value.

⌂ |●| LE LION D'OR**

pl. du Général-d'Espagne (Centre).
☎ 05.55.66.13.88 ➡ 05.55.66.84.73
Closed Sun evening and Mon out of season. **TV**. **Car park**.

A provincial inn without a great deal of charm. The bedrooms are all the same but they're at least comfortable and well-maintained; doubles with shower/wc or bath €43–46. The rooms with bath tend to be larger so it's worth paying the extra. Courteous reception. The classic cooking uses fresh ingredients and menus start at €14.

⅍ ⌂ |●| HÔTEL DE FRANCE – RESTAURANT AU RENDEZ-VOUS DES GOURMETS**

6 rue des Déportés (Centre).
☎ 05.55.66.10.22 ➡ 05.55.66.88.64
TV. **Disabled access**. **Car park**.

An establishment in the best tradition of provincial hotel-keeping. The comfortable and spacious rooms have all been renovated (doubles €46–91), but the new management could do with lightening up a bit. In the restaurant there are menus to suit all tastes and budgets at €14–43. There's even a little *brasserie* on the ground floor. Free apéritif.

BLESSAC   23200 (4KM NW)

⅍ ⌂ |●| LE RELAIS DES FORÊTS*

route d'Aubusson.
☎ 05.55.66.15.10 ➡ 05.55.83.87.91
Closed Fri evening; Sun evening; the February and All Saints' school holidays. **TV**. **Car park**.

A simple, easy-going and honest place – if you like generous portions of simple home cooking, this is where to come. Menus from €9 and one at €15 which offers a balanced selection of regional dishes with a decent potato pie and a very tasty ribsteak of Limousin beef. The décor in some rooms is old-

fashioned and a bit kitsch but the others have been refurbished. They're all clean and quiet. Doubles €24 with basin/wc (the shower is along the corridor) and €38 with shower/wc and TV. Nice welcome, though they don't accept credit cards. Free coffee.

VILLENEUVE (LA)   23260 (23KM E)

⅍ |●| LE RELAIS MARCHOIS

It's on the N141.
☎ and ➡ 05.55.67.35.78
Closed Tues evening and Wed; the last week in June; Jan.

The description "country inn" suits this traditional little place perfectly and the setting, with its interesting collection of fans and old coffee pots, creates the right atmosphere for the cooking. Dishes include grilled rib of beef with potato cake, *fricassée* of chicken with crayfish, *millefeuille* of scallops with whisky and an irresistible *nougat glacé* with coconut milk and *petits fours*. All the menus, from the regional one at €13 to the others up to €40, are good value. The food is generously served and well-presented and the service is charming. Free house apéritif.

SAINT-MARC-À-LOUBAUD   23460 (24KM SW)

⅍ |●| RESTAURANT LES MILLE SOURCES

It's in the centre; take the N141 towards Limoges, then the D7 towards Royère, turn left at Vallières in the direction of Saint-Yrieix and follow the signs for Saint-Marc-à-Loubaud.
☎ 05.55.66.03.69 and ➡ 05.55.66.09.69
Closed Mon Jan–April; Dec; Jan. **Garden**. **Car park**.

Located way up in the north of the Millevaches plateau, this place is very popular, so it's advisable to book. The quality of the cooking is quite astonishing and although the prices are a little high, it shouldn't be missed. Philippe Coutisson is a great chef as his duck *à la ficelle* will attest, and his specialities – duck and leg of lamb chargrilled over the open fire – also hit the spot. Set menus from €22. To complete the picture, you'll get a warm welcome, the décor is delightful and the lovingly tended garden is always full of flowers. Free coffee.

BEAULIEU-SUR-DORDOGNE   19120

⌂ |●| HÔTEL LE TURENNE**

1 bd. Saint-Rodolphe-de-Turenne (Centre).
☎ 05.55.91.10.16 ➡ 05.55.91.22.42
Closed mid-Nov to mid-March.

TV. Car park.

An eleventh-century Benedictine abbey which has been elegantly converted into a delightful hotel and restaurant. The arcaded dining room leads onto a terrace and shady garden and the turetted dwelling is festooned with creepers. You find your way to the spacious bedrooms up a stone staircase. The rooms have been tastefully renovated and each is furnished and decorated differently. They all have en-suite bathrooms, satellite TV and phone – a few even have period fireplaces. Doubles €39–54. And the restaurant is no disappointment. The cooking is inventive – try duck *foie gras* with ceps, *crépinette* of pig's trotters with violet mustard and any of the excellent desserts, particularly the *crème brûlées* flavoured with vanilla, walnuts and liquorice. There is a weekday menu at €12 and others €17–33. Professional welcome with a smile.

BOUSSAC   23600

|●| CAFÉ DE LA PLACE

4 pl. de l'Hôtel-de-Ville (Centre).
☎ 05.55.65.02.70
Closed Sun in June; Christmas Day; New Year's Day; Easter Mon. **Car park**.

Paulette Roger is a warm and welcoming figure. She posts just one set menu at €10, which gets you a starter, two dishes and a dessert. A typical meal might consist of melon, shellfish, meat *en paupiette* and potatoes, with pear tart to finish. Good value but they don't accept credit cards.

|●| LE RELAIS CREUSOIS

Route de la Châtre (Nord).
☎ 05.55.65.02.20
Closed Tues evening and Wed except July–Aug; 17 Oct–1 Nov dinner by reservation only; Jan; Feb; a week in June. **Car park**.

The cooking is good and the chef prepares lots of local dishes, but he also dreams up his own specialities – such as artichoke stew with marrowbone, lacquered duck thigh and cream beaten with spices. Menus €20–55. He also prepares dishes to take away.

GENOUILLAC   23350 (20KM W)

🌳 🛏 |●| LA PETITE MARIE

Lieu-dit Montfargeaud.
☎ 05.55.80.85.60
Disabled access. TV. Car park.

A charming, welcoming little country inn with

five rooms. Doubles for €35 including breakfast. Eat in the warm dining room with its sturdy beams and stone walls in winter, or out in the garden in summer. It's a place to take the time to savour the food and enjoy the view of the valleys and mountains. Honestly prepared dishes include house *foie gras*, duck *confit* and beef steak with pickled nettle cream. *Formule* at €9 and menus €15–22. Martial is something of a virtuoso on the accordion. A convivial place. Free house apéritif.

BRIVE-LA-GAILLARDE   19100

🌳 🛏 |●| HÔTEL-RESTAURANT LA CRÉMAILLIÈRE**

53 av. de Paris; it's 100m from the market.
☎ 05.55.74.32.47 ➡ 05.55.74.00.15
Closed Sun evening; Mon; the second week in in Feb; the first week in July.

Pascal Jacquinot, the new owner, had a hard act to follow after Charlou Raynal, but he's definitely succeeded. Although the décor is a bit garish, the cooking is splendid and dishes change regularly: duck carpaccio with a drizzle of vanilla olive oil, grated truffles, farm-raised pigeon with morels, cream and grilled bacon. Or you could be tempted by his summer truffles with scrambled eggs or the perch with salted butter and fresh sorrel in a light cream sauce. The milk-fed veal cutlet is simple and perfect. Menus €16–40. There are a few decent rooms with bath at €42. Free coffee.

|●| LA TOUPINE

11 rue Jean Labrunie.
☎ and ➡ 05.55.23.71.58
Closed Sun; Wed evening; the Feb school holidays; a fortnight in Aug.

This place is on the up. The dining room is rather dull, the welcome a tad brisk but the cooking makes up for everything: pig's trotters served on a *gallette*, saddle of rabbit, polenta pancake with girolle mushrooms, bread and butter pudding terrine. It's very, very good and prices are honest. *Formule* of the day €10, menus at €15 and €22 or around €23 *à la carte*. Best to book.

|●| BISTROT DE BRUNE

13 av. de Paris; (Centre).
☎ 05.55.24.00.91

A new-look brasserie – though they still use a blackboard to scribble up all their tempting, cheap dishes: soup of the day, marinated sardines, duck *andouillette* with Brive mustard, finely sliced calves' head, quality Limousin beef. Weekday lunch menu €11 or around €18 *à la carte*. The young, convivial, chatty owner has a good selection of local wines and some fine vintages besides. This good place that achieves that rare combination of relaxed atmosphere and really excellent food.

❘●❘ CHEZ FRANCIS

61 av. de Paris; (Centre)
☎ 05.55.74.41.72
Closed Sun; Mon evening; Feb school holidays to Whitsun; 3–20 Aug.

Lunch until 1.30pm, dinner until 10pm. The flattering comments scribbled on the walls of this delightful place add up to one thing – it's successful and popular, so much so that you have to book. Francis gives free rein to his imagination; his approach to cooking is thoughtful and he produces wonderfully executed dishes, prettily presented: rib of beef grilled over the coals with pickled shallots, John Dory *à la plancha*, vegetables and mushrooms sautéed in a wok, skewers of white scallops, hot *foie gras* cooked over salt and flavoured with rare peppers, tartlet of semi-preserved fruits. All the meats come from the Limousin and they're very tasty. Dish of the day €8 and menus €14 and €20.

USSAC   19270 (1KM N)

☎ ❘●❘ LE PETIT CLOS

Le Pouret.
☎ 05.55.86.12.65 ➡ 05.55.86.94.32
TV. Car park.

By common consent, this is the best place to eat in Brive – and it has a few fully equipped bedrooms in a modern annexe for €73. It's just out of town in a magnificent Corrèze house, originally a coaching inn; there's a lovely terrace and a pretty dining room. The cuisine is excellent and sticks to the classics, and you'll enjoy attentive service. It's a place that draws the well-to-do but if you want to talk sport, get the owner talking about rugby – it's his thing.

MALEMORT-SUR-CORRÈZE   19360 (3KM NE)

⅔ ☎ ❘●❘ AUBERGE DES VIEUX CHÊNES**

31 av. Honoré-de-Balzac.
☎ 05.55.24.13.55 ➡ 05.55.24.56.82
Closed Sun. **TV. Car park**.

This establishment isn't much to look at from the outside, but take a glance at the menus

(€11–26). It's a good place to experience inventive country-style cooking with a hint of the exotic: creamy risotto with pan-fried *foie gras* and parmesan *tuiles*, ling fillet with Brive violet mustard, upside-down tart with sweetbreads, capers and chestnuts, leaves of bitter chocolate *croustillant* with raspberry and *créme chantilly*, fresh fruit tarts. You'll enjoy both the food and the atmosphere in the bright dining room. The rooms have modern facilities – they're similar to the ones you'd find in a chain hotel but cheaper; doubles €37 with shower or bath/wc. Very good welcome. Free coffee.

DONZENAC   19270 (10KM N)

☎ ❘●❘ HÔTEL LA GAMADE – RESTAURANT LE PÉRIGORD**

Le bourg; take the D920.
☎ 05.55.85.72.34/05.55.85.71.07 ➡ 05.55.85.65–83

There's a rather elegant dining room, a tiny terrace (though the road runs past it) and a nice bar where you can also eat. Mme Salesse keeps a stern but benevolent eye on the regulars who drop in for a drink and a bite. There's a *menu du jour* at €13 and others €17–45, listing dishes such as black pudding salad with caramelized apples, calf's head *ravigote* and duck *confit Périgourdine*. The hotel is in another building, swathed in Virginia creeper, and has nine bedrooms, each of them different. Doubles €44 with shower/wc to €49 with big bathroom and a terrace with a view of the village.

CHÂTEAUPONSAC   87290

⅔ ☎ ❘●❘ HÔTEL-RESTAURANT DU CENTRE

pl. Mazurier; take the D1 and it's opposite the tourist office.
☎ 05.55.76.50.19
Closed Sun except July–Aug; a fortnight end Oct.

This popular, modest hotel with a bar/restaurant has clean, cheap rooms. Doubles €20 with basin (wc in the corridor) and €29 with shower/wc. The €12 menu includes cheese and dessert. Good value. Free coffee.

ROUSSAC   87140 (11KM SW)

❘●❘ LA FONTAINE SAINT-MARTIAL

Le bourg; by the D771.
☎ 05.55.60.27.42
Closed Wed evening. **Disabled access**.

A very attractive bar-restaurant which also

serves as a grocer's and tobacconist's. Marc Foussat, the modest young proprietor-chef, does a marvellous job. You can eat in the spick-and-span dining room or on the terrace. Several menus, €9–17, which list wholesome dishes: carp mousse with sorrel, *roulade* of plaice, ling with *hollandaise* sauce, hare stew, home-made raspberry *charlotte*. You'll find decent and inexpensive bottles on the short wine list. Classic cooking and friendly professional service. The bar is the meeting place for local football fans, so things really heat up on match nights. It's a convivial, relaxed place.

CHÉNÉRAILLES 23130

⌂ |●| LE COQ D'OR**

7 pl. du Champ de Foire (Centre).
☎ 05.55.62.30.83
Closed Sun evening; Mon; the first fortnight in Jan; 10 days in June; a week in Sept. **TV**. **Pay car park**.

Squeezed between Château Villemonteix and Châteaux Mazeau, this place has a reputation for quality cuisine. The chef's style updates local dishes for today's tastes – go for the potato tart with *fromage frais* or the fillet of trout with black wheat spaghetti. Weekday lunch menu €10 and others up to €32. They have a few double rooms for €27 with shower and up to €28 with shower/wc.

CLERGOUX 19320

⌂ HÔTEL CHAMMARD*

Le bourg; at Roche-Canillac get onto the D18 then take the D978 in the direction of Tulle.
☎ 05.55.27.76.04
Garden. **Car park**.

Old-style place filled with a lovely aroma of beeswax and home-made jam. Georgette is a delightful woman who'll welcome you into her home – where the *cantou*, the inglenook fireplace, dominates. The rooms, €24 with basin and €32 with shower, are very well-maintained and most of the doubles look onto the garden at the back.

COLLANGES-LA-ROUGE 19500

|●| LE CANTOU

It's in the centre of the village.
☎ 05.55.25.41.05
Closed Sun evening; Mon and Tues except in Jul-Aug; the last week in June; mid-Dec to mid-Jan.

There's a weekday menu at €15 and others

€19–27. At first glance these prices look a bit steep but the truth is they'll sort your hunger out well before they've emptied your wallet – the portions are vast and the quality of the cooking high. It's right in the middle of Collange and has a magnificent, shady terrace; there's also a superb dining room with rough-hewn stone walls furnished in a rustic style. The recipes are old, and they've been lovingly and respectfully recreated here: simmered, braised or grilled Limousine meat dishes, potatoes Collonges-style and an economically-priced local Corrèze wine to keep the bill down. There's the warmest of welcomes.

MEYSSAC 19500 (3KM SE)

⅍ ⌂ |●| LE RELAIS DU QUERCY**

av. du Quercy (Centre).
☎ 05.55.25.40.31 ✆ 05.55.25.36.22
Closed last week in Jan and 23 Nov–10 Dec.
Swimming pool. **TV**. **Garden**. **Car park**.

The village is built predominantly from the red sandstone that made Collonges famous. The hotel is in a large building with a stylish dining room that leads onto a terrace overlooking the pool. Duck, a local speciality, figures a lot on the menu, but alongside classic dishes (*cassoulet* with duck *confit*, for example), you'll find more inventive ones like chilli *à l'aiguillette*. Menus €11 or around €21 *à la carte*. The friendly, easy-going team are generous with those little extras. The rooms have good facilities and cost €33–50 – the most expensive one overlooks the pool. Half board is compulsory in July–Aug in €38 per person per day. Free coffee.

DUN-LE-PALESTEL 23800

⌂ |●| HÔTEL-RESTAURANT JOLY**

square Fernand-Riollet; it's opposite the church.
☎ 05.55.89.00.23 ✆ 05.55.89.15.89
Closed Sun evening; Mon lunchtime; 5–25 March; 1–20 Oct. **Disabled access**. **TV**.

This hotel is real *Vieille France* – the rooms are quiet, and the traditional cuisine and discreet service complete the picture. Double rooms for €35 with bath or shower. In the huge rustic dining room they serve faultless traditional cooking: duck *rillettes*, *terrine* of veal sweetbreads and St George Argaric mushrooms, *civet* of chamoix deer in Champigny wine. The €13 menu is more than adequate and there are others at €18–32 if you want to spend a little more. The owners also organize bike and walking trips for one or more days.

CROZANT   23160 (11.5KM N)

|●| RESTAURANT DU LAC

Lieu-dit Pont de Crozant; it's on the banks of the Creuse.
☎ 05.55.89.81.96
Closed Mon and Feb.

Don't miss this place. It has an exceptional
location on the water's edge, with a splendid
view of the cathedral and the bridge that links
two départments – and though it's on the
Indre bank of the river, it's actually in Creuse.
Well-executed, often inventive cooking using a
lot of fish. Menus €15–24. It's built a solid reputation so it's best to book.

ÉVAUX-LES-BAINS   23110

🐾 🛏 |●| GRAND HÔTEL**

Les thermes: it's down the hill from the town centre
beside the spa.
☎ 05.55.65.50.01 ➡ 05.55.65.59.16
Closed Nov–March. **TV**. **Car park**.

This is a grand hotel with old-fashioned charm
that's been going since 1900. It has high ceilings and wide red-carpeted corridors and is
full of people who come to take the waters.
The guests enjoy the comfort of the large, well-
heated rooms, all of which are equipped with a
bell to call the staff. It's peaceful. Doubles €36
with basin/wc and €51 with with bath/wc. The
ones which have been done up recently are
impeccable. There's also a restaurant with
menus at €12–24. Free apéritif.

FONTANIÈRES   23110 (8KM S)

|●| LE DAMIER

Le bourg; go along the D996 towards Auzances and it's
on the left hand side of the road.
☎ 05.55.82.35.91
Closed Mon evening and Tues.

It's not often that you find a pretty little inn like
this around here. It has a quiet, stylish atmosphere, with background music and quality
regional cuisine. Weekday lunch menu €10
and others €15–29, listing house *terrine* of
duck with *foie gras*, slabs of beef cooked in
different ways according to the season, local
cheeses and *nougat* ice with raspberry
coulis. It's a very pleasant place.

GENTIOUX-PIGEROLLES   23340

🛏 |●| LA FERME DE NAUTAS

Pigerolles; take the D982, the D35 and then the D26.

☎ 05.55.67.90.68 ➡ 05.55.67.93.12
e les-nautas@wanadoo.fr
Closed weekdays out of season.

This place, a working farm run by the hospitable François Chatoux, is a winner. He
used to be an engineer but took up farming
instead, and he runs an original place brimming with warmth and hospitality. His wife
does genuine local cuisine, using first-rate
ingredients and serving generous helpings of
tasty regional dishes – potato pie, cep tarts
and superb meat. Menus at €13 and €17
but you have to book in advance. The double
rooms are rustic in style, comfy and welcoming; they're €40 with shower/wc, breakfast
included. They don't accept credit cards.

GUÉRET   23000

🐾 🛏 |●| HÔTEL DE POMMEIL

75 rue de Pommeil.
☎ and ➡ 05.55.52.38.54
Closed Sun; 15 June–7 July. **Car park**.

A very simple, clean and welcoming hotel with
good prices. There are just nine rooms, so it's
best to book; doubles €30–33 with shower
and basin or shower/wc – some have been
renovated. They have two menus at €12 and
€15, which list veal *escalope* with a mushroom and cream sauce and scallops with saffron. Friendly atmosphere. 10% discount on
the room rate for a two-night stay Sept–June.

🛏 HÔTEL AUCLAIR

19 av. de la Sénatorerie; (Centre); it's near pl. Bonnyaud.
☎ 05.55.41.22.00 ➡ 05.55.52.86.89
Swimming pool. Pay car park.

About thirty rooms with good facilities and
furnished with rattan. Doubles €31–48 with
shower or bath. The small swimming pool
adds a hint of luxury. You must reserve your
parking space in advance.

🐾 |●| LE PUB ROCHEFORT

6 place Rochefort; it's in a pedestranized street.
☎ 05.55.52.61.02
Closed Sun and Mon lunchtime.

This place is right in the heart of the town and
has an intimate, warm setting with old stone
walls and ancestral beams. The food won't
get Michelin stars but it's honest, the value
for money is fair and the service comes with
a smile. Lunch menu at €11 or €14 in the
evening. There's a nice terrace in the interior
courtyard that gets full very quickly. Free
house aperitif.

SAINTE-FEYRE 23000 (7KM SE)

|●| RESTAURANT LES TOURISTES

pl. de la Mairie; take the D942 in the direction of
Aubusson
☎ 05.55.80.00.07
Closed Tues evening and Wed out of season. **Disabled
access**.

Tasty, classic local cooking prepared by
Michel Roux and served in generous portions. There's a quiet atmosphere and the
surroundings are lovely. You will get the measure of the excellent cooking from the menus
(€14–34). His specialities include *foie gras*
with prunes and old Armagnac, slivers of
duck with balsamic vinegar and veal fillet
wisth cream and cep sauce. Good local meat
dishes and skilfully prepared fish. Friendly
welcome.

JOUILLAT 23220 (14KM NE)

|●| L'AUBERGE DU CHÂTEAU

How to get there: follow Route de la Châtre, turn right
when you get to Villevaleix and it's beside the church.
☎ 05.55.41.88.43
Closed Sun evening; Mon; 24 Aug–9 Sept; 30 Dec–22
Jan.

Don't expect one of those touristy olde-
worlde inns that you often find in the neighbourhood of a château. *L'Auberge du
Château* fulfils an important role in holding
the local community together – it serves as a
grocer's and tobacconist's as well as a
restaurant. There's a rustic dining room and a
terrific paved garden with an awning at the
back. The two menus, €13 and 19, list
starter, main course, cheese and dessert; on
a Sunday there's only one (€22) but it lists
two main courses. If you like, call the day
before to check what the chef plans and he'll
make you something else if you don't like
what's available. And think about booking in
advance because it's very popular locally and
has a friendly atmosphere.

LIMOGES 87000

SEE MAP OVERLEAF

🎋 ☗ HÔTEL FAMILIA

18 rue du Gal-du-Bessol (North). **MAP C1-1**
☎ 05.55.77.51.40 ➡ 05.55.10.27.69
TV.

Just a short walk away from the centre in a
quiet street. Though the district has no great
appeal, this modest establishment is a find.

The owner welcomes you with a smile. You
get to the rooms across a pretty, shaded
courtyard. They are simple, spacious, perfectly maintained and at fair prices: doubles
with shower/wc €38. 10% discount.

🎋 ☗ HÔTEL DE LA PAIX**

25 place Jourdan. **MAP C2-2**
☎ 05.55.34.36.00 ➡ 05.55.32.37.06
Pay car park.

Well located in the corner of a quiet square –
and it's not far from the station or the old
parts of town. Between the entrance and the
breakfast room there's a small museum displaying the owner's impressive collection of
phonographs and mechanical music. The
rooms are huge; they're well maintained, regularly redecorated and variously furnished –
one has a fireplace, another a big bathroom.
You couldn't call it luxury but there's an
appealing retro style. It's reliable and offers
good value for money: doubles €43–46 with
shower or bath/wc. 10% discount on the
room rate.

🎋 ☗ LE RICHELIEU***

40 av. Baudin. **MAP B3-3**
☎ 05.55.34.22.82 ➡ 05.55.34.35.36
Disabled access. **TV**. **Pay car park**.

A quiet three-star where there's a deep
understanding of what professional service
means – matchless welcome, service and
cleanliness. The rooms have everything you
need, though the junior suites are a tad tight
for space; those in the annexe at the rear are
very quiet. The facilities are what you would
expect in a hotel such as this: proper bathrooms and attractive breakfast room with a
trompe l'œil painting. €51–85 for a double
with shower/wc or bath is a shade pricey,
though. Free car parking space.

|●| RESTAURANT CHEZ COLETTE

pl. de la Motte **MAP B2/3-10**
☎ 05.55.33.73.85
Closed evenings; Sun and Mon; July.

This little place is in the lively area of the covered market. It serves simple dishes that are,
naturally enough, inspired by fresh produce.
There's only one menu at €8 offering starter,
main course and dessert – quite a feat for
the price. If you're having a late night or an
early morning, they also serve snacks
8–10am – this is your chance to try some of
the local "peasant" dishes such as *giraud*, a
sausage made from sheep's blood and
cooked in the animal's intestine. Colette will

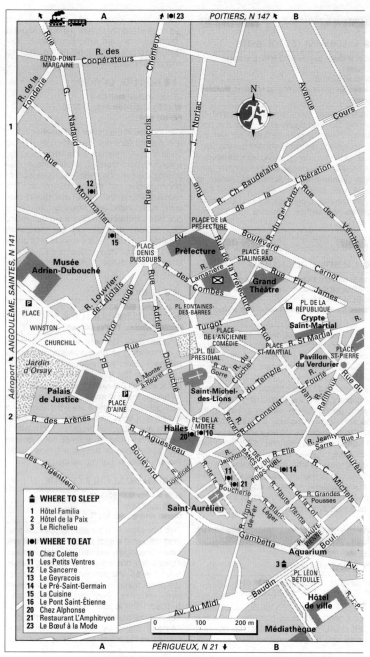

WHERE TO SLEEP

1 Hôtel Familia
2 Hôtel de la Paix
3 Le Richelieu

WHERE TO EAT

10 Chez Colette
11 Les Petits Ventres
12 Le Sancerre
13 Le Geyracois
14 Le Pré-Saint-Germain
15 La Cuisine
16 Le Pont Saint-Étienne
20 Chez Alphonse
21 Restaurant L'Amphitryon
23 Le Bœuf à la Mode

0   100   200 m

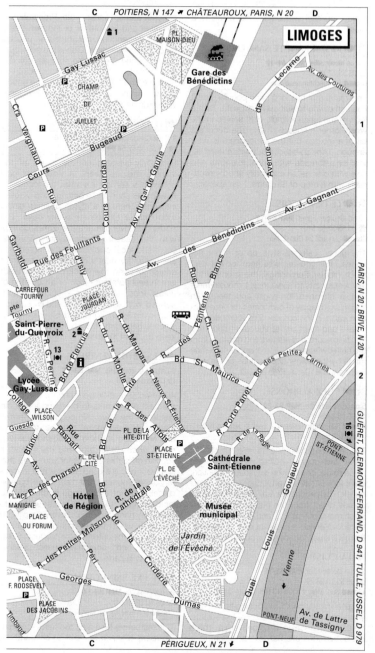

LIMOGES

PL. MAISON-DIEU

Gare des Bénédictins

Gay Lussac

CHAMP DE JUILLET

Crs Vergniaud

Cours

Rue

Bugeaud

Cours Jourdan

Av. du Gal de Gaulle

d'Isly

Av. des Coutures

Locarne

Avenue

Av. J. Gagnant

Av. des Bénédictins

Garibaldi

Rue des Feuillants

CARREFOUR TOURNY

pte Tourny

PLACE JOURDAN

Av.

Rue des Pénitents Blancs

Ch. Gide

Saint-Pierre-du-Queyroix

R. du 71e Mobile

R. du Maupas

Bd St Maurice

Bd des Petites Carmes

Lycée Gay-Lussac

R. G. Perrin

Bd de Fleurus

Cité

R. Neuve St-Étienne

R. Porte Panet

Collège

Guesde

PLACE WILSON

Rue

Raspail

Bd de la R. des Allois

PL. DE LA HTE-CITÉ

R. de la Règle

PONT ST-ÉTIENNE

Av.

Blanc

L.

R. des Charseix

PLACE DE LA CITÉ

PLACE ST-ETIENNE

PL. DE L'ÉVÊCHÉ

Cathédrale Saint-Étienne

PLACE MANIGNE

PLACE DU FORUM

Hôtel de Région

Bd

R. de la Cathédrale

Musée municipal

G.

Péri

R. des Petites Maisons

de la

Corderie

Jardin de l'Évêché

Quai

Louis

Vienne

Goujaud

PLACE F. ROOSEVELT

Georges

PLACE DES JACOBINS

Timbaud

Dumas

PONT-NEUF

Av. de Lattre de Tassigny

C   D

make you feel welcome. This place is a must.

☆ |●| RESTAURANT LE SANCERRE

18 rue Montmailler. **MAP A1-12**
☎ 05.55.77.71.95
Closed Sat lunchtime and Sun.

This restaurant has long been popular, and it has something to suit every appetite. Take a look at the lunch *formule* (€8) served in the week; other menus €13–21. The décor's a bit of a mixture but the atmosphere is lively enough. They do *boudineaux* with chestnuts, veal sweetbreads with ceps, *foie gras* and sole with orange, all especially good – especially with a drop of Sancerre. Free apéritif.

☆ |●| LE GEYRACOIS

15 bd. Georges-Perrin. **MAP C2-13**
☎ 05.55.32.58.51
Closed Sun and 24 Dec–2 Jan.

The garish cafeteria-style décor might not appeal, but you eat well here for not very much money. Surprisingly, this is one of the few restaurants to serve local Limousin meat that is stamped for origin and there's an impressive display of certificates for prize-winning cattle in the corridor. The *tournedos*, rib steaks and fillets are all succulent and juicy. You help yourself to starters and desserts from the buffet where you'll find a wonderful *terrine* made by the owner and pastries by his wife. Set menus €10–14. Free apéritif.

☆ |●| CHEZ ALPHONSE

5 place de la Motte. **MAP B3-20**
☎ 05.55.34.34.14
Closed Sun; public holidays; a week in Jan; the first 3 weeks in Aug.

This feels and looks like a bistro but it's also rather fashionable – *Chez Alphonse* is *the* place to go. The cuisine is also an attraction: calf's feet or calf's head Alphonse-style, beef cheek. The produce is really fresh because it comes direct from the market. There's one lunch menu only at €12 and others €15–21 *à la carte*. Service is pleasant and, in summer, there's a small terrace. Free house apéritif.

|●| LA CUISINE

21 rue Montmailler. **MAP A2-15**
☎ 05.55.10.28.29
Closed Sun; Mon; 27 Jan–13 Feb; 28 Jul–21 Aug.

Original, highly personal cooking from a chef who uses only the very freshest ingredients: breast of pigeon in a spiced crust, rolled calf's liver Venetian-style, monkfish in a coconut and coriander broth. Preparation of the meat and fish dishes or the desserts is taken very seriously, but there's an unusual touch of inventiveness. Dishes are generously served and the waiting staff are efficient and kindly. Lunch *formule* €13, or reckon on paying €23–30 *à la carte*. It would be good if the wine list had a few more wines from small vineyards, though.

|●| LE PONT SAINT-ÉTIENNE

8 pl. de Compostelle. Off map **D2/3-16**
☎ 05.55.30.52.54 ➡ 05.55.30.56.07

Beautifully situated on the banks of the Vienne, this restaurant is virtually a local community service: it's a bar, tobacconist's, newspaper shop and a betting shop all rolled into one. There is a stylish upstairs dining room and a terrace for sunny days. The cooking is inventive and the dishes change with the season. Portions are generous, you'll find local cuisine and the ingredients are fresh. Try goat's cheese with beetroot *coulis* followed by chicken breasts with lemon and potato *pallison* or a Colombo of meats (ribs, cheek and shoulder of pork cooked with a mix of West Indian spices). Menus €13–30. Wine is a bit pricey, and when it gets busy the service can't always keep up. Best to book.

|●| LES PETITS VENTRES

20 rue de la Boucherie. **MAP B3-11**
☎ 05.55.34.22.90

An attractive, half-timbered house with one of the best restaurants to be found in the old district of the town. Although *Petit Ventres* means "little stomachs", you can forget the diet when you eat here: black sausage with mash, *andouillette*, tripe and calf's head. If you like offal, this place is for you – one dish is a feast of calf's head, tongue and mesentery (a membrane that keeps the guts in place). Less of a challenge is the smoked lamb's tongue, a local dish that's very hard to find. They print the name of every supplier on the menu, which says everything you need to know about the quality of the produce. Great desserts and attractive rustic setting. €15–23 *à la carte*.

|●| LE PRÉ SAINT-GERMAIN

26 rue de la Loi. **MAP B3-14**
☎ 05.55.32.71.84
Closed Sun evening and Mon.

This restaurant tries a bit too hard – the dining room is kitsch rather than chic and the service is rather self-important. But the food makes up for all that: it's fine and light and full of lovely surprises. The young chef delights in colourful ingredients and plays with different textures. The cheapest menu is quite remarkable, especially since it costs only €16: *tartare* of chopped baby vegetables followed by beef with perfectly cooked mushrooms and a selection of memorable desserts. A good place.

I●I LE BŒUF À LA MODE

60 rue François-Chénieux. **Off map A1-23**
☎ 05.55.77.73.95
Closed Sat lunchtime; Sun; the first fortnight in Aug.

A restaurant in a butcher's shop run by master butcher Claude Lebraud, who's proud of his trade. He's a real pro and knows how to choose his meat and serve it perfectly prepared: sirloin of beef in cider, *épigramme* of lamb (cooked on one side only) with honey and spices, Chateaubriand with bone marrow. Pleasant décor, white linen. À *la carte* only; you'll spend €20–30.

⅍I●I RESTAURANT L'AMPHITRYON

26 rue de la Boucherie. **MAP B3-21**
☎ 05.55.33.36.39
Closed Sun; Mon and Sat lunchtimes; a fortnight in Aug.

You'll find this reliable restaurant which offers consistent quality across from the delightful chapel of Saint-Aurélien, the patron saint of butchers. Try *foie gras*, *tajine* of pigeon with dates, *roulé* of langoustine and fresh tomatoes or fillet of beef with marrow bone and *sauce bordelaise* – they're all nicely cooked and original without being eccentric. Prices are increasing while portions are not: weekday lunch menu €20, then others at €24–30 or €46 à *la carte*. But maybe that's what you have to pay to eat in an authentic Limoges atmosphere. There's a terrace in summer. Free house apéritif.

AIXE-SUR-VIENNE   87700 (13KM SW)

I●I AUBERGE DES DEUX PONTS

2 av. du Général-de-Gaulle; take the N21.
☎ 05.55.70.10.22
Closed Sun and Mon evenings except June–Sept.

First-rate, reasonably priced restaurant on the banks of the Vienne. The décor is cheery, with lots of yellow and navy blue, and there are flowers everywhere. They do lots of seafood, including grilled bream, as well as good charcoal-grilled steaks and duck breast

with Roquefort sauce. Weekday lunch *formule* €11, menus €20–30 and à *la carte*.

SAINT-GENCE   87510 (13KM NW)

⅍I●I LE MOULIN DE CHEVILLOU

How to get there: take the route de Bellac (N147), turn left towards Nieul and Saint-Gence is only 3km away. Go through the village and turn right 300m further on. It's signposted.
☎ and ➡ 05.55.75.86.13
Closed Mon–Thurs Oct–March.

Lovely place hidden in a secluded valley beside the Glane, in a park filled with donkeys, goats, ponies and birds. Children can play on the swings and the slide. Enjoy a pancake and a flagon of cider as you're lulled by the splashing sound of the watermill. In the restaurant, go for trout with country ham and ceps or saddle of rabbit with girolles. Menus €15–22. Service is efficient and staff are delightful. Best to book. Free apéritif.

SAINT-PRIEST-TAURION   87480 (13KM NE)

🏠 I●I LE RELAIS DU TAURION**

2 chemin des Contamines.
☎ and ➡ 05.55.39.70.14
Closed Sun evening, Mon and mid-Dec to mid-Jan. **TV**. **Car park**.

This is a beautiful ivy-covered house from the beginning of the twentieth century, set in a park. The place is memorable for its charm and excellent location on the banks of the Taurion river. The rooms, €41 with shower/wc and €47 with bath, are comfortable enough and well-maintained. There's a restaurant, but it's a bit pricey for what you get: weekday menu for €17 and others €24–32.

PEYRILHAC   87510 (15KM NW)

I●I AUBERGE DE LA QUEUE DE VACHE

It's on the N147.
☎ 05.55.53.38.11
Closed Sun–Thurs evenings except June–Sept. **TV**.

Sadly this attractive farm is right on the main road. Inside, though, it's pretty and welcoming and the noise isn't too intrusive. Typical local cooking using many ingredients from the owners' organic farm. Unusually for the Limousin, it's Scotch beef that appears on the menu – they have a Highland herd. The fruit and vegetables are local, however, and so are the cheeses. Starters include chicken with herbs, warm goat's cheese on green salad and Périgord salad with truffles; main courses include oxtail or beef cheek *confit*, pan-fried sirloin and an amazing semi-cooked home-grown *foie gras*. Good home-made chips, and baked vegetables that change with the seasons. The dessert list includes fruit tarts or melon preserved in honey. Menus €10–23. There's a small terrace at the back, open in summer. Reasonably priced wines.

SOLIGNAC   87110 (15KM S)

🎄 🏠 |⦿| LE SAINT-ÉLOI

66 av. Saint-Éloi.
☎ 05.55.00.44.52 ➡ 05.55.00.55.56
Closed Sun evening; Mon lunchtime; Jan. **TV**.

A handsome hotel in a peaceful village run by a young couple – they've completely refurbished the place inside and out. The attractive rooms have fine linen and are tastefully decorated in warm tones; some have a terrace and a whirlpool bath. Doubles €43–58. The elegant dining room has leaded lights and a splendid fireplace and the tables are perfectly dressed. Service is diligent. The cooking is modern and generously served – amounts are practically double what you'd expect in town. Wonderful *grenadins* of veal, perfectly prepared fish dishes with well-balanced sauces and the desserts are beautifully presented. Weekday menu €13 and others up to €38. Free apéritif.

ROYÈRES   87400 (18KM E)

🎄 🏠 |⦿| HÔTEL BEAU SITE**

hameau de Brignac; take the N141 towards Saint-Léonard-de-Noblat, then turn left onto the D124.
☎ 05.55.56.00.56 ➡ 05.55.56.31.17
Closed 1 Jan–1 April. **Swimming pool**. **TV**. **Car park**.

You can rely on good facilities in this hotel, which is set in peaceful greenery in country surroundings. The comfortable bedrooms are decorated with Madame's ornamental hand-painted designs and they're all different. Doubles with bath/wc or shower €44–51; the nicest have a view over the grounds and the pond. There's a nice garden with a wonderful heated pool. The restaurant offers a number of regional specialities such as *fricassée* of snails with ceps, mignon of pork with prunes and ginger, fillet of zander with champagne and scallops with leeks. For dessert try the marvellous chestnut *sabayon*. The €17 weekday menu is good, and there are others €21–38. Attentive service. Free coffee.

THOURON   87140 (22KM NW)

🎄 🏠 |⦿| LA POMME DE PIN

Hameau de La Tricherie; take the N147, then turn right onto the D7.
☎ 05.55.53.43.43 ➡ 05.55.53.35.33
Closed Mon; Tues lunchtime; Feb school holidays; Sept.
TV. **Disabled access**. **Car park**.

One of the best places in Haute-Vienne, in an old mill in the forest near a small lake. Weekday lunch menu €13 with others €20–30. Appealing dishes and delicious charcoal grills cooked over the fire; specialities include sweetbread and *foie gras* salad and chargrilled Limousin beef. There's a remarkable list of excellent wines. The rooms are comfortable and very clean with views of the river; doubles with shower/wc €46–53. Free house apéritif.

MAGNAC-LAVAL   87190

🎄 |⦿| LA FERME DU LOGIS

How to get there: go as far as Magnac-Laval,in the centre turn right in the direction of Bellac; the restaurant's 2km along on the left-hand side.
☎ 05.55.68.57.23 ➡ 05.55.68.52.80
eetiennemuller@aol.com
Closed Sun evening; Mon; Jan to mid-Feb. **Garden**. **Car park**.

This inn is in a converted building near a small lake. Generous portions of tasty local dishes are served by accommodating staff. They specialize in beef and venison which come from the family farm. Appetizing and satisfying menus at €13 (weekday lunch) and €11–24. The wines on the list are fairly priced. If you feel like hanging around, there's space for eight tents and room for two in a caravan equipped with shower. Free apéritif.

MORTEMART   87330

🎄 🏠 |⦿| HÔTEL LE RELAIS*

1 pl. Royale.
☎ and ➡ 05.55.68.12.09
Closed Tues evening except July–Aug; Wed; Feb. **TV**.

A pleasant and very attractive country hostelry in a beautiful village. There are a few pretty rooms for €46 with shower/wc, and a stylish stone-walled dining room. Attentive service and plenty of flavour in dishes such as *foie gras* with morel turnovers, duck breast with caramelized pears and *gratin* of wild strawberries. Set menus €15 (except Sun) and €21–32. You can also choose *à la carte*. Free apéritif.

CIEUX   87520 (13KM SE)

🖈 🛏 🍽 AUBERGE LA SOURCE**

av. du Lac; take the D5 as far as Blond, then turn right for Cieux.
☎ 05.55.03.33.23 ➡ 05.55.03.26.88
📧 awaldbauer@aol.com
Closed Sun evening; Mon; 10 Jan–15 Feb. **TV. Car park**.

A renovated former posthouse which commands a marvellous view of the Cieux lake, the valleys and the Blond mountains. The charming owners are highly experienced and make you feel totally welcome. The restaurant is light and airy and the cuisine, which is classic in style, is confidently and meticulously cooked. The fish is startlingly fresh and if you ask for your meat to be done in a particular way it will be cooked to perfection. There's a €13 weekday lunch menu and others €18–48. The décor in the rooms doesn't have the same charm, though, and the bathrooms look as if they belong in a chain hotel. Even so there's lots of space and they're well-maintained. And, of course, there's that wonderful view. Doubles €54 with shower/wc and €69 bath. 10% discount on the room rate Oct–March.

NEUVIC   19160

🛏 🍽 CHÂTEAU DU MIALARET

It's on the D991 in the direction of Égletons.
☎ 05.55.46.02.50 ➡ 05.55.46.02.65
Closed Jan to Easter. **TV. Car park**.

This nineteenth-century château, set in a gorgeous park, has been turned into a modestly luxurious hotel but has maintained many of its original features. Some bedrooms are in the towers; the largest ones, which are superb, have monumental fireplaces. Their conference centre (built in the grounds and rather a blot on the landscape) brings in the bulk of the income, so they can charge modest prices: doubles €30 with no toilet to €58 with full en-suite facilities. The dining room is impressive and they serve good regional dishes at fair prices: warm fish salad, zander with *beurre rouge* and onion chutney, fillet of beef with green peppercorns. Menus €14–29.

PEYRAT-LE-CHÂTEAU   87470

🖈 🛏 🍽 AUBERGE DU BOIS DE L'ÉTANG**

38 av. de la Tour; take the D940 in the direction of Bourganeuf.
☎ 05.55.69.40.19 ➡ 05.55.69.42.93
📧 serge.merle@wanadoo.fri
Closed Sun evening and Mon Nov–March; 15 Dec–20 Jan. **TV. Garden. Car park**.

Set in a magnificent, peaceful area a few kilometres from Lake Vassivière. You'll get a very warm welcome. Decent doubles at €27–46; those in the annexe have been recently done up and are the quietest. The restaurant is very nice indeed, and offers inventive dishes like *escalope* of *foie gras* with sherry and apples, warm blinis with raspberry caviar and red mullet with garlic purée. €12 lunch menu (except Sun) and others €14–31 – there's real innovation on the costlier ones. Half board, compulsory in July–Aug, costs €28–39 per person (there's a minimum three-night stay with that option). Free apéritif.

🖈 🛏 🍽 LE BELLERIVE**

29 av. de la Tour; take the D940 in the direction of Bourganeuf.
☎ 05.55.69.40.67 ➡ 05.55.69.47.96
Closed Sun evening; Mon out of season; end Jan to early Feb. **TV. Car park**.

This establishment owes its name to its location on the shores of Lake Peyrat. Delightful and well-maintained rooms with balconies and terraces cost €36–44 with shower/wc or bath; there are some big ones sleeping four or five. They serve good regional cooking in the restaurant: potato cake, warm asparagus salad with calf's liver, local meats, chestnut tart. Set menus €12–36. Free apéritif.

AUPHELLE   87470 (8KM E)

🖈 🛏 🍽 AU GOLF DU LIMOUSIN**

How to get there: take the D13 towards Vassivière then the D222 as far as the lake.
☎ 05.55.69.41.34 ➡ 05.55.69.49.16
📧 joel.lucchesi@voila.fr
TV. Car park.

This is one of the few hotels that almost overlooks Lake Vassivière. The building is constructed out of stone, surrounded by greenery and just 200m from the beach. The bedrooms are clean and very comfy with doubles at €43. Good, classic regional cuisine in the restaurant: home-made *terrine*, fillet of beef with ceps, zander with *beurre blanc*, sweetbreads with morels, mutton tripe and a fine selection of cheeses. Weekday lunch menu €13 and others €19–27.

Half board at €42 per person per day is compulsory July–Aug. There are tennis courts and a crazy golf course across the road. Free house apéritif.

NEDDE   87120 (10KM E)

☎ |O| AUBERGE LE VERROU

Lieu-dit de bourg-Nedde
☎ 05.55.69.98.04
Closed Wed in winter.

A warm, atmospheric establishment with several dining rooms. One has a beautiful old counter where you can prop yourself up while you have an apéritif; another has a pancake corner, and in summer they open up a charming little terrace. It's very popular locally. The short menu offers dishes cooked with fresh market produce, good Limousin meat, a choice of salads and sweet or savoury pancakes. Expect to pay €14–25 for a meal; in winter there's one menu only. There are a few pleasant rooms at €32–36. Friendly welcome.

AUGNE   87120 (12KM SW)

⅔ ☎ |O| LE RANCH DES LACS

Lieu-dit Vervialle. Take the D14 towards Bujaleuf and go through Chassat. At the next junction go left towards Négrignas; just before the small group of houses take the little road to the left to Vervialle.
☎ 05.55.69.15.66 ➡ 05.55.69.59.52
Open all year but telephone out of season.

An attractive establishment run by a Belgian couple. It used to be a riding school, and the walls and beams are decorated with old saddles. Nowadays it's a cross between a hotel and a hostel with a bar-restaurant. They serve a choice of about thirty Belgian beers and the menus (€14–22) feature a selection of special national dishes such as the *coffret du boulanger* (a loaf filled with scrambled eggs flavoured with herbs), *coucou de Malines* (chicken breast stuffed with chicory), veal cutlet with Gouda and, if you order in advance, as many helpings of mussels and chips as you like. There's a €10 *formule* including wine and coffee. From the veranda you'll get a view of the unspoiled Vienne valley. If you want accommodation, they have two doubles with bath for €30 and four very basic hostel rooms with three or four beds in each and communal washing facilities (€11 a head). Children, who are particularly welcome in this truly fabulous place, have a special games area all to themselves.

SAINT-HILAIRE-LE-CHATEAU   23250

☎ |O| HÔTEL DU THAURION**

10 Grand-Rue; take the D941 or the N41.
☎ 05.55.64.50.12 ➡ 05.55.64.90.92
Closed Wed and Thurs lunchtimes; 30 Nov–28 Feb. **TV. Car park.**

An attractively restored coaching inn owned by Gérard Fanton – the chef by whom all others in the Creuse are judged. His cooking is executed to perfection and he serves a mix of traditional and original dishes. His specialities include braised hock of pork, oxtail pancake, stuffed pig's trotter with Brive mustard sauce and crayfish-tail ravioli. There's a set menu of the day for €15 and others €24–61.The service is a bit slow. On the hotel side of things, the rooms are attractive and cost €50–76 for a double, but there are also a few guest rooms in the château next door in the same sort of price-range.

SAINT-JUNIEN   87200

⅔ ☎ |O| LE RENDEZ-VOUS DES CHASSEURS

leiu-dit Pont-à-la-Planche.
☎ 05.55.02.19.73 ➡ 05.55.02.06.98
Closed Fri; Sun evening; a fortnight in Jan.

This place is renowned for its famous gourmet menu – but it's not as pricey as you might expect. There's a menu at €12 (not served on Sunday) and others go up to €37. The dining has all the charm of *Vieille France* and there's a terrace in summer. Well maintained double rooms €33 with shower /wc or bath. Free *digestif*.

⅔ ☎ |O| LE RELAIS DE COMODOLIAC**

22 av. Sadi-Carnot.
☎ 05.55.02.27.26 ➡ 05.55.02.68.79
Restaurant closed Sun evening. **TV. Car park. Garden.**

The building is modern but they've created a very pleasant feel to it. The rooms are huge but well-maintained; the ones overlooking the road are a bit noisy, while those at the back are quieter but a little more expensive. Doubles with bath €41–49. The restaurant looks onto a little corner of greenery. The cooking is well-prepared and the fresh ingredients change with the seasons: salmon, sea bass, local meat and chicken, excellent sauces and wild mushrooms. Prices are fair, with menus at €14–30. Reliable service. Free house apéritif.

⅍ |●| LE LANDAIS

6 bd. de la République (Centre).
☎ 05.55.02.12.07 ➡ 05.55.02.90.95
Closed Tues and 15–30 Sept.

As soon as you cross the threshold, you sense you're going to be looked after. The restaurant adjoins the bar and it's easy to get comfortable. Honestly prepared dishes include rib of beef *Bordelaise*, duck stew, terrine of quail with juniper berries, scallops with ceps, *salmis* of wood-pigeon and *cassoulet*. Menus €9–33. Engaging welcome. Free coffee.

SAINT-AUVENT   87310 (14KM S)

⅍ |●| AUBERGE DE LA VALLÉE DE LA GORRE**

pl. de l'Église; it's on the D58.
☎ and ➡ 05.55.00.01.27
Closed Sun and Mon evenings.

A lovely little inn in a lovely little village. The dishes are devised and prepared by Hervé Sutre, the creative young chef. Try *foie gras* with Guérande salt, stuffed ceps, medallions of veal with crayfish or fresh fruit *croustillant*. Menus €11 (except on Sunday) and €17–38. There's a pleasant covered terrace for sunny days and it's best to book at the weekend. Free coffee.

SAINT-LÉONARD-DE-NOBLAT   87400

⅍ |●| LE GAY-LUSSAC

18 bd. Victor-Hugo; it's in the old town, about 30m from Place de la République.
☎ 05.55.56.98.45
Closed Sun evening and Mon; a fortnight end Sept to early Oct.

Newish restaurant, tastefully renovated, which offers traditional home cooking that reflects the changing seasons. There are welcoming dining rooms on the first floor. Lunch *formule* for €10 and other menus at €15–30. Specialities include *marbrée* of *foie gras*, salmon turnover, veal sweetbreads with ceps and snails. The menu changes every month. It can be difficult to get a table as prices are so reasonable. Staff are attentive and friendly. There's a little terrace onto the square. Free coffee.

⅍ |●| LES MOULINS DE NOBLAT – L'AUBERGE DE MATTRE-PIERRE

It's in the southwest of town.
☎ 05.55.56.29.73

At the lower end of Noblat, going towards

Limoges, there are several water-mills, most of which date from the twelfth century. They make a harmonious group and have been restored in order to serve as gallery spaces for pictures and local crafts; one has been turned into an inn with a lovely terrace on the bank of the Vienne. It's particularly lovely in fine weather, even though the noise of the wheel is hard to ignore. Fine, traditional cuisine with some good grills. Menus from €13. From June to September they organise giant barbecues.

CHÂTENET-EN-DOGNON (LE)   87400 (10KM N)

⅍ 🏠 |●| LE CHALET DU LAC**

Pont-du-Dognon; it's on the D5.
☎ 05.55.57.10.53 ➡ 05.55.57.11.46
Restaurant closed Sun evening and Jan. **Garden. Car park.**

This impressive but inexpensive chalet overlooks a charming lake where you can enjoy all sorts of watersports. Comfortable bedrooms €38 with the lake view – others look over the road. Very pleasant, traditional food. Set menus at €14–35 list dishes like *pavé* of Limousin beef, *cassolette* of beef *du Chalet*, *foie gras* omelette and salmon cooked in Guérande salt. There's also a gym and sauna. Free coffee.

SAINT-MARTIN-LA-MÉANNE   19320

⅍ 🏠 |●| HÔTEL LES VOYAGEURS**

pl. de la Mairie; it's in the middle of the village.
☎ 05.55.29.11.53 ➡ 05.55.29.27.70
Closed Sun evening and Mon out of season; Nov to mid-Feb. **TV. Car park. Garden.**

This typical Corrèze village house has been turned into a family inn with lots of character. Local produce is much in evidence in the cooking, which includes *fricassée* of frogs' legs and snails with parsley, zander with *beurre blanc*, veal sweetbreads with ceps, hot *escalope* of *foie gras*, fillet of char, veal *escalope* with morels and *crêpe soufflé* with orange. Set menus €14–30. The rooms are attractive and affordable, and doubles with shower cost €37–48; some have a view over the countryside. Free apéritif.

SAINT-MERD-DE-LAPLEAU   19320

⅍ 🏠 |●| HÔTEL-RESTAURANT FABRY**

pont du Chambon; it's 8km from Saint-Merd-De-Lapleau via the CD13.

☎ 05.55.27.88.39 ➡ 05.55.27.83.19
e faby@medianet.fr
Closed Fri evening and Sat lunchtime 1 Oct–30 April.

A substantial building in a magnificent setting on the banks of the Dordogne – many rooms have a view of the river. Lots of sea- and freshwater fish on the menus including roast cod with Puy lentil stew and zander in *beurre blanc*, as well as tasty meat dishes such as venison with bilberries and duck breast with Périgueux truffle sauce. The chocolate *fondant* with mint ice-cream is the star dessert. Menus start at €13 in the week, with others up to €33. The eight rooms (doubles €38–43) are smart and prettily decorated. Half board is compulsory in high season at €40 per person. Free apéritif.

SAINT-PARDOUX-LA-CROISILLE   19320

🏠 |●| HÔTEL-RESTAURANT BEAU SITE***

How to get there: take the D131.
☎ 05.55.27.79.44 ➡ 05.55.27.69.52
Closed 15 Oct–15 April. **Swimming pool**. **Garden**. **Car park**.

Hotel and leisure complex with a large garden, fishing pond, swimming pool, tennis courts and mountain bikes for hire – a place for people who like sporty holidays, good food and comfortable surroundings. Doubles with shower/wc cost €53; the rooms lack soul but they're well-maintained. The establishment is roomy enough to accommodate a lot of groups, especially out of season, without them taking over the place. The country cooking in the restaurant is fine: *foie gras*, zander with walnut stock, veal sweetbreads in pastry with truffle *jus* and raspberry *soufflé*. Menus €13–39.

SAINT-ROBERT   19310

🏠 |●| LE SAINT-ROBERT

It's in the centre.
☎ 05.55.25.58.09 ➡ 05.55.25.55.13
Swimming pool.

A charming place that's as appealing for a family stay as it is for a romantic break. This lovely residence was built on a hillside on the border between the Limousin and Périgord by a rich banker in the nineteenth century and boasts breathtaking views over the valley – enjoy them from the terrace and the swimming pool. The rooms are simple and soberly furnished, retaining all their charm and style; doubles €43–53. The restaurant offers

dishes using local produce and succulent meat. Menus €11–16.

SAINT-YRIEIX-LA-PERCHE   87500

🏃 🏠 |●| HOSTEL DE LA TOUR BLANCHE**

74 bd. de l'Hôtel-de-Ville.
☎ 05.55.75.18.17 ➡ 05.55.08.23.11
Closed Sunday and the Feb school holidays. **TV**. **Car park**.

The bedrooms are adequate enough, and although those in the rafters are a bit cramped they're comfortable. Doubles with bath or shower/wc €38. You won't be disappointed by the restaurant. The first of the two dining rooms is the more traditional, serving fresh *foie gras* either as a terrine or panfried, *millefeuille* of Canadian lobster, good meats, home-made Limousin tripe and saddle of rabbit stuffed with snails (menus €16–29). The other is more like a New York snack bar: the cooking is simpler but still pleasant and you get big helpings. They do great salads and a reasonably priced dish of the day with vegetables. Free apéritif.

🏃 |●| À LA BONNE CAVE

7 pl. de la Pierre-de-l'Homme (Centre); it's near the church.
☎ and ➡ 05.55.75.02.12
Closed Mon except July–Aug.

A pleasant restaurant in an old white stone buildling. The cooking is simple and good, prices are reasonable and service comes with a smile. Weekday lunch *formule* for €9 and others €10–21. Dishes include snail *profiteroles*, veal *tourtière* with ceps and apple *croustade* with caramel sauce. They have some good bottles of wine, too. Free coffee.

🏃 |●| RESTAURANT LE PLAN D'EAU

Le Plan d'Eau-d'Arfeuille; it's on the outskirts of town, head for the campsite.
☎ 05.55.75.96.84
Closed Tues evening and Wed; Jan. **Car park**.

This is a very nice restaurant with a view of Lake Arfeuille. Proprietor Jean Maitraud always has time for a chat with his guests and prepares special menus for important dates like Mother's Day. On less festive occasions there's a dish of the day and menus at €10–23. Traditional cooking and local dishes including Limousin beef, zander fillet and strawberries flambéed with Grand Marnier. Free soup starter.

COUSSAC-BONNEVAL   87500 (11 KM E)

≙ |●| LES VOYAGEURS **

21 av. du 11 Novembre.
☎ 05.55.75.20.24 ➡ 05.55.75.28.90
Closed Sun evening and Mon out of season, and Jan.
TV.

The façade is smothered in creepers, but despite the undisturbed appearance it's recently changed ownership. Five of the nine superb rooms look over the garden, and they're all clean and comfortable. Doubles with bath €38–44. Traditional cuisine featuring *foie gras*, ceps and *confits*. Try the fillet of beef with truffle sauce – it's equal to the best. Weekday menu at €10, but *à la carte* things get pricey. One of the best places in the area.

SERRE-DE-MESTES (LA)   19200

|●| BAR-RESTAURANT LA CRÉMAILLÈRE

Le bourg; take the D982.
☎ 05.55.72.34.74
Closed Mon; evenings; the last week in June; a week end Aug–Sept. **Car park**.

Go through the bar to get to the restaurant, where you'll be welcomed by the friendly smile of the owner. The cooking is simple and generously served, with regional specialities and dishes such as rabbit stew, calf's head, *coq au vin*, *confits* and *foie gras*. There are terrific home-made fruit tarts for dessert. Menus €14–21. This is a simple-looking place from the outside, but you'll certainly get your money's worth. Attentive service.

VALIERGUES   19200 (3KM S)

|●| LES MOULINS DE VALIERGUES

Betines; take the D982 then the D125.
☎ 05.55.72.81.31
Closed Sun evening; Mon, Tues lunchtime out of season; Jan and Sept. **Garden**. **Car park**.

Philippe studied at the hotel school in Dijon, then spent several years as a *sommelier* in an establishment on the shores of Lake Geneva before returning home. He and his wife created this delightful country restaurant in a charming little stone house way out in the countryside. Everything is prepared by Philippe; he's an inventive chef who makes good use of locally grown ingredients and mushrooms that he picks himself. His menus are sensitive to seasonal ingredients: semi-cooked *foie gras* with plum brandy, free-range lamb with fruit butter, Limousin beef

with sea salt, caramelized pork with spices, iced walnut *soufflé*. Set menus €18–29. The stylish dining room is dominated by a huge fireplace. They sell their own *foie gras* and a selection of quality wine.

SOUTERRAINE (LA)   23300

≙ |●| HÔTEL MODERNE

11 pl. de la Gare (Centre).
☎ 05.55.63.02.33
Closed Sat lunchtime and Sun; a fortnight in Aug.

This is a perfect example of a 1970s hotel-restaurant – it doesn't have great facilities but it's perfectly fine. The prices are old-fashioned, too: rooms €18–23 with shower but wc on the landing. The convivial bar, *le Pot de l'Amitié*, well deserves its name, which roughly means "A drink among friends". There's one menu only, the *menu ouvrier*, and it costs €8. Great place if you're on a tight budget.

SAINT-ÉTIENNE-DE-FURSAC   23290 (12KM S)

≙ |●| HÔTEL NOUGIER**

2 pl. de l'Église.
☎ 05.55.63.60.56 ➡ 05.55.63.65.47
Closed Sun evening and Mon out of season and on public holidays; Mon lunchtime in season; Dec to mid-March. **TV**. **Garden**. **Car park**.

A very appealing, typically Limousin country inn with twelve bedrooms, some looking onto the garden. Doubles with bath €47. The elegant dining room serves local dishes updated for modern tastes: *terrine* of crayfish tails, duck thighs in mushroom sauce, *croustillant* of pig's trotters. Menus €16–33 and *à la carte* options. The prices seem a little high for what you get, though, and the welcome is hardly engaging. There's also a pretty terrace.

BÉNÉVENT L'ABBAYE   23210 (2KM S)

≙ |●| HÔTEL DU CÈDRE**

rue l'Oiseau (East).
☎ 05.55.81.59.99 ➡ 05.55.81.59.98
Swimming pool. **TV**. **Disabled access**.

A magnificent eighteenth-century building which has been carefully restored. The bright rooms are all different and have been decorated with taste; the nicest have a view of the grounds and a majestic cedar tree. Doubles are €41–107, and have good facilities. In summer the attractive terrace serves as the setting for the gourmet restaurant. Menus €20–27; dishes change with the seasons. It's one of the most appealing places in the region.

TARNAC 19170

⅍ ≜ I●I HÔTEL DES VOYAGEURS**

It's in the centre.
☎ 05.55.95.53.12 ➡ 05.55.95.40.07
Closed Sun evening and Mon out of season; 20 Dec–10 Jan.

A huge stone house in the heart of the village near the church. It's wonderfully maintained by the Deschamps: Madame runs the restaurant with an easy charm while her husband practises his culinary arts in the kitchen. He produces local dishes with a deep knowledge of the region and uses only the freshest produce – fish, Limousin beef, mushrooms picked in the woods in season. Try the calf's head, the fillet of char with chive butter or the veal with girolles. Set menus €13–25 and *à la carte* dishes at reasonable prices. The large, bright bedrooms upstairs are very pleasant and cost €39 with shower/wc or €41 with bath. Excellent value all round. 10% discount on the room rate except July–Aug.

TULLE 19000

⅍ ≜ I●I HÔTEL DU BON ACCUEIL*

8–10 rue Canton.
☎ 05.55.26.70.57
Closed Sat evening and Sun except July–Aug; a fortnight Dec–Jan. **TV**.

A welcoming hotel-restaurant in a quiet street that you probably wouldn't find unless you knew about it. There are several cosy dining rooms where you can eat excellent duck or chicken *confits*, potato pies and, in season, cep omelettes. Set menus €12–22; the one at €16 offers two starters and would satisfy even the most ravenous of appetites. The bedrooms are quite large and very well-maintained – this place deserves more than one star. Doubles €27–33 with shower or bath. Free Kir.

≜ I●I LA TOQUE BLANCHE**

28 rue Jean-Jaurès, pl. Martial-Brigouleix (Centre).
☎ 05.55.26.75.41 ➡ 05.55.20.93.95
Closed Sun evening; Mon; 20 Jan–10 Feb; 1–10 July. **TV**.

The restaurant is one of *the* places to eat in the town. The welcome is much more informal and relaxed than the smart dining room might lead you to expect. And you eat extremely well. You'll find classic cuisine which is wonderfully executed, generously served and attractively presented: delicate poached sole with mushrooms, *mignon* of veal with apples and walnuts, rack of lamb with sweet garlic ravioli, warm apple tart with almond cream. Wine by the glass. Menus €20–45. Spacious, pretty double rooms with en-suite bathroom, TV and phone for €40–45 a night. Good value for money.

⅍ ≜ I●I HÔTEL-RESTAURANT DE LA GARE**

25 av. Winston-Churchill; it's opposite the station.
☎ 05.55.20.04.04 ➡ 05.55.20.15.87
Closed 1–15 Sept. **TV. Car park**.

A classic station hotel with a restaurant that's popular with the locals. The restaurant has been completely refurbished. The kitchen has a good reputation: rabbit *chasseur*, crayfish salad, duck fillet stuffed with morels. Menus at €15–17 and €21 for Sunday lunch. The rooms are comfortable and well-soundproofed, though the decoration may not be everyone's choice; doubles €33 with basin or €44 with shower/wc. Free apéritif.

I●I LE PASSÉ SIMPLE

6 rue François Bonnelye.
☎ 05.55.26.00.75
Closed Sat lunchtime and Sun; a week in Sept.

A cosy establishment serving delicious dishes: mosaic of artichokes with tomato *coulis*, warm *terrine* of beef cheek pickled in red wine, zander with watercress sauce, grilled duck breast with a sweet-and-sour sauce, a deliciously sticky rum baba. Weekday lunch menu €15 or three *formules* €16–20. Slick service and friendly welcome.

SAINTE-FORTUNADE 19490 (10KM S)

I●I LE MOULIN DE LACHAUD

How to get there: take the D940 to Ste-Fortunade then the D1 for Cornil; 4km further turn onto the D94 towards Chastang, Beynat and Aubazin. It's 2km from there.
☎ 05.55.27.30.95
Closed Mon and Tues excluding public holidays; 15 July–15 Aug; end Dec to end Jan.

This old mill is way out in the country. The owners are a delightful young couple from Burgundy. Monsieur works wonders in the kitchen, producing inventive dishes from local produce and local recipes, which he redefines in his own way. Weekday *formules* €13–20 and menus €25–40. Try the *émincé* of veal kidney pan-fried with Brive violet mustard and don't miss out on the desserts, especially the apricot tart with redcurrant and almond jelly. There's a terrace with a lovely view of the lake. You could learn to fish for trout if you fancy catching your own lunch.

LAGARDE-ENVAL   19150 (11KM S)

⋔ ☎ |●| LE CENTRAL**

Le bourg; it's opposite the church.
☎ 05.55.27.16.12 ➡ 05.55.27.13.79
Closed Mon out of season and Sept. **TV. Disabled access. Car park**.

This large house, smothered in Virginia creeper, has been in the same family for four generations. It's across from the church and the pretty manor, both of which are sadly overshadowed by modern buildings. Regional and gourmet dishes – cep omelette, *confit* and *farcidur* (vegetable dumplings) – are served in a rustic dining room. €11 lunch menu and others at €15–23; on Sunday there's only one at €20. Very clean, comfortable rooms go for €24–33 depending on the facilities. It's an pleasant establishment and the staff make sure you enjoy your stay. Free coffee.

GIMEL-LES-CASCADES   19800 (12M NE)

☎ |●| L'HOSTELLERIE DE LA VALLÉE**

Le bourg.
☎ 05.55.21.40.60 ➡ 05.55.21.38.74
Closed 1 Oct–31 March. **TV**.

A charming hotel. Crowds of people come to see the Gimel waterfalls, and since the sunny dining room has a fine view of them and the terrace is idyllic in warm weather, you need to book in summer. Doubles €33–36 with shower or bath; some rooms have views of the valley. Good cuisine in the restaurant using local produce – Limousin beef, duck thighs with ceps, zander with leeks, *grenadins* of veal. Menus €13–23.

SEILHAC   19700 (15.5KM NW)

☎ |●| HÔTEL-RESTAURANT LA DÉSIRADE

Le bourg; take the N120.
☎ 05.55.27.04.17
Closed Sun out of season and a week beginning of Sept.

This unassuming roadside hotel-restaurant is

made more attractive by the friendliness of the owner, who will give you a warm welcome. The dining room has a particularly lovely, unadorned parquet floor. Simple, uncomplicated dishes: Limousin steaks, pizza, mixed salads and meat grilled over the open fire at night. Weekday lunch menu €8 and others up to €14. The old-fashioned bedrooms have an undeniable charm. Doubles €17–23 with washbasin or shower (wc on the landing). A good place for travellers on a budget.

QUATRE-ROUTES-D'ALBUSSAC (LES)   19380 (16KM S)

⋔ ☎ |●| HÔTEL ROCHE DE VIC**

Les Quatre-Routes; it's at the junction of the N121 and the D940, 26km from Brive.
☎ 05.55.28.15.87 ➡ 05.55.28.01.09
e roche.vic@wanadoo.fr
Closed Mon out of season; public holidays; Jan to 15 March. **Swimming pool. TV. Disabled access. Garden. Car park**.

Service noon–2pm and 7–9pm. The large stone building is a 1950s-style manor with towers. Most of the bedrooms are at the back, overlooking the extensive grounds, the play area and the swimming pool. Doubles €26 with washing facilities and up to €59 with bath – they could be prettier but at least they're good value. The restaurant offers a large choice of regional dishes such as *foie gras* with ceps, duck with morels, zander with *beurre blanc* and a pancake *gâteau* with orange. *Formule* at €10 and menus €13–27. Free apéritif if you're staying in the hotel.

CORRÈZE   19800 (22KM NE)

⋔ |●| LE PÊCHEUR DE LUNE

pl. de la Mairie.
☎ 05.55.21.44.93
Closed Sun evening and Mon.

An atypical restaurant, where local dishes are served with a twist – the duck thigh is cooked with bilberries, the skate salad is freshened with asparagus and the cucumber salad has a tang of goat's cheese and pears. The veal *escalope* with girolles and the pigeon braised with horn of plenty mushrooms are particularly delicious. €11 weekday *menu du jour* and others €15–24. Free coffee.

CHAMBOULIVE   19450 (24KM N)

⋔ ☎ |●| L'AUBERGE DE LA VÉZÈRE

pont de Vernéjoux (East); take the D26.

☎ 05.55.73.06.94 ➡ 05.55.73.07.05
Garden. Car park.

A charming riverside inn popular with local anglers. It's a good idea to book in high season as there are only seven bedrooms under the eaves; they cost €30 for a double with shower/wc. On the ground floor there's a friendly, dimly lit bar with a *cantou* (inglenook fireplace) as its focal point, and also a bright, sunny dining room overlooking the river. Duck features quite prominently on the menus (as *civet*, *confit* and *foie gras*) but there's also good Limousin meat. There's a €9 weekday lunch menu and two others at €14 and €20. You'll get a cheery welcome from the proprietress, and after your meal you can go for a quiet stroll along the banks of the beautiful River Vézère. Free apéritif.

TURENNE   19500

🏠 ◉ LA MAISON DES CHANOINES

Route de l'église; take the D38 then the D150.
☎ and ➡ 05.55.85.93.43
Closed Mon and Tues lunchtimes; Wed, Thurs lunchtime

from 1 Nov to Palm Sunday.

Turenne is a beautiful old town and this hotel is quite delightful. You'll find it at the start of the lane that leads up to the church and the château built by the Knights Templar. The dining room has a vaulted ceiling, or you can eat under the awning on the lovely terrace. Imaginative cooking and nicely presented dishes: *foie gras* marinated in truffle vinegar served with home-made walnut bread, chargrilled veal with morels and lots of desserts with walnuts. Menus €26–32 and you can also enjoy the delights of the truffle menu – but that's to order. There are six comfortable, stylish bedrooms for €57–77. You'll get a lovely welcome.

◉ LA VICOMTÉ

Place de la Halle; (Centre).
☎ 05.55.85.91.32
Closed Sun evening; Mon; Oct–March.

Annie runs this place and she serves all the great classics of the local area at modest prices: menus €12–19. The delightful dining room has a parquet floor and windows opening onto the valley. There's a lovely terrace on the village square.

LORRAINE

54 Meurthe-et-Moselle

55 Meuse

57 Moselle

88 Vosges

ABRESCHVILLER   57560

🏃 🏠 |●| HÔTEL-RESTAURANT LE DONON*

57 rue Pierre-Marie (Centre).
☎ 03.87.03.74.90 📠 03.87.03.78.64
Closed Mon all year, Tues in winter, and 24 Dec–15 Jan. **TV**. **Car park**.

A small family hotel for walking enthusiasts, within easy reach of the forest trails and mountain tracks. There are five homely bedrooms; doubles with shower/wc or bath go for €29. They serve simple, filling local and traditional dishes in the restaurant: sea trout with *anise*, wild boar haunch with girolles, trout fillet with Riesling, and flambéed tarts on weekend evenings. Menus, ranging from €10–24, prove good value for money. Good service and friendly welcome. Free coffee.

SAINT-QUIRIN   57560 (5KM SW)

🏠 |●| L'HOSTELLERIE DU PRIEURÉ

163 rue du Général-de-Gaulle; take the D96.
☎ 03.87.08.66.52 📠 03.87.08.66.49
Closed Wed, Feb and All Saints' school holidays. **TV**. **Disabled access**. **Car park**.

In the eighteenth century, the Church did not have a reputation for modesty – witness the imposing sandstone priory which now houses this restaurant. The cooking is rich and inventive and has won the restaurant a "Moselle Gourmande" award – try *baechoffen* of snails in white wine sauce, fish *pot-au-feu* with fresh mushrooms, breast of chicken glazed with honey and spicy sauce, rabbit marinated in white wine with prunes and bacon, or lamb chops *à la provençale*. There's a weekday lunch menu for €11, with others from €15–46. You could do worse than stay the night here, too. The new rooms, in an annexe, have modern bathrooms but lack the charm of the restaurant. You'll pay €37–40 for doubles with shower or bath. Number 5 is very spacious and has a pretty balcony where you can eat breakfast.

LUTZELBOURG   57820 (22KM NE)

🏃 🏠 |●| LES VOSGES**

149 rue Ackermann (Centre); take the RN4, the A4 and then the CD38.
☎ 03.87.25.30.09 📠 03.87.25.42.22
Closed Thurs evening and Fri out of season, mid-Jan to mid-Feb, and 12 Nov–8 Dec. **TV**. **Pay car park**.

In a delightful village in the crook of the pretty Zom valley, this hotel is on the bank of a small canal. The long-established family hotel has lost none of its charm over the years. All the bedrooms are furnished with antiques, and the beds have lace eiderdowns. Large doubles with basin/wc go for €30, with shower/wc €41, and with bath €49. The traditional dining room suits the classic cooking. During the hunting season, try the sautéed deer with prunes, pheasant with mirabelle plums, or young wild boar with berries. Menus €15–30. Free parking.

BACCARAT   54120

🏠 |●| HÔTEL-RESTAURANT DE L'AGRICULTURE

54 rue des Trois-Frères-Clément (Northwest).

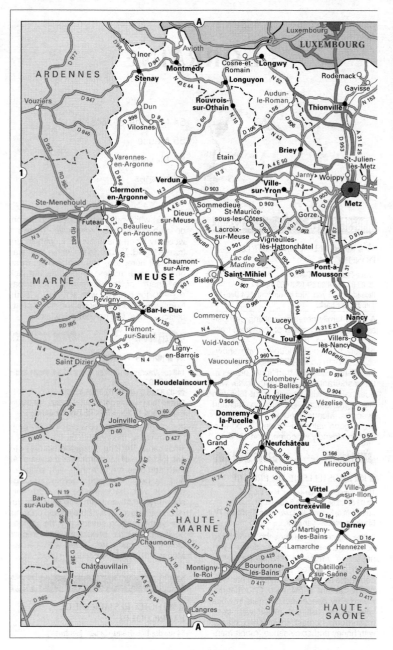

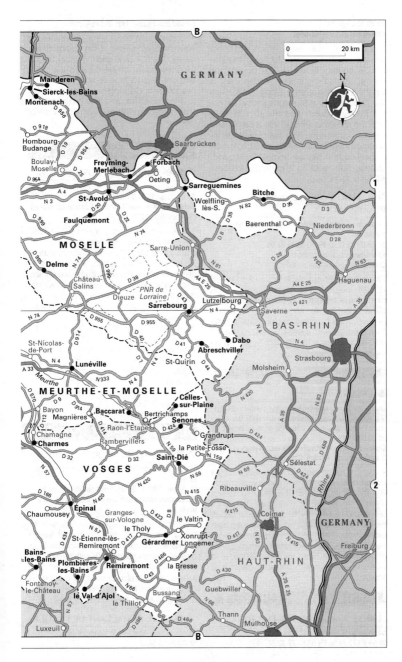

☎ 03.83.75.10.44
Closed Sat and Sun evenings.

You'll see colourful window boxes and bright flowers tumbling down the façade of this irresistible country hotel. It's just outside the centre, with its famous glass museum, and is a perfect place to stop on a long hike through the Santois or the Mortagne valley. Simple but freshly decorated rooms start at €29, with the shower squeezed into a corner and the wc along the landing. The convivial family atmosphere in the restaurant attracts a lot of local custom. Menus, from €10, list good, unpretentious cooking – you'll spend about €24 *à la carte*.

🏃 ⬧ |●| HÔTEL-RESTAURANT LA RENAISSANCE**

31 rue des Cristalleries (Centre); it's opposite the glassworks.
☎ 03.83.75.11.31 ➡ 03.83.75.21.09
e renaissance.la@wanadoo.fr
Closed Mon, Fri and Sun evenings.

This is a convenient place to stay if you want to visit the Baccarat glass museum. The rooms have been simply but tastefully refurbished; doubles with shower/wc or bath start at €45. The classical cooking uses fresh farm produce, with a weekday lunch menu at €10 and others €13–26. 10% discount on the room rate.

BERTRICHAMPS   54120 (5KM E)

|●| L'ÉCURIE

Les Noires-Terres; take the N59 in the direction of Saint-Dié, and as you leave Bertrichamps turn right. Don't cross the railway line, but follow the signs on the left.
☎ 03.83.71.43.14.
Closed Sun evening; Mon; Feb; the second week in July.
Disabled access. Garden. Car park.

A very fine, unpretentious restaurant run by a classy chef. Old mill and farm implements line the white walls of the beautiful dining room. The menus, at €10 (weekday lunch only) and €14–37, list tasty specialities including home-prepared *charcuterie*, delicious *croustillant* of ham with mushroom sauce, stuffed saddle of rabbit with mirabelle conserve, calf's head *sauce gribiche*, and veal sweetbreads with balsamic salad and shrimp.

MAGNIÈRES   54129 (15KM W)

🏃|●| LE WAGON DU PRÉ FLEURY

Ancienne gare: take the D47 from Baccarat.
☎ 03.83.72.32.58 ➡ 03.83.72.32.77

Closed Sun evening, Mon and early Jan.

This restaurant occupies a genuine old railway carriage, parked at the station of Magnières. The station is also the departure point for *draisines*, which are like pedalos on rails, and which go for trips up and down the local branch lines. Cooking is a mixture of French and foreign styles, and they sometimes host theme evenings. Menus from €13. Free coffee.

BAINS-LES-BAINS   88240

🏃 ⬧ |●| HÔTEL DE LA POSTE**

11 rue de Verdun (Centre); it's next to the spa.
☎ 03.29.36.31.01 ➡ 03.29.30.44.22
Hotel closed mid-Oct to March. **Restaurant closed** evenings except Mon and Sat. **TV**.

This establishment has a somewhat forbidding façade, but it's undoubtedly the best place in the area. There are fourteen attractive rooms at €26 with basin, €36 with shower/wc, or €39 with bath. You have a choice of two restaurants: the *Carré Bleu*, which is quite intimate, or the *Relais*, which is plusher and much bigger. The cuisine is innovative and subtly flavoured: dishes include *foie gras* deglazed with raspberry vinegar, and tripe with Toul snails. There's a €11 menu (weekdays only) and others from €16; reckon on around €29 *à la carte*. The dishes change regularly depending on what's good at market and the inspiration of the chef. 10% discount on the room rate or, if you're dining only, free coffee.

BAR-LE-DUC   55000

🏃 ⬧ |●| HÔTEL-RESTAURANT BERTRAND*

19 rue de l'Étoile (Centre-North); it's behind the train station.
☎ 03.29.79.02.97 **e** hotel-bertrand@wanadoo.fr
Restaurant closed Sun evening. **Garden. TV. Car park.**

A friendly, warm, no-frills guesthouse with a family atmosphere. Menus start at €8. The rooms are ordinary but well maintained; doubles with basin go for €20, with shower €23, and with shower/wc or bath €35. Some rooms have a balcony over the garden. The gorgeous Parc Marbeaumont is just a couple of minutes away. Free house *digestif*.

🏃|●| GRILL RESTAURANT DE LA TOUR

15 rue du Baile (East); it's in the upper town.
☎ 03.29.76.14.08

Closed Sat lunchtime, Sun and public holidays.

This sixteenth-century building is quite magnificent. You eat in a tiny room where they grill great *andouillettes* and black puddings over the open fire. The cooking, like the setting, is simple and authentic. Specialities include house duck *terrine*, grilled meats, and *tarte Tatin*. Lunch menu €11, others €14–19. Dinner is served only until 8pm. Free apéritif.

I●I PATATI ET PATATA

9 rue Brandfer (Centre).
☎ 08.00.50.90.31
Closed Sat lunchtime and Sun, except evenings of public holidays.

Lots of garnished and *gratinéed* dishes, many of them potato-based, and salads served in this young, cool place where you can eat quickly, cheaply and late into the night. Reckon on around €15 for a meal.

REVIGNY-SUR-ORNAIN   55800 (15KM W)

𝕬 ≜ I●I LES AGAPES–LA MAISON FORTE***

6 pl. Henriot du Coudray; take the D994 in the direction of Reims.
☎ 03.29.70.56.00 ➡ 03.29.70.59.30
Closed Sun evening, evenings of public holidays, Mon lunchtime, a week in Feb and a fortnight in Aug. **TV. Garden. Car park**.

The owners of the *Agapes* made such a success of their restaurant that they bought the rooms in *La Maison Forte* and transformed this ancient fourteenth-century building into a charming hotel-restaurant. It's quite splendid and is the only starred place in the *département*, but all in all, prices are reasonable. The main building, housing the restaurant, is at the end of a tree-lined avenue. It has been thoughtfully decorated and has bare stone walls, old floor tiles and a fireplace. The cuisine is fresh and inventive, using unusual incredients like dandelions and molasses. Menus €25–49 or around €43 *à la carte*. The guest rooms are in the wings to the left and right of the main building; they're all very comfortable with old-style furnishings. Doubles with bath range from €56 to €107; some of those in the towers have beds on a mezzanine floor, and there are a few suites sleeping three. Free coffee.

CHAUMONT-SUR-AIRE   55260 (20KM N)

≜ I●I AUBERGE DU MOULIN HAUT

How to get there: take the N35 then the D902.

☎ and ➡ 03.29.70.66.46
Closed Sun evening, Mon, and 15 Jan–15 Feb.

The wheel of this eighteenth-century mill turns gently to supply electricity to the restaurant and the noise is masked by the tinkling of a 1910 pianola. It's a peaceful and delightful place, run by a welcoming couple who have travelled widely in Africa, and the cuisine is balanced and full of flavour. The weekday lunch menu costs €14 and there are others from €22 to €46, variously featuring duck specialities, regional dishes and, at the top of the scale, a gastronomic menu. Keep some space for dessert, especially the *croustillant flambé* of mirabelle plums There are two double rooms in an annexe, costing €46.

BITCHE   57230

≜ I●I HÔTEL-PENSION DE LA GARE

2 av. Trumelet-Faber; it's near the station.
☎ and ➡ 03.87.96.00.14
Closed Sat, Sun, 10–26 Aug and 22 Dec–7 Jan. **Car park**.

Service noon–2pm and 7–8.30pm. This is the only cheap hotel in town, and though the rooms are modest they're very clean. Doubles with basin from €21, or €24 with shower. The *patronne* is so kind that you won't notice the slightly fading décor; sometimes the guests even lend a hand behind the bar. You'll eat unpretentious country cooking with a weekday set menu at €8; half board is €22. It's advisable to book early.

I●I L'AUBERGE DE LA TOUR

3 rue de la Gare; it's close to the Vauban citadel.
☎ 03.87.96.29.25
Closed Mon evening, Tues and Feb. **Car park**.

Atmospheric and cosy with its Belle Époque décor, this place has a popular brasserie atmosphere; the local paper, the *Républicain Lorrain*, lies about on the tables, and locals talk politics while they drink and eat. There's a weekday lunch menu for €10, and others from €19–37. Interesting food combinations include prawns *marinières* with vegetable broth, or pike-perch and salmon *terrine*. Try the home-made sorbets for dessert. The welcome is a little reserved but not offputting.

BAERENTHAL   57239 (20KM SE)

𝕬 ≜ LE KIRCHBERG**

8 rue de la Fôret; it's opposite the post office.

☎ 03.87.98.97.70 ➡ 03.87.98.97.91
Closed Jan. **TV**. **Disabled access**. **Car park**.

This unpretentious hotel is in a modern, very quiet building where it's easy to get a good night's sleep. Double rooms go for €47–55 with shower or €59 with bath; even the smallest rooms are spacious and comfortable. They also have studios sleeping two or four that they rent by the week or weekend. Free house apéritif.

BRIEY   54150

🛏 |●| HÔTEL ANCONA**

63 rue de Metz; it's near the bridge.
☎ 03.82.46.21.00 ➡ 03.82.20.29.85
TV.

Benefitting from its efficient double glazing, which effectively blocks out the passing traffic noise, this place offers comfortable rooms that are modestly priced at €40. The very friendly welcome makes it a pleasure to stay here. Decent, traditional food is served in the restaurant.

🛏 HÔTEL ASTER**

rue de l'Aurope; it's on the edge of the Sangsue lake.
☎ 03.82.46.66.94 ➡ 03.82.20.91.76
🅔 spitoni@wanadoo.fr
Disabled access. **TV**. **Car park**.

A large, modern block that bears no resemblance to that charming inn you could be looking for. But the modern and comfortable rooms are bright and sunny and the surrounding greenery is appealing. Doubles €43–47.

CELLES-SUR-PLAINE   88110

🛏 |●| HÔTEL DES LACS**

It's opposite the campsite.
☎ 03.29.41.17.06 ➡ 03.29.41.18.21
TV.

A rose-painted house that with its pleasant holiday décor would look more in keeping at a seaside resort than in the Vosges. The piano and old furnishings give it personality and create an intimate atmosphere. Doubles €34–41. Good cooking in the restaurant, where menus change frequently, and prices are reasonable.

CHARMES   88130

🛏 |●| HÔTEL LES REMPARTS**

4 rue des Capucins (Centre); it's near the town square.

☎ 03.29.38.02.40 ➡ 03.29.38.01.58
Closed Sun evening, Mon, end Feb, and middle fortnight in July. **Disabled access**. **TV**. **Car park**.

This is a charming place. The rooms are rather chic, and all have en-suite bathrooms. A double will cost €42. Even the most demanding palate will be satisfied by the cooking, which is prepared using fresh, seasonal market produce – go for the *turban* of trout with leeks and Pinot Noir, pike-perch with special mashed potatoes, or shellfish in season.

CLERMONT-EN-ARGONNE   55120

🌂 🛏 |●| HÔTEL-RESTAURANT BELLEVUE**

14 rue de la Libération (Centre).
☎ 03.29.87.41.02 ➡ 03.29.88.46.01
Closed Sun evening out of season and Wed. **TV**. **Garden**. **Car park**.

The hotel has been totally refurbished. The rooms are functional and anonymous but the façade and the dining room are ravishing. The dining room, which retains all its original Art Deco features from 1923, leads onto a balcony overlooking the garden and the countryside. The cooking is simple, and portions are generous: in season they offer game dishes such as *navarin* of wild boar with *fricassée* of wild mushrooms. The €14 menu is served daily except for Sunday, and there are others from €21–34. There are seven rooms, ranging from €40 with shower/wc to €46 with bath. Peace and quiet are guaranteed, especially in the rooms at the back. Free apéritif or coffee.

FUTEAU   55120 (10KM SW)

🌂 🛏 |●| HÔTEL-RESTAURANT L'ORÉE DU BOIS***

How to get there: take the N3; at Islettes, turn right onto the D2 and it's on the left, 500m beyond Futeau.
☎ 03.29.88.28.41 ➡ 03.29.88.24.52
🅔 oreedubois@free.fr
Closed Mon and Tues lunchtimes in season, Sun evening, Mon and Tues from Nov–March, Jan, and All Saints. **TV**. **Disabled access**. **Car park**.

This place is quietly set on the edge of a wood, so you'll sleep well. The fifteen large bedrooms all have en-suite bathrooms; doubles go for €70–120. They serve a weekday menu at €20 and others from €50–65. The local pigeon with coriander is particularly good. The *patronne* has two passions: cheese and wine and there's a good selection of vintages to choose from. Staff are friendly and enthusiastic. Free house *digestif*.

CONTREXÉVILLE   88140

🗢 🏠 |●| HÔTEL DE LORRAINE*

122 av. du Roi-Stanislas (Centre); it's near the train station.
☎ 03.29.08.04.24
Closed 15 Oct–1 March. **Car park**.

A big, pleasant old place with a bit of style. The cooking is traditional, though special diets can be catered for. Set menus start at €11 and rise to €21 – the last features Lorraine specialities. Try the roast fillet of perch, the snail ravioli with smoked bacon, frogs' legs with parsley, or snails in pastry. Double rooms €23 with washing facilities and €32 with shower/wc or bath. Half board from €33. The trains don't run at night, so it isn't too noisy. Free coffee.

🗢 🏠 |●| HÔTEL DES SOURCES**

rue Ziwer-Pacha; it's opposite the town hall.
☎ 03.29.08.04.48 ➡ 03.29.08.63.01
📧 hsources@club-internet.fr
Closed Oct–April. **TV**. **Disabled access**.

An elegant building very close to the esplanade with its colourful fountains. The atmosphere is just what you'd expect in a spa, with guests playing scrabble or cards together. The rooms are comfortable and have been decorated with care. On the third floor they've got a few attic rooms with basin for €29; otherwise doubles with shower go for €61, and those with bath cost €51. The restaurant isn't bad at all, with set menus starting at €14. Free breakfast.

🏠 |●| VILLA BEAUSÉJOUR**

204 rue Aizer-Pacha.
☎ 03.29.08.04.89 ➡ 03.29.08.62.28
TV.

A charming hotel with a cosy salon and reception area. The rooms are individually decorated and furnished with period pieces and old mirrors. Those looking over the tranquil garden are the nicest. Doubles €46. The restaurant provides good (fattening) food; try the house gizzard stew or rolled free-range chicken. Menus €15–32.

🏠 HÔTEL DE LA SOUVERAINE***

Parc thermal (Centre).
☎ 03.29.08.09.59 ➡ 03.29.08.16.39
Closed 15 Oct–25 March. **TV**. **Car park**.

This elegant building, which used to be the

residence of the Shah of Persia, looks onto the spa's park. It's a little formal, with beautifully renovated rooms, but they've kept the prices reasonable. Comfortable rooms start at €55 with shower/wc or bath.

DABO   57850

|●| RESTAURANT ZOLLSTOCK

11 route Zollstock, La Hoube; it's 6km from Dabo on the D45.
☎ 03.87.08.80.65 ➡ 03.87.08.86.41
Closed Mon and Christmas to New Year.

Looking across a forested valley, this restaurant doesn't get much passing trade, and most of the customers are regulars. There's a short lunchtime menu for €9 and others from €14–19, listing simple but tasty specialities. Plump for venison haunch and fresh *charcuterie* in season, salmon in champagne sauce and, for dinner, frogs' legs and *mignon* of veal with morels. It's small and extremely pleasant with an appealing family atmosphere, and is especially popular for Sunday lunch.

DELME   57590

🗢 🏠 |●| HÔTEL-RESTAURANT À LA XIIᴇ BORNE**

6 pl. de la République (Centre).
☎ 03.87.01.30.18 ➡ 03.87.01.38.39
📧 xll@omfpmoe.fr
Disabled access. **TV**. **Garden**. **Pay car park**.

Lunch until 2pm and dinner until 9.45pm. Delme was once a Roman encampment at the twelfth marker or *borne* on the road from Metz to Strasbourg – hence the establishment's name. The hotel has been refurbished and rooms cost €40 with bath or shower. There's also a sauna, free for all guests. Menus in the "Roman" dining room go for €15–38, while in the other, gastronomic dining room they feature dishes such as *foie gras escalope* with mirabelle plums or pike-perch and perch fillets with *beurre blanc*. There's a good list of local wines. 10% discount on the room rate.

DOMRÉMY-LA-PUCELLE   88630

🏠 HÔTEL JEANNE D'ARC

1 rue Principale (Centre); it's next to the church.
☎ 03.29.06.96.06
Closed mid-Nov to March. **Car park**.

A little hotel with seven rooms, very near St

Joan's house. Little has changed over the years, and that includes the prices: you'll pay €26 for a quiet, clean double with shower/wc. Breakfast, €4, is brought to your room.

AUTREVILLE   88300 (14KM NE)

🏠 |●| HÔTEL RELAIS ROSE**

24 rue de Neufchâteau (Southeast); take the D19 then the N74.
☎ 03.83.52.04.98 ➡ 03.83.52.06.03
TV. Disabled access. Garden. Car park.

The hotel, right on the main road, is not an obvious place to stop, but it's worth it. Inside it's a charming old family house with quite lovely rooms; some have balconies or views over the garden and the countryside beyond. With bath or shower they go for €40–53. The weekday lunch menu costs €11 and there are others from €15–25. They offer excellent rabbit with *vin gris* from Toul, veal sweetbreads with morels, and a number of dishes from the southwest – where Madame comes from – including *foie gras*, *cassoulet* and duck *confit*. Excellent wines from the ancient cellar.

ÉPINAL   88000

🏠 AZUR HÔTEL**

54 quai des Bons-Enfants (Centre).
☎ 03.29.64.05.25 ➡ 03.29.64.00.40
e vosgeshotels.com/azurhotel/index.htm
Closed 25 Dec–1 Jan. **TV.**

Excellent, soundproofed rooms at €29–43 with shower/wc or bath. Number 16 is split-level, with a small sitting room, and some rooms have a view of the canal so you can watch the canoes and the kayaks go by. You'll receive a hospitable welcome, and they'll take good care of you. Child's bed available for free.

🍴 🏠 HÔTEL KYRIAD**

12 av. du Général-de-Gaulle (West); it's opposite the train station.
☎ 03.29.82.10.74 ➡ 03.29.35.35.14
e hotel-kyriad-epinal@libertysurf.fr
Closed 23 Dec–2 Jan. **TV. Lock-up garage.**

This is part of a chain but you'd never guess so from its appearance. It has the charm of a family-run station hotel where they make you feel very welcome. The whole place has been gutted and renovated – there's a new bar – and they've put in soundproofing, which is essential to block out the noise of the road and passing trains. Doubles with shower/wc or with bath cost €50–55; there are also

three suites. 10% discount at weekends.

|●| RESTAURANT LE PINAUDRÉ

10 av. du Général-de-Gaulle (West); it's opposite the train station.
☎ 03.29.82.45.29
Closed Sat lunchtime, Sun and Aug.

A discreet restaurant that's easy to miss. The large, attractive dining room has been done up to look like a modern bistro, and the cooking is traditional with a few modern touches. There's an excellent weekday lunchtime menu at €11, and others at €14–25. Fish and seafood predominate, both on the menus and *à la carte*: typical offerings include roast salmon fillet with bilberries, John Dory in parsley, and fillet of sea bass with morels. As for the local dishes, try the warm *andouillette* salad or the pan-fried *escalope* of foie gras with mirabelle plums.

|●| LE PETIT ROBINSON

24 rue Raymond-Poincaré.
☎ 03.29.34.23.51
Closed Sat, Sun and mid-July to mid-August.

A fairly classic restaurant offering light, inventive cuisine that's good value for money. The €16 menu offers salad leaves with diced bacon, duck thigh with olives, cheese and dessert, and there are other menus up to €30. Try the excellent red mullet with anchovy if it's listed. The décor – all wood panelling and light colours – is soothing, as is the gentle jazz in the background.

🍴 |●| RESTAURANT LES FINES HERBES

15 rue La Maix (Centre); it's near place des Vosges.
☎ 03.29.31.46.70 ➡ 03.29.34.82.98
Closed Sun evening, Mon and the third week in Aug.

The décor is streamlined and modern while managing to feel intimate, and the unusual cooking is served with care and attention. Menus change every month and are reasonably priced; the lunchtime menu costs €17, with others up to €27. They do quite a lot of fish dishes; try the monkfish *tournedos* with morels or one of the seafood platters. They close at 10pm. Free coffee.

CHAUMOUSEY   88390 (10KM W)

|●| LE CALMOSIEN

37 rue d'Épinal; take the N460 in the direction of Darney.
☎ 03.29.66.80.77
Closed Sun evening. **Car park.**

From the outside you might mistake this

place for a country station, but inside the dining room is more Belle Époque than waiting room. In the summer they set a few tables out in the garden. The imaginative chef comes up with classic cuisine and a few local dishes: pigeon breast with spice bread sauce and duck thigh *confit* served on a salad dressed with hazelnut oil. Menus €14–44. There's a great wine list, with a few pleasant surprises. Since it has such an excellent reputation locally, it's best to book.

FAULQUEMONT   57380

🏃 🏠 HÔTEL LE CHÂTELAIN**

1 pl. Monroë (Centre); it's next to the church.
☎ 03.87.90.70.80 ➡ 03.87.90.74.78
TV. Disabled access. Car park.

This place looks less than appealing from the outside, but inside you'll find 25 comfortable rooms around a wonderful winter garden dotted with pot plants and troughs. Doubles €44 with shower/wc. It's all very new and lacks that lived-in feeling, but the boss is friendly and very enthusiastic. Best to book. Free coffee.

FORBACH   57600

🏠 HÔTEL LE PIGEON BLANC

42 rue Nationale (Centre).
☎ 03.87.85.23.05
Closed Sun. **Disabled access. Car park**.

This establishment is one of the best unstarred hotels in the area – the rooms in the annexe, which are very spacious and quiet, are particularly good. Doubles range from €15 with basin to €26 for very big, quiet rooms with large bathrooms. The only drawback is that you have to vacate your room by 10am.

🏃 🏠 HÔTEL DE LA POSTE**

57 rue Nationale (Centre).
☎ 03.87.85.08.80 ➡ 03.87.85.91.91
Car park. TV.

This is the oldest hotel in Forbach and it's been providing decent accommodation for a hundred years. Rooms have been fully renovated and decorated in blue, yellow or pink depending which floor they're on. Doubles with basin €23, with shower/wc or bath €41. It's set back from the street so you won't be disturbed by noise. Staff are friendly and unobtrusive. 10% discount July–Aug.

OETING   57600 (2KM S)

🏃 ❚●❚ RESTAURANT À L'ÉTANG

386 rue de Forbach; it's near the church.
☎ 03.87.87.33.85.
Closed Tues evening, Wed, and mid-Aug to early Sept. **Car park**.

Service noon–2pm and 7–10pm. A restaurant in a big, pleasant house with country-style décor and a little pond. The cheapest menu costs just €9 in the week, but it's a little uninspiring. The others run from €17–34; not surprisingly, the top-priced one is the gastronomic choice, with dishes like carp fillet with sorrel, pike-perch in Pinot Noir and game in season. Free coffee.

FREYMING-MERLEBACH   57800

🏠 ❚●❚ HÔTEL-RESTAURANT AU CAVEAU DE LA BIÈRE

2 rue du 5-Décembre; it's opposite the music conservatory.
☎ 03.87.81.33.45 ➡ 03.87.04.95.95
Closed Sat and Sun evenings. **Car park**.

A few regulars come to the bar for a beer, but above all this is a business hotel. Rooms are clean and functional at €20 with basin, €27 with shower, and €38 with bath. They prepare simple traditional dishes like *quiche lorraine*, grilled *andouillette* or tripe in Riesling, which you can wash down with a glass of Amos, one of the few beers that are still brewed locally. Weekday menu €9 and others from €12–30.

❚●❚ SAINTE-BARBE

23 rue de Metz; it's on the edge of town on the way to Metz, opposite the unmissable Houillères du Bassin Lorrain building.
☎ 03.87.81.24.24 ➡ 03.87.04.15.98
Closed Sat evening. **Disabled access**.

A good local restaurant that's ideal if you want a quick midday meal. Business workers pile into the big, old-fashioned – not to say kitsch – dining room at lunchtime, when they can enjoy huge helpings of hearty family cuisine. Menus €10–21. Service is cheery.

GÉRARDMER   88400

🏠 ❚●❚ AU P'TITS BOULAS* .

4 place du Tilleul (Centre).
☎ 03.29.27.10.06 ➡ 03.29.27.11.91
Closed Wed evening. **Car park**.

A charming family hotel with three bright,

very well-maintained double rooms at €26–40 with shower and shared wc. The restaurant provides good local dishes including sirloin steak with Münster cheese sauce, trout in Riesling and so on. Menus from €10.

🎄 🏠 HÔTEL DE PARIS**

3 rue de la Gare (Centre).
☎ 03.29.63.10.66 ➡ 03.29.63.16.47
TV. Car park.

A very simple little hotel located in the ski resort's busiest street. It's not a luxurious place, but the rooms have recently been redecorated and are reasonably priced; doubles go from €27 with basin, €37 with shower or bath/wc. The ones overlooking the interior courtyard are the quietest. The hotel fills up at the weekend so you should secure your room by sending a deposit. There's a separate brasserie on the ground floor, and a lively bar with a selection of ninety beers, ten of which are on draught. 10% discount.

🎄 🏠 ◖◗ HÔTEL VIRY – RESTAURANT L'AUBERGADE

pl. des Déportés (Centre); 200m from the lake.
☎ 03.29.6302.41 ➡ 03.29.63.14.03
Closed Fri evening out of season. **TV. Car park**.

The hotel has been around for a good forty years, during which time the common areas, landings and bathrooms have all been renovated. Double rooms €41–53 with shower/wc or with bath. The rustic-looking dining room offers particularly good value, and in summer you can eat on a covered terrace on the square. They serve sound regional cuisine: *vigneronne* salad, brawn with *ravigotte* sauce, chicken *fricassée* with Riesling or tripe in Sylvaner *à l'ancienne*. There's a decent *menu du marché* at €12; *à la carte* you'll pay around €24. Friendly welcome and courteous service. Free house apéritif.

🎄 🏠 HÔTEL GÉRARD D'ALSACE**

14 rue du 152è R.I. (Southwest).
☎ 03.29.63.02.38 ➡ 03.29.60.85.21
Restaurant closed a fortnight in Nov.
Swimming pool. TV. Car park.

This substantial Vosges house, just 150m from the lake on a small track, is a peaceful place. It's got a retro feel – the hotel opened in the early 50s – but it's not unattractive, and it does have a heated swimming pool. The rooms are modest but most of them have double glazing, and all of them overlook the garden. You'll pay €38–43 for a double with shower/wc or €53 with bath/wc. Guests can

hire mountain bikes at a special rate. 10% discount except in Feb, July and Aug.

🏠 ◖◗ HÔTEL-RESTAURANT CHÂLET DU LAC**

97 chemin de la droite du lac (West); it's beside the lake, 1km from the town centre on the D147 in the direction of Épinal.
☎ 03.29.63.38.76 ➡ 03.29.60.91.63
Closed Oct. **TV. Garden. Car park**.

A historic wooden chalet overlooking the lake and the road, which is far enough away not to be distracting. Though the rooms have been renovated, they've kept their antique furniture and have a really nice, old-fashioned feel. All of them have bath or shower and a balcony overlooking the lake, and they each cost €52. There's an annexe in another chalet a few metres away on the edge of the forest. As for the restaurant, the food is traditional with regional influences; cockerel in Riesling or quail with morels, for example. Seven set menus €15–52. Half board, which is often compulsory, costs €50 per person. Lovely garden.

🏠 LE GRAND HÔTEL***

place du Tilleul (Centre).
☎ 03.29.63.06.31 ➡ 03.29.63.46.81
Disabled access. TV. Two swimming pools. Car park.

A grand hotel in the old style, with a huge hall, glorious oak staircase and sweeping corridors. One of its earliest guests was Napoleon III who passed this way when he came to open the route over the Schlucht pass. The spacious rooms are attractively decorated and all have good bathrooms; some have balconies or terraces where you can have breakfast in summer. Doubles go for €76–128, and they have a few suites, too. There are two swimming pools – the heated indoor one has a Jacuzzi, with a fitness room and beauty salon. Make sure to have a beer in the cosy Louis XIII bar.

🎄 ◖◗ LE BISTROT DE LA PERLE

32 rue Charles-de-Gaulle (Centre).
☎ 03.29.60.86.24
Closed Wed out of season, Tues evening, and the last three weeks in Oct.

This place, which used to be a butcher's shop, retains its original, picturesque façade. The light, pleasant dining room offers friendly service and no-fuss food, including snail *cassolette*, grilled bacon salad, chicken in *civet*, fillet of pike-perch in Côte de Tout and grilled *andouillette*. Choose the €9 *formule* for good, freshly cooked dishes; there are also menus from €14–18. There's a patio planted with flowers at the back. Free apéritif.

🎿 |●| LES RIVES DU LAC

1 av. de Vichy; it's near the landing stage on the lake.
☎ 03.29.63.04.29
Closed 31 Oct–31 Jan, and lunchtimes 1 July–31 Aug.
Disabled access. Car park.

This restaurant, on the shores of the most famous lake in the Vosges, is a touristy place serving good, simple food at prices that are extremely reasonable given the location and the gorgeous terrace. The drawback is that the service is often slow. Menus €13–15. Do the done thing and go for the great *fumé vosgien* (salted pork with potatoes and *fromage frais*), or choose the *choucroute alsacienne* for €10. Free coffee.

|●| L'ASSIETTE DU COZ À L'ÂNE

place du Tilleul (Centre).
☎ 03.29.63.06.31
Closed Tues and Wed outside school holidays. **Disabled access.**

Although this is a fairly new place they've created the atmosphere of a local farm and done it successfully. The floor tiles, high, beamed ceiling and fireplace are all pleasantly rustic, and the local cuisine – pressed duck with lentils for example – suits the setting well. You dine well here, for fair prices; there's a single set menu for €15.

XONRUPT-LONGEMER   88400 (7KM NE)

☎ |●| HÔTEL LE COLLET – RESTAURANT LAPÔTRE***

9937 route de Colmar (Southeast); it's beyond Xonrupt on the D417 in the direction of col de la Schlucht Munster.
☎ 03.29.60.09.57 ➡ 03.29.60.08.77
Restaurant closed Wed outside school holidays, Thurs lunchtimes, 7–12 April and 11 Nov–8 Dec.
TV. Car park.

This is a big traditional chalet, set at 1100m in the heart of the Vosges nature reserve; it's near the cross-country ski trails and the ski lifts. The welcome is simple yet special and there's a luxurious feel to the place. Pretty double rooms with shower/wc or bath go for €66; the nicest ones have a balcony with a view of the forest. The very good regional cuisine has been revamped by a young chef bursting with ideas and enthusiasm: duck *confit* with a light *choucroute*, or pork fillet coated with spices and served with potato

galettes. Menus, €15–24, include *bibelaskas* (fresh cheese flavoured with horseradish and herbs), *lewerknepfla* (*quenelles* of liver), and poached trout. The wine list features a lot of Alsace wines along with a few gems from other regions.

THOLY (LE)   88530 (11KM W)

🎿 ☎ |●| L'AUBERGE AU PIED DE LA CASCADE*

12 chemin des Cascades; take the D11 to Tholy, and continue for 5km until you get to the Tendon waterfall.
☎ 03.29.33.21.18 ➡ 03.29.33.29.42
Closed Wed except school holidays, and mid-Nov to Christmas. **TV. Disabled access. Car park.**

A typical old Vosges inn buried in the countryside, right by the forest and the famous Tendon waterfall. Its attractions extend beyond the setting, the terrace and the ancient dining room; it's a tiny, peaceful place, often booked up, so you'd do best to reserve. Doubles €24 with basin, €30–47 with shower or bath. The food is delcious, too; they're known for serving the best trout in the area, caught fresh in the nearby pool. Menus €12–34 or around €15 *à la carte*. 10% discount on the room rate.

BRESSE (LA)   88250 (13KM SE)

🎿 ☎ |●| HÔTEL-RESTAURANT LE CHEVREUIL BLANC**

3 rue Paul-Claudel (Northwest); as you arrive in the resort coming from Gérardmer on the D486.
☎ 03.29.25.41.08 ➡ 03.29.25.65.34
Restaurant closed Sun evening outside school holidays; Spring holidays, and All Saints holidays. **TV. Car park.**

Maria Pia will greet you to this freshly painted inn with a friendly smile, and once you try the food, you'll be hooked. It's sophisticated without being pretentious, with lots of local dishes and a great fish stew. There's a weekday menu at €13 and others €15–33. They have just nine rooms, all with shower or bath, wc and telephone; you'll pay €47 for a double with bath. Half board costs from €38 per day per person; there are special rates for children. The owner is a rock 'n' roll fan, as the photos of Gene Vincent and Buddy Holly testify. Free coffee.

VALTIN (LE)   88230 (13KM NE)

☎ |●| AUBERGE DU VAL JOLI**

12 bis le Village (Centre); follow the signs to Saint-Dié out of Géradmer, turn right onto the D23 in the direction

of Colmar, then left at Zonrupt over the mountain road to Le Valtin.

☎ 03.29.60.91.37 ➡ 03.29.60.81.73

Closed Sun evening; Mon except for public holidays; 8–16 Jan; 19–27 March; 3–16 June. **TV**. **Car park**.

A superb place in one of the region's prettiest villages, set near pine forests and mountains. This is a real old-fashioned inn, with a warm and friendly atmosphere. The rooms vary from old and simple with shower/wc to modern and smart with balconies that look onto the mountains; if you want a view, ask for numbers 17–20. Doubles go for €23–43, but there is renovation work planned, and prices are expected to rise. Half board is compulsory during the school holidays. The dining rooms vary, too: one of them is wonderfully rustic, with a superb ceiling, while the other is huge and modern with enormous windows. In each you can eat good cooking and traditional local dishes. There's a weekday menu at €14, with others up to €47, listing dishes such as *pâté lorrain* (a sort of pie filled with pork mince), trout *au bleu* with butter sauce, smoked trout with a sorrel sauce, *blanc de sautret* (chicken in cream and Riesling sauce), *choucroute garnie*, and a fairly strong Münster cheese and bilberry tart.

HOUDELAINCOURT   55130

🏃 🛏 |O| L'AUBERGE DU PÈRE LOUIS**

☎ 03.29.89.64.14 ➡ 03.29.89.78.84
Closed Sun evening, Mon and Sept. **TV**. **Car park**.

Service till 2pm and 9pm. For anyone who likes good food, this is one of *the* places to eat in the region. The cooking is innovative and exciting, with dishes like roast pike-perch with *beurre rouge*, pan-fried *foie gras* with mirabelle plums, veal kidneys wich cream sauce and home-made sorbets. Menus start at €18, culminating in the truffle menu at €53. There are six quiet, pleasant rooms with shower/wc, which go for €38. 10% discount on the room rate.

LONGUYON   54260

🛏 |O| HÔTEL DE LA GARE–RESTAURANT LA TABLE DE NAPO*

2 rue de la Gare; it's next to the train station.
☎ 03.82.26.50.85 ➡ 03.82.39.21.33
Closed Fri evening except July–Aug; first fortnight in March, and three weeks in Sept. **Car park**.

The good-natured owner creates a family atmosphere in her establishment. It feels like an old guest house with pretty pieces of furni-

ture and bright, comfortable rooms; a double will cost €40 with shower/wc. The entrance to the hotel is on the station platform, and some rooms look over the tracks – sadly, the double glazing doesn't cut out all the noise. If you're worried about not sleeping well, ask for a room looking onto the street. The restaurant serves dishes cooked with fresh market produce, listed on menus from €11–40.

🛏 |O| HÔTEL DE LORRAINE – RESTAURANT LE MAS**

pl. de la Gare.
☎ 03.82.26.50.07 ➡ 03.82.39.26.09
e mas.lorraine@wanadoo.fr
Closed Mon, Oct–June. **TV**. **Pay garage**.

This *belle époque* hotel has an attractive façade and a lovely lounge boasting old beams and ceiling mouldings. The rooms, however, are completely different – though bright, they lack the style of the common areas. Doubles with shower/wc or bath cost €50. In the winter there's a blaze in the open fireplace and in summer they open up the terrace and plant troughs of flowers. The restaurant, with menus at €18 (weekdays) and €19, has a good reputation, but sadly, the welcome can be frosty.

LONGWY   54400

🛏 |O| HÔTEL DU NORD**

pl. Darche; it's right in the middle of the upper town.
☎ 03.82.23.40.81 ➡ 03.82.23.17.73
Restaurant closed Sun. **TV**. **Car park**.

Many towns in France have a bar-hotel like this, but this one has particular charm because of its unique location on the impressive square. The modern rooms are clean and quiet; they cost €43–46 with shower/wc or bath. The brasserie offers traditional dishes with set menus starting at €19.

COSNES ET ROMAIN   54400 (5KM W)

|O| LE TRAIN BLEU

How to get there: from Longwy-Haut, take the N18 in the direction of Longuyon for 4km, turn right at the sign.
☎ 03.82.23.98.09
Closed Sun evening, Mon, and Sat lunchtimes.

They've joined two railway carriages together to create this attractive dining room, and you have to push a button to open the door. Inside, the décor is plush and the cooking is great: try the *cassolette* of sweetbreads and girolles, or sole fillets stuffed with smoked salmon. Menus offer something for every budget, starting with the lunchtime menu at €12 and ranging up to €35. It's particularly popular at weekends.

🧍🍴 AUBERGE DES TROIS CANARDS

69 rue de la Lorraine-Romain; take the D43 in the direction of Cosnes-et-Romain.
☎ 03.82.24.35.36 ➡ 03.82.25.66.40
Closed Mon; Thurs and Sun evenings; a fortnight in the Feb school holidays, and a fortnight Aug/Sept. **Car park**.

The Virginia creeper has smothered this house to the point of camouflage – it's so dense that you can't even see the walls let alone the sign. There's a warm, rustic feel to the place, and they serve good country food like monkfish with tarragon sauce, *foie gras*, house *confit*, roast leg of duck *Henri IV* and quails with mirabelle plums. Menus start at €18, or you'll spend about €26 *à la carte*. On public holidays the prix fixe menu is too expensive to justify. Free Kir or Aligoté.

LUNÉVILLE   54300

🏨 HÔTEL DES PAGES***

5 quai des Petits-Bosquets; it's across the river from the château.
☎ 03.83.74.11.42 ➡ 03.83.73.46.63
TV. Car park.

This quiet hotel is enclosed by a large courtyard, not far from the river. The rooms that have been refurbished now have a contemporary "design" feel and modern facilities; the décor is subtle and unusual. Double rooms €49.

🧍🍴 MARIE LESZCZYNSKA

30 rue de Lorraine (Centre); it's behind the château.
☎ 03.83.73.11.85
Closed Sun evening and Mon.

This restaurant, named after the wife of King Louis XV, offers a friendly welcome and elegant cuisine: try the pan-fried duck *foie gras* with spced bread or the pork *filet mignon* in beer sauce, listed on menus from €13–35. The pretty dining room is refined and understated, with an intimate setting, and there's a pleasant terrace in a pedestrianized street – lovely when the sun shines. Free coffee.

MANDEREN   57480

🏨🍴 LE RELAIS DU CHÂTEAU MENSBERG**

15 rue du Château; it's on the D64.
☎ 03.82.83.73.16 ➡ 03.82.83.23.37

Closed 1–20 Jan. **TV. Disabled access. Garden. Lock-up garage**.

The château of Mensberg – known as the "Château de Malbrouck" – was built in the 7th century and, according to legend, rebuilt in the fifteenth with the help of the devil. Today the impressive building, which dominates the village, offers fifteen comfortable, pretty double rooms with shower/wc for €53. There's an extremely handsome dining room where you can enjoy a number of carefully prepared specialities that change with the seasons; menus €14–40.

METZ   57000

SEE MAP OVERLEAF

🧍🏨 HÔTEL MODERNE**

1 rue Lafayette. Off map **B3-4**
☎ 03.87.66.57.33 ➡ 03.87.55.98.59
✉ hotelmoderne@wanadoo.fr
TV. Private car park.

A classic station hotel with a predominantly business clientele. Rooms are modern and functional but not impersonal; the ones at the back are the quietest, while those with two double beds, like number 7, are terrific value. You'll pay €26 for a double with washing facilities or €41–49 for a room with bath. The owner is a charming woman with a ready smile. 25% discount and free breakfast at the weekend.

🧍🏨 HÔTEL LA PERGOLA**

13 route de Plappeville. Off map **A1-2**
☎ 03.87.32.52.94 ➡ 03.87.31.41.60
TV. Garden. Car park.

The hotel, with a 1950's-look façade, is some way from the centre and its sign is not very obvious. It's worth the effort of getting there, though; rooms, which are all furnished differently, feature brass beds and period furniture, and you are woken by the birds singing in the wonderful garden. Rooms up in the eaves have sloping ceilings, and some of the bathrooms are as big as the rooms themselves. Doubles €34–41. Ask for one overlooking the garden, where afternoon tea is served under the trees. 10% discount.

🏨 HÔTEL DU CENTRE**

14 rue du Pont-des-Loges. **MAP B2-8**
☎ 03.87.36.06.93 ➡ 03.87.75.60.65
✉ hotel-du-centre-metz@wanadoo.fr
TV. Pay garage.

Ideally located on a pedestrianized street and

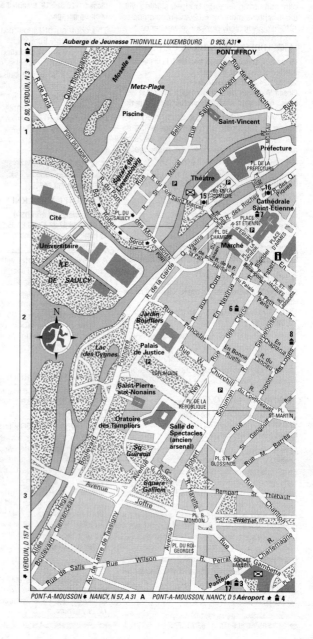

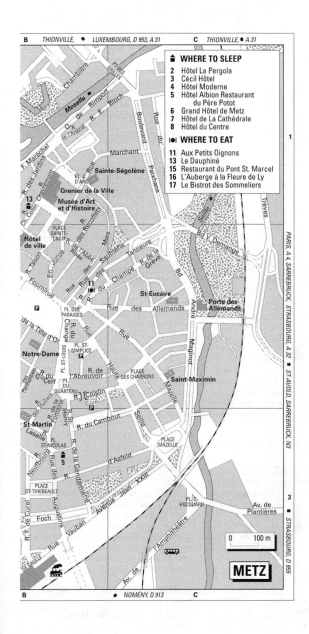

WHERE TO SLEEP

2 Hôtel La Pergola
3 Cécil Hôtel
4 Hôtel Moderne
5 Hôtel Albion Restaurant
   du Père Potot
6 Grand Hôtel de Metz
7 Hôtel de La Cathédrale
8 Hôtel du Centre

WHERE TO EAT

11 Aux Petits Oignons
13 Le Dauphiné
15 Restaurant du Pont St. Marcel
16 L'Auberge à la Fleure de Ly
17 Le Bistrot des Sommeliers

– hardly surprisingly, given the name – in the centre of the town. An old wooden staircase (no lift) takes you to the attractively arranged, charmiing rooms; those on the top floor, under the roof, have nice sloping ceilings. Doubles with shower/wc €40. The breads and pastries served at breakfast are cooked on the premises.

🐾 🛏 CÉCIL HÔTEL**

14 rue Pasteur. MAP B3-3
☎ 03.87.66.66.13 ➥ 03.87.56.96.02
📧 cecil-hotel@wanadoo.fr
Closed 26 Dec–2 Jan. TV. Disabled access. Pay garage.

The hotel is in a handsome early 20th-century building between the station and the centre. Prices for the modern and well-equipped – if slightly soulless – rooms, decorated in a 70s style, range from €49 for a double with shower/wc to €50 with bath. Free use of garage.

🐾 🛏 ﮩ﮳ HÔTEL ALBION – RESTAURANT DU PÈRE POTOT**

8 rue du Père-Potot. MAP B3-5
☎ 03.87.36.55.56 ➥ 03.87.36.39.80
📧 albionmetz@online.fr
TV. Disabled access. Pay car park.

Centrally located but looking a bit out of place in this particular neighbourhood, this hotel offers freshly refurbished rooms. They're all alike but not unpleasant, with TV and video, phone and mini-bar; doubles with shower/wc or bath go for €50. Note that the odd-numbered ones look onto the courtyard of an old abbey. The restaurant is good, too, with a weekday menu for €11 and others from €12–21. Free apéritif or free breakfast.

🐾 🛏 GRAND HÔTEL DE METZ**

3 rue des Clercs. MAP B2-6
☎ 03.87.36.16.33 ➥ 03.87.74.17.04
TV. Lock-up car park.

This hotel, in a pedestrianized street in the old part of town, boasts an ultra-modern entrance with a superb staircase. The clean, comfortable rooms are decorated in pastels and flower-patterned fabrics, and overlook the inner courtyard; doubles €53 with shower/wc or €69 with bath. 10% discount Fri–Sun.

🛏 HÔTEL DE LA CATHÉDRALE***

25 pl. de la Chambre. MAP B1-7
☎ 03.87.30.27.25
📧 hotel-cathedrale-metz@wanadoo.fr
TV. Disabled access. Garden.

Chateaubriand and Madame de Staël stayed in this coaching inn, which was built in 1627, and various other famous people have stayed here since. Monsieur Hocine restored the building himself and Madame undertook to decorate it – they've done it beautifully, and the period beams, iron work, casements and interior courtyard are all amazing. The rooms, too, are full of character and charm; each is decorated differently, but they're all bright with elegant fittings, and some have a view of the cathedral. Doubles €61–64 with shower/wc or €69 with bath. Booking strongly advised.

ﮩ﮳ AUX PETITS OIGNONS

5 rue du Champé (Centre). MAP B2-11
☎ 03.87.18.91.33
Closed Sun.

In a small street just off the centre, this restaurant has an intimate dining room that's perfect for a dinner for two. The simple, well-prepared dishes come from various regions in France: Lorraine of course, but also Provence and the Southwest. Menus go for €10 (lunchtime only) then €15–30. You'll spend more than that *à la carte*. It's best to book.

🐾 ﮩ﮳ RESTAURANT LE DAUPHINÉ

8 rue du Chanoine-Collin. MAP B1-13
☎ 03.87.36.03.04
Closed evenings except Fri–Sat, Sun, and Aug.

An unpretentious restaurant and tearoom with exposed beams. There's a €12 menu (not Sun), and others from €16–19, including a *menu campagnard*. Simple cooking but generous helpings: paella to order, calf's head and *quiche Lorraine*. The service is a bit casual. Free coffee.

ﮩ﮳ LE BISTROT DES SOMMELIERS

10 rue Pasteur. MAP B3-17
☎ 03.87.63.40.20
Closed Sat lunchtime, Sun.

Youthful, good-value place with leatherette-covered benches and wine-bottle candlesticks. There's an interesting selection of wines to drink, too, by the glass or the jug, and traditional dishes that are as simple as they are tasty. The single menu goes for €13, while if you eat *à la carte* (suggestions of the day are scribbled on the slate) you'll spend about €23. Terrace in summer.

🐾 ﮩ﮳ RESTAURANT DU PONT SAINT MARCEL

1 rue du Pont Saint Marcel. MAP A1-15
☎ 03.87.30.12.29

Disabled access. Car park.

This seventeenth-century building has a terrific location on the banks of the Moselle, with a breathtaking view of the cathedral and the town; there's no other place like it in Metz. The restaurant is decorated with frescoes portraying old city scenes, and the dining staff are dressed in period costume. Menus, €15 and €26, list delicious regional dishes based on recipes from a nineteenth-century collection: suckling pig in aspic, carp with white wine, *potée lorraine* and eel *en matelote* in Toul wine sauce. To accompany your meal, try one of the excellent Moselle or Lorraine wines. There's a lovely terrace too, with pots overflowing with flowers. Free apéritif.

|●| L'AUBERGE À LA FLEURE DE LY

5 rue des Piques. **MAP B1-16**
☎ 03.87.36.64.51
Closed Sat lunchtime, Sun and a fortnight in Aug.

Suzy welcomes you with her bright smile, reeling off the dishes of the day as she leads you to your table. You can go into the cellar to select your own wine from the new vintages and buy the odd bottle to take away, too. Try the *foie gras* in a cloth or the snail *matelotte*. Weekday menu €18, then others €26–35.

SAINT-JULIEN-LÈS-METZ   57070 (3KM NE)

⅔|●| RESTAURANT DU FORT SAINT-JULIEN

Route de Thionville; it's in the restored part of the fort right in the middle of the wood.
☎ 03.87.75.71.16
Closed Wed; Sun evening; 1–10 Jan, and 24 Jul–10 Aug. **Garden. Car park.**

The town has been traded between France and Germany several times since 1870, so it has a sort of dual nationality. You'll be welcomed by Coco, the owner's mynah bird, who might whistle his version of *The Marseillaise* or *Bridge over the River Kwai*. The place is impressively decorated to resemble a cellar and has the kind of relaxed atmosphere that makes you want to get your friends together for a blow-out. They serve substantial dishes like black pudding, *quiche lorraine* or *choucroute* with Riesling. Weekday menu €12 with others up to €21, or around €20 *à la carte*. Free *Kir lorrain*.

WOIPPY   57140 (4KM N)

⅔|●| L'AUBERGE BELLES FONTAINES

51 route de Thionville; take the Woippy exit on the A31.

☎ and ➡ 03.87.31.99.46
Closed Sun evening; Mon and Tues evenings; the last week in July; the first three weeks in Aug.
Disabled access. Garden. Car park.

A restful inn just minutes from the centre of Metz. It's decorated in classical fashion in the same shades of green as the trees in the park, and there's a terrace. Customers are mainly regulars. Substantial menus €16–42. Free apéritif.

GORZE   57680 (20KM SW)

⅔ ⛫ |●| HOSTELLERIE DU LION D'OR**

105 rue du Commerce (Centre); take the Fey exit on the A31.
☎ 03.87.52.00.90 ➡ 03.87.52.09.62
Closed Sun evening and Mon. **Disabled access. TV. Garden.**

You'll find this establishment in the narrow main road of this sleepy town. Once a post house, it still has character and charm, with hand-made floor tiles, timbered walls, a small interior pond, and a huge bay window that lets lots of light into the restaurant. All in all, it's an appropriate setting for the traditional cuisine; the €15 menu (weekdays, hotel guests only) and those from €21–35 list such dishes as calf's head, trout *au bleu*, and house *foie gras*. It's silver service, but you don't need to dress formally. The peace is sometimes shattered by the low-flying military jets, but the soundproofing does a pretty good job of cutting down the noise. Doubles with shower/wc go for €30, or €46 with bath. Free apéritif.

MONTENACH   57480

⛫ |●| HÔTEL-RESTAURANT AU VAL SIERCKOIS

3 pl. de la Mairie.
☎ 03.82.83.85.20 ➡ 03.82.83.61.91
Closed Mon evening, Tues and 17 July–5 Aug. **TV. Car park.**

Among the valleys and woods of northern Moselle, where France meets Luxembourg and Germany, this delightful, friendly inn is the ideal place to recharge your batteries. You'll be woken by birdsong and you can go for long walks in the forest. The cooking is unpretentious with menus of Lorraine specialities for €14–27. This is hunting country, so try the haunch of venison *Grand Veneur*. They have seven pretty rooms, €30 with shower or €41 with bath.

|●| L'AUBERGE DE LA KLAUSS

1 rue de Kirschnaumen; take the D956.
☎ 03.82.83.72.38
Closed Mon and 24 Dec–7 Jan. **Disabled access**.
Garden. **Car park**.

Friendly place serving quality cooking prepared on the spot using fresh ingredients. You can eat in one of four dining rooms; one is decorated with clocks and old time pieces and another looks like a hunting lodge. The lunch menu, €18, lists Lorraine specialities, but the others, up to €43, are considerably more substantial. The owner raises pigs and ducks – you can visit his farm and buy homemade treats – and the game comes from the nearby forest. There's an excellent wine cellar, too.

MONTMÉDY   55600

● |●| HÔTEL-RESTAURANT LE MÂDY**

8 pl. Raymond-Poincaré; it's in the main square.
☎ 03.29.80.10.87 ➡ 03.29.80.02.40
e noel.l@wanadoo.fr
Closed Sun evening, Mon except on public holidays and in summer, and Jan. **TV**. **Car park**.

Functional, characterless double rooms with bath cost €38 here, and the restaurant serves generous helpings of good regional dishes. Plump for specialities such as duck breast with raspberries, calf's head *vinaigrette*, or snails *en meurette* with red Toul wine sauce. There's a weekday menu at €12 and others from €19–34. Everything is done in the classic style, from the welcome and the décor to the background music and the cuisine.

NANCY   54000

SEE MAP OPPOSTIE

🛁 ● HÔTEL CARNOT**

2 cours Léopold. **MAP A2-2**
☎ 03.83.36.59.58 ➡ 03.83.37.00.19
TV.

The façade of this hotel had to be rebuilt after the war and is somewhat charmless, but the rooms are decent and the prices attractive; double with shower €24, €29–40 with a bath. Numbers 25 and 34 are the best: bigger, brighter and quieter than the others. You'll need to book in April, when there is a country fair in the square. Free welcome drink.

● GRAND HÔTEL DE LA POSTE**

56 pl. Monseigneur-Ruch. **MAP B2-5**

☎ 03.83.32.11.52 ➡ 03.83.37.58.74
TV.

This aged building, once a convent, offers 44 regularly redecorated rooms; some of them have pretty wardrobes made locally by Majorelle. Doubles with basin for €28, or €33–40 with bath. It's extremely good value for money when you consider that Place Stanislas is so close, and you'll be wakened by the cathedral bells.

● HÔTEL LE STANISLAS**

22 rue Saint-Catherine.
☎ 03.83.37.23.88 ➡ 03.83.32.31.02
TV.

The street is very busy, but has the advantage of being near the place Stanislas, and the double glazing efficiently stifles the noise outside. Don't be put off by the ordinary look of the hotel, either; rooms are bright and spacions with well-designed bathrooms with separate wc. Doubles with shower/wc go for €37–45.

🛁 ● HÔTEL LE JEAN-JAURÈS**

14 bd. Jean-Jaurès. **Off map A3-4**
☎ 03.83.27.74.14 ➡ 03.83.90.20.94
e jjaures.hotel@wanadoo.fr
TV. **Garden**. **Pay garage**.

This place was built as a craftsman's house and has retained a pleasant old-fashioned atmosphere enhanced by the mouldings and tapestries. The rooms over the street have been soundproofed, but you may still prefer the quieter ones over the garden. Whichever you choose, be prepared for a bit of exercise – there are four floors here and no lift. Double rooms with shower/wc cost €40 and you'll get a hospitable welcome from the young, energetic owner. 10% discount.

● HÔTEL DE GUISE**

18 rue de Guise. **MAP A1-3**
☎ 03.83.32.24.68 ➡ 03.83.35.75.63
Closed 9–24 Aug and 20 Dec–2 Jan. **TV**. **Pay car park**.

The Countess of Bressey used to live in this mansion in the heart of the old Nancy, and it has a romantic atmosphere reminiscent of a Dumas novel. A magnificent monumental eighteenth-century staircase leads to the rooms, some of which have monumental fireplaces and impressive beamed ceilings. Doubles with shower/wc or bath go for €46 and there are some small suites for €69. Great value.

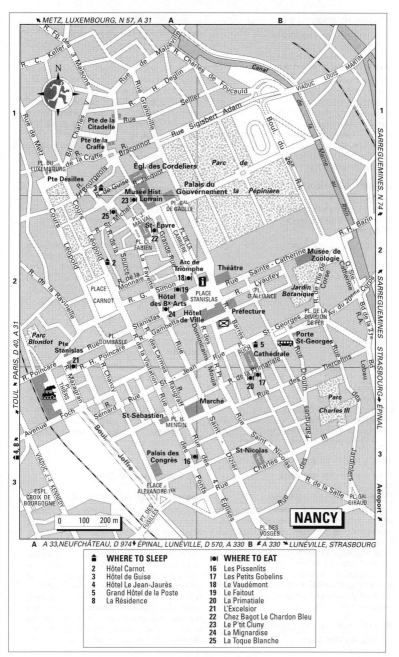

NANCY

A A 33, NEUFCHÂTEAU, D 974 ↓ ÉPINAL, LUNÉVILLE, D 570, A 330 **B** ↙ A 330 ↘ LUNÉVILLE, STRASBOURG

	WHERE TO SLEEP		**WHERE TO EAT**
2	Hôtel Carnot	16	Les Pissenlits
3	Hôtel de Guise	17	Les Petits Gobelins
4	Hôtel Le Jean-Jaurès	18	Le Vaudémont
5	Grand Hôtel de la Poste	19	Le Faitout
8	La Résidence	20	La Primatiale
		21	L'Excelsior
		22	Chez Bagot Le Chardon Bleu
		23	Le P'tit Cluny
		24	La Mignardise
		25	La Toque Blanche

♠ HÔTEL LA RÉSIDENCE***

30 bd. Jean-Jaurès. **Off map A3-8**
☎ 03.83.40.33.56 ➡ 03.83.90.16.28
e hotel.la.residence.nancy@wanadoo.fr
Closed 31 Dec and 1 Jan. **TV**. **Pay car park**.

The fact that you're greeted by someone in a station master's uniform gives you a clue about the owner's obsession. The hotel has been cleverly decorated to continue the theme – train magazines are scattered about all over the place and even the bedrooms haven't escaped. Doubles with shower/wc or bath €52–60. No restaurant, but you can order a meal on a tray.

♠ HÔTEL CRYSTAL***

5 rue Chanzy.
☎ 03.83.17.54.00 ➡ 03.83.17.54.30
e hotelcrystal.nancy@wanadoo.fr
TV. **Pay car park**.

Conviently located near the station with small, cosy rooms that are very comfortable and tastefully decorated. The quality beds and linen will ensure you have a good night's sleep. Doubles €73–99.

|●| LE VAUDÉMONT

4 pl. Vaudémont. **MAP A2-18**
☎ 03.83.37.05.70
Closed Mon and a fortnight in Oct.

Service noon–11pm. You'll get value for money in this cosy restaurant. Simple, tasty, cooking is listed on menus from €12–20, whild during the week the four-course lunch *formule*, €8, gets you a starter, a main course such as chicken in Riesling or ham with *choucroute*, cheese plus dessert. They have one of the best terraces in town, opening onto the pretty square.

|●| LES PETITS GOBELINS

18 rue de la Primatiale. **MAP B3-17**
☎ 03.83.35.49.03
Closed Sun, Mon and a fortnight in Aug.

A gourmet restaurant in a lovely building with an old, gleaming parquet floor. There's an assortment of furniture and collectables about the place and paintings and photos by local artists on the walls. Try the crisp *mille-feuille* of smoked salmon, the fillet of turbot with orange, and follow with the baked Alaska with sour cherries. At weekday lunchtimes there's a €13 *retour du marché* menu; others range from €16–34.

|●| CHEZ BAGOT – LE CHARDON BLEU

45 Grande-Rue. **MAP A2-22**

☎ 03.83.37.42.43 **e** chez.bagot@wanadoo.fr
Closed Sun evening, Mon, and three weeks in Aug.

It's a fair way from the shores of Brittany to the streets of Nancy, but that doesn't deter Breton Patrick Bagot from offering his customers authentic fish and shellfish from back home. He also serves quail in white pudding, unusual lamb *charcuterie* and *andouillette* of sole and crayfish. The elegant dining room is brilliantly light and the décor has a maritime feel to it. Weekday lunch menu at €13 and others at €21–30; you'll spend around €30 *à la carte*, which is a bit expensive.

|●| LA MIGNARDISE

28 rue Stanislas. **MAP A2-24**
☎ 03.83.32.20.22 ➡ 03.83.32.19.20
Closed Sun evening; Mon; Wed evening; a week in Jan; three weeks mid-July/Aug, and a week at All Saints.

Just round the corner from the place Stanislas, this salmon-coloured restaurant has just a few tables. The menus, €14 at lunchtime, and €21–40, list refined cuisine such as pike-perch, snails and frogs' legs; dishes change with the season. There's a shady terrace for sunny days. Efficient, unobtrusive service.

|●| RESTAURANT LA PRIMATIALE

14 rue de la Primatiale. **MAP B3-20**
☎ 03.83.30.44.03.
Closed Sat lunchtime, Sun and Christmas.

On a pedestrianized street and opposite *L'Échanson*, a wine bar where you can stop for an apéritif, this is a friendly, appealing restaurant. The cooking is original, light and delicate, and they've designed a really attractive wine list with a huge selection by the glass. There's an agreeable terrace on the street. Menus from €15.

|●| LE FAITOUT

7 rue Gustave-Simon. **MAP A2-19**
☎ 03.83.35.36.52
Closed a week in Jan and a week in Sept.

Le Faitout is in a pretty street that the tourists tend to ignore, even though it's just a couple of streets from place Stanislas. The red, black and white décor looks rather unappealing but the proprietress gives you a jovial welcome and the cooking is simple and generous. You'll usually find a few unexpected dishes on the menus: try the *terrine* of trout with cucumber, the leg of lamb in a herb crust, the seafood *pot-au-feu* and the banana and chocolate tart which is the house speciality. Menus from €15, with one designed specifically for vegetarians.

|●| LA TOQUE BLANCHE

1 rue Monsieur Trouille. **MAP A2-25**
☎ 03.83.30.17.20 ➡ 03.83.32.60.24
Closed Sun evening; Mon; the first week in Jan; Feb
school holidays; a fortnight July–Aug.

A refined place with a fresh-feeling, though
not desperately original, dining room and
some of the best cooking in town. It's popular locally for the interesting, good-value
lunch menu, €15, but they have a range of
others from €20–49 – try the ravioli with
frogs' legs and cheese. À la carte features
delicious specialities like pancake of pig's
trotters with potatoes, and the excellent wine
list offers a carefully chosen selection at fair
prices. This is just the place for a celebration.

|●| LES PISSENLITS

25 [bis] rue des Ponts. **MAP A3-16**
☎ 03.83.37.43.97 ➡ 03.83.35.72.49
Closed Sun and Mon. **Disabled access**.

Les Pissenlits is the younger sibling of La
Table des Mengi next door and the cooking is
just as good. It's a good-looking place, with
marble tables in the large dining room and a
handsome dresser showing off a collection of
Longwy porcelain. As for the food, they do
the most wonderful pastry cases with snails
and mushrooms, or try the slivers of duck in
honey and spices, fish fillets à la bouillabaisse, or the memorable calf's head
gribiche. The dish of the day costs €8, while
the menus range form €16–20. Danièle Men-
gin, one of France's best sommeliers, is
responsible for the quite exceptional cellar
and there is always a specially chosen selection of splendid wines available by the glass
at €1–2. Extremely popular and often full.

|●| RESTAURANT L'EXCELSIOR

50 rue Henri-Poincaré. **MAP A2/3-21**
☎ 03.83.35.24.57
Closed Christmas Eve dinner.

Service 8am–12.30am (11pm on Sun). An
institution in Nancy, known as the "*Excel*",
this is something of a historic monument with
its Art Nouveau décor; all the greatest names
of the Nancy School are represented, with
mahogany furniture by Majorelle and stained
glass by Gruber. The cooking and service are
in the best brasserie style, with menus starting at €20. Don't miss the fresh oysters,
Strasbourg choucroute or the pike-perch
with snails.

|●| LE P'TIT CLUNY**

97–99 Grand-Rue. **MAP A1/2-23**

☎ 03.83.32.85.94
Closed Sun and Mon.

A typical rustic Alsace wine cellar with walls of
rough-hewn stone and tankards and other
drinking utensils suspended from the ceiling.
Among the local specialities you should try
the tasty flammeküche – which are enough to
satisfy a big appetite. Standards are high, as
you will find if you order the choucroute, the
barbecued suckling pig or the calf's head. À
la carte you'll spend around €23.

NEUFCHÂTEAU   88300

🎋 🏠 |●| LE RIALTO**

67 rue de France (Centre).
☎ 03.29.06.09.40 ➡ 03.29.94.38.51
Closed Sun except July–Aug. **TV**. **Car park**.

You'll get a pleasant welcome from the
young proprietors of this long-standing hotel
on the edge of the historic old town. It's been
fully renovated and rooms are clean; those
overlooking the river are particularly nice.
Doubles cost €34 with shower/wc. Good
cooking in the restaurant – nothing fancy –
with a €9 lunch menu and others at €14 and
€20. There's a nice terrace open on sunny
days. Free house apéritif.

🏠 |●| LE SAINT-CHRISTOPHE**

1 av. de la Grande-Fontaine (Centre).
☎ 03.29.94.68.71 ➡ 03.29.06.02.09
e saint-christophe@relais-sud.champagne.com
TV.

Rooms here are on the small side but comfortable nonetheless; doubles range from
€48–53. Go for one that overlooks the River
Mouzon or the Saint Christophe church,
which is illuminated at night. The breakfast is
very good and there's lots of it. Along with a
brasserie, there's a classic restaurant with
wood panelling typical of this leafy region.
Very decent cooking; menus €11–39.

🎋 |●| RESTAURANT LE ROMAIN

74 av. Kennedy (West); it's on the Chaumont road, as
you leave town.
☎ and ➡ 03.29.06.18.80
Closed Sun evening; Mon; the Feb school holidays, and
25 Aug–8 Sept. **Car park**.

It's the décor rather than the food which
recalls ancient Rome. The chef shows considerable flair in his approach to traditional
dishes. Cooking times are judged perfectly
and he has an intuition for balancing flavours
– you'll feel that you're tasting standard dish-

es for the first time. Try the pig's trotters with potatoes and mushrooms, the pan-fried pike-perch with garlic cream, or saddle of rabbit with mirabelle plums. There's a weekday lunch menu for €12 and others from €19–30, listing dishes such as such as *terrine* of guinea fowl with onion marmalade, fillet of *rascasse* (scorpion fish) with fennel seeds, and beef skirt with shallots. You can eat on the terrace in summer. Great wine list with a few wines by the glass. Free coffee.

PLOMBIÈRES-LES-BAINS   88370

⚲ ☎ |●| HÔTEL DE LA FONTAINE STANISLAS**

Fontaine Stanislas – Granges de Plombières; it's 4km north of Plombières on the route d'Épinal via Xertigny.
☎ 03.29.66.01.53 ➥ 03.29.30.04.31
Closed 15 Oct–1 April. **TV. Garden. Car park**.

The same family has owned this hotel for four generations. It's miles out in the forest overlooking the valley, with a lovely terraced garden and footpaths through the woods. Bedrooms are regularly decorated and have an old-style charm; doubles go for €35 with shower, €45 with shower/wc and €49 with bath. Numbers 2, 3 and 11 have their own terrace while 18 and 19 have a corner sitting area. Half board from €45. There's a fantastic view from the restaurant, where they're strong on traditional cuisine and regional dishes: *chiffonade* of smoked salmon with poached egg, turbot with leek *fondue*, duck fillet with bitter cherries, *andouille* from Val d'Ajol, braised trout with sorrel, kirsch *soufflé*, and home-made ice-creams. Menus €15–35. Free coffee.

PONT-À-MOUSSON   54700

⚲ ☎ HÔTEL BAGATELLE***

47–49 rue Gambetta; you'll find it as you enter the town from the east.
☎ 03.83.81.03.64 ➥ 03.83.81.12.63
Closed Christmas to New Year. **TV. Pay car park**.

This modern hotel is brilliantly located near the abbey and the banks of the Moselle. It's a bit mournful, but the rooms are functional; a double with en-suite bathroom will cost €49–55. Free use of car park.

REMIREMONT   88200

⚲ ☎ HÔTEL DU CHEVAL DE BRONZE**

59 rue Charles-de-Gaulle (Centre).

☎ 03.29.62.52.24 ➥ 03.29.62.34.90
TV. Pay car park.

Once a coaching inn, this old hotel, which you enter under the arcade in the centre of town, has retained a lot of its charm. The clean rooms are quiet and the ones overlooking the road have all been soundproofed. Others look over the flowery courtyard. Doubles with shower or bath, €25–50. 10% discount for a three-night stay and free use of car park.

|●| RESTAURANT LE CLOS HEURTEBISE

13 chemin des Capucins (South); from the town centre go down rue Charles-de-Gaulle; after the big crossroads turn right and follow the signs.
☎ 03.29.62.08.04
Closed Wed and Sun evenings and 8–22 Jan. **Garden. Car park**.

This rather stylish restaurant stands at the edge of a wood in the hills that circle the town. The décor is chic and classically provincial and the service is impeccable. You'll eat excellent cuisine using fresh ingredients; try house specialities such as pan-fried *foie gras* with blueberries, pigeon, twice-cooked bream and frogs' legs in season. There's a trolley of wicked desserts, too. The €16 menu is served during the week and on Saturday lunchtimes; others range from €24–30. The wine list will delight connoisseurs. In summer you can eat outdoors.

ST-ÉTIENNE-LES-REMIREMONT   88200 (2KM)

☎ |●| LE CHALET BLANC**

From Remiremont, take the road in the direction of Bresse; it's next to the Centre Leclerc (Northwest).
☎ 03.29.26.11.80
Closed Sat lunchtime, Sun evening, Mon, the Feb school holidays and a fortnight in Aug. **TV. Car park**.

Despite its grim surroundings, with the Leclerc centre and a motorway to contend with, the restaurant serves finely prepared food on excellent-value menus (€18–52) and *à la carte*; the pollack fillet with shrimp crayfish and the fruit *au gratin* are very good indeed. If you don't want to face the motorway to get back into town after a good dinner, they have a few comfortable rooms for €53.

ROUVROIS-SUR-OTHAIN   55230

|●| LA MARMITE

☎ 03.28.85.90.79
Closed Sun evening; Mon; Tues in winter; 2–10 Jan,

and 19–25 Aug.

This bourgeois gastronomic restaurant is typical of its type; good quality ingredients are cooked to perfection and servings are very generous. There's an excellent welcome and you get good value for money. There's a weekday menu for €21 and others up to €41.

SAINT-AVOLD 57500

⚕ ≜ I●I HÔTEL-RESTAURANT DE PARIS

45 rue Hirschaue (Centre).
☎ 03.87.92.19.52 ➡ 03.87.92.94.32
Hotel closed Mon mornings. **Restaurant closed** Sat and Sun evenings. **TV**.

In the sixteenth century, this building belonged to the counts of Créhange, who were Protestants. They built a small chapel at the back of the inner courtyard where they could practise their religion without hindrance. That courtyard is now the dining room and the chapel, now an art gallery, retains its sculpted keystones and a fine vaulted ceiling. The restaurant's not that great, with menus from €11–38, but the rooms are decent and freshly refurbished. Doubles with shower/wc or bath go for €47. Free coffee and 10% discount on the room rate at weekends.

SAINT-DIÉ 88100

⚕ ≜ HÔTEL DES VOSGES**

53–57 rue Thiers (Centre); it's near the cathedral.
☎ 03.29.56.16.21 ➡ 03.29.55.48.71
TV. **Disabled access**. **Pay garage**.

A welcoming, well-managed hotel with seventeen rooms with different facilities at various prices. Doubles with shower €27 or €38–46 with shower/wc. The ones overlooking the road are noisy. It's open 24 hours – they have a night porter – which is convenient for late arrivals. No restaurant. 10% discount and free use of garage.

⚕ ≜ HÔTEL DE FRANCE**

1 rue Dauphine (Centre); it's next to the post office.
☎ 03.29.56.32.61 ➡ 03.29.56.01.09
Closed Sun. **TV**.

A well-located hotel with a courtyard. The rooms that look out onto it – numbers 3, 6 and 9 – are particularly quiet and also have a view of the cathedral. Don't be put off by the wallpaper in the staircase; most of the rooms

have been renovated. They go for €37 with shower/wc. 10% discount.

⚕ I●I RESTAURANT EUROPE

41 rue des Trois-Villes (Northwest).
☎ 03.29.56.32.03
Closed Sun evening; Mon; a fortnight in mid-Jan, and end July/three weeks in Aug.

In a dining room decorated fairly conventionally in shades of salmon and blue, the nice owner here offers a selection of dishes from different culinary traditions: pasta, couscous, a steak *tartare* that they shred with a knife rather than a mincer, and a few Balkan specialities including goulash. The food is invariably good and there are prices to suit all pockets. Set weekday lunch menu €11, then €14–21. Free coffee.

PETITE FOSSE (LA) 88490 (17KM NE)

⚕ ≜ I●I AUBERGE DU SPITZEMBERG**

2 av. Spitzemberg; when driving towards Strasbourg, take the Provenchères-sur-Faure exit, turn left and go through La Petite-Foss up to the Col d'Hermampaire, turn left and go on about 1km to the end of the road.
☎ 03.29.51.20.46 ➡ 03.29.51.10.12
Closed Tues and Jan. **TV**. **Garden**. **Lock-up garage**.

A lovely inn in an isolated spot in the Vosges forest where you can relax in peace and quiet. Comfortable double rooms cost €43–47 with shower/wc or bath. The dining room is very attractive, and they serve traditional cooking; try the trout in white Alsace wine, the Münster cheese flambéed in Marc or in cumin-flavoured alcohol, and, for dessert, the bilberry soup. There's a cheap set menu at €18, not served on Sunday lunchtimes, then others up to €21. Free use of garage and free round of mini-golf.

SAINT-MIHIEL 55300

⚕ ≜ I●I HÔTEL-RESTAURANT RIVE GAUCHE**

pl. de la Gare; it's near the old station bridge.
☎ 03.29.89.15.83 ➡ 03.29.89.15.35
Disabled access. **TV**. **Garden**. **Car park**.

They've done a wonderful job of restoring the old station house. The en-suite doubles have shower/wc or bath, cable TV and phone; they go for €39, which is fair given the facilities and the atmosphere. You'll get good traditional cooking in the restaurant, and fairly generous portions; the €10 menu is served daily except on Saturday evening and Sunday lunch, and there are others from €15–25. There's a children's play area outside and plans to build a swimming pool. 10% discount on the room rate Sept–April.

BISLÉE   55300 (5KM N)

|●| LA TABLE DES BONS PÈRES**

Chemin de Pichaumé; take the Bislée turning off the D964 between St. Mihiel and Commercy.
☎ 03.29.89.09.90 ➡ 03.29.89.10.01
Closed 14–26 Jan.

This restaurant, in a restored farmhouse by the River Meuse, is on the side of a road that is not too busy in summer. You dine in a bright airy room overlooking the meandering river, or on a delightful terrace on the bank. The cuisine has a light touch and there are a few regional specialities with lots of freshwater fish – perch, pike and pike-perch often feature. The lunchtime menu, €9, is served in the brasserie; other menus, €21–27, use plenty of seasonal produce including wild mushrooms. Hospitable welcome and stylish service.

LACROIX-SUR-MEUSE   55300 (10KM S)

⚶ 🏠 |●| AUBERGE DE LA PÊCHE À LA TRUITE

Route de Seuzey; take the D964 then the D109 after Lacroix.
☎ 03.29.90.10.97
Closed Tues out of season and the second fortnight in Jan. **Disabled access. Garden. Car park.**

This is more than a hotel-restaurant – it's a concept. You come here to catch the trout and ling that they let out of the fish ponds at 9am and 2pm daily – rods are available for hire. There are lots of facilities, including outdoor games for the children, so it's a good spot for families. The restaurant itself is a converted paper mill and they've built a terrace with an arbour. Naturally, they serve a lot of trout and other fish dishes: trout *rillettes*, trout *à la lorraine* and char with Belle de Meuse beer sauce are typical offerings. There's a weekday menu at €15 and others from €21–27. There are a few rooms; they go for €27 with basin, €40 with shower, €46 with shower/wc. Free half-day fishing if you stay for three days, and free house apéritif.

VIGNEULLES-LÈS-HATTONCHÂTEL   55210 (17KM NE)

⚶|●| L'AUBERGE LORRAINE

50 rue Poincaré; it's on the D901.

☎ 03.29.89.58.00 ➡ 03.29.39.58.00
Closed Mon.

A quiet restaurant in a peaceful village in the Lorraine regional park, north of the Lac de Madiane. Simple, good, nourishing fare is listed on the weekday lunch menu (€10) and on others from €15–21. You'll find dishes such as country *terrine* with mirabelle plums or fish flambéed with mirabelle brandy; in the evening they also offer pizzas and various cheese-topped dishes. Free coffee.

SAINT-MAURICE-SOUS-LES-CÔTES   55210 (22KM NE)

⚶ 🏠 |●| HÔTEL-RESTAURANT DES CÔTES DE MEUSE**

av. du Général Lelorrain; on the D901 turn left for Vigneulles-lès-Hattonchâtel, then take the D908.
☎ 03.29.89.35.61 ➡ 03.29.89.55.50
Closed Sun evenings, Mon, and three weeks at the beginning of Nov. **TV.**

This modest hotel is in a village where they produce Côtes de Meuse wines, which have a refreshing flinty flavour. The hotel itself has no distinctive charm but the owner goes out of his way to make guests feel comfortable, and the quiet, well-maintained rooms all have good bathrooms. Doubles with shower/wc or bath cost €34. In the restaurant there's a weekday lunch menu for €9 and others from €14–27. They feature carefully prepared fish dishes, including trout and pike-perch, carp fillet with walnuts, and scallops and Dublin Bay prawn kebabs. To finish, try the *chaud-froid* of mirabelle plums. There's a bar, too, with a billiard table. Free breakfast.

SARREBOURG   57400

⚶ 🏠 HÔTEL DE FRANCE**

3 av. de France (Centre).
☎ 03.87.03.21.47 ➡ 03.87.23.93.57
TV. Lock-up car park.

This is a big hotel with fifty well-maintained rooms. Though they're somewhat lacking in charm, they are a good size and ideal for families. Double rooms with basin €23, with shower €30, €42–45 with shower/wc or bath. The restaurant next door is run by the same family. 10% discount on the room rate.

🏠 |●| HÔTEL-RESTAURANT LES CÈDRES**

Zone de Loisirs-chemin d'Imling (West); there are signs on the N4 to the zone de Loisirs.

☎ 03.87.03.55.55 ➡ 03.87.03.66.33
Hotel closed 22 Dec–2 Jan. **Restaurant closed** Sat lunchtime and Sun evening. **TV**. **Disabled access**. **Garden**. **Car park**.

The architecture looks good in this rural setting and the spacious dining rooms are bright and peaceful. There's a piano with a see-through lid for the guests to play after a game of snooker. Chef Monsieur Morin cooks good food; à la carte try frogs' legs, fillet of pike-perch with *choucroute* or scampi and scallop ravioli. They do a weekday lunch menu for €10, and others €18–32. Expect to pay €55 for a double room with a bath or shower, or €46 per night at the weekends.

|●| L'AUBERGE MAÎTRE PIERRE

24 rue Saint-Martin (Northeast); head in the direction of the motorway, cross the railway bridge at the Sarrebourg exit towards Morhange, then follow the arrows.
☎ 03.87.03.10.16 ➡ 03.87.23.99.44
Closed Mon, Tues, and 20 Dec–10 Jan. **Garden**. **Car park**.

This place has changed its name for the nth time; its last incarnation, as the *Auberge de Zoo*, was flummoxed when they closed the zoo. They serve good, family-style Lorraine cooking, with tasty specialities; a past owner, Marguerite Pierre, invented *flammenküche*, an open bacon and cream tart, which is still on the menu along with ham in pastry and meats grilled on the open fire. A meal won't break the bank, either, with menus from €14 to €30. There's a convivial atmosphere and late on it can get riotous. In a completely different vein, there's a Tex-Mex restaurant in the basement.

SARREGUEMINES   57200

♠ HÔTEL AMADEUS**

7 av de la Gare (Centre).
☎ 03.87.98.55.46 ➡ 03.87.98.66.92
TV.

As the station hotel this place was getting very down at heel, but since its face-lift it's looking a lot better. The façade has a vaguely Art Deco appearance, and the rooms are beyond reproach – contemporary and attractive with good facilities including hair dryers. Doubles with shower/wc or bath go for €43–53.

⚘ ♠ |●| HÔTEL-RESTAURANT L'UNION**

28 rue Alexandre-de-Geiger; take rue du Maréchal-Foch and take the second on the left.
☎ 03.87.95.28.42 ➡ 03.87.98.25.21

✉ hotelunion@free.fr
Closed Sat, Sun and 23 Dec–2 Jan. **TV**. **Car park**.

A classic hotel set slightly away from the centre. The decoration in the rooms is nothing to shout about, but the facilities are good. You'll pay €49–58 for a comfortable room with shower/wc or bath. The restaurant at least has some style, with a display of minerals in the window, and Sarreguemines plates on the walls. Food is traditional and perfectly judged, with menus from €12–23. Free breakfast.

⚘ |●| RESTAURANT LAROCHE

3 pl. de la Gare (Southeast).
☎ 03.87.98.03.23
Closed Fri evening, Sat, 5–25 Aug, and 23 Dec–5 Jan. **Disabled access**.

There are two dining rooms, one of which offers a speedier service than the other. The décor is rustic and beginning to feel a bit tired, but it's as clean as can be. Dishes are nicely presented and good value; there's a weekday menu at €10 and set menus €13–18. Free coffee.

|●| RESTAURANT LA BONNE SOURCE

24 av. de la Gare (Southeast).
☎ 03.87.98.03.79
Closed Sat lunchtime, Sun evening, Mon, and 14 July to 15 Aug. **Car park**.

A traditional looking restaurant with wood panelling and a display of Sarreguemines china, proper tablecloths and cloth napkins. You'll be offered good Alsace and Lorraine specialities here – *flammenküche* (bacon, cream and onion flan), *lever knepfle* (liverballs with bacon and cream), home-made *charcuterie*, *choucroute* and spare ribs. They serve a lunch menu for €11 on weekdays and others at €12–20. Good value.

|●| LE CASINO DES SOMMELIERS

4 rue du Coloneol Cazal.
☎ 03.87.02.90.41 ➡ 03.87.02.90.28
Closed Sun evening, Mon, and a fortnight in Jan.

Located in the middle of a small park inside the town's old casino, a unusual building from the late nineteenth century, this classy bistro is decorated with wood panelling and porcelain. In summer there's a lovely terrace under the arcade looking towards the river. As for the food, it's tasty and well-priced, listed on menus from €13 or around €23 à la carte. There's an attractively priced wine list, too, with a good number of wines by the glass.

WOELFING-LÈS-SARREGUEMINES 57200 (12KM SE)

I●I PASCAL DIMOFSKI

113 route de Bitche; it's on the N62 going in the direction of Bitche.
☎ 03.87.02.38.21 ➡ 03.87.02.21.36
Closed Mon evening, Tues, two weeks in winter and three weeks in summer.

This may look like an ordinary roadside restaurant from the outside, but owner Pascal Dimofski has turned a simply run family establishment into a gastronomic restaurant that's been rated by the "Moselle Gourmande". The dining room has a refined, quiet atmosphere and it's full of businesspeople and regulars. Weekday lunch menus cost €20 or €24, and there are others from €33–64: choose dishes such as veal *terrine* with white port, tuna *carpaccio*, fresh pan-fried cod, iced strawberry *soufflé*, and lemon and mandarin sorbet. If you're lucky with the weather, eat in the garden.

SENONES 88210

🏂 🛌 I●I HÔTEL-RESTAURANT AU BON GÎTE**

3 pl. Vaultrin (Centre).
☎ 03.29.57.92.46 ➡ 03.29.57.93.92
Closed Sun evening; Mon evening on public holidays; the Feb school holidays, and a fortnight end-July/ Aug.
TV. Car park.

This lovely old house has been renovated inside and out and the resolutely modern décor complements the texture of the old walls. Monsieur and Madame Thomas, the owners, are very welcoming. There are about ten attractive rooms which are most comfortable; doubles go for €38 with shower or bath. Numbers 2, 5, 6, and 7 are the quietest. In the dining room you'll eat reliable regional cooking with lots of imagination: salmon, trout and mussel *demi-lune*, pork cheek ravioli, and bread and butter pudding with rhubarb *compote*. There's a weekday menu at €10 then others from €14–27. It gets busy at weekends. Free coffee.

🏂 I●I LA SALLE DES GARDES

7 pl. Clémenceau (Centre).
☎ 03.29.57.60.06
Closed Mon–Thurs evenings; three weeks in June, and a fortnight at Christmas. **Disabled access. Car park**.

A simple, attractive brasserie run by a friendly woman with a light culinary touch. Prices are reasonable; there's a short lunch menu at €10 and others up to €14. She specializes in meats grilled over the open fire; try kebabs of *filet mignon*, or cockerel accompanied by potatoes with bacon. It's a favourite with young people from all around the area. Free coffee.

GRANDRUPT 88210 (8KM)

🛌 I●I HÔTEL-RESTAURANT LA ROSERAIE*

3 rue de la Mairie.
☎ 03.29.41.04.16 ➡ 03.29.41.04.74

The perfect place if you're looking for tranquility and mountain walks in the forest. Simple but comfortable rooms go for €32–43. The pretty dining room is the ideal setting for their tasty food: home-made chicken liver *terrine*, rabbit thigh with pine kernels and herbs, and good sorbets. Menus €9–22. You get a nice welcome, not least from the resident Saint Bernard.

SIERCK-LES-BAINS 57480

🏂 I●I RESTAURANT LA VIEILLE PORTE

8 pl. Jean-de-Morbach (Centre).
☎ and ➡ 03.82.83.22.61
Closed Tues evening; Wed; Feb school holidays, and 24 July–8 Aug.

Sierck was a refuge for Cistercian monks during the religious wars, and there's an underground tunnel leading from the château to the eleventh-century tower. You reach the restaurant courtyard through an old gate dating from 1604. As for the food, you'll be offered confident dishes from chef Jean-Pierre Mercier who has a good reputation in these parts and further afield. The signature starter, hot trout with almonds, is well worth a try, and the peppered fillet of Charolais beef flambéed in Cognac is a little marvel. Weekday menu €13, then others from €30–53. Free apéritif.

GAVISSE 57570 (9KM W)

🏂 I●I RESTAURANT LE MEGACÉROS

19 pl. Jeanne-d'Arc (Centre); it's on the D64.
☎ 03.82.55.45.87
Closed Mon, Tues, 26 Dec–5 Jan. **Disabled access. Car park**.

The *megacéros* is an extinct ancestor of the deer, but there's nothing prehistoric about this restaurant. The cuisine is innovative and the chef creates subtle combinations with local ingredients – try the veal kidneys with dandelion wine, the salmon *unilatérale* (seared on one side only), and the mirabelle plum ice-cream. Menus €15–40. Free apéritif.

RODEMACK   57570 (13KM W)

🏃🍽 RESTAURANT LA MAISON DES BAILLIS

46 pl. des Baillis; take the D64 then the D62.
☎ 03.82.51.24.25
Closed Mon, Tues and the Feb school holidays. **Garden**. **Car park**.

The first lords of Rodemack settled in this handsome village in the twelfth century, and at the end of the fifteenth century the Austrians confiscated the estate. In the sixteenth century, the new owner, bored with being so far from the Viennese court, went home and left a bailiff in the house to manage the place. The restaurant is in this magnificent building. They serve good food in the glorious dining rooms. The menus, €14–30, are built around a robust, local dish such as ham cooked in a hay box with two different sauces. You'll spend about €23 *à la carte*. Free house apéritif.

STENAY   55700

🏠🍽 HÔTEL-RESTAURANT LE COMMERCE**

9 rue Aristide-Briand (Centre).
☎ 03.29.80.30.62 ➦ 03.29.80.61.77
Closed Fri evening, and Sun evening in winter.
TV.

Comfortable, spacious rooms with mini-bar and good bathrooms. Doubles cost €27–69 with shower or bath and wc. The dining room serves simple, generous dishes and an array of starters; there's a weekday menu at €11, another at €15, which includes wine, and others up to €38. À la carte there are a few specialities cooked with beer.

INOR   55700 (7KM N)

🏠🍽 AUBERGE LE FAISAN DORÉ**

rue de l'Écluse; take the D964, going north.
☎ 03.29.80.35.45 ➦ 03.29.80.37.92
Closed Fri. **Swimming pool**. **TV**. **Garden**. **Car park**.

This place, by the river in a village in the Meuse forest, is popular with hunters. You will eat well – try duck *confit* with mirabelle plums, monkfish with girolles, sirloin with local morels and game and wild mushrooms

in season. The weekday menu costs €10, and there are themed menus, focusing on Lorraine specialities or tradional dishes, from €17–27. There's a bar, too. The hotel is decent, though the timbers are fake. Doubles cost €31, all of them en-suite.

VILOSNES   55100 (20KM S)

🏃🏠🍽 HÔTEL-RESTAURANT DU VIEUX MOULIN

rue des Petits Ponts; it's on the D123b.
☎ 03.29.85.81.52 ➦ 03.29.85.88.19
Closed Tues lunchtime out of season, Jan, and Feb. **TV**. **Car park**.

The hotel is in the very heart of this quietest of quiet villages. The mill wheel stopped turning years ago but you can watch the Meuse flow peacefully by from the lovely terrace and from some of the guest rooms. Rooms with shower or bath go for €40–47. They are each different, though some of the beams are fake. They serve wholesome family cooking in the restaurant, with good traditional dishes listed on menus from €11–26. 10% discount on the room rate Nov–April. Free breakfast.

THIONVILLE   57100

🏠🍽 HÔTEL-RESTAURANT DES AMIS**

40 av. de-Bertier; leave the motorway at exit 40 and turn right at the fifth set of lights.
☎ 03.82.53.22.18 ➦ 03.82.54.32.40
Hotel closed Sun until 5pm. **Restaurant closed** Fri. **TV**. **Car park**.

A large establishment covered in Virginia creeper and geraniums. The proprietress, who will treat you like an old friend, keeps the hotel extremely clean. Doubles with shower/wc or bath go for €40–47. The dining room has been redecorated and redesigned; Monsieur painted the fresco himself and the place is lit by ornamental Alsatian lamps in highly carved wood. Go for the €10 *repas campagnard*, which is a real treat; you get *crudités*, smoked country ham, house *terrine*, garlic sausage, *fuseau lorrain*, roast potatoes, and cream cheese with herbs.

🏠 HÔTEL CENTRAL**

1 rue du Four Banal.
☎ 03.82.53.70.27 ➦ 03.82.53.23.34
📧 hotelcentral@bplorraine.fr
TV. **Car park**.

Really nice, central hotel on a pedestrianized street. Rooms have been prettily decorated with orange-tinted walls and floral fabrics;

some have micro-computers connected to the Net. There are also some family suites that sleep 4. Doubles with shower/wc or bath start at €47.

⅍ ≙ |●| HÔTEL L'HORIZON***

50 route du Crève-Coeur (Northwest); take exit 40 on the A31 onto the Thionville ring-road then straight on towards Bel Air hospital.
☎ 03.82.88.53.65 ➡ 03.82.34.55.84
e info@lhorizon.com
Hotel closed Jan and Feb. **Restaurant closed** Sat and Mon lunchtimes.
TV. Disabled access. Car park.

The striking façade of this luxurious hotel marks the building out from others nearby. In the restaurant, the dishes are finely prepared with a sure hand, but offer no surprises. Weekday menu €28 then others from €33–48. The real luxury is in the rooms; take number 3, which has the softest feather bed ever. In the bathroom you are spoilt with perfumes, soaps, shampoos and other extras. Doubles with shower go for €73, €88 with shower/wc and with bath, €104. Free apéritif or coffee, and 10% discount on the room rate Oct–March.

|●| LES SOMMELIERS

23 place de la République.
☎ 03.82.53.32.20 ➡ 03.82.53.47.84
Closed Sat lunchtime, Sun and Christmas–New Year's Day.

This reasonably priced restaurant has filled a gap in the market. The frontage is impressive (the building used to be a bank) and the dining room is a lovely space, decorated in brasserie style. They offer really tasty little dishes and a skilfully selected choice of wines, including some served by the glass. Menus start at €13, but you'll spend around €23 *à la carte*. It's simple and good, and the service is just as it should be.

HOMBOURG-BUDANGE 57920 (15KM SE)

⅍ |●| L'AUBERGE DU ROI ARTHUR

48 rue Principale; it's on the D918 to Bouzonville.
☎ 03.82.83.97.15
Closed Sun–Tues evenings, and a week from 14 July.

Nothing to do with the legend of King Arthur, but worth a trip anyway. It's a popular place, with lots of regular customers. They have a series of portraits on the walls from the château, and display a splendid porcelain dish made in Sarreguemines. Good country cooking is listed on menus from €11–23: try

croustade of snails with Moselle wine, fillet of beef with crayfish, frogs' legs or steak *tartare*. Free coffee.

TOUL 54200

⅍ ≙ LA VILLA LORRAINE**

15 rue Gambetta (Centre).
☎ 03.83.43.08.95 ➡ 03.83.64.63.64
TV. Pay car park.

The style of this building was influenced by the École de Nancy. It's central, clean, charming in an old-fashioned way, and inexpensive. Really nice doubles with shower go for €26, €33 with shower/wc, and €36 with bath. 10% discount for two nights.

⅍ ≙ HÔTEL DE L'EUROPE**

35 av. Victor-Hugo (Centre); it's near the station.
☎ 03.83.43.00.10 ➡ 03.83.63.27.67
Closed Christmas and New Year. **TV. Pay car park.**

This place is paradise for fans of 1930s style; almost everything dates from that period, including the doors, carpets, furniture and the bathrooms. Some rooms have been redecorated, but what they may have lost in authenticity they have maintained in charm. Room 35 is particularly splendid. Doubles with shower or bath €35–38. Free car park space.

|●| PIZZA REMI

10 av. Victor-Hugo; it's by the station, practically opposite the Hôtel de l'Europe.
☎ 03.83.6318.18
Closed Sat lunchtime and Sun.

A friendly and unaffected restaurant looking onto a little garden where you can eat breakfast in summer. The team of young cooks produce really tasty Italian food including home-made pasta and a wide variety of inexpensive pizzas and meat dishes. Menus €8–16. The wines aren't pricey either. A quality place.

LUCEY 54200 (9KM NW)

|●| L'AUBERGE DU PRESSOIR

rue des Pachenottes; it's on the D908 (known as the route des Vins et de la Mirabelle).
☎ 03.83.63.81.91
Closed Sun evening, Mon and 16 Aug–3 Sept. **Disabled access. Car park.**

It's essential to book at this popular place at the weekend and in summer – not least because of its beautiful countryside setting.

It's in what used to be the village station, and there's a genuine antique winepress in the courtyard. All the menus, even the cheapest, offer high quality food, delightfully presented and generously served. The cooking is regional and eclectic, with a number of specialities, including *profiteroles* with snails, *filet mignon* with mirabelle plum vinegar, and trout cooked in *vin gris* from Toul. There's a weekday menu at €12, then others from €23–26. The wine list features a good variety, including a Côtes de Toul, and you can pick up a few bottles at the wine merchant's next door.

ALLAIN   54170 (20KM S)

☎ LA HAIE DES VIGNES

Lieu-dit; La Haie des Vignes.
☎ 03.83.52.81.82 ➡ 03.83.52.04.27
Car park.

Honest, well-run little hotel just south of Toul and just off the motorway. Twenty fairly ordinary rooms, all at ground level, are reasonably priced at €35. The decoration isn't great, and there's no real charm to the place, but the friendliness of the owner makes up for a lot.

VAL-D'AJOL (LE)   88340

⚥ ☎ |●| HÔTEL-RESTAURANT LA RÉSIDENCE***

5 rue des Mousses (Centre); at the church take the D20 signposted to Hamaunard.
☎ 03.29.30.68.52 ➡ 03.29.66.53.00
Closed Sun evening and Mon from Oct–April except during the school holidays. **Swimming pool**. **TV**. **Garden**. **Car park**.

Since 1960, this handsome nineteenth-century master craftsman's house has been developed into a very pleasant establishment by three generations of the same family. You make your way through a maze of corridors and passageways to get to the comfortable, cosy bedrooms where you sleep in complete quiet. In addition to the main building there are two three-star annexes set in a green park where you'll also find the pool and the tennis court. Double rooms, all with shower or bath, cost €49–73. The cooking is equally good, with menus from €14 (weekdays only) up to €46. You should definitely try the famous Val d'Ajol *andouille*, which is served in its own dish, and the free-range chicken with Kirsch. Impeccable service. It's best to book. Free apéritif.

VERDUN   55100

⚥ ☎ |●| HÔTEL LE SAINT-PAUL**

12 pl. Saint-Paul (North).
☎ 03.29.86.02.16
Restaurant closed Sun evening and Nov–April.

This well-situated hotel offers moderate prices, a good standard of comfort, peace and quiet, and a pleasant family atmosphere. It's often occupied by people coming to visit the World War I graves. Rooms range from €25 with basin to €36 with shower/wc or bath; there are also a couple of rooms for families. For half board, reckon on paying €59 per person. The restaurant serves good traditional dishes from the Lorraine with a lunch menu at €10 and others up to €27. Free apéritif or coffee.

⚥ |●| RESTAURANT LE PICOTIN

38 av. Joffre (East).
☎ 03.29.84.53.45
Closed Sun evening. **Disabled access**.

If you prefer to eat in peace, opt for the dining room, as the terrace can get fairly noisy. Wherever you eat, you'll get good-quality, inventive cooking. There's a €10 weekday lunch menu, and others at €14 and €20. Try the goat's cheese pancake, or if you like steak, go for the excellent *tournedos 1900*. This place is popular with theatre people and night-owls, because it stays open late. Free apéritif.

|●| LE FORUM

35 rue des Gros-Degrés (Centre).
☎ 03.29.86.46.88
Closed Wed evening, Sun, and a fortnight July/Aug. **Disabled access**.

Good value, and with a strong local following, this restaurant has a lovely dining room tastefully decorated with subtle watercolours – the vaulted basement, however, is best avoided if you're claustrophobic. Cooking is simple but fresh and light, adapting traditional regional recipes with a modern twist. There's a lunch menu at €10 during the week, and others from €14–23.

⚥ |●| LE POSTE DE GARDE

47 rue Saint Victor (Centre-East).
☎ 03.29.86.38.49
Closed Mon–Fri lunchtimes, Fri and Sat evenings, public holidays and Aug. **Disabled access**.

This establishment was set up to employ young people coming out of custody as a way of helping them back into the world of work – ironically, it's in an old guard room. It has been brightly restored in pastel shades with green shutters, but, despite their best efforts, it is still a rather cold building. Happily, the atmosphere is excellent and the guests all seem to be satisfied. Simple, straightforward cooking, which doesn't attempt to be subtle, is served in large portions that will satisfy your appetite. Lunch *formule* for €8, menus €10–17, and various options *à la carte*. Free apéritif or coffee.

DIEUE-SUR-MEUSE 55320 (12KM S)

🛌 🏠 |●| CHÂTEAU DES MONTHAIRONS***

Les Monthairons; take the D34.
☎ and 📠 03.29.87.78.55
📧 chateau-des-monthairons@wanadoo.fr
Closed 1 Jan–10 Feb. **Disabled access. TV.**

A nineteenth-century château in a walled park with the Meuse meandering gently through it, this hotel is a member of the classy *Château-Hôtels-Indépendants* group. It's undeniably stunning to look at, but although the rooms are extremely comfortable they don't have any traditional charm. However, at a price of €82–156 for a double room – hardly a king's ransom – you will spend the night in a lovely place where you get lots of little extras such as dressing gowns and toiletries. The restaurant has a good reputation; you'll pay €20 for the weekday lunchtime menu and €30–70 for other set menus. Specialities include *tourte* of rabbit with truffles, pigeon breast, snail *cassolette* with duck's gizzards and redcurrant *soufflé*. Free coffee, and 10% discount on the room rate 15 Sept–15 Jan excluding weekends.

SOMMEDIEUE 55320 (15.5KM SE)

🏠 |●| LE RELAIS DES ÉPICHÉES

7 rue du Grand-Pont; take the D964 as far as Dieue then turn left onto the D159; it's near the war memorial.
☎ 03.29.87.61.36 📠 03.29.85.76.38
Closed Sun evening and 20 Dec–10 Jan. **TV. Car park.**

Service noon–2.30pm and 7.30–10pm. The bar is populated by regulars sipping a glass of something or calling into the tobacconist's to buy their fix. In the restaurant they serve good, simple cooking. The *quiche lorraine* and calf's head are first class; they may be listed on the weekday menu at €11 or any of the others from €13–24. The rooms are clean and have views of the Dieue stream; a

double with basin costs €27, €34 with shower/wc or bath. Pity about the fake beams.

ÉTAIN 55400 (20KM NE)

🛌 🏠 |●| HÔTEL-RESTAURANT LA SIRÈNE**

22 rue Prud'homme-Navette.
☎ 03.29.87.10.32 📠 03.29.87.17.65
Closed Sun evening, Mon out of season, and Jan. **TV. Garden. Car park.**

Apparently, Napoleon III dined in this handsome house after the battle of Gravelotte in 1870. The interior is very rustic in style and it's filled with antiques – in the bar there's an elegant old French billiard table. You'll get a pleasant welcome, the atmosphere is hushed and the customers are well-to-do. Rooms are quite comfortable, all of them double-glazed; doubles go for €35–53 with shower/wc or bath. The cheapest menu, €11, is served daily except Sunday, and there are others up to €38. You'll eat good, bourgeois cooking with dishes like salmon with tarragon, ham with peaches, and *foie gras*. There are two tennis courts and a place to play *boules*. Free coffee.

VILLE-SUR-YRON 54800

🛌 |●| LA TOQUE LORRAINE

1 rue de l'Yron; it's on the D132.
☎ 03.82.83.98.13
Closed Sun evening, Wed, Thurs and the second fortnight in July.

This pretty village is undergoing major restoration work. The restaurant, in one of the cottages opposite the carpenter's, has several dining rooms, one of which has a proud fireplace. It's got a farmhouse atmosphere, refined but formal, with stone walls beautifully shown off by discreet lighting. The cooking is full of flavour, and will set you up for a good walk round the village. There's a weekday lunch menu at €11 and others from €14–34; try tripe with Toul *vin gris*, brawn, snails in pastry cases, frogs' legs, kidneys with morels and Lorraine cake. Free *digestif* – but don't clink your glasses too hard, they're made of the finest crystal.

VITTEL 88800

🛌 🏠 HÔTEL LES OISEAUX

54 rue de Sugène (Centre); it's near the spa.

☎ 03.29.08.61.93
Closed Three weeks in Jan. **TV**. **Garden**. **Car park**.

This is not so much a hotel as a pretty little house that's been turned into a B&B by an extremely nice woman. Rooms with basin cost €22, with shower €37, and with bath €40. It's quiet and pleasant, with a tiny garden. 10% discount.

🏃 🛏 |●| HÔTEL-RESTAURANT LA CHAUMIÈRE

196 rue Jeanne-d'Arc (Centre).
☎ 03.29.08.02.87
Closed Sun in winter. **Car park**.

A tiny hotel with a bar and restaurant. It's not much to look at, but the proprietress is delightful, and the chef, who's been in the business for thirty years, cares about what he's doing. They give the impression that they are enjoying themselves, which makes a nice change from the health farm-style strictness that pervades the rest of the town. Rooms, €27 a night, are simple and clean, with washing facilities only. There's a lunch menu for €9, and others up to €15, listing a selection of local, regional or international dishes. 10% discount on the room rate.

🏃 🛏 |●| HÔTEL DE L'ORÉE DU BOIS**

L'Orée du Bois (West); it's 4km north on the D18 opposite the race course.
☎ 03.29.08.88.88 ➡ 03.29.08.01.61
e oree-du-bois@dial.oleane.com
Closed Sun evening, and Nov to end Jan. **TV**.
Swimming pool. **Disabled access**. **Garden**. **Car park**.

A modern hotel and conference centre in a quiet spot. They specialize in getting guests back into shape, and sports facilities include a gym, tennis courts, indoor heated swimming pool and a sauna. The rooms are comfortable; reckon on paying €49 for a double with bath. The restaurant serves menus from €11–30. Though dishes change regularly, you can expect constants like salmon *à l'unilatérale*, grilled on one side only, trout and frogs' legs in red Toul wine, fillet of beef and *chaud-froid* of mirabelles. Free coffee.

🏃 🛏 |●| HÔTEL-RESTAURANT D'ANGLETERRE***

rue de Charmey
☎ 03.29.08.08.42 ➡ 03.29.08.07.48
Closed mid-Dec to mid-Jan.
Disabled access. **TV**. **Car park**.

The classic, imposing spa hotel with a pink frontage and an all-pervading air of faded grandeur. In general, and particularly the rooms, everything has been done up. To guarantee peace and quiet, take a room at the back – the railway isn't that far. Doubles €76–89. The restaurant provides simple yet tasty and unusual dishes – marshland salad, red mullet fillets and duck with arabica beans – on menus from €14–26. Free apéritif.

|●| LE RÉTRO

158 rue Jeanne d'Arc.
☎ 03.29.0805.28
Closed Sat lunchtime, Sun evening and Mon.

Tasty southern dishes served year round in this easy-going, warm dining room: frogs' legs *à la provençale*, chicken *andalouse* and, in contrast, a milder creamy-sauced chicken *à la poulette*. They also grill meats over the huge wood fire, which is greatly appreciated by the loyal local clientele. Menus €10–21.

Midi-Pyrénées

AIGNAN · 32290

♙ |●| LE VIEUX LOGIS

rue des Arts; it's behind the town hall.
☎ and ➡ 05.62.09.23.55
Closed Sun evening. **TV**.

An unobtrusive establishment near the town square with period furniture and a cheery dining room. Good food on €10–20 menus which offer soups, salads, shrimps *à la provençale*, lamb kebab and desserts. The specialities, produced only when the ingredients are available at market, are fresh *foie gras* salad, zander with *beurre blanc*, ceps with parsley and prawns flambéed with Armagnac. There's a terrace but a rather stern welcome. Rooms with shower/wc or bath €34.

ALBAN · 81250

|●| RESTAURANT DU MIDI**

9 pl. des Tilleuls (Centre).
☎ 05.63.55.82.24
Closed Tues evening and the last week in Aug.

This unassuming little restaurant on the village square serves surprisingly high-quality food – the chef trained on some of the great local kitchens before taking over his grandmother's bistro. Several menus at €11–24 offer good value for money. Quality ingredients and fresh produce go into dishes such as veal tripe with potato; the standard menu changes at least twice a year. The desserts are made in-house. Warm and genuine welcome.

ALBI · 81000

♙ ♙ LA RÉGENCE**

27 av. Maréchal-Joffre (South); it's 150m from the train station.
☎ 05.63.54.01.42 ➡ 05.63.54.80.48
TV. Garden. Pay garage.

This quiet hotel feels like a friendly family guesthouse. There's a nice garden at the back where they serve breakfast in good weather. Bedrooms are decorated in floral style with co-ordinated prints. Doubles with basin €22 and €40 with shower/wc or bath: good value for money. 10% discount for the second night.

♙ HÔTEL SAINT-CLAIR**

8 rue Saint-Clair (Centre); it's near the cathedral.
☎ 05.63.54.25.66 ➡ 05.63.47.27.58
Closed one month Dec–Jan. **Garden. TV. Pay garage**.

A pretty, recently renovated two-star hotel in the old part of town which is maintained with care. Doubles with shower/wc €39 or €49 with bath. There's a non-smokers' floor – ask when you book. Nice owner.

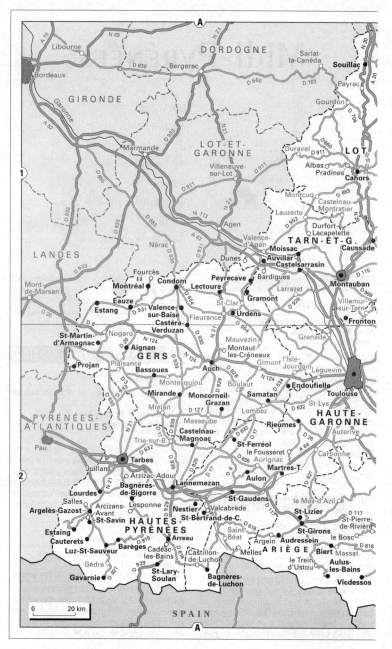

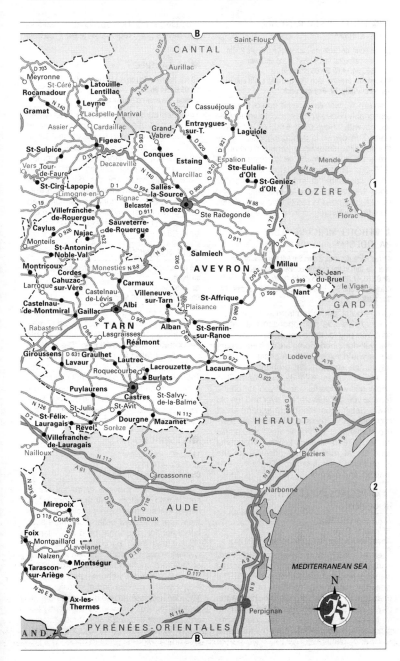

☎ |●| HÔTEL-RESTAURANT DU VIEIL-ALBY**

25 rue Henri-de-Toulouse-Lautrec (Centre); it's 200m from the cathedral in the heart of the old town.
☎ 05.63.54.14.69 ➡ 05.63.54.96.75
Closed Sun evening, Mon, Jan and a fortnight end June–early July. **TV. Pay car park**.

This simple, well-run hotel is one of the most reasonably priced in this part of town: Double rooms with shower/wc €40, or €49 with bath. The owner is very congenial, but he doesn't allow smoking anywhere in the hotel. Weekday lunch menu €12, with others €15–38. The cooking is excellent, with house specialities such as radish and salted pork liver salad, tripe *à l'Albigeoise* and monkfish braised in red Gaillac wine. Wines from the Gaillac region from €12 a bottle.

☎ |●| HÔTEL MERCURE ALBI BASTIDES***

41 rue Porta (Centre); it's on the left after the bridge over the Tarn in the direction of Paris-Carmaux.
☎ 05.63.47.66.66 ➡ 05.63.46.18.40
Closed Sat and Sun lunchtimes. **Disabled access. TV. Car park**.

Luxury hotel, converted from an eighteenth-century riverside mill, opposite the cathedral. You pay for the comfort, of course, but the well-equipped rooms are a bit impersonal, as you'd expect from a chain. You also pay for the view, which is probably the finest in Albi. Doubles €74–82 with bath. The cooking is wonderful – and if you eat on the terrace you get views of the river and the old town. Set menus €22–24; *à la carte* you'll pay about €34. The specialities include *marbré* of *foie gras* with duck *aiguillette*, house *cassoulet* and fillet of zander. Wonderful wine list at rock-bottom prices – try the restaurant's own Mercure. The service is amiable and efficient.

⍟ |●| RESTAURANT LE PETIT-BOUCHON

77 rue de la Croix-Verte.
☎ 05.63.54.11.75
Closed Sat evening; Sun; public holidays; 1–20 Aug.

There's a warm atmosphere in this clean, Parisian-style brasserie, which is decorated with the works of great photographers. The weekday menu (€9) consists of a starter, dessert and a choice from the dishes of the day – veal skirt, steak, duck *confit*, stuffed mutton tripe, *cassoulet*, sirloin, *coq au vin*, gizzard stew *en daube*. Other menus up to €20 and platters for €10. Fast, rather

brusque service. They specialize in cocktails and have a good regional wine list. Free coffee.

|●| LE LAUTREC

13 rue Henri-de-Toulouse-Lautrec (Centre).
☎ 05.63.54.86.55
Closed Sun evening and Mon.

This restaurant, located in the most touristy part of town, is sited in converted stables that belonged to the painter, Henri de Toulouse-Lautrec. Some tables are up on a gallery, while others are more spread out. The regional dishes are cooked exceedingly well. Try the pan-fried *foie gras*, scallops with garlic zander with truffle *jus*, duck *confit*, duck breast flambéed with Calvados or any of the excellent meat dishes. €11 lunch menu and others €14–35.

|●| LE TOURNESOL

rue de l'Ort-en-Salvy; it's in a side street leading to pl. du Vigan.
☎ 05.63.38.38.14
Closed Sun and 1–15 May.

This is the best vegetarian restaurant in the Tarn region, and it serves good food at realistic prices. The airy dining room is simply decorated and air-conditioned. The cooking is uncomplicated and very tasty: vegetable *pâté*, courgette flan, falafel. The *assiette Tournesol* gives you lots of variety and wonderful desserts like apple crumble or cheesecake with vanilla and honey. They serve apple juice and organic beer. A meal costs about €17.

|●| L'ESPRIT DU VIN

11 quai Choiseul (Centre).
☎ 05.63.54.60.44
Closed Sun eveing and Mon.

The dining room provides a tranquil, sober setting with old stone walls and modern furniture. For summer there's a lovely terrace; for winter, a vaulted cellar. The chef has a penchant for traditional produce – lamb, poultry and fresh baby vegetables – reworked in his own skilful way. He pays great attention to cooking times and produces a dish of milk-fed Pyrenean lamb which is crispy on the outside and gloriously inside. The desserts are splendid – try the *crème brûlées*, variously flavoured with mint, tea and lavender. There's a sumptuous cheese trolley. Menus €30–50. Lots of superb Gaillacs on the wine list. Best to book.

CASTELNAU-DE-LÉVIS   81150 (8KM SW)

|O| LA TAVERNE

rue Abijoux, Castelnau-de-Lévis; from Albi, take the
D600, after 4km turn left onto the D1 and Castelnau is
3km further on.
☎ 05.63.60.90.16 ➡ 05.63.60.96.73
Closed Mon, Tues, the Feb and All Saints' school
holidays.

Heaven on earth for lovers of good food and
definitely worth the trip. The "chef's suggestions" include raw marinated salmon salad
with herbs, red mullet served with prawn
mousseline, superlative roast duck stuffed
with raspberries and escalope of *foie gras*
with figs. The desserts are out of this world,
and the extensive wine list includes a terrific
Buzet. Menus from €21–41. You eat either in
the air-conditioned dining room, with its
country-style décor, or on the terrace, which
is enclosed. The service is as good as the
food.

ARGELÈS-GAZOST   65400

⊁ 🏠 |O| HÔTEL BEAU SITE**

10 rue du Capitaine-Digoy
☎ 05.62.97.08.63 ➡ 05.62.97.06.01
e hotel.beausite@wanadoo.fr
Closed 5 Nov–5 Dec. **Garden**.

A characterful hotel with an ivy-laden façade
brightened up with flowers. Genuine welcome, cosy atmosphere and period furniture. The rooms are all different and the
ones overlooking the huge and luxuriant
garden are particularly appealing. Doubles
€36–37 with shower or bath. The menu,
€14, offers two starters, main course,
cheese and dessert. And you can enjoy
your meal seated on the terrace, which has
a splendid view of the garden. Free house
apéritif.

⊁ 🏠 |O| LE MIRAMONT***

44 av. des Pyrénées (South); at the first roundabout,
take the road to Cauterets and it's opposite the spa.
☎ 05.62.97.01.26 ➡ 05.62.97.56.67
e hotel-miramont@sudfr.com
Closed Sun evening and Wed Jan–June and Oct; 5
Nov–20 Jan. **TV. Garden**.

A fine Art Deco hotel set in a park planted
with rose gardens and hydrangeas. The
rooms are spacious, elegant and calming,
with up-to-date facilities and en-suite bathrooms. They have balconies with views of
the old town or over the Pyrenees. Rooms 114,
121 and 122 are larger than standard; dou-

bles with shower/wc or bath €69. The
restaurant deserves a mention in its own
right. The chef, Pierre, is the owner's son,
and his wife runs the dining room. Dishes
change with the season and include good
fish specialities and light versions of regional
dishes: *fricassée* of veal sweetbreads, truffle
salad with poached eggs, pan-fried monkfish
with prawns, half-pigeon with Madeiran
sauce. He has a particular gift for preparing
desserts – try the iced *nougat* with honey
and almonds or the strawberry and redberry
sabayon. Menus €15 (not Sun or public holidays) and €24–37. The service is ultra-pro-
fessional without being too formal. Free coffee.

SAINT-SAVIN   65400 (3KM S)

⊁ 🏠 |O| LE VISCOS**

☎ 05.62.97.02.28 ➡ 05.62.97.04.95
e leviscos@wanadoo.fr
Closed Sun evening and Mon except in school holidays;
16–27 Dec. **TV**.

A lovely hotel with attractive rooms for
€32–50 with shower/wc or bath; half board
€47 per person. The cooking is based on
fresh local produce and it's pretty creative
with fish as the speciality: pimentos stuffed
with squid and prawns, duck *sushi* with *foie
gras*, duck *fondant*, pigs' trotters with ceps,
macaroon stuffed with almond ice-cream.
There's a *formule* for €14 (Mon–Sat), and
menus at €20–46 but *à la carte* is rather
expensive. They've already established a
good reputation but sometimes the welcome
is more off-hand than it needs to be. 10%
discount on the room rate except during
school holidays.

ARCIZANS-AVANT   65400 (4KM W)

⊁ 🏠 |O| AUBERGE LE CABALIROS**

16 rue de l'Église (South).
☎ 05.62.97.04.31 ➡ 05.62.97.91.48
Closed Tues evening; Wed out of season; 20 Jan–5 Feb;
8 Oct–8 Dec. **Garden. TV. Car park**.

This attractive inn has a terrace with views
over the valley. You'll get a good-hearted
welcome. Some of the rooms are under the
eaves and are lovely but others are not that
attractive – though they do have decent facilities. Doubles with shower or bath €40–46.
Traditional regional cooking with menus at
€14–26. The *à la carte* menu includes an
authentic *garbure*, a broth with pickled
goose and stuffed neck of duck.

SALLES 65400 (4KM N)

🏃 🏠 |O| LA CHÂTAIGNERAIE

It's in the centre of the village.
☎ 05.62.97.17.84 ➡ 05.62.97.93.14
Closed Jan. **Garden. Car park**.

Open only for bookings. A very beautiful dining room in a renovated farm. Grills are a speciality, and they are prepared in front of you: grilled Pyrenean lamb with beans, braised pigeon *confit*, pan-fried *foie gras* with grapes and bilberry tart. Menus €22–38. There's a lovely terrace in summer. There are rooms available in the *gîte* – €38 for a double – and if you book for a week, half board is available for €34 per person. Free coffee and 10% discount on the room rate.

ARREAU 65240

🏃 🏠 |O| HÔTEL D'ANGLETERRE**

Route de Luchon (South).
☎ 05.62.98.63.30 ➡ 05.62.98.69.66
Closed Mon 15 Sept–30 June; 30 Sept–26 Dec; 15 April–20 May. **Swimming pool. Garden. TV. Car park**.

A seventeenth-century coaching inn which has been tastefully restored to create a warm, comfortable hotel with quality furnishings and service. There's a nice family atmosphere and a warm welcome. Doubles with shower/wc €43–49, or €44–52 with bath. Half board is compulsory in high season at €43–52 per person. There's a pretty garden and a pool behind the hotel. Good regional cooking in the restaurant: duck *foie gras* cooked in a cloth, duck stew, salmon turnovers, medallions of monkfish with sliced red cabbage, *sabayon* of fruit *au gratin*. Menus €15–27. Free house apéritif.

CADÉAC-LES-BAINS 65240 (3KM S)

🏃 🏠 |O| HOSTELLERIE DU VAL-D'AURE

Route de Saint-Lary; it's on the D929.
☎ 05.62.98.60.63 ➡ 05.62.98.68.99
📧 hotel@hotel.valdaure.com
Closed 1 April–15 May and 25 Sept–20 Dec. **Disabled access. Swimming pool. Garden. TV. Car park**.

An appealing riverside establishment in a huge shady park. Double rooms with shower/wc or bath €36–50; some have a terrace. Half board, at €37–47 per person, is compulsory in season. The €10 lunchtime *menu-express* is a classic, but it's not served on Sunday. Other menus €15–20. Attentive, unobtrusive service from the owners, Chris-

tine and Claude, who give good advice about local walks. You can hire mountain bikes, play tennis and swim in the heated pool or in the sulphur spring – where people have been taking the waters since Roman times. Free house apéritif.

AUCH 32000

🏃 |O| LA TABLE D'HÔTE

7 rue Lamartine; it's between the cathedral and the Jacobin museum
☎ 05.62.05.55.62
Closed Sun evening; Wed; Jan. **Disabled access**.

A discreet little place with space for only twenty in the cosy and rustic cosy dining room. The *menu du jour* at €10 is particularly good value, and it's best to book if you're determined to taste their famous speciality – Hamburgers Gascon (lunch or dinner). Other menus €15 and €20. Terrific welcome from the young owners. Free house apéritif, coffee or *digestif*.

🏃 |O| LE JARDIN DES SAVEURS***

2 pl. de la Libération (Centre).
📧 auchgarreau@intelcom.fr
☎ 05.62.61.71.99

This place has a big reputation but you can enjoy the quality of the cooking on the very cheapest set menu (€20), which lists the likes of duck *terrine* with green peppercorns and herbs and farmhouse chicken roasted with bacon. The more you spend, the more luxurious the ingredients. There are *formules* with 2 dishes for €20 and €30, versions with 3 dishes for €23 and €38 and a fish menu for €59. *À la carte*, prices go off the scale but they don't mind if you order only one dish: platter of duck *foie gras*, crayfish with Greek vegetables, duck breast in a salt crust cooked in a hay box, chocolate and ginger *fondant royal*. There's also a coffee menu. The quality of the welcome and the service are of the standard you'd expect in a place like this. Free apéritif, coffee or *digestif*.

MONTAUT-LES-CRÉNEAUX 32810 (10KM E)

🏃 |O| LE PAPILLON

How to get there: it's on the N21, 6km from the centre of town, in the direction of Agen.
☎ 05.62.65.51.29. 📧 lepapillon@wanadoo.fr
Closed Sun evening and Mon; a week in the Feb school holidays; a fortnight Aug–Sept. **Disabled access. Garden. Car park**.

Good restaurant in a modern building. Mainly meat dishes here, though there are also few fish ones. Try the sole stuffed with *foie gras*, *cassoulet* with Gascon beans, squid salad with ginger vinaigrette or crab ravioli. The €12 weekday lunchtime menu includes wine, then there are others €15–39 – the middle-range ones are particularly good value. Free house *digestif*.

AUDRESSEIN — 09800

🎿 🏠 |●| AUBERGE D'AUDRESSEIN**

Route de Luchon (Centre); it's12km from Saint-Girons, at the mouth of the vallée du Biros.
☎ 05.61.96.11.80 ➡ 05.61.96.82.96
Closed Sun evening, Mon, 3 weeks in Jan and a week in Nov.

The sturdy walls of this nineteenth-century forge contain one of the area's better restaurants. The new owners are still feeling their way so the welcome remains a little reticent. It's still a very charming place with a terrace overlooking the confluence of two rivers. The cuisine is interestingly unusual – try the trout *soufflée*. Menus €17–43. Pleasant double rooms with basin or bath €30–40. 10% discount on the room rate April, June and Oct.

ARGEIN — 09800 (3KM W)

🎿 🏠 |●| HOSTELLERIE DE LA TERRASSE**

It's on the Portet-d'Aspet road.
☎ 05.61.96.70.11
Closed 15 Nov–1 Feb.

A nice little mountain hotel offering a lovely welcome and good food. The main attractions here are the owner's welcome and his excellent local cuisine – trout and ham cooked on a heated stone with ceps. There's a €11 weekday menu, then others at €15 and €27 with supplements for some dishes. A few modest rooms at €47 – ask for one with a view of the mountain. Free apéritif.

AULON — 65240

🎿 |●| AUBERGE DES ARYELETS

How to get there: from Arreau, take the D929 in the direction of Saint-Lary as far as Gauchen then turn right onto the D230
☎ 05.62.39.95.59
Closed Sun evening–Tues out of season; 5 Nov to 20 Dec.

A typical mountain dining room with timbers and beams, a mezzanine floor and a fireplace.

The décor has been brightened by Provençal tablecloths and napkins and a few watercolours. Cuisine is rooted firmly in the local tradition: *garbure* (broth with pickled goose), lamb steak with shallots and honey, duck breast with bilberries, *foie gras*, goat's cheese with ceps in pastry cases. Menus €15–24. The place is impeccably clean and the service is friendly and swift. They put a few tables on the terrace in fine weather. It's best to book. Free house apéritif.

AULUS-LES-BAINS — 09140

🎿 🏠 |●| HÔTEL DE FRANCE**

rue Principale (Centre).
☎ 05.61.96.00.90 ➡ 05.61.96.03.29
Closed mid-Oct to mid-Dec.
Garden. Lock-up car park.

A quiet, charmingly old-fashioned country hotel where you get a warm welcome. Reasonable rooms €27–38 with basin, shower or bath. Good home cooking with menus at €10–24 and half board for €33. À la carte, there's grilled duck breast, duck *confit*, trout with almonds and calf's sweetbreads with morels. The garden leads down to a mountain stream. Free apéritif or coffee.

🏠 |●| AUBERGE LES ORMEAUX

Trein d'Ustou.
☎ 05.61.66.53.22

A nice hotel in the Ustou valley with a few pleasant rooms and a library-cum-sitting room where you can while away the time. Doubles €64. The owner creates a lovely agmosphere and welcomes you with genuine friendliness. Menus €12–15.

AUVILLAR — 82340

🏠 |●| HÔTEL-RESTAURANT L'HORLOGE**

pl. de l'Horloge (Centre).
☎ 05.63.39.91.61 ➡ 05.63.39.75.20
Closed Fri, Sat lunchtime mid Oct to mid April.

The pretty village is one of the pilgrimage stops on the way to Santiago de Compostela. The restaurant caters for all appetites and all pockets. It's a charming place and has a superb terrace under the shady plane trees. For lunch, the *formule bouchon* is ideal, but, if you can afford it, go for the gourmet option. The young chef has real class – try his southwest specialities à la carte. Menus €24–49. It's also an ideal spot to stay, with very clean doubles at €40–46. Free apéritif.

BARDIGUES   82340 (4KM S)

🏃 I●I AUBERGE DE BARDIGUES

The village is on the D11, a 5-min drive off the motorway.
☎ 05.63.39.05.58
Closed Sat lunchtime; Sun evening; Mon; Jan; a fortnight in Oct.

A typical restaurant in a charming village, run by a young couple called Camille and Cyril. The dining room on the first floor has contemporary décor with splendid stone walls, and there's a beautiful and shady terrace opening onto the village and the surrounding countryside. The cuisine is intelligently prepared, light, tasty and fresh: semi-cooked *foie gras* with onion marmalade, *millefeuille* of salmon and artichoke and veal *blanquette*, tasty chocolate *moelleux*. The weekday lunch *menu du jour* for €10 includes wine and there are *menu-cartes* €17–22. As you would expect, the dishes change frequently and the wine isn't too expensive. Free house apéritif.

DUNES   82340 (12.5KM W)

I●I RESTAURANT LES TEMPLIERS

1 pl. des Martyrs; it's under the arcades. Take the D12 for Donzac then the D30.
☎ 05.63.39.86.21
Closed Sat lunchtime; Sun evening; also Mon and Tues Nov–April.

A nice local restaurant prettily set on a lovely village square. The dining room is bright and cosy. The €18 lunch menu (not served weekends and public holidays) offers refined local dishes at very affordable prices: quail salad with sour cherries, sea trout *tartare*, plaice *soufflé* with crayfish cream sauce, *crépinette* of stuffed guineafowl with cabbage and warm apples in cinnamon *coulis*. Others up to €50.

AX-LES-THERMES   09110

🏠 I●I LE CHÂLET**

avenue Turrell; it's opposite the thermal baths of Le Teich.
☎ 05.61.03.55.60 ✉ lechalet@club-internet.fr
Closed the last week in Feb; Nov. **TV. Car park**.

A really nice young couple have taken over this appealing hotel. All the rooms are bright and clean and some look over the Oriège that runs alongside the thermal spa of Le Teich. Doubles from €39. The restaurant is

beautiful and has a reputation as one of the gourmet tables in the Ariège. Menus €13–37 – tasty specialities include chicken stew with mushrooms.

🏃 🏠 I●I L'ORRY LE SAQUET

It's on the N20, 1km from Ax-les-Thermes going towards Andorra.
☎ 05.61.64.31.30 ➡ 05.61.64.00.31
Closed Tues evening and Wed except during school holidays; Jan; All Saints'. **TV. Car park**.

The steep climb to the top is well worth the effort. The twenty or so rooms in this hotel have all been refurbished and have names of flowers rather than numbers; doubles €40 with bath. It's a homely, lived-in kind of place. The €16 weekday menu is very good, listing rabbit in jelly flavoured with ceps, shoulder of lamb with whisky in a potato crust and *clafoutis* (custard baked with fresh fruit). Other menus, €24 and €55, contain excellent surprises including their speciality, twice-cooked pigeon. Free apéritif.

🏃 🏠 I●I LE GRILLON**

rue Saint-Udaut (Southeast); it's 300m from pl. du Breihl.
☎ 05.61.64.31.64 ➡ 05.61.64.25.48
✉ info@hotel-le-grillon.com
Restaurant closed Tues; Wed except in the school holidays; and mid-Oct to early Dec. **TV. Car park**.

A lovely mountain lodge run by Nanette and Philippe, an energetic young couple who know the area well and can organize hikes or snowshoe expeditions in winter. Comfortable rooms are €39–43 for a double with shower/wc or bath. You can have half board or full board, and hiking and skiing packages are available. The cooking is excellent: several dishes have subtle combinations of sweet and savoury flavours such as duck *confit* with a cider-flavoured *caramel*, salmon with vanilla and *croustillant* of duck with mountain honey. Menus €15–26, and the restaurant is always open for residents. 10% discount Sept–June.

BAGNÈRES-DE-BIGORRE   65200

🏃 🏠 I●I HÔTEL D'ALBRET**

26 rue de l'Horloge (Centre); it's on a corner with place d'Albret.
☎ 05.62.95.00.90 ➡ 05.62.91.19.13
✉ eric-coel@wanadoo.fr
Closed Nov–Jan.

The hotel has a pretty Art Deco façade and it's on a corner of the quiet and attractive place d'Albret. Old-style rooms, quite large and painted in fresh colours; the bathrooms have old-fashioned shoe-box baths. There's no double glazing but the road is not noisy. Rooms with washing facilities €21 (shower along the landing at a charge of €4), or bath €31 with bath. The Franco-Belgian couple who run the place make you feel very welcome. Good value for money. 10% discount on the room rate.

🛏 |●| HÔTEL DE LA PAIX**

9 rue de la République; (Centre).
☎ 05.62.95.20.60 ➡ 05.62.91.09.88
Closed 8 Dec–10 Jan. **Garden. TV.**

With sparkling white and pink fabrics in the hall, it's as kitsch as you like but the facilities are very good and the welcome can't be faulted. The rooms are all different (ask to see more than one) and offer good value for money. They're set around a sunny patio or look onto the garden; numbers 19 and 20 even have small balconies. Doubles cost from €23 with basin and €37–53 with shower/wc or bath. There are three dining rooms serving reassuring traditional dishes: scallops with ceps, trout fillet with giroles, steak with morels and duck breast with fruit sauce. Lunch menu at €11 and others €16–23; it's around €23 *à la carte*. The place sometimes hosts business seminars, so it's best to book.

🧗 |●| CRÊPERIE DE L'HORLOGE

12 rue Victor-Hugo, (Centre); it's in the old quarter in a pedestrianised street.
☎ 05.62.95.37.12
Closed Wed–Sat out of season; Nov

The décor is very pretty – musical scores, old typewriters, clocks, pots of preserves, blue hydrangeas – and gives this place the feel of a Parisian bistro. The dish of the day, which costs around €7, is often surprisingly original: duck mince with mashed potato, *tajine* of lamb, braised beef cheek, fish curry with Thai rice. They also offer a wide choice of *crêpes* for €2–5 each. Nice terrace in summer. Free house apéritif.

🧗 |●| LE BIGOURDAN

14 rue Victor-Hugo.
☎ 05.62.95.20.20
Closed Mon out of season.

This place is on the first floor of an old house in a pedestrianized street, so it's not noisy. Hefty beams, rough-cast walls, floral fabrics and still lifes on the walls. Good regional specialities are cooked using fresh produce – and the menu's as long as your arm. There's

a huge choice but quite a lot of supplements on the first menu (€11). Others cost €15–46 and list ravioli with horn of plenty mushrooms, *terrine* of pig's trotters and *foie gras*, *gâteau* of scallops and ceps, duck breast and rasperries *au gratin*. Free house apéritif.

LESPONNE   65710 (10KM S)

🧗 🛏 |●| DOMAINE DE RAMONJUAN**

How to get there: take the D935 from Bagnères to Baudéau and turn right onto the D29; leaving Lesponne in the direction of Chiroulet, it's on the right.
☎ 05.62.91.75.75 ➡ 05.62.91.74.54
e ramonjuan@wanadoo.fr
Closed Sun evening, Mon, Easter and All Saints' school holidays. **Disabled access. Swimming pool. Car park.**

This farm, at a height of 800m, has been turned into a nice hotel without losing its homely feeling. The pleasant rooms are named after flowers. Doubles with shower/wc €43; half board in high season costs €41–49 per person. They offer a host of activities including tennis, ping-pong, rafting, ballooning and billiards, and there's a gym with sauna and Jacuzzi in an old riverside barn. In May 2002, they're opening the granary, which will provide 15 holiday flats. They hold a good number of conferences so it's advisable to book. Free apéritif and 10% discount on the room rate.

BARÈGES   65120

🧗 |●| AUBERGE DU LIENZ, CHEZ LOUISETTE

How to get there: 3km from Barèges, going in the direction of Tourmalet, follow the road to the Plateau de Lienz.
☎ 05.62.92.67.17
Closed a week end April; Nov.

One of the nicest spots in the valley; it's surrounded by trees and is to be found at the beginning of the route around lakes Gière and Néouvielle. In winter, this is where the ski runs finish. It's a bit like the sort of country inn you might find near a big town, not least because of its glorious summer terrace. The *Petit Menu Randonneur* at €14 gives you a starter, a main course such as braised ham and cream cheese to finish. The more expensive ones, €21–30, have a wider choise of more interesting dishes: pan-fried duck *foie gras* with spiced rhododendron honey, *marbré* of duck *confit* with lentils and green peppercorns, trout salad or, *à la carte*, lamb chops. Desserts are on the pricey side. Free house apéritif.

BASSOUES 32320

⚇ 🏠 |O| HOSTELLERIE DU DONJON*

Centre; take the D943 through Montesquiou.
☎ 05.62.70.90.04
Hotel closed the first week in Sept; Jan. **Restaurant closed** Sat. **Garden. Car park**.

Bassoues is a delightful twelfth-century fortified town and this is an attractive, welcoming hotel. The owner checks you in personally, while his wife and a young chef dish up good family dishes at reasonable prices. The rooms are charming and cost €23 with basin, €30–33 with shower or shower/wc and €37 with bath and corner sitting room. Country-style dining room and Belgo-Gascon cooking in the restaurant; weekday menu at €10 and others at €15–30. There's a peaceful terrace for good weather. Free apéritif.

BELCASTEL 12390

🏠 |O| HÔTEL-RESTAURANT DU VIEUX PONT***

It's near the castle.
☎ 05.65.64.52.29 📠 05.65.64.44.32
📧 hotel-du-vieux-pont@wanadoo.fr
Closed Sun evening; Mon; Tues lunchtime; 1 Jan–15 March. **Disabled access. TV. Car park**.

Sisters Michèle and Nicole Fagegaltier have turned their beloved childhood home into a much-admired establishment, serving some of the best cooking around. Their approach is to update old family recipes to show off quality local produce: artichokes and asparagus with cream and vanilla oil, grilled duck *foie gras*, pigeon breast in ginger breadcrumbs and juniper, ceps with garlic, crispy spinach and parsley, bream stuffed with mussels, roast kid with cress *coulis*, caramel tart with juniper. Some of the dishes come at a price but there's a range of menus €23–41. The accommodation is as good as the cooking – the rooms are bright and well maintained and full of little extras that make all the difference. Doubles €69 with shower/wc and €73 with bath. Outstanding welcome and service.

BIERT 09320

|O| AUBERGE DU GYPAÈTE BARBU

pl. de l'Église (Centre); it's 4km from Massat on the road from St. Girons and Tarascon-sur-Ariège.
☎ 05.65.53.97.02 📠 05.65.35.95.92
Closed Sun evening; Mon; the last week in June; the last week in Sept.

Camille Coutanceau and his his wife took over this village bistro on the square, refurbished it beautifully and then gave it the name of a rare scavenging bird which has been recently re-introduced into the wild round here. The menus, €13–27, are simple and superb: trout with ceps, pan-fried *foie gras* with tart apples, goat's cheese *soufflé*. There's a pretty terrace.

CAHORS 46000

⚇ 🏠 HÔTEL DE FRANCE***

252 av. Jean-Jaurès (Centre); the avenue leads to (or from) the station.
☎ 05.65.35.16.76 📠 05.65.22.01.08
Closed a fortnight late Dec–early Jan. **Disabled access. TV. Private garage**.

Modern, functional architecture in this eighty-room hotel. Doubles with shower/wc €39 and €58 with bath. The ones overlooking the courtyard are quieter. They all have a direct phone and mini-bar and some have air conditioning too. 10% discount Oct–Mar.

⚇ 🏠 HÔTEL À L'ESCARGOT**

5 bd. Gambetta.
☎ 05.65.35.07.66 📠 05.65.53.92.38
Closed Sun evening and Mon out of season; 5 weeks in winter. **TV**.

A banal exterior but an attractive interior; the rooms, in an annexe away from the main building, are comfortable and have good facilities. There are beautiful views of the church or private gardens. Doubles €46 with shower/wc. Number 9 sleeps three and has a mezzanine and a big bay window. Hearty buffet breakfast for €5. Informal and very friendly reception. It's advisable to book. 10% discount on the room rate Sept–June.

🏠 |O| LE GRAND HÔTEL TERMINUS***

5 av. Charles-Freycinet (West); it's 50m from the train station.
☎ 05.65.53.32.00 📠 05.65.53.32.26
📧 terminus.balaudre@wanadoo.fr
Restaurant closed Sun, Mon and a fortnight in Nov. **Disabled access. TV. Car park**.

This delightful hotel was built at the turn of the last century by the current owner's grandfather and has never been out of the family. It's seen thorough renovation, though they've taken care to preserve its period style. The rooms are large, pleasant and air-conditioned; doubles from €56 with bath/wc. There's an award-winning restaurant with menus from at €30–76, or a cheaper *formule* served in the bar.

|O| BATEAU-RESTAURANT AU FIL DES DOUCEURS

90 quai de la Verrerie (East).; it's next to the Cabessut bridge.
☎ 05.65.22.13.04
Closed Sun evening, Mon and Jan.

The restaurant looks over the Lot river. The chef has his produce brought in from outlying farms and cooks everything with precision and artistry. He used to be a pastry cook, so try any of his pastry dishes – such as *foie gras* upside-down tart. Also available are light scrambled egg enriched with truffles and duck kebab with *foie gras*, and the desserts are delicious. Lunch *formule* at €11 and other menus €16–38. Efficient, friendly service.

|O| RESTAURANT LA GARENNE

It's on the N20 in the direction of Souillac, 5km outside Cahors.
☎ 05.65.35.40.67
Closed Mon and Tues evening; Wed (except mid-July to end Aug); mid-Feb to Easter. **Garden**. **Car park**.

This is a substantial private house built in 1846 and wonderfully decorated in the style of a country inn. Reception is pleasant and courteous. The cooking is full of imagination, originality and flair and the chef uses the finest of ingredients: scallops with truffle butter, pan-fried *escalope* of *foie gras*, rack of lamb with unpeeled cloves of garlic, eggs scrambled with truffles. Menus €14–43.

|O| RESTAURANT LE RENDEZ-VOUS

49 rue Clément-Marot.
☎ 05.65.22.65.10 ➡ 05.65.35.11.05
Closed Sun and Mon out of season, Sun and Mon lunchtime July–Aug, 29 April–14 May and 4–21 Nov.

An attractive, small, modern dining room with a mezzanine where they exhibit works by local artists. The cuisine is simple but uses fresh produce inventively and it's full of flavour and colour. Try the *foie gras* ravioli, the zander with baby vegetables or the *marbré* of goat's cheese. Weekday lunch menu at €15 or €21.

PRADINES   46090 (3KM NW)

⅍ 🏠 |O| LE CLOS GRAND**

Laberaudi; take the D8 in the direction of Pradines Luzech.
☎ 05.65.35.04.39 ➡ 05.65.22.56.69
Closed 24 Dec–31 Jan; 17–23 Feb; 1–6 May; 1–15

Oct. **Swimming pool**. **Garden**. **TV**. **Car park**.

A provincial inn with a lush garden and a lovely swimming pool. The rooms are very pleasant and comfortable and cost €40 with shower, €50 with shower/wc and €52 with bath; those in the annexe have views over the countryside. The restaurant has a very good reputation and specialities include *chaud froid* of duck *foie gras*, duck breast with honey and fisherman's platter. The cheapest set menu costs €13 (not served Sun), and others are €21–30. Free house apéritif.

ALBAS   46140 (25KM W)

⅍ |O| IMHOTEP

à Rivière Haute (East).
☎ 05.65.30.70.91
Closed Sun evening; Mon; a week in Jan.

Wonderfully located on the banks of the Lot, this restaurant is definitely out of the ordinary. Strains of jazz float through the pretty dining room, which is decorated with some splendid photographs of the region. It's run by a father-and-son team: Dad is in charge in the kitchen. Duck, cooked simply and skilfully, is his speciality: duck breast kebab with sautéed potatoes and ceps, duck brochette with curry, duck *civet*. Menus €15–39. There's a small terrace. You can also buy *foie gras* to take away. Free house apéritif.

CAHUZAC-SUR-VÈRE   81140

|O| LA FALAISE

Route de Cordes; it's 15km north of Gaillac.
☎ 05.63.33.96.31
Closed Fri and Sun evenings and Mon except public holidays; 15 Dec–20 Jan.

Refined cuisine from Guillaume Salvan, who has a real talent for introducing unexpected flavours to regional dishes. Dishes change with the seasons: snails with artichokes and ham, red peppers stuffed with salt cod, haunch of veal and so on. They give well-judged advice about the wine; their list is interesting and features good local Plageoles. The desserts are also excellent. Weekday menu €18 and others up to €38. Best to book.

CARMAUX   81400

|O| RESTAURANT LA MOUETTE

4 pl. Jean-Jaurès.
☎ 05.63.36.79.90 ➡ 05.63.76.40.76

Closed Sun; Mon evening; 10 days in Oct.

This is the best gastronomic restaurant in Carmaux. Monsieur Régis has devised a series of interesting menus: a weekday lunch menu at €9, a menu "Jaurès" and a "surprise" menu priced at €24; there's also a *formule* at €8. Specialities include grilled calves' feet, ravioli stuffed with smoked duck breast, *petit-gris* snails in flaky pastry and *millefeuille* of spiced-bread ice cream. Practically everything is prepared on the premises.

CASTELNAU-DE-MONTMIRAL   81140

⅍ ≙ |●| AUBERGE DES ARCADES

It's on the place des Arcades, the main square.
☎ 05.63.33.20.88
Closed 15–31 Jan.

Decent, very simple rooms for €27–37 with shower or bath. Some overlook the medieval village square and there are some really nice ones under the eaves. Downstairs there's a straightforward, hearty weekday *menu du jour* at €10 including cheese, wine and dessert. Or you could opt for a more expensive one; they go up to €31. The house specialities are wild boar stew and duck *confit*. They finish serving at 9pm. 10% discount on the room rate Sept–June.

LARROQUE   81140 (14KM NW)

⅍ |●| AU VAL D'ARAN

Centre.
☎ 05.63.33.11.15
Closed evenings out of season; Sat; 24 Dec–18 Jan.

A typical village inn with a comfortable dining room and terrace. The weekday lunch menu, €11, starts with a lavish plate of *charcuterie* and is followed by *crudités*, a main course, cheese and dessert. Other menus, €15–24, list boar *civet* or stew, snails Spanish-style, grills over the open fire and so on. Free coffee.

CASTELNAU-MAGNOAC   65230

⅍ ≙ |●| HÔTEL DUPONT**

pl. de l'Église; take the D929 from Lannemezan.
☎ 05.62.39.80.02 ➡ 05.62.39.82.20
Swimming pool (July–Aug only). **Disabled access**.

The hotel has celebrated its 150th anniversary and is a fantastic example of everything that it's worth hanging on to in traditional hotel-keeping. The spacious rooms, €27–34, are very welcoming, scrupulously clean and

good value; you'll be woken by church bells. Generously flavoured local dishes in the large, rustic dining room, with menus €9–18. Specialities include casserole of duck breast, thigh of duck with orange, fresh liver with three fruits, sautéed chicken *paysanne* and a delicious mussel soup. Free apéritif.

CASTELSARRASIN   82100

⅍ ≙ HÔTEL MARCEILLAC**

54 rue de l'Égalité; it's in a road off the pl. de la Liberté.
☎ 05.63.32.30.10 ➡ 05.62.32.39.52
Garden. **TV**. **Garage**.

There's a surprise when you walk into this seemingly ordinary hotel, purpose-built in the early nineteenth century. The rooms overlook a small interior courtyard with a glass roof and the reception area is in a kind of glass cage; the whole place is light and airy. The rooms are delightful and the furniture, though it's as old as the hotel, looks cared-for. Doubles with shower/wc €32–33 or €38–41 with bath. Delightful welcome. 10% discount on the room rate Sept–June.

CASTERA-VERDUZAN   32410

⅍ |●| LE FLORIDA

☎ 05.62.68.13.22 ➡ 05.62.68.10.33
Closed Sun evening and Mon except public holidays; the Feb school holidays. **Disabled access**.

A very old establishment which used to be run by the current owner's grandmother. Go for the fresh *foie gras* with fruit sauce, the upside-down tart with duck *foie gras* and caramelized sauce or the fresh duck liver with Gascon Floc. An excellent weekday lunch menu for €12; others €21–40. Free coffee.

CASTRES   81100

⅍ ≙ HÔTEL RIVIÈRE**

10 quai Tourcaudière (Centre); it's on the banks of the Agout, opposite the old tanners' houses.
☎ 05.63.59.04.53 ➡ 05.63.59.61.97
TV. **Pay garage**.

The attractive décor – reproductions of Impressionist paintings – and the congenial staff make this a pleasant hotel. The pretty rooms smell fresh and clean. You'll pay €26–39 with shower/wc. Buffet breakfast. The rooms overlooking the embankment can be noisy even though they have double glazing, and the terrace gets very busy in summer. Free breakfast after the second night and free use of garage.

☎ |●| HÔTEL DE L'EUROPE***

5 rue Victor-Hugo (Centre); 30m from pl. Jean-Jaurès.
☎ 05.63.59.00.33 ➡ 05.63.59.21.38
Restaurant closed Aug. **TV**.

This glorious seventeenth-century house was discovered and restored by a group of young people with a passion for art and architecture; it has the feel of an artist's studio. Each room is wonderful – a subtle balance of glass and warm brick, splendid beams and designer furniture, dressed stone and modern bathrooms. Doubles (€51) all have bathrooms and phones, and some have a mini-bar. In the restaurant, you select what you want from buffet dishes: lunch costs €8 and dinner €10. Specialities include *cassoulet* cooked in duck fat with sausage and duck *confit* and huge dessert platters. An extremely good hotel.

|●| RESTO DES HALLES

Place de l'Albinque; (Centre).
☎ 05.63.62.70.70

A good brasserie on the first floor of the Halle Baltard, specializing in meat – rib of beef, *pot-au-feu* with marrowbone, *andouillette* with mustard. Dish of the day €7, weekday menu for €11 or around €23 *à la carte*. Good wine at fair prices and friendly welcome, even if you turn up late.

⅍ |●| RESTAURANT LA MANDRAGORE

1 rue Malpas (Centre); it's near pl. Jean-Jaurès.
☎ 05.63.59.51.27
Closed Sun; Mon lunchtime; Jan.

A fashionable restaurant renowned for its futuristic designer décor and meticulous cooking. The lunch menu costs €11 and there are others up to €37 – warm salad of skate with herbs, duck breast in wine, *millefeuille* of seasonal fruit. À *la carte*, dishes include a delicious crab *parmentier*, veal *piccata* with noodles and asparagus and pan-fried crayfish with balsamic vinegar. The proprietor used to work at *Le Grand Écuyer* and was chosen as Belgium's best *sommelier* in 1975 and 1976; no surprise that the wine list is as thick as a mail-order catalogue. Free apéritif.

|●| LE PESCADOU

20 rue des Trois-Rois
☎ 05.63.72.32.22
Closed Sun and Mon.

When there's no space left in this little restau-

rant they set extra tables in the fish shop – the owner is a fishmonger first and a restaurateur second. The only dishes that are always on the menu are *bouillabaisse* or fish soup because everything else depends on the catch of the day. There are no menus but expect to pay around €20 *à la carte*. Everything is good, fresh and generously served. The service is full of charm and good humour – which explains why the place is always so full.

BURLATS   81100 (10KM NE)

⅍ ☎ |●| LE CASTEL DE BURLATS

8 pl. du 9-Mai-1945; take the D89 or the D4 then follow the signs to Burlats.
☎ 05.63.35.29.20 ➡ 05.63.51.14.69
Disabled access. **TV**. **Car park**.

A splendid château built between the fourteenth and sixteenth centuries. The owners have retained the natural charm of the building and the interior, and the comfortable rooms are lovely; some floors are laid with hand-made tiles. Doubles €61 with shower/wc or bath. The tearoom is in the huge salon, which also has a handsome billiard room. Menus €20–27. The extensive gardens are attractive. Free aperitif.

ROQUECOURBE   81210 (10KM N)

⅍ |●| LA CHAUMIÈRE

14 allée du Général-de-Gaulle; coming from Castres, go through the village and it's on the right.
☎ 05.63.75.60.88
Closed Sun evening; Mon; 3 weeks in Jan; the first week in July.

A family-run restaurant on a pretty square. You will be welcomed with kindness and the cuisine is excellent. There's a huge, peaceful dining room with a family atmosphere at the rear. Dish of the day €9 and menus €15–33. Specialities include semi-cooked duck *foie gras*, zander with shallot butter, *tournedos* with morels, duck breast with raspberry vinegar and a whole host of good local dishes. The *patronne* is sometimes willing to share her recipe for two dishes called *melsa* and *bougnette*. If you're there in raspberry season, ask for the raspberry *gratin*. Free apéritif.

SAINT-SALVY-DE-LA-BALME   81490 (16KM E)

⅍ |●| LE CLOS DU ROC

Centre; take the D622 in the direction of Brassac for 15km then turn right into the lane sign-posted to Saint-Salvy.

☎ 05.63.50.57.23
Closed Wed and Sun evenings; the first fortnight in Feb.
Disabled access.

A reliable restaurant in a solid granite house – it's popular locally, so it may be best to book. The spacious dining room is in a converted barn with enormous beams and the décor is stylish and charming. The cuisine has a good reputation and prices are affordable. They do a weekday lunch menu for €9, which includes cheese, dessert and wine, and others at €14–33. Specialities include trout gougons, duck thigh in Banyuls wine, knuckle of pork *confit* with peaches and *croustades*. Free aperitif.

CAUSSADE   82300

⅍ 🖹 |◉| HÔTEL LARROQUE**

av. de la Gare (Northwest); it's opposite the train station.
☎ 05.63.65.11.77 ➡ 05.63.65.12.04
e hotel.laroroque@club-internet.fr
Restaurant closed Sat lunchtime and Sun evening out of season. **Swimming pool**. **Garden**. **TV**. **Lock-up car park**.

A family business that goes back five generations and has a solid reputation. Guests and atmosphere are both rather elegant and the décor is plush; there's a very pleasant swimming pool and a solarium. Double rooms with en-suite bathrooms with shower/wc €38 or €41 with bath – one has a small terrace onto the swimming pool. The restaurant offers regional cuisine with a touch of style in dishes such as zander with three preserves, corn biscuits with *petit-gris* snails flavoured with flat parsley and iced *nougat* with walnuts. Menus €11–20. Free apéritif.

MONTEILS   02300 (2KM N)

⅍ |◉| LE CLOS DE MONTEILS

It's just 2km from the motorway exit.
☎ 05.63.93.03.51
Closed Sat lunchtime; Sun evening; Mon; mid-Jan to mid-Feb.

It's minutes from the motorway to this gourmet restaurant. It's run by chef Bernard Bordaries, who has worked in some of the greatest restaurants in France – and indeed the world – before settling in this lovely priory, swathed in Virginia creeper, out in the country meadows. He and his charming wife have created a place of refined charm. *Menu-express* €11, €14 lunch menu and others €22–27. Dishes include tart with farm bacon, *charlotte* with goat's cheese and artichokes,

jellied oxtail and cheek, sea bream with fennel marmalade and light *anchoïade*, stuffed chicken wing and luscious desserts. There's a terrace for sunny days. Free house apéritif.

CAUTERETS   65110

⅍ 🖹 |◉| HÔTEL DU LION D'OR**

12 rue Richelieu (Centre).
☎ 05.62.92.52.87 ➡ 05.62.92.03.67
e hotel.lion.dor@wanadoo.fr
Closed 1 Oct–20 Dec.

The *Lion d'Or*, run by sisters Bernadette and Rose-Marie, is the oldest hotel in this spa town – the ancient yellow-and-white façade is a bit of a clue. It's gradually been renovated with the utmost attention to detail: the lift is camouflaged by a wooden door and there's a wonderful percolator in the bar. The rooms are plush and cosy, with elegant light fittings, old beds and working antique phones; doubles with shower/wc are €37–50 and €53–62 with bath. Good home cooking is served in the pleasantly old-fashioned dining room, which is almost the last vestige of the old hotel. Half board €36–46 per person. 10% discount on the room rate except during school holidays.

🖹 |◉| LE SACCA**

11 bd. Latapie-Flurin.
☎ 05.62.92.50.02 ➡ 05.62.92.64.63
Closed Oct and Nov.

The clientele here mainly come for the waters. The décor is modern and somewhat uninspiring but the chef, Jean-Marc, produces excellent cuisine, the best in Cauterets. He's refined the regional recipes and given pride of place to vegetables – a pretty rare occurence. Try his upside-down tart of *foie gras*, the sea bream *à l'Espagnole*, *cassoulet* or the duck *confit*. You're served a dish of *amuse-bouches* while you're waiting to order. The plates are hot and the service is very professional. Menus €13–17. Half board, €37 per person, is compulsory July–Aug. The rooms have shower/wc or bath and cost €38–49; some have balconies with a view of the mountains.

⅍ |◉| LA FERME BASQUE

It's on the road to Le Cambasque, 4km from Cauterets or 1.2km from the ski resort on the road to Lac d'Ilhéou.
☎ 05.62.92.54.32
Open by reservation only out of season. **Closed** Nov–Dec.

Lots of *crêpes* and sandwiches are served in

this old farm, which has been going since 1928. The new owners have added some more elaborate dishes, too, using mutton, lamb and vegetables that they grow themselves: *garbure* with wild spinach, black pudding with onions, *blanquette* of lamb, lamb chops, lamb stew. Menus €13–17. In season meals are served on the huge terrace, which has a fabulous view down to Cauterets. Léon is a real shepherd and he likes to talk about his work; Chantal spent twenty years abroad and speaks lots of languages. She's brilliant at managing even the most difficult guests without losing her sense of humour. Free coffee.

CAYLUS   82160

🏠 |●| HÔTEL RENAISSANCE**

av. du Père-Huc.
☎ 05.63.67.06.26 ➡ 05.63.24.03.57
Closed Sun evening; Mon; a fortnight in Jan; 10 days in May.

The restaurant is in the main street of this very pretty hamlet. The rooms are modern and comfortable – doubles €34 with shower or €40 with bath. Weekday lunch menu €11, others €17–24. Dishes such as zander in veal *jus*, pan-fried *foie gras* with apples and duck breast with spices.

CONDOM   32100

🎋 🏠 HÔTEL LE LOGIS DES CORDELIERS**

rue de la Paix; it's near the bandstand, heading towards Agen.
☎ 05.62.28.03.68 ➡ 05.62.68.29.03
📧 le-logis-des-cordeliers@wanadoo.fr
Closed 3 Jan–3 Feb. **Garden. Swimming pool. TV. Garage.**

A quiet, modern hotel in the centre of town; it's surrounded by greenery. Joëlle and Pierre go out of their way to take care of you and can give you information about the locality. Very comfortable and spacious rooms with en-suite bathrooms; the ones above the street cost €41 while those overlooking the garden and the swimming pool are bigger and cost €64. 10% discount 15 Oct–15 April.

🎋 |●| L'ORIGAN

4 rue du Cadeo; it's on the way to the church, opposite the church school.
☎ 05.62.68.24.84

Closed Sun; Mon (Mon lunchtime in July); Sept.

Popular pizzeria in the old quarter. At "Jacques' place" you feel as if you're eating with friends. Congenial welcome, attentive service and tasty cooking – pizzas, pasta and huge salads, *escalope* of veal *à la parmigiana*, house steak. Set menus €10 at lunch for a main course and a dessert or €15–20 *à la carte*. The tables outside on the street are always full when the weather's good. Free apéritif.

🎋 |●| MOULIN DU PETIT GASCON

Route d'Eauze; it's on the outskirts of town, on the river bank opposite the stadium.
☎ 05.62.28.28.42
Closed Sun; Mon except mid-June to mid-Sept; 3 weeks in Nov.

A very special place which is so picturesque you could almost believe it was built as a film set; the terrace is surrounded by greenery on all sides. The cooking is light and prices are reasonable: duck breast in pastry, semi-cooked *foie gras* and home-made *cassoulet*, *osso bucco*, veal sweetbreads, a delicious bitter chocolate *gâteau*. Weekday lunch menu €11, others €16–24. In summer, you dine by candlelight to live music – book your table in advance. Ask the *patronne* about river cruises. Free apéritif.

CONQUES   12320

🏠 |●| AUBERGE SAINT-JACQUES**

rue Principale (Centre); it's near the abbey.
☎ 05.65.72.86.36 ➡ 05.65.72.82.47
Closed Mon out of season and Jan. **TV. Disabled access. Car park.**

The one hotel in Conques that everyone can afford – it's great value. Pleasant staff. Clean rooms, some of them very lovely indeed. Doubles €30–46. The restaurant serves local dishes but don't expect miracles. *Formule brasserie* at €13 and menus from €16.

🎋 🏠 |●| LE DOMAINE DE CAMBELONG***

It's at the bottom of the village next to the Dourdou.
☎ 05.65.72.84.77 ➡ 05.65.72.83.91
📧 domaine-de-cambelong@wanadoo.fr
Closed Sun (except public holidays and July–Aug); 10 Nov–12 Dec; 1–15 March. **Swimming pool. TV. Car park.**

One of the few remaining water-mills on the Dourdou. Very comfortable rooms, some with balconies or private terraces overlooking the river. Doubles €84 with shower/wc and €89–99 with bath. You eat as well as you sleep: foie gras with fig compote, zander with potatoes, duck with mashed potato and fondant foie gras, tart with cep caviar. This inspiration extends to the desserts – try meringue millefeuille with chestnuts. Lunch menu at €21 (except Sun) including apéritif and wine, then others up to €38. Half board is compulsory from Easter to All Saints' and costs €90 per person. 10% discount apart from long weekends over Easter, Whitsun, Christmas and New Year.

GRAND-VABRE   12320 (5.5KM N)

|●| CHEZ MARIE

How to get there: by the D901.
☎ and ➡ 05.65.69.84.55
Closed Tues–Thurs evenings except in high season; Jan. **Garden**. **Car park**.

A delightful little inn in this tiny village in the wilds of the Aveyron – Marie, the owner, is the niece of the village grocer. It's decorated simply, with a covered terrace. Staff are amiable and the service is attentive. Quality produce and traditional dishes: chicken with girolles, roast kid with sorrel, omelette with girolles and foie gras, aligot to order, estofinado in season. Nothing wildly out of the ordinary, but they're delicious anyway. Menus €12–20. It's best to book.

CORDES   81170

♈ ♙ HÔTEL DE LA CITÉ**

rue Haute; it's in the upper town.
☎ 05.63.56.03.53 ➡ 05.63.56.02.47
Closed 15 Oct–1 April.

Eight charming and characterful rooms in this complex of medieval buildings with high ceilings and stout beams. Some have fantastic views over the countryside, and all have modern facilities. Prices are very affordable for a tourist town – €45 for a double with shower/wc or bath. Free coffee.

♙ |●| LES ORMEAUX – RESTAURANT ET CHAMBRES D'HÔTES

3 rue Saint-Michel.
☎ 05.63.56.19.50
Closed Tues and 20 Dec–end Jan. **TV**. **Car park**.

The nicest establishment in the old town. It's a substantial medieval house with a cool courtyard and a dining room supported by huge old beams. The charming owner will advise you which local wine suits the dishes you have chosen from his wife's menus (€15–30). The produce she uses is of the highest quality and the cuisine is both original and true to the region – the tripe à l'albigeoise has a touch of saffron to give it a medieval flavour. There are a few double rooms for €52.

♈ ♙ |●| HOSTELLERIE DU PARC**

Les Cabannes.
☎ 05.63.56.02.59 ➡ 05.63.56.18.03
Closed Sun evening and Mon out of season. **Disabled access**. **TV**. **Swimming pool**. **Garden**. **Car park**.

This substantial stone country house, which overlooks an old park and garden, has a large rustic dining room. Menus at €19–45 with a children's menu for €10; kids under 6 eat free. Chef Claude Izard is a force to be reckoned with. He chairs an enormous number of associations and is a champion of authentic local cooking. His specialities prove the point – try rabbit with cabbage, petit-gris snails à la tarnaise, fresh foie gras. A few simple, quite comfortable rooms for €53 with shower/wc or €58 with bath. Free apéritif and 10% discount on the room rate Nov–March.

DOURGNE   81110

♈ ♙ |●| RESTAURANT DE LA MONTAGNE NOIRE

15 pl. des Promenades.
☎ 05.63.50.31.12
TV.

Take a seat on the pleasant terrace overlooking the long village square and enjoy the wonderful dishes created by David and Frédéric Gely. Their cooking gets away from the kind of thing you find everywhere in the region and interprets a few traditional dishes with unusual combinations of flavours – a remarkably light aumônière of gizzards confits and duck breast, quail breasts in a potato crust, pot-roast pigeon, bass with pickled tomatoes. Excellent desserts include homemade tiramisù, strawberry gratin and an orange pancake gâteau. Menus €12 (not Sunday) and €18–26. A few newly opened double rooms from €34. 10% discount on the room rate out of season.

SAINT-AVIT   81110 (5KM NW)

♙ |●| LES SAVEURS DE SAINT-AVIT

It's on the D14 between Soval and Mussagrel.

☎ and ➡ 05.63.50.11.45
Disabled access.

The newest gourmet restaurant in the Tarn. Mrs Scott is from the area; her husband Simon was voted the best young British chef in 1991 and worked at the Savoy in London before being persuaded to try his skills out here. His golden duck with honey and his risotto with fresh truffles are wonderfully light. And for cooking of this quality, the prices are very reasonable; menus €17–29 and around €40 *à la carte*. At the moment the wine list is rather short but with time it'll improve.

EAUZE 32800

🛏 |●| AUBERGE DU GUINLET*

Route de Castelnau-d'Auzan; take the D43.
☎ 05.62.09.80.84 ➡ 05.62.09.84.50
Closed Fri and Jan. **Disabled access. Swimming pool. Garden. TV. Car park.**

A huge holiday complex in beautiful countryside offering various options: hotel rooms at €40, bungalows 1km away on the lakeside for around €300 a week and camping spaces. The restaurant provides simple family cooking. The €10 weekday menu includes wine, while others up to €26 feature local specialities: duck *confit*, *civets* or *croustade*. Half board €34. They offer loads of activities, including tennis, swimming and golf.

ENDOUFIELLE 32600

|●| LA FERME DE MANON DES HERBES

It's on the D634 between Lombez and Isle-Jourdain.
☎ and ➡ 05.62.07.97.19.
Closed Wed and the New Year's holidays. **Swimming pool. Garden. Car park.**

This farm has been lovingly decorated with straw-seated chairs, dried flowers hanging from the beams, flowers and candles on the tables and an open fireplace; it has an intimate, warm ambience. Double rooms have good bathroom facilities for around €58. Menus, €19–27, list regional dishes, fish and house specialities: *foie gras* grilled or as a terrine, sea bass with *Noilly* sauce, pan-fried scallops *à la Provençale*, fish *papillotes*, *carpaccio* with fresh herbs and tasty desserts.

ENTRAYGUES-SUR-TRUYÈRE 12140

⚕ 🛏 |●| LA TRUYÈRE*

60 av. du Pont-de-la-Truyère (Northeast).

☎ 05.65.44.51.10 ➡ 05.65.44.57.78
Closed Mon and 15 Nov–30 March. **Disabled access. Garden. Private car park.**

Service 12.30–1.45pm and 7.30–8.45pm. A nice inn near the Gothic bridge with a pleasant garden.There are 25 double rooms, €31 with shower and €33–43 with bath; some have a view of the river and the valley. The cooking is good, with set menus at €10–30. Try the *marbré* of chicken in a chive cream, the *cassolette* of snails with a pastry crust or the rabbit *terrine*. À *la carte* they offer roast monkfish with paprika, lamb tripe *Aveyronnais* and green salad with ham and smoked duck breast. A good little family restaurant. 10% discount on the room rate Sept–June.

🛏 |●| HÔTEL DU LION D'OR*

Tour de Ville (Centre); it's in the main street.
☎ 05.65.44.50.01 ➡ 05.65.44.53.43
Disabled access. TV. Swimming pool. Garden. Car park.

Large, solid, stone-built hotel with fifty nice rooms; doubles €43–67 with shower/wc or bath. Some have whirlpool baths and balconies overlooking the garden. There's a sauna, a gym, and a pleasant garden where you can swim in the pool or play tennis or crazy golf. The restaurant is separate from the hotel; in it you enjoy good traditional dishes such as stuffed cabbage or trout, and a few more inventive dishes too. Weekday lunch *formule* €8 and menus €11–49.

ESTAING 12190

⚕ 🛏 |●| HÔTEL-RESTAURANT AUX ARMES D'ESTAING*

quai du Lot; it's across from the Gothic bridge.
☎ 05.65.44.70.02 ➡ 05.65.44.74.54
Closed a day and a half per week out of season; 15 Nov–1 March. **TV. Lock-up car park.**

A delightful hotel with provincial charm. The rooms in the main building have been renovated; doubles with washing facilities cost €27, €38 with shower/wc and €43 with shower/wc or bath. The cooking is good, tending towards the classic but with one or two unexpected dishes: wild duck with ceps, salad of lamb sweetbreads and girolles. Set menus €11–30. In summer they prefer you to stay on a half board basis – €33 per person. Free coffee.

🛏 |●| AUBERGE SAINT-FLEURET*

rue François-d'Estaing.

☎ 05.65.44.01.44 ➡ 05.65.44.72.19
e auberge.st.fleuret@wanadoo.fr
Closed Sun evening and Mon out of season; Dec–Feb.
Garden. **TV**. **Garage**.

The exterior of this building has been renovated, as have the rooms – those overlooking
the garden are particularly pleasant. Doubles
€32–40 with shower/wc or bath. The chintzy
dining room is cosy and decorated in shades
of blue. The cooking is traditional: snails with
walnut butter, roast pigeon breast with cep
jus, tomato and snail tart topped with Tomme
cheese, roast duck breast with spices. This is
no place for frugal eaters. Fair prices:
€11–26 with a gourmet menu with three
main courses for €43. Best to book in season.

ESTANG · 32240

⅍ 🏠 |●| HÔTEL-RESTAURANT DU COMMERCE*

pl. du IV Septembre. It's in the centre of the village, near
the arena.
☎ 05.62.09.63.41 ➡ 05.62.09.64.22
Closed Sun, Mon and Wed; the last week in Aug; the
last week in Dec.

This venerable establishment has had a
facelift. The rooms have been completely renovated and are ideal for an overnight stay;
doubles €33–36. The restaurant has a reputation for fine regional cuisine, serving calf's
head *sauce gribiche*, duck breast stuffed with
ceps, *foie gras* with fruit and leg of fattened
duck in Madeira wine. Set menus at €12–26
or around €27 *à la carte*. Free coffee.

FIGEAC · 46100

⅍ 🏠 HÔTEL CHAMPOLLION**

3 pl. Champollion (Centre).
☎ 05.65.34.04.37 ➡ 05.65.34.61.69
TV.

Ideally located right in the middle of the town,
this place is a bit of a change from traditional establishments. Rooms are bright, spacious and attractive with quality beds and
linen and tastefully decorated bathrooms;
doubles €41. There's a beautiful staircase in
a small atrium, a friendly bar and a pleasant
terrace. 10% discount on the room rate.

⅍ |●| RESTAURANT LA CUISINE DU MARCHÉ

15 rue Clermont.
☎ 05.65.50.18.55

Closed Sun.

The open-plan kitchen lets you watch the
chefs preparing tasty dishes that are much
lighter and more refined than most of the
local specialities. The colours, flavours and
smells really show off the fresh market produce: duck, *foie gras*, fresh fish such as sea
bream fillet, delicate desserts such as the
croustillant of summer fruit. Menus €14–
29 and a high-quality wine cellar. Joël Cen-
teno, the man in charge, is an experienced
hotelier. He acts more like a teamleader than
a manager, and creates a delightfully convivial atmosphere. Best to book. Free apéritif.

|●| LA PUCE À L'OREILLE

5 rue Saint-Thomas (Centre); it's in the heart of the old
town near the covered market and the Champollion
museum.
☎ 05.65.34.33.08
Closed Mon except July–Aug; a week around All Saints'
Day.

Located in a pretty fifteenth-century house in
a narrow, picturesque side street, this split-
level restaurant looks out onto a walled garden. The cooking has a great reputation.
There's a lunch *formule* for €12 and menus at
€15–32 (the cheapest options aren't served
on Sun or public holidays). Dishes – duck
breast with a honey and pepper sauce, fillet
of red mullet in oil, zander with vanilla-
flavoured hazelnut oil, duck breast with onion
marmalade – are attractively presented. The
service is swift and smiling. It's best to book.

FOIX · 09000

⅍ 🏠 HÔTEL PYRÈNE***

"Le Vignoble", rue Serge-Denis (South); it's on the N20
about 2km from the centre of town on the Soula-
Roquefixade road, going towards Spain.
☎ 05.61.65.48.66 ➡ 05.61.65.46.69
Closed mid-Dec to mid-Jan. **Disabled access**.
Swiming pool. **Garden**.

This hotel is modern compared to others in
town, and it is perfectly placed to catch
tourists as they migrate south to the Spanish
border. Take a dip in the pool in the garden
and you'll forget all about the journey. Doubles with shower/wc or bath €38–52. Free
apéritif.

🏠 |●| HÔTEL LONS***

6 pl. G.-Duthil (Centre); it's in the old town near Pont-
Vieux.
☎ 05.61.65.52.44 ➡ 05.61.02.68.18
e hotel-lons-foix@wanadoo.fr

Closed Fri evening; Sat lunchtime out of season; 20 Dec–20 Jan. **Disabled access**. **TV**.

Comfortable double rooms for €43–58 with en-suite bathroom/wc. Traditional, local dishes in the restaurant – fresh *foie gras*, *cassoulet* with duck *confit*, duck breast with pepper sauce. *À la carte* expect to pay about €20.

⦿ LE SAINT-MARTHE

21 rue Noël-Peyrévidal (Centre).
☎ 05.61.02.87.87 ➡ 05.61.05.19.00
e restaurant@le-saintemarthe.fr
Closed Tues evening; Wed out of season; Feb.

Although this is a grand restaurant in a very chic part of town, it's actually relatively affordable: menus €22–40 or around €44 *à la carte*. You get classic regional dishes for your money – *cassoulet* with duck *confit*, warm goat's cheese with cumin-flavoured whipped cream, scallops with shellfish *coulis*, upsidedown tart with black pudding and mushrooms. Serious stuff.

MONTGAILLARD 09330 (2KM S)

⦿ LE POÊLON

14 av. de Paris.
☎ 05.61.03.54.24
Closed a week around 15 July and three weeks in Jan. **Garden**.

This restaurant is always packed because of the quality of the tasty cuisine – excellent fish or meat. And with menus at €15–20, it offers good value for money.

SAINT-PIERRE-DE-RIVIÈRE 09000 (5KM W)

⋇ 🏠 ⦿ HÔTEL-RESTAURANT LA BARGUILLÈRE**

Centre; take the D17.
☎ 05.61.65.14.02 ➡ 05.61.02.62.16
Closed Wed and Nov–Feb. **Garden**.

Pleasant little village hotel with a nice garden; doubles with bath from €35. Regional and classic dishes with specialities such as pork trout with chive and crayfish sauce, pork *filet mignon* with prunes, fresh *foie gras* with apples flambéd in Hypocras, kid fricassée with morels. The €12 set menu includes cheese, dessert, wine and coffee, and there are others up to €33. Free coffee.

BOSC (LE) 09000 (12KM W)

⋇ 🏠 ⦿ AUBERGE LES MYRTILLES**

Col des Marrous; take the D17 from Foix.
☎ and ➡ 05.61.65.16.46

e aubergelesmyrtilles@wanadoo.fr
Closed Mon, Tues and public holidays out of season; mid-Nov to end-Jan. **Swimming pool**. **TV**. **Car park**.

A lovely chalet 1000m up and just 4km from the ski runs at the Tour Laffont. In summer it's wonderful for walkers – and all year round it's good for people who enjoy their food. Double rooms €44 with shower/wc and €52 with bath. In the dining room you'll find delicious dishes including trout with almonds, omelette with ceps and bilberry tart. Menus €14–21. Half board is compulsory July–Aug. There's an indoor pool, a sauna and Jacuzzi. Free apéritif.

NALZEN 09300 (19KM SE)

⦿ LES SAPINS

route de Foix.
☎ 05.61.03.03.85
Closed Mon; Wed; Sun evening; a fortnight in Nov; 3 weeks in Jan.

An excellent restaurant offering gourmet cuisine, now back in family hands. The dining room is very attractive. Stylishly presented dishes include duck breast *tournedos* with Hypocras and the cooking uses exclusively regional produce. Menus €11–24.

FRONTON 31620

⋇ 🏠 ⦿ LOU GREL

49 rue Jules Bersac.
☎ 05.61.82.03.00 ➡ 05.61.82.12.24
Closed Sat and Sun evenings and Mon. **Swimming pool**. **Garden**. **TV**.

This place has been renovated with scrupulous taste; double rooms €37–64 with bath. The cuisine has an excellent reputation and you're received warmly. Specialities include *foie gras* in salt, *salmis* of pigeon, duck breast Rossini (with *foie gras*), *osso bucco* and beef fillet with ceps. The €14 menu is served weekdays (apart from public holidays), and there are others €17–34. There's an all-duck menu and an all-fish menu, both including apéritif, wine and coffee. The dining room is pretty and there's a very pleasant garden terrace with a view of the park and the swimming pool where they serve salads and grills. It's a local institution, so it's best to book. Free coffee.

GAILLAC 81600

⋇ 🏠 ⦿ LA VERRERIE**

1 rue de l'Égalité (West); it's on the road to Montauban

and well signposted.
☎ 05.63.57.32.77 ➡ 05.63.57.32.27
e verrerie@club.internet.fr
Disabled access. **TV**. **Garden**. **Swimming pool**. **Car park**.

This is a newish place, but it's housed in a splendid nineteenth-century building which used to be a glass factory. The interior design is remarkably tasteful, retaining the original character while establishing a warm modern style. All the rooms are really pleasant and comfortable and have a personal feel; some have a view over a huge park. Prices are very reasonable considering all of the above; doubles €43 with shower/wc or €56 with bath. The staff are extremely welcoming. You'll find the best in local cooking in the restaurant – there's a *formule* for €12 and menus €18–30. Free Kir.

|●| LES SARMENTS

27 rue Cabrol (Centre); it's near the tourist office.
☎ 05.61.57.62.61 **e** sarments@spray.fr
Closed Sun evening and Mon; Wed evening Oct–April; mid-Dec to mid-Jan; mid-Feb to mid-March.

Located in a narrow medieval street in the old quarter, this restaurant has built a reputation by word of mouth. The setting is splendid – it's an old cellar with fourteenth- and sixteenth-century vaulting which has retained its original character and style. The tables are well-spaced and the welcome is friendly, though the atmosphere's a bit starchy. The cooking is good and takes its inspiration from the local produce, combining tastes and flavours in intriguing ways. Try the pan-fried *foie gras* with puréed lentils, the sea bass braised with baby vegetables or the duck thigh *confit*. Menus €23–33.

GAVARNIE   65120

🏃 🏠 COMPOSTELLE HÔTEL**

rue de l'Église (South).
☎ and ➡ 05.62.92.49.43
e compostelle@gavarnie.com
Closed 30 Sept–26 Dec and beginning of Jan to beginning of Feb. **Disabled access**. **Car park**.

Sylvie and Yvan, who are keen hikers, travelled a fair bit before taking over this pleasant little family hotel. Rooms are named after mountain flowers; you get the best view from the one called "Lys", which has a balcony. Those on the second floor have skylights. Doubles €32 with shower, €33–36 with shower/wc or €42–43 with bath – unfortunately the soundproofing isn't great, even in

the section of the hotel that's been renovated. Yvan knows the area well and can organize walks. 10% discount for a two-night stay, except during school holidays.

GIROUSSENS   81500

🏃 🏠 |●| HÔTEL-RESTAURANT L'ÉCHAUGUETTE

Centre.
☎ 05.63.41.63.65 ➡ 05.63.41.63.13
Closed Sun evening; Mon except July–Sept; 1–21 Feb; 15–30 Sept.

An "échauguette" is a corner turret on a house – in this case a thirteenth-century house in wonderful surroundings. Five rooms with bath for €43. The restaurant has a good reputation and the dining room is as delightful as the cooking. There's a good choice of menus, €11–43, and a splendid list of dishes *à la carte*: *marbré* of chicken livers, duckling with cep *jus*, *blanquette* of lamb, beef *daube* stew in Madiran and so on. Wines start at about €10 and you'll get half a bottle of Gaillac for €4. Claude Canonica will make you feel welcome and fill you in on the history of the village and the region. Free apéritif or coffee, or 10% discount on the room rate.

SAINT-SULPICE   81370 (9KM W)

🏃 |●| LE BERSY

It's on the main square opposite the post office.
☎ 05.63.40.09.17
Closed Sun; Feb school holidays; 15 Aug to the start of Autumn school term.

An excellent bar-restaurant-pizzera that's always full. Ask them to show you the blackboard where they list dishes of the day, and *à la carte* there's quite a good choice – duck breast with mushrooms, mixed salads and lots of good pizzas. The speciality is *daube* of gizzards stewed in Gaillac wine. Weekday lunch menu €9 and others up to €27. Friendly welcome and swift service, but they don't rush you. Free apéritif.

GRAMAT   46500

🏃 🏠 |●| LE RELAIS DES GOURMANDS**

2 av. de la Gare.
☎ 05.65.38.83.92 ➡ 05.65.38.70.99
e gcurtet@aol.com
Closed Sun evening; Mon lunchtime; the Feb school holidays. **Swimming pool**. **Garden**. **TV**. **Car park**.

An enormous house in immaculate condition

with a swimming pool, an outside bar and a flower garden. Bright, modern but rather anonymous rooms with bathrooms and direct-dial phone go for €45–73. You'll get a polite and attentive welcome from Susy, the British owner. The restaurant has a good reputation for light, inventive cooking: lamb sweetbread salad with sweet-and-sour sauce, scorpion fish with shellfish and mushroom sauce with Noilly, duck hearts *en brochette*, stuffed free-range chicken with a garlic *jus*. Good cheeses and fine desserts, particularly the *couronne* of chocolate with orange mousse. Weekday menu €14 (not served Sun), and others €15–34. Inexpensive local wines. 10% discount on the room rate Sept–June.

☎ |●| LE LION D'OR***

8 pl. de la République.
☎ 05.65.38.73.18 ► 05.63.65.38.84.50
e lion.d.or@wanadoo.fr
Closed Mon and Tues lunchtimes; 15 Dec–15 Jan. **TV**.
Car park.

One of the best restaurants in the region, with rooms in the best tradition of French hotel-keeping. Excellent reception and service. The décor is ultra-classic, with cream walls, chandeliers, oil paintings and the finest table linen. The superb chef has experience in France, the Far East and the West Indies, and offers duck liver and apple *tarte tatin*, snail stew with ceps and ham, gently braised local veal, apple and *quince crumble and vanilla ice cream with liquorice milk. Menus €18–58. The well-chosen wine list features good-value bottles from the region. Rooms are comfortable and splendidly maintained. Doubles with shower/wc €50 and €58–69 with bath.

GRAMONT   82120

⅔ |●| LE PETIT FEUILLANT

It's next to the château.
☎ 05.63.94.00.08
Closed Sun evening and Wed; Mon and Tues in winter; Feb.

This place is wonderfully friendly. No *à la carte* options, but six menus at €14–30 list the likes of home-made pasta, roast pork with prunes, *cassoulet*, gizzard salad, tart with garlic and cheese, duck *confit*, stuffed chicken (for 4), house *foie gras* and duck with sea salt. Everyone gets a complimentary apéritif, and you can enjoy it on the terrace with a view of the château. The good local cuisine is a big draw in the area, so it's important to book. Free *digestif*.

GRAULHET   81300

⅔ |●| LA RIGAUDIÉ

Route de Saint-Julien-du-Puy (East); it's 2km east of the town centre.
☎ 05.63.34.50.07 ► 05.83.34.29.27
Closed Sat lunchtime, Sun evening and Mon.

This restaurant, in a fabulous setting in a nature park, has an enormous air-conditioned dining room with a magnificent beamed ceiling. The cooking is excellent and the service professional. Weekday lunch menu €12 and others €18–37. Start with an appetizer then opt for sole or, even better, cod with *tapenade*. Other dishes include roast scallops with braised cabbage, pot-roast pigeon with ceps, rib steak with ceps and small tarts of duck with apples and honey sauce. Free apéritif.

LASGRAÏSSES   81300 (8KM NE)

⅔ |●| CHEZ PASCALE

Centre; it's on the D84, in the direction of Albi.
☎ 05.63.33.00.78
Closed Sun–Thurs evenings; the last fortnight in Aug.

This classic village bistro has old photographs on the walls, trophies in the cabinet and old-fashioned glazed-cotton tablecloths. It's a lively place. Weekday menu €11 and others up to €28. The cheapest one starts with your own choice of starters from the buffet, followed by a well-prepared local dish, a cheese course and a dessert. This is one of the rare establishments that know how to cook a steak *bleu* – seared on the outside, raw in the middle but hot right through. Good cheese board, but leave some space for the house flan. Excellent service. Free coffee.

LACAUNE   81230

⅔ ☎ |●| HÔTEL CALAS**

4 place de la Vierge
☎ 05.63.37.03.28 ► 05.63.37.09.19
e hotelcalas@wanadoo.fr
Closed Fri evening and Sat lunchtime Oct–March; mid-Dec to mid-Jan. **Car park**.

Four generations of the same family have run this old house and it's one of the best-known places in the region. The rooms are various sizes but are regularly renovated; doubles €33–40. It's renowned for a cuisine which is regional but which has an edge of inventiveness: guineafowl with ceps, twice-cooked pigeon. Menus €11–37. If you want to have

Sunday lunch (when they serve a special menu for €23), it's essential to book. The dining room is pleasant and decorated in shades of yellow. 10% discount on the room rate.

LACROUZETTE   81210

⌂ |●| L'AUBERGE DE CRÉMAUSSEL

How to get there: from Castres, take the D622 in the direction of Lacaune; 2km after Lafontas turn left in the direction of Lacrouzette-Rochers du Sidobre. The inn is signposted from here.
☎ and ➡ 05.63.50.61.33
Restaurant closed Wed, Sun evening and Jan. **Hotel closed** Nov–March. **Car park**.

Friendly country restaurant with a solid reputation and five spotless rooms with wooden floors (€30). The dining room has stone walls and a fine fireplace. Specialities – cheese soup in winter and crayfish in summer – have to be ordered ahead, but they serve a very good Roquefort salad at any time. Menus €14–20; *à la carte*, prices are fair. Finish with the local pastry known as *croustade*, which is sheer heaven.

LAGUIOLE   12210

⅍ ⌂ |●| HÔTEL RÉGIS***

pl. de la Patte-d'Oie.
☎ 05.65.44.30.05 ➡ 05.65.48.46.44
Closed 20 Nov–25 Dec.
TV. **Swimming pool**. **Car park**.

This is one of the oldest hotels in Laguiole, with big reception rooms, sitting rooms, a piano and a lot of atmosphere. The tastefully refurbished rooms are huge, comfortable and modern; doubles €34–40 with shower/wc, €37–64 with bath. The corridors are enlivened by beautiful art photographs. Good traditional cooking in the restaurant: *tripou*, rib of beef, duck breast with chestnuts, *aligot*. Menus €11–21. The welcome can be rather brusque. 10% discount on the room rate except weekends and school holidays.

⌂ |●| GRAND HÔTEL AUGUY***

2 allée de l'Amicale.
☎ 05.65.44.31.11 ➡ 05.65.51.50.81
e grand.hotel.auguy@wanadoo.fr
Closed Sun evening; Mon and Tues lunchtimes; 20 Nov to 28 March. **Disabled access**. **Garden**. **TV**. **Car park**.

A very good establishment with a solid reputation. Pleasant, well-equipped doubles for €46 with shower/wc and €56 with bath. The large dining room is bright, if a bit garish, and the cooking first-rate. Traditional local dishes hold their own: try the *galette* of pig's trotters in meat stock with ceps and potato cake, the stuffed tripe, the grilled rib of beef with *aligot*, the medallions of hare with juniper berries or the salmon trout in a Laguiole cheese sauce. Then indulge yourself with one of the wonderful desserts. Menus €25–61. Half board is available at €69–76 per person. The welcome and service are very pleasant.

CASSUÉJOULS   12210 (10KM NW)

⅍ |●| CHEZ COLETTE

How to get there: take the D900 in the direction of the Sarrans dam.
☎ 05.65.44.33.71
Closed Wed out of season.

Reservations are essential at this lovely little country bistro. Colette will ensure that you fall in love with the region, first by talking about it with passion and warmth and second by serving you simple, invigorating and filling meals. The setting couldn't be less pretentious or the atmosphere more relaxed and friendly. Menus from a modest €9: oyster mushroom flan, sausage with *aligot*, blue cheese and walnut tart, *truffade*. Free coffee.

LANNEMEZAN   65300

⅍ |●| CHEZ MAURETTE

10 rue des Pyrénés (Centre).
☎ 05.62.98.06.34
Closed Sun except public holidays and early Sept.

The inauspicious frontage of this restaurant, located in a dreary town, wouldn't make you slam on the brakes to stop – but that would be an error. The house speciality is the prize-winning tripe, and there's excellent *daube* of beef and calf's head. The owner and her daughters serve you. *Formule* (dish and dessert) for €7, or menus at €9 and €14. Wednesday is sheep market day – simply everybody piles in for lunch. Free coffee.

LATOUILLE-LENTILLAC   46400

⌂ |●| RESTAURANT GAILLARD**

It's in the village.
☎ 05.65.38.10.25 ➡ 05.65.38.13.13
e contact@hotel-gaillard.fr
Closed Nov. **Disabled access**. **TV**. **Car park**.

The place was thoroughly renovated a year or two back, and the rooms are all pleasantly decorated, simple, clean and air-conditioned; doubles with shower/wc €35 or €41 with bath. The restaurant enjoys an excellent reputation and draws in a regular local crowd. Dishes include *foie gras*, trout and duck *confit*, wild mushrooms, local lamb and terrific desserts. Set menus €13 (not Sun lunch) and up to €26. You get a particularly warm welcome.

LAUTREC   81440

|●| LE CHAMP D'ALLIUM

4 route de Castres (Centre).
☎ 05.63.70.05.24
Closed Sun evening; Mon; Tues lunchtime (except July–Aug).

The cooking here is considered to be among the most imaginative in the Tarn. It's not cheap for the area, but it is well worth it. The chef buys his ingredients from local farmers and producers or fresh from the market, and the dishes are fine as a result. They also change frequently: it's hard to choose between the cocks' combs with little onions and the gazpacho with roast crayfish and smoked bacon. And the suckling lamb in a herb crust, the fillet of beef with bonemarrow and the pot-roast pigeon are simply delicious, as is the turbot spiked with bay leaves. Menus €21–46. The dining room is pleasant and comfortable.

LAVAUR   81500

🏠 |●| HÔTEL LE JARDIN**

8–10 allée Ferréol-Mazas (Centre); it's next to the cathedral.
☎ 05.63.41.40.30 ➥ 05.63.41.47.74
e hotel.du.jardin@wanadoo.fr
Disabled access. TV. Garden.

The best hotel in town, beautifully situated in the centre. It's a grand house with comfortable rooms – €38 for a double. The staff make you feel welcome. The restaurant lists classic dishes using fresh produce: duck with cherries, pigeon in Gaillac wine, rack of lamb with thyme, fish stew. They make their own bread. Menus €14–35.

LECTOURE   32700

🎿 🏠 |●| HÔTEL DE BASTARD**

rue Lagrange (North).
(☎05.62.68.82.44 ➥ 05.62.68.76.81

e hoteldebastard@wanadoo.fr
Closed 20 Dec–1 Feb. **Swimming Pool. TV. Garden. Car park**.

This marvellous hotel is a fine example of eighteenth-century architecture. It's furnished and decorated with taste and is ideal for a romantic weekend. Pleasant welcome and incredible value. Doubles €43–61 with shower/wc or bath; half board, €49–66, is compulsory in July/Aug. In summer they serve meals on the terrace, which has a wonderful view over the rooftops, the swimming pool and the cypresses. Superlative chef Jean-Luc Arnaud is in charge in the kitchen. Menus €15–25. There's a *formule à la carte* which allows you to try some of the chef's specialities: iced cream of prawns with chives or asparagus in flaky pastry to start, then wing and thigh of roast pigeon with a salad, and, for dessert, prune soufflé or a *millefeuille* of soft fruit. The exceptional gourmet menu features three special *foie gras* dishes served with three different regional fruit brandies. 10% discount on the room rate for a minimum three-night stay Sept–June.

LEYME   46120

🎿 🏠 |●| HÔTEL-RESTAURANT LESCURE**

Route de St-Céré.
☎ 05.65.38.90.07 ➥ 05.65.11.21.39
Closed Sun evening out of season; Christmas school holidays; New Year's Day. **TV. Car park**.

This characterful hotel-restaurant, which has been run by the same family for more than fifty years, offers comfy accommodation at reasonable prices: doubles €30 with shower/wc. Breakfast costs €6 and half board starts at €40 per person. The large dining room overlooks a pond; you'll find terrific regional dishes like smoked wild boar with local mushrooms alongside classics such as smoked salmon with blinis, *tournenos Rossini* (fillet steak with *foie gras*) and duck breast flambéed with plum brandy. Weekday menu for €11, then others at €14–27. There's a good selection of wines. The decoration is thoughtful and tasteful, with a genuine Picasso and a number of Matisse reproductions. Free house apéritif.

LOURDES   65100

🎿 🏠 |●| HÔTEL RELAIS DES CRÊTES**

72 av. Alexandre-Maqui; it's on the right as you come

into Lourdes from Tarbes.
☎ 05.62.42.18.56
Closed 11 Nov–20 March

The location of this small family guesthouse, at the end of a side street behind a pretty hedge, protects it from the noise of the near-by main road. There are eleven tasteful, simple rooms looking out onto the courtyard; they're all spotlessly clean. In warm weather, breakfast is served on the hydrangea-filled terrace. Double with shower for €20 and €26–31 with bath. Lovely welcome from the charming *patronne*. 10% discount on the room rate April–Nov.

🛏 🏠 |O| HÔTEL MAJESTIC**

9 av. Maransin (Centre); it's a ten-minute walk from the shrines at the corner of the avenue and a cul-de-sac where you can park.
☎ 05.62.94.27.23 ➡ 05.62.94.64.91
Closed 15 Oct–15 April. **Disabled access. TV**.

Service at lunchtime and from 7.30pm. A classy establishment run by the friendly Cazaux family. The rustic rooms are extremely comfortable and have all mod cons including direct-dial phones and en-suite bathrooms with hairdriers; some have balconies. Doubles with shower or bath up to €44. Family cooking served in the chic dining room: duck breast, salmon *en papillote*, veal escalope with cream and morels, stuffed cabbage with Armagnac. The €8 *formule* is served daily and there are others €15–18. The *patronne* takes a lot of trouble for her guests; the only drawback, in fact, is the traffic noise. Free apéritif, coffee or *digestif* and 10% discount on the room rate.

🛏 🏠 |O| HÔTEL D'ALBRET**

21 pl. du Champs-Commun (Centre).
☎ 05.62.94.75.00 ➡ 05.62.94.78.45
Restaurant closed Sun evening and Mon out of season, 6 Jan–9 Feb and 25 Nov–31 Dec.
Hotel closed 6 Jan–10 March and 25 Nov–31 Dec **TV**.

The hotel is opposite the covered market and is in the part of Lourdes which looks more like a normal town. It offers comfortable rooms; those at the back are quiet and have a view of the mountains. Doubles with shower or bath €30–45. The cuisine in the restaurant is traditional with a regional basis; menus €11–15. Try the *garbure* with duck thigh, the *foie gras escalope* caramelized with apples or the iced Grand Marnier soufflée with egg custard. The boss is welcoming and generous. 10% discount on the room rate or 5% discount on half board, except in Aug.

🛏 🏠 |O| HÔTEL BEAUSÉJOUR***

16 av. de la Gare.
☎ 05.62.94.38.18 ➡ 05.62.94.96.20
e beausejour.p.martin@wanadoo.fr
Disabled access. Garden. TV.

A reasonably priced three-star, conveniently near the station. Classy rooms all have direct-dial telephones and safes as well as bathrooms with wc and hairdryer. The ones overlooking the station itself are big but poorly soundproofed; the ones at the back are smaller but they have a view over the town and towards the distant Pyrenees. Doubles with shower/wc or bath from €52. There's a pleasant garden where you can eat in good weather. The brasserie is open for lunch and dinner and offers a *formule brasserie* at €13 and menus €17–23. 10% discount on the room rate 15 Oct–30 March.

LUCHON   31110

🛏 🏠 |O| L'AUBERGE DE CASTEL-VIELH

Route de Superbagnères.
☎ and ➡ 05.61.79.36.79
Closed during the week Nov–Jan; Wed March–June and Sept. **Garden. TV. Car park**.

A pretty little house in the regional style, set on a small hill; it has a big garden and an appealing terrace. The cuisine has a good reputation: prawns with mushrooms, *fricassée* of lamb's sweetbreads with morels, *tripounet* of lamb in the old style and *pain brûlé*. Menus €15–34. The rooms are spacious and have mountain views; doubles €38–46. Free house apéritif.

🛏 |O| LE PAILHET

12 av. du Maréchal-Foch; it's next to the station.
☎ 05.61.79.09.60
Closed Tues evening, Wed and 15 Nov–1 Dec. **Car park**.

There's a *bar-tabac* attached to this little house and its dining room is always busy with locals. The regional cuisine is straightforward and tasty: frogs' legs with garlic, escalope of *foie gras* with green apples and duck breast with *foie gras*. Menus €13–25. Free apéritif.

MONTAUBAN-DE-LUCHON   31110 (2KM E)

🏠 |O| LES CASCADES**

How to get there: follow the signs for the Herran forest road and head for the hillside church of Montauban.
☎ 05.61.79.79.16 ➡ 05.61.79.83.09

Closed mid-Oct to end March. **TV. Garden**.

It's advisable to book at this exceptional establishment. The house is a listed building and it's in a wonderful location, clinging on to the mountainside in the middle of an enormous park just 50m from a gushing waterfall. You have to leave your car at the bottom and walk up, but you'll enjoy the scenery and the peace and quiet. In summer you eat outside and enjoy the superb views over the valley; otherwise it's the elegant dining room. Wonderful traditional cooking, with *pétéram* (stew of sheep's trotters and tripe) and *pistache* (braised leg of mutton with haricot beans). Their meat specialities include beef with ceps and duck breast with pickled shallots. Lunch menu €17, with others at €21 and €26 (on Sunday only). À *la carte* you can expect to pay €33 per person. There are a few double rooms; €32 with washing facilities and €38 with shower/wc. Half board, available if you stay for three nights or more, is €36–41. There are some lovely walks in the forest and, for a small charge, the owners can take you on a fifteen-minute hike.

CASTILLON DE LARBOUST   31110 (8KM W)

⅍ 🏠 |●| HÔTEL L'ESQUÉRADE**

How to get there: take the D618, the road to the Payresourde pass, for about 6km. 500m after Saint-Aventin, the hotel is at the bottom of the road.
☎ 05.61.79.19.64 ➡ 05.61.79.26.29
e info@esquerade.com
Closed 15 Nov–15 Dec.

The village is 954m up in gorgeous green countryside. The hotel itself is comfortable, and the building typical of the locality – it's built of stone with wooden balconies. Most of the rooms overlook the valley. Doubles €39 with shower and €49 with bath/wc; you can stay half-board on request. A young and gifted chef recently took the place over and he produces excellent dishes. The menu changes with each season, because he uses only fresh local produce: frogs' legs with parsley, crayfish with tomato *concassée* and so on. Menu prices start at €14 and go all the way up to €53. There's an excellent wine list with a selection of 150 different wines, mostly coming from the area between Biarritz and Narbonne. 10% discount on the room rate for a minimum three-night stay and free house *digestif*.

MELLES   31440 (30KM NE)

🏠 |●| AUBERGE DU CRABÈRE

How to get there: take the D618 then the N230.

☎ 05.61.79.21.99 ➡ 05.61.79.74.71
Closed Tues evening and Wed in winter (except during the school holidays).

The imposing house is right in the middle of the village, on the route of the GR10 walking trail. There are a few spacious, country-style rooms, with half board compulsory at €30 per person. Patrick Beauchet toiled long and hard as a chef on transatlantic cruise liners before going for this post. He's made the mountains his home and his cuisine is bursting with local goodies such as wild mushrooms, crayfish, snipe and other game in season. There's mountain soup, crayfish with corander sauce, lacquered pigeon and pigs' trotters with morels. He's become so expert that he's even written a recipe book called *Mes recettes de Comminges et des Pyrénées Centrales*. Menus €18–26 and a short menu "randonneur" for €11 – ideal if you're walking.

LUZ-SAINT-SAUVEUR   65120

⅍ 🏠 |●| HÔTEL LES TEMPLIERS**

pl. de la Comporte; opposite the church of Saint-André in the old part of town.
☎ 05.62.92.81.52 ➡ 05.62.92.93.05
Closed 1 Oct–1 Dec and 30 Apr–15 June.

Rooms are simple but spacious and not without charm – there's some wonderful and highly polished local furniture. Doubles with shower €32–40 or €34–43 with shower/wc; numbers 1 and 2 sleep three people and have shutters opening onto the fortified church and the square. There's a welcoming *crêperie* at street level. Monday is market day, when the front of the hotel is transformed into a Spanish-style flower stall. Free apéritif.

⅍ |●| CHEZ CHRISTINE

rue d'Ossun prolongée.
☎ 05.62.92.86.81
Closed lunchtimes; 24 May–10 June; 1 Oct–15 Dec.

The setting is welcoming and the décor most attractive: the hangings come from as far afield as Mali and Madagascar, and there are dried flowers, Bedouin keffiyehs and Toureg turbans. On the food front you'll find snacks and full meals – mixed salads, *noisettes* of lamb, duck breasts, pizzas, pasta, Pyrenean specialities to order and desserts that change regularly. No set menu; a meal *à la carte* costs around €17 and they do small portions for children. Even so, it's not exactly cheap for what it is. Free apéritif.

MARTRES-TOLOSANE   31220

🏕 🏠 |●| HÔTEL-RESTAURANT CASTET**

av. de la Gare
☎ 05.61.98.80.20
Hotel closed Nov school holidays. **Restaurant closed** Sun evening and Mon. **Swimming pool**. **TV**.

A quiet house just opposite the station. Double rooms with bath €35. There's a €11 menu (not served Sat evening or Sun lunchtime), others at €21 and €24 and good choices *à la carte*. They do duck specialities and a rib of beef cooked in a salt crust alongside other classic dishes using fresh local produce. Things change with the seasons – game in autumn, good fresh fish in summer. There's a wonderful shady terrace. Free house apéritif.

LE FOUSSERET   31430 (15KM NE)

🏕 |●| RESTAURANT DES VOYAGEURS

Grand Rue; take exit 23 off the A64 motorway as far as Fousseret and it's on the road up to the central square.
☎ 05.61.09.53.06
Closed Sat; Sun evening; 7 Aug–7 Sept; Christmas to New Year.

A grey house with green shutters. The welcome is as charming as the interior. Family-style cooking and dishes influenced by the region: *pot Gascon*, beef fillet, ravioli with *foie gras* in cep broth. The menu at €9 is excellent value and there are others €19–33. In summer you dine on the terrace behind the house. Free apéritif.

MAZAMET   81200

🏠 |●| HÔTEL JOURDON**

7 av. Albert Rouvière (Centre).
☎ 05.63.61.56.93 ➡ 05.63.61.83.38
Restaurant closed Sun evening and Mon. **TV**. **Car park**.

Robust, tasty food. On the menus (€14–38) you'll find specialities like cep ravioli, rack of lamb lacquered with Armagnac, *cassoulet*, vegetable *gratiné à l'ancienne* and *millefeuille* of monkfish with shellfish cream. The restaurant is popular with workers at lunchtime – the atmosphere may be very relaxed but the service is up to scratch, even if there isn't much elbow room. Some of the rooms are a bit cramped, too, but they're clean and air-conditioned. Doubles €43 with shower/wc or €46 with bath.

MILLAU   12100

🏠 |●| INTERNATIONAL HÔTEL-RESTAURANT***

1 pl. de la Tiné (Centre).
☎ 05.65.59.29.00 ➡ 05.65.59.29.01
Disabled access. **TV**. **Private car park**.

This place looks for all the world like it's part of a chain – it's hard to believe that it has been run by the Pomarède family for three generations. There are 110 rooms in all, so there's a good chance of finding a vacancy. They're all soundproofed and some have air conditioning. Prices are reasonable: doubles with shower/wc €43 and €73 with bath. If you have the choice, take a room facing south with a splendid view over the countryside. The plush restaurant has an excellent reputation and the dishes are elaborate. Menus from €21 with a decent range of local dishes.

🏕 🏠 |●| HÔTEL-RESTAURANT LE CÉVENOL**

115 rue du Rajol (South); 500m from the centre of town.
☎ 05.65.60.74.44 ➡ 05.65.60.85.99
Closed Sun, Mon–Wed lunchtimes except Easter Mon and Whit Mon, Mon and Tues lunchtime July to mid-Sept and 22 Nov–7 March. **Disabled access**. **Swimming pool**. **TV**. **Car park**.

A pleasant, modern establishment on the edge of the town. Menus, €17 and €25, are served in the restaurant or on the extremely pleasant terrace. Classic and carefully prepared dish: lamb sweetbreads with grapes, Roquefort sorbet with toasted walnut bread, fillet of beef with marrowbone, fruit soufflé with verbena parfait and coffee caramel. Children's menu €8. Doubles cost €45–55 with bath/wc. Half board, €48–53, is compulsory during the world pétanque competition. The place is quiet in spite of the busy road nearby. Free coffee.

🏕 |●| RESTAURANT CHEZ CAPION

3 rue J.-F. Alméras; it's close to bd. de la République, near the town hall.
☎ 05.65.60.00.91 ➡ 05.65.60.42.13
Closed Tues evening and Wed out of season; the Feb school holidays; early July.

This restaurant is highly respected by the people of Millau, who use it for all kinds of celebratory meals. The delicious cooking is mainly regional and uses a great deal of local produce. The dining room is bright with slightly old-fashioned décor, and prices are very reasonable given the quality of the cooking. There's an €11 weekday lunch menu and others €15–30. *À la carte*, choose from home-smoked salmon, duck breast with seasonal fruit and lamb sweetbreads *persillade* and help yourself as often as you like from the sweet trolley. Friendly welcome. Free coffee.

|●| AUBERGE OCCITANE

15 rue Peyrollerie (Centre).
☎ 05.65.60.45.54
Closed Sun except July–Aug; the last fortnight in March.

This restaurant is in an extremely old house. The menus cost €11–18; expect dishes such as *salade du berger*, *aligot*, duck breast, lamb fillet and Aubrac beef. Excellent regional specialities include cabbage with spelt (a kind of wheat), beef in red wine and trout fillets with sorrel sauce.

MIRANDE 32300

🎿 🏠 |●| AUBERGE DE LA HALLE

rue des Écoles; (Centre).
☎ 05.62.66.76.81
Closed Fri evening; Sat; 15 Aug–7 Sept. **Garden**.

A totally simple place where you feel relaxed right away. Traditional cuisine in handsome portions on a range of appetizing menus for €10–23. There are also a few rooms in a separate building – some overlooking the road, others the garden. They're modest and clean and cost €27 with basin and €30 with shower or shower/wc. The young owners are lovely.

MIREPOIX 09500

🎿 |●| RESTAURANT PORTE D'AVAL

cours Maréchal-de-Mirepoix (South).
☎ 05.61.68.19.19
Closed Sun evening and Mon; Tues lunchtime in winter and spring; 3 weeks in Nov.

It's a real surprise to find such a bright, modern restaurant so close to the medieval town. You'll get a splendid welcome and enjoy good cooking that shows off local produce and fish to their best advantage: duck breast with apples, *foie gras* with peaches and almonds, roast sea bream and trout with fresh herbs and prawns. Honest prices, too – the lunch menu costs €14 with others at €19–27. Nice terrace for summer. Free coffee.

COUTENS 09500 (6KM W)

🎿 |●| LE CLOS SAINT-MARTIN

How to get there; it's on the D119, between Mirepoix and Perriers.
☎ 05.61.68.11.12 ✆ le.clos.stmartin@wanadoo.fr
Closed Tues and Wed out of season; 31 Dec– 14 Feb.
Disabled access. Garden. Car park.

A convivial place. The ancient house has been respectfully brought up-to-date, and has warm yellow colour-washed walls with lavender windows and doors. Traditional cuisine and regularly changing dishes such as lamb cutlets cooked over the coals and duck breast. They claim that Tony Blair is a regular when he holidays in the area. Lunch menu €8, others €16–20. Lovely welcome. Best to book in season. Free rum and ginger.

MOISSAC 82200

🎿 🏠 |●| LE PONT NAPOLÉON

2 allée Montebello; it's just by the bridge.
☎ 05.63.04.01.55 ➡ 05.63.04.34.44
Closed Sun evening;Mon lunchtime; Wed; a fortnight at the beginning of Jan. **TV. Car park**.

The hotel is a dream, with fair prices and amazing bathrooms which, like the bedrooms, have been redecorated and insulated against the noise of the road. Doubles €34–52. Despite that, the restaurant is better-known. The *formule "34 Bis'trot"* provides for all appetites with old-fashioned dishes such as veal *blanquette* and *pot-au-feu*. At €7 or €12, it's pretty good value for money, but the gastronomic cuisine of Michel Dussau is what's made the restaurant's reputation, and it's better sampled on menus at €23–53. Free apéritif.

DURFORT-LACAPELETTE 82390 (6KM NE)

🎿 🏠 |●| HÔTEL-RESTAURANT AUBE NOUVELLE**

How to get there: take the D16 out of the village in the direction of Cazes-Mondenard or the D2 in the direction of Lauzerte.
☎ 05.63.04.50.33 ➡ 05.63.04.57.55
✆ aubenouvelle@chez.com
Closed 23 Dec–5 Jan. **Garden. Private car park**.

Owner Marc de Smet's parents moved from Belgium to the Quercy in 1955, and he and his wife Claudine took over their business. It's an idyllic spot surrounded by fields, which you can admire from the lovely terrace and garden. The clean, well-maintained rooms have been renovated to a high standard and cost €44 with shower/wc or bath. Half board, €41 per person, is compulsory May–Sept. The cooking is regional in flavour and Belgian in influence – saddle of rabbit *à la flamande*, shellfish *waterzooi*, beef in brown ale sauce and snail stew with creamed garlic. And all are in decent portions; menus €9–30. 10% discount on the room rate after the third night Sept–June.

MONCORNEIL-GRAZAN   32260

|●| RESTAURANT L'AUBERGE D'ASTARAC

It's between Masseube and Simorre.
☎ 05.62.65.48.81
Open evenings; Sun lunch; **Closed** Dec–Jan.
Garden.

This inn has been lovingly restored by two exceptional people who fell in love with the area. There's an old bar, a delightful dining room and a glorious terrace. At the bottom of the flower garden you'll see Christian Ter-mote's kitchen garden, full of vegetables and herbs. He taught himself to cook and uses those herbs with great subtlety. Try the apple stuffed with *foie gras*, the pigeon breast with a reduction of Madeiran wine, the cep and snail stew and the rhubarb tart. Set menus €23–46. There's an excellent choice of wine, with a particularly good selection from the south. Lucie is the genial lady of the house; she even lets her clients choose their own bottle from the cellar. You have to book.

MONTAUBAN   82000

⅍ ✿ |●| HÔTEL MERCURE***

12 rue Notre-Dame (Centre).
☎ 05.63.63.17.23 **e** mercuremontauban@wanadoo.fr
TV. Car park. Pay garage.

As a rule chain hotels don't appear in this guide, but this is an exception. The *Mercure* is simply the best hotel in town, very well-managed and with real charm. Inevitably it's also the most expensive – double rooms €75–85 with shower/wc or bath. The décor is bright and warm and the rooms are spacious and decorated in contemporary style with particularly splendid bathrooms. In the eighteenth century, the building was a private mansion. They also do food; menus €14–32. Free house apéritif and 10% discount on the room rate.

⅍ |●| LE SAMPA

21 and 21 [bis] rue des Carmes (Centre).
☎ 05.63.20.36.46
Closed Sun.

The trendy décor may have been inspired by the Wild West, but the cooking is 100% French and solidly regional: omelettes, grilled meat, duck *confit*. One weekday lunch menu for €10, *à la carte* you'll pay around €18 and there's a selection of dishes of the day. It's all good stuff and helpings are enormous. From May to mid-October they serve grills and salads on the lovely terrace. The welcome and service are congenial, and the warm, friendly atmosphere at the bar extends to the dining room. Free apéritif.

⅍ |●| AUX MILLE SAVEURS

6 rue Saint-Jean (Centre).
☎ 05.63.66.37.51
Closed Sun evening; Mon; the last fortnight in Aug; a week in Jan.

It's hard to find a restaurant offering better value for money in town. Although the setting is a tad impersonal, it's pleasant and relaxing. For a quick lunch, opt for the speedy *menu du marché*, €11, but to make more of an occasion of your meal choose from the menus at €17–31. The chef has travelled a good deal, and you'll taste flavours from faraway places in dishes which are otherwise rooted in the cuisine of the southwest. The service, though generally attentive, suffers when the place gets full. Free coffee and 10% discount June–Aug.

⅍ |●| RESTAURANT LE VENTADOUR

23 quai Villebourbon (West); it's on banks of the Tarn, opposite the Ingres museum.
☎ 05.63.63.34.58
Closed Sat and Mon lunchtimes; Sun; 1–15 Jan; 3 weeks in Aug.

Incredibly popular restaurant with a vaulted brick dining room done up to look like the inside of a castle. The place gets flooded whenever the Tarn bursts its banks, but on the other hand it's always cool whatever the temperature outside. This is cooking at its most refined and the service is first-rate. Prices are reasonable – weekday lunch menu €15 and others €21–40. Dishes include *fricassée* of mushrooms and gizzards *confit* in a pastry case with sesame seeds, canelloni with smoked and fresh salmon and duck breast stuffed with *foie gras*. Excellent desserts, too: *crêpe Suzette* with banana and liquorice cream. Free house *digestif*.

MONTRÉAL · 32500

|O| CHEZ SIMONE ·

It's in the village.
☎ 05.62.29.29.44.40
Closed Mon and sometimes Sun evening.

There are two entrances – one goes into the old-fashioned bistro, the other leads via the terrace to a main dining room which has all the attributes of a modish, gourmet restaurant. In the middle there's a display showing off all the bottles on the wine list and an impressive collection of Armagnac flagons – more than thirty vintages. There are three menus at €19–31. The top-price one starts with goose and duck *foie gras*, which is sliced in front of you and served without adornment. The cuisine is essentially regional but has quite a lot of sauces and they also do good fish. The owner has a nice bar under the arcades in the square where you can knock back a glass or two of Armagnac.

FOURCÈS · 32250 (6KM N)

👫 🏠 |O| CHÂTEAU DE FOURCÈS***

It's in the village.
☎ 05.62.29.49.53
Closed Oct–April. **Swimming pool. Garden. TV. Car park.**

A smart, charming place in a twelfth-century chateau in the middle of the village. It has been magnificently restored and has all the modern facilities you could wish for. The rooms are in soft colours and elegantly co-ordinated. There's a river running through the garden and a swimming pool nearby. High-season prices are €111 for doubles with shower or shower/wc and €148 with bath. Very good cooking to match, with dishes that change regularly: house *foie gras*, fillet of beef with Roquefort, duck breast with morels and monkfish with saffron sauce. Menus at €16 for weekday lunch then others at €22–43. Formal, stylish welcome and attentive service. Free house apéritif.

MONTRICOUX · 82800

👫 🏠 |O| LE RELAIS DU POSTILLON*

Le Bugarel; coming from Montauban, take the D115, before the village turn right.
☎ 05.63.67.23.58 📠 05.63.67.27.68

e relaisdupostillon@wanadoo.fr
Closed Fri evening and Sat lunchtime Sept–June; 15–30 Nov. **Garden. Car park.**

A pleasant inn providing good regional cooking. The dining room is cosy and they do some wonderful house specialities. Set menus from €14 (not Sun) up to €27. À la carte try cep omelette, frogs' legs *civet* of hare, *cassoulet*, *foie gras*, salmon with sorrel in flaky pastry, zander with saffron or the home-made pastries. There's a pleasant shady terrace and a garden. The rooms aren't particularly attractive but they're well-maintained; doubles with washing facilities €20 and €23 with shower (wc along the landing). Free house apéritif.

MONTSÉGUR · 09300

🏠 |O| HÔTEL-RESTAURANT COSTES**

52 rue Principale.
☎ 05.61.01.10.24 📠 05.61.03.06.28
e hotel-costes@post-club-internet.fr
Closed Mon out of season; Sun evening; mid-Nov to end March. **Garden.**

The building is covered in Virginia creeper and it's a nice place to stop if you're planning an assault on the peak of Montségur. A dozen simple rooms, fairly priced at €31 with shower and €33 with shower/wc. There's a family feel to the restaurant where they serve very good home cooking: *civet* of wild boar, duck breast with figs, game *pâtés*, duck *confit* with chanterelle mushrooms. Menus €15–29. There's a pleasant terrace and garden.

NAJAC · 12270

👫 🏠 |O| L'OUSTAL DEL BARRY**

pl. du Bourg.
☎ 05.65.29.74.32 📠 05.65.29.75.32
Restaurant closed Mon, Tues lunchtime and Nov–March. **Disabled access. Garden. TV. Car park.**

This lovely inn is an appealing place to stop and you'll be warmly received. The décor is plush and the rooms are very elegant while retaining an authentic rustic feel. Doubles with basin €32, with shower/wc and bath €48–51. The restaurant serves largely regional dishes using seasonal ingredients. Menus €19–46: chicken with cabbage, ox cheek in red wine, sweetbreads with ceps, *astet najacois* (roast pork stuffed with fillet steak, parsley and garlic). And the desserts are mouthwatering. Catherine Miquel is the passionate sommeliere who created the wine list, and she'll help you find the perfect vintage to complement to your meal. Free apéritif.

🏃 🏠 |●| LE BELLE RIVE**

le Roc du Pont (Northwest); it's 2km from the village.
☎ 05.65.29.73.90 ➔ 05.65.29.76.88
e hotel-bellrive.najac@wanadoo.fr
Closed Sun evening and Mon lunchtime April–Oct; Nov to early April. **Disabled access**. **Swimming pool**. **Garden**. **TV**. **Car park**.

A pleasant hotel in green, leafy surroundings on a bend in the river. The swimming pool and tennis court make it feel something like a family holiday centre. Rooms are bright and pleasant; doubles with shower/wc or bath cost €47. The cooking is good – house specialities include Roquefort *croustillant* with walnut salad, veal steak with garlic, crayfish *à l'ancienne, astet najacois* (roast pork stuffed with fillet steak, parsley and garlic), zander with veal *jus* and beef with truffle *jus*. Menus are €14–33, and you can eat outside in good weather. Free coffee.

NANT   12230

🏠 |●| HÔTEL DES VOYAGEURS – RESTAURANT LE MÉNESTREL*

pl. Saint-Jacques.
☎ and ➔ 05.65.62.26.88
Car park.

The lovely little town is an ideal base for hikers and this pleasant hotel, right in the centre, provides good bed and board. There's a simple, fresh look to the bedrooms; doubles with washing facilities €23, €25 with shower, €29 with shower/wc and €40 with bath/wc. The restaurant has a pretty terrace hung with wisteria in summer and serves plain, honest food: trout with Roquefort, stuffed cabbage, *émincé* of rabbit *en papillote*, a fish menu including stuffed mussels, cuttlefish with *rouille* (spicey garlic), stuffed queen scallops and all sorts of shellfish. Good choice of home-made desserts. Menu of the day €12, and others €14–26. Pleasant welcome and service. They lend guests mountain bikes. You have to book in advance in winter.

SAINT-JEAN-DU-BRUEL   12230 (7KM E)

🏠 |●| HÔTEL-RESTAURANT DU MIDI-PAPILLON**

☎ 05.65.62.26.04 ➔ 05.65.62.12.97
Closed 11 Nov to Palm Sunday. **Swimming pool**.

Garden. **Car park**.

This hotel in the depths of Aveyron welcomed its first guests in 1850 and has been since run by successive generations of the Papillon family. The rooms are exceptionally pleasant, particularly those overlooking the Dourbie, and they've recently been redecorated. Prices are reasonable: doubles with shower/wc €29 or €32–54 with bath. The dining room is decorated with flowers and overlooks the river and there's a pretty and pleasant terrace which is often full. The owner, Jean-Michel, uses only the freshest produce – he grows his own fruit and vegetables, rears his own chickens, fattens his own pigs and gathers his own mushrooms, so the cuisine is full of authentic flavours: home-made charcuterie, Roquefort and walnut tart, duck *confit*, goose fillet with morel sauce and an exquisite gentian jelly accompanied with *tuiles* and wild blackberries. Menus from €12 (weekday lunchtimes) up to €33. Pleasant staff; the service is unobtrusively efficient. Best to book.

NESTIER   65150

🏃 🏠 |●| LE RELAIS DU CASTERA**

Centre.
☎ 05.62.39.77.37 ➔ 05.62.39.77.29
Closed Sun evening and Mon; 3–21 Jan; 1–8 June.

The *Relais* looks pretty uninteresting outside but there's nothing remotely dull about the cooking of Serge Latour: he's one of the best chefs in the Hautes-Pyrénées. He assembles and presents dishes with elaborate care. You discover all kinds of new flavours at excellent prices: lunch menu €15 and others €23–40. Regional specialities include duck *foie gras* in many different settings, *cassoulet* with Tarbais beans, *fricassée* of crayfish with artichokes, *garbure* with *confit* of duck and a chocolate dessert platter. You can also create your own menu if you order in advance. Lots of local wines. There are a few comfortable rooms, €37–40 with shower/wc or €44 with bath/wc. Free coffee.

PEYRECAVE   32340

🏃 |●| CHEZ ANNIE

How to get there: it's halfway between Lectaure and Castelsarrazin on the Tarn and Garonne border.
☎ 05.62.28.65.40
Closed Sat lunchtime; Sun evening; the second fortnight in Sept.

Annie runs this stunning little inn and she also

does the cooking: house *cassoulet*, *daube* with prunes, *poule-au-pot*, chicken *galantine*. Set menus €8–15. Free house aperitif.

PROJAN   32400

⅍ ≙ LE CHÂTEAU DE PROJAN**

It's on the road from Saint-Mont to the N134.
☎ 05.62.09.46.21 ➡ 05.62.09.44.08
Closed Jan. **Car park**.

A genuine château standing alone on a hill. The family who've owned it since 1986 have transformed the place, letting in light and colour and filling the rooms with contemporary art. The salon, which has been decorated in a modern style, looks out over the countryside. Prices are about right for such a wonderful place: double rooms with basin €52 or €84–104 with shower/wc or bath. It's not a fully-fledged restaurant but they offer a *table d'hôte* menu to order in advance at €21. There's a baby grand if you fancy practising your scales. Free apéritif.

PUYLAURENS   81700

⅍ |●| CHÂTEAU CAP DE CASTEL**

It's in the village.
☎ 05.63.70.21.76 ➡ 05.63.70.21.76
Swimming pool. **TV**.

The château dates back to 1258 and rooms are in some of the outbuildings – this is an admirably run and appealing hotel. Doubles €38–76 depending on size, but all have large bathrooms. There's a swimming pool surrounded by a terrace and there are views looking over the valley. The cuisine served in the restaurant is typical of the region and in winter they do grills over the open fire. Menus €13–27. A lovely place.

RÉALMONT   81120

⅍ |●| LES ROUTIERS – CHEZ RICHARD ET PATRICIA

bd. Armengaud (Centre); it's on the N112 halfway between Castres and Albi.
☎ 05.63.55.65.44
Closed Sun; a week mid-Aug; 25 Dec–2 Jan. **Car park**.

A *Routier* restaurant with a great reputation. There's a huge dining room with attractive stone walls where they serve typical family dishes. The good €10 menu lists a self-service buffet of *hors-d'oeuvres*, main course,

cheese, dessert and wine; the €15 version is almost too huge to finish. Free apéritif.

|●| LES SECRETS GOURMANDS

72 av. du Général-de-Gaulle; (Centre).
☎ 05.63.79.07.67
Closed Sun evening.

The chef, Franck Augé, creates traditional but delicate and creative dishes – the pigeon braised in red wine is a perfect example. The menus (€16–44) are huge but you can opt for a dish from the *à la carte* list, which is imaginatively conceived and changes regularly. There's a special Sunday menu with four courses for €23. Service in the large, bright, pastel dining room is attentive. A good place.

REVEL   31250

⅍ ≙ |●| HÔTEL-RESTAURANT DU MIDI**

34 bd. Gambetta (Northwest).
☎ 05.61.83.50.50 ➡ 05.61.83.34.74
Restaurant closed Sun evening Nov to Easter; mid-Nov to early Dec. **Garden**. **TV**. **Car park**.

Elegant early nineteenth-century coaching inn, now a pleasant hotel with smart rooms for €40–64 with bath – the most expensive ones look over the garden. The nice dining room is bright and in summer you can eat outside. Weekday lunch menu of the day is €13; others €18–40. Dishes include *cassoulet* with duck *confit*, pot-roast pigeon breast, pan-fried *foie gras* and veal *grenadin* with spices and wine sauce. The very affordable wines including Corbières, Gaillac and Bordeaux. Free apéritif.

RIEUMES   31370

⅍ ≙ |●| HÔTEL LES PALMIERS**

13 pl. du Foirail.
☎ 05.61.91.81.01 ❷ albert.fernandez@free.fr
Closed Sun evening and 1–30 Sept. **Disabled access**. **Garden**. **TV**.

Swathed in Virginia creeper and fronted by a lovely plane tree, this old building sits on a vast square. The interior has been totally refurbished and the spacious rooms are tastefully decorated and prettily furnished. Doubles €37–46 with bath; the cheapest look onto the square, others onto an internal garden planted with palm trees (hence the hotel's name). In summer you can eat out there. The €11 lunch menu includes wine, while others, €17–30, offer more elaborate dishes: *carpaccio* of monkfish and salmon with basil and lemon, *carpaccio* of duck breast with olive paste, seafood *marinière*, *émincé* of duck breast, duck thigh *confit* with Toulouse *aillade*. On Sunday there's a single menu which includes *foie gras*, or you can eat *à la carte*. The owner is originally from Cuba and he adds some unusual spices to his dishes; in summer, he sometimes organizes jazz concerts. Free house apéritif.

ROCAMADOUR   46500

🕴 🏠 |O| HÔTEL-RESTAURANT LE LION D'OR**

It's in the medieval town.
☎ 05.65.33.62.04 📠 05.65.33.72.54
📧 liondor.rocamadour@wanadoo.fr
Closed 6 Nov–29 March.

A traditional hotel-restaurant which offers a lovely view of the old town. The comfy bedrooms are reasonable value – €32–46 for a double with shower/wc or bath. Recent renovation work has retained the character and the spirit of the place. In the restaurant, menus go for €11–30 and list specialities such as *foie gras tarte tatin* with morel sauce, *confit* of duck, duck breast with ceps and truffle omelette. Brilliant desserts – it's impossible to resist the walnut *gâteau* with egg custard. 10% discount on the room rate (except Aug).

🕴 🏠 |O| HÔTEL-RESTAURANT BEAU SITE***

rue de Rocamadour, it's on the only street in the medieval town; access to the hotel permitted by car.
☎ 05.65.33.63.08 📠 05.65.33.65.23
📧 hotel@bw-beausite.com
Closed 1 Jan–12 Feb and 12 Nov–31 Dec. **TV. Car park**.

The *Beau Site* is very appropriately named – it's in the heart of Rocamadour. Some of the well-maintained, attractive bedrooms have a breathtaking view of the abbey perched on the hill; doubles €48–60 with shower/wc, €60–80 with bath. Tasty, refined, aromatic dishes are served in a beautiful, flowery dining room; menus from €19. Specialities include leg of free-range lamb and house duck *foie gras*, duck breast cooked over the coals and sea bass with tomatoes preserved in olive oil. The terrace is shaded by lime trees. An excellent establishment in its category. 10% discount on the room rate Feb–April, 1–13 July and Oct–Nov.

🕴 🏠 |O| HÔTEL-RESTAURANT LES VIEILLES TOURS**

Lieu-dit Lafage (West); take the D673 2.5km in the direction of Payrac.
☎ 05.65.33.68.01 📠 05.65.33.68.59
📧 les.vieillestours@wanadoo.fr
Restaurant closed Mon–Sat lunchtimes, Sun evening, evenings of public holidays and 15 Nov–23 March.
Disabled access. Swimming pool. Garden. TV. Car park.

A splendid sixteenth-century manor house with a beautiful garden and a swimming pool. The rooms, all with phone and bathroom, are large and extremely pretty, and each is furnished in a different style; doubles €50 with shower/wc or up to €92 with bath. TV available on request. Predominantly regional dishes in the restaurant: duck *foie gras* poached in spiced Cahors wine, veal chop in a cep crust with potato, ham cake with beef *jus*. Menus €21–54 with half board (compulsory July–Aug) priced at €61–82. It's a good idea to book. In summer there are hikes or bike rides in the wild. 10% discount on the room rate out of season (but not during public holiday weekends). Free house apéritif when you have a meal.

MEYRONNE   46200 (14KM N)

🕴 🏠 |O| HÔTEL-RESTAURANT LA TERRASSE**

How to get there: take the D673 for 4km then turn left onto the D15.
☎ 05.65.32.21.60 📠 05.65.32.26.93
📧 terasse.liebus@wanadoo.fr
Closed Tues out of season, and Dec–Feb. **Swimming pool. Garden**.

Meyronne is an adorable little village up in the hills and this establishment was at one time the summer residence of the bishops of Tulle. The building is full of charm and character: the stone walls are covered in ivy and it has beams and turrets with sloping roofs. Prices are reasonable, with comfortable rooms going for €46–76 in the hotel or the castle proper. Those in the latter are deliciously cool in summer, which is a considerable plus in this part of the world – if you want a room here you must book well in advance. The terrace is shaded by a pergola and overlooks the valley. The restaurant specializes in regional dishes, including veal sweetbreads with morels, lamb cutlet with juniper and zander with tarragon. Menus €15–43. 10% discount on the room rate for the second night of your stay Sept–June. Free coffee.

CARENNAC   46110 (25.5KM NE)

🏕 🏠 |●| AUBERGE DU VIEUX QUERCY**

Centre.
☎ 05.65.10.96.59 ➡ 05.65.10.94.05
📧 vieuzquercy@medianet.fr
Closed Mon out of season, 15 Nov–15 March.
Swimming pool. Garden. TV. Car park.

Handsome tourist complex – with hotels, gardens and swimming pool – built around an old coaching inn in an idyllic setting. The main building is pretty ancient and has character; you can have a room there or in one of the annexes around the pool. Pleasant doubles €43–58 with shower/wc or bath. Half board, compulsory July–Aug, costs €47–55 per person. The dining room has views of the garden and a maze of rooftops. Set menus, €13–33, list local dishes: roast lamb in pastry with shallot *jus*, duck *confit* with cabbage and mushrooms, poached *foie gras* with fruit, lamb stew. Good Cahors wine. 10% discount on the room rate 4 May–9 Oct.

🏕 🏠 |●| HOSTELLERIE FÉNELON**

rue Principale.
☎ 05.65.10.96.46 ➡ 05.65.10.94.86
Closed Fri out of season, Sat lunchtime and 7 Jan–15 March and 25 Nov–20 Dec.
Swimming pool. Garden. TV. Car park.

Service lunchtime, and evening until 9pm. A conventional hotel with very decent, cosy rooms furnished in country style. Doubles with shower/wc €43 and €55 with bath. The cooking is good, with menus at €17–47. Half board, compulsory July–Sept, costs €46–55 per person. To whet your appetite, how about pan-fried scallops with ceps, zander with potatoes, veal chop with girolles prawns and saddle of rabbit? The dining room looks over the garden and swimming pool and some tables have views of the river. Free coffee.

RODEZ   12000

🏕 🏠 HÔTEL DE LA TOUR-MAJE***

bd. Gally (Centre).
☎ 05.65.68.34.68 ➡ 05.65.68.27.56
📧 bernard.lacaze@wandoo.fr
Closed the last fortnight in Dec. **Disabled access. TV.**

This classic hotel incorporates a fourteenth-century tower, a remnant of the old ramparts. The rooms are pleasant, modern and attractively decorated; doubles cost €53 with shower/wc and €61 with bath. Some rooms

sleeping 2, 3 or 4 are available in the tower and there are apartments for €107. There's a billiard room on the first floor. 10% discount 15 Jan–15 April and 15 Oct–15 Dec.

🏕 |●| RESTAURANT LA TAVERNE

23 rue de l'Embergue (Centre); it's near the cathedral.
☎ 05.65.42.14.51
Closed Sat lunchtime out of season; Sun; public holidays; the first week in May. **Garden**.

A vaulted basement dining room where you'll be served traditional and regional food – rib steak with Roquefort cheese, oxtail, stuffed cabbage, duck breast, *aligot*, *choucroute*, *fondue*, *tripoux*, *raclette*, wonderful homemade tarts. Prices are very reasonable: weekday lunch menu €10 and an extensive *menu-carte* for €15 with a selection of starters and main courses. There's a terrace at the back, overlooking the garden. Free apéritif.

🏕 |●| RESTAURANT WILLY'S

3 rue de la Viarague; it's near the church of Saint-Amans.
☎ 05.65.68.17.34
Closed Sun and Mon; a week in Spring; a week in Sept.

The building is painted blue and the dining room is in warm, pleasant colours. It's a friendly restaurant specializing in regional cooking with a touch of originality and exoticism. Good fresh produce is used: chicken liver salad with pickled garlic, fish *choucroute*, cod with *ratatouille*, braised free-range chicken with crayfish and *mignon* of pork braised with ginger, cinnamon and nutmeg. The €12 weekday lunch menu changes daily, there's another menu for €18 or you'll pay around €27 *à la carte*. You'll be welcomed without fuss and the atmosphere is young, informal and relaxed. Free house apéritif.

|●| RESTAURANT GOÛTS ET COULEURS

38 rue de Bonald (Centre); it's in one of the streets leading to pl. de la Cité.
☎ 05.65.42.75.10 ➡ 05.65.78.11.20
Closed Sun and Mon; 5–30 Jan; 1–8 May; 5–20 Sept.

Service until 9.30pm. Best to book. The dining room is painted in pastel shades and there's a warm atmosphere – perfect for an intimate dinner. The chef is a culinary artist, and his cooking from around the Mediterranean seaboard is truly inspired: jellied *tajine* of chicken with pickled lemons and olives, fresh sardine *gâteau* marinated with fennel, a *sushi* of wild strawberries with coconut milk and orange salad with almond milk and orange-flower water. Weekday lunch menus

€17, then others €23–56. Attentive but relaxed service. One of the best places hereabouts.

SAINTE-RADEGONDE　　　12850 (5KM N)

🏠 |◉| SALOON GUEST RANCH***

Landrevie-Sainte-Radegonde.
☎ 05.65.42.47.46 ➡ 05.65.78.32.36
Closed Mon–Sat lunchtimes to non-residents; 10 days in Feb. **TV**. **Swimming pool**. **Car park**.

Alain Tournier has created a little corner of the American Wild West, complete with horses and saloon. The latter is authentic down to the smallest detail, with mahogony furniture, red wallpaper and lots of photographs. Not surprisingly, meat looms large on the menu, and it's some of the best in the area; very generous set menus at €17. Rooms are spacious and the décor, of course, is cowboy-style – the luxury version, that is. Doubles €46 with shower/wc and €53 with bath. The staff are friendly and considerate. You can ride or take part in any of the many other activities if you're staying full board.

SALLES-LA SOURCE　　　12330 (10KM NW)

🍴 |◉| RESTAURANT DE LA CASCADE

How to get there: take the D901 and it's next to the museum.
☎ 05.65.67.29.08
Closed Wed evening out of season; Mon evening in season; Jan. **Disabled access**.

The small dining room is in pinkish tones and has a ravishing view of the surrounding valleys. Honest cuisine with a €9 weekday lunch option that changes every day and offers two starters, main course, cheese and dessert. Others €13 and 18. Free coffee.

SAINT-AFFRIQUE　　　12400

🍴 🏠 |◉| HÔTEL MODERNE**

54 rue Alphonse-Pezet; it's beside the disused train station.
☎ 05.65.49.20.44 ➡ 05.65.49.36.55
e hotel-restaurant-le-moderne@wanadoo.fr
Closed 1–27 Jan and the second week in Oct. **TV**. **Pay car park**.

This is a fairly dull part of the town away from the centre, but at least it's quiet. The frontage of *Hôtel Moderne* has a dome and is painted in fresh colours with a lovely old-fashioned feel. The family who run the place give you an extraordinarily warm welcome. Rooms are clean and decent; in the annexe a double

with shower (wc along the landing) costs €23, €38 with shower/wc or €49 with bath. Local dishes feature on the menu, but they've been reworked with a lot of imagination – good cooking like this is a rarity in this town. A fair few local specialities use Roquefort, among them the salad and the soufflé, and there's *charcuterie* and *foie gras*. Set lunch menus €12 and €11 and others at €17–44. 10% discount on the room rate Sept–June.

SAINT-ANTONIN-NOBLE-VAL　　　82140

🏠 |◉| HÔTEL DES THERMES**

1 pl. des Moines; if you're coming from the gorges, it's after the bridge on the left.
☎ 05.63.25.06.08 ➡ 05.63.25.06.06
Closed Thurs out of season. **TV**.

The prices and the waterside location are the best things about this place. Rooms look suspiciously like those you'd find in a chain, and can only just be described as comfortable – the young owners are considering renovations. Doubles with bath from €35. Some have a view of the river and the Anglars cliffface. Weekday lunch menu €9, others from €10.

|◉| LA SOURCE

Route de Marsac (South).
☎ 05.63.30.60.28

A lovely stone house with painted shutters on the banks of the Aveyron – a great place if you love your food. The €11 menu offers duck soup, a choice of starters and main courses and dessert. They don't put the food on plates but bring you a dish to serve yourself. If you have a huge appetite, opt for the €20 menu which adds a gizzard salad, omelette or trout and cheese. And if you just want a snack, no problem – choose a salad *à la carte*. The table water comes direct from the spring.

SAINT-BERTRAND-DE-COMMINGES　　　31510

🏠 HÔTEL DU COMMINGES**

pl. de la Cathédrale.
☎ 05.61.88.31.43 ➡ 05.61.94.98.22
Closed 1 Nov–31 March. **Garden**. **Car park**.

It's great to spend a night in this fantastic village built on a rocky promontory huddled round the cathedral. The hotel is a quite delightful old family house opposite the cathedral, swathed in ivy and wisteria with a small courtyard garden: the whole place is utterly charming. Large rooms with period furniture; doubles €27 with shower, €35–38 with shower/wc or €43–46 with bath.

🛏 🏠 |●| L'OPPIDUM**

rue de la Poste; near the cathedral on the road down to the post office.
☎ 05.61.88.33.50 ➦ 05.61.95.94.04
ⓔ oppidum@wanadoo.fr
Closed 15 Nov–20 Dec and 10–25 Jan. **TV**. **Disabled access**.

A small, pretty hotel that's been beautifully arranged. The rooms are comfortable but rather small and priced at €42 with shower/wc or €44 with bath – one is big enough to be a honeymoon suite. Menus from €14 (not Sun or public holidays) up €29, offering decent cuisine. There's a tearoom. Welcoming staff; they'll lend you a bike if you want to tour this wonderful area. 10% discount on the room rate Jan–April and free coffee to finish your meal.

|●| CAFÉ-RESTAURANT CHEZ SIMONE

☎ 05.61.94.91.05
Closed evenings out of season and All Saints' to Christmas.

It's worth making the effort to get here simply for the view, but the cooking, kindly welcome and friendly dining room add to the appeal. The €13 lunch menu is a really full meal from soup to pudding. There's one for €11 in the evening and a Sunday version for €15. Their speciality is stuffed chicken but you have to order in advance. Credit cards not accepted.

VALCABRÈRE   31510 (1.5KM E)

|●| LE LUGDUNUM

How to get there: after Valcabrère, join the N25, turn right and it's 400m further on.
☎ 05.61.94.52.05 ➦ 05.61.94.52.06
Closed Sun and Mon evenings; Tues and Wed out of season. **Car park**.

An unusual restaurant which resembles a Roman villa. It has a terrace overlooking the maize fields and a fantastic view of Saint-Bertrand. Renzo Pedrazzini, whose family comes from Lombardy, serves traditional local dishes, but the real attraction here are the recipes he has taken from the ancient Romans: sea bream with grapes, boar with *sauce bouillante*, salad *à l'hypotrima*, Lucanie sausages. He mixes honey and vinegar, won't use tomatoes or lemons because they were unknown to the ancients and gets his spices from a local herbalist – he regards

himself as an apprentice of Apicius, who wrote a treatise on cooking two millennia ago. The *menu antique* offers a precious haul of forgotten recipes. Take his wife's advice and have a spiced wine with your meal and try the rose or violet apéritif. A meal for two will cost €27–31.

SAINT-CIRQ-LAPOPIE   46330

🛏 🏠 |●| AUBERGE DU SOMBRAL**

pl. du Sombral (Centre).
☎ 05.65.31.26.08 ➦ 05.65.30.26.37
Closed Tues and Wed except July–Aug; 11 Nov–1 April.

A charming inn with a pitched roof and elegant décor. The rooms are appealingly furnished and decorated in soft, warm colours.; doubles €53 with shower/wc and €72 with bath. Traditional cooking with a justified reputation: ceps in pastry cases, leek *gratin* with truffles and splendid semi-cooked *foie gras*. Menus €12–35. A reliable establishment. Free coffee.

|●| RESTAURANT L'ATELIER

Centre; it's right next to Saint-Cirq.
☎ and ➦ 05.65.31.22.34 **ⓔ** latelier46@hotmail.com
Closed Tues evening and Wed except school holidays; Jan–Feb.

Right at the top of the hill you'll find this old building. There's a warm, cosy atmosphere so you'll quickly feel at home and the hearty cooking will delight gourmands and your average traveller alike. Menus (€11–24) list plenty of courses, with dishes like black Guercy duck, *cassoulet* and good *foie gras* served with a glass of white wine – excellent value for money.

TOUR DE FAURE   46330 (3KM W)

🏠 HÔTEL LES GABARRES**

Le bourg; take the D662 towards Figeac.
☎ 05.65.30.24.57 ➦ 05.65.30.25.85
Closed Nov–April. **Disabled access**. **Swimming pool**. **Car park**.

It isn't the most beautiful building but the excellent reception and the bright, clean, spacious bedrooms more than make up for that. Half the rooms overlook the swimming pool and in some parts of the establishment you get great views of the valley. Doubles with shower/wc €38–43 or €58 for rooms sleeping three people. There's a hearty buffet breakfast. The couple in charge can tell you all about the various walks around.

SAINT-FÉLIX-LAURAGAIS 31540

▲ |●| AUBERGE DU POIDS PUBLIC***

Faubourg Saint-Roch (West).
☎ 05.61.83.00.20 ▬► 05.61.83.86.21
Closed Sun evening Oct–April, and Jan. **TV**. **Garden**.
Car park.

Delightful rooms – some with views of the Lauragais hills. Doubles €43–53 with shower/wc or bath and direct phone. There are several little sitting rooms and a large, rustic dining room with fine exposed stonework and panoramic views. The atmosphere is classy. Set menus €21–53 – there's a basic one, a vegetarian one and the menu "Auberge", which includes *foie gras* cooked in a cloth, milk-fed lamb, Aquitaine sturgeon and summer fruit *croustillant*. You'll find comparatively unknown wines as well as great vintages on the wine list, priced from affordable to astronomical. The terrace is extremely pleasant in summer.

SAINT-JULIA 31540 (6KM N)

⌖ |●| L'AUBERGE DES REMPARTS

rue du Vinaigre.
☎ 05.61.83.04.79
Closed Sun and Mon evening.

A village inn with a growing reputation. The appetizing €10 menu of the day includes soup, *crudités*, *charcuterie*, dish of the day, cheese, dessert, wine and coffee. In the evening, the young chef shows his colours with more elaborate, refined cooking on menus at €14–21. Try the raw salmon marinated with dill, the *croustillant* of sea bream or the guineafowl with cabbage. In good weather they serve meals on the shady terrace. Free apéritif and coffee.

SAINT-FERRÉOL 31350

▲ |●| HÔTELLERIE DU LAC

av. Pierre-Paul-de-Riquet.
☎ 05.52.18.70.80 ▬► 05.62.18.71.13
Closed Sun evening except July–Aug. **Swimming pool**. **Garden**. **Car park**.

The hotel has been beautifully renovated since Chabrol used it for shooting most of his film *L'Enfer*: it's plush but colourful. The rooms, €53, are comfortable and some have views of the lake. The ground floor, dining rooms, sitting room and bar have also had a facelift. The swimming pool is heated and there's a sauna and a charming conservato-

ry overlooking the garden. The cuisine, unfortunately, doesn't reach the same high standard on menus at €18–29: duck *terrine*, lamb shank or red mullet fillets *à la Provençale*. Friendly welcome.

SAINT-GAUDENS 31800

⌖ |●| RESTAURANT DE L'ABATTOIR

bd. Leconte-de-Lisle (South); it's opposite the abattoir.
☎ 05.61.89.70.29
Closed Sun evening–Wed.

One of the best restaurants in the region. Nowhere else will you get meat that's as fresh, tender and downright delicious as at Christian Gillet's place. He's at the abattoirs every morning at dawn, choosing cuts of meat to feed the dealers who arrive from the country to sell their animals at market. The dining room is always packed. Try calves' head with *ravigote* sauce, tripes *à la Provençale*, flank of beef, rib of beef with bone marrow or grilled Arbas black pudding. Weekday lunch menu €11, others €14–20 and around €18 *à la carte*. The large dining room is bright and pleasant and the atmosphere is matey. Free house apéritif.

SAINT-GENIEZ-D'OLT 12130

⌖ ▲ |●| HÔTEL DE LA POSTE**

3 pl. Charles-de-Gaulle.
☎ 05.65.47.43.30 ▬► 05.65.47.42.75
Closed Tues and Wed Oct–March; Jan–March.
Swimming pool. **Garden**. **TV**. **Lock-up car park**.

A traditional village inn with an old sectioin, *La Réception*, and modern annexe, *Le Parc*. The former, furnished with superb antiques, is comfortable and cosy and the rooms are pleasant; €30–47 with shower/wc or bath. The restaurant, across the road in the annexe, is well-known for its quality cooking. You can eat in the dining room, on the veranda surrounded by greenery or in the glassed-in terrace on the first floor. Set menus €13 (except Sun), then €16–43. The house classics include *foie gras* upside-down tart, roast zander with meat juices and ceps and medallion of veal with liquorice. 10% discount on the room rate Sept–June.

SAINTE-EULALIE-D'OLT 12130 (3KM W)

⌖ ▲ |●| AU MOULIN D'ALEXANDRE**

Centre.
☎ 05.65.47.45.85 ▬► 05.65.52.73.78
Closed Sun evening from All Saints' to Easter; 7–20

May; the first fortnight in Oct; 22 April–5 May. **Garden**. **Car park**.

A delightful country inn in a renovated seventeenth-century water mill. The setting is idyllic and very restful. Pretty rooms for €38 with shower/wc or €43 with bath. The cooking's good and prices are reasonable, with a €10 menu (not served Sun or public holidays) and others up to €22 as well as good *à la carte* choices. The restaurant specializes in regional dishes like home-made *tripoux*, stuffed ceps, chanterelle omelette and stuffed breast of veal – the strawberry *millefeuille* they do in season is quite something. Half board, €43 a head, is compulsory July–Sept. Boats and mountain bikes are available for hire. They don't accept credit cards. Free *digestif*.

SAINT-GIRONS   09200

⅍ 🏠 |O| HÔTEL-RESTAURANT LA CLAIRIÈRE**

av. de la Résistance (Southwest); it's on the outskirts of town in the direction of Seix-Massat.
☎ 05.61.66.66.66 ➡ 05.34.14.30.30
e hotel.laclairiere@wanadoo.fr
Closed Sun evening and Mon Dec–April; the last fortnight in Nov. **Disabled access**. **Garden**. **TV**. **Swimming pool**. **Lock-up car park**.

A really wonderful place away from the traffic, camouflaged by a row of trees and a leafy park. Rooms are bright and comfortable and have views of the grounds. Doubles €43. In the pleasant restaurant menus cost €13 for lunch and €19–64 at dinner, listing delicious shellfish *tartare* with *aïoli* and a very good monkfish stew. In winter the atmosphere changes – they light a fire in the huge fireplace and have menus full of regional dishes. 10% discount on the room rate Sept–June.

SAINT-LARY-SOULAN   65170

⅍ 🏠 |O| HÔTEL-RESTAURANT LA PERGOLA**

It's in the main street.
☎ 05.62.39.40.46 ➡ 05.62.40.06.55
e jean-pierre.mir@wanadoo.fr
Closed a fortnight in May and early Nov to early Dec. **Garden**. **TV**. **Car park**.

A pleasant establishment dating from 1957 with a pretty garden and, of course, a pergola. The spacious rooms are comfortable, with wonderful beds, en-suite bathrooms, hairdriers and TV; the ones facing southwest have a view of Le Pla-d'Adet. Doubles €43–61.

They sometimes have to be pressed to let you have a room without breakfast (an extra €6), but the talent of the chef somewhat makes up for that. Lunch *formule* €11 and menus €16–34. Free house apéritif.

SAINT-LIZIER   09190

🏠 |O| HÔTEL DE LA TOUR

Route du Pont; it's at the foot of the old town on the banks of the Salat.
☎ 05.61.66.38.02

This historic hotel, the only one in the capital of the Couserans, has nine lovely rooms for €29–38; some look over of the river and others even have little balconies. The chef is creative – his *foie gras* and apple tart are gorgeous – but also does simple grills. Weekday menu €9 and others €13–25.

SAINT-MARTIN-D'ARMAGNAC   32110

🏠 |O| AUBERGE DU BERGERAYRE

How to get there: take the right turning off the D25.
☎ 05.62.09.08.72 ➡ 05.62.09.09.74
Closed Tues and Thurs; lunchtimes in winter (but book in the evening). **Disabled access**. **Swimming pool**. **Garden**. **TV**. **Car park**.

A wonderful inn deep in the countryside, complete with garden and swimming pool – you'll revel in the peace and quiet. The extremely comfortable rooms are all at ground level, and distributed between two buildings; they're €46–53 with shower/wc or €76 with bath. The top-price ones are in the old granary and have real character and luxurious facilities. Half board, obligatory in July/Aug, costs €39–60. The restaurant has a very good reputation, and you'll eat in a warm, friendly dining room with rustic décor. Menus €18–34. Dishes change through the seasons as and when fresh produce becomes available – *cassoulet*, *salade Gasconne*, chicken cooked in a caul, potatoes *au gratin*, *foie gras* cooked over vine cuttings. Best to book.

SAINT-SERNIN-SUR-RANCE   12380

⅍ 🏠 |O| HÔTEL CARAYON**

pl. du Fort; it's on the D999 between Albi and Millau.
☎ 05.65.98.19.19 ➡ 05.65.99.69.26
e carayon.hotel@wanadoo.fr
Closed Sun evening; Mon; Tues lunchtime (except July–Aug). **Disabled access**. **Swimming pool**. **TV**.

Lock-up car park.

The *Carayon* is a quality place and something of an institution. The owners are on first-name terms with all the local worthies. Some of the comfortable rooms have a balcony looking over the grounds and the country beyond; doubles €34–61 with shower/wc or bath. The cuisine has a great reputation and the chef gives you plenty of opportunity by offering seven menus: they start at €14 (not served Sunday lunchtime) and continue at €21–54. À la carte you can get pot-roast quail, pigeon in *salmis* sauce, lamb sweetbreads with garlic and parsley, goose heart kebabs, cep omelette and tempting desserts. If the weather's good, you can sit on the terrace and enjoy the panoramic views or swim in one of the two pools. You can also play tennis or golf, have a sauna or take a pedal boat on the river – all free of charge for guests. 10% discount on the room rate Oct–April.

SALMIECH   12120

⚥ ♠ |●| HÔTEL-RESTAURANT DU CÉOR

☎ and ➟ 05.65.46.70.13
Closed Sun and Mon evenings out of season.

This nineteenth-century coaching inn offers terrific value. There are thirty pleasant rooms costing €25–29; it's €28–37 a head for half board. Regional dishes dominate in the pretty, rustic dining room: *tripou*, *aligot*, duck breast cooked over a fire of vine shoots, crayfish with the chef's special sauce. Desserts include walnut tart and chocolate profiteroles. Menus €10–30. You can sit out on the terrace in good weather and admire the view of the village. Very welcoming owner. Free chestnut liqueur.

SAMATAN   32130

|●| AU CANARD GOURMAND

La Rente; It's on the road to Lombez.
☎ 05.62.62.49.81 **e** canard@canard-au-soulon.com
Closed Mon evening; Tues; a week in March; 3 weeks in Oct.

Ingenious interpretations of local cuisine. Lots of different *foie gras* dishes: one with dill, another pan-fried with vanilla sauce and an amazing one with liquorice. The dishes change with the seasons and the fresh market produce. Menus start at €15 and there are two *menu-cartes* at €21 and €26. The dining room is warm and pleasant. Efficient service but reserved welcome.

SAUVETERRE-DE-ROUERGUE   12800

♠ |●| LA GRAPPE D'OR

It's a stone's throw from pl. des Arcades.
☎ 05.65.72.00.62.
Closed Wed out of season
Hotel closed 15 Oct–14 April. **Garden**.

A small village hotel which is well-run and has double rooms with shower/wc for €24–26. The restaurant offers simple, robust country cooking. *Menu du jour* at €10, one with regional dishes at €13 and a "celebration" menu at €15 (served Sun and public holidays). Good-quality, simple, filling local dishes: *tripou*, chicken and duck *confit*, and gizzard salad. The garden is very nice and the setting alone is worth stopping for.

⚥ ♠ |●| LE SÉNÉCHAL***

It's north outside the fortifications.
☎ 05.65.71.29.00 **e** le.senechal@wanadoo.fr
Closed lunchtimes except at the weekend and public holidays; early Jan to mid-March. **Swimming pool**.
Disabled access. **TV**. **Car park**.

Local boy Michel Truchon loves his region – he talks about it with passion and will fill you in on its history. He also cares about quality produce, and sets about his cooking like an artist, creating wonderful dishes which are sophisticated and subtle. Set menus €23–92. Try the lentil *terrine* served with pig's ears or the braised veal and local potatoes drizzled with olive oil and served with aubergine caviar. For dessert go for an iced coffee *parfait* with endive seeds. You also get *amuse-bouches* and a lovely welcome. The rooms are quite magnificent, with terracotta floors and designer décor. Doubles with shower €119 or €150. Service is faultless yet unpretentious and friendly. Free apéritif.

SOUILLAC   46200

⚥ ♠ |●| GRAND HÔTEL***

1 allée Verninac (Centre).
☎ 05.65.32.78.30 ➟ 05.65.32.66.34
Closed Wed April and Oct; and Nov–March. **TV**. **Car park**.

This hotel is owned by the family of Roger Couderc, a popular rugby commentator. There are lots of comfortable rooms, some overlooking an atrium; doubles with shower/wc €31–73 or €50–78 with bath. There's also a solarium and a nice terrace with panoramic views. The restaurant, classical in style and understated in décor, has a good reputation for dishes from the Quercy region. The cheapest menu is €12 and there are others €20–40, including a truffle menu – house specialities include *Périgourdine* tripe with capers, flash-fried sole with truffle oil and creamy sauce and roast fillet of zander with ceps. A *trompe l'oeil* mural forms the backdrop for a shady terrace, which is pleasant in summer. 10% discount on the room rate April and Oct.

🎿 🏠 |◉| LA VIEILLE AUBERGE***

1 rue de la Recège (Centre).
☎ 05.65.32.79.43 ➡ 05.65.32.65.19
Closed Sun evening and Mon Jan–March; mid-Nov to mid-Dec. **Swimming pool**. **TV**. **Car park**.

This "old inn" is in fact a very modern hotel with a gastronomic restaurant. All rooms have satellite TV and video, and there's a gym, sauna, solarium and heated swimming pool. Doubles with shower/wc or bath €48–60. Chef Robert Véril is a staunch traditionalist who uses only local produce to create dishes from the Quercy and Périgord: artichokes with pan-fried *foie gras* and truffle sauce, pan-fried *escalope* of *foie gras* with walnuts, *estouffade* of potatoes with truffles, *galette* of cabbage with duck *confit*, fig profitrolles with vanilla ice-cream. He's even unearthed some almost-forgotten recipes such as *vermicelle Quercynois*, a garlic soup with eggs. Menus €20–55. The wine list leans heavily towards Cahors and other southwestern wines. The staff have been well-trained but sometimes it sounds as if they're repeating their lines by rote. 10% discount on the room rate in May and 20% in Oct.

TARASCON-SUR-ARIÈGE   09400

🎿 🏠 HÔTEL CONFORT**

3 quai Armand-Sylvestre (Centre).
☎ and ➡ 05.61.05.57.79
Closed 8–19 Jan. **TV**. **Garden**. **Pay garage**.

This welcoming place is right in the centre of town but, being on the banks of the Ariège, it's quiet. There are fourteen rooms, all overlooking the garden – some are particularly roomy and also have a view of the river. Doubles €27 with basin and up to €35 with bath. There's a €5 charge for use of the garage. 10% discount on the room rate and free breakfast (normally €5), except during school holidays.

TARBES   65000

🎿 🏠 HÔTEL DE L'AVENUE**

78–80 av. Bertrand Barère; 50m from the train station.

☎ and ➡ 05.62.93.06.36
Disabled access. **TV**. **Car park**.

This is a quiet little hotel, despite being near the station. The rooms are a bit bland but they're good value for money – doubles with shower/wc €26 and €30 with bath – and as clean as can be. The ones looking into the courtyard are the quietest. There's a family atmosphere and the owner's father, who retired some time ago, still welcomes the guests occasionally. 10% discount.

🎿 🏠 |◉| L'ISARD**

70 av. du Maréchal-Joffre (North); it's near the station.
☎ 05.62.93.06.69 ➡ 05.62.93.99.55
Closed Sun evening. **Garden**. **TV**.

A tiny, likeable hotel on a main road, with eight pleasant rooms; doubles with shower/wc €27 or €32 with bath. Some overlook the garden and are really quiet. The owner is delightful and very accommodating. In the restaurant there are menus and *formules* to suit all budgets – €10–30. Dishes include *foie gras*, scrambled eggs with fresh liver, *cassoulet* with Tarbes beans and prune ice cream with Armagnac. In fine weather meals are served in the garden under the awning. 10% discount on the room rate for a two-night stay Oct–April.

🎿|◉| CHEZ PATRICK

6 rue Adolphe d'Eichtal; on the corner of rue Saint-Jean.
☎ 05.62.36.36.82
Closed evenings; Sun; a fortnight in Aug. **Car park**.

A wonderful local restaurant just out of the centre, with a clientele of regulars who work round the corner or live nearby. It's run by a big family – they keep a cheery atmosphere in the dining room. The cooking is generously flavoured and prices are reasonable: the €9 menu includes soup, starter, dish of the day, wine and dessert. It's best to arrive early at lunchtime as it quickly gets full. Free coffee.

|◉| LE FIL À LA PATTE

30 rue Georges-Lasalle.
☎ 05.62.93.39.23
Closed Sat lunchtime; Sun evening; Mon; the second fortnight in Jan; the last 3 weeks in Aug.

A tiny and chic little restaurant looking for all the world like a Parisian bistro. New-style, inventive cuisine with lots of fish and local dishes given fresh interpretations. Weekday lunch menu at €15 and one other at €23 – which is also what you'll pay *à la carte*. Polite, slightly distant service.

JUILLAN   65290 (5KM SW)

♠ |●| L'ARAGON**

2 ter route de Lourdes; it's on the D921A.
☎ 05.62.32.07.07 ➡ 05.62.32.92.50
✉ hotel-restaurant-aragon@wanadoo.fr
Closed Sun evening; a fortnight in the Feb school
holidays; the first fortnight in Aug; 26 Dec–4 Jan.
Disabled access. TV. Car park.

Lovely double rooms, thematically decorated
and with efficient double glazing at €45 with
shower/wc and mini-bar and €49 with bath.
There's a bistro with a €15 menu, and a
rather plush dining room where the service is
impeccable and the cooking rightly enjoys its
reputation. *Menu du marché* for €27, a fish
menu for €40 and a gourmet one for €52 –
gazpacho with crayfish, scrambled eggs with
caviar, duck and goose *confit* with kidney
bean stew, a soufflé of pears and fruit brandy.

ARCIZAC-ADOUR   65360 (11KM S)

⅍|●| LA CHAUDRÉE

10 route des Pyrénées; it's on the D935 in the direction
of Bagnères.
☎ 05.62.45.32.00
Closed Sun evening; Mon; a fortnight in Feb; 3 weeks
from late July to mid-Aug.

A classic little establishment that, despite its
unassuming appearance, is one of the best
places to eat locally. The dining room has a
rustic feel with solid beams and a splendid
walnut buffet table – very *Vieille France*.
There's a €10 lunchtime menu (not served
Sun), and others €15–26: veal sweetbreads,
duck *foie gras* with apple and bilberry sauce,
garbure (broth with *confit*). Free house apéritif.

TOULOUSE   31000

SEE MAP OVERLEAF

♠ HÔTEL ANATOLE-FRANCE*

46 pl. Anatole-France. **MAP B2-2**
☎ 05.61.23.19.96 ➡ 05.61.21.47.66
TV.

You'll get a wonderful welcome in this good-
value hotel; reception is on the first floor. All
rooms have direct-dial phones and are exceptionally clean; doubles €19 with basin to €28
with shower/wc or bath.

♠ HÔTEL DES ARTS*

rue des Arts, 1 [bis] rue Cantegril. **MAP C2-4**
☎ 05.61.23.36.21 ➡ 05.61.12.22.37

In a picturesque neighbourhood in the middle of town, this hotel has a maze of corridors leading to pleasant, spacious, renovated rooms. Some of them have fireplaces,
some overlook the courtyard and all but three
overlooking the street have been double-
glazed. Doubles with washing facilities €22
and up to €28 with shower/wc. You order
your breakfast the night before; it's served in
your room – there's no breakfast room – or
you can have it in one of the numerous cafés
nearby.

⅍ ♠ HÔTEL DU GRAND BALCON*

8 rue Romiguières. **MAP C2-3**
☎ 05.61.21.48.08 ➡ 05.61.21.59.98
Closed three weeks in Aug. **TV**.

The pilots who used to fly the mail planes in
the early days of air-mail used to stay here
before taking off for Alicante, Africa or South
America. The hotel has hardly changed since
and it's full of photos of those intrepid days.
The Marquès sisters ran the place for place
for fifty years, and Monsieur Brousse, who
took over from them, was here more than
forty, so there's a solid feeling of tradition. It's
only just changed hands again and the new
owners are gradually updating it but with
respect for its history. Doubles €27 with
basin and up to €37 with bath/wc. Breakfast
€4. Rooms overlooking the street are noisy.

♠ HÔTEL CROIX-BARAGNON*

17 rue Croix-Baragnon. **MAP C3-1**
☎ 05.61.52.50.10 ➡ 05.61.52.08.60

Right in the centre, near the cathedral. The
hotel itself is very charming and has an exter-
nal staircase entwined with plants. You go up
to the first floor to find reception where a
warm welcome awaits. The rooms comfortable rather than amazing – some have windows over the courtyard – but the atmosphere is lovely. Doubles €31 with shower/wc
and TV. Best to book.

⅍ ♠ HÔTEL TRIANON**

7 rue Lafaille. **MAP C1-8**
☎ 05.61.62.74.74 ➡ 05.61.99.15.44
✉ hotel-trianon@wanadoo.fr
TV. Pay car park.

A delightful little hotel with pleasant, comfortable rooms; doubles €41 with shower/wc or
€44 with bath. The ones at the rear are quieter, though some at the front have double
glazing. In summer you have breakfast on the
patio; in winter you eat in the magnificent
vaulted wine cellars. The owner's so keen on
wine that he's named the rooms after great

vineyards. 10% discount on the room rate for the first night.

♠ HÔTEL VICTOR-HUGO**

26 bd. de Strasbourg. **MAP C1-14**
☎ 05.61.63.40.41 ➡ 05.61.62.66.31
℮hotel-victor-hugo@wanadoo.fr
Closed Christmas to New Year's Day. **Disabled access**.
TV.

This is one of the better hotels in this category in Toulouse. It's good value for money, though it's more functional than charming. The spotless rooms cost €41 with shower/wc or bigger ones at €51 with bath. Some have air conditioning and the triple glazing in the rooms over the street is efficient. Warm welcome.

⚘ ♠ HÔTEL SAINT-SERNIN**

2 rue Saint-Bernard. **MAP C1-11**
☎ 05.61.21.73.08 ➡ 05.61.22.49.61
TV. **Pay car park**.

A lovely, comfortable hotel which has been completely renovated. Reception is on the first floor and the staff will welcome you with a smile. Attractive rooms with shower/wc cost from €47–61; they're €49–64 with bath, direct phone and mini-bar. There are four rooms with a stunning view of the basilica. The bar on the ground floor isn't fantastic but they serve the best *croque-monsieurs* in town. It's very noisy at the weekend because of the local flea market. 10% discount on the room rate.

⚘ ♠ HÔTEL CASTELLANE**

17 rue Castellane. **MAP D2-9**
☎ 05.61.62.18.82 ➡ 05.61.62.58.04
℮ castellanehotel.com
Disabled access. **TV**. **Pay garage**.

Very new hotel in an excellent location in a quiet street. Built around a patio, it's full of light. The pleasant rooms are a little small but have modern facilities and air-conditioning; doubles with shower or bath are €48. There are also family rooms sleeping up to seven and studios with kitchenettes which can be rented by the night. Nice breakfast room and pleasant, professional welcome. 10% discount except at weekends and in the school holidays.

⚘ ♠ HÔTEL ALBERT-1ER**

8 rue Rivals and 7 rue John Fitzgerald Kennedy. **MAP C2-6**
☎ 05.61.21.17.91 ➡ 05.61.21.09.64
℮ hotel-albert-1er@wanadoo.fr **TV**. **Car park**.

A small hotel in a quiet street in the com-

mercial centre. Excellent, professional welcome but with a family feel: the owner produces home-made jams for breakfast. The pleasant foyer is decorated with mosaics and pink Toulouse bricks. You'll pay €52 for a double with shower/wc or €59 for bath/wc. They're all comfortable and most have air conditioning. They can get you preferential rates in the neighbouring car park. 10% discount on the room rate except at weekends and during school holidays.

♠ HÔTEL L'OURS BLANC-WILSON**

2 rue Victor-Hugo. **MAP C2-10**
☎ 05.61.21.62.40 ➡ 05.61.23.62.34
TV.

This district is full of mid-range hotels and this one, in a beautiful 1930s building, has excellent facilities like TV, telephone and air conditioning. Bedrooms all have en-suite bathrooms but the décor is rather disappointing: doubles €54–60. Breakfast €7. They've modernized the foyer but have kept the very old wooden lift cage. There are 75 rooms in total.

♠ HÔTEL DES BEAUX-ARTS****

1 pl. du Pont-Neuf. **MAP C3-12**
☎ 05.61.23.40.50 ➡ 05.61.22.02.27
℮ contact@hotelesbeauxarts.com
TV. **Car park**.

This classy hotel is a favourite with visiting politicians and actors staying in Toulouse. It's in the heart of the historic centre on the edge of the Garonne. The façade is eighteenth-century but the décor inside is up to modern standards. Doubles with shower/wc €76 or €99–167; there's one on the top floor with a terrace and a wonderful view of the Garonne. Buffet breakfast €14.

♠ HÔTEL MERMOZ***

50 rue Matabiau. **MAP D1-13**
☎ 05.61.63.04.04 ➡ 05.61.63.15.34
Disabled access. **TV**. **Pay garage**.

This hotel is protected from the noisy street by an interior courtyard; it's a modern, vaguely Neoclassical building with an elegant flight of stairs. The décor makes lots of references to the air-mail service which operated from the city, with Art Deco furniture and drawings of aeroplanes on the walls. Fifty very well equipped, spacious bedrooms; doubles €81. They have attractive weekend deals. Buffet breakfast €9.

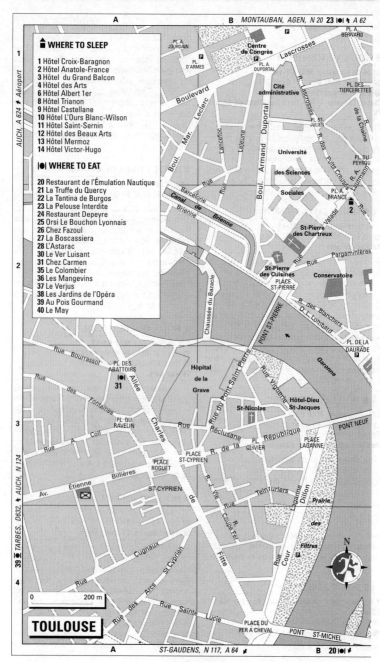

MONTAUBAN, AGEN, N 20 **23** |●| ↟ A 62

🛏 WHERE TO SLEEP

1 Hôtel Croix-Baragnon
2 Hôtel Anatole-France
3 Hôtel du Grand Balcon
4 Hôtel des Arts
6 Hôtel Albert 1er
8 Hôtel Trianon
9 Hôtel Castellane
10 Hôtel L'Ours Blanc-Wilson
11 Hôtel Saint-Sernin
12 Hôtel des Beaux Arts
13 Hôtel Mermoz
14 Hôtel Victor-Hugo

|●| WHERE TO EAT

20 Restaurant de l'Émulation Nautique
21 La Truffe du Quercy
22 La Tantina de Burgos
23 La Pelouse Interdite
24 Restaurant Depeyre
25 Orsi Le Bouchon Lyonnais
26 Chez Fazoul
27 La Boscassiera
28 L'Astarac
30 Le Ver Luisant
31 Chez Carmen
35 Le Colombier
36 Les Mangevins
37 Le Verjus
38 Les Jardins de l'Opéra
39 Au Pois Gourmand
40 Le May

TOULOUSE

A ST-GAUDENS, N 117, A 64 ↡ B **20** |●| ↡

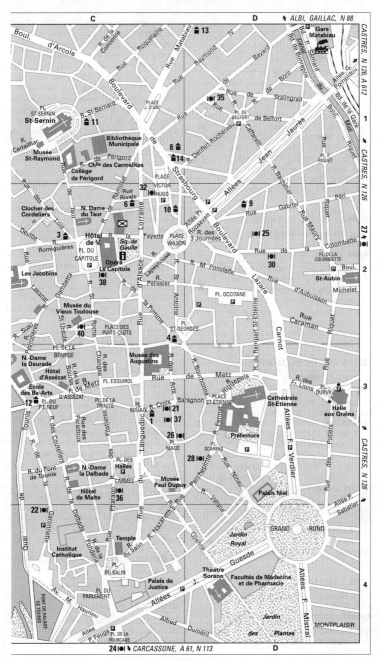

夫 |○| LE MAY

4 rue du May. **MAP C2-40**
☎ 05.61.23.98.76
Closed Sun lunchtime.

Right in the heart of the old town you'll find this restaurant with its two small, warm dining rooms. In summer they add a pleasant terrace. It's often packed because the food is good, cheap and excellent value for money: two-course lunch *formule* for €7, a three-course version for €8 and, in the evening, menus at €12 and €14. Freshly cooked dishes using local produce: house *confit*, duck breast with *foie gras*, vegetarian platter, marinated fish dishes in summer and casseroles in winter. Free house apéritif or *digestif*.

夫 |○| LA TRUFFE DU QUERCY

17 rue Croix-Baragnon. **MAP C3-21**
☎ 05.61.53.34.24
Closed Sun, public holidays and 27 July–27 Aug.

Renovated country décor and a relaxed family atmosphere in a real local restaurant. Good, traditional dishes from recipes that have been handed down from father to son over seventy years. Menus €8–19, individual dishes from €6. À la carte, you can get home-made *cassoulet au confit* and a few Spanish specialities. Free house apéritif.

|○| LES RESTOS DU MARCHÉ

pl. Victor-Hugo. **MAP C2-32**
Closed evenings and Mon.

A real Toulouse special. On market days at lunchtime, go up to the first floor of this concrete shed. There you'll find an amazingly lively and colourful scene, with half a dozen small restaurants providing plates of wholesome food cooked using the freshest market produce for the cheapest prices – menus start at around €10 including wine. The names give you a clue to the style of cuisine on offer: *Le Méditerranée*, *Le Magret*, *Chez Attila* (which specializes in fish and *zarzuela*, a sort of Spanish *bouillabaisse*). *Le Louchébem* offers a broad bean cassoulet on the first Saturday in the month, while at *Samaran* you can buy your *foie gras* fresh or cooked.

夫 |○| L'ASTARAC

21 rue Perchepinte. **MAP D3-28**
☎ 05.61.53.11.15
Closed Sat lunchtime; Sun; mid-July to mid-Aug.

Service lunchtimes and evenings until 10pm. This excellent restaurant is tucked away in a

narrow street in the old town; the tall room has sturdy beams and red brick walls hung with attractive paintings. There are discreet booths with comfy benches where you can have an intimate dinner for two. Tremendous Gascon cooking, with dishes such as salad of duck legs with *foie gras* and *paupiettes* of chicken with a cep cream sauce. Weekday lunch menu €10; others €16–24. They also offer two types of *foie gras*, *tournedos* of duck with a cep sauce and *poêlée Gasconne*. Sensibly priced wines like Fronton and Côtes-de-Saint-Mont. Free Pruneau à l'Armagnac.

夫 |○| RESTAURANT DE L'ÉMULATION NAUTIQUE

allée Alfred-Mayssonière. **Off map B4-20**
☎ 05.61.25.34.95
Closed Sun and Mon evenings; evenings if it's raining; Christmas to mid-Jan. **Garden**.

The best of the sailing club restaurants on the island of Ramier, just south of the town centre. It has a beautiful terrace, shaded by plane trees and looking out over the water. Weekday lunch menu €10; à la carte in the evening and at weekends for around €20. The grills are enormous: try their roast beef, the rack of lamb or the lamb shank, or go for one of the tasty salads. A wonderful place in summer. Free apéritif.

|○| LA BOSCASSIERA

1 rue Saint-Paul. Off map **D2-27**
☎ 05.61.20.34.11.
Closed Sat–Mon and mid-July to early Sept.

Nicolas used to run a mountain cabin in the Ariège but came to town to open this restaurant. The dining room is vast – this is where the first French jet engine was designed. It's beautifully furnished and you can see into the kitchen. Nicolas is a big man who cooks dishes from all over the region as they are intended to be cooked. Specialities include *confit* and *fricandeaux* of duck, *garbure*, Baltic herrings and a spectacular cod *cassoulet*. Lunch menu €13, or roughly €18 à la carte.

夫 |○| CHEZ CARMEN – RESTAURANT DES ABATTOIRS

97 allée Charles-de-Fitte. **MAP A3-31**
☎ 05.61.42.04.95
Closed Sun and Mon; public holidays; Aug.

The local abattoirs have gone – they've been turned into a contemporary art centre – but the meat here is as good as ever. The bistro (it's been going forty years) buzzes with life. Efficient if brusque service under the watchful eye of the owner, José-Antoine Carmen. Great plates of grilled meat or local dishes *à la carte* – calf's head, pig's trotters, steak *tartare*, rib of beef, roast duck breast with garlic. One menu at €14 (starter, meat dish and dessert) or about €23 *à la carte*. There are a few tables outside in summer. Free apéritif.

🖈 ❙●❙ LA TANTINA DE BURGOS

27 av. de la Garonnette. **MAP C4-22**
☎ 05.61.55.59.29
Closed Sun and Mon.

Service 7pm–1am. Very popular, a bit bohemian and decidedly Spanish. The terrace is pleasant in fine weather, while inside there is a large, lively dining room where you can sit at large tables or have a few tapas at the long bar – dishes cost between €4 and €6. They've opened a second, smaller, dining room which serves a mixture of French and Spanish dishes at very reasonable prices including *chicano* or chicken, squid, sea bass *tourte*, prawns, *empanadas* and *paella*. Expect to pay around €15 *à la carte*. Free aperitif.

❙●❙ LE VER LUISANT

41 rue de la Colombette. **MAP D2-30**
☎ 05.61.63.06.73
Closed Sat lunchtime; Sun; the week between Christmas and New Year; 3 weeks in Aug.

The restaurant is popular with theatre people and artists – it's smartish but bohemian. The cooking is classic and portions are generous, with excellent, inventive meat and regional dishes: grilled duck, salads, kebabs and so on. In winter they produce hearty dishes like *daube*, salt pork with lentils and *confits*. Reckon on €15-ish *à la carte*, with dishes of the day at €5. Great atmosphere and a nice bar.

🖈 ❙●❙ RESTAURANT DEPEYRE

77 route de Revel. **Off map C4-24**
☎ 05.61.20.26.56
Closed Sun and Aug.

It's 3km out of town on the edge of a road but both the *Vieille France* décor and the cuisine here are really attractive. Jacques Depeyre is a Maître-Cuisinier de France – clearly he's no slouch – while his wife used to run a restaurant in Brial. They're real professionals and have only recently come to Toulouse. Menus reflect the changing seasons and the course of the sun: *pâté* of three

kinds of fish with a sorrel *mousseline*, beef braised in Quercy wine, scallop stew with vegetables, fine fruit tart, iced Grand Marnier *bombe*. Lunch menu €15, others €26–49 – not bad when you consider the quality of the food. A very good restaurant

🖈 ❙●❙ LA PELOUSE INTERDITE

72 av. des États-Unis. Off map **B1-23**
☎ 05.61.47.30.40
Closed Oct–April and when it's raining. **Garden**.

An unusual place – the corners of the extraordinary garden are illuminated by numerous candles, furnished with junk-shop tables, chairs and large armchairs, table football and even hammocks and beds. Inside, in winter, there's a brilliantly coloured bar with a DJ who plays in the week. Delicious, inventive cuisine: goat's cheese and honey turnover, chicken with crayfish, curry · with coconut milk, Japanese-style beef, duck breast. It's essential to book. When you get there, ring the bell and wait. There's a *menu-carte* for €16 and a two-course *formule*. Free *digestif*.

🖈 ❙●❙ CHEZ FAZOUL

2 rue Tolosane. **MAP C3-26**
☎ 05.61.53.72.09
Closed Sun. **Disabled access**.

This restaurant has been serving good food for some time in its lovely and rather elegant seventeenth-century dining room. The €10 weekday lunch menu includes wine, service and a self-service buffet of *hors d'œuvres*. Other menus at €16–25 list good regional dishes, particularly grilled steak, duck breast and *foie gras* cooked old-style. Free house apéritif.

🖈 ❙●❙ LE COLOMBIER

14 rue de Bayard. **MAP D1-35**
☎ 05.61.62.40.05
Closed Sat lunchtime, Sun and Aug.

You'll come here for the *cassoulet*, which contains a goose *confit* that's been renowned for several generations – the recipe is top-secret. They offer a lunchtime *formule* during the week for €16 or menus €26–29; *à la carte* it costs an average of €38. You'll find salad of *lardons* with *confit*, medallion of duck *foie gras au torchon*, duck *foie gras* in goose fat and *croustade* of apples in Armagnac. Free cocktail.

🖈 ❙●❙ ORSI LE BOUCHON LYONNAIS

13 rue de l'Industrie. **MAP D2-25**
☎ 05.61.62.97.43

Closed Sat lunchtime or Sun.

This establishment is named after a famous gourmet chef from Lyons and is run by his brother. He produces specialities from his adopted region: the menus list dishes like *tablier de sapeur* (a slab of breaded ox tripe), pig's trotters and sliced *andouillette*, and the one listing,Gascon cuisine features one of the best *cassoulets* in town. Menus €18–29. The décor is classy *belle époque* and they open a terrace in summer. Free apéritif.

|●| LE VERJUS

7 rue Tolosane. **MAP C3-37**
☎ 05.61.52.06.93
Closed Sun, Mon, and July–Aug.

Service until 11pm. This place is popular for its unpretentious atmosphere and good bistro cooking. The dishes change constantly, though the chef's style is always evident: anchovies *au gratin,* scorpion fish stew with cider, mussels in red wine with zest of orange, beef *carbonnade* with sweet spices, mutton curry, tripe in tea, Portuguese pork *Alentejo*. There are also some surprising Thai dishes. Around €24 for three courses.

|●| LES MANGEVINS

46 rue Pharaon. **MAP C3-36**
☎ 05.61.52.79.16
Closed Sat, Sun and Aug.

Gérard opened this place mainly to sell and enjoy wines. He's a real connoisseur, and to show off the variety he has on sale he serves excellent *terrines* with very good bread. The dishes include vast salads with *foie gras*, *andouillette*, duck breast and some simple specialities like *foie gras* with sea salt and roast beef. The fish is sold by weight. Dishes around €9 or about €26 for a full meal.

⚒|●| AU POIS GOURMAND

3 rue Émile-Heybrard (off av. Casselardit). **Off map A3-39**
☎ 05.34.36.42.60 ➡ 05.34,36,42,08
e pois-gourmand@pois-gourmand.com
Closed Sat and Mon lunchtimes; Sun; a week in Feb; a fortnight in Aug.

It's not easy to find this place but it's worth the effort. It's a lovely house, built in 1870, which stands on the banks of the Garonne. There's a weekday lunch menu at €20 and three other menus €30–58. The cooking certainly deserves its excellent reputation: just try the brill fillet *à la badiane.*, the red mullet fillets in fig leaves or the pressed apples with figs. The dining room is magnificent, and

there are green plants all round the terrace. Free Kir.

⚒|●| LES JARDINS DE L'OPÉRA

1 pl. du Capitole. **MAP C2-38**
☎ 05.61.23.07.76 ➡ 05.61.23.63.00
e toulousy@wanadoo.fr
Closed Sun; Mon lunchtime; public holidays; 1–7 July; 3 weeks in Aug. **Garden**.

The cooking here is refined and inventive, and it's long since made a name for itself – so it's not surprising that a meal costs what it does. Menus start at €35 for lunch during the week then shoot up to €46 and €61 at dinner; there's also a vegetarian menu for €21. Dominique Toulousy is one of the great chefs in town and he changes the dishes regularly: foie gras ravioli with truffle *jus*, cassoulet, lasagne with vegetables, crayfish and oysters with caviar, pigeon in a spiced crust, maize flour pancakes with iced apricot mousse. The wines are reasonably priced given their quality and that of the food. Staff are very attentive. The garden has been wonderfully planted and is even more beautiful at night than during the day. Free apéritif.

URDENS   32500

⚒|●| L'AUBERGE PAYSANNE

pl. de l'Église.
☎ 05.62.06.25.57
Closed Mon in summer; Sun evening and Mon in winter; March; Oct. **Disabled access**. **Car park**.

Authentic rustic inn in converted stables. The terrace is particularly lovely in the summer, and really peaceful. The inn is famous for good local dishes such as stuffed chicken, duck thigh with peaches, Gascon salad, *émincé* of duck with wild mushrooms and *crème brûlée* with prunes. The €10 lunch menu includes wine, and there are others €14–27. Free apéritif.

VALENCE-SUR-BAÏSE   32310

⚒🏠|●| LA FERME DE FLARAN**

route de Condom; it's on the outskirts of the village on the D930.
☎ 05.62.28.58.22 ➡ 05.62.28.56.89
e ferme-de-flaran@mintel.net
Closed Mon except July–Aug; Sun evening; 15 Nov–15 Dec; Jan. **Swimming pool. Garden. TV. Car park**.

This old farm has been successfully converted into a hotel. The small rooms are very comfortable and go for €45 for a double with shower/wc or bath. Fresh produce from the markets and local producers are used for good regional specialities like *fricassée* of sole with ceps, pan-fried *foie gras*, *carpaccio* of duck breast, veal sweetbreads with morels and a hamburger of monkfish with *foie gras*. Menus €16–21. 10% discount on the room rate Sept–June.

VICDESSOS   09220

🛏 |●| HÔTEL DE FRANCE**

route d'Avzat.
☎ 05.61.64.88.17
Closed Oct.

A haven of peace between two valleys. Foaming waters course beneath the terrace, where you can sit enjoying a drink or a substantial meal. There's lots of choice on the menus which start at €10. You can enjoy the view of the mountains from your bedroom. Doubles from €31.

VILLEFRANCHE-DE-LAURAGAIS   31290

🛏 |●| HÔTEL DE FRANCE**

106 rue de la République (Centre).
☎ 05.61.81.62.17 ☛ 05.61.81.66.04
Closed Sun evening and Mon. **TV. Car park.**

This attractive nineteenth-century inn is in Villefranche-de-Lauragais, one of the best places to eat *cassoulet*, the famous local dish made with dried beans and goose and duck *confit*. Unsurprisingly, it's the house speciality. Menus €9 (not Sat, Sun or public holidays), then €12–43. Rooms, decorated in period style, cost €26 for a double with shower/wc or €33 with bath. They're quieter at the back. Number 32 has lovely floor tiles and an eighteenth-century fireplace.

VILLEFRANCHE-DE-ROUERGUE   12200

🌿 🛏 |●| HÔTEL-RESTAURANT BELLEVUE*

3 av. du Ségala (South); it's just behind the station near the town centre.
☎ 05.65.45.23.17 ☛ 05.65.45.11
Closed Sun, Mon lunchtime except July–Aug. **Garden. Car park**.

The building won't attract your gaze and the interior décor is pretty dated but you shouldn't pass up the chance to enjoy the food here – quality cooking at reasonable prices. Fresh local produce is used exclusively, and prices are good given what you get: menus

€13–43. *Foie gras* in pastry with melting pears, lamb sweetbreads with paprika, prawn ravioli with shellfish sauce, lobster. The hotel is clean, simple and unpretentious; doubles cost €15 with shower/wc and €26 with bath. The ones overlooking the street are a bit noisy. 10% discount on the room rate out of season.

🛏 |●| HÔTEL DE L'UNIVERS**

pl. de la République (Centre); it's on the north bank of the Aveyron.
☎ 05.65.45.15.63 ☛ 05.65.45.02.21
Restaurant closed Fri evening; Sat out of season (except before a public holiday). **Disabled access**. **TV. Car park**.

A fine-looking building. Rooms are clean and have been recently refurbished. Doubles are €28–53 with shower or bath – the nicest ones overlook the Aveyron. The cooking is simple and includes dishes like *tripou*, calf's head *ravigotte*, duck legs and medallions of lamb in a game sauce. Menus €12–45.

🌿 🛏 |●| LE RELAIS DE FARROU***

Farrou (North); head for Saint-Rémy, 3km on the Figeac road.
☎ 05.65.45.18.11 ☛ 05.65.45.32.59
Restaurant closed Sun evening and Mon out of season; 9–25 Feb; 26 Oct–4 Nov. **Disabled access**. **Swimming pool. Garden. TV. Car park**.

A small tourist complex with a park, pool, Turkish bath and hot tub. The rooms, all comfortable and air-conditioned, cost €44–52 with shower/wc or €55–75 with bath. The décor in the restaurant is a bit showy but the cooking has a good reputation. There's a range of menus: €13 at lunch (except Sun), a *menu terroir* for €20 and others €27–35. Specialities include *foie gras* cooked with spices, pike with celery mousseline, duck tounedos roasted with spices and pigeon breast with truffle. Try a glass of plum brandy if you don't fancy dessert. Free house apéritif.

|●| RESTAURANT DE LA HALLE – CHEZ PINTO

pl. de la Halle; (Centre); it's near the cathedral.
☎ 05.65.45.07.74

This workman's restaurant is one of the few remaining examples of that dying breed. You'll get a cordial welcome and be served substantial helpings of home cooking. There's a set menu for €8.

|●| L'ASSIETTE GOURMANDE

pl. A.-Lescure (Centre); it's beside the cathedral.

☎ 05.65.45.25.95
Closed Sun, Tues and Wed evening out of season; 6–22 April; a week in Sept; 27 Oct–5 Nov. **Car park**.

The décor is fairly clichéd, all wooden beams and copper pots, but the cooking is good. Set menus €12–27. They grill on an open fireplace fuelled with oak from the Causse chalk plateau, which gives the dishes a distinctive flavour – pan-fried *foie gras* with apples, *aligot* and *tripou*. The terrace is nice in summer.

MONTEILS   12200 (11.5KM S)

🎿 🏠 I●I RESTAURANT LE CLOS GOURMAND

☎ 05.65.29.63.15 ➡ 05.65.29.64.98
Open by reservation only.

This substantial master craftsman's house is lovely to look at and you'll get a friendly welcome from Anne-Marie Lavergne, who's well-known for the excellent regional specialities she serves her guests. Menus start at €11 and there are others €15–27, listing regional dishes such as stuffed duck's neck with walnuts, trout with *lardons* and beef with Roquefort. She also has a few rooms for €43 with bath/wc. Free apéritif.

VILLENEUVE-SUR-TARN   81250

🎿 🏠 I●I HOSTELLERIE DES LAURIERS**

au bourg (Centre); it's on the D77, 32km east of Albi.
☎ 05.63.55.84.23 ➡ 05.63.55.89.20
Closed Sun evening and Mon out of season; Nov to mid-March.

An absolutely delightful village hotel right next to the church, with a lawn running all the way down to the riverbank. It's brilliantly run by a lovely young couple. There are eight good rooms, a lovely dining room and a bar which is popular with the villagers. Weekday menu €12 then others €17–38. Several house specialities, including zander fillet, slow-cooked veal in its own juices, fillet of beef with cream and ceps and roast lamb with cloves of garlic. The boss really knows his way around the region and is a mine of information. There's a lovely terrace overlooking the grounds. They offer games for the kids. Free apéritif.

Nord-Pas-de-Calais

59 Nord

62 Pas-de-Calais

ARRAS   62000

⋏ 🏠 |●| CAFÉ-HÔTEL DU BEFFROI

28 pl. de la Vacquerie (Centre); it's behind the bell-tower.
☎ 03.21.23.13.78 ➡ 03.21.23.03.08
Closed Sun.

You'll find this establishment at the end of a cluster of typical Flemish houses. It's a classic bistro at street-level, jammed with locals, where you can get good food on the €14 menu. The rooms, reached by a steep staircase, are charming and well-maintained; they cost €39 with shower/wc or €32 with shower only. Number 10 overlooks the square, so you have a perfect view of the Golden Lion of Artois on the 75m bell-tower. Free house apéritif.

⋏ 🏠 HÔTEL DES TROIS LUPPARS**

49 Grand-Place (Centre).
☎ 03.21.07.41.41 ➡ 03.21.24.24.80
TV. Car park.

This fifteenth-century listed building, on one of the finest squares in northern France, houses a really charming hotel. The décor may be a touch modern given the surroundings, but rooms are very comfortable and all have shower/bath. They're fair value at €49 for a double with shower/wc or €56 with bath. The two new owners show you a genuinely warm welcome. 10% discount on the room rate 1 Nov–28 Feb.

⋏ 🏠 |●| HÔTEL-RESTAURANT AUX GRANDES ARCADES**

8–12 Grand-Place (Centre).

☎ 03.21.23.30.89 ➡ 03.21.71.50.94
TV.

Following a total overhaul, rooms here are comfortable, modern, clean and well-sound-proofed – and you couldn't possibly be more central. Doubles €49–53. The main dining room is one of the most beautiful in town, in the style of a 1900s brasserie with a lofty ceiling and gleaming dark wood panelling – there's a second room decorated more traditionally. Menus range from €13–29, including a regional menu listing Maroilles cheese tart, Arras *andouillette* with mustard and pancakes with brown sugar to finish. Free coffee.

⋏ |●| RESTAURANT CHEZ ANNIE

14 rue Paul-Doumer (Centre); it's 200m behind the bell-tower.
☎ 03.21.23.13.51
Closed weekday evenings; Sun open by reservation only.

This fun little establishment is like a miniature brasserie, with a staircase of almost monumental proportions given the size of the place. Climb the steps to the mezzanine, where you can watch the regulars propping up the bar while you feast on good home cooking. There's a generous *menu du jour* for €9; if you prefer to go *à la carte* you'll spend around €12. Free coffee.

⋏ |●| LE BOUCHOT

3 rue de Chanzy; it's near the station.
☎ 03.21.51.67.51
Closed Mon.

A bright, freshly decorated canteen-style restaurant with a marine theme – there's a boat in the middle of the dining room – which specializes in huge portions of good mussels

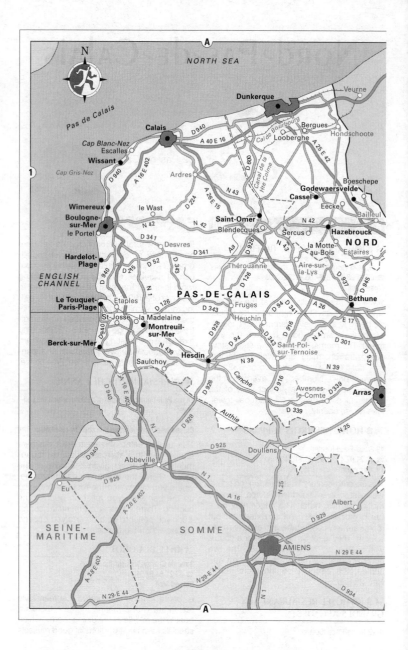

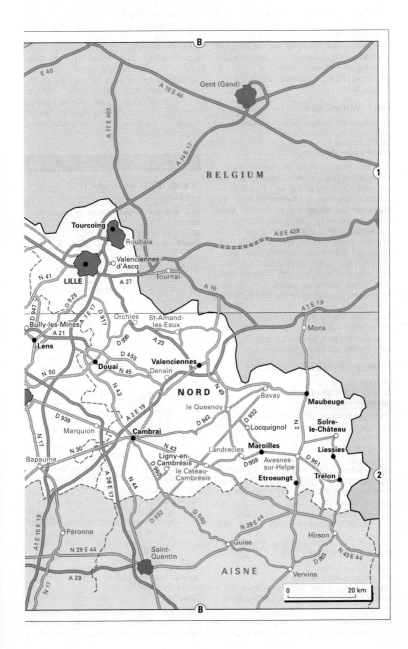

prepared in a fifteen different ways: with Maroilles cheese, *à la marseillaise*, with cream and dill, and so on. The chips are up to scratch, as they should be, and they also get full marks for their honestly cooked, inexpensive regional dishes. Menus €10–15, or around €13 for a complete meal *à la carte*. Free coffee.

|●| LE TROUBADOUR

29 av. du Général-de-Gaulle (Centre); it's opposite the casino.
☎03.21.71.34.50
Closed Sun and Mon evening.

The *bouchon* (Lyonnais restaurant) atmosphere in this place is very appealing; you feel almost as if you're dining with friends in the country. The warm welcome from the *patronne* has something to do with it, as does the cooking. Choices of the day are scrawled up on a blackboard (three lots of starters, main courses and desserts), with traditional dishes such as calf's head *sauce gribiche*, *pot-au-feu* (boiled beef and veg), and pan-fried scallops with fresh noodles. The house *terrine* is served with pickled onions and gigantic gherkins, and the bread is a peasant-style loaf. You'll pay €12 or so for a meal. The desserts are expensive given the context – €5 for a fresh fruit salad with strawberries and kiwi fruit – and so is the wine by the jug. It's worth booking.

⏏|●| RESTAURANT LA RAPIÈRE

44 Grand-Place (Centre).
☎ 03.21.55.09.92 ➡ 03.21.22.24.29
Closed Sun evening.

This friendly restaurant is hidden away under the sandstone arcades of one of the 155 houses enclosing the Grand-Place. It has a contemporary décor but serves solid, traditional cuisine – salmon *en papillote* and fillet of beef with Roquefort – and local specialities like Maroilles cheese flan, house *foie gras*, beef fillet with Maroiles and *andouillette* in pastry. Menus at €14–32 include regional wine. You'll need to be on expenses to dine in the vaulted seventeenth-century cellar. Free coffee.

|●| LA FAISANDERIE

45 Grand-Place (Centre).
☎ 03.21.48.20.76 ➡ 03.21.50.89.18
Closed Sun evening; Mon; the first week in Jan; a week of the Feb school holidays; the first three weeks in Aug.

Michelin may have taken away their star, but this is still generally acknowledged to be the best gourmet restaurant in town. Jean-Pierre Dargent still creates joyous dishes that are full of flavour and exquisitely prepared; just taste the fresh cod in a breadcrumb crust with a shellfish *jus*, the suckling pig roast with sage or the pan-fried artichokes and *crépiau* of fresh cream cheese with girolle mushrooms. Menus €22 (not Sat night), €34 and €51. The *sommelier* gives informed advice and doesn't push the pricey bottles, and at the end of the evening the chef comes round to bid his customers goodnight.

BERCK-SUR-MER 62600

⏏ 🏠 |●| HÔTEL-RESTAURANT LE VOLTAIRE

29 av. du Général-de-Gaulle (Centre); it's opposite the casino.
☎ 03.21.84.43.13 ➡ 03.21.84.61.72
Closed Tues out of season and 13–25 Feb. **TV**.

The renovated rooms here are spacious, spotless and efficiently soundproofed, with practical, modern décor. Doubles with basin go for €24, €29–41 with shower/wc or bath, and there's a good buffet breakfast costing €5. The warm, friendly welcome and youthful ambience extends to the ground-floor bar, which specializes in beers. Apart from a few local specialities such as *ficelle picarde* (stuffed pancake) and charcoal-grilled beef, the food is not that impressive. Menus €10–18. Free coffee.

⏏|●| L'AUBERGE DU BOIS

149 av. Quetier.
☎ 03.21.9.03.43
Closed Mon out of season and Jan.

Everyone in town calls this convivial place "Chez Ben" because the owner is so well-known. His bar-restaurant has a huge, simple and pleasant dining room decorated in warm tones, with menus from €14–31. The house speciality, fish *choucroute*, is good and there's plenty of it; if you want one of their impressive seafood platters, €56 per person, you'll need to order in advance. Free apéritif.

⏏|●| LA VERRIÈRE

Casino de Berck-sur-Mer, pl. du 18-Juin.
☎ 03.21.84.27.25
Closed Tues.

There are two entrances to this restaurant – the one that takes you past the rows of jangling slot machines will give you the wrong impression. The other offers the casino's classier face – a spacious, elegant restaurant where they serve the best cooking in town and probably along this stretch of the Opale coast. The chef uses only fresh produce, so dishes change all the time, and service is perfect. Menus €21–38. Free coffee.

BÉTHUNE 62400

⚐ 🏠 |●| HÔTEL DU VIEUX BEFFROI**

48 Grand-Place (Centre)
☎ 03.21.68.15.00 ➡ 03.21.56.66.32
Disabled access. TV. Car park.

A vast hotel, with turrets and gables, opposite the fourteenth-century bell-tower. You are woken by the bells in the morning, but thankfully they don't ring at night. Some of the old-fashioned rooms have been renovated and they're not short on charm – doubles with shower/wc or bath go for €43. Meals are served in a lively brasserie, where dishes include duo of fish with basil sauce, house smoked salmon and Périgord salad. You can choose from a range of menus between €12 and €23. Free *digestif*.

⚐|●| RESTAURANT LA TAVERNE

1 pl. de la République (Centre).
☎ 03.21.56.80.80 ➡ 03.21.65.77.00
Closed Sat lunchtime and Sun evening.

One of the best places in town, this traditional, unpretentious brasserie serves regional dishes to an appreciative local crowd. Choose from the menus (€14–23) or the varied *à la carte* selection. Specialities include various kinds of *choucroute* and an excellent and substantial fisherman's platter. Free coffee.

⚐|●| LA RIPAILLE

20 Grand-Place (Centre).
☎ 03.21.56.22.33
Closed Sat, Sun evening, and 24 Dec–8 Jan.

Though there's little to see from the outside – just a narrow, very ordinary frontage – this place is usually crammed with regulars who are very obviously enjoying themselves. The portions are big, the sauces and broths are appetizing and the fish and meat invariably splendid; this is a good place indeed. The dish of the day, €11, is always worth trying; otherwise go for the poultry *viennoise*, *crepinette* of pigs' trotters or cod with beer and

Mimolette cheese – to follow, the *moelleux* with bitter chocolate is superb. You're looking at around €23 *à la carte*. Free coffee.

BOULOGNE-SUR-MER 62200

🏠 HÔTEL FAIDHERBE**

12 rue Faidherbe (Centre).
☎ 03.21.31.60.93 ➡ 03.21.87.01.14
Disabled access. TV.

Near the harbour in a charmless part of town rebuilt after the War. If the weather's fine, Victor, the resident mynah bird, might decide to say a few words. There's a small, comfy Victorian-style lounge, and individually decorated rooms with good facilities. Doubles with shower €35, €39 with bath.

🏠 HÔTEL L'ALEXANDRA**

93 rue Thiers (Centre); it's near the port.
☎ 03.21.30.52.22 ➡ 03.21.30.20.03
Closed 28 Dec–31 Jan. **TV. Car park.**

A small, unfussy hotel in a street which manages to escape the worst of the town centre's heavy traffic. Rooms are brightly decorated and have good facilities; doubles with shower/wc go for €37–43. It's best to book in high season and during public holidays.

⚐|●| L'ESTAMINET DU CHÂTEAU

2 rue du Château (East); it's in the old town opposite the basilica of Notre-Dame.
☎ 03.21.91.49.66 ➡ 03.21.31.92.96
Closed Wed evening; Thurs; 23 Dec–23 Jan.

On a picturesque street in the fortified thirteenth-century part of the town, this is a reliable bet in a rather touristy area. It's a cosy little restaurant where traditions are respected – accordion music hasn't given way to techno and the bar is still inhabited by regulars. No complaints as far as the food is concerned, either – menus are reasonably priced at €11–27. Specialities include monkfish kebabs, skate wings, poached cod and Dublin Bay prawns. Free apéritif.

|●| CHEZ JULES

pl. Dalton (Centre); it's in the lower town.
☎ 03.21.31.54.12
Closed Sun evening.

This is *the* Boulogne brasserie, with a huge terrace on the square. It's been around for aeons so the service is efficient and the cooking tasty and reliable. Good bets include *moules marinières*, beef tripe, ham on the bone and calf's head *sauce gribiche*. They also have a second dining room and a pizzeria.

PORTEL (LE)   62480 (4.5KM SW)

斥 ❘●❘ LE PORTELOIS

42 quai Dugay-Trouin; take the D119 and at Portel
follow the signs to the beach.
☎ 03.21.31.44.60 ➡ 03.21.31.34.83
Closed Mon except July–Aug.

A seaside restaurant with a panoramic view
of the Channel interrupted only by the ruins
of a Napoleonic fort. Unsurprisingly, the
food's influenced by the sea, and there are
no fewer than 22 mussels specialities – try
them *à l'ancienne*, or in Flemish, Pekinese
or Hungarian style. As for the fish, the
waterzoï fish casserole is well worth a try.
Menus from €11 or around €23 *à la carte*.
Free coffee.

WAST (LE)   62142 (15KM E)

斥 ❚ ❘●❘ HOSTELLERIE DU CHÂTEAU DES TOURELLES**

How to get there: take the N42 towards Saint-Omer then
take the D127 to Le Wast.
☎ 03.21.33.34.78 ➡ 03.21.87.59.57
Disabled access. **TV**. **Car park**.

As you enter the village you'll see the hotel,
which is housed in a very elegant nineteenth-
century mansion, hidden behind the trees in
a small park. There's a modern annexe next
to the tennis courts. Ideally, you should stay
in the superb rooms of the "château" with
their Louis-Philippe furniture and small balconies. If your funds won't stretch to that, go
for an attic room. Doubles with shower/wc or
bath €46–49. Tennis, table tennis and billiards are all free for residents, and the
restaurant serves menus at €13–38. Free
coffee.

CALAIS   62100

斥 ❚ HÔTEL WINDSOR**

2 rue du Commandant-Bonningue (Northeast); head for
the harbour, and you'll find it on the extension of the pl.
d'Armes.
☎ 03.21.34.59.40 ➡ 03.21.97.68.59
TV. **Lock-up car park**.

In a quiet part of town, not far from the marina, the *Windsor* is owned by an Englishman
who'll give you a warm, polite welcome.
Attractive rooms from €27. 10% discount for
two nights.

斥 ❚ HÔTEL PACIFIC**

40 rue du Duc-de-Guise (North); it's near Notre-Dame
cathedral.
☎ 03.21.34.50.24 ➡ 03.21.97.58.02
TV. **Lock-up car park**.

A small, friendly hotel that's centrally located
but gratifyingly peaceful. The owners are renovating it floor by floor, and it proves good
value for this part of the world; doubles with
shower go for €29 or €38–39 with bath/wc.
They have family rooms that sleep up to four
people. The lounge and bar have a very retro
look. 5% discount.

斥 ❚ LE RICHELIEU**

17 rue Richelieu (North); it's opposite Richelieu park.
☎ 03.21.34.61.60 ➡ 03.21.85.89.28
Closed Christmas and New Year's Day. **TV**. **Lock-up
car park**.

Bright, comfortable rooms at €43 for a double with shower/wc or bath. Nine of them
have balconies looking over the huge, lush
Richelieu park – a soothing contrast to the
garish neon signs in the adjacent streets. It's
easy to relax here; the welcome is low-key,
though perhaps too much so, and the street
is very quiet. 10% discount.

CAMBRAI   59400

❚ HÔTEL DE FRANCE*

37 rue de Lille; it's 100m from the train station.
☎ 03.27.81.38.80 ➡ 03.27.78.13.88
Closed Sun. **TV**.

A typical station hotel – neat and tidy and
quaintly old-fashioned, though many rooms
have had a makeover. It's remarkably quiet,
even in the rooms overlooking the tracks –
few trains run at night. Doubles €31–42 with
shower/wc. You'll get a charming welcome
from the owner, who's something of a wine
buff.

❚ ❘●❘ LE MOUTON BLANC***

33 rue d'Alsace-Lorraine; it's about 200m from the train
station, in the street opposite.
☎ 03.27.81.30.16 ➡ 03.27.81.83.54
Restaurant closed Sun evening and Mon. **TV**. **Car
park**.

Solidly built nineteenth-century house with a
great deal of charm and a genuine family
atmosphere. The rooms exude a certain opu-
lence without going over the top, and cost
€53 for a double with shower/wc or €61
with bath. They serve good and interesting
dishes in the large dining room. Winners

include gnocchi with Maroilles cheese, *fric-assée* of scallops and Dublin Bay prawns, baby chicory cooked in lemon and boned pigeon with acacia honey. Menus €16–34. Breakfast is free, but it's not all that great.

🏂 |●| LE GRILL DE L'EUROPE

pl. Marcellin-Berthelot (Southwest); it's in the port district.
☎ 03.27.81.66.76
Closed Sat lunchtime; Sun evening; a fortnight July–Aug.

A popular haunt of truck drivers, sailors and fishermen, this is a simple, warm and lively bar where they serve straightforward home cooking. The €11 menu offers steak, dessert, a $1/_4$-litre of wine and coffee; other menus €17–36. There's also a self-service *hors d'œuvre* buffet, dishes of the day and an *à la carte* choice of frogs' legs *provençale*, beef steak with morels or *andouillette* flambéed with juniper. Free coffee.

🏂 |●| LE RESTO DU BEFFROI

4 rue du 11-Novembre; take the avenue opposite the town hall, and it's the second turning on the right.
☎ 03.27.81.50.10
Closed Sat lunchtime; Sun; the first fortnight in Feb; three weeks in Aug.

A friendly, if rather unusual, restaurant tucked away in a little street behind the Grand-Place. The décor is a mixture of traditional bistro and night club, and some of the cuisine takes its influence from the southwest, where chef Yves Galan used to breed ducks. Today he prepares good robust food, including duck breast and *cassoulet* with duck *confit*, veal sweetbreads *toulousaine* and chicken with cream and morel sauce. Menus €16–23. Free house Kir.

LIGNY-EN-CAMBRÉSIS   59400 (15KM SE)

🏠 |●| LE CHÂTEAU DE LIGNY

2 rue Pierre-Curie; take the N43 in the direction of Cateay-Cambrésis, and in Beauvois turn off to Ligny.
☎ 03.27.85.25.84 ➡ 03.27.85.79.79
Closed a fortnight in Feb.

This rural hideway is a stylish, tasteful place. The round tower is part of the original twelfth-century château, and the salons have ornamental ceilings. Each guest room has its own personality – you could lose yourself in the biggest one – and prices reflect the quality: you're looking at paying anything from €99–229. The restaurant, which is open to non-residents, has a huge reputation and

enjoys a magnificent setting; cooking is tasty, light and inspired. The menu, €43, lists frequently changing dishes such as fillet of beef with sautéed duck *foie gras* and stewed Breton lobster with verbena.

CASSEL   59670

🏂 |●| LA TAVERNE FLAMANDE

34 Grand-Place; it's opposite the town hall.
☎ 03.28.42.42.59 ➡ 03.28.40.51.84
Closed Tues evening; Wed; a week in Feb; a week at the end of Aug; a week at the end of Oct.

You'll get an authentic Flemish meal here. Try Flemish *croustillons*, chicken casserole Ghent style (cooked in a home-made bechamel-type sauce), veal kidneys flambéed with gin, Flemish apple tart sprinkled with brown sugar or *crêpes* flambéed in Houlle. Menus €10 (not Sun) and up to €21. Sit on the veranda, which is perched on the slopes of Mont Cassel, and enjoy the same panorama that so delighted the Romantic poet Lamartine. Free coffee.

🏂 |●| ESTAMINET 'TKASTEEL HOF

8 rue Saint-Nicolas; it's opposite the mill.
☎ 03.28.40.59.29 ➡ 03.28.42.43.23
Closed Mon–Wed from Oct to end March. **Car park**.

This tavern, at the top of Mont Cassel, is at the highest altitude in French Flanders – a mere 175.90m. There's a splendid view from upstairs. It's a wonderful little place, stuffed full of spoils from junk shops, with a tiny bar, a few tables, wooden chairs, a fireplace and baskets hanging from the beams. Typical offerings include various kinds of soup with endives, *cœur casselois* (pork mince with cubes of smoked bacon), *waterzoï* (fish stew), *potjevfleisch* (a local *pâté* of veal, chicken and rabbit) and apples in flaky pastry. Cheeses include *zermezeelois* or *mont-des-cats*, and even the mineral water is Flemish, hailing from Saint-Amand. This is hop country so there's a list of traditional beers rather than wine. You'll pay around €15 for a meal, or you could settle for one of the filling platters of local cheeses or *pâtés*. Free *digestif* or coffee.

EECKE   59114 (10KM SE)

|●| BRASSERIE SAINT-GEORGES

5 rue de Castre; take the D933 then the D947 and it's halfway between Cassel and Bailleul.
☎ 03.28.40.13.71
Closed Mon–Thurs lunchtimes; Mon–Thurs evenings

except July–Aug and on public holidays; Fri lunchtime; last week in Aug; Christmas Day. **TV**. **Car park**.

This bastion of Flemish culture has its own newsletter. The building started out as a farm in the sixteenth century, after which it became a mill, and then a posthouse, and the jumbled architecture and décor combine elements from this varied past. They began brewing beer here in the 1970s and now sell 63 specialist beers – *des Chênes*, brewed locally, is the most popular. Good traditional Flemish cooking includes *andouillettes*, grilled pork chitterlings with *standevleech* (potatoes cooked in coals), melted Maroilles cheese with cumin, grilled pork fillet and ham *à la 3 Monts* (ham on the bone marinated in beer with potatoes and Maroilles cheese *au gratin*). Prices are reasonable with menus from €17 or €18 *à la carte*.

BOESCHEPE   59299 (15KM E)

🏃 🏠 |●| AUBERGE DU VERT MONT**

Route du Mont-Noir; take the D948 towards Steenvoorde then the N348 to the Belgian border, and finally the D10 towards Bailleul; it's signposted from Boeschepe.
☎ 03.28.49.41.26 ➡ 03.28.49.48.58
Closed Mon and Tues lunchtimes. **TV**. **Car park**.

This small tourist complex, next to a hop field, used to be a farm. It retains a rural feel, with ducks splashing about in the pond and goats and sheep bleating in the fields. They offer games for children and there are a couple of tennis courts. The rooms are adorable too; they're €52–58 for a double with shower/wc or bath. There are flowers everywhere in the restaurant, which offers a range of tried-and-tested, well-prepared regional dishes: try fish stew, scallops *à la Hoegarden* or *potjevfleisch* (veal, chicken and rabbit *pâté*), and wash it down with one of their many Belgian and French beers. Menus €19–27. Free coffee.

DOUAI   59500

🏠 |●| HÔTEL LE CHAMBORD**

3509 route de Tournai; it's in Frais-Marais, 4km from the centre of Douai on the D917.
☎ 03.27.97.72.77 ➡ 03.27.99.35.14
Hotel closed a week in Feb and a fortnight in Aug.
Restaurant closed Sun evening and Mon.
TV. **Car park**.

Frais-Marais, a suburb of Douai, still feels like a village, though the main road runs past the

hotel – don't take a room on that side of the building. The comfortable, attractive rooms here are reasonably priced for the area – oddly enough, hotels in Douai cost a lot. Doubles with bath €43. The restaurant offers a €14 weekday menu with others up to €40.

🏃 🏠 |●| HÔTEL VOLUBILIS***

bd. Bauban; coming from Tournai, it's where the road comes to the Pont de Lille.
☎ 03.27.88.00.11 ➡ 03.27.96.07.41
🅔 hotelvolubilis@nordnet.fr
Closed Sun evening. **TV**. **Car park**.

Despite all appearances – at first glance it looks like a chain hotel – this is a very pleasant establishment with a fresh, brightly coloured interior and double rooms from €53. The restaurant has more than adequate menus starting at around €15. Free coffee.

🏃 🏠 |●| HÔTEL-RESTAURANT LA TERRASSE****

36 terrasse Saint-Pierre.
☎ 03.27.88.70.04
TV. **Car park**.

This is a four-star place and a member of the *Châteaux et Hôtels Indépendants* organization. It's beautifully situated near the collegiate church in a charming old house. Serious and traditional, run by very professional staff, it nevertheless offers reasonably priced rooms at €72–95 with shower/wc or bath. With its red brick and white stone walls hung with paintings, the dining room evokes traditional France; the ideal setting to enjoy beautifully presented, classic dishes. Fish, including lobster fresh from the tank, dominates, but they also do game in season and good *foie gras* dishes – and prices are more than honest. Set menus from €20 (including wine), to €66. There's a spectacular wine list of 900 different *appellations*; the proprietor owns vineyards in Burgundy. Free coffee.

|●| RESTAURANT AU TURBOTIN

9 rue de la Massue (Centre); it's near the Scarpe river, opposite the law courts.
☎ 03.27.87.04.16
Closed Sat lunchtime; Sun evening; Mon; the last week in Feb; Aug.

Au Turbotin is primarily a fish and seafood restaurant, though they also offer other regional dishes. Try the turbot with Maroilles cheese, lobster *brioche*, or specialities like fish *choucroute*, zander stuffed with pike mousse, fish *pot-au-feu*, pike *cannelloni* or lamb charlotte with cream and garlic. The weekday menu costs €15, with others at €24–40. With chic yet low-key surroundings, courteous and refined service and customers who don't have to watch the pennies, it's one of the town's classiest establishments.

DUNKERQUE   59240

� ⌂ TRIANON HÔTEL**

20 rue de la Colline (Northeast); follow the signs for the beach and the hotel is signposted.
☎ 03.28.63.39.15 ➡ 03.28.63.34.57
TV. Car park.

In a quiet district inhabited predominantly by retired people, this place is typical of the picturesque seaside villas that were built along this coast in the mid-nineteenth century. The hotel is quite charming and the rooms are pleasant, as is the tiny indoor garden next to the breakfast room. Doubles €40 with shower/wc or bath. The owner, who knows the area well, is always ready to help. One free breakfast per room and free bike loan.

⚫ ⌂ |●| HÔTEL-RESTAURANT L'HIRONDELLE**

46–48 av. Faidherbe (Northeast); from the centre head towards the beach, where it's signposted.
☎ 03.28.63.17.65 ➡ 03.28.66.15.43
Restaurant closed Sun evening; Mon; a fortnight from 20 Aug. **TV. Disabled access. Car park.**

Right next to a lovely little square – sadly marred by the thunder of the traffic – and not far from the sea, this is a faultless establishment with modern décor. The functional rooms, priced from €54, all have shower or bath. Reassuringly conventional dishes are served in the restaurant: poached turbot with Hollandaise sauce, seafood platters and *pot-jevleesch* (veal, rabbit and chicken in aspic cooked in white wine and vinegar). There's a weekday menu at €10 and others at €15 and €20; you'll spend around €22 *à la carte*. The small bar is a nice place to drink. Free apéritif.

⚫ |●| LE PÉCHÉ MIGNON

11 pl. du Casino; across the square from the casino.
☎ 03.28.66.14.44
Closed Sat lunchtime, Sun evening and Mon. **Garden.**

A cosy little dining room in pastel shades with soft armchairs. If you've lost your shirt in the casino across the square, you will probably still be able to afford the cheapest menu, modestly priced at €12. If you're dining before making for the gaming tables, howev-

er, there are others up to €31. Generously flavoured dishes include splendid house *foie gras*, smoked duck breast, good fish and regional desserts such as spiced bread ice-cream. When it's sunny, make for the little terrace in the garden – a consolation for the lack of sea view. The welcome is also excellent. Free apéritif, coffee or *digestif*.

⚫ |●| AU PETIT PIERRE

4 rue Dampierre (Centre).
☎ 03.28.66.28.36
Closed Sat lunchtime, Sun and Mon evenings.

This is one of the town's very few eighteenth-century residences that wasn't shelled in World War II. The owners have lovingly renovated it, creating an elegantly sober setting with varnished wooden furniture and salmon-pink walls. The smiling welcome is warm and the cooking is some of the best along the coast, with inspired regional dishes such as *gratin* with Bergues cheese, leek tart and cod with saffron. The meat dishes are splendid, particularly the *tournedos* with three peppers and the veal kidneys flambéed with beer. On the fish list, try the *waterzoï* or the stuffed sole, while for dessert you should plump for *crème brûlée* with endive or rhubarb with preserved stawberries. Menus €14–26. Free coffee.

BERGUES   59380 (10KM SE)

⚫ ⌂ |●| HÔTEL-RESTAURANT AU TONNELIER**

4 rue du Mont-de-Piété.
☎ 03.28.68.70.05 ➡ 03.28.68.21.87
Closed Mon lunchtime; the New Year holidays.
TV. Car park.

An attractive, quiet, ochre-yellow brick inn at the heart of the medieval village. It's opposite the Mont-de-Pié, a superb seventeenth-century building which has been converted into a museum. Doubles with basin go for €29 or €37–55 with shower/wc. The rooms looking onto the lovely little paved courtyard are the quietest, and get the most light – in summer this is where they serve meals. The good, regional cooking seems very in keeping with the opulent surroundings of the dining room. There are a number of regional specialities, including a terrific *potjes vleesch* (veal, rabbit and chicken in aspic cooked in white wine and vinegar). Menus from €14 (not Sun lunchtime) to €22. Free coffee at the end of your meal and one free breakfast per room Nov to mid-March.

LOOBERGHE   59630 (15KM SW)

⚥ |O| LE CAMPAGNARD

456 rue de Cassel; it's at the D11-D3 crossroads.
☎ 03.28.29.81.97
Closed evenings and the second fortnight in Nov.

A nice village restaurant run by a young local couple. They serve excellent country cooking amid a friendly atmosphere with eclectic music playing in the background in a pretty dining room decorated with images of old windmills. The €11 menu proves good value, and there are two more at €13 and €15. In the week there's a dish of the day for €7. Free coffee.

ETROEUNGT   59219

⚥ |O| FERME DE LA CAPELETTE

La Capelette; it's 7km south of Avesnes.
☎ 03.27.59.28.33
Closed Wed.

Naf and Dany Delmée converted their farmhouse into a country inn with splendid results. There's a pleasant dining room, and a vast terrace high above the Helpe valley. Best of all is the superb local cuisine, prepared with passion and professionalism. Nothing but fresh produce is used – the delicious oyster mushrooms are grown right here on the farm. The *terrines* are always good, particularly the one with duck and shiitake mushrooms. Other hits include the suckling pig *civet* prepared with dry cider, duck with sweet and sour sauce and baby onions, roast lamb with caramelized honey and guinea fowl flambéed with apple brandy. The apple tart is made with crisp pastry and fruit picked from the orchard. Dishes change with the seasons. Menus €14–29. Booking essential. Free coffee.

GODESWAERSVELDE   59270

⚥ |O| HET BLAUWERSHOF

rue d'Eecke (Centre); it's between Steenvoorde and Bailleul on the D18.
☎ 03.28.49.45.11
Closed Mon; a fortnight in Jan; the first fortnight in July.

The most famous tap-room in Flanders, and one of a dying breed. The bar and dining room have enormous charm – old furniture, rustic pots and long wooden tables where a happy group of patrons sit round enjoying the convivial atmosphere. You can also play traditional bar games. If you're hungry, it's well worth ordering here: herring fillets, leek tart, mustard tart, *potjevleesh* with chips and beef *carbonade* are all good. For pudding, there's *clafoutis* with apples or ice-creams. Dishes start at €5. One free 75cl bottle of Blauwersbier per table.

⚥ |O| LE ROI DU POTJE VLEESCH

31 rue du Mont-des-Cats.
☎ 03.28.42.52.56
Closed Mon, Tues in winter, and Jan.

The dining room here is warm and welcoming; odd to think that it used to be the family-run abattoir (you can still see the tethering rings on the walls). It's a characterful place, decorated with old domestic objects, plates, tools and photographs, and the cuisine is resolutely Flemish. Try *pâté* with garlic, *carbonade* or cockerel in beer. You'll eat excellent meals at very modest prices, starting at €7 for a Flemish platter and rising to around €18 for a meal *à la carte*. It's best to book at the weekend. They also have a shop selling regional delicacies made on-site – delicious *terrines* with *andouillettes* and a superb *potjevleesch*. Free coffee.

HARDELOT   62150

⚥ 🏠 |O| LA RÉGINA**

185 av. François 1er; it's 1.5km from the town centre.
☎ 03.28.41.98.79 ➦ 03.28.43.11.06
Closed Sun evening and Mon except July–Aug; Whitsun and Easter; Nov to mid-Feb.

A handsome, two-storey, modern establishment in a quiet residential district surrounded by wooded countryside. It's quiet, and not bad value given the facilities; doubles with shower/wc or bath are €54. The restaurant, *Les Brisants*, has a bright, elegant dining room and offers, fresh, assured cooking; good bets include cream of mussel soup and fish stew with mussel *jus*. Weekday menu €20, and others up to €34. Tennis, golf and stables are all close by, and the beach is 1km away. Free house apéritif.

HAZEBROUCK   59190

⚥ 🏠 HÔTEL LE GAMBRINUS**

2 rue Nationale (Centre); it's between the Grand-Place and the train station.
☎ 03.28.41.98.79 ➦ 03.28.43.11.06
TV. Car park.

This is Hazebrouck's only hotel, so it's here or in the car. Inside, the substantial nineteenth-century house is bright and well-decorated; pleasant doubles with shower/wc cost €47–52. The owners really know how to make you feel welcome. 10% discount on the room rate after the third night.

🕺 |●| RESTAURANT LE CENTRE

48 Grand-Place (Centre); it's opposite the town hall.
☎ 03.28.48.03.62
Closed Tues evening and Wed.

Regional specialities are the thing to go for here: *vleesch*, herring with warm apples, *gratin* with Maroilles cheese, *carbonade flamande* (beef and onions braised in Leffe beer). Alternatively, try any of the well-prepared *à la carte* dishes such as leg of duck with oyster mushrooms. Weekday lunch menu €10, regional menu €18 and others up to €36. Free house apéritif.

🕺 |●| RESTAURANT-ESTAMINET LA TAVERNE

61 Grand-Place (Centre).
☎ 03.28.41.63.09
Closed Sun evening and Mon; a week in Feb; three weeks in Aug. **Car park**.

This convivial restaurant has a warm atmosphere, elegant Flanders décor and good, local cooking: Maroilles cheese and leek quiche, juniper and apple tart, *potjevfleisch* (a veal, rabbit and chicken *pâté*), veal kidneys flambéed with juniper and *carbonnade flamande* (beef braised in beer). You'll get generous portions, dished up by good-natured staff. They offer occasional specials, too – mussels and chips on Friday, say, or *fondues* in the evening. Menus €12–22 and *à la carte*. There's also a tearoom. Free house apéritif.

MOTTE-AU-BOIS (LA)   59190 (5KM S)

🏠 |●| AUBERGE DE LA FORÊT**

Centre; it's five minutes from Hazebrouck on the D946 heading towards Merville.
☎ 03.28.48.08.78 ➡ 03.28.40.77.76
Closed Sat lunchtime; Sun evening; Mon; end Dec to end Feb; Aug. **TV. Garden. Car park**.

This 1950s hunting lodge, almost buried under foliage, is situated in the heart of a village deep in the vast Nieppe forest. The panelled rooms are simple but pleasant, particularly those with latticed windows opening onto lovely little gardens. Doubles with shower or bath go for €35–40. The restaurant is rustic in style, naturally enough, and offers regional specialities along with some exceptionally inventive cooking that justifies the

rather high prices. Weekday menu €22 or €37–46 on Sun. There's a good wine list – the cellar is one of the best in the region. Customers are well-heeled, and service can be snooty.

SERCUS   59173 (6KM W)

🕺 |●| ESTAMINET-AUBERGE AU SAINT-ÉRASME

18 route de Blaringhem; take the D106 or the N42 and turn off at Wallon-Capel.
☎ 03.28.41.85.43
Closed Mon; Sun–Thurs evenings; a week in Feb; and a fortnight Aug–Sept.

A spruce country inn with a pretty façade. Inside, it's snug and convivial, with a terrace open in summer. They serve home cooking in generous portions, with local dishes including *flamiches* with Maroilles cheese, a tasty chicken in beer and chips as crispy as can be. Go for the sugar tart for dessert. Prices are very reasonable: there's a €7.60 *menu du jour* served on weekdays and another at €11 at the weekend. You can even play traditional bar games. Free coffee.

HESDIN   62140

🕺 🏠 |●| HÔTEL DES FLANDRES**

20–22 rue d'Arras (Centre).
☎ 03.21.86.80.21 ➡ 03.21.86.28.01
Closed ten days June–July and ten days Dec–Jan.
TV. Car park.

No-fuss hotel with a family atmosphere in the midst of the "Seven Valleys" area. The rooms are straightforward and comfortable; doubles with shower/wc or bath €46. It's the same story in the restaurant, which serves traditional local dishes like chicken in beer and salmon *flamand*. The weekday *formule*, €14, includes main course, dessert and a glass of wine or beer, and there are menus at €15–21. Free house apéritif.

SAULCHOY   62870 (22.5KM SW)

🕺 |●| LE VAL D'AUTHIE

60 La Place; take the D928 towards Abbeville, then turn right onto the D119, which follows the River Authie.
☎ 03.21.90.30.20
Closed Thurs out of season and the first week in Sept.

A good, friendly old country inn with character. You'll get good home cooking here; tried and tested recipes include *vol au vent*, *coq au vin*, duck breast and leg of lamb. Weekday menu €12, then others from €20–28. In season they serve copious portions of game: hare casserole, wild boar stew, venison in cream sauce, pheasant in port. They also have some attractive guest rooms with shower/wc – €35 for two including breakfast – and a *gîte* (sleeping 4–6) to rent. Free coffee.

LENS 62300

|●| RESTAURANT LA DÉCOUVERTE

11 rue des Déportés; it's not far from the train station.
☎ 03.21.42.70.00
Closed Sun and Mon evenings.

A discreet restaurant in a little street without much traffic. They've divided the huge dining room with partitions prettily decorated with flowers. Menus, €11–21, list lots of offal dishes: pig's trotters in *vinaigrette* or coated in breadcrumbs and fried, *rillettes* (potted pork and goose meat), liver *meunier* (coated in flour and fried), grilled kidneys. *À la carte* a meal costs around €20. If you opt for a bottle of *réserve maison* wine you'll be charged only for what you drink. The clientèle tends to be elderly.

BULLY-LES-MINES 62160 (5KM W)

🏂 🏠 |●| L'ENFANT DU PAYS

152 rue de la Gare.
☎ 03.21.29.12.33 📠 03.21.29.27.55
e m.verbrugge@nordnet.fr
Closed Sun evening; three weeks over the Feb school holidays; 12–27 Nov. **TV**.

This place, despite its unprepossessing location at the back of the slag heaps, has got a good reputation for serving generous helpings of straightforward, authentic dishes made with fresh produce. The local and regional dishes change with the seasons; *millefeuille* of Maroilles cheese is always a good bet. Menus €9–27. You can also stay the night, in recently refurbished bedrooms that go for rock-bottom prices: doubles with basin and TV go for €14, or €21 with shower/wc or bath. 10% discount on the room rate or free house apéritif.

LIESSIES 59740

🏠 |●| LE CHÂTEAU DE LA MOTTE**

How to get there: take the D133 towards the lac du Val-Joly.
☎ 03.27.61.81.94 📠 03.27.61.83.57

e chateaudelamotte@aol.com
Closed Sun out of season and 19 Dec–5 Feb. **TV**. **Car park**.

Backing onto the Bois-l'Abbé national forest, this château was built in 1725 as a place of retreat for the monks of Liessies Abbey. It's a good-looking place, made from unusual pink brick and slate. The rooms, which offer the peace and silence the monks sought, cost €36 for a double. Menus, €18–40, include pork haunch *pot-au-feu*, fish stew with white wine, rack of lamb with beer sauce, zander fillet with sweet and sour sauce and farm-raised chicken *waterzoï*. They also host gastronomic evenings and weekends.

🏂 |●| CHEZ LOUIS

25 rue Roger Salengro; it's on the D133 on the road from Avesnes.
☎ 03.27.61.82.38
Closed Mon.

Despite the sign, which calls it a *friterie*, this is in fact a good restaurant with a pretty dining room. The building is an old farmer's house with hefty beams, tiled or stone floors and a wide hearth, and you eat communally at long wooden tables. Everything is homemade and tasty – including the wonderful chips – and they use only the freshest local produce to prepare devilishly good *terrines*, *andouillette*, *carbonade* stews, tripe, white pudding and Maroilles cheese tart. A meal here won't break the bank, either – you can get a snack for around €6, and only the *entrecôte* steak costs more than €8. There's a splendid terrace in summer, and children are well catered for with a playground and special pony and buggy rides. Free coffee.

|●| LE CARILLON

It's in the centre of the village, opposite the church.
☎ 03.27.61.80.21
Closed Sun evening except July–Aug; Tues evening; Wed; a fortnight in Nov.

A beautiful Avesnois house which has been tastefully restored. It's run by a couple of young professionals who have enhanced the gastronomic reputation of this region with their simple, skilled cooking. All the dishes change with the seasons and their desserts are spectacular. There's a weekday menu for €13, and others at €18–30. The wine cellar next door sells a selection of *vins de pays* and vintages at all sorts of prices, as well as a good range of whiskies.

LILLE   59000

SEE MAP OVERLEAF

♠ HÔTEL DE FRANCE**

10 rue de Béthune; M° Rihour. **MAP C2-4**
☎ 03.20.57.14.78 ➡ 03.20.57.06.01
Closed a week from Christmas to New Year. **TV**.

This unspectacular place is right in the centre of town, close to the Grand-Place; it can get pretty noisy, and unfortunately only the rooms on the first floor have been soundproofed. It lacks charm but there's nothing particular to find fault with and the staff are friendly. Spacious rooms with basin for €30, €40 with shower/wc, €43 with bath and direct-dial telephone.

⚲ ♠ LE GRAND HÔTEL**

51 rue Faidherbe. **MAP C2-6**
☎ 03.20.06.31.57 ➡ 03.20.06.24.44
Closed first three weeks in Aug. **TV**.

Typical of the sort of hotels France is famous for, this comfortable establishment near the station has attractive rooms decorated with a feminine touch. Very nice female owner and efficient staff. Doubles €58 with shower/wc or bath. They also have a few family rooms sleeping three or four. Free breakfast at weekends except over the Lille antiques weekend in Sept.

⚲ ♠ HÔTEL FLANDRE-ANGLETERRE**

13 pl. de la Gare. **MAP D2-3**
☎ 03.20.06.04.12 ➡ 03.20.06.37.76
TV.

Despite being opposite the station (in a dull part of town), this place isn't too noisy, with unfussy, well-soundproofed rooms with nice bathrooms and modern décor. Doubles €60 with bath. It's used mainly by businesspeople, and rates drop at the weekend if you stay at least two nights. 10% discount at the weekend.

⚲ ♠ LE BRUEGHEL**

5 parvis Saint-Maurice. **MAP C2-5**
☎ 03.20.06.06.69 ➡ 03.20.63.25.27
✉ hotel.brueghel@wanadoo.fr
TV. Pay car park.

This hotel, in an enormous brick building near the St-Maurice church, has personality and – better still – soul. The décor shows excellent taste, with antique furniture everywhere and nice prints on the wall; doubles go for €60–69 with shower/wc or bath. The rooms at the rear are very pleasant and quiet. The welcome

couldn't be better – the staff love their work and the night porter practically has a fan club. It's a favourite meeting place for actors performing in shows in town so it's best to book. One free breakfast per double room.

⚲ ♠ HÔTEL DE LA PAIX**

46 [bis] rue de Paris. **MAP C2-7**
☎ 03.20.54.63.93 ➡ 03.20.63.98.97
TV.

Beyond the grand reception of this hotel there's an eighteenth-century staircase that's so superb it's a shame to use the lift. The rooms are tastefully furnished and spacious; doubles with shower/wc €66 or €73 with bath. The owner gave up painting when she entered the hotel business, but it has remained a passion. She has devoted each room to a different contemporary artist and put reproductions on the walls. Number 12 has a terrace and a garden and they all have internet access. 10% discount at the weekend except in Aug and during the Lille antiques fair.

❙●❙ RESTAURANT LA PÂTE BRISÉE

65 rue de la Monnaie. **MAP C1-15**
☎ 03.20.74.29.00 ➡ 03.20.13.80.47

In the face of stiff competition, this restaurant is still *the* place for sweet and savoury tarts – Roquefort, Maroilles cheese or *tarte Tatin* – and regional baked cheese dishes like *tartiflette* with potatoes, diced bacon, braised onion and melted Maroilles cheese. The various reasonably priced *formules*, €7–16, include drinks, and portions are generous. There's a relaxed atmosphere, with a mainly student clientèle, and it's packed at lunchtime so it's best to arrive early. After 3pm, it also doubles as a tearoom.

⚲❙●❙ RESTAURANT LE SQUARE

52 rue Basse. **MAP C2-17**
☎ 03.20.74.16.17 ➡ 03.20.93.21.49
Closed Sun; Mon evening; the first three weeks in Aug.

The dining room is pleasant and quite intimate and both the welcome and service are friendly. *À la carte* they serve warm or cold salads and generous portions of regional dishes that change with the seasons: scallops with pale ale, rump steak with Maroilles, duck breast with honey, lasagne with salmon and so on. During the week, menus start at €9; the regional menu costs €14. The wine list has decently priced choices starting at around €12 for a bottle of full-bodied Pinot Noir. Free coffee.

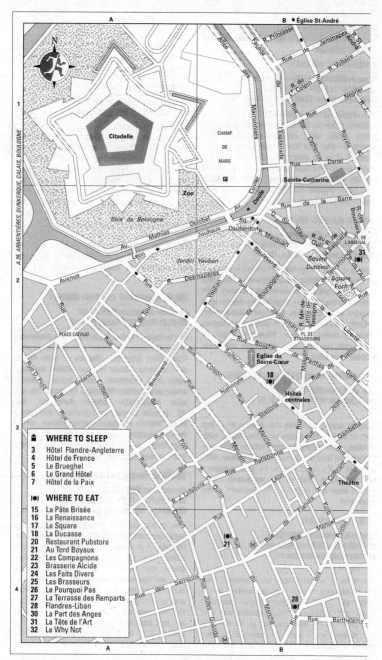

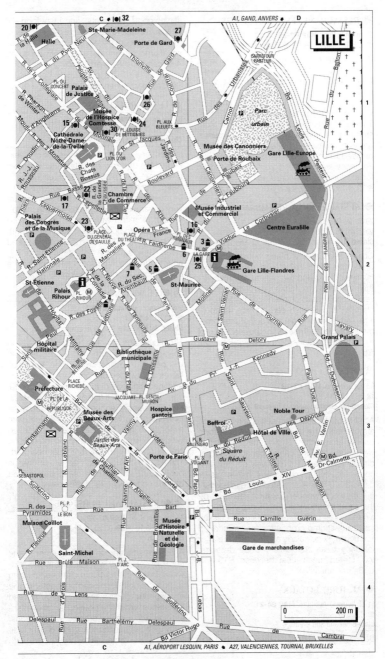

LILLE

Ste-Marie-Madeleine

C ◆ |●| 32

20 |●|

R. de la Halle

Halle

R. du Pont Neuf

Porte de Gard

27

A1, GAND, ANVERS ◆ D

CARREFOUR PASTEUR

Parc urbain

1

PL. DU CONCERT

Palais de Justice

26

Musée de l'Hospice Comtesse

15 |●|

24

Cathédrale Notre-Dame-de-la-Treille

PL. LOUISE DE BETTIGNIES

30

PL. AUX BLEUETS

Musée des Canonniers

Gare Lille-Europe

Porte de Roubaix

R. des Chats Bossus

22

Chambre de Commerce

17

Palais des Congrès et de la Musique

23

PLACE DU GENERAL DE GAULLE

Opéra

Musée Industriel et Commercial

Centre Euralille

16

3

6

25

Gare Lille-Flandres

St-Étienne

7

5

St-Maurice

2

Palais Rihour

4

Bibliothèque municipale

Hôpital militaire

Grand Palais

Préfecture

PLACE RICHEBÉ

Musée des Beaux-Arts

Hospice gantois

Noble Tour

Beffroi

Hôtel de Ville

3

Jardin des Beaux-Arts

Porte de Paris

PL. R. SALENGRO

Square du Réduit

PL. SEBASTOPOL

Maison Coilliot

LE BON

Saint-Michel

Musée d'Histoire Naturelle et de Géologie

Gare de marchandises

4

0   200 m

|O| RESTAURANT LES 3 BRASSEURS

22 pl. de la Gare. **MAP D2-25**
☎ 03.20.06.46.25 ➡ 03.20.06.46.29

If only there were more places like this lively, friendly pub. You can choose from several brews including amber, Scotch, Lille white and a pale ale, all brewed on the premises using the best barleys and hops – count on €2–11 for a pitcher containing 1.8 litres. There's an extensive menu, too, from a Munster cheese sandwich to more substantial grills and brasserie dishes – you'll be hard pressed to finish the ham hock *choucroute*. *Formules* start at €9; if you're famished go for the *formule Choucroute 3 Brasseurs* for €12, which includes a ¹⁄₂-litre of beer.

|O| RESTAURANT LA RENAISSANCE

29 pl. des Reignaux. **MAP D2-16**
☎ 03.20.06.17.56
Closed Sun, Mon and Tues evenings; 15 July–15 Aug.

Cheap and cheerful place with the atmosphere of a Parisian bistro, serving excellent family cooking and regional specialities. Try their mussels, ox kidneys, *potjevfleisch* (a veal, rabbit and chicken *pâté*), Maroilles cheese tart, Flemish *carbonnade*, *andouillette* flambéed with gin and any of the homemade desserts. Prices vary, but as a rule of thumb, meat dishes range in price from €6–8.

⅍|O| LA DUCASSE

96 rue Solférino. **MAP B3-18**
☎ 03.20.57.34.10
Closed Sat lunchtime; Sun; a fortnight in Aug.

An old-style local restaurant with a really warm atmosphere. The team who have run it for a quarter of a century or more have left things well alone – the long carved benches, the traditional tables and a truly lovely counter. In a corner there's a mechanical music player dated 1910 that is activated once in a while, but the huge wooden jukebox seems to be there just for show. The authentic bistro cuisine features *cassolette* of seafood, chicken *fricassée*, shrimp *croquettes*, prawn cooked in Gueuze, huge salads and a Flemish platter featuring three specialities. Good desserts, too. Grilled meats cost between €10 and €15. Free apéritif.

|O| AU TORD BOYAUX

11 pl. Nouvelle-Aventure. **MAP B4-21**
☎ 03.20.57.73.67
Closed Sat and Sun evenings.

Based in Wazemmes, this family place serves good, substantial and tasty food – if pheasant *choucroute* is on the menu, order it. Monique, the lovely owner, uses fresh seasonal produce, and the food is always great. À la carte dishes start at €7 and there's a menu for €10. It's particularly popular for Sunday lunch when you may have to book.

|O| LE POURQUOI-PAS

62 rue de Gand. **MAP C1-26**
☎ 03.20.42.12.16 ➡ 03.20.55.93.83
Closed Sat lunchtime; Sun; 2–3 weeks in Aug.

Dinner served until 11pm, midnight at weekends. One of a row of restaurants in an old Lille street, this place is nicely refined, with well-spaced tables and mood lighting. Dishes reveal various influences and servings are very generous; good options include medallions of monkfish with smoked bacon, snail *croustade* with puréed leek, duck breast with raspberries, shellfish and perfectly cooked steak. There's a lunch dish of the day for €7, an €11 lunch *formule* and a €17 menu in the evening or you could go *à la carte*.

⅍|O| LE WHY NOT

9 rue Maracci. **Off map C1-32**
☎ 03.20.74.14.14
Closed Sat lunchtime; Sun by reservation only.

The affable and attentive welcome is quite in keeping with the authentic, warm décor in this beautiful vaulted cellar. There are small tables for two or big ones for groups, all arranged higgledy-piggledy around a central bar. Dishes are traditional and regional, though inventive enough to satisfy the most exacting of foodies: roast goat's cheese with almonds, baked Maroilles cheese flambéed with gin, ostrich fillet with pickled shallots, *crème brûlée* with chicory and beer tart. There's something for all budgets on menus priced €12–28. Lots of reasonably priced options on the wine list. Free apéritif.

⅍|O| RESTAURANT PUBSTORE

44 rue de la Halle. **MAP C1-20**
☎ 03.20.55.10.35 ➡ 03.20.24.48.93
Closed Sun.

A busy restaurant on a busy street in the north of the old town – it's even full midweek. Inside the lights are dimmed, creating a sort of old-fashioned gangster-movie atmosphere, but it's bright enough to read the menus, which list poetically named dishes and their more prosaic explanations. They've been serving the same quality food for the past thirty years: grilled ham with pineapple, grilled steak with vegetables, veal chop with mushrooms and noodles with grated cheese, and a wide range of desserts to finish you off. The lunch menu, at €13, is the cheapest; a meal *à la carte* will cost around €21. Decent wine, too, with a house red for around €10. Free coffee.

⚒ |O| LA TERRASSE DES REMPARTS

Logis de la Porte de Gard, rue de Gard (North). **MAP C1-27**
☎ 03.20.06.74.74.

This place combines a softly lit seating area with red brick walls and a veranda on two levels that opens onto a terrace in good weather. Warm welcome and efficient, attentive service. The menu lists appetizing dishes that change with the seasons, and plenty of regional specialities: potato pie with crab and horn of plenty mushrooms, brill with pickled chicory, venison haunch with aubergine. The dessert buffet offers a panoply of pastries and home-made sorbets. Lunchtime menu €15, with others up to €24. Free coffee.

⚒ |O| RESTAURANT FLANDRES-LIBAN

125–127 rue des Postes. **MAP B4-28**
☎ 03.20.54.89.92
Closed Sun evening.

A Lebanese restaurant on the edge of Wazemmes, the last working-class part of Lille. The décor, with its delicate panels of carved wood, fountains and hangings, is a far cry from the usual places around here. They do a very good *mezzé*, and the waiters, whose polite demeanour is impeccable, explain the secrets of the twenty or so specialities: hummus, *shwarma*, *kofte* kebabs, cucumber and yoghurt, chicken kebab with three flavours, *kebbé* (a beef rissole with ground wheat). Menus start at €15; *à la carte* you'll pay around €20. These are reasonable prices for what is definitely the best Lebanese restaurant in or around Lille. Free *digestif*.

|O| LES FAITS DIVERS

44 rue de Gand. **MAP C1-24**
☎ 03.20.21.03.63 ⇥ 03.20.31.48.53
Closed Sun, Mon lunchtime, and 1–20 Aug.

There's a convivial, dynamic atmosphere in this brightly coloured, vaguely retro restaurant and welcoming, attentive service – you'll have a great evening. The customers are cool and youthful, but the food is classic bourgeois fare: scallops in pastry cases with

baby vegetables and curry-cream sauce, smoked salmon with scrambled eggs, a selection of fish with a cream and saffron sauce, duck leg *confit* with Salard potatoes, *croustillant* of banana and chocolate *fondue*. Menus €17–21. There's a choice of exotic coffees.

⚒ |O| LA PART DES ANGES

50 rue de la Monnaie. **MAP C1-30**
☎ 03.20.06.44.01
Closed Sun evening.

A noisy Parisian-style wine bar in the busiest street in the middle of the old town. There's a selection of at least twenty wines, some of which come from unusual shippers, and a few foreign wines including a Pinot Blanc from Egypt. The split-level dining room, all paint effects and voluminous green plants, buzzes with businesspeople, yuppies and students enjoying decent bistro food. A blackboard lists the dishes of the day – these might be chicory *au gratin*, steak, salmon with spinach or *terrine*. At lunchtime on Sundays, you can have a *charcuterie* or cheese platter, and snacks are always served at the bar. It's generally heaving, and thus service can be a bit slapdash. Expect to pay €18–23 for a meal. Free house apéritif.

⚒ |O| LES COMPAGNONS DE LA GRAPPE

22 rue Lepelletier. **MAP C2-22**
☎ 03.20.21.02.79
Closed Sun and Mon evening out of season.

Hidden in a narrow passage, this is one of the nicest restaurants in Lille. The terrace is crammed in sunny weather while the two dining rooms have lovely wood panelling and designer lighting. They're great places to eat handsome portions of well-cooked bistro classics with a modern twist. The bread deserves a special mention, too. Menus start at €19 with a lunch dish of the day for €8. There's an extensive wine list, with many offered by the glass. Free apéritif, coffee or *digestif*.

|O| LA TÊTE DE L'ART

10 rue de l'Arc. **MAP B2-31**
☎ and ⇥ 03.20.54.68.89
Closed Sun; Mon–Thurs evenings; Aug.

It's worth booking a table at this quiet little restaurant in a quiet little street. They serve an excellent *formule-carte* comprising starter, main course, cheese, dessert and as much wine as you like, all for €18. There are others for €19 and €23. They specialize in offal and regional dishes; star turns include snails with red wine *meurette* sauce, *andouillette* casserole with mustard, Maroilles cheese *craquant* with slivers of chicory, ling *blanquette* with Breton seaweed, pan-fried pig's kidneys with mustard, orange *terrine* with warm chocolate sauce and juniper sorbet with blackcurrant *coulis*.

|●| BRASSERIE ALCIDE

5 rue des Débris-Saint-Étienne. **MAP C2-23**
☎ 03.20.12.06.95
Closed 24 and 25 Dec.

Come here to experience the discreet charm of the bourgeois brasserie; uniformed waiters standing in line, an oak bar, large mirrors – and an equally discreet middle-aged clientele. Menus from €20 and dishes of the day around €11; chicken or scallop *waterzoï*, *cassoulet* with meat *confit*, salmon and leek *andouillette*, fisherman's stew and so on. The *formule* offers *moules marinières*, a choice between three regional dishes – including a very good char-grilled steak – and three beers.

VILLENEUVE-D'ASCQ · 59650 (8KM SE)

🏕 |●| RESTAURANT LES CHARMILLES

98 av. de Flandre (North).
☎ 03.20.72.40.30
Closed Wed and three weeks in Aug.

A very spacious dining room, painted pale and olive green, ideal for intimate meals for two. The cooking is creative, withmenus at €11, €13 and €19, and *à la carte* for around €21. The chef's special is stuffed sole, but try also local dishes such as Maroilles tart, *carbonade* of rabbit, *tournedos* flambéed with whisky and prawn sauce, fish of the day, *waterzoï* and slivers of pear with Roquefort. Free coffee.

MAROILLES · 59550

🏕 |●| L'ESTAMINET

83 Grand-Rue (Centre); it's opposite the church.
☎ 03.27.77.78.80
Closed Sun, Mon and Tues evenings.

A typical village restaurant in the town that produces the famous local cheese. Over the years this place has established a solid reputation for good, reliable local and regional dishes. The €10 weekday menu offers two courses, and there are others from €15–25,

along with *à la carte* choices. The dishes of the day are listed on a blackboard. You might get steak with Maroilles cheese sauce, mushroom tart, *andouillette* or a good selection of cheeses. Wines are reasonably priced. It's best to phone for a weekend reservation out of season. Free *digestif*.

LOCQUIGNOL · 59530 (4KM N)

🏕 🏠 |●| AUBERGE DU CROISIL

Route de Maroilles; from Maroilles or Le Quesnoi, follow the D233, and it's signposted 3km from Maroilles.
☎ 03.27.34.20.14 ➡ 03.27.34.20.15
Closed Sat evening and Mon except public holidays; 23 Dec–14 Feb.

This inn, way out in the Mormal forest, serves splendid traditional dishes, prepared by the boss, in a tranquil atmosphere. The *terrines* and goose *cassoulet* are winners, not to mention the scallops *à la provençale*, pigeon *chasseur* and calf's liver *à la lyonnaise*. The menus, €11–23, change every week; in the hunting season they do a lot of game, including wild boar cutlets with green peppercorns and delicious venison steak with raspberry. They also offer a couple of simple rooms, €23, with shared washing facilities. Free coffee.

MAUBEUGE · 59600

🏕 🏠 |●| LE GRAND HÔTEL – RESTAURANT DE PARIS**

1 porte de Paris; it's near the station.
☎ 03.27.64.63.16 ➡ 03.27.65.05.76
e grand.hotel.maubeuge@wanadoo.fr
TV. Disabled access. Lock-up car park.

The best restaurant in the area, a place for family celebrations and business lunches. Menus from €12–43 list lots of local produce: fish, seafood and game in season. Renovated rooms go for €41 with basin, €49 with shower/wc or bath. Free house apéritif and 10% discount on the room rate.

MONTREUIL-SUR-MER · 62170

🏠 |●| LE DARNÉTAL

pl. Darnétal (Centre).
☎ 03.21.06.04.87 ➡ 03.21.86.64.67
Closed Mon and Tues; Mon evening and Tues July–Aug.
Car park.

Traditional hotel on a lovely little square in the old town. The restaurant, which boasts a collection of great antiques, serves lots of delicate, delicious fish dishes: try the poached turbot with hollandaise sauce, lobster in *pastis* or warm oysters in champagne. Menus at €16 (weekdays only), €23 and €31. The four spacious, if rather bare, guest rooms are decorated in late nineteenth-century style. Ask to see them before handing over your money, because they're very different. Doubles €38–46.

🏠 |●| LE CLOS DES CAPUCINS**

46 pl. du Général-de-Gaulle (Centre).
☎ 03.21.06.08.65 📠 03.21.81.20.45
Closed Sun evening; Mon; Thurs evening in winter; a fortnight at beginning of Feb; a fortnight end-Nov.
Car park.

A neat, pretty dining room and a lovely welcome – you just know you're going to have a good meal. It's a particular favourite of English foodies who've popped across the channel for a gourmet experience. Start with the house smoked salmon or Saint-Vaast oysters, following with grilled crayfish with herbs from Provence or *pot-au-feu* of pork shoulder with cabbage. They have a choice of good, well-matured cheeses to finish. Menus €15–35, and good wines from €15 a bottle. Above the restaurant, there are a few rooms for €58 with shower/wc – a tad pricey.

MADELAINE-SOUS-MONTREUIL (LA) 62170 (5KM W)

🏠 |●| LA GRENOUILLÈRE*

It's in the centre of the village by the river.
☎ 03.21.06.07.22 📠 03.21.86.36.36
e auberge.la.grenouillere@wanadoo.fr
Closed Tues except July and Aug; Wed; Jan.
Garden. **Car park**.

This old coaching inn, down in the Canche valley, has several rooms where you can have a drink and a dining room with real charm – low beams, a fire, copper pots and decorative frogs (have a look at the murals). In summer you dine in a pretty flower garden. The chef has reinvented local dishes to create delicate, interestingly seasoned food, and has been awarded a Michelin star for his trouble: the house speciality is frogs' legs, but you should also try *fricassée* of *petit-gris* snails served with pig's trotters in licorice *jus*, potted chicken with coconut milk and veal with honey and spices. Weekday menu €26 with others up to €64, and affordable wines. There are four perfectly charming rooms in the old stable block for €69 with bath.

|●| AUBERGE DU VIEUX LOGIS

pl. de la Mairie; take the D139 or the D917 and it's at the foot of the walls.
☎ 03.21.06.10.92
Closed Mon; Tues; 1–20 Feb.

Rustic country inn serving traditional dishes using quality produce: house *cassoulet* with goose fat, veal kidneys *Vieux Logis* and excellent grilled beef. There are a few modish selections, too, including *carpaccio* of raw fish. Menus for €12, €18, €24 and €28, or *à la carte*. In fine weather you can eat on the terrace.

SAINT-OMER 62500

🏠 🏠 |●| HÔTEL-RESTAURANT LE VIVIER

22 rue Louis Martel (Centre).
☎ 03.21.95.76.00 📠 03.21.95.42.20
Closed Sun evening and Jan. **TV**.

A charming hotel situated in the pedestrianized centre of this attractive town. Good-looking, clean rooms with all facilities; doubles cost €44 with shower/wc or bath, hair drier, mini-bar, TV and phone. Appetizing dishes and regional specialities are served in the pleasant dining room: try pork fillet with celery cream, fresh fish or any of the numerous shellfish and seafood platters. Menus at €14 (not Sat evening or Sun), then €21–30. Friendly, efficient service. Free coffee.

🏠 🏠 |●| HÔTEL SAINT-LOUIS – RESTAURANT LE FLAUBERT**

25 rue d'Arras (Centre).
☎ 03.21.38.35.21 📠 03.21.38.57.26
e contact@hotel-saintlouis.com
Closed Sat and Sun lunchtimes and 24 Dec–2 Jan.
Disabled access. **TV**. **Car park**.

The hotel has been around since the 1920s, though it has been attractively renovated since. Calm, comfortable rooms from €53 with shower/wc or €56 with bath/wc. The restaurant has a brasserie menu, plus a €12 weekday one; those at €16, €21 and €25 list more elaborate and upmarket dishes. Specialities include fish *choucroute*, duck and *cassoulet*. Friendly, retro bar. Free apéritif.

|●| AUBERGE DU BACHELIN

12 bd. de Strasbourg (Northeast).
☎ 03.21.38.42.77
Closed Sun evening; Mon; Thurs evening except for reservations for a minimum of 15.

A classic restaurant with flowery décor and a

friendly atmosphere. Menus €12–21. On Friday they make *couscous*; other specialities include perch fillet with garlic, fish stew and beef *carbonade* with beer. The service is pleasant and efficient.

BLENDECQUES 62575 (4KM SE)

🕏 🛏 |●| LE SAINT-SÉBASTIEN**

2 Grand-Place (Centre); take exit 4 off the A26.
☎ 03.21.38.13.05 ➡ 03.21.39.77.85
Closed Sat lunchtime and Sun evening. **TV**.

Stone-built inn on a pretty square, with pleasant, comfortable rooms; doubles €39 with shower/wc or bath. In the nice rustic restaurant you'll find dishes like *andouille* salad, chicken *fricassée* with vinegar, *croustillant* of pigs' ears, pan-fried pigs' tripe, veal kidneys with Houlle juniper and local ale pie. Menus €12–27 or €34 *à la carte*. Free coffee.

TOUQUET (LE) 62520

🕏 🛏 HÔTEL LE CHALET**

15 rue de la Paix (Centre); it's 60m from the sea.
☎ 03.21.05.87.65 ➡ 03.21.05.47.49
Closed Jan. **TV**.

This hotel offers spick and span rooms at prices that are more than reasonable for Le Touquet. Doubles with basin or shower go for €29–35 or €41–55 with shower or bath/wc and there's a family room for €66. Some rooms look onto a small patio. You'll pay the top price if you want TV and a view of the sea – though it's more of a glimpse than a view. Free breakfast.

🕏 🛏 |●| HÔTEL BLUE COTTAGE**

41 rue Jean-Monnet (Centre); it's behind the market place.
☎ 03.21.05.15.33 ➡ 03.21.05.41.60
Closed Sun evening; Mon; mid-Nov to mid-Feb. **TV**. **Car park**.

Reasonably priced hotel with pretty blue and yellow rooms. Doubles with basin €38, €31–61 with shower/wc and €53–63 with bath. It's one of the few places in pricey Touquet to offer half board, which costs €37–50 per person and is compulsory July–Aug. Buffet breakfast €6. In the restaurant a dish of the day costs €9 and there are menus at €11–25. Third night free if you arrive on Sun, Mon or Tues from 11 Nov–31 March. Free coffee.

🕏 🛏 HÔTEL LE NOUVEAU CADDY**

130 rue de Metz (Centre); it's opposite the covered market and 150m from the beach.
☎ 03.21.05.83.95 ➡ 03.21.05.85.23
Closed Jan. **Disabled access**. **TV**.

Tastefully decorated hotel with four floors (and a lift), each painted a different colour to represent a different season. All the rooms are pleasant and comfortable with en-suite bathrooms; doubles €40–58. They also have studios with kitchenettes. 10% discount, except weekends from April to mid-Nov, school holidays and July–Aug.

🕏 🛏 HÔTEL LES EMBRUNS**

89 rue de Paris (Centre).
☎ 03.21.05.87.61 ➡ 03.21.05.85.09
Closed 15 Dec–15 Jan. **Disabled access**. **Garden**. **TV**.

In a quiet situation set back from the road and not far from the sea. The simple, comfortable rooms are clean and attractive; some look onto the garden, others have terraces. Doubles €41–55 with shower or bath, €53 for a triple or €64 for a room sleeping four. The breakfast room is charming. You can park bikes or motorbikes in the garden. 10% discount for a two-night stay Sept–June.

|●| AUBERGE L'ARLEQUIN

91 rue de Paris; it's near rue Saint-Jean and the seafront.
☎ 03.21.05.39.11 ➡ 03.21.06.13.06
Closed Wed May–Sept; Wed and Thurs Oct–April; end Dec to end Jan.

A classic, small restaurant where the owner cooks straightforward dishes: monkfish kebab with cabbage, veal *blanquette à l'ancienne* and skate with olive and raspberries. The cheap weekday menu, €14, is well-balanced, and there are others at €15 and €22.

|●| RESTAURANT AU DIAMANT ROSE

110 rue de Paris (Centre).
☎ 03.21.05.38.10 ➡ 03.21.05.89.75
Closed Tues evening except July–Aug; Wed; Jan.

This pastel pink restaurant attracts a loyal crowd of regulars and quiet holidaymakers who lap up the traditional, honest French cuisine. Typical dishes include poached monkfish with sorrel, duck thigh *confit* in goose fat, *foie gras* and *fruits de mer* – and they've got a good wine list. Dish of the day €9, menus €15–22 and *à la carte*.

🕏 |●| LES DEUX MOINEAUX

12 rue Saint-Jean (Centre).
☎ 03.21.0509.67
Closed Mon and a fortnight in June.

This brick-walled dining room has a warm,

intimate atmosphere, with gentle jazz playing in the background. The owner will welcome you pleasantly and the staff are equally kind. Try the snail stew or the cockerel in wine sauce, finishing with an array of well-matured regional cheeses. Weekday menu €15 and others up to €24. The wine list has a few reasonably priced bottles. Free coffee.

SAINT-JOSSE   62170 (7KM SE)

⅍ I●I LE RELAIS DE SAINT-JOSSE

Grand-Place; follow the D143 for 5km, take the D144 and it's near the church.
☎ and ➡ 03.21.94.61.75
Closed Sun evening; Mon; the first week in Jan; a week in the Feb school holidays.

Set on a pretty square in a village festooned with flowers, *Le Relais* has window boxes overflowing with geraniums. From first thing in the morning the proprietor, Étienne Delmer, who's a butcher's son, offers excellent rabbit *pâté*, scrambled eggs, cold meats in aspic, a wonderful *pâté de campagne*, smoked fish and, in winter, a good brawn. Those who prefer more conventional mealtimes can dine in the restaurant where there's a €16 weekday menu and others up to €33. Free coffee.

⅍ I●I L'AUBERGE DU MOULINEL

116 chaussée de l'Avant Pays, in Moulinel; take the road to Moulinel, go under the motorway and 2km further there's a sign where you turn left.
☎ 03.21.94.79.03
Closed Mon and Tues except for school holidays; 2–24 Jan; 24 June–3 July.

One of the best restaurants along the Opal coast, housed in a restored farmhouse way out in the countryside between Le Touquet and Montreuil-sur-Mer. It's run by Alain Lévy who produces deftly prepared dishes. He likes to use strong flavours and unusual but intriguing flavour combinations using lobster, hare and pigeon – try the richly flavoured hare *à la royale* with poached pear. The fish dishes show similar expertise. Menus €24–44 and affordable wines. Book to avoid disappointment. Free coffee except in July and Aug.

TOURCOING   59200

⅍ I●I RESTAURANT LE RUSTIQUE

206 rue de l'Yser (North); from the town centre follow rue de Gand for 3km which leads into rue de l'Yser.
☎ 03.20.94.44.62

Closed Mon; Tues–Thurs evenings except by reservation. **Car park**.

The surroundings have a rustic feel – logs burn in the fireplace and copper pans hang from the walls – but the service and food are rather more refined. Dishes include steak with *Carré du Vinage* cheese, ham on the bone, scallops on the shell, house *foie gras*, rack of lamb with herbs and some regional specialities. This is gourmet food at modest prices. Weekday menu €11, with others from €15–40 or around €23 *à la carte*. You can eat on the terrace when the weather is fine. Free house apéritif.

TRÉLON   59132

⅍ I●I LE FRAMBOISIER

1 rue F-Ansieau (Centre).
☎ 03.27.59.73.34
Closed Sun evening; Mon; a fortnight end Feb; last three weeks in Aug; a fortnight in early Sept. **Disabled access**.

A rare oasis of quality in a culinary desert, run by a couple who wanted to improve the region's gastronomic reputation. The dining room is fresh and pleasant, with sturdy beams, pink paint, pictures on the walls and classical music playing in the background. Service is quietly efficient. The dishes are full of new flavours and often inspired, changing depending on what's available in the markets. Try home-smoked salmon, fresh fish – sardines, skate, turbot, scallops – game in season and the horse *tournedos* with five peppers flambéed in Cognac. The homemade desserts are great, too: *crème brûlée* with raspberries, iced nougat and tarts. There's a €15 *formule* (not Sun or public holidays) and menus from €24–37. It's best to book at the weekend. Free coffee.

VALENCIENNES   59300

⅍ 🏠 LE BRISTOL**

2 av. de-Lattre-de-Tassigny (North); it's near the train station.
☎ 03.27.46.58.88 ➡ 03.27.47.34.39
Disabled access. TV.

There's nothing original about this hotel, but it's quiet and clean, the pleasant staff have ready smiles and there's a bar. Some of the light, spacious rooms overlook a courtyard and others the street – fortunately you don't hear the trains. Good-value doubles with basin go for €31, €37 with shower, €41 with shower/wc or bath. One free breakfast per room after the third night of your stay.

🕅 🏠 HÔTEL NOTRE-DAME**

1 pl. de l'Abbé-Thellier-de-Poncheville (Centre); it's opposite the basilica of Notre-Dame.
☎ 03.27.42.30.00 ➡ 03.27.45.12.68
📧 hotel-notredame@wanadoo.fr
Disabled access. TV. Pay car park.

Charming little hotel in a converted convent. The interior decoration is chic but not flashy, and staff are pleasant. Doubles with shower cost €38, with shower/wc or bath €46–55. Number 36, on the ground floor, looks out onto the indoor garden and is superb. 10% discount.

🕅 🏠 HÔTEL LE CLÉMENCEAU**

39 rue du Rempart; it's 300m from the Grand-Place and 200m from the train station.
☎ 03.27.30.55.55 ➡ 03.27.30.55.56
Closed Jan and Feb. **Disabled access. TV**.

Right near the station, this is a solid red-brick hotel with about twenty rooms, all with double glazing, fully equipped bathroom, hair drier and safe. Doubles €43, which is good value but doesn't compensate for the slightly off-putting welcome. 10% discount on the room rate at weekends.

🕅 🏠 |●| LE GRAND HÔTEL – RESTAURANT DU GRAND HÔTEL***

8 pl. de la Gare (Centre).
☎ 03.27.46.32.01 ➡ 03.27.29.65.57
Restaurant ☎ and ➡ 03.27.29.65.57
📧 grandhotel.val@wanadoo.fr
TV.

In a superb 1930s building just opposite the station, this thoroughly refurbished hotel boasts an elegant interior and spacious, attractive rooms. Doubles with shower/wc or bath are €77; if you want a whirlpool bath you're looking at €99–105. The splendid dining room has a lofty ceiling, a Tiffany stained-glass dome, columns, heavy curtains, old-fashioned lighting and long banquettes – totally beguiling. Great cooking, too. They offer a splendid selection of regional dishes and classic family favourites: home-made *potje vleesh*, pig cheek *confit* in a stew served with lentils, calf's tongue *à la flamande*, beef *carbonade*, calf's head, shepherd's pie, *mousselline* of pike with Riesling, barbecued pigeon, flambéed veal kidneys with cream and a trolley of home-made desserts. Menus €18–38, including a special *choucroute* menu, and good wines at all prices. Free coffee and one free breakfast per room from 13 July–15 Sept.

🕅 🏠 |●| AUBERGE DU BON FERMIER****

64 rue de Famars (Centre).
☎ 03.27.46.68.25
TV. Pay car park.

An old coaching inn in a splendidly preserved listed building. Inside, the corridors are skewed and tilted, and the staircases are narrow; the place resembles a museum, with ornaments and trinkets displayed in the smallest nooks and crannies. The rooms are equally charming, decorated in medieval or classical style. Doubles €87–98. The restaurant offers menus from €19 to €43, with a number of local dishes: *millefeuille* with Maroilles cheese, *carbonade flamande* and local pear *du hainaut*. 10% discount on the room rate Sat and Sun. Free coffee.

🕅 |●| RESTAURANT AU VIEUX SAINT-NICOLAS

72 rue de Paris (North).
☎ and ➡ 03.27.30.14.93
Closed Sun and Mon evenings and 14 July–15 Aug.

The décor in this peaceful little place is fresh, clean and modern, with a statue of a bishop contemplating the Klee and Kandinsky reproductions. Simple, tasty cooking includes *andouille* with juniper, chicken in beer, duck breast in honey and orange, *paella* and big salads. Menus range from €11–21, and wines are affordable. Free coffee.

🕅 |●| LE BISTROT D'EN FACE

5 av. d'Amsterdam (Centre).
☎ 03.27.42.25.25
Closed Sun evening.

This is the bistro belonging to the gastronomic restaurant *Rouet* opposite. It's cheaper and more relaxed and the décor is fresh and pleasant. They serve wholesome home cooking, and there's a huge choice: *navarin* of lamb with spring vegetables, bowls of mussels, frogs' legs, fresh scallops, *blanquette de veau à l'ancienne*, *cassoulet*, *gratin* of *andouille* with Chablis, duck legs with wine and blackcurrants, beef steak and oysters . . . Menus €12 and €16. Free house apéritif.

🕅 |●| LA PLANCHE À PAIN

1 rue d'Oultreman (Centre); it's 50m from the Place d'Armes.
☎ 03.27.42.25.25
Closed Sun evening, Mon and 5–25 Aug.

A solid establishment in a quiet street. The dining room is cosy, and you feel cossetted as soon as you arrive. Everyone comes here for the quality traditional cooking – they prepare dishes from the region and from the Mediterranean, including scallop and bacon kebab, cockerel with Chianti, warm king prawn salad with oyster mushrooms and *foie gras*, *rösti* or coddled eggs with Maroilles cheese, and a divine home-made combination of *foie gras* and smoked tongue. Menus €12–21. Free house apéritif.

🎋 |◉| RESTAURANT LA TOURTIÈRE

34 rue E-Macarez (East); it's just out of the town centre, near the tax office.
☎ 03.27.29.42.42 **e** latourtiere@evropost.org
Closed Mon and Wed evenings; Sat lunchtime.

The outside is really dreary, but it's much more friendly inside, with a relaxed, lively atmosphere. There's a *menu du Nord* and a *menu d'Italie*, both priced at €14, and in general the food is a mixture of regional favourites and Italian specialities – sometimes they're even combined, as in the macaroni with Maroilles cheese. Good bets include Avesnois veal and *tarte à la cassonade*. À la carte you'll find pizza and pasta, cheese and onion quiches and so on. Everything is served in vast portions. Free apéritif.

🎋 |◉| L'ORANGERIE

128 rue du Quesnoi (Centre).
☎ 03.27.42.70.70
Closed Sun; Mon; weekday lunchtimes; Aug.

Old local restaurant that's been transformed into a popular, lively, modern place. It has an easy-going, relaxed atmosphere with a warm setting and soft lighting. They serve fresh bistro dishes at affordable prices; menus, starting at €15, list such dishes as veal *blanquette à l'ancienne*, grilled shoulder of lamb with thyme, salmon *escalope* with leek *fondue* and various salads and *terrines*. On Thurs, Fri and Sat nights they hold dances after dinner and don't close until at 3am. Free *digestif*.

🎋 |◉| ROUET

8 av. d'Amsterdam (Centre).
☎ 03.27.46.44.52
Closed Sun evening and a fortnight in Aug.

Well-established gastronomic restaurant that just keeps on going. The faded, classic décor shows its age, but no one minds. It's a classy crowd – businesspeople, well-off retired folk, local dignitaries and the like – but everyone is treated the same and the service is so friendly that occasionally the waiters spend more time chatting than serving. The seafood – turbot, sea bream and king prawns – is

wonderfully fresh, and all the dishes are brilliantly prepared. Menus from €16 and seafood platters upwards of €34. Free house apéritif.

WIMEREUX   62179

🎋 🏠 |◉| HÔTEL DU CENTRE

78 rue Carnot (Centre).
☎ 03.21.32.41.08 **➡** 03.21.33.82.48
Closed Mon; 1–22 Jan; 17–31 Dec. **TV. Car park**.

A well-established, seriously run establishment in the centre of the town, just two minutes from the beach. Clean, comfortable double rooms (all due to be refurbished and some to be enlarged) go for €43 with shower/wc, €53 with bath. The dining room is cheery; they offer a *formule* with two dishes for €14 and menus from €16–27, listing traditional dishes like rabbit in jelly, sole, fish soup, local mussels and poached skate with *beurre noisette*. 10% discount on the room rate Sun–Thurs nights except July–Aug and public holidays.

🏠 |◉| L'ATLANTIC***

Digue de Mer (Centre).
☎ 03.21.32.41.01 **➡** 03.21.87.46.17
e alain.delpierre@wanadoo.fr
Closed Sun; Mon lunchtime; Feb. **TV. Car park**.

An impressive seafront place in one of the prettiest resorts on the Opal coast. There are just eight spacious, bright rooms, some of which look over the pedestrianized esplanade and the sea; doubles start at €60. Just the place for a truly relaxing weekend – but it's best to book. There are two restaurants – of which *La Liégoise* is the more stylish, with a good reputation – plus a brasserie with an airy dining room and a terrace serving good, honest fish dishes like fish soup and seafood platters. Menus start at €16, with others from €28 to €61.

WISSANT   62179

🏠 |◉| HÔTEL-RESTAURANT LE VIVIER**

pl. de l'Église (Centre).
☎ 03.21.35.93.61 **➡** 03.21.82.10.99
e le.vivier@wanadoo.fr
Restaurant closed Tues and Wed. **Disabled access. TV. Car park**.

Fronted by a *flobart*, or local fishing boat, this place specializes in seafood and fish, listed on menus from €15 to €30. The little rooms upstairs are really pretty, but those in the annexe further along the Boulogne road are even better, their balconies affording wonderful sea views over Cap Gris-Nez, the bay of Wissant and, on a clear day, the English coast. Doubles with shower €34, with bath €59.

ESCALLES-CAP BLANC-NEZ 62179 (5.5KM NW)

🏠 |●| HÔTEL-RESTAURANT À L'ESCALE**

rue de la Mer; take the D940.
☎ 03.21.85.25.00 📠 03.21.35.44.22
📧 hotel-lescale@hotel-lescale.com
Restaurant closed Wed Oct–March; mid-Dec to 27

Dec; Jan to early Feb. **Disabled access**. **TV**. **Car park**.

Ivy-smothered hotel in a tiny village at the foot of the magnificent chalk cliffs of the Cap Blanc-Nez. The rooms are charming; doubles with washing facilities go for €31, with shower/wc €46, with bath €50. To reach the restaurant you cross the tiny road leading to the fossil-strewn beach. The dining room is big and lively, and the cooking makes skilful use of seafood, with dishes such as fisherman's stew and a seafood platter. They do good regional dishes, too. A range of menus €13–32. Facilities include a tennis court and mountain bikes for hire.

Basse-Normandie

14 Calvados

50 Manche

61 Orne

AIGLE (L')   61300

|●| LA TOQUE ET LE VIN

35 rue Pasteur (Centre).
☎ 02.33.24.05.27
Closed Sun; Mon and Tues evenings.

The cooking is done by an experienced chef who opened this small wine bar with a colleague who takes care of the wine. He serves wholesome dishes at reasonable prices in a bright dining room. Fresh seasonal produce is used and dishes are full of flavour. There's a *formule* – dish of the day with a glass of wine – at €10 then menus €15–25.

CHANDAI   61300 (8.5KM E)

🎄 |●| AUBERGE DE L'ÉCUYER NORMAND

It's on the N26.
☎ 02.33.24.08.54
e ecuyer-normand@wanadoo.fr
Closed Mon (but reservations accepted in winter); Wed evening.

A stone and brick building fronted by evergreens. There's an inviting atmosphere in the hushed dining room with its open fire, beams and whitewashed walls. The talented chef adds a personal, modern touch to the dishes he prepares: prawn charlotte, boned pig's trotters with *jus*, lacquered duckling with Calvados-caralemized apples, pears with a honey *sabayon*. His fish dishes are similarly well-judged. Menus €13–50. Very warm welcome and attentive service. Free *trou Normand*, a shot of Calvados.

FERTÉ-FRÊNEL (LA)   61550 (14KM NW)

🎄 🏠 |●| HÔTEL DU PARADIS**

Grande-Rue.
☎ 02.33.34.81.33 📠 02.33.84.97.52
e choplin.le.paradis@wanadoo.fr
Closed Mon. **Disabled access. TV**.

This attractive little village inn lives up to its name and has a homely, friendly atmosphere. The most romantic room is number 16, which has a delightful bathroom and sweet little windows. Doubles €27–43 with shower/wc or bath. The restaurant serves generous portions of lovingly prepared, traditional dishes: mussels in cream sauce, seafood platter, fillet of beef with Roquefort cheese sauce, *tarte Tatin* flambéed with Calvados. €10 weekday menu and others €11–36. It's a very pleasant place to spend a summer or autumn evening. American Express not accepted. 10% discount on the room rate Oct–May.

ALENÇON   61000

🏠 HÔTEL DE PARIS*

26 rue Denis-Papin; it's opposite the station.
☎ 02.33.29.01.64 📠 02.33.29.44.87
TV.

Modest, extremely clean rooms with double glazing and the lowest rates in town – €20 for a double with basin and telephone, €24–27 with shower or €27–31 with shower/wc. Easy-going but courteous welcome. The little bar is frequented by lots of regulars.

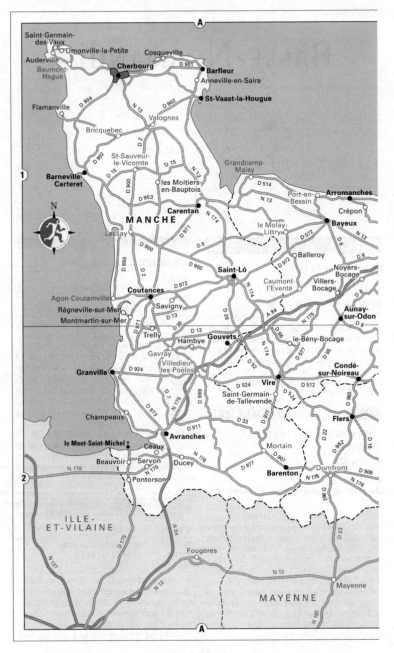

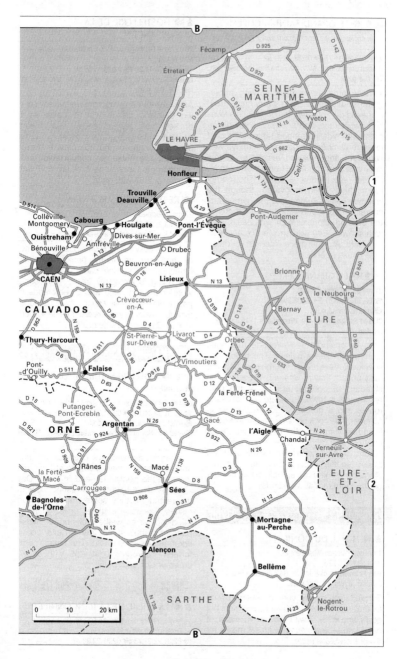

🏃 🏠 |O| LE GRAND SAINT-MICHEL**

7 rue du Temple; it's near the corn exchange (Halle aux Blés).
☎ 02.33.26.04.77 ➡ 02.33.26.71.82
Closed Sun evening; Mon; the Feb school holidays; July.
TV. Car park.

A handsome stone building with apple-green shutters situated in a very quiet street in the old part of town. Inside there's a lovely provincial feel and a large friendly dining room with nicely arranged tables. The chef loves to flambée things – veal kidneys with vermouth and mustard, escalope of *foie gras* with port, or fillet of beef *vieille mode*. Decent set menus €15–43. The comfy rooms have been renovated, though the imitation half-timbering and the garden furniture don't particularly suit the character of the building. Doubles €24 with basin, €27 with shower, €40 with shower/wc and €43 with bath. An ideal place – central yet quiet. Free house apéritif.

🏃 🏠 |O| LE GRAND CERF**

21 rue Saint-Blaise (Centre).
☎ 02.33.26.00.51 ➡ 02.33.26.63.07
e lgcert@wanadoo.fr
Closed Sat lunchtime, Sun evening and 1–15 Jan. **TV**.
Garden.

With its splendid 1830 façade this hotel looks rather like a palace. The rooms are spacious, have been refurbished and are fairly priced; they're €44–47. There's a high standard of cooking at one of the best restaurants in town. There are several dining rooms and a garden where they serve in summer. The cooking is well-regarded locally and is vying to be the best in town. Specialities include ballotine of guineafowl, "Grand Cerf" pigeon with morels and red mullet soufflé with Dublin Bay prawns. Menus €16–34. Free apéritif. 10% discount on the room rate at weekends.

ARGENTAN   61200

🏠 |O| HÔTEL DU DONJON*

1 rue de l'Hôtel-de-Ville (Centre).
☎ 02.33.67.03.76
Hotel closed 10 days in Feb. **Restaurant closed** 3 weeks in Aug. **TV**. **Car park**.

Simple, clean rooms, very reasonably priced for the area. Doubles €20 with basin/bidet but no TV, and €26–27 with shower/wc or bath. It has a brasserie-restaurant with set menus for €8 or there's *à la carte*.

🏠 |O| HOSTELLERIE DE LA RENAISSANCE**

20 av. de la Deuxième 2e-D-B (Southwest); it's on the road to Flers.
☎ 02.33.36.14.20 ➡ 02.33.36.65.50
Closed Sun evening; Mon; a week in Feb; a fortnight in Aug. **TV**. **Car park**.

An excellent contemporary restaurant serving delicious dishes with a novel slant: braised veal sweetbreads, sea bream cooked on its skin and a *moelleux* of bitter chocolate with coconut ice cream. Menus €15–38. The hotel has comfortable, well-soundproofed rooms; doubles are €57 with shower or €57 with bath.

|O| RESTAURANT D'ARGENTAN

22 rue du Beigle (Centre).
☎ 02.33.36.19.38
Closed Sun; Tues evening; a week in Feb.

The three cosy dining rooms buzz with activity and are frequently packed, making demands the service can't always meet. Everything is incredibly fresh. They serve wonderful calf's head and sweetbreads in pastry with Pommeau sauce. The €12 menu, available every day, is excellent value. Others at €14–31. A good little place.

ARROMANCHES-LES-BAINS   14117

🏃 🏠 |O| HÔTEL-RESTAURANT DE LA MARINE**

quai du Canada; it's on the sea shore by the harbour wall.
☎ 02.31.22.34.19 ➡ 02.31.22.98.80
e hotel.de.la.marine@wanadoo.fr
Closed mid-Nov to mid-Feb. **Disabled access**. **TV**. **Car park**.

The large bay windows overlook the sea and the beach, where you can still see the relics of the pontoons used in the D-Day landings: it's a haunting, arresting view. In the restaurant they serve mainly seafood dishes – seafood platters, grilled or flambéed lobster as well as savoury or sweet pancakes, but some aren't quite up to scratch. Menus €15–30. The clean, comfortable bedrooms cost €55 with shower/wc or €61 with bath.

CRÉPON   14480 (7KM SE)

🏠 |O| LA FERME DE LA RANÇONNIÈRE**

route d'Arromanches; take the D12 towards Cruelly –14km on, turn left onto the D65.
☎ 02.31.22.21.73 ➡ 02.31.22.98.39

🔞 www.ranconniere.com
TV. Garden. Car park.

The oldest parts of this beautiful and imposing fortified farmhouse date from the 13th century. The place is charming and not at all stuffy, offering a friendly, sincere, family welcome. All the rooms are individually decorated and tastefully furnished in traditional style. Some look onto a large, peaceful garden. Doubles €45–120 with shower/wc or bath. Half board, compulsory in high season, costs from €52 per person, which is good value – though it has to be said that the restaurant is not fabulous. The dining room has vaulted ceilings and the cuisine is typical of the region: *parfait* of chicken livers, fish and shellfish stew, *mignon* of pork with lemon, veal sweetbreads with prawns, duck breast. Menus €15–30; there's a children's menu for €9.

AUNAY-SUR-ODON   14260

🕌 🏠 |●| HÔTEL-RESTAURANT SAINT-MICHEL**

6–8 rue de Caen (Centre).
☎ 02.31.77.63.16 ➡ 02.31.77.05.83
Closed Sun evening and Mon (except July–Aug and public holidays); 15 Jan–15 Feb. **Disabled access. TV. Car park**.

This large hotel is in a village that's surrounded by marshes and was badly bombed during World War II so it doesn't look great from the outside. Inside, though, it's pleasant, with a modern dining room that contrasts nicely with the traditional cooking they serve. The chef uses all the good things that Normandy produces: *civet* of monkfish (a slow-cooked casserole) with fresh noodles, salad of warm seafood, beef skirt with Pont l'Évêque cheese, monkfish medallions with *fine champagne* sauce and chocolate *moelleux* with pears. Menus €12–35, and they also do a children's menu for €8. Decent, basic bedrooms cost €23 with washing facilities and €37 with shower/wc. Half board, €40, is compulsory at the weekend. 10% discount on the room rate.

AVRANCHES   50300

🏠 |●| HÔTEL DE LA CROIX D'OR**

83 rue de la Constitution (North).
☎ 02.33.58.04.88 ➡ 02.33.58.06.95
Closed Sun evening from mid-Oct to mid-March; Jan. **TV. Garden. Car park**.

This delightful seventeenth-century coaching inn sits beside the monument to General Patton. It has a superb garden with a stone urn and an old cider press. Inside, it's like a museum with its stone walls, beams, enormous fireplace and walls hung with copper, pewter and earthenware pots – all very charming. Doubles with shower/wc €43 to €61 with bath. Service is impeccable in the attractive dining room. Try the *millefeuille* of crab with basil and peas, the small lobster casserole with sweetbread ravioli, the *moelleux* of pink trout with bacon or the turbot fillet in a potato crust. The lunch menu is priced at €14 and they have others €21–38. The nicest restaurant in town.

|●| LE LITTRÉ

pl. de la Mairie; it's opposite the town hall.
☎ 02.33.58.01.66
📧 nivard.littre@wanadoo.fr
Closed Sun and Mon (except July–Aug); a fortnight end June to early July.

This place doesn't look like much from the outside, but it's one of the nicest restaurants around and has a beautiful dining room. The traditional cuisine is consistently good – you could order the dish of the day with your eyes shut and depend upon it being great. Fish *choucroute* is the house speciality, or go for the eggs *en meurette* and the veal chops with artichokes. Menus €13–20. Good desserts, including apple *clafoutis* (baked apple custard) and *pavé au chocolat*.

DUCEY   50220 (10KM SE)

🕌 🏠 |●| AUBERGE DE LA SÉLUNE**

2 rue Saint-Germain; take the the Ducey exit off the N176, and you'll find it on the left just before you get to the bridge.
☎ 02.33.48.53.62 ➡ 02.33.48.90.30
🔞 www.selune.com
Closed Mon Oct–March; 10 Jan–5 Feb; 18 Nov–15 Dec. **TV. Garden. Car park**.

Originally a hospice, this huge inn is located on the old road to Mont-Saint-Michel. The attractive bedrooms are individualistically decorated and you'll pay €49–52 for a comfortable double with shower/wc or bath. A lucky few will get a view of the garden that runs down to the slow-moving Sélune, one of the best trout and salmon rivers in France – it draws lots of fishermen, so pack your fishing rod. Carefully planned and executed menus at €14–34. They serve specialities such as salmon with perry, trout *soufflé*, stuffed saddle of rabbit with cider vinegar, fillet of sole with Vermouth and crab pie. Friendly staff. 10% discount on the room rate Oct–March.

BAGNOLES-DE-L'ORNE   61140

⚓ 🏠 |●| LA POTINIÈRE

rue des Casinos.
☎ 02.33.30.65.00
Closed Mon and Tues 1 Nov–31 March; 15 Dec–10 Feb.
TV.

It's hard to miss this place because the façade is one of the prettiest and most striking in town. There's a view of the lake from the dining room and most of the bedrooms – the others look onto a main road which is very quiet at night. This is a nice place and prices are modest: doubles with basin €20 and up to €40 with shower/wc or bath. There's a turret room, which is rather special. The cooking is simple, light and tasty and perfectly prepared: hot Camembert, *andouillette de Vire* with mustard, ham in cider, ostrich fillet. Menus 13–27. Free coffee.

⚓ 🏠 |●| LE CELTIC**

14 rue Pierre-Noal; it's on the outskirts of Tessé-la-Madeleine, opposite the château.
☎ 02.33.37.92.11 ➡ 02.33.38.90.27
📧 leceltic@club-internet.fr
Closed Tues evening and Wed out of season; 26 Dec–1 March. **TV.**

Michèle and Erick Alirol make you feel very welcome in this seaside house, which is typical of the region. The pleasant bedrooms all have telephone. Doubles with shower/wc €37 or €40 with bath. Menus €15–27 or you can dine *à la carte*. Lots of fresh local ingredients and seasonal produce are used: butterfly prawn fritters, lacquered duckling fillet with honey and *moelleux* of spiced crab. The rustic dining room is just right and the friendly staff serve with a smile. There's a snooker table. 10% discount on the room rate and free apéritif.

⚓ 🏠 |●| MANOIR DU LYS***

route de Juvigny-sous-Andaine; take the D235 and it's 3km from Bagnoles.
☎ 02.33.37.80.69 ➡ 02.33.30.05.80
🌐 www.manoir-du-lys.fr
Closed Sun evening and Mon 1 Nov–Easter; 2 Jan–14 Feb. **Disabled access. Garden. Swimming pool TV. Car park.**

A delightful manor deep in the Andaines forest, built as a hunting lodge by a fervent royalist. You'll hear cuckoos in the springtime and glimpse deer straying into the orchard. The rooms are bright and tastefully decorated; some have balconies overlooking the garden. Doubles €58–99 with shower/wc or bath. The staff and the cooking are as wonderful as

the setting. The restaurant uses fresh local produce and revives traditional flavours – *croquant* of Camembert with apples, zander smoked over beech, flat sausage made from pigs' trotters with sage and divine desserts. Menus €24–59. Free apéritif. 10% discount on the room rate Nov to mid-March.

RÂNES   61150 (20KM NE)

⚓ 🏠 |●| HÔTEL SAINT-PIERRE**

6 rue de la Libération; it's on the D916.
☎ 02.33.39.75.14 ➡ 02.33.35.49.23
Restaurant closed Fri evening out of season.
TV. Car park.

This place, housed in a substantial stone building, is run by very friendly staff. You can relax in their deep sofas and the dining room is painted in pistachio and red. The cooking is excellent and prices are reasonable – the house speciality is tripe, which has won countless prizes and awards (check out the certificates on the walls). Other hits include the roast chicken, which is perfectly cooked and seasoned, the *bœuf à la ficelle* (where the meat is tied with string, cooked in stock and served with a Camembert sauce), veal *escalope* with artichokes and frogs' legs. There's a weekday menu at €12 and others €17–30. Pleasant bedrooms €37 with shower/wc or €43 with bath. Ask for one overlooking the courtyard; you'll get absolute peace and quiet. 10% discount on the room rate 1 Nov–Easter.

BARENTON   50720

|●| RESTAURANT LE RELAIS DU PARC

46 rue Pierre-Crestey (West).
☎ 02.33.59.51.38
Closed Mon and weekday evenings; Christmas–New Year; the Feb school holidays.

If you get here early enough, you'll be able to listen to the Swedish chef issuing orders in the kitchen in jovial but commanding tones. He prepares attractive dishes using local produce with imagination, like a *fricassée* of cockerel with cider vinegar and a range of typical Normandy dishes featuring apples and cream. Menus €11–27. The dining room centres on a very attractive fireplace and an antique clock.

BARFLEUR   50760

⚓ 🏠 |●| LE MODERNE

1 pl. du Général-de-Gaulle; it's opposite the post office, 50m from the harbour.

☎ 02.33.23.12.44 ➡ 02.33.23.91.58
Closed Tues evening and Wed except July to mid-Sept; Jan to mid-Feb.

A colourful, pretty place with lots of flowers – it's only a shame that there's no sea view from the clean, simple bedrooms (doubles €34–49). In the restaurant they serve carefully prepared dishes on a range of menus: a weekday lunch one for €16 and others up to €53. The house speciality is fish *choucroute* with *beurre blanc* and there's also a good grilled seafood cocktail. The salmon and duck breast are smoked on the premises and the bread and *foie gras* are also home-made. Marvellous desserts. Free coffee.

♠ I●I LE CONQUÉRANT**

16–18 rue Saint-Thomas-Becket; it's 50m from the port
☎ 02.33.54.00.82
Hotel closed 15 Nov–15 March. **Restaurant open** evenings, and only for residents. **TV. Garden. Car park.**

A handsome seventeenth-century building with a sizeable formal garden at the back. The rooms range from simple to comfortable and €53–75 with shower/wc or bath – the best ones overlook the garden, though none has a sea view. Breakfast €5–9. You'll pay €13–23 for a meal in the stylish dining room, also a *crêperie*.

I●I CAFÉ DU CADRAN GPLM

It's in the village; take the D902 in the direction of Quettehou.
☎ 02.33.54.61.89
Closed evenings; weekends; 15 Aug–15 Sept. **Car park.**

This place is almost hidden by the crowd of tractors and juggernauts on their regular round of delivering and collecting the fruit and veg produced in the Val de Saire. The talk is all of cabbages and cauliflowers, yields and set-asides. If a glass of white wine at 11am is tempting, so is the menu of the day: steak and mash, lamb stew – solid classics and cheap as you like. Including wine, it's a snip at €9.

I●I AU BOUQUET DE COSQUEVILLE

Hameau Remoud; it's on the coast road to Cherbourg.
☎ 02.33.54.32.81 ➡ 02.33.54.63.38
Ⓦ www.boquetdecosqueville.com
Closed Tues and Wed out of season; Jan; the last week in June.

A big house in a little hamlet where you'll find one of the best tables in the Nord-Cotentin area. Chef Éric Pouhier specializes in carefully-judged fish and seafood dishes: cod fillet with tomato cream sauce, oyster and prawn soup with herbs, lobster with dry cider. Stylish, unobtrusive service and menus €17–53. In the same establishment there's another restaurant, the *Petit Gastro*, which is run by the same team. The atmosphere is less self-important and prices are more accessible with menus €10–14 but the chef takes equal care over the quality of the dishes – mussels with sorrel *au gratin*, russet apples with cider sauce.

🎋 ♠ I●I L'HERMITAGE**

promenade Abbé-Lebouteiller; it overlooks the port.
Hotel ☎ 02.33.04.46.39 ➡ 02.33.04.88.11
Restaurant ☎ 02.33.04.96.29
Closed Sun evening and Mon (except July–Aug); 12 Nov–20 Dec; 10–30 Jan. **TV. Pay car park.**

There's a delightful view of the sea and Carteret's little fishing port from the dining room and the terrace. Menus €14–40. There are a few pleasant bedrooms which cost from €30 with washing facilities to €53 with shower/wc and the harbour view. Free Calvados and 10% discount on the room rate.

♠ I●I HÔTEL DE LA MARINE***

11 rue de Paris.
☎ 02.33.53.83.31 ➡ 02.33.53.39.60
Closed Mon lunchtime April–June and Sept; Sun evening and Mon Feb–March and Oct; 12 Nov–1 Mar. **TV. Car park.**

There are breathtaking views from this large white building overlooking the harbour. Some bedrooms have a balcony, others a tiny terrace, and the décor throughout is fresh and stylish. Doubles €74–104. The good reputation of this establishment is due mostly to its restaurant, where the cooking is sophisticated, imaginative – and very elaborate. The elegant dining room has a rather chic atmosphere: Monsieur and Madame Cesne run the place smoothly, and the service is just so. Their son Laurent is the chef and he has put together a series of appetizing and imaginative menus – a weekday one for €25, another at €40 and a *menu dégustation* for €71. They feature dishes such as oysters *en nage* glazed with gherkins, plaice lacquered with honey and thyme with an onion and apple preserve, fillet of duck with shallots, *terrine* of goat's cheese with pickled aubergines and iced mousse with orange liqueur.

BAYEUX 14400

☎ |●| HÔTEL-RESTAURANT NOTRE-DAME*

44 rue des Cuisiniers (Centre); it's near the cathedral.
☎ 02.31.92.87.24 ➡ 02.31.92.67.11
Establishment closed 15 Nov–20 Dec. **Restaurant closed** Sun evening and Mon lunchtime Nov–Easter. **TV. Car park**.

A comfortingly traditional hotel where the décor in the rooms has a timeless quality – without being in any way opulent, they're comfortable. Prices for double rooms start at €31 with basin, around €46 with bath. Fancy, succulent cooking with mainly local dishes – shellfish *timbale* or *fricassée* of rabbit in cider. Menus from €14 to €27. Half board is compulsory in July–Aug and weekends in high season.

🏃 ☎ HÔTEL MOGADOR**

20 rue Alain-Chartier, pl. Saint-Patrice (North).
☎ 02.31.92.24.58 ➡ 02.31.92.24.85
Closed Feb school holidays. **Pay car park**. **TV**.

A discreet hotel on the edge of the touristy centre of town. The rooms are elegant and comfortable, and those around the courtyard are very quiet. Doubles with shower/wc €39 or €44 with bath; there's a charge of €12 extra per person in family rooms. Welcoming, friendly owner. 10% discount Nov–March.

🏃 ☎ HÔTEL D'ARGOUGES**

21 rue Saint-Patrice (Centre).
☎ 02.31.92.88.86 ➡ 02.31.92.69.16
e dargouges@aol.com
TV. Garden. Car park.

A lovely eighteenth-century mansion, built for the Argouges family with a delightful, large courtyard. The dining room is majestic and, behind the house, there's a big tree-filled garden and it's wonderful to have breakfast there when the weather's good. All the rooms have shower/wc or bath, TV and mini-bar and cost €47–73. Rooms 1–5 have a view of the garden. 10% discount.

🏃 |●| LA TABLE DU TERROIR

42 rue Saint-Jean (Centre); it's in the pedestrianized area.
☎ and ➡ 02.31.92.05.53
Closed Sun evening and Mon 1 May–15 Oct. **Disabled access**.

Louis Bisson has translated the notion of the

country *table d'hôte* to his home town. He was a butcher by trade before deciding to return and indulge his passion for cooking. He has set out a few tables in a beautiful room with stone walls and serves traditional, local, uncomplicated dishes: house *terrines*, rib of beef for two, grilled flank or skirt, calf's head with *sauce gribiche* or tripe. There are four menus €10–25, with a children's one for €7. This is a good, friendly little place which appeals to tourists and locals – anyone who wants a decent lunch. Free coffee.

|●| LE PETIT BISTROT

2 rue Bienvenue (Centre); it's beside the cathedral.
☎ 02.31.51.85.40
Closed Sun and Mon; mid-Dec to end Jan.

This is a genuine little bistro, chic yet very pleasant. The cooking is fresh-tasting and flavoursome, emphasizing the taste of the local ingredients: duck *terrine*, veal kidneys, fisherman's casserole and duck *foie gras*. Set menus – €15 and €27 – change with the seasons. A very good restaurant. Dogs not admitted.

COLOMBIERS-SUR-SEULLES 14480 (14KM E)

☎ |●| CHÂTEAU DU BAFFY**

How to get there: exit 7 from the Caen ring-road in the direction of Creully; turn right after Pierpont.
☎ 02.31.08.04.57. ➡ 02.31.08.08.29.
Restaurant closed 1 Nov–1 Feb.

This pretty château, which dates from the Enlightenment, is a lovely and romantic spot, with a river running through the beautiful garden. The bedrooms are comfortable, though prices are a little high – doubles with shower/wc or bath/wc go for €59–85 including breakfast. In the restaurant there's a €21 weekday menu, with others up to €32. They do typical home cooking and some more refined dishes – *grenadin* of veal, stuffed duck leg with a Pommeau sauce or prawn *croquants* scented with vanilla. There's a gym and tennis courts, and you can try your hand at mountain biking, archery and horse riding.

BELLÊME 61130

☎ |●| LE RELAIS SAINT-LOUIS**

1 bd. Bansard-des-Bois (Centre).
☎ 02.33.73.12.21 ➡ 02.33.83.71.19
Closed Sun evening, Mon; the second and third weeks in Feb. **TV. Car park**.

This is a good old-fashioned kind of inn. It's a

long, white building with pillars constructed on the old fortifications of this tiny village. The large dining room, its waiters sporting bow ties, is terribly old-fashioned but rather pleasant. The chef, Ghislaine, prepares classic dishes which take their inspiration from local recipes. Weekday menu €15 and others up to €29. Specialities include *foie gras* from Normandy, fresh scallops and the famous black pudding from Perche. The bedrooms are tastefully decorated; some overlook the gardens at the back of the inn. Doubles €46 with shower/wc or bath.

⬆ |●| DOMAINE DU GOLF DE BELLÊME

Les Sablons
☎ 02.33.73.00.07 ➡ 02.33.73.00.17
Ⓦ www.belleme.com
Disabled access. **TV**. **Car park**.

Service until midnight. Despite being part of a golf club, this restaurant is actually located in the old convent of the sixteenth-century priory of Saint-Val. The excellent menus, starting at €16, list perfectly cooked fish and inventive desserts. Specialities include guineafowl *terrine* with smoked bacon and Calvados, trout with smoked bacon and Pommeau butter, and the plum *terrine* with gingerbread and cinnamon ice cream is heavenly. They also serve grills and salads. Attentive service and a relaxed atmosphere. There are a few comfortable rooms in the outbuildings which have modern facilities. Doubles €64–90, but if you stay for a week in high season, rooms are charged at €79 per night.

⬆ |●| MOULIN DE VILLERAY****

Villegray; take the D203.
☎ 02.33.73.30.22 ➡ 02.33.73.38.28
ⓔ moulin.de.villeray@wanadoo.fr
Swimming pool. **Garden**. **TV**. **Car park**. **Disabled access**.

A charming establishment with several little mills – the biggest still with its wheel – dotted around the garden, terrace and swimming pool. The rooms are pricey (doubles €75–115) but the place is terribly romantic. And you can enjoy it just as much if you come for a meal. The chef has talent and offers a *menu du marché* of dishes concocted from that day's fresh produce: pigeon and artichoke *terrine*, fish *pot-au-feu*, strawberry soup. All the dishes are delicate and flavourful, with a particularly imaginative selection *à la carte* – go for the marrowbone with snails and mushrooms, the calf's cheek stew or any of the divine desserts. Menus €22–56. The chef's particular obsession is mushrooms

and in the autumn he arranges special mushroom weekends that include picking, cooking and tastings. The clientele is well-heeled, but everyone is very relaxed. Attentive welcome.

CABOURG   14390

⬆ LE BEAURIVAGE**

allée du Château (West); it's 800m from the centre of Cabourg on the route du Hôme.
☎ 02.31.24.08.08 ➡ 02.31.91.19.46
Ⓦ www.hotel-beaurivage-cabourg.fr
Closed 15 Nov–15 Dec. **TV**. **Car park**.

A large ochre-coloured building beside the sea. The décor and the clean bedrooms are certainly adequate but since this is the seaside you pay a bit extra. Doubles €49 with shower/wc, €57 with bath. Breakfast €6.

⬆ HÔTEL LE COTTAGE**

24 av. du Général-Leclerc; it's opposite the church.
☎ 02.31.91.65.61 ➡ 02.31.28.78.82
TV. **Garden**. **Car park**.

It's easy to fall under the spell of this delightful hotel in a charming, traditional Normandy house with a pretty flower garden. The owner will greet you like an old friend, and the bedrooms are cosy and charming with their floral décor. Doubles from €64 with shower/wc or bath. Although it's beside the road the double glazing is good and the bedrooms are quiet. Facilities include a billiard room, sauna and sunbed – so there's something to do even when it rains.

DIVES-SUR-MER   14160 (2KM S)

⅍ |●| RESTAURANT CHEZ LE BOUGNAT

29 rue Gaston-Manneville.
☎ 02.31.91.06.13
Closed evenings except Fri and Sat, but Tues and Wed lunchtimes only in season.

When the old owner retired, no one knew what would become of this established restaurant. But the new owner wisely decided to change very little – not the metro signs, not the 1950s advertising posters, nor even trinkets that would turn a junk dealer green with envy. The food is excellent – taking its inspiration principally from the region, it's prepared from fresh produce and first-rate ingredients. Dishes are firmly traditional, very simple and excellent: *pot-au-feu*, lamb with haricot beans, calf's head. There's only one menu at €13; it includes starter, main dish, cheese *and* dessert. You can also choose *à la carte*, which will set you back about €23. This is the best value for money locally so it's best to book. Free *digestif*.

AMFREVILLE   14860 (10KM SW)

☎ |●| AUBERGE DE L'ÉCARDE

19 route de Cabourg; it's on the D514.
☎ and ➡ 02.31.72.47.65
Closed Sun evening, Mon and Tues lunchtime; Dec–Jan. **Garden. Car park**.

A small and rather unassuming stone house on the side of the road, run by a kind, welcoming couple. The dining room is attractive and the garden terrace is peaceful in summer. Best of all, the simple country cooking is produced using only the freshest ingredients: pollack fillet with sorrel, skate with chive cream, veal kidneys with grain mustard, steak with Camembert and Roquefort sauce, *entrecôte* flambéed with Calvados. Good-value weekday menu €14, a *formule* at €12 and other menus up to €26, with a children's option for €8. Simple rooms – double with basin €27, or €32–37 with shower and garden view.

BEUVRON-EN-AUGE   14430 (14KM SE)

☎ |●| AUBERGE DE LA BOULE D'OR

pl. Michel Vermughen.
☎ 02.31.79.78.78 ➡ 02.31.39.61.50
Closed Tues evening and Wed (except July–Aug); Jan.

Right in the middle of one of the loveliest villages in the Auge, this superb half-timbered house was built in the eighteenth century. The beautiful façade is such a fine example of local architecture that it was photographed for a full-page publicity shot in *Le Monde*. The dining room is stylishly rustic, intimate yet friendly. They serve good local cooking, with tasty dishes at honest prices – go for the hot *andouille de Vire* with cider, the veal kidneys with grain mustard, and the apple tart to finish. Menus €15–30. Free coffee.

CAEN   14000

SEE MAP OVERLEAF

☎ |●| HÔTEL SAINT-ÉTIENNE*

2 rue de l'Académie. **MAP A2-3**
☎ 02.31.86.35.82 ➡ 02.31.85.57.69
Ⓦ www.hotel-saint-etienne.com
TV.

Characterful hotel in a peaceful street. It was built before the Revolution and much of the stonework and wood panelling is original. The

bedrooms are pretty; doubles are €21 with basin or €26–35 with shower/wc and telephone, making it the cheapest hotel in Caen so it's often full. The staff are very friendly. It doesn't have a restaurant, but there are plenty nearby. 10% discount on the room rate.

☎ |●| HÔTEL DES CORDELIERS**

4 rue des Cordeliers. **MAP B2-4**
☎ 02.31.86.37.15 ➡ 02.31.39.56.51
Closed Sun afternoon. **TV. Garden**.

A seventeenth-century town house with great charm in a street that leads to the castle. It's charming and quiet. The bedrooms are decorated in contemporary style with white walls and pale wooden furniture, and they look out over the pleasant patio or a narrow pedestrianized street. Doubles €26 with basin; €35 with shower/wc or bath. 10% discount on the room rate.

☎ |●| CENTRAL HÔTEL*

23 pl. Jean-Letellier. **MAP B2-2**
☎ 02.31.86.18.52 ➡ 02.31.86.88.11
Ⓦ www.centralhotel-caen.com
TV.

This 1960s building has no charm whatsoever, but at least the square is quiet and you get a friendly welcome. The rooms are bright and attractive and prices are reasonable: doubles €29 with shower, €37 with shower/wc or €40 with bath. Some have a view of the William the Conqueror's castle. It's a very good hotel considering it's only got one star. 10% discount Oct–Mar.

☎ |●| HÔTEL BERNIÈRES*

50 rue de Bernières. **MAP C2-5**
☎ 02.31.86.01.26 ➡ 02.31.86.51.76
Ⓦ www.hotelbernieres.com
TV.

This hotel is in a gruesome postwar building in a busy street, but the double glazing keeps out unwelcome noise and inside it's more like a guest house than a traditional hotel. Clean, attractively decorated rooms and a cordial welcome from the proprietress – who takes great care of her guests. Memorable €6 breakfast which includes ham and cheese. Doubles €37 with shower/wc and €40 with bath. The rooms under the eaves sleep four or five and cost €46. A one-star hotel that thoroughly deserves to be upgraded. 10% discount Oct–March.

|●| RESTAURANT MAÎTRE CORBEAU

94 rue Buquet. **MAP B1-11**
☎ 02.31.93.93.00.

Closed Sat and Mon lunchtimes; Sun; Aug; Christmas–New Year.

The décor is bizarre at this cheese restaurant – as if somebody had decided to redecorate Heidi's chalet through a haze of hallucinogens. There's a cow on the ceiling and a motley collection of cheese adverts and packets dotted around the place. They serve cheese *fondues* using local cheese or goat's cheese, *tartiflette*, coddled eggs with cheese and *escalopines* of Roquefort flambéed with Calvados. Weekday lunch menu €10 and others up to €19. Informal, enthusiastic welcome and service. There's nowhere quite like it in the region.

|●| LA PETITE AUBERGE

17 rue des Équipes d'Urgence. **MAP C2-17**
☎ and ➥ 02.31.86.43.30.
Closed Sun and Mon; first 3 weeks in Aug; a fortnight from 24 Dec.

The dining room is small and cosy, with *faux*-rustic décor; it's extended by a glassed-in terrace. Low-key welcome, peaceful atmosphere and professional service. The good local dishes change with the seasons. Highlights include tripe *à la mode de Caen*, grilled saddle of lamb with butter and fresh thyme, and salmon *rillettes* made from fresh and smoked fish. *Formule du jour* €10 and *menu-carte* €15.

⚗|●| LE BOUCHON DU VAUGUEUX

12 rue du Graindorge. **MAP C2-14**
☎ 02.31.44.26.26
Closed Sun and Mon.

This little place stands out in an area where restaurants do a thriving trade – many of which don't deserve to survive. You choose from a list of tasty dishes chalked up on big blackboards; winners include rabbit *terrine* with prunes, guineafowl *pastilla*, poached beef with vegetables and cod roast in its skin with a bacon crust. The salads are huge and enough for a whole meal; served in half-portions as a starter they go for half-price. Set menus €11 or €15. The staff are genuinely warm and friendly, just like the atmosphere, so it's not surprising that it's always very busy – best to book. Free *digestif*.

|●| RESTAURANT ALCIDE

1 pl. Courtonne. **MAP C2-13**
☎ 02.31.44.18.06 ➥ 02.31.94.47.45
Closed Sat and 21–31 Dec.

The outside is painted sky-blue and the décor inside isn't exactly earth-shattering,

but the warm atmosphere makes up for it. This is not the place to come if you're on a diet – they serve honest, robust local cuisine including calf's head, John Dory on a bed of *choucroute*, ham hock with lentils and tripe *à la mode de Caen*. Menus €13–21. One of the town's classics.

⚗|●| L'EMBROCHE

17 rue Porte-au-Berger. **MAP B1-12**
☎ 02.31.93.71.31
Closed Sat and Mon lunchtimes; Sun; 25 Sept–7 Oct; 24 Dec–6 Jan.

Pretty little dining room where you can see through into the kitchen; the atmosphere is enlivened by cool jazz and bebop. Charming, efficient service. Chalked up on the board you'll find local dishes cooked with fresh produce and bags of imagination – try *andouilles* with apples and cider vinegar or tripe with cider and Calvados. Lunch menu €14, others up to €16. All the wines on the short but interesting list are the same price. Free house apéritif March–Sept.

|●| RESTAURANT LE ZODIAQUE

15 quai Eugène-Meslin. **MAP C3-16**
☎ 02.31.84.46.31
Closed Mon–Wed evenings, Sun, public holidays, end of July and three weeks in Aug.

This cosy restaurant, decorated on the theme of the zodiac, has made a reputation for the meats they grill on the open fire – T-bone steak, duck breast and steak fillet. There are terrific home-made pastries for dessert. No set menus but expect to pay about €15 *à la carte*.

|●| LE GASTRONOME

43 rue Saint-Sauveur. **MAP A2-18**
☎ 02.31.86.57.75 ➥ 02.31.38.27.78
Closed Sat lunchtime; Sun.

The name of this restaurant is a challenge for any chef. The one here interprets classic dishes with a very individual touch, using local ingredients to produce dishes like warm oysters on an apple and pear *compôte*, turbot *gratiné* with clams, tripe *croustillant* with cream and Calvados, fillet of duck with artichokes with a sauce thickened with *foie gras* and a *gratin* of fresh fruit with Pommeau. Very decent menus €15–38. The dining room is sober and rather chic, and service is attentive, efficient and unobtrusive.

|●| LE CARLOTTA

16 quai Vendeuvre. **MAP C2-15**

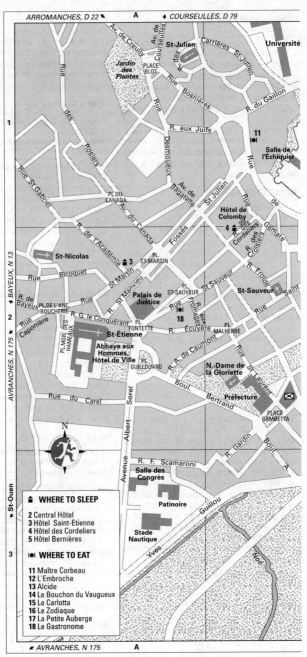

St-Julien

Université

Jardin
des
Plantes

PLACE
BLOT

R. du Gaillon

Rue aux Juifs

11

Salle de
l'Echiquier

PL DU
CANADA

Hôtel de
Colomby

4

R. de l'Académie

St-Nicolas

PL
ST-MARTIN

3

St-Sauveur

Rue Bicoquet

PL
ST-SAUVEUR

St-Sauveur

PL DE L'ANC.
BOUCHERIE

**Palais de
Justice**

18

PL
FONTETTE

PL
MALHERBE

R. G. le Conquérant

PL MGR DES
HAMEAUX

St-Étienne

**Abbaye aux
Hommes,
Hôtel de Ville**

PL
GUILLOUARD

N.-Dame de
la Gloriette

Préfecture

Rue du Caret

PLACE
GAMBETTA

R. F. Scamaroni

**Salle des
Congrès**

N

Patinoire

**Stade
Nautique**

⌂ WHERE TO SLEEP

2 Central Hôtel
3 Hôtel Saint-Etienne
4 Hôtel des Cordeliers
5 Hôtel Bernières

⦿ WHERE TO EAT

11 Maître Corbeau
12 L'Embroche
13 Alcide
14 Le Bouchon du Vaugueux
15 Le Carlotta
16 Le Zodiaque
17 La Petite Auberge
18 Le Gastronome

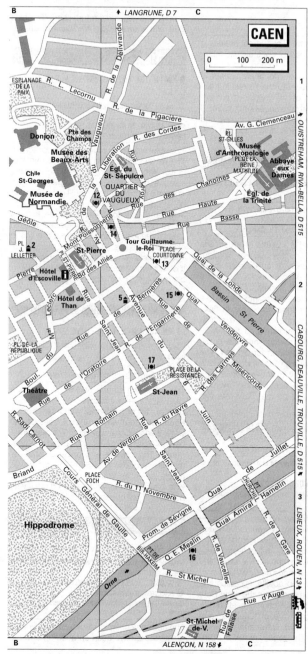

CAEN

0   100   200 m

☎ 02.31.86.68.99
Closed Sun.

Service until 11pm. The name makes it sound like a pizza parlour but the white table-cloths, the waiters in starched aprons and the rather plush, tasteful décor are pure Belle Époque – even down to the moleskin *banquettes*. This is a good, genuine, Parisian-style *brasserie* with provincial prices. You'll get first-rate cooking (good fish dishes and tasty meat) without spending a fortune. Set weekday menu €16 and others up to €31.

NOYERS-BOCAGE   14210 (12KM SW)

🎿 ✿ |●| HÔTEL-RESTAURANT LE RELAIS NORMAND**

How to get there: take the D675 or the N175.
☎ 02.31.77.97.37 ➡ 02.31.77.94.41
Closed Tues evening and Wed. **TV**. **Car park**.

The proprietor-chef is a Grand Master of the *Confrérie de fins Goustiers du Pré-Bocage*, an association which defends "real" food. Unsurprisingly, he's punctilious over the preparation of local dishes. Set menus €32–58 or *à la carte* – dishes include oysters poached in champagne, *foie gras* in flaky pastry, duck *à l'orange*, *blanquette* of fish with baby vegetables, flambéed *tarte Normande* with aged Calvados and the prize-winning *bonneau Normand* for dessert. The attractive, plush dining room is decorated in rustic style. Doubles with shower/wc or bath €36–43. It's a very peaceful, out-of-the-way place. 10% discount on the room rate late Oct–June.

VILLERS-BOCAGE   14310 (26KM SW)

✿ |●| AUBERGE LES TROIS ROIS**

2 pl. Jeanne-d'Arc; it's on the A84 in the direction of Mont St Michel.
☎ 02.31.77.00.32 ➡ 02.31.77.93.25
Closed Sun evening; Mon; Jan; the last week in June. **TV**. **Car park**.

This classic stone inn on the large village square has an elegant restaurant. Though the décor is a tad pompous and the staff a little formal the cooking is full of lively invention. The chef has run the kitchens for thirty years – his tripe *à la mode de Caen* is award-winning. He uses top-quality ingredients in every dish: recommended are the John Dory with fresh sorrel, the selection of seafish with oyster butter, pigeon breast "Lucullus" and hot apples with iced cinnamon caramel. Menus €18–47. The rooms are well main-

tained and regularly refurbished. Doubles €32 with shower and €47–58 with bath.

CARENTAN   50500

✿ |●| HÔTEL DU COMMERCE ET DE LA GARE*

34 rue du Docteur-Caillard; it's opposite the train station.
☎ 02.33.42.02.00 ➡ 02.33.42.20.01
Closed 30 Nov–1 March. **TV**. **Car park**.

The hotel has a beautiful, ivy-covered façade. The restaurant is attractive too: it's an intimate place with low lighting, a soothing colour scheme, and a polished parquet floor. There's a piano bar, too. You'll get very good home cooking on the set menus at €13–22. Meat and fish specialities include kebabs grilled on a wood fire, Camembert fritters, *moules marinières* and they do a fine line in elaborate salads. Children's menu €6. There's a sign encouraging customers to tell the chef what they thought of the food. Double rooms €29 with shower/wc or €36 with bath.

MOITIERS-EN-BAUPTOIS (LES) 50360 (20KM NW)

🎿 |●| AUBERGE DE L'OUVE

Village Longuérac; it's 16km south-west of Sainte-Mère-Église.
☎ 02.33.21.16.26
Open 30 Sept to Easter (by reservation only)

This lovely inn stands on the banks of the Ouve; it's miles from anywhere, surrounded by a cluster of old farms, with a few horses frolicking about and a line of trees at the water's edge. Great welcome. The restaurant has an attractive décor and a warm atmosphere. The cuisine is wonderful and the menus – very cheap at €11–19 – feature as much *terrine* as you can eat, potato stew with cream, eel *à la normande* and duck with potatoes. Free house *digestif*.

CHERBOURG   50100

🎿 ✿ HÔTEL DE LA CROIX DE MALTE**

5 rue des Halles (Centre); it's near the harbour, the theatre and the casino.
☎ 02.33.43.19.16 ➡ 02.33.43.65.66
e hotel.croix.malte@wanadoo.fr
Closed first week of Jan. **Disabled access**. **TV**. **Car park**.

The hotel has been totally refurbished and its quiet rooms have been spruced up and are extremely comfy. You'll get a very warm welcome from the owners. Doubles with shower/wc cost €25; they're €45 with bath, direct telephone and TV. If you book in advance, ask for room numbers 3, 6, 8 or 15 – they're the biggest. Excellent value for money. 10% discount Sept–June.

♨ HÔTEL DE LA RENAISSANCE**

4 rue de l'Église (Centre); it's opposite the church of La Trinité.
☎ 02.33.43.23.90 ➡ 02.33.43.96.10
TV. Pay car park.

The hotel has a great location in front of the wonderful church of La Trinité – if you're into frothy, frivolous architecture, you'll love the sugar-candy façade. All the comfortable bedrooms have been well-refurbished and they're very pleasant; every one has a view of the port. Doubles €45–52 with shower/wc or bath; there's a substantial breakfast on offer for €6. The smiling owner provides a lovely welcome and looks after her guests.

●I LE FAITOUT

25 rue Tour-Carrée; it's 100m from church of La Trinité.
☎ 02.33.04.25.04
Closed Sun; Mon lunchtime.

The attractive basement dining room is constructed in wood and stone and has a relaxed atmosphere. It's the archetype of a small, reliable restaurant that does precisely what it's supposed to – consequently it's often full. Good traditional cooking at prices that won't give you indigestion: the *formule* of the day lists dishes such as duck *croustillant*, calf's head *gribiche*, *andouillette* with Calvados and grilled salmon. *Pot-au-feu* is the house speciality, which you should accompany with a bottle of dry cider. The menu at €18 gives you starter, dish of the day, cheese and dessert; the dish of the day on its own costs €9. It's best to book for dinner and at weekends.

●I LE COTENTIN

30 quai de Caligny.
☎ 02.33.43.51.80
Closed Sun (except June–Aug); the first 3 weeks of Jan.

An ample brasserie-restaurant located near Cherbourg's pleasure port. No surprise to find that fish and seafood are the specialities. Service is good-natured and efficient and the waiting staff are friendly. There's plenty of choice *à la carte* and a huge choice of fixed-price menus. The cooking and dishes are

unusually interesting and use good local ingredients; menus change every three months to take account of the seasonal availability of produce. Two menus for €20 and €26, and the €15 and €21 *formules* offer a choice of two main courses. If you're making a booking, be sure to ask for a table on the first floor to get an impressive view over the port.

OMONVILLE-LA-PETITE   50440 (20KM NW)

♨ ♨ LA FOSSARDIÈRE**

hameau de la Fosse; take the D901 or the quiet, coast-road, the D45.
☎ 02.33.52.19.83 ➡ 02.33.52.73.49
Closed 15 Nov–15 March. **Car park.**

You'll find this lovely hotel in a hamlet just 500m from the sea, and you'll be treated to a warm welcome from owner Gilles Fossard. The bedrooms are comfortable and are reasonably priced at €40–56 – some have a whirlpool bath (which costs a little more). There's a tiny sauna. Free breakfast after the second night except in July–Aug.

AUDERVILLE   50440 (28KM NW)

●I L'AUBERGE DE GOURY

port de Goury; it's on the D901.
☎ 02.33.52.77.01
Closed Mon; the first week in Jan; the Feb school holidays. **Car park.**

The restaurant is located at the very tip of La Hague. It's a fishermen's inn and there's a wide fireplace in the old dining room; the new one has enormous windows that give you a marvellous vista of the sea. The owner is a robust character, and it's hardly surprising that this place is popular in high season – appreciative comments from movie and theatre stars decorate the visitors' book. The specialities are fish and meat grilled over an open wood fire and lobster, though you'll also find more intricate dishes like monkfish with leeks in flaky pastry and seafood platters. Menus €15–55; the most expensive one includes lobster and will do for even the largest appetites.

FLAMANVILLE   50340 (28KM SW)

♨ HÔTEL BEL AIR***

It's in the village; take the D4 and you'll find it 300m from the château.
☎ 02.33.04.48.00 ➡ 02.33.04.49.56
€ hotelbelair@aol.com
Closed 20 Dec–10 Jan. **Disabled access. TV.**

Car park.

An attractive hotel in the countryside near the magnificent Flamanville headland. The friendly welcome will instantly make you feel at home. Rooms are comfortable and have a certain charm for €47–70. The larger ones are in the main building, while those in the annexe are small and cosy. They either overlook the fields or the garden.

SAINT-GERMAIN-DES-VAUX   50440 (29KM NW)

|●| RESTAURANT LE MOULIN À VENT

Hameau de Danneville; it's on the D90 Port-Racine road.
☎ 02.33.52.75.20
Closed Sat and weekday evenings Dec–March; Sun evening and Mon, April– Nov. **Car park**.

Booking strongly advised. A gastronomic restaurant high above the bay beside the ruins of an old mill. The large, pleasant, softly-coloured dining room overlooks a little garden full of exotic plants, and beyond to Saint-Martin's cove. Superb cooking using the freshest produce. The good-value €15 menu, served in the week, includes eight oysters. Others go up to €26. À la carte dishes are pricier: boned roast pigeon, duck breast with sage, salmon fillet à l'unilatérale (grilled on one side only) and lobster stew with fresh pasta.

CONDÉ-SUR-NOIREAU   14110

⚙ ≘ |●| HÔTEL-RESTAURANT DU CERF**

18 rue du Chêne; it's 500m from the centre on the Aunay-sur-Odon road.
☎ 02.31.69.40.55 ➡ 02.31.69.78.29
● www.le-cerf.com
Closed Sun evening, Mon; the Feb school holidays; a week in the Nov school holidays. **TV**. **Garden**. **Car park**.

A traditional country hotel which has moved with the times. You'll be greeted like an old friend by Mme Malgrey, a lovely woman who knows all there is to know about the Suisse Normande and can advise you where to go. Her husband's domain is the kitchen, where he specializes in traditional local cooking. The €11 weekday menu – not available on public holidays – is fine as far as it goes but the better dishes are on the more expensive ones (up to €28): warm foie gras salad, boeuf à la ficelle with Camembert sauce, haddock fillet with chicory salad and honey dessert with Pommeau jelly. Doubles €31–37 with shower/wc or with bath; make sure you ask for a room overlooking the garden. Free coffee.

COUTANCES   50200

≘ |●| RELAIS DU VIADUC

25 av. de Verdun (South); it's beside the service station on the outskirts of Coutances on the Granville road.
☎ 02.33.45.02.68 ➡ 02.33.45.69.86
Closed Fri evening; Sat out of season; the first fortnight in July; the second fortnight in Dec. **TV**. **Car park**.

Rooms are basic but pleasant and numbers 4, 6 and 8 have a pretty view of the upper town and the cathedral; doubles are €26 with basin or €29 with shower. Half board costs €30 per person. The restaurant is really a good Relais Routier with all that implies – big helpings of decent grub. Weekday menu €9 and others up to €23. Good dishes include duck foie gras, lemon sole fillets in vanilla butter, sea food and apple terrine with cider caramel. Children's menu €6.

|●| LE RÂTELIER

3-bis rue Georges Clémenceau; it's near the cathedral.
☎ 02.33.45.00.67
Closed Sun and Mon; the Feb school holidays.

A nice little crêperie with a bright and pleasant dining room with a few attractive engravings and decorative plates on the wall. There's a choice of at least fifty different pancakes made with black wheat and almost as many made with rye. Menus €7–15.

MONTMARTIN-SUR-MER   50590 (10KM SW)

⚙ ≘ |●| HÔTELLERIE DU BON VIEUX TEMPS**

7 rue Pierre-des-Touches (Centre); it's opposite the post office.
☎ 02.33.47.54.44 ➡ 02.33.46.27.12
Closed Sun evening and Mon lunchtime out of season; 10 days end of Jan; 10 days end of Oct. **TV**. **Car park**.

This inn, just a couple of kilometres from the sea, is appropriately named. There's a definite feeling of old times in the spacious wood-panelled dining room, hung with paintings. They serve good country cooking using lashings of cream and cider: grilled lobster to order, warm andouille with Pommeau sauce, fillet of salmon stuffed with poached oysters and served with a Benedictine sauce. Weekday lunch menu €11, and others €17–32. Double rooms €24–40 with basin, shower/wc or bath. Everything is very well-run. Free coffee.

REGNÉVILLE-SUR-MER   50590 (10KM SW)

⚙ |●| LE JULES GOMMÈS

It's in the village; take the D20 towards Granville, then

7km further turn onto the D49.
☎ 02.33.45.32.04
Closed Tues and Wed (except Christmas, Easter and Summer holidays); 5 Nov–18 Dec.

The drive along the D49 gives you splendid views of the sea. Part-restaurant, part-*crêperie* and part-Irish pub, this is one of the cosiest places in the area and it has magnificent sea views. The first-class décor includes beautiful furniture and walls covered in gorgeous watercolours of the region. It's run by a nice young couple. They serve terrific *crêpes* and *galettes* – try the *crêpe* flambéed with Calvados. Reasonably priced menus at €11 and €22. The pub is convivial. Free house apéritif.

SAVIGNY   50210 (10KM E)

⚛ 🏠 |●| LA VOISINIÈRE

8 route des Hêtres; it's signposted on the Saint-Lô–Coutances road. Take the D52 or the D380.
☎ 02.33.07.60.32 ➡ 02.33.46.25.28
Closed Sun evening; Mon; Tues lunchtime; the first fortnight in Jan; Feb; a fortnight end Oct to early Nov. **TV. Car park**.

A large, charming building right out in the country. They've planted superb Brazilian plants in the large garden. The four bedrooms, €37 for a double, are attractive and traditionally furnished, and the cooking has quite a reputation locally. Menus at €16–35 list dishes such as *escalope* of salmon with leek fondue and *fricassée* of guineafowl with mushrooms; they also grill meat over the open fire and prepare lots of good seafood. Booking is essential for Sunday lunch. Free house *digestif*.

MESNILBUS (LE)   50490 (12KM NE)

⚛ 🏠 |●| AUBERGE DES BONNES GENS

It's in the village; go to Saint-Sauveur-Lendelin and then take the D53.
☎ 02.33.07.66.85
Closed Sun evening and Mon Oct–Easter; a fortnight in Oct; a fortnight in Jan. **Car park**.

A good little village inn in beautiful countryside. They have four pleasant bedrooms with shower for €31 and a rustic dining room where they serve generous portions of traditional Normandy dishes cooked with plenty of cream. Menus at €14–23: they list dishes such as fish soup, local ham with cider or tripe, *méli-mélo* of kidneys, veal sweetbreads with Pommeau, warm oysters *au gratin* with cider, monkfish stew, fillet of bass cooked in red wine and a Normandy pudding. 10% dis-

count on the room rate (except July–Aug) and free house apéritif with a meal.

TRELLY   50660 (13KM S)

🏠 |●| VERTE CAMPAGNE**

Le Hamel au Chevalier; take the D7 or the D971 south from Coutances.
☎ 02.33.47.65.33 ➡ 02.33.47.38.03
Closed Sun evening except July–Aug; Mon; the first week of Dec; the first fortnight in Jan. **Car park**.

This magnificent old building is swamped with ivy and located in a tiny village deep in the country. The lovely interior features enormous beams and stone walls and there are lots of decorative objects dotted around. The staff are a little formal in their welcome but the cooking is some of the very best you'll taste. Menus €21–35, or a good deal more *à la carte*: roast pigeon with spices, lamb from the salt marshes served with pearl barley, red mullet and artichokes in a warm *vinaigrette*, and, for dessert, *moelleux* of chocolate. The wine list is interesting and prices are reasonable. Very pleasant double rooms with washing facilities are €34 or €58 with shower/wc.

HAMBYE   50450 (20KM SE)

⚛ 🏠 |●| AUBERGE DE L'ABBAYE D'HAMBYE**

route de l'Abbaye
☎ 02.33.61.42.19 ➡ 02.33.61.00.85
Closed Sun evening; Mon; the Feb school holidays; 1–15 Oct. **Car park**.

In a beautiful country setting you'll find this quiet little hotel with charming and comfortable bedrooms – €50 with shower/wc or €53 with bath. The place is meticulously run, and Micheline and Jean Allain welcome you in a friendly, courteous fashion. The menus, from €18 to €49, list appetizing and delicious dishes from different regions: Burgundy or Alsace snails, fish soup, seafood platters, lamb kebabs grilled over the coals and good *crêpes*. 10% discount on the room rate.

DEAUVILLE   14800

⚛ 🏠 LE PATIO**

180 av. de la République (Centre); it's between the beach and the racecourse.
☎ 02.31.88.25.07 ➡ 02.31.88.00.81
Closed 6–27 Jan. **Disabled access. TV**.

The bedrooms in this large, white hotel have recovered their old charm since the refurbishment was completed; some overlook the shaded flower-filled patio. Prices are reasonable for Deauville, with doubles at €32–43 with shower and wc on the landing or €44–68 with bath, TV and phone. There's a gym. 10% discount on the room rate (excluding weekends and school holidays).

≜ HÔTEL LE CHANTILLY**

120 av. de la République (Centre); it's 500m from the train station.
☎ 02.31.88.79.75 ➡ 02.31.88.41.29
📧 hchantilly@aol.com
TV.

This hotel has been renovated throughout and has modern facilities. It radiates a certain charm and it's advisable to book. Doubles with shower/wc or bath are €46–53 – not too bad for Deauville. You'll get a nice welcome from the friendly, chatty proprietress.

FALAISE   14700

⅍ ≜ |O| HÔTEL-RESTAURANT DE LA POSTE**

38 rue Georges-Clémenceau (Centre).
☎ 02.31.90.13.14 ➡ 02.31.90.01.81
Closed Sun evening; Mon; the second fortnight in Nov; 2–20 Jan. **TV**. **Lock-up car park**.

This is a very pleasant inn, the kind of place where you feel immediately at ease. The owners provide good cooking and comfortable, nicely decorated rooms. The chef uses lots of local ingredients and cooks simple traditional dishes such as calf's head *sauce ravigote*, sautéed veal kidneys with morels, tripe kebabs, and monkfish *à la Normande*. Weekday menu €14 and others up to €36. Bedrooms are well-maintained and double-glazed; they go for €44 with shower/wc and €55 with bath. Efficient, friendly service. 10% discount on the room rate and free house apéritif with a meal.

⅍ |O| LA FINE FOURCHETTE

52 rue Georges-Clémenceau (Centre).
☎ 02.31.90.08.59
Closed Tues evening and 16–28 Feb.

Bright, cheerful restaurant. Every year the chef goes off to work with great chefs in different parts of the country, so his cooking is always innovative and dynamic. He picked up the pan-fried zander with orange zest from the *Ritz*; his crab canelloni with cream comes from his days at the *Grand Véfour*. You get a good idea of the cooking even on

the €13 menu and a better one on the others up to €31. Efficient service by genuinely friendly staff. Free *digestif*.

PONT-D'OUILLY   14690 (18KM W)

⅍ ≜ |O| HÔTEL DU COMMERCE**

rue de Falaise (Centre).
☎ 02.31.69.80.16 ➡ 02.31.69.78.08
Closed Sun evening and Mon; mid-Jan to mid-Feb; the first week of Oct. **TV**. **Car park**.

Although it's surrounded by pastureland and little farms, this country inn is in a rather characterless building. The dining room is large and bright, however, and the staff genuinely friendly. Good ingredients are used to make mainly local dishes – try prawns flambéed with *sauce thermidor*, steak with Camembert sauce and veal with apple and cream sauce. Menus €11 (except Sunday) to €30. Quiet comfortable rooms: doubles €31 with washing facilities and €38 with shower/wc or bath. Free apéritif.

⅍ ≜ |O| AUBERGE SAINT-CHRISTOPHE**

How to get there: take the D511 towards Pont-d'Ouilly for 17km then the D23 in the direction of Thury-Harcourt.
☎ 02.31.69.81.23. ➡ 02.31.69.26.58
Closed Sun evening; Mon; the Feb and Nov school holidays; the last fortnight in Aug. **TV**. **Garden**. **Car park**.

Lovely inn with Virginia creeper winding around the façade. The owners make you feel welcome, and the pretty décor gives the place an undeniable charm; when summer comes you can eat out in the garden. The chef serves traditional dishes wtih a touch of something extra: farm-raised chicken with cider, *bœuf à la ficelle*, poached eggs with mussels, beef with Camembert cream, *fondant* with apples, caramel ice-cream. The menus, €17–35, will satisfy any appetite. Staff are welcoming and attentive. The pretty little bedrooms overlook the garden; doubles cost €44 with shower/wc or bath. Half-board is compulsory in summer, at €46 per person. Free coffee and 10% discount on the room rate Sept–March.

FLERS   61100

≜ HÔTEL OASIS**

3 [bis] rue de Paris (Centre).
☎ 02.33.64.95.80 ➡ 02.33.65.97.76
TV. **Pay car park**.

This town was destroyed by bombing in

World War II and had to be rebuilt; it doesn't have the charm of a country inn but behind the ordinary exterior is a little haven. You'll get a nice welcome. The décor verges on the kitsch, but the bedrooms are comfy, well-maintained and good value. Doubles from €21 with washing facilities up to €42 with bath and cable TV. There are also rooms sleeping three or four.

|●| RESTAURANT AU BOUT DE LA RUE

60 rue de la Gare (Southwest).
☎ 02.33.65.31.53 ➡ 02.33.65.46.81
e lebouleux@wanadoo.fr
Closed Sun and public holidays.

The jazzy retro décor works well in this excellent place, and the attentive staff make you feel welcome. The cooking is as imaginative as the surroundings, featuring dishes such as marinated raw salmon with herbs, salad with warm *andouille*, salmon with Camembert cream sauce, steak tartare finely chopped (not minced) and chocolate *moelleux*. *Formule* at €14 and menus €18–22. Good selection of wines at reasonable prices, and interesting coffees from Costa Rica, Ethiopia and Guatemala.

|●| AUBERGE DES VIEILLES PIERRES

Le Buisson Corblin; take the Argentan road and it's 3km from the centre.
☎ 02.33.65.06.96 ➡ 02.33.65.80.72
Closed Mon and Tues; the Feb school holidays; the first 3 weeks in Aug. **Disabled access**. **Car park**.

Bright, attractive restaurant, owned by a team of talented young people who give it an informal, natural feel. The cooking is superb and dishes are skilfully prepared. The brilliant €13 weekday menu lists salt cod with leeks and braised guineafowl with cabbage; the other menus, €19–34, are equally good.

FERRIÈRE-AUX-ÉTANGS (LA)   61450 (10KM S)

|●| AUBERGE DE LA MINE

Le Gué-Plat; take the D18, then the D21 route de Domfront and turn left 1.5km further.
☎ 02.33.66.91.10 ➡ 02.33.96.73.90
Closed Tues, Wed, 2–24 Jan and 16 Aug–3 Sept. **Car park**. **Disabled access**.

Apparently this large ivy-covered brick house was once a miners' canteen – as the nearby slag heaps attest. But times have moved on and this delightful little place with its stylish décor is now a chic, intimate restaurant. The chef is an artist and his dishes are as beautiful to look at as they are delicious to eat: *fricassée* of prawns served in a buckwheat

crêpe with cider butter, pan-fried duck *foie gras* coated with spiced breadcrumbs, caramelized apple on a sponge base. Menus €17–43. Cheerful, friendly staff.

GOUVETS   50420

⚲ |●| RESTAURANT LES BRUYÈRES

It's on the RN175.
☎ 02.33.51.69.82
Closed Sunday. **Car park**. **Disabled access**.

A fairly new building sitting by the side of the road. It's not especially attractive from the outside, but the welcome, the springtime décor and the value for money make it worth stopping. The chef changes the dishes on the menu every week to take account of the fresh produce or the fish that's been landed. The array of pastries is immensely tempting. The lunch menu costs €11, the €12 *formule* comprises and main dish and dessert, and there are other menus €15–21. Free coffee.

GRANVILLE   50400

⚲ LE MICHELET**

5 rue Jules-Michelet; it's on the seashore, near the casino.
☎ 02.33.50.06.55 ➡ 02.33.50.12.25
TV. **Car park**.

Near the sea, a few minutes from the casino and the thalassotherapy centre, this little hotel has an attractive white façade. It's run by a charming young couple who give you a marvellous welcome. The bedrooms are simple, bright and well maintained. Doubles €21 with basin up to €46 bath.

⚲ |●| CRÊPERIE L'ÉCHAUGUETTE

24 rue Saint-Jean; it's in the upper town over the Grand port and the bridge.
☎ 02.33.50.51.87
Closed Tues and Wed out of season; Tues in holiday periods; a fortnight in March; mid-Nov to early Dec.

A special little *crêperie* secreted in the old town's maze of pretty little streets. The unobtrusive staff and cosy atmosphere provide a perfect setting. The very simplest *crêpe* with butter is delicious, as is the *crêpe gratinée* with scallops. A meal costs about €10. Free house Kir Normand.

⚲ |●| RESTAURANT LE PHARE

11 rue du Port; it's on the harbour.
☎ 02.33.50.12.94
Closed Tues and Wed (except July–Aug); 20 Dec–15

Jan. **Disabled access**.

The view of the harbour from the first floor dining room is splendid, and the fish market, just footsteps away, supplies the restaurant with ultra-fresh seafood. The medley of fish with a butter sauce is typical of the freshness of the chef's approach, just like the fish *pot-au-feu*, the stuffed yellow pollack with Cardinal sauce and the seafood platter. The cheapest menu costs €11 (except at weekends): it includes *moules marinière* or 9 oysters with a jug of wine. If you're feeling hungry – and flush – go for the €58 one, which includes a huge lobster. All the desserts are home-made. Free house apéritif.

CHAMPEAUX   50530 (15KM S)

🏂 ☎ |●| HÔTEL LES HERMELLES – RESTAURANT AU MARQUIS DE TOMBELAINE

How to get there: take the D911 that runs along the Channel coast between Carelles and Saint-Jean-le-Thomas.
☎ 02.33.61.85.94 ➡ 02.33.61.21.52
Closed Tues evening and Wed (except July–Aug); Jan; a few days in Feb and Nov. **Disabled access**. **TV**. **Car park**.

You'll find this lively hotel atop the Champeaux cliffs and across the bay from Mont-Saint-Michel. Comfortable double rooms €46–54. The intimate dining room is a successful combination of stonework, panelling and beams. The chef is a disciple of Auge Escoffier, the classic French cook, so the dishes are rich: fillet of cod with hot *andouille*, oysters cooked in cider, lobster Thermidor. Menus €17–41. Half board €47–54 per person. 10% discount on the room rate Nov–March.

HONFLEUR   14600

🏂 ☎ |●| LES CASCADES*

17 pl. Thiers (Centre); it's just off the old harbour.
☎ 02.31.89.05.83 ➡ 02.31.89.32.13
Closed Mon evening and Tues except in the Feb school holidays, Easter and July–Aug, and 11 Nov to Feb. **TV**.

A rather basic hotel in a good location which has been run by the energetic Mme Cogen for a good thirty years. Doubles with shower/wc or bath €31–46. The simple, classic cooking revolves around fresh fish and seafood. Menus €11–28. Half board is compulsory at weekends and in season at €46 per person. Phone reservations not accepted. 10% discount on the room rate.

🏂 ☎ |●| HÔTEL LE BELVÉDÈRE**

36 rue Émile-Renouf (Centre).
☎ 02.31.89.08.13 ➡ 02.31.89.51.40.
Closed Sun evening and Mon 1 Oct–30 March. **TV**.

This hotel is away from the summer hurly-burly of the town centre and the marina; it's a lovely master-craftsman's house with a look-out on the roof, set in a peaceful garden. There are about ten bedrooms, all of which have been completely refurbished – €44–55 with shower or bath. It's often fully booked at the weekend. They serve creative dishes such as pan-fried scallops with artichokes *au gratin*, veal medallions with mushroom and aubergine caviare and a parsley coulis and seafood with vanilla. Menus €10 (out of season), with others €16–30. Free apéritif.

|●| THÉ ET TRADITION

20 pl. Hamelin.
☎ 02.31.89.17.42
Closed evenings Sun–Fri; Tues and Wed from May–Oct (Tues only in season); Dec–Jan.

Tea-room in a splendid building dating from just after the French Revolution. They serve continental or English breakfast from 8.30am, and at lunchtime offer a good selection of dishes such as tomato and basil tart, rabbit turnover, *quiche*, apple tart flambéed with Calvados, and cider ice-cream with Calvados caramel. Menus €15–18, or €24 *à la carte*. There's a splendid dessert and pastry menu (they have an in-house pastry chef) – the Bourbon mousse with egg custard is spectacular. All dishes are made to order.

🏂 |●| LA TORTUE

36 rue de l'Homme-de-bois (Centre); it's near the church of Sainte-Catherine.
☎ 02.31.89.04.93
Closed Tues out of season and Jan.

This is a friendly place – though when they get busy at the weekend the welcome and the speed of service suffer. Other than that, this is an excellent restaurant offering good value in a town where it's not always to be found. Pretty dining room and traditional cuisine: prawn salad, fresh *foie gras* terrine, fillets of sole *gratinée* with saffron, apple turnover with caramel sauce. Mouthwatering menus €16–29, including a vegetarian one. Free coffee.

HOULGATE   14510

🏂 ☎ |●| HOSTELLERIE NORMANDE**

11 rue E.-Deschanel (Centre); it's off la rue des Bains.

☎ 02.31.28.77.77 ➡ 02.31.28.08.07
TV.

This beautiful nineteenth-century building is the oldest hotel in Houlgate and has been thoughtfully renovated. They've decorated it in a pseudo-Baroque style and have considerably improved the rooms without pushing up the prices too much. Doubles €38–76 with shower/wc or €48–92 with bath. You'll get a nice welcome, and there's a lovely garden where you can have a very leisurely breakfast. In the restaurant they serve simple, satisfying dishes like calf's head and *andouille* wih mustard. Weekday menu €10 and up to €21. Free shot of house Calvados, and 10% discount on the room rate excluding weekends and public holidays.

♣ SANTA CECILIA**

25 allées des Alliés; it's 100m from the beach
☎ 02.31.28.71.71 ➡ 02.31.28.51.73
TV.

A pretty villa with an atmosphere dating from the 1880s; the dining room is decorated with finely painted murals. You'll get a wonderful welcome from the owner. The bedrooms are faultless and individually decorated – some have been furnished in period style. Doubles €50 with shower/wc or €60 with bath.

LISIEUX   14100

♣ HÔTEL DE LOURDES**

4 rue au Char (Centre); t's near the town hall and the theatre.
☎ 02.31.31.19.48 ➡ 02.31.31.08.67
Closed Sun in winter. **TV**. **Lock-up car park**.

A hotel that's popular with pilgrims who come to the shrine. The rooms are on three floors (there's a lift) and have all been renovated. They're bright and well maintained and most of them have TV. Doubles €34–38 with shower/wc or €41 with bath. 10% discount for a two-night stay Nov–Easter.

♣ I◉I LA COUPE D'OR**

49 rue Pont-Mortain (Centre).
☎ 02.31.31.16.84 ➡ 02.31.31.35.60
Closed Fri and Sun evening out of season and the first fortnight in Jan. **TV**.

A classic, well-run hotel. The bedrooms are clean, the bathrooms are lovely and the 1970s décor has a certain kitsch appeal. Doubles €44 with shower/wc or bath. Half board, from €43, is compulsory at long weekends. The cooking is fairly classical and

reliable with dishes such as *foie gras* with apples and Pommeau, turbot with ceps and iced soufflé with Calvados. Weekday lunch menu €10 and others up to €29. Free house apéritif.

♣ AZUR HÔTEL***

15 rue au Char (Centre).
☎ 02.31.62.09.14 ➡ 02.31.62.16.06
e resa@azur-hotel.com
TV.

A three-star hotel, recently refurbished. Pleasant well-equipped bedrooms; doubles €46–73 with shower/wc or bath. They provide welcoming little extras like a bathrobe, a hair drier and a chocolate on your pillow to make your stay more relaxing. The breakfast room is very pretty. Free breakfast (usually €8) out of season.

♣ I◉I RESTAURANT AUX ACACIAS

13 rue de la Résistance (Centre).
☎ 02.31.62.10.95
Closed Sun evening and Mon (except for public holidays); the last week in Nov. **Car park**.

An appealing, centrally located restaurant with a cosy décor – spring colours, vases of dried flowers and little ornaments. It's fresh and pleasant, just like the cooking: pan-fried *escalope* of foie gras with apples and Pommeau sauce, pan-fried king prawns with Mediterranean vegetable compote, apple tart with ice-cream. Sadly the desserts are a bit heavy. Menus from €15 (not served Saturday evening) to €44. Efficient service with a smile. Free coffee.

MONT-SAINT-MICHEL (LE)   50170

♣ I◉I HÔTEL DU GUESCLIN**

Grande-Rue.
☎ 02.33.60.14.10 ➡ 02.33.60.45.81
Closed Tues evening, Wed and 5 Nov–31 March.
TV. **Car park**.

A well-maintained hotel offering reasonable value for money when you compare it to the local competition. Comfortable, very clean doubles at €49–69. There are two dining rooms; if you want quick service and *formules express* for €9–11, head for the brasserie downstairs. Upstairs you get a breathtaking view over the bay, and they serve classic regional and fish dishes. Set menus €14–30. The service and the welcome don't always keep up when the tourist hordes descend, however. Free apéritif.

BEAUVOIR   50170 (4KM S)

🏃 🏠 HÔTEL LE GUÉ DE BEAUVOIR*

Route de Pontorson: it's next to the Gué de Beauvoir campsite.
☎ 02.33.60.09.23
Closed 30 Sept to Palm Sunday. **Car park**.

This place is in complete contrast to the dull hotels that proliferate around here: it's a handsome house standing in flower-filled grounds. The bedrooms are simple but have great charm and go for €35 with basin and €42 with shower/wc or bath. Breakfast (€5) is served in the pleasant conservatory. 10% discount April–June.

PONTORSON   50170 (9KM S)

🏃 🏠 🍽 HÔTEL-RESTAURANT LE BRETAGNE**

59 rue Couesnon (Centre); it's on the main street.
☎ 02.33.60.10.55 ➡ 02.33.58.20.54
📧 debretagne@destination.bretagne.com
Closed Mon out of season and 5 Jan–5 Feb. **TV. Car park**.

A lovely 18th-century coaching inn where you'll be welcomed warmly. The bedrooms are all very pleasant and cost €38–61 with shower/wc or bath. A crowd of regulars inhabits the restaurant, where the dishes are prepared with care and the chef uses only fresh ingredients. Classical, local and simple food – oysters gratinées with Camembert, rillettes of mackerel with cucumber coulis, salmon tartare with grapefruit, ox-cheek with a foie gras sauce and fresh noodles, rack of lamb with rosemary, duck breast with spiced pear, nougat with two chocolates and coffee cream. Weekday menu €15 and others up to €43. Very good value. 10% discount on the room rate 1 Oct–30 March.

🏃 🏠 🍽 HÔTEL MONTGOMERY**

13 rue Couesnon.
☎ 02.33.60.00.09 ➡ 02.33.60.37.66
📧 hotel.montgomery@wanadoo.fr
Closed Sat, Sun in low season and 8–22 Feb. **TV. Car park**.

This sixteenth-century house was the seat of the Counts of Montmgomery; nowadays it provides the setting for 32 rooms with exceptional furniture. Doubles with bath or shower/wc €57–72. Buffet breakfast €8. The restaurant is exclusively available for hotel guests and serves dinner only (not Saturday), priced at €15 or à la carte. 10% discount on the room rate Jan–March and 3 Nov–13 Dec.

SERVON   50170 (10KM SE)

🏃 🏠 🍽 AUBERGE DE SERVON**

Centre; on the road from Pontaubault to Pontorson on the D107.
☎ 02.33.60.17.92 ➡ 02.33.60.35.26
Closed Wed except July–15 Sept, Sat lunchtime, mid-Nov to mid-Dec and the Feb school holidays. **TV. Car park**.

A charming hotel with pretty grounds in a tranquil village. The friendly young owners have created a peaceful, tasteful atmosphere. All the rooms have been attractively refurbished and they're named after famous musicians and composers. In the old presbytery there are six lovely doubles and one that sleeps four, or you can stay in the annexe; €44–55 with shower/wc or bath. They serve wonderful Périgord specialities in the pleasant dining room – semi-cooked foie gras and breast of duck with honey – along with seafood stew, salmon with green cabbage and monkfish with vanilla. Menus €15–40. Free house apéritif.

CÉAUX   50220 (15KM E)

🏃 🏠 🍽 HÔTEL-RESTAURANT AU P'TIT QUINQUIN**

Les Forges; take the D275 in the direction of Avranches, then the D43, it's only 2km after the village of Courtils.
☎ 02.33.70.97.20 ➡ 02.33.70.97.42
Closed Sun evening, Mon out of season and 5 Jan–15 Feb. **TV. Car park**.

This place is miles from the hurly-burly, but the road can be noisy – so you'd do well to choose a room at the back. Doubles €32 with washing facilities, €40 with shower/wc or bath. The €11 menu offers good value for money – fish terrine with two sauces, zander with thyme – while another lists half a dozen oysters or the chef's terrine with cognac, followed by salmon with sweet peppers or creamed spinach.10% discount on the room rate 12 Nov to the end of March.

MORTAGNE-AU-PERCHE   61400

🏃 🏠 🍽 HÔTEL DU TRIBUNAL**

4 pl. du Palais (Centre).
☎ 02.33.25.04.77 ➡ 02.33.83.60.83
📧 hotel-du-tribunal@wanadoo.fr
Closed a fortnight Dec/Jan. **TV**.

The oldest parts of this handsome, traditional Percheron house date from the thirteenth century, though most of it is younger than that. The square and the façade have hardly changed since the end of the nineteenth century, when the inn was called "John who laughs, John who weeps", perhaps in reference to the fate of those processed by the law courts which stood next door. Renovations have not diminished the character of the interior and there's a lovely annexe at the back where the rooms are even quieter and overlook a tiny flower-filled courtyard. Doubles €43–73 with shower or bath. The food is very good and features interesting cuisine alongside classical dishes: *croustillant* of black pudding, *millefeuille* of sole and wild mushrooms, smoked salmon and raw marinated salmon, chicken *fricassée* with Camembert, *aumonière Normande*. Menus €14–29. A delightful, quite stylish place where the welcome is so warm. 10% discount on the room rate for a two-night stay Oct–March.

LONGNY-AU-PERCHE 61290 (18KM E)

●I LE MOULIN DE LA FENDERIE

Route de Bizou; from Mortagne, take the D8 through the forest of Rénovaldieu.
☎ 02.33.83.66.98
Closed Mon evening and Tues. **TV**.

A restaurant housed in a superb watermill which has been patiently restored by the two owners. You are pleasantly welcomed and there is a terrace by the water's edge. The cuisine is delicate, perfumed and original, and the chef gives local dishes a touch of exotic spice. Weekday menu €15, and others €25–46.

OUISTREHAM-RIVA-BELLA 14150

⅔ ▲ ●I HÔTEL-RESTAURANT LE NORMANDIE-LE CHALUT**

71 av. Michel-Cabieu; it's near the harbour
☎ 02.31.97.19.57 ➡ 02.31.97.20.07
e hotel@lenormandie.com
Closed Sun evening and Mon from Nov–March; 20 Dec–20 Jan. **TV. Car park**.

Two classic hotels opposite each other, run by an energetic young couple. Both have been tastefully refurbished. Doubles cost €52–58 with shower/wc or bath and telephone. You'll find wonderful food in the stylish dining room. Choose from delicate, refined versions of traditional dishes such as pan-fried duck *foie gras* nougat, peppered John Dory fillet with apples and pears and braised knuckle of veal. The service is a tad

uptight, though. Weekday menu at €15 and others up to €55. 10% discount on the room rate except in high season and public holidays.

●I RESTAURANT LE MÉTROPOLITAIN

1 route de Lion; it's near the post office.
☎ 02.31.97.18.61
Closed Mon evening and Tuesfrom Oct–April, and a week at the end of Nov. **Car park**.

Decorated to look like a 1930s Parisian *métro* station, this place offers local produce and seafood cooked to perfection and attractively presented – try the smoked cod with cider, the grilled turbot with hollandaise sauce, the sole with chives or the cod steak with cider and apple *terrine*. Menus €11–29.

COLLEVILLE-MONTGOMERY 14880 (4.5KM N)

●I RESTAURANT LA FERME SAINT-HUBERT

3 rue de la Mer; take the D35.
☎ 02.31.96.35.41
Closed Sun evening and Mon except in season and on public holidays; 24 Dec–15 Jan. **Disabled access. Car park**.

A large Normandy house where you can lunch either in the cosy rustic dining room or the bright conservatory. Good, traditional food includes monkfish in cider, duck, *fricassée* of kidneys and a monkfish joint with cider and seaweed – enough to satisy the heartiest appetites. Weekday lunch menu €15 or €24–40. Free coffee.

BÉNOUVILLE 14970 (5KM S)

⅔ ▲ ●I HÔTEL-RESTAURANT LA GLYCINE**

In the village; it's on the Ouistreham road, opposite the church.
☎ 02.31.44.61.94 ➡ 02.31.43.67.30
Closed Sun evening out of season; 20 Dec–5 Jan. **TV. Car park. Disabled access**.

This is a beautiful stone building covered in wisteria. Refurbished bedrooms with shower/wc and telephone go for €7; breakfast is €6. The smart-looking restaurant is a perfect setting for good food, imaginatively and carefully prepared – the young chef is in a class of his own. Dishes such as half-lobster with Dublin Bay prawns *au gratin*, duck breast with five peppers and baby vegetables, fillet of sole, pan-fried *foie gras* with balsamic vinegar and *crêpes aumonières* with fresh fruit. Menus €15 (not served Sun), then others €20–36. Children's menu €15. Free *sorbet Normand*.

PONT-L'ÉVÊQUE · 14130

☎ HÔTEL DE FRANCE

1 rue de Geôle (Centre).
☎ 02.31.64.30.44 ➡ 02.31.64.98.90
Closed Christmas and New Year's Day; a fortnight in the Feb school holidays. **TV. Car park**.

A small hotel in a quiet street close to the town centre. The young owners have decorated the rooms in country style, with individuality, personality and charm; some have a view over the fields full of grazing cows. Doubles with basin go for €26 or up to €40 with shower/wc or bath. The breakfast menu changes each day and the jams and preserves are home-made.

|●| RESTAURANT LA POMME D'OR

52 rue Saint-Michel (West); it's near the town hall.
☎ 02.31.64.01.98
Closed Tues except in summer; a week in Oct. **Car park**.

This little bar-restaurant presents a startling array of fresh, plain cooking in its old-fashioned dining room. The affable chef prepares ten different dishes – the star turns are salt pork with lentils, duck with cider and tripe cooked in the local style – and the desserts are excellent too. Set menus €9–14.

⚚ |●| AUBERGE DE LA TOUQUES

pl. de l'Église (Centre); it's 1km from the autoroute exit.
☎ 02.31.64.01.69
Closed Mon evening and Tues except in Aug; 2–26 Jan; 3–26 Dec. **Car park**.

This is a handsome Normandy building on the bank of the Touques river near the village church. The chef prepares all the Norman classics: chicken *Vallée d'Auge* with apples and cream, house tripe, brill with apples, lobster flan, caramelized apple mousse. €15 weekday menu with others €20–31. Attentive service. Free glass of Calvados.

DRUBEC · 14130 (8KM SW)

|●| LA HAIE TONDUE

How to get there; take the D58 and it's 2km south of Beaumont-en-Auge at the N175 junction.
☎ 02.31.64.85.00
Closed Mon evening except public holidays and Aug; Tues except public holidays; a fortnight Jan–Feb. **Car park**.

This restaurant, in a beautiful old house covered in ivy, offers very good food at reasonable prices – in fact, it's the best value for money in the area. The setting is most agreeable, the service is faultless and there's a good wine list. As for the cuisine, it's perfectly prepared, even on the cheapest of the menus (from €19). Dishes change regularly but the following are typical: *compote* of rabbit with onion marmalade, chicken with balsamic vinegar, *paupiettes* of sole with lettuce *coulis*, fillets of duck with apricots. It's popular with coach parties and can get crowded.

SAINT-LÔ · 50000

☎ |●| L'AUBERGE NORMANDE

20 rue de Villedieu (Centre).
☎ 02.33.05.10.89 ➡ 02.33.05.37.26
Closed Mon and Sat lunchtime, a fortnight Dec/Jan and the second fortnight in July.

Élisa and Sylvain Maquaire completely refurbished the inn when they took it over and will make you feel very welcome. Sylvain is a thoughtful, creative cook with a stylish repertoire. Try his perch in *beurre blanc*, the ravioli stuffed with sea bass, the veal fillet with ceps or the duck breast with Pommeau and honey. Weekday lunch menu €13 and others up to €27. Doubles €27 with basin, €30 with shower and shared wc on the landing, and €37 with shower/wc.

☎ ARMORIC HÔTEL*

15–17 rue de la Marne (North).
☎ 02.33.05.61.32 ➡ 02.33.05.12.68
TV.

You'll get a very warm welcome in this quiet, out of the way, good-value hotel – though it can cool off in the hectic tourist season. The comfy bedrooms are tastefully decorated and all have phone and TV (even if some are on the small side); doubles €40 with bath. If you've had a tiring journey, you'll love numbers 16 and 21 which have a whirlpool bath and cost a bit more. Even considering the rather frugal breakfast, this is one of the best places in the Manche.

⚚ |●| LE BISTROT DE PAUL ET ROGER

42 rue du Neubourg (Centre); it's halfway between the town hall and the church of Sainte-Croix.
☎ 02.33.57.19.00
Closed Sun, Mon evening and a fortnight July/Aug.

This little restaurant, the gathering place for Caen football fans, has a genuine bistro look and atmosphere. Food is quick and good. There's lots of home cooking – shepherd's pie, calf's head *gribiche* and *tarte Tatin*. €11 for a main course and dessert, €9 for a main course or €11 for the dish of the day. Free coffee.

📉 |●| LE PÉCHÉ MIGNON

84 rue du Maréchal-Juin (East); go towards Bayeux. It's well away from the town centre.
☎ 02.33.72.23.77 📠 02.33.72.27.58
Closed Mon, Sat lunchtime, Sun evening, 1–10 Jan and 25 July–15 Aug.

The service in this comfortable restaurant is impeccable and the food is marvellous – top-class gourmet cuisine prepared by a talented young chef. Stellar dishes include zander with saffron and cocoa beans, veal sweet-breads with morels and *sabayon* of apples and cinnamon. Menus €14–33. Free house apéritif and 10% discount on the *Normand* and *Gastronomique* menus.

SAINT-VAAST-LA-HOUGUE   50550

🏠 |●| HÔTEL DE FRANCE – RESTAURANT LES FUCHSIAS**

20 rue du Maréchal-Foch; it's less than two minutes from the harbour.
☎ 02.33.54.42.26 📠 02.33.43.46.79
📧 france_fuchsias@wanadoo.fr
Closed Mon and Tues except in July–Aug; Jan; Feb.

Most of the pretty bedrooms overlook a little garden – the fuchsia there gave its name to the restaurant and is a hundred years old. Double rooms €27–76 with basin, shower/wc or bath and there's also a little suite. Half board is compulsory in July–Aug for €41–64. This is also one of the best restaurants in the area. Ask for a table on the veranda, which is decorated with *trompe l'oeil* murals. Weekday menu (€14) and others (€21–51) list delicious dishes: hot oysters with *beurre rouge*, roast brill with crab *coulis* and apples in puff pastry with Calvados cream sauce. Every year in the last ten days of August they give chamber music concerts in the garden.

SÉES   61500

📉 🏠 THE GARDEN HÔTEL**

12 [bis] rue des Ardrillers; it's 400m from the cathedral.
☎ 02.33.27.98.27 📠 02.33.28.90.07
TV. Garden. Car park.

The Australian who used to run the hotel has since gone home, but the English name stuck. Things are remarkably quiet around here; there's a convent next door. As a mark

of respect, none of the bedrooms looks onto it; they overlook a flower garden instead. The basic bedrooms are excellent value for money: doubles €26 with basin and €38 with bath. The staff are perfectly lovely. In keeping with the spiritual atmosphere, there's an amusing collection of religious knick-knacks. 10% discount.

THURY-HARCOURT   14220

📉 🏠 |●| HÔTEL DU VAL D'ORNE

9 route d'Aunay-sur-Odon.
☎ 02.31.79.70.81 📠 02.31.79.16.12
Closed Sat lunchtime in season, Fri evening, Sat out of season and a week in the Feb school holidays.
Car park.

Everyone's image of a country hotel – even down to the ivy clambering up the walls. Courteous welcome and simple, fresh-looking rooms at €20 with basin or €31 with shower/wc or bath. In tune with the style, the rustic dining room has paintings of rural scenes on the wall. Simple, straightforward local dishes: calves' head with *ravigote* sauce and beef cheek with Camembert sauce. Weekday lunch menu €9 and others up to €15. Free house apéritif.

TROUVILLE-SUR-MER   14360

🏠 LA MAISON NORMANDE**

4 pl. de Lattre de Tassigny (Centre).
☎ 02.31.88.12.25 📠 02.31.88.78.79
TV.

Two old shops that have been made into a charming hotel, in a half-timbered house fronted by carved stone columns. Lovely welcome and cosy sitting room; any modernization is in keeping with the style of the building. The rooms are distributed here and there throughout the maze of passageways; doubles €49 with shower up to €58 with en-suite bath.

📉 🏠 LES SABLETTES**

15 rue Paul-Besson (Centre); it's near the casino.
☎ 02.31.88.10.66 📠 02.31.88.59.06
📧 hotelsablettes@post.club-internet.fr
Closed Jan. **TV**.

The frontage of this place is perfect and the hotel itself is as pretty as can be. It has a very cosy atmosphere, almost like a guesthouse, with a comfortable lounge and a lovely old wooden staircase. The whole place is sparklingly clean and it's run by a charming woman. Quiet, stylish doubles are €41 with basin/wc, €53 with shower/wc and €61 with bath – good value for Trouville. 10% discount except during school holidays or weekends.

⚜ |●| RESTAURANT LES MOUETTES

11 rue des Bains (Centre).
☎ 02.31.98.06.97 ➡ 02.31.88.42.22

A fish restaurant in a busy little street. The décor is reminiscent of a Parisian bistro and there are two terraces – one in the shade and one in the sun. Pleasant welcome and enjoyable cooking. Particularly good choices inlcude *fricassée* of whelks, oyster mushrooms with Camembert, haddock with cream sauce, duck fillet with apples and fish *pot-au-feu*. Menus €11–22. Free *digestif*.

|●| RESTAURANT LE CHALUTIER

3 rue de Verdun (Centre); it's opposite the fish market in a steep little street.
☎ 02.31.88.36.39
Closed Tues evening and Wed out of season; Jan.

Cosy little restaurant with a maritime theme that runs through all three tiny dining rooms. They serve fish, seafood and a few good regional specialities. Set menus €14–27. Best to book in season.

⚜ |●| LES VAPEURS

160 bd. Fernand-Moureaux (Centre); it's next to the town hall, opposite the fish market.
☎ 02.31.88.15.24 ➡ 02.31.88.20.58.

This, the best-known brasserie in Trouville, opened in 1927 but has more of a 1950s atmosphere thanks to the neon signs that were added back then. All the American actors who come to the Deauville film festival eat here and the chef, Gérard Bazire, is vigilant in keeping standards high. Try the house specialities – steamed local mussels and freshly cooked prawns. Everything is fresh as can be; after all, the fishing boats land their catch only minutes away. The tripe's particularly good, too, especially with a nice glass of Saumur, and you'll get a genuine welcome – even if you're not a celebrity. There's a set menu at €19 or a meal will cost about €23 *à la carte*. You'll have to book at the weekend. Free *digestif*.

⚜ |●| RESTAURANT LA PETITE AUBERGE

7 rue Carnot (Centre); it's in a little street off pl. du Maréchal-Foch, in front of the casino.
☎ 02.31.88.11.07
Closed Tues and Wed except in July–Aug.

There's no *à la carte* menu and the set

menus, €22–33, change with the season. Given the quality of the food, these represent good value for money, listing such dishes as fish soup, plaice fillet *soufflé* braised in cider and *crêpes* with apples. They also have tasty specialities such as flash-fried salmon with sorrel, *aiguillettes* of duck with roast apples and *andouillette* with grain mustard. Nice welcome and efficient service. Free coffee.

|●| BISTROT LES QUATRE CHATS

8 rue d'Orléans (Centre).
☎ 02.31.88.94.94
Closed Wed and Thurs out of season, and from Nov (after the arrival of the Beaujolais Nouveau) to mid-Dec.

This place is favoured by Parisians and celebrities alike. The dining room has little bistro tables and rose-coloured walls – it's packed with books, postcards, photos and newspapers and has a wonderful percolator sitting on the counter. The chef has spiced up a range of classical dishes by adding a few unexpected flavours – good ones include crab and avocado *pâté*, breast of duck with ginger, *carbonnade flamande* (beef braised in beer) and lamb curry. Their speciality, however, is the *gigot de 7-heures* – a leg of lamb that's cooked for seven hours. Expect to pay €31 *à la carte*.

VIRE   14500

⚜ 🛏 |●| HÔTEL DE FRANCE**

4 rue d'Aignaux (Centre).
☎ 02.31.68.00.35 ➡ 02.31.68.22.65
Closed 20 Dec–15 Jan. **TV.**

A large, plush-looking hotel built of local grey granite. Comfy bedrooms are decorated in rococo style; doubles cost €38–46 with shower/wc or bath. Rooms at the back are quieter and have marvellous views of the wooded valleys. In the restaurant try the local *andouille*, which is made in Vire. Set menus, €9–34, offer classic dishes such as *cassolette* of scampi with pink peppercorns, warm *andouille* in a pastry turnover, *savarin* of fish with a warm chive sauce and veal sweetbreads. Free coffee.

SAINT-GERMAIN-DE-TAILLEVENDE
14500 (5KM S)

|●| L'AUBERGE SAINT-GERMAIN

How to get there: take the D577.
☎ 02.31.68.24.16 ➡ 02.31.68.83.57
✉ le.castel.normand@wanadoo.fr

Closed Sun evening and Mon.

A pretty granite house, typical of the architectural style of the Virois marshes, on the square of a charming village. The dining room is warm and welcoming with its low-slung beams and open fire and you'll experience smiling, speedy service. The chef puts a lot of local dishes on the menu: leek and haddock flan, ham braised in Pommeau, farm-raised chicken *fricassée* in cider and flambéed apple tart. These are attentively prepared and offer good value for money: menus €11–31. They open a small terrace in summer.

BÉNY-BOCAGE (LE)　　14350 (14.5KM N)

⚵ ☗ I●I LE CASTEL NORMAND**

How to get there: take the D577 Caen road for about 9km, then turn left onto the D56 for 2km.

☎ 02.31.68.76.03 ➡ 02.31.68.63.58
e le.castel.normand@wanadoo.fr
Closed Sun evening, Mon, and 1–10 Feb. **TV**. **Car park**.

A lovely stone building with lots of character near the handsome covered market on the town square. Refined rustic décor and first-class service. The cooking is full of flavour and the chef combines unusual ingredients to produce dishes that would flatter a grander establishment: *andouille* with Pommeau, *profiteroles* of prawns, veal sweetbreads in a pastry case, duck breasts with dried fruit, monkfish threaded with smoked bacon, *foie gras* with apples and veal with watercress sauce. Weekday menu €20 and others up to €50. Doubles €49 with shower/wc or bath. 10% discount on the room rate.

Haute-Normandie

27 Eure

76 Seine-Maritime

ANDELYS (LES) 27700

☎ |●| HÔTEL DE NORMANDIE**

1 rue Grande, Le Petit Andely.
☎ 02.32.54.10.52 ➡ 02.32.54.25.84
Closed Wed evening; Thurs; Dec. **Garden**. **TV**. **Car park**.

Run by the same family for several decades, this large hotel, in a traditional Normandy building on the banks of the Seine, is the ideal place for a pleasant wekend. You'll get a warm welcome and enjoy good cooking. Menus, €16–43, list dishes such as monkfish stew with Pommeau, duck with apples, soft-boiled eggs with Roquefort and a Calvados sorbet presented as a variation on the *trou normand* (a shot of Calvados served between courses). Doubles €31 with basin, €49 with shower or bath.

💤 ☎ |●| HÔTEL DE PARIS – RESTAURANT LE CASTELET**

10 av. de la République; from the main square follow the signs to Le Petit Andely.
☎ 02.32.54.06.33 ➡ 02.32.54.65.92
℮ thierry.augustin@libertysurf.fr
Restaurant closed Sun evening and Wed. **TV**. **Garden**. **Car park**.

A young, dynamic owner has taken over this small castle hotel with pointed roofs. Some evenings he plays his accordion or hosts poetry readings. The rooms have been redecorated and are very comfortable. Those over the garden are quieter, though even the ones at the front don't get much traffic noise at night. Doubles €39 with basin, €43–51 with shower/wc or bath. The restaurant,

which has a huge terrace in summer, specializes in good regional cuisine made with fresh ingredients: duck *foie gras* cooked in a cloth, say, or *croustillant* of duck breasts with honey and monkfish *blanquette*. Menus €14–38 – some supplements are expensive. Free apéritif and 10% discount on the room rate Oct–April.

☎ |●| HÔTEL DE LA CHAÎNE D'OR***

27 rue Grande, Le Petit Andely; it's opposite the church on the banks of the Seine.
☎ 02.32.54.00.31 ➡ 02.32.54.05.68
Closed Sun evening; Mon; Tues lunchtime; end Dec to end Jan. **TV**. **Garage**.

This solidly constructed hotel has a quiet riverside location. Built in 1751, it gets its name from the chain that once stretched from the riverbank to the nearby island. Anyone wishing to pass the chain had to pay a toll; it became known as the "Chaîne d'Or" because it made a fortune. The hotel is luxurious but the easy-going staff make you feel welcome. Doubles, €74–120, have all facilities. Those overlooking the Seine are tastefully decorated and classically furnished, while others are more modern. You get a view of the barges on the river from the wonderful dining room where a fire is lit when it gets cold. It's one of the best restaurants in this part of the world, serving dishes such as farm-raised chicken with a vanilla and cinnamon infusion, creamed scallops and Norman oysters with Camembert, roast duck with apples and Pommeau jus, fillet of zander with a coriander and olive infusion with artichoke purée and, for afters, a hot chocolate dessert with jasmin syrup. Menus €25, €39 and €54.

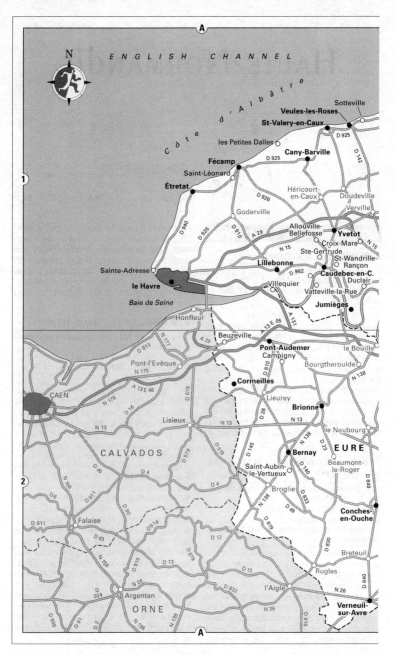

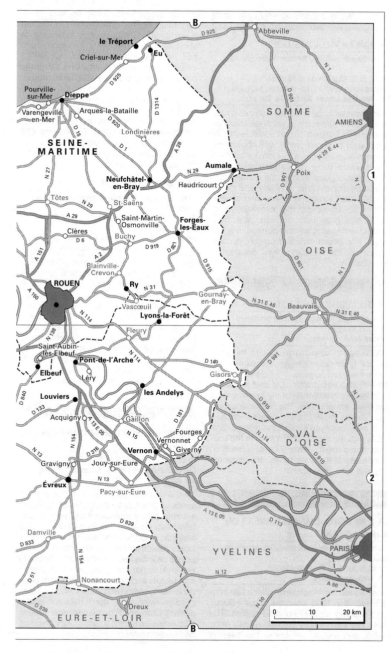

AUMALE   76390

🧍🛏️|●| LA VILLA DES HOUX**

av. du Général-de-Gaulle; the street is opposite the station.
☎ 02.35.93.93.30 ➡ 02.35.93.03.94
Closed Sun evening 15 Oct–15 March; a fortnight in Jan. **Disabled access. Garden. TV. Car park.**

This two-star hotel is run so well that it really deserves three. It's in an Anglo-Norman house with thirteen rooms. Doubles €52– with basin or shower, €69 with shower/wc or bath/wc – one has a four-poster bed and costs a little more. The stylish restaurant, which has a good view of the garden, lists attractive dishes on its weekday €16 menu; there's also a regional menu and others, from €22–45, which offer excellent value: duck *foie gras* with apricots and quail stuffed with *foie gras* and cooked in a salt crust. Half board, €55 per person, is compulsory at the weekend. 10% discount in low season.

VILLERS-HAUDRICOURT   76390 (5KM SW)

🧍|●| L'AUBERGE DE LA MARE-AUX-FÉES

route de Forges; it's on the D8 in the direction of Forges.
☎ 02.35.93.41.79
Closed Sat, Sun and Aug.

You'll need to keep an eye open for this pretty, half-timbered house on the side of the road; there are no signs. It's an authentic little inn, decorated with style and simplicity, and serves traditional family cooking in a convivial atmosphere. The €11 menu gets you starter, main course, cheese, dessert and wine, and you'll sit round a large farm table with the regular customers. In the second dining room, where you eat more conventionally at separate tables, the cheapest menu is €16. Free apéritif.

BERNAY   27300

🧍🛏️|●| HÔTEL D'ANGLETERRE ET DU CHEVAL BLANC*

10 rue du Général-de-Gaulle (West); it's opposite the post office.
☎ 02.32.43.12.59 ➡ 02.32.43.63.26
TV. Lock-up car park.

They added the "Angleterre" after a visit from Edward VII in 1908 when the "Cheval Blanc" had stabling for 300 hundred horses. The hotel has been run by the same family since 1926, and the current owner has been in charge since 1948. Little by little he is upgrading the numerous rooms in this old building which, though it is beginning to show its age, is still lovely. The rooms with baths are the nicest, especially number 23 which is on a corner overlooking the music school garden. Doubles €28 with shower, €36 with bath. Madame does the cooking, using fresh produce to prepare classic dishes like guineafowl with cream and apple sauce, lobster with orange, sole *meunière* and home-made desserts. The €9 and €12 menus are served daily except Sunday, and there are others going up in price to €28. Free apéritif.

🧍🛏️|●| LE LION D'OR**

48 rue du Général-de-Gaulle (Centre); it's in the main street.
☎ 02.32.43.12.06; ☎ restaurant 02.32.44.23.85
➡ 02.32.46.60.58
Restaurant closed Sun evening in winter; Mon lunchtime. **TV. Disabled access. Car park.**

Extremely clean and welcoming hotel with tasteful, if not desperately original, rooms at €36 with shower/wc and €40 with bath. The restaurant, which is under separate management, offers a €10 weekday menu and others at €16–30. The chef's love of his work is clearly evident: all *terrines*, *foie gras*, stocks for sauces and pastries are made on the premises. Specialities include fillet of trout with Camembert, pan-fried oyster mushrooms and fresh fish from Cherbourg or Caen. 10% discount on the room rate 1 Oct–1 June.

SAINT-AUBIN-LE-VERTUEUX   27300 (4KM S)

🧍🛏️|●| L'HOSTELLERIE DU MOULIN FOURET

☎ 02.32.43.19.95 ➡ 02.32.45.55.50
Closed Sun evening and Mon except July and Aug. **Car park.**

This sixteenth-century windmill stands in spacious grounds on the banks of the Charentonne. It's a gorgeous setting, and you can go fly-fishing nearby. François Deduit creates imaginative dishes and sauces using fresh local produce and offers very simple choices alongside more elaborate options. Specialities include hot *foie gras,* pot-roast pigeon with carrots and braised sea bass with pickled lemons, saffron and cumin. And for a surprise to finish with, don't miss the *grand dessert Chauvel*. Top-class service. Menus €20 (weekdays only) to €51. 10% discount on the room rate.

SAINT-QUENTIN-DES-ISLES   27270 (4KM S)

☆ |●| RESTAURANT LA POMMERAIE

It's on the N138.
☎ 02.32.45.28.88 ➡ 02.32.44.69.00
Closed Sun evening and Mon. **Garden**.

This long, low building, just set back from the road, has a Neoclassical façade and stylish décor throughout. The huge, bright dining room overlooks the pretty garden where you can watch the ducks splashing about in the pond – all very relaxing. You'll be served warm appetizers as you wait for your meal. Menus, €13 (weekday lunchtimes) up to €45, list dishes like pan-fried *foie gras* with redcurrants, veal braised with morel cream sauce, steamed lobster and fruit *bavarois*. Free apéritif.

BEAUMONT-LE-ROGER   27170 (17KM E)

☆ |●| LA CALÈCHE

54 rue Saint-Nicolas.
☎ 02.32.45.25.99
Closed Tues evening; Wed; a fortnight in Jan; a fortnight in July.

The chef's creativity extends beyond the kitchen – when there's a festival or a holiday, he decorates the front of the building. His cooking revels in a host of influences, and includes dishes such as *fricassée* of seafood, house *terrine* with onion preserve, chicken fritters with *pousse* spinach and house apple tart. There are a number of fish specialities, and all desserts are cooked on the premises. Menus €12–26. Free coffee.

BRIONNE   27800

☆ 🏠 |●| HÔTEL-RESTAURANT L'AUBERGE DU VIEUX DONJON**

pl. Fremont-des-Essarts (Centre); it's the market square.
☎ 02.32.44.80.62 ➡ 02.32.45.83.23
Closed Sun evening; Mon. **TV. Garden. Car park**.

A large half-timbered inn with rooms overlooking the garden; €45 with shower/wc, €46 with bath. Have breakfast, an apéritif or a meal on the terrace in the courtyard. There's a classic menu at €13 and other, more imaginative, ones for €22–33. Regional dishes include seafood, *foie gras* with onion preserve, seafood platter, duck breast with peaches or apples and beef fillet with morels. Free house apéritif.

☆ 🏠 |●| HÔTEL AQUILON**

9 route de Calleville.

☎ 02.32.44.81.49 ➡ 02.32.44.38.83
Disabled access. TV. Car park.

You'll find this large brick-built building by the 11th-century keep. No two rooms – doubles €46–58 with shower/wc or bath – are alike: those in the main building are lovely (especially number 3, which has a double aspect of the valley and the grounds), and there's a nice mini-suite with sloping ceilings. Family atmosphere and attentive staff. There's a €16 menu, and others listing regional specialities. 10% discount on the room rate.

☆ 🏠 |●| LE LOGIS***

1 pl. Saint-Denis.
☎ 02.32.44.81.73 ➡ 02.32.45.10.92
Closed Sat lunchtime; Sun evening; Mon; a fortnight in the Feb school holidays; 12 days in Aug. **Disabled access. TV. Car park**.

This hotel building has been completely refurbished and offers up-to-date comfort. You'll pay €52 for a double with shower/wc, €60 with bath. The cooking is fresh and full of flavour, and dishes change with the season. There's a weekday menu at €17 (€25 at the weekend), then others €34–54. 10% discount on the room rate Oct–March.

CANY-BARVILLE   76450

☆ |●| L'AUBERGE DE FRANCE

73 rue du Général-de-Gaulle; it's in the main street, beside the bridge across the River Durdent.
☎ 02.35.97.80.10
Closed Sun evening; Tues; ten days in Feb; a fortnight in Sept.

This large white building, which looks more like a café than a restaurant, features seasonally changing dishes – fillet of plaice with *langoustines*, *grenadins* of veal with morels, John Dory with creamed peas. Weekday lunch menu €14, others from €21 up to the *menu dégustation* at €37. Superb wines. Free coffee.

CAUDEBEC-EN-CAUX   76490

☆ 🏠 |●| LE CHEVAL BLANC*

4 pl. René-Coty; from the town hall on the banks of the Seine, go towards Saint-Arnoult-Lillebonne; pl. René-Coty is a few metres further on.
☎ 02.35.96.21.66 ➡ 02.35.95.35.40
Restaurant closed Sun evening out of season; four weeks in Jan–Feb. **TV. Car park**.

Friendly staff, tasty cooking and attractive décor. Pretty, comfortable double rooms go for €31 with basin/wc and up to €45 with bath. Regional dishes are served in the restaurant, like ox tripe *à la normande*, the speciality of the house, *foie gras* with apple jelly, salmon ravioli and *millefeuille* of preserved apricot with vanilla. There's a lunch menu at €12 then others €19–28. The kitchen closes at 9.30pm. 10% discount Sept–June.

SAINTE-GERTRUDE 76490 (3KM N)

|●| RESTAURANT AU RENDEZ-VOUS DES CHASSEURS

It's opposite the church.
☎ 02.35.96.20.30
Closed Wed; Sun evening; the Feb school holidays; 20–30 Aug. **Disabled access**. **Garden**.

This quiet little restaurant nestling between the forest and the small village church serves good regional cooking at prices to suit all pockets. Hunters and travellers have been coming here for more than 150 years. Menus, €15–23, might feature calf's head *sauce gribiche* or roulade of salmon with crayfish, while in winter the chef makes a delicious game stew with pheasant, venison and hare. You can eat out on the terrace in the garden in fine weather.

SAINT-WANDRILLE-RANÇON 76490 (3KM E)

🎋 |●| RESTAURANT LES DEUX COURONNES

☎ 02.35.96.11.44
Closed Sun evening; Mon except public holidays; the Feb school holidays.

A seventeenth-century inn virtually in the precincts of the famous abbey. Tempting dishes include roast crayfish with *herbes de Provence*, *panaché* of kidneys and veal sweetbreads and apple pancakes served with cinnamon ice-cream. There's a €14 *formule* served in the week, and menus €21–26 or, *à la carte*, €31–39. Free coffee.

VILLEQUIER 76490 (4.5KM SW)

♠ |●| HÔTEL DU GRAND SAPIN

quai de Seine; it's on the outskirts of Villequier going towards Caudebec.
☎ 02.35.56.78.73 ➡ 02.35.95.69.27
Closed Tues evening and Wed except July–Aug; 5 Feb–5 March; the second fortnight in Nov. **TV**. **Car park**.

Magnificent Normandy house on the banks of the Seine, with a lovely flower garden featuring an enormous magnolia – unusual in

these parts. Throughout, the place is friendly and cosy, with a new terrace for summer. Double rooms €42; all of them overlook the river. In the large rustic dining room menus go for €19–32; there's also a short €11 menu served during the week and at Saturday lunchtime. Excellent value for money. It's essential to call and make reservations.

VATTEVILLE-LA-RUE 76490 (8KM S)

|●| AUBERGE DU MOULIN

Quesnay: taking the D65 from the bridge over the Brontonne, don't go into Vatteville but take the road to Aizier; the hamlet of Quesnay is on the left.
☎ 02.35.96.10.88
Closed evenings and Wed.

Other villages still have places like this multi-purpose establishment – restaurant-bar-tobacconist's-grocer's – but they're not usually as nice. The dining room offers a rustic setting with checked tablecloths, hunting trophies and wild boars' heads on the wall, and a wide, open fire. The few tables are usually taken. Food here is just what you might expect from the setting – lots of rugged, hearty, traditional dishes at inexpensive prices: go for calf's head with *sauce gribiche*, scallops *à la provençale*, trout *meunière* or *andouillettes*. Menus €10–21.

CONCHES-EN-OUCHE 27190

🎋 ♠ |●| HÔTEL-RESTAURANT LE CYGNE**

36 rue du Val.
☎ 02.32.30.20.60 ➡ 02.32.30.45.73
Restaurant closed Sun evening and Mon.

This hotel has a few comfortable rooms with classic décor. Doubles cost €41 with basin or €49 with bath. The restaurant, meanwhile, is refined but rustic – the ideal backdrop for traditional, well-flavoured cooking. Dishes change with the seasons: try oxtail in jelly, medallions of pork with cider or pineapple with red fruit *coulis*. Good-value menus from €15 to the *menu terroir* at €26. Free apéritif.

CORMEILLES 27260

🎋 |●| LE FLORIDA

21 rue de l'Abaye; it's opposite the town hall.
☎ 02.32.57.80.97
Closed Mon; Sun–Fri evenings; 15 Oct–31 March; 15 June–1 July.

This good little restaurant offers reliable cuisine made with quality local produce, efficient service and a friendly welcome. The *terrine* is excellent, while other specialities include rabbit in cider and veal *escalope normande*. Menus are good value, with a weekday lunch menu for €10, and others at €14 and €20. Free coffee.

DIEPPE 76200

☎ |●| HÔTEL AU GRAND DUQUESNE*

15 pl. Saint-Jacques (Centre); it's in the street opposite the church of Saint-Jacques.
☎ 02.32.14.61.10 ➡ 02.35.94.89.83
TV.

This hotel, which has been entirely refurbished in a tasteful, modern style, has pretty, well-equipped bedrooms. They start at €29 with basin and rise to €39 with bath. The restaurant serves mainly fish and seafood with menus from €11 to €22.

🍴 ☎ LES ARCADES DE LA BOURSE**

1–3 arcades de la Bourse (Centre); it's on the marina.
☎ 02.35.84.14.12 ➡ 02.35.40.22.09
TV.

Modern, comfortable rooms – nothing over the top – some of which have wonderful views over the marina. Doubles €43 with shower/wc, €57 with a view. Free apéritif.

|●| LE BISTROT DU POLLET

23 rue de Tête de Bœuf (Centre); it's on the quai, between Ango bridge and Colbert bridge, opposite the post office.
☎ 02.35.84.68.57
Closed Sun and Mon.

A small, friendly restaurant with a cosy interior – lots of old photographs on the walls and old-fashioned music in the background. It may be wise to book, especially at lunchtime, when it fills up with loyal regulars. Fish is a speciality here – the grilled bass and sea bream are wonderful – along with *foie gras du pêcheur*, a typical Dieppois recipe of marinated, puréed monkfish liver. Prices are more than reasonable, with a lunch menu at €11 during the week, or around €20 *à la carte*.

🍴 |●| À LA MARMITE DIEPPOISE

8 rue Saint-Jean (Centre); it's just by quai Duquesne.
☎ 02.35.84.24.26
Closed Sun and Thurs evenings; Mon.

A classic Dieppoise restaurant serving fine food. Menus revolve around fish dishes pre-

pared with cream; their superb signature dish is *marmite diéppoise*, a tasty stew of monkfish, ling, brill, sole and scallops, with mussles and crayfish, all cooked together in a pan. Menus €16–37. Free house apéritif.

POURVILLE-SUR-MER 76550 (4.5KM W)

|●| L'HUÎTRIÈRE

rue du 19-Août; it's west of Dieppe on the seashore.
☎ 02.35.84.36.20 ➡ 02.35.84.38.09
Closed end Sept to Easter. **Car park**.

Service from 10am to approximately 8pm. A seafood restaurant above the store where oysters are sold direct from the oyster beds. It specializes in oysters, of course, along with clams, whelks, winkles, cockles and *crêpes*. The décor is appealing, with sea-blue walls, oyster baskets hung from the ceiling and an ancient diving suit in the corner, and the bay windows open right onto the beach. In summer, they set up a huge terrace. Though the food is good, prices are high for such a simple place.

VARENGEVILLE-SUR-MER 76119 (8KM SW)

☎ |●| HÔTEL-RESTAURANT LA TERRASSE**

route de Vasterival.
☎ 02.35.85.12.54 ➡ 02.35.85.11.70
📧 françois.delafontaine@wanadoo.fr
Closed mid-Oct to mid-March. **Car park**.

This cosy family hotel snuggling among the pine trees is a regular favourite with British visitors. It's in a remarkable location on the cliffs and the veranda is a superb spot to admire the Channel over a drink. The 22 attractive rooms, all with shower/wc or bath, go for €45–49. The restaurant serves lots of fish; for a tasty, light meal try the house *terrine* with dried fruit, the scallops marinated in herbs and the apple pancake. Menus €13–26. Because of its popularity, management often expects guests to stay half-board.

ARQUES-LA BATAILLE 76880 (9KM SE)

🍴 ☎ LE MANOIR D'ARCHELLES

Archelles; it's on the D1, Neuchâtel road, on the edge of town, next to *l'Auberge d'Archelles*.
☎ 02.35.85.50.16
TV. Car park.

This stunning sixteenth-century manor house, built of a mosaic of brick and flint stones, offers doubles for €28–31 with shower/wc, €39–46 with bath; they also have a suite that sleeps four. The décor is more rustic than chic but that doesn't diminish its charm. The rooms in the fortified gatehouse, reached by a spiral stone staircase, are particularly attractive, giving good views of the château. Have a wander round the orchard and carefully tended vegetable garden. 5% discount on the room rate.

🔆 |●| L'AUBERGE D'ARCHELLES

Archelles; it's on the D1, Neuchâtel road, on the edge of town, next to *Le Manoir* (above).
☎ 02.35.83.40.51
Closed Fri; Sat lunchtime; Sun evening; the third week in Feb; a fortnight in Aug/Sept. **Car park**.

This good-value restaurant, owned by the same people as *Le Manoir*, is housed in beautifully converted old stables. The cuisine is as attractive as the setting, featuring regional and gastronomic dishes on the superb €14 menu and other excellent menus from €18–32. Try crab *briquette* with spices, caramelized quail salad, cod charlotte with herbs or the house *foie gras*. Free coffee.

ELBEUF 76500

🛏 |●| LE SQUARIUM*

25 rue Pierre-Brossolette (Southeast); it's opposite the cinema.
☎ 02.35.81.10.52
Closed Sun and Aug. **Car park**.

It's advisable to book if you're planning on coming to this cosy little hotel-bar. The spacious bedrooms are freshly painted and well-maintained, proving good value for money; doubles cost €23 with basin, €31 with shower and €39 with bath. The restaurant is open for lunch, offering *à la carte* and two set menus at €9 and €12.

🔆 🛏 |●| LE PROGRÈS**

47 rue Henry (Centre); it's almost opposite the town hall.
☎ and ➡ 02.35.78.42.67
Closed Sun and Fri evening. **TV**.

A quiet hotel, nicely situated between the Seine and the shopping streets. Prices are good; doubles go for €25 with basin/wc, €34 with bath. There's a pleasant brasserie offering menus from €9; if that's not your scene, try the simple, regional dishes in the prettily decorated dining room. Menus at €12 and €16–30. One free breakfast per double room, or coffee after a meal.

|●| RESTAURANT LE JARDIN SAINT-LOUIS

24 rue Proudhon (Centre); the entrance is on pl. de la République.
☎ 02.35.77.63.22
Closed Sun evening. **Car park**.

The friendly people who run this restaurant will make you feel very welcome before plying you with classic dishes such as *tartare* of salmon with fresh herbs, roast *langoustine* with lemon butter or braised beef marrow with sea salt – try the local speciality, *caille aux monstrueux d'Elbeuf*, quail with leeks. Weekday lunch menu €9, others up to €20, or around €23 *à la carte*.

SAINT-AUBIN-LÈS-ELBEUF 76410 (2KM N)

🔆 🛏 HÔTEL DU CHÂTEAU BLANC**

65 rue Jean-Jaurès; cross the bridge over the Seine and it's on the corner of the first street on the right.
☎ and ➡ 02.35.77.10.53
Closed Sun afternoon. **TV**. **Garden**. **Car park**.

A large house, which despite being rather noisy in the morning on account of the nearby main road, has plenty to recommend it. There's a walled garden with parking space and a large, pleasant lounge where you can relax and read the paper. The spacious rooms are double-glazed and very well maintained; €34 with shower/wc and €37 with bath. There's no restaurant, but they'll rustle you up snack food on request. 10% discount Feb–April.

ÉTRETAT 76790

🛏 HÔTEL D'ANGLETERRE

35 av. George-V (Centre); it's 100m from the sea on the Le Havre road that starts at the tourist office.
☎ 02.35.27.01.34 ➡ 02.35.25.76.28

A clean, welcoming, reasonably priced hotel, well away from the touristy part of town – in other words, something of a find. The reception is in the Hôtel de la Poste in the same street. Doubles €37 with shower/wc, €43 with bath/wc. Buffet breakfast.

🛏 |●| L'ESCALE**

pl. Foch (Centre); it's opposite the old market.
☎ 02.35.27.03.69 ➡ 02.35.28.05.86
TV.

This completely refurbished hotel-brasserie is a really nice place. The wood-panelled bedrooms are a bit small but pleasant enough; doubles with shower/wc go for €45. The lively ground-floor restaurant-brasserie serves simple dishes – mussels and chips, omelettes, salads, pizzas and *crêpes*, along with a few gourmet dishes, with menus from

€12. Sit on the terrace and watch the world hurry by in the square.

🔒 |O| HÔTEL LE CORSAIRE**

rue du Général-Leclerc.
☎ 02.35.10.38.90 ➡ 02.35.28.89.74
TV.

One of the few hotels on the seafront, with a pretty red-brick façade and a magnificent view of the famous cliffs. The modern bedrooms are all decorated in different styles, and range from €61 with shower/wc to €68–90 with bath; you'll pay most for a sea view. The restaurant, which has a terrace, also has good sea and cliff views, and offers simple, unfussy food. They specialize in seafood and fish. Menus €12–30.

|O| L'HUITRIÈRE

rue Traz-Perrier; it's on the seafront, towards Aval cliffs.
☎ 02.35.27.02.82

An extraordinary circular dining room with a sensational panoramic view over the beaches and cliffs. They specialize in seafood and fish and take great care over the preparation of each dish. The €15 menu – also served at the weekend – proves very good value, listing dishes such as mussels *marinière*, fillet of cod with tomato and basil and *tarte Tatin*. Other menus go for €23–37; you'll spend around €27 *à la carte*. Every diner receives a complimentary *trou normand* – a shot of Calvados – between courses.

🍴 |O| RESTAURANT LE GALION

bd. René-Coty (Centre).
☎ 02.35.29.48.74 ➡ 02.35.29.74.48
Closed Tues evening; Wed except during Easter school holidays and summer; 20 Dec–20 Feb.

Cosy restaurant with seventeenth-century décor – enormous fireplace, little tinted window panes, old beams – and high-class service. The €19 menu is beautifully balanced, listing velvety smooth fish soup, escalope of salmon with Muscadet and oysters poached in champagne. Other menus €27–36. Free coffee.

EU   76260

🍴 🔒 |O| HÔTEL-RESTAURANT MAINE**

av. de la Gare.
☎ 02.35.86.16.64 ➡ 02.35.50.86.25
@ hotelmaine@aol.com
Restaurant closed Sun evening except public holiday weekends and 16 Aug–8 Sept. **TV**. **Car park**.

Bright and peaceful establishment in a master-craftsman's house opposite the old station. Though some have been refurbished more recently than others, the bedrooms have all facilities, with en-suite bathrooms, TV and telephones. Doubles with shower/wc cost €48, with bath €51. Half board, obligatory over holiday weekends from Easter to September, costs €51 per person, which, given the quality of the cuisine, is good value. Indeed, it's worth coming just for a meal. The *Maine* has been serving food since 1867, and the dining room is an exceptional example of Art Nouveau. Dishes are modern yet firmly rooted in local and traditional cuisine. The weekday menu costs €14 with two others – one for fish and the other for meat – at €22. Free apéritif.

ÉVREUX   27000

🍴 🔒 |O| HÔTEL-RESTAURANT DE LA BICHE**

9 rue Joséphine, pl. Saint-Taurin (West).
☎ 02.32.38.66.00. ➡ 02.32.33.54.05
Restaurant closed Sun and July–Aug. **Disabled access**. **TV**. **Car park**.

An amazing hotel-restaurant on the edge of an extremely pretty square. The building – where Louis Malle shot his film *Le Voleur* – started its days as the hunting lodge of François I before becoming the most sophisticated brothel in the area. It's built around an interior patio and has a gloriously retro feel. The bedrooms, which lead off a gallery, go for €23 with basin, €38 with shower/wc and €41 with bath. You'll either get a view of place Saint-Taurin, which is very quiet in the evening, or the river. The first-rate restaurant serves imaginative home cooking with dishes such as marrowbones with sea salt on toast, Portuguese *aïoli* with fish *pot-au-feu* or flambéed veal kidneys and sweetbreads. Menus €12–22 or *à la carte*. 10% discount on the room rate.

|O| RESTAURANT LA CROIX D'OR

3 rue Joséphine (West).
☎ 02.32.33.06.07
Closed 24 Dec–1 Jan.

Fine food intelligently prepared by people who care about what they do. The chef regularly makes the trip to the Paris food markets so the ingredients are super-fresh, and you get none of the pretentious mini-portions typical of nouvelle cuisine. In the large, bright dining room, waiters dressed as sailors race between tables that are often taken up by locals. The signature dishes are crayfish *clafoutis* and *bouillabaisse*, but you might want to take advantage of the superb weekday lunch menu instead; for €10, you can choose from genuine innovations like *terrine* of half-cooked salmon with a *coulis* of tomato, olives and basil, *clafoutis* with asparagus and langoustines, fresh shellfish or game in season. Other equally impressive menus range from €13 to €30. It's a shame that the terrace is on such a noisy road.

GRAVIGNY   27930 (4KM N)

|●| LE SAINT-NICOLAS

38 av. Aristide-Briand (Centre); it's on the D155 towards Louviers, on the right.
☎ 02.32.38.35.15 ➡ 02.32.31.19.34
Closed Aug. **Car park**.

This unobtrusive house conceals a number of lovely little dining rooms decorated in a simple, sophisticated style – intimate ones for candlelit dinners, larger ones for lively groups and a terrace for outside dining. Chef Claude Sauvant uses only the best ingredients he can find on the market. The boned pig's trotters with truffles are delicious, as are the perch fillets with Saint-Nicolas butter and the warm oysters with cream and shallot sauce. Superb wine list. Menus from €14.

JOUY-SUR-EURE   27120 (12KM E)

|●| LE RELAIS DU GUESCLIN

pl. de l'Église; take the N13 in the direction of Pacy-sur-Eure, then the D57.
☎ 02.32.36.62.75
Closed evenings except for reservations; Wed; Aug. **Car park**.

A little Normandy inn with a church on one side and fields on the other. Peace and quiet are guaranteed, so you can have an undisturbed lunch outside. The daily *formule*, €14, gets you a main course plus starter or dessert, and there are other menus up to €29; dishes include *bonhomme normand*, foie gras, ox kidneys and warm tarts – the best of Normandy cuisine and good dry cider to boot.

FÉCAMP   76400

🍴 🛏 |●| LE MARTIN

18 pl. Saint-Étienne (Centre); it's next to the church.
☎ 02.35.28.23.82 ➡ 02.35.28.61.21
Hotel closed first fortnight in March; last fortnight in

Sept. **Restaurant closed** Sun evening and Mon except public holidays. **TV**.

A good little restaurant that resolutely ignores the whims of fashion. You'll get typical Normandy dishes and classic cuisine here, served in a rustic dining room with exposed beams. The €12 menu is good value, but it's not available on Saturday evening, Sunday or public holidays. Others range from €14 to €42. The hotel rooms – €24 with basin and €28 with shower – are rudimentary, but good enough if you're stuck for a bed. 10% discount on the room rate Sept–June.

🍴 🛏 HÔTEL DE LA PLAGE**

87 rue de la Plage (Centre); it's 30m from the beach.
☎ 02.35.29.76.51 ➡ 02.35.28.68.30
TV. **Disabled access**. **Garage**.

A charming, well-equipped hotel very close to the beach. Most rooms have been refurbished – doubles go for €35 with shower or €45 with shower/wc or bath. Breakfast, €5, is served in an attractive room, and you'll get a good-natured welcome. 10% discount Nov–April except weekends and public holidays.

🛏 |●| HÔTEL D'ANGLETERRE**

93 rue de la Plage (Centre); it's near the casino.
☎ 02.35.28.01.60 ➡ 02.35.28.62.95
Closed Christmas. **TV**. **Car park**.

This hotel has a variety of bright and colourful rooms in the main building, and decent rooms in the annexe. Rates range from €38–55 – the cheaper ones are those which have yet to be done up – with some family rooms for €49–67. The whole place has a family-friendly feel, and the youthful staff make everyone feel welcome. There's a pub-style restaurant where you can get a meal for about €12.

|●| LE VICOMTÉ

4 rue du Président-Coty; it's 50m from the port, behind the Palais Bénédictine.
☎ 02.35.28.47.63
Closed Wed evening; Sun; public holidays; a fortnight in Aug; a fortnight Dec–Jan.

A very welcoming, and rather unusual, retro bistro with checked tablecloths and posters from the *Petit Journal* adorning the walls. They serve just one set menu at €14, but the dishes – regional cooking, based on fresh produce – change every day. Excellent value and impeccable service.

🍴 |●| LE MARITIME**

2 pl. Nicolas-Selles; it's across from the marina.

☎ 02.35.28.21.71

Very good seafood restaurant with a jaunty white and blue frontage. It's been afloat for a number of years, and has definitely found its sea legs: climb aboard with confidence for seafood platters, *blanquette* of salt cod, fish paella and good meat dishes. Menus €15–32. Take-away available. Free coffee.

SAINT-LÉONARD — 76400 (2KM S)

☎ |⦿| AUBERGE DE LA ROUGE**

route du Havre; it's on the D925.
☎ 02.35.28.07.59. ➡ 02.35.28.70.55
e auberge.rouge@wanadoo.fr
Closed Sun evening; Mon; and three weeks Jan–Feb. **Disabled access. Garden. TV. Car park.**

This large, delightful inn is just over a hundred years old, and the new owners are carrying on in the tradition laid down by their predecessors. It's a high-quality establishment where you can eat beside the fountain in the garden and listen to the birds. Dishes change with the seasons: try grilled sole in oyster stock, duck *à la rouennaise*, frogs' legs in a pastry turnover and *crêpes soufflés*. Menus start at €16 (except Sun lunch), with others €25–46. There are also a few comfortable bedrooms, €53 for a double, but they look over the road and are a tad noisy.

FORGES-LES-EAUX — 76440

☎ LE CONTINENTAL***

110 av. des Sources; it's near the casino.
☎ 02.32.89.50.50 ➡ 02.35.90.26.14
TV. Car park.

An impressive half-timbered building that's been thoroughly renovated. With its large foyer and balconies it still has the nicely old-fashioned atmosphere of old casino hotels, and offers well-equipped bedrooms for between €60 and €64. Guests can use the nearby Club Med facilities by arrangement.

SAINT-MARTIN-OSMONVILLE — 76680 (23KM W)

🎿 |⦿| AUBERGE DE LA VARENNE

2 route de la Libération; take the D919 to Buchy, then the D41.
☎ 02.35.34.13.80
Closed Sun evening and Mon Nov–March; Sun evening only March–Nov.

They stick firmly to traditional, local cooking in this pleasant roadside inn – try the *cassolette* of fresh scallops with cream, the black pudding served in a pancake or the Calvados *soufflé*. Weekday menu at €16 and others €19–39. With very attentive service and a warm welcome, it's a good place to eat after visiting the old market in Buchy. There's an open fire in the winter, and a lovely terrace in good weather. Free coffee.

HAVRE (LE) — 76600

SEE MAP OVERLEAF

☎ |⦿| HÔTEL LE MONACO

16 rue de Paris. **MAP B4-3**
☎ 02.35.42.21.01 ➡ 02.35.42.01.01
TV. Car park.

This is one of the nearest hotels to the ferry, and it's pretty well-maintained. Doubles go for €23 with washing facilities and €31–38 with shower or bath. There's also a brasserie serving menus between €10 and €14 and a restaurant where specialities include smoked salmon and *foie gras*; menus here go for €18–33.

🎿 ☎ HÔTEL-CELTIC**

106 rue Voltaire. **MAP B3-1**
☎ 02.35.42.39.77 ➡ 02.35.21.67.65
Closed Christmas school holidays. **TV. Car park.**

Delightfully located hotel with views of the Niemeyer theatre and the merchant port. Double rooms are brightly painted, with modern bathrooms; those with shower go for €31; with shower/wc or with bath they're €43. 10% discount on the room rate.

☎ LE PETIT VATEL**

8 rue Louis Brindeau. **MAP A3-4**
☎ 02.35.41.72.07 ➡ 02.35.21.37.86
e hotel.celtic@wanadoo.fr
Closed Christmas school holidays.

A central hotel where the brightly painted, clean rooms have modern facilities and bathrooms; €37 with shower, €41 with shower/wc and €46 with bath. There's nothing special about the view but the hotel offers very good value.

|⦿| RESTAURANT LE LYONNAIS

7 rue de Bretagne. **MAP C3-12**
☎ 02.35.22.07.31
Closed Sat lunchtime; Sun; a fortnight in mid-July.

Successfully recreating the atmosphere of a typical Lyonnais bistro, this place has a copper chimney breast, checkerboard floor tiles and brick walls. Dishes include *gâteau*

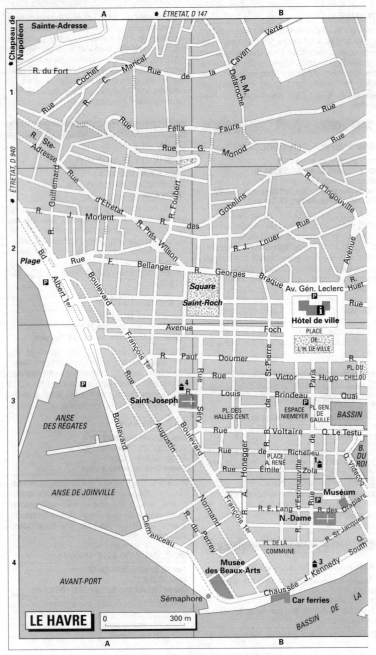

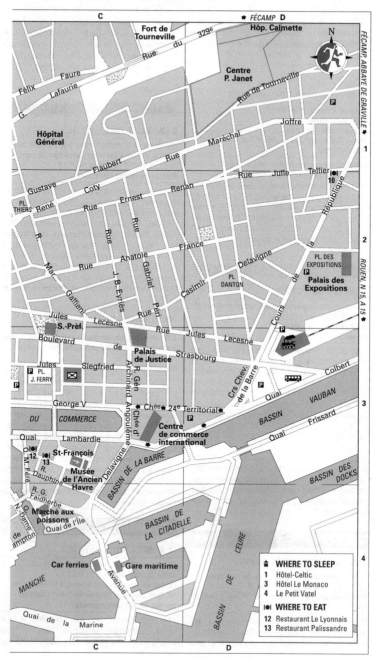

of chicken livers and *andouillette lyonnaise* with boiled potatoes, though the warm upside-down apple tart is a more local dish. The €10 menu is served during the week only, but the others, from €15–20, are good too.

🎍 |●| RESTAURANT PALISSANDRE

33 rue de Bretagne. **MAP C3-13**
☎ 02.35.21.69.00
✉ olivierboutron@aol.com
Closed Wed evening; Sat lunchtime; Sun; one week in Feb; 15–30 Aug.

Great food served in a sober, dark-wood interior reminiscent of a boat. Try the fish with cider or the mussels; if seafood doesn't tempt you, go for the *andouillette* or one of the meat dishes. Menus start at €13, which is very good value for the old town, and go all the way up to €23. The "Oh! le pressé" menu, €10, is served in twenty minutes flat. Free Kir.

SAINTE-ADRESSE   76310 (2KM NW)

🎍 |●| LES TROIS PICS

promenade des Régates; it's at the northernmost end of Le Havre beach.
☎ and ☛ 02.35.48.20.60.
Closed Sun and Mon out of season; Dec; Jan.

This place, standing on the quay, looks for all the world like a liner in dry dock. The large wooden dining room has a wonderful, panoramic view of the mouth of the Seine and the maritime décor is imaginative and refined. From the ship's rail you can see Deauville, ten miles off in the distance. They do very decent brasserie cooking: oysters cooked in cider, perhaps, or fish *à l'andouille*. Menus start at €12 (weekdays), rising to €18 or €29; *à la carte* will set you back €29 per head. Have a drink on the terrace in summer – when dusk falls and the lights are turned on across the bay, you can almost imagine you're out at sea. Free house apéritif.

JUMIÈGES   76480

🎍 🏠 |●| AUBERGE DES RUINES

pl. de la Mairie (Centre); it's opposite the monastery.
☎ 02.35.37.24.05 ☛ 02.35.37.87.34
Closed Sun and Tues evenings; Wed; 25 Aug–5 Sept; 20 Dec–5 Jan. **Car park**.

The best restaurant in town, where you can snuggle up in front of the fire in winter or relax under the awning in summer. If you

regard yourself as a foodie, try the *émincé* of snails with garlic, courgettes *en anchoïade,* pigeon with vanilla or oyster and smoked salmon *tartare.* The weekday menu goes for €14, with others €21–41. Four basic bedrooms with basin only at €26. Free coffee.

DUCLAIR   76480 (9KM NW)

🏠 |●| HÔTEL DE LA POSTE**

286 quai de La Libération (Centre); take the D982, follow the river, and you'll see it just across from the ferry.
☎ 02.35.37.50.04 ☛ 02.35.37.39.19
Restaurant closed Sun evening.

A simple, welcoming place that deserves its excellent reputation. Comfortable doubles with shower/wc are €32, or €43 with bath/wc; they all have a lovely view over the water. You also get wonderful views from the two dining rooms. You're in duck-rearing country here – indeed, despite Rouen's claims to the contrary, this is the place that invented the recipe for pressed duck *de Duclair,* which is the house speciality. Menus €12–31.

|●| RESTAURANT AU VAL DE SEINE

380 quai de la Libération (Centre); take the D982, follow the river, and you'll see it just across from the ferry.
☎ 02.35.37.99.88
Closed Mon evening; Tues; Oct.

The décor at this high-class *crêperie* is simple and pleasant, if ordinary, with a panoramic view of the Seine and the ferries from the first-floor dining room. As well as the *crêpes,* you can also enjoy carefully prepared fish dishes – warm salad of queen scallops, mussels with raspberry vinegar, John Dory with basil, seafood platter – all at very reasonable prices, with menus from €11 to €24. They're open all day on Sunday, when they serve cakes as well as savoury snacks.

LILLEBONNE   76170

🎍 🏠 |●| LA P'TITE AUBERGE

20 rue du Havre (Centre); it's behind the church.
☎ 02.35.38.00.59 ☛ 02.35.38.57.33
Closed Sat lunchtime; Sun evening; a fortnight in the Feb school holidays; three weeks in Aug. **Disabled access. TV. Car park opposite.**

This hotel, under new management, is in a large, half-timbered house. Most of the bright rooms have had new bathrooms fitted; doubles go for €28 with basin (the wc is along the landing) and €42 for shower/wc or bath. The rustic dining room is a good place to eat traditional cuisine such as house *foie gras*, veal sweetbreads *Rossini* and chocolate *moelleux*, with a lunch menu for €11 and others €14–24. There's a shady terrace open during warm weather. Free coffee.

LOUVIERS   27400

⅍ 🏠 I●I LE PRÉ-SAINT-GERMAIN***

7 rue Saint-Germain (Centre); it's northeast of pl. Ernest-Thorel.
☎ 02.32.40.48.48 ➡ 02.32.50.75.60
Bistro closed Sun evening **Restaurant closed** Sat lunchtime and Sun evening. **Disabled access**. **TV**. **Car park**.

Built in the middle of an old orchard, this Neoclassical-style hotel boasts all the facilities you should expect from a three-star establishment, with doubles at €75–90 with bath/wc. You can be sure of eating well, too, with dishes such as *fricassée* of lobster and King prawns with curry and coconut, duck with apple brandy and cinnamon and a fine apple tart with vanilla ice-cream flambéed in Calvados. Menus €30–53, with a bistro *formule* at €14. Nice terrace in summer. Free apéritif.

⅍ I●I RESTAURANT LE JARDIN DE BIGARD

39–41 rue du Quai; it's on the corner of rue du Coq.
☎ 02.32.40.02.45
Closed Wed and Sun evenings.

A centrally located, unpretentious restaurant with a bright, airy dining room offering simple but carefully prepared dishes at reasonable prices. The weekday lunch menu costs €9, and there are others from €12 to €25. Specialities include scallops in cider, calf's head *sauce gribiche*, fillet of trout with Camembert and cockerel in cider. Free house apéritif with dinner.

⅍ I●I LE CLOS NORMAND

rue de la Gare–chaussée du Vexin (Northeast); cross the Eure by rue des Anciens-Combattants d'AFN and it's right there.
☎ 02.32.40.03.56 ➡ 02.32.40.61.24
Closed Mon and four weeks July–Aug.

Rustic décor and traditional, though imaginative, cooking. They do a number of fish specialities and lots of dishes using cream and locally grown produce – try the trout with

Camembert, duck with grapes or the salmon in cream sauce, finishing off with a *charlotte* of apples and Calvados. Menu €12 during the week, with others at €15–22. Free house apéritif.

ACQUIGNY   27400 (5KM S)

⅍ I●I LA CHAUMIÈRE

15 rue Aristide-Briand (Centre); it's opposite the town hall.
☎ 02.32.50.20.54
Closed Tues and Wed. **Car park**.

A really nice restaurant with rustic décor and a relaxed atmosphere. The chef produces new dishes every day, but typical offerings might be chicken liver *terrine*, ceps on toast, veal chops *à la normande*, game in season and chocolate *terrine*. When it's chilly, they grill meat and fish over the fire. No menus, but the *à la carte* prices are reasonable at €17–46. There's a very good selection of wines available by the glass. Free *digestif*.

LÉRY   27690 (7KM NE)

I●I LA FONTAINE SAINT-GABRIEL

2 pl. de l'Église.
☎ 02.32.59.09.39 📧 a.fontaine@wanadoo.fr
Closed Mon except public holidays and in summer. **Car park**.

A delightful, tree-shaded square, a pretty Romanesque church and the banks of the Eure just a stone's throw away (great for post-prandial strolls) – all in all a quite charming setting for this welcoming restaurant. Madame runs the dining room, while Monsieur, the chef, produces exquisite food such as *foie gras* in a cloth, roast duck with thyme cream and home-baked Vacherin pastry. Menus €20–28 and some *à la carte* options.

PONT-DE-L'ARCHE   27340 (11KM N)

⅍ 🏠 HÔTEL DE LA TOUR**

41 quai Foch (Centre); take the N15 over the bridge and it's on the left on the Eure riverbank.
☎ 02.35.23.00.99 ➡ 02.35.23.46.22
TV. **Garden**. **Car park**.

The old façade is perfectly in keeping with the pretty houses along the quay, but the interior has been expertly refurbished by the charming owners, Monsieur and Madame Helouard. Everything about it – the colours, the décor, the little details that make for a comfortable stay and the friendly welcome – gives this place a quality not normally found in a hotel in this category. If they're not full, you can tour the empty rooms and choose the one you want. Doubles cost €50, and whether you opt for one overlooking the ramparts and the church of Notre-Dame-des-Arts or one with a view of the lush riverbank, they're all equally quiet. One free breakfast per double room.

LYONS-LA-FORÊT 27480

🕉 🏠 |●| HOSTELLERIE DU DOMAINE SAINT-PAUL**

It's 800m out of the village on the D321.
☎ 02.32.49.60.57 ➡ 02.32.49.56.05
📧 domaine-saint-paul@liberty.fr
Closed 2 Nov–1 April. **Swimming pool**. **TV**. **Car park**.

A substantial house, built as a hunting lodge in 1815, with various annexes around the main building. It's been in the same family since 1946. The grounds are quiet, planted with flower beds, and there's an open-air swimming pool. Simply decorated rooms go for €49–72; half or full board is compulsory. The restaurant serves typical regional cooking with a few original touches: Camembert *croquettes*, prawn cocktail, salmon with creamed garlic, duck *fricassée* with cider and Pommeau and delicious house desserts. There's a weekday lunchtime menu at €19 and others from €23 to €32, including a *menu terroir*. Reservations are recommended, especially at the weekend. Free house *digestif*.

NEUFCHÂTEL-EN-BRAY 76270

🕉 🏠 |●| HOSTELLERIE DU GRAND CERF**

9 Grande-Rue-Fausse-Porte (Centre); go down the main street and it's beyond the church.
☎ 02.35.93.00.02 ➡ 02.35.94.14.92
📧 grand-cerf.hotel@wanadoo.fr
Closed Fri; Sat lunchtime; Dec. **TV**. **Car park**.

You'll be spoiled rotten here, and you'll need a good excuse ready for the waitress if you don't eat every scrap. This is traditional Normandy cooking, with a variety of menus ranging from €12 to €25. The rooms are well maintained, with doubles going for €37–43. Free apéritif, and fruit juice for the children.

PONT-AUDEMER 27500

🕉 🏠 |●| RESTAURANT LE CANEL – HÔTEL DU PALAIS ET DE LA POSTE

14 rue Alfred Camel; it's near the post office.
☎ 02.32.41.50.74
Closed Tues; Sun evening; the last week in Feb; the first fortnight in Sept. **Car park**. **TV**. **Disabled access**.

The deliciously retro dining room is a perfect setting for local dishes served with a few original touches: skate *terrine*, fillet of duck *à l'eunoise*, *méli-mélo* of fish with tartare sauce. The weekday menu, €10, is served lunchtime and evenings until 8pm, and there are others at €15–29. The hotel is less appealing, though the rooms are good value; doubles with basin go for €21, or €37 with shower or bath/wc. Free house *digestif*.

🕉 🏠 |●| AUBERGE DU VIEUX PUITS**

6 rue Notre-Dame-du-Pré (Centre).
☎ 02.32.41.01.48 ➡ 02.32.42.37.28
📧 vieux.puits@wanadoo.fr
Closed Mon all year; Mon and Tues in summer; 16 Dec–25 Jan. **Car park**. **TV**. **Disabled access**.

This magnificent, half-timbered seventeenth-century building has just twelve bedrooms, and people dining at the inn get priority. The rooms in the oldest part are cheaper and more typically Norman than those in the modern part, but the soundproofing's not as good. Doubles start at €50 with shower/wc, increasing to €53–72 with bath; half board is compulsory. They serve traditional, refined Normandy cooking, which you can eat either in the cosy dining room or in an intimate sitting room. Menus change frequently; there's a weekday lunch *menu express* at €27, and others from €53–72. Specialities include mussel and Parmesan *soufflé*, trout Bovary with champagne sauce and apple tart. 10% discount on the room rate Oct–March.

🕉 |●| RESTAURANT HASTING

10 rue des Cordeliers (Centre); from pl. Victor-Hugo take pl. Louis-Gillian, then rue des Cordeliers.
☎ 02.32.42.89.68
Closed Tues and Nov.

This is a little country restaurant right in the centre of town. The dining room is small, with checked tablecloths, while the kitchen serves simple but tasty dishes including chops with cream and apples, duck with Madeira sauce, John Dory with sorrel sauce and couscous. Menus cost €9, €11 and €13, with a *formule brasserie* available on weekdays only. Free apéritif.

CAMPIGNY   27500 (6KM SE)

🏃 🏠 |●| RESTAURANT L'ANDRIEN – HÔTEL LE PETIT COQ AUX CHAMPS****

La Pommeraie sud.
☎ 02.32.41.04.19 ➡ 02.32.56.06.25
e le/petit.coq.aux.champs@wanadoo.fr
Closed three weeks in Jan. **Swimming pool. TV. Car park**.

Beautifully located in glorious Normandy countryside, this welcoming restaurant has a relaxed atmosphere. That said, it's fairly sophisticated, and the food is excellent. Chef Jean-Marie Huard is constantly inventing new dishes that delight both the palate and the eye. His speciality is a terrific *foie gras pot-au-feu* with crunchy cabbage, but it doesn't come cheap. Menus go for €30–60; the one at €37 includes apéritif, wine and coffee. Rooms with bath cost €106–140, except from May–Aug, when half board is compulsory at €107–134 per person. 10% discount on the room rate.

BEUZEVILLE   27210 (12KM W)

🏠 |●| AUBERGE DU COCHON D'OR**

pl. du Général-de-Gaulle; it's opposite the town hall.
☎ 02.32.57.70.46 ➡ 02.32.42.25.70
e Auberge-du-Cochon-Dor@wanadoo.fr
Closed Mon; Mon and Sun evening Oct–March; 15 Dec–15 Jan. **Garden. TV. Car park**.

This inn, which has been well-known for a couple of centuries, owes its continuing reputation to the chef who's been marshalling his forces in the kitchen since 1962. He specializes in Normandy dishes like eels stewed in cider, chicken *quenelles* with a Camembert sauce and skate wings with cabbage, all of which you can enjoy in the large rustic dining room. There's a weekday menu at €13, another at €18 (not Sun lunch), and others rising to €38. As for the rooms, doubles go for €34 with shower/wc and €38–51 with bath. There's an annexe across the road called the *Petit Castel*; here the quiet rooms overlook a garden where you can have breakfast.

🏃 🏠 |●| HÔTEL DE LA POSTE**

60 rue Constant-Fouché; it's opposite the town hall.
☎ 02.32.20.32.32 ➡ 02.32.42.11.01
Restaurant closed Thurs and 15 Oct–22 March. **TV. Garden. Car park**.

This authentic coaching inn, which dates back to 1844, has a garden and a terrace at the back. Bedrooms with shower or bath go

for €41–49; if you're there at the weekend, half board, €50 per person, is a good deal. Menus start at €12 (weekday lunchtime) and €15 (which includes cheese and dessert) and rise to €30. The chef cooks a good number of regional speacialities such as *foie gras*, and has a particular weakness for *andouille*, which he prepares in several ways. 10% discount for a two-night stay Sept–June, except bank holidays and weekends.

ROUEN   76000

SEE MAP OVERLEAF

🏠 HÔTEL DU PALAIS**

12 rue du Tambour. **MAP B2-8**
☎ 02.35.71.41.40
Closed Sun noon–7pm. TV.

In a tiny street between the law courts and the Gros Horloge, right across from the underground station, this hotel has two trump cards – its central location and its modest prices. Don't go expecting any great luxury, but the make-believe courtyard and the slightly random décor will appeal to the young at heart. Doubles €30 with shower or €34 with shower/wc.

🏃 🏠 |●| HÔTEL BRISTOL

45 rue aux Juifs. **MAP B2-6**
☎ 02.35.71.54.21
Closed Sun and the first fortnight in Aug. **TV**.

A beautifully restored half-timbered building with nine bedrooms, €34–43 for a double with bath and phone. They serve a weekday lunch menu at €12. House specialities are rabbit with mustard, and apple *tarte Tatin*. 5% discount on the room rate.

🏃 🏠 HÔTEL CÉLINE**

26 rue de Campulley. **Off map B1-1**
☎ 02.35.71.95.23 ➡ 02.35.89.53.71
Closed Sun 1–5pm and 25 Dec–2 Jan. **TV**.

A large white building in remarkably peaceful surroundings. The bedrooms are modern and clean; some of those on the top floor are particularly big, but they get a little too hot in the height of summer. Reasonably priced doubles with shower €35–46. One free breakfast per room.

🏃 🏠 HÔTEL BEAUSÉJOUR*

9 rue Pouchet. **MAP B1-2**
☎ 02.35.71.93.47 ➡ 02.35.98.01.24
TV.

One of the best places near the station, this

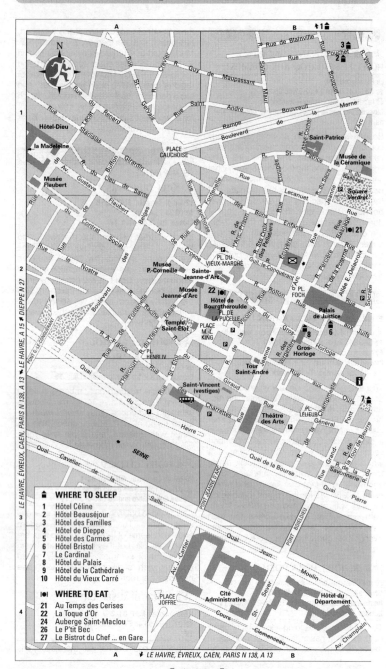

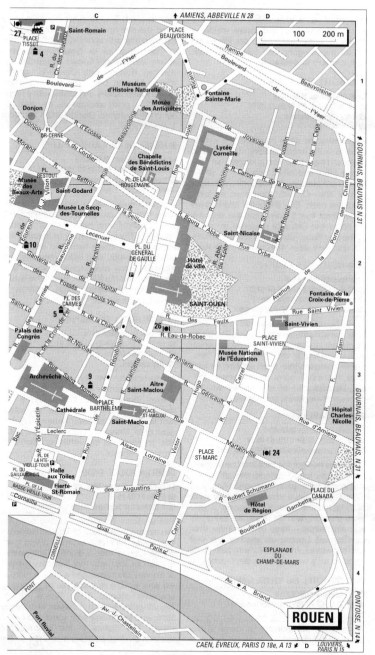

ROUEN

quiet hotel has a smart exterior with freshly renovated, well-equipped rooms inside, a charming garden and a salon-bar. Prices are fair for the category, with doubles at €38. 10% discount at weekends.

⚘ ⌂ HÔTEL DES CARMES*

33 pl. des Carmes. **MAP C2-5**
☎ 02.35.71.92.31 ➡ 02.35.71.76.96
e h.des.carmes@mcom.fr
TV.

A very attractive place on one of the liveliest squares in the middle of town. The décor is bright and new, full of circus imagery, and the young team welcomes you with a smile. Rooms are pleasant and colourful, with doubles at €40–43 with shower/wc or bath. Breakfast costs €5 – the butter and yoghurt come direct from the farm and the jams (try the apple and Calvados preserve) are made by the best Rouen companies using old methods. Excellent value. 10% discount Oct–April.

⚘ ⌂ HÔTEL DES FAMILLES*

4 rue Pouchet. **MAP B1-3**
☎ 02.35.71.88.51 ➡ 02.35.07.54.65
e francoixe.bretagnolle@wanadoo.fr
Closed 22 Dec–10 Jan. **TV**. **Pay car park**.

An old house that's been turned into a lovely hotel, conveniently near the station. The bright rooms are delightful, and the décor, which evokes the turn of the eighteenth and nineteenth centuries, has been assembled with taste. All the bathrooms are completely modern. Doubles €43–46 with shower/wc. 5% discount at weekends and July–Aug.

⚘ ⌂ LE CARDINAL**

1 pl. de la Cathédrale. **MAP C1-7**
☎ 02.35.70.24.42 ➡ 02.35.89.75.14
Closed three weeks Dec/Jan. **TV**. **Pay car park**.

This place has got the best location in town. Almost every room overlooks the cathedral – a splendid sight, particularly when floodlit at night – and there's a terrace where they serve breakfast in fine weather. The owner is perfectly charming and the rooms are extremely well-maintained – three of them have their own terraces. Doubles are good value at €49 with shower/wc and €53–62 with bath. 10% discount for a two-night stay Sept–June.

⚘ ⌂ |●| HÔTEL DU VIEUX CARRÉ**

34 rue Ganterie. **MAP C2-10**
☎ 02.35.71.67.70 **e** vieuxcarre@mcom.fr
TV.

There are a few characterful rooms in this pretty, half-timbered house in the centre of the old town. They're inevitably quite small given the size and age of the building, but they're pretty, with soothing décor, and some of them overlook a delightful courtyard ablaze with colourful flowers. Prices are reasonable: doubles with shower/wc go for €50, €55 with bath. The tearoom offers savoury tarts, salads and cakes, with a menu for €11; in good weather you can take tea out in the courtyard. One breakfast per room 1 Jan–31 April.

⌂ HÔTEL DE LA CATHÉDRALE**

12 rue Saint-Romain. **MAP C3-9**
☎ 02.35.71.57.95 ➡ 02.35.70.15.54
e contact@hotel.de.la.cathedrale.fr
Closed Christmas–1 Jan. **TV**.

In a good, quiet location, on a pedestrianized street that runs alongside the cathedral, this is a delightful little hotel with an internal courtyard. The rooms are not all as attractive, however. They range from €50 with shower/wc up to €60 with bath. There's a tearoom offering a wide choice of unusal teas and, if you feel like a snack, they serve quiches with lots of different fillings. Breakfast is served on the terrace.

⚘ ⌂ |●| HÔTEL DE DIEPPE***

pl. Bernard-Tissot. **MAP C1-4**
☎ 02.35.71.96.00. ➡ 02.35.89.65.21
e hotel.dieppe@wanadoo.fr
TV. **Pay car park.**

A large hotel run with style by a family who've been in the business longer than anyone else in town. The rooms, comfortable but a little impersonal, cost €82–98, while the restaurant is famed for pressed Rouen duck and good grills. Menus €21–35. If you like to eat late, try the hotel bar, which is open until 1am. Free apéritif.

⚘ |●| LA TOQUE D'OR

11 pl. du Vieux-Marché. **MAP B2-22**
☎ 02.35.71.46.29
Grill closed Sat evening and Sun lunchtime.

This attractive Normandy building is on the very square where Joan of Arc was burned at the stake. The stylish beamed dining room on the ground floor is dignified and peaceful, with an €8 menu (not Saturday evening or Sunday lunchtime) and a couple more at €9 and €10; à la carte you're looking at spending around €16. Typical dishes include grilled salmon escalope with *beurre blanc* and lemon sole with sorrel and cream sauce. The dishes in the informal grill upstairs are less sophisticated than on the ground floor, but they prove good value for money. Free coffee.

|●| AU TEMPS DES CERISES

4–6 rue des Basnage. MAP B2-21
☎ 02.35.89.98.00
Closed Sat and Mon lunchtimes, and all day Sun.

The décor – a kitsch dairy theme – tells you immediately what this place is about. No other restaurant in Rouen offers such a wide range of cheese dishes. Don't miss the grilled Camembert with sour cherry preserve, veal escalope with Pont l'Évèque cheese or cream cheese ice-cream with caramel sauce. Lunch menu for €10, others €14–20. The low prices and good food make this a popular haunt for young locals.

⚗ |●| AUBERGE SAINT-MACLOU

224–226 rue Martainville. MAP D3-24
☎ 02.35.71.06.67
Closed Sun and Mon except public holidays.

Housed in a timber-clad building, with genuine rustic décor, a nice bar and a little terrace open in summer, this restaurant serves comforting food like rabbit *terrine* with onion marmalade, veal chop *à la normande* and various sorbets. The weekday lunch menu, €11, includes a Kir and ¼ litre of wine, and there are others from €13–21. Free coffee.

⚗ |●| LE P'TIT BEC

182 rue Eau-de-Robec. MAP C2-26
☎ 02.35.07.63.33
Closed Mon–Thurs evenings, Fri and Sat.

Lovely, bright tearoom that also does delicious home-made lunches, including *gratins*, coddled eggs and pastries. Delightful service from the waitresses who race about to keep the regulars happy. There's just one set menu, at €12, but it's well put together and satisfying; *à la carte* you can eat for around €17. In fine weather, sit out on the terrace, which is on one of the prettiest streets in Rouen. Free apéritif.

⚗ |●| LE BISTROT DU CHEF… EN GARE

pl. Bernard-Tissot (North). MAP C1-27
☎ 02.35.71.41.15 ➔ 02.35.15.14.43
✉ media-restauration@wanadoo.fr
Closed Sat lunchtime; Sun; Mon evening; Aug.

Chef Arnaud Guerpillon is reviving the tradition of good station food. On the floor above the buffet, there's a large, hushed dining room that's always full of regulars. Dishes such as duck *terrine*, veal escalope with cream and apples, *andouillette* and rice pud-

ding are served both on the €14 menu and *à la carte* (for which you'll pay around €18). Free coffee.

CLÈRES — 76690 (18.5KM N)

⚗ |●| LE FLAMANT ROSE

pl. de la Halle (Centre); take the D27 and turn off onto the D6 at Boulay.
☎ 02.35.33.22.47
Closed Tues; every evening except by reservation; 15 Nov–15 Dec.

This simple place serves regional dishes and a few brasserie classics such as calf's head *sauce ravigotte*, home-smoked salmon, perch fillets, duck breasts with cider and tripe in Calvados. There's a lunch menu for €8, with others at €11–15. Reservations essential for dinner. Free house Kir.

RY — 76116 (20KM E)

|●| RESTAURANT LE BOVARY

Grande-Rue.
☎ 02.35.23.61.46
Closed Mon and Tues evenings; the Feb school holidays.

Flaubert went into raptures over the church and the covered market at Ry. He was also delighted by this restaurant, which has a cosy atmosphere and wonderful timber façade. They do a weekday lunch menu for €9, with others up to €26. Staff are welcoming and the service is hard to fault, which is pretty amazing at these prices. In the evening, the €18 menu is sheer delight, listing dishes such as calf's head, scallops with Benedictine sauce and *délice rouennais*, a local dessert with apples. The main courses change with the seasons, but you can expect something along the lines of duck breast, *coq au vin* or scallops.

SAINT-VALÉRY-EN-CAUX — 76460

⚗ 🏠 HÔTEL HENRI IV**

16 route du Havre (Southwest); from the centre take the Fécamp–Cany-Barville road; it's several hundred metres along on the left.
☎ 02.35.97.19.62 ➔ 02.35.57.10.01
TV.

Owner Michèle loves taking care of her guests, and she creates a cheerful atmosphere in this large, ivy-covered, brick-built hotel with patio. Comfortable bedrooms go from €28 with basin to €45 with bath; those at the back are the quietest. Michèle also loves flying; if you'd like a trip along the coast, she can arrange it with her friends at the flying club. Free apéritif.

🛏 |●| HÔTEL-RESTAURANT LA MARINE

113 rue Saint-Léger (Southwest); from the bridge go past the Maison Henri IV, the tourist office; it's on the first road on the left.
☎ and ↦ 02.35.97.05.09
Closed Fri in winter; Dec; Jan. **TV**.

You'll be made to feel very welcome in this quiet family-run hotel and restaurant. The whole of the ground floor – the two dining rooms, the entrance, the bar and the breakfast room – has had a face-lift. Otherwise, there are no fancy trimmings, but facilities are perfectly adequate. You'll spend €31 for a room with shower/wc or €39 with bath and TV. Weekday menus at €10, and others from €15–28, are served in two charming, old-fashioned dining rooms where regional specialities include skate in cider and apple tart with a Calvados custard. Half board from €30.

|●| LE RESTAURANT DU PORT

18 quai d'Amont (Centre).
☎ 02.35.97.08.93 ↦ 02.35.97.28.32
Closed Sun and Mon out of season.

As you can guess from the name, this seafood restaurant stands right by the harbour. It's the most refined establishment in town, and the prices reflect that. The €18 menu is simple and classic, while the more interesting one at €32 features *bouillabaisse* using fish from the Channel, mackerel tart and smoked salmon *terrine*. They also do a seafood platter and a few meat dishes. Everything is freshly cooked and the service can't be faulted. Ask for a table by the wide window with a view over the port.

SOTTEVILLE-SUR-MER   76740 (10KM E)

🎋 🛏 HÔTEL DES ROCHERS**

pl. de l'Église.
☎ 02.35.97.07.06 ↦ 02.35.97.71.73
Closed 1 Feb–5 March. **Disabled access**. **Garden**.

A big building, which used to be a presbytery, with a delightful walled garden. They have ten or so quiet, comfortable rooms with shower or bath €38–44. Free coffee.

|●| RESTAURANT LES EMBRUNS

pl. de l'Église; go towards Dieppe and turn left onto the D68 at Veules-les-Roses.

☎ 02.35.97.77.99
Closed Sun evening; Mon out of season; 20 Jan–10 Feb; a few weeks after the end of the season. **Disabled access**.

This used to be a bar and tobacconist's, but has since been transformed into a gourmet restaurant. Weekday lunch menus cost €11 or €14 with a starter, main course, and dessert or coffee. There are others from €21–39. Specialities are drawn from the local region and further afield: fish stew, *noisettes* of lamb *à la provençale*, lobster with fresh basil and duck breast with cider.

PETITES DALLES (LES)   76540 (17KM W)

🎋 🛏 |●| HÔTEL-RESTAURANT DE LA PLAGE

92 rue Joseph-Heuzé; take the D925 towards Fécamp and it's in the main street 50m from the beach.
☎ 02.35.27.40.77
Closed Sun and Mon evenings and Wed out of season; a period during the Feb, Easter and Christmas school holidays.

Monsieur and Mme Pierre will welcome you warmly to this handsome brick establishment with its wooden balconies and delightful turrets. The whole place is very quiet, with cosy, inexpensive rooms; doubles with shower/wc cost €35 or €38 with bath. It's rare to find such a reasonably priced hotel of such quality on the coast. The little dining room, meanwhile, a mixture of traditional and modern styles, is also a good bet. It's great food, prepared with the best produce; the starters are recommended, as is the house speciality of warm oysters wrapped in lettuce – or try *civet* of winkles and oysters with cider and *coulis* of beetroot with apples. Menus €14–29. 5% discount if you stay half-board.

TRÉPORT (LE)   76470

🎋 🛏 HÔTEL DE CALAIS

1-5-11 rue de Paris; from the quay, head up towards the church.
☎ 02.35.86.07.46 ↦ 02.27.28.09.00
Car park.

This former coaching inn, perched above the harbour, was built almost two centuries ago. Previous guests have included Victor Hugo. It's lost a little of its character through the most recent refurbishments but the rooms are nice and bright, and the bathrooms have been re-fitted. Only some of the rooms overlook the harbour, and they're not all the same size, so it's worth asking for what you want. Doubles

€30–65 with shower/wc and €45–60 with bath. They also have furnished rooms and apartments. One free breakfast per room per night, except public holidays and July–Aug.

|●| MON P'TIT BAR

3–5 rue de la Rade (Centre); it's on the port.
☎ 02.35.86.28.78

A nice, authentic, unstuffy little place that's less a conventional restaurant than a bar which serves food all day until late. Dishes are cooked using fresh market produce, prices are low and you get a friendly reception. Good seafood platters. Menus €10–15.

⅔ |●| LA MATELOTE

34 quai François-1er (Centre); it's on the harbour.
☎ 02.35.86.01.13
Closed Tues evening; Christmas–New Year holidays.
Disabled access.

Come here to enjoy a wide choice of wonderfully fresh fish and seafood. From the first-floor dining room you can watch the boats plying the harbour and the waves breaking on the jetty while feasting on fish stew *tréportaise*, fish *choucroute*, grilled sea bream, mussels *au gratin* or tasty seafood platters. There's a €12 menu (not weekends or public holidays) and others at €19–38. Service can be formal. Free *digestif*.

CRIEL-SUR-MER   76910 (8.5KM SW)

⅔ 🏠 |●| HOSTELLERIE DE LA VIEILLE FERME**

Mesnil-Val-Plage; take the cliff road, and it's in the main street, 300m from the beach.
☎ 02.35.86.72.18 ➡ 02.35.86.12.67
Closed Sun evening and Mon out of season; 2 Dec–7 Jan. **TV. Garden. Car park**.

An enormous, traditional Normandy building with a terrace, manicured lawn, a large garden with twittering birds and an old cider press. Very comfortable, quiet bedrooms go for €49 with shower/wc and €58 with bath. The dining room is decorated in a beautiful, traditional style and the menus, €17–37, feature dishes like seafood *pot-au-feu*, crayfish and Dublin Bay prawns with sherry vinegar, veal sweetbreads with mushroom sauce and Grand Marnier *soufflé*. Half board, compulsory in season, starts at €54 per person. Free coffee.

VERNEUIL-SUR-AVRE   27130

⅔ 🏠 |●| HÔTEL LE SAUMON**

89 pl. de la Madeleine; it's on the church square.
☎ 02.32.32.02.36 ➡ 02.32.37.55.80
Closed Sun evening Nov to Easter; 18 Dec–5 Jan.
Disabled access. TV.

A good, reliable provincial hotel. Rooms have a view of the old city walls of the square and the magnificent church tower – they're all quiet. Doubles €38 with shower/wc and €42–48 with bath. The restaurant is very good, serving dishes typical of this part of Normandy such as salmon, scallops with orange, lobster, seafood, veal sweetbreads and leg of duck *à la normande*. Menus at €10 (weekdays only) and €14–45; *à la carte* you'll spend around €30. There's also a substantial self-service buffet breakfast for €6. Free coffee.

VERNON   27200

⅔ 🏠 |●| HÔTEL D'ÉVREUX – RESTAURANT LE RELAIS NORMAND***

11 pl. d'Évreux (Centre); it's opposite the post office.
☎ 02.32.21.16.12 ➡ 02.32.21.32.73
📧 hotel-dévreux@libertysurf.fr
Restaurant closed Sun evening except Easter and Whitsun. **Car park**.

This hotel may look like a typical Normandy house from the outside, but inside, where the Austrian owner has decorated the place to remind her of home, it's slightly different – witness the rustic bar, collection of Bavarian beer mugs and imposing fireplace. The French chef, passionate about good food, has a number of specialities – roast Normandy oysters, *saucisson* of pig's trotters with truffle *jus*, pan-fried *foie gras* with apples and a thin-crusted apple tart with an iced Pommeau soufflé. Menus €21–25. Rooms, which are good, clean, and quiet, will set you back €44 with shower/wc, €53 with bath. In the summer there's a conservatory open. Reservations are recommended. 10% discount on the room rate for a two-night stay Nov–March.

⅔ |●| LA HALLE AUX GRAINS

31 rue de Gamilly; it's near the pl. de la République.
☎ 02.32.21.31.99
Closed Sun evening; Mon; a fortnight in Aug; the New Year holiday.

The welcome at this restaurant is warm, the setting attractive and the service diligent – no wonder it's packed year-round. Everything – including the pizza dough – is prepared from the freshest produce on the premises. The grilled meat is first-rate, as are the snails in pastry cases, the *soufflé* with scallops, the fisherman's platter and the orange and Grand Marnier soup. Dishes of the day average at around €6, and you'll pay €12–15 for a meal *à la carte*. The wine list is attractively priced and varied, with some vintages offered by the glass. Free apéritif.

VERNONNET   27200 (1KM N)

|●| LE RELAIS DES TOURELLES

rue de la Chaussée (Northeast); it's opposite Vernon on the other side of the Seine.
☎ 02.32.51.54.52
Closed Mon; Sun evening. **Car park**.

This charming restaurant serves a range of regional specialities including sweetbreads with morels, veal kidneys in mustard and warm oysters on a leek *fondue*. The €20 menu is a bit special; serve yourself from the *hors d'œuvre* buffet as many times as you like, then proceed with a main course, cheese and dessert. Dish of the day €9, other menus €14 and €26, and good choices *à la carte*.

GIVERNY   27620 (5KM E)

🏃 🏠 |●| HÔTEL LA MUSARDIÈRE**

123 rue Claude-Monet (Centre); it's just beyond the Monet museum.
☎ 02.32.21.03.18 ➡ 02.32.21.60.00
Closed Dec. **TV. Garden. Car park**.

A large house with a veranda and a huge garden, near Monet's house. The restaurant can get very full, so you may have to wait a long time to be served. Dishes of the day cost €8, menus €21 and €23. There's also a *crêperie*. For most of the year, the spacious double rooms go for €47–63 with shower/wc or bath. Breakfast €6. Free coffee.

|●| RESTAURANT LES NYMPHÉAS

rue Claude-Monet (Centre); it's across from the Monet museum.
☎ 02.32.21.20.31
Closed Mon except public holidays; 1Nov–30 March. **Car park**.

An ideal place for a snack after visiting Monet's house and garden. The marble tables create a bistro atmosphere and there are two terraces: one opposite the car park and a covered one on the other side of the building. They serve substantial salads and daily changing menus for €14–23; you can order a plate of cheese, a simple dish or just an ice-cream.

🏃 |●| LES JARDINS DE GIVERNY

1 rue du Milieu (chemin du Roy); take the D5 from Vernon and it's on the left 1km beyond the petrol station.
☎ 02.32.21.60.80 ➡ 02.32.51.93.77
Closed Mon; Sun evening; Dec; Jan–Feb. **Car park**.

This typical Normandy building isn't quite as idyllic as the name suggests, but it's not lacking in charm – and Monet did eat here, as did a host of other famous people including Clémenceau and Aristide Briand. Here you can get classic Normandy dishes served in a Louis XVI dining room: roast organic chicken, organic duck, sole fillet with prawns and iced *diplomate normand* with spiced bread. Menus, €20–38, all feature an unusual *trou normand* – this is usually a shot of Calvados served to aid digestion, but here you get a refreshing cider and Calvados sorbet. Excellent local specialities and fish dishes, some of them delicately infused with the flavour of seaweed. They're happy to advise on which wine to choose. Free coffee.

FOURGES   27630 (15KM NE)

🏃 |●| LE MOULIN DE FOURGES

38 rue du Moulin; take the D5 towards Magny-en-Vexin and follow the signposts in Fourges.
☎ 02.32.52.12.12 ➡ 02.32.52.92.56
Closed Sun evening and Mon April–Oct; 1 Nov–25 March.

It's worth coming to this splendid mill on the banks of the fast-flowing Epte for the romantic setting alone. Menus, €25–54, list finely cooked dishes: rabbit with *choucroute*, frogs' legs, veal sweetbreads with cream, John Dory *gratiné* with mushrooms and chocolate *profiteroles*. The shaded terrace is enjoyable in summer, but try to avoid coming at the weekend when the tour buses and cars fight over the parking spaces – the groups themselves are catered for in a separate dining room in a restored barn. Free house apéritif.

VEULES-LES-ROSES   76980

🏠 |●| RÉSIDENCE DOUCE FRANCE***

13 rue du Docteur Girard (Centre).
☎ 02.35.57.85.30 ➡ 02.35.57.85.31
Closed Tues evening out of season; 15–30 Nov; 5–30 Jan. **Disabled access. Garden. TV**.

This exceptional place is an absolute winner. It's become a hotel only recently after considerable refurbishment of the original seventeenth-century coaching inn. An immense fortified building built of brick and pale-coloured wood, with the coach yard in the middle, it's a quiet, restful and romantic place. The extremely spacious and comfy rooms, more like mini-suites, go for €72–99. Their *campagnard* breakfast, €7, includes all sorts of *charcuterie*, breads and sweet buns, and they serve a brunch for €12. If the weather is good, you can eat in the garden, which is delightful.

YVETOT   76190

⚏ |●| LA MAISON NORMANDE

18 av. Clémenceau (Northeast).
☎ 02.35.56.50.38
Car park.

This coaching inn is situated, unsurprisingly, on the edge of the N15, just a few minutes off the motorway. It's a particularly attractive seventeenth-century Normandy building, built round a huge stable yard, and with gorgeous décor – little seems to have changed since Napoleon III stayed here. The restaurant serves delicious, beautifully presented dishes such as home-made *foie gras terrine*, veal kidneys and sweetbreads with Pommeau, duck stuffed with ceps and chocolate cake with caramel sauce. There's a €10 *formule* – starter, main course and dessert – and menus at €14–21. Free coffee.

⚏ |●| LE SAINT-BERNARD

1 av. Foch; it's on the N15 in the direction of Le Havre.
☎ 02.35.95.06.75
Closed Mon and Tues evenings; Wed; the Feb school holidays.

Well-known restaurant with idiosyncratic décor – old radio sets, photos of local kids and French comics on the wall – with country music in the background. The cuisine is imaginative too, and there's a *table d'hôte* with an amazing *formule* at €10. Start by helping yourself from the *hors d'œuvre* buffet, follow with a tasty dish of the day such as sautéed lamb and finish with *millefeuille*. Other menus €12–24. House specialities include *foie gras*, cooked oysters and chocolate *moelleux* dessert. Free *digestif*.

CROIX MARE   76190 (5KM SE)

🏠 |●| AUBERGE DU VAL AU CESNE

How to get there: it's 3km beyond Yvetot, on the D5.
☎ 02.35.56.63.06 📠 02.35.56.92.78
📧 valcesne@chateauxhotels.com
Disabled access. **TV**. **Car park**.

The ducks and beautiful doves outside this cosy old Normandy inn create a perfect pastoral setting. You can eat outside in summer, and the bantams will come and peck up the crumbs. The food is excellent; try the sole stuffed with prawn mousse, the *escalope* of turkey made to a peasant recipe or the juicy steak. They offer a €25 menu with starter, main course and dessert, or you'll pay at least €38 *à la carte*. The delicious food and the unusual setting make the prices a bit easier to swallow. There are a few new rooms with en-suite bathrooms at €76.

⚏ |●| AUBERGE DE LA FORGE

How to get there: it's on the N15 between Le Havre and Rouen.
☎ 02.35.91.25.94
Closed Tues evening and Wed except when they fall on public holidays or the day before public holidays.
Disabled access. **Car park**.

A discreetly decorated country restaurant serving traditional regional dishes. The service is friendly and professional. Menus €16–41, some of which include wine. There are lots of tasty treats on offer here, including *fondant* of two salmons with lemon, sliced braised shoulder of beef, guineafowl *confit* and broccoli *bavarois*. Free Calvados sorbet.

ALLOUVILLE-BELLEFOSSE   76190 (6KM W)

⚏ |●| AU VIEUX NORMAND

How to get there: take the N15 or the D34.
☎ 02.35.96.00.00

You'll find this country inn next to a grand old oak tree on the village square and most of the local population sitting at the tables. There's a great atmosphere around the fire. They offer a huge choice of dishes which change constantly: black pudding *gâteau*, skate with cream, steak, *marmite dieppoise* (fish stew), seafood platters and house tripe, which is a must. Substantial menus €9–17. They serve red wine by the jug and cider on tap. Free apéritif.

Pays-de-la-Loire

44 Loire-Atlantique

49 Maine-et-Loire

53 Mayenne

72 Sarthe

85 Vendée

ANGERS 49000

SEE MAP ON PP.578–579

🏃 🏚 |●| HÔTEL DES LICES

25 rue des Lices. **MAP B3-3**
☎ 02.41.87.44.10
Closed Aug. **TV**.

A pleasant hotel with thirteen rooms on a city-centre road. It's an old private residence which has been renovated, and it offers pretty little rooms decorated in fresh colours. Double glazing is fitted in the ones that overlook the road and they're all very well maintained. Doubles €20 with basin, €27 with shower/wc. They also serve snacks – savoury tarts, quiches – and a meal costs around €11. Warm, natural welcome. Best to book. Free apéritif.

🏚 HÔTEL MARGUERITE D'ANJOU

13 pl. Kennedy. **MAP B3-4**
☎ 02.41.88.11.61 ➡ 02.41.87.37.61
Closed Mon morning; 24–31 Dec. **TV**.

Brilliantly located opposite the impressive château of Angers. It's essential to book and they even ask for a deposit. There are eight rooms, all of which are spotlessly clean and have double glazing and en-suite bathrooms – doubles €35–40. Breakfast, served in the bar, is the real thing, with as much bread as you like.

🏃 🏚 CONTINENTAL HÔTEL**

12–14 rue Louis-de-Romain. **MAP B2-8**
☎ 02.41.86.94.94 ➡ 02.41.86.96.60
e le.continental@wanadoo.fr
Closed Sun 12.30–5pm. **Disabled access. TV**.

The pretty frontage has an old-style sign out-side. The communal areas are warm and bright and the whole place has been refurbished; there's a pleasant little lounge and breakfast room. Comfortable rooms cost €43 with shower/wc or €47 with bath. Friendly welcome by the owners, who are justifiably proud of their hotel. 10% discount Fri–Sun.

🏃 🏚 HÔTEL SAINT-JULIEN**

9 pl. du Ralliement. **MAP C2-9**
☎ 02.41.88.41.62 ➡ 02.41.20.95.19
e s.julien@wanadoo.fr
TV.

You'd be hard pushed to find anything more central, and you'll get a nice welcome here. The thirty comfortable air-conditioned rooms are pleasantly decorated – and most have been nicely refurbished. Doubles cost €45–51 with shower/wc or bath. The rooms overlooking the square are the most expensive; those on the second floor are smaller. The small interior courtyard is ideal for breakfast on a fine day. When you book, you could ask them to book a table at the *Provence Caffé* next door (☎ 02.41.87.44.15), which specializes in tasty cooking from the south. 10% discount.

🏃 🏚 HÔTEL DU PROGRÈS**

26 rue Denis-Papin. **MAP B2-10**
☎ 02.41.88.10.14 ➡ 02.41.87.82.93
Closed Christmas Day and New Year's Day. **TV**.

This comfy hotel offers good value for money in a district which is a bit dreary but handy for the train station. The rooms are decorated in tones of blue with identical furnishings, though they're of varying size; doubles

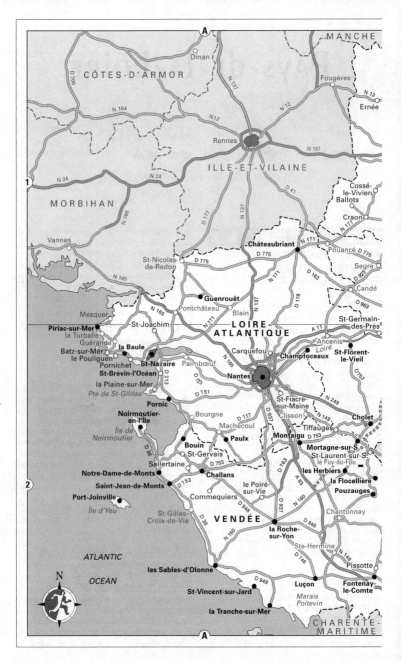

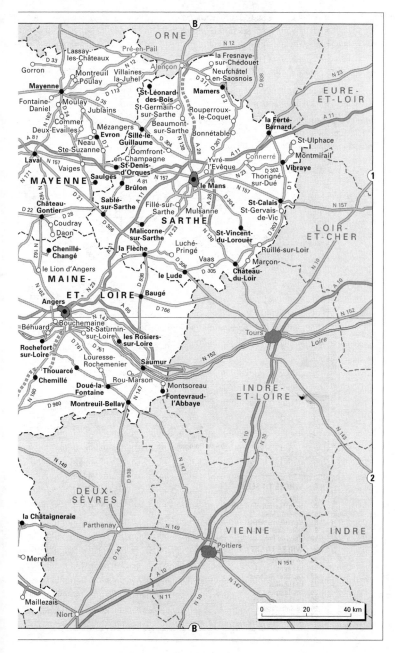

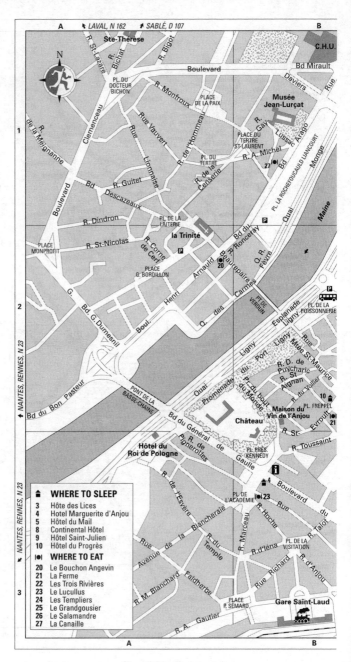

WHERE TO SLEEP

3   Hôte des Lices
4   Hotel Marguerite d'Anjou
5   Hôtel du Mail
8   Continental Hôtel
9   Hôtel Saint-Julien
10   Hôtel du Progrès

WHERE TO EAT

20   Le Bouchon Angevin
21   La Ferme
22   Les Trois Rivières
23   Le Lucullus
24   Les Templiers
25   Le Grandgousier
26   Le Salamandre
27   La Canaille

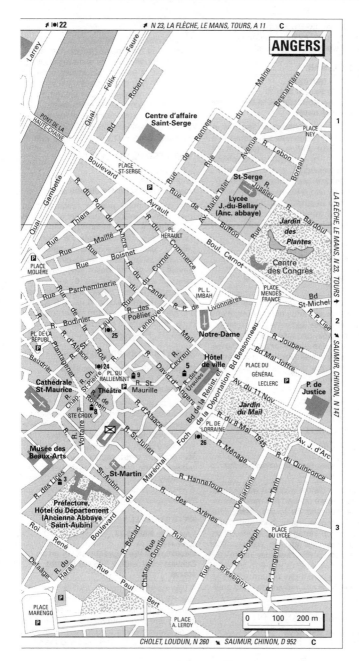

€46–47 with shower/wc or bath. Excellent facilities and very friendly reception. 10% discount at weekends July–Aug.

⌂ HÔTEL DU MAIL**

8 rue des Ursules. **MAP C2-5**
☎ 02.41.88.56.22 ➡ 02.41.86.91.20
Closed Sun noon–6.30pm and public holidays. **TV. Pay car park. Disabled access.**

There isn't another hotel quite like this in Angers – it's a 17th-century townhouse in a very quiet street with a definite touch of *Vieille France*. The atmosphere is sophisticated and pleasingly conventional. Refurbished bedrooms are furnished and decorated tastefully and €46–49 with shower/wc or bath. In fine weather, a buffet breakfast is served on the terrace in the shade of an ancient lime tree. Essential to book.

⚞⦿ LES TEMPLIERS

5 rue des Deux-Haies. **MAP B2-24**
☎ 02.41.88.33.11
Closed Sun, Mon lunchtime and a fortnight at Christmas.

A bright dining room with medieval décor. Lances, old swords and pennants ornament the walls, which are illuminated by torchlight. It's best to book, because the tasty, traditional cooking has a lot of local fans. Dishes are classics and well prepared using fresh produce from the daily market. Weekday lunch menu €9, *menu du templier* at €17 and *menu du Roy* at €23. There's not a dress code exactly, but they're not keen on jeans. Free Kir.

⚞⦿ LA CANAILLE

8 bd. Arago. **MAP B1-27**
☎ 02.41.88.56.11
Closed Sat lunchtime; Sun; public holidays; the first three weeks in Aug.

This run-down district is on the way up and the young owners opened this restaurant to add some sun and life to the scene. The cooking is simple, tasty and appealing: steak or scallop kebabs, simple grilled fish and puddings with childish names. The cheapest menu is €10 (weekday lunch), rising to €13 on weeknights and €15 and €23 at other times; you'll pay around €20 *à la carte*. Free glass of Crémant de Loire after your meal.

⚞⦿ LE BOUCHON ANGEVIN

44 rue Beaurepaire. **MAP A2-20**
☎ 02.41.24.77.97

Closed Sun; Mon; Aug.

A wine cellar with a restaurant at the back in the heart of the Doutre district. Two small, characterful dining rooms and a big fireplace. Menus €10 at weekday lunchtimes, or others at €12–15. An interesting selection of dishes *à la carte* – deep-fried Camembert, salad with hot *rillauds*, grilled *andouillette*, duck thigh *confit*, home-made pastries and an Angers speciality of potted, shredded pork. You'll pay about €21 *à la carte*. Free apéritif.

⚞⦿ RESTAURANT LA FERME

2–4 pl. Freppel. **MAP B2-21**
☎ 02.41.87.09.90
Closed Sun evening and Wed. **Disabled access.**

One of the most popular restaurants in town, with a terrace in the quiet shadow of the cathedral and a stunning dining room. It's stayed successful over the years by offering reliable cooking and generously flavoured dishes – but when it's crowded the service can get slapdash. Weekday lunch menu at €10, then others €14–27. They specialize in poultry: *poule-au-pot*, escalope of *foie gras* and breast of duck with apples. *À la carte* you can try warm *rillauds d'Anjou*, duck *choucroute* or calf's head. Main courses €9–11. Free coffee.

⚞⦿ LES TROIS RIVIÈRES

62 promenade de Reculée. **Off map B1-22**
☎ 02.41.73.31.88
Disabled access. Car park.

This famous riverside fish restaurant with its panoramic dining room is always full, even on weekdays, so it's best to book. The welcome and service are efficient but not formal. They specialize in fish and the cooking is excellent: surf and turf salad, salmon *tournedos* with red Anjou wine, fillet of perch in butter sauce. Weekday lunch menu €13 with others €16–30. Lots of good dry white wines – try the Domaine de Brizé. Free apéritif.

⦿ LE LUCULLUS

5 rue Hoche. **MAP B3-23**
☎ 02.41.87.00.44
Closed Sun and Mon (except Mother's Day and the Christmas school holidays); 1–23 Aug. **Disabled access.**

A very good restaurant in 15th-century cellars. Faultless service and carefully prepared dishes: eggs with morels, ox cheek, fillet of zander and chocolate *millefeuille*. The €18 weekday *formule* is a good way of investigating the region's specialities and the dishes are accompanied by local wines. You'll find a weekday lunch menu at €13 and gastronomic menus from €18 to €46; there's a minimum charge of €21 at weekends.

⚘ |●| LE GRANDGOUSIER

7 rue Saint-Laud. **MAP B2-25**
☎ 02.41.87.81.47
Closed Sat and Wed lunchtimes, Sun.

The beautiful dining room dates from the 16th century and has walls made of local stone and sturdy beams. Regional cuisine with literary inspiration: *Pantagruel* or *Gargantua* salads and *Maître Alcofridas terrine* made from chicken livers and grapes marinated in Coteaux de l'Aubance. The €14 menu, available at lunchtimes and dinner until 10pm, includes an apéritif and Anjou wine. The huge €23 menu, which offers a different wine with each dish, offers *andouillette* and potato *salade de mémé Gargamelle* followed by duck *tournedos*. There's a terrace. Free coffee.

|●| LA SALAMANDRE

1 bd. du Maréchal Foch. **MAP C3-26**
☎ 02.41.88.99.55
Closed Sun (also Mon in Aug).

This restaurant, on the premises of the *Hôtel d'Anjou*, has a reputation for consistently good cuisine. The well-proportioned dining room has an elegant, classic décor, with a portrait of François I on a wooden medallion. Smart clientele and perfect service. The dishes speak for themselves: *sabayon* of pan-fried oysters with Layon wine, grilled sea bass with basil and cream sauce and a *tian* of vegetables. Lunch menu €21 with others at €28 and €38. Excellent wine list.

BOUCHEMAINE   49080 (11KM SW)

⚘ |●| RESTAURANT LA TERRASSE

pl. Ruzeboucla, La Pointe-de-Bouchemaine.
☎ 02.41.77.11.96
Closed Sun evening out of season. **Disabled access**.

The dining room offers one of the most wonderful panoramic views of the Loire that there is. It's well-known for its cooking and the sauces in particular are heavenly. Menus start at €15 (weekday lunchtime), with others from €21 to €53. There are dishes like fish *terrine* with a Savenières jelly, leek terrine with *foie gras* and zander with *beurre blanc*. The quality of service sometimes slips. Best to book. Free apéritif.

SAINT-SATURNIN-SUR-LOIRE 49320 (17KM SE)

|●| AUBERGE DE LA CAILLOTTE

2 rue de la Loire (Centre); it's on the bank of the Loire.
☎ 02.41.54.63.74
Closed Mon and Tues in winter; just Mon in summer.
Disabled access. Car park.

In autumn and winter you eat in the ravishing rustic dining room; for summer there's a spacious, shady terrace. Hospitable welcome with a touch of humour. Best of all, though, are the cooking and the appealing wine list. Menus, €19–28, list an ever-changing selection of dishes: zander with *beurre blanc*, crayfish, pan-fried eels and river fish. *À la carte* you'll pay €29 – and it's worth it. You'll feel very relaxed here.

BÉHUARD   49170 (18KM SW)

|●| RESTAURANT LES TONNELLES

rue Principale.
☎ 02.41.72.21.50
Closed Sun and Weds evenings; Mon; Jan–Feb. **Car park**.

The terrace is delightful in summer, when you sit under the arbour and enjoy the wonderful food. Weekday lunch *formule* €23, menus €29–60. The specialities are principally fish dishes – roast zander with *beurre blanc*, eel, pike and *cotriade* (stew of white fish with mussels) – but also try their roast pigeon with elderflower *jus* or the rabbit *confit*. Very tasty.

SAINT-GERMAIN-DES-PRÉS 49170 (23KM W)

|●| LA CHAUFFETERIE

How to get there: take the D15 between Saint-Germain-des-Prés and Saint-Augin-des-Bois or the A11, leaving at the Beaufreau-Chalonnes exit.
☎ 02.41.39.92.92
Closed Mon–Wed (except group bookings). **Car park**.
Disabled access.

This little farmhouse, deep in the country, was taken over by a Parisian couple a few years ago. There are two gorgeous dining rooms with fireplaces and the chairs are decorated in antique style. They offer good, simple cooking: snails in a pastry case, pigeon with cep stuffing and blancmange perfumed with orange blossom. Menus €16–24. You'll get attentive service from the owner – who's a trained astrologer – while his wife runs the kitchen.

BAUGÉ   49150

沐 🏠 IOI HOSTELLERIE DE LA BOULE D'OR**

4 rue du Cygne (Centre).
☎ 02.41.89.82.12
Closed Sun evening, Mon and 18 Dec–10 Jan. **TV**. **Car park**. **Disabled access**.

A friendly little hotel with ten attractively decorated rooms overlooking an internal courtyard. Doubles with shower/wc and TV are €47–26. Half board costs €63. The restaurant specializes in good regional cooking; menus are €14–29. It's best to book. Free apéritif.

BAULE (LA)   44500

沐 🏠 HÔTEL MARINI**

22 av. Clémenceau (Centre); it's between the tourist office and the railway station.
☎ 02.40.60.23.29 ➡ 02.40.11.16.98
🌐.hotel-marini@wanadoo.fr
TV. **Swimming pool**. **Car park**.

Recent renovation work has given this little hotel a pleasantly fresh, youthful appearance and added an indoor heated swimming pool. The comfortable, tastefully furnished rooms are particularly good value for money: doubles with shower/wc are €47, or €66 with bath. Hospitable owners. 10% discount Sept–June.

沐 🏠 IOI HÔTEL LUTÉTIA – RESTAURANT LE ROSSINI**

13 av. des Evens (South); it's near the town hall.
☎ 02.40.60.25.81 ➡ 02.40.42.73.52
Closed Sun evening and Mon out of season; Tues lunchtime; Jan. **TV**. **Car park**.

An elegant restaurant which is a real classic, with a dining room decorated in 1930s style. You'll get a welcoming smile from *la patronne*, while her husband, the chef, creates stylish, fresh dishes – try fillet of beef Rossini with goose *foie gras*, fish cooked in a salt crust or roast salmon in *beurre rouge*. The desserts are delicate and unusual, such as fig *au gratin* with almond cream. €26 weekday menu; others 26–38. Double rooms €49–63. Free coffee with a meal and a surprise gift if you stay overnight.

沐 🏠 HOSTELLERIE DU BOIS**

65 av. Lajarrige (Centre).
☎ 02.40.60.24.78 ➡ 02.40.42.05.88
🌐 www.hostellerie-du-bois.com

Closed 1 Jan–1 April. **Garden**. **TV**. **Pay car park**.

Set back from a lively street, this hotel is shaded by pine trees and has a flower garden. There are fifteen bedrooms, which go for €55–64 with shower/wc. It's a delightful and pleasantly cool place filled with souvenirs of Southeast Asia. 10% discount on the room rate Sept–June.

IOI RESTAURANT CHEZ L'ÉCAILLEUR

av. des Ibis; it's near the market.
☎ 02.40.60.87.94
Closed evenings, Mon out of season, a fortnight in the Feb school holidays and a fortnight in Nov.

Undiluted pleasure here: treat yourself to a dozen plump Brittany oysters or clams with a $1/2$ litre of Gros-Plant wine – or there's a *formule* at €8. Enjoy it all at the relaxed bar.

沐 IOI LA FERME DU GRAND CLOS

52 av. de Lattre-de-Tassigny; it's opposite the riding school.
☎ 02.40.60.03.30
Closed Tues and Wed out of season. **Disabled access**.

The poshest *crêperie* in town – it's delightful and not at all stuffy. The wheat and buckwheat *crêpes* are equally delicious and the farm itself is really attractive. They also produce delicious, home-cooked dishes – *cassoulet* with duck *confit* or calf's head *sauce gribiche* – with *formules* from €12. Free coffee.

POULIGUEN (LE)   44510 (3KM W)

沐 IOI RESTAURANT L'OPÉRA DE LA MER

promenade du Port; it's by the jetty.
☎ 02.40.62.31.03
Closed Wed and Thurs out of season; Jan; 15 Nov–1 Dec. **Car park**.

Families strolling by the harbour stop under the trees to watch the relaxed crowd and pirouetting staff at this popular restaurant – the terrace is chock-a-block in summer. They serve fresh salads, nice fish soup and good oysters. Menus €17–25. Free apéritif.

PORNICHET   44380 (6KM E)

沐 🏠 IOI HÔTEL-RESTAURANT LE RÉGENT**

150 bd. des Océanides; it's on the seafront.
☎ 02.40.61.05.68 ➡ 02.40.61.25.53
🌐 www.le-regent.fr
Closed Mon in winter; Dec–Jan. **TV**. **Car park**.

A family hotel facing the sea. It's bright and colourful, if a little bland. Doubles €53 with shower/wc, €65 with bath. Half board, at €46, is compulsory July–Aug. The restaurant specializes in fish and seafood: the yellow ling *charlotte* with shellfish *coulis* and the duo of zander and pike with a Saumur red wine sauce are particularly good. Menus €15–30. Free apéritif.

⅔ ☎ |●| VILLA FLORNOY

7 av. Flornoy.
☎ 02.40.11.60.00 ➡ 02.40.61.86.47
Ⓦ www.villa-flornoy.com
Closed Nov–March. **Garden. TV.**

A charming hotel in a quiet street just 300m from the beach. It feels like a family house and has been decorated with taste. The sitting room is pleasant and comfortable and attractively furnished with period furniture, and there's a lovely garden where you can relax with a book. Doubles €56–69 with shower/wc or €56–84 with bath. They serve meals, costing €18, in the evening only. Free apéritif.

⅔ |●| RESTAURANT LA BRIGANTINE

How to get there: it's on the harbour.
☎ 02.40.61.03.58
Closed Mon, Tues evening and Wed (except school holidays); 11 Nov–8 Feb. **Car park.**

Though it's surrounded by dour, grey concrete, this is the only *crêperie* in town with a terrace on the harbour. Pleasant décor and a log fire in the dining room. They do good *crêpes*, a range of grills over the open fire – rib of beef, duck breast, or baron of lamb – and some more exotic dishes such as tandoori chicken and Creole black pudding from the French Antilles. Menus €14–22, but *à la carte* is the better option. Free apéritif.

BATZ-SUR-MER   44740 (8KM W)

⅔ |●| RESTAURANT LE DERWIN

rue du Golf; it's on the seafront between Batz and Le Pouliguen.
Closed Tues (all year round); Wed and Thurs (except school holidays); and Oct–1 April. **Car park.**

This place is popular with the sailing fraternity. It has no telephone or electronic till – cash or cheque only – but it's always full. The ideal place for a plate of mussels, seafood and *crêpes* while you gaze out to sea. Expect to pay €12–18 per person. Free coffee.

BOUIN   85230

⅔ ☎ |●| HÔTEL LE MARTINET**

1 pl. de la Croix-Blanche; it's beside the church.

☎ 02.51.49.08.94 ➡ 02.51.49.83.08
Ⓦ www.lemartinet.com
Restaurant closed Jan–Feb. **Garden. Swimming pool. TV. Car park.**

This large and beautiful 18th-century house offers a choice of bedrooms – old-fashioned ones overlooking the square or newer rooms at ground level that give direct access to the garden and swimming pool. Doubles €46–55. Françoise has redecorated the place and also takes care of reception. Her sons also have a role: Emmanuel looks after the kitchen garden and does the cooking while Jean-François supplies the fish and seafood. Breakfast is served in the old dining room, which smells delightfully of beeswax. In the evening, typical choices include a dozen oysters, terrine of *foie gras*, *panaché* of eel and frogs' legs, grilled sea bream and carpaccio of marinated salmon. Menus €15–19. 10% discount on the room rate 1 Oct–30 April.

⅔ |●| RESTAURANT LE COURLIS

15 rue du Pays-de-Monts; it's on the edge of town.
☎ 02.51.68.64.65
Closed Mon, Wed evening except July–Aug.

A white, rather squat building which is typical of the area. The flower-filled dining room is a nice place to enjoy the mouthwatering cuisine and a range of specialities that change with the seasons and the fresh fish that's landed – poached sea bream with *beurre blanc*, sole *meunière* with five spices, turbot with bacon and oyster and *foie gras* turnover with samphire. Weekday menu €13 and others €18–54. Free coffee or apéritif.

BRULÔN   72350

⅔ ☎ |●| HÔTEL-RESTAURANT LA BOULE D'OR

26 place Albert Liebault (Centre).
☎ 02.43.95.60.40 ➡ 02.43.95.07.78
Ⓔ labouledor@freesurf.fr
Closed Sun evening. **TV.**

Nothing seems to have changed in this sturdy village house over the past three decades – the owner, the customers and the atmosphere have all stayed the same. The aromas wafting from the plates as they're carried into the dining room are still wonderful, and the cuisine is traditional and uses only fresh produce. You can feast without breaking the bank, too – the weekday menu costs €10, and others go up to €20. You'll get half a dozen oysters, scorpion fish served with sorrel sauce, a delicious *noix* of rib steak, a cheese platter and dessert. Try the chef's specialities: *suprême* of chicken with pineapple and fillet of zander with cream and mussels. Clean, comfortable bedrooms are €27 with basin or €35 with shower/wc. Free coffee.

CHALLANS 85300

🏃 🏠 HÔTEL DE L'ANTIQUITÉ

14 rue Gallieni.
☎ 02.51.68.02.84 ➡ 02.51.35.55.74
ⓦ www.hotelantiquite.com
Swimming pool. TV. Car park.

Very ordinary from the outside but inside it's charming, with refined period furniture shown off to best advantage. The rooms are spacious and most of them have been tastefully renovated. The rooms – €46–61 with shower or bath/wc – are all set around the swimming pool which is where you have breakfast. It's a blissful place and run by a nice, energetic couple. 10% discount Sept–June.

🏃 |●| RESTAURANT LA GITE DU TOURNE PIERRE

route de Saint-Gilles; it's 3km on the D69, between Challans and Soullans.
☎ 02.51.68.14.78
Closed Sat lunchtime; Sun evening; a fortnight in March; three weeks in Oct.

Time seems to have stopped at this beautiful house, but you'll discover new flavours in the dishes. Lobster occupies pride of place but the home-made *foie gras* is much in evidence too – duck *Rossini* with truffles and *foie gras*, *fricassée* of sole with mushrooms and *foie gras*. Menus €30–43. Faultless, unpretentious service. A good place if you're feeling flush. Free apéritif.

SALLERTAINE 85300 (8.5KM NW)

🏃 |●| RESTAURANT LA COURONNE

Route de Beauvoir-sur-Mer; take the Beauvoir road and turn left after 2km.
☎ 02.51.49.11.33
Closed Sun and Mon evenings out of season. **Parking.**

Good food at affordable prices. You eat either in the panelled dining room with its old cartwheel or at the large counter with its impressive model boat. Menus, €11–26, list dishes like fillet of duck, fish wrapped in crisp pancakes and pear caramel with raspberry juice. You'll get smiling service, well-presented food and excellent value. Free apéritif.

COMMEQUIERS 85220 (12KM SE)

🏃 🏠 |●| HÔTEL DE LA GARE

rue de la Morinière; take the D32 then the D82.
☎ 02.51.54.80.38 ➡ 02.28.10.41.47
Restaurant closed Mon, Jan and All Saints' holidays.
Hotel closed 1 Oct–31 May. **Swimming pool. Car park.**

In the early twentieth century, when the railway network extended into the remotest parts of France, this substantial Victorian house was built. No trains now – but at least the nights are quiet. The rooms here are inviting, pleasant and attractively decorated; doubles are €27 with shower and €32 with shower/wc. The dining room is fresh and bright, too, with lots of green and a railway theme running through it – old photographs, station lanterns, ticket punchers. Good, simple dishes are served in ample portions: seafood platters, fish, scallops with saffron and veal kidneys with port sauce. Menus €11–23. There's a shady garden where you can relax after a swim.

SAINT-GERVAIS 85230 (12KM NW)

|●| RESTAURANT LA PITCHOUNETTE

48 rue Bonne-Brise (West); it's on the D948 in the direction of Beauvoir and Noirmoutier.
☎ 02.51.68.68.88
Closed Mon out of season.

A really welcoming and pretty house with flowers everywhere – but Gérard Thoumoux's cooking outshines the décor. There are many tempting dishes: duck *foie gras* with a hot *brioche*, fresh catch of the day and snails according to Grandma Marguerite's recipe. If you fancy the seafood platter, you'll need to order 48 hours in advance. Weekday lunch menu €9 and others €15–26. There's a terrace in the flower garden in summer.

CHAMPTOCEAUX 49270

🏃 🏠 |●| HÔTEL-RESTAURANT LE CHAMPALUD**

promenade du Champalud; it's in the centre of town.
☎ 02.40.83.50.09 ➡ 02.40.83.53.81
Restaurant closed Sun evening out of season. **TV.**
Disabled access. Car park.

The hotel is in a charming village on the banks of the Loire and it's been completely overhauled. There are a dozen comfortable rooms for €43–49. The restaurant has a good reputation; the *menu du jour* (€10) includes cheese, dessert and wine, and there are others at €14–34. À la carte, try *terrine*, zander fillet with *beurre blanc* or frogs' legs. They offer various sports facilities – tennis courts nearby, a gym and mountain bikes – and a sitting room filled with board games. Friendly, very energetic owner and a place which is good value for money. 10% discount on the room rate 1 Nov–31 Mar.

CHÂTAIGNERAIE (LA)　　85120

𝕵 🏠 |●| L'AUBERGE DE LA TERRASSE**

7 rue de Beauregard (Centre).
☎ 02.51.69.68.68 ▶ 02.51.52.67.96
Closed Fri and Sun evenings and Sat lunchtime from Sept to mid-June; a week at All Saints'. **TV**. **Disabled access**.

This hotel, which occupies a well-restored, substantial house in a quiet road, has a family atmosphere and a quality restaurant. Double rooms are €50 with shower/wc. The owner, Monsieur Leroy, provides a culinary voyage of discovery through the Vendée marshes and the sea – specialities include eel with butter and bacon and snails prepared in many different ways. Menus €10–27. There's a shady terrace which has a lovely view. One free breakfast per room except June–Aug.

CHÂTEAUBRIANT　　44110

|●| LE POÊLON D'OR

30 [bis] rue du 11-Novembre (Centre); it's near the post office and the town hall.
☎ 02.40.81.43.33
Closed Sun evening, Mon, a fortnight in Feb and three weeks in Aug.

The service is nicely formal and the rustic décor has a very French feel. You'll find gourmet dishes like tender, succulent Châteaubriand with curry sauce, John Dory with *beurre blanc*, fillet of bass *en écailles* and a sensational apple tart with lavender. Menus €16–46.

CHÂTEAU-DU-LOIR　　72500

𝕵 🏠 |●| HÔTEL-RESTAURANT LE GRAND HÔTEL**

59 av. Aristide-Briand (Centre).
☎ 02.43.44.00.17 ▶ 02.43.44.37.58
Closed mid-Nov to mid-Dec. **TV**. **Car park**.

This old coaching inn has stood the test of time. It offers doubles with bath for €43 and the superb cuisine adds to the establishment's reputation. Meals are served in a charming old-style dining room with a painted ceiling, and include dishes such as calf's head *ravigotte*, duck *foie gras*, *terrine* of young rabbit in aspic and *marmite sarthoise* (a stew of chicken, rabbit, ham and mushrooms). Menus €17–38. Free coffee.

VAAS　　72420 (8KM SW)

𝕵 🏠 |●| HÔTEL-RESTAURANT LE VÉDAQUAIS**

pl. de la Liberté (Centre); take the D305 or the D30.
☎ 02.43.46.01.41 ▶ 02.43.46.37.60
e vedaquais@aol.com
Closed Fri and Sun evenings; Mon; the Feb school holidays. **TV**. **Car park**. **Disabled access**.

This old-fashioned village hotel occupies the old schoolhouse. Daniel Beauvais is a very good chef who doesn't talk much, while his wife Sylvie is a very good hostess who chats away quite happily. They offer a *menu du marché* for €9, and others at €13–34 or à la carte. Each is a real treat – fresh-tasting, straightforward and brimming with creativity: *rillette* of zander with marinated eel, chicken breast with morels, leg of duck with pears and a few little treats such as apple tart with rosemary honey for dessert. The rooms – €38 with shower/wc or €53 with bath – are every bit as pleasant. 10% discount on the room rate and free apéritif.

MARÇON　　72340 (8.5KM NE)

𝕵 |●| RESTAURANT DU BŒUF

21 pl. de l'Église (Centre); take the N138, then head onto the D305.
☎ 02.43.44.13.12
Closed Sun evening and Mon (only Mon lunchtime July–Aug); 20 Jan to 5 March.

Creole dishes take pride of place on the menus here; there's a weekday menu at €11, then others €12–30. Dishes include chicken with crayfish, prawn *fricassée* with coconut milk, pork stew and lamb *colombo*. Have some punch and a few fritters to start with and round things off with a house liqueur. Free coffee.

RUILLÉ-SUR-LOIR　　72340 (16KM NE)

🏠 |●| HÔTEL-RESTAURANT SAINT PIERRE

42 rue Nationale (Centre); take the D305, it's 6km from La Chartre-sur-le-Loir.

☎ 02.43.44.44.36
Closed Sun evening; 15 Dec–5 Jan.

This appealing little village hotel, with an unassuming façade and a cosy, friendly atmosphere, is one of a dying breed. The proprietress fusses over all her customers and nobody around these parts can rival her €8 *menu ouvrier* – the dozens of plates of *hors-d'œuvres* are even served out ahead of time to deal with the rush. A bottle of red wine is included in the price. On Sunday there is a choice of leg of lamb, duck with pepper, salad, cheese platter and dessert. They offer a few simple doubles with basin for €20.

CHÂTEAU-GONTIER 53200

≜ |●| HÔTEL DU CERF**

31 rue Garnier (South); it's opposite the Champion supermarket on the N162, the Laval-Angers road.
☎ 02.43.07.25.13 ➡ 02.43.07.02.90
Garden. TV. Secure parking.

The frontage of this hotel, which is in the centre of town and near the river, has had a facelift. As you would expect, the rooms overlooking the garden are quieter than the others: €31–34 for a double with shower/wc or bath. They do lunch and dinner from Mon to Friday lunchtime.

⚒ ≜ |●| HOSTELLERIE DE MIRVAULT**

rue du Val-de-Mayenne; it's signposted, about 2km from the town centre.
☎ 02.43.07.13.17 ➡ 02.43.07.66.90
Restaurant closed Mon and Wed lunchtime in summer. **TV.**

Way out in the countryside on the banks of the Mayenne, this relaxing place is run by an English couple. There are eleven rooms with full facilities and river views. Doubles with bath or shower cost €43–46, which is remarkable value given the quality of the establishment. They've even set aside a reading room. The cooking is also high quality: roast zander with *beurre blanc*, mignon of pork with cider and guineafowl *terrine* with Pommeau. Weekday menu €14 and others €20–27. Free *digestif*.

|●| RESTAURANT L'AQUARELLE

route de Ménil (South), in Pendu-en-Saint-Fort. It's 400m from the centre; follow the road that runs along the north bank of the Mayenne towards Sablé, and at the roundabout take the Ménil road.
☎ 02.43.70.15.44
Closed Sun evening out of season, Mon, 15–31 Jan and

the last week in Sept. **Car park**.

Situated outside town on the banks of the Mayenne, this place will set you dreaming. The terrace is beautiful on summer days, and the panoramic dining room, air-conditioned in summer, offers a magnificent view of the river. The light, creative cooking includes dishes like grilled freshwater fish served with lime butter, a medley of lamb with *langoustine* and thyme. Menus €14–27.

COUDRAY 53200 (7KM SE)

|●| RESTAURANT L'AMPHITRYON

2 rue de Daon (Centre); take the D22 and it's opposite the church.
☎ 02.43.70.46.46
℮ lamphitryon@wanadoo.fr
Closed Tues evening, Wed and Sun evening Nov–March; the Feb school holidays; 1 May; the first fortnight in July; 24–25 Dec. **Disabled access. Car park**.

This place might look like any other inn, but it's gained a reputation as one of the most delightful places in the *département*. There's something invigorating about both the cooking and the décor. Dishes are light and colourful: *terrine* of sardines and shrimps with cardamon, fillet of trout with potatoes, *millefeuille* of Camembert and *fine* apple tart. Set menus €14–21. If you have a big appetite, go for the regional one.

DAON 53200 (11.5KM SE)

≜ |●| HÔTEL-RESTAURANT À L'AUBERGE

10 rue Dominique-Godivier; take the D22.
☎ 02.43.06.91.14
Closed Sat out of season.

A good country inn specializing in fish and seafood dishes. It's popular with fishermen because the menus are good and cheap – €8 (Mon–Sat) and up to €20. Basic bedrooms with basin go for €23.

BALLOTS 53350 (30KM NW)

⚒ |●| RESTAURANT L'AUBERGE DU MOUILLOTIN

9 pl. de l'Église (Centre); take the D22, and 9.5km beyond Craon turn onto the D25 towards La Guerche-de-Bretagne.
☎ 02.43.06.61.81
Closed Tues and Thurs evenings and Wed (except groups); 8 days in Feb; a fortnight in Aug. **Garden. Disabled access**.

This restaurant serves delicious omelettes with all sorts of rich and tasty fillings – *foie gras* and snails – along with mouthwatering dishes like fillet of perch with cider, veal *escaloppe* Mouillotin and a warm apple tart with cinammon. Weekday menu €9, with others €12–21. As a change from the rich gourmet dishes, they also serve savoury or sweet *crêpes*. The pretty dining room overlooks the garden. Free apéritif.

CHEMILLÉ   49120

⚥ ♨ |●| L'AUBERGE DE L'ARRIVÉE**

15 rue de la Gare.
☎ 02.41.30.60.31 ➡ 02.41.30.78.45
Restaurant closed Sun evening out of season and the first week in Jan. **TV**. **Car park**.

A private mansion offering decent doubles with shower/wc or bath for €40–46. Half board is compulsory over weekends in Jul–Aug at €32 per person, but that's no hardship because the food, served in a plush dining room, is very good. Menus start at €11 and continue at €14–26. À *la carte* there's *ballotine* of duck with *foie gras*, escalope of zander with wild nettle shoots, braised swordfish with herbs, prawn kebabs with lime and wild rice and pork fillet with spices. Pleasant terrace filled with pot plants. Excellent reception. Free coffee or breakfast if you have an evening meal and stay overnight Sept–June.

CHENILLÉ-CHANGÉ   49220

⚥ ♨ |●| AUBERGE LA TABLE DU MEUNIER

How to get there: take the N162 north from Lion-d'Angers, then the D78.
☎ 02.41.95.10.98 ➡ 02.41.95.10.52
e maine.anjou.rivieres@wanadoo.fr
Closed Sun evening, Mon, Tue and Wed 1 Nov–31 March; Mon evening, Tue and Wed 1 April–30 June; 1 Sept–30 Oct. **Disabled access**. **Car park**.

Situated in a village full of flowers with a gentle river running nearby and a huge statue in the entrance, this dreamy place offers guaranteed peace and quiet. There are six charmingly decorated dining rooms and a huge panoramic terrace. Really tasty local cuisine with a good reputation: house *foie gras*, zander with *beurre blanc*, duck breast with apples and *beurre blanc*, *nougat glacé* with a raspberry *coulis*. Menus from €15 (except Sun lunchtime and public holidays) and up to €41. They have a few rooms on a boat nearby, where you'll be lulled to sleep by the sound of the flowing water. Free apéritif.

CHOLET   49300

⚥ |●| AU PASSÉ SIMPLE

181 rue Nationale.
☎ 02.41.75.90.061
Closed Sun (lunchtime only on public holidays); Mon; the first week in Jan; 2 weeks in Aug.

Fish dishes are the speciality in this bright and modern restaurant. There's a weekday lunch *formule* for €11, a menu at €12 and others €17–28. Specialities include zander with *beurre blanc*; for dessert try the *sabayon* of caramelized apples with acacia honey, served on a heavy slate block. Free apéritif.

DOUÉ-LA-FONTAINE   49700

|●| LE CAVEAU

4 [bis] pl. du Champde-Foire; it's signposted from the town centre.
☎ 02.41.59.38.28
Closed Mon–Thurs and Fri lunchtime out of season.

A warm, welcoming place in the heart of the village, which started life a medieval cellar before becoming a famous dance hall. People head here for their *fouaces*, or hearth-cakes – a sort of unleavened bread traditionally cooked in cinders. Try them with *rillettes*, goat's cheese or smothered with sweet local butter. Several *formules* are on offer (generously served and easy on the pocket), as well as a €9 lunch menu and another at €18 including wine and coffee. The place is run by three smiling young people who will fill you in on all manner of activities in the region; once in a while they have a theatrical evening.

LOURESSE-ROCHEMENIER   49700 (6KM N)

⚥ |●| LES CAVES DE LA GÉNÉVRAIE

13 rue du Musée-Rocheménier (Centre); take the D761 or the D69 north from Doué-la-Fontaine.
☎ 02.41.59.34.22
Closed Mon July–Aug; Mon–Thurs, Fri lunch and Sun evening Sept–June;.a fortnight in early Jan **Disabled access**. **Car park**.

This gallery, hewn out of the rock, was used as a hiding place during the Wars of Religion. Nowadays there are several small dining rooms and, when it's hot outside, the stone keeps them cool. They offer the local speciality *fouaces* (wheat cakes cooked in cinders), which they stuff with *rillettes*, beans or mushrooms and serve with *hors-d'œuvres* and Layon wines. There's one menu only, at €19, which includes wine and coffee.

Reservations only – and smoking is not permitted. Free coffee.

ÉVRON   53600

♠ |●| HÔTEL-RESTAURANT BRASSERIE DE LA GARE**

13 rue de la Paix (Centre); it's opposite the station.
☎ 02.43.01.60.29 ➡ 02.43.37.26.53
Restaurant closed Sun **Establishment closed** 3–22 Aug. **TV**.

This establishment looks like something out of another era and you'd probably hesitate before deciding to give it a go. It's a good place, however, and offers quiet, comfortable bedrooms with shower or bath for €33–37. They serve generous portions of good regional cooking in the restaurant – the €10 weekday menu lists dishes like house *terrine*, rib steak *façon vallée de l'Erve* and rhubarb tart. There's another menu at €15.

MEZANGERS   53600 (6KM N)

⅔ ♠ |●| RELAIS DU GUÉ DE SELLE***

Route de Mayenne; it's on the D7.
☎ 02.43.91.20.00 ➡ 02.43.91.20.10
ⓦ www.relais-du-gue-de-selle.com
Closed Fri and Sun evenings and Mon 16 Oct–31 May; 22 Dec–10 Jan. **Garden. Swimming pool. TV. Car park**.

Though this farmhouse – which is located in the middle of the country with the forest at its back and a pond at the front – has lost nearly everything of its original atmosphere, it's been restored and converted into a welcoming inn. It offers great menus from €18 (weekdays only) to €41. Try the lobster and *foie gras* turnover, the marbled rabbit *pâté* with onion marmalade, the chicken with morels and the warm apples with caramel. You'll get absolute peace and quiet in the pleasant, comfortable bedrooms (€59–86), which overlook either the garden, the swimming pool or the countryside. 10% discount on the room rate.

NEAU   53150 (6KM W)

♠ |●| HÔTEL-RESTAURANT LA CROIX VERTE**

2 rue d'Évron (Centre); from Évron, head towards Laval.
☎ 02.43.98.23.41 ➡ 02.43.98.25.39
Restaurant closed Sun and Fri evenings Nov to end March. **Establishment closed** Feb school holidays. **TV. Car park**.

Your heart might sink when you catch sight of

this place – it's set on an unattractive junction and sports a dreary façade. But you'll be pleasantly surprised when you step inside, and might even be tempted to stay longer than you planned. Superbly refurbished bedrooms with shower/wc or bath are €36–37, and there's a nice bar. The *à la carte* menu is full of tasty specialities – mussels with Pommeau, duck *foie gras*, scallops in Noilly, fillet of trout with Pommeau and delicious rib steak with girolles. Weekday menu €11, with others €17–27.

SAINTE-SUZANNE   53270 (7KM SE)

⅔ |●| RESTAURANT L'AUBERGE DE LA CITÉ

7 pl. Hubert-II (Centre); take the D7.
☎ 02.43.01.47.66
Closed Mon and Tues evenings (except July–Aug); Jan.

This restaurant, housed in a fourteenth-century building, serves very good food, some of it concocted from medieval recipes. (The *patronne* will even prepare medieval menus to order for groups.) Otherwise, people usually go for the *crêpes* and *galettes*. If those don't appeal, there are menus from €10 to €21. Free apéritif or coffee.

DEUX-ÉVAILLES   53150 (12KM NW)

⅔ |●| LA FENDERIE

site de la Fenderie; it's on the D129 between Jublains and Montsurs, at the edge of the village.
☎ 02.43.90.00.95
Closed Mon. **Car park. Disabled access**.

This place stands in forty acres of grounds; normally the birds have the place to themselves but at the weekends picnickers crowd in – so avoid the scrum by relaxing on the terrace opposite the pond. Menus at €13–30 (or from €9 during the week) list local dishes that change daily. Good bets include the warm chicken and apple salad with cider vinegar and the pike with *beurre blanc*. When skies are grey, enjoy the dining room with its fireplace and exposed beams. Free *coupette* served with your dessert.

JUBLAINS   53160 (17KM NW)

|●| CRÊPERIE-GRILL L'ORGÉTORIX

9 rue Henri-Barbe.
☎ 02.43.04.31.64
Closed last week of the summer holidays. **Open** by reservation only out of season.

Here, Monsieur takes command of the stove

and Madame oversees the dining room. They're obviously doing something right – after 12.30pm there's hardly a seat left. The menus are delicious and very cheap: two-course *formule* for €6, three-course menu at €8 including drink. They also serve *crêpes*. Perhaps follow your meal with a stroll around this old Gaul village.

FERTÉ-BERNARD (LA)   72400

🎿 🏠 |●| HÔTEL-RESTAURANT DU STADE

21–23 rue Virette.
☎ 02.43.93.01.67 ➡ 02.43.93.48.26
Closed Fri and Sun evenings; a week from Christmas to New Year's Day; Aug. **Car park**. **TV**. **Disabled access**.

A small establishment in a little side road – you feel you've gone back twenty years. It's clean and well maintained. Doubles from €38–43. Nice family-style cooking on a good weekday menu at €9 (including coffee); others go up to €28. Free coffee.

🎿 🏠 |●| HÔTEL-RESTAURANT LA PERDRIX**

2 rue de Paris.
☎ 02.43.93.00.44 ➡ 02.43.93.74.95
e restaurantlaperdrix@hotmail.com
Closed Mon evening; Tues; Feb. **TV**. **Pay car park**.

Serge Thibaut's establishment is as pleasing to the eye as it is to the palate. Menus (€17–35) list masterpieces such as pan-fried duck *foie gras* with raspberry vinegar, braised monkfish *osso bucco*-style with spaghetti, pigeons with potato pancakes and sliced pineapple with sabayon. The wine cellar boasts almost six hundred vintages. Doubles are €38–49 with shower/wc, and there's a duplex that sleeps five. Fortunately, the exceptional talent here goes hand in hand with great modesty and outstanding hospitality. Free coffee.

🎿 |●| LE BOCAGE FLEURI

14 pl. Carnot, galerie Carnot.
☎ 02.43.71.24.04
Closed Sun; Tues evening; Aug. **Garden**.

A little place in the middle of town, much praised by the locals. The terrace is ideal when the weather's fine. Really professional cuisine and they don't stint on the helpings; menus from €8 in the week. There's a lovely interior garden. Free coffee.

|●| LE DAUPHIN

3 rue d'Huisne (Centre); it's in a pedestrianized street.

☎ 02.43.93.00.39
Closed Sun evening; Mon; the last fortnight in Aug.
Disabled access.

This delightful restaurant is dominated by a huge fireplace. It's located in a historic building near the porte Saint-Julien and is popular with couples and gourmands alike. Menus €15–37. The dishes, including fillet of beef with *foie gras* or chocolate *moelleux* with pistachios, change regularly.

SAINT-ULPHACE   72320 (14KM SE)

🎿 |●| LE GRAND MONARQUE

5 pl. du Grand-Monarque (Centre); it's right in the heart of the village.
☎ 02.43.93.27.27
Closed Sun evening; Tues.

This place is a hit with the locals – who enjoy long, convivial Sunday lunches here. Menus are priced from €8 to €35 and offer good solid cuisine: house *foie gras*, scallop and Dublin Bay prawn salad. There's a covered terrace in summer and in winter they have themed evenings – based around dishes such as paella, *choucroute*, seafood and so on. Free coffee.

MONTMIRAIL   72320 (15KM SE)

|●| CRÊPERIE L'ANCIENNE FORGE

11 [bis] pl. du Château.
☎ 02.43.71.49.14
Closed Sun evening; Tues; a week in Sept; a fortnight at New Year.

A pretty little restaurant with a terrace overlooking a château. The good food includes wonderful salads and *galettes*, delicately flavoured *taboulé*, rib steak and ice cream with strawberries. It'll cost you around €11 for a meal. Soft background music and friendly smiles.

BONNÉTABLES   72110 (20KM W)

🎿 🏠 |●| HÔTEL-RESTAURANT LE LION D'OR

1 rue du Maréchal-Leclerc (Centre).
☎ and ➡ 02.43.29.38.55
Closed Sun in Aug. **TV**. **Car park**.

This charming building, which dates back to the eleventh century, is situated in the centre of the town. It has fifteen delightful rooms, which cost from €30 with basin to €38 with shower or bath. There's a restaurant and a *crêperie*, too: in the former the cooking is from the Sarthe region and dishes are sophisticated. Weekday lunch menu €8, others €14–26. They make all their own pastries – try the *tarte Tatin*. Very warm welcome. Free apéritif and 10% discount on the room rate.

FLÈCHE (LA)   72200

🏃 🏠 |●| RELAIS HENRI IV

It's on the Le Mans road, the N23.
☎ 02.43.94.07.10 📠 02.43.45.97.33
Closed Sun evening; Mon; the Feb and All Saints' school holidays. **TV**.

The inn is on the edge of the town and set back from the road. The rooms are bright, clean and soundproofed; doubles €32–40. Good food, also: the duck breast in a salt crust is excellent, and – since the chef is really passionate about chocolate – make sure to try his *millefeuille*. The walls in the dining room are plastered with 200 chocolate moulds and figurines. Menus €13–€27. Nice welcome. Free apéritif.

🏃 🏠 RELAIS CICERO***

18 bd. d'Alger (Centre); it's near pl. Thiers, close to the Prytanée.
☎ 02.43.94.14.14 📠 02.43.45.98.96
Closed Sun evening, 12 Dec–6 Jan and 27 July–13 Aug. **Garden. Car park TV**.

A beautiful residence in a sixteenth-century building (modified in the eighteenth century), well away from the crowds and noise of the town. There's an English bar, a reading room, a comfortable breakfast room and an open fire. Bedrooms in the main house are so stylish and comfortable that they're well worth splashing out on, but the hotel proper is actually on the other side of the flower garden. There you get cosy doubles with shower or bath for €66–103. This place oozes charm. 10% discount Sept–June.

🏃 |●| LE MOULIN DES QUATRE SAISONS

rue Gallieni (Centre); it's opposite the town hall.
☎ 02.43.45.12.12
Closed Sun and Wed evenings; Mon; the middle two weeks in Jan.

This restaurant has a great riverside location opposite the Château des Carmes, and with the country inn décor and the syrupy background music you could almost imagine yourself on the banks of the Danube. There's a wonderful terrace, too. Tasty, good-value food on menus from €14 (including coffee and wine). Dishes change regularly but might include *pastilla* of oxtail with horseradish sauce and salmon with fresh noodles. Free coffee.

🏃 |●| RESTAURANT LA FESSE D'ANGE

pl. du 8-Mai-1945 (Centre).
☎ 02.43.94.73.60
Closed Sun and Tues evenings; Mon; the first week of Feb; 1–20 Aug.

An extremely good establishment, with bold modern décor. Menus go from €17 to €33 and dishes change regularly but might include *foie gras* with dried apricots, *suprême* of guineafowl in nettle sauce, *escalopines* of warm *foie gras* with peppered pears, fillet of zander with white Jasnières and warm raspberry *soufflé*. Free coffee.

LUCHÉ-PRINGÉ   72800 (13KM E)

🏃 🏠 |●| AUBERGE DU PORT-DES-ROCHES**

Le Port-des-Roches (North).
☎ 02.43.45.44.48. 📠 02.43.45.39.61
Closed Sun evening; Mon; 27 Jan–10 March. **TV. Car park**.

This inn is run by an energetic, hard-working young couple who are bringing the place back to life. Brightly coloured bedrooms cost €38–47 for a double. In the cosy dining room they serve skilfully prepared dishes at good country prices – set menus are €18–32. There's an impressive selection of dishes and they change three times a year: *gratin* of goat's cheese gnocchi with beetroot sauce, poached char with walnuts, braised veal sweetbreads with pig's ears, tart of fresh sardines, *Paris-Brest* (a large choux pastry ring with almond and butter cream) served with candied pineapple. The superb flowery terrace overlooks the river, as do some of the bedrooms. Free apéritif.

FLOCELLIÈRE (LA)   85700

🏃 🏠 |●| CHÂTEAU DE LA FLOCELLIÈRE

La Flocelière; follow the signposts from Saint-Michel.
☎ 02.51.57.22.03 📠 02.51.57.75.21
🌐 www.flocellierecastle.com
Swimming pool. Garden. TV. Car park.

A luxurious hotel occupying a neo-Gothic castle, renovated by the Vignal family some years ago. Given the spaciousness of the superb rooms, it's not overly expensive at €99–160, and you'll have to book a long time in advance. Guests have access to the large park and swimming pool and can nose round the ruins of the 13th-century castle as well. The proprietors also rent out the dungeon, which is big enough for three families, and there are *gîtes* costing €381–1068 according to size and the length of your stay. They serve an evening meal for €38, which you enjoy in the company of the owners. 10% discount on the room rate and free apéritif Sept–June.

FONTENAY-LE-COMTE   85200

🕭 🏠 |●| HÔTEL FONTARABIE – RESTAURANT LA GLYCINE**

57 rue de la République (Centre).
☎ 02.51.69.17.24 ➡ 02.51.51.02.73
📧 fontarabie@aol.com
Closed 20 Dec–8 Jan. **Disabled access. TV. Car park**.

A long time ago, it was traditional for Basque merchants to travel to Fontenay to trade horses during the Feast of St John. They stayed in this very coaching inn – though the handsome white stone building with its slate roof has been restored somewhat since then. The new décor is tasteful, if a touch too modern, and the bedrooms are clean with adequate facilities. Try to avoid the ones overlooking the street – they're smaller and noiser. Doubles €43–49 with shower/wc. The restaurant, which is named after the wonderful wisteria over the front door, offers good regional cooking and generous portions of dishes like grilled *andouillette*, grilled calf's liver with bacon and a mouthwatering chocolate mousse. Menus €7–23 or around €15 *à la carte*. You'll get a cheerful reception from young, smiling staff. 10% discount on the room rate Sept–June.

🕭 |●| AUX CHOUANS GOURMETS

6 rue des Halles (Centre).
☎ 02.51.69.55.92
Closed Sun evening; Mon; a week in Jan; the last fortnight in March.

Service noon–2pm and 7–9.30pm. A solidly built house with a noble façade; the dining room has splendid rough-hewn stone walls and there's a covered terrace overlooking the Vendée. Perfectly pitched welcome and service. You'll find traditional and gourmet cuisine that uses fresh ingredients purchased from the market on the doorstep. Dishes change with the seasons: ham *de Vendée* with *ballotine* forcemeat; pan-fried crayfish with shellfish *jus* and fried parsley. Menus €13–34. Free coffee.

PISSOTTE   85200 (4KM N)

🕭 |●| CRÊPERIE LE POMMIER

9 rue des Gélinières (Centre); take the D938.
☎ 02.51.69.08.06
Closed Mon; 12 days at the end of Sept. **Disabled access. Garden. Car park**.

This serene old building is next to an ancient wine cellar. It has a garden and a conservatory, and is covered in wisteria and Virginia creeper. They do *crêpes* served with a generous side dish – try the *Bretonne* with *andouillette*, apples and salad, the *Caprine* with goat's cheese and thyme or the *Syracuse* with smoked breast of duck, pan-fried apples and orange sauce. Wash it all down with a nice bottle of local rosé. Menus start at €7. Free apéritif.

MERVENT   85200 (11KM NE)

🕭 |●| CRÊPERIE DU CHÂTEAU DE LA CITARDIÈRE

Les Ouillères; take the D99 from Mervent.
☎ 02.51.00.27.04
Closed Wed in season, Mon–Fri (except public holidays) Oct to May.

Pretty place in a rather strange seventeenth-century castle. Parts of it have been converted to provide accommodation for walkers. There's a gorgeous rustic dining room which smells of wood smoke and pancake batter, or you can enjoy the fresh air out on the terrace in summer. They serve the most wonderful *crêpes* filled with everything from duck breast to mushrooms, or there's a sweet one with flambéed apples. Expect to pay about €12 for a complete meal. There's a cellar where they hold exhibitions and musical evenings. Free coffee.

VELLUIRE   85770 (11KM SW)

🕭 🏠 |●| L'AUBERGE DE LA RIVIÈRE**

How to get there: take the D938 as far as Nizeau, then the D68.
☎ 02.51.52.32.15 ➡ 02.51.52.37.42
Closed Sun evening and Mon out of season; Mon only 1 Jul–20 Sept. **Disabled access. TV. Car park**.

This place is ideal if you're after quiet, luxury and fine cooking. The attractive dining room, all yellow tablecloths, beams, pot plants and tapestries, makes a great setting to eat bass with artichokes, prawns in flaky pastry or young pigeon with morels. Weekday menu €19; others €31–39. The charming country-style bedrooms cost €69–82 with bath;

number 10 is the only one without a river view. 10% discount on the room rate for a two-night stay mid-Sept to mid-June.

MAILLEZAIS   85420 (15KM SE)

⚐ ☎ HÔTEL SAINT-NICOLAS**

rue du Docteur-Daroux (Centre).
☎ 02.51.00.74.45 ➡ 02.51.87.29.10
Closed 15 Nov–15 Feb. **TV**. **Lock-up garage**.

The young owner of this friendly little hotel looks after everything – from the simple rooms (€35–52 with shower or bath) to the terrace with its tiny gardens. He knows the area like the back of his hand and will show you his own walks through the Poitou marshlands; it's an excellent base from which to explore the area. 10% discount except during school holidays.

FONTEVRAUD-L'ABBAYE   49590

⚐ ☎ |●| HÔTEL LA CROIX BLANCHE**

7 pl. des Plantagenêts; it's beside the abbey.
☎ 02.41.51.71.11 ➡ 02.41.38.15.38
e snc.lacroixblanche@wanadoo.fr
Closed 13 Jan–10 Feb; 18–29 Nov. **Disabled access**. **TV**. **Car park**.

A delightful hotel in an elegant building, right next to the abbey of Fontevraud. They have 21 bedrooms set around a quiet, flower-filled courtyard. Doubles with shower/wc or bath are €40–79. Some have a fireplace made of local stone. The restaurant, well known for its good cooking, offers a vegetarian menu for €15 and others €23–40. A typical list might include salad of black pudding with walnuts and fried apples, lamb chops with onions, followed by cheese and dessert. On the most expensive menus – which include two main courses – you might see wild mushrooms with asparagus, *goujons* of sole, beef *tournedos* with truffle sauce and duck *foie gras* with figs and Calvados. Nice welcome. One free breakfast per room Oct–March and free house apéritif.

GUENROUET   44530

⚐ |●| LE JARDIN DE L'ISAC

31 rue de l'Isac; it's 6km east of Saint-Gildes-les-Bois.
☎ 02.40.87.66.11
e cuisineries@relais-saint-clair.com
Closed Mon and Tues except June–Aug; a week in Jan; a week in Feb. **Disabled access**.

This place is actually two restaurants run by

the same couple – a gastronomic establishment upstairs and this one below offering unbeatable prices. In summer you eat on the flower-filled terrace in the shade of a magnificent wisteria. Menus are at €10 and €14, or you can dine *à la carte*. You could easily be satisfied with the *hors-d'œuvre* buffet, which offers a wide selection including fish *terrine*, *charcuterie* and all sorts of *crudités*. For a main course, opt for grilled meat or fish of the day and then head straight back to the buffet for dessert. There are two dining rooms, the best of which looks onto the river – the other one, where the buffets are, is somewhat gloomy. Professional service and welcome. Free coffee.

HERBIERS (LES)   85500

☎ |●| HÔTEL-RESTAURANT LE CENTRE**

6 rue de l'Église (Centre).
☎ 02.51.67.01.75 ➡ 02.51.66.82.24
Closed Fri evening; Sat out of season; 10 days at the end of July; the Christmas school holidays. **TV**.

This place is located in the middle of the town, but it's quiet enough and warmly welcoming – ideal as a base from which to explore the region. Doubles €41–46. Half board is compulsory during the Puy-du-Fou show and over the weekend. This is no hardship because the owner is a good chef and produces dishes using fresh produce and lots of fish. Menus €11–24.

☎ |●| HÔTEL-RESTAURANT LE RELAIS**

18 rue de Saumur (Centre).
☎ 02.51.91.01.64 ➡ 02.51.67.36.50
Closed Sun evening, Mon lunchtime, 30 July–8 Aug. **TV**.

This good hotel, with its beautiful, well-renovated façade, offers 26 luxurious bedrooms; doubles are €44 with shower/wc or bath. Although it's by the roadside, the double glazing is effective. In the dining room, which is as swanky as the bedrooms, you can choose between traditional brasserie dishes or gourmet cuisine such as medallions of hind sautéed in thyme butter, Saint-Paul snails with *foie gras*, lobster *blanquette*. Menus at €11 for weekday lunch and others €15–48.

SAINT-LAURENT-SUR-SÈVRE   85290 (20KM NE)

⚐ ☎ |●| HÔTEL-RESTAURANT L'HERMITAGE**

2 rue de la Jouvence (Centre); take the D752 and it's on the river Sèvre, by the bridge opposite the basilica.

☎ 02.51.67.83.03 ➦ 02.51.67.84.11
Closed Sat out of season; Sun evening 1 May–30 Sept; a week in the Feb school holidays; 1–15 Aug. **TV. Car park**.

A nice family inn with a terrace overlooking the river. The chef/proprietor gets up at the crack of dawn to pick what he needs from his kitchen garden and sometimes fishes for zander in the river below the terrace. The menus, €12–24, list good dishes, and you'll get generous portions: Vendée ham, zander with sorrel, chocolate *charlotte*. The dining room has changed little since the 1960s and the rooms are comfortable but perhaps need updating. The nicest ones look over the river Sèvre. Doubles €34–41. Free coffee.

LAVAL 53000

⚲ ⌂ MARIN HÔTEL**

100–102 av. Robert-Buron (Northeast); it's opposite the train station.
☎ 02.43.53.09.68 ➦ 02.43.56.95.35
℮ decouacon@wanadoo.fr
TV. Pay car park. Disabled access.

This establishment, which belongs to the *Inter-Hôtel* chain, is modern, functional and an ideal place to stop if you've just got off the TGV. Doubles €42 with shower/wc or bath – the ones overlooking the road are noisy. There are lots of restaurants in the area. No credit cards. 10% discount Fri–Sun.

⚲ |◉| L'AVENIO

38 quai de Bootz.
☎ 02.43.56.87.51
Closed Sat, Sun and the first three weeks in Aug. **Car park**.

This is a haunt of local fishermen and people on their lunch-break. The place is decorated with old fishing lines, reels and hooks and conversations often focus on the ones that got away. Home cooking: it's delicious and served in gargantuan portions. There's only one menu, at €11, but it includes wine and a coffee. A place which feels genuine. No credit cards. Free house apéritif.

⚲ |◉| L'ANTIQUAIRE

5 rue des Béliers (Centre); it's behind the cathedral.
☎ 02.43.53.66.76
Closed Wed; Sat lunchtime; a week in the Feb school holidays; 6–27 July.

The food here is simply magnificent. The cheapest menu is a bargain at €15 and there are others up to €35. They list dishes like *foie gras* terrine with apple and cider preserve,

gras terrine with apple and cider preserve, zander fillet with shallots and cider vinegar, steak with Camembert *au gratin* and Port Salut cheese sauce and *moelleux* of chocolate with pistachio ice-cream. The house speciality is crayfish tail lasagne with local *andouillette*. Free coffee.

|◉| LA BRAISE

4 rue de la Trinité (Centre); it's in the old town, near the cathedral.
☎ 02.43.53.21.87
Closed Sat lunchtime; Sun; Mon; a week at Easter; a week around 15 Aug.

A cute little place with beautiful furniture, wooden beams and hand-made hexagonal floor tiles. You receive a wonderful welcome. The simple, authentic dishes are skilfully cooked, many of them over charcoal. Grilled fish and meat are the specialities, as you would expect – try the scallop kebabs, the knuckle of pork with Armagnac or the red mullet kebab. Menus from €17. If it's sunny, sit on the terrace.

|◉| RESTAURANT LE BISTRO DE PARIS

22 quai Jehan-Fouquet (Centre); it's on the banks of the Mayenne.
☎ 02.43.56.98.29
Closed Sat lunchtime; Sun evening; Mon; 10–28 Aug. **Disabled access**.

This is the best restaurant in town and can be the most expensive – unless you choose the *menu-carte*, which costs €21 in the week. At the other end of the scale, there's a *menu dégustation* for €40. Lots of wonderful dishes are served: sole fillet with lobster *jus*, roast saddle of lamb with nettles and a selection of home-made desserts. Guy Lemercier comes up with creative ideas to delight his regulars, who get a good-natured but not overly effusive welcome. Old-fashioned brasserie décor with rows and rows of mirrors, good service and fine wines.

CHANGÉ 53810 (4KM N)

⚲ |◉| LA TABLE RONDE

pl. de la Mairie (Centre); it's near the church.
☎ 02.43.53.43.33
Closed Sun and Wed evenings; Mon **Car park**.

The upstairs restaurant is impressive and expensive; downstairs there's an attractive bistro with '30s décor, smiling waitresses and low prices. On a fine day you can sit on the terrace, which faces the town on one side and the park on the other. There's a weekday *menu du jour* for €13 and others up to €36, listing dishes like zander and shrimp *ballotin*, cockerel ham with cider vinegar and pear *terrine* with caramel. Everything is skilfully prepared, rich in flavour and colourful – it's well worth leaving Laval to get here. Free apéritif.

GENEST-SAINT-ISLE (LE)   53940 (12KM W)

⚐ |●| RESTAURANT LE SALVERT

Route d'Olivet.
☎ 02.43.37.14.3
Closed Sun evening and Mon. **Disabled access**. **Car park**.

Just ten minutes from Laval on the Olivet lake, this restaurant has a terrace open in summer and an open fire when the weather is cooler. It's classy, too – this isn't a place to come wearing shorts or hiking boots. Menus (€15–29) list local dishes scupulously prepared using seasonal vegetables: *salade gourmande*, *foie gras*, smoked salmon, stuffed saddle of rabbit steamed in thyme and a wonderful selection of desserts. Their bread is home-made, just like everything else. Free coffee.

COSSÉ-LE-VIVIEN   53230 (18KM SW)

⚑ |●| HÔTEL-RESTAURANT L'ÉTOILE**

2 rue de Nantes (Centre); take the N171.
☎ 02.43.98.81.31 ➡ 02.43.98.96.64
Closed Sun evening; Mon; the second week of Feb; a fortnight in Aug. **TV**. **Car park**.

The seven bedrooms here are perfectly adequate, but the décor's pretty tacky. Doubles €24–34 with shower/wc or bath. The restaurant serves good traditional cooking, with a weekday menu at €10 and three others (€12–21), listing dishes like *croustillant* of pigs' ears, *fondant* of oxtails and *craquant* of starfruit. Best to book at weekends.

VAIGES   53480 (22KM E)

⚐ ⚑ |●| HÔTEL DU COMMERCE***

Rue du Fief-aux-Moines (Centre); take exit 2 off the A81.
☎ 02.43.90.50.07 ➡ 02.43.90.57.40
ⓦ www.hotelcommerce.com
Closed Fri and Sun evenings Oct–April; 1 May; evenings of 24 and 25 Dec; 4–27 Jan. **Disabled access**. **TV**. **Car park**.

Since 1882, when the Oger family first started running this successful hotel, their only concern has been that their guests should sleep soundly and eat well. You can quite happily spend a night or two in one of their quiet bedrooms – €52 with shower or bath – and dine in the conservatory where they serve good food based on local produce: duck *foie gras*, rabbit thigh in cider, cheeses and apple tart. There's a *formule* for €14 and menus €16–43. Free coffee.

ERNÉE   53500 (30KM NW)

⚑ |●| LE GRAND CERF**

17–19 rue Aristide-Briand (Centre); it's on the N12 in the direction of Mayenne.
☎ 02.43.05.13.09 ➡ 02.43.05.02.90
Closed Sun evening and Mon out of season; 15–31 Jan. **TV**. **Car park**.

A good hotel in northern Mayenne, a region of dolmens and standing stones. The establishment is known for its hospitality, facilities and good food. The restaurant is fairly sombre, but it's more relaxed in the bistro corner. The dishes are intelligently planned around seasonal produce and offered on various menus: crayfish tails roasted with cubes of pig's trotter, fillet of beef in a spiced bread crust and fresh fruit soup with ginger sorbet. Weekday lunch *formule* at €16, then others €21–28. Beautiful bedrooms are €40 with bath.

⚐ |●| LA TABLE NORMANDE

3 av. Aristide-Briand (Centre); it's on the N12 in the direction of Mayenne.
☎ 02.43.05.13.09 ➡ 02.43.05.02.90
Closed Tues–Thurs evenings; a fortnight in the Feb school holidays; a fortnight in Aug.

Even if the lunch or dinner service is finished, they never refuse to serve you here. The owners are deeply committed to what they do. Their restaurant has a nice atmosphere and is popular with local workers, travelling salesmen and passing tourists. Delicious homemade dishes. Lunch menu €9 or others €12–18 – good value. Free house apéritif.

LUÇON   85400

⚐ ⚑ |●| HÔTEL-RESTAURANT LE BŒUF COURONNÉ**

55 route de La-Roche-sur-Yon (West).
☎ 02.51.56.11.32 ➡ 02.51.56.98.25
ⓔ boeufcouronne@wanadoo.fr
Closed Sun evening and Mon. **TV**. **Car park**.

Though it's a little close to the road, this is an attractive place, with a flower-laden pergola, a delightfully cosy lounge and several dining rooms. Good cooking: duck *foie gras* in port, *grenadin* of veal with chanterelles, *paupiettes* of sole with langoustine, duck breast with peaches. Set menus €11–26. It's a delight to watch them preparing the flambéed dishes. Four rather plush bedrooms at €43 with shower/wc or bath. Free coffee.

LUDE (LE)   72800

⅍ |●| LA RENAISSANCE**

2 av. de la Libération.
☎ 02.43.94.63.10
Closed Sun evening and Mon. **TV. Car park**.

Though this is a pretty grand place, the atmosphere is in no way formal and men don't even have to wear ties. There is a bewildering choice of dishes on the menu, but the chef is happy to help you decide. He uses the freshest produce and monitors the cooking of each dish meticulously. Service is also good and comes with a smile. Weekday menu at €10 and others €13–33. Free house apéritif.

MALICORNE-SUR-SARTHE   72270

⅍ |●| RESTAURANT LA PETITE AUBERGE

5 pl. Du-Guesclin.
☎ 02.43.94.80.52
e lellio@club-internet.fr
Closed Sun–Fri evenings out of season; Mon in season; 15 Feb–15 March. **Disabled access. Car park**.

Set on a riverbank, this restaurant has a rather attractive terrace where you can treat yourself to pike *terrine*, fillet of sea trout, cheese and dessert for €14. Prices go up a little on Sunday and there's a choice of other menus from €20 to €32. À *la carte*, dishes change according to what's in season and which fish is available at the market. The elegant flower-filled dining room has a fireplace and is ideal for grey days. Free coffee.

MAMERS   72600

⬕ |●| HÔTEL-RESTAURANT LE DAUPHIN**

54 rue du Fort.
☎ 02.43.34.24.24
Closed Fri and Sun evenings. **TV. Car park**.

Pay a visit to this unpretentious little hotel if you want to try *rillettes* – a delicacy made from shredded pork cooked in its own fat – at their best. À *la carte* you'll come across specialities such as omelette with *rillettes* and *marmite sarthoise*; menus at €10–26. They

also have perfectly adequate bedrooms: €27–40 with shower, shower/wc or bath.

NEUCHÂTEL-EN-SAOSNOIS   72600 (9KM W)

⬕ |●| RELAIS DES ÉTANGS DE GUIBERT

How to get there: in the village turn right by the church into rue Louis-Ragot and it's 800m further on.
☎ 02.43.97.15.38 ➡ 02.43.97.66.42
Closed Sun evening and Mon (except public holidays). **Disabled access. Car park**.

Set at the edge of the Perseigne forest near the pond, this place comes to life as soon as the sun shows its face. It's got it all – pleasant décor, wonderful welcome and good prices – and you may find it difficult to get a room at the weekend. Rooms are decorated with sailing or hunting themes. Doubles €41. In the restaurant they serve lots of fish and house *foie gras*; there's a weekday lunch menu for €13 and others up to €29.

ROUPERROUX-LE-COQUET   72110 (18KM SE)

⅍ |●| LE PETIT CAMPAGNARD

It's on the D301.
☎ 02.43.29.79.74
Closed Mon and Weds; Tues and Thurs evenings (except for group bookings for 15–20 people). **Disabled access. Car park**.

A pretty little place, especially popular on Sundays. The unbeatable €11 menu offers *rillettes* (shredded pork cooked in its own fat), chicken with cider, cheese and dessert. The €9 weekday menu is also a good deal, as are the others, €17–27 – they list interesting dishes like scallops with leeks, fillet of red mullet with lemon sauce, ostrich flambéed with Calvados and venison flambéed with whisky. Free coffee.

FRESNAYE-SUR-CHÉDOUET (LA)   72600 (22KM NW)

⅍ ⬕ |●| L'AUBERGE SAINT-PAUL

La Grande Terre; take the D3 and the D234.
☎ 02.43.97.82.76 ➡ 02.43.97.82.84
Closed Mon and Tues except public holidays. **Disabled access. Car park**.

This former stud farm is an ideal place to come if you like to eat in peace. There are four little bedrooms for €30 with bath – although they don't have quite the same timeless charm as the inn, with its fireplace and red floor tiles. Pascal Yenk's cooking is skilfully prepared and full of flavour. He offers dishes like duck *foie gras* with shallot preserve, *suprême* of bass in a potato crust, medallions of lamb with *confit* of vegetables and roast *langoustine*. Wonderful set menu at €20. Very professional service. 10% discount on the room rate.

MANS (LE)   72000

⅍ ≙ HÔTEL LA POMMERAIE**

314 rue de l'Éventail (East); follow signs for the N23 to Paris, turn into rue de Douce-Amie at auberge Bagatelle.
☎ 02.43.85.13.93
Garden. Disabled access. TV. Car park.

Though just a short car journey from the city centre, this hotel, which is set in a large, flower-filled garden, is wonderfully peaceful. Concentrate on the garden, the hospitality and the feeling of luxury and you might even be able to forget the bland postwar architecture. Doubles from €31 with basin to €42 with bath. The energetic young hotelier lets you choose your own room. Free coffee.

⅍ ≙ ANJOU HÔTEL

23 bd. de la Gare; it's opposite the train station.
☎ 02.43.24.90.45 ➡ 02.43.24.82.38
Closed 20 Dec–2 Jan. **TV. Pay car park.**

A practically located hotel opposite the station. The young couple who have taken it over really care for their guests and give you a warm welcome. They have redecorated the rooms and put in double glazing: they go for €47 with shower or bath. One free breakfast for each night's stay.

⅍ ≙ |●| HÔTEL GREEN 7**

447 av. Georges-Durand (Southeast); it's in the south of the town on the road to Tours.
☎ 02.43.40.30.30 ➡ 02.43.40.30.00
e le.green.7@wanadoo.fr
Closed Fri and Sun evenings. **TV. Car park. Disabled access.**

A pleasant hotel less than 2km from the 24-hour Le Mans circuit. Comfortable, well-decorated rooms with shower or bath cost from €45, including a splendid breakfast. Though the restaurant is not brilliant, it produces more than adequate traditional dishes using fresh produce if you don't want to go into town for a meal: pan-fried scallops with herbs, saddle of lamb with rosemary. Menus €13–30. There's also a fitness room with a Jacuzzi and sauna. Free apéritif.

⅍ ≙ |●| HÔTEL CHANTECLER***

50 rue de la Pelouse (East); it's between the train station and the conference centre.

☎ 02.43.14.40.00 ➡ 02.43.77.16.28
ⓦ www.hotelchantecler.fr
TV. Car park.

Just a short distance from the station, this hotel offers peace and comfort within easy reach of the old part of Le Mans. The welcome is sincere, the parking easy and the breakfast, which is served in the conservatory, rather good. Decent doubles with shower or bath, €59–63 There is a restaurant on the ground floor, but it doesn't compare to the rest of the establishment. 10% discount on the room rate in August.

⅍ |●| AUBERGE DES 7 PLATS

79 Grande-Rue (Centre); it's in the old town.
☎ 02.43.24.57.77
Closed Sun and Mon.

The large half-timbered house has real style – there are several in the street but this is one of the best you'll find in the old part of Le Mans. Their other claim to originality, as you'll guess from the name, is that they offer seven hot dishes on the same menu. The youthful, relaxed welcome adds considerably to the appeal. There's a brigade of staff in the kitchen producing beef Rossini-style with *foie gras* and cep sauce, local ham or duck breast with peppercorns, duck *confit* and *paupiettes* with a great deal of care and attention. To top it all, it's good value for money: €11 for a main course and a dessert, with another menu at €14. *Appellation* wines are sold by the carafe and all the apéritifs cost €3. Probably advisable to book. Free *digestif*.

|●| L'ATLAS

80 bd. de la Petite Vitesse (Southeast).
☎ 02.43.61.03.16
Closed Mon and Sat lunchtime. **Disabled access.**

Open until 11.30pm. Close to the station, in an area otherwise lacking in good restaurants, this Moroccan restaurant is a real find. The proprietor has done his country proud with both the opulent decor and the cuisine – try the excellent *tajines* and fresh Moroccan pastries. There's an €11 menu and you'll pay about €17–23 *à la carte*. Live music at weekends.

⅍ |●| LE NEZ ROUGE

107 Grande-Rue (Northwest).
☎ 02.43.24.27.26
Closed Sun and Mon; three weeks from mid-Aug to 7 Sept.

This old-town gourmet restaurant is the place to come for a *mongolfière* of mussels and cockles in a leek sauce, poached turbot in champagne, fillets of grenadier served in a butter and wine sauce or quails with figs. Weekday menu at €17, with others €25–37. For a more relaxed atmosphere try the same establishment's charming gourmet *crêperie*, which is on pl. du Hallai nearby. Free coffee.

🏃 |●| LE FLAMBADOU

14 [bis] rue Saint-Flaceau (West); it's near the town hall.
☎ 02.43.24.88.38
℮ le.flambadou@wanadoo.fr
Closed Sun; a week at Easter; a week around 15 Aug.

The owner-chef of this highly recommended restaurant prepares specialities from his native region of the Landes and Périgord: casserole of snails with ceps, goose casserole *à la lotoise* and *fricassée* of duck. The main courses are so generous that you may not be able to manage a dessert. Allow around €27 *à la carte*. You can dine in the sweet little dining room or out on the shady terrace. Warm, hearty welcome. Free apéritif.

YVRÉ-L'ÉVÊQUE   72530 (5KM E)

🏃 🏠 HÔTEL-MOTEL PAPEA**

Bener; leave Le Mans on the N23 and follow signs to Papea.
☎ 02.43.89.64.09 ➡ 02.43.89.49.81
TV. Car park.

This motel is set in lovely grounds near the abbey of Epau. Some twenty comfortable chalets, separated from each other by bushes and trees, cost €31–43 for two. Ideal if you want to stay in the country but also be very close to the city. You can get meals on a tray, €8, to order in advance. Lower prices for weekends, long stays and commercial travellers are on offer. Friendly welcome. One free breakfast per room per night.

MULSANNE   72230 (8KM S)

🏠 |●| HÔTEL-RESTAURANT ARBOR – AUBERGE DE MULSANNE**

route de Tours; it's 10 minutes from town near the race circuit.
☎ 02.43.39.18.90 ➡ 02.43.39.18.99
🌐 www.aubergemulsanne.fr
Restaurant closed Sat lunchtime; Sun; 3 weeks in Aug. **Swimming pool. TV. Car park. Disabled access**.

This hotel, used by the competing teams during the 24-hour Le Mans race, is worth visiting any time of the year. The impeccable rooms cost €50 with bath, and there's a

sauna and swimming pool. Weekday menu €15, €23 at weekends, and others €29–56.

FILLÉ-SUR-SARTHE   72210 (15.5KM SW)

🏃 |●| RESTAURANT LE BARRAGE

rue du Passeur; it's the last house past the church.
☎ 02.43.87.14.40
Closed Sun evening; Mon; the All Saints' school holidays.

This restaurant is very popular locally, so if you want a table on the terrace looking directly onto the towpath and the Sarthe river, you should reserve. It's a serene, rural setting, and a perfect place to enjoy the good food – *foie gras* flan with port sauce, salmon *escalope* roasted with fresh herbs, roast cod with lemon butter. Weekday menus €9 and €13–24. Warm welcome. Free coffee.

DOMFRONT-EN-CHAMPAGNE 72240 (18KM NW)

🏃 |●| RESTAURANT DU MIDI

33 rue du Mans; it's on the D304, towards Mayenne.
☎ 02.43.20.52.04
Closed Mon; Tues; Wed–Sun evenings; Fri and Sat lunchtimes.

The dining room is comfortable, the surroundings are classy and the service is attentive. The cuisine has an excellent reputation, too – the weekday lunch menu, €12, lists mixed meat stew braised with Chinon wine, zander with smoked bacon, cheese and dessert. Other menus, €12–31, offer *foie gras* ravioli with morels, duck breast *à l'ancienne*, mussel stew, swordfish steak and Calvados sorbet with *tarte Tatin*. Reasonably priced wines on a generally good list. Free glass of sparkling wine with dessert.

BEAUMONT-SUR-SARTHE   72170 (25KM N)

🏃 🏠 |●| HÔTEL-RESTAURANT DU CHEMIN DE FER**

pl. de la Gare, Vivoin. Turn off the N138 onto the D26 towards Vivoin; the hotel is less than 1km from the town centre.
☎ 02.43.97.00.05 ➡ 02.43.97.87.49
℮ hotel-du-chemin-de-fer@wanadoo.fr
Closed Fri evening; Sat lunchtime; Sun evening (Nov–Easter). **Garden. TV. Car park**.

Cheerful staff welcome you and mouthwatering aromas waft from the kitchens. With the garden behind the house and the pastoral atmosphere in the large dining room you could almost be in the country. Treat yourself – scallops flambéed in whisky, *marmite* sarthoise (local hotpot), rib of beef, pike *terrine*, sautéed rabbit with mushrooms and fillet of pork in cider. Weekday *menu du jour* is €10. Fifteen pleasant rooms €35–46 with shower/wc or bath. Free apéritif.

THORIGNÉ-SUR-DUÉ 72160 (28KM E)

🅰 🔒 |◐| HÔTEL-RESTAURANT SAINT-JACQUES***

pl. du Monument; take the N23 and D302.
☎ 02.43.89.95.50 ➡ 02.43.76.58.42
✉ hotel-st-jacques.thorigne@wanadoo.fr
Closed Mon and Sun evening Sept–Jun; 1–15 Jan; 18–28 Jun. **Disabled access. Garden. TV. Secure parking**.

This family hotel celebrated its 150th anniversary in 2000, and the comfort, courtesy and good food it offers are an excellent example of traditional hotel-keeping. Doubles €52–69. Menus €14–53. Specialities include roast prawns on a bed of leeks, chicken with morel cream sauce, scallops with vanilla butter, whole steamed ox kidney with sweet garlic cream and iced nougat with raspberry *coulis*. 10% discount on the room rate.

SAINT-GERMAIN-SUR-SARTHE 72130 (35KM N)

🅰 |◐| RESTAURANT LE SAINT-GERMAIN

La Hutte. Take the N138; it's at the crossroads.
☎ 02.43.97.53.06
Closed Sun and Tues evenings, Mon.

It doesn't look promising from the outside, but in spite of the traffic rushing past on the main road this is a lovely place. Madame makes sure there are fresh flowers in the dining room and Monsieur keeps up the high standards of French sauce-making in the kitchen. Try the rabbit *terrine*, a splendid *cassolette* of fish, grilled rib of beef *béarnaise*, *salade gourmande*, fresh oysters, *gratin* of lobster or *fondant* of veal with morels. Dish of the day €10, with menus €11–35. Free apéritif.

MAYENNE 53100

🔒 |◐| L'AUBERGE DES TROIS ÉPIS

15 rue de la Madeleine; it's on the Laval road.
☎ 02.43.04.87.34 ➡ 02.43.04.83.60
Hotel closed 1 week in Dec; 1 week in Feb; 2 weeks in Aug. **Restaurant closed** Friday evening and Sat lunchtime. **Disabled access. TV. Car park**.

Quiet, peaceful old-fashioned hotel. Doubles have shower or bath (wc on the landing), which will cost you €24–26. Dishes in the restaurant include *trout à la normande* and

andouillette in cider. Weekday menu €9, with others €12 and €20.

🔒 HÔTEL LA TOUR DES ANGLAIS**

13 [bis] pl. Juhel (Centre).
☎ 02.43.04.34.56 ➡ 02.43.32.13.84
🌐 www.latourdesanglais.com
Restaurant closed lunchtimes and Sat–Sun. **Disabled access. TV. Car park**.

Very close to Château de Mayenne, this hotel has one wonderful room in a fortified tower with a dramatic view of the Mayenne river. The other rooms are comfortable but more modern; they're €41–43 with shower or bath. Weekday menu €11 and another at €15. There's an English-style bar with a billiard table and impressive wooden beams.

🅰 🔒 |◐| LE GRAND HÔTEL**

2 rue Ambroise de Loré (Centre); it faces the Mayenne river.
☎ 02.43.00.96.00 ➡ 02.43.32.08.49
Hotel closed Sat Nov–April. **Restaurant closed** Sat and Sun lunchtimes; 5–18 Aug. **Establishment closed** 21 Dec–6 Jan **Car park. TV**.

If only the rest of the town could be renovated and maintained as well as this hotel. Tourists arriving by car, bike and even boat are greeted with a cheery smile. Well-appointed rooms are €49–72 with shower/wc or bath. In the restaurant you get Breton or Norman cuisine in a quaint ambience, with menus €15–33; expect house *foie gras* with Muscat, red mullet fillets with aubergine caviar, duck breast with Coteau Layon sauce and apples with Calvados ice-cream. Round off the evening with a good whisky in the bar. 10% discount on the room rate (except Jun and Sept).

FONTAINE-DANIEL 53100 (4KM SW)

🅰 |◐| RESTAURANT LA FORGE

La Place (Centre).
☎ 02.43.00.34.85
Closed Wed; Sun evening; the Feb school holidays.

This lovely restaurant on the main square of this pretty village boasts a very nice terrace where you can enjoy excellent cuisine – such as marinated salmon *terrine* with leeks and rack of lamb *pot-au-feu* with baby vegetables. Menus €15–32. Best to book. Free coffee.

MOULAY 53100 (4KM S)

🔒 |◐| HÔTEL-RESTAURANT BEAU RIVAGE

How to get there: it's on the N162 between Mayenne and Moulay.
☎ 02.43.00.49.13 ➡ 02.43.04.43.69

Closed Mon and the Feb school holidays. **TV**. **Car park**.

This lovely hotel-restaurant, set on the bank of the Mayenne river, is quite a sight. The dining room and the terrace (which stretches right down to the water), are often full, so make sure you reserve a table. The €11 weekday menu and others up to €27 offer rabbit and prune *terrine*, calf's head *ravigotte* served with a spicy *vinaigrette*, *cassolette* of queen scallops, lacquered pork spare ribs, cheese and *crème brûlée*. Three rooms with shower/wc are €43.

⅍ 🏠 |❍| LA MARJOLAINE**

Le Bas-Mont; it's on the way out of Moulay heading towards Laval.
☎ 02.43.00.48.42 ➡ 02.43.08.10.58
Closed Sun evening, Mon lunchtime. **TV**. **Car park**.

A hotel with a dozen brand-new and comfortable rooms that have been soothingly decorated. Doubles €49–66 with shower/wc or bath. The restaurant is up-and-coming and you should dress smartly. The quality of the cuisine and freshness of the ingredients is exemplary – try oysters cooked with celery seeds, veal cutlets with a cardamon-scented *jus*, stuffed pigeon with blackberry *jus* and the tasty desserts. Menus €15, €22 and €30. 10% discount on the room rate.

COMMER   53470 (9KM S)

⅍ 🏠 CHAMBRE D'HÔTE LA CHEVRIE***

How to get there: 5km south of Mayenne on the N162 towards Laval, follow the signposts to La Mayenne.
☎ 02.43.00.44.30 ➡ 06.84.17.17.29
Car park. **TV**.

This farmhouse is at least a hundred years old. Natural, kind welcome, and the room price hasn't increased for nine years – it's an affordable €30–34, breakfast included. There's a wonderful view over the countryside and neighbouring organic farm. The towpath is close by and a good place for an outing on foot, bike or horseback. 10% discount except July–Aug.

MONTREUIL-POULAY   53640 (12KM N)

|❍| L'AUBERGE CAMPAGNARDE

Le Presbytère.
☎ 02.43.32.07.11
Closed Sun evening; Mon. **Disabled access**. **Car park**.

You'll get a kind welcome in this restaurant, and the service is friendly without being overfamiliar. They serve apéritifs and coffee on the terrace even when the weather isn't quite fine enough to eat a full meal outside. You'll find astonishing selection of local dishes, traditionally made: *terrine* of duck and Pommeau in winter or of baby vegetables in summer, pike in a wine and butter sauce, sea bream with chervil, duck in cider in summer and goose in winter. Weekday menu €9, with others €16–20. Best to book.

LASSAY-LES-CHÂTEAUX   53110 (16KM NE)

⅍ |❍| RESTAURANT DU CHÂTEAU

37 rue Migoret-Lamberdière.
☎ 02.43.04.71.99
Closed Sun (reservations only); Mon evening; and the second and third weeks in Aug.

Béatrice and Hervé have a mixed clientele of made up of regulars and British tourists passing through. They've set aside a special dining room for the locals, who lunch on the €8 *menu ouvrier* (including ¼ litre of wine). Others are €11–14. There's a great atmosphere so try and get a table in there. The dishes are all freshly cooked in the kitchens: they're simple, tasty and prepared by a real pro. Best to book. Free coffee.

GORRON   53120 (25KM NW)

⅍ 🏠 |❍| HÔTEL-RESTAURANT LE BRETAGNE**

41 rue de Bretagne (East); take the D12 to Saint-Georges-Buttavent and then the D5.
☎ 02.43.08.63.67 ➡ 02.43.08.01.15
Closed Sun evening and Mon. **TV**. **Car park**.

A good village restaurant where you can get a hearty meal and gourmet cooking. Menus, €13–29, offer *mousseline* of zander with crab sauce, shellfish casserole with vermouth, honey-glazed roast breast of duck with Perry and apple turnover with cider caramel. The décor is spruce in pastel colours, and the dining room looks over the river Colmont. Double rooms €40. 10% discount on the room rate.

VILLAINES-LA-JUHEL   53700 (28KM E)

⅍ 🏠 |❍| L'HOSTELLERIE DE LA JUHEL

27 rue Jules-Doitteau (Centre); take the D113.
☎ 02.43.03.23.24 ➡ 02.43.03.79.87
Closed Fri and Sun evenings; 3 weeks in the Feb school holidays. **TV**.

The enthusiastic chef offers superb grilled meat dishes and guineafowl braised in cider. It's excellent value for money, with a weekday menu at €8, another at €13 and an average meal *à la carte* costing €18. Double rooms €27 with basin and up to €40 with shower or bath. 10% discount on the room rate.

MONTAIGU   85600

♠ |●| HÔTEL-RESTAURANT LES VOYAGEURS**

9 av. Villebois-Mareuil; it's in the centre of town.
☎ 02.51.94.00.71 ➡ 02.51.94.07.78
Ⓦ www.hotel-restaurant-les-voyageurs.fr
Disabled access. **Swimming pool**. **Car park**.

A long pink hotel with a flag flying above it, made up of three buildings constructed around a swimming pool – each facing wall is painted in a different colour and there's definitely a Mediterranean feel. The rooms are comfortable and of varying sizes; doubles €34–69. In the basement there's a fitness room. The dining room is on the ground floor and looks over the swimming pool. It's huge and bright and the cooking is very tasty. Menus €11–30. Breakfast €5. Nice staff.

⅍|●| LE CATHELINEAU

3 [bis] pl. du Champ-de-Foire.
☎ and ➡ 02.51.94.26.40
Closed Sun evening; Mon. **Disabled access**. **Car park**.

Michel Piveteau is the chef here. His cooking is original, combining unusual flavours, and his menus change every three weeks. Expect dishes like grilled lobster with *beurre blanc*, oysters cooked with liquorice, veal medallions with morels and a gratin of seasonal fruit with chocolate *Marquise*. Menus €14–46. There's a tank with fresh lobsters in it. Free coffee.

MONTREUIL-BELLAY   49260

⅍ ♠ |●| SPLENDID'HÔTEL**

139 rue du Docteur-Gaudrez (Centre); it's near the château.
☎ 02.41.53.10.00 ➡ 02.41.52.45.17
Ⓔ contact@splendid-hotel.fr
Closed Sun evening out of season. **Disabled access**. **Swimming pool**. **TV**. **Car park**.

This convivial establishment has everything you could ask for. The beautiful building comprises adjoining fifteenth- and seventeenth-century wings with a wide range of conventional, clean rooms – doubles with basin are €41, and €44–50 with shower or bath/wc. In the mornings the only sound you'll hear is the

fountain, while in the evening you can join locals at the lively bar. There's a pleasant dining room where they serve freshly prepared dishes in copious portions. Menus €12 (lunch) to €32. There's a big choice of fish dishes and the house speciality is pike black pudding. There's free use of the fitness facilities at the *Hôtel-Relais du Bellay* (below). 10% discount on the room rate.

⅍ ♠ HÔTEL-RELAIS DU BELLAY**

96 rue Nationale (Centre); it's behind the château.
☎ 02.41.53.10.10 ➡ 02.41.52.45.17
Closed Sun evening Oct–Easter. **Swimming pool**. **Garden**. **TV**. **Car park**.

Owned by the same people as the *Splendid'Hôtel* and sharing its reception area, this hotel – which used to be the local girls' school – has a similarly relaxed, friendly welcome. In the main building, the comfortable and spacious rooms, which have been completely renovated, go for €44–67 with shower, €69 with bath. Some look out onto the château and the fortifications. There's no restaurant but a buffet breakfast costs €7. There's a large, pleasant garden with swimming pool, as well as a fitness room, sauna, Turkish bath and Jacuzzi. 10% discount.

|●| LA GRANGE À DÎME

rue du Château (Centre).
☎ 02.41.50.97.24 Ⓔ grange.a.dime@wanadoo.fr
Open every evening from 8pm; Sun lunchtime in season; Fri–Sun evenings out of season. **Closed** 15 Dec–15 Jan.

The setting is a 15th-century barn (and former tax office) with a fantastic beamed ceiling which looks rather like the upturned hull of a boat. The single menu, €19, includes wine and coffee and lists stuffed mushrooms, *fillettes*, knuckle of pork, duck *confit*, salad, goat's cheese and a freshly baked pastry. Coffee is also included. You are definitely advised to arrive feeling very hungry. Nice welcome – the waiting staff are dressed in period costume.

MORTAGNE-SUR-SÈVRE   85290

⅍ ♠ |●| HÔTEL-RESTAURANT DE FRANCE ET LA TAVERNE**

4 pl. du Docteur-Pichat; it's at the crossroads of the Nantes-Poitiers/ Paris-Les Sables roads.
☎ 02.51.65.03.37 ➡ 02.51.65.27.83
Closed evenings, Sat and Sun 15 Oct–1 April. **TV**. **Swimming pool**.

The *Hôtel de France*, built in 1604, was renovated in 1968, and since then, nothing has changed. You can't miss this beautiful and noble building as you arrive in the main square – it's smothered in ivy. Inside, endless corridors and odd little corners lead to plush, comfortable rooms. Doubles €44 with shower/wc, €53 with bath and covered terrace with garden view. *La Taverne* has a sumptuous medieval-style dining room with period-looking furniture and collections of copper pans around the fireplace. The food is a festival of delicate, surprising flavours: crayfish in *verjus*, turbot with nettles, slivers of veal kidneys with green peppercorns. Other than the €13 menu of the day, prices are high, but justifiably so – menus are €25–50. During the week, the *Petite Auberge* next door offers more affordable menus: €13 and €15. There's a swimming pool in the old *curé*'s garden. Impeccable service. Free coffee.

NANTES   44000

SEE MAP OVERLEAF

🧍 ♨ HÔTEL SAINT-DANIEL*

4 rue du Bouffay. **MAP C2-2**
☎ 02.40.47.41.25 ➡ 02.51.72.03.99
Garden. TV. Car park.

A remarkable little hotel in the Bouffay district, clean and well-run. Doubles €24 with shower or €27 with shower/wc or bath. The nineteen rooms all have telephones and alarm clocks, though you'll pay a €3 surcharge if you want a TV. Some rooms face the pedestrianized street; others look onto the garden and the charming Sainte-Croix church. The prices attract younger travellers especially, so it's essential to book. 10% discount.

🧍 ♨ HÔTEL FOURCROY*

11 rue Fourcroy. **MAP B3-3**
☎ 02.40.44.68.00
Closed 22 Dec–3 Jan. **TV. Pay car park**.

Plain but quiet and decent. Doubles €28 with shower/wc. Some look onto a private courtyard. 10% discount 15 July–15 Aug.

🧍 ♨ |●| HÔTEL DUCHESSE ANNE**

3–4 pl. de la Duchesse Anne. **MAP D2-8**
☎ 02.40.74.78.78 ➡ 02.40.74.60.20
Restaurant closed Sat lunchtime and Sun. **TV. Pay car park**.

This is one of the finest hotels in Nantes, located in a palatial building behind the château – but it's by no means the most expensive and deserves more than its two stars. There are around sixty rooms: the simple ones are fully equipped but the opulent rooms have one (or even two) stone balconies looking out to the château, massive bathrooms with vast tubs and acres of space. Doubles with shower/wc €49–60 or up to €75 with bath/wc. Prices are more modest in the restaurant: you'll find menus at €10–30 and dishes such as marinated red peppers, duck breast in cider and a tulip of fruit. 10% discount on the room rate.

🧍 ♨ HÔTEL AMIRAL**

26 [bis] rue Scribe. **MAP B2-5**
☎ 02.40.69.20.21 ➡ 02.40.73.98.13
🌐 www.hotel-nantes.fr
Disabled access. TV. Pay car park.

This brand-new chain hotel has everything a businessperson could want: pleasant rooms, double glazing, mini-bars and so on, but it still has appeal for the leisure traveller. Doubles €61. Friendly welcome. 10% discount for a two-night stay, and there's special promotional rate at weekends.

🧍 ♨ L'HÔTEL***

6 rue Henri-IV. **MAP D2-7**
☎ 02.40.29.30.31 ➡ 02.40.29.00.95
🌐 www.ligneplus.com/lhotel
Disabled access. TV. Pay car park.

A pleasant, easy-going business hotel that's very comfortable and perfectly located opposite the château of Anne de Bretagne. Well-soundproofed doubles go for €60 with shower/wc or bath – some have private terraces with view over the garden. A professional, cheerful welcome. 10% discount on the room rate or free use of the car park.

🧍 ♨ HÔTEL LA PÉROUSE***

3 allée Duquesne. **MAP B2-6**
☎ 02.40.89.75.00 ➡ 02.40.89.76.00
🌐 www.hotel-laperouse.com
Disabled access. TV.

There's no middle ground with this contemporary hotel – you either love it or loathe it. A large block of heavy, compact white granite, echoing a Nantais mansion, it has large windows looking over the cours des Cinquante-Otages and the rooftops. Inside there is plenty of wood, designer furniture, space and tranquility – not a place for those nostalgic for the hotels of yesteryear. Doubles €76–92 with shower/wc or bath; breakfast is on offer at €8. One free breakfast per room.

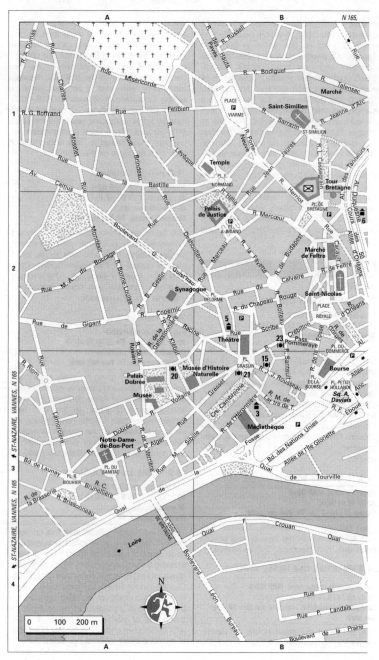

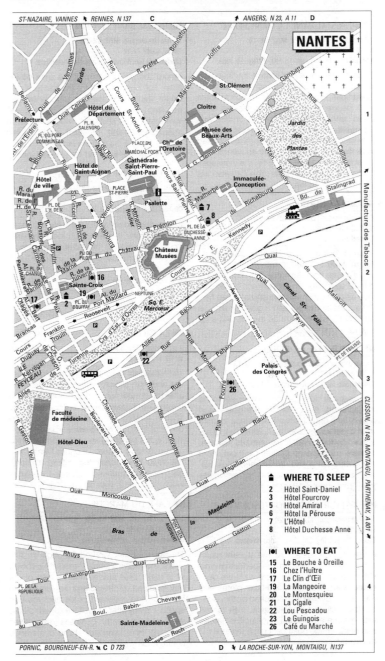

🎄 |●| RESTAURANT LA MANGEOIRE

16 rue des Petites-Écuries. **MAP C2-19**
☎ 02.40.48.70.83
Closed Sun; Mon; 1 Jan–15 Feb; 7 May–10 June.

Cuisine that combines French tradition with creativity: house *foie gras* with a compote of dried fruits, duck thigh *confit*, fish *choucroute* with *beurre blanc*, pan-fried prawns flambéed with whisky and *crème brûlée* with Cointreau. Weekday lunch menu at €9; others up to €23. The surroundings are choked with family photographs and souvenirs, and customers are invited to write little messages on the 400-year-old walls. You can also eat outside. Free coffee.

|●| CHEZ L'HUÎTRE

5 rue des Petites Écuries. **MAP C2-16**
☎ 02.51.82.02.02
Closed Sun.

A small bistro in the Bouffay district with rough walls covered in old metal signs. As you'll gather from the name, the youthful proprietor specializes in salmon and oysters as well as platters of seafood and smoked fish. Try a plate of oysters and a glass of wine as an apéritif. Fish platters go for €8, and a full meal will cost about €12.

|●| LE BOUCHE À OREILLE

14 rue Jean-Jacques-Rousseau. **MAP B3-15**
☎ 02.40.73.00.25
Closed Sat; Sun; public holidays; 29 July–15 Aug.

Situated very close to the opera house, this is a gathering place for theatre-goers and sports fans alike. It's more of a place to drink than a restaurant, and the cuisine isn't fancy: black pudding with caramelized apples, *tabliers de sapeurs* (grilled ox tripe), ham hock with lentils and, in summer, huge salads. Set lunch menu at €11, or *à la carte* you'll pay about €18.

|●| RESTAURANT LE MONTESQUIEU

1 rue Montesquieu. **MAP A3-20**
☎ 02.40.73.06.69
Closed Fri evening; Sat; Sun; public holidays; Aug.

A friendly local restaurant and student haunt in a quiet spot beyond the pedestrianized Graslin area. The dining room walls are decorated with Rouen and Moustier plates and the tables covered with checked cloths. Specialities include tuna with *aïolli*, leek *terrine* with onion marmalade, Dauphinois potatoes and home-made pastries. Lunch menu €11; the evening equivalent is €12.

|●| RESTAURANT LE CLIN D'ŒIL

15 rue Beauregard. **MAP C2-17**
☎ 02.40.47.72.37
Closed Sat lunchtime, Sun and Mon lunchtime.

Ignore the tiny, gloomy dining area downstairs and head instead for the first floor. The bright décor and friendly atmosphere are equalled by the charming, good-hearted service. Very good and fresh food which is an imaginative blend of local and oriental favourites – try the banana *tarte Tatin*. Lunch *formule* €11, or €13 and €17 in the evening.

|●| RESTAURANT LE GUINGOIS

3 [bis] rue Santeuil. **MAP B2-23**
☎ 02.40.73.36.49
Closed Mon, Sun and July.

One of the hubs of social life in Nantes, open until midnight. It offers good food prepared from fresh market ingredients at decent prices. The menus (€14–25) and the lunch *formule* (€11) list home cooking which is without fuss or flourish. Dishes of the day are chalked up on the blackboard: ham hock with lentils, grilled *andouillette*, veal sweetbreads *à l'ancienne* – all the classics.

|●| LA CIGALE

4 pl. Graslin. **MAP B3-21**
☎ 02.51.84.94.94

The restaurant to be seen in – visiting celebrities and high-society types come for supper after the theatre (which is just opposite). The cuisine isn't particularly brilliant and the speedy service is a little tiresome, but the decor of this 1900s brasserie – painted ceilings, wood panelling and coloured ceramics – is undeniably superb; Jacques Demy used the place in his classic movie *Lola*. It's actually not too expensive to dine – weekday lunch menu €12, with others €15–24.

|●| CAFÉ DU MARCHÉ

1 rue de Mayence. **MAP D3-26**
☎ 02.40.47.63.50
Closed evenings; weekends; Aug.

The formula has worked for nigh-on fifty years: they serve a single menu with a choice of at least three starters then a dish of the day, followed by cheese and dessert – yours for €15. Add a decent bottle and you can spend a lovely afternoon. It's a superb place, very popular with business executives escaping from seminars at the conference centre nearby.

☆ |●| LOU PESCADOU

8 allée Baco. **MAP C3-22**
☎ 02.40.35.29.50
Closed Sat lunchtime; Sun; Mon evening.

It's a good idea to book here, since this is one of the best seafood restaurants around and it gets pretty busy. The chef is a real enthusiast and a Muscadet aficionado – anything that he prepares in a white wine and butter sauce (*beurre blanc*) is a surefire winner. The sea bass baked in a salt crust is magnificent, too, as are specialities such as sole *meunière*, wild sea bream in salt and, if you can afford it, lobster and crayfish from the tank. Menus €19–58. Free apéritif.

CARQUEFOU   44470 (10KM N)

|●| RESTAURANT L'AUBERGE DU VIEUX GACHET

Le Gachet.
☎ 02.40.25.10.92
Closed Sun evening; Mon; Weds evening Jan–Feb.

An attractive country inn with a terrace on the banks of the Erdre which isn't allowing old habits to die – dishes are still served under a cloche. Inventive, delicious poultry and fish present you with the best of France: quail salad, hot *foie gras*, mushrooms stuffed with crab, roast pigeon with sauce thickened with liver and roast sea bream with olive oil. The fish is good, too, and prices are very affordable. Weekday menu €15 and others up to €40. To walk here from Nantes, simply follow the path along the Erdre – it'll take about two hours. The Château de la Gacherie is just opposite.

SAINT-FIACRE   44690 (18KM SE)

☆ |●| LE FIACRE

1 rue d'Échirens; take the D59 towards Clisson.
☎ 02.40.54.83.92
Closed evenings and weekends except for reservations; 1–21 Aug.

Small country restaurant where you eat at scrubbed wooden tables. Very well-known locally for its good wine and food, it offers just one lunch menu for €9 with a choice of two starters, a main dish (veal *blanquette* or *coq-au-vin*), cheese, dessert, coffee and wine. If you have an interest in wine, corner the proprietor, who has over a hundred Muscadets in the cellar – he knows them all individually and can talk to you for hours. Free apéritif.

MESSAN   44640 (20KM W)

|●| LE TISONNIER

50 rue Messan; it's on the D723 Saint Brévin-Painbœuf road on the way into Messan.
☎ 02.40.64.29.83
Closed evenings; 11 Aug–2 Sept.

Plain restaurant-café (also a tobacconist's and newsagent's) where the €8 *menu ouvrier* gets you a tasty meal: sausage in Muscadet plus cheese or dessert and a ¼ litre of wine. Other menus are priced at €10–28 and offer dishes which are a little more elaborate: half a cockerel, scallops, frogs' legs or sirloin steak. It would be hard to find better value for money and swifter service.

NOIRMOUTIER-EN-L'ÎLE   85330

☆ 🏠 |●| HÔTEL-RESTAURANT LES CAPUCINES**

38 av. de la Victoire (North); it's on the Bois de la Chaize road.
☎ 02.51.39.06.82 ➡ 02.51.39.33.10
Closed Wed and Thurs out of season; 1 Jan–12 Feb; 1 Nov–31 Dec. **Disabled access. TV. Swimming pool. Car park.**

This hotel is set between the forest and the ocean and offers peace and quiet. It's run by Anne and Jean-Luc David, whose watchwords are quality and modernity. The wholesome food and comfortable rooms make it well worth a visit. Doubles are €37–52 with shower and €55–75 with bath. There's a weekday menu at €12 and others €17–34; dishes include fisherman's stew, eel, frogs' legs and hot *andouillette* with onion *compote*. They prefer it if you stay half board in July–Aug or on spring public holidays, but it's not compulsory. Free breakfast per room in low season and at the spring public holidays.

☆ 🏠 |●| LE CHÂTEAU DE PÉLAVÉ***

9 allée de Chaillot; it's on the edge of the Chaize forest.
☎ 02.51.39.01.94 ➡ 02.51.39.70.42
🌐 www.chateau-de-pelave.fr
Restaurant closed 6–14 Jan; 12 Nov–25 Dec. **TV. Car park. Disabled access.**

This vast 19th-century house is set in lovely wooded grounds. It's been renovated recently but its Victorian charm is undiminished. Comfortable, spacious rooms available for €48–120 with shower/wc – book well in advance. The cuisine is of good quality and mainly traditional with a balance between meat and fish dishes: crayfish ravioli, half-duck with a turnip *tarte Tatin*, cod *tournedos* wrapped in country ham. There's a *formule* for €17 and other menus at €22–45. You'll also find an excellent selection of wines, purchased by the patron directly from the producers. It's preferred if you stay half board in season, priced €63–97 per person. Free apéritif or coffee and 10% discount on the room rate out of season (except weekends).

☎ |●| HÔTEL LES DOUVES**

11 rue des Douves (Centre); it's opposite the château.
☎ 02.51.39.02.72 ➡ 02.51.39.73.09
Closed Jan. **Swimming pool**. **TV**. **Car park**.

This plush hotel nestles below the château in a very peaceful spot, and it's quiet with a family atmosphere. The rooms are fresh and pretty with floral décor, and all have modern facilities; they go for €50–70 with shower/wc or bath. There's a swimming pool for people who are too lazy to make it as far as the beach. The restaurant, *Le Manoir*, located in the next building, is run by the owners' son.

☎ |●| HÔTEL DU GÉNÉRAL-D'ELBÉE***

pl. d'Armes; it's at the foot of the château near the canal port.
☎ 02.51.39.10.29 ➡ 02.51.39.08.23
e general-delbee@wanadoo.fr
Closed Jan–March. **Swimming pool**. **Disabled access**.

A marvellous hotel in an historic 18th-century building. VIP types stay here but it's quite unspoilt and still affordable to people who prefer refined places with a bit of character. Some of the rooms are in a modern part of the building and overlook the pool; doubles are €60–190 depending on location and size. There's a bar-sitting room.

☎ |●| HÔTEL-RESTAURANT FLEUR DE SEL***

rue des Saulniers, BP 207 (Southwest); follow the signs from the château.
☎ 02.51.39.09.07 ➡ 02.51.39.09.76
⊕ www.fleurdesel.fr
Closed Mon lunchtime (except public holidays); 3 Nov–15 Mar. **Restaurant closed** Tues (except school holidays) **Swimming pool**. **Car park**. **TV**. **Disabled access**.

A magnificent place now classified as a *Châteaux et demeures de tradition* hotel, built some twenty years ago in a style which is typical of the island. It's set apart from the town in the middle of a huge estate with

Mediterranean landscapes, and has a lovely swimming pool. All 35 rooms are different but equally well-equipped; the ones overlooking the pool are cosy and have English pine furniture, while those with private flowery terraces have yew furniture and a maritime feel. Doubles €70–125 with bath/wc. The restaurant is one of the best on the island if not in the Vendée. Everything is prepared on the premises: crayfish baked in their skins, mussels with garlic *au gratin*, duck fillet with olives. Menus €23–40. Half board, at €66–104, is available for a two-night minimum stay. You can hire bikes or go on excursions. All in all, ideal for a relaxing stay.

|●| RESTAURANT CÔTÉ JARDIN

1 [bis] rue du Grand-Four (Centre); it faces the château at the top of the old town.
☎ 02.51.39.03.02
Closed Mon; Thurs and Sun evenings; Mon–Fri from mid-Nov to end Jan.

This elegant restaurant in a splendid building has a beautiful dining room with stone walls and hefty beams. It offers gourmet fish and seafood: potato tart with crayfish and prawns with celery *julienne*, roast sea bream with sea salt and green asparagus butter. Delicate desserts such as *millefeuille* of pineapple with soft fruit *coulis*. There's a €15 two-course *formule* and menus for €21–34. Friendly welcome.

NOTRE-DAME-DE-MONTS   85690

🏊 ☎ |●| HÔTEL DE LA PLAGE***

145 av. de la Mer; it's on the corner of the main street, at right angles to the beach.
☎ 02.51.58.83.09 ➡ 02.51.58.97.12
Closed Oct–March. **TV**. **Car park**.

If you're going to splash out you might just as well do it properly. Ask for a room with a sea view and you'll get a terrace thrown in too. The prices aren't outrageous given the quality of the place, the nice welcome and the rooms: doubles €30–35 with basin, €54–79 with shower/wc or bath. Lots of fish is served in the restaurant, but it does other things too: savoury pancakes with local lobster, duck thigh with Muscadet sauce, sea bream on a bed of sea salt with *beurre blanc*, frosted cherries flambéed with Poissy. Free *digestif*.

PAULX · 44270

🏕 |●| RESTAURANT LES VOYAGEURS

1 pl. de l'Église (Centre); it's opposite the church.
☎ 02.40.26.02.76
Closed Sun and Tues evenings; Mon; a fortnight in
March; the last week in Aug; the first fortnight in Sept.

Call up the day before and they will create
carefully prepared dishes to order. At
lunchtime it's the haunt of businesspeople
who enjoy classic cuisine, while in the evening
the dishes are more unusual and they change
frequently with the seasons – pike or zander
with *beurre blanc*, veal kidneys flambéed with
blackcurrant berries, chocolate *moelleux*. The
produce is selected with meticulous care –
free-range chicken, locally raised meat and
exceptionally fresh fish. Menus €17–45 or *à la
carte* expect to pay around €38. Free coffee.

PIRIAC-SUR-MER · 44420

🏕 🛏 |●| HÔTEL-RESTAURANT DE LA POINTE

1 quai de Verdun (North); it's by the sea wall.
☎ 02.40.23.50.04 ➡ 02.40.15.59.65
Closed Tues evening and Wed out of season. **Car park**.

A relaxed hotel. Doubles with basin €31,
with shower/wc €40. They're not exactly the
last word in style but some have a view of the
harbour and beach. The dining room, decorated like a traditional bistro, offers substantial salads, fish and seafood. Weekday menu
€8; others €15 and €23. Friendly welcome.
Half board at €44 is compulsory July–Aug.
10% discount on the room rate Sept–June.

🏕 |●| CRÊPERIE LACOMÈRE

18 rue de Kéroman (Centre).
☎ and ➡ 02.40.23.53.63
Closed Mon and Tues in mid-season; throughout winter
(except in the school holidays).

This restaurant is a little more inventive than
the standard *crêperie*, with a menu which is
inspired by the owner's travels around the
world. Try the fish *tajine*, the red mullet
escabèche or the fish *choucroute*. Menus at
€9 and €12. There are only ten tables so it's
best to book. Free apéritif.

PORNIC · 44210

|●| RESTAURANT L'ESTAMINET

8 rue du Maréchal-Foch (Centre).

☎ 02.40.82.35.99
Closed Sun evening and Mon Sept–June.

This restaurant in a busy street doesn't look
out of the ordinary, but once you're inside,
the *patronne's* delightful manner and the
chef's fresh cuisine will convince you that it
is. Menus €15–23. Try scallops with baby
vegetables or skate with queen scallops, nut
butter and cider vinegar.

|●| RESTAURANT BEAU RIVAGE

plage de la Birochère.
☎ 02.40.82.03.08 📧 info@restaurant-beaurivage.com
Closed Sun and Wed evenings, Mon out of season;
Jan; 10–26 Dec.

A friendly, colourful restaurant in a beautiful
spot looking right over the beach. Seafood is
the speciality here, and the chef thoughtfully
crafts excellent dishes from fresh ingredients: Atlantic *bouillabaisse*, sea bream
grilled on its skin with olive oil and lobster
salad with herbs. Good menus €19–54, and
there's an excellent wine list too.

PLAINE-SUR-MER (LA) · 44770 (9KM W)

🏕 🛏 |●| HÔTEL-RESTAURANT ANNE DE BRETAGNE★★★

port de la Gravette.
☎ 02.40.21.54.72 ➡ 02.40.21.02.33
🌐 www.annedebretagne.com
Closed Mon, Tues lunchtime, Sun evening from mid-
Sept to mid-May; 7 Jan–end Feb. **Disabled access**.
Swimming pool. **TV**. **Car park**.

A charming hotel with lovely rooms that have
garden or sea views. The location is splendid
and it's very quiet. Doubles with shower/wc
€59–99 or €82–122 with bath. There's a
fancy little bar and a gourmet restaurant with
a good reputation. You'll experience a large
selection of menus from €36 to €76, including themed ones based on seasonal ingredients. There's also a *formule* (main course
and dessert) for €21. Specialities include
roast monkfish with red wine and sole
cooked in its skin. Superb cellar with 15,000
bottles. Excellent welcome. 10% discount
on reservations made out of season (except
at weekends).

PORT-JOINVILLE (ÎLE D'YEU) · 85350

🏕 🛏 HÔTEL L'ESCALE

rue de la Croix-du-Port.
☎ 02.51.58.50.28 ➡ 02.51.59.33.55
📧 yeu.escale@voila.fr
Closed 15 Nov–15 Dec. **Garden**. **TV**. **Car park**.

Disabled access.

Painted white with yellow shutters, this is the prettiest place on the Île d'Yeu. Despite having thirty rooms, it retains a guesthouse atmosphere, with cool marine décor. Doubles €29–32 with shower or shower/wc, and €46–53 with bath. Breakfast, at €5, is served around the old well in the middle of the bright dining room – you can the garden through French windows. The owner gives good advice about where to visit and what to see in the area. 10% discount Oct–March.

⚒ 🏨 ATLANTIC HÔTEL***

quai Carnot (Centre).
☎ 02.51.58.38.80 ➡ 02.51.58.35.92
Closed 6–29 Jan. **TV**.

Fifteen cute and comfortable little rooms. Half of them face the fishing harbour, the focus of local activity, while the others look out over the village – both views are pleasant. You'll pay €37 out of season for a double with the village view, and up to €60 in summer for one with a view of the harbour. Breakfast €5. 10% discount on the room rate (except July–Aug).

⚒ 🏨 |●| FLUX HÔTEL – RESTAURANT LA MARÉE**

27 rue Pierre-Henry.
☎ 02.51.58.36.25 ➡ 02.51.59.44.57
Closed Sun evening. **Disabled access**. **Garden**. **TV**. **Car park**.

Away from the bustle of Port-Joinville, this hotel's peaceful grounds, bordering the seashore, give it a delightful aspect. Well-kept double rooms overlooking the garden cost €38–53; number 15, set away from the main hotel, is especially spacious and has a fireplace. The restaurant, *La Marée*, is run by different people, so you'll pay for your meal separately. The enormous dining room has a huge fireplace for winter evenings and a lovely terrace for dining out beneath the shade of the trees in summer. Creamy soups are a house speciality, as are the mussels *sauce poulette*. Set menus €14–30 and smiling, friendly service. 10% discount on the room rate Sept–June (excluding spring public holidays).

⚒ |●| RESTAURANT DU PÈRE RABALLAND – L'ÉTAPE MARITIME

6 place de la Norvège; it's on the harbour.
☎ 02.51.26.02.77
Closed 7 Jan–4 Feb.

A bar-brasserie decorated to look like the

inside of a boat. The cuisine is refined and they serve seafood accompanied by wines bought direct from the vineyards. If you want more intimacy, go for the "gastronomic" dining room upstairs, but the food is the same – *blanquette* of cuttlefish *à l'ancienne*, scallop stew and so on. Mussels with Patagos are the house speciality. Menus €12–26: it's excellent value for money. Père Raballand is well-known in town and the atmosphere in his bistro in summer or at the weekend is unmatched. Free apéritif.

⚒ |●| LES BAFOUETTES

8 rue Gabriel Guist'hau (Centre); it's 100m from the port, past the tourist office.
☎ 02.51.59.38.38
Closed Tues Sept–June except for school holidays.

The dining room is freshly decorated with pictures by local artists, and the cuisine is delicious and served by really enthusiastic staff. Menus start at €13 and go up to €34; dishes include fricassée of monkfish with ginger, pan-fried and flambeéd crayfish with curry, tuna *tartare* and other seafood goodies. In summer there's a lobster menu for €69. Free coffee.

POUZAUGES   85700

|●| RESTAURANT PATRICK

rue de la Baudrière (South); it's on the D752, at Puzauges-Gare just after Fleury-Michon on the left.
☎ 02.51.65.83.09
Closed Sun and Mon evenings; the first 3 weeks in Aug; a week in Mar.

A long modern house, painted pink. Everyone round here knows the place because the Patrick in question is a talented chef who has made a great name for himself. He gets his fish from the coast and certainly knows how to use it. His €18 menu lists a choice between ten oysters or salmon *tartare*, then *confit* of duck or roast zander followed by dessert. Others are €9–25; they're all good.

ROCHEFORT-SUR-LOIRE   49190

⚒ 🏨 |●| LE GRAND HÔTEL**

30 rue René-Gasnier.
☎ 02.41.78.80.46 ➡ 02.41.78.83.25
📧 legrandhotel@libertysurf.fr
Closed Wed; Sun evening; Tues evening out of season; 18 Dec–18 Jan. **Garden**.

A nice old house with a garden, located in the main street. It's ideal as a base for exploring the Layon area. The ground-floor dining room is decorated in shades of yellow and green. Carefully prepared dishes feature lots of local specialities with dishes changing regularly. Menus €17–34. The lady owner is a passionate wine-lover which explains the well-researched wine list. The rooms are fairly big but quite simple and cost €30 with shower or €37 with shower/wc; the nicest are on the first floor overlooking the garden. Nice welcome. Free glass of Coteau du Layon.

ROCHE-SUR-YON (LA)　85000

🕭 🏠 |◉| MARIE STUART HÔTEL**

86 bd. Louis-Blanc (Centre); it's opposite the station.
☎ 02.51.37.02.24 ➠ 02.51.37.86.37
Restaurant closed Sat lunchtime and Sun. **TV**.

This hotel overflows with Scottish trappings, including tartans, coats of arms and a portrait of Mary, Queen of Scots. The spacious rooms are rather chic and have stylish furniture; doubles €47 with shower/wc or bath. The restaurant serves good, simple food with some quasi-Scottish specialities: Highland steak, Scotch eggs and dumplings but also fisherman's stew. Menus are €12–€29; the bar menu gives you a starter and a main course. They have a good selection of malts. Free Irish coffee.

🕭 🏠 HÔTEL LE LOGIS DE LA COUPERIE***

route de Cholet. It's five minutes from the town centre – take the main road to Cholet and then the D80.
☎ 02.51.37.21.19 ➠ 02.51.47.71.08
TV. **Car park**.

In a stately 14th-century mansion hidden away in the depths of the countryside, this is one of the most appealing hotels in the Vendée. The atmosphere is a combination of refinement and simplicity. There are just seven cosy rooms, each named after a flower and decorated in English style with canopy beds and antique furniture. Doubles €49 with shower/wc or €58 with bath. The only sounds to wake you are the ducks and the frogs in the pond. Don't miss the lovingly prepared breakfast. A cordial welcome from a charming host. Free coffee or tea.

|◉| LE CLÉMENCEAU

40 rue Georges-Clémenceau (Centre).
☎ 02.51.37.10.20
Closed 1 Jan, 1 May and 25 Dec.

This is a genuine brasserie and it has an attractive terrace. It's well-known for the freshness of its shellfish, seafood and fish – the names of the suppliers are even inscribed on the menu. There's a substantial seafood platter for €24 and very tasty fish soup. Full meals from €13. Nice staff and friendly atmosphere.

🕭 |◉| SAINT CHARLES RESTAURANT

38 rue du Président-de-Gaulle (Centre).
☎ 02.51.47.71.37
✉ mail@restaurant-stcharles.com
Closed Sat lunchtime; Sun; Aug.

Photos of jazz musicians and instruments adorn the walls, jazz plays softly in the background and even the menu features jazz references. In this relaxed atmosphere the chef produces creations such as *carpaccio* of duck with *foie gras* and sea bream steamed over seaweed. Menus, €15–32, offer good value for money. Free coffee.

POIRÉ-SUR-VIE (LE)　85170 (13.5KM NW)

🕭 🏠 |◉| HÔTEL-RESTAURANT LE CENTRE**

19 pl. du Marché (Centre); take the D6.
☎ 02.51.31.81.20 ➠ 02.51.31.88.21
Closed Fri and Sun evening out of season. **Disabled access**. **Swimming pool**. **TV**. **Car park**.

This welcoming hotel, right in the middle of the village, has clean, comfortable rooms. Doubles are €28 with basin, €54 with bath. The restaurant offers simple authentic regional cooking, with dishes like fillet of zander in a butter and white wine sauce, country ham *à la crème* and home-made *foie gras* – all at reasonable prices. There's a brasserie menu for €10 and others at €15–25. Free coffee.

MACHÉ　85190 (22KM NW)

🕭 |◉| AUBERGE LE FOUGERAIS

How to get there: take the D948 for 22km; after Aizenay turn left beyond the river Vie bridge and follow the signposts.
☎ 02.51.55.75.44
Closed Mon–Wed evenings except July–Aug; a fortnight in Oct. **Car park**. **Disabled access**.

A lovely converted barn covered in ivy and with a shady terrace. It's a peaceful place, where unfussy, tasty food is served at simple tables. The chef adds a few vine stems to the open fire when he grills eel, salmon, rib of beef or quail and roasts monkfish with citrus fruit. Weekday lunch menu at €10 and others €18–23, offering good value for money. Free apéritif.

ROSIERS-SUR-LOIRE (LES) 49350

🏃 |O| LA TOQUE BLANCHE

2 rue Quartz; it's on the way out of the village on the
Angers road, after the bridge.
☎ 02.41.51.80.75
Closed Tues evening and Wed. **Car park.**

It is becoming increasingly necessary to
book a table at this up-and-coming restaurant – and it's absolutely essential for Sunday
lunch. Inventive cuisine is served in an elegant, air-conditioned dining room. There's a
€17 menu including wine (not served Sun)
and others at €22–37. Dishes are cooked
using fresh produce chosen from the market
by the chef himself: home-smoked salmon,
red mullet *mousse* and caviar sauce, liver
parfait in port accompanied by a glass of
Layon, *langoustine* tails sautéed with vanilla
pods, poached chicken à l'*angevine*, sweet-
and-sour duck and much more. Friendly welcome. Free coffee.

SABLES-D'OLONNE (LES) 85100

🏃 🏠 HÔTEL DE LA TOUR**

46 rue du Docteur-Canteteau, La Chaume (West).
☎ and ➡ 2.51.95.38.48

This nice little place is in a typical street in the
Chaume district, and it's run by a young couple who make guests feel like friends.
Madame has decorated each room in a different theme, with colours inspired by the
sea. Doubles €31–46 with shower or show-
er/wc; some rooms have a view of the port.
There's also an interior garden full of flowers
where you can have breakfast, or you can eat
in the breakfast room accompanied by
Madame's singing. A very unusual place.
10% discount for a minimum 3-night stay
Sept–June (except long weekends).

🏃 🏠 |O| HÔTEL LES EMBRUNS**

33 rue du Lieutenant-Anger, La Chaume (North).
☎ 02.51.95.25.99 ➡ 02.51.95.84.48
Ⓦ www.hotel-lesembruns.com
Closed Sun evening Oct–April; Nov–Feb. **TV. Car park.**

You can spot the yellow frontage of this
building with its green shutters from the
other side of the harbour. The rooms are
very pretty and painted in attractive colours,
and they're brilliantly maintained by the welcoming young pair who run the place. Some
of the rooms overlook the port, while the
ones looking onto a small side street are
cooler in summer. Doubles €38–48. 10%

discount Sept–June except holiday weekends.

🏃 🏠 |O| HÔTEL ANTOINE**

60 rue Napoléon (Centre).
☎ 02.51.95.08.36 ➡ 02.51.23.92.78
ⓔ antoinehotel@club-internet.fr
Closed 15 Oct–20 March. **Garden. TV. Pay car park.**

A delightful haven right in the centre of town
which has undergone a face-lift inside and
out. Quiet rooms, some of which look out
over the garden, cost €43–53 with show-
er/wc in the annexe or in the main hotel and
they've all been updated with new bathrooms, carpets and curtains. Prices are a little lower out of season. Half board, compulsory July–Aug, is €40–46 per person. Even
the dining room has had a makeover and the
food is excellent, prepared from the freshest
market produce. 10% discount on the room
rate Sept–June except for public holiday
weekends.

🏃 🏠 |O| HÔTEL LES HIRONDELLES**

44 rue des Corderies (Centre).
☎ 02.51.95.10.50 ➡ 02.51.32.31.01
ⓔ leshirondelles@wanadoo.fr
Closed end Sept to end March. **TV. Pay car park.**

This hotel doesn't look particularly attractive
from the outside but the rooms have a fresh,
modern décor. Some have balconies which
are ideal for breakfast and others lead onto a
pretty white patio planted with exotic, perfumed plants. Doubles €49–56 with show-
er/wc. Menus, €12–22, list fish and seafood
dishes: fish *choucroute*, prawn kebabs and
mussel stew. The kindness of the hostess is
completely winning. Free coffee.

🏃 |O| L'AFFICHE

21 quai Guiné; it's near the port, opposite the dock for
the boats to the Île d'Yeu.
☎ 02.51.95.34.74
Closed Sun and Thurs evenings; Mon; and Jan.

The outside is painted yellow and beckons
you in. The menus change three times a year
but list dishes such as marlin with sweet garlic, *gratin* of asparagus and Dublin Bay
prawns, sautéed lamb sweetbreads with
crayfish and duck breast with honey – with
gratin of strawberries and pistachio nuts for
dessert. Menus €11–25. A flavourful treat and
good value for money. Free coffee.

|O| LA FLEUR DES MERS

5 quai Guiné; it's on the seafront facing the harbour.
☎ 02.51.95.18.10

Closed Sun evening, Mon, Tues morning in winter; Mon Jul–Aug.

Chic and spruce with the ambience of a luxury liner; as you go up to the top floor, you get a splendid view of the harbour. The dining room is fresh, bright and spacious, and the cuisine is delicate: *gratin* of seafood, delicious grilled sardines, fresh *moules marinière* and *parmentier* of duck *foie gras* (that is to say, served with mashed potatoes). Weekday lunch menu €11 (July–Sept) with others at €14–30.

🎿 |●| RESTAURANT GEORGE V

20 rue George-V, La Chaume.
☎ 02.51.95.11.52
Closed Sun evening and Mon out of season.

Both elegant dining rooms look out to the harbour entrance. Chef Olivier Burban prepares excellent food – not surprisingly, fish is the main ingredient, but it's imaginatively prepared. Unexpected flavours pop up in dishes such as *gateau* of crayfish and oysters with *foie gras* sauce. Leave room for the *pain perdu* (France's answer to bread-and-butter pudding) or the hot apple tart. Menus start at €12 and continue at €18–23. Free coffee.

🎿 |●| RESTAURANT LE CLIPPER

19 [bis] quai Guiné.
☎ 02.51.32.03.61
Closed Tues evening and Wed; Mon July–Aug; 10–26 Dec; 14–27 Feb

The wooden room with its hurricane lamps and portholes makes you feel like you're in a clipper. The menu features unusual fish dishes: subtle yet astonishing combinations include John Dory with vanilla and saffron, sea bream with a salt crust, monkfish *blanquette* with vegetables stewed in butter and roast pears with caramel. €15 lunch menu and others €22–30. There are many local regulars who obviously appreciate the considerate, attentive service. There's a terrace in summer. Free coffee.

SABLÉ-SUR-SARTHE   72300

🎿 |●| LES PALMIERS

54 Grande-Rue (Centre).
☎ 02.43.95.03.82
Closed Tues; Sat lunchtime.

The Moroccan hospitality and cuisine you'll encounter here offers quite an antidote to the *rillette* and fish stew that otherwise abounds in these parts. Abdou mans the kitchens while his French wife greets the guests.

There is little passing trade in this run-down street in the old part of town, and the owners depend on the restaurant's reputation for its survival. Fortunately, that seems safe. The two large dining rooms are smart and very well decorated, offering comfortable surroundings in which to enjoy the best of Moroccan cuisine. They offer large helpings of aromatic stews, vegetables and excellent meat: superb *tajines* cost €10–11, *couscous* with a selection of meats is €10–15, and there are delicious home-made pastries. You'll pay €12–18 for a meal *à la carte*. Free coffee.

|●| L'HOSTELLERIE SAINT-MARTIN

3 rue Haute-Saint-Martin (Centre); it's in a small street leading off the town hall square towards the château.
☎ 02.43.95.00.03 📧 st-martin4@wanadoo.fr
Closed Sun and Wed evenings; Mon.

This town-centre restaurant seems to be in a clement microclimate – or so the palm tree across the street would suggest. The high-ceilinged dining room has an antiquated charm and traditional décor, with a dresser, Normandy clock, heavy red velvet curtains, copper pots and pans and fresh flowers on every table; the parquet floor creaks underfoot. You'll find good local food; there's a menu for €15, or expect to pay about €30 *à la carte*. You can also eat on the terrace.

DUREIL   72270 (16KM E)

|●| L'AUBERGE DES ACACIAS

Centre; take the D309 to Parcé-sur-Sarthe or the D23 to Malicorne, then turn down the small road that follows the Sarthe river.
☎ 02.43.95.34.03
Closed Sun evening; Mon; weeknights Nov–Feb; a fortnight in March; a fortnight in Oct.

It may not be smothered in Virginia creeper these days but it's still worth a visit. Dishes change seasonally and their speciality is duck breast with elderflower – the dessert platter is a must. The terrace is delightful, and in winter you can eat beside the cosy fireplace. Menus €14–23.

SAINT-CALAIS   72120

|●| À SAINT-ANTOINE

8 pl. Saint-Antoine (Northeast).
☎ 02.43.35.01.56
Closed Sun and Wed evenings, Mon in winter. **Car park**.

The Achard brothers – wine waiter at

Maxim's and chef at *Plaza Athénée* – caused quite a stir when they took over an old bistro in place Saint-Antoine and turned it into a "real" restaurant. Despite that, it's a good, unfussy place, where locals meet for lunch at the bar before returning to their occupations; the small dining room soon fills up. Eric the chef has moved on, leaving Christophe to poach another colleague from the *Plaza*. The personality of the cooking has changed but the quality hasn't: expect colourful, tasty dishes on the menus. Weekday menu €11 or others €15–37. Good, affordable local wines.

SAINT-GERVAIS-DE-VIC — 72120 (4KM S)

🧖 |●| LE SAINT-ÉLOI

1 rue Bertrand-Guilmain; it's near the church.
☎ 02.43.35.19.56
Closed Sun evening out of season; the second fortnight in Jan; the first fortnight in Aug.

The proprietors of this restaurant used to be pork butchers, but now their dining room is full every Sunday. The €9 weekday menu gets you a buffet of starters, *blanquette* or *coq au vin*, cheese, tart, coffee and wine. Other menus are €20–23, the most expensive of which offers three dishes – a starter, a fish course and breast of duck with green peppercorns. Free apéritif.

SAINT-DENIS-D'ORQUES — 72350

🧖 |●| L'AUBERGE DE LA GRANDE CHARNIE

rue Principale (Centre); it's on the N157, halfway between Laval and Le Mans.
☎ 02.43.88.43.12
Closed Mon; Sun–Thurs evenings; end Jan to early Feb. **Car park. Disabled access.**

An exquisite dining room and excellent local cuisine at prices that won't break the bank. They offer a dish of the day – such as chicken breast stuffed with *foie gras*, *croustillant* of crayfish with a fish *coulis* or fish stew *sarthoise* – but always take the advice of the *patronne* who will tell you what's best. Menus €14–35. Free coffee.

SAINT-FLORENT-LE-VIEIL — 49410

🧖 🏠 |●| L'HOSTELLERIE DE LA GABELLE**

12 quai de la Loire.
☎ 02.41.72.50.19 ➡ 02.41.72.54.38

Closed Sun evening, Mon lunchtime, Fri evening Oct–May; 23 Dec–1 Jan. **TV**.

A traditional provincial hotel, well-located on the banks of the Loire – it's a good spot to stop if you're travelling between Nantes and Angers. Most of the rooms have been redecorated in various themes; doubles €40–43 with shower/wc or bath. The cuisine is simple but tasty: Loire eels *à la Provençale*, zander in *beurre blanc* and house *foie gras*. Menus €12 in the week, with others at €18–37. Free coffee.

SAINT-JEAN-DE-MONTS — 85160

🧖 🏠 |●| HÔTEL-RESTAURANT LE ROBINSON**

28 bd. Leclerc (Centre).
☎ 02.51.59.20.20 ➡ 02.51.58.88.03
Ⓦ www.hotel-le-robinson.com
Closed Dec–Jan. **TV. Swimming pool. Car park.**

This family business has become a substantial tourist complex over the years. The original hotel has changed considerably with many extensions and additions, but quality has been maintained. There are several types of room, all comfortable – some overlook the leafy avenues, others have a view of the road. Doubles €32–66. Traditional, pleasant, carefully prepared cuisine: scallop kebabs and other seafood dishes, duck breast with honey and apples. There's a €12 menu (not Sun lunch) and others at €18–30. As ever for this part of the world, reserve well in advance. Free coffee.

SAINT-LÉONARD-DES-BOIS — 72590

🧖 🏠 |●| TOURING HÔTEL***

How to get there: follow the Alpes Mancelles route.
☎ 02.43.31.44.44 ➡ 02.43.31.44.49
Ⓔ tng@forestdale.com
Swimming pool. TV. Car park.

A good place to stay, near the Sarthe river in the heart of the hills known as *les Alpes Mancelles*. Although the building is constructed from concrete, the atmosphere, hospitality, cuisine and swimming pool soon make you forget the dull architecture – it's the only outpost of the English *Forestdale* chain in France. Quiet, well-appointed rooms with shower/wc or bath/wc cost €69–84. There's a weekday lunch menu at €18, with others €22–46. Dishes are tasty – haddock fillet with cockles, smoked salmon, duck breast, charlotte with goat's cheese and seasonal fruit turnover. 10% discount on the room rate.

SAINT-NAZAIRE 44600

🏃 🛏 HÔTEL DE TOURAINE*

4 av. de la République (Centre); it's near the town halll.
☎ 02.40.22.47.56 ➡ 02.40.22.55.05
📧 hoteltouraine.free.fr
Closed 18 Dec–8 Jan. **TV**.

It's hard enough to find a reasonably priced and pleasant hotel in Saint-Nazaire – let alone one that offers a substantial breakfast (served in the garden in good weather) and a free ironing service to boot. Doubles €20 with basin, €33–36 with bath. 10% discount on the room rate 1 Oct–31 March.

🏃 🛏 |●| KORALI HÔTEL**

pl. de la Gare (Centre).
☎ 02.40.01.89.89 ➡ 02.40.66.47.96
TV. Disabled access.

This welcoming establishment is in a modern building and all the rooms have good facilities. Doubles with shower/wc are €44–53 or €53–99 with bath. Menus €15–21. Breakfast is served, rather incredibly, from 2am to noon. 10% discount on the room rate 1 Sept–31 May.

SAINT-JOACHIM 44720 (10KM N)

🏃 🛏 |●| L'AUBERGE DU PARC – LA MARE AUX OISEAUX

162 Ile de Fédrun.
☎ 02.40.88.53.01 ➡ 02.40.91.67.44
🌐 auberge-du-parc.com
Closed Sun evening and Mon and March.

The inhabitants of île de Fédrun have adopted Éric Guérin – an alumnus of the famous *Tour d'Argent* in Paris – as their favourite chef. He's full of ideas and produces inspired dishes: snails and cuttlefish with wild nettles, lacquered zander, frogs on a bed of seaweed. Menus €30, 40 and 46. Four rooms with bath/wc are under the reed-thatched roof – in keeping with the local *Brièronne* atmosphere – cost €61. 10% discount on the room rate.

SAINT-VINCENT-DU-LOROUËR 72150

🏃 |●| L'AUBERGE DE L'HERMITIÈRE

sources de l'Hermitière; it's 4.5 km south of Saint-Vincent-du-Lorouër.
☎ 02.43.44.84.45

Closed Mon evening, Tues and Wed Oct–April; Mon and Tues May–Sept; mid-Jan to end Feb. **Disabled access**.

The setting of this house is splendid: it's in a wood, just by the river, and there's a terrace under the trees. It's one of the great tables in the Sarthe (even the Queen Mother has been here), yet it still serves a menu for €15 – others are €23–34. Free apéritif.

SAINT-VINCENT-SUR-JARD 85520

🛏 |●| HÔTEL-RESTAURANT DE L'OCÉAN**

rue Georges-Clémenceau (West); it's next to musée Clémenceau.
☎ 02.51.33.40.45 ➡ 02.51.33.98.15
🌐 www.hotel-restaurant-ocean.com
Closed Wed out of season and mid-Nov to end Feb. **Disabled access. Swimming pool. Garden. TV. Car park**.

This prewar hotel continues to grow in reputation and hospitality. The rooms, which look onto a quiet garden, cost €40–69 with shower or bath; the six set menus (€13–38), should satisfy seafood-lovers. Half board, compulsory June–Sept, is €42–62 per person. Friendly welcome; they'll let you use the pool even if you've just dropped in for a drink.

SAULGES 53340

🏃 🛏 |●| HÔTEL-RESTAURANT L'ERMITAGE***

pl. Saint-Pierre.
☎ 02.43.64.66.00 ➡ 02.43.64.66.20
Closed Sun evening and Mon Oct to mid-April; All Saints'; Feb. **Swimming pool. TV. Car park. Disabled access**.

A modern hotel with bright, spacious, comfortable rooms overlooking the park, swimming pool and countryside (€50–84 with shower/wc or bath). The restaurant serves traditional dishes with a modern twist: fresh crab *soufflé* with lobster cream, duck *terrine* with *foie gras*, beef in Chinon, rabbit kidneys with Pommeau, apple tart with gingerbread ice-cream. A wide selection of menus, at €18–40. Free house apéritif.

SAUMUR 49400

🛏 HÔTEL LE CANTER

pl. de la Sénatorie, Saint-Hilaire-Saint-Florent; it's 2km from the centre on the D751 in the direction of Chênehutte.

☎ 02.41.50.37.88
Car park.

A friendly, good-value little hotel just outside the town – you feel as if you're in a village but you can get into the centre very quickly. The whole place is very clean and well maintained; doubles cost from €21 to €27. The owner will be happy to supply any information you might need. No credit cards.

⚘ 🏨 HÔTEL LE VOLNEY**

1 rue Vonley; it's near the post office.
☎ 02.41.51.25.41 ➡ 02.41.38.11.04
ⓦ www.le-volney.com
Closed 7–22 Dec. **TV**. **Car park**.

The rooms are spotless, homely and comforting and will calm you down if you're feeling stressed. The prices have been remarkably stable over recent years – €24 for a double with basin, €34 with shower/wc and €40 with bath. Excellent welcome from the mistress of the house. 10% discount Nov–March.

⚘ 🏨 HÔTEL DE LONDRES**

48 rue d'Orléans (Centre).
☎ 02.41.51.23.98 ➡ 02.41.51.12.63
ⓦ www.lelondres.com
TV. **Car park**.

Friendly hotel in a busy location, but don't worry – the soundproofing cuts out the noise of the street. It's been redecorated in a charming English style and is well-maintained. Room numbers 25 and 28 have particularly lovely new décor, and there are a few family rooms, too. Doubles €34 (with basin) and €40–46 with shower/wc or bath. Very warm welcome. Copious buffet breakfast for €6. 10% discount.

⚘ 🏨 CENTRAL KYRIAD**

23 rue Daillé (Centre); from quai Carnot take rue Fidélité and it's the first on the left after rue Saint-Nicolas.
☎ 02.41.51.05.78 ➡ 02.41.67.82.35
ⓔ kyriad.saumur@motte-mieux.com
TV. **Pay car park**.

This modern building, to be found in a quiet street, offers pleasant, rather refined décor with exposed beams. The 27 rooms are spacious and some surprise with their flights of stairs, sloping ceilings and stylish furniture. There are some family rooms with spacious bathrooms. Doubles with shower/wc or bath cost €45–60. Affable, welcoming host. 10% discount in low season.

⚘ 🏨 ❙●❙ HÔTEL ANNE D'ANJOU***

32–33 quai Mayaud (Centre); it's below the château,

beside the Loire.
☎ 02.41.67.30.30 ➡ 02.41.67.51.00
ⓦ www.anneanjou.com
Disabled access. **TV**. **Pay car park**.

An elegant and charming eighteenth-century building with a flower-filled internal courtyard and a superb (listed) staircase. Comfortable doubles with antique furniture go for €72 with shower/wc or €92 with bath. Some are under the eaves; there's also an opulent, Empire-style bedroom ideal for a special treat or a honeymoon, as well as suites costing up to €159. Professional welcome. Breakfast €9. There's also a restaurant serving good local dishes: zander with a herb *compote*, carpaccio of scallops with vinaigrette and pigeon with cocoa seeds. Menus €17–55. 10% discount mid-Oct to mid-April.

❙●❙ AUBERGE SAINT-PIERRE

6 pl. Saint-Pierre and 33 rue de la Tonnelle.
☎ 02.41.51.26.25
Closed Sun except July–Aug; Mon; the first week in April; the second and third weeks in Oct.

This fifteenth-century house is half-timbered and hung with flowers. There are several dining rooms but they're often full to bursting – so it's just as well that you can eat outside in summer. You'll enjoy simple, appetizing cuisine: roast zander with Champigny wine sauce, *bœuf bourguignon*. There's a *formule brasserie* at €11 and menus €13–23. It's very reasonably priced and really shouldn't be missed.

⚘ ❙●❙ L'AUBERGE REINE DE SICILE

71 rue Waldeck-Rousseau (Northeast); it's on île d'Offard, between the two bridges.
☎ 02.41.67.30.48
Closed Sun evening; Mon; Aug. **Car park**.

This welcoming and quiet restaurant, situated beside a charming medieval building, is away from the usual tourist circuit. They specialize in meat and fish grilled over the wood fire but there's a good selection of other dishes to try as well: fish *terrine*, *moules marinière*, eels stewed in a wine sauce, zander in a white wine and butter sauce, home-made *foie gras*, rib of Charolais beef, *andouillette*, duck *confit*, leg of lamb. Menus €17–31. It's worth booking. Free apéritif.

⚘ ❙●❙ LES MÉNESTRELS

11–13 rue Raspail; it's next to the law courts.
☎ 02.41.67.71.10
Closed Sun (in mid-season, Sun evening only).

The best restaurant in the area, boasts a rustic setting, original beams and exposed stonework. As for the food, the set menus at €18 (lunchtimes Mon–Sat) and €29–65 offer fine combinations of complex flavours. Specialities change frequently, but typically you might be offered joint of zander with *Guémené andouille* or pigeon breast wrapped in cabbage with *foie gras* and truffle *jus*. Excellent welcome. Free coffee.

ROU-MARSON   49400 (6KM W)

⅍ |●| LES CAVES DE ROU MARSON

1 rue Henri Fricotelle; leaving Saumur on the N147, head for Cholet, take the D960, and it's signposted after 6km.
☎ 02.41.50.50.05. **e** cavesdemarson@aol.com
Closed 25 Dec–15 Jan. **Open** Tues–Sat evening and Sun lunchtime 15 June–15 Sep; Fri and Sat evening, Sun lunch 16 Sept–14 June. **Car park**. **Disabled access**.

The best-known restaurant in Saumur: it's a labyrinth of dining rooms in a cave, lit by candles and with a unique charm. The food is fantastic, too – they serve mouthwatering *fouées* (a kind of *galette*) filled with beans, *rillettes*, goat's cheese and *foie gras*. As a starter you could try a flambéed tart with a glass of Coteaux-du-Layon, and to finish, a salad and a delicious *gratin* of seasonal fruit. Accompany it with an excellent bottle of red Anjou. Menus start at €18, then there's a *formule rillettes de canard* at €21 and a *formule foie gras* for €26 as well as a children's menu at €9. It's not at all expensive given the quality. You have to book a table several days in advance in high season. Free glass of sparkling wine with dessert.

MONTSOREAU   49730 (11KM SE)

⅍ |●| RESTAURANT LE SAUT-AUX-LOUPS

route de Saumur; coming from Saumur on the D947, it's on the edge of the village.
☎ 02.41.51.70.30 **e** sautauxloups@fr.st
Open lunchtimes; Sun only June and Sept; Tues–Sun July–Aug. **Disabled access**.

This was the first restaurant in the region to relaunch an almost-forgotten local speciality called the *galipette*. It's made by stuffing three big mushrooms with *rillette* or *andouillette* and *crème fraîche*, snails or goat's cheese. Then they're browned gently in a bread oven fuelled by vine cuttings and served with a light, fruity Gamay. Here you can get the platter of mushrooms for €11, a main course and a dessert for €14 and a full meal including apéritif, wine and coffee for

€18. Excellent welcome delivered by the young owner; in summer he puts tables outside. Free coffee.

SILLÉ-LE-GUILLAUME   72140

⅍ ⋔ |●| LE BRETAGNE**

1 pl. de la Croix d'Or (Centre); it's near the station.
☎ 02.43.20.10.10
Closed Fri–Sun evening April–Sept; Fri evening, Sat lunchtime and Sun evening Oct–March; the second fortnight in Aug. **TV**. **Car park**.

Inside this crumbling family hotel there's a superb restaurant offering fresh-tasting and exciting dishes that change with the seasons: leek *terrine*, *foie gras* salad with walnut oil, lightly smoked salmon, green lentils, *fondant* of oxtail, scorpion fish with lemongrass, and a delicious *Paris-Brest* filled with butter icing. Weekday menu at €12, and others €20–30. Decent rooms €31–41. 10% discount on the room rate.

THOUARCÉ   49380

|●| LE RELAIS DE BONNEZEAUX

How to get there: take the D24 for about 2km from Thouarcé heading towards Angers; it's in the old train station.
☎ 02.41.54.08.33 **e** relais.bonnezeaux@wanadoo.fr
Closed evenings Sun–Tues and three weeks in Jan. **Car park**. **Disabled access**.

Though this restaurant is housed in a nineteenth-century station, there's little of the old atmosphere left. Nevertheless, the dining room, with its panoramic view, is an elegant setting for the refined cuisine. There's a €15 menu served on weekdays and others €21–40. They specialize in delicious, original fish dishes. À *la carte* try milk-fed lamb, zander *suprême* in red Anjou wine and *nougat glacé* with Cointreau. The wine list includes some amazing old vintages. There's a shady terrace and playground for the children.

TRANCHE-SUR-MER (LA)   85360

|●| RESTAURANT LE NAUTILE

103 rue du Phare.
☎ 02.51.30.32.18
Closed Sun evening and Mon out of season; Jan.

Anonymous-looking restaurant with a terrace, hidden away in the residential part of La Tranche. The setting is characterless, but this is one of the region's most fashionable venues. Cyril Godard's fine, flavoursome cuisine makes it worth a visit – as do the grounds and the veranda. Try the salmon *aumônière* with saltwort, the fisherman's casserole and the duck lacquered with spices. Menus €15–28.

VIBRAYE   72320

🎋 🏠 I●I L'AUBERGE DE LA FORÊT**

rue Gabriel Goussault (Centre).
☎ 02.43.93.60.07 ➡ 02.43.71.20.36
⊛ www.auberge-de-la-foret.fr
Closed Sun evening and Mon; 15 Jan–15 Feb. **TV**. **Car park**.

Peaceful, central hotel with comfortable rooms at €42–46 with shower/wc or bath. There's a weekday menu for €15, a *menu du terroir* for €18 and others €26–43. They list mainly local dishes, including Guérande salad with warm crayfish, a half-lobster flambéed with Cognac and served with crab butter, fillet of beef marinated in port and pan-fried with *foie gras*, veal kidneys and *marmite sarthoise* with Jasnière.

You can also get more elaborate cuisine like hot oysters on a bed of leeks and roast duck in cream and cider. Free apéritif.

🏠 I●I HÔTEL-RESTAURANT LE CHAPEAU ROUGE**

pl. de l'Hôtel-de-Ville.
☎ 02.43.93.60.02 ➡ 02.43.71.52.18
Closed Sun evening (except by reservation). **Disabled access**. **TV**. **Car park**.

Reliable and appealing hotel covered in Virginia creeper. The chef prepares good traditional and classic dishes – authentic *tournedos Rossini*, good local meat, fish fresh from La Rochelle, classic *crème caramel* – which are served in a dining room packed with hunting trophies. Weekday menu €14 and others at €18 and €29. Everything they serve is made in their own kitchens – from the bread to the desserts. There's a good atmosphere guaranteed in the bar on market days. The sixteen bedrooms, five of them with mini-bar, are very quiet. They cost €43–50 with shower/wc or bath.

Picardie

02 Aisne

60 Oise

80 Somme

ALBERT   80300

♠ |●| HÔTEL DE LA PAIX**

43 rue Victor-Hugo; it's near the Basilica.
☎ 03.22.75.01.64 ➡ 03.22.75.44.17
Closed Sun evening. **TV**.

This hotel's period wood panelling and bar do a lot to retain the distinguished atmosphere of the 1925 building it's situated in. The rooms have been prettily refurbished and are comfortable. Doubles with handbasin €34, or €45–49 with shower or bath. The dining room is pleasant and simple, and appealing family cooking is on the menu: potatoes with snails and Camembert cream sauce, calves' head sauce *gribiche*, steak with shallots. Menus from €12. The proprietor offers a winning welcome.

⚘ ♠ |●| HÔTEL DE LA BASILIQUE**

3–5 rue Gambetta (Centre).
☎ 03.22.75.04.71 ➡ 03.22.75.10.47
Ⓦ http://perso.wanadoo.fr/hotel.de.la.basilique
Closed Sat evening and Mon Easter–All Saints'; Sun out of season; three weeks in Aug; Christmas. **TV**.

This hotel near the red-brick basilica offers a friendly welcome, comfortable rooms and good regional cooking. Doubles €44–28. The conventional dining room makes a matching set with the rooms; weekday *formule* €10 or menus €12–23; try the home-made duck *pâté en croûte* and the rabbit with prunes. Free coffee.

AMIENS   80000

SEE MAP ON P.621

♠ HÔTEL DE NORMANDIE

1 [bis] rue Lamartine. **MAP C2-2**
☎ 03.22.91.74.99 ➡ 03.22.92.06.56
TV. Car park.

Thirty ordinary and very simple rooms. The wallpaper is dreary and the plumbing is inadequately hidden – but if you're stuck for a bed it will do. Doubles with basin, shower or bath/wc €28–46. In contrast the 1930s breakfast room has splendid stained glass and the Parisian couple who own the place are lovely and welcoming.

♠ HÔTEL VICTOR HUGO*

2 rue de l'Oratoire. **MAP C2-3**
☎ 03.22.91.57.91 ➡ 03.22.92.74.02
TV.

This very old establishment in a lovely quarter of the town, has retained some of its original charm and its natural wood staircase, despite extensive renovations. Some rooms are more comfortable than others, and each one is different. The smaller attic rooms have a romantic view over the roof tops and cost the same as the others. Some of the carpetting is due for a change. Doubles 33.54€ with shower/wc or 38.11€ with bath. Welcoming owner. Best to book.

⚘ ♠ HOTEL ALSACE-LORRAINE**

18 rue de la Morlière. **MAP C1-6**
☎ 03.22.91.35.71 ➡ 03.22.80.43.90

Just away from the centre in a quiet area, there's a delightful little hotel behind a lovely blue door. Thirteen rooms are painted brilliant white and simply but thoughtfully decorated. Some rooms are accessible from the interior courtyard. Doubles with shower/wc or bath

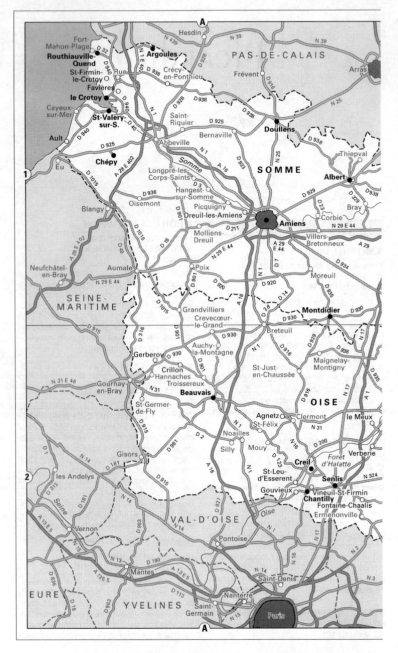

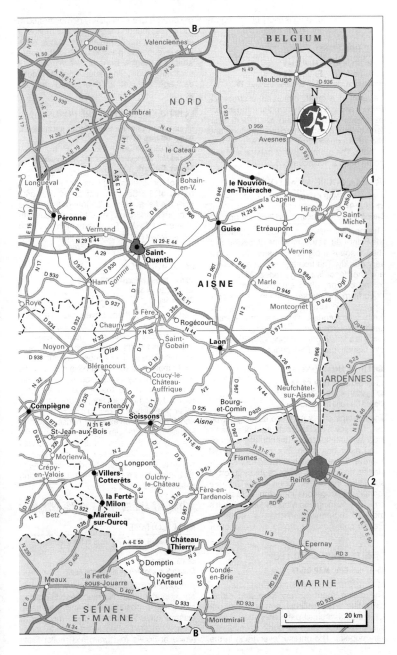

€49–61. The welcome is every bit as charming. 10% discount on the room rate.

♠ LE PRIEURÉ**

6 and 17 rue Porion. **MAP B1-4**
☎ 03.22.92.27.67 ➡ 03.22.92.46.16
Restaurant closed Sun evenings and Mon. **TV**.

Situated in a quiet, picturesque street, *Le Prieuré* and the main building and the annexes have all been renovated. Each room is different with carefully chosen furniture and thoughtful decoration; €49–61 with shower or bath. The problem is that service and welcome need a makeover too.

⚒ |●| LA SOUPE À CAILLOUX

place du Don. **MAP C1-10**
☎ 03.22.91.92.70
Closed Mon except in season; end Dec–early Jan.

This popular restaurant is ideally situated in the Saint-Leu district near the cathedral, and the terrace is a big draw in summer – it fills very quickly. The frontage is stone-coloured and the décor is orange tones. Nice, comforting cuisine, often employing fresh produce from the market: salmon with bacon, slow-cooked lamb (it takes 7 hours) and lamb with prunes, almonds and sesame seeds. Weekday lunch menu €12–€19. À la carte is a little more – around €23. It's a simple, friendly place. Free coffee.

|●| LE T'CHIOT ZINC

18 rue de Noyon. **MAP C2-14**
☎ 03.22.91.43.79
Closed Sun, and Mon lunchtime.

The frontage of this Art Deco building is typical of the town and the restaurant has been a local favourite for ages. The cooking is not as good as it has been, but maybe that will improve. There are several dining rooms; specialities include suckling pig, *caqhuse* (a sort of stew) and, in summer, rabbit in jelly.There's a *formule* with couscous (including wine) served on Friday evening and Monday lunchtime. It's more of a Spanish inn than an authentic French one. *Formule rapide* €11 and other menus €14–26.

⚒ |●| LE PORC SAINT-LEU

45–47 quai Bélu. **MAP C1-11**
☎ 03.22.80.00.73

The dining room is very long and rather cabin-like – low ceilings, soft lights, check table cloths, a small patio and a terrace for sunny weather. Best to book because it's very popular. The phrase "everything in the

pig is good to eat" is clearly demonstrated in this place, though there aren't any menus; *à la carte* will cost you around about €23. Dishes such as pork knuckle with trotter attached, marrow bone or *filet mignon* with mirabelle plums. The side dishes are ideal: cabbage peasant style or good mashed spuds.

⚒ |●| RESTAURANT LE PRÉ PORUS

95 rue Voyelle; it's on the edge of Camon just before the bridge. **Off map C1-16**
☎ 03.22.46.25.03
Closed Mon and Tues evenings, and Feb. **Disabled access. Car park**.

One of the loveliest settings for lunch on the banks of the Somme, just a few moments from the fields. Menus list lots of fish dishes and grills, and begin at €14 (not Sun) with others at €25–35. The quality of the cooking is not always high enough to justify the price of the more expensive menus. Free coffee.

|●| LE BOUCHON

10 rue Alexandre-Fatton. **MAP C2-13**
☎ 03.22.92.14.32
Closed Sun.

Service until 10.30pm. Lovely, old-style bistro with red benches and a zinc-topped bar. There are plans to refurbish but it would be a shame if its friendly nature were lost. It's a stylish little place with an atmosphere and cooking to match. As you might have guessed, it's modelled on a Lyonnais "Bouchon", basically a brasserie, where the fare is always of a robust type: hot sausage, *andouillette* and other offal dishes. Here you'll also find a seasonal menu and an excellent house speciality – snail casserole with thyme. There's also a menu where they serve a different wine with each course. Steer away from the wine list because the prices are heady. Lunch menu €12 and others €19–38. Smiling, easy-going welcome and service.

DREUIL LES AMIENS   80730 (6KM NW)

|●| LE COTTAGE

385 bd. Pasteur; it's on the N235 in the direction of Picquigny.
☎ 03.22.54.10.98
Closed Sun and Mon evenings, and Aug.

A good little roadside restaurant. It features an unpretentious Normandy-style dining room with exposed beams and they serve classic, refined cuisine. Lunch menu €12 then €19–34. Dishes listed include *millefeuille* of house *foie gras*, red mullet fillets

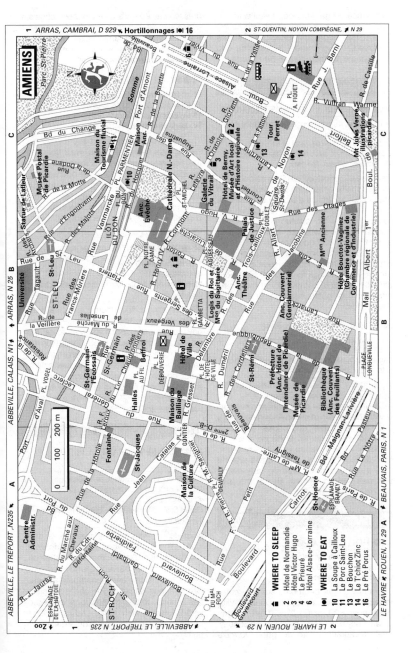

AMIENS

WHERE TO SLEEP
1 Hôtel de Normandie
2 Hôtel Victor Hugo
3 Le Prieuré
4 Hôtel Alsace-Lorraine

WHERE TO EAT
10 La Soupe à Cailloux
11 Le Porc Saint-Leu
13 Le Bouchon
14 Le T'chiot Zinc
16 Le Pré Porus

with sauce vierge, knuckle of veal with ink-cap mushrooms or zander fillet with *beurre blanc*. The hours of service are strictly observed, though, and the welcome and atmosphere are more formal than need be.

ARGOULES   80120

⚘ ☎ |●| AUBERGE DU GROS TILLEUL***

pl. du Château; it's in the village square opposite the 18th-century château.
☎ 03.22.29.91.00 ➡ 03.22.23.91.64
Closed Mon except public holidays; Sun evening; Jan.
TV. Disabled access. Car park.

Because of its history – Sully is said to have planted the lime tree the restaurant's named after and it served as a branch of a Sienese bank – not to mention its delightful sur-roundings, this inn is listed in all the guide books. There's a weekday *formule express* at €11 and a €35 gourmet menu. The cui-sine is traditional with heavy sauces and not especially delicate. Rooms have a view of the grounds, and go for €58–89 for a dou-ble. Half board is compulsory at the week-end and over public holidays, at €53–58. Free coffee.

|●| AUBERGE LE COQ EN PÂTE

route de Valloires; it's 500m from the abbey.
☎ 03.22.29.92.09
Closed Sunday evening and Mon in Jan and a fortnight at the end of Sept. **Disabled access**.

They serve excellent local dishes in this pretty establishment. There's only one menu in season but dishes change regular-ly with the season and depending on what's fresh in the market; cod pricked with pink garlic, chicken with *vin jaune* or, in winter, cockerel in beer sauce or a pastry crust. Menus start at €14 and it costs around €30 *à la carte*. The charming lady owner provides smiling service. By far the best cooking in the area.

BEAUVAIS   60000

☎ |●| HÔTEL DE LA POSTE

19–21 rue Gambetta (Centre).
☎ 03.44.45.14.97 ➡ 03.44.45.02.31
Closed Sun. **TV. Pay car park**.

The small, bright bedrooms are very com-fortable and well equipped. Doubles with basin cost €22, or up to €31 with show-er/wc. They don't serve breakfast on Sunday. The restaurant offers a good *formule*

brasserie at €9 – it's a very popular choice, especially at lunchtimes. Other menus €13–19, also offer good value for money. The daily special is nicely presented and changes frequently.

⚘ ☎ HÔTEL LA RÉSIDENCE**

24 rue Louis-Borel (Northeast); it's on the N1.
☎ 03.44.48.30.98 ➡ 03.44.45.09.42
ⓦ www.hoteldelaresidence.fr
TV.. Lock-up car park.

This hotel is on a very quiet street in a resi-dential area twenty minutes' walk from the town centre, where the only thing disturbing the silence is the sound of the odd passing bicycle. You'll get a jokey, good-natured welcome, a modern, well-equipped room and good value for money. Doubles with shower €37, or €46 with bath. 10% dis-count.

⚘ |●| RESTAURANT LE MARIGNAN

1 rue de Malherbe (Centre).
☎ 03.44.48.15.15
Closed Sun evening and Mon except on public holidays; 20 July–2 Aug.

On the ground floor there's a typical bar-brasserie where they serve a decent week-day menu for €10. But if you want to get the most out of this place, head instead for the plush first-floor dining room. Here you can sample well-prepared Picardie specialities, including fish dishes, coddled eggs, veal *fric-assée*, scallops *Dieppois* and *crème brulée*. Menus €16 and €28 and there's *à la carte*. Free house apéritif.

CRILLON   60112 (15KM NW)

⚘ |●| BAR-RESTAURANT LA PETITE FRANCE

7 rue du Moulin. At Troissereux, on the Beauvais-Abbeville road, fork left onto the D133 to Crillon.
☎ 03.44.81.01.13
Closed Sun and Mon evenings, Tues and mid-Aug to mid-Sept.

A rustic inn with hunting trophies on the walls. The food is very good, made with only fresh ingredients – even the dishes on the €11 *formule*, served at lunch and din-ner, are delicious and generously served. Other menus €13–28. The chef's speciali-ties include *foie gras escalope* deglazed with Sauternes, fish dishes and game. One of the best places in the region. Free apéri-tif.

AGNETZ 60600 (20KM E)

⚘ |●| AUBERGE DE GICOUR

Forêt de Hez-Gicourt; head for Gicourt and take the Gicourt Zone Hôtelière turning.
☎ 03.44.50.00.31
Closed Sun evening and Mon. **Disabled access**.

This popular, pleasant inn has recently changed hands but doesn't seem to have suffered as a result. The best evidence of this is that the locals still pile in at the weekend. There's a menu *terroir* at €17 (not at weekends), a menu *gourmand* at €24 and one for the kids at €11. Free apéritif.

GEREBOY 660380 (21KM NW)

⚘ |●| L'AMBASSADE DE MONTMARTRE

2 allée du Jeu de Tamis, (Centre); take the D133 in the direction of Abbeville.
☎ 03.44.82.16.50
Closed Sun evening, Mon and Tues evening and beginning of Dec to mid-Feb.

This place is sited at the foot of the old city walls right at the end of this wonderful village – which is listed as one of the most beautiful in France. Both it and the restaurant are worth making the effort to visit. The pretty half-timbered house is owned by Jean-Pierre, the son of a former President of the République de Montmartre and he makes you feel welcome. The spacious, rustic dining room has a mezzanine where he holds art exhibitions. Decent local dishes with menus €15–22. When the weather gets warm you can sit on the terrace out front and savour your (free) apéritif.

CHANTILLY 60500

|●| RESTAURANT LE GOUTILLON

61 rue du Connétable (Centre); it's near the château.
☎ 03.44.58.01.00

This restaurant has an old-fashioned décor with exposed beams and stone walls covered with vintage advertisements. The waiter brings a blackboard to the table and places it on a chair and you make your choice from the dishes listed on it. A variety of tasty starters and house specialities including *andouillette 5A*, *steak tartare au poivre à l'ancienne* Lyonnais sausage and lamb shank *confit*. There's a three-course lunch *formule* for €14, à la carte reckon on €23.

|●| AUX GOÛTERS CHAMPÊTRES

Hameau du parc du Château; it's inside the grounds of the château where you have to pay to get in.
☎ 03.44.57.46.21
Closed mid-Nov to mid-March.

A lovely place to eat when it's fine but at the weekend you have to book to have any hope of getting a table. You eat outside in nicely maintained little gardens, under sun-shades – utterly charming. Take a peak at the murals in the Prince de Condé's tea room. Friendly welcome and service. The €15 menu offers a dish and a pudding which are very filling while the €24 menu is the more popular with dishes such as a "crown" of duck breasts, duck or pork confit, cheese and crème Chantilly for dessert.

VINEUIL-SAINT-FIRMIN 60500 (4KM NE)

|●| RESTAURANT LES GRANDS PRÉS

route d'Avilly.
☎ 03.44.57.71.97
Closed Sun evening and Mon, Mon lunchtime only in June–Aug. **Garden. Car park**.

This place is out in the country, a five-minute drive from Chantilly. The straightforward, traditional cuisine includes dishes like marbled *foie gras* and duck *confit*, poached scallops and mussels with *anise*, and ox kidneys with oyster mushrooms. Menus at €15 (not weekends) and €23 and one for the kids for €10. There's a terrace, where you can enjoy the fresh country air.

GOUVIEUX 60270 (5KM W)

⌂ |●| HÔSTELLERIE DU PAVILLION SAINT-HUBERT

chemin de Marisy, lieu-dit Toutevoie.
☎ 03.44.57.07.04 ➡ 03.44.57.75.42
Closed Sun evening and Mon Nov–Easter, and 15 Jan–15 Feb. **TV. Car park**.

This old fisherman's house is set in a charming spot on a bend in the Oise river and it's a lovely place to bring family, friends or a special person. From the terrace you can watch the barges slip by or simply listen to the birds. The cooking is traditional, with a €24 menu (€27 at weekends) listing a choice of nine starters, and à la carte dishes such as snail *profiteroles* with Roquefort and the house speciality, veal kidneys with mustard. Double rooms, €49 to €66, come with shower/wc. The rooms overlooking the river are the most popular and they're often booked at the weekend.

SAINT-LEU-D'ESSERENT 60340 (5.5KM NW)

⚘ ⌂ |●| HÔTEL DE L'OISE*

25 quai d'Amont (East); take the N16 then follow the D44.

☎ 03.44.56.60.24 ➡ 03.44.56.05.11
Restaurant closed Fri and Sun evenings, Sat, and the first three weeks in Aug. **TV**. **Car park**.

A dream of a riverside hotel: it's quiet, peaceful and offers friendly hospitality. Double rooms at €46 with shower/wc or bath. The restaurant has a rustic décor and boasts a superb painting of Claude Monet's garden at Giverny. The three-course menu, €11, is served to guests at lunchtimes (not Sun); other menus €20–32. Excellent specialities *à la carte* and the pastries are home-made. A great little place even though it has only one star. 10% discount Fri, Sat and Sun nights from Oct to March.

CHÂTEAU-THIERRY   02400

⅍ ☎ |●| **HÔTEL-RESTAURANT HEXAGONE****

50 av. d'Essômes; take the Paris road from the centre of town then follow the signs for Charly-sur-Marne.
☎ 03.23.83.83.42 ➡ 03.23.83.64.17
Closed Sun except for groups and 22–29 Dec. **TV**. **Disabled access**. **Car park**.

You'll get a warm welcome in this modern hotel, and you will also be well looked-after. Comfortable doubles with shower or bath €40. There is a hearty buffet-style breakfast – cereals, cheese, *charcuterie* and so on – at €5. The restaurant's cheapest menu, €12, is perfectly adequate, and there are four others up to €26. Good traditional home cooking, scallops in champagne sauce, pepper steak and a notable *tarte Tatin*. The River Marne flows past the bottom of the garden. 10% discount on the room rate.

DOMPTIN   02310 12KM SW)

⅍ ☎ |●| **HÔTEL-RESTAURANT LE CYGNE D'ARGENT**

24 rue de la Fontaine; take the N3 west from Château-Thierry, then the D11 and it's in the main street.
☎ 03.23.70.79.90
Closed Mon evening. **TV**. **Car park**. **Disabled access**.

Lovely country hotel on the Champagne wine route. Fine local cuisine – house terrines, panfried scallops with preserved leeks, duck breast roasted with local grapes, champagne sorbet with home made Ratafia (a fortified wine) and game in season. There's a weekday menu for €12 and others €18–34. The bedrooms have fully-equipped bathrooms (shower or bath/wc), TV and minibar, all priced at €38. One of the best places in the area. Free apéritif.

CHÉPY   80210

☎ |●| **L'AUBERGE PICARDE****

pl. de la Gare; it's opposite Chépy-Valines train station.
☎ 03.22.26.20.78 ➡ 03.22.26.33.34
Restaurant closed Sat lunchtime and Sun evening. **TV**. **Disabled access**. **Car park**.

The large, modern building is more motel than charming inn, but it has one of the best restaurants in the region. The dining room has ample proportions and is decorated in traditional style. They serve good seafood and typical local dishes using seasonal produce: *ficelle Picarde*, salmon and asparagus tips with *vinaigrette*, fried fish with seaweed butter. There's a weekday menu at €14 and others are €20–31. It's best to book at weekends. The rooms are standardized but comfortable, with doubles for €41–46.

COMPIÈGNE   60200

⅍ ☎ **HÔTEL DE FLANDRE****

16 quai de la République (Centre).
☎ 03.44.83.24.40 ➡ 03.44.90.02.75
Closed a fortnighe end Dec/early Jan. **TV**.

An enormous classical building on the banks of the Oise. The hotel offers good facilities at reasonable prices: €32 for a double with basin, €50–53 with shower/wc or bath. Rooms are spacious and the double glazing guarantees peace and quiet. Pleasant welcome. 10% discount.

|●| **LE PALAIS GOURMAND**

8 rue Dahomey (Centre).
☎ 03.44.40.13.13
Closed Sun evening, Mon and a fortnight in Aug.

An old baker's transformed into a modern restaurant with lots of corners and little dining rooms. The sky filters through the stained glass and sets off the attractive décor, which strikes a nice balance between bold colour and restrained design. Lovely old hand-made floor tiles. The cuisine offers both seasonal dishes and modern interpretations; *formules* and menus €12–27. Wine by the jug is sold at fair prices. Overall, it's excellent value for money.

|●| **LE BISTROT DES ARTS**

80 Cours Guynemer; it's on the riverbank.
☎ 03.44.20.10.10
Closed Sun.

The easy-going, professional service perfectly suits the setting of this bistrot, which is where the gourmands in town come to eat. There's no short menu, the weekday lunch *formule* costs €18 or the set menu €21 which is fair given the quality. *À la carte*, a meal costs around €26. Typical brasserie and local dishes – wholesome and generously served. Sadly there are no wines by the jug so it's hard to keep the price down. Best to book.

❙●❙ LA FERME DU CARANDEAU

route de l'Armistice; take the N31 in the direction of Soissons.
☎ 03.44.85.89.89
Closed Sun evening and Mon.

This half-timbered inn, near the clearing where the Armistice was signed, has come up with a very attractive formula. On the single menu, €23, you're served *kir royal*, a huge choice of *hors d'œuvre* from the buffet, spit-roasted meat, cheese, dessert, as much wine as you like and coffee. There's lamb on Friday, and pork on Saturday evening and Sunday lunch. It's become so successful that you'd do well to book. Good food, generous helpings and a convivial atmosphere.

MEUX (LE)   60880 (10KM S)

🍴❙●❙ LA MAISON DU GOURMET

1 rue de la République; it's on the D13
☎ 03.44.91.10.10
Closed Sat lunchtime, Sun and Mon evenings, 10 days in Feb and three weeks end July/Aug.
Disabled access. Car park in the courtyard.

The owner-chef isn't new to this game – seven years at *Maxim's* in Paris and a few at the Château de Raray. The €15 menu alone makes it worth a visit; a typical selection might be panfried *foie gras* with honey, duck breast with Morello cherries, *filet mignon* with cider sauce, strawberry *croustillant* and warm soufflé with soft fruit. There's more choice on the €23 menu and a wide range of dishes *à la carte*. The chef strives to give you value for money and succeeds. You'll be greeted and served in a friendly, efficient manner. It's worth booking. Free coffee.

VERBERIE   60410 (15KM SW)

🏠 ❙●❙ AUBERGE DE NORMANDIE

26 rue de la Pêcherie; take the D200 or the D932 near the Oise river.
☎ 03.44.40.92.33 ➡ 03.44.40.50.62
📧 christiane.maleties@wanadoo.fr

Closed Sun evening, Mon and the last three weeks in July.

A nice country inn with a classic dining room furnished with imitation rustic furniture and a pleasant terrace festooned with flowers. Double rooms €35–52. The unexpectedly interesting cuisine uses quality produce which is produced with art and craft. From the meat specialities, try the stuffed pig's trotters and the desserts are delicious. Weekday menu €15 and others €18–27. Lovely welcome.

SAINT-JEAN-AUX-BOIS   60350 (20KM SE)

🍴 🏠 ❙●❙ AUBERGE À LA BONNE IDÉE***

3 rue des Meuniers (Southeast); take the D332 then turn left onto the D85.
☎ 03.44.42.84.09 ➡ 03.44.42.80.45
🌐 www.a-la-bonne-idee.fr
Closed Sun evening and Mon except public holidays and 14 Jan–10 Feb. **TV. Disabled access. Private car park.**

This is a picture-postcard inn with wooden shutters and striped blinds, in the middle of splendid village in the Compiègne forest. The €15 menu is served at the bar and there are other menus for €20–58. Specialities include duck *terrine*, Bresse chicken with mushroom sauce and *foie gras* escalope with honey and cider vinegar. You can eat on the terrace in fine weather. The prettily decorated rooms, €58–69, feature a number of personal touches along with en-suite bath/wc and direct-dial telephone. Nice terrace in summer and they have wild deer and an aviary in the grounds. Free apéritif.

CROTOY (LE)   60100

🍴 🏠 ❙●❙ LES TOURELLES*

2–4 rue Pierre Guerlain; take the A16; it's by the beach.
☎ 03.22.27.16.33 ➡ 03.22.27.11.45.
🌐 www.lestourelles.com
Closed three weeks in Jan. **TV.**

This red-brick turreted building, erected on the Somme estuary, was once the mansion of perfumier Pierre Guerlain. Perhaps appropriately, everything is done meticulously, from the charming bedrooms with their wonderful views of the estuary to the relaxing lounge-bar and the children's playroom. There are only 24 rooms so book well in advance. Doubles €44–58; room number 33 is in the tower. The welcome, setting, décor and cuisine are all top quality. Local specialities are served in the smart dining room – star dishes include the fish *matelotte* and the seafood platter. Menus €19–43. Free apéritif.

|O| LA GRIGNOTINE

5 rue Porte-du-Pont
☎ 03.22.27.07.49
Closed Wed out of season.

A drearily-decorated restaurant which is always overflowing with people because the food is so good. Smiling, easy-going welcome. The lunchtime *formule*, €9, is as simple as could be. It's mussels with 25 different sauces – garlic, Portuguese-style, Hungarian-style or simply *marinières*. They're served in a huge pot with fresh chips. Very filling, brilliantly cooked and cheap. They also offer dishes *à la carte* and a meal will cost around €15. Note that because the place is so small, push-chairs and pets are not allowed.

FAVIÈRES   80120 (4KM NE)

🏠 |O| RESTAURANT LA CLÉ DES CHAMPS

pl. des Frères-Caudron (Centre); take the D140.
☎ 03.22.27.88.00
Closed Sun evening and Mon (except public holidays); a fortnight in Jan, 10 days in Feb and 10 days end Aug–early Sept. **Disabled access**. **Car park**.

If you want to get away from it all, come to this well-known inn set among the salt meadows. It provides a refined, comfortable setting. The specialities are fish, landed at the local harbour, and dishes based around fresh produce from the market. Madame makes you feel very welcome. Weekday menu €14 and others €23–38. Free coffee.

SAINT-FIRMIN-LÈS-CROTOY   80550 (7KM N)

🏠 |O| AUBERGE DE LA DUNE**

rue de la Dune; take the D104 in the direction of Saint-Firmin, at the D204 turn-off and take the signs to the Marquenterre bird sanctuary.
☎ 03.22.25.03.06/03.22.25.01.88 ➡ 03.22.25.66.74
Closed Tues evening and Wed from Oct to mid-March. **TV**. **Car park**.

This small farmhouse has been nicely restored and belongs to the nearby bird sanctuary. The eleven brightly-painted bedrooms are cosy as you like and, though they're not big, they're comfortable; all come with shower/wc, TV and phone. Doubles from €46. They serve decent food in the restaurant and a menu of Picardy specialities. Menus from €13. Friendly welcome.

DOULLENS   80600

🏠 |O| LE SULLY**

45 rue Jacques-Mossion (Centre); it's beside the train station.
☎ 03.22.77.10.87 ➡ 03.22.77.31.01
Closed Mon, a fortnight in Jan and the last fortnight of June. **TV**.

A fairly modern building, with seven modest rooms at €33. They're very clean and well-equipped but they don't have much character. The restaurant has good menus at €10, €14 and €21; they list regional specialities such as potato terrine, *caqhuse* (a kind of stew) and preserved rhubarb with *grenadine*. The chef makes you feel welcome.

FERTÉ-MILON (LA)   02460

🏠 🏠 HÔTEL RACINE**

pl. du Port-au-Blé (Centre).
☎ 03.23.96.72.02 ➡ 03.23.96.72.37
e ileauxpeintres@free.fr
Closed the first fortnight in Jan. **TV**. **Garden**. **Car park**.

A superb little hotel in a 17th-century building. The eight rooms have been tastefully decorated and they're reasonably priced: double with shower/wc €46, €49 with bath. Outside there's a garden with a paved courtyard and a pretty corner tower overlooking the banks of the Ourcq. The owners organize art courses. Pleasant welcome. Free apéritif.

|O| RESTAURANT LES RUINES

2 pl. du Vieux-Château (South).
☎ 03.23.96.71.56
Closed Mon, evenings except Sat, and Aug. **Garden**. **Car park**.

A good inn. It's owned by a landscape gardener; you dine outside in a lovely garden next to the ruined château, so you get to admire his handiwork. Traditional, good-value cooking; there's an €11 *formule rapide*, served during the week, and other menus are €17–25. Dishes such as rabbit with girolles, ostrich escalop with morels and cider, lamb with olives and monkfish fillet with spiced prawns.

GUISE   02120

🏠 🏠 |O| HÔTEL-RESTAURANT CHAMPAGNE-PICARDIE**

41 rue André-Godin (Centre).
☎ 03.23.60.43.44 ➡ 03.23.61.37.85

Closed Sun evening, Mon and Christmas to 2 Jan. **TV. Garden. Lock-up car park.**

This is a beautiful residence, encircled by a little park and overlooked by the château belonging to the duc de Guise. The twelve comfortable bedrooms are spacious and bright. Doubles with shower/wc or bath are €38. Service in the restaurant is pleasant, as is the food – hearty regional dishes that are not too expensive. The weekday *menu du jour*, €9, is simple but delicious, and there are more elaborate ones €13–21. The most expensive lists *foie gras*, sole *meunière* and a choice of cheese and desserts. Courteous welcome. Free coffee.

LAON   02000

⋔ HÔTEL LES CHEVALIERS**

3–5 rue Sérurier (Centre); it's in the middle of the medieval town.
e hotelchevaliers@aol.com
☎ 03.23.27.17.50 ➡ 03.23.23.40.71
Closed Sun and Mon except on public holidays and in the tourist season and 15 Nov–15 March. **TV.**

Fourteen attractively decorated bedrooms with low ceilings and exposed beams in a stylish old building. It's a breath of the past. Doubles €52 with shower, €60 with bath (including breakfast). Some have an extraordinary view over the surrounding countryside. The welcome from the owner could be friendlier.

I●I BAR-RESTAURANT LE RÉTRO

18 bd. de Lyon; it's the main street in the lower town.
☎ 03.23.23.04.49
Closed Sun lunchtime (unless you book).

A friendly, busy place that is particularly popular with local workers at lunchtimes. Marie-Thérèse, the owner, has a loyal following. The cheapest menu (€12) has superb traditional dishes: *onglet* and *entrecôte* steak from the local area, Maroilles cheese tart, home-made *terrine* and calf's-head *ravigote*. There's also a list of freshly made salads. The slightly kitsch dining room is festooned with green plants and artificial flowers.

⋇ I●I RESTAURANT LA PETITE AUBERGE

45 bd. Brossolette (Centre); it's near the train station.
☎ 03.23.23.02.38
Closed Sat lunchtime, Sun and Mon evening except on public holidays and a fortnight in Aug.

Laon's gourmet restaurant. The cooking is modern and the owner's son, Willy Marc Zorn, introduces a touch of originality to tasty

dishes such as sea bass with pumpkin *coulis*, *crème au lard* and pan-fried veal sweetbreads in pale ale with a chicory *fondue*. Menus – at €20, €23 and €34 – are appropriately priced. The same team runs *Le Saint-Amour* (☎ 03.23.23.31.01), next door, which offers home-style Lyonnais cooking and excellent Beaujolais. Free apéritif at *La Petite Auberge* only.

ROGÉCOURT   02800 (15KM E)

⋔ I●I TABLE ET CHAMBRE D'HÔTE DE ROGÉCOURT

Le Mont Rouge (South); take the N44 in the direction of Fère.
☎ 03.23.56.32.31 ➡ 03.23.56.32.31
Car park.

This place is to be found in a 17th-century castle on a private estate near the St-Gobin Forest. They provide lots of activities: a sitting room with TV, snooker, a library; outside there's a lake, a putting range, a children's play area, ping-pong and *boules*. Spacious doubles with washing facilities/wc for €46–53. If you want a meal, you have to book a place at the Table d'Hôte.

MAREUIL-SUR-OURCQ   60890

I●I AUBERGE DE L'OURCQ

7 rue de Thury (Centre); take the D936 from La Ferté-Milon.
☎ 03.44.87.24.14
Closed Mon, evenings except Fri and Sat, three weeks in Jan and a fortnight end-July.

The skilful chef in this high-class restaurant makes good use of local produce. *Menu du jour* at €12 served weekday lunchtimes, regional menus around €22 and others up to €32. There's a wide choice of meat dishes from home and away, and good fish too – roast scallops and croustilland of monkfish. Affordable wines. Smiling welcome and efficient service.

MONTDIDIER   80500

⋇ ⋔ I●I HÔTEL DE DIJON**

1 pl. du 10-Août-1918; it's on the Beauvais road.
☎ 03.22.78.01.35 ➡ 03.22.78.27.24
Restaurant closed Sat, Sun evening, a fortnight in the Feb school holidays and the first three weeks in Aug.
TV. Lock-up car park.

This hotel has been completely renovated, with comfortable rooms painted in "modern" colours which unfortunately already seem a bit passé. Doubles at €46–52 with shower/wc or bath. The restaurant specializes in meat dishes, either grilled or more elaborately prepared: *ficelle Picarde* or grilled steak with *Maître d'Hôtel* butter. Menus at €14–23. Free coffee.

🕸 |●| RESTAURANT LE PARMENTIER

11 rue Albert-1er; it's opposite the post office.
☎ 03.22.78.15.10
Closed evenings, Aug and a week Christmas–New Year.

Very popular restaurant, where you can get generous portions of reasonably priced home cooking. Most dishes are prepared from fresh local produce. The menus, €11–21, offer dishes such as seafood pancake stuffed with ham, mushrooms with crème fraîche sauce, and *ficelle Picarde*; *hachis Parmentier* (shepherd's pie) is often the dish of the day. They serve good locally-brewed beers. Cheerful staff. Free apéritif.

NOUVION-EN-THIÉRACHE (LE)   02170

🕸 🏠 |●| HÔTEL DE LA PAIX**

37 rue Mont-Vicary (Northwest).
☎ 03.23.97.04.55 ➡ 03.23.98.98.39
✉ la.pierre.pierrart@wanadoo.fr
Closed Sun evening, Mon lunchtime, the Feb school holidays and the last fortnight in Aug. **TV. Lock-up car park.**

This is a good country hotel with friendly staff and it's been renovated. The restaurant is a delight and the cooking out of the ordinary. They offer regional dishes such as steak with Maroilles cheese sauce, seafood specialities including prawn ravioli with a shellfish *coulis* and turbot soufflé with basil and saffron, followed by tasty desserts to satisfy even the most demanding palate. Weekday menu at €15, then two more at €22 and €28. The large, comfortable bedrooms cost €43 with shower/wc and €53 with bath. Number 1 faces south and has a private terrace. Free apéritif or breakfast.

ÉTRÉAUPONT   02580 (19KM SE)

🕸 🏠 |●| LE CLOS DU MONTVINAGE ET L'AUBERGE DU VAL DE L'OISE**

8 rue Albert-Ledent; it's on the N2.
☎ 03.23.97.91.10 ➡ 03.23.97.48.92
🌐 www.clos-du-montvinage.com
Hotel closed a week in Feb and a week in Aug.
Restaurant closed Sun evening and Mon lunchtime.
TV. Disabled access. Car park.

A huge 19th-century bourgeois residence in

relaxing grounds with tennis courts. The rooms are spacious and comfortable. The ones on the second floor have exposed beams. Doubles €55 with shower/wc and €66 with bath. The welcome is charming. In the *Auberge du Val de l'Oise* restaurant, run by the same family, you can enjoy very tasty cooking: stewed scallops with lobster stock, green pepper steak and iced Vacherin with soft fruit. Menus €15–20. There's a new restaurant in the hotel, the delights of which are yet to be experienced. Free apéritif and 10% discount on the room rate on Fridays, except during public holidays.

PÉRONNE   80200

🕸 🏠 |●| HOSTELLERIE DES REMPARTS**

23 rue Beaubois; it's 100m off the main street.
☎ 03.22.84.01.22 ➡ 03.22.84.31.96
Disabled access. TV. Lock-up car park.

A country inn with a post-war feel in peaceful grounds on a quiet street. But it's had a makeover and forty renovated rooms are due in 2002; doubles with shower/wc and bath €42–76. They serve traditional local dishes with a creative touch in the cosy dining room. €14 menu in the week, then others up to €38; *à la carte* a meal gets expensive. Free house apéritif.

ROUTHIAUVILLE-QUEND   80120

🏠 |●| AUBERGE LE FIACRE***

Hameau de Routhiauville.
☎ 03.22.23.47.30 ➡ 03.22.27.19.80
Closed Tues lunchtime, Tues Nov–April, and 15 Jan–15 Feb. **TV. Garden. Disabled access. Car park.**

The inn is in a pleasant half-timbered building which is quite classy but more bourgeois than bohemian – jackets and ties are *de rigueur*. The restaurant is very cosy and it's well known locally for its cooking. The menu, which changes with the seasons, features fish and seasonal, regional specialities (using scallops, ceps or morel mushrooms). Menus start at €18 in the week with others up to €36. They also offer ten or so comfortable rooms, all of which overlook the garden, from €58–69 a double.

SAINT-QUENTIN   02100

🏠 |●| HÔTEL-RESTAURANT DE GUISE*

93 rue de Guise (Southeast); it's some distance from the

town centre, on the way to La Capelle.
☎ 03.23.68.27.69 ➡ 03.23.68.05.13
TV. Disabled access. Secure parking.

The rooms are clean, comfortable, and cheap; doubles with shower cost €26. They offer a weekday lunch *menu express* for €8, which is more fuel than cuisine, but they really specialize in *couscous*, priced €10–13, and paella for €13.

🎋 ♠ |●| LE FLORENCE**

42 rue Émile-Zola (Centre).
☎ 03.23.64.22.22 ➡ 03.23.62.52.85
Ⓦ www.hotel-le-florence.fr
Restaurant closed Sun and Mon lunchtimes. **TV. Car park**.

This hotel offers simple, clean doubles for €22 with basin, €33 with shower/wc and €36 with bath. Ask for a room overlooking the courtyard – Émile-Zola is a busy street. The restaurant has two dining rooms, one for non-smokers. It specializes in good Italian dishes such as *osso bucco*, pizza, lasagne and fresh pasta. Menus at €12 and €14, or about €15 *à la carte*. There's a shady terrace and an Italianate fountain. Free apéritif.

♠ |●| HÔTEL DE LA PAIX**

3 pl. du 8-Octobre (Centre); it's near the train station.
☎ 03.23.62.77.62 ➡ 03.23.62.66.03
Ⓔ hoteldelapaix@webonline.fr
TV. Car park.

An impressive 1914 building which has been pleasantly modernized. Doubles with shower/wc €46 and €49 with bath. There are two restaurants on the ground floor. *Le Brésilien* serves traditional specialities and a gourmet menu, while *Le Carnotzet* (open evenings until midnight) serves Savoy dishes. There's a two-course menu at €12 and another at €26, or – if you want to spend less – both restaurants offer inexpensive pizzas. Children's menu €9.

♠ |●| HÔTEL DES CANONNIERS***

15 rue des Canonniers (Centre).
☎ 03.23.62.87.87 ➡ 03.23.62.87.86
Ⓦ www.hotel-canonniers.com
Closed Sun evening except for reservations and 4–18 Aug. **TV. Garden. Car park**.

Originally a private residence built in the 18th and 19th centuries, this hotel is located in the quiet central area of Saint-Quentin. The spacious rooms are extremely comfortable, and feature many personal touches. The cheapest rooms at €49 have shower only; others, €64–100, have bath. Breakfast is served in the pretty internal garden. The female owner will greet you very kindly.

|●| RESTAURANT LE GLACIER

28 pl. de l'Hôtel-de-Ville (Centre).
☎ 03.23.62.27.09
Closed Mon, Sun evening and a week Christmas–New Year. **Car park**.

Service until 11pm. This small, nicely decorated restaurant has a fresco on the wall, checked tablecloths and opalescent glass lamps. It opens onto the pretty, pedestrian l'Hôtel-de-Ville square, and in summer you can sit on the terrace. They serve ice cream, of course, along with house specialities such as mussels *en cocotte* with chips, steak *tartare* and *choucroute* with ham hock or fish. Menus at €13–21, children's menu €7. Good value.

SAINT-VALÉRY-SUR-SOMME 80230

🎋 ♠ |●| LE RELAIS GUILLAUME DE NOR-MANDIE**

46 quai Romerel.
☎ 03.22.60.82.36 ➡ 03.22.60.81.82
Ⓔ relais-guillaume@wanadoo.fr
Closed Tues except July–Aug; 20 Dec–31 Jan. **TV. Garden. Lock-up car park**.

This tall, narrow manor house, set in a garden by the water's edge, is a bit of an architectural mish-mash. Quite stylish, but some bedrooms feel a bit tired – though they're comfortable enough. Doubles €46–53 with shower/wc or bath. Ask for a room with a sea view or go for number 1, which has a delightful little terrace. The restaurant breathes "Vieille France", and serves appropriately traditional fare which is filling but not hugely tasty. Menus, €14–35, list regional specialities and meals are served in a beautiful dining room. Free apéritif.

♠ |●| HÔTEL DU PORT ET DES BAINS***

1 quai Blavet; it's in the lower town, on the river mouth.
☎ 03.22.60.80.09 Ⓔ hotel-hdb@wanadoo.fr
Closed Wed, Oct–May, the first fortnight in Jan and a week in Nov.

A nice little place with a freshly painted façade, situated in a town that features lots of different architectural styles and which is surrounded by varied landscapes. The establishment has been remodelled and upgraded to a three-star. The rooms aren't huge but they've been well refurbished and painted in bright colours. They all overlook the Somme. Doubles with shower/wc €53 or €69 with bath. The seafood is good and both dining rooms get very busy. Menus €14–30.

≘ HÔTEL PICARDIA***

41 quai du Romerel; it's opposite the Hôtel Guillaume de Normandy.
☎ 03.22.60.32.30 ➥ 03.22.60.76.69
e perso@wanadoo.fr

This is a place that will appeal to families or those with a bit of cash. It's a pretty village house which has been thoroughly refurbished so the rooms are bright and the furnishings are stylish – if anything, it feels just a tad overdone. Fairly luxurious bathrooms. Doubles €64 and there's duplex at €93 (which sleeps families or groups). Lovely welcome.

AULT   80460 (21KM SE)

≘ IOI HÔTEL-RESTAURANT VICTOR HUGO

25 rue de la Pêche; it's 100m from the centre of town.
☎ 03.22.60.40.40 ➥ 03.22.6040.00
TV. Car park.

You can't miss this place: it's painted a startling blue and located in the upper part of the village overlooking Onival beach. The hotel is attractive inside, too, and the 12 rooms are decorated brightly. Double rooms €47 with shower or bath. Engaging welcome. They serve a few Russian specialities in the restaurant – *brotsch*, beef stroganoff – alongside the turbot with morels and the shrimps with flambéed vodka. There's a menu at €19 and a *menu dégustation* for €29.

IOI RESTAURANT L'HORIZON

31 rue de Saint-Valéry; in upper Ault-Onival on top of the cliffs.
☎ 03.22.60.43.21
Closed Wed evening and Thurs out of season.

A little restaurant with a rather banal maritime theme which amounts to a few post-Impressionist watercolours, a collection of coffee mills and a tide chart. But there's a fabulous view overlooking the beach – even if only three tables have it. The seafood platters and seafood are better than the other dishes. Menus €12–23; all dishes are freshly made. Lovely welcome.

SENLIS   60300

🎋 ≘ IOI HOSTELLERIE DE LA PORTE BEL-LON**

51 rue Bellon; it's just off rue de la République.
☎ 03.44.53.03.05 ➥ 03.44.53.29.94
Closed 20 Dec–10 Jan. **TV**.

A superb old house, set back from the road,

with 18 comfortable and spacious rooms, €50 with shower/wc and €64 with bath. The restaurant is attractively decorated or you can eat in the shady garden in good weather. Weekday menu for €19 or others €21–30. The chef's speciality is duck breast with honey and cider vinegar. Just ask to enjoy your free apéritif in their 13th-century cellar.

FONTAINE-CHAALIS   60300 (8KM SE)

≘ IOI L'AUBERGE DE FONTAINE**

22 Grande-Rue (Centre); take the D330 towards Nanteuil-le-Haudoin.
☎ 03.44.54.20.22 ➥ 03.44.60.25.38
Closed Mon and Tues from Nov to end Feb; 4–24 Jan.
Disabled access. TV.

This well-known inn has a justifiably fine reputation. Dominique the chef trained with the great Bocuse and he'll captivate you with his enthusiasm as well as his food. He offers a weekday *formule* for €15 and menus at €22–24. His specialities include *foie gras* with pickled garlic and prunes and smooth pea sauce with roast shrimps. Eight attractive, perfectly comfortable rooms decorated in Provençal colours; doubles €42 with shower/wc, €47 with bath. There's a very attractive, big garden.

SOISSONS   02200

≘ LE CLOVIS*

7 rue Ernest-Ringuier (Centre); it's near the town hall gardens.
☎ 03.23.59.26.57
Disabled access. Lock-up car park.

This hotel is not particularly special, but it has a certain style. The friendly owner will happily advise his guests on places to go and things to see. There are just eight bedrooms; some have a view of the Aisne river while others look onto a private courtyard where parts of the walls are the old, ruined city ramparts. Doubles cost €21 with basin and washing facilities (wc is on the landing), and up to €28 with bath.

IOI LE CHOUANS

1 rue Pétrot-Labarre; (Centre); it's round the corner from the town hall square.
☎ 03.23.93.02.01
Closed sun evening and Mon..

The dining room is in the cellar of a 19th-century convent; no hint of a chill, though, in its warm and convivial atmosphere. There are ten set menus in all, starting with the weekday lunch ones for €11 and €13 (not available on public holidays) then ranging from €15 to €27.

FONTENOY   02290 (10KM W)

🎣 🛏 |O| AUBERGE DU BORD DE L'EAU

1 rue Bout du Port.
☎ 03.23.74.25.76 **F➔** 03.23.74.25.76
Closed Wed, 23 Sept–7 Oct and 14–31 Jan. **TV**.

A charming hotel on the banks of the Aisne. Weekday lunch menu at €14 and others €19–30. They bake their own bread, smoke their own salmon and make their own *foie gras* – everything is absolutely fresh. All seven rooms have bathrooms with shower/wc (€38) and some have a lovely, peaceful river view. Free coffee.

BOURG-ET-COMIN   02160 (25KM E)

🛏 |O| AUBERGE DE LA VALLÉE**

6 rue d'Oeuilly; take the N31 in the direction of Reims then turn left at Fisme in the direction of Laon. It's in the centre of the village.
☎ 03.23.25.81.58 **F➔** 03.23.25.38.10
Restaurant closed Tues evening and Wed except for hotel guests. **TV**.

Evelyne is the owner and she will welcome you warmly. Her establishment is near the local tourist sites such as the Chemin des Dames, the Caverne du Dragon and the Ailette pleasure park. Her rooms are clean and tidy and you'll pay €38 for a double with shower/wc – if you need an extra bed it will cost €5. She provides good traditional cuisine using good local produce. Weekday lunch menu for €10 then others €15 and €20.

VILLERS-COTTERÊTS   02600

🛏 HÔTEL LE RÉGENT***

26 rue du Général-Mangin (Centre).

☎ 03.23.96.01.46 **F➔** 03.23.96.37.57
e hotel.le.regent@gofanet.com
Closed Sun evenings Nov–March, except public holidays. **Disabled access. TV. Lock-up car park**.

There's an authentic 16th-century coaching inn behind the 18th-century façade and it's run by a distinguished and charming owner. The seventeen rooms are all different – some of them have been classifed as historic monuments, in fact. The cheapest double with shower costs €46 and there are others up to €66. A charming little hotel which is value for money.

|O| L'ORTHOGRAPHE

63 rue du Général-Leclerc.
☎ 03.23.96.30.84
Closed Sun evening and Mon. **Disabled access. Car park**.

A restaurant that sets the local standard, and it has friendly service too. The chef prepares mouth-watering dishes: *foie gras terrine* with Sauternes jelly, iced shrimps with tomato and basil *vinaigrette*, grilled brill with Guérande salt and *fondant* with three chocolates. The specialities are scallops with bacon and duck Rossini cooked with *foie gras*. Weekday menu €14 or €19. All the fish is fresh and landed nearby.

LONGPONT   02600 (11.5KM NE)

🛏 |O| HÔTEL DE L'ABBAYE**

rue des Tourelles (Centre); turn off the N2 onto the D2.
☎ and **F➔** 03.23.96.02.44
TV. Lock-up car park.

Gorgeous ivy-covered inn in a romantic setting on the edge of the Retz forest. Rooms cost €43 for a double with bath. Number 111 has a view over the fortified port. Excellent, fresh local produce is served in the restaurant, and there is game in season. Menus €18–29. In the afternoons they serve delicious pancakes.

Poitou-Charentes

16 Charente

17 Charente-Maritime

79 Deux-Sèvres

86 Vienne

AIX (ÎLE DE)   17123

♠ I●I HÔTEL-RESTAURANT LE NAPOLÉON ET DES BAINS RÉUNIS**

rue Gourgaud (Centre).
☎ 05.46.84.66.02 ➥ 05.46.84.69.70
Closed Sun evening and Mon Oct–March; mid-Nov to mid-Jan. **Swimming Pool. TV. Car Park**.

This comfortable establishment, which has fifteen attractive rooms, is the only hotel on the island. Doubles go for €35–52 with shower/wc and €43–58 with bath; half board, €43 per person, is compulsory in July and August. There's a pleasant sitting room where you can have a drink, and the restaurant serves fish dishes like salmon *tartare* or roast cod stew in red wine. *Formule* €11 and menus €14–27. The welcome and service are somewhat erratic.

ANGLES-SUR-L'ANGLIN   86260

⚖ ♠ I●I LE RELAIS DU LION D'OR

rue d'Enfer
☎ 05.49.48.32.53 ➥ 05.45.84.02.28
℮ thoreau@lyondor.com
Restaurant closed Mon and Tues lunchtime in season; Mon and Tues out of season **Hotel closed** three weeks in Nov; Jan to mid-Feb. **Car park**.

Guillaume and Heather met when he worked as a banker in London; since then they've made their home in this fifteenth-century inn and restored it with great style. The ten welcoming guest rooms are individually decorated and comfortable, with nice furnishings and a fresh, period feel. Doubles €49–75 with bath/wc. Meals are served in the regal surroundings of the restaurant where there's a weekday lunch menu for €14 and two more for €17 and €29. Specialities include a *foie gras* flan with shellfish *coulis*, duck breast with preserved lemons and garlic and, for dessert, apple *croustillant* or chocolate *fondant*. The wine cellar is stocked by Augé, a highly reputed supplier; fine wines cost less than €15. There's also a relaxation centre where you can get a massage, a steam bath, facials and so on or, if you feel more active, they even run short courses in interior design. Free house apéritif.

ANGOULÊME   16000

♠ I●I LE PALMA

4 rampe d'Aguesseau (Centre); it's between the train station and the town centre.
☎ 05.45.95.22.89 ➥ 05.45.94.26.66.
Closed Sat lunchtime and Sun.

Located on the edge of old Angoulême in a rather ordinary-looking area, this hotel has an attractive frontage, and the classic local food makes it worth seeking out. The restaurant is pleasant, with a corner bodega, and offers good value, too, with a menu at €11 and others up to €21. Rooms are pleasant enough, with bedrooms for €24 for a double with shower and €32 with shower/wc – the best ones are at the back.

⚖ ♠ I●I LE GASTÉ

381 route de Bordeaux (South); it's 3km from the centre if you're travelling towards Bordeaux.
☎ 05.45.91.89.98 ➥ 05.45.25.24.67

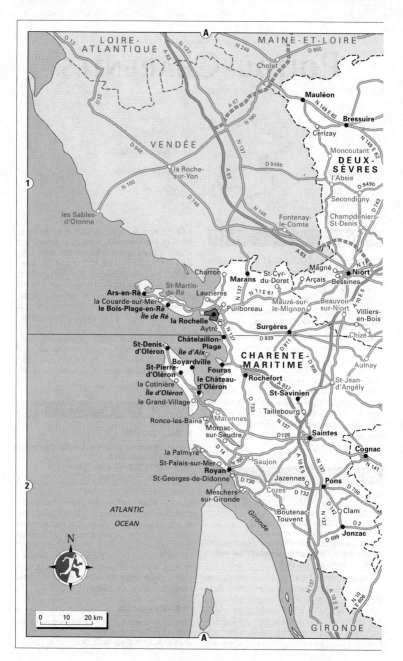

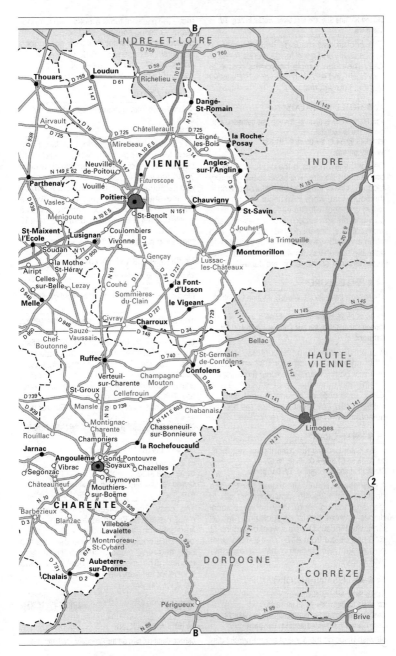

Closed Sat and Sun; the first three weeks in Aug. **TV**. **Car park**.

This unobtrusive roadside hotel, known for its hospitality and good food, offers a menu at €12. The clean, simple bedrooms cost €26 with basin and €27 with shower/wc. Pleasant terrace. Free apéritif.

🎝 🏠 HÔTEL DU PALAIS**

4 pl. Francis-Louvel (Centre); it's near the cathedral and next to the law courts.
☎ 05.45.92.54.11 ➡ 05.45.92.01.83
TV. **Pay garage**.

One of the few hotels in the old town, looking onto a pretty square. The seventeenth-century façade is one of the most beautiful of its kind in the southwest, while the interior has an air of faded grandeur with its wide staircase, high-ceilinged breakfast room, wood panelling and worn carpets. Decent doubles go for €31 with basin and €43–54 with shower or bath. Some have big balconies with views of the old town. 10% discount on the room rate June–Aug.

🎝 🏠 🍴 LE FLORE**

414 route de Bordeaux (Southwest); it's 1km from the town centre.
☎ 05.45.25.35.35 ➡ 05.45.25.34.69
Closed Sat and Sun; the first three weeks in Aug. **TV**. **Car park**.

A short distance from the centre, this hotel offers comfortable rooms for €32 with shower/wc or bath. There's a *formule* (two dishes) for €8 and other menus at €13, €19 and €25. Good choices include the *papillotte* of salmon with baby vegetables and the braised guineafowl with tarragon. Free coffee.

🎝 🏠 🍴 LE CRAB**

27 rue Kléber-La-Grand-Font (East); it's near the station.
☎ 05.45.95.51.80 ➡ 05.45.95.38.52
Closed Sat and Sun evening. **TV**. **Car park**.

A peaceful family inn with a quiet bar. Spruce doubles cost €38 with shower/wc or bath. In the large dining room they serve regional dishes such as breast of duck and braised crab with Pineau. There's a weekday menu at €10 and others from €15–27. 10% discount on the room rate Fri–Sun unless there's a festival in town.

🎝 🏠 🍴 LE SAINT-ANTOINE**

31 rue Saint-Antoine (Northwest).
☎ 05.45.68.38.21 ➡ 05.45.69.10.31
Restaurant closed Sat lunchtime; Sun evening; 24 Dec–1 Jan. **TV**. **Disabled access**. **Car park**.

Newish place on the edge of a commercial dis-

trict – the pleasant terrace looks onto a roundabout – offering soundproofed bedrooms with shower/wc or bath for €52. It's got a good restaurant with menus at €12 (not weekends) and €18–37, and a number of choices *à la carte*. 10% discount on the room rate.

🍴 CHEZ PAUL

8 place Francis-Louve (Centre); it's opposite the law courts.
☎ 05.45.90.04.61

Open from noon to midnight. A large and very long dining room which has been sucessfully decorated to keep you cosy even when the weather is bad. On warmer days, you can choose from the veranda, a terrace on the square and a cool garden with a stream. The food is nicely prepared, with a weekday menu for €10 and others at €15 and €18. It's a great spot for a drink, and they even have a café theatre.

🎝 🍴 RESTAURANT LA CITÉ

28 rue Saint-Roch (Centre).
☎ 05.45.92.42.69
Closed Sun; Mon evening; Feb school holidays; three weeks in Aug.

The smiling owner is very efficient, the tables are attractively set and all the fish is exceptionally fresh. Try the seafood platter, shellfish, home-made fish soup, home-made squid fritters, *fricassée* of mussels, or the house speciality, *brochette la cité*, a kebab of mussels, prawns and scallops. There's a meat menu, too. The weekday lunch menu costs €11, and there are others at €18 and €24. Free coffee.

GOND-PONTOUVRE (LE)　　16160 (2KM N)

🎝 🍴 L'ENTRECÔTE

45 route de Paris; it's on the N10.
☎ 05.45.68.04.52
Closed Sat lunchtime and Sun. **Disabled access**. **Car park**.

This cosy, friendly tavern houses the best meat restaurant in the area, with a wood-fired grill. They'll show you your slab of meat before it's cooked, in case you think it's too big, and will prepare it exactly as you request. The mega-rib of beef is a good choice for families. Menus €13–27. Free coffee after dinner.

SOYAUX　　16800 (2KM SE)

🎝 🍴 LA CIGOGNE

Cabane Bambou; turn off the Périgueux road after the

tunnel, on rue Aristide-Briand, follow the noticeboards and it's 1.3km further on.
☎ 05.45.95.89.23
Closed Sun evening and Mon. **Car park**.

Superb, good-value restaurant with a shady terrace and a lovely view. The owners, who spent some years overseas, have introduced a few exotic influences into their refined cuisine, but offer classic dishes as well: snails *à la charentaise*, medallion of monkfish with orange butter and duck with honey and Pineau. Dishes change with the seasons. Weekday lunch menu for €11 and others from €17–26. Free coffee.

PUYMOYEN   16400 (7KM S)

🏃 🏠 |●| L'AUBERGE DES ROCHERS

It's opposite the church.
☎ 05.45.61.25.77 ➡ 05.45.61.25.77
Car park.

Friendly country house hotel next to a deer farm. It's simple, peaceful and inexpensive, with doubles at €15 with basin, €18 with shower. Half board is €23. You get generous portions in the restaurant, where the menu at €9 offers a choice of starters, main course, cheese and dessert. Prices for other menus vary seasonally. Free coffee or *digestif*.

CHAMPNIERS   16430 (9KM NE)

🏃 🏠 |●| RESTAURANT LE FEU DE BOIS**

It's on the N10 in the direction of Poitiers.
☎ 05.45.68.69.96 ➡ 05.45.69.73.10
Closed Sun evening. **Disabled access**. **TV**. **Car park**.

Large octagonal dining room where they grill meat over a fire fuelled by vine cuttings. They offer a few local dishes such as grilled ham with shallots. Menus €13–29. Free Kir.

MOUTHIERS-SUR-BOËME   16440 (13KM S)

🏃 |●| CAFÉ-RESTAURANT DE LA GARE

pl. de la Gare; take the N10 in the direction of Bordeaux then take the fork to Blanzac.
☎ 05.45.67.94.24
Closed Sun and Mon evenings. **Disabled access**. **Car park**.

This is the type of easy-going, popular place you might have have found here fifty years ago. There's a gravel terrace under the plane trees, an old zinc-topped bar and a beautiful old-school dining room. The food is of a high standard, with an astonishingly good-value €10 menu (not Sun) which gets you soup,

starter, main course, cheese, dessert, coffee and a ¼-litre of wine! Other menus €13–23. Free apéritif.

CHAZELLES   16380 (20KM E)

🏃 |●| RESTAURANT LES GROTTES DU QUEROY

How to get there; take the D699, at Queroy, follow the signs to Grottes du Queroy.
☎ 05.45.23.53.85
Closed Mon except from Easter to 1 Nov; the Nov school holidays. **Disabled access**. **Car park**.

In the middle of the Bois-Blanc forest, far from the hassle of urban life, this restaurant has a huge, tranquil terrace 50m from the prehistoric caves. Have the *foie gras,* the cep stew, the *gratin* of prawns with Pineau or the *foie gras* with port. Menus €11–26. Free coffee.

VIBRAC   16120 (22KM W)

🏃 🏠 |●| LES OMBRAGES**

Route Claude-Bonnier; take the N141, and 3.5km from Hiersac, turn left to Vibrac.
☎ 05.45.97.32.33 ➡ 05.45.97.32.05
Closed Sun evening Mon; the Christmas school holidays. **TV**. **Garden**. **Swimming pool**. **Car park**.

Though the building itself is pretty charmless, it does boast a fantastic location. In a shady garden in the countryside near Bassac abbey – and close to a delightful beach – it also has an outdoor pool, tennis courts and table tennis facilities. Rooms, which are quiet and comfortable, cost €43 with shower/wc and €46 with bath. In the restaurant – which has a veranda overlooking the garden – you can't go wrong with the fish: try monkfish fillet with citrus fruit or scallops with asparagus tips. There's a €11 weekday lunch menu and others from €17–29, and a range of choices *à la carte*. Free apéritif and 10% discount on the room rate.

VILLEBOIS-LAVALETTE   16320 (28KM SE)

🏠 |●| HÔTEL-RESTAURANT DU COMMERCE

How to get there: take the D939.
☎ 05.45.64.90.30
Closed Tues afternoon; ten days in June; Christmas–1 Jan. **Car park**.

An attractive old hotel in a nice hillside village, run by a young, hard-working couple. Rooms are very simple but well-maintained, going for €15 with basin, €27 with shower/wc. The menus are straightforward, too: you'll get a starter, main course, cheese, dessert, coffee and a ¼-litre of wine for all of €9 (€10 in the evening). Other menus €15 and €21.

SAINT-GROUX   16230 (30KM N)

⚕ ☎ ❘●❘ HÔTEL-RESTAURANT LES TROIS SAULES**

How to get there: take the N10 to Mansle then the D739 towards Aigre; it's 3km further, on the right.
☎ 05.45.20.31.40 ➡ 05.45.22.73.81
e lestroissauleshotelrest@minitel.net
Closed Sun evening; Mon lunchtime out of season; 17 Feb–4 March; 27 Oct–12 Nov. **Disabled access. TV. Car park.**

The village, on a bend in the River Charente, was named after a hermit who lived in Angoumois in the sixteenth century. The inn itself is cosy and attractive with a family atmosphere and attentive staff. Rooms are simple, located in a modern building which, though lacking charm, is very quiet and next to a stream. They go for €35 with shower/wc, €39 with bath. In the restaurant, which you'll find in the older building, there's a €9 menu (not Sun), and others from €14–26; all of them list flavoursome traditional and regional dishes. Try their scallops in Pineau. Free apéritif.

ARS-EN-RÉ   17590

⚕ ☎ HÔTEL LE SÉNÉCHAL*

6 rue Gambetta; it's in the town centre by the church.
☎ 05.46.29.40.42 ➡ 05.46.29.21.25
Closed Jan.

All the rooms in this serene, welcoming place have been superbly renovated, with natural floors, stone walls and wooden ceilings, old furniture and sleek, modern lighting. Doubles range from €46 to €122 for the suite with a terrace. There's also a flower-filled patio where you can read in peace, and board games available in the sitting room, which has an open fire. It's best to book at least two months in advance. 10% discount on the room rate out of season.

❘●❘ CÔTÉ QUAI

9 quai de la Crée; it's on the port.
☎ 05.46.29.94.94
Closed Tues out of season except for the school holidays; Jan. **Disabled access.**

Well-deserving of its good reputation, this small dining room is simplicity itself, exuding a seaside ambience and with a small terrace

overlooking the port. The menu, unsurprisingly, features a lot of fish dishes, all of which are delicately judged and tasty. The chef's inventions will keep you guessing – which herb does he use in the cuttle fish *fricassée*? How does he make the hot chocolate *fondant* truffles? There are no menus; dishes range from €12 to €20.

SAINT-CLÉMENT-DES-BALEINES   17590 (4KM NW)

☎ HÔTEL LE CHAT BOTTÉ**

pl. de l'Église.
☎ 05.46.29.21.93 ➡ 05.46.29.29.97
Closed early Jan to mid-Feb and end Nov to mid-Dec. **Disabled access. Garden. TV. Car park.**

A quiet, charming hotel on the church square. The bright rooms feature lots of natural wood and some are panelled throughout. Traditional breakfast is served on the flowery patio. There's a health complex, which offers mineral baths and various treatments, a couple of tennis courts and a number of sun-loungers dotted around the vast, beautiful grounds. Double rooms cost €55–85 with shower; with bath they're €62–98. They don't accept credit cards, and you'll need to book in advance.

❘●❘ RESTAURANT LE CHAT BOTTÉ

2 rue de la Mairie; it's 30m from the church.
☎ 05.46.29.42.09 ➡ 05.46.29.29.77
Closed Mon out of season; mid-Jan to mid-Feb; 20 Nov–20 Dec. **Disabled access.**

Beyond a doubt, this is one of the best restaurants on the island and the prices are more than reasonable, given the location. The huge dining room is decorated with lots of natural wood, and they light a fire in the open hearth in winter; in summer there's a south-facing terrace to enjoy. As for the food, you're looking at top-notch fresh fish dishes such as *mouclade* and sea bass in pastry with *beurre blanc*. They're classical, but prepared with flair. The cheapest menu costs €21, and there are others at €30–59 with a children's menu for €11.

PORTES-EN-RÉ (LES)   17880 (10KM N)

⚕❘●❘ RESTAURANT LE CHASSE-MARÉE

1 rue Jules-David.
☎ 05.46.29.52.03 ➡ 05.46.29.62.10
e restaurant.chasse.maree@wanadoo.fr
Closed Wed; mid-Nov to early April.

A delightful, elegant restaurant on the square

of the island's smartest village. The walls are hung with paintings, there's an old piano and a trombone in a corner and an intriguing collection of second-hand objects scattered about the place. Menus, €21 (not Sun and public holidays) and €27–41, are beautifully presented and full of delicious flavours. The chef is particularly proud of his plaice fillets *au blanc*, fillet of beef with warm oysters and orange ice with hot chocolate sauce. Free house apéritif.

AUBETERRE-SUR-DRONNE 16390

☎ |●| HOSTELLERIE DU PÉRIGORD**

It's in the pleasure port area on the Ribérac road.
☎ 05.45.98.40.46 ➡ 05.45.98.50.46
e hpmorel@aol.com
Closed Sun evening and Mon out of season; Sun evening in season; 10–26 Jan; a fortnight in Nov.
Disabled access. **Swimming pool**. **TV**. **Car park**.

This is an old establishment that was saved from ruin by an Anglo-French couple – take a look at the "before" photographs in reception. The rooms have been very nicely renovated and are as lovely as you could wish for. Doubles with shower or bath/wc cost €38–69. There's a quiet sitting room where you can read peacefully, and a pleasant dining room with a veranda opening onto the garden (with a pocket-size pool). The cuisine is modern, and bursting with ideas; the weekday lunch menu goes for €15 with others from €23 to €34.

BOIS-PLAGE-EN-RÉ (LE) 17580

⅔ ☎ |●| HÔTEL-RESTAURANT L'OCÉAN**

172 rue Saint-Martin; it's 50m from the church.
☎ 05.46.09.23.07 ➡ 05.46.09.05.40
Restaurant closed Wed except in school holidays; early Jan to early Feb. **TV**. **Car park**.

This wonderful hotel is in a typical island house, on a quiet street away from passing traffic. There's a string of delightful little sitting rooms furnished with antiques, and the charmingly decorated guest rooms are set round a huge flower-filled patio with an ancient pine tree growing in the middle. Doubles go for €61–91 with shower/wc or bath. The dining room is equally delightful, with a terrace on the patio. Dishes, prepared from fresh market produce, change seasonally. Try the *chaudrée charentaise* (the local fish soup) and the cod with thyme butter for their finely balanced flavours. Menus €21–30. Free apéritif.

|●| RESTAURANT AU PETIT BOIS

23 rue de l'Église (Centre).
☎ 05.46.09.37.21
Closed Sun and Mon evening out of season.

This is a friendly place with flowery oil-cloth table coverings. The menus are good value, offering starter, main course and dessert; they start at €10 (lunchtime only) then rise from €14 to €20. All fish is bought direct from local fishermen and couldn't be fresher; *à la carte* you'll find prawns on skewers, eel *fricassée*, sole stuffed with crab served with locally grown potatoes, clams with garlic butter and so on. Unique to the island is Le Royal, a fresh, light white wine that's well worth a taste.

⅔ |●| LA BOUVETTE GRILL DE MER

Moulin de Morinand (North); take the Saint-Martin-de-Ré bypass, then the road to Le Bois-Plage, and it's about 1km further.
☎ 05.46.09.29.87 ➡ 05.46.09.96.05
Closed Sun evening; Mon lunchtime; Wed out of season; a fortnight in Jan.

One of the island's most interesting restaurants, partly because it's housed in an old garage in magnificent surroundings (with a terrace and barbecue) but also because the seafood is wonderfully fresh. Suggestions are chalked up on the board – *salade terre-mer*, oysters, langoustine *fricassée*, monkfish on skewers, grilled bass and, for afters, warm goat's cheese, fruit tarts, fresh pineapple and meringue. Star choices include the mouthwatering *salade bouvette*, with salmon, scallops and cuttlefish, the *éclade* of mussels served on pine needles with a dash of raspberry vinegar, and the glorious stuffed crab. There's a weekday lunch menu for €15, or you'll spend around €27 *à la carte*. It's best to book several days in advance in season. Free apéritif, coffee or *digestif*.

COUARDE-SUR-MER (LA) 17670 (3KM N)

⅔ ☎ |●| HÔTEL-RESTAURANT LA SALICORNE

16 rue de l'Olivette (East); it's near the main street.
☎ and ➡ 05.46.29.82.37
Closed Thurs lunchtime July–Aug; from All Saints' to Easter.

Long dining room with a terrace that runs the full length of the establishment. The menus, €15 (weekday lunch only) and €21, offer just a glimpse of the chef's great talent. To experience the real quality of Luc Dumond's gifts, order *à la carte*: the *clafoutis* of prawns with mushrooms, lobster stew with shellfish and crayfish with *foie gras* show his deft use of spices and flavours. You'll end up paying about €38 a head, which isn't all that bad for this pricey island. The modest rooms, which are due for decoration, cost €30 for a double with basin. Free coffee after a meal.

🕯 🛏 |●| HÔTEL-RESTAURANT LES MOUETTES

28 Grande-Rue (Centre).
☎ 05.46.29.90.30 ➡ 05.46.29.05.41
Closed Sun afternoon Oct–March. **TV**.

One of the most charming places on the island, yet one of the least expensive. Some ten rooms look over the interior terrace, with another twelve in an annexe on a very quiet street. Doubles with shower/wc cost €44–59. Book early if you want to stay in summer, as there are regulars who return every year. The terrace is open all day, with affordable menus at €9–20. Try the local oysters with a glass of Muscadet, the *mouclade* or any of the fish, all of which is freshly caught. 10% discount on the room rate.

🕯 🛏 |●| HÔTEL LE VIEUX GRÉEMENT

13 pl. Carnot; it's behind the church.
☎ 05.46.29.82.18 ➡ 05.46.29.50.79
Closed Wed and Jan–March. **Disabled access**. **TV**.

This hotel has been tastefully restored, drawing inspiration from the colours of the sea. The well-appointed rooms go for €48–96 with bath; those overlooking the square are charming. Be sure to book in advance. They no longer have a proper restaurant but they do serve oysters and tasty filled sandwiches. Eat them out the terrace or in the courtyard, which is shaded by a vine-covered arbour. Free apéritif and 10% discount on the room rate out of season.

|●| RESTAURANT LA CABINE DE BAIN

Grande-Rue (Centre).
☎ 05.46.29.84.26
Closed Sun evening and Mon except Easter and July–Aug; Oct to end March except over the All Saints' public holidays.

The fairy-tale dining room is a kaleidoscope of colours and the terrace is equally appealing. There's lots of fish on the menu, as you would expect, but the dishes aren't limited to local traditions; try grilled salmon with olives, *meagre* (which is something like sea bass) with orange butter, mussels with Pineau or, for an exotic touch, salmon *sashimi*. There's a lunch

menu for €14; *à la carte* it's easy to run up a bill of €30–38 per person for a full meal.

🕯 |●| LA ROUE TOURNE

It's on the left of the road from Boyardville to Sauzelle, practically opposite the fish ponds of the Surine.
☎ 05.46.47.21.47
Closed Nov to Easter.

An unusual and delightful out-of-the-way place, run by the same family for more than thirty years. It's a stone house with beams and a huge open fireplace, and big communal tables with benches (plus cushions). Menus go for €27, with dishes of the day at around €6–9. Seafood is the speciality here, along with fish caught directly from the ponds across the road. Around 11pm, when you've struggled your way through a vast seafood platter, the atmosphere hots up as the owner gets out his guitar and leads the gathering in a chorus of *Viva España* and other cheesy '80's classics. There's no other place like it on the island. You should book for dinner, but it's not necessary at lunchtime. Free apéritif.

🕯 🛏 |●| HÔTEL-RESTAURANT LA BOULE D'OR**

15 pl. Émile-Zola (Southwest); it's near the station.
☎ 05.49.65.02.18 ➡ 05.49.74.11.19
Closed Sun evening; Mon lunchtime. **TV**. **Lock-up car park**.

Quality, if not particularly original, traditional dishes served in a plush, comfortable dining room. Service is speedy, the food is tasty and helpings are ample. Menus €11–30. You get a really warm welcome and the female owner is very jolly. Double rooms €36 with shower/wc or bath. Free apéritif.

🛏 |●| HÔTEL DU CHEVAL BLANC

33 ave. du 25 Août; it's in the centre of the town on the St-Mesmin road.
☎ 05.49.80.05.77 ➡ 05.49.80.08.74
Closed Sat and Sun out of season; Sun in season; three weeks over the Christmas and New Year holidays.

Rooms here are comfortable, with all facilities; most of them open onto a small mossy garden. Doubles cost €38 and €45. In the dining room there's a majestic chimney breast where they grill fish and meat over the open fire. Specialities include sirloin steak and lamb steak with thyme, and though the portions are not over-generous, the meat is very flavoursome. Menus €10–20.

CHALAIS 16210

|●| LE RELAIS DU CHÂTEAU

Château 15 rue du Château.
☎ 05.45.98.23.58
Closed Mon evening except in summer; Wed; a fortnight in Oct. **Car park**.

The restaurant occupies the old guard room of the enormous fourteenth-century château of the Talleyrands, which dominates the valley of the Tude and the Vivonne rivers. You reach it across a working drawbridge. There's a period interior, with a vaulted ceiling that gives the dining room real style. The new chef, committed to using only fresh produce, has made some changes to the menus and adopts an innovative approach to typical local dishes. Weekday lunch menu €14 and €20–26.

CHARROUX 86250

🛏 |●| HOSTELLERIE CHARLEMAGNE**

7 rue de Rochemeaux (Centre); it's next to the ruined abbey, opposite the covered market.
☎ 05.49.87.50.37
Closed Sun evening and Mon except in July–Aug. **TV**. **Car park**.

The décor of this inn, built from stone from the ruined abbey, takes you back to a romantic past. The rooms are comfortable – number 8, with its bathroom of dressed stone, is very special. Doubles go for €30 with shower/wc or bath. As for dining, tasty dishes include goat's cheese salad, rack of lamb with unpeeled garlic cloves and beef steak with Cognac and crushed peppercorns. Prices are fair, with menus from €14 to €30.

CHÂTEAU-D'OLÉRON (LE) 17480

🛏 |●| HÔTEL DE FRANCE – RESTAURANT LA FLEUR DE SEL**

11 rue du Maréchal-Foch (Centre); it's very near the main square.
☎ 05.46.47.60.07 ➡ 05.46.75.21.55
Restaurant closed Sun evening and Mon out of season; six weeks in Dec–Jan. **TV**.

This typical central hotel in a historic village is comfortable and welcoming. Doubles cost €30–47 with shower/wc or bath; none has a

sea view. Half board is optional. The restaurant is excellent, with good-value menus – they start at €10 (weekday lunch) and rise to €25 with a children's menu for €7 – and the chef has bags of imagination. Try his sirloin with port, red mullet with meat juices or Dublin Bay prawns flambéed with Cognac.

GRAND-VILLAGE 17370 (11KM S)

🌲|●| LE RELAIS DES SALINES

port des Salines.
☎ 05.46.75.82.42
Closed Sun evening and Mon out of season; mid-Oct to mid-March.

You'll find this attractive restaurant in one of a cluster of brightly painted wooden huts beside the canals in the marshes. Wherever you dine, be it inside or at one of the tables on a boat moored on the quay, the food is delicious and good value, with superb fish and seafood specialities including warm oysters with *fondue* of leeks or langoustines flambéed with Pineau. The short lunch menu (not Sunday) lists half a dozen oysters, pan-fried *céteaux* (which resembles sole) and a delicious *crème brûlée*, all for €11. Going *à la carte* will set you back around €23. Free coffee.

RONCE-LES-BAINS 17390 (18.5KM S)

🌲 🛏 |●| HÔTEL LE GRAND CHALET – RESTAURANT LE BRISE-LAMES**

2 av. de la Cèpe (Centre).
☎ 05.46.36.06.41 ➡ 05.46.36.38.87
Closed Mon lunchtime and Tues out of season; mid-Nov to mid-Feb. **Garden**. **Car park**.

An attractive, classic seaside hotel on the edge of the ocean, near the fine sandy beaches that run all the way to Royan. The nicest rooms – those which lead onto the garden, or come with sea view or terrace – are the most expensive, but all of them have shower/wc or bath; rates range from €35 to €60. The superb chef adapts the menus according to season and whatever's fresh at the market, but you can count on being offered lots of fish and seafood. There's a lunch menu (not Sun) for €14, and others at €20–40 with a children's menu for €8. The bread and pastries are all home-made. Free house apéritif.

CHÂTELAILLON-PLAGE 17340

🌲 🛏 HÔTEL D'ORBIGNY**

47 bd. de la République (North); it's between the town

hall and Fort Saint-Jean.

☎ 05.46.56.24.68 ➡ 05.46.30.04.82

Closed Dec–Feb. **Swimming pool**. **TV**. **Car park**.

This reliable hotel began life as a holiday home at the start of the twentieth century. It's a large, typical seaside building just 100m from the beach – and there's a swimming pool so you can take a dip when the tide goes out (it can recede a good kilometre hereabouts). The rooms, decorated simply but attractively, prove fair value, though those with carpeted walls are inevitably rather dull and dark. Doubles go for €32 with basin, €40–43 with shower/wc or bath. Though the rooms over the street have good double glazing, those on the swimming pool side are quietest. Note that there's a charge for the car park in July and August. 10% discount except July–Aug and public holiday weekends.

🏃 🏠 HÔTEL VICTORIA**

13 av. du Général-Leclerc (Centre).

☎ 05.46.30.01.10 ➡ 05.46.56.10.09

Closed mid-Dec to end Jan. **Car park**.

Typical late eighteenth-century seaside building that has been vigorously brought back to life by the owners. They've refurbished the pleasant rooms in good taste, and offer doubles at €46 with shower/wc or €54 with bath. The station is just across the road but there are very few trains at night and the place is large enough for you to find a quiet room. Free apéritif.

🍴 BAINS DES FLEURS

76 bd. de la Mer; it's on the seashore.

☎ 05.46.56.00.58

Closed Wed in season; Mon–Thurs out of season; Nov–Jan. **Disabled access**.

A genuine *crêperie* with an appealing terrace that looks out to sea. They offer 125 different *crêpes* with classic, daring and unusual fillings and fanciful names like Juju or Marco. Ingredients are the freshest available, and all tastes are catered for. A meal will cost between €14 and €19. It can get very full so you may have to wait for a table.

🍴 LES FLOTS

52 bd. de la Mer; it's on the seashore.

☎ 05.46.56.23.42

Closed Wed; Christmas to end Jan. **Car park**.

A quietly charming restaurant with a lovely parquet floor and attractive wooden furniture. Savour the aromas of high-class bistro cuisine, with a preponderance of fish dishes

and traditional recipes, and try the wonderfully fresh eel *fricassée* and seafood platters. Pastries are cooked in-house, and they serve wine by the glass. There's a €21 menu; *à la carte* you can expect to pay around €30.

CHAUVIGNY   86300

🏠 🍴 HÔTEL-RESTAURANT LE LION D'OR**

8 rue du Marché (Centre); it's on the N151.

☎ 05.49.46.30.28 ➡ 05.49.47.74.28

Closed 24 Dec–2 Jan. **Disabled access**. **TV**. **Car park**.

A traditional hotel in the heart of town next to the church. The bedrooms – some in the main building, others situated in an annexe overlooking the quiet car park at the back – have all been done up, and there's one family room. They charge €24 for doubles with shower/wc or bath. In the good-looking dining room, you'll eat tasty dishes like lamb *noisette* with warm goat's cheese, sole with chipped courgettes and *gâteau de crêpe soufflées* with raspberry *coulis*. Menus €15–31.

🏠 🍴 LE CHALET FLEURI**

31 av. Aristide-Briand; take the Poitiers road out of Chauvigny then first left after the bridge over the Vienne.

☎ 05.49.46.31.12 ➡ 05.49.56.48.31

Restaurant closed Mon lunchtime except public holidays. **Disabled access**. **TV**. **Car park**.

This hotel is a fairly modern building surrounded by gardens and trees on the banks of the River Vienne, just outside the village. It's very peaceful, and the spacious interior is nice and bright. Guest rooms are impeccable, with comfortable beds and views either of the river or of the medieval town. Doubles €43–49 with shower or bath/wc. They serve appealing, traditional cuisine in the large, attractive dining room: try veal *blanquette* or frogs' legs *à la provençale*. Weekday menu at €12 and others €15–31.

🏃 🍴 LES CHOUCAS

21 rue des Puys, Ville Haute; it's in the medieval town.

☎ 05.49.46.36.42

Closed Wed Sept–March; the second fortnight in Nov.

The setting is welcoming with lots of character, and as you go up the splendid medieval staircase to the first floor you'll smell glorious aromas emanating from the kitchens. Try *farci poitevin* (green vegetables and herbs mixed with pork fat, cream and eggs, wrapped in cabbage leaves and poached in ham and pork stock), rabbit stew and scallops with citrus fruit. Menus €11–22. They also offer good local wines by the jug and an apéritif known as "courtisane", made to a medieval recipe using rosé wine steeped with cinnamon and ginger. Truffle tastings Nov–March. Free house apéritif or coffee.

COGNAC   16100

♦ ♠ HÔTEL LA RÉSIDENCE**

25 av. Victor-Hugo (Centre); 100m from pl. François 1er.
☎ 05.45.36.62.40 ➡ 05.45.36.62.49
e la.residence@free.fr **TV. Pay car park.**

This charming little hotel has smart, well-soundproofed bedrooms at €30 or €37 with washing facilities or shower, €41–44 with shower/wc and €49 with bath. If you want a really quiet night, ask for room 109; if you like a lot of space ask for number 201, which has a sitting room and sleeps three. 10% discount except July–Aug.

♦ ♠ ● L'ÉTAPE**

2 av. d'Angoulême; it's on the N14 on the way to Jarnac.
☎ 05.45.32.16.15 ➡ 05.45.36.20.03
Closed Sat lunchtime and Sun evening. **TV. Car park.**

With its informal welcome and homely atmosphere, this is an ideal base if you want to visit the Hennessy or Martel Cognac houses. Comfy doubles with basin and shower go for €32–38 with basin or shower, €43 with shower/wc or bath. There are two dining rooms here; the one on the ground floor is a brasserie offering a €9 *menu rapide* (weekdays only), while in the basement a more traditional dining room features a range of sophisticated menus, €11–22, with local dishes such as chicken *confit* with Pineau or steak with Cognac. Free house apéritif.

♦ ● RESTAURANT LA BONNE GOULE

42 allée de la Corderie (Centre).
☎ 05.45.82.06.37 ➡ 05.45.36.00.76
Closed Sun out of season and a fortnight in May. **Car park**.

Typically Charentes – a quiet cosy atmosphere, characterful country-style décor and good home-made food. Portions are generous – try the local snails or rib of beef in Cognac. The cheapest menu costs €10 (not Sun) while others cost €13–19. Musical evenings Fri and Sat. Free apéritif or coffee.

♦ ● RESTAURANT LA BOÎTE À SEL

68 av. Victor-Hugo (Southeast).
☎ 05.45.32.07.68 ➡ 05.45.32.37.20
Closed Mon and 20 Dec–5 Jan.

The chef in this converted grocer's store is committed to promoting regional produce and he changes his menus with the season. He's kept the shop's original shelves and windows, using them now to display a range of fine wines and cognacs, many of which can be served by the glass. Excellent cooking: rolled sole fillets stuffed with Dublin Bay prawns, fillet of beef flambéed with Cognac and traditional *crème brûlée*. Menus €11–35, or €30 *à la carte*. Whatever you eat, start with a glass of iced Cognac. Free house apéritif.

♦ ● LE COQ D'OR

33 pl. François 1er (Centre).
☎ 05.45.82.02.56

This is a Parisian-style brasserie right in the middle of town. Quick service, friendly welcome, a good range of prices and lots to choose from *à la carte*: salads, *choucroutes*, platters of shellfish, grills, calf's head, snails and so on. There are also some very delicious specialities such as veal chops with ceps deglazed with Cognac. Go for the Charentais desserts: *jonchet* (cream cheese, drained on rush mats) or *caillebotte* (soured milk served with sugar and a Cognac chaser). Portions are large. Menus €12–38. Free coffee.

SEGONZAC   16130 (14KM SE)

● LA CAGOUILLARDE

How to get there: take the D24 towards Barbezieux.
☎ 05.45.83.40.51
Closed Sat lunchtime and Sun evening. **Garden**.

The unusual décor in this old hotel combines rustic and modern styles. To judge by the décor the first dining room was probably the old bistro, but nowadays it needs a crowd to achieve any kind of atmosphere. The second, more intimate room has a large fireplace fuelled with vine cuttings for the grills. There's also a terrace for the summer. Food is good – though portions aren't over-generous – with lots of regional specialities like stuffed Cagouille snails (a local variety), ham with shallots and vinegar or grilled lamb cutlets with walnut oil. They also offer a nice selection of Pineau wines. Weekday lunch menu at €12, with others at €18 and €24, or around €24 *à la carte*.

CONFOLENS   16500

⬥ |●| LA MÈRE MICHELET**

19 allées de Blossac.
☎ 05.45.84.04.11 ➡ 05.45.84.00.92
Closed Mon from Nov to end April. **TV**.

A dynamic family-run business that's become something of a local institution. In the restaurant try the Saint-Barthélemy veal sweetbreads or the lamb cutlets *confolentaise*; the home-made pastries are tempting, too. Menus €11–35 and *à la carte*. Classic, clean bedrooms go for €20 with basin, €35–40 with shower/wc or with bath.

⚹ ⬥ |●| HÔTEL-RESTAURANT DE VIENNE**

rue de la Ferrandie.
☎ 05.45.84.09.24 ➡ 05.45.84.11.60
Closed Sun evening; Mon from Oct–end March; 2–15 Nov; 21 Jan–3 Feb. **TV**. **Car park**.

This beautiful hotel with a large waterfront terrace on the Vienne is in one of the narrow alleys in the old neighbourhood around the church of Sainte-Maxime. The years are beginning to tell, but it still has lots of charm, with spacious, rustic bedrooms and good, inexpensive food. Try the *terrine* of chicken livers with Pineau and any of the home-made pastries. Menus €12–24. Some rooms have a view of the river; doubles €29 with washing facilities, €37 with shower/wc or bath. Free coffee.

DANGÉ-SAINT-ROMAIN   86220

⚹ ⬥ |●| LE DAMIUS**

16 rue de la Gare.
☎ 05.49.86.40.28 ➡ 05.49.93.13.69
Closed Sun evening; Mon; the last fortnight in Sept. **TV**. **Garden**. **Car park**.

A little family hotel, lovingly run by Michel and Martine Malbrant, with a restaurant overlooking the terrace and a garden especially designed for kids. The cooking is good, with menus from €13–29. Try the zander with *beurre blanc* or the shoulder of lamb with chives. Double rooms cost €43 with shower/wc or €47 with bath; they also have some rooms sleeping four. The hotel is soundproofed but light sleepers should note that the TGV line does run past. Friendly welcome. 10% discount on the room rate.

FONT-D'USSON (LA)   86350

⚹ ⬥ |●| AUBERGE DE L'ÉCURIE**

How to get there: it's on the D727, 3.5km from Usson-du-Poitou.
☎ 05.49.59.53.84
Closed Sun evening except public holidays; a fortnight in Oct. **Disabled access**. **TV**. **Car park**.

In a wonderfully remote rural location, this place is in a beautifully converted stable that's been decorated in rustic style. The simple dishes, cooked using quality ingredients, include eel stew, parsley snails or *civet* of kid with wild garlic. Menus at €12, €27 and €30. In summer there's a tearoom where you can enjoy home-made pastries and cakes. The ten comfortable double rooms, all with shower/wc, go for €36. Free apéritif or coffee.

FOURAS   17450

⬥ GRAND HÔTEL DES BAINS**

15 rue du Général-Brüncher (Centre); it's 50m from the Vauban fort and the beach.
☎ 05.46.8403.44 ➡ 05.46.84.58.26
e hoteldebains@wanadoo.fr
Closed Nov–Jan **TV**. **Garden**. **Pay lock-up car park**.

Attractive old coaching inn right in the middle of Fouras. The classic rooms have some style, and most of them look out onto the pretty garden where you eat breakfast in the summer. Doubles with shower but no wc cost €33–44, or €41–55 with bath. The beach is just a short walk away.

⬥ HÔTEL LA ROSERAIE**

2 av. du Port-Nord (Northwest); follow the signs for port de la Fumée.
☎ 05.46.84.64.89
TV. **Garden**. **Disabled access**.

Monsieur and Mme Lacroix lavish lots of attention on their little hotel, a detached house with an unlikely-looking entrance hall done up to look like a 1950s nightclub. Prices are reasonable for the area bright, clean doubles, all of which overlook the sea or garden, cost €38–53 with shower/wc or bath. Dogs are welcome.

JARNAC   16200

⚹ |●| RESTAURANT DU CHÂTEAU

15 pl. du Château (Centre).
☎ 05.45.81.07.17 ➡ 05.45.35.35.71

Closed Sun and Wed evenings; Mon; 1–31 Jan; 5–28 Aug.

With a cosy dining room painted yellow and blue, this the best restaurant in the area, and the cooking is taken very seriously indeed. Dishes change with the seasons and what's fresh at the market, but specialities include duck *foie gras*, pan-fried *langoustine* tails with orange, *tournedos Rossini*, iced *soufflé* with Cognac. They offer a weekday lunchtime menu at €16, with others from €24–37 and various options *à la carte*. The wine list is as impressive as the cooking and includes more than one hundred Bordeaux vintages. Free apéritif.

JONZAC   17500

🧍 🛏 |●| LE CLUB**

8 pl. de l'Église (Centre).
☎ 05.46.48.02.27 ➡ 05.46.48.17.15
Closed Fri evening; Sat; 25 Dec–10 Dec. **TV. Car park**.

This little hotel, which stands on the church square, offers large, clean, well-equipped bedrooms. Numbers 1, 2, 3 and 4 are the biggest. Doubles with shower/wc are €38 or €43 with bath – excellent value for the location. The dining room serves good-quality brasserie and bistro food, with a weekday menu for €10 and others at €18–22. It's popular with locals, and you'd do best to book. Free coffee.

CLAM   17500 (6KM N)

🛏 |●| HÔTEL-RESTAURANT LE VIEUX-LOGIS**

How to get there: take the D142 in the direction of Pons.
☎ 05.46.70.20.13 ➡ 05.46.70.20.64
Closed Sat lunchtime and Sun evening out of season 14 Dec–11 Feb. **Disabled access. Swimming pool. TV**.

You'll feel as you've been invited to a friend's house when you walk into this welcoming country inn. The owner used to be a photographer and his prints decorate the walls. Madame's cooking is first-rate, with lots of traditional family dishes and regional specialities. Try the pan-fried veal sweetbreads flambéed in Cognac, the gratineéd oysters with *foie gras* or the house *foie gras*. They offer a €14 menu (not served Sun), and others up to €30. The guest rooms, which all overlook a small garden, are in a separate, modern building; doubles cost €38 with shower and

€41–47 with bath. There's a small swimming pool and you can even borrow mountain bikes. Reservations are recommended.

LOUDUN   86200

🛏 |●| HOSTELLERIE DE LA ROUE D'OR**

1 av. d'Anjou (North).
☎ 05.49.98.01.23 ➡ 05.49.22.31.05
Closed Sun evening Oct to Easter. **Disabled access. TV. Car park**.

This cosy former coaching inn stands at a quiet crossroads, its faded pink walls swathed in Virginia creeper. In the restaurant, really good regional dishes include *fricassée* of Petit Gris snails with butter and chervil, pigeon with grapes, roast monkfish with thyme and girolles and girolles *au gratin* with Kirsch. There's a €13 menu served during the week, with others up to €33. The bedrooms are in the same provincial vein as the restaurant; the more characterful ones have beamed ceilings, while the ones on the side of the building are quietest. All doubles €43.

🛏 |●| LE RICORDEAU

bd. de la Boeuffeterie.
☎ 05.49.22.67.27 ➡ 05.49.22.53.16
Closed Sun evening and Mon in high season; a week in Feb. **TV**.

An enthusiastic young couple have taken over this characterful establishment right in the middle of old Loudun. They offer just three simple, spruce rooms, each of which is very spacious – though not perfectly soundproofed. Doubles with bath/wc are €35. The large, bright dining room is an attractive setting for a meal, and in summer you can eat on a flowery terrace right next to the Saint-Pierre church. It's very high-class cuisine here, with tasty, subtle dishes like beef cheek *millefeuille* with tomato *coulis*, zander fillet with saffron, duck breast with mashed potato and a delicious chocolate *craquant*. The *formule express*, €11, gets you a main course, choice of starter or dessert and a drink, while other menus range from €14–32. The prices for the wines are a little high but, all in all, given the quality of the welcome, the tasty dishes and the good value, that's a mere quibble.

LUSIGNAN   86600

🧍 🛏 |●| LE CHAPEAU ROUGE**

1 rue de Chypre.

☎ 05.49.43.31.10 ➡ 05.49.43.31.20
Closed Sun evening; Mon; public holidays except in summer; a fortnight in Oct; the Feb school holidays. **TV**. **Car park**.

This former coaching inn, built in 1643, has a large fireplace dominating the beautiful dining room. The quality cooking emphasizes fish dishes like pike balls *à la dugléré* and joint of cod with a herb crust; other good options include the house *terrine* with onion marmalade and the *Petit Gris* snails. The €12 menu is served during the week only, while those from €18–26 are available any time. Pleasant bedrooms have good facilities, going for €38 with shower/wc and €47 with bath. Numbers 4 and 10, which overlook the courtyard, are the quietest. it's a pity about the bar, which has been redecorated to look particularly characterless. Free coffee.

COULOMBIERS 86600 (8KM NE)

☎ ❚◉❙ LE CENTRE POITOU**

39 route Nationale; take the N11 towards Poitiers.
☎ 05.49.60.90.15 ➡ 05.49.50.05.84
Closed Sun evening and Mon from Oct–June; the Feb school holidays. **TV**. **Car park**.

This large, charming restaurant is a gourmet's dream, serving subtle, refined cuisine – duckling with spiced caramel, poached chicken, warm *foie gras tartelettes* with sautéed truffles and autumn fruit tart flavoured with vanilla. The menus, €18–61, are named after queens – "Clothilde", "Diana" and "Aliénoir" – and you eat like a king. The rooms have been enlarged and impressively renovated; doubles cost €46 with bath. The *formule*, which gets you the dish of the day and wine for €7, is served on the terrace with an awning.

MARANS 17230

☎ ❚◉❙ ☎ LA PORTE VERTE

20 quai Foch (Centre).
☎ 05.46.01.09.45
Closed Wed; Sun–Tues evenings out of season; 15 Sept–15 June; the Feb and Nov school holidays. **Garden**.

This place, in the most attractive part of Marans, has a pocket-handkerchief garden overlooking the Pomère canal – a nice place to dine on a warm evening. Inside, there are two charming, cosy dining rooms; the larger one has a magnificent fireplace with a roaring fire in winter. The cuisine is of a high standard, putting an inventive spin on the best regional

dishes; choose rabbit *terrine* with Muscadet or the eel with parsley. Menus €13–21. There's a good wine list, too. As for the guest rooms, they're rather magnificent, with enormous bathrooms, and prove good value at €46–53 including breakfast. 20% discount on the room rate out of season.

SAINT-CYR-DU-DORET 17170 (14KM SE)

❚◉❙ LA POMMERIE

Take the D116 in the direction of Taugon; 150m after the *lieu-dit* Margot, look out for the sign to turn left.
☎ 05.46.27.85.59
Closed Sun evening and Mon; weekdays in Jan; Feb. **TV**. **Garden**. **Disabled access**.

In a peaceful location surrounded by an apple orchard, this nice country restaurant offers lovingly prepared local food: try the house *terrine*, pan-fried snails, parsleyed eels or zander *paupiettes*. Portions are massive, and it's excellent value, with a range of set menus; the weekday lunch menu, €15, includes an apéritif and a carafe of wine, and there are others €22–33.

MAULÉON 79700

⚘ ☎ ❚◉❙ HÔTEL-RESTAURANT L'EUROPE**

15 rue de l'Hôpital (Centre); it's the continuation of la Grand-Rue.
☎ 05.49.81.40.33 ➡ 05.49.81.62.47
Closed Fri and Sun evenings Sept–April; Sun evening and Mon May–Aug; mid-Dec to mid-Jan. **Disabled access**. **TV**. **Car park**.

This former coaching inn has been operating for more than a hundred years, but the combination of modern décor and Jacques Durand's generous portions of elaborate dishes has given it a new lease of life. Menus, €11–27, list oysters cooked in cider, pear with goat's cheese, sautéed farm chicken with crayfish and a lovely apple turnover. Elegant bedrooms from €40 with shower/wc. Free coffee.

MELLE 79500

⚘ ☎ ❚◉❙ HÔTEL-RESTAURANT LES GLYCINES**

5 pl. René-Groussard (Centre).
☎ 05.49.27.01.11 ➡ 05.49.27.93.45
Closed Sun evening except July–Aug; Mon; two weeks in Jan. **TV**.

Housed in an impressive nineteenth-century

building, this hotel takes its name from the wisteria that smothers it. Expect to pay €40 for a double with shower/wc or €46 with bath. The kitchen has a great reputation locally, and the warm, traditional dining room is a nice place to eat dishes such as eel stew, roast rabbit with wild garlic, shortcake with caramelized apples and rosemary ice-cream. There's a €12 menu served during the week only, then others from €14–34. The cooking may be refined, but you'll get an informal, relaxed welcome and service. Free apéritif.

CELLES-SUR-BELLE   79370 (8KM)

♠ |●| AUBERGE DE L'HOSTELLERIE

1 pl. des Époux-Laurant; it's opposite the church.
☎ 05.49.32.93.32 ➡ 05.49.79.72.65
TV. Car park.

Offering good value and attentive service (maybe overly so), this inn enjoys a nice setting and a peaceful little terrace from where you can watch them preparing your food in the kitchens. The elegant, original dishes show off fascinating flavours while keeping in the traditional mould; try bream with a *courgette-colombo* coating or the *mignon* of veal. Menus start at €11 and rise to €34. The cocktails are excellent, too, and they offer a good wine list. Guest rooms are spotless, with a warm, refined décor; they go for €37–49. It's essential to book in advance.

MONTMORILLON   86500

⅔ ♠ |●| HÔTEL DE FRANCE – RESTAURANT LE LUCULLUS**

4 bd. de Strasbourg; it's opposite the Sous-Préfecture.
☎ 05.49.84.09.09 ➡ 05.49.84.58.68
Brasserie closed public holidays; Sat evening and Sun lunchtime from May–Sept; Sat and Sun Oct–April.
Restaurant closed Sun evening and Mon except public holidays. **Disabled access. TV. Car park.**

Ten air-conditioned doubles with shower/wc from €40. In the bistro, they serve a three-course lunch *formule* for €13 including wine and coffee, along with a range of salads and grills, while the restaurant offers five menus ranging from €18 to €40. This is a place for anyone who takes their food seriously; the chef takes great care in preparing the elaborate, seasonal dishes, and everything, even the bread, is made in-house. Star dishes include deer with thyme, braised turbot with cream and paprika, zander fillet with watercress, and in spring, suckling lamb *montmorillonnais*. Free coffee.

|●| LE ROMAN DES SAVEURS

2 rue Montebello.
☎ 05.49.91.52.06
Closed Sun evening except July-Aug.

The young couple who run this restaurant fell in love with the area and decided to sell their restaurant in Paris to settle here. They've done a good job of restoring the eighteenth-century mansion, part of which was once a prison; different staircases lead to four small dining rooms with venerable wooden beams and tasteful pictures all around the stone walls. There's nothing fussy to distract you from your food, which is simple, fresh and ungimmicky, listed on menus ranging from €13 to €25. Ask for a table in the bay window that looks down on the Gartempe.

NIORT   79000

♠ HÔTEL SAINT-JEAN*

21 av. Saint-Jean (Centre); it's on the Saintes road.
☎ 05.49.79.20.76 ➡ 05.49.35.03.27
Car park.

A basic, well-run hotel just a stone's throw from the centre of town, run by a new owner. With doubles from €20 with basin and €27 with bath and telephone, it's one of the best deals in town, and you'll get a very friendly welcome.

⅔ ♠ FRANCE HÔTEL**

8 rue des Cordeliers; it's in the town centre.
☎ 05.49.24.01.34 ➡ 05.49.24.24.50
TV. Car park.

Some of the rooms have been renovated, others haven't, but they're all quiet and many of them overlook the charming interior courtyard. Doubles €24–35. There's a cupboard-full of comics in the lobby, and Internet access for guests. Free breakfast and parking space.

⅔ ♠ HÔTEL DE PARIS**

12 av. de Paris
☎ 05.49.24.93.78 ➡ 05.49.28.27.57
Closed Christmas and New Year's Day. **TV. Car park.**

This is a nice-looking, welcoming building with identical double rooms which have all been repainted. Doubles €30–46. It's near the centre, with lots of restaurants nearby. Free parking.

♠ HÔTEL DU MOULIN**

27 rue de l'Espingole; it's on the river bank on the Nantes road.

☎ 05.49.09.07.07 ➡ 05.49.09.19.40
Disabled access. TV. Car park.

This recently built hotel, overlooking the River Sèvre, offers very comfortable double bedrooms with bath, telephone and radio for €37–41. Two of them are designed especially for disabled visitors and nine have a balcony overlooking the neighbouring gardens. This is where the performers stay when they're appearing at the cultural centre across the river; if you want to know if anybody famous has stayed in your room, you can check the list pinned up at reception.

♠ LE GRAND HÔTEL-BEST WESTERN***

32 av. de Paris (Centre); it's near pl. de la Brèche and well signposted.
☎ 05.49.24.22.21 ➡ 05.49.24.42.41
Closed week at the end of the year. **Garden. TV. Pay garage.**

This hotel has been refurbished and returned to its former glory with a charming dining room, a nice bar leading onto a patio, and a pretty garden with terrace. They owners go to a great deal of trouble for their guests – offering sweet or salt butter at breakfast, say – and the prices are good, with doubles at €63–72 with bath. Rooms with numbers ending in a 5, 6 or 7 overlook the internal garden, where you can have breakfast.

⦿ LA TARTINE

2 rue de la Boule d'Or (Centre).
☎ 05.49.28.20.14
Closed Sat lunchtime and Sun.

Just off Niort's noisy main square, this charming place is housed in the old stables of a nineteenth-century coaching inn. They serve a huge choice of salads, tarts, meat and fish dishes, along with tasty sandwiches made using country bread; menus range from €9 to €23. (Watch out for the desserts, though, which can be pricey.) There's a fine wine list – hardly surprising, since the restaurant is next door to the most famous wine merchant in town. It's safest to book a table.

⦿ RESTAURANT LES QUATRE SAISONS

247 av. de La Rochelle (South).
☎ 05.49.79.41.06
Closed Sun and Aug. **Disabled access.**

A family-run restaurant offering sound, traditional, and often regional, cooking – dishes like stuffed snails, eel stew with wine from the Haut-Poitou, pork *filet mignon* with Pineau des Charentes, goat's cheeses and angelica

soufflé. The cheapest menu costs €9, there's a good *menu du marché* at €11, and another at €24.

🍴⦿ RESTAURANT LA CRÉOLE

54 av. du 24-Février; it's near the tourist office.
☎ 05.49.28.00.26
Closed Sun; Mon; Tues and Wed evenings; Fri and Sat lunchtimes.

An exotic restaurant for this rural part of the country – it's brightly coloured and fun, with spicy dishes that smack of the Caribbean. The €14 menu gets you rum with *accras* (spicy appetizers), followed by Creole black pudding or *massalé* of pork from Réunion. They also do a €10 menu at lunchtime. Free *accras* cocktail.

⦿ LA TABLE DES SAVEURS

9 rue Thiers.
☎ 05.49.77.44.35 ➡ 05.49.77.44.46
Closed Sun except public holidays.

An efficient, refined place in the centre of town, where classic food – lots of fish – is served with good wines. Menus, €12–36, list such dishes as chicory tart, monkfish salad with tarragon and sole *blanquette.*

BESSINES   79000 (4KM SW)

♠ REIX HÔTEL

av. de La Rochelle; it's on the right after the Macif building.
☎ 05.49.09.15.15 ➡ 05.49.09.14.13
Closed Christmas–New Year's day. **Garden. Swimming pool.**

This decent hotel makes an ideal place for an overnight stay on the way to your holiday destination. You'll get a nice welcome, and there's a comfortable sitting room with sofas and a piano, a pretty garden to relax in and even a pool for when the weather's warm. Doubles with bath €52.

MAGNÉ   79460 (7KM W)

🍴⦿ L'AUBERGE DU SEVREAU

24 rue du Marais-Poitevin; it's halfway between Niort and Coulon.
☎ 05.49.35.71.02
Closed Sun evening and Mon.

This attractive restaurant, with lots of wood and wonderfully high ceilings, serves good quality cuisine such as *brioche* stuffed with snails, eel stew, zander fillet and chicken breasts. There's a weekday menu for €9 and others up to €26. Enjoy your meal on the terrace overlooking the river, and you couldn't be anywhere but the marshes of the Poitou. Free coffee.

COULON   79510 (13KM W)

🏃 🏠 |●| HÔTEL-RESTAURANT LE CENTRAL

4 rue d'Autremont; it's opposite the church.
☎ 05.49.35.90.20 ➡ 05.49.35.81.07
Closed Sun evening; Mon; 15–31 Jan; 1–17 Oct.
Disabled access. Car park.

Typically local establishment where they serve snail *cassolette forestière*, eel *fricassée*, roast zander in Anjou wine and desserts such as *crème brûlée* with angelica or Pineau sorbet. There's a good, tasty menu at € 15, and the others, € 21–32, are very substantial. The small guest rooms, € 40 with shower/wc or bath, will do fine if you're stuck for somewhere to stay. 10% discount on the room rate.

🏠 HÔTEL AU MARAIS***

46–48 quai Louis-Tardy; it's on the tow path.
☎ 05.49.35.90.43 ➡ 05.49.35.81.98
Closed Jan. **Disabled access. TV. Car park**.

A classic riverside hotel where you can really relax. Bright cheerful doubles go for € 55–70 with shower/wc or bath; some have river views. The owners organize enjoyable walks through this intriguing area of lakes and marshes. It's best to book.

ARÇAIS   79210 (20KM W)

|●| AUBERGE DE LA VENISE VERTE

14 route de Damoix.
☎ 05.49.35.37.15 ➡ 05.49.35.32.54
Closed Wed; Thurs; Nov–Feb.

Nicely renovated restaurant with a family atmosphere and muted décor. They offer a wealth of regional dishes, including good sliced country ham, with menus from € 13–30 and a nice (rather pricey) wine list. There's a grassy play area for the kids and they serve up to 10pm. Try the house apéritif, the *troussepinette* – it's delicious.

VILLIERS-EN-BOIS   79360 (23KM SE)

🏠 |●| L'AUBERGE DES CÈDRES

How to get there: take the Zoorama road in Chizée.
☎ 05.49.76.79.53 ➡ 05.49.76.79.81
🅮 pascale-regis@wanadoo.fr
Closed Sun evening; Mon. **Disabled access. TV. Car park**.

The new owners, who arrived in January 2001, are still finding their feet, but they're committed to improving everything, and the inn's setting on the edge of the Chizé forest is as lovely as ever. The rooms are peaceful, sizeable and comfortable, though a few details need attention – tired décor, neon lights and snowstorms on the TV when it rains. Doubles € 27–38. The new team in the restaurant work hard, but the dishes are somewhat lacking in imagination. Weekday menu € 10 and others up to € 33.

PARTHENAY   79200

|●| LA TRUFFADE

14 pl. du 11 Novembre.
☎ 05.49.64.02.26
Closed Tues evening; Wed; 15 March–1 April; a fortnight end Nov–Dec. **Car park**.

This place has a strong taste of the Auvergne, from the décor and the cuisine right down to the cubes of Tome de Laguiole cheese and the apéritif. There's accordion music in the background and an occasional shout from the boss, all tempered by the good-natured serving staff. Specialities are full of flavour and precisely prepared – try the *truffade* (garlic, potato and cheese bake), tripe, Auvergne sausage or cabbage stuffed with duck *confit*, and round it off with one of the home-made desserts. Menus € 13–27. They have a nice terrace on the square.

POITIERS   86000

🏃 🏠 |●| HÔTEL DE PARIS*

123 bd. du Grand-Cerf (West).
☎ 05.49.58.39.37
Restaurant closed Sun. **TV**.

The 1960s architecture may be dated, and the location a touch noisy, but this place is one of the better examples of old-school hotel-keeping. You'll be pampered by the staff, who know the area well, and you can eat good food at reasonable prices. Try the *fricassée* of small eels caught in the marsh, duck fillet with pears or the local lamb. Menus € 10–19. Doubles € 23 with basin, € 30 with shower/wc. 10% discount on the room rate.

🏃 🏠 HÔTEL DU CHAPON FIN**

pl. du Maréchal-Leclerc (Centre); it's near the town hall.
☎ 05.49.88.02.97 ➡ 05.49.88.91.63
🅮 hotel.chaponfin-Poitiers@wanadoo.fr
Closed Fri evening in winter and 22 Dec–12 Jan. **TV**.

Pay car park.

The quiet bedrooms here are spacious and each one is decorated differently. They start at €32 with shower, rising to €41 with shower/wc and €46 with bath. Free parking and 10% discount 15 Nov–15 March for a minimum two-night stay.

♠ LE PLAT D'ÉTAIN**

7–9 rue du Plat-d'Étain; it's next to the town hall.
☎ 05.49.41.04.80 ➡ 05.49.52.89.04
TV. Car park.

A restored coaching inn hidden away in a narrow side street in the centre. The rooms are comfortable, quiet and spotless, and each one is given a name rather than a number. "Basilic", "Absinthe" and "Aneth" in the eaves have lovely views of the bell tower of Saint-Porchaire, and some look into the interior courtyard. Doubles with shower/wc cost €40, with bath €46.

⅔ ♠ CITOTEL LE TERMINUS**

3 bd. Pont-Achard (West).
☎ 05.49.62.92.30 ➡ 05.49.62.92.40
TV. Pay garage.

A large hotel, lovingly run by a charming couple. The quiet bedrooms – some of them rustic, with sloping ceilings, and others more modern – have all been soundproofed to block out the noise of the station opposite. Doubles €40 with shower, €44 with shower/wc and €49 with bath.There's a bar for guests. 10% discount.

⅔ ♠ INTER-HÔTEL CONTINENTAL**

2 bd. Solférino (West); it's opposite the station.
☎ 05.49.37.93.93 ➡ 05.49.53.01.16
e hotel-continental@wanadoo.fr
Disabled access. TV.

Classic hotel with clean, well-planned bedrooms. Doubles with shower/wc or bath €40–49; rates drop slightly at the weekend. Buffet breakfast €6. 10% discount.

⅔ ♠ HÔTEL DE L'EUROPE**

39 rue Carnot (Centre); it's opposite the Carnot car park.
☎ 05.49.88.12.00 ➡ 05.49.88.97.30
Disabled access. TV. Car park.

Attractive, individual and well-equipped rooms. Opt for those in the small courtyard, where some look onto a garden. Doubles with shower/wc or bath cost €52–57, and the buffet breakfast will set you back €7. 10% discount on the room rate.

⅔ ♠ LE GRAND HÔTEL***

28 rue Carnot (Centre); it's opposite the Carnot car park.

☎ 05.49.60.90.60 ➡ 05.49.62.81.89
e grandhotelpoitiers@wanadoo.fr
Disabled access. TV. Car park.

A quiet, decent hotel in the heart of the city, with Art Deco-style interior and spacious, well-equipped rooms with air conditioning. Doubles with shower/wc are €70, €78 with bath, and the buffet breakfast costs €8. Free breakfast.

⅔ |O| RESTAURANT LES BONS ENFANTS

11 [bis] rue Cloche-Perse (Centre).
☎ 05.49.41.49.82
Closed Sun; Mon; 1–15 Aug; Christmas to 1 Jan.
Disabled access.

This place, in Poitiers' delightful sixteenth-century walled city, is straight out of a fairy tale. The walls are decorated with a large fresco of Alice in Wonderland, there are angel clocks and old photographs of school children dotted around. The food's good too, with a €9 *formule* and menus from €18 to €21. Try the semi-cooked *foie gras*, calf's head with chive sauce or the fish stew, and round it off with a scrummy schocolate *soufflé*. Free coffee.

⅔ |O| LE POITEVIN

76 rue Carnot (Centre); it's near the Carnot car park.
☎ 05.49.88.35.04 ➡ 05.49.52.88.05
Closed Sun; Easter school holidays; a fortnight in July.
Disabled access.

This intimate restaurant has a pleasing décor with criss-cross beams. It's popular with businesspeople at lunchtime and with couples who want some quiet, intimate time together in the evening. There's a choice of five different dining rooms, all lit by candles. Menus, starting at €11 for the lunch *formule* and rising to €35, list classic regional dishes including eel *rillettes*, roast kid with wild garlic, lamb with three cheeses, Dublin Bay prawns and fillet of beef with *foie gras*. Free house apéritif.

|O| RESTAURANT CHEZ CUL DE PAILLE

3 rue Théophraste-Renaudot (Centre).
☎ 05.49.41.07.35
Closed Sun; public holidays; Aug.

The walls of this institution, yellowed with age, have scrawled messages from famous people all over them and strings of garlic and chilli peppers hanging from the beams. You sit on straw-seated stools and eat at wooden tables where they serve authentic regional cooking ranging from brains *meunière* to the local *farci poitevin*, a tasty variation of stuffed cabbage. Pork is a speciality. There's a weekday menu at €17, or you'll spend around €24 à la carte. It's open till late, but order before 11pm when prices shoot up.

IOI RESTAURANT MAXIME

4 rue Saint-Nicholas.
☎ 05.49.41.09.55
Closed Sat in summer; Sat lunch in winter; Sun; mid-July to mid-Aug. **Garden**.

Serving the best food in Poitiers, this fine restaurant is a gourmand's dream. There's a warmly decorated dining room where you can eat inspired, inventive food prepared with fresh produce. The *menu fraîcheur* goes for €18, while others range from €24–43. The convivial atmosphere just goes to show you don't have to lock yourself in an ivory tower to appreciate quality food, while the perfect service manages to be at once attentive and unobtrusive.

SAINT-BENOÎT   86280 (2KM S)

🎋 🏠 IOI LE CHALET DE VENISE***

6 rue du Square (Centre); it's not far from the ruins of the Roman aqueduct.
☎ 05.49.88.45.07 ➡ 05.49.52.95.44
Restaurant closed Sun evening; Mon; Tues lunchtime; the Feb school holidays. **Disabled access**. **TV**. **Garden**. **Car park**.

Wonderful, chic hotel with a lovely garden dotted with riverside fountains and vast, spreading trees, and a bright, uncluttered restaurant boasting a large bay window. The modern bedrooms go for €53 with terrace and shower/wc or bath. As for the food, every dish is skilfully prepared by Serge Mautret, a talented chef who's always searching for new flavours and combinations. Depending on the season, try the fine tart with rabbit and *foie gras* laced with Cognac, the Poitou snail ravioli or a *nage* of fish scented with anise. There's a weekday lunch menu for €21 and others at €28–48. Free apéritif.

VIVONNE   86370 (14KM SW)

🎋 🏠 IOI LE SAINT-GEORGES**

12 Grand-Rue; it's beside the church.
☎ 05.49.89.01.89 ➡ 05.49.89.00.22
Disabled access. **TV**. **Car park**.

A very old hotel in the centre of Vivonne. It's slightly lacking in character since being entirely refurbished, but time will do its job, and the owner is extremely friendly and welcoming. There are 26 modern doubles with

trouser press, hair-drier and TV; they go for €35–40 with shower/wc, €43–49 with bath. Buffet breakfast costs €5. It's very near Futuroscope, so if you want a room you should book in advance. There are plans to upgrade the restaurant, so although the menus are currently €10 (not Sunday) and €13–21, this may all change. 10% discount on the room rate Oct–May and free coffee.

🎋 IOI RESTAURANT LA TREILLE

10 av. de Bordeaux (South); it's opposite the park de Vonnant.
☎ 05.49.43.41.13 ➡ 05.49.89.00.72
Closed Wed evening and the Feb school holidays. **Car park**.

Napoleon paused long enough on his long march south to Spain to dine in this inn. Panic broke out as staff tried to prepare a dinner fit for the emperor. They served *farci poitevin*, a local variation on stuffed cabbage, and apparently he loved it. Today the inn is as welcoming as ever, though service can be slow, and the cooking is invariably good, rich in traditional flavours. The €12 menu, which includes wine, is served during the week only; if you want to try the famous *farci poitevin*, you'll have to go for the €19 *saveurs régionales* menu. Those with giant appetites will appreciate the €27 *Festival de Vivonne* – it lists lamb cutlets with fresh basil, *mouclade*, zander with Borgueil, *compote* of duck *à l'ancienne* and a pear flan with apricot *coulis*. Free apéritif.

DISSAY   86130 (15KM NW)

🎋 🏠 IOI HÔTEL-RESTAURANT BINJAMIN**

It's on the N10.
☎ 05.49.52.42.37 ➡ 05.49.62.59.06
Closed Sat lunchtime; Sun; Mon. **Swimming pool**. **TV**. **Car park**.

The unusual architecture – a slightly uneasy marriage between a cube and a round building – houses a nice establishment with a pretty dining room where you can enjoy appealing, subtle cuisine. Try the pan-fried *foie gras* with apples deglazed with beetroot juice, the zander with honeyed, sliced potato, or the red mullet with spiced *jus*. There's also an impressive wine list with a good selection of clarets, Burgundies and Loire wines. Weekday menu at €18, others at €28–43, and various options à la carte. If you want to stay the night, doubles with good soundproofing and shower/wc go for €43; some overlook the pool. Free breakfast.

🏂 |●| RESTAURANT LE CLOS FLEURI

474 rue de l'église (North); it's on the road to Saint-Cyr.
☎ 05.49.52.40.27
Closed Sun and Wed evenings. **Car park**.

Across the road from the fairytale château de Dissay, this restaurant has been run by Jean-Jack Berteau for nearly three decades. Scouring the region for genuine Poitou produce, he prepares a famously good calf's head *gribiche*, along with delicious eel stewed in Chinon wine and lamb stew with vegetables. There's a weekday menu at €14, with others from €21–30. The wine list has a careful selection of local vintages. Free apéritif.

NEUVILLE-DE-POITOU   86170 (15KM NW)

🏂 ≙ |●| L'OASIS**

2 rue Daniel-Ouvrard (Centre).
☎ 05.49.54.50.06 ➡ 05.49.51.03.46
e oqsis-hotel@wanadoo.fr
Restaurant closed lunchtimes; the Feb school holidays.
TV. Car park.

A good place, not too far from Futuroscope, with bright, spring-like rooms. Those looking onto the street are soundproofed – in any case, the street is quiet at night. Doubles cost €46 with shower/wc including breakfast. The restaurant, open in the evenings only, offers simple, unpretentious dishes like *colombo* of frogs' legs, *farci poitevin* and steak with *foie gras*. Menus are €11 (not Sun) and €13–15. 10% discount on the room rate 12 Nov–31 March and free coffee.

🏂 |●| RESTAURANT SAINT-FORTUNAT

4 rue Bangoura-Moridé (Centre).
☎ 05.49.54.56.74
Closed Sun evening; Mon;16–30 Aug; Jan.

A rustic building with exposed stonework, a veranda and a well-laid-out courtyard. The saint after whom the inn is named was an epicurean – doubtless he would have approved of the good food and excellent regional wines here. The cooking combines simplicity and sophisticated flavours. Try the crayfish salad with preserved apple, the kid with wild mushrooms or the veal kidneys with fresh herbs and spices. There's a €15 menu, served daily, and others at €19–28. Faultless service, though the atmosphere can be a bit solemn. Free apéritif.

VOUILLÉ   86190 (17KM NW)

🏂 ≙ |●| HÔTEL-RESTAURANT LE CHEVAL BLANC**

3 rue de la Barre (Centre); take the N149 towards

Parthenay.
☎ 05.49.51.81.46 ➡ 05.49.51.96.31
e LeChevalBlancClovis@wanadoo.fr
TV. Car park.

A family-run waterside hotel overlooking the river with a terrace on the bank. The restaurant specializes in regional dishes and has a fine list of Loire, Burgundy and Bordeaux wines. Specialities include eel stewed in wine, kid cooked Poitou-style and pike with *beurre blanc*. Weekday menu at €12, others €15–40, and *à la carte*. It's good value, but the service is a bit slow. Doubles with basin €27, €41 with shower/wc. 10% discount on the room rate Sept–June.

≙ |●| LE CLOVIS**

pl. François-Albert (Centre).
☎ 05.46.51.81.46 ➡ 05.49.51.96.31
e LeChevalBlancClovis@wanadoo.fr
Disabled access. TV.

Owned by the people who run the *Cheval Blanc*, 50m up the street, and sharing the same restaurant, this place offers modern rooms with good facilities. Doubles go for €41 with shower/wc or bath.

PONS   17800

🏂 ≙ |●| HÔTEL-RESTAURANT DE BORDEAUX**

1 av. Gambetta; from Saintes, take the N137 in the direction of Bordeaux or exit 36 from the A10, signposted to Pons.
☎ 05.46.91.31.12 ➡ 05.46.91.22.25
e hotel.de.bx@hotel.de.bordeaux.com
Closed Sun evening; Mon lunchtime; Sat evening Oct–April. **TV. Car park**.

The austere façade may not promise much, but appearances are misleading. It's actually a welcoming place, with a classy dining room and immaculate service. The young owner has returned to his home town after working in some of the great kitchens of France, and the food he prepares is outstanding, using only the freshest ingredients. Menus, €19–37, list a range of fine dishes that change with the seasons. There's an English-style bar where you can extend your evening and in good weather you can dine out on the rose-bordered patio. The rooms are simple but elegant, and some look onto the patio. Doubles with shower/wc or bath cost €38. All in all, you'll get everything you'd expect to find in a luxury establishment – except for the prices. 10% discount on the room rate Oct–April.

JAZENNES 17260 (9KM W)

|●| LA ROZÉ

La Foy; it's on the D732 about 1km from Gemozac.
☎ 05.46.94.55.90
Closed Wed evening.

Charming restaurant in a wonderful old Charentais house with a glorious courtyard – a fabulous place to dine in summer, with a play area for the kids. Inside there's a gentle family atmosphere. Good gourmet dishes appear on the menus – duck breast, for example, and duck *confit* – with a variety of options using fresh, seasonal ingredients. There's a *formule* for €9 and menus at €14–18.

ROCHEFORT 17300

🎋 ☎ HÔTEL ROCA FORTIS**

14 rue de la République (Centre).
☎ 05.46.99.26.32 ➡ 05.46.99.26.62
Closed 27 Dec–5 Jan. **Garden. TV. Car park.**

This quiet hotel, in an old townhouse on a street lined with beautiful buildings, is particularly lovely in the soft evening light. The whole place has a slightly old-fashioned charm and is very comfortable, with rooms looking onto the internal courtyard or a pretty flower garden where you can relax with a book. Doubles with basin €27, €39 with shower/wc, €42 with bath. Incidentally, *Roca Fortis* is Latin for Rochefort. Credit cards not accepted. 10% discount Sept–June.

|●| LE CAP NELL

1 quai Bellot; it overlooks the pleasure port.
☎ 05.46.87.31.77
Closed Tues in May; Wed May–Sept; three weeks in Oct.

A bunch of friends banded together to open this wine bar-cum-fisherman's tavern, where the decent local cooking – lots of seafood – isn't fettered by finesse. There's a *formule* for €9, which includes the dish of the day, and menus from €13 to €20, with a children's menu at €6. If you're after a drink, make for the terrace; it's the perfect place to relax with a glass of something cold. The tavern's mysterious name refers to a legend that's revealed in the pages of the menus.

ROCHEFOUCAULD (LA) 16110

🎋 ☎ |●| LA VIEILLE AUBERGE DE LA CARPE D'OR***

1 route de Vitrac (Centre).

☎ 05.45.62.02.72 ➡ 05.45.63.01.88
Disabled access. TV. Car park.

This quiet old inn is an attractively converted sixteenth-century coaching stop in the centre of town. The bedrooms have been done up without losing the style of the house: doubles are €35–45. In the dining room, which is rustic and cosy with relatively formal service, you'll eat generous servings of traditional cuisine. Menus start at €10 (not on weekends) with others at €15–49. Free apéritif.

CHASSENEUIL-SUR-BONNIEURE 16260 (11KM NE)

☎ |●| HÔTEL DE LA GARE*

9 rue de la Gare (Centre); take the D141.
☎ 05.45.39.50.36 ➡ 05.45.39.64.03
Closed Mon; Sun evening; three weeks in Jan; three weeks in July. **TV. Car park.**

A no-nonsense, good-value place. In the restaurant, go for the specialities — *noisette* of lamb *à la charentaise*, fillet of trout with Pineau or fillet of beef with a shallot *fondue*. Menus at €10 (not Sun) and €14–24. If you're staying, reckon on €24 for a double with basin, and up to €40 with bath.

ROCHELLE (LA) 17000

SEE MAP OVERLEAF

☎ |●| HÔTEL LE TRANSATLANTIQUE – LYCÉE HÔTELIER

av. des Minimes. **Off map C4-2**
☎ 05.46.44.90.42 ➡ 05.46.44.95.43
Hotel closed Sat, Sun and school holidays.
Restaurant closed Mon. **Disabled access. TV. Car park.**

The district, near Minimes port, is frankly unappealing, but the hotel-restaurant is extremely attractive and beats all competition hands down. Run by La Rochelle's hotel school and staffed by eager trainees, it offers unbeatable prices, with doubles at €23 with shower/wc and €27 with bath. There are only eight rooms so it's imperative to book early. The restaurant, on the other hand, seats sixty – but it's so great and such good value that you need to arrive early or be prepared for a wait. There's a lunch menu for €13; you'll pay around €20 in the evening *à la carte*.

🎋 ☎ HÔTEL LE BORDEAUX*

43 rue Saint-Nicolas. **MAP C4-3**
☎ 05.46.41.31.22 ➡ 05.46.41.24.43

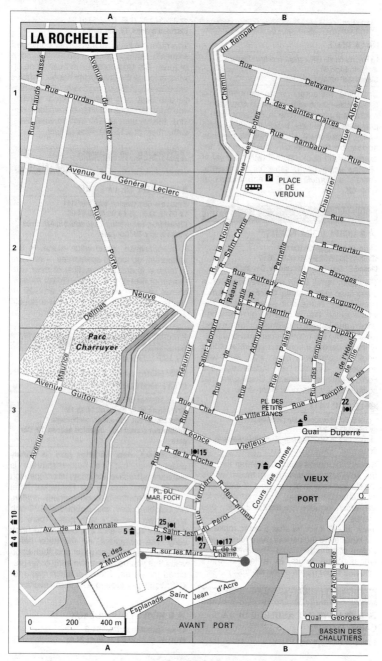

LA ROCHELLE

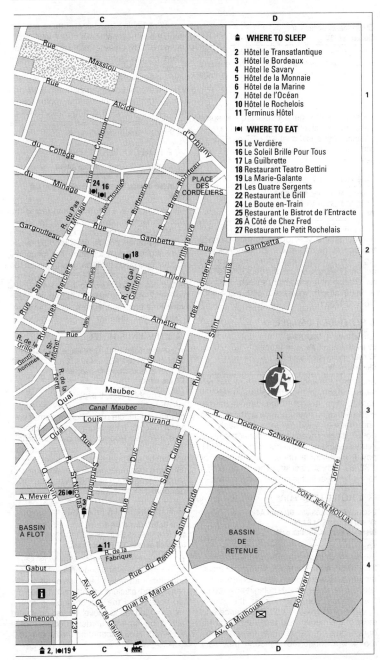

WHERE TO SLEEP

2 Hôtel le Transatlantique
3 Hôtel le Bordeaux
4 Hôtel le Savary
5 Hôtel de la Monnaie
6 Hôtel de la Marine
7 Hôtel de l'Océan
10 Hôtel le Rochelois
11 Terminus Hôtel

WHERE TO EAT

15 Le Verdière
16 Le Soleil Brille Pour Tous
17 La Guilbrette
18 Restaurant Teatro Bettini
19 La Marie-Galante
21 Les Quatre Sergents
22 Restaurant Le Grill
24 Le Boute en-Train
25 Restaurant le Bistrot de l'Entracte
26 À Côté de Chez Fred
27 Restaurant le Petit Rochelais

e hbordeaux@wanadoo.fr
Closed Dec. **TV**.

This small, pretty hotel, decorated with colourful windowboxes, is in the fisherman's district of the old town. It's like a quiet village during the day but gets very lively at night. The rooms are colourful and well-maintained, each one different, with a variety of sizes. Those in the attic get a lot of light, and some even have a balcony. They're fair value, too: doubles with basin cost €29–37 or €35–46 with shower/wc or bath. 10% discount in low season.

🏖 🏨 HÔTEL DE L'OCÉAN**

36 cours des Dames. **MAP B3-7**
☎ 05.46.41.31.97 ➡ 05.46.41.51.12
TV.

This place is wonderfully situated on the old harbour with a view of the towers. Despite the double glazing, it can be very noisy at night – which is fine if you like being in on the action. Quieter rooms at the back offer a better chance of a good night's sleep. Doubles €29–56, all with shower/wc. 10% discount 1 Nov–30 March.

🏨 HÔTEL DE LA MARINE**

30 quai Duperré. **MAP B3-6**
☎ 05.46.50.51.63 ➡ 05.46.44.02.69
e hotel.marine@wanadoo.fr
Closed Jan. **TV**.

Squeezed between the terraces of two different establishments, this pleasant hotel is easy to miss. It's got thirteen spruce rooms, some with a really lovely view of the old port and the sea in the distance, but sadly the double glazing doesn't keep out all the noise in the evening when the port gets busy. You'll pay €35–39 for a double with shower, or €38–62 with shower/wc. There's no dining room, so breakfast is served in the rooms.

🏖 🏨 HÔTEL LE SAVARY

2-bis rue Alsace-Lorraine. **Off map A4-4**
☎ and ➡ 05.46.34.83.44
Disabled access. **TV**. **Car park**.

This hotel is a good fifteen-minute walk from the centre of town in a quiet residential area. It's a white, concrete block, the type of architecture that was considered modern in the late '50s, and is currently being renovated by the young couple who own the place. They've already done up the entrance and most of the rooms; next in line are the corridors – and not before time. Generally, the rooms are comfortable, though they vary considerably in size; some of them are in a separate house that looks over a well-planted garden where you can take breakfast. There are also some family rooms with bunk beds. Bathrooms are good throughout, all of them equipped with hair-driers. Doubles with shower/wc or bath cost between €38 and €53. 10% discount on the room rate 1 Oct–30 June except during public holidays and long weekends. There's a charge for use of the car park in high season.

🏖 🏨 HÔTEL LE ROCHELOIS**

66 bd. Winston-Churchill. **Off map A4-10**
☎ 05.46.43.34.34 ➡ 05.46.42.10.37
Disabled access. **Swimming pool**. **TV**. **Pay car park**.

Modern hotel in a good position facing the Atlantic. Guests have free use of the sports facilities – the gym, Jacuzzi, sauna, Turkish bath and tennis courts. Or you could take it easy and lounge by the pool. The functional rooms have good facilities, and those on the first floor have a terrace. Rooms with shower/wc but no sea view cost €38–47; you'll pay €62–84 for a room with bath and sea view. Free breakfast, except during the major holidays and July–Aug.

🏖 🏨 TERMINUS HÔTEL

pl. du Commandant-de-La-Motte-Rouge. **MAP C4-11**
☎ 05.46.50.69.69 ➡ 05.46.41.73.12
e hotel.terminus@tourisme-français.com
TV. **Car park**.

As you might guess, this place is close to the rail station, but it's also close to the Gabut district and the old port. There are small personal touches in the décor here, and furnishings are rustic. Rooms at the back are simple and quiet while those overlooking the road are bright and spacious but noisier. Prices are more than reasonable, with doubles with shower/wc at €41–53, €61 with bath. 10% discount 1 Oct–31 March.

🏖 🏨 HÔTEL DE LA MONNAIE

3 rue de la Monnaie. **A4-5**
☎ 05.46.50.65.65 ➡ 05.46.50.53.19
Disabled access. **TV**. **Pay car park**.

This seventeenth-century Mint was saved from ruin in 1988 and converted into a hotel. Facilities – attractive bathrooms, air conditioning and efficient sound insulation – are top-notch, and the modern-looking rooms are arranged round a lovely paved courtyard with a pocket-size garden. Double rooms €84–100. 10% discount on the room rate 1 Oct–1 April.

❘●❘ LE VERDIÈRE

6 rue de la Cloche. **MAP A/B3-5**
☎ 05.46.50.56.75
Closed Sun evening in winter; Mon.

If you happen upon this place, you'll find it hard to drag yourself away. The décor might be tired, but the cooking more than makes up for it; the owner creates invariably fine food that extends to even the cheapest *formules* and menus. Intelligently prepared dishes use only the freshest produce, with lots of fish; the cuttlefish stew is a speciality, as is the *foie gras* deliciously prepared with fresh fruit and the roast duck breast with acacia honey. Desserts are no letdown, either. Weekday *formules* €9, or €11 in the evening before 9.30pm, with two other menus at €16 and €24.

❘●❘ LE SOLEIL BRILLE POUR TOUS

13 rue des Cloutiers. **MAP C2–16**
☎ 05.46.41.11.42
Closed Sun and Mon.

In addition to the small dining room, which has mosaic-encrusted walls and tables tightly packed around the open kitchen, there's a sunny terrace with two to three tables in summer. Everything is made in-house with fresh, organic ingredients and subtle mixtures of herbs and spices, and portions are more than generous. The *formule* — starter and dish of the day accompanied by fresh vegetables — is good value at €9, while the small *à la carte* menu offers tasty, well-seasoned dishes, including a few vegetarian options, for €8–9 each. No credit or debit cards.

🎄❘●❘ LA MARIE-GALANTE

35 av. des Minimes. **Off map C4–19**
☎ 05.46.44.05.54
Closed Mon–Thurs evenings Nov–Easter.

The cuisine here is simple, with an emphasis on classic fish dishes: oysters, fish soup, *moules marinières*, whelks with mayonnaise, and an attractively priced fish dish of the day. The weekday lunch *formule express*, €10, gets you salad, dish of the day and coffee, and there are menus at €13–18. Free house apéritif.

🎄❘●❘ RESTAURANT TEATRO BETTINI

3 rue Thiers. **MAP C2–18**
☎ 05.46.41.07.03
Closed Sun; Mon; 25 Sept–1 Oct; 22 Dec–2 Jan.

Pizza might not be the first thing that springs to mind in La Rochelle, but they're well above average at this popular joint, cooked in a real wood-fired oven. It's worth trying the pasta, too, and the *escalope corrado* – whatever you choose, you'll want to wash it down with one of the large selection of Italian wines. Menus €11 and €13, and a children's menu at €6. Free house apéritif.

🎄❘●❘ LES QUATRE SERGENTS

49 rue Saint-Jean-du-Pérot. **MAP A4-21**
☎ 05.46.41.35.80 ➡ 05.46.41.95.64
Closed Sun evening and Mon. **Disabled access**.

In a townhouse dating from 1842, this dining room is in a wonderful winter garden with a glass roof. It's a superb setting, and the formal service perfectly in keeping. The chef doesn't limit himself to classic brasserie food, and enjoys adding contemporary twists to some dishes. Try the trout with Calvados and apples, snail *profiteroles* in wine lees sauce or the *blanquette* of hake with pistachios and orange zest. The €13 menu is good value, and there are others at €18–32, with a children's menu for €6. Expect to pay at least €30 *à la carte*. Wine is served by the glass. Free glass of Pineau des Charentes.

❘●❘ RESTAURANT LE GRILL

10 route du Port. **MAP B3-22**
☎ 05.46.41.95.90
Closed Sat and Mon lunchtimes; Sun.

If you're not lucky enough to get one of the very few tables at this local favourite, sit at the bar (which itself has only ten places), and sink your teeth into a thick steak, fresh from the grill. This is a great place for tasty Basque and Spanish dishes; you'll pay somewhere between €15 and €21 for a complete meal. Wines by the glass and scrumptious desserts.

❘●❘ LA GUILBRETTE

16 rue de la Chaîne. **MAP B4-17**
☎ 05.46.41.57.05

Though this is a new place, it's already made an impression. The chef uses exclusively fresh produce – which is by no means typical in La Rochelle – in his well-executed, creative and generous dishes; the *menu-cartes* (from €23) change every couple of months. There's also a lunch menu for €20, which gets you a choice of starter or dessert with the main course. They also host regular theme evenings with a single menu laden with dishes from a selected region.

🎄❘●❘ LE BOUTE-EN-TRAIN

7 rue des Bonnes Femmes. **MAP C2-24**

☎ 05.46.41.73.74
Closed Sun; Mon; the second fortnight in Oct; the third week in Feb.

A really attractive bistro which, painted in shades of blue with bronzed, aged wood, manages to be bright and intimate at the same time. It's as good for a hasty lunch as it is for a family supper – they provide crayons, felt-tips and paper to keep the little ones happy and there's a collection of this infant art on the walls. You'll eat good hearty home cooking such as marrowbone on toast with Guérande sea salt, Dublin Bay prawn stew and apple crumble. The *menu-carte* is €20, and there are a variety of house specialities for around €12. Free coffee.

|●| RESTAURANT LE PETIT ROCHELAIS

25 rue Saint-Jean-du-Pérot. **MAP B4-27**
☎ 05.46.41.28.43
Closed Sun.

A friendly bistro with waxed cotton tablecloths and good Lyonnais cuisine. The kitchen produces seasonal dishes using the freshest local produce, and menus change often; typical dishes include calf's head *sauce gribiche* and seven-hour lamb. Desserts are delightful, featuring such treats as chocolate soup with banana and orange and vanilla *millefeuille* with a caramel sauce. They don't do set menus, but the dishes of the day are chalked up on the board. A meal costs around €23, which is good value.

|●| RESTAURANT LE BISTROT DE L'ENTRACTE

22 rue Saint-Jean-du-Pérot. **MAP A4-25**
☎ 05.46.50.62.60
Closed Sun.

The restaurant is run by Didier Cadio, an experienced chef formerly number two at *Coutances*, La Rochelle's grandest establishment. He offers a single *menu-carte* – main course and dessert – for €24. Try the *gâteau* of langoustines with tarragon cream sauce, sole with almonds and pistachios or *tournedos* of roast cod with buttered cabbage. There's lots of choice, with good desserts and an impressive wine list.

|●| À CÔTÉ DE CHEZ FRED

30–34 rue Saint-Nicolas. **MAP C4-26**
☎ 05.46.41.65.76
e chezfred@rivages.net
Closed Sun; Mon; three weeks after All Saints' Day.

Fred, a well-known local character, runs the neighbouring fishmonger's as well as the

restaurant; what's on the menu depends on what has been landed that day. It's best to opt for the simplest, seasonal dishes. There are no set menus, but you can expect to pay around €25 for a good meal *à la carte*. It gets very full, so reservations are recommended whether you want to eat in the simple, unadorned dining room or the terrace.

AYTRÉ — 17440 (3KM S)

⚶ 🏠 |●| HÔTEL-RESTAURANT LES PLATANES*

29 av. du Commandant-Lysiak; from La Rochelle take the bypass towards Aytré.
☎ 05.46.44.29.91 ➡ 05.46.31.06.90
Closed Sun and Chrismas–10 Jan. **Disabled access.**
TV. Car park.

Simple, exceptionally good-value food served in a large country-style dining room run by Mme Lechat and her smiling staff. At lunchtime it's popular with regulars from the neighbouring industrial park, who are treated to different dishes every day; with its huge portions and good seafood, the place is full in the evenings and at weekends as well. Menus €10–23. There are also a few simple, affordable rooms at €26–27 for a double with basin, €28–29 with shower/wc. Half board, around €40 per person, is compulsory June–Sept. 10% discount on the room rate out of season.

PUILBOREAU — 17138 (5KM E)

⚶ 🏠 |●| AUBERGE DE LA BELLE ÉTOILE**

12 rue de la Belle Étoile; take the N11 in the direction of Nantes, take the Chagnolet exit and follow the signs.
☎ 05.46.68.01.43 ➡ 05.46.68.06.10
Closed Sat lunchtime and Sun. **Car park.**

A nice family affair installed in an old sugar-beet store. The owner, who used to be a pastry cook, now follows the seasons for his inspiration: you might try *foie gras* cooked in a cloth, salmon with Pineau des Charentes sauce or fine-sliced deer. The dish of the day costs around €11, and there are menus at €14 (hotel guests only) and €20, with a children's menu for €6. The guest rooms, in the seventeenth-century outbuildings, vary; some are simple, bright and colourful, while others bask in the muted charm of the old stone walls. Each of them looks onto the beautifully maintained garden. Doubles €30–46; half board, €30–41, is compulsory from July to mid-Sept. Free apéritif.

LAUZIÈRES   17137 (7KM N)

🛉 |O| BAR PORT LAUZIÈRES

port du Plomb; it's at the seafront facing the île de Ré.
☎ 05.46.37.45.44
Closed Tues except July; Oct to mid-March. **Car park**.

An old fisherman's hut converted into a shell-fish bar. Local oyster farmers gather at the old-fashioned zinc-topped bar; on the other side, the dining room has a sea view and a cosy fireplace ideal for wintry evenings. Choose from shellfish, mussels and grilled sardines or fish platters with oysters, langoustines, prawns and sardines. Add a splash of wine and you're looking at not much more than €15 for a meal. Free apéritif.

CHARRON   17230 (16KM N)

🛉 |O| RESTAURANT THEDDY-MOULES

72 rue du 14-Juillet; on the port road known as le Pave.
☎ 05.46.01.51.29 ⇨ 05.46.01.57.31
Closed Oct–April.

People come to Charron for one reason — to eat mussels at *Theddy-Moules*. Theddy, a mussel farmer, came up with the bright idea of arranging a few tables in a kind of large shed, putting a terrace out front and serving the freshest seafood you can imagine. It's right on the edge of the road and the setting is rudimentary, but customers flock here for the quality seafood at affordable prices. Try the mussels *spécial Theddy* with Pineau and cream or an *assiette dégustation* of langoustine, oysters, whelks, winkles and prawns. They serve fish *à la carte*, too: sole, perhaps, or sea bass, or a simple plate of grilled sardines. A full meal will set you back around €18, a seafood selection €10, and a generous seafood platter around €16. Reservations are recommended in the evening. Free apéritif.

LEIGNÉ-LES-BOIS   86450 (19KM SE)

🛉 |O| HÔTEL-RESTAURANT BERNARD GAUTIER

pl. de la Mairie (Centre); take the D14 and the D15.
☎ 05.49.86.53.82 ⇨ 05.49.86.58.05
Closed Sun evening; Mon; Feb; the second fortnight in Nov. **Car park**.

In an extremely secluded spot in the remotest part of northern Vienne, this modest-looking establishment offers some of the best food in the region. Here you'll enjoy sub-tle flavours and exciting combinations: typical offerings include fresh cod with herbs, *gâteau* of young rabbit with tartare sauce, *tartare* of fresh salmon, zander with a light *beurre blanc* and *tournedos*. If you like *andouillette à la ficelle* you're in for a real treat, and the *crème brûlée* is fabulous. Menus cost between €21 and €40; portions are so huge that you'll struggle to finish. There's a good wine list, too. If you want to stay, there are a few clean, simple bedrooms, costing €24 for a double with basin. Good food, good rooms and a cheerful owner – you'd be pushed to find better.

🛏 HÔTEL DE L'EUROPE

1 av. des Fontaines (Centre).
☎ 05.49.86.21.81 ⇨ 05.46.86.66.28
Closed mid-Oct to March. **TV. Car park**.

A bulky building with a slim garden at the back and around thirty simple rooms that have been carefully improved. There's a convivial, family atmosphere, and it doesn't cost a fortune: doubles are €30–34 with shower or bath/wc.

ROYAN   17200

🛉 🛏 VILLA TRIDENT THYRSÉ

66 bd. Frédéric-Garnier (Southeast).
☎ 05.46.0512.83
Closed Sun afternoon out of season. **TV. Car park**.

There *have* been a few alterations since this place was built, but that doesn't stop it looking like something from a timewarp. Vivid colours, a set of bongo drums next to the Formica bar and salsa music wafting out onto the terrace that looks out to sea – blink and you could be in an Art Deco hotel in Miami Beach. All the rooms are simple and pleasant, with vintage 1950s décor; you'll pay €27–36 for doubles with basin, €35–52 with shower or bath. They also have a few self-contained studios available for rent by the week or for an out-of-season weekend. The sandy beach is just across the road. 10% discount.

🛏 HÔTEL BELLE-VUE**

122 av. de Pontaillac (Southwest); it's on the D25 from Saint-Palais.
☎ 05.46.39.06.75 ⇨ 05.46.39.44.92
Closed Nov–March. **TV. Garden. Car park**.

Starting out as a family guest house in the 1950s, this place has grown into a cosy hotel with antiques in the comfortable rooms and, as the name suggests, a lovely view over

Pontaillac bay. Some rooms have a balcony while others look onto the garden. Doubles €30–57 with shower/wc or bath.

🏂 🏠 |O| HÔTEL ABYSSE – RESTAURANT L'ANJOU**

17 rue Font-de-Cherves (Centre); near the market, 200m from the beach.
☎ 05.46.05.30.79 ➡ 05.46.05.30.16
Restaurant closed Sun evening and Mon out of season; Mon in summer; last week in Jan; last week in Sept. **TV**.

The restaurant here serves generous portions of good traditional food, and naturally they do lots of fish. The dining room is decorated rather fussily but the owner welcomes you enthusiastically and the service is efficient and unpretentious. Menus go for €10 (weekday lunchtimes) and €14–32; the children's menu is €7. Brightly decorated rooms, some with balcony, cost €49–64 with shower/wc or bath. There are also a few apartments, perfect for families: you'll pay from €56 for three or four people. Free apéritif and 10% discount on the room rate for a two-night stay.

🏂 |O| RESTAURANT LE CHALET DE ROYAN

6 bd. de la Grandière. it's at the eastern end of the seafront opposite the tourist office.
☎ 05.46.05.04.90 ➡ 05.46.22.31.84
Closed Tues evening and Wed except July–Aug.

A towny version of a country inn with rustic décor, local cuisine and slick service. It's built up its reputation over the years with dishes like eel *fricassée* with olives and cod joint with sweet pepper sauce. Menus €18–51. Free glass of champagne.

SAINT-GEORGES-DE-DIDONNE   17110 (4KM S)

🏂 🏠 |O| HÔTEL-RESTAURANT COLINETTE ET COSTABÉLA*

16 av. de la Grande-Plage (Northeast).
☎ 05.46.05.15.75 ➡ 05.46.06.54.17
e info@colinette.not
Restaurant closed Sun evening out of season; mid-Dec to early Feb.

Located in the Vallières pine forest, the *Colinette* has had a face-lift – out with the florals and in with the brilliant white paint and double glazing. In the next street, the *Costabéla* is more like an anonymous 1970s villa with flowery wallpaper and chenille bedspreads. Doubles €40–66 with shower/wc or bath. The menus, €17–26 or €6 for children, list safe

family favourites such as *terrine, mouclade* and seafood stew in white sauce. Half board, €79–98, is compulsory in July–Aug. 10% discount on the room rate Sept–June.

|O| L'ESCAPADE

7 rue Autrusseau (Centre).
☎ 05.46.06.24.24
Restaurant closed Mon; Tues; April–Oct.

Seafood bistro with really nice décor, a terrace and a sweet little patio with vines climbing all over the awning. The fish dishes are simple but carefully prepared and, like the seafood, they're fresh as can be. Specialities include fish *choucroute* and beautifully presented seafood platters. Menus €14–26. Nice wine list.

SAINT-PALAIS-SUR-MER   17420 (6KM W)

|O| LE PETIT POUCET

La Grande Côte; it's on the coast road to La Palmyre.
☎ and ➡ 05.46.23.20.48
Closed Wed from Oct–March; Jan.

This concrete 1950s block used to be a real eyesore, but it's since been camouflaged by Virginia creeper and ivy, and the trees and shrubs planted around it make it much more attractive. Inside, in the spacious dining room, you get a magnificent view of the Grande Côte beach and the ocean beyond. The decent cooking is good value, if not always tip-top quality; it's best to plump for for the seafood – pan-fried scallops with cider, Dublin Bay prawns with Pineau, hot oysters with leek *fondue*. Menus €12–30, and a children's menu at €7.

MESCHERS-SUR-GIRONDE   17132 (12KM S)

🏂 🏠 |O| LES GROTTES DE MATATA**

bd. de la Falaise.
☎ 05.46.02.70.02 ➡ 05.46.02.78.00
Restaurant closed Sun evening Nov–Feb.

Touristy place on the pathway through the Matata grottoes. It's a modern, clifftop building, with a few rooms: doubles with shower/wc cost €46, €53 with bath. The terrace, which affords breathtaking views of the turbulent grey-blue waters of the Gironde estuary, is a great place for breakfast; you get the same view from the *crêperie*, which is set up in one of the troglodyte dwellings in the cliffs – check out the walls, made of compacted rock packed full of fossils. You'll pay around €18 for a meal. 10% discount on the room rate Sept–June.

MORNAC-SUR-SEUDRE   17113 (13KM N)

🏃 |O| LE TAHITI

1 route de Sandre; it's opposite the harbour.
☎ 05.46.22.76.53
📧 letahiti@libertysurf.fr
Closed Tues and Wed lunchtimes out of season;
Nov–March.

A simple dining room, a popular bar and a terrace on the harbour of this picturesque and charming village. The fish and seafood dishes are very straightforward: oysters, grilled mullet with tarragon butter, whitebait, grilled sardines. Menus €7–24 and children's menu €7. It's very popular with coach parties. Free coffee.

PALMYRE (LA)   17570 (18KM NW)

🏃 🏠 |O| PALMYROTEL**

2 allée des Passereaux (Centre); it's near the zoo
☎ 05.46.23.65.65 📠 05.46.22.44.13
📧 palmyrotel.m.c.@wanadoo.fr
Closed Nov–Easter. **Disabled access**. **Garden**. **TV**. **Car park**.

This vast hotel offers good value for money for the region. It's a contemporary, alpine-style building surrounded by a Mediterranean-style garden on the edge of the pine forest. There are 46 identical, functional rooms, all with en-suite shower/wc or bath; doubles cost between €46 and €78 depending on the season. Although half board is not compulsory, they do advise you to take that option; you'll pay around €47. Menus are €15–34, with children's menus at €6 and €7. 10% discount on the room rate Sept–June.

BOUTENAC-TOUVENT   17120 (28KM SE)

🏃 🏠 |O| LE RELAIS DE TOUVENT**

4 rue de Saintonge (Centre); it's on the D730.
☎ 05.46.94.13.06 📠 05.46.94.10.40
Closed Sun evening and Mon except in summer and
15–31 Dec. **Disabled access**. **Garden**. **TV**. **Car park**.

This dreary building, plonked down on a roundabout, doesn't immediately appeal, but it has an absolutely enormous garden and nice, newly decorated rooms. Better still, the prices are attractive for the region. Bedrooms are classic in style though the colours can be garish; they're €38 for a double with shower/wc and €43 with bath. Also, they serve good, honest cooking, with plenty of regional dishes; try the *mouclade*, lobster salad with *foie gras* or lamprey. The cheapest

menu goes for €14, with others at €21–46. Check out the interesting wine list. Free coffee.

RUFFEC   16700

🏃 |O| LE MOULIN DE CONDAC

Condac; take the Confolens road.
☎ 05.45.31.04.97 📠 05.45.31.29.74
Closed Mon and Tues evenings in winter; Mon
lunchtime in summer. **Disabled access**.

This welcoming restaurant, in an attractively restored eighteenth-century mill on the banks of the Charente, offers traditional, local cooking of quality. There's a weekday lunch menu for €11, with others for €15–29 and a children's menu listing regional dishes for €10; it'll set you back around €27 *à la carte*. Eat on the beautiful shaded terrace or, if you're feeling energetic, enjoy the pedalos and the mini-golf. They even host a disco at the weekends. Free apéritif.

VERTEUIL-SUR-CHARENTE   16150 (10KM SW)

🏠 |O| LA PALOMA**

14 rue de la Fontaine.
☎ 05.44.29.04.49 📠 05.45.29.51.31
📧 lapaloma@worldonline.fr
Closed Sun evening and Mon out of season; a fortnight
in Feb; a fortnight in Nov. **TV**. **Car park**.

There's a goat and some Vietnamese pigs roaming around the garden, a talking parrot and an iguana in a corner of the bar and some pedigree hens clucking away in the back. The rooms have been pleasantly and sensitively renovated by the young couple who own the place – number 7 has a terrace and deck chairs. Doubles with shower are €30, or €38–46 with bath/wc. The cooking is tasty, too; the weekday menu proves good value at €11, and there are others from €14–27.

SAINT-DENIS-D'OLÉRON   17650

🏃 🏠 |O| HÔTEL-RESTAURANT LE MOULIN DE LA GALETTE*

8 rue Ernest-Morisset (Centre); it's on the town square,
near the church.
☎ 05.46.47.88.04 📠 05.46.47.69.05
Closed Oct–March. **Disabled access**.

You can't miss this florid seaside villa on the town square. It's a genuine family guesthouse with large rooms decorated in period style; doubles are €35–46 with shower/wc, while half board, compulsory in July–Aug, costs €36–41 per person. You'll find the same old charm in the dining room, where a few tables are laid on the terrace facing the market square. Menus range from €14–24, with a seafood menu for €27. The exacting owner-chef won't use anything but the freshest ingredients. No credit cards. 10% discount on the room rate Sept–June.

SAINT-MAIXENT-L'ÉCOLE 79400

🏡 🔝 |●| HÔTEL-RESTAURANT LE LOGIS SAINT-MARTIN***

chemin de Pissot (Southeast); head for Niort, turn left at the last set of lights in the town, and follow the signs.
☎ 05.49.05.58.68. ➡ 05.49.76.19.93.
Closed Sat lunchtime; Mon; Tues evening; Jan. **TV**. **Car park**.

A huge seventeenth-century riverside residence set in its own grounds. Peace and quiet are guaranteed, even though you're just a few hundred metres from the town centre. The rooms have been decorated in keeping with the style and charm of the building, featuring fine fabrics and furniture, with glass from Bohemia and Murano. Doubles €79 with shower/wc, €110 with bath. In the restaurant most dishes involve fish or seafood; there's a lunch menu at €28 and others €40–80. Given the environment, the welcome is splendidly relaxed. 10% discount on the room rate Nov–March.

SOUDAN 29800 (7.5KM E)

🔝 |●| L'ORANGERIE

It's on the N11.
☎ 05.49.06.56.06 ➡ 05.49.06.56.10
Closed Sun evening and Wed from 1 Oct–31 March; three weeks from mid-Nov. **Car park**.

Tasty and refined regional cooking at really affordable prices. The dining room is cosy, bright and spacious, with windows opening onto a small garden, and service is swift, attentive and friendly. Menus €15–37; don't miss the delicious home-made desserts. Should you need to stay, their double rooms are not at all bad for €30–37.

AIRIPT 79260 (10KM S)

🏡 🔝 |●| L'AUBERGE DU PORT D'AIRIPT

How to get there: take the N11 Niort road and at La Crèche, and follow the signs to Aiript.
☎ 05.49.25.58.81 ➡ 05.49.05.33.49

Restaurant closed Mon. **Swimming pool**. **Car park**.

This old farm, located in a peaceful, pretty valley, has been converted into a superb inn with lots of quiet corners and a warm atmosphere throughout. With two hectares of land and three buildings, a Hollywood-style swimming pool and a small spring with resident ducks, this place delights everyone from young couples to families – and even better, there are just five guest rooms (€36 with shower/wc or bath). The dining room has plain stone walls and a terrace that looks down on an old wash house. Specialities include frogs' legs, duck breasts and quail fillet, and they serve *crêpes* and grills by the pool in summer. Menus start at €14; *à la carte* you'll pay around €34. They don't accept credit cards. Free apéritif.

MOTHE-SAINT-HÉRAY (LA) 79800 (11KM SE)

🏡 🔝 |●| HÔTEL-RESTAURANT LE CORNEILLE**

13 rue du Maréchal-Joffre (Centre).
☎ 05.49.05.17.08 ➡ 05.49.05.19.56
ℰ corneille@wanadoo.fr
Hotel closed 20 Dec–10 Jan.
Restaurant closed Fri evening out of season; Sun evening. **TV**. **Car park**.

Based in the home of Dr Pierre Corneille, who was the last descendant of the famous seventeenth-century tragedian, this charming old family hotel provides a pleasing rustic setting for a series of small dining rooms. Good quality local dishes are listed on all the menus, €14–27, which you can enjoy inside or out in the garden. Most of the rooms are comfortable, though some are less good than others; doubles start at €35. Don't miss breakfast – it's unusually delicious. Free coffee.

SAINT-PIERRE-D'OLÉRON 17310

🏡 🔝 LE SQUARE**

pl. des Anciens-Combattants (Centre).
☎ 05.46.47.00.35 ➡ 05.46.75.04.90
Closed 30 Nov–1 April. **Swimming pool**. **TV**. **Car park**.

An unpretentious little hotel with a certain style. It's far enough away from the centre to be peaceful, and it has some real attractions, among them a pretty courtyard, a swimming pool surrounded by flowers and a sauna. The rooms offer no surprises; those in the renovated part of the hotel are the nicest, and the owners are in the process of refurbishing the rest. Doubles €43–64 with shower/wc or bath. 10% discount April and May.

🏊 |●| FRANÇOIS

55 rue de la République (Centre).
☎ 05.46.47.29.44 ➡ 05.46.47.02.33
Closed Sun evening and Mon out of season; Dec.

A lovely classical dining room, service that's beyond reproach and quite simply the best food in town. Dishes are traditional and attentively prepared; highlights include artichoke *pâté* with smoked bacon and cuttlefish stew. Extremely reasonable prices, too; the €12 menu is a real treat, and there are others from €15–26. Free coffee.

COTINIÈRE (LA)   17310 (3KM S)

🏨 |●| HÔTEL FACE AUX FLOTS**

24 rue du Four (Centre); it's 300m from the port.
☎ 05.46.47.10.05 ➡ 05.46.47.45.95.
Closed mid-Nov to mid–Feb, except Christmas holidays.
Disabled access. Garden. Swimming pool. TV.

A haven of peace away from the exhausting throng jostling around the little fishing harbour, this place is run by a smiling, efficient woman who takes the job of looking after her customers seriously. Double rooms with shower/wc or bath cost €38–70. Some of them have a clear view of the silvery sea – which is just as well because the cream-coloured wall carpet is dreadful. Half board, compulsory in season, costs €44–66 per person. The restaurant, which has a panoramic view and a bar, is good; specialities include seafood platters, sole fillet with morels, roast sea bream with truffles and truly delicious chocolate *délices*. Menus €15–30, with a €11 option for children. There's a small garden and a swimming pool.

🏊 |●| L'ASSIETTE DU CAPITAINE

It's on the port.
☎ 05.46.47.38.78
Closed Mon evening and Tues out of season; mid-Nov to mid-Feb.

Overlooking the port where fish are sold direct from the boats, and decorated with old sea charts and a lovely collection of mussel baskets, *L'Assiette* serves seafood which is fresh as can be. Dishes are creative, original and change with the seasons: highlights include *mouclades* and shark with banana, and, unusually for a seafood restaurant, their desserts are great – try the chocolate dessert with cream. Menus €11–26. Free coffee.

SAINT-SAVINIEN   17350

🏊 |●| AUBERGE DU QUAI DES FLEURS

53 quai des Fleurs; it's the continuation of the main street.
☎ 05.46.90.12.59
Closed Nov–Jan. **Disabled access**.

An unexpected establishment in an old riverside house with two terraces. Old pedal sewing machines are used as table bases and hastily knotted sack cloth covers the chairs; meanwhile Billie Holiday croons in the background. It's run by a Swedish woman so most of the mouthwatering dishes hail from her homeland – choose from a summer weekday lunch menu at €11 or go *à la carte* and spend €14–18. They also host occasional live jazz or blues concerts, when menus run from €20 to €30, and in August there's a week-long festival of eclectic music. Free apéritif or coffee.

SAINT-SAVIN-SUR-GARTEMPE   86310

🏨 |●| HÔTEL DE FRANCE

38 pl. de la République (Centre).
☎ 05.49.48.19.03 ➡ 05.49.48.97.07
Closed Sun evening except July-Aug; a fortnight Nov–Dec.

A pleasantly traditional hotel behind a welcoming façade, with fifteen good rooms. The three in the eaves are charming and cheaper than the others. Even though the rooms at the front are double-glazed the road is noisy so opt for the ones at the back. Doubles with shower cost €40, €44 with bath. Good traditional cuisine is served in the flowery dining room, where you can choose from a variety of menus (€14–22) or *à la carte*.

SAINTES   17100

🏊 🏨 HÔTEL BLEU NUIT**

1 rue Pasteur (West); go along cours National towards the A10.
☎ 05.46.93.01.72 ➡ 05.46.74.43.80
📧 aubleunuit@t3a.com
Closed Sun evening from 1 Oct–15 April. **Disabled access. TV. Pay car park.**

The well-run family-friendly hotel is located on a busy crossroads, but they've installed excellent double glazing and there are quieter rooms at the back. All the rooms are simple and tasteful, and they offer good value for money; doubles with basin cost €29, with shower/wc €37, €38 with bath. 10% discount.

☐ HÔTEL DE L'AVENUE**

114 av. Gambetta; it's near the Abbey aus Dames.
☎ 05.46.74.05.91 ➡ 05.46.74.32.16
Closed Christmas holidays.

A friendly, colourful hotel with some fifteen pleasant rooms. They're all different, but none of them looks over the street, so they're all quiet, and there's a peaceful calm in the breakfast room to ease you into the day. Doubles range from €30–44 with bath/wc. Good value.

☐ HÔTEL DES MESSAGERIES**

rue des Messageries (Centre).
☎ 05.46.93.64.99 ➡ 05.46.92.14.34
Closed 22 Dec–5 Jan. **TV. Pay garage.**

Very comfortable, · classic hotel in a quiet street in the old town. It started its days as a coaching inn, but today only a few of the stones from the original building are visible in the very old staircase. It has two wings, which enclose a pretty paved courtyard, and the rooms are very quiet. Air-conditioned doubles €46 with shower/wc or €53 with bath.

☐ RESTAURANT LA CIBOULETTE

36 rue Pérat (Centre); go down cours National and cross the Charente, follow av. Gambetta and, after the bridge, turn into the third street on the left.
☎ 05.46.74.07.36 ➡ 05.46.94.14.54
Closed Sat lunchtime and Sun.

The restaurant has a pretty dining room that's recently been redecorated and had air conditioning installed. The young chef, who comes from Brest, prepares lots of fish and shellfish – his successes include plaice *en papillote* with Roscoff seaweed and a shellfish *jus*, a tasty mixed "fisherman's platter" and fish smoked over beech chippings. He also pays culinary homage to the Charente with dishes such as *jaud* (chicken marinated in Cognac), *fricassée* of eel *à la charentaise* and *mouclade*. He makes all the bread and the desserts, too. The €15 menu is served daily except Sunday and public holidays, and there are others €23–28 with a children's option at €9. There's a reasonably priced wine list with lots of regional choices.

☐ LE PISTOU

3 pl. du Théâtre (Centre).
☎ 05.46.74.47.53 ➡ 05.46.91.13.52
Closed Sun and Jan.

A centrally located restaurant where the prices won't break the bank. The cooking

goes back to basics, and some of the dishes have a Mediterranean flavour: mussels with *pistou* (the French version of Italian pesto), sea bass flambéed in *pastis, paella*. There's always a fish dish of the day and lots of salads in summer. *Menu-carte* from €18 to €22 or *à la carte*. Free apéritif.

TAILLEBOURG   17350 (12KM N)

☐ AUBERGE DES GLYCINES

How to get there: it's by the riverside on the Saint-Savinien road coming from Saintes.
☎ 05.46.91.81.40
Closed Wed; first fortnight in Nov; a fortnight at the end of Feb. **Garden.**

This inn stands on the banks of the Charente in an unknown but absolutely delightful riverside town. On warm days you eat in the old flower garden or on the shady first-floor terrace. It gets busy at weekends but during the week you're disturbed only by the splash of the carp in the river. The place has recently been overhauled and offers slightly different food: try the snails, zander *terrine*, cockerel in Cognac or any of the seasonal specialities. Menus at €17 or €22, or about €27 *à la carte*. Reservations are recommended. Free apéritif.

SURGÈRES   17700

☐ HÔTEL-RESTAURANT GAMBETTA*

49 rue Gambetta (North); its on the Niort road.
☎ 05.46.07.03.64 ➡ 05.46.07.37.32
Closed Sun lunchtime in July–Aug; Sat evening and Sun Sept–June; Christmas to 1 Jan. **TV. Garden. Car park.**

This place, popular with sales reps and travelling businesspeople, offers clean, standard doubles for €26 with basin and up to €37 with shower/wc. Those on the garden side are quietest. There is a simple menu at €11 and another at €17, while choices *à la carte* list Burgundy specialities as well as local dishes. The proprietress comes from Beaujolais country and the wine list features good wines from her region, all at very decent prices. Half board €38 per person. Free apéritif.

VIGEANT (LE)   86140

☐ HÔTEL VAL DE VIENNE – RESTAURANT LA GRIMOLÉE

Port de Salles; it's 5km south on the D110.

☎ 05.49.48.27.27 ➡ 05.49.48.47.47
Restaurant closed Sun evening; Mon; Jan–Feb. **TV**.
Garden. **Car park**.

In the hollow of a green valley, on the banks of the Vienne, this hotel stands in three hectares of grounds and provides twenty functional rooms. The modern architecture gives it the look of a stylish motel, which works well, and there's a private terrace opening onto a heated swimming pool. The setting is enchanting and quiet as can be – it's been awarded a *Relais du Silence* badge. Doubles range from €59 to €67. In the restaurant, the imaginative cuisine has a good reputation: try roast fillet of lamb with sweet garlic sauce, turbot spiked with Szechuan peppers or orange salad in a mint-scented infusion. There's a weekday menu for €14 and others at €21–30.

THOUARS 17300

❙●❙ RESTAURANT DU LOGIS DE POMPOIS

Sainte-Verge (Centre).
☎ 05.49.96.27.84 ➡ 05.49.96.13.97
Closed Sun evening; Mon; Tues; a fortnight in Jan; a week in July. **Disabled access**. **Car park**.

A remarkable restaurant housed in a magnificent old wine house. You dine in a huge room with beams and unadorned stone. The cuisine is top of the range and the welcome is outstanding. Weekday lunch menu €14, and others up to €40 – try the *marbré* of duck *foie gras*, the rabbit with ginger and lime, the asparagus *charlotte* or the caramelized crab and lobster.

PROVENCE-ALPES-CÔTE d'AZUR

04 Alpes-de-Haute-Provence

05 Hautes-Alpes

06 Alpes-Maritimes

13 Bouches-du-Rhône

83 Var

84 Vaucluse

AIX-EN-PROVENCE 13100

SEE MAP ON P.670

⌂ HÔTEL LE PRIEURÉ**

It's on the N96. **Off map B1-5**
☎ 04.42.21.05.23 ➡ 04.42.21.60.56
Pay car park.

Some time ago, this old priory was converted into a lovely hotel with 23 cosy rooms. All of them look out onto the ornate Pavillon Lanfant park. Doubles €50–69 with bath. Breakfast, €6, is served in your room or on the terrace. The proprietress welcomes you with a smile.

⌂ LES QUATRE DAUPHINS**

54 rue Roux-Alphéran. **MAP B2-6**
☎ 04.42.38.16.39 ➡ 04.42.38.60.19
TV.

A quiet, charming hotel named after the nearby fountain. The small, tastefully furnished rooms, spaced across three floors, all have telephone. Doubles €53 with shower/wc, €61–64 with bath. The place is full of Provençal prints and charming painted wooden furniture.

冬 ⌂ HÔTEL CARDINAL**

24 Rue du Cardinal. **MAP B2-7**
☎ 04.42.38.32.30 ➡ 04.42.26.39.05
TV.

There's an appealing atmosphere in this quiet, comfortable hotel. Some of the rooms have been refurbished and they're much in demand – though people who know the place opt for the bigger ones in the annexe;

doubles for €58. Relaxed, friendly welcome. 10% discount on the room rate.

冬 ⌂ |●| HÔTEL SAINT-CHRISTOPHE – BRASSERIE LÉOPOLD**

2 av. Victor Hugo. **MAP A2-8**
☎ 04.42.26.01.24 ➡ 04.42.38.53.17
Restaurant closed Mon and 3–28 Aug. **TV**.

Slap-bang in the centre of town. It's one of *the* places in Aix because of its Art Deco design. Doubles, €67–74, are air-conditioned and have full en-suite bathrooms; some even have small terraces. A few suites at €90. The trump card is the *brasserie* on the ground floor – a real institution crammed with tables and with waiters in long aprons. Try the steak *tartare* or the stuffed Provençal vegetables. Menus €13–28. A pleasurable place. Free house apéritif.

|●| RESTAURANT LE CARILLON

10 rue Portalis. **MAP B1-11**
Closed Sat evening, Sun, a week in Feb, and Aug.
Disabled access.

They don't have a telephone here, so you can't reserve: you have to turn up early and take a seat with the regulars, many of them pensioners, who appreciate the home cooking. A completely unpretentious place which is ideal for lunch or dinner. Menus €9 and €12.

|●| RESTAURANT LA BROCHERIE

5 rue Fernand-Dol. **MAP B2-14**
☎ 04.42.38.33.21 📧 labrocherie@aol.com
Closed Sat lunchtime, Sun and Aug.

Pleasant, rustic atmosphere, with a huge

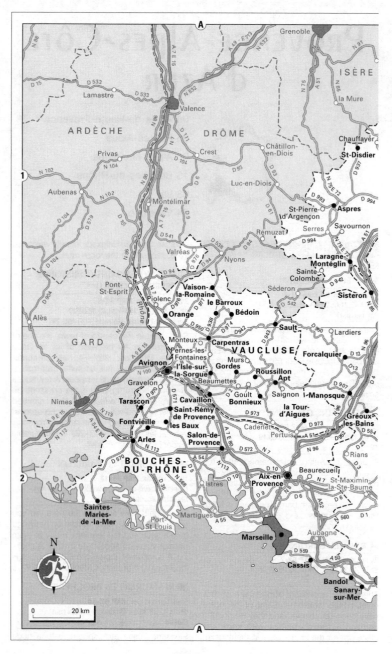

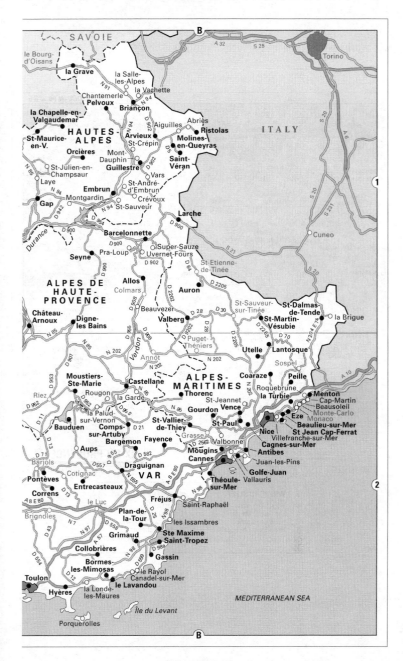

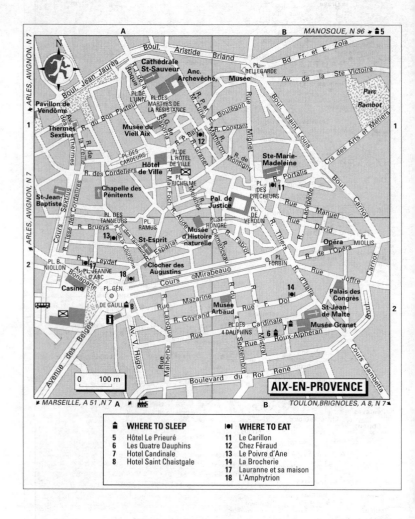

AIX-EN-PROVENCE

⌂ WHERE TO SLEEP	|◉| WHERE TO EAT
5 Hôtel Le Prieuré	11 Le Carillon
6 Les Quatre Dauphins	12 Chez Féraud
7 Hotel Candinale	13 Le Poivre d'Ane
8 Hotel Saint Chaistgale	14 La Brocherie
	17 Lauranne et sa maison
	18 L'Amphytrion

Renaissance fireplace where they cook whole chickens on the spit. There's an excellent choice of meat dishes, though people come here mainly for the grilled fish. There's an original *menu grillade* for €14 with a self-service *hors d'œuvre* buffet, main course from the spit and dessert of the day. *Formule* €12 at lunchtime and a tasty Provençal dinner menu for €21.

🕏 |●| LAURANNE ET SA MAISON

16 rue Victor-Leydef. **MAP A2-17**
☎ 04.42.93.02.03
Closed Sun; Mon evening; Jan; 1–15 Nov.

An enticing-looking, friendly place in a lovely and sunny setting. Fresh, inventive cooking, showing off the flavours of the south. Dishes change all the time but could include stuffed vegetables, tart with duck *confit* and ceps and a *tajine* with figs and apricots. Lunch menu for €12, others up to €27 or about €29 *à la carte*. Free house *digestif*.

🕏 |●| LE POIVRE D'ÂNE

7 rue de la Couronne. **MAP A2-13**
☎ 04.42.93.45.56
Closed Sun; Mon; the first 3 weeks in Aug.

The décor is as colourful as the food in this warm, welcoming place. They serve original, attractive dishes in generous portions; menus change every two months. The prices are really good value: weekday lunch menu for €14 or you'll pay an average of €22 *à la carte*. As a guide, starters include raviolis or *caillettes* (rather reminiscent of haggis); for main courses try the fish *tian*; and don't miss the orange-scented *crème brûlée* for dessert – they bring it to your table and use a red-hot brand to caramelize the sugar in front of you. Take a look at the grocer's at number 10 across the road: it's run by the same people. Free coffee.

🕏 |●| L'AMPHYTRION

2 rue Paul Doumer. **MAP A2-18**
☎ 04.42.26.54.10

The chef, Bruno Ungar, loves Provençal cuisine – and you certainly experience it in his cooking, which lists local dishes which are highly coloured and richly flavoured. Menus €17–45. There's plenty of space to be comfortable on the terrace and the *menu du marché* is an ideal option for lunch. The speciality is rack of lamb in an olive paste crust. Free apéritif.

🕏 |●| CHEZ FÉRAUD

8 rue du Puits-Juif. **MAP A1–12**
☎ 04.42.63.07.27

Closed Sun; Mon lunchtime; Aug.

Right in the centre of old Aix – you get a real feel of old Provence. The home cooking is prepared attentively by the father and served by the son under the watchful eye of the mother: try the *soupe au pistou*, *pieds et paquets* (lamb's tripe and trotters) or the slowly cooked *daube* (braised beef in wine sauce). Menus €19–24. Ask to be shown the secret cellars; there's also a terrace. Free house apéritif.

BEAURECUEIL · · · · · · · · · 13100 (10KM E)

🕏 🏠 |●| RELAIS SAINTE-VICTOIRE***

It's in the village.
☎ 04.42.66.94.98 ➡ 04.42.66.85.96
📧 relais-ste-victoire@wanadoo.fr
Closed Mon; Fri lunchtime; Sun evening; a week in Jan; the Feb school holidays; All Saints'. **Swimming pool**. **TV. Car park**.

This establishment, at the foot of Mont Sainte-Victoire, is one of the best restaurants in the region, and it's run by a family of real characters. The décor is brightly coloured and there's a collection of unusual paddles on the walls. René Berges' cooking is full of sun-drenched, southern flavours: poached eggs with truffle cream, preserved tomato tart served with grilled sardine fillets, rack of lamb glazed with local honey. *Formule-cartes* €26–61. Rooms, €61–122 with bath, overlook the grounds or the countryside. Free house apéritif.

ALLOS · · · · · · · · · · · · · · 04260

🕏 🏠 |●| HÔTEL-RESTAURANT LES GENTIANES**

Grand-Rue.
☎ 04.92.83.03.50 ➡ 04.92.83.02.71
Closed Tues out of season; 17 April–10 May; 12 Nov–4 Dec.

Small inn, popular with skiers in winter and walkers in summer. It's got a friendly atmosphere. Really pretty rooms with doubles €32 with shower/wc; full board is €58. The menus, €11 weekday lunchtimes and €14–24, list honest, hearty dishes including rib steak with ceps, spaghetti *carbonara*, *daube* with polenta and salmon fillet on a bed of ravioli. Free house *digestif*.

BEAUVEZER · · · · · · · · · 04370 (13KM S)

🕏 🏠 |●| HÔTEL LE BELLEVUE**

pl. du Village; take the D908 towards St André des Alpes

and it's on the village square.
☎ 04.92.83.51.60 x04.92.83.51.60
e bellevue@wanadoo.fr
Closed 1 Nov–23 Dec. **Car park**.

A charming place to stop between Provence and the Alps – a haven of peace and tranquillity behind an ochre façade. The comfortable double rooms, tastefully decorated in warm colours and Provençal prints, go for €40 with basin and €44–47 with bath. Six rooms have views of the mountains, and there's a suite sleeping four to six. You eat heartily in the restaurant – lunch menu €13, others €18–24. Delicious regional dishes: aubergine and garlic flan, bass en papillote, cep ravioli, duck with olives. 10% discount on the room rate 3 March–1 May and 1–31 Oct. Free apéritif.

ANTIBES   06600

𝕏 ☗ HÔTEL DE L'ÉTOILE**

2 av. Gambetta (Centre); it's 5 minutes from the station.
☎ 04.93.34.26.30 ➡ 04.93.34.41.48
e omfp@hotel-etoile.com
TV. Pay car park.

The only hotel of this category in the centre of Antibes. Although modern and comfortable, it's better for an overnight stop than as a place to spend a holiday. Spacious rooms with good sound insulation; doubles €43–47 with shower/wc or €49–53 with bath. It's a friendly place, but the requirement to pay for your room in advance is a little tiresome. 10% discount Sept–June.

𝕏 ☗ LE MAS DJOLIBA***

29 av. de Provence (Centre).
☎ 04.93.34.02.48 ➡ 04.93.34.05.81
e info@pcastel-djoliba.com
Closed Nov–Jan. **Swimming pool**. **TV**. **Car park**.

A pretty Provençal house surrounded by greenery. The delightful rooms, decorated in the local style, cost €70–75 with shower/wc or €82–98 with bath. They prefer you to stay half-board in season but it's not compulsory; it costs €61–77 per person. There's a relaxing swimming pool so you don't have to fight your way to the crowded beach. It's the only hotel in its category to offer such good facilities at these prices. Friendly, professional welcome. Free coffee.

|●| RESTAURANT LE SAFRANIER

1 pl. du Safranier.
☎ 04.93.34.80.50
Closed Sun evening and Mon in winter; Mon and Wed

lunchtime in season; 15 Dec–15 Jan.

It's astonishing that places like this still exist on the Côte d'Azur. You feel as if you're in an small Provençal village in this haven of tranquillity with its lovely terrace covered in greenery. Friendly welcome and good service. There's a menu at €10, or you'll pay around €23 à la carte. Excellent fish soup and a superb bouillabaisse, which you have to order in advance. Grilled fish always available. Credit cards not accepted.

JUAN-LES-PINS   06160 (1KM W)

𝕏 ☗ LA JABOTTE*

13 av. Max-Maurey: it's off bd. James-Wyllie which borders Cap d'Antibes.
☎ 04.93.61.45.89 ➡ 04.93.61.07.04
Closed Sun afternoon and 15 Nov–15 Dec. **Disabled access. Car park**.

This hotel offers good value for money: spotless rooms with shower or bath at €44–62. The bungalows looking onto the terrace are particularly nice. Half board is competitively priced at €38–56 per person. There's a suite with two double rooms – good for families or groups of four – and it has a view of the mountain. Friendly welcome, but you should avoid arriving between 1pm and 6pm on a Sunday, when they take a break. Relaxing atmosphere and a gentle pace. 10% discount for a minimum three-night stay Nov–March, excluding school holidays.

𝕏 ☗ HÔTEL SAINTE-VALÉRIE***

rue de l'Oratoire.
☎ 04.93.61.07.15 ➡ 04.93.61.47.52
e sainte-valerie@juanlespins.net
Closed 30 Sept–15 April. **Garden**. **Swimming pool**. **TV. Car park**.

A stylish hotel, ideal for a romantic holiday. Set in a quiet part of Juan-les-Pins just a short distance from the Gould pine woods and the sea, it has a pool and a pretty, shady garden where you can take refuge from the heat. Meals are served in the garden – one menu at €21. Modern, tastefully decorated double rooms €88–107 with shower/wc and up to €146 with bath. 10% discount on the room rate out of season.

APT   84400

𝕏 ☗ |●| HÔTEL-RESTAURANT LE PALAIS**

24 pl. Gabriel-Péri (Centre); it's opposite the town hall.
☎ and ➡ 04.90.04.89.32

Restaurant closed Mon. **Establishment closed** 4 Nov–15 Dec.

A relatively characterless hotel, best described as modest, in an old house in the centre of town. Hotels are not Apt's strong point, so this will do well enough for an overnight. Doubles €27 with basin, €35–40 with shower/wc or bath. Straightforward Provençal cooking – soup with pesto and aubergine *tian aïoli* – on menus €10–20. Free coffee.

ARLES 13200

♠ HÔTEL LE CLOÎTRE**

16 rue du Cloître (Centre); it's between the amphitheatre and Saint-Trophime.
☎ 04.90.96.29.50 ➡ 04.90.96.02.88
e hotel_cloitre@hotmail.com
Closed 1 Nov–15 March. **Car park**.

A charming, really tranquil hotel which is supported by thirteenth-century vaulted arcades. The largest rooms, which date from the thirteenth and seventeenth centuries, have big beams and are decorated with gleaming tiles. Simple doubles €38 with shower, €41–55 with shower/wc and €44–60 with bath. Remarkably kind owner.

⅔ ♠ HÔTEL CALENDAL**

5 rue Porte de Laure.
☎ 04.90.96.11.89 ➡ 04.90.96.05.84
e contact@lecalendal.com
Disabled access. **Garden**. **TV**. **Pay garage**.

This hotel, situated in the middle of the town, is decorated with local fabrics and dotted with huge vases of stunningly coloured flowers. Arles is famous for photography and the stairwell is hung with lots of unusual photographs. There's a cool patio where you can shelter from the sun. The arena where they still hold bull-fights is close by. Air-conditioned rooms €39–45 with shower/wc and €68–74 with bath; three have a terrace. They've enlarged the reception and built a private garage but if you want a space, €10, it's essential to book. By way of food, they offer a buffet *formule* for €14 (lunchtime only in season, dinner out of season), snacks and salads are served in the garden, and there's a tearoom. A lovely place. 10% discount Nov–March.

⅔ ♠ HÔTEL DE L'AMPHITHÉÂTRE**

5 rue Diderot (Centre); it's near the Roman theatre.
☎ 04.90.96.10.30 ➡ 04.90.93.98.69
e contact@hotelamphitheatre.fr
TV.

Previously known as *Hôtel Diderot*, this place

has been totally renovated and has a charming new look. All the bedrooms have been decorated in Provençal style; doubles cost €44–55 with bath or shower/wc. The charming owner serves an unusually good breakfast. 10% discount Nov–March.

⅔ ♠ ⅠⅠ HÔTEL MIREILLE***

2 pl. Saint-Pierre; it's the other side of the Rhône in the Trinquetaille district.
☎ 04.90.93.70.74 ➡ 04.90.93.87.28
e contact@hotel-mireille.com
Closed Nov–March. **Garden**. **Swimming pool**. **Car park**. **Garage**.

A curtain of trees screens off the swimming pool, which is presided over by a watchful old statue. Doubles overlooking the garden and pool cost €60–105. Half board is compulsory during the *Feria* and at Easter. There's a huge and pleasant dining room. Lovely seafood (including *bouillabaisse provençale*) and quality meat dishes on menus €18–27. Good welcome. 10% discount if you stay a week half-board and free house apéritif, coffee or *digestif*.

ⅠⅠ L'ESCALADOU

23 rue Porte-de-Laure (Centre).
☎ 04.90.96.70.43
Closed 24–25 Dec; 1 Jan.

If you want a taste of authentic Arles, this is the place. It's a local haunt – as well as running it, Jean-Charles Signoret also makes traditional costumes for popular festivals, which the waitresses wear. Menus €13–21. Real fish soup and *bouillabaisse*.

ⅠⅠ LE JARDIN DE MANON

14 av. des Alyscamps; it's a little way from the town centre, at the bottom end of bd. des Lices, beyond the police station.
☎ 04.90.93.38.68
Closed Wed; Sun evening Nov–March; the Feb and All Saints' school holidays. **Garden**.

A friendly restaurant with a small garden at the back (watch out for the mosquitoes in the evening). Excellent, creative cuisine; there's a €13 lunch menu and others €16–34. The extensive wine list offers good value for money.

⅔ ⅠⅠ LA CHARCUTERIE

51 rue des Arènes (Centre).
☎ 04.90.93.44.44

A genuine Lyon-style bistro right in the centre of Arles. The owner, François, drives all the way to Lyon to supply the kitchen with authentic produce like the *andouillette de Bobosse* – a must. His restaurant is on the premises of an old *charcuterie* dating back to the 1940s, and Regouya cooks very tasty dishes in front of you on an old marble counter. François is also a painter: his canvasses cover the walls. In summer, the menu lists salads, grills and *tapas* and there's a welcoming terrace seating about a dozen customers. About €14 for lunch and €20 for dinner. Free house apéritif.

|●| LA GUEULE DU LOUP

39 rue des Arènes (Centre).
☎ 04.90.96.96.69

You're practically in the kitchen as soon as you walk into this place; the dining room is upstairs. There are magic charts and documents about sorcery on the wall – the owner used to be a magician but decided to become a restaurateur and gave it all up (well, almost: he still does a gourmet dinner show on a Friday night). Delicious dishes such as ravioli with basil, fine tart with red mullet and anchovy, duckling breast *à la badiane* and lamb from Provence. The dining room is so small, it's best to book. Gastronomic menu from €23 and they do a special one for €24 during the *Feria*. *À la carte*, expect to pay around €32.

🎄 |●| CÔTÉ COUR

65 rue Amédée-Pichot.
☎ 04.90.49.77.76
Closed Wed and 10 days in Jan.

A superb dining room with walls of chiselled stone, hand-made floor tiles, sturdy beams and air conditioning. The tables are laid with Provençal tablecloths. The dishes come in huge portions but are resolutely classic: aubergine *charlotte*, leg of lamb *à la provençale*, *fricassée* of fish with rosemary butter. Menus €24–31 (all include cheese and dessert). *À la carte*, dishes include sweet-and-sour scallops, tuna *daube* and fillet steak Côté Cour (with *foie gras*). Nice dessert menu. Charming, if slightly diffident, welcome from the young team. Free house *digestif*.

ARVIEUX   05350

🎄 🏠 |●| LA FERME D'IZOARD***

Hameau de la Chalp; it's 30km northwest of Saint-Véran in the direction of Brançion over the col de l'Izoard or via Guillestre in winter when the col is closed.
☎ 04.92.46.89.00 ➡ 04.92.46.82.37

e j.fryehet@laferme.fr
Disabled access. Swimming pool. TV. Car park.

A family-run establishment with good facilities including a heated pool. The building is rustic, but the décor is elegant and stylish. Prices are fair considering the high standards: prices range from €45 to €133 for doubles, studios or self-contained two-roomed apartments with kitchenette and bathroom. Half board €45–90. Simple but tasty cooking, with lots of grills on the open fire, and menus €13–30. It's a lovely place to relax in superb countryside. 12% discount in the first week in July and the week before Christmas.

ASPRES-SUR-BUËCH   04150

🎄 🏠 |●| HÔTEL DU PARC**

Route de Grenoble (Centre).
☎ 04.92.58.60.01 ➡ 04.92.58.67.84.
e info@hotel-buech.com
Closed Sun evening and Wed out of season; 6 Dec–6 Jan. **Garden. Car park.**

It's very pleasant to lunch on the terrace near the rose garden or the patio– in spite of the main road that passes in front. Lunch menu for €15 and decent *menus express* listing mixed salad, chicken *basquaise* and a dessert such as strawberry *bavarois*. Other menus up to €32. Doubles with basin €29 and up to €46 with bath. All the rooms are clean and have good facilities. 10% discount for a three-night stay.

AURON   06660

🎄 🏠 |●| HÔTEL LAS DONNAS**

Grande-Place (Centre); it's next to the ice-rink.
☎ 04.93.23.00.03 ➡ 04.93.23.07.37
Closed end April to mid-July; end Aug to mid-Dec. **TV.**

A pleasant, peaceful hotel with some forty sunny rooms, €33–104, half of which have balconies overlooking the ski runs. The restaurant serves good wholesome food – menus, €16–21, offer beef *fondue* and *raclette*, *mousseline* of fish, *rillettes* of young rabbit and so on. Around €22 *à la carte*. Half board at €30–65 is compulsory during school holidays. Lovely glassed-in terrace. Free apéritif or coffee.

AVIGNON   84000

SEE MAP OVERLEAF

🎄 🏠 HÔTEL MIGNON*

12 rue Joseph-Vernet. **MAP B2-4**
☎ 04.90.82.17.30 📠 04.90.85.78.46
📧 hotel.mignon@wanadoo.fr
TV.

Though the décor in this well-kept and welcoming place is a little busy, it's not unattractive. The rooms are tastefully furnished, and have double glazing and efficient insulation; doubles €36 with shower/wc. Each room has a telephone, cable TV and a whole host of services you wouldn't expect in a one-star hotel. Breakfast €4. There are three flights of stairs and no lift. 10% discount Nov–Feb.

🎄 🏠 🍴 HÔTEL-RESTAURANT LE MAGNAN**

63 rue du Portail-Magnanen. **MAP C3-6**
☎ 04.90.86.36.51 📠 04.90.85.48.90
📧 magnan@wanadoo.fr
Garden. **TV**. **Car park**.

Though not particularly attractive, this hotel is conveniently situated close to the station and the city walls. There are good points inside, too, like the quiet, relaxing patio with a cool garden and the clean rooms with modern facilities. Doubles with shower/wc €40–46. Breakfast €5. Children under twelve stay free. The restaurant is adequate if you don't want to head into town. Menus €13 in the week and up to €19. One free breakfast per room.

🎄 🏠 HÔTEL DE BLAUVAC**

11 rue de la Bancasse. **MAP B2-8**
☎ 04.90.86.34.11 📠 04.90.86.27.41
📧 blauvac@aol.com
Closed 3–17 Jan. **TV**.

A very good hotel in an elegant seventeenth-century mansion, ideally located in a narrow street in the historic centre close to place de l'Horloge. It's retained some of the original features of the house, which was the residence of the Marquis de Blauvac – the elegant wrought-iron staircase and some of the arched stone doorways. The décor is a happy combination of old stones and modern design. Well-appointed doubles at €47–55 with shower/wc or €50–61 with bath. Attentive service. 10% discount for a two-night stay.

🎄 🏠 HÔTEL DE GARLANDE-CITOTEL**

20 rue Galante. **MAP B2-9**
☎ 04.90.85.08.85 📠 04.90.27.16.58
📧 hotel.carlande@avignon-et-provence.com
Closed Sun out of season. **TV**.

An old house, beautifully situated near the Saint-Didiert bell tower. Michèle Michelotte has gone to great lengths to make her establishment comfortable and welcoming; hers is a delightful place that feels more like a guesthouse than a hotel. Attractive, well-maintained rooms cost €50–53 with shower/wc and €58–69 with bath. 10% discount for a two-night stay, except during the festival.

🎄 🏠 HÔTEL BRISTOL***

44 cours Jean-Jaurès. **MAP B3-7**
☎ 04.90.16.48.48 📠 04.90.86.22.72
📧 bristol.avignon.best.western@wanadoo.fr
Disabled access. **TV**. **Pay garage**.

A modern, rather stylish and very welcoming hotel. All the rooms have air conditioning and efficient double glazing. Doubles with shower or bath €58–85. There's a charge for the garage and you'll need to book in advance. 10% discount Aug–June.

🎄 🍴 LE WOOLLOOMOOLOO

16 [bis] rue des Teinturiers. **MAP C3-21**
☎ 04.90.85.28.44

Striking, very trendy restaurant in a converted printworks. The only light comes from a central hanging chandelier. It's a fusion of a colonial eatery in Sumatra and an arty New York loft and feels somewhat surreal – the old printing press is still there and petals are strewn over the tables and floor. They serve tasty world cuisine: *taramasalata*, chicken *yassa*, red mullet *ceviche* with cardamom, beef *maffe* and sea bream *à la brésilienne*. Menus €10, €13 and €16 or around €23 *à la carte*. Free punch with spice syrup, free coffee or free *digestif*.

🎄 🍴 RESTAURANT ROSE AU PETIT BEDON

70 rue Joseph-Vernet. **MAP B2-18**
☎ 04.90.82.33.98
Closed Sun; Mon lunchtime; 6–14 Aug; a fortnight in winter.

The welcoming atmosphere in this friendly restaurant is due in good part to Rose, the owner – she's turned it into a local institution. The resolutely Provençal cuisine features mouthwatering dishes that change with the seasons: ravioli in cream and herb sauce, sea bream with lemon, lamb with olive paste, shoulder of lamb *confit* with whole cloves of garlic and *pain Martegau* (bread with potatoes, green beans, garlic mayonnaise and cod). Lunchtime *menu-carte* at €17 or €27 in the evening and around €29 *à la carte*.

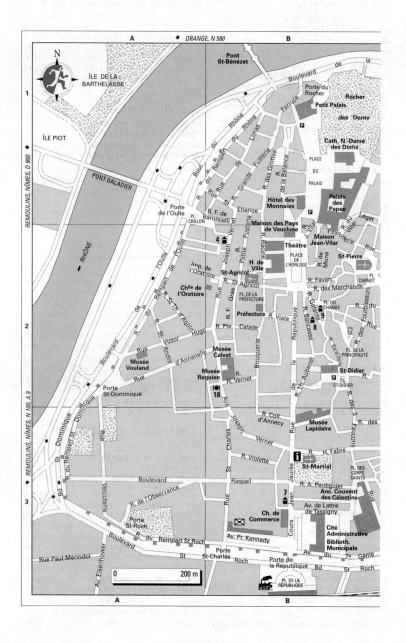

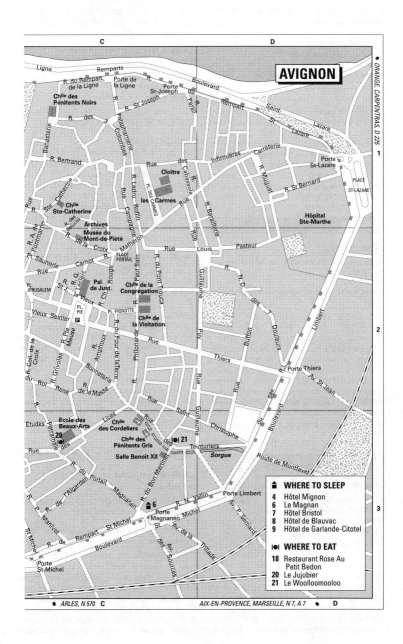

AVIGNON

⌂	WHERE TO SLEEP
4	Hôtel Mignon
6	Le Magnan
7	Hôtel Bristol
8	Hôtel de Blauvac
9	Hôtel de Garlande-Citotel

|◉|	WHERE TO EAT
18	Restaurant Rose Au Petit Bedon
20	Le Jujubier
21	Le Woolloomooloo

⊳ ARLES, N 570 C   AIX-EN-PROVENCE, MARSEILLE, N 7, A 7 ⊳ D

Attentive service and friendly welcome. Free apéritif or *digestif*.

🎿 |O| LE JUJUBIER

24 rue des Lices. **MAP C3-20**
☎ 04.90.86.64.08
Closed evenings except festival time; Sat; Sun; Aug.

Fresh Provençal cuisine served in a dining room which is delightfully decorated to resemble a local farmhouse. The menus are written by hand and list dishes made from recipes passed down through the generations: nettle soup, tuna with *sauce verte*, stuffed aubergines, rabbit *bouillabaisse*, lamb with spelt, preserved octopus, lambs' tongues. The list of dishes changes weekly. One menu for €18 or around €21 *à la carte*. Free coffee.

BANDOL   83150

🎿 |O| L'OULIVO

19 rue des Tonneliers; it's 100m from the port beside the church.
☎ 04.94.29.81.79
Closed Sun lunchtime in summer; weekday evenings in winter.

Very simple, very good restaurant, where a wonderfully kind *patronne* serves fresh, authentic Provençal cuisine. They offer a weekday lunch menu at €11 for starter, main course, dessert and coffee, or others at €15 and €19. There's a remarkable evening menu which includes aubergine turnovers, lamb tripe and trotters and a notable dish called *alouettes sans tête*. In summer they do a magnificent platter of a dozen different tapas. There's a pleasant terrace in summer. Free coffee.

BARCELONNETTE   04400

🎿 🏠 |O| HÔTEL DU CHEVAL BLANC**

12 rue Grenette (Centre).
☎ 04.92.81.00.19 ▶ 04.92.81.15.39
Closed Sun out of season and 1 Oct–20 Dec.
TV. Car park.

This hotel-restaurant has been in the Barneaud family for three generations, and the fourth is waiting eagerly in the wings. Double rooms with shower/wc and TV €44–46. Dish of the day €11 and a single menu at €14. The traditional cooking features game, fresh noodles and spinach pie. It's a very popular place with cycle tourists; you can store bikes in the stables, and they

prepare special "sporty" breakfasts (normal breakfast €5) and packed lunches on request. Free coffee.

🎿 |O| AZTÉCA HÔTEL***

3 rue François-Arnaud.
☎ 04.92.81.46.36 ▶ 04.92.81.43.92
ℯ hotel-azteca@wanadoo.fr
Closed 3 Nov–1 Dec. **Garden**.

From the outside you could mistake this place for a rather chic private clinic. The rooms are prettily decorated, three of them in an unusual Mexican-Alpine style – the people who built the villa at the end of the nineteenth century made their fortune in Mexico. Doubles €49–56 with shower/wc, €55–79 with bath. It's a quiet place with a peaceful garden where you can have a buffet breakfast for €8. In summer the breakfast is laid out on the dresser in the Mexican-style salon. Friendly welcome. There's a shuttle up to the slopes. Free house apéritif.

🎿 |O| LA MANGEOIRE GOURMANDE

pl. des 4-Vents; it's near the church.
☎ 04.92.81.01.61
Closed Sun evening and Wed out of season; 15 Nov–30 Dec.

The seventeenth-century vaulted dining room of this restaurant is genuinely welcoming. Loïc Balanec, a young chef bursting with talent, has brought new life to the restaurant, and his tasty food strikes a good balance between tradition and innovation. Delightful dishes include skate *provençale* with mint, salted chicken and a Potence with beef flambéed in whisky (for two). This is a restaurant with a reputation, so you should book. Weekday lunch menu €15, others €25–33. Free coffee.

UVERNET-FOURS   04400 (4.5KM SW)

🎿 |O| RESTAURANT LE PASSE MONTAGNE

How to get there: take the D902 towards Pra-Loup, and turn before the junction for col d'Allos.
☎ 04.92.81.08.58
Closed Tues evening; Wed; 15–30 June; 15 Nov–15 Dec. **Car park**.

This place has the warm atmosphere of a wooden chalet, and you can admire the peaks of Pain de Sucre and Chapeau de Gendarme from the terrace. It's a relaxed place: the menu looks as if it has been written by a schoolchild on a sheet from an exercise book. The peaceful atmosphere is heightened in winter when they light a roaring fire in the huge fireplace. The chef has rediscovered Provençal cooking from his grandmother's era but used his talent to adapt it to the present day – dishes include fresh ewe's milk cheese with *cébettes* (tiny Provençal onions), stuffed baby vegetables, lasagne with snails, *tarte aux sanguins* (a type of mushroom) and roast capon with cream and morels in pastry. Set menus €15–26. Free coffee.

SUPER-SAUZE   04400 (5KM SE)

⛺ LE PYJAMA**

It's at the foot of the ski runs.
☎ 04.92.81.12.00 ➡ 04.92.81.03.16
Closed 6 weeks May/June and mid-Sept to 20 Dec.**TV**. **Car park**.

The rooms are furnished with old pieces of furniture and ornaments, and they look out onto a peaceful panorama of larches. All have wide terraces, and some have mezzanines; doubles €15–41. There are places where you can curl up with a book in winter and tables outside where you can have a cool drink in summer. And there's an interesting junk shop on the ground floor. Pets very welcome.

PRA-LOUP   04400 (6KM SW)

🌿 ⛺ |●| LE PRIEURÉ***

Les Molanes
☎ 04.92.84.11.43 ➡ 04.92.84.01.88
Closed May and Oct–Nov. **Swimming pool**. **TV**. **Car park**.

An eighteenth-century priory which has been converted into a very warm, rustic hotel with breathtaking views of the Pain de Sucre and Chapeau de Gendarme mountains. Doubles €49–73. Appetizing cooking – trout with Génépy butter, *charbonnade*, lamb with Génépy as well. Menus €15–33 or around €24 *à la carte*. Free *digestif*.

🌿 ⛺ |●| AUBERGE DU CLOS SOREL**

Les Molanes; it's next to the train station entrance.
☎ 04.92.84.10.74 ➡ 04.92.84.09.14
📧 info@seolan.com
Closed 15 April–15 June and 1 Sept–15 Dec.
Swimming pool. **TV**. **Car park**.

A charming mountainside inn in a very old farmhouse. It's very close to the ski slopes and there's a lovely pool. Cosy rooms with beams and stone walls €61–137. You can have tea by the fireside, and they serve honest dishes in the candlelit restaurant, where there's a *menu-carte* for €24. Friendly welcome. Free house apéritif.

BARGEMON   83830

🌿 |●| RESTAURANT LA TAVERNE

pl. Philippe-Chauvier (Centre); it's on the village square.
☎ 04.94.76.62.19
Closed Sun evening; Mon; 15 Nov–1 March.

Charming, old-fashioned inn in an amazing village which clings tenaciously to the hillside. Fresh produce gathered from small local growers is used for Provençal cooking infused with a few fresh ideas: snail stew in pastry, lamb *confit* with dried tomatoes, local *caillette* from the Haut Var. It's where the locals come for Sunday lunch. Menus €17–27. Shaded terrace. Free coffee.

BARROUX (LE)   84330

⛺ |●| HÔTEL-RESTAURANT LES GÉRANIUMS**

pl. de la Croix.
☎ 04.90.62.41.08 ➡ 04.90.62.56.48
Closed 15 Nov–1 April. **Car park**.

A village hotel in a handsome white stone building which has been beautifully renovated. The terrace and some rooms have sweeping views of the plains; it's a quiet spot where only the cicadas disturb the silence. Traditional comfort without fuss. Doubles €42 with shower/wc, €47 with bath. Menus, €15–46, list traditional Provençal cooking with no frills. Specialities include quail *pâté* with onion marmalade, rabbit with savoury, duck breast with Muscat de Beaumes de Venise, pigeon with apples and *crème brûlée* with liquorice.

BAUDUEN   83630

🌿 ⛺ |●| L'AUBERGE DU LAC**

rue Grande (Centre).
☎ 04.94.70.08.04
📧 auberge.lac@wanadoo.fr
Closed 15 Nov–15 Mar.

This rustic inn is located in a charming little village on the banks of lake Sainte-Croix. The owner has been pampering his guests here for more than twenty years. The rooms are attractive and pleasant, particularly those which look onto the lake; they cost €64 with bath. The restaurant serves delicious menus €20–46; half board, €61 per person, is compulsory June–Sept. In summer, you can eat on a little terrace wreathed with vines, while in the winter the warm dining room is very welcoming. Good local cuisine, game in season, fish and local wine. Free coffee.

BAUX-DE-PROVENCE (LES)   13520

⅍ 🏠 I●I HOSTELLERIE DE LA REINE-JEANNE

It's in the village.
☎ 04.90.54.32.06 ➡ 04.9-.54.32.33
Closed 20 November–20 Dec; Jan. **TV**.

When the main street is heaving with tourists in the summer, all you want to do is get out of town – but this is a charming refuge when they've all gone. The old house has been lovingly and astutely renovated. The rooms are pleasant and individual. Doubles €45 with basin or shower and €50–60 with shower/wc or bath; the most expensive one is more like an apartment with an amazing view and incredible terrace. In the restaurant they serve quality local dishes. Lunch *formule* for €15 and others €20–26, listing roast lamb with pickled garlic and vegetable tart with olive paste. Free coffee.

BEAULIEU-SUR-MER   06310

⅍ 🏠 HÔTEL SELECT*

1 pl. du Général-de-Gaulle (Centre); it's 100m from the station.
☎ 04.93.01.05.42 ➡ 04.93.01.34.30
Closed Nov. **TV**.

This very cosy hotel is as friendly as a family guesthouse. It's the best value for money in town, though rooms facing the square are slightly noisy. Doubles €43–49 with shower/wc or bath. The proprietor is friendly and genuinely helpful – he can tell you anything you need to know about the region. Stay six nights (including breakfast) and get the seventh free.

⅍ 🏠 HÔTEL LE HAVRE BLEU**

29 bd. Maréchal-Joffre (North).
☎ 04.93.01.01.40 ➡ 04.93.01.29.92
📧 hotel.lehavrebleu@wanadoo.fr
Disabled access. **TV**. **Car park**.

A nineteenth-century hotel with a quiet family atmosphere. The clean, simple décor, white paintwork and bright blue shutters are very Mediterranean. Doubles €46–51 with shower/wc or bath; some have a terrace. 10% discount.

⅍ 🏠 HÔTEL COMTÉ DE NICE***

25 bd. Marinoni; coming from Nice, don't follow the road down to the sea but turn off towards the market square.
☎ 04.93.01.19.70 ➡ 04.93.01.23.09
TV. **Pay garage**.

You immediately feel good when you walk into this hotel. The family will greet you warmly and the rooms are well-appointed, with air-conditioning, telephone, mini-safe and hairdrier; doubles €60–88 with bath. Good breakfasts for €7, and you pay €7 for the garage too.There's a sauna and fitness centre. The beach and the harbour are five minutes away. 10% discount except during holiday time and the Monaco Grand Prix.

BÉDOIN   84410

⅍ 🏠 HÔTEL LA GARANCE**

Sainte-Colombe; it's 3km from the village on the Mont Ventoux road.
☎ 04.90.12.81.00 ➡ 04.90.65.93.05
Disabled access. **Swimming pool**. **TV**. **Car park**.

"Garance" is the French word for madder, a type of plant which used to be grown in the area. It was used to dye the trousers of the French soldiers in the 1870 wars, and brought prosperity to the region for many years. You'll love the décor and the tranquility of this captivating hotel. Clean, stylish doubles €40–44 and €46 with shower/wc or bath. The pleasant terrace, which overlooks Mont Ventoux, is the ideal place for an invigorating outdoor breakfast. Low-key welcome, but efficient, attentive service. There's no restaurant, but if you go half board you take meals at *La Colombe*, which is directly opposite. 10% discount Sept–June.

⅍ I●I RESTAURANT LA COLOMBE

Sainte-Colombe.
☎ and ➡ 04.90.65.61.20
Closed Sun evening and Wed; 11 Nov–31 March. **Car park**.

Bustling yet relaxed restaurant in an enchanting location at the foot of Mont Ventoux. It's decorated in bright Provençal colours, and there's a congenial, sunny terrace. The proprietress settles you down with a broad smile and the proprietor prepares fresh, tasty food. Menus €19–43. In summer they do pesto soup and kid stew, and in autumn there's venison steak with truffles, spit-roasted game and stews. The red wines come from the Côte du Ventoux. Free house apéritif.

BONNIEUX 84480

◉ RESTAURANT DE LA GARE

chemin de la Gare (Northwest); it's on the D145 in the direction of Goult.
☎ 04.90.7582.00
Closed Sun evening, Mon and Jan. **Disabled access**.

The old station was turned into an art gallery by the grandmother of the current owner. The huge dining room has an old-fashioned charm and there's a gorgeous terrace overlooking the garden and beyond to a ruined château. The lunch menu, €10, which includes a $^1/_4$-litre of wine, lists *hors d'œuvres* from the buffet and a freshly cooked dish of the day. The cuisine is distinctly Provençal in flavour: good fresh fish, a *bouillabaisse* that you have to order three days in advance, Lubéron lamb and so on. Menus €19–26 or about €23 for a meal *à la carte*. Easy-going welcome.

◉ LE FOURNIL

5 pl. Carnot (Centre).
☎ 04.90.75.83.62
Closed Mon; Tues lunchtime; Mon and Tues Oct–March; 1 Dec–1 Feb.

This establishment, which has a pleasant terrace, stands right in the heart of the village next to the fountain. It's building a solid reputation, so you might need to book. Good traditional cooking: *galette* of pig's trotters, ravioli with a filling of lamb's brains, twice-cooked kid, roast milk-fed lamb, *pot-au-feu* of new vegetables with basil. There's a very decent €16 lunch menu served during the week and others at €22–32.

BORMES-LES-MIMOSAS 83230

♙ ☎ HÔTEL PARADIS**

62 impasse de Castellan (South); it's on the right as you go down from the village.
☎ 04.94.01.32.62 ➡ 04.94.01.32.60
Closed 1 Oct–30 March. **Garden. Car park**.

This peaceful hotel is well off the tourist track. Clean, simple, pleasantly decorated doubles for €42 with shower and €55–66 with with shower/wc or bath. They also have a separate building, which looks onto the wonderful garden (of which the owner is justly proud) – perfect for families or groups. 10% discount on the room rate, out of season and excluding public holiday long weekends.

♙ ☎ ◉ L'HÔTEL DE LA PLAGE**

rond-point de la Bienvenue-La Favière; take the road in the direction of the port, then turn off to La Favière.
☎ 04.94.71.02.74 ➡ 04.94.71.77.22
Closed Oct–March. **TV. Car park**.

Other than a few concessions to fashion and some improved comforts, this place has barely changed since opening in 1960, and it still has the same regular guests – there are games of *pétanque* in the evening after the guests have dined. Rooms €43–49 with shower/wc or €55–61 with bath. Half board, €55–61, is compulsory July–Aug. Good selection of menus at €15–28. The only blots on the landscape are the concrete blocks on the way to the beach. Free apéritif and 10% discount on the room rate out of season and excluding public holiday long weekends

BRIANÇON 05100

♙ ☎ ◉ L'AUBERGE DE L'IMPOSSIBLE**

43 av. de Savoie (Nord).
☎ 04.92.21.02.98 ➡ 04.92.21.13.75
e auberge.impossible@wnadoo.fr
Closed Mon out of season; lunchtimes in winter; Nov.
TV. Car park.

An unpretentious hotel-restaurant with fifteen or so decent rooms. Doubles €29 with basin and €44 with shower/wc – reasonable prices for the area. Simple, nourishing family cooking is served in the restaurant: fish *fondue* and *tartiflette*. Lunch menu €10 and others €14–18. In summer you dine on the terrace. There's a good atmosphere in the evenings, and in the winter they sometimes host *crêpe* parties or karaoke evenings for the residents. They also offer half board, weekly rates and ski packages. 10% discount on the room rate May–June and Sept–Oct.

♙ ◉ L'AUBERGE DU MONT PROREL**

5 rue René Froger (East); it's at the foot of the ski lifts.
☎ 04.92.20.22.88 ➡ 04.92.21.27.76
e aubergemontprorel@worldonline.fr
Closed Nov. **TV. Car park**.

At the lower end of Vauban fortress, this chalet is at the foot of the Prorel ski lift, which leads up to the Serre-Chevalier area, and there's easy access to the town. Rooms are clean and cosy, and about half have a balcony. Doubles €53–66 with shower or bath/wc. Half board costs from €56; they offer weekly rates. The restaurant serves classic regional cooking on menus at €11 (lunch) and €17. Live music on Sunday evenings – great atmosphere. Free house apéritif.

🕍 🛏 HÔTEL EDELWEISS**

32 av. de la République (Centre).
☎ 04.92.21.02.94 ➡ 04.92.21.22.55
Closed Nov. **TV**.

A small hotel, located very near Vauban's magnificent fortress, opposite the cultural centre and the conference centre. The east-facing rooms have a lovely view of the local woods; those facing west overlook the town. It's clean and quiet, though the décor is dull. Doubles €49–53 with bath. 10% discount out of season.

🕍 |●| LE PÉCHÉ GOURMAND

2 route de Gap.
☎ 04.92.21.33.21
Closed Christmas and a week at the end of April.
Disabled access. Car park.

Though it's set on a corner of a huge junction, this restaurant has a shaded terrace well away from the streams of cars and two elegant dining rooms. The excellent menus list goat's cheese ravioli with green pea *purée* and roast guineafowl breast with rosemary *jus* – both quite delicious. There's a respectable selection of cheeses, good desserts and an extensive list of coffees. Weekday lunch menu €12, then others €21–40. Free apéritif.

🕍 |●| LE PIED DE LA GARGOUILLE

64 Grande-Rue; it's in the old town opposite the municipal library.
☎ 04.92.20.12.95
Closed except for Fri–Sun evenings out of season; lunchtimes in season; Oct.

This restaurant centres on an open fire where the host keeps an expert eye on the delicious grilled dishes. The walls are adorned with antique skis and snowshoes. Excellent sweet and savoury *tourtons*; other specialities include mountain dishes and steak grilled over the embers. One menu at €16; *à la carte* around €21. Enthusiastic welcome. Free apéritif or coffee.

🕍 |●| RESTAURANT LE RUSTIQUE

rue du Pont-d'Asfeld (Centre); coming down from the Grande Gargouille take the first left after the fountain and it's 300m further on.
☎ 04.92.21.00.10
Closed Mon out of season;Tues except public holidays; a fortnight end June to July; end Nov–mid-Dec.

Country décor, good quality cooking and a warm welcome. The speciality is fresh trout served with all manner of sauces – try it with apples flambéed in Calvados, leek *coulis*, garlic and cream or Roquefort cheese. The generous salads are good, too, and they do a tasty *fondue savoyarde* with morels. Menus €17–25, and *à la carte* around €26. Slow service, however. Free apéritif.

VACHETTE (LA)   05100 (4KM NE)

🕍 |●| LE NANO

Route d'Italie, Val des Près; it's on the N94, in the direction of Montgenèvre and Italy.
☎ 04.92.21.06.09
Closed Sun and Mon except July–Aug.

The warm, pleasant setting, the quietly efficient service and above all the quality of the cooking make this one of the best places to eat in the area. The fine, classical dishes are skilfully seasoned – *roulade* of rabbit with basil, boned cockerel with spiced sauce – and there are very good desserts. Menus €23–41.Their wine list is expertly chosen with quality vintages. Free coffee.

CHANTEMERLE   05330 (7KM N)

🕍 🛏 |●| LA BOULE DE NEIGE***

Route de Grenoble; it's in the centre of the village.
☎ 04.92.24.00.16 ➡ 04.92.24.00.25
Closed end April–1 July; 1 Sept to mid-Dec. **TV**.

Prices aren't the cheapest, but this is a wonderfully comfortable establishment and you won't want to leave. Doubles with shower/wc or bath at €70–119; half board (compulsory during the school holidays) costs €55–78. The restaurant is very pleasant and the cooking is delicate – fillet of pork *mignon* with endive sauce and rack of lamb with garlic cream sauce. Menus €24–27.The ski-lift for the Serre-Chevalier slopes is 100m away. Free coffee.

SALLE-LÈS-ALPES (LA)   05240 (8KM N)

|●| LA MAROTTE

36 rue de la Guisane; it's in the main street.
☎ 04.92.24.77.23
Closed lunchtimes; Sun; Oct–Nov; May–June.

A really nice restaurant which has been here for years. The boss prepares delicious dishes; there's one menu only at €15, or *à la carte* expect a bill of around €24. Try the vegetable *terrine*, the house speciality. The herring and shallot bread and the apple *tarte Tatin* also deserve a mention. It's best to book.

CAGNES SUR MER 06800

♠ LE VAL DUCHESSE**

11 rue de Paris; it's 50m from the beach.
☎ 04.92.13.40.00 ➡ 04.92.13.40.29
Garden. Swimming pool. TV. Car park.

Set in a quiet street, away from the traffic and the impersonal high-rises down by the sea, this place has a pretty garden planted with palm trees, a swimming pool, a ping-pong table and games for the children. The décor is full of southern colour and you can rent studios from €38 to €56. Apartments sleeping four, with bathrooms and south-facing terraces, go for €53–79. Prices go down if you stay a week or more. Warm reception.

♠ LE MAS D'AZUR

42 av. de Nice, Cros-de-Cagnes.
☎ 04.93.20.19.19
Garden. TV. Car park.

At first sight, this hotel, set on the edge of the main road, doesn't look very promising. But inside you travel back in time about 25 years. It's a charming old Provençal house with a courtyard, and you're welcomed warmly by the kindly owners. On top of that, it's just three minutes' walk from the beach. Fifteen quiet rooms and an appealing garden. Doubles with shower/wc €47–51.

|O| LE RENOIR

10 rue J.-R.-Giacosa; it's opposite les Halles.
☎ 04.93.22.59.58
Closed Sun and Thurs evenings; Mon; 15 Dec–15 Jan; July.

The outside of the restaurant, across from the covered market, looks dreary, but the sumptuous first-floor dining room is cheerily decorated in shades of yellow. The food is equally appealing: rabbit with *tapenade*, *sanguins* (mushrooms that grow in pine woods) cooked with red peppers, *daube* with ceps and *fricassée* of fish. The *patronne*, who is wonderfully kind, will help you choose. Menus €13 and €22.

|O| LA TABLE D'YVES

85 Montée de la Bourgade, Vieux Cagnes
☎ 04.93.20.33.33
Closed Tues and Thurs lunchtimes; Wed; the Feb and All Saints' school holidays.

Yves Merville has twenty years of experience in the finest kitchens behind him, and today, although he's working in a pocket-sized restaurant, he and his wife run it with professionalism and charm. The décor – blue and ochre walls with bleached beams – is welcoming. Two menus only, at €21 and €26. Dishes change frequently, allowing the chef to give full flight to his imagination: *cappuccino* of little crabs, chicken risotto with curry, lamb with Provençal courgettes, bread and butter pudding with pan-fried fruit.

CANNES 06400

♠ HÔTEL CHANTECLAIR

12 rue Forville; it's near the Palais des Festivals and the Midi beach.
☎ and ➡ 04.93.39.68.88
Closed mid-Nov to around 21 Dec.

Though it's ideally located (100m from the liveliest part of town), this hotel is nonetheless perfectly quiet. Functional rooms with white walls and simple pine furniture cost €33–40 – though sometimes they're not as clean as a real stickler might hope. There's a charming patio where you can have breakfast. You'll get a warm welcome from the chatty host, who will explain where you can park for free in the town.

♠ HÔTEL MOLIÈRE**

5–7 rue Molière (East); it's 100m from La Croisette.
☎ 04.93.38.16.16 ➡ 04.93.68.29.57
Closed 15 Nov–25 Dec. **Disabled access. Garden. TV.**

This hotel is housed in two adjoining buildings; one of them nineteenth-century, with a pretty façade, and the other modern. Each is furnished in the appropriate style. Lovely rooms with shower or bath €69–107. Although the hotel is very close to the town centre, the location is quiet and there is a large garden in which to enjoy breakfast. Friendly welcome. 10% discount.

♠ HÔTEL DE FRANCE***

85 rue d'Antibes (Centre).
☎ 04.93.06.54.54 ➡ 04.93.68.53.43
✉ infos@h-de-France.com
Closed 22 Nov–26 Dec. **TV. Lock-up car park.**

This place has been completely refurbished without losing its Art Deco style. It's in the busiest part of town, right on the main thoroughfare, and has thirty rooms with modern facilities – air conditioning, safe, hairdrier and the rest – for €71–102. Rooms 501–508 have a view of the sea. 10% discount Sept–July excluding 31 Dec.

♠ LE SPLENDID***

4–6 rue Félix Faure.

☎ 04.97.06.22.22 ➡ 04.93.99.55.02
Disabled access. TV.

It's not a palace such as you find on La Croisette but it's pretty close. Behind the majestic turn-of-the-century façade, there's one of the town's loveliest hotels, wonderfully run by Annick Cagnat and her family. The beautiful rooms have antique furniture and all sorts of little extras to make your stay feel really luxurious. The prices – €98–137 for a double – are fair. Free breakfast.

☆ ❙●❙ LE JARDIN

15 av. Isola.
☎ 04.93.38.17.85
Closed Sun evening and Mon.

This is one of the most popular restaurants in town among locals. It's a simple little place, far from the tourist areas and the boisterous crowds of the Croisette. The district is a little depressing, as is the bar, where a TV flickers in the corner. But walk through it to reach a hidden garden where you can dine in peace on simple, tasty food: *daube provençale*, grilled sole, breast of duck with green peppercorns or sardines, bass or sea bream grilled over embers. Prices are gratifyingly low – menus €11–17 – and the welcome is pleasant. Free apéritif.

☆ ❙●❙ LE COMPTOIR DES VINS

13 bd. de la République (Centre).
☎ 04.93.68.13.26
Closed Mon–Tues evenings; Wed; Sun; Feb.

You enter via the cellar, selecting your wine first, then choose food to suit. It took the owner some time to get the local Cannois used to the idea of a bistro-cellar, but he succeeded. It's busy and buzzy, especially in the evening. Good, wholesome dishes: sausage with pistachios, *blanquette* of veal, a huge range of sandwiches and some Savoyard specialities. Weekday lunch menu €13, €22 in the evening or €18 *à la carte*. Wine, by the glass or the bottle, is good value. Free house apéritif.

❙●❙ RESTAURANT AUX BONS ENFANTS

80 rue Meynadier (Centre); it's opposite Forville market.
Closed Sat evening except in season; Sun; Aug and New Year.

There's no telephone, so the regulars pop in during the morning to reserve a table while the staff are still peeling the vegetables bought in the Forville market. Home cooking and regional dishes: goat's cheese *terrine* with tomato *confit*, sole *meunière*, aubergine

and sardine fritters, *aïoli*, tarts and home-made iced *nougat*. One menu at €14. Good-natured greeting and service.

☆ ❙●❙ LE BOUCHON D'OBJECTIF

10 rue Constantine (East).
☎ 04.93.99.21.76
Closed Sun evening and Mon out of season except when there are conferences.

Each month this friendly restaurant stages an exhibition of a different photographer's work. The simple, original food includes snails with dill in flaky pastry, rabbit *terrine* with grapes and pistachios and suckling pig with honey. Menus €14 and €22. There's a pretty terrace facing onto a modern pedestrianized area. Free apéritif.

☆ ❙●❙ RESTAURANT AU BEC FIN

12 rue du 24-Août (Centre); it's between the train station and the rue d'Antibes.
☎ 04.93.38.35.86
Closed Sun; the first week in July; the first fortnight in Nov. **Disabled access**.

This restaurant gets very full, so don't arrive too late. The menus, €16 and €19, offer a staggering choice with nearly twenty starters and almost as many mains. Mostly local cuisine: *daube provençale* (a slowly braised beef stew), vegetable *soupe au pistou*, scorpion fish *à la pêcheur*. Good daily specials, too – you won't even notice the bland décor. Free apéritif.

☆ ❙●❙ CÔTÉ JARDIN

12 av. Saint-Louis (Northwest); it's behind the Palais de Justice.
☎ 04.93.39.98.38
Closed Sun and Mon; Feb.

A very good restaurant outside the touristy part of Cannes, beyond the railway line in a discreet cul-de-sac. It's a charming Provençal villa in a lovely garden. The cooking is wonderfully fragrant: ginger soup, chicken with coconut, duck *confit* topped with celeriac purée and orange zest, caramel *croustillant*, pan-fried apples with sesame seeds. Menus €19 (lunch) and €31. Free apéritif.

☆ ❙●❙ RESTAURANT LOU SOULEOU

16 bd. Jean-Hibert (Southwest); it's on the road to Mandelieu.
☎ 04.93.39.85.55
Closed Mon out of season; Mon–Wed lunchtimes in summer; Nov.

This restaurant is behind the old harbour in a district where few tourists venture. The menus are excellent value for money, listing dishes such as *blanquette* of monkfish with mussels, fillet of sea bass with watercress and *bourride du pêcheur*, a fish soup full of monkfish, lobster, mussels, garlic *croûtons* and *rouille*. Dishes of the day €19 and menus from €22. Sip a Kir as you admire the view of the Estérel hills. Free apéritif.

GOLFE-JUAN 06220 (4KM NE)

🛉 🏠 HÔTEL CALIFORNIA*

222 av. de la Liberté (East); it's on the N7, 800m from the station, close to the seashore.
☎ 04.93.63.78.63
Closed 1 Nov. **TV**. **Car park**.

This 1930s house, set back from the main road, has been converted into a hotel with pretty double rooms available for €23–30 in low season and €38–43 in high season. Studio apartments also available. 10% discount except July–Aug.

🏠 🍽 LE PALM-HÔTEL

17 av. de la Palmeraie.
☎ 04.93.63.72.24 ➡ 04.93.63.18.45
Restaurant closed 15 Oct–1 March. **Car park**.

Unfortunately, the N7 passes close by (a definite minus), but this beautiful old house has lots of charm and the owners have a real sense of hospitality. Spruce rooms which have been done up in style cost €58–73 each. There's a terrace where you can eat reliable local dishes. Menus €15 and €23, and half board from €44. Free apéritif.

VALLAURIS 06220 (8KM NE)

🛉 🍽 LE MANUSCRIT

224 chemin Lintier (Centre); it's in the centre of town off the bd. du Tapis-Vert.
☎ 04.93.64.56.56
Closed Mon and Sun evening in season; Mon and Tues out of season; 15 Nov to early Dec.

The interior of this fine stone building, which used to be a perfume factory, is exceptional, and the food is pretty good too. You can eat in the dining room (where there's a wonderful display of prints and canvases), in the conservatory (full of subtropical flowers) or on the terrace beneath the hundred-year-old magnolia tree. The weekday lunch menu, €16, and others at €21–28, all offer a wide range of dishes: seafood *terrine*, pan-fried *andouillette* in champagne, fish stew, veal sweetbreads and other such delights. Affordable wines. Free apéritif.

VALBONNE 06560 (11KM N)

🛉 🍽 LA FONTAINE AUX VINS

3 rue Grande; it's in the old down.
☎ 04.93.12.93.20
Closed Wed except in season.

Predominantly a wine bar, this place also serves "Provençal tapas" – little dishes of tasty morsels – along with original sandwiches and attentively prepared dishes. Around €12 *à la carte*. Wines are carefully selected and affordable, and they also offer a good pale ale. If you want to buy some of the products they serve, you can get them at *Olivier and Co* next door. Free coffee.

🍽 L'AUBERGE FLEURIE

1016 route de Cannes (South); it's on the right, 1km before you get to Valbonne, coming from Cannes.
☎ 04.93.12.02.80
Closed Sun evening; Mon July–Aug; Dec. **Disabled access**.

A very good restaurant in a pretty, wisteria-covered building with huge mirrors in the dining rooms. Inventive, sunny dishes are made from the best ingredients with the simplest flavours: *croustillant* of fish with *ratatouille*, rolled quail with ceps and girolles, John Dory with salt and *crème brûlée*. Menus €20–25. Lots of regular patrons and service with a smile.

CARPENTRAS 84200

🛉 🏠 HÔTEL LE FIACRE**

153 rue Vigne (Centre).
☎ 04.90.63.03.15 ➡ 04.90.60.49.73
TV. **Pay car park**.

This eighteenth-century convent, located in a quiet street in the centre of town, was converted into a town house and then, some forty years ago, into a hotel. You go up a monumental staircase to the rooms, which are all individually decorated and look out onto a delightful courtyard. €44 for a double with shower/wc and €59 with bath. Breakfast €6. 10% discount for two nights Sept–June.

MONTEUX 84170 (5KM SW)

🛉 🏠 🍽 LE SELECT HÔTEL***

24 bd. de Carpentras.
☎ 04.90.66.27.91 ➡ 04.90.66.33.05
Closed Sat and Sun evening out of season; 15 Dec–8 Jan. **Swimming pool**. **TV**. **Car park**.

You'll get a really friendly welcome from the Dutch couple who own this characterful old famhouse. Doubles with bath €52. The simple, original food is fine, light and of excellent quality – menus €14–22. In summer, eat on the terrace in the shade of the plane trees beside the swimming pool. Try the delicious locally grown wines. Free apéritif.

PERNES-LES-FONTAINES 84210 (5.5KM S)

⅍ |●| DAME L'OIE

56 rue Troubadour; it's on the D938.
☎ 04.90.61.62.43

There's a fountain in the middle of the dining room, where the décor is English country style. Kindly welcome and service. The cuisine is typically southern – simple but nicely prepared, with stunning flavours. Try salad Landaise with *foie gras*, sardines, roast lamb with Provençal herbs or grilled duck breast with sweet-and-sour sauce. It's good value, with a weekday lunch menu €11 and others €18–23. Dishes change regularly with seasonal produce. Good local wines. Free apéritif or coffee.

CASSIS 13260

⅍ ☋ |●| LE CLOS DES ARÔMES**

10 rue Paul-Mouton; it's a two-minute walk from the town centre.
☎ 04.42.01.71.84 ➡ 04.42.01.31.76
Closed Mon–Wed lunchtimes except public holidays; 10 Nov–10 March. **Car park**.

An elegant restaurant, just ouside the centre of town, that looks like a Provençal dolls' house. Enjoy sophisticated dishes in the large, shady, flower-filled courtyard. Menus €19 and €26. Specialities include beef *daube à l'ancienne*, fish *pot-au-feu*, baked sea bream flambéed with Pastis, stuffed sardines and *bouillabaisse*. There are fourteen peaceful rooms; doubles €59 with shower/wc and €72 with bath. Free apéritif.

☋ |●| LE JARDIN D'EMILE

plage du Bestouan.
☎ 04.42.01.80.55 **e** provence@lejardindemile.fr
Closed a fortnight in early Jan and a fortnight at the end of Nov. **Garden**. **TV**. **Car park**.

A charming, enjoyable place with a great view. Seven ravishing rooms – including a honeymoon suite and two attic rooms – go for €61–84 with shower/wc or €69–99 with bath. The chic but relaxed restaurant serves creative Mediterranean cooking: *pieds et paquets* (lamb tripe and trotters), joint of beef tied with string, *façon Ludovick Bal* with rosemary mash, flaked fresh cod with potatoes and gar-

lic. There's a weekday lunch menu at €27 and others all the way up to the €45 *menu découverte*. Dine in the garden if at all possible, under ancient pines, olives, figs and cypresses.

CASTELLANE 04120

☋ |●| MA PETITE AUBERGE

pl. Centrale (Centre); at the foot of Notre-Dame-du-Roc.
☎ 04.92.83.62.06 ➡ 04.92.83.68.49
Closed Wed out of season. **Garden**. **TV**. **Car park**.

A old-style hotel which has been sensitively renovated. Comfortable, appealing doubles for €40–52 with shower/wc or bath. Traditional, unfussy food: starling *pâté*, simply grilled red mullet, lamb chops with herbs, a splendid *crème caramel*. There's a veranda and a garden with huge, ancient, shady lime trees. Menus €14–30.

GARDE (LA) 04120 (3KM SE)

⅍ ☋ |●| AUBERGE DU TEILLON**

Route Napoléon; it's on the N85 towards Grasse.
☎ 04.92.83.60.88 ➡ 04.92.83.74.08
Closed Mon except July–Aug; 15 Dec–15 March. **TV**.

People come here from all along the coast at the weekend. You feel cocooned in the rustic little dining room, where chef Yves Lépine uses Provençal ingredients to produce flavoursome dishes on menus at €17–37: snails in *brioche* with vermouth and *foie gras*, smoked lamb, veal kidneys with morels, roast pigeon with ceps, rack of lamb *à la provençale*. Prolong the pleasure by staying the night; doubles cost €30 with basin, €35 with shower and €44 with shower/wc. Half board at €48 is compulsory July–Aug. Rooms facing the main road can be noisy, so ask for ones at the back if you want a lie-in. 10% discount on the room rate.

ROUGON 04120 (17KM SW)

⅍ ☋ |●| AUBERGE DU POINT-SUBLIME**

How to get there: it's on the D952 at the entrance to the Verdon Gorges.
☎ 04.92.83.60.35 ➡ 04.92.83.74.31
e point.sublime@wanadoo.fr
Closed Wed except July–Aug; 15 Oct–30 March. **TV**.
Car park.

There are two small dining rooms here, one non-smoking. Whichever you choose, there is quite a treat in store: checked tablecloths, tiled floors, green plants and photographs of the Verdon around the rooms. *Formule* with dish of the day €18, menus €21–33. Fresh local dishes flavoured countryside herbs: hot goat's cheese salad, rabbit *caillette*, *civet* of lamb and regional dishes like trout and scrambled eggs with truffles. The desserts alone are worth a visit – particularly the fig *crème brûlée* – and there are some wonderful local apéritifs flavoured with oranges, walnuts, honey, blackberry and herbs. Doubles, at €40 with shower and €45 with shower/wc or bath, are blissfully peaceful. Half board, €45, is compulsory in summer, and you'll need to reserve during July and August. 10% discount on the room rate except weekends and school holidays.

PALUD-SUR-VERDON (LA) 04120 (25KM SW)

♠ |●| HÔTEL-RESTAURANT LE PROVENCE**

route La Maline; take the D23, it's 50m from the village.
☎ 04.92.77.38.88 ➡ 04.92.77.31.05
🖂 hotelleprovence@aol.com
Closed Nov to Palm Sunday. **Disabled access**. **TV**. **Car park**.

This hotel has wide views of the route des Crêtes. Doubles with shower/wc €38–55, or €42–56 with bath; half board costs €38–53 per person. Menus €15–26. Specialities include toasted goat's cheese salad, duck with honey, cockerel with shrimps, rabbit *à la provençale*, salmon with sorrel and lamb tripe and trotters. There's a relaxing lounge, or you can sip a cool drink on the terrace and savour the peace and quiet. Babysitting service.

⚘ ♠ HÔTEL DES GORGES DU VERDON***

How to get there: take the D952, the road north of the gorges.
☎ 04.92.77.38.26 ➡ 04.92.77.35.00
Closed 28 Oct–30 March. **Swimming pool**. **TV**. **Car park**.

This hotel is in the heart of the Verdon Gorges, on a hillside facing the village and the surrounding countryside. The spectacular scenery helps you forget the hotel's rather brutal architecture. The rooms are similarly modern, but they're well-equipped, clean and comfortable and decorated in Provençal style. Doubles with shower/wc or bath €69–99. They serve very decent food, mostly traditional Provençal dishes: *anchoïade*, artichokes *en barigoule* (stuffed with mushrooms and ham), lamb chops with tarragon, fillet of salmon with olive oil and savoury, scrambled eggs with truffles. Menus from €21. Half board, compulsory in season and at weekends, costs €69–99. Free apéritif.

CAVAILLON 84300

♠ HÔTEL BEL-AIR

62 rue Bel-Air (Centre).
☎ 04.90.78.11.75

An archetypal hotel for travellers on a budget who like an old-fashioned atmosphere and who value friendliness and good company more than comfort. The seven pleasant rooms are simply decorated. Doubles with basin/wc €32, or €35 with shower/wc. Each room has a bowl of sweets and an information pack about Cavaillon and its environs. Breakfast, with fresh fruit and home-made jam, is served at a big communal table for €6. They prefer to be paid by cheque, travellers' cheques or in cash.

♠ HÔTEL DU PARC**

183 pl. François-Tourel (West); it's near the tourist office.
☎ 04.90.71.57.78 ➡ 04.90.76.10.35
🖂 hotel-du-parc.fr
TV. **Pay car park**.

A huge old house opposite the Roman arch. Good hospitality and family atmosphere. The rooms are classically decorated and fit in well with the architecture. If you choose one facing the park at the side of the hotel you'll be awoken by birdsong. Doubles €44 with shower/wc and €47 with bath. Breakfast €6.

⚘|●| LA CUISINE DU MARCHÉ

pl. Gambetta (Centre).
☎ 04.90.71.56.00
Closed Tues evening and Wed.

It's quite a job to find this place: it's on a square that looks like a roundabout, and you have to look up to see the sign at first-floor level. But climb the stairs and you'll find an attractive, unfussy dining room with a view over the main square. Chef Olivier Mahieu prepares excellent fresh dishes with a strong southern French accent: marinaded salad fillets, cod with olive paste crust, rack of lamb, duck breast with *Marchand de Vin* sauce and lamb tripe and trotters *à la provençale*. Weekday lunch menu €12, then others €16–32. Free apéritif.

CHAPELLE-EN-VALGAUDEMAR (LA) 05800

⚘ ♠ |●| HÔTEL-RESTAURANT DU MONT-OLAN**

☎ 04.92.55.23.03 ➡ 04.92.55.34.58
Closed 15 Sept–1 April. **TV**. **Car park**.

Chalet-style hotel where all the rooms look

out towards the soaring peaks that dominate the village. Monsieur and Mme Voltan's large dining room has a panoramic view of the fast-flowing Navette river; you'll consume huge quantities of ravioli with honey, potato pie and sturdy platters of robust food to build up your strength for an assault on the mountains. Menus €11–22. Doubles €39–46 with shower/wc. Free coffee.

CHÂTEAU-ARNOUX   04160

|●| L'OUSTAOU DE LA FOUN

How to get there: it's 1.5km north on the N85.
☎ 04.92.62.65.30
Closed Sun evening and Mon, a week at the end of Nov.

This restaurant, which occupies a Provençal hacienda, manages to be chic yet relaxed. The chef, who comes from a family of farmers and *charcutiers*, really knows his stuff, and he organizes cookery courses. His dishes balance fine ingredients and create delightful flavour combinations: braised and pan-fried calf's head served on potatoes and goat's cheese, sardine and herb fritters, rabbit and artichoke casserole with rosemary and juniper, pigeon *croustillé* with ceps, upside-down lamb tart with herbs and fresh goat's cheese. If you have any room for dessert, try the *crème brûlée* with thyme or the strawberry salad with liquorice ice-cream. The side dishes are unusual while remaining simple. Weekday lunch menu €15 and others €18–32.

|●| AU GOÛT DU JOUR

It's on the N85, opposite the château.
☎ 04.92.64.48.48 ✉ info@bonneetape.com
Closed Mon and Tues lunchtime out of season; 3 Jan–12 Feb; 26 Nov–12 Dec.

This relaxed bistro is the cheaper sibling of the upmarket *Bonne Étape* next door. The sunny décor creates an elegant, refined atmosphere, but the food is very reasonably priced: menus €15 and €23. The main courses, displayed on a slate, change with the seasons and what's freshest in the market. Try mussel and saffron soup, fresh anchovies marinated in fennel, duck leg with olives or the delicious *tarte alsacienne* with strawberries.

CHAUFFAYER   05800

♠ |●| LE BERCAIL**

It's on the N85, the route de Napoléon, on the right on the road to Gap.
☎ 04.92.55.22.21 ➡ 04.92.55.31.55
Closed Sun evening and Nov.

This hotel-restaurant offers good value for money, with prettily decorated, comfortable rooms – doubles €30–46 with shower/wc or bath. The large dining room has a lovely Provençal feel and there's a shaded terrace filled with glorious geraniums. The cuisine is regional and classic, with menus at €12–30; pan-fried *noisette* of lamb, trout *meunière* and raviolis are the specialities.

🛤 ♠ |●| LE CHÂTEAU DES HERBEYS***

It's on the N85, the route de Napoléon.
☎ 04.92.55.26.83
Closed Tues except in school holidays; Nov–March.
Garden. Swimming pool. TV. Car park.

Looking down the route that Napoleon took on his return from Elba, this noble and beautiful residence surrounded by substantial grounds. The rooms are high-ceilinged and luxurious, with parquet floors, plush and tasteful fabrics and splendid bathrooms. The "Roy" room is a truly royal suite with a canopied bed, sitting room and Jacuzzi; it's also the most expensive. Doubles with bath €69–114. In the park there is a tennis court and a swimming pool. The restaurant offers *foie gras* and goose. Menus €19–36. Half board from €61. Free coffee or *digestif*.

COARAZE   06390

🛤 ♠ |●| LE RELAIS DE LA FEUILLERAIE

3037 route du Soleil.
☎ 04.93.79.39.90 ➡ 04.93.79.39.95
Car park.

This isn't in Coaraze itself – it's on the way up, about 2.5km before you get there. The owner used to live in Paris but he was wearied by the relentless pace of life so he settled down south. His wife does the cooking and creates good, inventive dishes which are finely prepared and tasty. Menus from €14. The rooms are pretty and painted in different colours – some have a terrace offering a restful view. Doubles €55.

COLLOBRIÈRES   83610

🛤 |●| HÔTEL-RESTAURANT DES MAURES

19 bd Lazare-Carnot
☎ 04.94.48.07.10.

A genuine family restaurant that's popular

with the locals – everyone crowds in to watch the football on weekday evenings. The rooms cost €18 with shower/wc and are simple, but at that price you can't argue. Nicely cooked Provençal cuisine served in gargantuan portions – the mushroom omelette spills ceps all over the plate and the chestnut ice-cream is a challenge to finish. There's a charming terrace by the river. Free coffee after our meal.

🕏 |●| LA PETITE FONTAINE

pl. de la République.
☎ 04.94.48.00.12
Closed Mon; the Feb school holidays; 15–30 Sept.

One of the best places for miles around, in a peaceful village in the Maures mountains. This rustic restaurant is decorated with old farming implements and the cooking is delicious: *fricassée* of chicken with garlic, rabbit in white wine, beef *daube à la provençale*, duck breast with ceps. Weekday menu €21 and a dinner version at €25. They serve wine from the local co-operative by the glass. Free *digestif*.

COMPS-SUR-ARTUBY   83840

🕏 🏠 |●| GRAND HÔTEL BAIN**

How to get there: it's between Draguignan and Castellane.
☎ 04.94.76.90.06 ➡ 04.94.76.92.24
✉ jmbain@wanadoo.fr
Closed 12 Nov–26 Dec. **TV**. **Car park**.

The Bain family has owned this hotel since 1737. Today it's frequented by local hunters, who relish the hearty local dishes: *pâté* studded with local truffles, omelettes served with truffles, trout with basil in pastry, rabbit with tomato and basil, *daube à la provençale*, roast rack of lamb and goat's cheese. Menus €13–30. Nice rooms cost €43–46 with shower/wc or with bath. Free coffee.

CORRENS   83570

🏠 |●| AUBERGE LE VAL D'ARGENS

place de l'Arenier.
☎ 04.94.59.57.02 ➡ 04.94.59.54.11

A really nice inn under shady plane trees with a truly charming terrace on the bank of the Argens. The cuisine has no pretentions to being "grand" but it's good enough; menus €15–20. There are three very pleasant rooms with shower/wc for €48–54. The owner loves Dubout posters and all manner of

brightly coloured souvenirs are scattered everywhere. From 15 April to 15 Nov, you can hire canoes or kayaks – €20–34 for a half-day or €31–46 for the whole day.

DIGNE-LES-BAINS   04000

🕏 🏠 |●| HÔTEL DU PETIT SAINT-JEAN*

14 cours des Arès (Centre); it's on the corner of pl. Charles-de-Gaulle.
☎ 04.92.31.30.04 ➡ 04.92.36.05.80
Closed 24 Dec–6 Jan. **Pay garage**.

Cosy, small and welcoming hotel with a nostalgic feel. Double rooms from €23 with basin to €38 with shower/wc. The cheerful host serves decent food in the first-floor restaurant: rabbit with onions, stew of suckling pig, *aïoli*, *bœuf en daubes*, *blanquette* of veal. Menus €9–21. Free coffee.

🕏 🏠 |●| L'ORIGAN

6 rue Pied-de-Ville (Centre); in the pedestrianised area.
☎ 04.92.31.62.13 ✉ rest-origan@wanadoo.fr
Closed Sun; Christmas week; the Feb school holidays.

A restaurant in the heart of the old quarter of the spa town. Chef Philippe Cochet prepares delicious food such as John Dory fillets with basil, a cold *aïoli* of cod and vegetables, *pieds et paquets* (lamb tripe and trotters), stuffed veal fillet and red mullet with chives. Menus €18–33. They have some simple rooms for €15 with basin and €21 with shower. Free house apéritif and 10% dicount on the room rate.

🕏 🏠 |●| HÔTEL DU GRAND PARIS****

19 bd. Thiers.
☎ 04.92.31.11.15 ➡ 04.32.32.82
✉ GrandParis@wanadoo.fr
Closed Sun evening and Mon out of season; 1 Dec–1 March. **TV**. **Car park**.

Stylish hotel that has been converted from a seventeenth-century convent. The welcome is slightly formal but the place oozes discreet charm. The chef prepares classic dishes using good ingredients: cod *brandade* with truffles, *émincé* of lamb with Châteauneuf du Pape vinegar, sea bream with meat juice, hot lime soufflé. Menus €23–64 or around €41 *à la carte*. Lovely, comfortable double rooms for €70. Breakfast €10. Free apéritif.

🕏 🏠 |●| HÔTEL VILLA GAÏA***

Route de Nice; it's 4km from the centre on the Castellane road.
☎ 04.92.31.21.60 ➡ 04.92.31.20.12

Closed Nov–March. **Disabled access**. **Car park**.

This quiet hotel, an impressive building set in shady, green grounds, was converted from an old convalescent home and still keeps to some of the old rules. Dinner is served at the same time every night, and there's a single menu (€21) featuring superb regional dishes: lamb with lemon, pesto soup and pear tart with goat's cheese. They use vegetables from the garden, local cheeses and meat and fish direct from the market. You dine on the terrace, in the library or the salon. Excellent breakfast for €8. Rooms €79; half board, which is compulsory July–Aug, costs €68. Free apéritif.

DRAGUIGNAN 83300

🔥 |●| RESTAURANT LE BARON

42 Grand-Rue (Centre).
☎ 04.94.67.31.76
Closed Mon except public holidays and for groups.

Though the white stone frontage of this building looks rather grand, inside it feels more like a doctor's surgery than a restaurant. The food is good, however, and the classics from the Mediterranean and Franche-Comté are listed on the menus €11–23: monkfish *bourride* (stew), cockerel in *vin jaune* or with morels. Free house apéritif, coffee or *digestif*.

|●| LE DOMINO

28 av. Carnot (Centre); it's on the main street.
☎ 04.94.67.15.33
Closed Sun; Mon; Sat lunchtime; 1–17Nov.

This building has a lot of character and so does the stylish Tex-Mex restaurant inside. Kindly welcome and attentive service. À la carte you'll pay around €20–23 per person for salads, spiced-up meat dishes and Mexican specialities such as chicken and beef *fajitas* and spare ribs. You can dine on the veranda or out under the palm trees.

EMBRUN 05200

🔥 🏠 |●| HÔTEL DE LA MAIRIE**

pl. de la Mairie or pl. Barthelon (Centre).
☎ 04.92.43.20.65 ➡ 04.92.43.47.02
Closed Sun evening and Mon in winter; a fortnight in mid-May; Oct–Nov. **Disabled access**. **TV**.

This hotel is a model of its type, with a convivial brasserie, high-quality food and competent, charming staff. It's a favourite with locals for an evening drink or Sunday lunch. Specialities include ravioli with morel sauce,

sautéed prawns *à la provençale* and an excellent duck *confit*. Menus €15–21. Best to book. Clean, bright rooms are €46–49 for a double – choose one which looks out onto the square. Free coffee.

🔥 🏠 |●| HÔTEL NOTRE-DAME**

av. Général-Nicolas – route de Chalvet; coming from Guillestre, turn right before the post office then right again.
☎ 04.92.43.08.36 ➡ 04.92.43.58.41
Closed Sun evening and Mon except for school holidays; Jan. **Garden**. **TV**. **Car park**.

Just five minutes' walk from the centre of town, this family hotel is a peaceful haven set at the far end of a large garden. After receiving a warm welcome you will be shown to extremely clean rooms with excellent beds. Doubles with shower/wc €46. Good quality cuisine using only local produce – duck breast, trout, lamb tripe and trotters – is served on menus at €18–26. Half board, compulsory in summer, costs €45. Free coffee.

|●| RESTAURANT PASCAL

Hameau de Caléyère.
☎ 04.92.43.00.69
Closed Sept.

It's not the place for a romantic tête-à-tête, but the family atmosphere is convivial and infectious – you'll leave in a good mood. The *patronne* greets all her customers by shaking their hand. There's only one menu, at €11, and it's substantial. The vegetables, eggs and meats all come from local farms. The local *digestif* is called *vipérine* – it bites like a snake.

SAINT-ANDRÉ-D'EMBRUN 05200 (6KM NE)

|●| RESTAURANT LA GRANDE FERME

Les Rauffes; it's on the Crévoux road.
☎ 04.92.43.09.99 ✉ lagrandeferme@wanadoo.fr
Closed evenings; Wed; Oct to mid-Dec.

Owners Nicole and Thierry will welcome you into a magnificent vaulted dining room that they restored themselves. This restaurant has a well-deserved reputation in the region and it serves excellent traditional cuisine – try the baked eggs with Queyras blue cheese and the pear *gratin* with brandy from the Hautes-Alpes. Menus €12 and 18. Good selection of wines. *Gîtes* available for rent.

SAINT-SAUVEUR 05200 (10KM S)

|●| RESTAURANT LES MANINS

Hameau des Manins; take the road to Les Orres and it's

sign-posted off to the left – don't take the ones for St-Sauveur.
☎ 04.92.43.09.27
Open July to mid-Sept noon–9pm; reservations only the rest of the year.

Fantastic restaurant with breathtaking views from the terrace looking down at Lac de Serre-Ponçon and Embrun. Architect Eric Boissel built this elegant wooden structure with his own hands, and designed all the furniture. The dishes are devised by Nicole, who's an attentive hostess. Try *grand mézé*, a complete Middle Eastern meal with individual dishes of red peppers, *tzatziki*, *hummus*, *köfte*, feta cheese, fresh onions, *tapenade* and the like. They also do mixed salads, substantial pizzas and good *crêpes*, and there's a splendid crumble for dessert. Pizzas are €9; expect to pay €19 *à la carte*.

CRÉVOUX   05200 (15KM E)

🏠 |●| L'AUBERGE

Le Chef-lieu; it's at the top of the village opposite the teleski.
☎ 04.92.43.18.18
Closed Oct. **Car park**.

An excellent spot at the foot of the ski runs run by a friendly, welcoming local couple. The clean rooms are freshly decorated and warm, though they're not all huge; €30 per person half board. The dining room is very spacious and the dishes are typical of the area: egg fondue with blue-cheese cream sauce, cheese turonvers, trout with creamed peppers, steak with ceps. Menus €11–18. If you want information about the walking trails, don't hesitate to ask.

ENTRECASTEAUX   83570

🎿🏠|●| LA FOURCHETTE

Le Courtil (Centre); it's next to the church.
☎ 04.94.04.42.78 **e** pierrelenicolas@lemel.fr
Closed Sun evening; Mon; Jan–Feb.

In the shadow of the famous château, this place attracts gourmet travellers who enjoy delicious food while admiring the wonderful view from the terrace. Chef Pierre Nicolas runs the kitchens while his American wife greets you. Simple, quality cooking and honest prices: €15 for the two-course lunch menu (weekdays), and a range of others up to €23. Dishes include *foie gras* cannelloni and sautéed king scallops with truffles. Free coffee.

ÈZE   06360

🎿🏠|●| HERMITAGE DU COL D'ÈZE**

Grande Corniche (North); from Èze, take the D46 and then the Grande Corniche; it's 500m on the left.
☎ 04.93.41.00.68 **F→** 04.93.41.24.05
Restaurant closed Mon; Thurs and Fri lunchtimes; 15 Oct–1 Feb. **Garden. Swimming pool. TV. Car park**.

Monsieur and Mme Bérardi's hotel is a place in which to relax in peace and quiet. The swimming pool will ease your aching limbs after a mountain walk – the location is at the start of a lot of trails. There is a splendid view of the southern Alps and the cooler air at this altitude provides relief from the heat of the coast. Doubles €25–47 with shower/wc or bath. The chef personalizes his recipes, working with only fresh produce and, in some seasons, fruit and vegetables from the garden. Menus from €15. Half board from €35 per person. Free coffee.

🏠|●| AUBERGE DES DEUX CORNICHES**

It's 1km along the D46 in the direction of Col d'Èze.
☎ 04.93.41.19.54 **F→** 04.92.10.86.26
Closed Thurs lunchtime and Nov to Easter. **TV. Car park**.

This hotel is in a quiet spot above the village of Èze, high enough up for you to get a view of the sea from your room. It's often full in summer. Charming welcome from the owner. Pleasant double rooms, some with balcony, €53. Carefully prepared food.

FAYENCE   83440

🎿🏠 HÔTEL LA SOUSTO

4 rue du Paty.
☎ 04.94.76.02.16 **e** guy.corteccia@wanadoo.fr
Closed the All Saints' holidays.

You get the best of Provence in this attractive little hotel in the centre of an old village above the valley. The simply furnished rooms have a hotplate, fridge and basin; some also have a shower. Each room has personality – number 5 has a sunny little terrace overlooking the valley. Doubles with shower/wc €41. 10% discount Sept–June.

FONTVIEILLE   13990

🎿🏠 HÔTEL LE DAUDET***

7 av. de Montmajour; it's on the way out of the village on the road to Arles.
☎ 04.90.54.76.06 **F→** 04.90.54.76.95

Closed Oct–March. **Swimming pool. Car park**.

This new hotel is named after the writer Alphonse Daudet, whose mill is nearby. Built around a patio, it has about fourteen straightforward rooms with their own terrace. There's a swimming pool among the pine trees. Doubles €50–58 with shower or bath. Free apéritif or coffee.

⅍ |●| LA CUISINE AU PLANET

144 Grand Rue; it's in the old village.
☎ 04.90.54.63.97
Closed Mon, Tues lunchtime out of season; Mon and Tues lunchtimes in season; a fortnight in Feb; a fortnight in Nov.

This charming, creeper-covered restaurant is run by a couple who are crazy about the area and prepare local dishes with a light touch all their own. Menus €23–29 – dishes such as stuffed fresh anchovies and swordfish with olive oil. Impressive wine list. Free coffee.

FORCALQUIER   04300

☗ AUBERGE CHARAMBEAU**

route de Niozelles; it's 3.5km out of town on the N100 in the direction of Niozelles.
☎ 04.92.70.91.70 ➡ 04.92.70.81.83
e contact@charambeau.com
Closed 15 Nov–15 Feb. **TV. Swimming pool. Car park**.

This hotel occupies a converted eighteenth-century farm in the middle of a seven-hectare expanse of hills and meadows. It's a lovely place to stay, looking down over the valley. Ten freshly decorated, attractive rooms; some have balconies, others wide terraces and all have good facilities. One room has been converted for disabled visitors. Doubles €49–76 with shower/wc or bath.

LARDIERS   04230 (18KM N)

|●| LE CAFÉ DE LA LAVANDE

How to get there: take the D950 towards Banon, and at Notre Dame turn right onto the D12 towards Saumane.
☎ 04.92.73.31.52
Closed Sun and Mon out of season; a fortnight in the Nov and Feb school holidays.

Old-fashioned country café in a village that looks out to the Lure mountains. Regulars drop in for a morning glass of white wine or a *pastis* in the evening, but its worth taking the time for a meal. It's simple food, all fresh and good: duck with cherries, lamb stew, creamed salt cod. Menus from €15.

FRÉJUS   83600

☗ HÔTEL OASIS

Impasse J.B. Charcot, Fréjus Plage.
☎ 04.94.51.50.44 ➡ 04.94.53.01.04
e info@hotel-oasis.net
Closed 10 Nov–1 Feb. **TV. Car park**.

A small, quiet 1950s building in a cul-de-sac five minutes from the beach. It's run by a young couple who welcome you like family friends. The rooms are varied – old-fashioned wallpaper in some, pretty Provençal décor in others – and though not big, they're more than adequate. Doubles with shower €37–49 or €41–63 with shower/wc. Breakfast is served on the terrace under an awning.

⅍ ☗ |●| HÔTEL ARENA***

139 rue du Général-de-Gaulle (Centre); it's next to pl. Agricola.
☎ 04.94.17.09.40 ➡ 04.94.52.01.52
e info@arena-hotel.com
Restaurant closed Sat and Mon lunchtimes; Jan.
Disabled access. TV. Garden. Swimming pool. Car park.

A lovely place if you're not on a tight budget. It's an old establishment that's been attractively and tastefully renovated, and the décor is pure Provence: warm colours on the walls, mosaic floors and painted furniture. The rooms aren't huge but they're very pretty, air-conditioned and efficiently soundproofed (you don't hear the trains on the lines nearby). They go for €69–115 with shower/wc or bath. There's a lush garden with luxuriant greenery and a swimming pool. The flavoursome cuisine consists of mainly Mediterranean dishes with a dash of individuality. Menus €22–42. Free coffee.

GAP   05000

⅍ ☗ |●| HÔTEL-RESTAURANT PORTE-COLOMBE**

4 pl. Frédéric-Euzières (West).
☎ 04.92.51.04.13 ➡ 04.92.52.42.50
Restaurant closed Fri evening and Sat; 30 April–19 May; 4–25 Jan. **TV. Car park**.

Don't let the electric shutters and cable TV distract you from the beautiful view of Gap and its cathedral. This hotel is in a modern, unappealing building but the rooms are individualized and comfortable with double-glazing. Doubles €43–58 with shower/wc or bath. Fine cuisine includes salmon *mousse-line* with crab *coulis*, ravioli *en tourtons* and succulent desserts. Menus €14–33. 10% discount Oct–June.

⅍ 🏠 |●| LA GRILLE***

2 pl. Frédéric-Euzière (Centre).
☎ 04.92.53.84 84 ⟾ 04.92.52.42.38
Closed during the Christmas holidays.

Though the building looks pretty dreary, inside the welcome is most affable and the rooms are spacious, quiet and comfortable. As in a lot of other hotels in Gap, the furnishings and décor look dated. Air-conditioned doubles with shower/wc or with bath and mini-bar for €44–55. Menus €14–30. 10% discount on the room rate.

⅍ 🏠 |●| LA FERME BLANCHE***

Route des Romettes (Northwest); from the station take the col Bayard road, turn right onto the Romettes road then turn first left, and it's at the end of the road.
☎ 04.92.51.03.41 ⟾ 04.92.51.35.39
e la.ferme.blanche@wanadoo.fr **TV**.

This charming hotel, away from the main road, has a nice sunny terrace. In the public areas, lovely furniture complements the vaulted rooms and the elegant fire place, and they've used an old bank counter as the bar. Rooms are bright and comfortable, though the decoration is looking a little tired; doubles with shower €44, or €49 with bath. Breakfast is served until noon. The cooking is typical of the region and elegantly prepared. Menus €14–49: kid stew and potatoes *Dauphinois* with ceps, crayfish stew, *marbré* of rabbit with prunes. The welcoming owner is a mine of information about walks and cultural events. 10% discount on the room rate.

⅍ |●| AU DEUXIÈME SOUFFLE

pl. de la Cathédrale (Centre).
☎ 04.92.53.57.87
Closed Sun–Wed evenings.

This unusual establishment next to the cathedral is a restaurant, tearoom, gallery and secondhand clothes store all in one. Lasagne is the house speciality, and they serve excellent savoury and sweet tarts and mixed salads. Original, tasty dishes of the day, such as roast pork with peaches and coconut chicken go for €7; you'll pay about €12 *à la carte*. Vegetarian dishes include pasta salad and ravioli with basil. Attractive, typical local décor in the dining room and on the terrace. Free apéritif, coffee or *digestif*.

⅍ |●| LES OLIVADES

Malcombe on the Veynes road. Take the Veynes/Valence road; at the second roundabout, look for the signs to Les Olivades on the right.
☎ 04.92.52.66.80
Closed Sun evening and Mon.

This place overlooks Gap and the neighbouring mountains. It has a huge terrace in dark brown wood, and above the tall trees provide shade. If the weather gets bad, you can take refuge in the old sheep shelter with its vaulted ceilings. The regional dishes are deliciously prepared and infused with Provençal flavours: cheese-filled ravioli with honey butter, cod with *anise*, peach salad with a mint *coulis*. Simple elegant fare which isn't too rich nor too heavy – just delicous. Menus €11–19.

⅍ |●| LE TOURTON DES ALPES

1 rue des Cordiers (Northeast).
☎ 04.92.53.90.91

A well-established, successful restaurant which serves the region's best *tourtons* – potato fritters, served here with green salad and raw ham. They're included in the menus at €15–18, or available to order *à la carte*. The setting is a large, vaulted dining room with bare stone walls. The simple décor is freshened by a fountain and enlivened by the smiles of the waiting staff. If you're tempted, there's a shop where they sell local specialities. Free coffee.

|●| LA MUSARDIÈRE

3 pl. du Revelly (Centre)
☎ 04.92.51.56.15
Closed Tues evening, Wed, 17–21 April and 1–15 July.

Many of the dishes at this spruce, pretty restaurant are traditional Alsatian specialities – the owners come from that part of the world. The substantial *menu Alsacien* includes knuckle of pork braised in beer, fish *choucroute* and zander in Riesling. Menus €17–25. Courteous service.

⅍ |●| RESTAURANT LE PASTURIER

18 rue Pérolière (Centre); it's in the pedestrianized area.
☎ 04.92.53.69.29
Closed Sun and Mon lunchtime July–Aug except public holidays.

The elegant, intimate atmosphere at this restaurant makes it ideal for a romantic dinner. The owners are lively and welcoming, and chef Pascal Dorche changes his menus frequently, sometimes producing unusual dishes. His honest cooking is more than satisfying – goat's cheese *nougat* with pistachios and lavender, wild boar ham, a *madeleine* with pike and prawns, artichoke bottoms and Banyuls wine vinegar, ravioli stuffed with leeks and morels, and unmissable white chocolate and coconut desserts. Menus €20–53; *à la carte* around €46. There's a small terrace open in summer. Free coffee.

LAYE   05500 (11.5KM N)

|●| HÔTEL AIGUILLE

It's in the Laye ski resort.
☎ 04.92.50.50.62 **e** pierrot@hotelaiguille.com
Car park.

Helen sorted out the décor and Pierrot creates the atmosphere – they make a lovely, welcoming couple. He's originally from Marseille, where he used to sell postcards on the Vieux Port. The rooms are pretty, elegantly wood-panelled and very clean. Doubles €44–52. And it has a great location at the foot of the ski slopes. Best to book.

|●| RESTAURANT LA LAITERIE DU COL BAYARD

How to get there: take the N85 from Gap to Grenoble and follow the signs.
☎ 04.92.50.50.06
Closed Mon except school holidays and public holidays; mid-Nov to mid-Dec. **Car park**.

The farmer, the farmer's son and the farmer's grandson run this place – and they've been running it since 1935. They serve platters of *charcuterie*, salads with blue cheese sauce, chese kebabs, the *plateau Champsaurin* (which offers a selection of ten different cheeses) and a variety of generous salads. Menus €12–20 or *à la carte*.

🎋|●| LE PETIT RENARD

It's in the ski-resort.
☎ 04.92.50.06.20 **e** lay@club-internet.fr
Closed Wed from Spring–Autumn; mid-Nov to mid-Dec. **Disabled access**.

The locals flood in to this restaurant which offers the best value for money in town. Speedy, friendly service. Classic regional dishes: *tourtons*, ravioli and house *foie gras* and salmon escalope with Maroilles cheese. The raclettes and fondues are good – the Savoyard cheese one has ceps in it. Menus €12–33. The large dining room has a lovely atmosphere: it's like a room in an ample chalet and it has a mezzanine. In summer, the terrace offers a ravishing view and there's a children's games corner. Free house apéritif.

MONTGARDIN   05230 (12KM E)

🎋|●| L'AUBERGE DU MOULIN

How to get there: take the N94 in the direction of

Embrun and it's on the right in the village.
☎ 04.92.50.32.98
Closed Sun evening and Mon; open by reservation only during the rest of the week.

Known locally as the Three Sisters, this place is run by three women who are wonderful cooks. Many of the superb local dishes feature duck or goose. The single menu at €21 is satisfying and skilfully prepared; it lists *gâteau* of spleen and duck liver, *fricassée* of whole duckling done like a *coq au vin*, fresh cheese with honey and a good *bavarois*. There's a family atmosphere. Free apéritif.

SAINT-JULIEN-EN-CHAMPSAUR   05500 (20KM N)

🎋 🏠 |●| LES CHÊNETS

How to get there: take the Grenoble road to Fare, then turn right towards Saint-Bonnet and Saint-Julien.
☎ 04.92.50.03.15.
Closed Wed and Sun evening out of season; 3–21 April; 13 Nov–27 Dec.

A mountain chalet with a warm family feeling. Simple double rooms with shower/wc or bath go for €35–41. The cuisine is better than good and focuses on regional dishes. At the cheaper end of the scale are *tourtons* (potato fritters with ham and salad) and *crème brûlée* for dessert. More pricey are duck *carpaccio* with grapefruit *vinaigrette* and braised lambs' tongues and cheeks. Perfectly ripened cheeses, excellent home-made desserts and a good wine list. Weekday menu €15 or others €24–31. Free apéritif.

GASSIN   83580

🏠 |●| HÔTEL BELLO-VISTO**

pl. des Barrys (East).
☎ 04.94.56.17.30 ➡ 04.94.43.45.36
Restaurant closed Tues and end Oct to end Dec.

This excellently situated little hotel, on the edge of the village, has a terrace with a superb view of the bay of Saint-Tropez. Rooms are smart, clean and well priced for the area – doubles with shower/wc €46–58. You'll need to book in July and August. Provençal cuisine dominates in the restaurant: roast rabbit with garlic or truffle galette. Menu at €23.

GORDES   84220

🏠 |●| AUBERGE DE CARCARILLE**

Les Gervais (South); it's 3km below Gordes on the D2.

☎ 04.90.72.02.63 ➡ 04.90.72.05.74
e cacaril@club-internet.fr
Closed Fri out of season and 15 Nov–28 Dec. **Disabled access. Swimming pool. TV. Car park.**

A welcoming inn which is modern but not obviously so. The dining room is quite elegant and creates the right atmosphere for the traditional Provençal cuisine: saddle of rabbit with sage, duck *foie gras* sausage, lamb's trotters and tripe, *bouillabaisse*, salad of *mesclun*. Menus €15 and €23–33. The pleasant rooms aren't cheap, but that's not surprising in the heart of Lubéron. Doubles €53 with shower/wc and €56–61 with bath. Breakfast €8.

⅍ ☎ HÔTEL LE MAS DE LA SÉNANCOLE***

Imberts; 5km outside Gordes on the D2.
☎ 04.90.76.76.55 ➡ 04.90.76.70.44
e gordes@mas-de-la-senancole.com
Closed Nov–March. **Disabled access. Garden. Swimming pool. TV. Car park.**

Though this is a completely new building, it has been built in the old Provençal style and fits well into the surroundings. The exceptionally comfortable doubles with shower/wc go for €92–107 or €137–€153 with bath. There are also two superb apartments with enclosed balcony and huge bathrooms. The swimming pool is surrounded by greenery. Quality place, quality welcome, quality service. Free apéritif.

GOULT   84220 (8KM SE)

⅍ |●| LE CAFÉ DE LA POSTE

pl. de la Libération; it's on the village square.
☎ 04.90.72.23.23
Closed Wed; evenings and Sun the restaurant is closed but the bar is open; Nov and Jan.

Dine in a friendly atmosphere in this pretty village. Good house specialities include rabbit *à la pebrade*, vegetable *terrine*, *crespéou*, *aïoli* and *anchoïade*. Dish of the day for €8, *menu du jour* €11 or options *à la carte*. Children's menu €8. Free coffee.

|●| AUBERGE LE FIACRE

quartier Pied-Rousset; it's 5km out of the village on the N100 in the direction of Apt.
☎ 04.90.72.26.31
Closed Sun evening out of season; Thurs lunchtime in season; 11 Nov–11 Dec. **Car park.**

An excellent restaurant serving light, inventive Provençal cooking using local produce. The owners will give you a kind, cheerful welcome; mother and daughter wait at table while father is in charge of the cooking. The vegetable soup with basil, the crayfish ravioli, the rack of Ventoux lamb and the lamb *tian* alone make a visit worthwhile, and they also do game in season. In summer you can dine outside under the lime trees, where you're serenaded by a chorus of cicadas. Menus, €17 at lunch and €24–27 at dinner, offer good value for money.

MURS   84220 (8.5KM NE)

⅍ ☎ |●| LE CRILLON

It's in the middle of the village.
☎ 04.90.72.60.31 ➡ 04.90.72.63.12
e crillon.murs@wanadoo.fr
Closed Thurs out of season; Thurs lunch in season; 15 Jan–29 Feb. **TV. Car park.**

This country hotel, in a characterful village in the Lubéron wilds, offers stylish doubles, some with terraces or mezzanines, for €45 with shower/wc and €46 with bath. Weekday menu for €12, then others at €17–21; there's also a children's menu for €8. There are some lovely dishes which are made using wild mushrooms or truffles: *tournedos* with morels, truffle omelette, stewed hare and local game. 5% discount for a minimum six-night stay half- or full-board.

BEAUMETTES   84220 (9KM SE)

⅍ |●| RESTAURANT LA REMISE

It's in the middle of the village.
☎ 04.90.72.23.05
Closed Wed; Tues evening out of season; mid-Jan to mid-Feb. **Disabled access.**

The unpretentious €14 menu is one of the most reasonably priced in the Lubéron. The others, €21–27, are significantly more elaborate, listing dishes such as fish soup, home-smoked salmon, king prawns flambéed with whisky and *fricassée* of lamb with creamed garlic. Meals are served on the shady terrace. Free coffee.

GOURDON   06620

⅍ |●| AU VIEUX FOUR

rue Basse; it's a turning off the main street.
☎ 04.93.09.68.60
Closed evenings; Sat; 1–15 June; mid-Nov to mid-Dec.

A pleasant place for a spot of lunch. Start with a plate of local *charcuterie* or shepherd's salad, then follow that with rabbit with thyme or meat grilled over the coals. Finish off with *clafoutis*. Menu €15, or *à la carte* around €18. Free *digestif*.

GRAVE (LA)　　05320

🏕 🏠 |⬤| L'EDELWEISS**

Centre.
☎ 04.76.79.90.93 ➡ 04.76.79.92.64
✉ edelweiss@wow.com
Closed lunchtimes in winter; end Sept to mid-Dec; early May to early June. **TV**.

This enjoyable hotel is owned by the organizers of the world-famous annual Mieje ski race. The modern hotel stands well away from the noise of the road. The clientele is international and sporty and there's always a riotous atmosphere late into the evening. You can relax on the terrace and gaze upon the summits of the 4000m Écrins, or enjoy the sauna and Jacuzzi. The place has been renovated recently but rooms are on the small side; they cost €47–52. Menus €14–20. 10% discount on the room rate.

GRÉOUX-LES-BAINS　　05320

🏕 🏠 |⬤| HÔTEL-RESTAURANT DES ALPES**

19 av. des Alpes; it's in the middle of the village.
☎ 04.94.74.24.24 ➡ 04.94.74.24.26
Closed Dec–Feb. **Swimming pool**. **TV**. **Car park**.

A bright, fresh house where the simple, tastefully decorated rooms have views over the village, the park or the pool. Doubles with shower/wc €41–62 and €48–62 with bath. The restaurant serves a good range of interesting dishes which change regularly: aubergine and sardine *millefeuille*, fresh salmon with drizzled olive oil, roast rabbit haunch with honey, sea bass baked with finely sliced potatoes. Menus €14–35. Warm welcome. Free *digestif*.

GRIMAUD　　83310

🏠 LE GINESTEL

Chemin des Blaquières; it's 3km outside Grimaud village and 1.5km from Port-Grimaud on the D61.
☎ or ➡ 04.94.43.48.45
Closed 10 Oct–1 April. **Disabled access**. **Swimming pool**. **Garden**. **Car park**.

When the dust has settled from the dirt track you'll negotiate in order to get here, you'll find yourself looking at an unpretentious hotel with eighteen rooms, each with a private ter-

race overlooking the park and swimming pool. If you want to arrive by boat, there's a pontoon on the River Giscle to tie up. Doubles with shower/wc €57–99.

🏠 |⬤| HÔTEL LA PIERRERIE***

Quartier du Grand Pont; it's 2km from Port-Grimaud on the D61.
☎ 04.94.43.24.60 ➡ 04.94.43.24.78
Closed 31 Oct–1 April. **Garden**. **Swimming pool**. **TV**.

An attractive little hotel way out in the countryside – yet it's above the gulf of Saint-Tropez. It's built like a typical Provençal *mas*, with lots of small stone buildings in the greenery and among the flowers. Rooms with shower/wc or bath €58–98. It's wonderfully quiet.

🏠 ATHÉNOPOLIS***

quartier Mouretti; it's 3km outside Grimaud on the road to la Garde-Freinet.
☎ 04.94.43.24.24 ➡ 04.94.43.37.05
Closed 1 Nov–1 April. **Disabled access**. **Swimming pool**. **Garden**. **TV**. **Car park**.

Attractively decorated, airy rooms with balconies or terraces. The swimming pool is inviting and the atmosphere peaceful – ideal if you want to relax. Doubles with shower/wc or bath €78–104. Very generous breakfast with fresh fruit; they also provide dinner for residents for €18. The garden and the surroundings are delightful.

GUILLESTRE　　05600

🏕 🏠 |⬤| LE CHALET ALPIN**

Route du Queyras; as you leave Guillestre, turn left onto the Queyras road.
☎ 04.92.45.00.35 ➡ 04.92.45.43.41
Closed 20 April–5 May; 15 Nov–20 Dec. **Car park**.

A family-run establishment with decent rooms at honest prices: doubles €35–41 with shower/wc or bath. The ones facing south over the park have a splendid view. Traditional, well-prepared cooking in the restaurant, on menus at €15–28: scallops with fresh fruit, *terrine* of duck *foie gras*, *crépinettes* of salmon with a saffron infusion, duck breast with sour cherries and Génépi wine. Half board available from €43. Free *digestif*.

MONT-DAUPHIN　　05600 (4KM NW)

🏠 |⬤| L'AUBERGE DE L'ECHAUGUETTE**

rue Catinat; it's on the main street
☎ 04.92.45.07.13 ➡ 04.92.45.14.22

e info@echauguette.com
Restaurant closed Mon out of season and Nov.
TV.

The building used to be the school for the children of the soldiers stationed here. The place was restored two years ago and has been impressively done. The welcome is very warm and at the weekend the staff wear local costume. There's a tavern, a restful garden at the back where you can eat or have a drink and an elegantly decorated dining room. Dishes include scallop tart, veal sweetbreads in pastry cases with Roquefort sauce and lots of local specialities. Menus €14–28 and in summer there's one for €10 served at lunchtime. The spacious rooms all have en-suite bathrooms and they've been charmingly decorated. Doubles €36–46; half board €43.

SAINT-CRÉPIN   05600 (9KM N)

|●| L'AMISTOUS

It's in the centre of the village.
☎ 04.92.45.25.30
Closed Mon and Tues out of season; Nov–Christmas.

This restaurant is popular with locals and tourists alike. Their pizzas are particularly good, and they serve a smoky *cassolette* of veal sweetbreads and an absolutely delicious trout *au bleu*. You must try the chef's *potence* ("gallows") – meat or his shellfish flambéed in whisky or *anis* and served with special homemade sauces. Weekday lunch menu €12, others €17–21. There's an extensive, varied and affordable wine list.

HYÈRES   83400

🏃 🏠 HÔTEL DU SOLEIL**

rue du Rempart (Northeast).
☎ 04.94.65.16.26 ➡ 04.94.35.40.40
e soleil@hotel-du-soleil.fr
TV.

A hotel absolutely engulfed by ivy in a very peaceful spot next to the medieval town. The rooms of this old building are haphazardly furnished and smell of lavender. Doubles €35–65 with shower/wc and €40–37 with bath. 10% discount except in school holidays and summer.

PORQUEROLLES   83400 (2KM SE)

🏠 |●| LES GLYCINES

Place d'Armes
☎ 04.94.58.30.36 ➡ 04.94.58.35.22

e auberge.glycines@wanadoo.fr

A charming hotel which has been renovated in the spirit of Provence. The time to come is in March when the "glycines" (wisteria) is in bloom; avoid it in high summer if you want to be pampered. They only do their rooms on a half-board basis – €50–135. The patio is the best place to eat and the cuisine leans heavily in the direction of fish and seafood: fish *tartare*, omlelette with sea urchins and tuna carpaccio. Menus €15–26. If you want to treat yourself, this is probably the best place on the island.

LALONDE-LES-MAURES   83250 (8KM E)

|●| LE JARDIN PROVENÇAL

15-18 av. Georges-Clémenceau
☎ 04.94.66.57.34
Closed Sun evening and Mon out of season; 15 Dec–15 Jan.

The dining room has a stylish Provençal décor – and comes with that essential ingredient, a pleasant terrace in the garden. Charming welcome with equally good service and local dishes: stuffed sardines with Provençal bread; free-range cockerel gently stewed in local wine. Menus €21–37 or around €38 *à la carte*.

ISLE-SUR-LA-SORGUE (L')   84800

|●| LE CARRÉ D'HERBES

13 av. des 4-Otages (Centre).
☎ 04.90.38.62.95
e provence@carredherbes.com
Closed Tues, Wed and Jan.

An idyllic spot in a town which is swamped by visitors as soon as the weather gets good – and it's getting taken over by antique shops as well. Dine in a room full of antique furniture and bric-à-brac, on the terrace or in a converted aviary. One menu at €24 or €30 *à la carte*; children's menu €8. The fresh food is full of original flavours – try *tartine de la bergère*, rabbit and olive stew, or pan-fried polenta and roast chicken with thyme, and finish with fruit crumble. Attentive, helpful service.

LANTOSQUE   06450

🏃 🏠 |●| L'AUBERGE DU BON PUITS**

Lesuquet de Lantosque; it's 5 km south of Lantosque on the D2565.

☎ 04.93.03.17.65 ➡ 04.93.03.10.45
Closed Tue except July–Aug; Nov–Easter. **TV. Car park.**

Best to ask for a room with a garden view to avoid the noise of the road. Doubles from €49. The restaurant serves substantial, tasty, family-style dishes prepared with care: live trout from the tank, Barbary duckling cooked on the rotisserie, tripe, ravioli *à la Niçoise*. Menus from €16. There's a shady terrace which provides welcome shade in the heat of summer. Across the road there's a large play area for children: ping-pong, tobaggons and so on. Free house apéritif or coffee.

LARAGNE-MONTÉGLIN   05300

⚄ 🏠 HÔTEL CHRISMA**

25 route de Grenoble (North); it's 300m from the town centre on the Serres road.
☎ 04.92.65.09.36 ➡ 04.92.65.08.12
e hotelchrisma@caramail.com
Closed 15 Nov–1 March. **Swimming pool. Garden. Car park.**

If you're simply looking for somewhere to stop for the night, this is a good place. Neat rooms with shower/wc or bath €35–40. The rooms overlooking the garden – where they do frequent barbecues – are lovely. You'll get a warm welcome. Free apéritif and 10% discount Sept–June excluding public holiday weekends.

⚄ 🍴 L'ARAIGNÉE GOURMANDE

8 rue de la Paix (Centre).
☎ 04.92.65.13.39
Closed Tues evening; Wed; 15 Oct–15 Nov.

Located in the centre of the town, this unpretentious place is pleasant and clean. Good traditional cooking and a range of set menus: weekday lunch €11 and others at €19 and €28. Dishes include *terrine* with juniper, lamb's tongue with *sauce gribiche* and fillet of red mullet on leek *fondue*. Attentive service. Free coffee.

SAINTE-COLOMBE   05700 (17KM W)

⚄ 🏠 🍴 LE CÉANS**

Les Bégües; take the N75 in the direction of Serres, then the D30 towards Orpierre, then take the Laborel road out of the village to Bégües.
☎ 04.92.66.24.22 ➡ 04.92.28.29
e le.ceans@infonie.fr
Closed Nov to mid-March. **Garden. Swimming pool.**

A family-run establishment halfway up the mountains in the Buech area, surrounded by orchards and lavender fields. Madame runs

the place while Monsieur and their son produce reliable, tasty regional dishes. *Menu du jour* €13 and others up to €29. Specialities include snail *profiteroles*, lamb chops with honey and *fricassée* of chicken with morels. The rooms are small but quiet; doubles with shower/wc €37–42. Garden, swimming pool, sauna, Jacuzzi – there's everything for a pleasant stay. Free house apéritif.

SAVOURNON   05700 (18KM N)

⚄ 🏠 🍴 L'AUBERGE DES RASTEL*

How to get there; take the D21 towards col de Laye.
☎ 04.92.67.13.05 ➡ 04.92.67.13.05
Closed Wed out of season; a week at Christmas; a week in early June.

A cheap, friendly inn away from it all in a village midway up the mountains. It's a perfect spot for walkers wishing to explore the area. Simple, functional double rooms €27 with shower/wc. The young owner-chef prepares delicious, no-frills dishes using only the freshest local produce; menus €12 and €18. There's a terrace and a bright, large dining room, and you'll get a slobbering 70kg welcome from Mao the dog. Credit cards are not accepted. Free coffee.

LARCHE   04530

🏠 🍴 AUBERGE DU LAUZANIER

It's on the D900, just before the Larche pass.
☎ 04.94.84.35.93
Car park.

An enticing hideaway in Haute Ubaye, between Barcelonnette and the Italian border, run by a trio who've made it wonderfully comfortable. The substantial, tasty cooking is ideal for skiers and walkers – they offer platters of *charcuterie*, *tourtons*, omelettes, roast lamb with a morel crust and fruit tarts with raspberries or bilberries. Weekday menu €8 and others for a bit more. There's a *gîte* with spotless rooms for €15 a night.

LAVANDOU (LE)   83980

⚄ 🏠 HÔTEL CALIFORNIA**

av. de Provence (Centre).
☎ 04.94.01.59.99 ➡ 04.94.01.59.28
e hotel.california@wanadoo.fr
Garden. TV. Car park.

The young couple who own the hotel – just eight minutes from the beach – have completely refurbished it. The husband is an architect who has put his talents to good use, while the wife is wonderfully welcoming. You'll feel immediately at ease, and you can spend hours gazing out at the bay and the islands. The rooms aren't huge, but they have been thoughtfully arranged. Doubles with shower/wc €34–64; the cheaper rooms look over the garden. Free breakfast in low and mid-season.

⬆ HÔTEL LE RABELAIS**

2 rue Rabelais (Southeast); it's opposite the old port.
☎ 04.94.71.00.56 �┝ 04.94.71.82.55
✉ hotel.lerabelais@wanadoo.fr
Closed 11 Nov to end of Jan. **Disabled access. TV. Car park.**

A small hotel with salmon-coloured walls and green shutters which is close to the centre and not far from the beaches either. Comfortable, pretty rooms with basin or with shower/wc at €44–65; some have a balcony overlooking the fishing harbour.

⚹ ⬆ |●| HÔTEL-RESTAURANT BEAU SOLEIL**

Aiguebelle-plage; it's 5km from the centre on the St-Tropez road.
☎ 04.94.05.84.55 �┝ 04.94.05.70.89
Closed Oct to Easter. **Disabled access. TV. Car park.**

A quiet little hotel, which on summer nights makes a peaceful respite from the cacophony in Lavandou. The dynamic young owners, Monsieur and Mme Podda, offer a kind and considerate welcome to tourists. Simple but pleasant rooms, all with sea view and air conditioning; with shower/wc or bath they go for €46–79. Half board, compulsory in high season, is €53–65 per person. Menus, €15–27, list a wide choice of local specialities, including stuffed capon, *bouillabaisse* and a very special *bourride* (fish stew). 10% discount on the room rate in June and Sept.

|●| LE RELAIS DU VIEUX SAUVAIRE

route des Crêtes.
☎ 04.94.05.84.22
Closed Oct–end April.
Swimming pool.

This four-hundred-year-old coaching inn is on a pretty road up to the mountain peaks and there's a lovely view over Lavandou below. You can have a dip in the pool before heading to your table. The dishes are typical of the region: sardines *provençales*, fish in salt crust, pizzas, grilled *langoustines* and a warm fruit tart to finish with – a range to sat-

isfy all tastes and all pockets. Menus €17–30.

RAYOL-CANADEL   83820 (13KM E)

⚹ |●| MAURIN DES MAURES

av. du Touring-Club (Centre); it's on the main street in the centre of the village.
☎ 04.94.05.60.11
Closed evenings 10 Nov–20 Dec.

The owner, Dédé Del Monte, paces up and down behind his bar while the locals, perched on their stools, exchange gossip over a *pastis* (drunk undiluted in these parts). Dishes in the restaurant include *bouillabaisse*, *millefeuille* of aubergines, a trio of grilled vegetables, mixed grill andgrilled fish. Weekday lunch menu at €11, then others at €18 and €23. Reserve a table by the window so that you can admire the view of the bay. Free apéritif – generally orange or lemon wine.

ÎLE DU LEVANT   83400 (20KM SE)

⚹ ⬆ |●| HÔTEL LE PONANT

It's on the island that's 30min by boat off Le Lavandou.
☎ 04.94.05.90.41 �┝ 04.94.05.90.41
✉ ponant@club-internet.fr
Closed 21 Sept–1 June.

It's a 30-minute crossing to get to the island from here – for information call ☎ 04.94.71.01.02. The 1950s building stands out like the prow of a ship on a crest of coastal cliffs. There are huge, wide terraces leading out from the rooms; each is personally decorated by Frets, the unusual boss of this unusual place. They're all different – a chunk of rock emerges in one bathroom while another is done entirely in wood. Rooms have shower/wc. Half board only, costing €76–91 per person. Free house apéritif.

MANOSQUE   04100

⚹ |●| RESTAURANT LE LUBERON

21 [bis] pl. Terreau (Centre).
☎ 04.92.72.03.09
Closed Sun evening; Mon except in July; the first fortnight in Sept.

The intense flavours of Provence are found in the food here – even though the chef comes from the north of France. He's got a creative imagination, and offers dishes such as artichoke and truffle salad, grilled pigeon with rosemary and lamb *daube* and uses lots of olive oil and basil. Weekday menu €11 and others €15–40. Tasteful rustic décor, and a terrace with a pergola. Free glass of Bon de Muscats from the Lure distillery.

⅍ |●| RESTAURANT DOMINIQUE BUCAILLE

43 bd. des Tilleuls (Centre).
☎ 04.92.72.32.28 **e** dbucaille@aol.com
Closed Wed evening and Sun; a week in the Feb school holidays; mid-July to mid-Aug. **Disabled access**.

This bright, modern place has been a brilliant success. The chef adds his own touch to classic dishes: poached egg with *foie gras* and crushed potato; roast John Dory with pepper served in a casserole of pickled tomatoes and *gnocchi*; vegetables pickled in olive oil in a pastry case. Menus €15–40. The wine list has a selection of excellent local vintages, particularly the Coteaux-de-Pierrevert from the Blaque domain. Decent prices. Free aperitif or *digestif*.

MARSEILLE   13000

SEE MAP OVERLEAF

1st arrondissement
☎ HÔTEL BEAULIEU-GLARIS*

1 pl. des Marseillaises; M° Arles. **MAP D1-15**
☎ 04.91.90.70.59 ➡ 04.91.56.14.04
e hotel-beaulieu@wanadoo.fr
Closed Christmas to 1 Jan. **TV**.

A stone's throw from the monumental steps of Saint-Charles station, where you get a breathtaking view of the city. The hotel is handy if you're travelling by train and while it's not the height of luxury, it's clean and well maintained. The rooms at the back are huge and quiet, and get lots of sun. Doubles €24 with basin, €38 with shower/wc.

⅍ ☎ HÔTEL DU COQ*

26 rue du Coq. **MAP D1-6**
☎ 04.91.62.61.29 ➡ 04.91.64.02.05

Unpretentious hotel just five minutes from Saint-Charles station; if you telephone, they'll come and collect you by car. You get an excellent welcome. Prices are reasonable: €25 for a room without shower, €30 for one with. The street is quiet, but for real peace opt for the rooms overlooking the courtyard at the back. 10% discount and free breakfast.

☎ HÔTEL AZUR**

24 cours Franklin-Roosevelt; M° Réformés-Canebière.

Off map D1-2
☎ 04.91.42.74.38 ➡ 04.91.47.27.91
TV.

A pleasant hotel with friendly owners on a steep, quiet street lined with handsome buildings. The rooms have been renovated and have air conditioning; doubles with shower/wc cost €38 or €52 with bath. The nicest look out onto little gardens at the back. Lovely breakfast with home-made pastries.

⅍ ☎ SAINT-FERRÉOL'S HÔTEL***

19 rue Pisançon; M° Noailles-Estrangin-Préfecture.
MAP C2-5
☎ 04.91.33.12.21 ➡ 04.91.54.29.97
e st.ferreol@wanadoo.fr
TV.

This hotel is in a good location, close to the old port. The glitzy rooms are named after famous painters – Van Gogh, Picasso, Monet and Cézanne – and decorated with appropriate prints. Doubles with good facilities €67–88. No charge for children under four. Breakfast €7 with fresh orange juice. Excellent welcome. 10% discount.

|●| LA PART DES ANGES

33 rue Sainte. **MAP C3-40**
☎ 04.91.33.55.70

Service 9am until 2am the following morning; Sun it's 1–6pm. A friendly wine bar where you come to buy your table wine from the barrel or for a good bottle as a treat. There's a little dining room at the back where you can eat salads for around €7. A full meal costs around €11. Lovely atmosphere.

⅍ |●| LES MENUS PLAISIRS

1 rue Haxo; M° Vieux-Port–Hôtel-de-Ville. **MAP C2-32**
☎ 04.91.54.94.38
Closed evenings and weekends.

Lunch only. A nice little place with lots of old clocks on the wall. The boss is a proud Marseillais who champions his town while taking orders and serving dishes. A really warm atmosphere and hordes of customers who appreciate good value. The menu changes daily and dishes are appetizing: small salads with chickpeas or feta, skate wing with *beurre blanc*, lasagne, sautéed pork with red kidney beans and some good little desserts like fig and custard tart. Menus from €8. Terrace. Free coffee.

|●| PIZZERIA AU FEU DE BOIS

10 rue d'Aubagne; M° Noailles. **MAP C2-33**

☎ 04.91.54.33.96
Closed Sun and a fortnight in Sept.

This place is well-known for its outstanding pizzas cooked in a wood-fired oven. They're coated with a range of toppings including *royale* (mushrooms, garlic, sausage and cheese) and *orientale* (meat, cream cheese, egg and tomatoes). *À la carte* you can get *pieds et paquets* (mutton tripe cooked with sheep's trotters) and lasagne. Menus from €8. Bland décor, regular customers and friendly service. If you're in a rush, get a portion of pizza to take away from the counter outside.

|●| LES COLONIES

26 rue Lulli. **MAP C2-41**
☎ 04.91.54.11.17
Closed Sun and Aug.

Service 8am–7pm. A warm, welcoming, original place where they don't allow smoking because it's too small. This is where you buy tea, chocolates and biscuits baked by "Le Petit Duc" from Saint-Rémy. It occupies an old bank building which has been decorated to within an inch of its life – voluminous curtains, elaborate chandeliers. Good for lunch: cannelloni with *brousse* (a local cheese), tarts, or cream cheese with honey and spiced bread. Menus from €8.

⅍|●| O'STOP

16 rue Saint-Saens. **MAP C2-20**
☎ 04.91.33.85.34

Service 8am–7am (23 hours out of 24). The snack bar opposite the opera is an institution; it attracts everyone from well-dressed gentleman to local shopkeepers, and it's not uncommon to bump into an opera singer or stagehand. The house specialities – *alouettes* (or meatballs), pasta with pesto and *daube à la provençale* – are very decent. The sandwiches have good fillings and should not be ignored. Great atmosphere in the early hours. Meals from €8 and average price *à la carte* about €15. Free apéritif.

⅍|●| L'OLIVERAIE

10 pl. aux Huiles; M° Vieux-Port–Hôtel de Ville. **MAP B2-22**
☎ 04.91.33.34.41
Closed Sat lunchtime; Sun; Jan. **Car park.**

A typical local bistro with a welcoming owner, good service and superb Provençal cooking. There's a good lunch menu at €16, and it's €21 in the evening including wine. Around €33 *à la carte*. Free coffee.

2nd arrondissement
⅍ ✿ HÔTEL HERMÈS**

2 rue Bonneterie; M° Vieux-Port–Hôtel-de-Ville. **MAP C2-16**
☎ 04.96.11.63.63 ➔ 04.96.11.63.64
e hotel.hermes@wanadoo.fr **TV.**

Superbly located on the Old Port. Don't let the name on the southern façade confuse you – they've kept the old Hôtel Bellevue sign. The rooms (with shower/wc) have air conditioning; the ones that look out on the side road don't have the view but are quieter while the ones over the port have a fantastic view of the town and the sea. Some even have a small terrace. They're very popular so you need to book in advance saying you want one of them. Doubles €55–64.

⅍ ✿ HÔTEL LA RÉSIDENCE DU VIEUX PORT***

18 quai du Port; M° Vieux-Port–Hôtel-de-Ville. **MAP B2-7**
☎ 04.91.91.91.22 ➔ 04.91.56.60.88
e hotel.residence@wanadoo.fr
TV. Disabled access.

This great family hotel, on the town hall side of the Vieux Port, has a good view of Notre-Dame. Rooms are large, light, air-conditioned and pleasantly furnished – though the bathrooms are a bit small. You can sit on your balcony and watch the boats chug past. Doubles €99; they've also got a suite sleeping four or five for €114. Friendly service and good breakfast. 10% discount.

|●| CHEZ MADIE – LES GALINETTES

138 quai du Port. **MAP B2-43**
☎ 04.91.90.40.87
Closed Sun.

Way out at the end of the quay you'll find this restaurant – it's the place to come for robust, authentic Provençal cooking. It's now run by Madie's granddaughter and, although she still serves the excellent chicken in Meunière sauce, her real speciality is meat (her father was a wholesale butcher). Authentic *pieds et paquets* – lamb tripe and trotters. The clams with thyme are also good. Lunch menu €13 with starter and main, and others up to €23.

|●| LE CAFÉ PARISIEN

1 pl. Sadi-Carnot. **MAP B1-42**
☎ 04.91.90.05.77
Closed Sun.

Service 4am–10pm. The last Marseille café to have retained its early twentieth-century décor and matching atmosphere. At break-

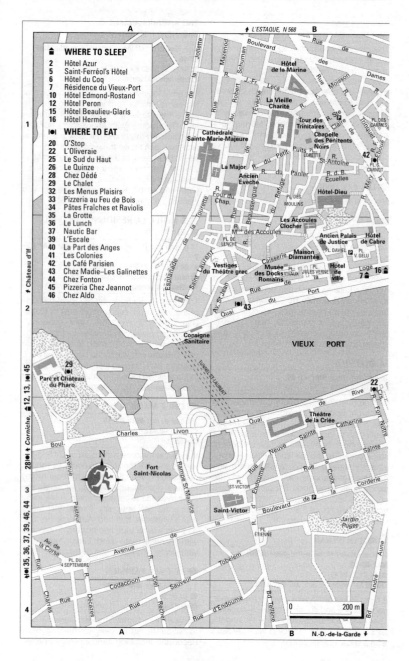

WHERE TO SLEEP

2 Hôtel Azur
5 Saint-Ferréol's Hôtel
6 Hôtel du Coq
7 Résidence du Vieux-Port
10 Hôtel Edmond-Rostand
12 Hôtel Peron
15 Hôtel Beaulieu-Glaris
16 Hôtel Hermès

WHERE TO EAT

20 O'Stop
22 L'Oliveraie
25 Le Sud du Haut
26 Le Quinze
28 Chez Dédé
29 Le Chalet
32 Les Menus Plaisirs
33 Pizzeria au Feu de Bois
34 Pâtes Fraîches et Raviolis
35 La Grotte
36 Le Lunch
37 Nautic Bar
39 L'Escale
40 La Part des Anges
41 Les Colonies
42 Le Café Parisien
43 Chez Madie–Les Galinettes
44 Chez Fonton
45 Pizzeria Chez Jeannot
46 Chez Aldo

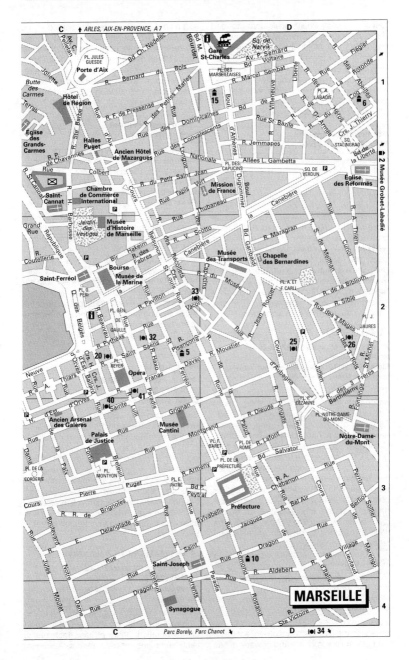

ARLES, AIX-EN-PROVENCE, A 7

MARSEILLE

Parc Borely, Parc Chanot ↘ |●| 34 ↘

fast time, this is where locals come to read the paper quietly on their way home with a *baguette*. And at lunchtime, people really swarm here – there's always a substantial dish of the day, around €10, and a dessert trolley. In the evening, especially at the weekend, *tapas* is the draw. There's always a hubbub of voices and plenty of lively discussion. It'll cost about €16 for a meal *à la carte*.

6th arrondissement
🎗 🏠 IOI HÔTEL EDMOND ROSTAND**

31 rue Dragon; M° Estrangin-Préfecture. **MAP D3-10**
☎ 04.91.37.74.95 ➡ 04.91.57.19.04
Garden. TV.

A well-kept family hotel in a quiet little street. It is named after the dramatist who wrote *Cyrano de Bergerac* – he was born in a house close by. The bright, modern rooms all have bathrooms and direct-dial phone. Doubles with bath €49, and they also have rooms that sleep four. Ask for one with a view of the garden, which is pretty and quiet. Breakfast, €5, includes excellent home-made jam, and there's a nice lunchtime menu for €13, listing grills and Provençal specialities. 10% discount on the room rate for long stays.

🎗 IOI LE SUD DU HAUT

80 cours Julien; M° Noailles. **MAP D2-25**
☎ 04.91.92.66.64
Closed Sun and Mon; Thurs–Sat evenings; Tues–Sat lunchtimes; 15 Aug–6 Sept.

The setting is like a bric-à-brac shop with its assorted holiday souvenirs. Outside, there's a terrace where you can admire the wonderful fountain in cours Julien, and the good atmosphere is enhanced by the Afro-Cuban-Carribbean music that plays in the background. Old recipes are revamped here, and a touch of finesse added to dishes – stuffed vegetables, roast goat's cheese with herbs, rib of beef with a Roquefort pancake, duck *confit* with a walnut crust, rack of lamb with herbs. Prices are reasonable: €10–14 *à la carte* at lunchtime, €22–27 for dinner. The service manages to be both attentive and relaxed. Free apéritif.

🎗 IOI LE QUINZE

15 rue des 3-Rois; M° Cours-Julien-Notre-Dame-du-Mont. **MAP D2-26**
☎ 04.91.92.81.81
Closed lunchtimes and 24 Dec.

Service from 7.30pm. This street, which runs parallel to the famous cours Julien, acts as a kind of overflow from it – and nowadays has

just as many restaurants. This particular one is lively, laid-back and has a great atmosphere. Despite its name, it's not the local rugby fifteen that everyone raves about here, but the football team, Olympique Marseille. Simple home cooking: *daube*, good barbecued meats and suckling pig in cider. Substantial menus €13–17. Free apéritif.

7th arrondissement
🎗 🏠 HÔTEL PERON**

119 corniche Kennedy (West). **Off map A3-12**
How to get there: take bus no. 83 from the Vieux Port and get off at the Corniche-Frégier stop.
☎ 04.91.31.01.41 ➡ 04.91.59.42.01
e marseillehotelperon@mintel.net
TV. Car park.

Irresistibly kitsch 1950s hotel, where each room is decorated in the style of a different French region with moulded plaster murals and dolls in traditional dress. The bathrooms teem with ceramic fish and sea creatures. Doubles with bath €49–52. As it's right beside the sea, you get a great view from the balconies at the front and the rooms are soundproofed – which keeps out some of the traffic flashing past on the Corniche. Rooms at the back, though lacking the view, are quieter. Cheerful welcome and attentive service. 10% discount.

IOI LE CHALET

Jardin du Pharo (West). **MAP A2-29**
☎ 04.91.52.80.11
Closed Nov–March.

Service noon–6pm. Outdoor café in the gardens of the palace built by Napoléon III for the Empress Eugénie. The traditional dishes cost between €8 and €13: grilled swordfish, cuttlefish *à l'armoricaine* (with onions and tomatoes), tuna *provençale*, salads. You'll pay €13–23 for a complete meal. In summer, when the centre of town can be unbearably hot, the shaded terrace gets a light, refreshing sea breeze. A lovely place for a quiet afternoon drink, with a very beautiful view of the old port.

🎗 IOI PIZZERIA CHEZ JEANNOT

Vallon des Auffes. **Off map A2/3-45**
☎ 04.91.52.11.28
Closed Sun evening in winter; 17 Nov–2 Dec; 22 Dec–13 Jan.

Nestling in the bottom of the picturesque Vallon des Auffes, this big pizzeria has a significant reputation. Tasty pizzas, fresh pasta, lamb tripe and trotters (not in summer), breaded mussel kebabs. Everything is incredibly fresh and it'll cost you around €18 a head. There are several terraces at the water's edge. It's in a friendly fishing port, unfortunately a little spoilt by the 1960s building craze. Free apéritif.

▮●▮ CHEZ FONFON

140 rue du Vallon-des-Auffes. **Off map A3-44**
☎ 04.91.52.14.38 **e** chez fonfon@aol.com
Closed Sun and Mon evenings and 2–23 Jan.

Service noon–2pm and 7–10pm. The glory days of this establishment were years ago – the tourists flooded in. And now, under its new management, it's come right back. It's in a superb location with an unbelievable view. The fresh fish is a feast, and there's an excellent *bouillabaisse*. Menus from €29; around €45 *à la carte*.

8th arrondissement
⅔ ▮●▮ PÂTES FRAÎCHES ET RAVIOLIS

150 rue Jean-Mermoz, on the corner of rue Émile Sicard (South); M° Rond-Point-du-Prado. **Off map D4-34**
☎ 04.91.76.18.85
Closed evenings; Sun; public holidays; Aug.

You have to go through the kitchens of this Italian deli to get to the veranda, where all the windows open out onto a gravel courtyard. Start with San Daniele ham or a mozzarella kebab before devouring one of the great pasta or ravioli dishes. Expect to pay around €15 for a meal. It's in a very quiet, middle-class area. Free coffee.

▮●▮ LA GROTTE

Calanque de Callelongue (South); M° Castellane. **Off map A3-35**
How to get there: take a no. 20 bus from the Métro station to Callelongue, the starting point for the Cassis–Calanques walk.
☎ 04.91.73.17.79

There's nothing here but are a few cabins, a tiny port with the occasional boat and *La Grotte*. The terrace, shaded by an awning, is very popular with Marseille locals at lunchtime when the patio gets too much sun – it's much nicer at dinner. Truly excellent pizzas, and more expensive grilled fish. It's a large place and feels a bit like a factory but it's still friendly. Between €18 and €38 *à la carte* but they don't accept credit cards. Don't forget mosquito repellent – there are quite a few at night. Best to book.

⅔ ▮●▮ CHEZ DÉDÉ

32 bd. Bonne Brise. **Off map A3-28**

☎ 04.91.73.01.03
Closed Sun evening; Mon; Tues and Wed lunchtime in winter.

The terrace juts out over the water, while the dining room is decorated with model boats. The menu is simple, listing oven-baked pizzas, pasta, mussel kebabs and grilled fish. One of the few places to offer grilled sardines – truly delicious. Around €22 *à la carte*. Free apéritif.

▮●▮ CHEZ ALDO

28 rue Audemar-Tibido. **Off map A3-46**
☎ 04.91.73.31.55
Closed Feb.

An insignificant-looking place, you might think, but it's packed day and night. The pizza and the fresh fish should explain why. The grilled fish is brilliant, or try fresh prawns, mussels and squid cooked over the embers. Around €24 *à la carte*. Friendly welcome and a lovely terrace with a gorgeous view over the bay.

⅔ ▮●▮ L'ESCALE

2 bd. Alexandre Delabre – Les Goudes. **Off map A3-39**
☎ 04.91.73.16.78
Closed Sun evening, Mon, and Jan.

This restaurant is on the edge of the fishing village. It's run by a man who used to be a fishmonger, so the quality and freshness of the fish can't be bettered. The setting is lovely, with a big terrace overlooking the sea and the fishing port, and a beautiful dining room with a big wooden bar. They offer excellent *bouillabaisse* and seafood *paella*. À la carte around €30. Free apéritif.

9th arrondissement
⅔ ▮●▮ LE NAUTIC BAR

Calanque de Morgiou; M° Rond-Point-du-Prado. **Off map A3-37**
How to get there: at the Metro stop, take a 23 bus and get off at the Morgiou-Beauvallon stop; it's a bit of a walk.
☎ 04.91.40.06.37
Closed Jan, but it's best to phone at any time.

This place, known as "chez Sylvie" to the locals, has a nice terrace that makes an ideal place to feast on seafood or whitebait, fish soup or fried *girella*, a brilliantly coloured local fish. There's a set menu at €21. Sip some chilled wine and enjoy the cool sea breeze in wonderful surroundings. It's got everything you could want after a morning's swimming and diving, but take some water with you if you're walking because there's no drinking water in the creeks. You have to phone in advance to arrange a pass – the area is closed to unauthorized vehicles June–Sept to avoid forest fires. Free *digestif*.

☆ |●| LE LUNCH

Calanque de Sormiou (West); M° Rond-Point-du-Prado.
Off map A3-36
How to get there: at the Métro stop take a no. 23 bus to La Cayolle and then hop on the free shuttle (7.30am–7pm).
☎ 04.91.25.05.37
Closed end end Oct to mid-March.

In summer, when the road is closed to cars and motorbikes, you have to phone the day before to sort out your pass. Going down towards the creek you get a magnificent view of the blue sea dotted with little spots of turquoise. All you have to do then is to sit on the terrace with a glass of chilled local Cassis and order a plate of sea bream or red mullet from the menu. Fish is sold by weight; expect to pay about €30. Good *bouillabaisse* – order it a day in advance. Free apéritif, coffee or *digestif*.

MENTON   06500

🏠 |●| HÔTEL BEAUREGARD*

10 rue Albert 1er; it's west of the city centre about 300m from the train station.
☎ 04.93.28.63.363 ➡ 04.93.28.63.79
TV.

The garden surrounding the hotel is planted with palms, lemon trees and bouganvillia; the building has charm and character and is over a hundred years old. It's a remarkable place well away from the bustle of the town. The rooms are fresh and quiet and offer good facilities; doubles €32. The man who runs the place will give you a warm, natural welcome.

☆ 🏠 HÔTEL CHAMBORD***

6 av. Boyer; it's next to the tourist office and the casino.
☎ 04.93.35.94.19 ➡ 04.93.35.30.55
TV. Car park.

A friendly family hotel on the main street in the centre of Menton. The spacious, really comfortable rooms go for €84–100, breakfast included. The doubles are at the rear of the building; the twin rooms have a view of the gardens. All just a stone's throw from the sea. Free breakfast.

☆ |●| LE MIDI

103 av. de Sospel.

☎ 04.93.57.55.96
Closed Sun and Wed evenings; July.

This unusual restaurant is well away from the racket of the centre. It's run by people who love traditional Menton dishes, and the menu lists them all in the local dialect – the easiest way to try the local delicacies is to order the *Assiette du Midi*. Alternatively, opt for the *formule-maison*, which gets you a panoply of dishes followed by a home-made fruit tart. All the produce is fresh and on Friday they offer home-made ravioli. Weekday lunch menu €11 and others up to €21; *à la carte* around €30. Free apéritif.

|●| A BRAÏJADE MÉRIDIOUNALE

66 rue Longue.
☎ 04.93.35.65.65
Closed lunchtimes in summer; Wed; 15 Nov–15 Dec.

The rustic dining room has exposed stonework and behind the bar there's a big wood-fired oven that gives a good flavour to the meat dishes. You know exactly what you're getting here – the range of set menus starts at €24. Lots of marinated and grilled meats, including garlic chicken kebabs and Provençal favourites such as beef stew *niçoise* with ravioli and fish *aïoli*. Everything is served in generous portions by nice, friendly staff.

ROQUEBRUNE-CAP-MARTIN   06190 (3KM S)

🏠 |●| LES DEUX FRÈRES

pl. des Deux Frères.
☎ 04.93.28.99.00 ➡ 04.93.28.99.10
📧 2frères@webstore.fr
Closed Mon; mid-Nov to mid-Dec. **TV. Car park**.

This special place, which stands on the outskirts of the old village, is housed in a belvedere that giving a marvellous view of the whole area. The young Dutch owner has entirely restored the house and redecorated it charmingly; you'll pay €91 for a double with sea or mountain view. The lovely dining room is the perfect setting to savour dishes that are full of flavour and prepared with imagination from high-quality produce: chilled mussel soup, *fricassée* of Bresse chicken with citrus fruit, lamb steaks in a herb crust, grilled fish. Lunch menu €18 and others up to €37.

BEAUSOLEIL   06240 (8KM S)

🏠 HÔTEL VILLA BOERI**

29 bd. du Général-Leclerc (Centre).

☎ 04.93.78.38.10 ➡ 04.93.41.90.95
TV.

A pretty hotel with geraniums in window boxes, surrounded by palm trees. It's tucked away among the high-rises in the suburbs of Monte Carlo. Very large, air-conditioned doubles, decorated in a restrained fashion, from €33–65 with shower/wc or with bath. You can just glimpse the sea from rooms 201, 202, 301 and 302.

⫚ 🏠 HÔTEL DIANA**

17 bd. du Général-Leclerc (Centre).
☎ 04.93.78.47.58 ➡ 04.93.41.88.94
TV. Pay car park.

This hotel has an amazing green *belle époque* façade, and is less expensive than a hotel on the other side of the street – this side is France, the other is Monte Carlo. You get to the rooms using an old lift; they're all air-conditioned and you'll pay €41 for a double with shower or €52 for one with bath. Good welcome. They don't accept credit cards.

MOLINES-EN-QUEYRAS 05350

⫚ 🏠 |●| LA MAISON GAUDISSARD**

Gaudissard (North). As you come into town, turn left after the post office; the hotel is 600m further on.
☎ 04.92.45.83.29 ➡ 04.92.45.80.57
e maison.gaudissard@wanadoo.fr
Closed 1 April to mid-June and mid-Sept to Christmas.
Car park.

This establishment has been a tourist centre since 1969 when Bernard Gentil transformed his home into France's first cross-country ski centre. He's constantly introducing new services and facilities. In winter, they offer courses in cross-country skiing and other ski-related activities, including treks through the mountains; in summer, hiking and paragliding bring the crowds in. After your exertions, relax on the terrace high above the village, where you get a wonderful view of the mountains. There's also a sitting room and a Finnish sauna. Doubles with en-suite facilities €48–57. The restaurant offers a single menu at €16. *Gîtes* are also available. 10% discount on the room rate except during school holidays.

ABRIÈS 05460 (10KM N)

|●| RESTAURANT GRAIN DE LUNE

Le Roux; take the D441 from Abriès for 3km.
☎ 04.92.46.70.05

A lovely place in a tiny hamlet run by two women who are passionate about cooking. They prepare your dish in front of you and cook it fresh in the old bread oven; flavours have a strong Italian accent, their cold dishes are composed of fresh produce and the bread itself is delicious. There's a mix of sweet-savoury dishes – both the toasted goat's cheese salad with diced bacon and the chesnut coulis are divine. Take your time here – you'll have to anyway because service isn't the speediest. *À la carte* only; a meal will cost around €25.

AIGUILLES 05470 (10KM N)

⫚ |●| LA TÊTE DE L'ART

How to get there: take the D5 in the direction of Château-Ville-Vieille, then the D947 to Aiguilles; it's on the village square.
☎ 04.92.46.823.49
Closed Sun evening and Mon out of season unless you book; a fortnight beginning of May; a fortnight beginning Nov.

This restaurant, run by a Parisian, is right in the middle of the village. The owner worked in the capital for twenty years or so before leaving the rat race to settle here. He collects pigs, and you'll spot porcine drawings, photos, oils, ornaments and statuettes all over the place. They serve pizzas, *pierrades* – where you cook your main dish yourself on a hot stone – *fondues* and mixed platters of sausage or cheese. Menus €12–18 or *à la carte*. It's best to book in high season, especially when they hold jazz, rock or other conconcerts (which they do a couple of times a month). Free apéritif.

MOUGINS 06250

⫚ 🏠 |●| LE MANOIR DE L'ÉTANG***

Les Bois de Fontmerle, route d'Antibes – it's not signposted.
☎ 04.92.28.36.00 ➡ 04.92.28.36.10
Hotel closed Nov–Feb. **Restaurant closed** Mon out of season. **Garden. Swimming pool**.

Jean Cocteau dreamed of turning this magnificent site, on the road from Antibes to Mougins, into a "cinema city". The project fell apart but the remarkable building was put to different use as a unique hotel. The huge rooms look onto the vast garden and the lake; doubles €91–137. The restaurant serves sophisticated, delicate cuisine which you can eat indoors or out on the terrace; €23 weekday lunch menu and another at €29. 10% discount on the room rate Oct, March and April.

⦿❘ RESTO DES ARTS

rue du Maréchal-Foch.
☎ 04.93.75.60.03
Closed Tues lunchtime out of season. **Disabled access**.

An appealing, homely place in a town full of glitzy establishments catering for celebs and millionaires. Denise prepares traditional dishes made to recipes handed down from her mother and grandmother; there have been six generations of cooks in the family. She goes off every morning hunting down the best ingredients, which she uses to prepare dishes such as *daube provençale*, *aïoli* (salt cod with garlic mayonnaise), fish *pot-au-feu*, *stouffi* of lamb with *polenta* and stuffed baby vegetables. Gregory, formerly hairstylist to the stars, now waits at table, having decided to settle in Mougins. He's easy-going and very relaxed. The €10 lunch menu at is a steal and the other one costs only €15.

⧗❘⦿❘ LES PINS DE MOUGINS

2308 av. Maréchal Juin, quartier Val de Mougins.
☎ 04.93.45.25.96
Closed Sun evening except July–Aug; Mon. **Garden**.

Escape the tourist masses in the centre and spend some quiet time in this attractive restaurant. Fresh, tasty food; the €15 menu lists scallop salad with avocado and fresh tomatoes, *aïoli* and *crème brûlée*, and there are others at €21 and €42. The dining room is brightly decorated in yellows and green and there's a terrace in the garden under the pine trees. Free coffee or *digestif*.

MOUSTIERS-SAINTE-MARIE 04360

⧗ 🏠 ❘⦿❘ LE RELAIS**

pl. du Couvert; (Centre).
☎ 04.92.74.66.10 ➠ 04.92.74.60.47
📧 le.relais@wanadoo.fr
Closed Fri out of season; Jan to 20 Feb. **TV**.

Located on the bank of a stream in the centre of the village, this inn is really popular in summer, when it's best to book. Very pretty rooms go for €43 with basin or shower, €53 with shower/wc and €73 with bath; if you're a light sleeper, avoid the ones that look out onto the pounding waterfall. The restaurant deserves special mention for traditional dishes such as *foie gras* cooked in a cloth, *mille-feuille* of aubergine, local lamb, red mullet *en chartreuse* (braised with cabbage) and trout

poached in walnut wine. There are some vegetarian options too. *Formule* €15, menus for €30 or around €33 *à la carte*. Slightly brusque welcome. 10% discount on the room rate March–June and Nov.

🏠 HÔTEL DE LA FERME ROSE***

chemin Embourgues; it's at the foot of the town.
☎ 04.92.74.69.47 ➠ 04.92.74.60.76
Closed 15 Jan–15 March and 15 Nov–15 Dec. **Disabled access**. **TV**. **Car park**.

This is a gem of a place, a typical Provençal farmhouse deep in the country. You'd expect traditional rustic décor, but not a bit of it. The owner, a real fan of the '50s and '60s, has decorated the bar and the bedrooms with a jukebox, bistro tables, coat-stands and lots of bric-à-brac dating from that era. Even the kitchen, where they prepare breakfast, continues the theme. It could so easily look a bit tacky, but everything fits in perfectly. The rooms are really quiet and the ones on the ground floor have a pretty terrace. Doubles €59–99 with shower/wc and €114–130 with bath. The copious breakfast will definitely set you up for the day.

NICE 06000

SEE MAP OVERLEAF

🏠 HÔTEL DANEMARK*

3 av. des Baumettes. **MAP A3-4**
☎ 04.93.44.12.04 ➠ 04.93.44.56.75

A quiet, ochre-coloured house, hidden behind a few pines in the old part of Nice. The area is full of residential blocks of flats but it's conveniently near the Promenade des Anglais and the owners are so nice that you won't mind the unprepossessing environs. The rooms are simple, tastefully decorated and clean. Doubles €33 with shower/wc or bath.

⧗ 🏠 HÔTEL LOCARNO***

4 av. des Baumettes. **MAP A3-7**
☎ 04.93.96.28.00 ➠ 04.93.86.18.81
TV. **Garage**.

Just minutes from the Promenade des Anglais, this comfortable modern hotel has fifty air-conditioned rooms, some with particularly good facilities. It's a place executives use when they're in Nice on business. There's a sitting room and snooker room. Doubles €43–64 with shower/wc and €55–89 with bath. You have to book space in the garage. 10% discount, except during the Monaco Grand Prix.

♨ |●| HÔTEL LES CAMÉLIAS**

3 rue Spitalieri. **MAP C3-5**
☎ 04.93.62.15.54 ➡ 04.93.80.42.96
Closed Nov. **Garden. Disabled access. Pay car park.**

A haven of tranquillity with a little garden full of exotic plants right in the heart of Nice. The regulars all have their own favourite room; these cost €46 with shower/wc and €61 with bath, breakfast included. There's a bar in the foyer for pre-dinner drinks, a TV room and a small selection of books. Half board is €38 and the guest's menu costs €11.

♨ HÔTEL DE LA BUFFA

56 rue de la Buffa. **MAP B3-14**
☎ 04.93.88.77.35 ➡ 04.93.88.83.39
e buffa.3soleils@informa.fr

A sweet little hotel with simple rooms at modest prices. Doubles €49–61, all of them air-conditioned. Warm welcome and efficient service. Reception is so packed with information about the area that it's almost a tourist office in its own right.

⚘ ♨ HÔTEL AMARYLLIS

3 rue Alsace-Lorraine. **MAP B2-6**
☎ 04.93.88.20.24 ➡ 04.93.87.13/25
Closed 20 Nov–20 Dec and 10–24 Jan. **TV.**

It's hard to tell whether you're in Nice or Manhattan because the décor is just like so many of the simple hotels one finds in New York. Fortunately the prices are from this side of the pond – €55 for a double with shower/wc and TV. Some rooms lead onto the quiet courtyard. Accommodating, friendly welcome. 10% discount out of season.

⚘ ♨ HÔTEL L'OASIS***

23 rue Gounod. **MAP B3-9**
☎ 04.93.88.12.29 ➡ 04.93.16.14.40
Garden. TV. Car park.

Set back a little, on a road near the Promenade des Anglais, this hotel is in a peaceful, shady garden – truly an oasis in the centre of town. Comfortable double rooms €62–72. This hotel once entertained Chekhov and his compatriot, a certain Vladimír Ilyich Ulianov – more commonly known as Lenin. 10% discount Sept–June.

♨ HÔTEL DE LA FONTAINE***

49 rue de France. **MAP B3-11**
☎ 04.93.88.30.38 ➡ 04.93.88.98.11
e hotel-fontaine@webstore.fr
Disabled access. TV.

Right in the centre of Nice, a short walk from the sea and the pedestrianized streets.

Though it looks unremarkable from the outside, inside it's a different story. The good-looking rooms are clean and pleasant, and you can breakfast on the patio accompanied by the rushing fountain. You'll get a warm welcome from the friendly owner, who does everything to make sure you enjoy your stay. He and his staff are all polite and friendly. Double rooms with shower/wc €84–90; ask for one overlooking the courtyard. Top marks for the €8 buffet breakfast.

⚘ ♨ |●| HÔTEL WINDSOR***

11 rue Dalpozzo. **MAP B3-10**
☎ 04.93.88.59.35 ➡ 04.93.88.94.57
e windsor@webstore.fr
Restaurant closed Sun. **Swimming pool. TV. Car park.**

With its marvellous Oriental-looking foyer, its tropical garden planted with brilliantly coloured bougainvillea, palms and bamboos and its little swimming pool, this place is truly something special. Guests can use the sauna, Turkish baths and massage rooms, and there's a relaxation room decorated with plants and Thai statuettes. The owners are keen on contemporary art and each room has been decorated by a different artist. Doubles go for €84 with shower/wc or €114 with bath. À la carte only in the restaurant – you'll pay about €23 for a good meal, which will be primarily southern in flavour. Afterwards, sit back and listen to the birdsong – some of it real, some of it recorded – and enjoy the paintings. Free apéritif.

|●| CHEZ PIPO

13 rue Bavastro. **MAP D3-21**
☎ 04.93.55.88.82
Closed lunchtimes; Mon Jan–May; 15–25 March.

A lovely place. Through the door, you glimpse the long wooden tables where customers sit side by side. They serve *socca*, the thin, flat cake made from chickpea flour which is a Nice speciality. Those in the know say that this place has the best *socca* in town; it's definitely worth trying, as is the *pissaladière* (onion tart) and the sweet Swiss chard pie. You won't spend much more than €7 on a full meal, including drink.

⚘ |●| THE JUNGLE ARTS

6 rue Lepante. **MAP C2-33**
☎ 04.93.92.00.18
Closed Sun and Aug.

Fashionable world cuisine restaurant offering traditional French food, African dishes, kangaroo steaks, horse-meat hamburgers,

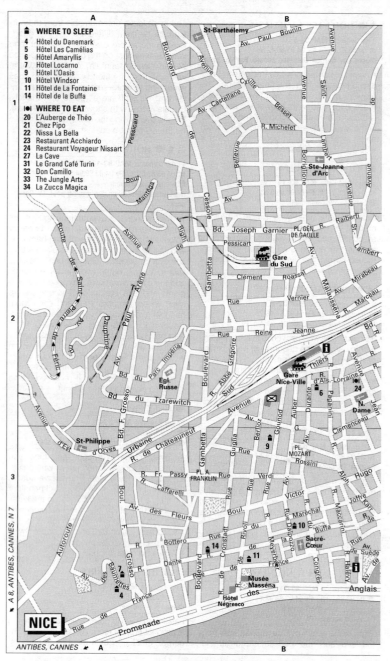

WHERE TO SLEEP
4 Hôtel du Danemark
5 Hôtel Les Camélias
6 Hôtel Amaryllis
7 Hôtel Locarno
9 Hôtel L'Oasis
10 Hôtel Windsor
11 Hôtel de La Fontaine
14 Hôtel de la Buffa

WHERE TO EAT
20 L'Auberge de Théo
21 Chez Pipo
22 Nissa La Bella
23 Restaurant Acchiardo
24 Restaurant Voyageur Nissart
27 La Cave
31 Le Grand Café Turin
32 Don Camillo
33 The Jungle Arts
34 La Zucca Magica

NICE

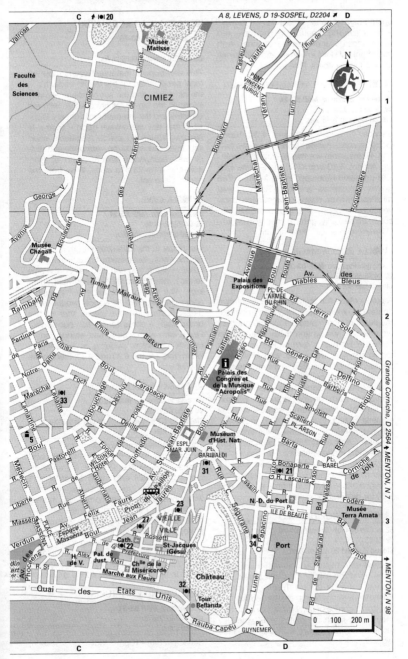

spare ribs and goose breast. Lunch *formule*
€10 or evening menu €14. The funky red
and orange décor evokes the savannah, with
lots of animal skins in frames and waitresses
dressed as panthers. Free apéritif.

🎋 |Ol RESTAURANT VOYAGEUR NISSART

19 rue Alsace-Lorraine. **MAP B2-24**
☎ 04.93.82.19.60
Closed Mon and 1–15 July.

Service 11.30am–2pm and 6.30–10pm.
Good regional cuisine served in a rustic setting. Restaurants like this are rapidly vanish-
ing. Menus €10 and €17; there's one with
well-prepared Nice specialities for €13. The
house specialities are *osso bucco*, wild
mushrooms in oil, ravioli, courgette tart, baby
vegetables, peppers *à la provençale* and
soupe au pistou (vegetable soup with pesto).
Different menus daily. Free apéritif.

🎋 |Ol LA ZUCCA MAGICA

4 [bis] quai Papacino. **MAP D3-34**
☎ 04.93.56.25.27
Closed Sun and Mon.

A quirky place run by Marco, the vegetarian
cousin of Luciano Pavarotti. When it opened,
the seers of doom predicted failure but they
were proved wrong and today Marco is so
busy that he has to turn people away. The
dining room is decorated with Halloween
pumpkins and illuminated by a small forest of
candles. There's no menu, so you eat what
you're given – lasagne, red peppers stuffed
with pasta, pumpkin and gorgonzola tart and
the like. The dining room is so dark that it is
sometimes hard to see what's on your plate,
but you can depend upon it being tasty and
inventive, and everything is prepared from
the freshest market produce. He uses a lot of
chickpeas, lentils and beans, and employs
seasonings that pay homage to his Roman
background. €14 at lunchtime and around
€20 for dinner. Free coffee.

🎋 |Ol L'AUBERGE DE THÉO

52 av. Cap-de-Croix. **Off map C1-20**
☎ 04.93.81.26.19
Closed Mon and 20 Aug–10 Sept.

Service until 11pm. An inn with a delightful
patio up in the hills of the Cimiez area. The
dishes betray a strong Tuscan influence:
fresh pasta with prawns, char-grilled meat or
fish and a choice of tasty pizzas so large that
they hardly fit on the plates. €14 weekday
lunch menu, and others €24 and €38. Free
digestif.

|Ol RESTAURANT ACCHIARDO

38 rue Droite. **MAP C3-23**
☎ 04.93.85.51.16
Closed Sat evening and Sun; Aug.

This very popular restaurant caters more for
local people than for the tourist trade. It's in
the old town, and the surroundings are very
informal: the big tables are covered with red
oilcloths and the atmosphere is cheery. Dishes of the day are always good – tripe *à la
Niçoise*, *soupe au pistou* (vegetable soup
with basil sauce), *daube*, *ratatouille* and ravioli with bolognaise sauce, pesto or Gorgonzola. €18–23 *à la carte*. Wine from the
barrel. Cash only.

🎋 |Ol LA CAVE

rue Francis Gallo. **MAP C3-27**
☎ 04.93.62.48.46.
Closed lunchtimes and Mon.

The décor in the little dining room is choco-
late-box cosy, but despite its name there's no
cellar in sight. You can also eat on the little
terrace, overlooked by old apartment buildings. The young chef turns out flavourful
cooking using fresh Provençal produce: red
mullet fillets with olive paste, fillet of sea
bream with a citrus sauce, fish *pot-au-feu*.
Finish with a chocolate and orange tart, a
creamy chocolate pudding or a wonderful
lemon tart. Menus €20 and €33. Free house
apéritif.

|Ol NISSA LA BELLA

6 rue Sainte-Reparate. **MAP C3-22**
☎ 04.93.62.10.20
Closed Tues; Wed (Wed lunchtime only in season); a
fortnight in June.

This restaurant serves typical dishes from
Nice that are full of the intense flavours and
aromas of Provence. Portions are so enormous that you'll only need to order one
course, whether you choose baked rabbit
with polenta, beef stew *provençal*, home-
made ravioli or stuffed baby vegetables. The
handsome ochre dining room has a relaxed
atmosphere – most of it is open to the street
– and there's a second dining room at the
back, which is cool in summer. You'll leave
feeling satisfied and generally well-disposed
towards the world. Around €21 *à la carte*.

|Ol LE GRAND CAFÉ TURIN

5 pl. Garibaldi. **MAP D3-31**
☎ 04.93.62.29.52
Closed June.

Service 8am–10pm out of season,

5pm–11pm July–Aug. This seafood restaurant is an institution in Nice, serving fresh oysters daily, copious platters of oysters, prawns and whelks, and sea urchins in season. The two dining rooms and the terrace are always full but you can simply stop by for a drink if you want. They don't accept cheques but they do take credit cards. €23–30 *à la carte*.

补 |◉| DON CAMILLO

5 rue des Ponchettes. **MAP C3-32**
☎ 04.93.85.67.95
Closed Sun and Mon lunchtime.

In an attempt to steer clear of the crowds while still remaining central, Stéphane Viano chose a quiet spot between the cours Saleya and the seafront to site his restaurant. The large dining room is attractively decorated in light colours, and the food is of high quality: risotto with courgette flowers, roast sea bream with anchovy *jus* and lemon zest, escalope of *foie gras* with sweet and sour summer fruits and onion conserve. The desserts are prepared by a talented pastry chef. *Menu du marché* at €28, or €38 *à la carte*. The service is both professional and affable. Free house apéritif.

VILLEFRANCHE-SUR-MER   06230 (7KM E)

补 ☎ |◉| HÔTEL RESTAURANT LE PROVENÇAL**

4 av. du Maréchal-Joffre.
☎ 04.93.76/53/53 ➡ 04.93.76.96.00
Closed 1 Nov–23 Dec. **Garden**.

A pretty house with blue shutters. The rooms are clean and pleasant, particularly those on the second and third floors – which also have views of the garden and the sea. Doubles €58–90 with shower or bath; all are air-conditioned. They're very popular, so you need to book well in advance. There's a delightful patio for breakfast or dinner – the delicious food includes fish soup, ravioli with pesto, stew of dried cod *en stofficada* (with garlic, tomatoes, potatoes and olives) and rabbit *provençal* flambéed in *marc de Bandol*. Menus €17–19. 10% discount on the room rate Sept–June.

补 |◉| RESTAURANT MICHEL'S

pl. Amélie-Pollonnais; it's on the port.
☎ 04.93.76.73.24
Closed Tues.

This is the "in" place at the moment, and the atmosphere's pretty laid-back. The large terrace comes into its own on summer evenings. There are no set menus, but the *à la carte* menu is full of wonderful dishes – fish and seafood, mostly, prepared with seasonal produce. There's salmon *chausson*, *terrine* of starling with juniper berries, monkfish and scampi kebab with a sweet and sour sauce, veal chop with apple and Calvados purée and strawberry cheesecake with egg custard. About €24 *à la carte*; dishes of the day €12. Friendly attentive service. Free apéritif.

补 |◉| LA MÈRE GERMAINE

quai Courbet (South); it's on the port.
☎ 04.93.01.71.39

This restaurant is in a perfect situation on the port and is undoubtedly one of the best places between Nice and Monaco. It has a magnificent view of Villefranche's natural harbour, a lovely dining room, and a terrace. There's an army of smart waiters. Dishes are prepared using only the freshest ingredients and the fish and seafood are nothing less than wonderful: *escabèche* of sardines, fillets of sole cooked to perfection. Like everything else, the desserts are prepared in-house. Menu €34. *À la carte*, prices climb steeply – from €46 to around €61. Free coffee.

ORANGE   84100

补 ☎ HÔTEL LE GLACIER**

46 cours Aristide-Briand (Centre).
☎ 04.90.34.02.01 ➡ 04.90.51.13.80
Closed Sun from Nov to Easter, and 23 Dec–1 Feb.
📧 hotelgla@aol.com
TV. **Car park**. **Lock-up garage**.

This comfortable hotel has been run by three generations of the Cunha family. All the rooms are decorated differently: some are in Provençal style, while others look more English. Doubles with shower/wc €44 and up to €61 with bath. There's a charming breakfast room. Musicians performing in the festival often stay here. 10% discount Sept–June.

补 ☎ HÔTEL ARÈNE***

pl. de Langes (Centre); it's in the historic centre, near the town hall.
☎ 04.90.11.40.40 ➡ 04.90.11.40.45
Closed 8–30 Nov. **TV**. **Pay garage**.

A quiet, delightful hotel in the pedestrianized area. The air-conditioned rooms are decorated in a pretty Provençal style. A few of them have a terrace, where you can eat breakfast, €8, with Provençal pastries and jam made locally. Doubles €67–92 with shower/wc or bath. It really is a pity there's no restaurant. One free soft drink from the minibar.

洗 |O| RESTAURANT LE YACA

24 pl. Silvain (Centre); it's by the Roman theatre.
☎ 04.90.34.70.03
Closed Tues evening except in summer; Wed; the first three weeks in Nov.

The exposed beams and stonework create an intimate and pleasant setting, and there are pretty pictures on the walls and fresh flowers on the tables. The classic dishes are thoughtfully prepared: seafood stew, home-made chicken liver *terrine* with onion marmalade, leg of lamb gratinéed with olive purée, snail and baby vegetables in pastry case and for dessert, chocolate *marquise* with egg custard or pear charlotte with raspberry *coulis*. Dish of the day €9 and menus €11–20. Free coffee.

|O| RESTAURANT LA ROSELIÈRE

4 rue du Renoyer (Centre); to the right of the town hall.
☎ 04.90. 34.50.42
Closed Sun evening, Mon and the last fortnight in Dec.

The décor is a mish-mash of enamel advertising signs from the '50s and '60s, cartoon characters, teddy bears and bits and pieces picked up in secondhand shops. If the weather's not good enough to eat outside, come inside and listen to the music, which ranges from Jacques Brel to Mahler. The single menu at €16 gives you a choice of four starters, four main courses and a few desserts. The banana tart is out of this world. Fred changes the menu each week depending on the seasonal produce: choices include *foie gras*, pig's trotters, herrings in oil and veal kidneys *à la provençale*. The cellar is full of good, inexpensive wines. Credit cards not accepted.

PIOLENC   84420 (4KM N)

洗 ☎ |O| AUBERGE L'ORANGERIE

4 rue de l'Ormeau; take the N7.
☎ 04.90.29.59.88 ➡ 04.90.29.67.74
e orangerie@orangerie.net
Closed Mon out of season and ten days in Nov.
Disabled access. TV. Car park.

A beautiful inn surrounded by trees. After working in various hotels around the world, Gérard and his wife decided to set up their own place, and have been here now for more than ten years. The six cosy rooms with rustic-style furniture go for €60–65 with shower/wc or bath; the one with a secluded private terrace is particularly lovely. The whole house is decorated with copies of masters

painted by Gérard himself. In the restaurant you'll find a lunch menu at €17 and others €25–33 – stuffed crab, *colombo* of fish, thin slices of kangaroo meat with ginger and orange and some good traditional Provençal dishes,. Gérard's cellar, which has more than 350 different vintages, is unbelievable, as is his selection of whiskies. Half board, compulsory Easter to 30 Sept, is €62 per person. 10% discount for the third night except at Easter, All Saints', Christmas and New Year.

PEILLE   06440

☎ |O| BELVÉDÈRE HÔTEL

3 pl. Jean-Miol; it's on the edge of the village.
☎ 04.93.79.90.45
Closed Mon, and 20 Nov–29 Dec.

The very friendly Mme Beauseigneur has five clean, simple rooms that each have a splendid view of the mountain. Doubles €33 with washing facilities. You get a bird's-eye view of the valley from the excellent restaurant, which offers appealing menus from €16. Specialities include lemon chicken, gnocchi and ravioli stuffed with ricotta cheese.

PELVOUX   05340

洗 ☎ |O| LE SAINT-ANTOINE**

How to get there: on the Briançon–Embrun road, turn off onto the D994 into the Vallouise valley and it's 11km on.
☎ 04.92.23.36.99 ➡ 04.92.23.45.20
e hotel.st.antoine@wanadoo.fr
Closed Sun evening; 1 May–5 June; 30 Sept–1 Dec.

The valley is on the edge of the Écrins national park and it's still wild. The hotel is a reliable, efficiently run establishment with a friendly atmosphere. The rooms are simple and clean and some have balconies overlooking the stream. Doubles with basin €27–34; €33–43 with shower/wc. Honest, tasty traditional dishes – including a Savoy *fondue*. Cheapest menu for €13 then €16–22. Half board for €36–42 per person. Free coffee and 10% discount on the room rate if you stay at least ten days.

PLAN-DE-LA-TOUR   83120

洗 ☎ MAS DES BRUGASSIÈRES**

☎ 04.94.55.50.55 ➡ 04.94.55.50.51
Closed 10 Oct–20 March **e** mas.brugassieres@free.fr
Swimming pool. TV. Car park.

A charming hotel in a pleasant village at the

heart of the Massif des Maures, just 5km from the sea and 12km from Saint-Tropez. It's run by a couple of ex-globetrotters who have decorated the place with oddments that they've picked up on their travels. Relaxing welcome, rooms for €69–87 and swimming pool. They do a special pool-side breakfast, served from 10am to 1pm. Easygoing welcome and ambience. Free apéritif, and if you stay more than three nights Sept–June you get two breakfasts free.

PONTEVÈS   83670

⅍ 🏠 |●| LE ROUGE GORGE**

Quartier les Costs; take the D560 2km east of Barjols, go over the bridge and drive up the hill to the village.
☎ 04.94.77.03.97 ➡ 04.94.77.22.17
Closed Tues out of season; 1 Jan–15 March; the All Saints' holidays. **Swimming pool. TV. Car park**.

Lively inn in a village that is typical of many between the Gorges du Verdon and the coast. The welcome is as warm as the climate. In the evening, you dine by the pool on good local dishes like soup with beans, stuffed vegetables, *aiguillettes* of lamb with rosemary, *daube* of beef *à la provençale* and salmon marinated with herbs and olive oil. Menus €15–23. Comfortable, unpretentious rooms with shower/wc or bath €49–56. Half board is compulsory in July–Aug and costs €45–49 per person. There are dozens of walks to do in the surrounding countryside. Free house apéritif.

RISTOLAS   05460

🏠 |●| LE CHALET DE SÉGURE**

How to get there: it's at the top of the village.
☎ 04.92.46.71.30 ➡ 04.92.46.79.54
Closed Mon; end March to end May; end Sept to Christmas. **Car park**.

This chalet, in the tree-covered mountains of Haut Queyras, is the ideal place to recharge your batteries. The owner, Jean-Marie, organizes outings in snow-shoes in winter and along tracks into the wilds of the mountains in summer. His hobby is carpentry and he's made a lot of the furniture for the hotel. Pascale, his wife, embroiders samplers and many of them are hung on the walls. In the dining room a mannequin will greet you dressed in traditional costume in winter and a turn-of-the-century school uniform in summer. Menus from €12 (not Sunday) to €20. Specialities include duck breast with honey

and spices and apples with caramel. Bright double rooms are priced at €43; half board is €47 per person.

ROUSSILLON   84220

⅍ |●| RESTAURANT MINCKA'S

pl. de la Mairie (Centre).
☎ 04.90.05.66.22
Closed Thurs; 11 Nov–25 Dec; 7 Jan to the Feb school holidays.

Prettily decorated little restaurant in a mountainous region of rich, rust-red rock. Good set menu for €17 and a selection of imaginative dishes with powerful flavours: beef *daube* with cardomom, pork stew with fresh ginger and honey. Service is easy-going – sometimes too much so. It's best to book. Free apéritif.

SAINT-DALMAS-DE-TENDE   06430

⅍ 🏠 |●| LE TERMINUS**

rue des Martyrs-de-la-Résistance; it's opposite the station.
☎ 04.93.04.96.96 ➡ 04.93.04.96.97
Closed 24 Oct to mid-Nov. **Garden. Car park**.

The friendly welcome makes you immediately feel at ease in this old family home. The nights are cool and restful in the mountains, and it'll most likely be the birds that wake you. Very pretty, simple rooms for €33–53. There's a pleasant pergola at the front and an attractive dining room with a fireplace and a wood-fired oven. Menus from €14 list dishes which are prepared on the spot by the *patronne* – her ravioli is unforgettable. Free house apéritif.

BRIGUE (LA)   06430 (3KM E)

|●| LA CASSOLETTE

20 rue du Général-de-Gaulle; it's between Place Saint-Martin and the Place de Nice.
☎ 04.93.04.63.82
Closed Sun evening and Mon except public holidays; a fortnight end of March.

This tiny, pretty, family-run restaurant serves good home cooking. The dining room is full of models and trinkets of chickens in all shapes and sizes. If they run out of things, the boss will go next door to the butcher to fetch an extra *tournedos* or breast of duck. Wholesome leek, potato and courgette tart, rabbit *à la provençale*, ravioli and grilled duck breast with *foie gras*. Menus from €13.

SAINT-DISDIER   05250

🏠 |O| AUBERGE LA NEYRETTE**

How to get there: it's where the Saint-Étienne-en-Dévoluy road crosses the road to Veynes.
☎ 04.92.58.81.17 ➡ 04.92.58.89.95
e info@la-neyrette.com
Closed a fortnight in mid-April; mid-Nov to mid-Dec.
TV. Car park.

Impeccable rooms in an old water mill standiing in solitary splendour at the bottom of a little valley. There are only twelve rooms, and they fill quickly so it's best to book. Number 1 has a splendid view. Doubles with shower/wc or bath €55. The restaurant is very good, offering trout from the nearby lake, house *terrine* and *tourtons* (rather like pancakes). Menus €17–26 or *à la carte*.

SAINT-JEAN-CAP-FERRAT   06230

🏠 HÔTEL LE CLAIR LOGIS**

12 av. Centrale (Centre); it's in the centre of the peninsula, on the corner of allée des Brises.
☎ 04.93.76.04.57 ➡ 04.93.76.11.85
Disabled access. Garden. TV. Car park.

Situated in a quiet residential area, this haven of peace and tranquillity has an exotic garden and all eighteen rooms have a balcony or a little terrace. General de Gaulle came here to relax back in 1952. It's not cheap, though it is reasonable for the peninsula – a millionaires' haunt. Doubles €68 with shower/wc, €99 with bath in peak season. Ideal for a romantic weekend on the Côte d'Azur. 10% discount Oct–May.

|O| LE SLOOP

It's on the new harbour.
☎ 04.93.01.48.63
Closed Tues evening and Wed out of season; Tues and Wed lunchtimes in season; 15 Nov–15 Dec.

This is by far the nicest of a whole string of fancy restaurants by the harbour. You'll receive a warm welcome. The chef produces sophisticated cooking – the single menu, €24, offers good choices and excellent value. Try fresh salmon *tartare* and *aïoli*, minestrone with saffron and fresh thyme, grilled sea bream, whole roast sea bass *à la Niçoise* or veal chop studded with truffles and served with its own juices. There's a pleasant terrace facing the harbour.

SAINT-MARTIN-VÉSUBIE   06450

🏠 |O| HÔTEL-RESTAURANT LA BONNE AUBERGE**

allée de Verdun; turn left as you leave Saint-Martin and head for Colmiane and Boreon.
☎ 04.93.03.20.49 ➡ 04.93.03.20.69
Closed mid-Nov to mid-Feb. **TV.**

This beautiful stone hotel is comfortable and well-run. Well-maintained doubles go for €43 with shower/wc and €46 with bath. Try to avoid the ones that look out onto the avenue – it gets particularly busy at the weekend. Menus, starting at €15, list traditional, delicious food such as grouper *terrine*, trout *meunière*, lamb stew, duckling with olives and quail casserole. Pleasant terrace, surrounded by a hedge. Half board €43. Free house apéritif.

SAINT-MAURICE-EN-VALGAUDEMAR   05800

🏠 |O| HÔTEL-RESTAURANT LE VAL DES SOURCES**

Les Barrengeards; before the village of Le Roux, turn right over the bridge then right again; it's on the left 300m on.
☎ and ➡ 04.92.55.23.75
e le.val.des.sources@wanadoo.fr
Closed 1 Nov to end March. **Swimming pool.**

Comfortable hotel located in a wild valley. Claude and his wife took it over and have improved the facilities in rooms which are simple but have good beds. Doubles €27 with basin, €43–55 with shower/wc or bath. The tasty food is nourishing and many of the dishes are local specialities: *oreilles d'âne* (a pastry case made in the shape of donkey's ears and filled with spinach and chard), ravioli with honey, *flozon* (potato tart with smoked bacon and shallots). Weekday menu for €12 then others €15–23 – it's best to book. In summer, half board, which costs €35–46, is compulsory. There are *gîtes* in the grounds and a covered, heated swimming pool. Free apéritif.

SAINT-PAUL-DE-VENCE   06570

🏠 AUBERGE LE HAMEAU***

528 route de la Colle; 1km from the village on the D7.
☎ 04.93.32.80.24 ➡ 04.93.32.55.75
Closed mid-Nov to mid-Feb. **Garden. Swimming pool. Car park.**

Set deep in the countryside, this place has a

superb view of the village of Saint-Paul. There's a pleasant terraced garden and a pool. Comfortable air-conditioned rooms with nice furniture go for €88–126. Ask for a room in the main building because the annexe has less character.

SAINT-RÉMY-DE-PROVENCE 13210

⚤ ⌂ HÔTEL VILLE VERTE**

pl. de la République (Centre).
☎ 04.90.92.06.14 ➡ 04.90.92.56.54
✉ contact@hotel-villeverte.com
Disabled access. Swimming pool. TV. Car park.

It is said that Charles Gounod, the composer of *Faust*, wrote the opera *Mireille* in this hotel and there's a plaque on the wall to comemorate the event. It's just minutes from the centre of town and has prices to suit all budgets: doubles with shower €33–37 and €40–46 with shower/wc or bath; some rooms have balconies. There are also studios with kitchenette for two people, rented by the week. There's an indoor swimming pool that's covered in winter, a courtyard and pleasant terraces. 10% discount on the room rate except during school holidays (not for the studios).

⌂ |●| LE CHALET FLEURI**

15 av. Frédéric-Mistral, route de Maillane.
☎ 04.90.92.03.62 ➡ 04.90.92.60.28
Restaurant closed Tues. Garden. Car park.

An old-style family guesthouse with a little garden where you can take a pre-prandial stroll among the topiary. Good, wholesome local dishes such as rabbit with olive paste and cuttlefish with parsley; menus change daily. Half board €47 per person. Double rooms for €38–46; they're practical and stuffed with ornaments. In the morning over breakfast, chat to the owner about the bull races.

⚤ ⌂ LE CHEVAL BLANC**

6 av. Fauconnet (Centre).
☎ 04.90.92.09.28 ➡ 04.90.92.69.05
Closed Nov–March. Disabled access. TV. Pay garage.

Refurbished rooms with shower/wc or bath and direct-dial telephone €44–49. There's a lovely terrace and a veranda. The private car park is a considerable asset in the centre of Saint-Rémy, but there's a charge of €4. 10% discount for a minimum three-night stay.

⌂ HÔTEL L'AMANDIÈRE**

av. Théodore Aubanel; it's 700m from the town centre, in the direction of Noves.

☎ 04.90.92.41.00 ➡ 04.90.92.48.38
Closed Nov to mid-March. Disabled access. Swimming pool. TV. Car park.

A young, vibrant hotel just outside Saint-Rémy. Comfortable, spacious rooms €47 with shower/wc and €52 with bath. With its wonderful breakfast (€7) and warm welcome, this place is one of the best of its type.

⌂ HÔTEL DU SOLEIL**

35 av. Pasteur (South).
☎ 04.90.92.00.63 ➡ 04.90.92.61.07
Closed Nov–March. Swimming pool. Garden. TV. Garage. Lock-up car park.

The hotel is set around a large courtyard. It also has a swimming pool, terrace and garden. All rooms have TV. Doubles €47–61 with shower/wc or bath – the ones with bath are bigger. There's a garage for bikes, motorbikes and a lock-up for the cars.

⌂ L'HÔTEL DES ATELIERS DE L'IMAGE***

traverse de Borry, 5 av. Pasteur (Centre).
☎ 04.90.92.51.50 ➡ 04.90.92.43.52.
Disabled access. TV. Car park.

What used to be the old Saint-Rémy music hall has been turned into a smart new hotel with 18 modern rooms; you'll pay €110–150 for en-suite facilities and €145–190 for *de luxe* ones. They're all decorated in a contemporary fashion, with stylish photos all over the walls. Photography is *the* topic of conversation in the bar and they hold conventions on the subject. Though it's right in the heart of the old town, this is a remarkably relaxing place.

|●| RESTAURANT LA GOUSSE D'AIL

25 rue Carnot (Centre).
☎ 04.90.92.16.87
Closed Thurs and Sat lunchtimes; 15 Nov–5 March.

Service until 11pm. Intimate atmosphere and food that offers value for money. Lunch menu €15 and others €16–34, with different dishes each day. House specialities include *pavé* of beef with creamy garlic sauce, snails *à la provençale* and a few vegetarian dishes. Tuesday is *bouillabaisse* day and on Friday it's *aïoli*. Great wine list. Jazz on Thursdays.

|●| LA SOURCE

13 av. de la Libération.
☎ 04.90.92.44.71
Closed Wed and Jan.

A serene, tranquil place – in the image of the couple who run it. It's best to book if you want a table on the terrace by the garden.

Monsieur produces tasty, traditional Provençal dishes such as red mullet fillets with a black olive *coulis* and *noisette* of lamb stuffed with truffles. Menus €15 and €25–36. There's a tempting swimming pool, but unfortunately you're not allowed in it.

|●| L'ORANGERIE CHABERT

16 bd. Victor-Hugo.
☎ 04.90.92.05.95
Closed Sun evening and Mon out of season; Mon and Tues lunchtimes July–Aug; 3 weeks in Nov; 3 weeks in March. **Garden**.

The clientele here includes a decent number of great and good, the odd general's widow and a smattering of well-to-do wine-growers. You can dine in the sizeable garden. There's a classy but relaxed atmosphere but there's nothing slapdash about the cuisine. Even the short menu is balanced and perfectly prepared: *marbré* of *brousse* cheese in olive oil, goujons of whiting with green apples and a low-calorie dessert. Menus €17, €25 and €33.

|●| LA MAISON JAUNE

15 rue Carnot (Centre).
☎ 04.90.92.56.14 **e** lamaisonjaune@wanadoo.fr
Closed Sun evening and Mon in winter; Mon, Tues lunchtime in summer; Jan–Feb.

Stylish place where you'll be served imaginative dishes at realistic prices. There's a weekday lunch menu for €18 (not public holidays), and gourmet versions at €27–49. House specialities include stuffed artichokes, sardine fillets with fennel and pickled lemon, roast fillet of lamb with olive paste, roast pigeon in Baux wine and hot walnut tart. There's a superb terrace.

|●| XA

24 bd. Mirabeau (Centre).
☎ 04.90.92.41.23
Closed Wed and Oct–March.

This place looks like a prettily decorated flat with its bistro chairs, mirrors and spotlights, not to mention its appealing terrace. There's only one menu for €23, or you can eat *à la carte*. The food is imaginative – *parfait* of aubergine, marinated fresh anchovy fillets, red mullet fillets with fennel seed, blanc-mange with almonds. They must be doing something right – they've been going more than 17 years.

GRAVESON   13690 (9KM NW)

♠ LE CADRAN SOLAIRE**

It's in the village.

☎ 04.90.95.71.79 ↦ 04.90.95.55.04
e cadransolaire@wanadoo.fr
Closed Jan. **Garden**.

An enchanting old posthouse in a quiet place. The rooms are comfortable and painted in contemporary colours; doubles €46–69. There's a shady garden and a terrace where you can munch on the snack you've bought at the Friday farmer's market. Breakfast is served until 10am.

♠ |●| LE MAS DES AMANDIERS**

route d'Avignon.
☎ 04.90.95.81.76 ↦ 04.90.95.85.18
e contact@hotel-des-amandines.com
Closed Wed lunchtime; 15 Oct–15 March.
Disabled access. **TV**. **Swimming pool**. **Car park**.

This hotel gets booked up in summer. It offers attractive, reasonably priced rooms for €52 with bath, and there's a little restaurant where you can have dinner – menus €14 and €22. Out of season, when they have more time, the owners might take you to the farmers' market with them or to visit the perfume museum; they know how to look after their guests.

♠ |●| HÔTEL DU MOULIN D'AURE**

quartier Cassoulen; it's just outside the village on the Tarascon road.
☎ 04.90.95.84.05 ↦ 04.90.95.73.84
e hotel-moulin-d-aure@wanadoo.fr
TV. **Swimming pool**. **Car park**.

A lovely place surrounded by vast grounds with pines and olive trees. The cicadas sing, the swimming pool awaits and the proprietress has a friendly smile. Pleasant rooms with bath €49–76. Nice, lazy atmosphere; in summer you can eat the Provençal or Italian dishes – fresh pasta, risotto – they serve by the pool if you really can't be bothered to move. Menu for €21. Ideal for families.

SAINT-TROPEZ   83990

♠ LOU CAGNARD**

18 av. Paul-Roussel (North); it's a couple of minutes from the port and 250m from the place des Lices.
☎ 04.94.97.04.24 ↦ 04.94.97.09.44
Closed 2 Nov–27 Dec. **Garden**. **TV**. **Car park**.

A large, typically Provençal house with nicely updated rooms for €45–48 with shower and €58–87 with shower/wc or bath. Pleasant terrace and flower garden. If you want a good night's sleep on summer nights you should reserve a room that looks onto the garden.

⅍ 🏠 HÔTEL LOU TROUPELEN***

Chemin des Vendanges (Centre).
☎ 04.94.97.44 88 ➡ 04.94.97.41.76
Closed mid-Oct to mid-April. **TV**. **Car park**.

This place doesn't pretend to be the most fashionable hotel in town, but it has a lovely family atmosphere and the prices are good value for Saint-Tropez – doubles €67–84 with shower/wc or bath. The free car park is a great advantage, and you're just minutes from the centre of town and a short drive from the beaches. Breakfast under the pine trees or in the garden is most enjoyable.

⅍ |◉| CANTINA EL MEXICANO

16 rue des Remparts (Centre); go up rue de la Mairie under the gateway and it's about 100m along on the right.
☎ 04.94.97.40.96
Closed lunchtimes; 15 Oct–1 April.

One of the few fashionable places in St-Tropez where the prices won't send a shiver down your spine. Out front there's a little mosaic-lined pond and a statue of the Virgin. They serve real Mexican dishes indoors: tacos, quesadillas, tortillas – and fantastic margaritas. It's delicious, generously served and the place has real atmosphere. Lots of local people come here regularly in high and low season. You'll pay about €24 à la carte. Free *Tequila rapido* at the end of your meal.

SAINT-VALLIER-DE-THIEY 06460

⅍ 🏠 |◉| HOSTELLERIE LE PRÉJOLY**

route Napoléon, pl. Rouguière (Centre); coming from Grasse it's at the beginning of the village on the right.
☎ 04.93.42.60.86 ➡ 04.93.42.67.80
Closed Sun evening and Mon except July–Aug; Dec–Jan. **Disabled access**. **Garden**. **TV**.

A chic establishment with reasonable prices. The charming hotel is set in a large, quiet garden, and it has a sauna and solarium. Most of the rooms have a terrace; doubles €38–53 with shower/wc or bath. The restaurant is the real draw, though; there's weekday menu €15 and another at €30, listing scampi omelette, pan-fried scallops with crayfish butter, honeyed breast of duck, rib steak with truffle-scented *jus*, rabbit stew, mutton tripe and sheep's trotters *à la provençale* and calf's tongue. Classic cuisine which sets greater store in quality than originality. Half board (€52–58) is compulsory in summer. Free apéritif.

SAINT-VÉRAN 05350

⅍ 🏠 |◉| AUBERGE-GÎTE D'ÉTAPE LE MONCHU

La Chalp-Sainte-Agathe.
☎ 04.92.45.83.96 ➡ 04.92.45.80.09
🅔 info@lemonchu.fr
Closed mid-April to mid-June; mid-Sept to 20 Dec. **Car park**.

In the highest village in France, at an altitude of 2040m, Nathalie and Philippe Babinet have converted their big farmhouse into a welcoming *gîte* with the comforts of a decent hotel. The cooking is traditional, and meals are served in a handsome dining room faced with larch and with a vaulted ceiling. Specialities include *fondue*, *tartiflette raclette* (to order in advance), Queyras cheese and onion marmalade and home-made pastries. Menu €15 or €22 *à la carte*. All the rooms are bright and comfortable and are let out only on a half-board basis at €29–47. Facilities include sauna, billiard room and table tennis. 10% discount Jan, June and Sept.

⅍ 🏠 |◉| LES CHALETS DU VILLARD***

Quartier Le Villard.
☎ 04.92.45.82.08 ➡ 04.92.45.86.22
🅔 info@leschaletsduvillard.fr
Closed Tues lunchtime; 20 April–20 June; 20 Sept–20 Dec. **TV**.

Exceptional place built entirely out of wood, with super-comfortable, spacious studios and two-roomed apartments with south-facing balconies. Each has a hi-fi, dishwasher and luxury bathroom, and some have whirlpool baths. There are even some studios adapted for people with allergies. Doubles €38–76 according to facilities and season. The restaurant-grill *La Gratinée* is on the ground floor; menus are €14–23 with dishes such as Saint-Véran cheese (*caillette*) and the house speciality, *Queyraflette*. Free house apéritif.

|◉| LA MAISON D'ÉLISA

Le Raux; it's in lower Saint-Véran.
☎ 04.92.45.82.48
Closed April to mid-June; Sept to mid-Dec.

Marie, Parisian by birth but two decades as Saint-Véranienne, is an artistic women who has invested the place with her strong personality – there's more than a hint of 1968 in the air. The terrace has a superb view of the valley to the majestic peak of Roche Brune in the distance, and the dining room has a splendid wooden floors. The place is stuffed with old photographs, hats, children's games and knick-knacks. The cuisine is creative, elegant and original: nettle soup, home-made tarts, spicy *fricassée* of veal and a chocolate *moelleux* dessert that melts in the mouth. It really doesn't matter that the service is slow. Lunch menu €15 or about €23 *à la carte*. She doesn't accept credit cards and it's best to book.

SAINTE-MAXIME   83120

🏠 ℹ️ L'ENSOLLEILLÉE**

29 av. Jean-Jaurès (Centre); it's on the corner of rue F-Martin, 50m from the beach.
☎ 04.94.96.02.27 📠 04.94.49.06.21
Closed Oct to Easter. **TV**. **Car park**.

Lovely welcome and décor in this old-fashioned hotel – the genuine kindness is fantastic, and the rooms are unpretentious, comfortable and clean. Rooms €38–44 with shower or €46–54 with shower/wc. Half board, compulsory July–Aug, costs €40. The restaurant is full of little surprises; menus €15–21. And the place is only 50m from the beach. 10% discount on the room rate out of season and excluding public holiday weekends. Free coffee.

🏠 ℹ️ HÔTEL-RESTAURANT-MONTFLEURI

3 av. Montfleuri (Northeast).
☎ 04.94.96.18.26
📧 montfleuri.ste.maxime@wanadoo.fr
Swimming pool.

You imagine from the outside that this is a deeply traditional seaside hotel. Inside, though it's full of energy, run by a young couple who create a terrific atmosphere. All the rooms are different, all equally pleasant. Doubles with shower/wc or bath, €54–114 with bathroom and €70–183 with a terrace and sea view. Good, family cooking served at tables set out around a Hollywood-esque swimming pool. Free house apéritif.

🏠 ℹ️ LE JAS NEUF

112 av. du Débarquement; it's 2km from the Nartelle beach in the direction of the Gulf of aint-Maxime.
☎ 04.94.55.07.30 📠 04.94.49.09.71
📧 info@hotel-jasneuf.com
Closed Nov–Christmas; Jan. **Garden**. **Swimming pool**.

A genuinely charming hotel run by a very nice couple who go to great lengths to look after their guests. Very comfortable air-conditioned rooms, deftly decorated in Provençal style; doubles for €78–160. The restaurant is very reliable and uses quality local produce –

the John Dory with spiced tomatoes and fennel is typical of the flavourful, delicate cuisine. *À la carte*, a meal costs €28–38. There's a wonderfully bright veranda and a smiling team. Life here is good, with the swimming pool, sun-loungers in the garden – miles from the turmoil and the crowds.

ℹ️ RESTAURANT LA MAISON BLEUE

24 [bis] rue Paul-Bert (Centre); it's in the pedestrianised area on the seafront.
☎ 04.94.96.51.92 📧 maisonbl@aol.com
Closed Wed in Oct; 27 Oct–26 Dec; 3 Jan–30 March.

A little house decorated in blue, ochre and yellow. The terrace, with its comfortable bench seats, is a lovely spot for a good meal: fresh fish soup, ravioli with a sardine filling, stuffed mussels, sea bream with fennel *en papillote*. Menus €15 and €21. This is a very good place, but the service could be more attentive.

🏠 ℹ️ AUBERGE SANS SOUCI

34 rue Paul-Bert (Centre).
☎ 04.94.96.18.26
Closed Mon out of season; 30 Oct–14 Feb.

This inn is a great place to eat. The food is typical of Provence – simple, tasty and full of the flavours of the *garrigue*, the local heathland. In summer you can dine on the pleasant terrace in the town's "gourmet" street or, if there's a nip in the air, in the cosy dining room. The menus, €15 and €22, feature lamb shank with mushrooms, roast sea bream with basil and *mérou* (a Mediterranean fish) fillet with vermouth sauce. Free apéritif.

ISSAMBRES (LES)   83389 (4KM NE)

🏠 ℹ️ LE PROVENÇAL***

How to get there; take the N98 towards Saint-Raphaël.
☎ 04.94.96.90.49 📠 04.94.49.62.48
📧 info@hotel.le.provencal.com
Closed Tues lunchtime;weekday lunchtimes 8 July–19 Aug except for public holidays; Nov–early Feb except over New Year. **TV**.

Just the place for an old-fashioned holiday, this charming hotel has a view over the gulf of Saint-Tropez and the beach. It's run by the Sauvan family, who are all smiles when you arrive – they can give you tips about what to do (watersports, golf courses, spas). Their cooking is superb, and you dine in the shade of the restaurant's terrace. Menus €23–35, or if you wish you can order a simple grilled fish and other tasty Provençal dishes *à la carte*. Rooms cost €52–95. There's a pretty terrace and a lovely beach with fine sand with a view of Saint-Tropez.

SAINTES-MARIES-DE-LA-MER `13460`

☎ HÔTEL MÉDITÉRRANÉE**

4 rue Frédéric-Mistral; it's in the middle of town near the arena.
☎ 04.90.97.82.09 ➡ 04.90.97.76.31
e hotel_le_mediterrannee@worldonline.fr

A tiny little hotel which is both clean and well-run. There are flowers and plants everywhere. Doubles €35 with shower to €53 with bath/wc – some of them overlook the little courtyard.

☎ |●| MAS DES SALICORNES**

rue d'Arles; at the beginning of the village on the D570.
☎ 04.90.97.83.41 ➡ 04.90.97.85.70
e linfo@hotel-salicornes.com
Closed 15 Nov–1 April. **Swimming pool. TV. Car park**.

Some evenings, the Merlins and their friend Jojo – a Provençal storyteller – entertain you once you've dined on delicious traditional dishes and drunk the invigorating local wine. They also organize flamenco evenings on the beach for only €24 (which you reach by horse-drawn carriage, no less) and run cookery classes. Comfortable double rooms with whitewashed walls €38–46. Menus €14 and €24. There's a lovely swimming pool.

☎ |●| LE MIRAGE**

14 rue Camille-Pelletan (Northeast); it's 200m from the beach.
☎ 04.90.97.80.43 ➡ 04.90.97.72.22
e stephan.monnet@wanadoo.fr
Closed lunchtimes except Mon and public holidays; 30 Oct–1 April. **Disabled access. Garden**.

This modern, comfortable hotel with a white façade was a cinema from 1953–63. Today it has a pretty sitting room on the first floor, and offers doubles with shower/wc at €41–49, or bath for €43–53. Avoid the ones on the ground floor – they're dreary. Nice restaurant Au Fond du Jardin, with colourful murals and good-value, tasty dishes; menus €17–26, offering skate wings with pesto, beef stew and terrine with aïoli. The terrace opens onto a little garden.

☎ HÔTEL LE BLEU MARINE**

av. du Docteur-Cambon.
☎ 04.90.97.77.00 ➡ 04.90.97.76.00
Closed 1Nov–29 March except Christmas and New Year holidays. **Disabled access. Swimming pool. TV**.

As you might have guessed from the name, the sea isn't far away. Tasteful décor, friendly welcome, and all 26 rooms face the swimming pool. Doubles €55–61. In summer,

light snacks and salads are served by the pool.

SALON-DE-PROVENCE `13300`

⅍ ☎ GRAND HÔTEL DE LA POSTE**

1 rue des Frères-Kennedy (Centre); it's at the end of the cours Carnot across from the Fontaine Moussue.
☎ 04.90.56.01.9 4 ➡ 04.90.56.20.77
e zap@zapsolu.com
Closed Sun end Oct to end Feb, and 15 Jan– 5 Feb. **TV. Pay car park**.

A good place to stay in the centre of town, with well-soundproofed rooms for €40 with shower or €47 with bath. The owners, keen to provide all sorts of services to their guests, act as an unofficial tourist information centre. 10% discount Oct–April.

☎ HÔTEL VENDÔME**

34 rue du Maréchal-Joffre (Centre).
☎ 04.90.56.01.96 ➡ 04.90.56.48.78
e hotelvendome@ifrance.com
TV.

The rooms in this hotel, decorated in intense Provençal colours, go for €40–47. All have huge bathrooms. Ask for one overlooking the cool, delightful patio. Attentive if slightly formal staff.

|●| LA SALLE À MANGER

6 rue du Maréchal-Joffre (Centre); it's next to the Fontaine Moussue.
☎ 04.90.56.28.01
Closed Sun evening and Mon.

The Miège family took over this nineteenth-century residence and transformed it into a vibrant, lively place which is renowned for gourmet cuisine. It's a real pleasure to sit on the terrace under the chestnut trees or in the Rococo salons. Two weekday lunchtime formules at €13 (two courses) and €20 (three) and €18–29 à la carte. Have a plate of Bouzigues oysters, a casserole of stuffed cuttlefish or lamb with tapenade. A good choice of desserts. They've made a big effort and searched out some interesting local wines with prices starting at €10 a bottle. Best to book.

SANARY-SUR-MER `83110`

⅍ ☎ |●| HÔTEL-RESTAURANT BON ABRI**

94 av. des Poilus; 200m from the harbour and beaches.
☎ 04.94.74.02.81 ➡ 04.94.74.30.01
Closed Mon, Sun eveing out of season, and end-Nov to

end Jan except for New Year'sl celebrations. **Disabled access**. **Garden**. **Pay car park**.

A very simple but quite delightful hotel in a lush garden full of greenery and bushes. The nine large rooms are well-designed and brightly decorated; doubles €39–50 with shower/wc or bath. Half board, compulsory during the school holidays, costs €35–42. The cuisine has had a makeover as well: try the veal sweetbreads in a pastry case or the *émincé* of duck with caramel. Lunch menu €11; others €17–22. Free apéritif and free use of the car park – out of season only.

🏕️ |●| L'OCÉAN JAZZ

74 route de la Gare; it's 500m from the town centre.
☎ 04.94.07.36.11 ➡ 04.94.34.68.62
Closed Sat lunchtime, and Sun evening Nov–March. **Disabled access**. **Car park**.

An excellent little restaurant with a weekday lunch *formule* at €12 including a $1/4$-litre of wine and others €17–27. They put a dish of olive paste and hunks of bread on the table to start you off; carefully prepared regional dishes made with fresh local produce and presentation worthy of a much grander place follow. Efficient, easy-going service and a truly friendly welcome. The dining room is charming and the terrace is splendid. There's music in the background, and live duos and trios on Friday and Saturday evenings. Free *digestif*.

SAULT   84390

🏕️ 🛏️ |●| HOSTELLERIE DU VAL DE SAULT***

Ancien chemin d'Aurel; it's 1.5km from the centre of the village – follow the signs.
☎ 04.90.64.01.41 ➡ 04.90.64.12.74
ℯ valdesault@aol.com
Closed Nov–March. **Disabled access**. **Swimming pool**. **TV**. **Car park**.

This fairly new hotel-restaurant is a haven in a gorgeous landscape of lavender and forests. It faces Mont Ventoux and has eleven spacious rooms, each with a little sitting area and a terrace. Doubles with bath/wc for €83 and half board at €79–99 per person. In the kitchen, Yves Gattechaut skilfully combines traditional ingredients to create innovative flavours. His *galette* made from spelt (a kind of wheat) with lamb offal and a *compote* of shallots is a real treat, as is his fish soup with pesto and saffron, and it's worth trying the lavender honey-roast leg of lamb. Weekday lunch menu €21 and from €30 in the

evening; there's a truffle menu for €45 and a children's menu at €12.

SEYNE-LES-ALPES   04140

🏕️ 🛏️ |●| LE VIEUX TILLEUL**

Les Auches; it's a ten-minute walk from the centre of the village
☎ 04.92.35.00.04 ➡ 04.92.35.26.81
Closed Sat lunchtime; Sun evening; Nov. **Car park**.

Near-perfect hotel near the ski slopes in a sweet village in the Vallée de la Blanche. In summer you can lounge around in the shade of the huge trees in the grounds. The rooms in the old farmhouse have been attractively and originally renovated; doubles €32 with basin and €40–47 with shower/wc or bath. Honest cuisine with some mountain dishes and others from further afield: lamb haunch with cream, veal chops with girolles, cod *à la provençale*. sheep's cheese salad, pork with Roquefort and the like. Weekday lunch menu €12, and others €17–22. 10% discount on the room rate.

SISTERON   04200

🏕️ 🛏️ |●| GRAND HÔTEL DU COURS***

allée de Verdun (Centre).
☎ 04.92.61.04.51 ➡ 04.92.61.41.73
ℯ hotelducours@wanadoo.fr
Closed Nov–March. **TV**. **Car park**.

A chic hotel with fifty rooms. Provincial atmosphere, courteous welcome and attentive service. The rooms are all very clean but some are noisier than others – avoid those that look out onto the main road and plump instead for one with a view of the château or the cathedral. Doubles €52–73 with shower/wc or bath. The lively, attractive restaurant serves sound local specialities: *fricassée* of lamb with basil, *fricassée* of monkfish with ceps, leg of lamb with pickled garlic and olive purée, lamb *daube à la provençale*. Menus €13, 19 and 24. Free apéritif.

|●| LES BECS FINS

16 rue Saunerie; it's in the centre of the lower town, parallel to the tunnel.
☎ 04.92.61.12.04 **ℯ** becsfins@aol.com
Closed Wed and Sun evening out of season; Tues evening; 13–27 June and 1–12 Dec.

A gourmet restaurant in a town that has a reputation for rearing excellent lamb. They're pretty serious about their cooking, but the atmosphere is relaxed, warm and friendly.

The menus are well-judged and in the best traditions of Provence – pan-fried *escalope* of *foie gras*, snail stew in white wine, sautéed lamb, duck breast prepared nine different ways and Châteaubriand prepared eight different ways. And as you would expect, lamb features in many dishes. Menus €20–49.

TARASCON   13150

🏋 🏠 |●| HOSTELLERIE SAINT-MICHEL

Abbaye de Frigolet; it's 12km from the centre of town.
☎ 04.90.90.52.70 ➥ 04.90.05.75.22
e abayedefrigolet@frigolet.com
Garden. **TV**. **Car park**.

A former abbey offering rooms with a variety of facilities; spacious doubles €28 with basin, €38 with shower/wc and €49 with bath. Meals are served in an old refectory – it's got a fantastic entrance – or in the garden. Appetizing *aïoli* with rabbit and sautéed veal in white wine. And you have to try the ice-cream served with Frigolet liqueur. Menus €10–20. Free house *digestif*.

THORENC   06750

🏠 |●| HÔTEL DES VOYAGEURS**

av. Belvédère (East).
☎ 04.93.60.00.18 ➥ 04.93.60.03.51
Closed Thurs out of season. **Garden**. **TV**. **Car park**.

Twelve faultlessly clean rooms, €43–46. Half board, compulsory in season, costs €43 per person. The good restaurant offers a weekday menu at €14 and another at €24; they list dishes such as calf's head *sauce ravigote* and sautéed rabbit *chasseur*. There's a pleasant terrace and garden with a view of the village.

|●| LE CHRISTIANA

L'Audibergue.
☎ 04.93.60.45.41
Closed evenings; 1–20 Dec.

Set at the foot of the Audibergue ski runs, this restaurant sees a lot of regulars from Cannes. The menus are substantial, and you can help yourself to the five starters – country ham, fried garlic bread, crudités, *terrines* and calf's head – as often as you like, following them with tripe *à la Niçoise*, roast lamb, wild boar or hare stew, cheese and dessert. All that for €18. Dish of the day €10. Booking essential at weekends and public holidays.

TOULON   83000

🏋 🏠 HÔTEL MOLIÈRE*

12 rue Molière (Centre); it's in the pedestrian area next to the theatre.
☎ 04.94.92.78.35 ➥ 04.94.62.85.82
Closed Jan. **TV**. **Car park**.

A very simple family hotel with unbeatable prices. The owners really know how to make you feel welcome and do their best to make sure you have a pleasant stay. Comfortable, clean, soundproofed doubles €19 with basin and €30 with shower/wc. Numbers 18, 19 and 20 have a great view of the harbour. An excellent place of its kind. 10% discount for a two-night stay, Sept–June.

🏋 🏠 HÔTEL LE JAURÈS*

11 rue Jean-Jaurès (Centre).
☎ 04.94.92.83.04 ➥ 04.94.62.16.74
TV.

A long-standing favourite which really should have two stars. It's friendly, clean and offers some of the best value for money in town. €29 for a double with shower/wc, €33 with bath. The rooms overlooking the courtyard are quiet. Covered storage for bikes. 10% discount Sept–June for a two-night stay.

|●| RESTAURANT LE CELLIER

52 rue Jean-Jaurès (Centre).
☎ 04.94.92.64.35
Closed Sat, public holidays, a week at Easter and a fortnight in Aug.

Warm, friendly restaurant where you get a choice of menus at €13–24, listing dishes like mussels with shallots, red mullet in Côtes-de-Provence wine and monkfish in cider. The décor contributes to the charm and appeal of this quiet little place.

|●| LE JARDIN DU SOMMELIER

20 allée Courbet; beside pl. d'Armes, behind the arsenal.
☎ 04.94.62.03.27 **e** jsommelier@infonie.fr
Closed Sat lunchtime and Sun.

The *sommelier* and chef who run the place believe that what's on your plate and what's in your glass are equally important. Their sunny restaurant is full of wonderful aromas and pretty colours; mouthwatering smells waft from the kitchens, where they prepare fabulous dishes such as fresh tomato and aubergine tart, crayfish *tartare*, guineafowl breast with cinnamon couscous and hot chocolate *moelleux* with vanilla cream. Lunch *formule* for €14 and menus €27–33; it's around €33 *à la carte*. Needless to say, you'll get a friendly welcome.

TOUR-D'AIGUES (LA)   84240

⚘ |●| AUBERGE DE LA TOUR

51 rue Antoine-de-Très (Centre); it's opposite the church.
☎ 04.90.07.34.64
Closed Mon, and Nov.

This good, friendly restaurant has a handsome, tastefully decorated dining room with a vaulted stone ceiling and a shaded terrace open in good weather. Menus, €11 (weekday lunchtime) and €15–28, feature fish and traditional Provençal dishes like lamb tripe, meatballs *à la provençale*, kid *blanquette* and crayfish *fricassée*. Free apéritif.

TURBIE (LA)   06320

🏠 |●| LE CÉSARÉE – LE CARPE DIEM

15 cours Albert 1er; just outside the village near the large public car park.
☎ 04.93.41.16.08 ➡ 04.93.41.19.49
TV. Car park.

This old restored inn has comfortable rooms with en-suite facilities and views over the hills. Doubles €52–76; from the most expensive you can see the sea in the distance. Courteous and attentive welcome. The restaurant is not very well-known yet but, since the chef uses only local organic produce, it won't be long before it is – even the house apéritif is supposed to be good for you. Menus from €13.

UTELLE   06450

⚘ |●| AUBERGERIE DEL CAMPO

route d'Utelle.
☎ 04.93.03.13.12

Just below the road climbing steeply up to Utelle, there's a lovingly restored shepherd's house dating from 1785. In the rustic dining room, with its handsome fireplace and olive-wood floors, you're served classic dishes like ravioli with duck and cep filling, king scallop *fricassée* with raspberry vinegar, trout braised with tarragon and splendid desserts. Lunchtime *formule* €12 and set menus €16–29. The beautiful terrace looks over the Gorges de la Vésubie. Friendly atmosphere. Dinner by reservation only. Free apéritif.

VAISON-LA-ROMAINE   84110

⚘ 🏠 HÔTEL BURRHUS**

1 pl. Montfort (Centre); take the Bollène exit off the A7.
☎ 04.90.36.00.11 ➡ 04.90.36.39.05
e info@burrhus.com
Closed Sun Jan–Feb; 1–21 Jan; 8–22 Dec. **TV. Car park**.

Attractive hotel, all ochre walls and wrought iron, with a billiard room. The bedrooms are distributed around a warren of corridors and they're all different – some are decorated in Provençal style, others are more basic. Doubles with shower/wc €43–46, with bath €44–49. There's a shaded terrace on the main square where you can enjoy a snack. Faultless welcome. The owners are into contemporary art and hold regular exhibitions. 10% discount on the room rate.

⚘ 🏠 |●| L'HOSTELLERIE DU BEFFROI***

rue de l'Évêché (South).
☎ 04.90.36.04.71 ➡ 04.90.36.24.78
e lebeffroi@wanadoo.fr
Hotel closed Feb–29 March. **Restaurant closed** weekday lunchtimes; end Jan to end March.
TV. Car park.

This exceptional hotel is housed in two residences from the sixteenth and seventeenth centuries. The salon has been magnificently furnished, and the bedrooms have good facilities. Doubles with shower/wc €75 or bath €91–107. Menus €42–38. The food is good – lamb *daube à l'avignonnaise*, *aigo-boulido* – and there's a salad bar on the terrace in summer. Free house apéritif.

VALBERG   06710

🏠 |●| HÔTEL LE CHASTELLAN**

rue Saint-Jean; it's behind the tourist office off the main square, up the road to the left.
☎ 04.93.02.57.41 ➡ 04.93.02.61.65

This is a family-run hotel for families to stay in. It boasts 37 lovely rooms, a large, airy dining room and a games room for the children. Doubles €58 and five suites for €88. They all have shower/wc or bath and direct-dial telephone, and prices include buffet breakfast. There's only one menu at €17, and half board is €51 per person.

|●| CÔTÉ JARDIN

It's behind the main square.
☎ 04.93.02.64.70

Closed Wed out of season. **Garden**.

You rarely think of gourmet food when you think about ski resorts, but here's the exception to the rule. True, you can get *tartiflette*, *raclette* and *fondue*, but it would be a pity to opt for dishes that are more typical of Savoy than of Provence. The dishes on the menus (€13–28) show off the talents of the chef: *croustillant* of scallops with oyster mushrooms, home-made *terrine* with *foie gras*, duck breast with spiced orange. Not only does the food taste good, but the presentation is exceptional. The dining room faces the garden. Friendly service.

VENCE   06140

☎ |●| AUBERGE DES SEIGNEURS**

pl. Frêne (Centre).
☎ 04.93.58.04.24 ➡ 04.93.24.08.01
Hotel closed 15 Nov–15 March. **Restaurant** closed Mon and Tues lunchtime.

This beautiful fifteenth-century building is situated on the ramparts at the entrance to the old town. The rooms, which are more like suites, are named after painters; some have mountain views. Prices are more than reasonable – €60–69 with shower or bath. The restaurant offers sophisticated, imaginative cooking on menus from €27. Warm welcome.

|●| LE P'TIT PROVENÇAL

4 pl. Clémenceau.
☎ 04.93.58.50.64
Closed Wed and Thurs out of season, Nov and March.

A new restaurant, with a relaxed informal atmosphere, in the centre of the old

town. The food is extremely imaginative and typically Provençal. Dishes change frequently, but typically include stew of cheek of suckling pig, ravioli *à la bouillabaisse*, leg and shoulder of rabbit with *tapenade* and stuffed baby vegetables. Weekday lunch menu €12 and other menus up to €25. If you eat on the terrace you can admire the view of the lively, historic town.

|●| LA FARIGOULE

15 av. Henri-Isnard.
☎ 04.93.58.01.27
Closed Tues and Wed lunchtime in summer; the school holidays.

You come here for the authentic atmosphere and tasty Provençal cooking with a touch of the exotic – sardine tart with coriander and pickled lime, sautéed rabbit with olives, suckling lamb roast with cardomom. Menus from €21 or *à la carte*. The chef trained with the great Alain Ducasse when he had his restaurant in Juan-les-Pins. Try his speciality dessert – a wonderful dish of roast figs.

SAINT-JEANNET   06640 (8KM NE)

☎ |●| HÔTEL L'INDICIBLE*

rue du Saumalier.
☎ 04.92.11.01.08 ➡ 04.92.11.02.06

A little hotel in the middle of the village – there are signs to get you there – run by a friendly yong couple. Peter and Els hail from Gand in Belgium. Their hotel is in an old house which has been very attractively renovated and it provides rooms which have views over Le Baou, the hills and the sea in the distance. Doubles €50. They also run a restaurant in the summer, up to 15 Sept.

Rhône-Alpes

AIX-LES-BAINS   73100

☎ |●| HÔTEL BROISIN*

10 ruelle du Revet (Centre).
☎ 04.79.35.06.15 ➡ 04.79.88.10.10
Closed 1 Dec to end Feb. **TV.**

A little hotel in a quiet side street in the centre of town, just a short walk from the spa. It's a very typical spa town hotel with the atmosphere of a family guesthouse; many guests have been coming here for years. The rooms have been freshened up and prices are modest: €24 for a double with basin, €32 with shower/wc. The restaurant doesn't merit a special visit; it offers one menu at €8.

☎ |●| HÔTEL-RESTAURANT LES PLATANES**

173 av. du Petit-Port (West); it's near the lake.
☎ 04.79.61.40.54 ➡ 04.79.35.00.41
Closed 1 Nov–1 Feb. **TV. Car park**.

Set in a residential area near the lake, this hotel has a lovely shaded terrace. At weekends, the owner organizes musical evenings – everything from New Orleans jazz to Django on a Friday, and French *chansons* from Brel to Brassens on a Saturday. The firmly classic cuisine features many Savoy specialities: deep-fried Reblochon cheese, *fricassée* of quail *à la mondeuse.* The chef also has a deft touch with fish dishes. Menus

€17–40. The décor in the bedrooms has seen better days, but the facilities are good, and they're very quiet. Doubles with shower/wc €35–43.

🍴 ☎ |●| HÔTEL-RESTAURANT AU PETIT VATEL**

11 rue du Temple (Centre).
☎ 04.79.35.04.80 ➡ 04.79.34.01.51
Closed Jan. **TV. Garden. Car park**.

In a quiet street in the centre of town, just next to the Anglican church of St Swithin, this charmingly old-fashioned establishment has an elegant atmosphere. The rooms at the back, complete with balcony, overlook a little garden with walls swathed in ivy. Doubles €46 with shower/wc. The dining room has a pleasant atmosphere and there's a delightful terrace in the garden. Tasty, classical cooking – the freshwater fish, particularly the trout, is good, as are the *osso bucco* and the Savoyard specialities of *fondues* and *raclette*. Dish of the day for €8 and menus €17–22. Free house apéritif and 10% discount on the room rate.

☎ |●| HÔTEL-RESTAURANT LE MANOIR***

37 rue Georges-1er; it's behind the spa.
☎ 04.79.61.44.00 ➡ 04.79.35.67.67
📧 info@hotel-lemanoir.com
Swimming pool. Garden. TV. Car park.

A reliable hotel set among the trees, which is

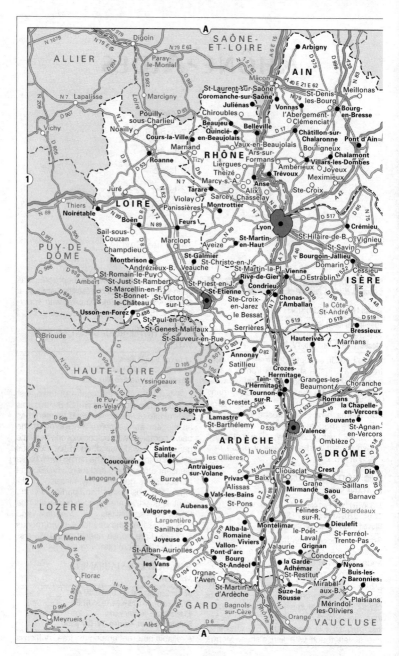

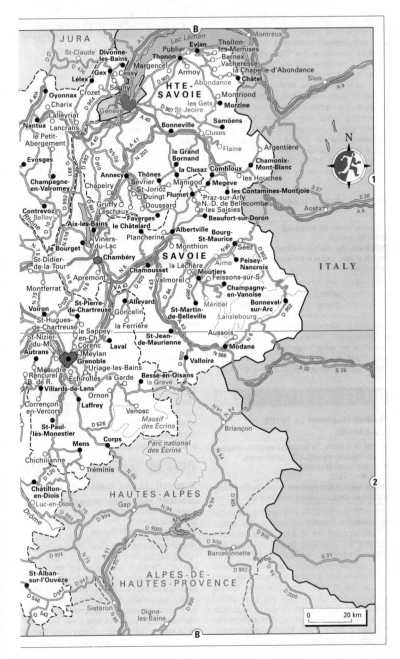

full of character – though not quite top of the range. The "manoir" is actually a series of outbuildings belonging to two *belle époque* mansions, the "Splendide" and the "Royal". The cosy, well-equipped rooms are decorated in a style that's in keeping with the building. Doubles €60–106 with shower/wc or bath. The sitting rooms are comfortable, the garden pleasant and the indoor swimming pool very 1930s Hollywood; there's also a Jacuzzi and a fitness room. Excellent regional cuisine – try the suckling pig *à la savoyarde* or any of the delicate freshwater fish. Menus €22–45. The young, relaxed staff create an easy-going atmosphere.

|●| RESTAURANT L'AUBERGE DU PONT ROUGE

151 av. du Grand-Port (Northwest).
☎ 04.79.63.43.90
Closed Sun, Mon and Tues evenings; Thurs; a week at the end of June; a week at the beginning of Sept; 20 Dec–10 Jan.

This restaurant is always busy. The dining room isn't particularly beautiful and the terrace in the gravel courtyard isn't that great, but the owners are friendly and the cooking is wonderful. Menus are a combination of southwestern dishes and fish – which depends on what's landed from the lake – and there are specialities from Périgord. Weekday lunch menu €10, others €15–30.

ALBA-LA-ROMAINE   07400

⅔ |●| RESTAURANT LA PETITE CHAUMIÈRE

Quartier de la Roche. It's signposted on the main square in Vieil Alba; take the road at the bottom to the preserved hamlet of La Roche.
☎ 04.45.52.43.50
Closed Tues and Wed lunchtime in summer; Mon–Thurs and Sun evenings; Fri and Sat lunchtimes Nov–Jan.

The setting is very unusual and the welcome is delightful. There are only a few tables inside, as most are on a lovely terrace overlooking an imposing tower of crumbling rocks. Traditional, old-fashioned, family cuisine – cream of carrot soup, sautéed lamb with spices and a real crème caramel – and it's served in handsome portions. Menus €10–14; they don't have set specialities, though the savoury tart, cream of vegetable soup, lamb sautéed with spices and chocolate tart make a pretty regular appearance. Booking advisable. Free house apéritif.

ALBERTVILLE   73200

⅔ ♠ |●| AUBERGE COSTAROCHE**

1 chemin Pierre-du-Roy (South); take the pont du Mirantin – it's near the medieval town of Conflans and the château in Costaroche.
☎ 04.79.32.02.02 ➡ 04.79.31.37.59
TV. Garden. Car park.

A large, rather dull building in a residential area surrounded by a tree-filled garden. The young couple who have recently taken it over are trying to give it more personality. For a start they give you a charming welcome, and the rooms have been gently renovated. Doubles with bath €33–46. The dining room is not very intimate but the cooking is decent: raviolis gratinéed with cheese, flambéed king prawns *à la Provençale*. scallops in Noilly sauce. Weekday lunch menu €11; others €14–30. 10% discount on the room rate.

MONTHION   73200 (8KM SW)

|●| LES SEIZE CLOCHERS

How to get there: on the D925, between Grignon and Notre-Dame-des-Millières, turn left onto the D64.
☎ 04.79.31.30.39
Closed Mon and Wed evening except July–Aug; 3 weeks mid-Dec to mid-Jan. **Car park**.

As the name suggests, there's a view of sixteen bell towers from the restaurant's bay window as well as on the terrace, and you can also see the Combe de Savoie. Good classic dishes, such as *diots* (vegetable and pork sausages in white wine), *tartiflette* and *fondue*, and a few more traditional ones like *fricassée* of snails *à la Savoyarde* (with cheese and potatoes) and chanterelles in puff pastry. €13 lunch menu (except Sun), others €17–27.

PLANCHERINE   73200 (10KM W)

⅔ |●| CHALET DES TRAPPEURS

Col de Tamié; from Albertville, follow the signs for Gilly-sur-Isère and then col de Tamié.
☎ 04.79.32.21.44
Closed Mon and Wed. **TV. Garden**.

The characterful, attractive chalet is sturdily built of wood and, as you might expect in a trapper's chalet, huge logs burn in the hearth, hunting trophies line the walls and animal skins are draped on the benches. They serve Savoy specialities like *tartiflette* and *fondue*, substantial omelettes and some remarkable local dishes: *fricassée* of rabbit with *trompette de la mort* mushrooms, country-style fillet of *féra* (which is a kind of salmon). Weekday lunch menu €11 and others €14–24. There's a large terrace and deckchairs in the garden. While you're in the area, buy some of the cheese made by the monks in the nearby abbey of Tamié. Free apéritif.

ALLEVARD   38580

🕴 🛏 |●| LES TERRASSES** NEW

29 avenue de Savoie; it's opposite the old train station.
☎ 04.76.45.84.42 ➡ 04.76.13.57.65
Closed Sun evening and Wed out of season; a week at the end of April; Nov.

A rather dull building from the outside, but it's been attractively renovated inside and decorated in shades of blue and white with posters of great artists' works on the walls. The corner bar in the veranda at the entrance is bright and the dining room is fresh and smart. They serve salads, a dish of the day, hot goat's cheese with honey and Chartreuse iced soufflé. Weekday *formule* for €8; menus in the week from €11 and one at €13 on Sunday. The lady owner takes the time to show you the rooms so you can choose. Doubles €32–35 depending on the facilities – some have a view over the garden. Free house apéritif or coffee.

GONCELIN   38570 (10KM S)

|●| RESTAURANT LE CLOS DU CHÂTEAU

How to get there: on the D525 from Allevard.
☎ and ➡ 04.76.71.72.04
℮ closchateau@netsysteme.net
Open lunchtimes; Fri and Sat evenings during the school holidays. **Disabled access. Car park**.

This thirteenth-century house, in the mountains of Chartreuse and Belledonne, is run by an extremely nice English couple who've given it a new lease of life. It's not easy to see it from the road because it's set in very extensive grounds. You dine in the shade of the hazels and ancient cedars with a view over the mountains, or in the restaurant which has a French-style ceiling. Bag a table by the fire in winter. Suzie Glayser is in charge of the service while her husband creates wonderful flavours in the kitchen: specialities include crayfish ravioli in a creamy broth, and beef Wellington with *foie gras*. There's a lunch *formule* at €15 and menus €27–38.

FERRIÈRE (LA)   38580 (17KM S)

🕴 🛏 |●| AUBERGE NEMOZ

Hameau La Martinette; take the D525 in the direction of

Fond-de-France.
☎ 04.76.45.03.10 ➡ 04.76.45.88.75
Closed Mon–Thurs during term-time; Mon evening in winter; weekends and public holidays out of season; mid-Nov to mid-Dec. **Car park**.

This chalet is at the end of a forest track in the little-known valley of Haut-Breda. It's a relaxed place with stone walls and a wide fireplace ready to cook real *raclette* or *tartiflette*. You'll find a few specialities on the menus – €14 weekday and €19–26 – including Breda salad with smoked fillet of trout; fresh trout with almonds, *en papillotte* or *au bleu*; fresh salmon; mutton *terrine* with *tapenade* or chicken with shrimps. There are a couple of charming rooms for €55–61 including breakfast. Best to book. Free apéritif.

ANNECY   74000

SEE MAP OVERLEAF

🛏 CRYSTAL HÔTEL**

20 rue Louis-Chaumontet. **MAP A1-4**
☎ 04.50.57.33.90 ➡ 04.50.67.86.43
℮ annecycrystal@aol.com
TV. Free car park and pay lock-up garage.

This concrete building is away from the town centre – a good fifteen minutes on foot – in a charmless district behind the station. But you don't hear the trains, you'll be made really welcome and the modern rooms, despite the 1970s décor, have good facilities. Doubles with shower/wc €36–45 or €39–47 with bath. It's more a place for an overnight stop than a longer stay.

🕴 🛏 ALÉRY HÔTEL**

5 av. d'Aléry. **MAP A2-6**
☎ 04.50.45.24.75. ➡ 04.50.51.26.90
℮ hotel.alery@wanadoo.fr **TV. Pay car park**.

Characterful traditional hotel in a good spot between the station and the old town. All the rooms are decorated in the Savoy style with pictures painted on wood and they have air conditioning. Doubles €37–56 with shower/wc or bath. The owners welcome you charmingly, the facilities are perfect and you'll have a quiet night in the rooms at the back. Good breakfast. One free breakfast per room per night.

🕴 🛏 |●| HÔTEL LES TERRASSES**

15 rue Louis Chaumontel. **Off map A1-9**
☎ 04.50.57.08.98 ➡ 04.50.57.05.28
℮ lesterrasses@wanadoo.fr
TV. Car park.

A stunning old house which has been trans-

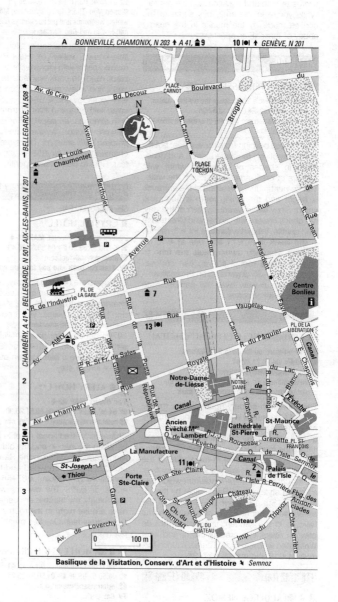

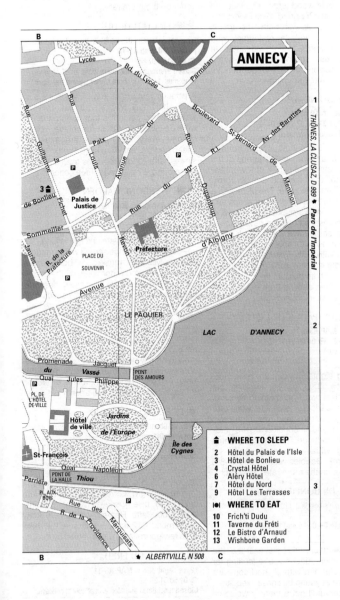

ANNECY

Lycée
Bd. du Lycée
Parmelan
Boulevard
St-Bernard
Av. des Barattes
THÔNES, LA CLUSAZ, D 999 ↑ Parc de l'Impérial
Rue Guillaume
Rue
Paix
la
Louis
Fichet
de Bonlieu
Avenue
du
Rue
du
30ᵉ
R.I.
de
Menthon
Dupanloup
Sommeiller
Jaurès
R. de la Préfecture
PLACE DU SOUVENIR
Rue
Revon
Préfecture
d'Albigny
Avenue
3 ♠
Palais de Justice
LE PÂQUIER

LAC   D'ANNECY

Promenade
du
Jacquet
Vassé
Quai
Jules
Philippe
PONT DES AMOURS
PL DE L'HÔTEL DE VILLE
Hôtel de ville
Jardins de l'Europe
Île des Cygnes
St-François
Quai
Napoléon III
PONT DE LA HALLE
Thiou
Perrière
PL AUX BOIS
Rue
des
R. de la Providence
Marquisats

♠ WHERE TO SLEEP

2 Hôtel du Palais de l'Isle
3 Hôtel de Bonlieu
4 Crystal Hôtel
6 Aléry Hôtel
7 Hôtel du Nord
9 Hôtel Les Terrasses

|●| WHERE TO EAT

10 Frich'ti Dudu
11 Taverne du Fréti
12 Le Bistro d'Arnaud
13 Wishbone Garden

♠ ALBERTVILLE, N 508

formed into a spruce, modern little hotel with a charming garden. The rooms are plain (white walls, pale wood furniture), quiet and comfortable and offer good value for money: €41–58 for a double with bath. The area is dull, however. There's a restaurant with menus at €10 and €13 – it's adequate. In July and August, staying on a half-board basis is compulsory at €41–47 per person. Excellent welcome. Free coffee.

⅍ 🏠 HÔTEL DU NORD**

24 rue Sommeiller. **MAP A2-7**
☎ 04.50.45.08.78 **F▶** 04.50.51.22.04
e annecy.hotel.du.nord@wanadoo.fr
TV. Car park.

This hotel is in a great location in one of the shopping streets in the centre of town, near to the station, the lake and the old town. You'll get a warm welcome. The place has a certain charm with its panelled reception and loggia. The rooms are pastel-pretty, with lovely bathrooms; half of them have air conditioning and some have lovely views of old Annecy. Doubles with shower/wc €42–50 and €45–55 with bath. The breakfast room provides a pleasurable setting in which to start the day with its parquet floor and modern furniture. Free parking 6pm–10am. 10% discount for a two-night stay Sept–June.

⅍ 🏠 HÔTEL DU PALAIS DE L'ISLE***

13 rue Perrière. **MAP B3-2**
☎ 04.50.45.86.87 **F▶** 04.50.51.87.15
e palaisle@aol.com
TV.

An imposing eighteenth-century residence, superbly located in narrow, winding old streets with the River Thiou running beneath. A few rooms overlook the palace, while others face the château and the old town. Soundproofing and air conditioning are gradually being introduced. The modern rooms are superb, with furniture designed by Philippe Starck. Doubles with bath €60–80. 10% discount on the room rate Oct–March.

⅍ 🏠 HÔTEL DE BONLIEU***

5 rue de Bonlieu; it's beside the Palais de Justice.
MAP B1-3
☎ 04.50.45.17.16 **F▶** 04.50.45.11.48
TV. Car park.

A good, dependable little hotel near the lake and the old town, ideal if you're looking for peace and quiet and with all mod cons. It's targeted more at young business execs than travellers, but you'll get a friendly welcome and prices are sensible: double rooms

€61–75 with shower/wc or bath. There's a charge for the car park July–Aug. 10% discount on the room rate.

⅍ 🍽 FRICH'TI DUDU

9 rue Louis-Armand (North); it's in the pedestrianized precinct. **Off map B1-10**
☎ 04.50.09.97.65
Closed evenings except reservations for 15 or more; weekends; 1–15 Aug. **Free underground car park.**

A popular restaurant in an area that's seriously short of good places to eat. This bizzarely named place fills that gap and is well worth a visit. It's full at lunchtime, dishes change every day, prices are incredibly cheap and you eat like a king. The cooking is simple, with various *formules* from €6; you'll pay around €9 *à la carte*. Free coffee.

⅍ 🍽 WISHBONE GARDEN

29 [bis] rue Vaugelas. **MAP A2-13**
☎ 04.50.45.25.96
Closed Sun and Mon.

An unusual place where chicken is king. The speciality is free-range served with a range of sauces: Mexican, mushroom, honey, raspberry vinegar. You order yours by the chunk: quarter, half or whole. Excellent desserts, particularly the crumble and the *fondant au chocolat*. In the evening it's *à la carte* only: choose from dishes such as chicken with *tartiflette* and grilled duck breast. The dining room is on two floors, and the terrace well away from the hurly-burly of tourists. The jovial British owner creates a realaxed atmosphere and really knows his stuff. Weekday lunch *formule* €8, including drink, or around €11 *à la carte*. Free house apéritif.

🍽 LE BISTRO D'ARNAUD

36 av. de Chambéry; it's at the entrance to town, near pont Neuf. **Off map A3-12**
☎ 04.50.45.51.42
Closed Sun and Mon.

This warm, friendly place lists dishes of the day on a blackboard. Specialities from Lyon feature strongly: calves' head, *pot-au-feu*, calf's head, pike *quenelles* (fish balls), frogs' legs, *andouillette*. Realistic prices – weekday lunch menu €12 and another at €18. There are a few good-value wines served by the jug.

🍽 TAVERNE DU FRÉTI

12 rue Sainte-Claire. **MAP A3-11**
☎ 04.50.51.29.52
Closed lunchtimes and Mon except school holidays.

The *Fréti* is one of the few places on this

touristy street that still offers quality at reasonable prices. It's a cheese shop, and naturally enough they specialize in dishes that use it: sixteen types of *fondue* (€10–15), *raclettes* (around €10), *tartiflette* (€10) and potatoes with blue or goat's cheese. *À la carte* you'll pay around €15. There's a pretty dining room upstairs – a 1970s version of rustic – where you can eat if the weather's not good enough to sit outside under the arcade.

SEVRIER   74320 (5KM S)

🌲 |●| AUBERGE DU BESSARD

525 route d'Albertville; on the N508.
☎ 04.50.52.40.45
Closed 21 Oct–19 March. **Car park. Disabled access.**

If you dream of sitting on the banks of the lake with the water lapping at the terrace while you dine on fine fresh fish, here's just the place. It's something of a local institution and has been run by the same family for the last fifty years. The atmosphere is warm and friendly. You'll pay about €23 *à la carte*; there's also a €15 weekday menu and a €20 one at the weekend. It could well list fish *terrine*, perch, *féra* (a kind of salmon) with sorrel and a choice of cheese or dessert. Free coffee.

SAINT-JORIOZ   74410 (9KM S)

🌲 🏠 |●| HÔTEL AUBERGE DE LA COCHETTE**

Lieu-dit "La Magne" à Saint-Eustache; go to St-Jorioz and follow the signs.
☎ 04.50.32.03.53 📠 04.50.32.02.70
📧 info@hotel-la-cochette.com
Hotel closed 15 Dec–15 March. **Restaurant closed** weekdays Sept to end April. **Car park**.

All you have to do is climb – straight up from Saint-Jorioz, following the arrows. The magnificent view over the lake of Annecy, 6km away, is breathtaking. The owner loves paragliding – you can go up with him and land just behind the hotel. He has nice rooms for €27–30 with basin, €34–37 with shower/wc and €37–40 with bath. The food is delicious, with great menus from €15–26 listing such delights as snails in flaky pastry with garlic cream and salad with chicken and crayfish. It's wonderful to eat on the terrace. Free *digestif* and 10% discount on the room rate Sept–June.

CHAPEIRY   74540 (11KM SW)

|●| AUBERGE LA GRANGE À JULES

Le Pélevoz; leave the A41 motorway at the Rumilly exit and take the N201 in the direction of Annecy. After Alby,

turn left towards Chapeiry and you'll find it after the bridge on the right.
☎ 04.50.68.15.07
Closed Sun; Mon and Tues evenings; Wed. **TV. Garden. Car park**.

This is a lovely little rustic place in the back of beyond. In summer, you can have lunch or dinner in the garden under the trees and among the flowers; in winter, the open fire takes the chill off the air. They produce good dishes using fresh ingredients: potato tart with *foie gras*, frogs' legs with parsley. The *navarin* of lamb in pastry is truly memorable. Weekday menu €17 and others up to €39.

DOUSSARD   74210 (12KM SE)

🌲 🏠 |●| À L'AUBERGE

Route de Chevaline.
☎ 04.50.44.86.28 📠 04.50.44.86.28
Closed Mon out of season and 15 Nov–15 Dec. **Car park**.

This old house is full of activity from dawn to dusk. It can seem a bit chaotic but the friendly owner runs the place well – the liveliness is all part of the charm. The regulars hang around the bar before choosing whether to eat in one of the two warm dining rooms or on the terrace. The straightforward regional cuisine is good and really affordable: there's a menu at €11 or it's around €15 *à la carte*. There's a little *crêperie* next door, run by the owner's husband. Attractive rooms at €33 with shower and €38 with shower/wc. For cyclists and walkers, there's a dormitory in a converted stable, which costs €8 per person per night. 10% discount on the room rate 15 Sept–15 March and free *digestif*.

DUINGT   74410 (12KM SE)

🌲 🏠 |●| HÔTEL-RESTAURANT DU LAC**

☎ 04.50.68.90.90 📠 04.50.68.50.18
📧 info@hoteldulac.com
Hotel closed 16 Oct–9 Feb. **Restaurant closed** Sun evening and Mon out of season; 1 Oct–27 April. **TV. Car park**.

The lovely hotel is far enough away from the road that you only see the lake and hear little but the birds. The rooms have all been completely refurbished; doubles with shower/wc €53–62 and €50–73 with bath. Half board is compulsory July–Aug, and costs €50–59 per person. The place is full of young people – the owners among them – and you're served with a smile in the bright, fresh restaurant, where the chef creates interesting, inventive dishes. You'll enjoy a skilful blend of colours, flavours and textures – try *féra* (a type of salmon from the lake) with sesame *vinaigrette* or *confit* of rabbit with mixed spices. Weekday lunch menu €15, others €21–59. Gorgeous terrace for sunny days and a private beach. 10% discount on the room rate out of season and free apéritif.

GRUFFY — 74540 (17.5KM SW)

🛠 🛏 ІОІ AUX GORGES DU CHÉRAN**

Pont de l'Abîme; take the N210 and 1km after Chaux turn onto the D5 – once you've passed Gruffy, it's a further 1.5km.
☎ 04.50.52.51.13 📠 04.50.52.57.33
Closed 11 Nov–23 March. **TV**. **Car park**.

This chalet practically clings to the cliff above the Chéran, near the bridge over the abyss. Rooms 1, 4, 5 and 6 have balconies overlooking the gorge. Newly refurbished rooms €38–46 with shower/wc, €56 with bath. The restaurant has the usual local specialities on menus at €14–24. The cooking isn't trying to win any awards but you'll eat well – try the trout with almonds, the fillet of beef with morels and the bilberry tart. You can eat on the terrace or inside. Perfect, attentive welcome. Free house apéritif.

LESCHAUX — 74320 (18KM S)

🛠 ІОІ LES QUATRE VENTS

Col de Leschaux; by the N508 which skirts lac d'Annecy and then the D912 in the direction of Col de Leschaux.
☎ 04.50.32.03.58
Closed Mon and Tues except July–Aug; Dec.

The restaurant is on the road over the peak, on the edge of the wild Bauges country. It's a nice little place which looks pretty ordinary – something between a roadside caff and a country inn. Inside you'll get a bright, friendly welcome and eat in a warm dining room with an open fire. The menus are substantial; there's a weekday one at €11 and others up to €22. Good home-cooked regional dishes: potatoes with snails and Reblochon cheese cream, *crudités*, steak and chips, *escalope bornandine*, goat's cheese with walnuts, frog's legs *à la savoyarde*. Free apéritif.

ANNONAY — 07100

🛠 🛏 HÔTEL DU MIDI**

17 pl. des Cordeliers (Centre); it's in the lower town.
☎ 04.75.33.23.77 📠 04.75.33.02.43
TV. **Car park**.

Set in a good location on a very lively square,

this hotel is a sturdy building of remarkable dimensions, with wide corridors, large rooms (especially the ones overlooking the square) and thick, plush carpets. There are pictures and engravings of hot air balloons all over the place – the Montgolfier brothers were born in Annonay. Doubles with basin €26, €30 with shower, €38 with shower/wc and €44 with bath. 10% discount on the room rate Oct–March.

ІОІ RESTAURANT MARC ET CHRISTINE

29 av. Marc-Seguin; it's opposite the old station.
☎ 04.75.33.46.97
Closed Sun evening and Mon; the Feb school holidays; 16–31 Aug. **Disabled access**. **Garden**.

The inventive cooking here is appreciated by an essentially local clientele. Christine gives her guests a warm welcome and ushers them into a sitting room decorated in peach tones. Marc does the cooking, and prepares dishes that combine classic and local ingredients. The menus change daily: crayfish and sweet onion soup, Burgundy snails with pig's trotters, sea bream *royale*, grilled tenderloin of beef. Main courses about €11 *à la carte* and menus from €28. A large selection of wines is available by the glass. In summer you can eat outside in the pleasant garden.

SATILLIEU — 07290 (14KM S)

🛠 🛏 ІОІ HÔTEL-RESTAURANT SAPET**

pl. de la Faurie; from Annonay, follow the signs first for the centre of town and then for Lalouvesc D578A.
☎ 04.75.34.95.42 📠 04.75.69.91.13
📧 hotelrestaurantchaletsapet@wanadoo.fr
Closed 26 Dec–2 Jan. **Swimming pool**. **TV**. **Lock-up car park**.

This place, situated in the centre of the village, has an excellent reputation. The welcome is really nice and the cooking first-rate. One of the specialities is *crique ardéchoise*, made with grated potatoes sprinkled with garlic, onions and parsley. €12 weekday menu and others €13–21. The recently renovated bedrooms are clean and comfortable; doubles with shower/wc or bath cost €37 and half board starts at €34. Arrangements can be made for mountain biking or hiking, and there's an open-air pool. Free house apéritif and 10% discount on the room rate Sept–June.

SERRIÈRES — 07340 (15KM NE)

🛏 ІОІ HÔTEL-RESTAURANT SCHAEFFER**

It's on the R86.

☎ 04.75.34.00.07 📠 4.75.34.08.79
📧 mathe@hotel-shaeffer.co
TV. **Pay car park**.

A substantial house on the banks of the Rhône. It's a gourmet restaurant which uses the best seasonal produce in menus at €21–29. Salivate over dishes such as envelopes of ravioli stuffed with mushrooms topped with pigeon livers and served in a rich, aromatic broth and pan-fried venison steak served with with a bitter chocolate *jus*. The cheeseboard is impressive and their desserts – such as bitter chocolate *au gratin* with pistachio ice-cream and sorbet – are inventive and delicious. The more expensive menus include appetizers and *petits fours*. The fine wine list includes a range of good Côtes-du-Rhônes and Hermitages but there are also some more modest bottles. There are modern, functional, air-conditioned and soundproofed rooms for €55; some have views of the river and the bridge. A high-quality place to stay, but one where you don't have to spend a fortune.

ANSE   69480

🏃 🛏 🍽 HÔTEL-RESTAURANT LE SAINT-ROMAIN**

Route de Graves; it's signposted, 200m off the main road.
☎ 04.74.60.24.46 📠 04.74.76.12.85
📧 hotel-saint-romain@wanadoo.fr
Closed Sun evening 1–30 Nov; 25 Nov–5 Dec. **TV**. **Car park**.

Traditional, classic *Logis de France* hotel with honest cooking in the restaurant – guineafowl breast with hazelnuts, game stew, numerous ripe cheeses and home-made desserts. The dining room has sturdy beams and there's a pleasant terrace for summer. Menus €15–44. Rooms are sizeable; they cost €47 with shower/wc and €43 with bath/wc. Free apéritif or coffee.

🏃 🍽 LE COLOMBIER

Pont de Saint-Bernard; it's 2km from the centre of town, in the direction of Trévoux, on the banks of the Saône.
☎ 04.74.67.04.68 📠 04.74.67.20.30
Closed Sun evening and Mon except April–Sept; Nov to end Feb. **Car park**.

Service from noon and 7pm. Cross the bridge and it's almost as if you've passed into a different time zone. This waterside restaurant, which looks like a *guinguette* (riverside café) from a hundred years ago, has been providing good food at reasonable prices for more than twenty years – delicious grilled pig's trotters, zander, frogs' legs, carp *goujons*. Menus from €15 – *hors d'œuvre* buffet, whitebait and tart – up to €30. Free apéritif, *digestif* or coffee.

MARCY-SUR-ANSE   69480 (7KM SW)

🍽 LE TÉLÉGRAPHE

How to get there; take the D79 for Lachassagne and turn left onto the D70.
☎ and 📠 4.74.60.24.73
Closed Sun evening and Mon; a fortnight in June; a fortnight in Nov. **Car park**.

You can order any of the menus with confidence – they cost €16 (not Sun) and €19–38. The house *terrine* and *andouillette* with mustard sauce are delicious, while the *croustille* of St Marcellin goat's cheese has a real tang. Great desserts and flavourful Beaujolais. The pleasant terrace is well away from the road, so it's quiet.

ALIX   69380 (10KM SW)

🏃 🍽 LE VIEUX MOULIN

Chemin du Vieux Moulin; take the D39 in the direction of Lachassagne, turn left for Marcy, and Alix is signposted to the right.
☎ 04.78.43.91.66 📠 04.78.47.98.46
📧 annic.umhauer@wanadoo.fr
Closed Mon and Tues (except public holidays); 12 Aug–10 Sept. **Car park**.

Service until 1.15pm, and in the evenings until 9.15pm. This mill built of pale gold stones has been converted into a charming restaurant with three cosy dining rooms and a barn for families or large groups. Menus at €20–44 list good, reliable dishes: sea-trout with sorrel, guineafowl with morels, duck *foie gras*, frogs' legs, *andouillette*, monkfish with cream and curry sauce and leek *fondue*. Portions are huge. Afterwards you can have a game of *boules* or relax on the terrace. Free coffee.

THEIZÉ   69620 (13KM W)

🏃 🛏 🍽 HÔTEL-RESTAURANT LE THEIZEROT*

Centre; take the D39 Lachassagne road and it's signposted to the right.
☎ 04.74.71.22.26 📠 04.74.71.25.37
Hotel closed 20 Dec–5 Jan. **Restaurant closed** Sun and Mon evenings; Tues and Wed. **Car park**.

This old village café has a few cheap, simple rooms from €20 with basin and €28 with shower. It's not the height of luxury but ideal if you've done too many miles on your bike or walked through one too many vineyards. Weekday menu €11 and others €13–21. Filling regional dishes: *lyonnais* salad, *andouillette*, pike *quenelles* and *choucroute* in winter. Free regional apéritif.

🎿 🛏 |●| HÔTEL-RESTAURANT LA FEUILLÉE

How to get there: take the D39 Lachassagne road and turn right to Theizé.
☎ and ► 04.74.71.22.19
TV.

The large café-restaurant serves honest home cooking – in summer there's a €10 including wine and coffee. Meals to order in the evenings and on Sunday. The five rooms have been attractively arranged, all with shower (wc along the landing), and go for €23 for a double. Good value so it's best to book. Free house apéritif.

ANTRAIGUES-SUR-VOLANE   07530

🎿 |●| LO PODELLO

It's on the village square.
☎ 04.75.38.71.48
Closed Jan–Feb.

The welcoming terrace is set on the typical village square, while the dining room is welcoming with stone walls and gleaming old wood. The jovial owner is happiness personified and he serves decent regional cuisine: excellent *caillette*, *mignon* of veal with goat's cheese and parsleyed potatoes. Finish off with a light cream cheese. Menus €13–25. Free house apéritif.

🎿 |●| RESTAURANT LA REMISE

Pont de l'Huile.
☎ 04.75.38.74
Closed Fri; Sun evening; 10 Dec–6 Jan.

An inviting dining room in rustic style and one of the best tables in the Volane valley. It's as busy in the week as it is on a Sunday. Menus €18 and €31, both including apéritif and *digestif*. Sadly the welcome is sometimes less than wonderful. Free house apéritif or *digestif*.

BURZET   07450 (18KM W)

🎿 🛏 |●| HÔTEL-AUBERGE LES MYRTILLES

pl. de la Confrerie (Centre); it's on the D245.
☎ 04.75.94.45.39 ► 04.73.94.48.77

e les.myrtilles@libertysurf.fr
Closed Sun evening and Mon except July–Aug; mid-Nov to mid-Dec. **Garden**. **TV**. **Car park**.

There's a sense of quiet confidence about this place. The rooms are quite simple but the facilities are regularly improved – though up to now there's only one with an en-suite bathroom. Two of them look over the quiet, sunny little garden. Doubles €29 with basin, €44 with shower/wc. Pleasant dining room and the terrace is on the square. The kitchen concocts tasty dishes using fresh produce: *caillette* (a sort of haggis) with bilberries, chicken stuffed with chestnuts, duck breast with ginger. *Formule* at €12 (main course with either starter or dessert), menus €15–19. Service and welcome conducted by a young, efficient team. Free coffee and 10% discount on the room rate Sept–June.

ARBIGNY   01190

🎿 🛏 |●| LE MOULIN DE LA BREVETTE**

How to get there: take the D37, then the D933, and turn right off the road from Arbigny to Pont-de-Vaux.
☎ 03.85.36.49.27 ► 03.85.30.66.91
e moulin.brevete@wanadoo.fr
Closed 15 Nov–15 Feb except for reservations.
Disabled access. **Car park**.

This old mill – minus its wheel – stands deep in the countryside. The bedrooms, in a converted farmhouse, are large, bright, comfortable and quiet. Doubles €53–64 with shower/wc or bath; numbers 15–19 and 29–32 have the best views. Nice welcome. They do simple meals in the restaurant – Bresse chicken, *coq au vin*, snails and the like. Menus €18–32. Free coffee.

AUBENAS   07200

🎿 🛏 |●| HÔTEL DES NÉGOCIANTS*

pl. de l'Hôtel-de-Ville (Centre); it's in the old part of town opposite the château.
☎ 04.75.35.18.74
Closed Sun, 15–31 March and 15–31 Oct. **TV**. **Car park**.

Advantages are the central location and the cheap prices. The clean rooms, most with TV, have decent beds. Doubles with basin €21, €33 with shower/wc and €37 with bath. The restaurant serves dishes from various regions: calf's head, rabbit stew, fish soup, Ardèche *caillette* (a bit like haggis), duck with olives, beef Ardèche-style. Menus €7–19. Free house apéritif.

🎿 🏠 |O| AUBERGE DES PINS

95 route de Vals.
☎ 04.75.35.29.36 ➡ 04.75.89.00.15
Hotel closed Oct. **Restaurant closed** Sun. **TV.**
Garden. Car park.

A charming, sprawling building in a pleasant setting with lots of pine trees in the garden. The rooms are big, clean and good value for money, and most have air-conditioning; doubles with shower/wc or bath/wc €37–44. The restaurant is sunset yellow, and serves dishes including country pâté with chestnuts and onion marmalade, *caillette*, omelette with ceps and the house speciality – Lyonnais dishes. *Menu du jour* €11, then others €14–18. A good few reasonable wines, fairly priced. Free house *digestif* and one breakfast per room Feb–April and Nov.

🎿 🏠 |O| LA PINÈDE**

route du camping Les Pins (Northwest); it's on the road to Lentillère, the D235, 1.5km from the town centre.
☎ 04.75.35.25.88 ➡ 04.75.93.06.42
ℓ la.pinede@wanadoo.fr
Closed 10 Dec–1 Feb. **Swimming pool. TV.**

A traditional holiday hotel in a very peaceful location, so it's probably best to book in summer. Doubles €44–46 with shower/wc or bath. Half board, compulsory July–Aug, costs €44 per person. The restaurant offers decent value for money, with a €14 menu (not served Sun) and others up to €18–29. There's a swimming pool with a panoramic view, a tennis court, and a climbing wall. Free coffee and one breakfast free per room.

|O| LES COLONQUINTES

rue du quai de l'Ardèche; it's on the RN104 in the direction of Privas.
☎ 04.75.93.88.33
Closed Sat and Mon in season; Sun evening and Mon out of season; a fortnight in Jan; a week in Sept.
Disabled access. Garden.

There's an appealing garden-terrace offering inviting shade as well as a charming dining room with a vaulted ceiling. The cooking is wonderfully fresh, thoughtfully prepared and attractively presented. The menu lists shoals of fish dishes – sea bream, salmon, squid, whiting. There's a €11 *formule rapide* served at lunch during the week, and several others from €15 to €33.

🎿 |O| LE CHAT QUI PÊCHE

6 pl. de la Grenette; it's near Saint-Benoît cathedral.
☎ 04.75.93.87.49
Closed Tues and Wed except July–Aug; 27 Oct–5 Nov;

1 Jan–31 March.

This restaurant is in a lovely seventeenth-century Ardèche house and serves strictly local dishes which are generously served and very good: chestnut flan with chicken *jus*, fresh duck *foie gras*, *fricassée* of snails, *caillettes* and *andouillettes ardéchoises* and *fondant ardéchois* – a delicious mixture of chocolate, chestnut and vanilla cream. Menus €15–25 or *à la carte*. Polite, charming welcome. Free coffee.

|O| RESTAURANT LE FOURNIL

34 rue du 4-Septembre (Centre); it's near Saint-Benoît cathedral.
☎ and ➡ 04.75.93.58.68
Closed Sun and Mon; the Christmas, Feb and Nov school holidays; the second fortnight in June.

This handsome fifteenth-century building with its patio and vaults is the ideal setting to try the exquisite dishes prepared by Michel Leynaud. His establishment is stylish, from the welcome to the gourmet food – rabbit with herbs and olive paste, lobster stew with morels. Menus €16–29, and *à la carte* about €27. Extensive wine list. Occasionally the service can be slow

SANILHAC   07110 (25KM SW)

🎿 🏠 |O| AUBERGE DE LA TOUR DE BRISON**

How to get there: take the D104, then the D103 in the direction of Largentière then follow the road to Montréal.
☎ 04.75.39.19.56
Closed Tues evening; Wed except July–Aug; 10 Jan–20 March. **Disabled access. Swimming pool. TV. Car park.**

This pleasant hotel, run by a nice couple, has twelve air-conditioned rooms, some with whirlpool bath and (on a clear day) a view of the Alps. Doubles €33–38 with basin, €43–49 with shower/wc and €51–54 with bath. There are some family rooms with fireplaces. The cheapest menu at €24 is very generously served. Dishes include chicken liver mousse with chestnuts and traditional *caillette*. There are tennis courts and a swimming pool on the spot and lots of other activities in the area. Free apéritif and garage for motorbikes. Free house apéritif.

SAINT-PONS   07580 (28KM E)

🏠 |O| HOSTELLERIE GOURMANDE MÈRE BIQUETTE**

Les Allignols (North); turn left off the N102 onto the

D293, at Saint-Pons you should start to see signs for the inn – it's 4km further.
☎ 04.75.36.72.61 ➡ 04.75.36.76.25
Closed Nov–31 March but reservations accepted.
Swimming pool. TV. Lock-up car park.

The natural setting for this old farmhouse is quite spectacular: the grounds are extensive and there are breathtaking views of the mountains and the valley. The country-style bedrooms are very handsome with lots of wood panelling. Prices reflect the quality – doubles €48–50 with shower/wc and €52–71 with bath. There's also a welcoming, refined restaurant serving good classics: *foie gras* in a pastry case, house *caillette*, snail stew with shallots, duck breast with honey and Calvados and local dishes. Menus €15–32. Half board is available for a minimum of two or four days, depending on the season. They can lend you a mountain bike.

AUTRANS 38880

⭑ |●| HÔTEL DE LA POSTE***

place de l'Église.
☎ 04.76.95.31.03 ➡ 04.76.95.30.17
Closed mid-April–10 May and 20 Oct–10 Dec. **TV.**

A local institution that's been run by the same family since before the Second World War. The thirty rooms all have good facilites; some have sitting rooms and balconies looking out over the front. Doubles €48–76; some rooms sleep four. There are splendid sporting facilities – take a look at the superb covered swimming pool with its exotic décor, which you reach via a private underground passageway. There's also a Jacuzzi, a fitness room and a sauna. Good cuisine with a *formule rapide* for €10, a weekday lunch menu for €13 and expect to pay upwards of €17 for dinner.

MÉAUDRE 38112 (6KM S)

🎿 ⭑ |●| LE PERTUZON

ave. du Vercors.
☎ 04.76.95.21.17 ➡ 04.76.95.26.00
✉ locana@club-internet.fr
Closed Sun and Tues eveings, Wed and 20 Nov–20 Dec.

An establishment with nine pleasant rooms, some of which have a garden view. Doubles €35. Smart yet warm dining room and cusine of excellent reputation. The regional menu (not served Sunday) lists appetizer, a Vercors salad, turban of trout with Royans ravioli then cheese and chocolate profiteroles – all that for €15. The chef worked in Réu-

nion and Egypt after qualifying from hotel school then came to Vercors. There's a nice garden and terrace in summer. Free apéritif.

BEAUFORT-SUR-DORON 73270

🎿 ⭑ |●| HÔTEL-RESTAURANT LE GRAND MONT**

pl. de l'Église (Centre); take the Albert-Beaufort road.
☎ 04.79.38.33.36 ➡ 04.79.38.39.07
Closed 24 April–9 May; Oct; the first week in Nov. **TV.**

A delightful hotel on the outskirts of the ancient village. The rooms look a little tired but they're comfortable; doubles with shower/wc €45–46. In the restaurant, which is a traditional bistro with an old-style dining room, they serve primarily regional dishes: *diots* with *crozets* (local vegetable and pork sausages cooked in white wine and served with square-shaped noodles), omelette with Beaufort cheese. Menus €10–25. Free house apéritif.

BEAUJEU 69430

🎿 ⭑ |●| HÔTEL-RESTAURANT ANNE DE BEAUJEU**

28 rue de la République (Centre).
☎ 04.74.04.87.58 ➡ 04.74.69.22.13
Closed Sun evening, Mon; mid-Dec to mid-Jan. **TV.**
Garden. Car park.

Though the hotel is named after the daughter of Louis XI (who lived in the late fifteenth century), the building is not of that era. It has a garden, a plush foyer and an impressive dining room. Doubles €49–55. The cooking isn't hugely creative, but they serve classic dishes such as *chartreuse* of pigeon braised with cabbage and monkfish with apples and vinegar. Menus €17–42. Free house apéritif and 10% discount on the room rate Nov–March.

BELLEVILLE 69220

🎿|●| LE BUFFET DE LA GARE

pl. de la Gare; it's near the train station.
☎ 04.74.66.07.36 ➡ 04.74.69.69.49
Closed evenings except for reservations; weekends; 3 weeks in Aug. **Car park.**

It's sometimes said that French train stations and their surroundings aren't as appealing as they once were. This restaurant is an exception: a cute little house full of flowers and plants, it's decorated with old posters, Art Deco light fixtures and quirky old mirrors. Hélène Bessy, the owner, always has a smile and a kind word for her customers. The €15 menu, which is chalked up on the blackboard, might include house-made *terrine*, leeks *vinaigrette*, stuffed tomatoes and courgettes, cheese and dessert; you'll pay around €18 *à la carte*. Her husband supplies the wine. Reservations necessary in the evening for groups. During the grape harvest, the place is still pretty busy at one o'clock in the morning. Free *apéritif*.

VAUX-EN-BEAUJOLAIS   69460 (15KM SW)

🏌 🏠 |●| AUBERGE DE CLOCHEMERLE**

rue Gabriel-Chevallier; take the D43 in the direction of Odenas, and at Saint-Étienne-des-Oullières, turn left in the direction of Vaux.
☎ 04.74.03.20.16 ➡ 04.74.03.28.48
e aub.clochemerle@netcourrier.com
Closed Tues evening and Wed in summer; Tues and Wed in winter; a fortnight in Feb; a fortnight in Aug. **TV**. **Disabled access**.

This village, which inspired Gabriel Chevallier's novel *Clochemerle*, is the only one in France where people come from far and wide to see the street urinal. The restaurant serves excellent food which is in evidence on all the menus (€16–50), and the prices are justified. As time goes on, the cuisine is favouring gourmet dishes yet still offers good value for money. Lovely shaded terrace for the summer. All the rooms have been freshly refurbished, though they have kept their charm because of the period furniture. Doubles €41–49 with shower or bath. Free house apéritif.

LIERGUES   69400 (24KM SW)

🏌 |●| AUBERGE DE LIERGUES

Centre; take the D35 in the direction of Tarare.
☎ and ➡ 04.74.68.07.02
Closed Tues evening and Wed; 10–30 Aug.

The owner likes to have a good laugh and will practically insist on your having a glass of Beaujolais as soon as you arrive – and it's hard to resist in a place like this, where there are more local winegrowers about than tourists. There's a pair of €10 *formules* at lunchtime, and three menus €14–20. There are lots of specialities from Lyon such as *andouille*, *coq au vin* in Beaujolais wine, home-made *terrine* and seasonal dishes like game. Eat in the bistro with its wooden tables rather than in the dining room. Free apéritif.

BESSE-EN-OISANS   38142

🏠 |●| HÔTEL ALPIN

How to get there: take the N91, then the D25.
☎ 04.76.80.06.55 ➡ 04.76.80.12.45
Lock-up for bikes and motorbikes.

In one of the most beautiful villages in the Oisan area, this chalet hotel offers genuine mountain hospitality. The simple, no-frills rooms are beautifully maintained and cost €37–42 for a double. It's well worth paying €37–40 per person and going half-board – and it's compulsory in season. The pleasant dining room has huge beams hewn from pine trunks and walls built from local stone. The good family cooking is generously served, but they eat early and there's no dinner menu – you get what the *patronne* feels like cooking. There's always a hearty soup, good *hors d'œuvres* and a tasty main dish. They can also prepare specialities to order, including *fondue*, *farcis* and *crozets*. Menus from €12. *À la carte* you can choose snacks such as omelettes or *tartiflette*. *Gîtes*, studios or small apartments also for rent.

VENOSC   38520 (19KM S)

🏌 🏠 |●| HÔTEL-RESTAURANT LES AMIS DE LA MONTAGNE*

Le Courtil; take the N91 then the D530.
☎ 04.76.11.10.00 ➡ 04.76.80.20.56
Closed 25 April–18 June and 5 Sept–20 Dec.
Swimming pool.

What the Durdan clan don't know about Venosc, a little mountain village 1000m up, isn't worth knowing. They run hotels, *gîtes*, restaurants, shops and boutiques, give skiing lessons and rent out rooms. Most of their efforts, however, are focused on this hotel, which is sheer delight if you're after peace and quiet. Rooms €42–77 with shower/wc or bath, some with balconies; half board costs €46 per person. You dine in the grill room, which has lots of atmosphere. Menus from €15 list regional food: the speciality is *grenaillade* (potatoes with Saint-Marcellin, a mild goat's cheese) but you'll also find scrambled eggs with morels, trout with walnuts, duck thigh with bilberries and so on. There are at least a dozen sorts of salads, grills, *fondues* and *raclette*. The desserts look good and taste better. The hotel has a pool, a Turkish bath and a sauna. Free house apéritif.

GARDE (LA)   38520 (29KM W)

⅍ ☎ |❶| LA FORÊT DE MARONNE*

It's in Maronne.
☎ 04.76.80.00.06 ➡ 04.76.79.14.61
Closed May and early Oct–20 Dec. **Swimming pool**

This is a nice, family-run hotel, sited way up at 1450m, on a promontory. Pleasant rooms (doubles €30–49) and excellent family cooking. Menus €14–21, and half board €41–46 per person. Very warm welcome. There's a teleski near the hotel that takes you up to the Alpe d'Huez ski runs and in summer, if you're a walker, the GR54 trail is close by. Lovely swimming pool. Free Kir.

⅍|❶| LES GORGES DE SARENNE

Centre; take the N91 then the D211.
☎ 04.76.80.07.85
Closed Sun evening in mid-season and Mon; a fortnight in May; the first fortnight in Oct. **TV. Car park**.

There are 21 bends in the road up to Alpe-d'Huez and this restaurant is the perfect rest stop, with a wonderful view of the gorges and the forest. Rose-Marie and Jacky greet you warmly. Service is swift, the atmosphere's friendly and the place is sparklingly clean. Weekday lunch menu €11. Their specialities are crab *au gratin*, salmon *escalope* with queen scallops and sorrel sauce and scallop salad. They also do delicious *raclette*, *fondue* and *gardette*, their own style of *fondue*. There's a little terrace for sunny days. They have a few guest rooms and half board is compulsory for €60 for two sharing a double room. They offer two-day ski packages for €85 per person. Free coffee.

ORNON   38520 (39KM S)

⅍|❶| RESTAURANT LE POTIRON

La Palud; take the D526 in the direction of La Mure.
☎ 04.76.80.63.27.
Closed Sun evening out of season. **Disabled access**. **Car park**.

You'll find this restaurant on a bend in the road; it has a warm décor and is always pretty busy. Good snacks are served all day – *casse-croûte campagnard*, raw ham, bacon omelette, fresh cream cheese, soup, salad, *terrine*. Menus €14–33 and around €27 *à la carte*. The €14 one gets you a plate of raw ham and the meat dish of the day served with vegetables prepared in Dany's own special way – in the form of a celery flan, say, or as courgette fritters with coriander. Try the homemade walnut or gentian wine. In winter,

it's best to call in advance or you might find it's closed. Free apéritif.

BOËN   42130

⅍|❶| LE CUVAGE

La Goutte des Bois; it's 1km out of Boën in the direction of Leignoux, on a narrow road overlooking the D8.
☎ 04.77.24.15.08
Closed Mon and Tues.

Whether you eat on the veranda or the terrace, you'll feast your eyes on the superb panoramic view. The menus are built for big appetites: there are menus for €13–19 listing *charcuterie*, house *terrine*, house *foie gras*, meats grilled over the embers and spit-roast suckling pig. On Saturday evenings they hold comedy events. Free apéritif.

SAIL-SOUS-COUZAN   42890 (6KM W)

⅍ ☎ |❶| LES SIRES DE SEMUR*

Les Promenades (Centre); take the N89.
☎ 04.77.24.52.40 ➡ 04.77.24.57.14
Closed Fri and Sun evenings; Sat lunchtime; a week in Aug. **TV. Car park**.

Situated on a village square dominated by the ruins of a medieval castle, this hotel is run by a very nice Burgundian man and his wife. The cooking is absolutely authentic but prepared by a chef who is always on the lookout for new ideas. One inspiration is ancient cookery – try his guineafowl in flaky pastry with a sauce from a recipe by Apicius, the Roman gourmet. Menus €10–36. The wine cellar is well-stocked. The hotel is a decent one-star with showers and wc on the landing, but it's being updated. Rooms from €24 with basin and up to €34 with bath. You'll get a very nice welcome and enjoy the homely atmosphere. Free house apéritif.

BONNEVAL-SUR-ARC   73480

⅍ ☎ |❶| HÔTEL LA BERGERIE**

It's 100m from the tourist office and the slopes.
☎ 04.79.05.94.97 ➡ 04.79.05.93.24
Closed 22 April–12 June and 30 Sept–20 Dec. **Car park**.

A startling concrete block of a building hidden amongst the trees some distance from the rest of the village. The owners are very friendly and offer excellent value for money. Classic rooms, most of which have south-facing balconies with views of the Evettes mountains, cost €49; half board at €51 is compulsory in winter and 10 July–20 Aug. Local dishes feature prominently on the menus: Beaufort cheese tart, trout, three-cheese turnovers. Menus €11; a meal *à la carte* costs about €18. 10% discount on full or half board in Jan and 25 March–25 April.

♠ I●I AUBERGE LE PRÉ CATIN

It's in the village.
☎ 04.79.05.95.07 ➡ 04.79.05.88.07
Closed Sun evening and Mon. **TV**.

A lovely stone house with a roof made of *lauzes*, flat stones which weigh about 70kg each. It was built only recently but it blends in well with the other buildings. The chef is mainly self-taught so while the cuisine is genuinely local it's very different from the standard *tartiflette* and *raclette*. He creates dishes based entirely around the best produce he can find – he cooks his *diots* in Cignin wine and does good ravioli. While the portions are adequate, prices are rather high: menus €19–26. Doubles with bath/wc for €53.

BONNEVILLE   74130

⅍ ♠ I●I HÔTEL DE L'ARVE**

70 rue du Pont (Centre).
☎ 04.50.97.01.28 ➡ 04.50.25.78.39
Closed Fri evening; Sat except in Feb and Aug; Sept. **TV**. **Lock-up car park**.

A conventional provincial hotel where the owner plays cards with his friends. The rooms are classic with good facilities – the ones at the back look onto the garden courtyard with its picturesque entrance and the medieval rue Brune. Doubles with shower/wc or bath €39. Menus start at €12 (weekdays only) and continue at €14–33. Good traditional dishes: *fricassée* of scallops with ceps, veal kidneys with girolle mushrooms, pan-fried scallops caramelized in orange juice, *langoustines* with bacon, breast of duck with quinces. Fast service with a smile. 10% discount on the room rate Sept–July.

BOURG-EN-BRESSE   01000

♠ I●I HÔTEL-RESTAURANT DU MAIL**

46 av. du Mail (West); from the centre of town, follow the signs for Villefranche-sur-Saône.
☎ 04.74.21.00.26 ➡ 04.74.21.29.55
Closed Sun evening and Mon; 20 July–9 Aug; 28 Dec–10 Jan. **TV**. **Pay lock-up garage**. **Free car park**.

The pretty, comfortable rooms in this hotel are decorated in contemporary style, and

you'll appreciate the air conditioning in summer. Those overlooking the garden are quietest – even the double glazing in the others can't cut out all the noise from the station. Good value doubles €36 with shower/wc and up to €46 with bath/wc. The rather smart restaurant is popular with the locals. Set menus at €15–46 list traditional local cooking such as frogs' legs and *poulet de Bresse*, and there's an impressive dessert trolley. Nice terrace. Essential to book.

♠ LE LOGIS DE BROU**

132 bd. de Brou (South); it's just before the monastery, on the right.
☎ 04.74.22.11.55 ➡ 04.74.22.37.30
Closed the last fortnight of the year. **TV**. **Lock-up car park**.

A bleak 1960s building that's hardly brightened up by its blue balconies. But inside it's a comfortable, attractive hotel. The hall is full of flowers and the owner greets you with a winning smile. The bright, clean rooms in soft colours are well-soundproofed. Doubles with shower/wc €49 or €53–61 with bath.

⅍ ♠ LE TERMINUS***

19 rue Alphonse-Baudin (Centre); it's 50m from the train station.
☎ 04.74.21.01.21 ➡ 04.74.21.36.47
TV.

This classic terminus hotel has a grand Napoleon III hall and a wonderful antique lift. It is set in superb grounds with a rose garden and ornamental ponds, so all the rooms are quiet. They vary in style – some have period furniture, others are modern. Doubles with shower/wc and TV €58 or €69 with bath. Breakfast €8. 8% discount on the room rate.

⅍ ♠ HÔTEL DE FRANCE***

19 pl. Bernard (Centre).
☎ 04.74.23.30.24 ➡ 04.74.23.69.90
e info@grand-hoteldefrance.com
TV. **Car park**.

Mid-nineteenth-century hotel in the centre of town, in a charming little square with a village atmosphere. The entrance is very grand, and you almost hesitate to walk on the beautiful mosaic floors. The whole place has been refurbished and provides modern facilities in a warm décor which has retained the hotel's character. Stylish doubles €69–72 with shower/wc and €74–79 with bath. The whole place has a chic feel, but the welcome is relaxed and friendly. The bar stays open late. 10% discount on the room rate 15 Nov–15 April.

|O| CHEZ TRICHARD

4 cours de Verdun (Centre); it's opposite the cinema.
☎ 04.74.23.11.24
Closed Sun; Mon; 3 weeks in July.

This bistro is a favourite in these parts. The short menu lists local specialities such as pike *quenelles*, Bresse chicken with cream and morels and steak with Roquefort or mustard sauce – and there are delicious sautéed potatoes served with every main course. Menus €12–30.

🎄|O| LA TABLE RONDE

126 bd. de Brou (Southwest); head for Brou monastery.
☎ 04.74.23.71.17
Closed Sat lunchtime; Sun; a fortnight in Aug.

In just a few years, this restaurant has become *the* place to eat around here. The cosy dining room is small so you should consider booking, though they've also added a terrace. You may well see a celeb or two, and photographs of stars who have eaten here line the walls. The rich cooking is a mixture of modern and classical – chicken, frogs' legs, calf's head *gribiche* and the like – and is full of interesting tastes and flavours. The menus, €12–25, are well within the reach of mere mortals and dishes change weekly. *À la carte* is a bit more pricey, but duck breast with creamed *foie gras* isn't something you eat every day. Courteous service. Free apéritif.

|O| CHEZ BLANC

Place Bernard; it's on the main square.
☎ 04.74.45.29.11

Like all the "Blanc" establishments attached to the great chef, the cooking here is refined, tasty, unusual and handsomely served. Lots of dishes feature local Bresse chicken but there's also zander fillet, pike fish balls, cream of lentils and kidneys *à la Mâconnaise*. The clientele is realaxed and the bill won't give you high blood pressure. There's a menu of the day for €17 or, *à la carte*, you'll pay around €27. There's little to add other than to remark that the swift service comes with a smile and that the modern decoration is light and fresh. If you really want to be picky, it's a little noisier than ideal.

|O| LA BRASSERIE DU FRANÇAIS

7 av. Alsace-Lorraine (Centre); it's near the tourist office.
☎ 04.74.22.55.14
Closed Sat evening and Sun; the first 3 weeks in Aug; the last week in Dec.

This splendid Second Empire dining room attracts a clientele of lawyers, journalists and Bourg notables. The ceiling mouldings and bevelled mirrors are lovely, and the service is as classy as the cooking. Excellent, honest regional cuisine and traditional brasserie dishes: *choucroute*, chicken in cream sauce, seafood platter, steak and chips. Menus €21–45 or around €38 *à la carte*. Terrace in summer.

SAINT-DENIS-LÈS-BOURG   01000 (5KM E)

🏠|O| HÔTEL-RESTAURANT DU LAC

1981 route de Trévoux; it's between Saint-Denis and Corgenon.
☎ 04.74.24.24.73
Restaurant closed Wed. **Hotel closed** end Oct–April.
Car park.

A roomy family house on the edge of the lake, set back from the road. Rooms are clean and modern with doubles for €23–30 depending on facilities. The restaurant is full of the flavours of the region – menus €13–32. There's a little bar, a wide terrace, a lake and the field behind is full of animals. It's ideal for families because the whole atmosphere is easy-going and unfussy.

MEILLONNAS   01370 (15KM NE)

|O| AUBERGE AU VIEUX MEILLONNAS

How to get there: take the N83 in the direction of Lons-le-Saunier, then the A40 to Meillonnas.
☎ and ➡ 04.74.51.34.46
Closed Tues evening and Wed. **Car park**. **Disabled access.**

This little village inn, a rustic stone house, is typical of this peaceful part of the world. It's worth making the trip for the chef's cooking. Dishes include raw ham from the Tarn, veal escalopes in lime juice, rabbit with rosemary in flaky pastry, medallions of monkfish with saffron, chicken with cream and morels and frogs' legs with a parsley garnish. Weekday lunch menu €10 and others €15–32. In fine weather you can eat in the delightful garden with its weeping willows, pine trees and banana plants.

SAINT-LAURENT-SUR-SAÔNE   01750 (29KM W)

|O| LE SAINT-LAURENT

1 quai Bouchacourt; it's on the riverbank leading to the old bridge.
☎ 03.85.39.29.19 **e** saintlaurent@georgesblanc.com

This is another restaurant in the proliferating empire of the great chef Georges Blanc – he has others in Bourg and Vonnas. You get the usual efficiency, kindness, originality and skill, and for only a little more than you might normally pay. Inspiring dishes such as rabbit *compote*, crayfish ravioli, Bresse chicken with vinegar and pears with bitter chocolate. Menus €15–35. There's a fine list of wines. The decoration is simple with a few old ornaments dotted elegantly around the dining room; black-and-white photographs and old adverts cover the walls. The peaceful terrace overlooks Villefranche. You won't be disappointed – unless you forget to book, that is.

BOURGET-DU-LAC (LE)   73370

♠ |●| HÔTEL-RESTAURANT LA CERISAIE**

618 route des Tournelles (North); it's 2.5km from Bourget, on the D42 in the direction of Les Catons.
☎ 04.79.25.01.29 ➡ 04.79.25.26.19
Closed Sun evening; Wed out of season; first week in Jan; Nov. **TV**. **Car park**.

The hotel stands at the foot of the Dent du Chat mountain, surrounded by fields planted with cherry trees. The proprietors are from Chamonix – Brigitte looks after the hotel while husband Philippe does the cooking. Some rooms have a splendid view of the lake which inspired Lamartine, one of France's greatest poets. Doubles €25 with basin, €35 with shower and €43 with shower/wc. Half board at €41 is compulsory July–Aug. The chef produces a lot of fish dishes – the €15 menu (not served Sun) lists *lavaret* (a salmon-like fish) roasted with morels, zander with crayfish tails and Saint-Marcellin (a mild cheese) *en chemise*. Other menus €21–34.

⅔ ♠ |●| HÔTEL DU LAC

bd. du Lac (Centre).
☎ 04.79.25.00.10 ➡ 04.79.25.34.57
Closed Wed. **Disabled access**. **Car park**.

This hotel, a pretty stone building standing close to the water, has recently been taken over by a new team. Simple doubles with basin €30 and up to €49 with shower/wc. In summer, sit on the flower-filled terrace and watch the comings and goings at the lake shore. Fish, including fried freshwater fish and *lavaret*, is much in evidence *à la carte* and on the set menus at €18–24. Free coffee.

VIVIERS-DU-LAC   73420 (3KM E)

|●| RESTAURANT LA MAISON DES PÊCHEURS

611 rive du Lac (East); follow the lakeshore in the

direction of Aix-les-Bains.
☎ and ➡ 04.79.54.41.29
Closed Mon evening and Tues. **Garden**.

If you wander into the garden of this waterside restaurant, you'll see all the fishing boats that have been hauled out of the water to dry. In the bar, fishermen compare the size of their catch over a drink. And fish dishes are the mainstay of the kitchen's reputation: fillets of perch and *lavaret*, trout, fried freshwater fish. Weekday menu €10, with others €18–30.

BOURGOIN-JALLIEU   38300

|●| L'AQUARELLE

19 avenue des Alpes; it's 100m from the train station on the left.
☎ 04.74.18.15.00
Closed Sun evening and Mon; the first fortnight in Jan; a fortnight in Aug.

It's only been going since autumn of 2000 but this place has already made a name for itself. It's inside a walled garden in a large, late nineteenth-century mansion; the décor is Art Nouveau with a collection of lovely oil paintings and a large oak staircase. Delicate and inventive cuisine; on the €19 menu (weekday lunch) you'll find appetizers, Roquefort and spiced bread *terrine*, roast rabbit with a cream and mustard reduction and a chocolate Marquise with preserved cherries and *petits fours*. Other menus €24–43. Welcoming smiles. There's a separate sitting room for smokers.

DOMARIN   38300 (0.5KM SW)

♠ HÔTEL DES DAUPHINS

8 rue Berrier; it's a road to the left opposite the station.
☎ 04.74.93.00.58
TV. **Car park**.

A very quiet place not far from the centre offering rooms with all facilities, some for non-smokers. Rooms are found in the main building and on the ground floor of an annexe, looking over the garden. Doubles €30; buffet breakfast €4. There's a terrace next to the lawn. Nice welcome.

SAINT-SAVIN   38300 (4KM N)

⅔ |●| RESTAURANT LE DEMPTÉZIEU

pl. du Château (Northwest); take the N6 in the direction of Bourgoin-Jallieu, then the D143 on the right.
☎ 04.74.28.90.49
Closed Mon evening; Tues; 1–15 Jan. **Car park**.

Yves and Corinne Bello have turned this old

village café into a wonderful gourmet restaurant. They'll give you a very natural welcome and unpretentious service with a smile. Dishes are elaborate and well-tuned to today's tastes: warm scallop salad with hazelnut oil, *fricassée* of fresh frogs' legs with cream sauce, pigeon with a shrimp *coulis*. Weekday lunch menu €10 including wine and coffee, and others €14–30. You're guaranteed a delicious meal. Free coffee.

CESSIEU   38890 (13KM E)

🏠 |O| LA GENTILHOMMIÈRE DU SAINT-BERNARD**

3 rue de Reval.
☎ 04.74.88.30.09 ➥ 04.74.88.32.61
Closed Sun evening and Mon; the All Saints' holiday week; a week in Jan. **TV**. **Lock-up car park**.

A huge ochre house with ivy climbing all over the front. Osane, the Saint Bernard dog, welcomes you. Rooms, priced at €43 for a double, have good facilities and en-suite bathrooms; most look out over the huge wooded park where there's a swing and deckchairs. The verandas and terraces also have the view. And there are two separate chalets in the park for €53 a night. Friday night is speciality night – frog's legs, fried smelt (pearly fish). Menu of the day €12; the one at €15 includes wine and coffee and there's a *menu terroir* for €21. They have dances on the third Saturday in the month. Natural, cordial welcome. The only negative is the occasionally slow service.

SAINT-DIDIER-DE-LA-TOUR   38110 (19KM E)

🏕 |O| AUX BERGES DU LAC

58 route du Lac.
☎ 04.74.97.32.82
Closed weeknights Sept–May and the Christmas school holidays. **Car park**.

This place has got it right. You can have a nice meal and enjoy yourself in an atmosphere so good that you scarcely notice the occasional noise passing trains. There's a huge bay window with a view of the lake and a terrace in summer. Menus are cheap at €8–25, and the chef prepares excellent frogs' legs and fried fish. It's perfect for Sunday lunch. Free apéritif.

VIGNIEU   38890 (22KM NE)

🏕 🏠 |O| CHÂTEAU DE CHAPEAU CORNU***

How to get there: take the D16 in the direction of Saint-Chef-Morestel.
☎ 04.74.27.79.00 ➥ 04.74.92.49.31
📧 chapeau.cornu@wanadoo.fr
Restaurant closed Sun evening. **Swimming pool**. **TV**. **Car park**.

An unusual name for an unusual place which occupies a thirteenth-century castle. It's now a charming hotel-restaurant offering bright, comfortable double rooms furnished with antiques and contemporary art from €65 (there are also some suites). The restaurant has vaulted dining rooms and a terrace; all dishes are prepared using local produce. The lunch menu of the day, which includes a ¼-litre of wine and coffee, costs €15, there's another lunch menu for €16 and others at €24–43. Specialities include goat's cheese and Sassenage blue cheese in a pastry case, red mullet fillets, Royan ravioli stuffed with snails, trout stuffed with oyster mushrooms, sweetbreads braised with morels and delicious fresh fruit *au gratin*. Out of season they offer an "Escapade" deal – one night, two meals including apéritif and wine and two breakfasts served in your room for €13. Free apéritif.

BOURG-SAINT-ANDÉOL   07700

🏕 🏠 |O| HÔTEL-RESTAURANT LE PRIEURÉ**

quais du Rhône.
☎ 04.75.54.62.99 ➥ 04.75.54.63.73
Closed Sat lunchtime and Sun evening out of season; Sun in summer; the last fortnight in Sept; Christmas. **TV**.

The oldest part of this imposing building on the banks of the Rhône dates from the twelfth century. Each bedroom is pleasantly furnished and the lounges and terrace overlook the Rhône. Doubles €53–58. The main road can be noisy so ask for a room around the side. Weekday lunch menu €12 and others up to €24. Free apéritif.

SAINT-MARTIN-D'ARDÈCHE   07700 (19KM SW)

🏕 🏠 |O| HÔTEL-RESTAURANT LE BELLE-VUE**

quai de l'Ardèche; it's opposite the port.
☎ 04.75.04.66.72. ➥ 04.75.04.61.37
TV. **Car park**.

The *Bellevue* has an elevated dining room and the terrace overlooks the port. The atmosphere is easy-going and they serve local Ardèche specialities without frills – *terrine*, various fish dishes, *caillette* with boiled potatoes and *crème caramel*. It's a nice, popular place. Menus €10–17. The rooms are of superior quality and have been recently updated with shower/wc and air conditioning. Doubles €40–55. Free house apéritif.

BOURG-SAINT-MAURICE 73700

🏃 🏠 |●| HÔTEL-RESTAURANT LA PETITE AUBERGE*

Le Reverset; it's 1km from the centre of town on the N90 in the direction of Moûtiers.
☎ 04.79.07.05.86. **Restaurant** ☎ 04.79.07.37.11
➡ 04.79.07.26.51
e hotel.lapetiteauberge@wanadoo.fr
Restaurant closed Sun evening and Mon; 15 Oct–15 Nov. **Hotel closed** 1 May–15 June. **Car park.**

This quiet little inn is away from the main road. Unpretentious if rather elderly rooms go for €35 with shower and €43 with bath. The restaurant, separate from the hotel, offers simple, pleasant food of consistent quality and fast and friendly service. You can eat in the low-ceilinged dining room in winter, or the tree-shaded terrace in summer. Set weekday menu €12 and others €20–24. Free apéritif and 10% discount on the room rate May to Oct.

🏃 🏠 HÔTEL ATLANTIC***

69 route d'Hauteville (Southwest). It's 2km from the centre of town; take the N90 in the direction of Moûtiers, then turn left onto the small road to Hauteville.
☎ 04.79.07.01.70 ➡ 04.79.07.51.55
Disabled access. TV.

This hotel is far enough out of town to be peaceful, and the garden leads out into the surrounding fields. It's a fairly recent building but it's hard to believe that the stone walls haven't been there for ever. Though it's a chic little place, you receive a genuinely warm welcome from the two sisters who own it. They divide their time between running this hotel and a hut up in the mountains. The atmosphere is spacious and bright, from the reception area to the rooms. Doubles with shower/wc €40 and €60 with bath; the nicest ones come with balconies and a mountain view. Free use of sauna.

SÉEZ 73700 (4KM E)

🏃 🏠 |●| RELAIS DES VILLARDS**

Villard-Dessus; it's 4km from the centre – take the N90 that goes up to the Petit-Saint-Bernard pass.
☎ 04.79.41.00.66 ➡ 04.79.41.08.13
e relaisdesvillards@wanadoo.fr
Closed Mon in winter; May; 1 Oct–20 Dec. **TV. Car**

park. **Disabled access.**

You're just 20km from Italy here, and this typical chalet provides the last stop before the border for many travellers. Ten pleasant, attractive rooms with shower/wc cost €44–50 or €58 with bath. You'll get a warm welcome and service with a smile. Cooking is traditional with a few Savoy specialities: *matafan* (a coarse pancake), *tartiflette*, *fondue* made with Beaufort cheese and so on. Menus €11–18 or around €17 *à la carte*. The hotel arranges sporting activities and courses in paragliding, riding, white-water rafting and mountain biking. They also offer a ski package at Les Arcs. Free apéritif.

🏃 |●| RESTAURANT L'OLYMPIQUE

rue de la Libération; take the N90 in the direction of Tignes-Val d'Isère for the Col du Pont Saint-Bernard.
☎ 04.79.41.01.52
Closed Wed and 17–30 June. **Disabled access.**

A very simple restaurant owned by a local man with an infectious good humour. Menus at €14 (lunchtime) and €19, or €21-ish *à la carte*. The choice is long and varied: fillets of sole in lemon sauce, veal kidneys in Madeira and chicken with crayfish. Their *fondue* is one of the cheapest around. You can eat here almost all year, which is unusual in this part of the mountains.

BOUVANTE 26190

🏃 🏠 |●| AUBERGE DU PIONNIER*

col du Pionnier
☎ 04.75.48.57.12 ➡ 04.75.48.58.26
Closed Tues out of season; Nov–Jan.

There's a "hôtel au naturel" classification in French hotels, and this one, on the edge of a forest and by the GR9 walking trail, qualifies. Its nine simple rooms look over the mountains, the pine forest and the meadows where wild animals come to feed. Doubles with basin €26, €41 with shower/wc. In the restaurant conversations turn to the woods, the wild and hunting. The amazing owner is both waitress and cook – her menus, €13–21, feature solid slices of *pâté*, chicken with cream sauce and potatoes and home-made tart. Her speciality is chicken with crayfish tails. Half board, compulsory in summer, costs €30–38. Free coffee.

BRESSIEUX 38870

|●| AUBERGE DU CHÂTEAU

It's at the top of the village; take the D71

☎ 04.74,20.91.01
Closed Mon and Tue.

A beautifully located inn at the foot of the ruined Château of Bressieux (dating back to the thirteenth century) with a superb panoramic view over the Bièvre plain. Tasty dishes such as *fricassée* of rabbit with mustard and side dishes such as *gratin Dauphinois* potatoes and *ratatouille*. Lunch menu (not Sun) at €11 and others €15–24. Modestly priced wines by the jug. In summer you eat on the terrace under a bamboo awning.

BUIS-LES-BARONNIES   26170

🎿 ♠ LES ARCADES – LE LION D'OR

pl. du Marché (Centre).
☎ 04.75.28.81.13 ➡ 04.75.28.12.07
Closed Jan. **TV. Lock-up garage**.

Well-located in the centre of town on a ravishing arcaded square. There's a family atmosphere and you get an excellent welcome. The furnishings in the hall are higgledy-piggledy but the rooms are smart with modern bathrooms and good beds. Doubles €35–58 with shower/wc or bath. In summer, they open the garden to guests. 10% discount on the room rate Oct–Nov and Feb–March.

♠ ESCAPADE CLOÎTRE DES DOMINICAINS

rue de la Cour du Roi Dauphin (Centre).
☎ 04.75.28.06.77 ➡ 04.75.28.13.20
Closed Jan–Feb.

Reception staffed 9am–noon and 5–7pm. Housed in a sixteenth-century Dominican convent in the centre of town, this is a good option if you want to be centrally located without paying a fortune. It's very well-run. Ask for a room looking out onto the cloisters; doubles with shower/wc for €45. Apartments for two to five people can be rented by the week for €327–450. There's no restaurant but you can order a meal for €11. Bikes can be parked in the courtyard.

|●| LE GRILL DU FOUR À PAIN

24 av. Boissis d'Anglas (Southwest); coming into town, it's before you reach the Mensonges bridge.
☎ 04.75.28.10.34
Closed Sun evening; Mon Sept–June; Mon lunchtime July–Aug; 15 Nov–15 Feb. **Car park**.

A nice little restaurant where the service is pleasant and the sophisticated food is good and inexpensive. Menus €13–22. Speciali-

ties include asparagus and artichoke *ratatouille*, scallop *cassolette* and lamb with creamed thyme sauce. They do a *plat du terroir* for €10 including a glass of wine, and the wines are very reasonably priced. There's a shaded terrace in the garden.

🎿|●| LA FOURCHETTE

Les Arcades, pl. du Marché; (Centre).
☎ 04.75.28.03.31 ✉ fourchette@faxvia.net
Closed Sun evening, Mon and Nov.

The chef started here over twenty years ago, and still approaches his work with the same serious professionalism. Delicious regional cuisine and a smiling, friendly welcome. Pleasant dining room with sponged walls hung with watercolours. The specialities include ravioli *de Royans au gratin*, lamb shank with herbs, *croustade* with morels and very tender meat. If you're lucky enough to find crayfish with cream and tarragon sauce on the menu, don't think twice about ordering it. Menus €13–29. A good selection of local wines at honest prices: €6–9. Free house apéritif.

PLAISIANS   26170 (8.5KM SE)

🎿|●| AUBERGE DE LA CLUE

How to get there: take the D72 then the D526.
☎ 04.75.28.01.17
Closed Mon–Fri and Sun evening out of season; Mon April–Sept; Oct. **Disabled access**. **Car park**.

Hordes of gourmands stream up the mountain to this place, especially at the weekend. The restaurant serves hefty portions of good, cheap food concocted by two brothers. Their mother, who's got a terrific laugh and a great line in conversation, looks after the dining room. She'll set a *terrine* on your table for you to help yourself until your meal arrives – you could do worse than to start with *caillette*, a delicious haggis-like preparation of baked pork and vegetables with herbs and follow it with home-made mutton tripe and sheep's trotters or kid stew, rabbit with olive paste, fresh monkfish or lamb's sweetbreads. For dessert, try the quince sorbet with quince liqueur – it's out of this world. Menus €21–26. You can see the Ventoux from the window. Free coffee.

MÉRINDOL-LES-OLIVIERS   26170 (9KM W)

🎿 ♠ |●| AUBERGE DE LA GLORIETTE

How to get there: on the D147.
☎ 04.75.28.71.08 ➡ 04.75.28.71.08
Closed Sun evening and Thurs out of season; Sun in

summer; Jan to early Feb. **Car park**.

On the left there's a baker's, on the right an old-style restaurant and in between the two is a wonderful terrace. Sit in the shade of the old plane tree for breakfast, relax to the sound of the nearby spring and gaze at the hillsides with their olive groves and apricot orchards. Doubles €38–46 with shower/wc, €46–53 with bath. The rooms at the back are particularly quiet. In the restaurant, snacks include good savoury tarts, sausage with olives, *terrine*, roast shoulder of lamb with a crusty bread-crumb coating and fruit tart straight from the oven. À la carte you'll pay around €23, and in the evening, there's a single menu at €15. Free apéritif.

CHALAMONT   01320

|●| RESTAURANT CLERC

Grande-Rue.
☎ 04.74.61.70.30 ➡ 04.74.61.75.00
Closed Mon and Tues; a fortnight at the beginning of Jan; the second fortnight in Nov. **Car park**.

The menu informs you that the restaurant has specialized in frogs' legs for three generations – in other words, the cooking is traditional. The chef is gradually introducing changes but doing so slowly so as not to upset the local people who've been coming here for years. The menus, €20–50, read like handbooks to local cooking – there's even one called the "menu tradition", just in case you weren't sure. It lists frogs' legs sautéed in butter with herbs, salad of fried carp *goujons* and chicken with morels.

CHAMBÉRY   73000

🎿 🏠 |●| HÔTEL DE LA BANCHE*

pl. de l'Hôtel-de-Ville (Centre); it's near the old town.
☎ 04.79.33.15.62
Closed 1–10 May and 1–15 Sept.

A popular place, well located on a pedestrianized square near the old town centre. The rooms are from another era and prices are attractive; double €30 with shower, €33 with shower/wc. Numbers 18, 19 and 20 look onto an extraordinary colonnaded alleyway. The restaurant is good and cheap, too: menus at €11–18 list *tartiflette*, frogs' legs and cod *Lyonnaise* with potatoes. Free coffee.

🎿 🏠 |●| HÔTEL-RESTAURANT AUX PERVENCHES**

600 chemin des Charmettes (Southeast); from the

centre of town head for vallon des Charmettes and the Jean-Jacques Rousseau museum.
☎ 04.79.33.34.26 ➡ 04.79.60.02.52
✉ info@pervenches.net
Closed Sun evening and Mon; a fortnight in Nov. **TV**. **Car park**.

In the late summer of 1736, Jean-Jacques Rousseau brought Mme de Warens to live in a country house in Les Charmettes. It's thanks to his reputation that this delightful little valley has been spared the worst excesses of the developers and has retained its country feel – this hotel is certainly like a country inn. In summer, you eat on the terrace in the shade of the trees with only the sound of birdsong to intrude on your enjoyment. Really traditional dishes form the basis of this cuisine: the €15 "tradition" menu lists *foie gras* with sea salt, duck breast with honey and spices and so on. Other menus €17–30. Double rooms with basin or shower go for €30 and €38 with shower/wc or bath. They're lovely and cool in summer. Free coffee.

🎿 🏠 |●| HÔTEL LE REVARD**

41 av. de la Boisse (Centre); it's opposite the train station.
☎ 04.79.62.04.64 ➡ 04.79.96.37.26
TV. **Pay garage**.

Very welcoming staff at your service in reception. The rooms are rather cold and almost aggressively functional – they resemble ones you'd expect to find in a chain. Some, happily, look onto the lovely grounds. Doubles with shower/wc €33–35 and €38–50 with bath. The restaurant serves traditional dishes such as *fondue*, *tartifflette*, salmon fillet and kidneys in Madiera sauce – it's good for a quick meal. Menus for €9, €10 and above. Free use of garage (usually €6).

🎿 🏠 |●| CITY HÔTEL**

9 rue Denfert-Rochereau (Centre); it's between carré Curial and Saint-François cathedral.
☎ 04.79.85.76.79 ➡ 04.79.85.86.11
TV. **Car park**.

The hotel is right in the centre of town, so the rooms overlooking the street are noisy. Even though the street has been pedestrianized the bars are lively, especially on Friday and Saturday nights. The rooms are functional and decorated in very contemporary style – which is a bit of a surprise in an eighteenth-century building. You'll get a friendly welcome and at least the room prices are decent. Doubles €34 with basin, €42 with shower or shower/wc and €47 with bath. 10% discount on the room rate.

🌲 🏠 |○| HÔTEL-RESTAURANT SAVOYARD**

35 pl. Monge (Southeast); it's on the square next to the carré Curial.
☎ 04.79.33.36.55 ➡ 04.79.85.25.70
Closed Sun except public holidays or for groups. **TV**.
Car park.

This is a big, friendly establishment with ten or so soundproofed rooms with geranium-filled window-boxes. Doubles with shower/wc €41. Half board is compulsory at the weekend in Feb. The owner is descended from a long line of restaurateurs. Menus at €12–21 feature Savoy specialities and regional dishes. Free coffee.

🌲 |○| EL MOSQUITO

153 carré Curial (Centre); it's behind the market.
☎ 04.79.75.28.00
Closed Sun.

Where most Mexican-style joints put all their effort into creating the right décor, this one concentrates on preparing the right food. The menu lists chilli and *tacos*, of course, along with some Inca and Aztec dishes that are quite remarkable. The desserts are just as good – beautifully presented and served with wide smiles. €8–20 for a complete meal.

|○| L'HYPOTÉNUSE

141 carré Curial (Centre).
☎ 04.79.85.80.15 ➡ 04.79.85.80.18
Closed Sun; Mon; a week in spring; 14 July–15 Aug.

This restaurant, situated on the peaceful old square, boasts a modern, stylish décor that provides an appropriate setting for the chef's sophisticated, flavourful cooking. Weekday lunch menu €14, and others €18–40 – good value for money. Try leek and Reblochon cheese turnover, rabbit *confit* with pine honey, steamed bass with hazelnut oil or sole *gratinée*. In the summer, they open up a terrace on the square.

🌲 |○| RESTAURANT LA VANOISE

44 av. Pierre-Lanfrey; it's near the main post office.
☎ 04.79.69.02.78
closed Sun evening and Mon.

The décor is bright, young and modern and the restaurant has a clientele of loyal regulars. In contrast, the cooking is traditional, but it does display brilliant, inventive touches. The menus are modified every two weeks and the dishes on the *à la carte* menu change even more frequently. The chef likes to cook all kinds of fish – such as char *meu-*

nière and red mullet with basi and *bouill-abaisse*. Menus €19–40 or €35 *à la carte*. The wine list is huge, listing both prestigious Burgundies and little-known Savoy wines. Best to book. Free coffee.

APREMONT   73190 (8KM SE)

|○| RESTAURANT LE DEVIN

Lieu-dit Au Devin; take the D201, and once you get to Apremont, follow the signs.
☎ 04.79.28.33.43
Closed Sun evening and Mon; a week in Jan; a week Aug–Sept.

Service noon–3.30pm and 7pm–midnight. This is a country restaurant of the finest kind, somewhat lost among the hills of the Apremont wine country. The dining room is rustic and pretty, and the menu features honest and interesting Savoy dishes that stray well beyond the standard tourist fare of *fondue* and *tartiflette*. The house speciality is *farçon savoyard* (potatoes baked with bacon, prunes, pears, raisins and eggs). You can choose *à la carte* or from the €11 weekday lunch menu or others up to €17.

CHAMONIX   74400

🌲 🏠 LA BOULE DE NEIGE*

362 rue Joseph-Vallot (Centre).
☎ 04.50.53.04.48 ➡ 04.50.55.91.09
📧 postmaster@hotel.laboule@claranet.fr
Closed Nov. **Car park**.

Very close to the centre, but off the tourist track. They have a few really nice rooms done up in traditional style; doubles with basin at €32–41, €37–46 with shower and €38–47 with shower/wc. You can help yourself to as much breakfast as you like from the buffet, and there are hearty breakfast dishes *à la carte*. The clientèle is young and international, and everyone gets a great welcome; the young owners are happy to give you any information you need. Free coffee.

🌲 🏠 HÔTEL DES LACS**

992 route des Gaillands (Southwest); it's five minutes from the centre of town in the Gaillands area.
☎ 04.50.53.02.08 ➡ 04.50.53.66.64
Closed 1 Oct–14 June. **Car park**.

This hotel, which faces Mont Blanc, is an old house with an old-fashioned bar – but it's a different story in the rooms, which have been entirely refurbished. They're tasteful, functional and good value for money. Some even have a balcony and a view of the mountain.

Doubles with shower or bath €44–48. Polite, friendly welcome. Free apéritif.

🍴 🏨 HÔTEL DU FAUCIGNY**

118 pl. de l'Église (Centre); it's opposite the tourist office.
☎ 04.50.53.01.17 ➡ 04.50.53.01.17
e hotel.faucigny@wanadoo.fr
Closed June and Nov. **TV**. **Garden**. **Car park**.

An unpretentious little hotel with a homely atmosphere in a quiet street. It's a family-run place and the neat rooms have facilities perfectly adequate facilities. Doubles €46 with shower and €46–53 with shower/wc. There's a small, interior courtyard and a pleasant garden. 10% discount on the room rate.

🍴 🏨 I●I HÔTEL LA SAVOYARDE***

28 rue des Moussoux (North); it's beside the Brévent cable car station.
☎ 04.50.53.00.77 ➡ 04.50.55.86.82
e lasavoyarde@wanadoo.fr
Closed Tues lunchtime; 9–23 May; 26 Nov–20 Dec. **TV**. **Car park**.

The little chalet, facing Mont Blanc, has been renovated and extended. There are fourteen charming but pricey rooms with all mod cons at €88–113. The restaurant serves very good food and the service is great. Menus €13–28, and even the cheapest one is superb: Reblochon (a mild local cheese) in flaky pastry or chicory salad for starters, *escalope* of sea trout with a creamed parsley sauce or the local version of cabbage soup as main courses, and cheese or pastry of the day to finish. If you'd rather just have one dish, try the jacket potatoes or the *raclette*. Free apéritif.

I●I LE PANIER DES QUATRE SAISONS

24 galerie Blanc-Neige.
☎ 04.50.53.98.77 **e** lepanierdes4saisons@cham.org
Closed Wed; Thurs lunchtime; 25 May–17 June; 15 Nov–5 Dec.

A flight of stairs off la rue Paccard leads to this small, really charming restaurant offering excellent cooking. For freshness and inventiveness it's unmatched by any of the touristy places – and it's good value for money. The €13 (weekday lunch) menu gives you a good meal and includes a glass of wine; other menus €18–30. The friendy, personal welcome is refreshing in a town where so many restaurants herd you in and out as fast as possible.

ARGENTIÈRE   74400 (8KM NE)

🍴 I●I LA CRÈMERIE DU GLACIER

766 route de la Glacière; in summer, take the dirt road

after the Lognan cable car; in winter take the chemin de la Rosière.
☎ 04.50.54.07.52 **e** claudyraunel@wanadoo.fr
Closed Tues evening and Wed in winter excluding school holidays; 15 May–15 June; 20 Sept–20 Dec.
Car park.

This restaurant, way out in the forest, is where people from Chamonix come to get back to nature and breathe some fresh air. They serve snacks and substantial plates of local dishes: *farçon* (potatoes with milk, eggs, bacon, raisins and prunes), which traditionally accompanies smoked ham or cured meat, simple omelettes, huge salads, *fondues* with ceps and a variety of cheese *croûtes*, some with morels. In winter there's a lunch menu at €10 and a children's menu at €6, and expect to pay €17 *à la carte*. Free house aperitif.

LES HOUCHES   74310 (8KM W)

🍴 🏨 AUBERGE LE MONTAGNY**

Lieu-dit Le Pont; as you come into the village from Chamonix, it's 450m further along on the left.
☎ 04.50.54.57.37 ➡ 04.50.54.52.97
Closed 1 Nov–15 Dec and 15 April–15 May. **TV**. **Car park**.

This farm was built in 1876 in the centre of a tranquil mountain hamlet. You'd hardly realize that now because of all the changes that have been made, but it still has a cosy charm and the wood panelling hasn't been tampered with. The rooms are huge and pretty, and all have superb, bright bathrooms; doubles €62. Warm welcome. The ski slopes are nearby. 10% discount except during school holidays.

CHAMOUSSET   73390

🍴 🏨 I●I HÔTEL-RESTAURANT CHRISTIN**

La Lilette (centre); take the N90 from Albertville in the direction of Chambéry, and when you reach Pont-Royal, follow the signs for Chamousset.
☎ 04.79.36.42.06 ➡ 04.79.36.45.43
Closed Sun evening and Mon; 1–10 Jan; 1–8 May; 15 Sept–5 Oct. **TV**. **Car park**.

A perfect country inn on a tiny square shaded by chestnut trees. You can hear a little brook flowing somewhere nearby, but you can't see it through the thick vegetation. The pleasant dining room has huge bay windows. The classic cuisine uses excellent ingredients and, given the huge portions, proves good value. There's a €13 menu (not served Sun) and others at €17–27. The rooms are in the annexe and, though somewhat lacking in charm, they're spacious and comfortable; doubles €30 with shower/wc and €33–38 with bath. If you're a light sleeper, you may be disturbed by the trains going by at night. The staff are helpful. Free apéritif.

CHAMPAGNE-EN-VALROMEY   01260

🖑 🏠 |❂| AUBERGE DU COL DE LA LÈBE*

How to get there: take the D8 and follow the signs for Col de la Lèbe.

☎ 04.79.87.64.54 ➡ 04.79.87.54.26

Closed Mon (Mon evening July–Aug) and Tues; 1 Jan–14 April; ten days at the end of June; 15 Nov–15 Dec. **TV. Swimming pool. Car park**.

Right out in the country, on the way up to the pass, this restaurant has a cosy dining room with lots of wood and houseplants. The service is stylish but not in the least pretentious, and the sophisticated cooking includes dishes like *pâté* of ox cheek with *foie gras*, fillet of beef *gourmandine*, zander with chive cream and *terrine* of pears and summer fruits. Weekday menu for €15 and others up to €32; half board starts at €42 per person. They also do grills over the coals. Rooms are fairly modest but their old-fashioned air gives them a degree of style and you're guaranteed lots of peace and quiet up here. Doubles up to €47. You get a wonderful view of the Valromey valley from the swimming pool. Free house apéritif.

PETIT-ABERGEMENT (LE)   01260 (15KM N)

🖑 🏠 |❂| LA SOUPIÈRE A DES OREILLES

How to get there: on the D31.

☎ 04.79.87.65.81 ➡ 04.79.87.54.46

e lasoupiere@free.fr

Closed Sun evening and Mon excluding school holidays; 1 Nov–27 Dec. **Car park**.

A substantial stone building in a quiet village 800m up. Claude Masclet left the French railways and moved here with his wife Colette some ten years ago. You quickly feel at home. The rooms are simple but pleasant and the only sound you'll hear are the bells from the Romanesque church next door. Doubles with shower/wc €26–29. The rustic dining room is a great place to eat good home cooking: excellent raw ham, *diots* (pork and vegetable sausages), *fondues*, chicken in cream and morel sauce. Menus €11–22. The terrace gets the full force of the sun; it's just off the bar, where there's always

an exhibition of paintings. Claude runs an annual painting festival, held at the beginning of August. And if you're here in winter and enjoy cross-country skiing, you'll be in your element. Free house apéritif and 10% discount on the room rate except during school holidays.

CHAMPAGNY-EN-VANOISE   73350

🖑 🏠 |❂| LES CHALETS DU BOUQUETIN****

Le Planay; head in the direction of Champagny-le-Haut.

☎ 04.79.55.01.13 ➡ 04.79.55.04.76

e info@bouquetin.com

Closed 15 Oct–15 Dec. **Disabled access**. **TV. Car park**.

The menus here change every day and you eat good, wholesome, local dishes. *À la carte* – around €23 – you can get *raclette*, *pierrade* (where your food is cooked on a hot stone), *fondue*, *pela* (potatoes, onions and Reblochon cheese) and *croûte savoyarde* (ham on a base of flaky pastry with cheese sauce). The large terrace under the birch trees affords a panoramic view of Courchevel. They have rooms and flats for two to twenty people, let on a daily or weekly basis. Doubles €53–64 with bath. Free house apéritif.

CHAPELLE-EN-VERCORS (LA)   26420

🖑 🏠 |❂| HÔTEL DU NORD

av. de Provence (Centre).

☎ 04.75.48.22.13

Closed Sun lunchtime Oct–April, and a fortnight in Nov.

A brilliant, understated, unpretentious hotel with seven rooms. Doubles €28 with shower and €38 with shower/wc. Rooms have views over the Vercors rather than the mountains. Family and regional cooking, including dishes like mushroom ravioli, roast lamb and cep omelette. There's a dish of the day for €8 including wine, another at €11 and *à la carte* for around €15. Half board from €30 per person. Free apéritif.

SAINT-AGNAN-EN-VERCORS   26420 (4KM S)

🏠 |❂| AUBERGE LE COLLET

It's on the D518, 1km outside the Chapelle-en-Vercors.

☎ 04.75.48.13.18 ➡ 04.75.48.13.25

e aubergelecolle@dubinternet.fr

Closed Mon evening and Tues; mid-Oct; a week in June. **Car park**.

This substantial mountain house is in the heart of the Vercors and provides an ideal spot for a well-earned rest. Lovely dining room, traditionally decorated – sturdy wooden beams, wooden floors and rough-cast on the walls ornamented by old photos. The warming log fire chases away the winter chill. Appropriate cuisine that's simple, filling and most welcoming. The menu of the day for €11 (starter, main course, cheese and dessert) is filling and excellent value for money and, surprisingly enough, they offer specialities from the Landes on other menus, €20–27. The owners spent some time in the southwest and brought back some good recipes with them: confits, foie gras, Salard potatoes and so on. It makes a nice change from local mountain food.The welcome is genuinely warm, the cuisine excellent. The simple, well-arranged rooms are meticulously maintained. Doubles €44 with shower/wc. Everything you need for a comfortable stay.

CHÂTEL 74390

☆ ✿ HÔTEL-RESTAURANT LES FOUGÈRES**

route du Petit-Châtel (Centre).
☎ 04.50.73.21.06 ➡ 04.50.73.38.34
Closed 20 April–5 July and 24 Aug–18 Dec. **Car park.**

This authentic old farm has been restored without losing its original style. It's a cheerful establishment run by a dynamic young couple. In summer it's a perfect place to unwind for a bit, while in winter everyone gets to know each other over fondue and croûte savoyarde. The bathrooms in the panelled bedrooms have been updated; doubles with shower/wc €42 in low season or €49 in high season – when half board at €40–50 per person is compulsory. The restaurant's not open in summer, though a good buffet breakfast is served until 11am. They don't take credit cards. Free apéritif.

☆ ✿ |●| HÔTEL-RESTAURANT LA PERDRIX BLANCHE**

Pré-de-la-Joux (Centre); it's 2.5km from the centre in the direction of le Linga, at the bottom of the cable lifts.
☎ 04.50.73.22.76 ➡ 04.50.73.35.21
❷ info@laperdrixblanche.com
Closed 1 May–15 June and 10 Sept–15 Nov. **TV. Car park.**

This delightful Savoy chalet stands well away from the resort in the fir trees at the foot of the ski runs. The whole place has had a makeover so rooms are fresh and have air conditioning – some have a balcony too. Doubles €58 with shower/wc or bath. Half

board, compulsory in the winter holidays, costs €40–61 per person. The typical local cooking – tartiflette, berthoud (marinated cheese baked in the oven) and fondue – is just the thing after a day's skiing or hiking, and the menus, €12–20, satisfy even the biggest of appetites. Free apéritif.

☆ |●| RESTAURANT LA BONNE MÉNAGÈRE

How to get there: it's one street north of the tourist office.
☎ 04.50.73.24.45
Closed lunchtimes in summer; May and June; mid-Sept to 20 Dec.

You'll get a delightful welcome here. The two dining rooms, decorated with old enamel plaques and little bunches of dried flowers, are popular with the local ski crowd. They serve starters like charcuterie and main dishes like berthoud, fondue, and croûte aux champignons (mushrooms on a layer of flaky pastry covered with cheese and then grilled). For dessert, try the pear sorbet with pear liqueur. The prices are fair; menus from €11 and à la carte around €25. Free house apéritif, coffee or digestif.

|●| RESTAURANT L'ABREUVOIR-CHEZ GINETTE**

hameau de Vonnes; head for Switzerland and you'll find the restaurant 1km out of town, very near lac de Vonnes.
☎ 04.50.73.24.89
Garden. Car park.

Berthoud de la vallée d'Abondance, the local speciality, is prepared very well at this authentic, country place. It's an absolutely delicious dish made from cheese, which is diced and marinated in white wine vinegar, Madeira and garlic before being put into the oven. They do other Savoy specialities and on holiday nights Louky gets his accordion out and everyone has a great time. Menus €12–24 or around €12 à la carte. From the garden, you get a great view of the mountain and the lake, which is lit up at night.

CHAPELLE D'ABONDANCE (LA) 74360 (5.5KM W)

☆ ✿ |●| L'ENSOLEILLÉE**

rue Principale (Centre).
☎ 04.50.73.50.42 ➡ 04.50.73.52.96
❷ info@hotel-ensoleille.com
Closed Tues; Easter to end May; end Sept to 20 Dec.
TV. Swimming pool. Car park.

The hotel, in a huge family house, thoroughly deserves its reputation. Most rooms have been renovated and have rustic, wooden furniture – and they've added a heated swimming pool and a Jacuzzi. Doubles with shower/wc or bath for €46–61. Half board, from €49 per person, is compulsory during the school holidays. Madame and her husband look after the dining room and the guests, one son runs the bar and the *Carnotzet* (where the *fondue* lovers gather) and the other is the chef. He uses only the finest ingredients, from the selection of various meats cooked on a hot stone – a local speciality – to the *cassolette* of calf's sweetbreads with cream and mushroom sauce. The dining rooms are welcoming and full of people enjoying themselves. There's a weekday menu at €18 and others €20–41. Free house apéritif.

𝒫 ≙ |●| LES GENTIANETTES**

Centre.
☎ 04.50.73.56.46 ➡ 04.50.73.56.39
℮ gentianettes@wanadoo.fr
Swimming pool. TV.

A lively new place run by professionals. It's in the centre of the village, away from the noisy road and just footsteps from the cross-country ski trails. Bright, comfortable rooms cost €53–69 with shower/wc or bath. Half board, priced at €40–66 per person, is compulsory in season. The restaurant, decorated like a mountain chalet, serves sophisticated cuisine that's unusually inventive for the region: mixed fish with wild chives, duck breast with bilberry vinegar, *escalope* of veal with cheese and potatoes. Lunch menu €16 (not Sun), others €18–41 or around €24 *à la carte*. There are lovely walks in the surrounding area and a pretty little indoor swimming pool. Free apéritif and 10% discount on the room rate.

CHÂTELARD (LE)　　73630

𝒫 ≙ |●| LE ROSSANE – CHEZ EVELYNE

Centre.
☎ 04.79.52.11.23 ➡ 04.79.54.83.44
℮ rossane@icor.fr
Restaurant closed evenings; reserve at all other times.
Disabled access. TV. Garden. Car park.

On the edge of a somewhat charmless town, this is a good place from which to explore the wild Bauges region. Évelyne the owner will give you a firm handshake as she welcomes you to her well-run establishment. The rooms have been well-refurbished with excellent facilities but modest prices – doubles with

shower/wc go for €34. Most have fantastic views over the countryside. The restaurant is utterly packed at lunchtime; there's a lunch *formule* for €8, a lunch menu at €11 and others €13–24. You can have a post-prandial snooze in a deck-chair in the garden, which is hardly distinguishable from the surrounding countryside. Free apéritif.

CHÂTILLON-EN-DIOIS　　26410

𝒫 ≙ |●| HÔTEL-RESTAURANT DU DAUPHINÉ

pl. Pierre Dévoluy (Centre); it's opposite the tourist office
☎ 04.75.21.13.13
Closed Tues evening and Wed; Sun evening Nov–June; the Christmas holidays; Feb.

An old hotel-café-restaurant right in the heart of the village. Its eight rooms are nicely old-fashioned but painted in fresh colours; the old furniture adds lots of charm and the floorboards creak. Room 7 has an iron bedstead and the bathroom is discreetly hidden in an alcove. Doubles €26 with washing facilities and €33 with shower/wc. There's a shaded terrace overlooking the road and an attractively decorated dining room (old mirror, bistro tables and friezes on the walls). The changing seasons and the whim of the chef are responsible for the frequent changes to the menu: fresh goat's cheese with pesto and pickled tomatoes, *bouillabaisse* Provençale, *aiguillette* of guineafowl with blackcurrants. The €12 *menu du jour* includes a glass of wine. You can choose with your eyes closed because everything is freshly cooked and the chef has real originality. Even if you're not eating you should try the home-made plant syrups – thyme, sage and lime – and the unusual "café du barman". Very friendly welcome from the dynamic young team. Free house apéritif and 10% discount on the room rate Sept–July.

CHÂTILLON-SUR-CHALARONNE　　01400

≙ |●| HÔTEL-RESTAURANT DE LA TOUR**

pl. de la République (Centre).
☎ 04.74.55.05.12 ➡ 04.74.55.09.19
Closed Sun evening, Wed and a fortnight in Dec.
Disabled access. TV. Lock-up garage.

A delightful establishment that stands out in a beautifully preserved medieval town. The hotel has exposed white stonework, half-timbering and a pepper-pot turret in pink brick; it was built in the fourteenth century and turned into a hotel three centuries later. The place has been renovated with great sensitivity and style, and is run by a young, welcoming team. In the restaurant menus start at €17 (not served Sun) and continue at €20–49. They list *gâteau* of chicken livers, stuffed chicken, chicken with cream and morel sauce, crayfish ravioli, pan-fried butterfly prawns and frogs *meunière*. Classic, spacious rooms, all recently redecorated. Doubles with shower or bath €50–64.

ABERGEMENT-CLÉMENCIAT (L') 01400 (8KM S)

|●| RESTAURANT LE SAINT-LAZARE

How to get there: take the D2 as far as Châtillon-sur-Chalaronne and go on another 5km.
☎ 04.74.24.00.23 ➡ 04.74.24.00.62
Closed Wed and Thurs; the Feb school holidays; the second fortnight in July; a week in Nov.

Even though the premises are on the ground floor of a substantial, fairly modern house in the centre of the village, this business has been going for ages. Christian Bidard, the young owner-chef, took over from his great-grandparents who opened a baker's-cum-grocer's-cum-café-cum restaurant in 1899. His is one of the best tables in the region and the setting in a large, bright dining room is ideal. Attentive service and inventive, delicate dishes with a good number of imaginative fish dishes: zander in season, sardines stuffed with minced chard, crayfish tails with grapefruit flesh and avocado *sabayon*. Also on offers are dishes using local, farm-raised chickens and meat. For dessert, try the pear *orientale*. Menus start at €23, then continue at €27–61. The wines are selected from local growers but there are also some from further afield.

CHOMAS L'AMBALLAN 38121

🏠 |●| DOMAINE DE CLAIREFONTAINE**

Chemin des Fontanettes;
☎ 04.74.58.81.521 ➡ 04.74.58.80.93
Closed Sun evening; Mon; Tues lunchtime; 20 Dec–20 Jan. **TV. Car park**.

A mansion in a magnificent estate which is more than three hundred years old. The very spacious rooms in the Domaine are furnished with taste. There are plans to update them so hurry to make the most of the prices before they go up: doubles €38–55 in the Domaine, but those in the Jardins de Clairefontaine are much more expensive at €91 per night. The cuisine is very stylish and prepared by

Philippe Girardon (voted the best trainee chef in France) but the menus are in the upper price bracket – weekday menu for €27 with others from €41. You'll receive the professional welcome you should expect in such a place. Tennis courts and boules.

CLUSAZ (LA) 74220

🎿 🏠 |●| LES AIRELLES**

Centre.
☎ 04.50.02.40.51 ➡ 04.50.32.35.33
📧 info@clusaz.com
TV.

A dream of a hotel in the centre of the village. It's been carefully renovated and offers bright, colourful doubles with all mod cons and shower/wc at €46–91. Half board at €56–76 is compulsory during school holidays. Guests have use of the Jacuzzi, sauna and swimming pool in the hotel *Les Sapins*, a bit further up, which belongs to relatives. Genuine, simple welcome, just like the food. Weekday lunch menu at €15 and others €20–24, listing all the regional specialities. Free house *digestif*.

|●| LE CHALET DU LAC

Lac des Confins; just before you get to the lake, take the dirt road on the right.
☎ 04.50.02.53.26 📧 chalac@club-internet.fr
Closed Tues except in school holidays. **Car park**.

This is a family business, and everybody is involved in running it smoothly. The menus (€11–14) feature Savoy specialities such as old-style *fricassée* of suckling pig, *tartiflette* and sautéed chicken with three types of vinegar. Try the platters of home-made *charcuterie*, fritters or *tomme blanche*. Around €19 *à la carte*. There's a sunny terrace with lake views. The atmosphere is informal – even a bit crazy some evenings.

COMBLOUX 74920

🎿 🏠 |●| LES GRANITS**

1409 route de Sallanches; it's 1.5km from the centre on the Sallanches road.
☎ 04.50.58.64.46 ➡ 04.50.58.61.63
Closed April–June inclusive and mid-Sept to Christmas. **Disabled access. TV. Car park**.

Double rooms with basin €43, or €53 with shower/wc or bath. Half board €47 per person. The hotel's quite close to a road – it's not very busy, but if you want to ensure a quiet night, ask for a room in the annexe or at the rear. In the attractive dining room you can choose from menus at €13–15 or *à la carte*, around €18. Typical Savoy dishes: *matafan, diotz, tartiflette* and *fondue*. Free coffee.

🏠 |O| HÔTEL-RESTAURANT LE COIN SAVOYARD**

300 route de la Cry; it's opposite the church.
☎ 04.50.58.60.27 ➡ 04.50.58.64.44
e coin-savoyard@wanadoo.fr
Closed Mon out of season; 14 April–1 June; and 15 Sept–10 Dec. **Swimming pool**. **TV**. **Car park**.

Lots of people come here year after year, so it's best to book well in advance. The cheerful, informal doubles, with shower/wc or bath, cost €67. You can have a drink or something light for dinner – a good omelette and salad, a steak with morels or a *fondue* – in a traditional Savoy setting. There are no set menus, so expect to pay about €23 *à la carte*. There's a sunny terrace facing Mont Blanc and the pool is great in the summer.

CONDRIEU   69420

🍴🏠 |O| HÔTEL-RESTAURANT LA RÉCLUSIÈRE**

14 route Nationale (Centre).
☎ 04.74.56.67.27 ➡ 04.74.56.80.05
Closed Mon evening and Tues; Feb school holidays.

Chef Martin Fleischmann enlarged this restaurant and added a few rooms, which are very comfortable and stylish. Doubles with shower/wc €50 or €69 with bath. In the restaurant, menus at €23–52 list minestrone with shellfish and saffron, duck breast with apples fried with smoked bacon and spiced *jus* and Armagnac ice-cream. Good wine list and attentive service. Free house apéritif.

CONTAMINES-MONTJOIE (LES)   74170

🏠 |O| LE MONT-JOLY*

La Chapelle.
☎ 04.50.47.00.17
Closed Oct–Nov. **Car park**.

This pretty gingerbread hotel on the outskirts of town is friendly and quiet and just 2km from the ski slopes. It offers simple, freshly decorated rooms and a few chalets next to the main building. Doubles cost €32 with basin, €37 with bath. Half board, €32–40, is compulsory in winter. The restaurant is pretty ordinary but offers set menus at €10 and €14 or *fondue* and *raclette* for around

€15 *à la carte*. There's a nice terrace surrounded by trees with a view of the mountains.

🍴🏠 LA CLEF DES CHAMPS*

route de la Frasse; it's above the village, in the street opposite the tourist office.
☎ 04.50.47.06.09 ➡ 04.50.47.09.49
e
Closed 22 April–20 June and 10 Sept–20 Dec. **Garden**. **Car park**.

An old restored farmhouse up the slopes in the resort. Reservations are essential in winter and advisable in summer. Doubles with shower/wc €38 – numbers 2, 3, 4 and 9 have balconies with views over the valley. Half board, compulsory during the winter and summer seasons, costs €33–36 per person. They offer special rates for children under eight. The restaurant is open to residents only. 10% discount Jan, April, June and Sept for full or half board.

🍴🏠 |O| HÔTEL-RESTAURANT LE GAI SOLEIL**

288 chemin des Layers; it's above the church.
☎ 04.50.47.02.94 ➡ 04.50.47.18.43
e gaisoleil@wanadoo.fr
Closed 15 April–14 June and 14 Sept–19 Dec. **Car park**.

Set in an old wooden farmhouse, built in 1823, this is a beautifully decorated hotel that's maintained with great care. You'll get a tremendous welcome. Handsome rooms, some with a mezzanine floor and all with direct-dial telephones and en-suite bathrooms, go for €43–64 with shower/wc or €53–67 with bath. Half board at €44–58 is compulsory during the school holidays. There's a set menu at €15 and another at €24 for residents only. 10% discount except during school holidays. Free house apéritif.

CONTREVOZ   01300

🍴 |O| L'AUBERGE DE CONTREVOZ – LA PLUMARDIÈRE

How to get there: on the N504.
☎ 04.79.81.82.54 ➡ 04.79.81.80.17
Closed Sun evening and Mon in winter; Jan. **Garden**.

A charming inn in a countryside village. This huge farmhouse has retained some of its original features, including the big fireplace and an enormous pair of blacksmith's bellows. There's a wonderful garden full of fruit trees where you can eat in good weather. Regional cuisine with an original twist is featured on the €14 weekday lunch menu – country salad, roast chicken with thyme and potatoes *dauphinoise*. But the cooking is so good that you might be tempted by the costlier menus at €20–33. Try the *foie gras*, and the home-smoked salmon and duck fillets are also sublime. Free coffee.

CORMORANCHE-SUR-SAÔNE   01290

🏊 🏠 |●| HÔTEL-RESTAURANT CHEZ LA MÈRE MARTINET

How to get there: take the N6 in the direction of Villefranche as far as Crêches-sur-Saône and then the D51; alternatively, take the D51 from Saint-Laurent-sur-Saône.
☎ 03.85.36.20.40 ➡ 03.85.31.77.19
Closed Mon and Feb. **TV. Garden. Car park**.

A nice little village inn where you'll receive a very warm welcome. Menus for €12–44 list delicious local cuisine: chicken breast with cream, fresh frogs' legs with parsley and garlic, Charolais beef steak with Bresse blue cheese sauce, hot sausage, home-made pastries. In fine weather you can sit out on the little terrace in the garden. A few double rooms with bath for €38. Free apéritif. 10% discount on the room rate.

CORPS   38970

🏊 🏠 |●| LA MARMOTTE

rue Principale.
☎ and ➡ 04.76.30.01.02
Closed Mon and Tues Sept–April; a week in Oct; the last fortnight in Dec.

An unpretentious little restaurant with some rooms that, though simple, are bright and comfortable, all with shower/wc. They're well maintained and some are attractively housed in the eaves. Doubles for €30 and half board for €30 per person. Regional cuisine with a personal touch at very reasonable prices in the restaurant. It's a comfortable setting and there's a small terrace in summer. Substantial dishes on menus €10–17 and there's a *for-mule* (main course with a choice of starter or dessert) for €9. Tasty dishes change often but a few old faithfuls are generally available: *pot-au-feu* with ravioli, home-made *caillette*, pastry parcels stuffed with vegetables, suckling pig stew, *fondue* with goat's cheese and walnuts. Free house apéritif or coffee

🏊 🏠 |●| HÔTEL DE LA POSTE**

pl. de la Mairie (Centre).

☎ 04.76.30.00.03 ➡ 04.76.30.02.73
Closed 3 Jan–14 Feb.

This hotel, in the centre of the village on the "route Napoléon", is one of the best-known places in the region. The heavy, fussy, old-fashioned interior décor may not be to all tastes, but the rooms are comfortable and cost €36–69 with shower/wc or bath. The cooking has a well-established reputation. There's a weekday menu for €17 and others €19–25. You get a wide choice *à la carte*: queen scallops with morels, joint of lamb cooked on a spit, wild boar stew, calf's sweetbreads with cream, trout braised with crayfish, wild duck *grand-mère*. There's a fight for tables on the terrace in good weather, even though the road goes past right in front. Free coffee or *digestif*.

🏊 🏠 |●| BOUSTIGUE HÔTEL**

route de la Salette.
☎ 04.76.30.01.03 ➡ 04.76.30.04.40
Closed 15 Oct–1 May. **Swimming pool. TV. Car park**.

Signs on the road leading to Notre-Dame-de-la-Salette, a place of pilgrimage, inform you "C'est par là" (This way) and "Vous approchez" (You're getting close), as they lead you towards this rather large hotel. You would be hard pushed to find a better place to relax than this, with its pool, its sauna and its putting green. It's on a plateau 1200m up, and it has a panoramic view of the village of Corps and lac du Sautet. The rooms are not very big but they're pleasant and cost €40 with shower/wc and €40–52 with bath. Bernard Dumas prepares modestly priced local dishes: ravioli with snails, calf's sweetbreads braised with mushrooms, pork cheek, wild mushrooms, chicken from Beaumont. Menus €15–30. Free *digestif*. 10% discount on the room rate in May, June and Sept.

COUCOURON   07470

🏠 |●| HÔTEL-RESTAURANT AU CARREFOUR DES LACS**

☎ 04.66.46.12.70 ➡ 04.66.46.16.42
Closed 1 Dec–1 Feb. **TV. Car park**.

An attractive mountain inn near a lake in the middle of the Ardèche plateau. Clean rooms €20 with shower, €28 with shower/wc and €42 with bath. Half board, compulsory July–Aug, costs €32 per person. The handsome dining room offers good food prepared from fresh ingredients, including fine *charcu-*

terie, delicious local cheeses and home-made desserts. Set menus €11–26.

COURS-LA-VILLE   69470

🏃 🏠 |❶| LE NOUVEL HÔTEL**

5 rue Georges-Clémenceau (Centre).
☎ 04.74.89.70.21 ➡ 04.74.89.84.41
Closed 25 Dec–3 Jan and a week in Aug. **TV**.

Good regional food at reasonable prices, served in a friendly dining room. Menus from €14 (except Sun) to €27. They also offer pretty rooms with direct-dial telephone – €26 with basin, €41 with bath. Free house apéritif.

🏃 🏠 |❶| LE PAVILLON**

Col du Pavillon; it's 3km from Cours-la-Ville on the D64 heading in the direction of Écharmeaux.
☎ 04.74.89.83.55 ✉ hotel-le-pavillon@wanadoo.fr
Closed Sat and Sun evening Nov–March; Sat only July–Aug; Feb. **Disabled access**. **TV**. **Car park**.

This hotel, surrounded by fir trees, stands absolutely alone at an altitude of 755m. The owners are keen travellers, and photographs of their expeditions to Morocco, India and the Arctic line the walls. The modern, comfortable rooms cost €52 with shower or bath, and the ground-floor ones have a private terrace and a view over the grounds. The pleasant restaurant offers a lunch *formule* for €13 then menus €18–20: haddock fillet, saffron-cream soup, gateau of chicken livers and crayfish and various platters – mushrooms, Chinese and seafood. Free house apéritif, coffee or *digestif*.

MARNAND   69240 (10KM S)

🏃 🏠 |❶| HÔTEL-RESTAURANT LA TERRASSE**

How to get there: from the centre of Thizy turn left for Marnand.
☎ 04.74.64.19.22 ➡ 04.74.64.25.95
Closed Sun evening and Mon; the Feb and All Saints' school holidays. **Disabled access**. **TV**. **Car park**.

Occupying a converted industrial building, this well-designed hotel looks great, and it's in a good location, with lovely views over the Beaujolais hills from each room. Brightly decorated doubles with bath go for €40. The restaurant is just as attractive, and features unusual dishes alongside traditional choices: pan-fried scallops with puréed leeks, fish fillets with chorizo, fresh fruit ice-cream with chocolate sauce. Menus €11–38. Easy-

going welcome. 10% discount on the room rate June–Sept.

CRÉMIEU   38460

🏃 🏠 |❶| L'AUBERGE DE LA CHAITE**

cours Baron-Raverat.
☎ 04.74.90.76.63 ➡ 04.74.90.88.08
Closed Sun evening, Mon, 2–31 Jan and the last week in April. **TV**. **Garden**. **Car park**.

This hotel has a beautiful setting, in a medieval village with ruined fortifications. Doubles €38 with shower, €41 with shower/wc, €46 with bath – those overlooking the garden have had a lovely make-over. You'll be treated like a king in the restaurant or on the terrace. Menus start at €13 (not Sunday), with others from €20: *terrine* of duck with orange, salmon *quenelles*, fried chicken with rum and ginger, roast duck with two kinds of peach. 10% discount on the room rate for a two-night stay Sept–June.

🏃 |❶| LES CASTORS

41 rue Porcherie
☎ 04.74.90.02.49
Closed Thurs and Sun evenings; Mon; a week at the end of March; a fortnight at the end of Sept and Christmas week.

One of those places that doesn't look much outside but the pleasant dining room offers the best food in town. Good, tasty dishes: ostrich fillet with green peppercorns, duck *foie gras* salad, veal chops with morels, and excellent savoury and sweet *crêpes*. Menus €9–28. Prices take off *à la carte*. Free coffee.

|❶| HÔTEL DE LA POSTE

21 rue Porcherie; it's opposite the covered market.
☎ 04.74.90.71.41
Closed Wed out of season; a fortnight in Feb; 3 weeks in Sept.

This wasn't a post office and it's not a hotel either – or rather, it's not a hotel any more. Rather, it's a typical, old-fashioned bistro, with flowers at every window, old ads on the walls and banquette seating. At lunchtime it attracts a young business crowd, who enjoy well-priced dishes of the day and set menus at €16–24. Fish and shellfish feature highly: mussels *poularde* (in cream sauce), fried smelt, fish *pot-au-feu*, fillet of beef Madagascar.

SAINT-HILAIRE-DE-BRENS   38460 (6KM SE)

🏃 |❶| AU BOIS JOLI

La Gare; coming from Crémieu, it's at the junction of the

Morestel and Bourgoin-Jallieu roads.
☎ 04.74.92.81.82 ➡ 04.74.92.93.27
Closed Tues–Sun evenings; a week in Jan; 18 Aug–18 Sept. **Garden. Car park**.

This renowned restaurant has been run for generations by the Vistalli family. It has two large dining rooms that can accommodate about a hundred people and it's decorated with pine cones and cowbells. Try frog's legs *provençale*, chicken with crayfish, zander fillet with sorrel or game including wild boar in season. The €11 lunch menu (not Sun) includes cheese and dessert, and there are others up to €25. Delicious wines. Free coffee.

CREST   26400

🏃 🏠 ❘●❘ LE KLÉBER**

6 rue Aristide-Dumont; it's in the centre of town by the town hall.
☎ 04.75.25.11.69 ➡ 04.75.76.82.82
Closed Sun and Tues evenings; Mon. **TV. Car park**.

This smart-looking little restaurant is decorated in ochre colours. It's known for its gourmet food and specializes in fish and regional dishes. There's a weekday menu at €15 and others up to €39: cep salad with slivers of duck, lobster stew with a verbena infusion, *aiguillette* of beef with *bordelaise* sauce. A few prettily decorated rooms at affordable prices: doubles cost €27 with shower and €37 with shower/wc or bath/wc. This is the most attractive place in town. Free apéritif.

🏃 ❘●❘ LA TARTINE

10 rue Peysson/13 rue de la République (Centre); it's near the church of Saint-Sauveur.
☎ 04.75.25.11.53
Closed Sat lunchtime; Sun and Wed evening; the All Saints' and Feb school holidays; the end of June.

The restaurant occupies the whole of the first floor of a very old house which is typical of the ones you find in old Crest. There's a piano in the large, lofty dining room – this place is popular with musicians, and your visit may well coincide with an impromptu jazz jam. Véronique the owner makes imaginative snacks and serves simple food – there's a dish of the day and various grills. *Menu du jour* €9 then others €15–19. It's very busy at lunchtime and at the weekend so it's advisable to book. Free coffee.

GRANE   26400 (8KM W)

🏃 🏠 ❘●❘ RESTAURANT GIFFON**

place de l'Église.

☎ 04.75.62.60.64
Closed Mon in season; Sun evening and Tues lunchtime out of season; no closures 1 June–1 Oct. **TV. Swimming pool. Car park**.

You get a choice of rooms: the older (and cheaper) ones are over the restaurant, the more individualized and spacious ones are around the swimming pool. Doubles €46 with shower and up to €104 with bath/wc. The décor in the restaurant is smart but slightly out-of-date. The food explains why the chef has made this restaurant such a local favourite: *foie gras* with honeyed pears and pink peppercorns, *noisette* of lamb with truffle medallions cooked in their juices, char with truffle butter and morels. Menus €20–58. Perfect welcome and service. Free coffee and 10% discount on the room rate 1 Oct–1 May.

SAILLANS   26340 (16KM E)

🏃 ❘●❘ LA PANTOUFLE RIEUSE

43 Grande Rue; it's the main street.
☎ 04.75.21.59.60
Closed Tues in season; Mon–Fri out of season; Dec–15 Jan.

A charming restaurant in a pretty village. The owner brings flavours from distant lands to her cuisine – there's a nice *formule assiette découverte* providing a dish from a different place each day, and an *assiette du monde* – a culinary journey overseas to destinations such as China, Portugal and Armenia. The dishes are tasty and often surprising and always prepared using fresh ingredients. There's a menu for €11 and a meal *à la carte* costs around €15. Free house apéritif, coffee or house *digestif*.

OMBLÈZE   26400 (29.5KM NE)

🏃 🏠 ❘●❘ AUBERGE DU MOULIN DE LA PIPE

How to get there: from Crest follow the road to Die, at Mirabel et Blacons, turn onto the D70 as far as Plan-de-Baix, then take the D578 for a further 5km.
☎ 04.75.76.42.05 ➡ 04.75.76.42.60
Closed 11 Nov–7 Feb. **Disabled access. Car park**.

This restored old mill lies at the far end of a valley with views of the gorges, a river and the waterfalls. It attracts outdoorsy people of all ages who come to Omblèze for the climbing school, flying trapeze and circus courses and the rock, blues and reggae concerts. The various *formules* include dishes such as *foie gras* ravioli, *caillette* with onion preserve, Dauphinois potatoes *au gratin* and chocolate fondant with lavender. Menus €13–25. Doubles €40 with bath/wc. There are three *gîtes* for groups and three furnished apartments to rent. 10% discount on the room rate Sept–June.

DIE   26150

🛏 HÔTEL DES ALPES**

87 rue Camille Buffardel (Centre).
☎ 04.75.22.15.83 ➡ 04.75.22.09.38
TV. Pay car park.

The wide staircase is all that remains from this former fourteenth-century coaching inn. Nonetheless the hotel offers a couple of dozen comfortable rooms with good facilities – the second-floor ones have a splendid view of the Glandasse mountains and are very quiet. Doubles €33–38 and with some family rooms sleeping 5 or 6 people. Some might find that the pink everywhere in the house is too much, though, and Madame's passion for puzzles adds to the kitsch. That said, the welcome is pleasant and it's a good base for exploring the town and the countryside.

🍴 |O| LA FERME DES BATETS

quartier des Batets; it's 3km from the centre of town on the D518 road to Crest.
☎ 04.75.22.11.45
Closed Sun evening and Wed; 15–31 Oct. **Car park**.

If you're footsore and weary from walking in the Vercors, this old farmhouse – the dining room is a converted seventeenth-century stable – will come as a welcome sight. Try the guineafowl with thyme or the boned quail with juniper and a glass of local wine like a Châtillon-Champassias from Cornillon. Menus €13–26. It can get very busy. Free glass of Clairette – a local sparkling wine – with dessert.

BARNAVE   26310 (13KM SE)

🍴 🛏 |O| L'AUBERGERIE

Grande-Rue.
☎ 04.75.21.82.13 ➡ 04.75.21.84.31
Restaurant closed Tues in season; Mon–Fri in winter.
TV.

You know you're here when you see the sheep sign. The large dining room occupies a converted stable, and upstairs there's an informal café where villagers come to play cards. They serve dishes such as savoury pie, goat's cheese pastries, guineafowl in a cream sauce and rabbit in Clairette de Die, a local sparkling wine. Menus €13–20. The oldest house in the village has been converted to provide five tasteful, simply decorated

rooms with kitchenettes; they go for €30. You can also rent them for the weekend or by the week. Free house apéritif.

DIEULEFIT   26220

🍴 |O| AUBERGE LES BRISES

Route de Nyons; it's 1.5km from the centre of town.
☎ 04.75.46.41.49
Closed Tues and Wed out of season; Jan–Feb.

This restaurant has quickly made a name for itself for its good food and friendly reception. Chef Didier le Doujet and his wife have created a little corner of their native Brittany in the Drôme, though they've swapped the flavours of the Atlantic for local ones – try the duck ham salad or the egg custard with *picodon* cheese. Very appealing menus at €19–32 list dishes such as *croustillant* of stuffed whiting with garlic, fish *blanquette* and veal kidneys with morels. There's also a *plat du terroir* at €9. Eat on the shady terrace in summer or in the rustic dining room. Free apéritif.

LE POËT-LAVAL   26160 (6KM NW)

🍴 🛏 |O| LES HOSPITALIERS***

It's halfway between La Bégude and Dieulefit.
☎ 04.75.46.22.32 ➡ 04.75.56.49.99
Closed Mon and Tues (except for residents); 1 Jan–15 March; 11 Nov–20 Dec. **Car park**.

The hotel looks down over one of the loveliest villages in the Drôme; it's an idyllic place for a romantic weekend. There are some twenty rooms at €46 with shower and €61–122 with bath, which offer sophisticated luxury. The salon and dining room are superb – pale wood, ancient beams and cosy furnishings. The superb terrace looks over marvellous countryside and is the place for dinner as the sun goes down. It's advisable to stick to the menus (€24–52), because *à la carte* can be pricey. After your meal take a wander along the windy roads or visit one of the local Protestant museums. Free house apéritif.

FÉLINES-SUR-RIMANDOULE 26160 (12KM NW)

🍴 |O| RESTAURANT CHEZ DENIS

How to get there: take the D540 then the D179.
☎ 04.75.90.16.73
Closed Mon and Tues evenings; Wed out of season; weekends in Jan; the first weekend in Feb; during the week 1 Dec–31 March. **Car park**.

Denis is actually the present chef's father, but there haven't been any drastic changes since he retired and the whole place quietly carries on just as it ever did. On Sunday and sunny days people flock to this handsome restaurant up in the hills to eat on a cool terrace in a relaxed atmosphere to the sound of a running stream. Set menus, €17–35, offer good value for money and specialities include *escalopes* of *foie gras* with blackcurrant sauce, snails *au gratin* with noodles and duck with olives. It's best to book at weekends. Free coffee.

DIVONNE-LES-BAINS 01220

🎿 🏨 |●| LA TERRASSE FLEURIE**

315 rue Fontaine (Centre); it's very near the casino.
☎ 04.50.20.06.32 ➡ 04.50.20.40.34
Closed 31 Oct–1 March. **TV**.

A very quiet and aptly named hotel with a flowery terrace and balcony. It's remarkably peaceful, despite being so close to the centre of town. The modern rooms have charm – doubles with shower/wc or bath €46–52 – while the restaurant offers simple, inexpensive home cooking. Menus start at €13, there's a Sunday one for €14 and a *menu terroir* at €20 and it costs around €18 *à la carte*. Excellent value for Divonne. 10% discount on the room rate Oct–May.

ÉVIAN 74500

🎿 🏨 HÔTEL CONTINENTAL**

65 rue Nationale (Centre).
☎ 04.50.75.37.54 ➡ 04.50.75.31.11
Closed 2–15 Jan.

The new owners of this hotel spend a lot of time in the USA, and they've turned this place into a place which shouts with life. Each room has personality and the atmosphere is genuinely friendly. Courteous welcome and great prices, considering the charm of the place and the size of the rooms: doubles €37–49 with shower/wc or €40–52 with bath. 10% discount on the room rate Sept–June.

PUBLIER 74500 (3.5KM W)

🎿 🏨 |●| HÔTEL-RESTAURANT LE CHABLAIS**

rue du Chablais; it's on the D11.
☎ 04.50.75.28.06 ➡ 04.50.74.67.32
Closed Sun in winter; 20 Dec–31 Jan; 1 May. **TV**. **Car park**.

A clean, tidy, efficient place with a Swiss feel. The hotel's right on the lake and half of the

rooms have a superb view of it. They're really attractive, though facilities are standard; doubles €25–28 with basin, €32–36 with shower and €37–46 with shower/wc or bath. Brasserie menu €14 at lunchtime; others €16–25. Free house apéritif or 10% discount on the room rate Sept–June.

BERNEX 74500 (10KM SE)

🎿 🏨 |●| L'ÉCHELLE

How to get there: it's beside the church.
☎ 04.50.73.60.42 ➡ 04.50.73.69.21
Closed Mon and Tues except school holidays; 15 Nov–15 Dec. **Car park**.

A restaurant where everyone takes time out to enjoy the finer things in life. Chef Pierre Mercier follows the methods of his mother, "la Félicie", who used to cook for the mountain walkers at Saint-Michel. Try the snail *brochettes*, duck *aiguillettes à la mondeuse* or the grilled meats. Weekday lunch menu €10 and others €22–30. Wine is from local vineyards. They have a few rooms for €41–49 per person. Free *digestif*.

|●| RESTAURANT LE RELAIS DE LA CHEVRETTE

Trossy; get there on the D21 and the D52 – go through Bernex and head for Dent-d'Oche.
☎ 04.50.73.60.27
Closed Wed except in school holidays; 5 Nov–20 Dec. **Disabled access**. **Garden**. **Car park**.

This picture-perfect chalet with red and white wooden shutters has a menu featuring typical Alpine produce: dried meat and ham, omelettes and bilberry tart. In winter you can sit by the open fire, while in summer you can enjoy the garden, which has a stream running through it. You'll pay €15 for a substantial meal *à la carte*. There's a good wine list featuring Savoy wines. Warm welcome.

THOLLON-LES-MÉMISES 74500 (10KM E)

🎿 🏨 |●| HÔTEL BON SÉJOUR**

Centre.
☎ 04.50.70.92.65 ➡ 04.50.70.95.72
Closed 15 Nov–20 Dec. **Garden**. **TV**. **Garage**.

This is a family hotel where everyone helps out. The younger Duponts are refurbishing the bedrooms one by one; doubles with shower/wc or bath cost €43–58. Good, tasty mountain cuisine in the restaurant, prepared with care and served generously. Prices are attractive, too, with menus at €14–21.

There's a terrace and a garden. Free apéritif.

VACHERESSE 74360 (20KM SE)

🌿 🏠 |●| AU PETIT CHEZ SOI

How to get there; take the D21 to Vinzier, the D32 to
Chevenoz then the D222 in the direction of Abondance.
☎ and ➡ 04.50.73.10.11
Car park.

You'll find this old house at the head of the
Abondance valley, between Lake Geneva
and the ski resorts. It's a very traditional,
friendly place, where you eat whatever has
been prepared that day on menus at €11
and €14. The daughters come in to lend a
hand – as, occasionally, do the guests. The
rooms look as if they're from another era, but
you'll get as good a night's sleep here. Doubles €30 with shower/wc. Free apéritif.

EVOSGES 01230

🏠 |●| L'AUBERGE CAMPAGNARDE**

How to get there: as you leave Saint-Rambert, head for
Belley; 1km from town, take the D34.
☎ 04.74.38.55.55 ➡ 04.74.38.55.62
e mano.merloz@wanadoo.fr
Closed Tues evening, Wed, Jan and Nov. **TV**.
Swimming pool. Lock-up car park.

The winding road up is gorgeous, threading
through steep vineyards and past huge white
rocks that erupt from the bushes. The inn is
like a holiday complex offering games for the
children and mini-golf. Most rooms have been
renovated and they're comfortable and quiet
– €27 with basin, €38 with shower/wc, €47
with bath. The dining room is cosy but they
could really do with offering a more modest
menu – the cheapest costs €21. It shows off
the top-quality produce used: guineafowl *fricassée* with balsamic vinegar, snail stew, quail
in Jeannette's style and hazelnut tart. Others
€24–40. The cuisine is full of flavour and
some of the dishes are very subtle.

PEZIÈRES-RESINAND (LES) 01110 (6KM NE)

🌿 |●| LE BOOMERANG

How to get here: take the N504 to Saint-Rambert and
then turn left onto the D34; it's signposted from the
village of Oncieu.
☎ 04.74.35.58.60 ➡ 04.74.38.58.32
e rpboomerang@aol.com
Closed Mon; Nov–Dec; whenever the boss goes
shopping in Australia.

Just one of a few scattered houses huddled in
one of Bugey's superb isolated valleys, this

astonishing inn is owned by Brent Perkins,
originally from Adelaide, who settled here with
his kangaroo after marrying a French woman.
You'll get a genuine barbie – even a vegetarian
one – along with steak and British and Australian sauces, ostrich fillets and roast emu
with bush herbs. Menus €16–25. The wine list
is divided between Australia and Bugey. They
open a tearoom in the afternoon. Free *digestif*.

FAVERGES 74210

🌿 |●| LA CARTE D'AUTREFOIS

25 rue Gambetta (Centre).
☎ 04.50.32.49.98
Closed Sun evening and Mon; first week in Jan; last
week in May; last week in Aug.

A little restaurant in a delightful spot not far
from the lake of Annecy, with a small ski
resort nearby. It has a nice dining room and
honest, flavourful cooking – about as far as
you can get from the standard fare dished up
in the local tourist traps. Try the home-made
ravioli or the kangaroo and ostrich. Menus
€13–19. Free apéritif.

FEURS 42110

|●| CHALET DE LA BOULE D'OR

42 route de Lyon (East); it's near the Feurs east exit.
☎ 04.77.26.20.68
Closed Sun evening, Mon, 15–30 Jan, and 1–22 Aug.

A gourmet restaurant that's not too expensive
– on weekdays, anyway. The staff are attentive
without being intrusive, the food is delicate and
the wines have been carefully selected (though
prices are quite high). All the dishes are good:
cod and parsley tart, zander with creamed
green lentils and *terrine* with artichoke hearts
and herb vinaigrette. The appetizers are full of
subtle flavours and the desserts are out of this
world. Menu at €15 (weekdays); the others at
€24–49 seem a bit overpriced.

MARCLOPT 42210 (11KM S)

🏠 |●| LE KHAN

☎ 04.77.54.58.40
How to get here: leave the A72 at the Montbrison-
Montrond exit and take the D115 to Marclopt.
Closed Thurs evening except in season; the second
week in Jan; a fortnight in Oct. **Car park**.

This modern inn prides itself on serving
authentic French food: home-made *foie gras*,
wine from local vineyards, home-made jam for
breakfast. The décor features stone walls built

by the owner's son and murals painted by local artists. The welcome you'll get from the proprietress couldn't be warmer, and her cooking is fresh and original – you serve yourself. Menus €17–29; the *foie gras* menu, which you have to order in advance, serves that delicacy in a variety of preparations. The spacious guestrooms, decorated in charming rustic style cost €18. Superb breakfast for €6.

PANISSIÈRES   42360 (12KM NE)

✿ |●| HÔTEL-RESTAURANT DE LA POSTE**

95 rue J-B Guerpillon; take the D89 then the D60 in the direction of Tarare (Centre).
☎ 04.77.28.64.00 ➡ 04.77.28.69.94
Restaurant closed Fri and Sat lunchtime. **TV**.

A popular hotel that the owners have completely restored. The rooms are simple but good value; doubles €29–38. Superb views over the Forez mountains, and an elegant dining room serving decent, good cooking. Weekday lunch menu €65, others €14–24. Excellent welcome.

VIOLAY   42780 (22KM NE)

⚝ ✿ |●| HÔTEL-RESTAURANT PERRIER**

pl. de l'Église; from Feurs, head for Balbigny then take the D1 in the direction of Tarare.
☎ 04.74.63.91.01 ➡ 04.74.63.91.77
Closed Sat and Sun evening; Jan–Feb. **Disabled access. TV. Lock-up car park**.

Jean-Luc Clot and his wife will make you feel very welcome when you arrive. The village is a popular centre for cross-country skiing and there's a pretty church over the road from the hotel. It's well-run and prices are affordable: €26 for a double with basin or €33–38 for a sumptuous room with bath. Much of the cooking in the restaurant is inspired by the cuisine of southwest France. Prices are reasonable – there's a weekday menu at €14 and others €17–22, among them a *menu terroir* which includes wine and coffee. Try the *confits* of duck or chicken, cockerel with tarragon, veal sweetbreads flambéed with Madeira or the scallops *Normande*. Free apéritif and 10% discount on the room rate.

FLUMET   73590

⚝ ✿ |●| HÔTEL-RESTAURANT LE PARC DES CÈDRES***

Centre.
☎ 04.79.31.72.37 ➡ 04.79.31.61.66

Closed April–May; Oct to 20 Dec. **TV**. **Car park**.

The family who have run this establishment for over a century belong to the old school of hotel-keeping. The building is surrounded by substantial grounds planted with cedar trees, there are club chairs in the sitting room and a snooker table in the bar. Some of the rooms were redecorated in the 1970s while others are more traditionally rustic. Doubles with shower/wc €44 or €58 with bath – some have terraces or balconies. In the restaurant, good-quality produce makes for good cooking: truffled *terrine*, oven-baked kidneys flambéed with Cognac, sautéed calves' liver with Apremont wine sauce and moka-chocolate slice. Menus from €15 or €27. The terrace under the cedar trees is wonderful in summer. 10% discount on the room rate or free coffee.

NOTRE-DAME-DE-BELLECOMBE   73590 (5KM S)

|●| LA FERME DE VICTORINE

Le Mont-Rond; take the N218 in the direction of Les Saisies and 3km before Notre-Dame-de-Bellecombe, take the left towards Le Planay.
☎ 04.79.31.63.46 ➡ 04.79.31.79.91
Closed Sun evening and Mon in spring and autumn; 25 June–5 July; 14 Nov–20 Dec.

The dining room has a huge fireplace for cold winter days and, in the summer, they open a bright, sunny terrace with a great view of the mountain. Menus – €17 at lunchtime in the week and €21–33 – list nicely prepared traditional Savoy dishes. Try mushroom *fondue*, *tartiflette* made with *tamié* (a local cheese), chicken with morels or *reblochonnade*. Even the biggest appetites will be satisfied with the *farcement* (potatoes baked with eggs, milk, raisins and prunes). Good Savoy wines also available.

SAISIES (LES)   73620 (14KM S)

⚝ ✿ |●| LE MÉTÉOR*

How to get there: in the village, follow the signs to the Village Vacances.
☎ 04.79.38.90.79 ➡ 04.79.38.97.00
Closed 28 April–7 July; 2 Sept–1 Dec.

This typical, wooden chalet built in a mountain meadow is quietly set apart from the ski resort but just 100m from the slopes. The rooms, nothing special but perfectly acceptable, cost €38 with shower/wc; in winter half board is compulsory and costs €39–47 per person. Lunch menu €11; it's €15 in the evening. They serve Savoy specialities such as *fondue*, *raclette* and *tartiflette*. Warm welcome and atmosphere. Free house apéritif.

🎿 |●| RESTAURANT LE CHAUDRON

Centre; take the D218, and it's beside the police station.
☎ 04.79.38.92.76
Closed 15 April–15 Dec.

Though the decoration at this restaurant is typical of hundreds of places in the mountains, the food is good. The good regional dishes are amply served and fortifying after a day's skiing: *diots*, *fondue*, *reblochonnade*, fillets of *féra* (a type of salmon), and beef topped with cheese. Menus from €11 at lunchtime up to €30 or around €22 *à la carte*. There's a nice terrace where you can get a good view of Mont Blanc on a clear day. Warm ambience and friendly service. Free *digestif*.

GARDE-ADHÉMAR (LA)   26700

🎿 🏠 |●| LOGIS DE L'ESCALIN

Northwest; take the Montélimar-Sud exit off the A7 then go 1.5km along the road to Donzère.
☎ 04.75.04.41.32 ➡ 04.75.04.40.05
ℯ info@lescalin.com
Closed Sun evening; Mon; the first fortnight in Jan. **TV**. **Garden**. **Car park**.

A little hotel on the side of a hill overlooking the Rhône Valley. The motorway is a couple of kilometres away as the crow flies, but seems much, much further. The hotel, a handsome building in local style painted white with blue shutters, provides seven fresh, refurbished rooms; doubles €53 with shower/wc and €61 with bath. There's a weekday menu at €20 and others up to €40. Dishes include fresh pan-fried *foie gras* with cinnamon apples, garlic braised ham and veal with cream and tarragon sauce. There are more than 200 vintages on the wine list and a pleasant garden in which to sample them. Free coffee and 10% discount on the room rate Sept–June except weekends.

GEX   01170

🎿 🏠 HÔTEL DU PARC**

av. des Alpes (Centre).
☎ 04.50.41.50.18 ➡ 04.50.42.37.29
Closed Sun and 1–15 Jan. **TV**. **Car park**.

This traditional, characterful hotel has been run by the same family for over seventy years. The park it's named after is across the road and the hotel itself has a huge, prize-winning garden full of geraniums, roses,

begonias and all sorts of colourful flowers. Rooms are being renovated one by one; they go for €43 with shower/wc and €61 with bath. 10% discount.

CESSY   01170 (2KM SE)

🏠 MOTEL LA BERGERIE

805 route Plaine (South); it's on the N5, Geneva–Paris road.
☎ 04.50.41.41.75 ➡ 04.50.41.71.82
TV. **Car park**.

This place is surrounded by fields, so peace and quiet are the order of the day. The rooms are large and have en-suite bath and good facilities; doubles €30 and some rooms for three at €40. It's far from luxurious but it offers value for money and the lady owner ensures you have a warm, smiling welcome. They do a substantial breakfast with home-made preserves for €4, served until noon.

SEGNY   01170 (6KM SE)

🏠 LA BONNE AUBERGE**

rue du Vieux-Bourg (Centre); take the N5.
☎ 04.50.41.60.42 ➡ 04.50.41.71.79
Closed Christmas to 15 March. **TV**. **Garden**. **Lock-up car park**.

An authentic country inn hidden from the road by the trees in the garden. There are flowers everywhere, even on the murals by the stairs. Attractive, well-maintained rooms for €27 for a double with shower/wc or €36 with bath – very good value for a hotel near Gex. Warm welcome and family atmosphere. There's no restaurant, though they do serve breakfast complete with home-made jam.

CROZET   01170 (8KM SW)

🏠 |●| LE BOIS JOLY**

route du Télécabine (South); take the D984 in the direction of Bellegarde and turn right onto the D89 as far as Crozet; it's 500m from the cable car.
☎ 04.50.41.01.96 ➡ 04.50.42.48.47
Closed Fri; Easter school holidays. **TV**.

This is a big establishment on the lower slopes of the Jura. There is a splendid view of the Alps from the terrace, where you can eat in fine weather. The rooms have good facilities – some of them with balconies – and are reasonably priced for the area: €30 with basin and €40 with bath. The restaurant provides generous portions of regional dishes such as frogs' legs or guineafowl with morel sauce. Menus €12–24. Half board and full board available.

GRAND-BORNAND (LE)   74450

♠ |●| HÔTEL-RESTAURANT LA CROIX SAINT-MAURICE**

Centre.
☎ 04.50.02.20.05 ➦ 04.50.02.35.37
✉ info@hotel-lacroixstmaurice.com
Restaurant closed Oct. **Disabled access**. **TV**. **Pay car park**.

This hotel, run by the same family for some thirty years, strikes the right tone in this family resort, and every year regulars come back for what amounts to a family reunion. The south-facing rooms look over the Aravis mountains; some have a balcony or terrace. All rooms are en-suite, with either shower/wc or bath and cost €33–53. Half board is obligatory in Feb and costs €37–56 per person. The restaurant, open only in winter, offers an €15 weekday menu and others up to €24. Lots of regional specialities *à la carte*, including rissoles of *reblochon* cheese with salad, *fricassée savoyarde* with *polenta* and potatoes *au gratin*.

♨ ♠ |●| HÔTEL-RESTAURANT LES GLAÏEULS**

Centre; it's at the foot of the slopes, where the cable cars start from.
☎ 04.50.02.20.23 ➦ 04.50.02.25.00
Closed 20 April–15 June; 20 Sept–20 Dec. **TV**. **Car park**.

A very well-run hotel. Though the façade is pretty ordinary, in summer the flowers at every window and on the terrace make it look lovely. It's a very traditional place, with cosy sitting rooms and classic décor. The owners are polite and friendly. Rooms have good facilities and cost €40–55 with shower/wc or bath. Good cooking in the restaurant, with unusual yet classic dishes such as freshwater fish poached in Savoy wines and *foie gras* escalope with apples. Menus €14–37. There's a sunny terrace. Free coffee.

♠ HÔTEL LES CIMES***

Le Chinaillon (Centre).
☎ 04.50.27.00.38 ➦ 04.50.27.08.46
✉ info@hotel-les-cimes.com
Closed 1 May–15 June and 10 Sept–20 Nov.

A stone's throw from the old village of Chinaillon and 100m from the pistes, this is a traveller's dream come true. The couple who run the place have converted an ordinary place above a chic boutique into a friendly

inn which is full of the fragrance of wood and polish. Bedrooms are wonderfully quiet, with comfortable feather beds. Doubles cost €74–114 with shower/wc or bath; the price includes a superb breakfast. Half board can be arranged with a restaurant nearby. And the owners look after their guests very well.

♨ |●| LA FERME DE LORMAY

Vallée du Bouchet; it's 7km from the village, in the direction of the col des Annes – turn right when you get to the little chapel.
Closed Tues in summer; Tues and weekday lunchtimes in winter; 1 May–20 June; 10 Sept and 15–20 Dec.

There's an authentic atmosphere in this old farmhouse-inn – in fact, in an attempt to keep the place for local people there was no sign outside the door until relatively recently. In summer, when they serve food on the terrace, try the chicken with crayfish, the trout or the house *quenelles*. When the weather gets cold the tables are put close together round the fireplace, and there is more *charcuterie* and pork on the menu – the roast pork and bacon soup are both delicious. It's cooking you want to linger over. About €23–33 *à la carte*. Free house apéritif.

GRENOBLE   38000

SEE MAP OVERLEAF

♨ ♠ HÔTEL DE L'EUROPE**

22 pl. Grenette. **MAP C3-1**
☎ and ➦ 04.76.46.16.94
✉ hotel.europe.gre@wanadoo.fr
TV.

The hotel is in a lively pedestrianized area right in the centre of Grenoble, but the rooms – some 50 of them – are well-soundproofed and noise isn't a problem. It's a comfortable place, the welcome is genuine and the prices are unusually modest for the town: €24 for a double with basin, €41–55 with shower/wc or bath. Rooms are all regularly renovated. There's also a gym and a sauna. 10% discount 15 July–15 Aug.

♠ HÔTEL DES PATINOIRES**

12 rue Marie-Chamoux; it's 500m south of the Palais des Sports, off av. Jeanne-d'Arc. **Off map D4-2**
☎ 04.76.44.43.65 ➦ 04.76.44.44.77
✉ infor@hotel-patinoire.com **TV**. **Pay garage**.

It may not be the easiest place in the world to find, but this is one of the best hotels in town and is good value for money. The owners are genial, attentive and full of information about where to go and what to do. Warm atmos-

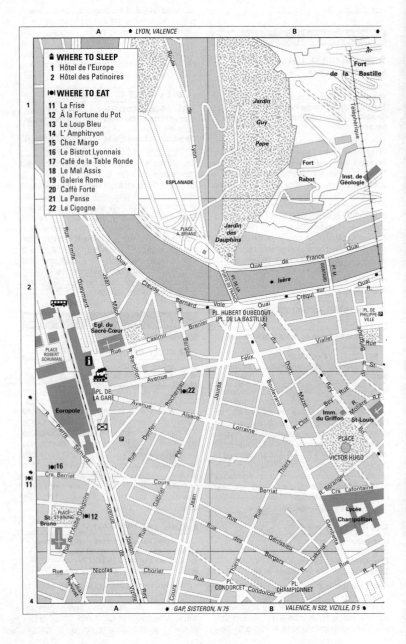

⌂ WHERE TO SLEEP
1 Hôtel de l'Europe
2 Hôtel des Patinoires

|●| WHERE TO EAT
11 La Frise
12 À la Fortune du Pot
13 Le Loup Bleu
14 L' Amphitryon
15 Chez Margo
16 Le Bistrot Lyonnais
17 Café de la Table Ronde
18 Le Mal Assis
19 Galerie Rome
20 Caffé Forte
21 La Panse
22 La Cigogne

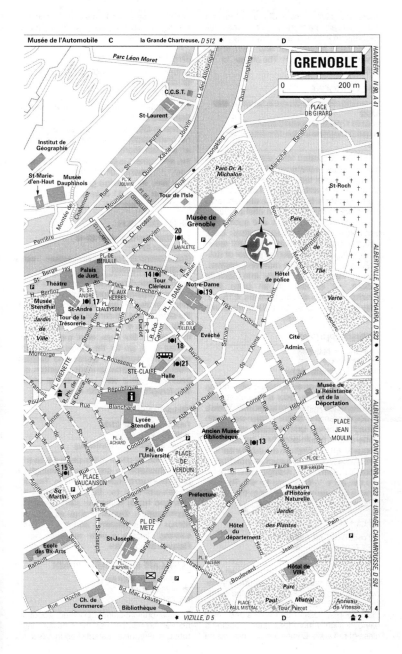

phere and décor – many of the pictures on the walls are painted by the owner. It's superbly maintained and extremely quiet. Comfortable rooms cost €42 with shower/wc and €46 with bath. The charge for the garage is €5.

|●| LA CIGOGNE

11 rue Denfer-Rochereau; it's next to the station. **MAP A3-22**
☎ 04.76.17.16.88 **e** bodelors@wanadoo.fr
Closed Sat lunchtime and Sun; Mon–Wed evenings; Aug.

A quirkily decorated little restaurant which quietly makes its presence felt. It's popular as a lunch place for local workers. The décor is slightly bizarre, with a fake roof to the bar, an old typewriter, a bread paddle and old radio sets stuck on the walls. The chef produces remarkable regional dishes and substantial portions – try the marvellous steak *bleu*, which is crisp on the outside but still red in the middle. There are also a number of delicious cheese dishes like *racleton* (potatoes, country ham, *crème fraîche* and Raclette cheese, all cooked on an open fire). Lunchtime menu €7, with others €15–18. They serve very early – by 1.30pm the dining room is practically empty.

🎐|●| L'AMPHITRYON

9 rue Chenoise. **MAP C2-14**
☎ 04.76.51.38.07
Closed Sun lunchtime and Aug.

An unusual place on a street lined with nothing but restaurants. The décor is minimalist, with an unexpected Roman wall at one end. There's an eclectic range of dishes – Italian ravioli with spinach or salmon, lamb delicately spiced with home-made, mouth-scorching *harissa* – on menus at €8–12. Portions are substantial: the "Brick" couscous, a mixture of several different types, is a meal in itself. A single menu for €14. You can get a ¹/₂-litre of red for €6. The welcome is very warm – in contrast to the coolest of cool atmospheres. Free *digestif*.

|●| LA FRISE

150 cours Berriat. **Off map A3-11**
☎ 04.76.96.58.22
Closed weekends and Aug.

Near the Magasin, the contemporary art centre, this place has a bright, colourful interior with pictures by local artists on the walls. Tasty dishes; the *formule* for €11 includes a main course, dessert and coffee and you'll pay only slightly more for a meal including a glass of red wine. Dishes are prepared using fresh ingredients and served in big portions, and the delicious desserts are home-made. Friendly welcome.

|●| À LA FORTUNE DU POT

34 rue de l'Abbé-Grégoire. **MAP A3-12**
☎ 04.76.96.20.05
Closed Sun and Mon; Aug.

This place is on the corner of the Marché Saint-Bruno, the most lively and popular market in Grenoble. The dry stone walls are hung with pictures, there's a Formica bar and an old clock that doesn't work any more and the atmosphere is great, aided by the genial host. It's always full of people recounting local tales and having a good time. There's a single menu at €11 at lunchtime; it goes up to €13 in the evening.

|●| LE LOUP BLEU

7 rue Dominique-Villars. **MAP D3-13**
☎ 04.76.51.22.70
Closed Sat lunchtime and Sun; public holidays; 3 weeks in Aug. **Disabled access.**

Service noon–2pm and dinner 8–10.15pm. This unobtrusive restaurant, with the old shutters still in place, is quiet and atmospheric, and the cooking and the service are both first-rate. Dishes on the €11 lunch menu change with the seasons. But if you want a slightly more refined meal, go for the others at €17–29, which offer traditional dishes and excellent meat and fish. Some are worth a mention: sea bass with walnut wine, duck breast stuffed with *foie gras*, scallops with roasted ceps.

|●| LA PANSE

7 rue de la Paix. **MAP C2-21**
☎ 04.76.54.09.54
Closed Sun and mid-July to mid-Aug.

The minimalist décor at this place will be a bit too fashionable for some tastes, though it's brightened up by colourful pictures. The welcome's a bit cool, too. But the cooking is reliable and highly distinctive with a touch of sophistication. Dishes change all the time. Menus €12 at lunchtime and €14–24 in the evening. There's a wide range of wines. Relaxed atmosphere.

🎐|●| CAFÉ DE LA TABLE RONDE

7 pl. Saint-André. **MAP C2-17**
☎ 04.76.44.51.41
Closed Sun.

Service until midnight. Located about as centrally as you can get, this café is an institution in Grenoble. Established in 1793, it's the second oldest café in France after *Le Procope* in Paris, and tradition, hospitality and conviviality are its watchwords. The terrace is a great vantage point from which to watch the world go by on the square, and the décor in the dining room is splendid. There are lots of good dishes *à la carte*: frogs' legs, grilled beef, *diot* with shallots, calf's head and so on. Menus €13–27 and affordable wines such as Gamay de Savoie and others are served by the glass or jug. Free apéritif.

|●| CAFFÈ FORTÉ

4 pl. Lavalette. **MAP C2-20**
☎ 04.76.03.25.30 ➡ 04.76.03.25.55
Closed Sun lunchtime.

This delightful place stands opposite the Grenoble museum in a quiet, wide road. The lofty dining room is vaguely baroque in style, and in summer the terrace is always full. The atmosphere is pretty easy-going but busy. The choice of dishes is eclectic and everything is freshly prepared: huge steak *tartare*, real *frites*, excellent salads and pasta. There's a lunch *formule* for €14; a meal *à la carte* costs in the region of €18. Pleasant welcome.

|●| CHEZ MARGO

5 rue Millet. **MAP C3-15**
☎ 04.76.46.27.87
Closed Sat lunchtime and Sun.

This restaurant, in a quiet little street, is often busy. Even on weekday evenings there's a reliable stream of regulars who drop in. The dining room is split-level, decorated in a smart rustic style and the atmosphere is very informal. The cooking is traditional, prepared with care and the regional dishes are quite substantial. There's a €15 lunch menu, and others up to €24. You get lots of choice: *fricassée* of scampi with ravioli, sliced veal sweetbreads with ginger and lime, *caillette* served on a potato cake, monkfish medallions with wild mushrooms, *confit* of duck thigh. Dishes of the day use fresh market produce – *fricassée* of kid with fresh tarragon, for example. Short but good wine list.

|●| LE BISTROT LYONNAIS

168 cours Berriat. **MAP A3-16**
☎ 04.76.21.95.33
Closed Sat lunchtime, 24 Dec–1 Jan.

Just opposite the Magasin, the contemporary art centre, this restaurant has a warm interior charmingly decorated in period style. In summer, there's a little terrace that's well

protected from the road by a fragrant wisteria and lots of greenery. Good Lyonnais dishes on the menus (€19–25). If you've got time for an extended lunch, try the Roquefort and scallop *terrine*, the fresh sardines marinated in lemon, the fillet of beef with a morel crust, the *sauté* of veal sweetbreads with port or the scambled eggs with truffles. Wine prices are reasonable and they serve Côtes-du-Rhône and Beaujolais by the jug.

⅍ |●| GALERIE ROME

1 rue Très-Cloîtres. **MAP D2-19**
☎ 04.76.42.82.01
Closed Sat lunchtime; Sun; Mon evening; the last 3 weeks in Aug.

The décor of this restaurant is colourful and original, with numerous paintings and brilliantly lit sculptures. There's also a quiet, charming patio. The *à la carte* menu is quite short, listing good *terrines*, tasty meat dishes, light sauces and interesting salads all at reasonable prices – about €23 for a meal.The €9 dish of the day is written up on the blackboard. In the evening they stop serving at 10.15pm. Free *digestif*.

⅍ |●| LE MAL ASSIS

9 rue Bayard. **MAP C2-18**
☎ 04.76.54.75.93
Closed Mon; Sun; 15 July–15 Aug.

This place, a local favourite, has wood panelling and a fireplace and charming service. There's a menu for €38; *à la carte* in the evening will cost you around €24. Dishes include *fondant* of vegetables, saddle of rabbit with *aïoli*, Provençal fish stew and plain chocolate *marquise*. Free apéritif.

MEYLAN   38249 (4KM NE)

⅍ |●| LA CERISAIE CLUB

18 chemin de Saint-Martin; leave Grenoble on bd. Jean-Paris, then follow av. de Verdun and av. des Sept-Laux. Before arriving in Montbonnet, turn right into le chemin de Saint-Martin.
☎ 04.76.41.91.29 ✉ lacerisaieclub@club.internet.fr
Closed Sat lunchtime; Sun evening.

A lovely private mansion in a big garden just minutes from Grenoble. The dining room has a high ceiling and the décor is luxurious. On sunny days you get a fabulous view from the superb terrace, which is surrounded by flowers. The place well deserves its good reputation, which has largely spread by word of mouth. A lunchtime *formule* at €14, and menus at €20–47 offering sophisticated dishes. À la carte, try *millefeuille* of pan-fried *foie gras*, salmon with citrus butter, rack of lamb with a herb crust, slivers of John Dory with oriental spices or duck breast with sour cherries. Best to book. The wine list boasts 150 vintages. Free apéritif, coffee or *digestif*.

CORENC 38700 (10KM N)

|●| CAFÉ-RESTAURANT DE LA CHAPELLE

12 route de Chartreuse; it's 3km after Corenc-Village – take the D512 in the direction of Saint-Pierre-de-Chartreuse.
☎ 04.76.88.05.40
Closed Mon unless it's a public holiday; Sun evening. **Disabled access**. **Car park**.

If you're here in summer, do what the locals do and head for the hills instead of sweltering in the centre of town. This unpretentious café-restaurant has a long-established reputation for its home cooking, friendly atmosphere and, best of all, its shady terrace. Menus €11–18. If you don't like local specialities like *gratin dauphinois*, *fondue* or bilberry tart, you could try their salads, trout with almond, *civet* stews or grills.

|●| LA CORNE D'OR

159 route de Chartreuse (Northeast).
☎ 04.76.88.00.02
Closed Sun evening in season and a fortnight in Jan.

This substantial house, dominating the valley, is a lovely cool place to come when Grenoble is blistering in the sun. You get superb panoramic views from the bay windows in the colourful dining room and from the terrace, which is surrounded by greenery. The reputation of the inspirational cuisine is growing and it's affordable. The appeal of the place is the *rôtisserie* but they also offer fried mozzarella and aubergines, pickled red peppers, house *terrine*, lasagne with salmon and ravioli. Menus €13 and €18; a jug of Lyonnais costs €6. Friendly welcome.

URIAGE-LES-BAINS 38410 (10KM SE)

⌖ ⌂ |●| AUBERGE DU VERNON

Les Davids; follow the signs for Chamrousse via col du Luitel.
☎ 04.76.89.10.56
Closed Sun evening and 1 Oct–1 April.

Service until 9pm. This country inn looks like something from a fairy story; it's a little farm with a pond, a huge tree, flowers all over the place and a phenomenal view of the mountains. The Girouds, who have run the place for thirty years, serve good home cooking in generous portions – this is real country food

– including *charcuteries* and omelette *paysanne*. €12 lunch menu (not Sunday), others from €18 and a small selection of specialities to order, including veal sweetbreads with ceps and chicken with morels. Six very pretty, tiny doubles go for €30–43 with basin or shower/wc. Peace and quiet guaranteed. Free coffee.

⌖ ⌂ |●| LES MÉSANGES**

route des Mésanges, Le Vachez; 1km along the Saint-Martin-d'Uriage road, turn right onto the Bouloud road.
☎ 04.76.89.70.69 ▐→ 04.76.89.56.97
e prince@hotel-les-mesanges.com
Hotel closed 20 Oct to end Jan; April. **Restaurant closed** Tues except to residents. **TV**. **Swimming pool**. **Car park**.

The Prince family, who have owned this place since 1946, have established a solid reputation. All the rooms have been refurbished; the loveliest ones have big balconies from which you can see down the valley as far as Vizille, while the smaller ones look across the fields. Doubles €46 with shower/wc and €58 with bath. In the restaurant, there's a lunch menu for €15 (not served Sun), and others €18–43 including a *menu terroir* of local dishes. Specialities include pigeon in a caul with caramelized spices, pig's trotters, duo of lamb with pickled garlic and ice-cream with Chartreuse. It's all very rich in flavours and calories. Heated swimming pool for the use of residents. 10% discount on the room rate Sept–June.

SAINT-NIZIER-DU-MARCHEROTTE 38250 (10KM S)

|●| AUBERGE LES HERBES SAUVAGES

Les Guillets; take the D106 from Sayssinet and it's after the Memorial to the Resistance, on the right just as you get to the village.
☎ 04.76.53.43.26
Closed Wed and Thurs; reserve on weekday evenings.

The windows peak through the ivy and there's a south-facing terrace providing a lovely view onto the Trois Pucelles peaks. The cosy interior is particularly warm and well-appointed: wood panelling, fireplace, reading room and library. Take a look at the bed in the alcove almost hidden in a corner of the dining room. The dishes are tasty and portions are substantial – toasted goat;s cheese salad, raw ham and potato cake. Fulsome platters for €12–13; prices include dessert. The owner keeps a watchful eye on everything.

SAPPEY-E-CHARTREUSE (LE) 38250 (10KM S)

|O| RELAIS SAINT-EYNAUD

It's at Fort Saint-Eynard; take the D512 from Grenoble.
☎ 04.76.85.25.24
Closed Sun evening and Mon; 1 Nov–1 May.

Service 11am–11pm. The restaurant is on the summit of Saint-Eynard at an altitude of 1340m. The belvedere is incorporated into the cliff face with an impressive view over Grenoble and the Grésilvaudan valley. There are two vaulted dining rooms with rough-hewn stone walls softened by a selection of pictures and wooden bistro tables swathed in tablecloths. Simple, uncomplicated fare: sandwiches, *crêpes* and cakes all at modest prices. The €11 menu lists a plate of charcuterie, omelette with chives, salad and dessert. Then there's another for €14. The Grenoblois swarm here for dinner in summer, when they put tables outside. It's also a bar.

GRIGNAN   26230

★ LE CLAIR DE LA PLUME***

pl. du Mail, (Centre); it's below the château, close to the town hall.
☎ 04.75.46.59.20 ➡ 04.75.91.81.31
📧 plume2@wanadoo.fr
Closed a fortnight in Feb. **TV**. **Garden**. **Car park**.

Super situation in the old town across from one of the most beautiful washhouses in the Midi. It's a very elegant eighteenth-century house with a serene atmosphere and a small, relaxing garden. The whole place emanates good taste, comfort and refinement. Urbane, polite welcome. All the rooms (€85–150) are different. You have breakfast in the old kitchen, which is full of original character.

|O| LA PICCOLINA

How to get there: it's below the château, close to the town hall.
☎ 04.75.46.59.20
Closed Mon and Tues out of season; Tues only June–Sept; 10 Dec–20 Jan.

This pizza place rivals many a gourmet restaurant. They serve good salads and tasty pizzas cooked in a proper wood-fired oven. There's also a choice of excellent grills. The dining room is small and, because it's good, it gets full quickly. There's a *formule rapide* at €9 (not available Sat, Sun or public holidays) and menus at €13 and €17. Modestly priced wines – €13 for a jug, €8 for a litre and €10 for a Vinsobres.

👣 |O| LE POÈME

Montée du Tricot; it's 50m from the town hall.

☎ 04.75.91.10.90
Closed Mon and Wed lunchtimes; Tues; Feb.

A new place that's speedily making a name for itself. The cuisine is very elaborate and has lots of creative verve. There are only four dishes on the menus (€17–35), but they change all the time: goat's cheese tarte, olive paste and basil, sea bream *en papillotte*, *croustillant* of pigeon with truffles. À la carte can get expensive. Faultless service. It's best to book at the weekend. Free coffee.

HAUTERIVES   26390

★ |O| LE RELAIS**

pl. de l'Église (West); it's opposite the church.
☎ 04.75.68.81.12 ➡ 04.75.68.92.42
Hotel closed Sun evening and Mon out of season; mid-Jan to mid-Feb. **Restaurant closed** Mon in summer. **Car park**.

The thick, sturdy walls of this handsome nineteenth-century building are lined with photos and engravings by Ferdinand Cheval – a local postman who constructed an extraordinary sculpture from stones he collected on his rounds. The large, rustic bedrooms cost €27–38 with washing facilities, €47 with shower/wc or bath, and the restaurant offers regional menus €13–24.

JOYEUSE   07260

👣 ★ |O| HÔTEL DE L'EUROPE**

Centre; it's on the D104.
☎ 04.75.39.51.26 ➡ 04.75.39.59.00
📧 contact@ardeche-hotel.net
Disabled access. **TV**. **Swimming pool**. **Car park**.

You get fair value for a place that's on the way to the gorges of the Ardèche and the Cévennes. The small refurbished bedrooms go for €33–41 with shower/wc or bath. They serve tasty, simple dishes such as omelettes with ceps, trout *meunière*, *charcuterie*, chestnut custard and pizzas of impressive size. Menus €9–27. The large heated indoor pool has a great view over the Cévennes. There's also a *boules* area. 10% discount on the room rate Oct –April.

|O| RESTAURANT VALENTINA

pl. de la Peyre (Centre).
☎ 04.75.39.90.65
Closed Mon, Jan–March and Oct–Dec.

This is the only restaurant in the old town, and

since it's well away from traffic, the terrace overlooking the nice little square is a pleasant place to sit. The owners are a nice Italian couple who are keen travellers – the lights are made from baskets they bought in Guatemala and there's a Lambretta they brought back from Italy. Authentic Italian cooking – pasta with pine nuts, tortellini with ceps and tagliatelli with smoked salmon and vodka sauce. The home-made desserts are seriously good. Menus from €20, or you'll pay €8 or so for a single dish. Good Italian wines.

SAINT-ALBAN-AURIOLLES　　07120 (10KM SE)

🏃 🏠 |●| HÔTEL DOUCE FRANCE**

It's on the D208.
☎ 04.75.39.37.08 ➡ 04.75.39.04.93
Closed Mon except in summer; Jan. **Disabled access**. **Swimming pool**. **Car park**.

It's best to book in summer if you want to stay in this reasonably priced hotel in the midst of the vineyards. In the main building, which lacks real character, doubles cost €35 with shower and €41–44 with shower/wc or bath. They also have bungalows by the swimming pool, which are better situated. Weekday lunch menu for €11 and €14–27, listing the choice of pan-fried *foie gras*, oysters *gratinée* with leek *purée* and grilled sea bass. Free apéritif.

JULIÉNAS　　69840

🏃 🏠 |●| CHEZ LA ROSE**

Centre.
☎ 04.74.04.41.20 ➡ 04.74.04.49.29
e info@chez-la-rose.fr
Hotel closed Feb school holidays and 1–15 Dec.
Restaurant closed Mon, Tues, Thurs and Fri lunchtimes (except on public holidays); 10–28 Feb; 10–19 Dec. **TV**. **Car park**.

With its elegant façade, this building has the look of an old posthouse. The main building houses comfortable, rustic bedrooms while those across the road are genuine suites with a sitting room – one even has a private garden. Doubles with shower/wc or bath cost €38–56. The magnificent dining room is a perfect setting for famously tasty regional cooking produced by a seriously good chef: *terrine* of pressed duck breast, *foie gras*, *coq au vin* and lobster stew. Menus €23–47. 20% discount on the room rate if you dine in the restaurant. Free coffee.

LAMASTRE　　07270

🏠 |●| HÔTEL DU MIDI – RESTAURANT BARATTÉRO

How to get there: from Lamastre, head for Le Puy; it's 2km further on the right.
☎ 04.75.06.41.50 ➡ 04.75.06.49.75
Closed Mon; Fri and Sun evenings; Christmas to mid-Feb. **TV**. **Car park**.

A gourmet restaurant that has enjoyed a good reputation for several decades. The dining room is classy and cosy. You get the measure of the cooking from the cheapest menu at €30, though the more you spend – €44–67 – the more unusual and luxurious the ingredients: Bresse chicken cooked in a bladder, a divine iced chestnut soufflé. The service is meticulous and old-style French: you feel rather as if you have to sit straight at your table and not clatter your cutlery. Rooms in the hotel are equally cosy and perfectly maintained; doubles €66 with shower/wc and €74 with bath. Free house apéritif.

CRESTET (LE)　　07270 (8KM NE)

🏃 🏠 |●| LA TERRASSE**

Centre; take the D534 in the direction of Tournon; Crestet is on the left.
☎ 04.75.06.24.44 ➡ 04.75.06.23.25
Closed Sat in winter and 25 Dec–3 Jan. **Disabled access**. **TV**. **Swimming pool**. **Car park**.

There's an air of serenity in this classic establishment – you get the feeling that the people here really know how to live. Acceptable rooms cost from €32 for a double with shower and from €35 with shower/wc. Menus, €10–15, list a good selection of regional dishes; it's worth trying *picodon*, the local goat's cheese, which has a slightly piquant flavour. The dining room has a lovely view of the Doux valley and, in summer, when the swimming pool area is ablaze with flowers, a rampant vine provides shade for the terrace. Free house apéritif.

SAINT-BARTHÉLMY-GROZON　　07270 (8KM S)

🏃 🏠 |●| HÔTEL GRÈVE**

Le Vaure; it's on the Valence-Le Puy road, in the village.
☎ 04.75.06.58.92 ➡ 04.75.06.58.92
Closed Feb. **Car park**.

The owner always takes time to chat with her clients and to make sure they're properly looked after. She has an equally straightforward approach to her cooking – it's honest and generously flavoured. Traditional dishes as well as *paëlla* and *couscous* – menus start at €10 – served inside or out on the shady terrace in summer. The simple rooms are clean and cheap at €23 for a double with basin, €27 with shower and €30 with shower/wc. There's a pleasant family atmosphere. Free coffee and 10% discount on the room rate.

LAVAL   38190

|●| CAFÉ-RESTAURANT DES SPORTS

From Grenoble take the N41 and turn off at exit number 24 signposted to Brignard, then the D528 in the direction of the Pré de l'Arc.
☎ 04.76.71.44.60
Closed Sun evening and Wed; out of season, it's best to phone in advance.

A village restaurant providing flavourful yet simple cuisine. Specialities include chicken with morels, veal with morels, suckling pig stew, frogs' legs with mustard sauce and excellent *gratin Dauphinois* potatoes. Their bread is baked in a wood-fuelled oven. Menus for €15–23 and dish of the day at €8 (not Sun). Crêpes and cakes served all day. In summer there's a terrace and a theatre on the lawn. Quiet but very attentive welcome. Free coffee. A good spot to stop if you're doing a walk.

LÉLEX   01410

⚰ ♠ |●| HÔTEL-RESTAURANT MONT JURA**

ancienne route de Mijoux (Centre); take the D991.
☎ 04.50.20.90.53 ➡ 04.50.20.95.20
Closed Tues out of season; a fortnight in Nov. **TV. Car park**.

This place is in the middle of a ski resort that's recently been named Mont-Jura but it's retained its village atmosphere. You'll get a good-natured welcome. The rustic rooms are spacious and comfortable, with doubles at €28 with washing facilities and €43 with shower or bath. The regional cooking is lavishly served and prices are affordable – menus €15–23. Try *fricassée* of suckling pig, *foie gras*, *gratin* of crayfish and game in autumn. Free apéritif.

LYON   69000

SEE MAP OVERLEAF

1st arrondissement

⚰ ♠ HÔTEL SAINT-VINCENT**

9 rue Pareille; M° Hôtel-de-Ville. **MAP B1-1**
☎ 04.78.27.22.56 ➡ 04.78.30.92.87
e hotel.st-vincent@wanadoo.fr
Closed Aug. **TV**.

This hotel is freshly painted and definitely not lacking in charm – all the rooms have parquet floors and some boast beautiful fireplaces. The hotel is made up of four different buildings with internal courtyards; you reach the rooms through a maze of corridors. Doubles cost €35 with shower, €44 with shower/wc and €47 with bath. There are also a few triples. An excellent welcome is guaranteed. Free breakfast. 10% discount.

⚰ |●| LA RANDONNÉE

4 rue Terme; M° Hôtel-de-Ville. **MAP C1-31**
☎ and ➡ 04.78.27.86.81
Closed Sun lunchtime; Mon; the last fortnight in Aug.

At the foot of a steep road going up to Croix Rousse, this restaurant (one of the least expensive in Lyon) is very popular with its penurious young customers. The nice owners prepare simple home cooking and typical Lyonnais dishes at very reasonable prices: there's a flock of *formules* and menus at €5–14; they've even got one for vegetarians. You'll find chicken with tarragon, prawns flambéd with cognac, squid *à la Provençale* and grilled duck breast. Wines are very cheap, too. It can be hard to find a table at times. Free parking in the Terreaux car park at night. Free *digestif*.

⚰ |●| ALYSSAAR

rue du Bât-d'Argent (Centre). **MAP D2-19**
☎ 04.78.29.57.66
Closed lunchtimes; Sun and Mon; the Christmas holidays.

Alyssaar is a Syrian whose genuine kindness makes his customers feel special. He will happily explain the various specialities served on the *assiette du Calife*, a selection of Syrian delicacies, and in which order you should eat them. The beef with cherries is amazing, as is the lamb kebab with aubergines. The "Thousand-and-one-nights" dessert is a revelation. Menus €12–17. Free *digestif*.

|●| RESTAURANT CHEZ GEORGES – AU P'TIT BOUCHON

8 rue du Garet; M° Hôtel-de-Ville or Louis-Pradel. **MAP D1-20**
☎ 04.78.28.30.46
Closed Sat, Sun and Aug.

Set this down alongside an old Paris bistro

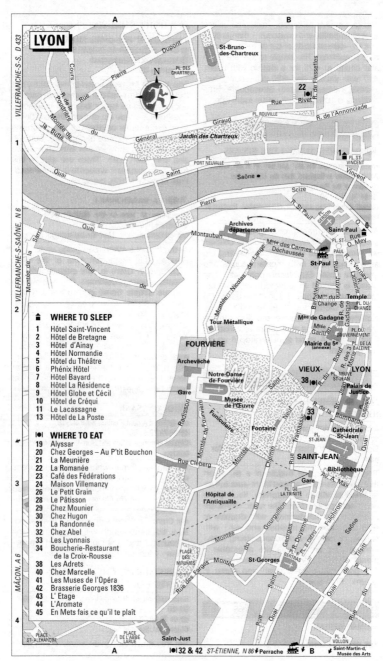

LYON

St-Bruno-des-Chartreux

PL. DES CHARTREUX

R. de Flessettes

22 Rivet

Rue

R. de l'Annonciade

Dupont

Pierre

R. de la Pouthère

Montée de la Butte

Cours

Rue

du

Général

Giraud

PL. ROUVILLE

Jardin des Chartreux

PL. PORT NEUVILLE

Saint

PL. ST-VINCENT

1

Quai

Saône

Scize

Montée de la Sarra

Rue

de

Pierre

R. St-Paul

R. GERSON

Saint-Paul

O. Mey

6

Archives **départementales**

Montauban

Mtée des Carmes Déchaussés

PL. ST-PAUL

St-Paul

R. Vernay

R. Lainerie

Barthélemy

Mtée du Change

Temple

PL. DU CHANGE

Tour Métallique

Mtée Nicolas de Lange

Mtée de Gadagne

Mtée Gartit

PL. DU GOUVERNEMENT

PL. DE LA BALEINE

FOURVIÈRE

Mairie du 5e (annexe)

Archevêché

Notre-Dame-de-Fourvière

Saint

VIEUX-

LYON

38

PL. NEUVE ST-JEAN

Palais de Justice

Gare

Musée de l'Œuvre

33

R. de la Bombarde

Radisson

Montée de Fourvière

Funiculaire

Fontaine

Neuf

Mtée Tramassac

Cathédrale St-Jean

Rue Cléberg

Montée

Chemin

PL. ST-JEAN

SAINT-JEAN

Bibliothèque

Gare

AV. A. Max

Hôpital de l'Antiquaille

PL. DE LA TRINITÉ

Montée

Gourguillon

Montée

Georges

PL. F. Doyenné

PL. E. Senard

Fulchiron

Saône

PONT

PLACE DES MINIMES

Montée

St-Georges

du

Rue des Farges

Quai

Tilsitt

PLACE ST-ALEXANDRE

PLACE DE L'ABBÉ LARUE

Saint-Just

Quai

PL. A. VOLLON

4

WHERE TO SLEEP ⚏

1 Hôtel Saint-Vincent
2 Hôtel de Bretagne
3 Hôtel d'Ainay
4 Hôtel Normandie
5 Hôtel du Théâtre
6 Phénix Hôtel
7 Hôtel Bayard
8 Hôtel La Résidence
9 Hôtel Globe et Cécil
10 Hôtel de Créqui
11 Le Lacassagne
13 Hôtel de La Poste

WHERE TO EAT ⦿

19 Alyssar
20 Chez Georges – Au P'tit Bouchon
21 La Meunière
22 La Romanée
23 Café des Fédérations
24 Maison Villemanzy
26 Le Petit Grain
28 Le Pâtisson
29 Chez Mounier
30 Chez Hugon
31 La Randonnée
32 Chez Abel
33 Les Lyonnais
34 Boucherie-Restaurant de la Croix-Rousse
38 Les Adrets
40 Chez Marcelle
41 Les Muses de l'Opéra
42 Brasserie Georges 1836
43 L'Etage
44 L'Aromate
45 En Mets fais ce qu'il te plaît

⦿ 32 & 42 ST-ÉTIENNE, N 86 ⬦ Perrache   B   Saint-Martin-d, Musée des Arts

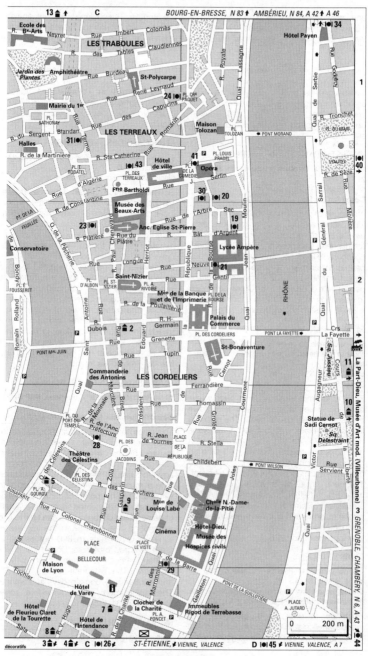

Ecole des
R. Bx-Arts
Neyret   Rue   Imbert   Colomès
LES TRABOULES   Claudiennes
des   Tables
Rue   Burdeau
Jardin des   Amphithéâtre
Plantes   Rue   St-Polycarpe
René Leynaud
24 ▮●▮ PL. CX.
PAQUET
Mairie du 1ᵉʳ   Capucins
PL.
SATHONAY   Rue   des
Rue   Romarin
R. du   Sergent   Blandan   **LES TERREAUX**
Halles   31▮●▮   Terme
R. de la Martinière   Rue Ste Catherine
PT. DE LA   ▮●▮43   Hôtel   PL. DES
FEUILLÉE   de ville   TERREAUX
Fne Bartholdi
Musée des
Beaux-Arts
23 ▮●▮   Anc. Eglise St-Pierre
Conservatoire

Hôtel Payen

34

Maison
Tolozan   PL.
TOLOZAN   ← PONT MORAND

41   PL. LOUIS
▮●▮   PRADEL
Opéra

30   Serlin
▮●▮   ▮●▮ 20

Sec.

19
▮●▮
d'Argent

Lycée Ampère

L'Autel
▮●▮ 40

RHÔNE

[775]

and you wouldn't be able to tell them apart – it's got the checked tablecloths, the imitation leather benches, the mirror-lined walls and the original, zinc-topped bar. The attentive but unobtrusive owner serves at table while his wife is busy in the handkerchief-sized kitchen. Well-balanced Lyonnais menus list sausage with lentils, grilled veal sausage, an astonishingly good Saint-Marcellin (a mild cheese from the Dauphiné) and a great upside-down apple tart. Set menus €14–19 and around €21 *à la carte*.

|●| RESTAURANT LA MEUNIÈRE

11 rue Neuve; M° Cordeliers or Hôtel-de-Ville. **MAP D2-21**
☎ 04.78.28.62.91
Closed Sun and Mon; 14 July to 15 Aug.

An exuberant place where you'll get a wonderful welcome, an abundance of good local dishes, a buffet of enticing starters and a friendly atmosphere. They serve traditional Lyons food: *cochonnaille* (pork sausage made from various parts of the animal), *tablier de sapeur* (ox tripe egged, crumbed and fried), and *andouillette* – perfect with a Beaujolais or Côtes-du-Rhône to wash it down. Lunch menu €15, with others €20–25. Best to book for dinner.

🔥 |●| LES MUSES DE L'OPÉRA

pl. de la Comédie; it's on the 7th floor of the opera house so take the lift beside the entrance to the opera. **MAP D1-41**
☎ 04.72.00.45.58
Closed Sun.

Service until midnight. This long, narrow seventh-floor dining room gives you great views of the street way down below. The décor is fashionably black, which means your eye is drawn outside to the large terrace which overlooks the square. Inside, you'll dine on the colourful, original, skilfully prepared food that is the hallmark of chef Philippe Chavent. The *menu du jour* offers typical Lyons dishes, while *à la carte* there's an astonishingly good *croustillant* of lamb with dried apricots and a *terrine* of lentils and chicken livers. Weekday lunch menu €16, another at €21 and an evening version for €26. Free house apéritif.

🔥 |●| L'ÉTAGE

4 pl. des Terreaux; M° Hôtel-de-Ville. **MAP C1-43**
☎ 04.78.28.19.59
Closed Sun and Mon; bank holidays; a few days in Feb; the last week in July; the first 3 weeks in Aug.

Push open the door and you find yourself in a wood-panelled salon draped in red. From the tables by the windows you get a good view of the fountain. The cooking is elegant, fine and precise, and though the dishes change frequently the quality remains the same: *marbré* of chicken with pickled onions and apple chutney, roast salmon with paprika, semolina and hazelnut oil, Saint-Marcellin goat's cheese. Dish of the day €11; menus €17–24. If you want a change from Lyonnais dishes, there's a lobster menu for €47 (you must order two days in advance). Lots of regulars. Free coffee.

🔥 |●| CAFÉ DES FÉDÉRATIONS

8 rue du Major-Martin; M° Hôtel-de-Ville. **MAP C2-23**
☎ 04.78.28.26.00
Closed Sat lunchtime; Sun; 3 weeks in Aug.

Scenes from the classic Tavernier movie, *L'Horloger de Saint-Paul*, were filmed in this local institution – and it hasn't changed a bit. It is one of the best Lyonnais *bouchons* (the name given to the city's popular brasserie-restaurants) and the perfect place to taste really good Lyonnais cuisine. The dishes are traditional: *gras-double* (marinated for two days in white wine and mustard), *tablier de sapeur* (ox tripe egged, crumbed and grilled), calf's head *ravigote*. Splendid *hors d'œuvres* include *charcuterie*, bowls of lentils, beetroot, brawn and calf's feet, mixed seasonal salads and sausage cooked in red wine. Lunch menu €18, and an evening *formule* with more choice at €23. Service is swift and friendly. Free house apéritif.

🔥 |●| RESTAURANT LA ROMANÉE

19 rue Rivet; 800m from M° Croix-Paquet. **MAP B1-22**
☎ 04.72.00.80.87
Closed Sat lunchtime, Sun evening, Mon and Aug.

This place has a long-standing reputation for good cooking; Élisabeth Denis is a fine chef inspired by the flavours of the south. She changes her menus every couple of months, and produces dishes of boundless invention – wild mushroom *terrine*, fish *choucroute* with *beurre blanc*, breast of duck with mushrooms and truffle-scented sauce and a variety of home-made desserts. You can't fail to find a tempting little vintage on the impressive wine list which runs to 800 bottles, all of them selected by Daniel Denis, the chef's husband. Prices run from cheap to very expensive. The restaurant can only seat 25, and is often fully booked days in advance. The dining room is a smoke-free zone. Menus €18–34. Free house apéritif.

|●| MAISON VILLEMANZY

25 montée Saint-Sébastien; M° Croix-Pâquet. **MAP**

C1-24
☎ 04.78.39.37.00
Closed Sun; Mon lunchtime; 1–15 Jan.

This unspoilt house, once the residence of a doctor-colonel, sits high above the city on the slopes of La Croix-Rousse. There's a magnificent terrace from where you can survey the town – the view's very popular, so it's best to book. Guillaume Mouchel, in charge in the kitchens, was a pupil of Jean-Paul Lacombe, one of Lyon's great chefs. You get lots of choice on the well-devised €21 *menu carte*, which changes every two days. To eat lightly, go for the dish of the day plus green salad for €11. A reasonably priced wine list.

⅍ |●| CHEZ HUGON

12 rue Pizay; M° Hôtel-de-Ville. **MAP D1-30**
☎ 04.78.28.10.94
Closed Sat and Sun; Aug.

As you wander around the town hall area, you'll find this authentic Lyonnais *bouchon* in a little alley. It's remained unchanged over the years. The dining room has only a few tables, covered with checked tablecloths, where you can eat excellent Lyons specialities like sheep's trotters, *tablier de sapeur* (ox tripe egged, crumbed and grilled), and *gâteau de foies de volaille* (chicken livers mixed with *foie gras*, eggs and cream). Menu €23 or *à la carte* around €21. Free coffee.

2nd arrondissement
≘ HÔTEL D'AINAY*

14 rue des Remparts-d'Ainay (South); M° Ampère-Victor-Hugo. **Off map C4-3**
☎ 04.78.42.43.42 ➡ 04.72.77.51.90
TV.

If you're on a budget, this very simple hotel will suit you down to the ground; it's in a quiet, rather delightful pedestrianized neighbourhood not far from the magnificent basilica. The friendly young couple who run it put a good deal of effort into creating a restful atmosphere. The rooms have good double glazing and look onto the road, the courtyard or the place Ampère. Doubles €27 with basin, €37 with bath. 10% discount Sept–July.

⅍ ≘ HÔTEL NORMANDIE**

3 rue du Bélier (South); M° Perrache. **Off map C4-4**
☎ 04.78.37.31.36 ➡ 04.78.40.98.56
TV.

This hotel, named after the great French liner, is in a quiet street. It has about forty small rooms for €39 with shower, €45 with shower/wc and €50 with bath. The double glazing keeps out most of the noise from the railway station. Some rooms have been spruced up, and more are due for the same treatment. Pleasant staff can tell you what to see. 10% discount in July sand Aug and 5% the rest of the year.

⅍ ≘ HÔTEL DE BRETAGNE*

10 rue Dubois; M° Cordeliers. **MAP C2-2**
☎ 04.78.37.79.33 ➡ 04.72.77.99.92
℮hoteldebretaghe-lyon@wanadoo.fr
TV.

This hotel, halfway between the Saône and place des Cordeliers, offers good value for money. The rooms are clean, smart and soundproofed – good for the ones overlooking the street which are big and bright. The ones over the courtyard are very gloomy. Doubles with shower/wc cost €40, and there are also rooms that sleep three or four. 10% discount.

≘ HÔTEL BAYARD**

23 pl. Bellecour; M° Bellecour. **MAP C4-7**
☎ 04.78.37.39.64 ➡ 04.72.40.95.51
TV. **Car park**.

Though they're all newly decorated, no two rooms in this hotel are alike . Some have lots of personality; several have canopied beds, polished parquet floors and a great view of the place Bellecour; number 5 has an enormous bathroom; number 15, which overlooks the courtyard, can sleep four. Doubles €40–58 with shower, €69–84 with shower/wc and €69–73 with bath. The little breakfast nook has a very rural feel. Follow the signs up the stairs to the reception on the first floor.

⅍ ≘ HÔTEL DU THÉÂTRE**

10 rue de Savoie; M° Bellecour. **MAP C3-5**
☎ 04.78.42.33.32 ➡ 04.72.40.00.61
TV.

The show starts as you walk through the door: a staircase, dressed like a stage set, leads up to reception on the second floor and sets the tone for the rest of the hotel. If you're lucky, you'll get one of the rooms overlooking the place des Célestins and the theatre – the view is stunning. It's best to book well ahead and ask for one of those rooms. There's a nice little breakfast room and the atmosphere is relaxed. Rooms €49 with shower/wc and €52 with bath. One free breakfast per double room.

🏃 🏠 HÔTEL LA RÉSIDENCE***

18 rue Victor-Hugo; M° Bellecour or Ampère-Victor-Hugo. **MAP C4-8**
☎ 04.78.42.63.28 **📠** 04.78.42.85.76
📧 hotel-la-residence@wanadoo.fr
TV. Disabled access.

Halfway between Perrache and Bellecour in a lively pedestrianized street with lots of shops. They practise old-style hotel-keeping here and it's one of the cheapest three-star places in town. The rooms have all had a makeover and are cosy and air-conditioned – they're €57 with shower/wc, €61 with bath. Professional welcome. 10% discount July–Aug.

🏃 🏠 HÔTEL GLOBE ET CÉCIL***

21 rue Gasparin; M° Bellecour. **MAP C3-9**
☎ 04.78.42.58.95 **📠** 04.72.41.99.06
📧 globe.et.cecil@wanadoo.fr
TV.

A top-notch three-star in the city centre. Each room has been decorated in a style appropriate to its size and has its own character – some have handsome marble fireplaces, balconies and air conditioning. The rooms that overlook the street are brighter than the others. The service can't be faulted, and it comes with a smile. Doubles €119–122 with shower/wc or bath, including breakfast. 10% discount on weekdays.

🏃 🍽️ LE PETIT GRAIN

19 rue de la Charité (South); M° Ampère or Bellecour.
Off map C4-26
☎ 04.72.41.77.85
Closed Sun; evenings after 8pm; 15–28 Aug.

A simple little snack bar in an old milliner's shop near rue Auge-Comte, the street with all the antique shops. It's prettily decorated with a scattering of objects picked up from street markets by the cheerful Vietnamese owner. You can have a substantial *bo bun* (stir-fried beef and noodles), a huge and delicious salad or a dish of the day – usually Vietnamese or Chinese. Terrific pear and chocolate or apple crumble and seasonal fruit *clafoutis*. Dish of the day €7, *formules* and menus from €8. Make a visit to the fabric museum or the decorative arts museum across the street after lunch. Free apéritif.

🍽️ RESTAURANT CHEZ MOUNIER

3 rue des Marronniers; M° Bellecour. **MAP C3/4-29**
☎ 04.78.37.79.26
Closed Sun evening and Mon; the last week in Aug; the first fortnight in Sept; the first week in Jan.

Lyon is famous for its puppets; the one in this restaurant window, smiling at passers-by and inviting them in, is the comic character Guignol. This is the most authentic of the *bouchons* in this touristy street, with two bare little dining rooms. There's a good atmosphere created by Christine Moinier, and the regional cooking has character: *gnafrons* (little sausages), *tablier de sapeur* (ox tripe egged, crumbed and grilled). For €10 you get three courses and there are another two menus for €13 and €15.

🏃 🍽️ LE PÂTISSON

17 rue du Port-du-Temple (Centre); M° Bellecour.
MAP C3-28
☎ 04.72.41.81.71
Closed Fri evening; Sat April–Sept; Sat lunchtime Oct–March; Sun; the third week in Aug.

Yves Perrin, owner of the only organic and vegetarian restaurant in the city, has been a finalist in two prestigious culinary competitions – his diplomas are proudly displayed on the walls. Try medallions of tofu with a *julienne* of saffron-flavoured vegetables or the millet and aubergine *provençale*. Dish of the day €8, menus €10–11 at lunchtime and €15–17 in the evening. No smoking. Free house apéritif.

🍽️ BRASSERIE GEORGES 1836

30 cours de Verdun; it's next to Perrache station.
Off map B4-42
☎ 04.72.56.54.54
Closed 1 May.

This cosmopolitan Art Deco brasserie, which has been open since 1836, is a barn of a place – it seats 1000 diners served by 200 staff. The cuisine is in the same grand tradition: sausage in *brioche*, *quenelle* of pike and, inevitably, *choucroute*. Weekday lunch menu €11 and others €16–23; ham with mashed potatoes is served free to children under three. They serve good beer and the atmosphere is cheery, with a lively jazz evening on Saturday. Sadly the ugly Perrache car park mars the view.

🏃 🍽️ CHEZ ABEL

25 rue Guynemer (South); M° Ampère. **Off map B4-32**
☎ 04.78.37.46.18
Closed Sat lunchtime; Sun; Aug.

This place, just a stone's throw from the Saône and 200m from the basilica, has very old wainscotting and a creaky parquet floor. It looks like a folk museum, full of oddments, hefty wooden tables and a beer pump from 1925. House specialities include liver, calf's head, *andouillette*, chicken with rice and *quenelles* of pike. Menus €14 and €21–28; *à la carte*, however, prices soar. Free *digestif*.

3rd arrondissement
☗ LE LACASSAGNE***

245 av. Lacassagne (East); M° Grange-Blanche; it's a fair distance from the centre, near the hospitals and the town of Bron. **Off map D2-11**
☎ 04.78.54.09.12 ➡ 04.72.36.99.23
TV. Disabled access. Car park.

You'll need a car to get to this pleasant hotel on the edge of town. It has big rooms; some overlook a garden. Nice welcome and reasonable prices. Doubles €37 with shower/wc and €54 with bath. Light meals provided on request – salad, *croque-monsieur*, cream cheese and so on – for €10–13.

⅍ ☗ |●| HÔTEL DE CRÉQUI**

158 rue de Créqui (East); M° Guichard; it's not far from the TGV station. **Off map D3-10**
☎ 04.78.60.20.47 ➡ 04.78.62.21.12
Closed Easter; Aug; the Christmas holidays. **TV.**

A spruce new hotel near the law courts, a ten-minute walk from the town centre. The bedrooms are comfortable, with cheerful yellow walls and blue carpets, but they're a bit of a squeeze. All rooms cost €59 with bath. Smiling, professional staff. They do simple meals – it's €9 for the dish of the day – and there's a wine bar (not at weekends). 10% discount on the room rate.

4th arrondissement
⅍ ☗ HÔTEL DE LA POSTE

1 rue Victor Fort (North); M° Croix-Rousse.
Off map C1-13
☎ and ➡ 04.78.28.62.67

One of the least expensive hotels in town and certainly one of the nicest, located in the heart of the marvellous Croix-Rousse neighbourhood. It's housed in a working-class block of flats and though the building doesn't exactly ooze charm, it's very well-maintained. The lovely proprietress has a friendly smile for everybody, but reserves half of her twenty rooms for her regulars. Rooms €15–24 with basin and €29 with shower. 10% discount July–Aug.

|●| BOUCHERIE-RESTAURANT DE LA CROIX-ROUSSE

3 pl. des Tapis; M° Croix-Rousse. **Off map D1-34**
☎ and ➡ 04.78.28.48.82
Closed Sun evening; Mon; Wed evening; May.

Proprietor Yves Daguin is a butcher first and foremost, and to get to the restaurant you have to go through his shop. And though he can turn his hand to a tasty *andouillette beaujolaise* (a type of sausage cooked in Beaujolais wine), his best dishes are simple and unadorned without sauce. For starters, share a platter of lamb kidneys and sweetbreads or the selection of *saucissons de Lyon* before moving onto the meat of your choice. There's a very good selection of reasonably priced wines from tiny vineyards in Beaujolais and Côtes-du-Rhône. Menus at €8–13; dish of the day at lunchtime for €7. Dinner *à la carte* will cost around €24. There's a big terrace in front of the shop.

5th arrondissement
☗ PHÉNIX HÔTEL***

7 quai de Bondy; M° Hôtel-de-Ville. **MAP B2-6**
☎ 04.78.28.24.24 ➡ 04.78.28.62.86
℮ phenixhotel@wanadoo.fr
Disabled access. TV. Car park.

The hotel, in a splendid seventeenth-century building, offers big, tastefully decorated rooms. It's also the only hotel in town to offer a view of the Saône; others look over the Croix-Rousse hill. They're beautifully appointed and impeccably maintained. Very professional welcome and an international clientele. Doubles €135–168 including breakfast.

⅍ |●| LES LYONNAIS

1 rue Tramassac; M° Vieux-Lyon. **MAP B3-33**
☎ 04.78.37.64.82
Closed Sun evening; Mon; 3 weeks in Aug. **Disabled access.**

An imitation Lyon *bouchon* that just about works. Since it opened this friendly place has drawn regular crowds for its efficient service, good food and affordable prices. Weekday lunch *formules* €8 and 10; menus €10–23 including a *menu du marché* which changes with the seasons and a *menu Lyonnais*. Dishes include *tabliers de sapeur*, hot sausages, calf's head with sauce *gribiche* and pike balls with shellfish sauce. Free coffee.

⅍ |●| LES ADRETS

30 rue du Bœuf; M° Vieux-Lyon. **MAP B2-38**
☎ 04.78.38.24.30
Closed Sat and Sun; Aug.

This typically Lyonnais place isn't at the forefront of fashion but it's always full of people. The lunch menu (€12) is brilliant: excellent dishes including as good a fish soup as you'll eat in Marseilles, scallop and prawn salad, grilled ravioli, pressed herrings with Jerusalem artichokes, marinated salmon and *croustillant* of zander fillet with spiced bread. It's perfectly accompanied by a jug of wine which, like the coffee, is included in the price. Other menus €18–37. Free apéritif.

6th arrondissement
⟨𝄞 |●| CHEZ MARCELLE

71 cours Vitton (East); M° Masséna. **Off map D1-40**
☎ 04.78.89.51.07
Closed Sat, Sun and Aug.

Scores of regulars come here not for the décor but for the marvellous food. Marcelle is one of the last genuine "mères" – the name given to the old-fashioned style of female cook – in the city. Her cooking is just as traditional. First comes the selection of *hors d'œuvres* – a series of salad bowls full of lentils, fresh green beans (in season), wonderful *cervelas* (a delicious pork sausage), bacon, cooked peppers and so on. Next, you can have an amazing *tablier de sapeur* (ox tripe egged and crumbed before being grilled), calf's liver or thick slabs of succulent meat. End the feast with a terrific *crème caramel* – a house rule insists customers should never claim to be full, so make sure you have no plans for the afternoon. Lunch menu €23, but it's *à la carte* only at dinner and can get pricey – up to around €34. Free apéritif.

7th arrondissement
⟨𝄞 |●| L'AROMATE

94 Grande-Rue-de-la-Guillotière (right bank); M° Saxe-Gambetta. **Off map A4-44**
☎ 04.78.58.94.56
Closed Sun and Mon; mid-July to mid-Aug.

The "La Guillotière" area is known for its range of foreign restaurants but this is a tiny place producing Camargue cuisine. The restaurant is classified as a "bio-mixte" establishment, meaning that they use organic meats, genuinely wild varities of tropical fish, edible marshland plants and other classified species. It's run by a brilliant couple who fuss over their clients like crazy. You'll find *taureau* (literally "bull") prepared in all ways imaginable: *andouillette*, haunch, grilled, pan-fried, *tartare* and so on. There's also a good range of carefully prepared fish and squid dishes. Start with an *améthyste* – a house apéritif that's as good as it is surprising – and finish with a heavenly dessert. Presentation, size of portions, seasonings and the service all make this an excellent

place. And when the bill comes, you pay as you have eaten – with pleasure. Menus €14 and €20; it's around €25–29 *à la carte*. Free house apéritif.

|●| EN METS, FAIS CE QU'IL TE PLAÎT

rue Chevreul; M° Jean-Macé. Off map A4-45
☎ 04.78.72.46.58
Closed Sat and Sun; Aug.

A really good restaurant with two dining rooms; you can see into the kitchen from the first one, which has a bar, while the second has metal grilles at the windows and tables lit by modern, colourful lamps. It's a relaxing place, with easy-going, attentive service. The menu changes every three weeks but they always have lots of fresh vegetables with olive oil, good duck, fresh fish and excellent seafood. The produce and ingredients are the freshest, and the attention paid to precise cooking is impressive. You'll pay €21–30 *à la carte*. There's a selection of good wines served by the glass.

CHASSELAY   69830 (10KM SW)

|●| GUY LAUSSAUSAIE

It's in the village; take the A6, then the N6 and the D16.
☎ 04.78.47.62.59 **e** guylaussausaie@wanadoo.fr
Closed Tues and Wed; Aug. **Car park**.

Guy Lassausaie studied with some of the great chefs before taking over the family business, determined to give it a new lease of life. The dining room is very chic, having been sumptuously decorated, and his cooking is classic with a subtle touch of modernity which takes it out of the ordinary – *cappuccino* of pickled chicory, roast quail with pistachio nuts, celery pie, oxtail braised with rosemary. The cheeses are ripened to perfection and there is a sumptuous dessert trolley. Menus €30–62. There's also an interesting wine list with grapes from round the world. Attentive service and decent prices for this quality of restaurant.

MEGÈVE   74120

⟨𝄞 ▲ |●| HÔTEL-CHALET DES OURS**

Chemin des Roseaux (Centre).
☎ 04.50.21.57.40 ▶ 04.50.93.05.73
e chaletdesours@aol.com
Closed Thurs evening; May–June; Nov. **Car park**.

It's a big surprise to find such a gem in the opulent surroundings of Megève. Owned by an English woman, this lovely place is a haven of refinement, simplicity and kindness. The panelled rooms are decorated simply with vases of flowers and soft feather beds. Doubles €58–75 with shower/wc; half board at €53–75 per person is compulsory in winter. There's a reading room with a beautiful fireplace and a TV, and a small dining room in the basement. They offer one menu at €15 and a rather exotic Thai version to order for dinner. It's sheer pleasure to have five different kinds of tea to choose from at breakfast. 10% discount on the room rate except in high season.

PRAZ-SUR-ARLY   74120 (5KM SW)

🏂 🏠 |●| LA GRIYOTIRE***

route de la Tonnaz (Centre); take the N212.
☎ 04.50.21.86.36 ➡ 04.50.21.86.34
📧 griyotire@wanadoo.fr
Hotel closed Mid-April to mid-June; mid-Sept to mid-Dec. **Restaurant closed** lunchtimes. **TV. Swimming pool. Garden. Car park**.

A dream of an Alpine chalet in the middle of a family resort not far from Megève, set well away from the main road that runs through the middle of the village. The rooms have been decorated in exquisite taste and each is different. There's lots of wood everywhere and the feather beds are gloriously soft; doubles with shower/wc €61–75. Half-board, compulsory during the winter school holidays, €60–62. Charming welcome and a family atmosphere – there's even a games room for the children. *Fondue* and *raclette* are served on winter evenings. Set menu €24. There's a lovely garden, a sauna, a steam bath, a massage room and a swimming pool open in summer. Free coffee.

MENS   38710

🏠 |●| AUBERGE DE MENS***

pl. du Breuil (Centre).
☎ 04.76.34.81.00 ➡ 04.76.34.80.90
Restaurant closed Feb; open by reservation only Oct–May. **Disabled access. TV. Car park**.

This huge renovated house offers comfortable rooms at €43 for a double with shower/wc or bath. The décor is fresh and colourful and there's a lovely garden where you can relax on quiet evenings. They serve traditional home cooking, with a menu at €15 including cheese and dessert. Nice welcome.

🏂|●| CAFÉ DES ARTS

rue Principale (Centre); from Grenoble take the N85 then the D526.
☎ 04.76.34.68.16
Restaurant closed Sun evening; Sept–June. **TV**.

This charming place is the most famous café in the Trièves and it's listed as a historic monument. In 1896, Gustave Riquet, a painter from Picardy, decorated the ceilings and walls with beautiful allegorical frescoes and views of the countryside. The self-taught chef-owner prepares superb dishes that vary according to what's good at market. The choice is limited, but you can be sure that whatever is on offer will be inspired. Try the house *terrine* of *foie gras* and the fresh fish if they're available. Menus €11 at lunch then €13–17 at dinner (which is by reservation only). Free coffee.

TRÉMNIS   38710 (15KM S)

🏂 🏠 |●| HÔTEL DES ALPES

hameau de Château-Bas: take the D66 from Mens then the D216.
☎ 04.76.34.72.94
Closed Sun evening and Mon out of season; Nov–Feb.

This is the type of hotel you'd expect to see on an old sepia postcard of the mountains. Set in marvellous countryside, it's been wonderfully run for generations. There's a vaulted café-bar and a grandfather clock ticking away in the dining room next to the buffet. In these comforting surroundings you can eat good family cooking from menus at very low prices: €11 (not Sunday) to €15. Doubles cost €30 with basin and €44 with shower. Free coffee.

CHICHILIANNE   38930 (20KM W)

🏂 🏠 |●| AU GAI SOLEIL DU MONT-AIGUILLE**

La Richardière; take the N75 then the D7, it's 2.5km from the village at the foot of Mont Aiguille, where the walking trails start.
☎ 04.76.34.41.71 ➡ 04.76.34.40.63
Closed All Saints' Day to end Nov.

Surrounded by a fantastic ring of mountains, this hotel is at the foot of Mont Aiguille among the woods, copses and wheat fields. The house, built in 1720, has its original stone staircase, and there has been a hotel here for fifty years. The *patronne* is warm-hearted and welcoming. Rooms are super-clean and reasonably priced: €33–46 with basin or shower/wc. Good classic dishes are served in the restaurant: chicken liver *soufflé*, pork stew, chicken with crayfish and various grilled meats. Menus €12 (not Sun), and half board at €36–44. Cheaply priced wines with a Cuvée at €8 and a Châtillon-en-Diois at €8. It's lively in high season.10% discount on the room rate Jan–April inclusive.

☎ |●| CHÂTEAU DE PASSIÈRES**

How to get there: take the D526 from Mens to Clelles, then the D7 to the foot of Mont Aiguille.
☎ 04.76.34.45.48 ➡ 04.76.34.46.25
Closed Sun evening and Mon except July–Aug; Dec–Jan. **Swiming pool**. **TV**. **Car park**.

A fifteenth-century château, owned by the mayor, in a magnificent location. All the rooms have up-to-date facilities, and the prices (€50–65) are attractive. Numbers 1, 4 and 5 are the most expensive because they have original wood panelling. You can sit and chat in the charming sitting room – a veritable picture gallery – well into the small hours. There's a good bar, and imaginative cooking is served in a large dining room. Menus from €18 list specialities such as *compote* of duck and trout with walnuts, turnovers studded with truffles on a creamed leek *fondue*, salmon steak with dandelion honey, *fricassée* of ceps and snails on a bed of ravioli. There's a nice swimming pool in the grounds.

MIRMANDE   26270

🍴 |●| RESTAURANT MARGOT

Centre; it's near the post office.
☎ 04.75.63.08.05 📧 margot@wanadoo.fr/margot
Closed Wed, and Jan–Feb.

This restaurant, like the listed village, is a mixture of stylishness and rustic simplicity. It's a place for people who love old-style cooking. In summer you can go inside to cool off in the tastefully decorated dining room, or sit out on a bench on the terrace in the shade of the climbing vines. There's a weekday lunch menu at €12 and others €17–22. You get a good choice of regional specialities but dishes constantly change: guineafowl *pot-au-feu*, braised veal *à la provençale*, lamb *Tonton Firmin*, chocolate *fondant*. Sometimes there are jazz evenings. Free apéritif.

CLIOUSCLAT   26270 (2KM N)

🍴 ☎ |●| LA TREILLE MUSCATE**

How to get there: it's 1km from Mirmande on the D57.
☎ 04.75.63.13.10 ➡ 04.75.63.10.79
Closed Wed and 15 Dec–1 March. **Disabled access**. **Garden**. **TV**. **Car park**.

A large, pretty house with green shutters and walls half-covered in ivy. Inside, the rooms have a sophisticated charm and some have a terrace with a view over the countryside; they cost €53 with shower/wc and €84 with bath. There's a lovely enclosed garden and the dining room is bright and roomy with a corner fireplace and a few stylish tables. The cuisine, which uses local produce, is typical of this sunny region: pressed chicken in a *pot-au-feu* with mustard, preserved lamb with garlic. The weekday lunch menu at €14 and others up €22 offer great value. Excellent welcome. Free coffee.

MODANE   73500

🍴 ☎ |●| HÔTEL-RESTAURANT LE PERCE-NEIGE**

14 av. Jean-Jaurès (Centre); it's opposite the station.
☎ 04.79.05.00.50 ➡ 04.79.05.12.92
Closed Sun out of season; 1–19 May; 1 Oct–6 Nov. **TV**.

This is an ideal place for an overnight stop in a town that is not sufficiently appealing for a longer stay. The rooms are simple and the welcome slightly brusque; doubles €38 with shower/wc and up to €51 with bath. All the rooms are well soundproofed, which is just as well since the hotel is on the road and opposite the railway track. The traditional cooking is good: *coq au vin* with Savoy wine, trout fillet with Apremont wine sauce. Menus €12–18. 10% discount outside the summer and winter seasons.

AUSSOIS   73500 (15KM NE)

🍴 |●| FORT MARIE-CHRISTINE

How to get there: take the D215 and turn right before getting to Aussois.
☎ 04.79.20.36.44 📧 fort.m.c.@wanadoo.fr
Closed Sun evening and Mon 15 Sept–15 Dec and 25 May–15 June; 20 April–20 May; 1 Nov–20 Dec. **TV**. **Car park**. **Disabled access**.

This sturdy fortress on an outcrop of rock, is part of a string of fortifications built by the crown of Piedmont and Sardinia to protect the kingdom from French invasion. The lofty halls and vaults have been extensively restored, though the interior still feels rather like a barracks. The restaurant is renowned for its splendid local cooking: pork *fricassée*, cockerel with bilberries, *agnelot* (home-made ravioli) with sage, *civet* of rabbit with Gamay wine served with polenta, *diots* (herb sausages cooked in wine). The prices won't have you up in arms, either, with menus at €13–21 and good local wines by the jug. The small terrace in the interior courtyard is roasting in summer. Free coffee.

MONTBRISON   42600

🏃 🏢 |●| HÔTEL-RESTAURANT DES VOYAGEURS

16 rue Simon-Boyer (Centre).
☎ 04.77.96.17.64 ➡ 04.77.58.95.02
Closed Sat and Sun evenings; 24–31 Dec. **TV**. **Car park**.

This hotel, set in a little street in the centre of town, has got old-fashioned charm. The spacious rooms, furnished in the '30s and '40s, go for €23 with shower and €32 with bath. You'll get traditional cooking in the restaurant, where they offer menus for €10 (not Sun), €13 and €19. 10% discount for a two-night stay and a free coffee.

🏃 🏢 |●| LE GIL DE FRANCE

18 [bis] bd. Lachèze; it's just beyond the centre.
☎ 04.77.58.06.16 ➡ 04.77.58.73.78
Disabled access. **TV**. **Car park**.

A modern hotel on the outskirts of town, situated in front of a big park. The rooms and bright and fresh with modern facilities and go for €44 with shower/wc. The friendly young team bring a personal touch to the place, and it's better than many of the hotels in the centre. Don't expect miracles in the restaurant, though – menus €9–24. Free coffee.

🏃 |●| LE GOURMANDIN

4 [bis] rue des Pénitents (Centre).
☎ 04.77.58.58.72
Closed Sun evening; Mon; a fortnight in Jan; a fortnight in July.

Christian Bellot decided to open his restaurant in a disused crockery warehouse in the town that was the capital of the counts of Forez. The modern décor feels very comfortable but the black ceiling won't be to everyone's taste. The restaurant undoubtedly deserves its two stars and the well-heeled customers certainly enjoy the cuisine. The chef prepares seasonal game particularly skilfully, his meat and fish dishes are finely judged. Try the house *foie gras*, the *foie gras gâteau*, the lobster *fricassée* with vanilla or game in season. Weekday menu €15 and others €21–47. Attentive, professional service. Free coffee.

🏃 |●| RESTAURANT YVES THOLLOT

93 route de Lyon; take the D496.

☎ 04.77.96.10.40
Closed Sun evening and Mon; the Feb school holidays; 3 weeks in Aug.

This place is on the outskirts of Savigneux in a craft zone, near a chain hotel and looking not dissimilar. Yves Thollot welcomes you with a wide smile and his delicious cooking is very good: frogs' legs and apple salad, pan-fried *foie gras* with green apples and raspberry *coulis*, grilled bream, zander with *beurre blanc* and house butterscotch ice-cream with hot chocolate sauce. Menus €17–24. Free apéritif.

CHAMPDIEU   42600 (5KM)

|●| HOSTELLERIE DU PRIEURÉ

Route de Boën; it's on the D8, away from the centre.
☎ 04.77.58.31.21
Closed Thurs except public holidays; a fortnight in Aug. **Car park**.

This place, on the border of the *département*, is run by a chef who's absolutely expert at traditional cooking techniques. He offers a simple option for €12 – a main course with a starter or dessert – and gourmet choices on the others menus (€16–37). Affordable wine.

SAINT-ROMAIN-LE-PUY   42610 (8KM S)

🏃 🏢 |●| AUBERGE LES TRABUCHES**

How to get there: take the D8 from Sury-le-Comtal to Montbrison, turn left before the Parot spring and follow the signs to the right.
☎ 04.77.97.79.70 ➡ 04.77.97.79.74
Closed Mon; a fortnight in Feb; a fortnight in Oct. **TV**.

Six simple rooms with basin (€35) share common bathing and toilet facilities; the five others at ground level in the annexe have en-suite shower/wc and TV and cost €44. Cheery welcome. In the restaurant they serve simple menus: rabbit *terrine* and meat dishes with sauce. You'll pay €11 for the weekday menu, with others at €15–23. Free house apéritif.

MONTÉLIMAR   26200

🏢 HÔTEL PIERRE**

7 pl. des Clercs (Centre); it's near the church of Sainte-Croix in the old town, next to a little square.
☎ 04.75.01.33.16
Closed Feb. **TV**.

This prettily renovated sixteenth-century town house on a small square is delightful. Its pretty porch, candelabra-studded corridor, paved courtyard, ivy-covered terrace and dressed stone staircase create a striking atmosphere. The twelve rooms – €24 with basin, €38 with bath – are fairly ordinary compared to the rest of the place, though some have been refurbished. The best is number 2, which has a balcony swamped in Virginia creeper. There's space to park bikes.

⚲ ☗ HÔTEL BEAUSOLEIL**

pl. d'Armes-Allées Provençales (Northwest).
☎ 04.75.01.19.80 ➡ 04.75.01.08.17
Garden. Pay car park.

A characterful hotel offering sixteen pleasant rooms for €27 with washing facilities along the landing and €43 with shower/wc or bath. It's well away from the traffic but close to the centre of the town. Breakfast is served in a lovely garden. Nice welcome. 10% discount on the room rate.

☗ SPHINX HÔTEL**

19 bd. Marre-Desmarais (Centre).
☎ 04.75.01.86.64 ➡ 04.75.52.34.21
ⓔ reception@sphinx-hotel.fr
Closed 20 Dec–5 Jan. **TV. Pay lock-up car park.**

Exceedingly well-located away from the traffic noise. The front of the building is covered with ivy and it's a lovely seventeenth-century private mansion with wood panelling and antique furniture inside. The superb salon has a tranquil atmosphere so it's a perfect place to relax. You get an appropriately stylish welcome. The rooms are adorable and have very good facilities: air conditioning, direct dial phone, mini-bar. Doubles €41–53. When it's sunny, breakfast is served on the terrace. There's a charge of €3 for the car park.

⚲ ☗ HÔTEL DU PARC**

27 bd. Charles-de-Gaulle (West).
☎ 04.75.01.00.73 ➡ 04.75.51.27.93
TV. Pay garage.

A classic hotel without a huge amount of character – but it is across from the park. The owners keep it spotless and welcome you most civilly. Bright, comfortable rooms with shower or bath cost €43–45 for shower/wc and €58–69 with bath. Free fresh orange at breakfast.

⚲ ❘●❘ LA PETITE FRANCE

34 impasse Raymond-Daujat (Centre).
☎ 04.75.46.07.94
Closed Sat lunchtime, Sun and public holidays.

You have to be quite determined to find this restaurant in a small cul-de-sac. It's worth making the effort because it's a nice little place with a fresh, friendly dining room and a vaulted ceiling, murals, pale wood, green plants and quiet music in the background. It's frequented by locals. Well-worked dishes and a good-value short menu for €13; others up to €25. Dishes include pan-fried monkfish with paprika and cream, *paupiette* of salmon and scallops, a duo of veal sweetbreads and hot *foie gras* with raspberry vinegar. Decent wines, starting at around €11 for a *Côteau de Tricastin*. Free house apéritif.

❘●❘ LE CHALET DU PARC

bd. Marre Desmarais, Allées Provençales (Northwest); it's next to the tourist office.
☎ 04.75.98.60.60 ➡ 04.75.98.63.44

A dynamic young couple took over this place with the express aim of turning it into a top-class gourmet restaurant. And the cooking is indeed inspired, produced by a chef who's bursting with ideas and enthusiasm. He puts together remarkable combinations of flavours and uses only fresh produce: scallops rolled in smoked ham, rabbit thigh in lemon caramel, grilled supreme of guineafowl with fresh herbs, a perfectly-judged salmon *unilatérale* (cooked on one side only). The luscious *dôme de chocolat* with iced vanilla will do for any chocoholic. Menus from €15. The downstairs dining room is still a little bare but they've put all the effort into what really counts – the cooking.

VALAURIE   26230 (19KM SE)

⚲ ☗ ❘●❘ DOMAINE LES MÉJEONNES***

How to get there: take the RN7, then the D133 in the direction of Grignan-Noyons; it's 1km from the village.
☎ 04.75.98.60.60 ➡ 04.75.98.63.44
Closed Sun evening out of season. **Swimming pool. TV. Car park.**

If you want to see this old farmhouse at its best, arrive in the mellow glow of late afternoon or in the evening when the floodlights illuminate the vines and the old stones. It's recently been renovated; the lovely, spacious, comfortable rooms go for €58 for a double with shower or bath. Menus at €15–28 list good, appetizing food with a few regulars: lamb shank braised in wine, roast supreme of goose, duck *foie gras* in Muscat de Beaume-de-Venise. You'll get a courteous welcome – and the swimming pool is superb. 10% discount on the room rate Sept–June.

☗ ❘●❘ LA TABLE DE NICOLE

Route de Grignan.

☎ 04.75.98.52.03 ➡ 04.75.98.58.45
Swimming pool. Car park.

A favourite spot for visiting Americans, way out in the country. It has everything you hope to find in the Midi – a charming dining room with dry stone walls, a wide fireplace, bright pictures, soft lights and Provençal tablecloths – and a relaxed atmosphere that suits its clientele. The *patron* is chatty and at ease and the food is delicious. The cheapest menu (€22) lets you choose from at least fifteen different *hors d'œuvres*, laid out on a table; the main course changes daily, but will list a local dish with tasty vegetables *au gratin*. Foie gras appears on the €30 menu and there's a truffle menu at €44. There's also an impressive selection of regional cheeses, but the menus are so generously served that you'll probably struggle for space. Lots of Côtes du Rhône wines on the remarkable wine list, with *vins de pays* – rich Cornas, Saint-Péray and Saint-Joseph – Crozes Hermitage, and many others. About ten rooms with excellent facilities from €58.

MONTROTTIER 69770

⚒ 🛏 |●| L'AUBERGE DES BLÉS D'OR**

La Curtillat – route de Saint-Julien-sur-Bibost. Take the N89, then the D7; after Saint-Bel, head for Bibost, then take the D246 and keep going until 2km before Montrottier.
☎ and ➡ 04.74.70.13.56
Closed Tues, evenings reservations only. **TV. Car park**.

It's best to book in season to be sure of a room or a table; out of season, check that they're serving meals. This country inn, which stands alone among the fields and is surrounded by flowers, has been superbly restored. The rooms with shower/wc (€49) are in an annexe and look over the valley. They boast all mod cons and total silence. The lovely, rustic dining room has a creaking parquet floor and vast beams. Flavoursome cuisine with a regional slant on menus from €20 with a children's menu at €10. You can sit on your terrace watching the sun go down behind the hills, with the church of Montrottier illuminated in the distance. 10% discount on the room rate or a pot of local honey.

MORZINE 74110

⚒ 🛏 |●| HÔTEL LES LANS***

quartier des Prodains; it's 300m from the cable car that goes to Avoriaz.

☎ 04.50.79.00.90 ➡ 04.50.79.15.22
Closed Sept–Nov and May–June. **TV**.

He used to be a ski instructor, she's mad about local history and culture – today, along with their two daughters, they put life into this huge newly-built chalet. The prices are unbeatable considering what you get. Half board is compulsory, costing €44 per person in summer and €53–73 in winter. Monsieur Mallurez happily takes care of the cooking but escapes from the kitchen once a week to take people on wildlife discovery trips, while Madame conducts guided tours. During some periods of the summer, trips are free for children under ten. Christmas and New Year are celebrated in style – at no extra charge for residents. 10% discount on the half-board rate.

🛏 |●| LES PRODAINS**

Prodains; it's 4km from the centre of Morzine at the foot of the Avoriaz ski-lift.
☎ 04.50.79.25.26 ➡ 04.50.75.76.17
📧 hotellesprodains@aol.com
Closed 20 April–25 June, 5 Sept–10 Dec. **TV**.
Swimming pool. Car park.

You'll get a very warm welcome at this friendly family establishment at the foot of the ski runs. The chalet has pretty rooms with balconies, all with a fantastic view of the slopes; doubles with shower/wc or bath cost €55. The huge terrace gets swamped by skiers as soon as the sun comes out. Menus €15–20; although you can certainly get a tasty *tartiflette*, the inventive cooking is not limited to mountain dishes. Try the *émincé* of duck with pineapple, the pan-fried scallops served in a crusty case or desserts such as iced drops of sour cherry with vanilla cream. Swimming pool for the summer, when the boss also takes guests up to the mountain hut where he serves tasty mountain dishes.

⚒ |●| RESTAURANT LA GRANGETTE

How to get there: it's near the Nyon cable car.
☎ 04.50.79.05.76
Closed Mon evening; 11 April–13 July; 1 Oct–20 Dec.

A little family business at the foot of the ski slopes where you can enjoy a tasty meal in a friendly atmosphere. The €10 lunch menu gets you the dish of the day – frogs' legs, house *terrine*, cheese-filled turnovers, beef *bourguignon* with mashed potato, say – and home-made tart for dessert. Other menus up to €23. The house speciality is frog's legs in cream sauce. Lots of walking trails start (and finish) here. Free coffee.

♨ |●| LA CHAMADE

Centre; it's near the tourist office.
☎ 04.50.79.13.91 **e** restaurant@lachamade.com
Closed Tues and Wed out of season; May; 15 Nov–10 Dec.

This is a local institution with a varied menu featuring everything from pizzas cooked in a wood-fired oven to regional specialities. It's recently been doing things differently now that son Thierry, who's a chef, has taken over in the kitchen – his wife runs the dining room. Thierry likes pork in all its guises, and offers *pâté* of pig's head, *atriaux* (a type of patty) and mountain suckling pig with apple fritters. There's one menu at €41 or expect to pay €30 *à la carte*. The terrace is really great in summer. Free *apéritif*.

MONTRIOND   74110 (6KM NE)

♨ |●| AUBERGE LA CHALANDE

Lieu-dit Ardent.
☎ 04.50.79.19.69
Closed Mon; 21 April–14 June; 16 Sept–14 Dec inclusive.

This old chalet feels like it's way out in a lost mountain hamlet – though it's actually at the foot of the ski lifts going up to Avoriaz. It used to belong to the owner's mother, and he hasn't changed the warm, rustic surroundings a bit. He turns out delicious dishes, whether you choose from the menus (€17–33), or go *à la carte* (around €30). On the cheapest menu, you'll get cheese *croûte*, braised sausage with leeks and potato fritters and bilberry tart. The more expensive menus feature salmon and crayfish. Wonderful welcome. It's best to book. Free house *digestif*.

MOÛTIERS   73600

♨ 🏠 |●| HÔTEL WELCOME'S**

33 av. Greyffié-de-Bellecombe; it's near the station.
☎ 04.79.24.00.48 **➡** 04.79.22.99.96
e hotel.welcome@wanadoo.fr
Closed 15 April–10 July and 30 Aug–20 Dec.
Disabled access. TV. Car park.

A comfortable station hotel where they pride themselves on giving a nice welcome. The pleasant, comfortable rooms cost €46–53 for a double – the ones at the rear are very quiet. You get traditional cooking in the restaurant, where they serve a few brasserie dishes and some good fish courses. Menus €14 (weekday lunch) and €21–24. The parking spaces for motorcycles and bikes are free

of charge. Free apéritif.

FEISSONS-SUR-SALINS   73350 (12KM SE)

♨ 🏠 |●| LE BALCON DES TROIS VALLÉES**

How to get there: take the D915 to Bozel then the D89.
☎ 04.79.24.24.34 **➡** 04.79.24.24.79
e b3v@club-internet.fr
Closed Wed out of season; Oct; Nov–15 Dec; May-June; All Saints'; a week from 15 Aug. **Car park**.

The population of this tiny isolated village grew all the way to 154 with the arrival of the four people who run this hotel. They renovated a squat chalet, taking great care to respect its style and proportions. It looks a bit functional from the outside, but that's made up for by the warm décor. Double rooms with basin go for €29–35 and €32–38 with shower/wc. It's a very friendly place and they serve lots of good Belgian beers. They also make local dishes like mountain ham and *génépi*, as well as old standards given an imaginative twist. Menus €14–20. You can hire cross-country skis, mountain bikes and tennis racquets. Free apéritif and 10% discount on the room rate May, Oct and Nov.

LÉCHÈRE (LA)   73260 (12KM N)

♨ |●| RESTAURANT LA VIEILLE FORGE

Bellecombe; take exit 37, signposted Valmorel
☎ 04.79.24.17.97
Closed lunchtimes; Tues; Jan and Feb. **Car park**.

You won't find the usual stultified spa town atmosphere in this restaurant. It used to be a blacksmith's, and the décor features some of the old smithy equipment and a jumble of musical instruments including a piano and a balafon (an African instrument something like a xylophone), which customers are free to use if they so desire. Tasty, traditional cooking, Savoy specialities, meat dishes in sauce, mushrooms and duck breast on set menus at €10–19 including wine. There's live music every Friday and they're open very late – until 4am in summer. Free apéritif or coffee.

VALMOREL   73260 (14KM W)

♨ 🏠 |●| CHÂTEAU DU CREY**

Les Avanchers, hameau du Crey; take the D95 and it's at the lower end of the resort.
☎ 04.79.09.87.00 **➡** 04.79.09.89.51
Closed 21 April–21 May and 1–30 Oct. **Swimming pool**.

A classic family-run chalet in an absolutely

authentic mountain hamlet. Everyone, especially the huge dog, knows how to give you a warm welcome. Rooms are well-appointed; there are family rooms sleeping four or five, and doubles with shower/wc or bath cost €46. In the restaurant, menus cost €11–20. They list mountain specialities and a few other dishes, including scallops with prawns, steak with morels and monkfish with oyster mushrooms. *À la carte*, you choose from a range of Savoy specialities. The vast swimming pool, open in summer, is rather unusual – it's inflatable. Free coffee and 10% discount on the room rate.

⍭ |●| RESTAURANT LE SKI ROC

Centre; it's in a pedestrianized street off the main street.
☎ 04.79.09.83.17 **e** denis/murat@worldonline.fr
Closed 20 April–20 June; mid-Sept to mid-Dec.

This is *the* place to eat in Valmorel. It's got a nice chalet-style interior and there's a great ambience in the wine bar, where the crowd comes to sample a selection of Savoy wines served by the glass or the bottle. Decent, straightforward, mountain fare is served by a young dynamic team in the restaurant – *fondue* and *braserade*, excellent *raclette* made with Reblochon, *carpaccio* of *foie gras* with a truffle vinaigrette, guineafowl *piccata* with morels. Weekday menu for €13 and others €15–20 – good value for money, in other words. Relax in a deckchair on the terrace when the sun shines. Free *digestif*.

NANTUA   01130

|●| RESTAURANT BELLE RIVE

23 route de la Cluse (Northwest); take the N84 from Cluse and it's just before you get to Nantua.
☎ 04.74.75.16.60
Closed Tues evening; Wed out of season. **Car park**.

This place, right by the lake, is equally popular with families doing big get-togethers and local workers for lunch. You'll need to book or get there early if you want a table on the pleasant veranda overlooking the lake. The €10 lunch menu is pretty decent, and others at €13–30 include the famous *quenelles de Nantua*. (meatballs served with a crayfish butter sauce). You have to wait a full fifteen minutes for them; they're freshly cooked and well worth it. Efficient service.

CHARIX   01130 (10KM S)

♠ |●| AUBERGE DU LAC GENIN

How to get there: take the N84 in the direction of Bellegarde, then turn left at Le Martinet onto the D95.
☎ 04.74.75.52.50 ➡ 04.74.75.51.15
Closed Sun evening; Mon; 15 Oct–1 Dec. **TV. Car park**.

The magnificent lake and the setting in the beautiful dark Jura forests makes the trip up here worthwhile. In summer, it's a paradise for fishermen and walkers, but be sure to have the right equipment and chains on your car tyres in winter – the weather can be really severe. Unsurprisingly, the best rooms have windows onto the lake. They aren't exactly luxurious, and prices are average: €20 with basin, €30 with shower and €40 with bath. The €11 menu is unimaginative, but there are others up to €18 listing mountain ham, meats grilled on the open fire, wine sausage and veal cutlet with mustard. It's substantial rather than gourmet cooking and there's a real family atmosphere. Nice welcome and in summer the place gets very full.

CHÂTILLON-DE-MICHAILLE   01200 (12KM SE)

⍭ ♠ |●| AUBERGE DE LA FONTAINE**

Ochiaz (East); take the N206, then the N84, turn off at the Ochiaz exit and take the D101 to Châtillon.
☎ 04.50.56.57.23 ➡ 04.50.56.56.55
e aubergefontaine@mintel.net
Closed Sun and Tues evenings and Mon out of season; three weeks in Jan; a week in June; a week at the beginning of Oct. **Lock-up car park**.

This pretty stone inn, festooned with flowers in summer, is just next to a bubbling fountain in a delightful village. It is a smart little place without being formal. The rooms are comfortable and quiet and you'll get a restorative night's sleep at reasonable prices – doubles €30 with basin, €35 with shower/wc or bath. You can eat very well – pike *quenelles*, duck in pastry cases and *gratin* of crayfish tails – though dishes could do with a little more imagination. Menus start at €15 (weekdays only) then continue at €19–46. Free coffee and 10% discount on the room rate.

LALLEYRIAT   01130 (14KM E)

⍭ |●| LES GENTIANES

How to get there: take the N84 in the direction of Bellegarde as far as Neyrolles and then the D55.
☎ 04.74.75.31.80
Closed Wed; Sun evening; the end of Jan.

Given that it's named after a mountain flower, you'd expect to find that this lovely stone-walled village inn specializes in traditional mountain food. The Parisian chef does serve regional cuisine, but he also offers novel dishes such as warm *foie gras* with three fruits in Armagnac, frogs' legscharlotte and *millefeuille* of scallops with nettle butter. Prices are fair with menus at €20–35. Free coffee.

LANCRANS 01200 (17KM SE)

🏃 🏠 |O| LE SORGIA**

Grande-Rue; take the D991 to Lélex and Mijoux.
☎ 04.50.48.15.81 ► 04.50.48.44.72
Closed Sun evening; Mon; Sat lunchtime; 20 Aug–15 Sept; 22–31 Dec. **TV. Car park**.

An old village bar-restaurant named after the mountain in front of it. Over the last century it has grown to become a hotel-restaurant with a balcony and veranda overlooking the valley. The rooms are comfortable and pleasant and filled with period furniture. Doubles €38 with shower/wc and €41 with bath. They serve simple, local dishes in generous portions: *féra* (freshwater salmon) cooked in Savoy wine, snails and baby mushrooms in flaky pastry. €12 weekday menu and others €17–30. Pleasant welcome. Free house apéritif.

NOIRÉTABLE 42440

🏃 🏠 |O| HÔTEL-RESTAURANT AU RENDEZ-VOUS DES CHASSEURS**

Route de l'Hermitage (Southwest); it's about 2km from the centre of the village on the D53.
☎ 04.77.24.72.51 ► 04.77.24.93.40
Closed Sun evening and Mon out of season, Sun in Jan and Feb, ten days during the Feb school holidays and three weeks from 15 Sept. **TV. Car park**.

Though the thundering motorway is just 6km away, all you can see from the dining room of this hotel are the Forez mountains. The inn has fourteen rooms – €24 with basin and €34 with shower/wc or bath. The cheapest menu in the week is at €9, and there are others at €15–30. All the scents and flavours of Forez can be found in the dishes here, which include home-made charcuterie, leek *terrine* with *Bleu d'Auvergne* cheese, *parfait* of chicken liver with bilberries, pigeon *pot-au-feu* and game in season. 10% discount on the room rate for a two-night stay Oct–June.

JURÉ 42430 (20KM NE)

🏃 |O| AUBERGE LE MOULIN

How to get there: take the D53 and turn right onto the D86 before you get to Saint-Just-en-Chevalet.
☎ 04.77.62.55.24
Open Sat and Sun; public holidays March–Nov;

Tues–Sun July–Aug. **Closed** 15 Nov–7 March. **Car park**.

This little inn in an old mill has an idyllic setting. Its electricity is supplied by the stream running underneath and apparently, the Lumière brothers made their first moving pictures here. It's a shame it's not open more. The country menus, €10–31, are delicious, and offer excellent home-made *terrines* cooked in a wood-fuelled oven, *rissoles*, free-range poultry, and home-made pastries that go down a treat with cider. They prefer you to order in advance. Very affordable wines. Free house apéritif.

NYONS 26110

🏠 |O| LA PICHOLINE***

Promenade de la Perrière; it's on the hilltop as you come into the town.
☎ 04.75.26.06.21 ► 04.75.26.40.72
Restaurant closed Mon and Tues Oct–April; Mon May–Sept; 4–27 Feb; 14 Oct–6 Nov. **TV. Swimming pool. Car park**.

The décor in the foyer and the restaurant is a bit chi-chi, but the owners make a real fuss of their guests. Big, light and pleasant rooms €47–62; numbers 1–10 have breathtaking views looking south. Half board, €47–59 per person, is compulsory July–Aug. Decent food – the regional menus at €21, €25 and €35 are extremely satisfying. The swimming pool is surrounded by olive trees.

🏠 |O| HÔTEL LA CARAVELLE***

8 rue des Antignans (South); from the pont de l'Europe, you go along the Promenade de la Digue.
☎ 04.75.26.07.44 ► 04.75.26.23.79
Closed 1 Nov–31 Jan. **Garden. TV. Lock-up car park**.

Just away from the centre, this hotel is surrounded by a huge, pleasant garden. It's an old *bastide*, a substantial private residence, with nine very comfortable rooms and a pair of small apartments (bedroom and a little sitting room with a child's bed). Really opulent atmosphere and polite welcome. The place for peace and quiet. Most of the rooms have a view over the garden, some have balconies. Doubles €65–69 with shower/wc or bath, breakfast €8. There's a shady terrace for a drink.

|O| RESTO DES ARTS

rue des Déportés (Centre).
☎ 04.75.26.31.49 📧 restodesarts@wanadoo.fr
Closed Wed; Tues also in low season; Nov.

Right in the heart of old Nyons. It's a rendezvous for local artists and gourmet wine-makers – it belongs to Claude and Monique Bonfils, wine-growers in the Drôme and real food-lovers as well. There's a relaxed yet fashionable atmosphere and the place is nearly always full. The cooking is tasty and generously served and while it's traditional, it has a personal touch – dishes such as goat's cheese salad with sesame oil, red mullet with *foie gras*, duck *confit* with wild mushrooms, slivers of duck with apricot honey, pan-fried *foie gras* with apples and a duo of king prawn and scallops. There's a dish of the day and a *menu du jour* for €11 andothers €17–22. As you would expect, the wine list has a host of good Côtes du Rhônes.

|●| LE PETIT CAVEAU

9 rue Victor Hugo; it's in the street at right angles to the Pavillon du Tourisme.
☎ 04.75.26.20.21
Closed Sun evening; Mon; 15 Nov–15 Dec.

Muriel Cormont is a graduate of the Suze-La-Rousse wine university and her husband used to work for the great chef Robuchon. It was Muriel's idea to offer three different glasses of wine (€11) that she selects to suit the dishes you have chosen. Her husband is a seriously good chef – try his roast saddle of rabbit with hazelnuts, roast lamb, *confit* of lamb chops, sweetbread and kidney kebabs or red pepper risotto. Good wine and excellent cuisine – you get the best of both worlds at reasonable prices. Weekday menu €17, others €26–37, and menus change every week.

MIRABEL-AUX-BARONNIES   26110 (7KM S)

⅍ |●| LA COLOQUINTE

av. de la Résistance; take the D538 in the direction of Vaison-la-Romaine.
☎ 04.75.27.19.89
Closed Wed; Thurs lunchtime; Sun evening Nov–March; the Feb, All Saints' and Christmas school holidays.

When the sun's out it's nice to sit on the lovely shaded patio; otherwise you dine in the colourful dining room with hefty beams and well-spaced tables. The food is good and only fresh seasonal produce is used. Menu €24, *à la carte* around €31. The colourful dishes are full of flavour, very carefully prepared and seasoned, and the fish is cooked to perfection: tasty *terrines*, pan-fried *foie gras* with clarified butter, roast kid with thyme, bream with *sauce vierge*, oyster mushroom *gâteau*, duck breast and wild mushrooms. A fine choice of perfectly ripe

cheeses and various desserts. The wine list has a good selection of Côtes-du-Rhones starting at around €11. Free Myro (the local version of Kir).

SAINT-FERRÉOL-TRENTE-PAS   26110 (10KM NE)

⊜ |●| AUBERGE DE TRENTE PAS

It's in the village; from Nyons, take the D94, then the D70 in the direction of Bourdeaux.
☎ 04.75.27.71.39 ➡ 04.75.27.71.39
e auberge30pas@wanadoo.fr
Closed Nov–March.

The village is typical of those found in the mountains of the Drôme. This straightforward establishment has very simple, clean rooms and family cuisine prepared with soul. You're served in the convivial dining room. There's a short lunch menu for €10, a Sunday lunch version for €17 and others from €14. Véronique makes you feel welcome; she's enjoying her country retreat after years in polluted Paris. Rooms start at €40 and you can stay half board if you wish.

CONDORCET   26110 (7KM E)

|●| LA CHARRETTE BLEUE

route de Gap.
☎ 04.75.27.72.33
Closed Wed and Thurs lunchtime; Sun evening Nov–March.

Word of mouth is always the best publicity – just follow the trail and you'll get here. Very professional, honest cooking: tradition with an individual twist. Fresh herbs from the hills and the heath are deliciously combined: pressed *pot-au-feu*, rack of lamb with a garlic crust and guineafowl with pickled lemons. Menus €15, €20 and €42. Dishes include *foie gras*, triology of local lamb and a platter of the chef's delectable desserts. Lots of Côtes-du-Rhône wines on the list, a Visan-Villages for €15 and a Vinsobres Domaine du Moulin for €11. The dining room is prettily arranged but there's a terrace for sunny days – the best tables are under the olive trees. Delectable cuisine, warm welcome and efficient service.

OYONNAX   01100

⅍ ⊜ NOUVEL HÔTEL**

31 rue René-Nicod (Centre); 150m fron the train station.
☎ 04.74.77.28.11 ➡ 04.74.77.03.71
TV. Pay car park.

Despite its name, this place is getting on a bit

– but it's not without individuality, as you'll see when you get to reception, where there's a display of the plastics for which Oyonnax is famous. The refurbished rooms are good value. Doubles cost €24–27 with basin, €27–30 with shower, while larger rooms with shower/wc or bath go for €36–39. It's the little things they do that make all the difference: you can have breakfast brought to your room for no extra charge. Free use of the garage.

🕺 🛎 |●| HÔTEL-RESTAURANT BUFFARD**

pl. de l'Église; it's in the middle of town, 100m from the train station.
☎ 04.74.77.86.01 ► 04.74.73.77.68
Restaurant closed Fri and Sun evenings; Sat; 25 July–15 Aug. **TV**. **Car park**.

This hotel-restaurant has maintained its excellent reputation for a hundred years – it celebrated its centenary in 1998. Rooms with period furniture cost €27 with basin, €41 with shower/wc and €49 with bath. In the restaurant they serve rich home cooking in generous portions. Menus €11–27. Some include regional specialities such as *quenelles Nantua*, *gratin* of crayfish tails, frog's legs, chicken with morels and *délice* of duck liver. Free apéritif, coffee or house *digestif*, and 10% discount on the room rate.

PEISEY-NANCROIX   73210

🕺 |●| RESTAURANT CHEZ FÉLIX

Plan-Peisey; it's between Les Mélèzes and Val Landry.
☎ 04.79.07.92.41
Closed 1 Sept–20 Dec; 21 April–1 July. **Car park**.

In a nineteenth-century Alpine chalet on the edge of the Vanoise park, this place serves *crêpes*, which you sprinkle with fresh, homemade raspberry juice. There are no set menus, but they offer all sorts of regional specialities *à la carte*. If you opt for *crêpes*, a meal will cost about €12 for a meal of pancakes, and around €23 for a Savoyard meal. There's a bird's-eye view of the Ponturin gorge from the terrace. Free house apéritif.

PONT-D'AIN   01160

🕺 |●| RESTAURANT-BAR LE TERMINUS

71 rue Saint-Exupéry (North); take exit 9 off the A42, then take the N75 in the direction of Bourg-en-Bresse.
☎ and ► 04.74.39.07.17
Closed Sun evening, Mon; evenings before public holidays. **Car park**.

This restaurant has two pretty little dining

rooms and a terrace for warm weather. The real effort goes into the cooking rather than the décor; you get generous portions of regional food at decent prices. Menus start at €11, with others at €14–24. Friendly welcome and efficient service. Free coffee.

PRIVAS   07000

🕺 |●| LE GOURMANDIN

cours de l'Esplanade (Centre); it's on the corner of rue Pierre-Fillat.
☎ 04.75.64.51.52
Closed Sun evening; Mon; Wed; 16 Aug–2 Sept.

This is the best place to eat in Privas – you could genuinely call it a fine table. Philippe Bourjas has a way of modernizing local dishes and refining old recipes with delicate and creative adjustments. And he doesn't stint on the portions, either – both the *cassolette* of cheese ravioli in a cep sauce and the duck *foie gras* are generously served. Menus €15–24. The setting is sober, the service conscientious and pleasant but without fuss. There's a good wine list. Free coffee.

ALISSAS   07210 (4KM SE)

🕺 |●| RESTAURANT LOUS ESCLOS

quartier Rabagnol (Southeast); it's beside the D2, which bypasses Alissas.
☎ 04.75.65.12.73
Closed Sun evening and Mon; 10 days in Aug; a fortnight at Christmas. **Car park**.

A rather stylish place in a slip-road. The air-conditioned dining room is quiet and the bay windows look out over the bare hills. Weekday menu for €10 and others €15–26 include pan-fried snails with s*auce Esclos*, chicken tart with crayfish tail jus, house *charcuterie* and *mignon* of pork with Madeira sauce. Nicely prepared and you can appreciate the quality of the seasonal produce. Incidentally, *esclos* is local dialect for "clogs". Free coffee.

BAIX   07210 (24KM E)

🛎 |●| L'AUBERGE DES QUATRE VENTS**

Route de Chomérac; it's on the D2.
☎ and ► 04.75.85.84.49
Closed Sat lunchtime and Sun evening out of season; the Feb school holidays. **TV**. **Car park**.

There's a soothing atmosphere in the large and light but soberly decorated dining room. Good, local dishes: duck thighs with girolles or fresh cream cheese with soft fruit and a fruit *coulis*. *Menu du jour* €11 and others €21–15 and menus change every two weeks. Fairly priced wines. Smart, quiet rooms cost €27–38 depending on facilities – they're clean and modern.

QUINCIÉ-EN-BEAUJOLAIS   69430

⚹ |●| RESTAURANT AU RAISIN BEAUJOLAIS

How to get there: take the D37 from Beaujeu in the direction of Saint-Vincent and it's on the right about 4km along the road.
☎ 04.74.04.32.79 ➡ 04.74.69.02.12
@cabannes-gerard@wanadoo.fr
Closed evenings; Sat; the first 3 weeks in Aug; the third week in Jan.

The food at this unpretentious bistro is just what you need to soak up all those wine tastings. The chatty proprietor looks after the dining room while his wife runs the kitchen, preparing the tasty, slowly cooked dishes. There's a weekday menu at €11 and others up to €22; dishes include duck breast *terrine*, frog's legs *persillade*, snails in garlic butter and *andouillette Bobosse* (a type of sausage) in Mâcon-Villages and local cream cheese. When it comes to the wine, you have a huge choice of Beaujolais *appellations*. There's an enclosed, air-conditioned terrace, which is great in summer. Free house apéritif.

⚹ |●| AUBERGE DU PONT DES SAMSONS

Le-Pont-des-Samsons; take the D37 in the direction of Beaujeu.
☎ 04.74.04.32.09
Closed Wed evening; Thurs; the first 10 days in Feb. **Car park**.

The crossroads is hardly an ideal location, and the restaurant doesn't look much from the outside. But the décor is nice and it's spotlessly clean. Better still, the excellent dishes are served in huge portions: frog's legs *à la Provençale*, *foie gras*, salad of snail *croustillant*, half cockerel with cider and prunes, zander with butter sauce, fan of red mullet fillets with almonds and basil sauce, duck breast with red fruits, *brioche* with morel sauce, steak with green peppercorns. Four menus €16–33 and around €30 *à la carte*. Attentive service from start to finish. Free coffee.

CHIROUBLES   69115 (11KM NW)

⚹ |●| LA TERRASSE DU BEAUJOLAIS

How to get there: take the D9 to Villié-Morgon, then turn left onto the D86.
☎ 04.74.69.90.79
Closed Mon evening; Mon–Fri from mid-Dec to 1 March; the Feb school holidays. **Car park**.

A gorgeous place on the winding road that leads you to the major Beaujolais vineyards. Blessed by a cool breeze year round, it also has a playground for children, and attracts lots of famililes at weekends. *À la carte* they do good mixed salads, great *terrines* and pastries filled with all manner of sweet and-savoury things. Menus €19–49. Free house apéritif.

RIVE-DE-GIER   42800

⚹ |●| RESTAURANT GEORGES PAQUET

Combeplaine; take the La Madeleine exit off the A47.
☎ 04.77.75.02.18
Closed Mon lunchtime; Tues–Thurs and Sun evenings; the Feb school holidays; mid-July to mid-Aug. **Car park**.

Set in a desolate area of factories and industrial wasteland between the motorway and the main road, this restaurant serves good food. It's got a hushed atmosphere and is decorated in bright, warm colours. The speciality is seafood and there are all sorts of fish served with tasty sauces. There are two weekday lunch menus at €13; the latter offers a choice of three starters and three main courses followed by cheese or dessert. It also includes a drink, so it's very good value for money. The other menus, €18–38, are a bit overpriced. On Friday evening, by reservation only, they can do a menu that offers nothing but desserts – perfect if you've got a sweet tooth. Free coffee.

SAINT-MARTIN-LA-PLAINE   42800 (8KM W)

|●| LE FLAMANT ROSE

How to get there: take the D37, and follow the signs to the Parc Zoologique.
☎ 04.77.75.91.13.
Closed Sun; Mon evening.

The beautiful terrace is the only lovely thing about this big building, which stands in front of a stretch of water opposite the zoo. Inside, however, the two dining rooms get lots of light – though admittedly the one reserved for the excellent and substantial €9 lunchtime menu isn't as attractive as the one where the others (€17–36) are served. The chef takes some risks, successfully combining sweet and savoury flavours, and prepares delicious desserts and home-made bread. They can also prepare you a picnic for about €8. Very warm welcome.

SAINTE-CROIX-EN-JAREZ   42800 (10KM E)

🏃 🏠 |●| LE PRIEURÉ*

How to get there: take the D30.
☎ 04.77.20.20.09 ➡ 04.77.20.20.80
Closed Mon; Jan–Feb. **TV**.

The road leading up to this delightful and beautiful place runs along the Couzon and past the dam. Here you get bed and board in the former guest quarters of a twelfth-century monastery – most of it dismantled during the Revolution, when its stones were used to build the village. The four rooms, €46 with bath, are simple but very well equipped and wonderfully quiet. The restaurant is on the first floor and has a beamed ceiling *à la Française*. Unpretentious, traditional cuisine and regional dishes: home-made *terrine*, tripe with tomato, tripes *au gratin*, *charcuterie* and fresh cheeses. Menus €12–40. The bar has a vaulted ceiling and in summer there's a terrace on the village square – you'll appreciate the freshness of the air up here. Kindly welcome. Free coffee.

ROANNE   42300

🏠 |●| HÔTEL DE L'ANCRE

24 pl. du Maréchal-de-Lattre-de-Tassigny (Centre).
☎ 04.77.71.22.70
Closed Sun and 1–15 Aug.

This modest hotel, in a lovely building of the kind you find in a 1930s seaside resort, doesn't seem to have changed much since that era – even the ashtrays advertise brands that no longer exist. If you're of a nostalgic bent and looking for cheap accommodation, then this is the place for you. Rooms €27 with bath. Home cooking is served in a magnificent dining room with a parquet floor. Menus €8 (weekday lunch) and €13.

🏠 HÔTEL DE LA GRENETTE

12 pl. Maréchal-de Lattre-de-Tassigny (Centre).
☎ 04.77.71.25.59 ➡ 04.77.71.29.69
TV.

A little hotel recently taken over by a lovely couple who've started to refurbish it. Rooms are basic but well maintained; €33 with shower, €37 with shower/wc. The reception may be shut on Friday, Saturday or Sunday afternoons, so it's best to phone in advance.

🏠 HÔTEL TERMINUS**

15 cours de la République (pl. de la Gare) (West); it's opposite the train station.
☎ 04.77.71.79.69 ➡ 04.77.72.90.26
TV. Car park.

A good hotel of its kind, well-located. It has about fifty rooms with bath (€35–40) – they're pretty standard. Ask for one overlooking the courtyard, where it's quieter. The terrace is nice in summer.

|●| LE CENTRAL

20 cours de la République; it's opposite the train station.
☎ 04.77.67.72.72
Closed Sun and Mon; 3 weeks in Aug; a week between Christmas and New Year's Day.

The Troisgros family – the nationally and internationally renowned chefs – have opened up this less expensive restaurant next door to their gourmet flagship, *Troisgros*. Rigged up to look like an old-fashioned grocery store, it sells smartly packaged pots of goodies, mustard with wine, duck *rillettes* and balsamic vinegar. There are photographs of the suppliers on the walls of the two dining rooms. Wonderfully inventive menus at €15 and €20–24, while the *à la carte* menu gives a glimpse of the imagination that goes into the cooking next door. The wine is affordable and served bistro-style, with the bottle uncorked.

🏃 |●| L'AVENTURE

24 rue Pierre-Despierre.
☎ 04.77.68.01.15
Closed Sun and Mon; 3 weeks in Aug; a week at Christmas.

Jean-Luc Trambouze is a young chef from Roanne who's on the way up. You'll find his restaurant in a small street near the Loire. The frontage is bistro-blue but inside there's a cosy dining room decorated in pale colours. The kitchen opens out into the dining room – not to be showy but to add to the friendly atmosphere. The chef's dishes are full of imagination and fresh ideas. There are no particular specialities: it's the dynamism of the cooking and the audaciousness of the seasonings that make the dishes so distinctive. Excellent lunch menu for €17 which includes wine and others €20–46. Affordable wine list. Free coffee.

POUILLY-SOUS-CHARLIEU   42720 (14KM N)

|●| AUBERGE DU CHÂTEAU DE TIGNY

How to get there: take the D487, it's east of the village

and is signposted.
☎ 04.77.60.09.55
Closed Mon and Tues; Wed and Thurs evenings 1 Oct–5 May; 25 Dec–18 Jan; 16 Sept–4 Oct.

This is undoubtedly a favourite spot in the Roanne region. Marie Blin and Jacques Rivière are sometime market gardeners who supplied the region's top restaurants. They both loved old buildings and good food, so they decided to give it all up to restore a magnificent little manor house and turn it into this delightful inn. The menus are exceptional, both for the wide choice offered and for the freshness of the innovative cooking, especially the fish. It's also the best value for money in the region. Weekday lunch menu for €13 and gourmet menus €21–33. When the weather's nice, you can dine on the pleasant terrace or in the cool interior. Marie will give you a charming welcome. The river and lake add to the wonderful setting.

NOAILLY   42640 (15KM NW)

🏃 🏠 |●| CHÂTEAU DE LA MOTTE***

La Motte; take the N7 to Saint-Germain-Lespinasse, then the D4 towards Charlieu. It's between Noailly and La Benisson-Dieu.
☎ 04.77.66.64.60 ➡ 04.77.66.64.38
Closed Sun evening and Mon except July–Aug; 1 Nov to Palm Sunday. **Swimming pool**. **TV**. **Car park**.

This romantic château is in the upper price bracket but it's very special. The absolutely charming rooms are decorated and furnished with imagination and taste. Doubles €69–92. Traditional local cuisine is listed on the weekday lunch menu, which at €14 is excellent value, and there are others €21–45. You can go horseriding with owner Sylvie Fayolle, there's a swimming pool in the grounds and a pergola down by the ornamental lake which is perfect for a few quiet hours with a book. If you stay four nights, the prices go down. 10% discount on the room rate Sept–June.

ROMANS-SUR-ISÈRE   26100

🏃 🏠 HÔTEL MAGDELEINE

31 av. Pierre Sémard (Centre); the road runs at right angles to the station.
☎ 04.75.02.33.53 ➡ 04.75.72.78.38
Closed Sun except for reservations; 2–20 Jan. **TV**.

A strategically placed hotel right near the station, the historic centre and the factory shops. The owner originates from the Vosges and he runs the place expertly. He does everything himself – reception, cleaning, breakfasts and even the ironing. The rooms are being renovated one after the other, they're quite big and have new bedding and efficient double glazing. Doubles with shower or bath €35. It's spotlessly clean and you get a genuinely warm welcome. 10% discount on the room rate.

🏃 🏠 |●| HÔTEL DES BALMES**

Hameau des Balmes; it's about 4km from the centre; take the D532, Tain road for 2km, then turn right in the direction of Les Balmes.
☎ 04.75.02.29.52 ➡ 04.75.02.75.47
📧 hoteldesbalmes@wanadoo.fr
Closed Sun out of season and a week in Jan **Restaurant closed** Mon lunchtime. **Swimming pool**. **TV**. **Pay car park**.

This hotel, in a sleepy little village, has twelve pretty rooms with bath and balcony for €43. In the restaurant, *Au Tahiti*, the owners have created an exotic décor with glass beads and shells. The cooking is strictly regional French – Drôme guineafowl, lamb from the Préalpes. Menus €13–18. The local council has introduced a tourist tax of €0.60 per person per day. Free *apéritif*.

🏃 |●| RESTAURANT LA CASSOLETTE

16 rue Rebatte (Centre); it's in a pedestrianized street near tour Jacquemart.
☎ 04.75.02.55.71
Closed Sun; Mon; 27 July–19 Aug.

An intimate restaurant in a charming, thirteenth-century building, where the three dining rooms have vaulted ceilings. There's a range of menus, €12–41, listing aubergine caviare with asparagus tips, red mullet fillets with puréed red peppers, saddle of lamb with thyme vinaigrette and scallop ravioli. Extensive wine list. Free coffee.

🏃 |●| LE CAFÉ DES ARTS

49 cours Pierre Didier (Centre).
☎ 04.75.02.77.23
Closed Sun.

The round dining room is encircled by a veranda. It's a bit smart but not formal because it's softened by lots of green plants and you can watch the chefs behind the glass. The dishes are substantial with lots of fresh fish dishes – try tuna and salmon *tartare*, roast sea bream with dilll *jus*, pan-fried king prawns on a bed of red peppers. Local dishes figure on the menus too, and carnivores are well-catered-for – duck breast with orange, *foie gras*, steak *tartare*. *Formule* (with choices of two out of three courses) €14 and menus €18–24. Wine by the glass.

The service is efficient and friendly. They open the terrace under the plane trees when the sun shines; it's cut off from the road (which can be noisy in the daytime) by a thick green hedge. Free house *digestif*.

GRANGES-LÈS-BEAUMONT   26600 (4KM W)

⚘ 🏠 |●| LES VIEILLES GRANGES**

Granges-lès-Beaumont; take the D53 Tain road for 3km then turn left at the sign.
☎ 04.75.71.50.43 ➡ 04.75.71.59.79
Closed Sun evening, Mon, and Tues lunchtime. **TV. Car park.**

This collection of old buildings overlooking the Isère, surrounded by mature fruit trees, has been renovated and turned into a romantic hotel-restaurant with a terrace shaded by lime trees. Comfortable double rooms go for €37–49 with shower/wc or bath – the more expensive ones have a river view. In the dining room you can eat tasty food, with menus at €13–30. It's easy to decide on the main course – ravioli, regional specialities such as *caillette* (pork and vegetable faggot) and frogs' legs – but more difficult to choose a wine from the extensive list. Luckily the staff are patient and helpful. Free house apéritif.

SAINT-AGRÈVE   07320

🏠 |●| DOMAINE DE RILHAC**

Lieu-dit Rilhac; from Saint-Agrève, follow the road to Le Cheylard for about 1km; take the D21 fork off the D120 and follow the arrows.
☎ 04.75.30.20.20 ➡ 04.75.30.20.00
Closed Tues evening to Thurs; Jan–Feb. **TV. Car park.**

A sixteenth-century farm that has been tastefully restored and converted into a delightful hotel-restaurant. It's a luxury place at affordable prices, set deep in the countryside in a stunning spot facing monts Mézenc and Gerbier. It has a dressed-stone façade, blue shutters and finely engraved wrought ironwork inside, which goes well with the ochre plaster and the exposed beams. Six double rooms from €64. Breakfast is served until 10.30am. Half board might be compulsory July–Aug, so it's best to check. A three-course weekday lunch menu at €21 and others €33–67. The *à la carte* menu changes with the seasons but the price can spiral out of control; specialities include ox tail with Cornas wine saude, trout salad, carpaccio of beef, duck breast with chestnut flower honey and iced nougat with *marrons glacés*.

SAINT-AUBAN-SUR-L'OUVEZE   26170

⚘ 🏠 |●| AUBERGE DE LA CLAVELIÈRE

It's in the main street of the village; on the D546, halfway between Buis-les-Baronnies and Séderon.
☎ 04.75.28.61.07 ➡ 04.75.28.60.30
Closed Sat lunchtime; a week in June; a week in Sept; 20 Dec–5 Jan.

A great mariner, François-Hector d'Albert, who fought for the Americans in the War of Independence, hailed from this charming village way off the beaten track. In its centre is this simple, warm and welcoming hotel in a solid stone house. There are the simplest of rooms but they're well maintained and have good beds; doubles €38. Between 1 July and 1 Sept, half board at €34 per person, is compulsory. In winter not all the rooms are open, so it's best to telephone in advance. The cooking offers stalwart family-style and regional dishes. Local workers and travelling salesmen head here at lunchtime to make the most of the €11 menu. The menus at €16 and €21 are more elaborate: sardines *escabèche*, duck breast with honey, smoked salmon ravioli salad, and honey and lavender flan. Free *digestif*.

SAINT-ÉTIENNE   42000

⚘ 🏠 HÔTEL LE CHEVAL NOIR**

11 rue François-Gillet (Centre).
☎ 04.77.33.41.72 ➡ 04.77.37.79.19
TV. Car park.

This old hotel, which had lost its original splendour, was bought by a couple of former bankers who completely renovated the place. Most of the numerous rooms have good, modern facilities, and prices are very modest considering its central location: doubles go for €29 with shower and €43 with bath, with cheaper deals during the week. 10% discount.

⚘ 🏠 |●| HÔTEL LE BALADIN**

12 rue de la Ville (Centre); it's in a busy pedestrianised street.
☎ 04.77.37.17.97 ➡ 04.77.37.17.17
Closed Snack bar on Sun; 23 July–23 Aug. **TV.**

This place fills up very quickly, especially during the theatre season when the actors appearing at the Comédie de Saint-Étienne stay here. It's a pleasant little hotel with fourteen small rooms for €30 with shower or €37 with bath. They serve food in the snack bar on the ground floor – dish of the day €6.

Free coffee and 10% discount on the room rate at weekends.

🏃 🏠 HÔTEL DES ARTS**

11 rue Gambetta (Centre).
☎ 04.77.32.42.11 ➡ 04.77.34.06.72
TV. Pay car park.

Not far from the museum of old Saint-Étienne, in a small square off the Grand-Rue where the trams run, this two-star hotel is good value for money. Doubles €46 with shower/wc or bath. Very friendly welcome and English spoken. 10% discount.

🏃 🏠 |●| HÔTEL TERMINUS DU FOREZ***

31 av. Denfert-Rochereau; it's opposite the Châteaucrux station, five minutes from the centre.
☎ 04.77.32.48.47 ➡ 04.77.34.03.30
✉ hotel.forez@wanadoo.fr
Closed 6–27 Aug. **TV. Car park**.

This is a big, classic three-star hotel, with stylish rooms with original paintings on the walls. Doubles €53 with shower/wc and €60 with bath. If you walk down the stairs you can pick up a guide to the local tourist attractions in the region. Excellent welcome. The restaurant, La Loco, is on the ground floor, where they serve seasonal dishes is more than satisfactory. Cheapest menu €11, then €18–35. 10% discount on the room rate Thurs–Mon.

🏠 |●| L'ALBATROS

67 rue Saint-Simon; turn left after the arms factory, opposite the golf course.
☎ 04.77.41.41.00 ➡ 04.77.38.28.16
Closed a fortnight in Aug; a fortnight Dec–Jan.
Disabled access. Swimming pool. TV. Car park.

A place to enjoy peace and greenery, overlooking the golf course, in the upper part of the town. The rooms here are modern and functional and cost €69. Good welcome.

🏃 |●| LA FOURCHETTE GOURMANDE

10 rue Francis Garnier (Centre).
☎ 04.77.41.76.86
Closed Sat lunchtime and Sun evening.

This place is a real favourite. It used to be the Saint-Étienne football team's favourite back in the glory days of the 1970s. But just like the team, the place went downhill more recently – until the new owner took over. He's friendly and professional, and has completely refurbished the dining room and revolutionized the menu: seafood pot with king prawns, salad of Fourme cheese with walnuts, shrimp *clafoutis* with asparagus tips, roast saddle of lamb with rosemary and *mille-*

feuille of caramelized apples – refined, luscious dishes. Lunch *menu du jour* €9, others €14–25. Free apéritif.

🏃 |●| CORNES D'AUROCHS!

18 rue Michel-Servet; it's 150m from the town hall.
☎ 04.77.32.27.27
Closed Sat and Mon lunchtimes; Sun; 20 July–30 Aug.

A fun bistro offering Lyonnais cooking and traditional specials including dishes with wild mushrooms – *andouillette*, *tablier de sapeur*, a "Gargantua" platter (which gives you a bit of everything), steak *tartare*, fillet steak with ceps, duck *confit*. The €12 lunch menu is a good deal with others at €16–32. The owner is jovial, his wife is smiling and welcoming. They don't like you to smoke in the restaurant. Free pear liqueur or Marc du Pays at the end of your meal.

🏃 |●| RESTAURANT LA RISSOLÉE

23 rue Pointe-Cadet (Centre); it's on the edge of the pedestrianised area.
☎ 04.77.33.58.47
Closed lunchtimes; Sun; Aug.

What's unusual about this restaurant, which is in a district that boasts lots of them, is is that it serves Belgian specialities – and, aptly, the menus are written on recycled *Tintin* albums. They do huge plates of food: mounds of rissoled potatoes, substantial helpings of mussels cooked in 33 different ways and served with chips. In the evening they offer superb *carbonade*. Menus €14–21, beer included. Try an "SB", the house cocktail – it'll blow your head off. Free house *digestif*.

|●| CARPE DIEM

6 rue Léon Nautin.
☎ 04.77.38.65.36
Closed Sun and Mon evenings. **Disabled access**.

You go along a small pedestrianized street in the old town to get to this restaurant, where the dining room is a pleasant mixture of old stone, ochre and blue. The cooking is a delight: foie gras cooked in three ways, *croustillant* of salmon and scallops, duck breast with morels, chocolate cream and soft fruit *au gratin*. Menus €14–42. The service is executed with great care and finesse. Superb wine list and another with Kirs, whiskies and even cigars.

🏃 |●| LE CERCLE

15 pl. de l'Hôtel-de-Ville (Centre).
☎ 04.77.25.27.27
Closed Sun and Mon evenings; 1–19 Aug.

This restaurant occupies part of the former

premises of the Saint-Étienne bridge club, in a superb building opposite the town hall. The owners have kept the panelling and the gilding in one of the most beautiful rooms, which is pure Napoleon III in style. The restaurant attracts local worthies but prices are nevertheless very reasonable, with a weekday lunch *formule* (main course and dessert) and menus €15–49. Decent food, pleasantly presented, and friendly service. Free apéritif.

🌴 |●| RESTAURANT À LA BOUCHE PLEINE

8 pl. Chavanelle; it's near the fire station.
☎ 04.77.33.92.47
Closed Sat and Sun; weekday lunchtimes; Aug.

Photos of the regulars cover the walls of the cosy little dining room, where you'll bump into actors and sundry nightowls congregating into the small hours. Like them, when you've finished a meal lovingly prepared by Henriette, you'll want to be told the recipe for the *diable au corps*, the explosive house cocktail – they actually set light to it. You get a really nice welcome from Marco. Menus €18–27. The cooking is the sort you get in a classic Lyonnais bistro: chicken with prawns, *tablier du sapeur*, cheese soufflé. Best to book. Free apéritif.

|●| NOUVELLE

30 rue St-Jean (Centre).
☎ 04.77.32.32.60
Closed Sun evening; Mon; the first fortnight in Jan; 3 weeks in Aug.

The fashionable place to eat in Saint-Étienne, right in the centre of town. It's got everything a gourmet restaurant should have – subtle décor, professional staff and the kind of menu you dream about – but it doesn't charge the prices you might expect. Menus €15 (weekday lunch) then €24–53. The young chef loves to revamp dishes like *brandade de morue* (salt cod pounded with garlic, olive oil and cream), and does creative things with pasta – ravioli stuffed with lamb or salmon lasagna. Portions are generous, and it's all very imaginative – even if some sauces are not as light as they could be. It's best to book.

SAINT-PRIES-EN-JAREZ   42270 (2KM N)

|●| RESTAURANT DU MUSÉE

Lieu-dit La Terrasse; follow the signs to the museum of modern art.
☎ 04.77.59.24.52
Closed Sun evening.

Stéphane Laurier (who runs the *Nouvelle*

restaurant in town), has taken over this restaurant inside the museum. His cooking is very inventive, skilfully using spices and mixing unusual flavours – try the *croustillant* of fish. Lunch menus €10 and €13 and *menu-cartes* at €14 and €18. Even the cheapest menu changes every month and you get excellent value for money. Efficient service. And there's a lovely terrace that opens in warm weather.

SAINT-GENEST-MALIFAUX   42660 (12KM S)

🌴 ▤ |●| AUBERGE DE CAMPAGNE LA DILIGENCE

Le Château du Bois; take the N82 to Bicètre then the D501 and it's 3km from the village.
☎ 04.77.39.04.99
Closed Mon and Tues except July–Aug; Jan. **Car park**.

This was orignially a farmhouse belonging to the thirteenth-century castle, which is still inhabited. Now it's a really nice restaurant and is part of the agricultural college of Saint-Genest. Good food and pleasant service with seasonal menus for €10 on weekdays then others at €15–23. The handsome dining room has a fireplace and there's a terrace in the farm courtyard. You can camp in the grounds for next to nothing and a night in a gîte costs €9 (breakfast not included). It's a horse farm so you can go riding. It's advisable to book. Free apéritif.

🌴 |●| RESTAURANT MONTMARTIN

18 rue du Velay; take the N82, then the D501 to Plafony.
☎ 04.77.51.21.25
Closed evenings except for reservations; Wed; a week in Jan; a week in July.

Located in one of the less attractive villages in this part of the world, this place was established after World War II by the grandmother of the present owners – they've kept the warm atmosphere and the creaking parquet. No nouvelle cuisine here; this is the place for generous portions of rich food including morels, frog's legs and *quenelles*. Weekday menu €12 and others €15–28. It's very popular with families for Sunday lunch. Free *digestif*.

SAINT-VICTOR-SUR-LOIRE   42230 (15KM W)

|●| LE CROQUE CERISE

Base Nautique de Saint-Victor; take the D3A.
☎ 04.77.90.07.54
Closed Sun and Wed evenings; Mon; Jan–Feb.
Disabled access. Car park.

The big building is not particularly elegant,

but the dining rooms with their large windows and the terrace by the harbour are really pleasant. Attentively prepared, simple dishes include whitebait, pizza cooked in a wood-fired oven and grapefruit *terrine*. Weekday menu €12 and others €21–27. The food, service and welcome are spot-on.

SAINT-PAUL-EN-CORNILLON 42240 (17KM SW)

🎿 |●| LA CASCADE

How to get there: go in the direction of Firminy, take the D3 and turn left onto the D46 before the bridge.
☎ 04.77.35.70.02
Closed Mon in winter; the first week in Sept. **Car park**.

No views of cascades, as it happens, but you do get the Loire instead. The classic dining room gets lots of light, and there's a very pleasant terrace shaded by plane trees and an impressive sequoia. It's a pity that the car park is so badly placed between the terrace and the river. The chef's speciality is king prawns grilled with saffron, and the menus provide dishes such as salad of Fourme de Montbrison cheese and trout *meunière*. Thoughtfully prepared, simple food, served with care. Menus €17–30. Free apéritif.

BESSAT (LE) 42660 (18KM SE)

🛏 |●| HÔTEL LA FONDUE – RESTAURANT CHEZ LE PÈRE CHARLES**

Grande-Rue (Centre).
☎ 04.77.20.40.09 ➡ 04.77.20.45.20
Closed Sun evening 1 March–3 Nov. **TV**. **Car park**.

A good restaurant way up at 1170m in the middle of the Pilat regional park, where the people of Lyon and Saint-Étienne come to get a bit of fresh air. Splendid gourmet dishes: goose *foie gras*, *tournedos* with paprika cream, veal chops with girolles, trout stuffed with ceps and a selection of sweets and home-made chocolate desserts. Dish of the day €10, and lots of menus at €11–39. Warm atmosphere. Doubles €32 with shower/wc and €43 with bath. The bathrooms are big but the rooms with shower have a rather strange arrangement – a revolving cupboard which hides the toilet and the shower.

🎿 🛏 |●| AUBERGE DE LA JASSERIE

La Jasserie; it's 6km after Le Bessat – follow the arrows from the village.
☎ 04.77.20.40.16 ➡ 04.77.20.45.43
Closed Wed in winter, except during school holidays. **Disabled access**. **TV**.

This old farmhouse, with its little bell tower, is

a bit of an institution. It's one of those simple country inns that hasn't changed for generations, where you sit at wooden tables and chairs in a huge old dining room. It's at the bottom of the ski runs so it's an ideal place to warm up over a hot chocolate and a slice of bilberry tart. The only drawback is that it's too crowded and noisy at the weekend. Menus €9–27. If you want to stay, you can sleep on a bunk-bed in their basic dormitory for €11; you have to share facilities and go half-board. Free house apéritif.

SAINT-JUST-SAINT-RAMBERT 42170 (20KM NW)

🎿 |●| RESTAURANT DU REMPART

2 rue de la Loire; take the turning westward off the D8, when you're going in the direction of St-Genest-Lerpt.
☎ 04.77.52.13.19
Closed Sun evening and Mon; 4–26 Aug.

A couple of rustic dining rooms up on the first floor of a very old house built in the town walls. There's a gifted, inventive chef at work – excellent *foie gras* in particular. Menus €14–31. Smiling, pleasant service. In summer, meals are served on the flowery terrace at the foot of the town walls. Free coffee.

SAINT-CHRISTO-EN-JAREZ 42320 (23KM NE)

🛏 |●| HÔTEL-RESTAURANT BESSON – LES TOURISTES*

route de la Combe; go to Saint-Chamond, then take the D2 in the direction of Valfleury and col de la Gachet.
☎ 04.77.20.85.01
Closed Wed and 1–15 Sept.

Far away from the hurly-burly of Saint-Étienne and Saint-Chamond, at an altitude of 800m on the south side of the Monts du Lyonnais, this quiet, old-fashioned hotel offers rooms with a view of the Pilat mountain range. Doubles €29 with bath and wc along the landing. It's pretty standard food in the restaurant, but they do have good *charcuteries*. You can get a country snack or choose from menus at €11–24. Disabled access in the restaurant.

SAINT-MARCELLIN-EN-FOREZ 42680 (25KM NW)

|●| MANOIR DU COLOMBIER

9 rue Carles-de-Mazenod; on the A72, take the Andrézieux-Bouthéon exit, the D8 to Bouson and the D498 to the village.
☎ 04.77.52.90.37
Closed Tues evening and Wed.

In a little village at the foot of the Forez mountains this beautiful sixteenth-century manor house clings to the past. There are three dining rooms, all decorated differently, and a wonderful courtyard where you can eat. The food is pleasant, if not particularly sophisticated, and portions are generous. The cheapest menu at €15 is good and there are others €21–41. If you can stretch to it, treat yourself to the tasty roast pigeon. Friendly welcome.

SAINT-SAUVEUR-EN-RUE   42220 (25KM S)

⚎ 🏠 |●| CHÂTEAU DE BOBIGNEUX

Bobigneux; take the N82 south to col du Grand-Bois, then the D22 for 11km; it's 2.5km from the village.
☎ 04.77.39.24.33 ➥ 04.77.39.25.74
e chateau-de-bobigneux@wanadoo.fr
Closed Wed and Jan–Feb. **Car park**.

After eighteen years in Greenland the owners moved here and took over this sixteenth-century stone manor house, which is right next to a farm belonging to Madame's brother. They've created a delightful place to stay and prices are reasonable. The farm provides them with all the fresh produce they need, and Monsieur, who is a talented chef, creates great dishes. There's a *menu campagnard* served in the week for €11 and others up to €23. The dining rooms have been pleasantly renovated, and the terrace and garden are both lovely. There are six pretty, bright, spacious country-style rooms for €35–38. The welcome is charming. Free apéritif.

SAINT-GALMIER   42330

|●| LA CHARPINIÈRE***

Lieu-dit la Carpinière.
☎ 04.77.52.75.00 ➥ 04.77.54.18.79
TV. Swimming pool. Car park.

A splendid establishment in substantial grounds that guarantee quiet. Pleasant and functional rooms €70. They have a range of facilities including a fitness centre, Turkish bath, sauna, tennis courts and a swimming pool. The restaurant is in a conservatory and offers high-quality cooking that's both original and refined. Menus €12–38. The service is particularly attentive. It's not the cheapest place, but you won't be let down.

|●| LE BOUGAINVILLIER

Pré Château; it's signposted from the Badoit source on the banks of the Coise.
☎ 04.77.54.03.31
Closed Sun and Wed evenings; Mon; the Feb school holidays; 3 weeks in Aug. **Car park**.

A pretty building swathed in Virginia creeper

in the rather stylish little town which is the source of Badoit mineral water. In the evening, the local inhabitants form a queue to collect their free fizzy water. The restaurant has three dining rooms, one of them a veranda overlooking a walled garden by the water's edge. Gérard Charbonnier is one of the most interesting young chefs in the area. He spent two years in Gagnaire's well-known restaurant, where he was encouraged to be creative. His fish dishes are delicate and skilfully prepared. The €20 menu isn't available at weekends, when there are others €28–45. Charming, low-key welcome. Well worth the fifteen-minute drive from Saint-Étienne.

VEAUCHE   42340 (6KM S)

🏠 |●| HÔTEL-RESTAURANT DE LA GARE

55 av. H.-Planchet; take the D12 – it's next to the train station and a huge factory.
☎ 04.77.54.60.10 ➥ 04.77.94.30.53
Closed evenings; Sun; public holidays. **Car park**.

A reliable neighbourhood restaurant providing good food at sensible prices. There's a weekday menu at €8 and others €11–38. The menus list fine, delicately prepared dishes: *compotée* of pig's trotters or salmon flan, *foie gras*, fish dishes and a good selection of desserts. Pleasant, conventional décor and a warm friendly welcome. The hotel has ten basic rooms for €18 with basin up to €25 with shower/wc. A place to bear in mind if you're stuck for somewhere to stay – under general circumstances, however, the view of the station and the factory is probably not quite what you're looking for.

ANDREZIEUX-BOUTHÉON   42160 (8KM S)

⚎ 🏠 |●| LES IRIS***

32 rue Jean-Martouret; take the D12.
☎ 04.77.36.09.09 ➥ 04.77.36.09.00
Closed Sun evening and Mon; a week in the Feb school holidays; a fortnight in Aug; a week at All Saints'.
Disabled access. Garden. Swimming pool. TV. Car park.

This handsome residence, which you reach by ascending two elegant flights of steps, stands on the outskirts of a rather industrial town near Saint-Étienne airport. The ten functional but pleasant bedrooms, named after flowers, are in the annexe. They overlook the swimming pool and the garden with its gigantic cedar trees; they go for €69 with bath. The restaurant serves conventional cuisine and has a décor to match. Menus at €18–50. It's a place to take the family, for a romantic weekend or even a business seminar. 10% discount on the room rate July–Aug.

CHAZELLES-SUR-LYON   42140 (10KM NE)

🎿 🛏 |O| CHÂTEAU BLANCHARD**

36 route de Saint-Galmier; very near the hat museum.
☎ 04.77.54.28.88 ➡ 04.77.54.36.03
Closed Sun evening, Mon and a fortnight in Jan.
Disabled access. TV. Car park.

This so-called castle, in France's millinery capital, is actually a 1930s folly that was once the home of a hat-maker. It lay neglected for forty years but has since been restored to its original splendour. The garish frontage is decorated with friezes, while inside the décor is a glorious confusion of neo-greco-classical-kitsch. Very well-equipped doubles from €47 with bath; number 6 (€62 per night) has original décor. The restaurant fits into its surroundings very nicely. You'll get a warm welcome and classic, well-presented menus starting at €17 on weekdays with others €21 or €20 à la carte. It specializes in fresh fish. You can eat on the terrace. Free *digestif*.

SAINT-JEAN-DE-MAURIENNE   73300

🎿 🛏 |O| HÔTEL-RESTAURANT DU NORD**

pl. du Champ-de-Foire.
☎ 04.79.64.02.08 ➡ 04.79.59.91.31
e info@hoteldunord.net
Closed Sun evening and Mon lunchtime except Feb and July–Aug; 15 Oct–15 Nov. **TV. Car park**.

A former coaching inn with a little tower. The restaurant, which has a vaulted ceiling and stone walls, is in the old stables. The cooking is well-judged and reliable, and although it's classic the chef has some original ideas – try home-made *foie gras*, guineafowl breast with cheese sauce, *chaud-froid* of home-smoked salmon or beef steak with morels. There's an €12 weekday menu, and others up to €32. The rooms are identical and offer good value for money. Doubles €42 with shower/wc. 10% discount on the room rate and free house apéritif.

SAINT-MARTIN-DE-BELLEVILLE   73440

🎿 🛏 |O| LE LACHENAL**

Centre; 50m from the ski-lifts.
☎ 04.79.08.96.29 ➡ 04.79.08.94.23
Closed mid-April to end June; 1 Sept–20 Dec.

A lovely doll's house of a place, with cosy rooms with flower-painted shutters and panelled walls. Doubles €53 with shower/wc or bath. Simple, flavourful dishes: fillet of Salers beef with mushrooms, *fondue* flavoured with Kirsch, duck *foie gras* cooked in a cloth and bilberries in flaky pastry. Menus €16–31. The Lemattre family are wonderful hosts. It's often full, so it's best to book. 10% discount on the room rate in summer.

🎿 |O| LA BOUITTE

Quartier Saint-Marcel; take the D117 towards Les Ménuires (about 2km).
☎ 04.79.08.96.77
Closed May–June and Sept–Dec. **Car park**.

Without doubt, this is the best restaurant in the valley. They combine simple ingredients in astonishing ways to create excellent dishes that are full of flavour: salad of lean bacon and *croutons*, hot *foie gras* escalope on a corn *galette*, calf's liver with spinach, rabbit tart with shallot conserve. The desserts are out of this world, as are the *petits fours* they serve with coffee. You'll have a first-class meal in the stylish country dining room. Attentive, faultless service. Menus €25–48 – well worth it for the wonderful cooking. Free coffee.

SAINT-MARTIN-EN-HAUT   69850

🎿 |O| RESTAURANT LES QUATRE SAISONS

pl. de l'Église (Centre).
☎ 04.78.48.69.12
Closed Tues and 1–15 Sept.

A surprising restaurant on the pretty square of a hilltop village at the edge of the Monts du Lyonnais. Generous portions of seasonal dishes are served in the fresco-lined dining room. Lunch menu €11, then others €15–27. The welcoming owners know how to take care of their customers. Free coffee.

AVEIZE   69610 (9KM NW)

🎿 🛏 |O| HÔTEL-RESTAURANT RIVOLLIER

Le bourg; take the D34.
☎ 04.74.26.01.08 ➡ 04.74.26.01.90
Closed Mon.

It's a wonder how a place this size can survive in such a small village. But once you've experienced the sheer professionalism, first-class welcome and service, and eaten a superb meal in the pleasant airy dining room, you'll be less surprised. They offer delectable menus at €10 (weekdays) and €14–23 and a wide selection of dishes of the day such as *ballotine* of duck with figs and pike soufflé with shrimps. If you're stuck for accommodation, they also have eight very basic rooms at €30 with shower or €33 with bath. Free apéritif.

SAINT-PIERRE-DE-CHARTREUSE   38380

🕏 🏠 |●| HÔTEL DU NORD**

It's on the main street.
☎ 04.76.88.61.10 ➡ 04.76.88.64.07
Closed a week in June. **Car park.**

A lovely atmospheric place with fresh, spruce rooms decorated with period furniture. Doubles €21 with basin up to €37 with shower/wc or bath/wc. All the rooms are different and a pair are split-level. The dining room has a fireplace, it's warm and there are lots of ornaments and paintings on the wall. Classic specialities in the restaurant: *fondues*, *tartiflette*, trout with almond, coconut tart. Menus €11 (not Sun) and up to €27. Decent Côtes-du-Rhone at modest prices. Shady garden. Free house apéritif and coffee.

🕏 🏠 |●| L'AUBERGE DU CUCHERON*

Col du Cucheron (north); it's 3km north of the town centre, on the D512.
☎ 04.76.88.62.06 ➡ 04.76.88.65.43
Closed Sun evening and Mon except during school holidays, and 15 Oct–25 Dec. **Car park.**

This nice old inn, surrounded by trees, is one of a dying breed. The views are magnificent and the *patronne* is charming. There are seven rooms at €27–38. Half board at €35–38 per person is compulsory in school holidays. Menus €16–27, or around €20 *à la carte* with specialities such as salmon and scorpion fish *terrine*, quail with sour cherry, veal with morels and iced nougat. You're just 20m from the ski runs in winter, and it's deliciously peaceful in summer. 10% discount on the room rate except in school holidays.

SAINT-HUGHES-DE-CHARTREUSE 38380 (4KM S)

🕏 |●| LA CABINE

It's next to the church-museum.
☎ 04.76.88.67.13
Open daily from Jan to mid-March and July–Sept; weekends only the rest of the year. **Car park.**

Service 10am–2am. The restaurant is in a converted school. There's a nice combination of white wood and rough-hewn stone.

There are some sculptures, tools, domestic implements and dried flowers to decorate the place. The pleasant terrace overlooks the forest and the beginning of the cross-country ski trails. Dishes such as *tartiflette* (to order an hour in advance), *fondues*, lots of salads, savoury tarts, omelettes, *crêpes* and icecreams. The €10 menu is served until 9.30pm and a meal *à la carte* costs around €14. They have live music in the evening – jazz, blues and French song. Free coffee.

SAINTE-EULALIE   07510

🕏 🏠 |●| HÔTEL DU NORD**

Centre; it's opposite the church.
☎ 04.75.38.80.09 ➡ 04.75.38.85.50
Closed Wed except July– Aug, and 11 Nov–11 Feb.
Disabled access. Car park.

This hotel has had a facelift. Half the rooms have been refurbished, and there are two new sitting rooms, one with a veranda; both have magnificent views over the Loire plain. Double rooms €36–38 with shower/wc or €40–43 with bath. Menus at €15–25 list interesting specialities such as duck thigh *confit* with bilberry sauce, trout *soufflé* with *beurre blanc* and pork *estouffade* in Ardèche wine. For dessert you absolutely must try the *crème brûlée* with bilberries and raspberries. This place is a magnet for fans of fly-fishing – the chef is smitten by the sport. Free apéritif.

SAGNES ET DOUDOULET   07450 (8KM SW)

🕏 🏠 |●| HOSTELLERIE CHANEAL**

It's in the edge of the village, on the Buzet road.
☎ 04.75.38.80.88 ➡ 04.75.38.80.54
Disabled access. TV.

Instead of leaving the country for the town, the young chef decided to stay and take over the family business – he's the fourth generation to run the place. The climate is harsh and the winters are long which doesn't make things easy, so business is seasonal – sometimes when the snow is deep, it's hard even to get deliveries up here. Inside the thick walls, the rooms are comfortable and the walls are built of stone and wood. Comfortable doubles with shower/wc or bath/wc for €38. The chef uses carefully selected local produce and he makes the *charcuterie* and bread himself, as well as the *terrines* of wild plants and local trout. Menus €15–23. Fantastically warm welcome. Free *digestif*.

SAMOËNS 74340

⚄ 🏠 |●| LE MOULIN DU BATHIEU**

Verclan: take the D4 in the direction of Morillon, then turn left to Samoëns 1600.
☎ 04.50.34.48.07 ➡ 04.50.34.43.25
📧 moulin-du-bathieu@wanadoo.fr
Closed 29 April–1 June; 4 Nov–21 Dec. **TV**. **Car park**.

The only thing to break the silence here is the babbling brook that used to turn the mill-wheel. The bedrooms, with their wood-clad walls, have a warm, soothing feel. Several of them are split-level, making them ideal for families. Doubles with shower/wc or bath €53–99. You have to book to eat in the restaurant. Menus €18 and others from €27, one featuring Savoyard specialities: *fondue*, *pela*, *féra*, meats cooked on a stone. Free coffee.

|●| LA FANDOLIEUSE

Centre.
☎ 04.50.34.98.28
Closed spring and autumn but it's worth telephoning.

In the fifteenth century the people of this valley spoke a poetic, sing-song dialect called Mourmé; *fandolieuse* is their word for "dancer". This pleasant little *crêperie*, in a sixteenth-century house with wainscotted walls, has given all its *crêpes* a Mourmé name: *Tapotu* means "drum", *violurin* means "musician", *crépioti* describes the crackling ice and *souffluche* the biting wind. They also do *fondue*s and a very substantial *soupe châtrée* made with bread, Tomme cheese and onions – it's a local speciality, traditionally eaten on the feast of Saint Christopher. *À la carte* only; expect to pay around €15.

SUZE-LA-ROUSSE 26790

⚄ 🏠 |●| HÔTEL LE COMTE**

route de Bollène (West); as you leave town on the Bollène road, it's on the right.
☎ 04.75.04.85.38 ➡ 04.75.04.85.37
Closed 31 Dec–16 Jan. **Disabled access**. **TV**.
Swimming pool. **Car park**.

A big Provençal farmhouse that's been wonderfully converted. It's got shady grounds and a swimming pool. Doubles with luxurious bathrooms and polished wood panelling cost €49–55 with shower/wc or bath. Some are in the tiny keep, and a few have a terrace overlooking the neighbouring vineyards. Excellent menus at €14–28: *caillette* (a local kind of haggis), lamb's trotters, tart with smoked cod mousse, braised beef *à la Provençale*, courgette *au gratin*, *gratin* of warm fruit. Free house apéritif.

SAINT-RESTITUT 26130 (8KM NW)

|●| RESTAURANT LES BUISSES

Southeast; leave Saint-Restitut by the Suze-la-Rousse road, go past the statue of the Virgin Mary, and follow the D218.
☎ 04.75.04.96.50
Closed Sat lunchtime and Mon out of season. **Car park**.

A beautiful country house way out in the truffle-oak forests with a Provençal garden. In summer the crickets sing, and you sit out on the terrace to enjoy robustly flavoured cooking from the south. There's also a spacious, newly decorated dining room with a working fireplace. Lovely welcome and a nice relaxed atmosphere. Lunch menu at €15 and another at €23, with a choice of five flavoursome starters and main courses. Specialities include lamb fondue, *assiette des Buisses* (a platter of aubergine, peppers, pickled tomatoes and courgettes drizzled with local olive oil), deep-fried courgette flowers and so on. Remarkable wine list.

TAIN L'HERMITAGE 26600

🏠 HÔTEL LES 2 COTEAUX**

19 rue Joseph Péla; it's on the bank of Rhône by the pedestrian bridge.
☎ 04.75.08.33.01 ➡ 04.75.08.44.20
Closed Sun and Mon lunchtimes Nov–Feb; end Dec–3 Feb. **TV**. **Pay garage**.

A family hotel in a superb location on the banks of the Rhône just by a bridge to the Ardèche. Though they're a little the worse for wear, the west-facing rooms have a magnificent view of the river and the Château de Tournon; one even has a small terrace. That said, those at the back also have a lovely view, this time over the Hermitage hills. Everything is being renovated progressively; doubles with hand basin or shower €24–26, €37–43 with shower/wc and €43–49 with bath. The breakfast terrace also has a gorgeous view of the Rhône flowing by. Nice welcome.

CROZES-HERMITAGE 26600 (3KM N)

⚄ |●| LE BISTROT DES VINS

How to get there: take the D153 and it's in the village.
☎ 04.75.07.18.03
Closed Wed.

This is serious wine country and this charming village is in the Hermitage vineyard hills. It's a bistro-style dining room with a small terrace, run by a very welcoming young couple. Tasty cuisine using fresh market produce and, naturally enough, you accompany your meal with a jug of the local vintage at knockdown prices. There's one menu only at €15, offering a choice of starters, dish of the day, cheese and dessert. It's doing well and has established a regular clientele so it's best to book. Free house apéritif.

TARARE   69170

🏃 |●| RESTAURANT JEAN BROUILLY

3 ter route de Paris.
☎ 04.74.63.24.56
Closed Sun and Mon; Feb school holidays; 3 weeks in Aug.

The Brouillys have been running things here for a good twenty years. The house, built by an industrialist, is pretty typical of the region and has beautiful grounds. Jean Brouilly is a considerable chef and a welcoming man. Whether you choose the fresh garden salad, the pan-fried *foie gras* with rhubarb, the quartet of scallops with caviar on salt cod mousse, the veal fillet with a magnolia flower, the red mullet with olives or the *millefeuille* with Bourbon vanilla, you'll appreciate his skilful handling of fresh produce and delicate balancing of flavours. He combines herbs, spices and wild produce to most original effect. Menus €24–58. On warm days you can eat on the veranda and admire the grounds. Free glass of Beaujolais.

SARCEY   69490 (12KM E)

🏃 🏠 |●| LE CHATARD**

1 allée du Mas; take the N7 in the direction of Lyon, turn left onto the D118.
☎ 04.74.26.85.85 ➡ 04.74.26.89.99
ⓔ le-chatard@wanadoo.fr
Closed Mon and 1–14 Jan. **Disabled access. Swimming pool. TV. Car park.**

A reliable, peaceful hotel-restaurant with a nice swimming pool. The restaurant attracts businesspeople and local families because of the prices and the top-quality traditional cuisine – €15 for lunch during the week, and others up to €40. Doubles €38–45 with shower/wc or bath/wc; they don't have huge charm but they do have all mod cons. 10% discount July–Aug except on Sat.

THÔNES   74230

🏃 🏠 |●| HÔTEL DU COMMERCE**

5 rue des Clefs (Centre).
☎ 04.50.02.13.66 ➡ 04.50.32.16.24
Closed Sun evening; Wed out of season; a week in April; a fortnight in Nov. **TV. Car park.**

The big attraction here is the food. The chef, Robert Bastard-Rosset, really knows his business, and creates a few inspired surprises – pike *quenelles* (a sort of light fish ball) with a crayfish *coulis* and the best *farcements* in the region. A good range of menus: €12 (weekday lunchtime) and €19–53. Perfect service in a cosy dining room with wood everywhere. The rooms have great views of the forest, even though the place is in the middle of the town. They're very colourful, sometimes a bit too much so, but can't be beaten for value. Doubles €36–66 with shower/wc or bath. The *patronne* has been taking care of her guests for over thirty years. Free *génépy*.

MANIGOD   74230 (6KM SE)

🏃 🏠 |●| HÔTEL-RESTAURANT DE LA VIEILLE FERME**

col de Merdassier; from Thônes, take the D12 then the D16 towards Manigod, go through La Croix-Fry and head for the resort of L'Étale.
☎ 04.50.02.41.49 ➡ 04.50.32.65.53
Closed Wed except in school holidays; 1 May–5 June; 30 Oct–18 Dec. **TV. Car park.**

An archetypal Alpine chalet at the foot of the Étale ski slopes. They have five pretty rooms, at €46–53 with shower or bath. The menus, €9–21, list food that's as typical and authentic as the place – try the *farcement* and leeks *au gratin*. Half board, compulsory during the school holidays, costs €47–53. Charming service. Free coffee.

THONON-LES-BAINS   74200

🏃 |●| RESTAURANT LE VICTORIA

5 pl. des Arts (Centre).
☎ 04.50.71.02.82
Closed Christmas to 1 Jan.

The lovely *belle époque* glass frontage is overrun by greenery, which makes the dining room pleasantly private. They serve good, traditional cooking using fine ingredients, and prepare tasty dishes of both freshwater and sea fish – try the sea bass in a salt crust. In summer they offer huge crispy salads.

Menus €11 (not Sun) and €17–25. Free apéritif.

MARGENCEL   74200 (5KM SW)

⅍ ⬧ |●| HÔTEL-RESTAURANT LES CYGNES**

port de Séchex; when you get to Margencel, head for the port of Séchex on the D33.
☎ 04.50.72.63.10 ➦ 04.50.72.68.22
Closed Tues out of season; Dec–Jan. **TV**. **Car park**.

Known simply as *Chez Jules*, this is a local institution in a small port by the side of Lake Geneva. It's been going since the 1930s. The restaurant is famous for fresh fish – try the soup of freshwater fish, fillets of perch, *féra* (a type of salmon) *à l'ancienne* or fish *pot-au-feu*. Menus €17–33. The rooms are delightful and some have a lake view; €46 with shower/wc. Free coffee and 10% discount in spring and autumn.

ARMOY   74200 (6.5KM SE)

⅍ ⬧ |●| HÔTEL-RESTAURANT LE CHALET**

L'Ermitage; it's on the D26.
☎ 04.50.71.08.11 ➦ 04.50.71.33.88
Closed out of season except for reservations.
Swimming pool. **Garden**. **Car park**.

This building, which does indeed resemble a Swiss chalet, stands at the top of a wooded slope high above the village and Lake Geneva. You get lots of peace and quiet and a superb view from most of the rooms, some of which have their own terrace. If you're here in summer, ask for one of the wooden chalets around the swimming pool. Doubles €27–29 with basin, €37–43 with shower/wc. Menus €14 (except Sun lunch) and €14–21. The cuisine is carefully prepared: home-made *charcuteries*, salmon with tarragon. There's a big garden and a fine view of the lake – you won't want to leave. Free house apéritif.

TOURNON-SUR-RHÔNE   07300

⅍ ⬧ |●| HÔTEL AZALÉES**

6 av. de la Gare (Southwest).
☎ 04.75.08.05.23 ➦ 04.75.08.18.27
Closed Sun evening 15 Oct–15 March; 23 Dec–5 Jan.
Disabled access. **TV**. **Car park**.

You can sit on the terrace and watch the steam train puffing its way through Haut-Vivarais en route to Lamastre. Comfortable, modern doubles €37 with shower or bath. Menus from

€14 list mainly regional cooking with a good goat's cheese flan and, for dessert, iced chestnut soufflé. 10% discount on the room rate.

|●| RESTAURANT AUX SABLETTES

187 route de Lamastre (West); go 3km along the Lamastre road, turn left, and it's opposite the Acacias campsite.
☎ 04.75.08.44.34
Closed Wed except July–Aug and Jan. **Car park**.

This restaurant and bar, which specializes in beer, is a bit out of the way, but it's popular with young locals and people from the nearby campsite. The décor doesn't have much character, but the menu lists a few original specialities: meats and even desserts like mousses and tarts cooked with beer. The less adventurous will be well satisfied with the ravioli, a delicious regional speciality or any of the pizzas baked in a wood-fuelled oven and grills. Menus €10–21.

|●| RESTAURANT L'ESTRAGON

6 pl. Saint-Julien; it's opposite the church.
☎ 04.75.08.87.66
Closed Wed except in summer; Feb–March.

In a great location, in the middle of a pedestrianized area very close to the Rhône, this place offers good, simple food at reasonable prices. Menus €10–17. There's a *pierre chaude* (hot stone) menu, comprising a salad, veal or steak, cheese and dessert. The salads are huge and the zander with red wine and pickled shallots is very tasty. Efficient, attentive service.

TRÉVOUX   01600

⬧ HÔTEL DES VOYAGEURS**

28 rue du Palais; it's near the Parliament building.
☎ 04.74.00.12.343 ➦ 04.74.00.64.24
Closed Aug. **TV**. **Car park**.

It's the only hotel in town but it doesn't rest on its laurels. It's been nicely and cleanly decorated. Doubles from €30. They have an arrangement with the café-bar on the ground floor so you can have a meal delivered during the week.

|●| JOËL CHARLOT

2 place du Pont; it's at the foot of the town on the banks of the Saône next to the tourist office.
☎ 04.74.00.27.23
Closed Sun evening; Mon and Wed Sept–Oct; Feb; 10 days in Aug. **Car park**.

A breath of sea air wafts through this restaurant specializing in fish – they've decorated it with fishing nets and models of sea gulls and created a bistro setting. It's somewhere between a brasserie and a rustic restaurant and is well-run and family-orientated. It looks over the Saône, there's a big terrace and it's set back from the main road. The cuisine is richly flavoured and generously served – take a glance at the kitchen itself, done out in white tiles and very '70s in style. The lunch menu of the day, €11, will revive the spirits for your onward journey but do make the most of all the fish dishes.

|O| CHEZ BRUNO

8 Grande rue; it's opposite the church.
☎ 04.74.00.20.57
Closed Sun, Tues and Thurs evenings; a week April–May; 3 weeks in Aug; a week at New Year.

On the face of things this is an ordinary-looking place but it has a lot going for it: a lovely smiling welcome, tasty dishes with menus that change all the time and lots of quick meals for not much money. Some specialities come from the Mediterranean – *bouillabaisse Sétoise* and *fondue Savoyarde* – but they're all full of flavour. There's a huge buffet table of starters and home-made desserts. Buffet *formule* for €12 and menus €13–19. The plates and serving dishes are made by Bruno's father-in-law, and the décor is bright with lots of paintings by Bruno's wife. It's simple, efficient and a real pleasure.

USSON-EN-FOREZ   42550

🕺 🛏 |O| HÔTEL RIVAL*

rue Centrale (Centre).
☎ 04.77.50.63.65 ➡ 04.77.50.67.62
Closed Mon Oct–June and the Feb school holidays. **TV. Car park**.

A typical family hotel in a little mountain village up in the Forez. The restaurant serves large portions of traditional dishes, with a weekday menu of €10 and others €17–30. Try the warm *galantine* with snails or the *génoise* with veal and morels. You can eat on the terrace. The rooms are clean and affordable, if lacking in character. Doubles €21 with basin and €38 with bath. Very friendly proprietress. Free apéritif and 10% discount on the room rate.

SAINT-BONNET-LE-CHÂTEAU   42380 (14KM NE)

🛏 |O| LE BEFRANC

7 rue d'Augel; it's on the edge of town on the road from

Usso-en-Forez.
☎ 04.77.50.54.54 ➡ 04.77.50.73.17
TV. Car park.

This beautiful town with a medieval centre is the capital of *pétanque*. The hotel is a short distance from the centre and offers spruce rooms that have been attractively decorated. Doubles €32. Regional dishes are the order of the day in the restaurant and menus are priced €13–38. Charming welcome.

VALENCE   26000

🕺 🛏 HÔTEL DE L'EUROPE**

15 av. Félix-Faure (Centre); it's near the tourist office and the station.
☎ 04.75.82.62.65 ➡ 04.75.82.66.66
Closed Sun 2–6pm. **TV. Car park**.

A conveniently located hotel with quiet, air-conditioned rooms that have been completely refurbished. The double glazing is very effective at keeping out the noise from the street below. Doubles with good facilities €33 with shower and €40–45 with bath. One free breakfast when two stay.

🕺 |O| RESTAURANT ONE TWO...TEA

37 Grande Rue (Centre).
☎ 04.75.55.96.31
Closed Sun; public holidays; 11–25 Aug.

The interior is a combination of brick and wood, there are pictures on the walls and vases full of flowers – all supposedly in a "British look". It's crammed at lunchtime and for dinner, though a small terrace takes the overflow in summer. You'll get a substantial meal for a modest €18: chicken liver gateau, *caillette* (a sort of haggis) with shallots and wine sauce, ravioli with cream and absinthe sauce, salmon fillet with anchovy butter, huge salads, steak with shallots, a *gâteau* of chicken livers with tomato *coulis*. It's tasty and filling, but leave room for a portion of the apple pie, crumble or *tarte Tatin*. Good value for money and welcoming staff. Free house apéritif.

🕺 |O| RESTAURANT L'ÉPICERIE

18 pl. Saint-Jean (Centre); it's next to Saint-Jean church.
☎ 04.75.42.74.46
Closed Sat lunchtime and Sun; Aug; Christmas; Easter. **Disabled access**.

It's some time since the grocer's shop closed, but the restaurant that took over the premises continues to flourish. Good, regional dishes: cream of lentil soup with diced *foie gras*, salad of grilled ravioli, roast mountain lamb with morels, monkfish with watercress, red mullet with Syrah wine sauce, Roseval potatoes with wind-dried ham. Menus €18–51. When the weather's nice, you can sit on the terrace on a little square opposite an old covered market and be at peace with the world. Free coffee.

|●| AUBERGE DU PIN

285 [bis] av. Victor Hugo (East); it's not far from the train station.
☎ 04.75.44.53.86
Closed Aug.

The Pic is a four-star deluxe establishment with a two-star restaurant, a Relais & Châteaux sign and prices to match. The *Auberge du Pin* next door is much more affordable. There's a *menu-carte* at €27 – the dishes are prepared in the same kitchen as in the fabulous restaurant next door. The dishes change very frequently. and the cooking is full of flavour and is a combination of local and more traditional choices – Vichyssoise of asparagus, half-cockerel with aromatic herbs and fish *au gratin*. A meal *à la carte* costs around €27. The bright yellow dining room is small, so you ought to reserve in autumn and winter when the terrace isn't open.

VALGORGE   07110

⬛ |●| HÔTEL LE TANARGUE**

chez Coste (Centre).
☎ 04.75.88.98.98 ➡ 04.75.88.96.09
Closed end Dec to beginning of March. **TV**. **Car park**.

Huddling at an altitude of 500m at the foot of Mont Tanargue on the edge of the Ardèche, this cosy hotel offers large pretty doubles for €35–40 with shower/wc and €45–53 with bath/wc. Ask for one with a view of the valley. There's a lunch menu of the day for €9 which includes a main course, dessert and a cup of coffee or glass of wine then others €14–27. Specialities include mountain *charcuterie*, *caillette* and salmon *terrine* with Puy lentils. Portions are generous and particular care is paid to preparing the vegetable dishes. The dining room is vast and there's an impressive pair of giant bellows hanging above the fireplace.

VALLOIRE   73450

⬛ ⬛ |●| HÔTEL CHRISTIANIA**

Centre.

☎ 04.79.59.00.57 ➡ 04.79.59.00.06
e info@christiania.hotel.com
Closed 20 April to mid-June and 10 Sept–10 Dec. **TV**. **Car park**.

Everyone in Valloire seems to drop in for a drink at the lively bar at some point during the day. They're all sports fans and express forthright views on stories in *L'Équipe*, the French daily sports paper. There's a relaxed, friendly, family atmosphere. The rooms are stylish with good facilities; €30 with basin, €44 with shower and €50–55 with shower/wc or bath/wc. Half board, compulsory in winter, costs upwards of €46 per person. The big dining room next to the bar offers home cooking and great traditional dishes including *diots* (pork sausages in white wine with vegetables) and *biscuit de Savoie* with *génépi* ice-cream. Menus €13–27. Free coffee.

⬛ ⬛ |●| HÔTEL LA SETAZ – RESTAURANT LE GASTILLEUR***

Centre.
☎ 04.79.59.01.03 ➡ 04.79.59.00.63
e info@la-setaz.com
Closed 20 April to beginning of June; 20 Sept–15 Dec. **TV**. **Garden**. **Swimming pool**. **Car park**.

Despite its unprepossessing exterior, this is a very classy place, admirably run by Monique Villard. Chef Jacques prepares the kind of dishes that take his French customers back to their childhood but adapts them to suit modern tastes: lobster biscuit with Bresse chicken, fillet of sea bass roasted *à la gardiane*, lamb noisette, chops *aumonière* and Grand Marnier soufflé. You will find some of his specialities making an appearance on the menus – €20 on weekdays and €24–23 elsewhere. Service is flawless and you'll get a pleasant welcome. In the summer, they open the heated swimming pool and often have barbecues in the garden. The hotel rooms are starkly contemporary, but they face due south and some have balconies or terraces. Doubles with shower/wc or bath €61–73. Half board is compulsory at Christmas and Feb–March and costs €61–76. Free coffee.

|●| L'ASILE DES FONDUES

rue des Grandes Alpes; it's near the church and the tourist office.
☎ 04.79.59.04.71
Closed May–June and Sept–Nov.

The restaurant has a charming country dining room with lots of style. The welcome you get is so lovely that you'll be tempted to come back time and time again – if you can cope with the touristy bits, that is. They offer at least ten types of *fondue*, as much *raclette* as you can eat and *diots*, the local pork and vegetable sausages in white wine.You can eat for €18–27 *à la carte*.

VALLON-PONT-D'ARC   07150

⚐ 🛏 |●| HÔTEL-RESTAURANT LE BELVEDÈRE

route des Gorges; it's 6km outside Vallon.
☎ 04.75.88.00.02 ➡ 04.75.88.12.22
Closed Wed lunchtime and end-Nov to end-March.

This is a traditional establishment with neat, functional rooms that are a bit small – though some have balconies. Doubles with shower/wc for €41. The long, bright dining room is painted pink and has a bay window. Appetizing, healthy, uncomplicated cooking, professionally served: house *terrine*, meat dishes in sauce and a platter of local cheeses. Honestly priced menus €14–18. There's a patio in summer. Free coffee.

⚐ 🛏 |●| HÔTEL CLOS DES BRUYÈRES – RESTAURANT L'OLIVETTE

route des Gorges; it's just on the outskirts of Vallon, by the roundabout.
☎ 04.75.37.18.85 ➡ 04.75.37.14.89
e clos.des.bruyeres@online.fr
Closed 1 Oct–31 March. **Garden. Swimming pools. Car park.**

A modern-looking, standardized type of building by the side of the road but this hotel offers good facilities and behind it there are nice green spaces with trees. Though the rooms are functional they have a touch of individuality. Doubles, depending on the facilities and the season, cost €44–55. The most expensive ones have a view of the garden and the two swimming pools; avoid those that overlook the *route des Gorges*. The dining room is airy but rather lacking in character. Menus €11–15. Free apéritif.

⚐ |●| RESTAURANT LE CHELSEA

bd. Peschère-Alizon (Centre); it's on the main street.
☎ 04.75.88.01.40
Closed Oct–April.

An Ardèche version of a trendy young restaurant. The little dining room, which leads out onto the garden, is decorated with pictures of cartoon characters. The salads (€6–8) and pastas are obviously the *Chelsea*'s thing, but they've added a few cooked dishes to their repertoire: duck breast with honey and mint, *croustillant* of salmon with curry (€9–15). Weekday menu at €15 others from €21. A reliable place. Free coffee.

ORGNAC-L'AVEN   07150 (23KM S)

⚐ |●| HÔTEL DE L'AVEN***

pl. de la Mairie (Centre).
☎ 04.75.38.61.80 ➡ 04.75.38.66.69
Hotel closed mid-Nov to mid-March. **Restaurant open** Sun lunchtime out of season. **TV.**

The affable, attentive owner welcomes you to his simple establishment. The corridors and rooms smell fresh; doubles with shower/wc €38–42. The regional cooking is straightforward and unaffected: *charcuterie*, omelette with ceps and truffles, guineafowl and local desserts. Service is in a rustic-style dining room or on the terrace. Menus €14–23. Free house apéritif and 10% discount on the room rate April–May and Oct.

VALS-LES-BAINS   07600

⚐ 🛏 |●| HÔTEL SAINT-JEAN**

112 [bis] rue Jean-Jaurès (Centre); it's just set back from the road, on the banks of the river Voltour.
☎ 04.75.37.42.50 ➡ 04.75.37.54.77
e hotel.st.jean@wanadoo.fr
Closed 1 Nov to mid-April. **TV.**

A tall nineteenth-century building with a slightly sad exterior but an exuberant welcome and comfortable rooms. They have all been renovated and are lovely, though they're very small. Doubles €38 with shower/wc and €41 with bath/wc. Neutral décor but the overall effect is faultless. There's a big dining room with wide bay windows – menus €13–22. It's a classic-style place that offers peace and quiet. 10% discount on the room rate.

⚐ 🛏 |●| GRAND HOTEL DE L'EUROPE**

86 rue Jean-Jaurès.
☎ 04.75.37.43.94 ➡ 04.75.94.66

A friendly welcome awaits you in this ochre-fronted hotel. The dining room is colourful, painted in blue and yellow, and there's a terrace under the pine trees. Doubles €40 with shower/wc or €43 with bath. And the cooking is both tasty and reliable – *foie gras* with apple, pan-fried scallops with *foie gras* and Sauternes cream sauce, deer stew with almonds. Menus €10–30. Free house apéritif.

🏨 |O| GRAND HÔTEL DE LYON***

11 av. Paul Ribeyre (Centre).
☎ 04.75.37.43.70 ➡ 04.75.37.59.11
e hotel.de.lyon@wanadoo.fr
Closed 1 Oct–22 April. **TV**. **Swimming pool**. **Pay car park**.

A solid, serious hotel built at the beginning of the twentieth century – a place that won't let you down. The rooms are big, painted in pastel shades and well-maintained. The bedding is cosy and smells of roses. Doubles €51–61. The swimming pool has a wave machine and a waterfall – plus it's heated. There's a TV room, a billard saloon and a pretty little dining room. You can stay half-board if you wish. Honest, fortifying dishes of quality food with a *formule* for €13 and menus €18–37.

🏨 |O| HÔTEL-RESTAURANT LE VIVARAIS

5 rue Claude Expilly (Centre).
☎ 04.75.94.65.85 ➡ 04.75.37.65.47
Closed Feb. **Swimming pool**. **TV**. **Car park**.

Easy to find: it's the most beautiful building in town and it's painted pink. Since 1930, they have been perfecting the art of providing good beds and good food for their guests. The décor is Art Deco, from the wallpaper and the colours to the furniture and even some of the baths. A high degree of comfort and luxury, with excellent service. Doubles €53 with shower/wc and €92 with bath. The standard at table is just as high and Madame is a wonderful advocate for her region's cuisine. There's a three-course *formule* at €15 including a glass of wine and coffee, and menus at €27–43. Free house apéritif.

🍴 |O| RESTAURANT CHEZ MIREILLE

3 rue Jean-Jaurès, (Centre); it's at the end of the main road.
☎ 04.75.37.49.06
Closed Tues evening and Wed out of season.

Mireille is run by Colette, whose cuisine is highly recommended. Everything is cooked in her kitchen – it seems odd to have to say this, but it's not always the case. The filling *menu ardéchois* has two starters, and is simply superb. While the cooking is certainly respectful of tradition, there's something individual about it, too: poached eggs with smoked salmon, frogs' legs *à la Provençale*, red mullet fillets with chives and iced nougat with chestnut pancake. Menus €8 (main course and dessert) and €12–21. Free house apéritif.

VANS (LES)   07140

🍴 🏨 |O| HÔTEL LES CÉVENNES

pl. Ollier (Centre); it's in the main square.
☎ 04.75.37.23.09
Closed Mon. **Car park**.

From the minute you walk in, you're aware of a very special atmosphere – a sort of gentle madness that's infected the place for nigh-on forty years. The highly individual décor is a real jumble, with flowers, paintings, photos and old documents all jostling for space. The restaurant serves generous portions – *crêpe* from the Cévennes, *coq au vin*, many regional dishes. Set menus €11–27. It is undoubtedly better-known for its cooking than as a hotel, but its double rooms with average facilities go for €24 with shower/wc on the landing. Half board at €38 is compulsory. Free house apéritif.

🍴 🏨 |O| HÔTEL-RESTAURANT LE MAS DE L'ESPAÏRE**

Bois de Païolive
☎ 04.75.94.95.01 ➡ 04.75.37.21.00
e espaire@wanadoo.fr
Closed lunchtimes, Jan–Feb. **Swimming pool**. **TV**. **Car park**.

There's a sense of calm in this sturdy, imposing building in a splendid setting, and you're put at your ease by the excellent welcome. All the facilities you need for a good stay are here: lots of space inside and out, a swimming pool and even cicadas chirruping in the background. Doubles with en-suite bathrooms €47–69. The cuisine offers a variety of traditional specialities from the Cévennes, the Ardèche and Lyons. Menus €14 and €20. You can go on wonderful walks through the magic Païolive forest, which adjoins the property. Free house apéritif.

|O| RESTAURANT LE GRANGOUSIER

rue Courte; it's opposite the church.
☎ 04.75.94.90.86
Closed Tues and Wed except July–Aug; 1 Jan–12 Feb.

This stylish restaurant serves both simple menus and gourmet ones which will delight even the most ardent foodie. The cooking is imaginative – stuffed rabbit with fresh noodles, *foie gras* with cream and nettle sauce, salad of pan-fried *foie gras* with chestnuts, Vacherin with chestnuts. The dining room, with its vaulted ceiling and dressed stone walls, is the perfect setting for these wonderful delicacies and although the place is smart, prices are fair: menus €17–22. The wine list includes a number of very affordable bottles.

VIENNE   38200

|O| RESTAURANT L'ESTANCOT

4 rue de la Table-Ronde (North).
☎ 04.74.85.12.09
Closed Sun and Mon.

Situated in a quiet side street in the old town near the Saint-André-le-Bas church, *L'Estancot* has a pretty façade with windowboxes laden with flowers and a long, beautiful dining room. Dishes of the day go for €7, menus are from €8 (weekday) and continue at €12–16. The house specialities are *criques* (made with potatoes, chopped parsley and eggs – only served Sat), and *paillassons* (plain potatoes) accompanied by all sorts of delicious things. Other delights include duck breast with five types of peppercorn, sea-urchin flan with shellfish sauce, veal kidneys with walnut wine and pears poached in vanilla with caramel sauce. Super-fast service. Reservations only.

ESTRABLIN   38780 (8KM SE)

🎿 ☎ LA GABETIÈRE***

How to get there: take the D502 and it's on the left after the crossroads that lead you to Estrablin.
☎ 04.74.58.01.31 ➡ 04.74.58.08.98
TV. Garden. Swimming pool. Car park.

You'll want to hide away forever in this lovely, luxurious sixteenth-century stone manor house – especially if you get a room with a view of the grounds. The décor is exquisitely tasteful and the welcome is simple, warm and attentive. Rooms €44 with shower/wc, €52–60 with bath; a suite in the tower sleeps four. There's a welcoming bar-cum-TV room, a heated pool and tables in the garden where you can have your picnic. This really is an unusually lovely place and the charming *patronne* will give you all sorts of information about what to see. 10% discount Sept–June.

🎿 |O| FRANTONY

ZA Le Rocher; take the D41 in the direction of Grenoble and it's by the huge roundabout.
☎ 04.74.57.24.70
Closed Mon and Tues except feast days and public holidays.

Though it's rather oddly located in a business park surrounded by roads and concrete buildings, the dining room here is attractive and the dishes are interesting and sometimes unusual. The chef used to work for an Emir, so his cuisine has a touch of sophistication and elegance. Try the Barbary duck with onions and coriander, frogs' legs and spinach lasagne, quail stuffed with olives and polenta or *marbré* of *foie gras* with aubergine. Menus €12–31 or €21 *à la carte*. Free house apéritif.

VILLARD-DE-LANS   38250

☎ VILLA PRIMEROSE**

147 av. des Bains.
☎ 04.76.95.13.17
Closed 1 Nov–20 Dec. **Car park**.

Here's a place where they really make you feel welcome. The quiet rooms in this beautiful building look out onto the Gerbier mountain range. €23–40 for rooms for a double; they have some communicating rooms ideal for families. There's no longer a restaurant, but the owner lets residents use the kitchens to cook meals which they are invited to eat in the dining room. Breakfast €4.

🎿 ☎ |O| À LA FERME DU BOIS BARBU**

How to get there: it's 3km from the centre in the direction of Bois-Barbu.
☎ 04.76.95.13.09 ➡ 04.76.94.10.65
✉ fermeboisbarbu@planete.vercors.com
Hotel closed 3 weeks in June and 3 weeks from mid-Nov. **TV. Car park**.

A real mountain inn on the edge of a forest and next to a quiet road. You can sit on the flowery terrace shaded by lime trees or relax in a nice comfy armchair while Nadine, your hostess, plays the piano. Rooms €41–48 with shower/wc – most have been refurbished. It's ideal for cross-country skiers, since the trails are just nearby, as well as for mountain bikers. Menus at €14–20 list delicious local dishes: stuffed breast of veal with walnuts, house *caillettes*, frog's legs in Diois wine sauce, steak with morels, Bleu du Vercors cheese croquettes, iced soufflé with Chartreuse. They prefer you to stay half-board at €40–46. 10% discount on the room rate in low season.

🎿 |O| MALATERRE

Lieu-dit Malaterre; from Villars, take the D215C, shortly after Bois-Barbu turn onto the forest road signposted to Malaterre.
☎ 04.76.95.94.34 ✉ supervielle@wanadoo.fr
Open daily noon–6pm July–Aug and Dec–March; Fri evening July–Aug; Sun Sept–Oct and April–June.

Closed Feb; March; Nov. **Car park**.

This is an excellent restaurant in an old wooden house in the forest. The building, once the home of a forester, dates from the 1900s; there's no electricity and water is still brought up by tanker. Lydia and Bernard, who run a farm nearby, decided to revive this place by providing good food and drink for cross-country skiers and walkers. There's a fantastic variety of foresters' implements ornamenting the walls, and the atmosphere is genuinely warm. When the weather's fine it's wonderful to sit out on the terrace, and when it's cold you can warm your hands around a bowl of good vegetable soup and munch on home-made bread baked in the wood-fired oven. Menus, €9–15, list genuine regional cuisine which relies on fresh produce from the farm – try the Vercors platter, Royans ravioli, *caillette*, blue Vercors cheese, mushroom omelette, *charcuterie*, *gratiné* of ravioli with cream or fillet of smoked trout. And leave space for pudding – there's home-made spice cake with honey, upside-down apple tart and *tarte du chef*. At tea-time they offer delicious ice-creams. To drink, you can choose between the local *rataplane* (sold by the litre jug), cider and local apple juice. On summer Friday evenings, your hosts recount the legends of the Vercors around the fire. Free *digestif*.

CORRENÇON-EN-VERCORS   38250 (5.5KM S)

🏠 I●I LE CARIBOU

Le Clos de la Balme. Take the D215c; it's 2km after the golf course practically at the foot of the ski runs.
☎ 04.76.95.82.82 ➡ 04.76.95.83.17
Closed April. **Swimming pool**.

The rooms are painted in yellow, green and red and all have en-suite bathrooms and telephone. Doubles €38. Some sleep three and they have 2-roomed studios starting from €275 a week in low season. The restaurant has a lovely wooden floor and is decorated with souvenirs from Africa and Indonesia. Menus €13–22 with half board costing €47 per person. The owners are lovely and they create a good-humoured atmosphere. There's lots to do – swimming pool, sauna, kids' games, ping-pong, pony and horse-riding in summer and painting classes. There's a cabaret at apéritif time. It's great for young families.

🏠 I●I HÔTEL DU GOLF – RESTAURANT DU BLOIS FLEURI***

It's on the D215c between the golf course and the village.

☎ 04.76.95.84.84 ➡ 04.76.95.82.84
Closed April and mid-Oct to mid-Dec. **TV**. **Swimming pool**.

This old farmhouse was restored by the present owners' grandparents and they've recently had it renovated. There's nothing to match it in the luxury category in town. It offers a dozen rooms, two with balconies and some sleeping up to 5. They're individually decorated and cosy with the bathroom and separate wc off the spacious entrance hall. Wood panelling and dried flowers complete the picture. And those added extras are provided – minibar and dressing gowns. €80–120 for a double room. The restaurant opens up onto the terrace in good weather. There's a *menu fraîcheur* for €15 (lunch but not Sunday) and others start from €24. In the grounds there's a heated swimming pool and sauna.

VILLARS-LES-DOMBES   01330

I●I RESTAURANT L'ÉCU DE FRANCE

rue du Commerce (Centre); it's on the main street, near to the church.
☎ 04.74.98.01.79
Closed Sun–Tues evenings; Wed; Jan.

A traditional restaurant serving regional dishes – lots of Bresse chicken but also frogs' legs and duck breast. It's an affordable place to eat in this somewhat touristy town: menus €14–33. Old photographs of the town hang on the wall.

BOULIGNEUX   01130 (4KM NW)

I●I LE THOU

How to get there: take the D2 Chatillon-sur-Chalaronne road.
☎ 04.74.98.15.25
Closed Mon, Tues and Feb. **Garden**.

A pleasant and appealing restaurant. The dining room walls are hung with a variety of pictures, and there's a mature garden with a terrace. The chef's speciality is carp served in many delicious guises: salad of warm carp with mustard, *goujons*, *profiteroles* of carp mousse. The cheeses and the desserts are perfect and the wine list is splendid. Menus from €27, or around €46 *à la carte*.

JOYEUX   01800 (8KM SE)

🚲 I●I LA BICYCLETTE BLEUE

How to get there; take the D904 from Villars in the direction of Chalamont then turn right onto the D61 for 2 kms and it's in the centre of the village.

☎ 04.74.98.21.48
Closed Tues evening; Wed except July–Aug; mid-Dec to mid-Jan. **Disabled access**.

An isolated country restaurant in a renovated farmhouse. It's fresh and friendly and smoothly run by a family and their donkey d'Artagnan. It's a lovely place to have lunch – fine in the dining room but even better under the awning. Lots of unpretentious local dishes, attentively prepared and thoughtfully cooked: farmhouse chicken with cream sauce, carp fillet with sorrel, fresh frogs' legs. Lunch menu for €9 and others €14–27. Try the house cocktail made with sparkling Bugey wine. You can hire a bike and take off through the countryside. Kids especially will love it.

SAINTE-CROIX   01120 (14KM SE)

🏠 |●| CHEZ NOUS**

It's in the village; take the D22 as far as Pizay, then turn right onto the D61.
☎ 04.78.06.60.60 ➡ 04.78.06.63.26
Closed Sun evening and Mon; Dec.

Set well back from the road in the countryside, this comfortable establishment offers very quiet rooms in a modern annexe; doubles with bath €45. Menus start at €13 (not served Sun), with others €17–45. Though you can get traditional cuisine, they also list interesting variations on the regional theme: fresh frogs' legs, chicken with cream sauce.

ARS-SUR-FORMANS   01480 (19KM W)

🎿 🏠 |●| HÔTEL-RESTAURANT LA BONNE ÉTOILE

It's on the D904.
☎ 04.74.00.77.38 ➡ 04.74.08.10.10
Closed Mon evening and Tues; Jan.

This village is where the relics of Saint Curé are to be found and it attracts many pilgrims. When the Pope visited, he had a meal in this very restaurant – the plate he used is hung up outside the door. This is a friendly, welcoming establishment and the clean rooms smell of the countryside. Doubles €33 with shower/wc. The owner collects all sorts of knick-knacks – dolls and coffee pots in particular. Simple, unpretentious dishes with menus at €11 and €20. 10% discount on the room rate.

VIVIERS   07220

🎿 |●| RESTAURANT DE L'HORLOGE

faubourg le Cire; it's on the RN86.

☎ 04.75.52.62.43
Closed Sun evening and Mon.

When you see the neon signs, it's hard to believe what awaits inside. The dining room is vast and decorated by huge murals from the nineteenth century, painted by passing artists. The robust, tasty cooking is prepared using fresh market produce. You eat well and cheaply: dish of the day €6 and three menus €9 (a steal) up to €16. You eat well for very little. Free coffee.

VOIRON   38500

|●| RESTAURANT LE BOIS JOLI

la Tivollière; take the Chambéry road for about 2km, and turn left.
☎ 04.76.05.22.25 ➡ 04.76.66.10.79
Closed Sun and Mon evening; also Tues and Wed evneings out of season; the first 3 weeks in Jan. **Disabled access**. **Car park**.

The tasty, hearty cooking ranges across quails with morels, liver gâteau, kidneys in Madeira sauce, kid with morels and chicken with crayfish. There's a lovely veranda where you can sit and relax while you survey the countryside. Weekday lunch menu €9 (dish of the day and dessert), then others up to €20.

MONTFERRAT   38620 (13KM N)

|●| AUBERGE FÉFETTE

Le Vernay (North); follow the lake road from Montferrat.
☎ 04.76.32.40.46
Closed Mon evening and Tues; 15–30 April; 15–30 Oct. **Car park**.

A nice little house way out in the countryside. It's a family affair run by the Groseilles; the son is the chef while his father runs the dining room. Good menus at €20–27, with dishes that change with the seasons: *papillote* of *foie gras* with raspberries, scallop salad with pan-fried girolles, roast monkfish with sea salt, potted lamb with apricots, *fricassée* of lobster in Banyuls wine. Dine on the terrace in good weather. Reliable and good so it's best to book.

VONNAS   01540

|●| L'ANCIENNE AUBERGE

pl. du Marché.
☎ 04.74.50.90.50 ➡ 04.74.50.08.80
Closed Jan.

Vonnas is the home town of star chef

Georges Blanc – his own restaurant is across the road from this old inn, still run by his family. It's full of old famly photographs and collections of lemonade bottles, and is opposite a romantic little wooden bridge over the Veyle. In summer you can enjoy the terrace and patio at the back. The service is polite, efficient and swift. You start with an appetizer and delicious cocktail, setting you up for your meal and the local regional wines. The recipes and produce used come from the region: eggs *en meurette*, onion *terrine*, salmon *tartare*, *poulet de Bresse* cooked to Grandmother Blanc's recipe. And the prices are reasonable: the menu of the day costs €15 and the others (€26–35) are simply amazing for what they cost. It's a tad over-commercialized – lots of "Blanc" produce on sale – but it's still superb and will more than do while you save up to go to the place opposite.

Index

D

M

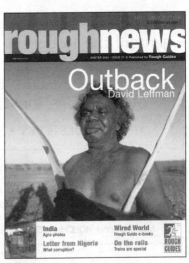

The ideas expressed in this code were developed by and for independent travellers.

Learn About The Country You're Visiting
Start enjoying your travels before you leave by tapping into as many sources of information as you can.

The Cost Of Your Holiday
Think about where your money goes - be fair and realistic about how cheaply you travel. Try and put money into local peoples' hands; drink local beer or fruit juice rather than imported brands and stay in locally owned accommodation. Haggle with humour and not aggressively. Pay what something is worth to you and remember how wealthy you are compared to local people.

Embrace The Local Culture
Open your mind to new cultures and traditions. Think carefully about what's appropriate in terms of your clothes and the way you behave. You'll earn respect and be more readily welcomed by local people. Respect local laws and attitudes towards drugs and alcohol that vary in different countries and communities. Think about the impact you could have on them.

Exploring The World – The Travellers' Code

Being sensitive to these ideas means getting more out of your travels - and giving more back to the people you meet and the places you visit.

Minimise Your Environmental Impact
Think about what happens to your rubbish - take biodegradable products and a water filter bottle. Be sensitive to limited resources like water, fuel and electricity. Help preserve local wildlife and habitats by respecting rules and regulations, such as sticking to footpaths and not standing on coral.

Don't Rely On Guidebooks
Use your guidebook as a starting point, not the only source of information. Talk to locals, then discover your own adventure!

Be Discreet With Photography
Don't treat people as part of the landscape, they may not want their picture taken. Ask first and respect their wishes.

Tourism Concern works with people the world over to promote tourism that benefits their communities, but we can only carry on our work with the support of people like you. For membership details or to find out how to make your travels work for local people and the environment, visit our website

www.tourismconcern.org.uk

TourismConcern
Campaigning for Ethical and Fairly Traded Tourism